Elliott Erwitt

Snaps

PHAIDON

non mint copy

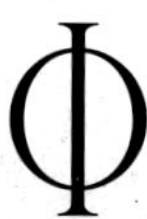

Read
Rest
Touch
Stand
Tell
Point
Look
Move
Play

14

56

118

172

244

296

338

412

480

The World and Elliott Erwitt

Murray Sayle

This book shows a rare talent, despite its modest title, and talent is a gift of the gods. Still, like film, it has to be developed. There's no other collection like it, and there never will be another. Treasure this book: it's destined to be a classic. How do I know? Because the times and technologies that made it possible will never come again.

Elio ('Hello Elio' twisted American tongues, so it became Elliott) Romano Erwitt was born in the American Hospital at Neuilly-sur-Seine, Paris (France) on 26 July 1928. If that wasn't romantic enough, his mother Evgenia, from a well-to-do family in Moscow, met his father Boris, an architectural student from Odessa, in Istanbul, Turkey. Those were the early, less strict days of the Soviet Union, before Stalin made his opponents run on time, and both were out to see the world. They caught the even more romantic Stamboul Train to Trieste, where they married. When Elliott and I were filming on the same train, we raised a glass in their honour. Boris resumed his studies in Rome (hence 'Romano'), tried his luck in Paris, and then with their only child the family moved to Milan, where Elliott grew up speaking Italian at school and Russian at home. Not liking, with Boris's Jewish background, the look of Europe, the Erwitts took the last peacetime voyage of the *Ile de France* on 1 September 1939, reaching New York five days into World War II.

The senior Erwitts' marriage was already on the rocks. Some people are not cut out to be married, especially to each other. Boris (he died in 1993) was an unworldly intellectual who never settled to a regular calling (he even tried photography, following, he said, in his famous son's footsteps). Evgenia was, in her inventive English, the 'artistical' one, dabbling in painting and drawing. Elliott inherited the talents of both parents, neither of much immediate use when, aged eleven, he was sent to an elementary school in New York, unable to speak English. Three years later, ever seeking the big opportunity, Boris Erwitt took his son to Los Angeles, where Elliott enrolled in Hollywood High School. When you are suddenly cast among foreigners jabbering in a language you barely understand, you have to use your eyes instead. What do you see? Comical, sad, happy humans, people rather like yourself. Does this explain Elliott's lifelong attraction to things visual? I put this theory to him years later, in Nepal, where we were shooting a game of polo played on elephants – so many of them that I had my personal polo-playing and commentary elephant, with a camera elephant for Elliott and a soft-footed sound elephant for our recordist, Lee Orloff. 'You may be right!' he shouted back. 'Action! Watch the ball!' As usual, we wrote the script that same evening, over a laugh-filled dinner. 'The ball is coloured orange to distinguish it from any droppings during a tense game' was, I recall, one of the better lines we came up with.

Elliott's ambition for a career in photography sharpened in 1944 after Boris left for New Orleans seeking opportunity as an antique dealer. This was not a case, Elliott recalls, of a father running away from home, but of escaping excessive alimony payments. Elliott chose to stay in their house in LA, supporting himself by soda-jerking, breaking eggs in a bakery, photographing weddings and babies (like many kids of those days, he'd taught himself developing and enlarging black-and-white photos) and a job in a commercial photography lab. In 1946, aged eighteen, he took a Greyhound bus to New York, camera in hand, and hit the streets shooting. A shot from that early trip (p.232) shows a tiny dog in a sweater beside the (relatively) enormous wedge-heels of a woman whose New Look skirt just gets into frame. The elements of an authentic Erwitt are already present: playful juxtaposition, a cute dog, a mystery (what does she look like?). So Elliott's gift is one he was born with, or developed early in life. And he still has it (p.70). But he bears other marks of his early years. He needed to earn a living, and photography offered the best prospects, but it was also a medium for self-expression, a hobby, if not an obsession. I have never worked with another photographer

who keeps the two aspects so separate. Or was so insistent that photographers keep their copyrights, thus opening the way for a lifelong career for himself and his colleagues.

We met, as I recall in 1977, as photographers and writers usually do – on a job, or 'an assignment' if the pay is more than $1 a word. The German edition of the travel magazine *Geo* had separately commissioned us to do a funny story about the two million Japanese who climb Mount Fuji every year, the less inhibited (*'der befreiet Japanische pinkler'*, as *Geo* put it) using the sacred mountain as an outdoor urinal. I found a bulldozer which took Elliott and his ladder, lights, cases of lenses and so on up the back side of Fuji, at night. I made two meaningful discoveries on this job. First, Elliott turned out to be the most amusing man I'd run across in years. Thinking about this, I realize I mean the most amusable man – he can see a joke, in words or images, better than anyone I know. Then I noticed that, as well as his 'business camera' as he put it, he usually carried his 'hobby camera', a well-worn Leica M3 with a 50mm standard lens, loaded (for anyone who hopes to be the new Elliottt Erwitt) with Kodak Tri-X or Ilford HP4, developed in Microdol – the standard black-and-white outfit with which most of the photos in this book were taken.

Of course I had seen some of Elliott's photos. Who hasn't? I knew his name, vaguely. I knew some of his dog snaps; one that stuck in mind was of a small terrier jumping for joy, four paws off the ground, in Ballycotton, Ireland, in 1968. A would-be photographer myself, like many writers, I wondered: how in the name of Niepce did he do that?

Especially, I remembered Richard Nixon stabbing Nikita Khrushchev's chest with a stern forefinger in their famous 'kitchen debate' at the American exhibition in Moscow in 1959, much used in the Republican campaign the following year. How did Elliott get that? Years later, in Africa, he told me the story. He was on assignment for Westinghouse, photographing their refrigerator in the model American kitchen. William Safire, subsequently the conservative political columnist, then PR man for Macy's department store, admitted Elliott to the kitchen. Nixon and Khrushchev began arguing in front of his Leica. 'Americans eat meat and Russian eat cabbage. Why?' Nixon demanded. 'Go and [expletive] your grandmother!' said Khrushchev, never short of witty retort. Understanding both sides, Elliott cracked up, but not before capturing the moment on film. A thank-you print he later sent Safire became a Republican poster campaign without his permission, especially galling as he voted Democrat. The photo, however, still tells us a lot about Russia, America, and politics.

Sheer luck, if you like, or 'F/8 and be there', as photojournalists describe their trade secret. But as his fellow Magnum photographer Ernst Haas often remarked, 'it's amazing how lucky some people can be'. After the Fuji trip, Elliott flew off to Hamburg to show his German editors, he said, which were the funny pictures. A number of journalistic jobs and a lot of laughs followed, and then, in the 1980s, we started to make films for TV, first a series for HBO called *The Great Pleasure Hunts*, which I wrote and in which I played (rather realistically, I thought) the part of a jaded journalist wandering the world in search of exotic entertaiment, food and drink, with Elliott as director and cameraman. We had great fun making movies and we hope it shows. Our message was satirical, puritanical, or both, and charmingly naïve: 'The search for pleasure,' my character warned, 'leads only to heartburn and herpes', the sexually transmitted disease of those innocent years. Scores of times I watched Elliott improve his luck. 'Something coming up here', he would say, reaching for his hobby camera, usually on the appearance of an appealing dog, a sweet old couple, or whatever. As the subject approached I could just about hear his shutter's preliminary clicks (rangefinder Leicas have unusually quiet actions). The subjects rarely even noticed. Not always, but quite often, BINGO!

Elliott had caught the impossible moment, what his friend Henri Cartier-Bresson called *'l'instante critique'* and for this book we might re-name *'l'instante hysterique'*. Many photographers try to improve their luck with noisy, wasteful motor drives, but I have never seen (or heard) Elliott use one. Every frame he shoots, as his contact sheets indicate, is usually well composed, a presentable picture in its own right. A lifetime's devotion to craftsmanship, and it shows.

Elliott uses his long-polished technique for improving his luck in the commercial and journalistc work which earns his living, finances his tireless globe-trotting and makes possible his photographic hobby, and thus most of this book. There's an example on the cover. The winsome small boy, his grandfather and the horizontal loaves of French bread set against vertical rows of trees all say 'Erwitt'. It could have been one of his hobby shots, every element timed and placed. It is, however, an advertising photo for French tourism. If you look closely you can see how Elliott has improved his luck: he composed the scene and focused his camera first, put a stone on the road to mark the spot, and pressed the release as the back wheel passed by. That, too is photography, imaginative and intelligent, just what his client wanted (Elliott calls this approach 'creative obedience').

Talent will out, but there remains a mystery about the endless fascination of this series of photos of the funny, the odd and the famous, most of them shot just because they were there. Partly it must lie in the sheer size of this collection. Photography's unit of expression is not a single photograph, but a sequence, and this surely must be the longest sequence ever made in one instantly recognizable style. But there has to be more to it than the grudging admiration we feel for someone who constructs a life-size Eiffel Tower out of matchsticks. Would this book be improved by colour? Somehow, no. With this clue I consulted my son Alexander, a computer science major. 'It's easy, dad,' he replied, 'all our memories are stored in black and white. Saves mind space. We have a paintbox in our heads and colour them in as needed. For anything that needs instant recognition – to get a joke, for instance, to identify the face of a friend, or one of our make-believe friends (the famous), to grasp an unexpected relationship of shape or pattern, to convey an emotion – colour just gets in the way. Too much unnecessary information. Nicéphore Niepce stumbled on to something new with black-and-white photography, a way of speaking simply and directly to our inner memory banks. Like radio for the eyes.'

'But,' I asked, 'why does it have to be a book of photographs? Wouldn't drawings do the trick?'

'Not quite,' he replied, 'drawings are someone else's artefacts. Our heads aren't full of drawings, unless we're Picasso. A black-and-white photograph reassures us that there was once something like that out there, stripped to essentials, ready to be grasped. Have you noticed how Elliott's pictures stick in the memory?'

I have, so I tried the theory on Elliott.

'Alexander may be right,' he said, 'I've sometimes used the by-line Snaps Pikazo.'

'But is he right about black and white?' I asked.

'I started in black and white, which certainly gives more control over the end result. Just stuck with it.'

It's not quite true that Elliott's photos have no captions and speak entirely for themselves. A photo not anchored in a time and a place is no longer an interesting design. Every photo in this book has at least two identifying marks: a place, often a city, and the year. Except, perhaps for 'I rub you truly', a line from one of our movies about Japanese massage parlours, dates and places must surely be the most economically evocative concepts in any language. 'We'll always have Paris'

Humphrey Bogart told Ingrid Bergman in *Casablanca*, and he hardly needed to add the year. Looking though this book, we see one man's dates, places and faces unreeling over more than a half century; the bizarre, hilarious, extraordinary, tender and touching scenes his Leica has caught. His vision belongs to no particular city or country, no race or ethnicity. Only a tireless citizen of the world, one with an extraordinary persistence of aim and effort, could have done it, and no one else has. Or, I think, ever will. Black and white is almost a lost art, electronic manipulation of images is casting doubt on the authenticity of all photographs, undermining the 'slice of reality' which makes them effective, even if it is an illusion. Even the contact sheet is no more. Elliott caught his world, by good luck, at a moment when technology and commerce combined to nourish his gift.

It is a kindly, optimistic, even an old-fashioned world. There's no violence, no war, no cruelty or pain; no slums, and only a few mansions. A world of many bright beginnings, and even a few happy endings. It is mostly a world of cities: no doubt because that's where the most people are. It's a world of laughs without malice, of sympathetic, more-than-half-human dogs, muscled men and fat ladies, Germans, Japanese, French, British, Americans, Russians and the rest of us, proving how much they all have in common. It is a selective view of life, of course; but then again, so is every view of life that will fit into a single head, or a book. Here we have one sharp-eyed man's sightings on his voyage down the river of life. As the commentary of one of our films (in a sequence about a Japanese 'love hotel' disguised to look like the liner *Queen Elizabeth II*) invites you: 'Hurro, and welcome aboard!'

Text by Charles Flowers

'It's good when you can't explain a picture,' Elliott Erwitt says, 'because that means it's visual.'

Friends, fans, family and some sharp-eared critics will recognize this comment as a characteristically nimble Erwitt riff: intentionally colloquial simple language is used to prick whatever intellectual pomposities might be lurking on the horizon, then the self-professed naif whips out a pun that is almost a sucker punch. A first glance rarely takes in an Erwitt photo, and a first hearing does not always sound the depth of his deceptively homely wordplays.

It is within the context of this remark, of course, that he asked me to write some comments here…Wily Elliott! But we have worked together, photog and scribbler, on many projects over the past fifteen years and have more than once heard together the chimes at midnight, so I will take him at his word, as it were.

A couple of housekeeping matters…Why *Snaps*? Elliott despises artsy, hyperaesthetic lingo about the nuts and bolts of the picture-taking trade (and, for all of his puckish charm, has been heard to speak unkindly of those who traffic in such bilge). The term 'snap' is straightforward. Since he bought his first camera at age fourteen, he has 'snapped' pictures; that's the act. There's another level of meaning: Elliott wants his snaps to capture the perfect millisecond, from his point of view. Frozen action or expression, precisely apt composition, bizarre or touching chance conjunction of real-life images…Snap. The story is in the caught moment…Snap.

And why divide these photos into nine sections? It's more for the eye than for the sense, a method of organizing the experience of some five hundred photos. It works well enough, as long as we don't mistake the terms for Elliott's original goals. Don't let our attempt to create a kind of playful order tyrannize your own conversations with these inimitable images.

These five decades' worth of photos include internationally famous shots as well as forgotten work he's dredged up recently from long-neglected files in his Manhattan office.

Throughout the book he has paired photos in order to make visual puns, even though each image can stand alone and has indeed done so quite nicely in other formats. Still, as pairs, they augment rather than diminish his original single intent. (More is more!) He may not even glimpse a possible connection until decades later, as he forages for the *n*th time through those steadily accumulating files of snaps.

Visual and verbal puns require a slight step backward from the meaning, a mental disconnect, a recognition that signs and symbols denote but do not embody. Perhaps this is the natural legacy of someone born in France in 1928 to Russian parents, raised in Italy, then brought to New York at age eleven speaking Russian, French, Italian and not a word of English. As he learned the meanings, he also heard the music of these languages, a survivalist's gift that is acutely tuned to dissonance. He cherishes fatuous circumlocutions and insane euphemisms. The peculiar utterances of George W. Bush are pure bliss to him. He will rush to the phone after a meeting with ad execs to pass along the latest sparkling gem of industry argot.

While he is most widely known, and even beloved, for the humorous or poignant pictures that capture an unposed moment in the flow of human or lower animal experience (especially at the canine level), Elliott is also a powerfully effective journalist and, when the occasion demands, tragedian. To understand how the same sensibility can portray the grieving widow of an assassinated US president and elsewhere record the surreal conjunction of Christ and a Pepsi ad – to submit to both types of image and see how they are emotionally kin – is to understand (though never, never state) the qualities of perception that are unique to Elliott's work.

Read

Since his early twenties Elliott has been a member of the rowdy, if prestigious, invitation-only photographers' collective Magnum. *Read* begins with the agency's most-requested image from the Civil Rights era in the US. A man who smiles often but rarely laughs, Elliott was horrified when I first saw this image and laughed aloud.

But I had been there, a boy in the South who, like many kids I knew then, was surprised and disappointed when the 'Colored' fountain in the downtown dry-goods store shot up water that was perfectly clear rather than hued like the rainbow. My laugh was ironic laughter at the absurdity of the entire segregation era, of course: for example, the fundamentalist preachers who said 'our Negroes' deserved a harsh life because God was punishing them for the sins of their Old Testament ancestor Ham. When staff members at my hometown's African-American Museum saw the photo, they laughed, too, in about the same way. They remembered the cruelty, but also the insanity that drove it. They also wanted to hang it high so that today's children and teens could see it, a testimony to a world this generation is fortunate to find antique.

That others might experience his image somewhat differently than he, that still others might be jerked in an instant into their past, that yet others might learn what is more powerfully shown than told – these are the kinds of readings, more experential than literary, that Elliott inspires in the indelible union of simple words and complex evoked narrative, not only here but in different moods elsewhere.

Throughout this section he plays around with word-related notions, such as the literary aspects of painting, signs that use words and signs that are visual symbols, various kinds of 'signage' (an ad-world term he finds hilarious and can somehow bring into a surprising variety of conversations), words that show up in the midst of contrary happenings, unintended messages and several portraits, wordless, of the people who live by putting words together. The last photo in *Read*, a delicious bit of mischief that Elliott typically presents to friends as their wedding gift, unforgettably requires the reading of the nonverbal (p.54).

Whether or not consciously, the boy who came to English already knowing several languages must have realized that the eccentric locutions of any tongue slightly colour experience in different ways; that real life makes its course unspoken through those imperfect thickets of signage, and cannot be explained in the words of any one language. Just like the photos, as we have been fairly warned…

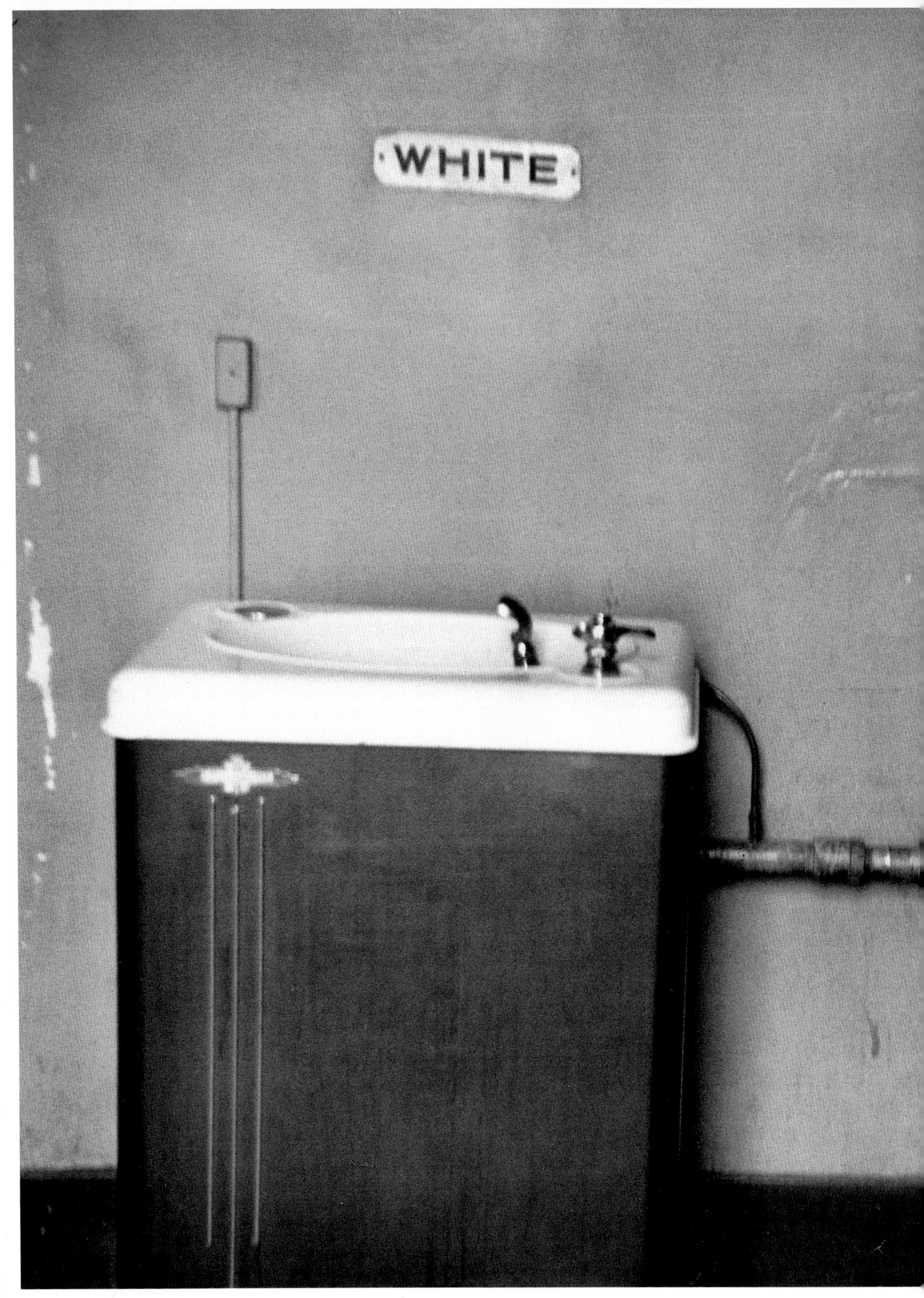

North Carolina, 1950

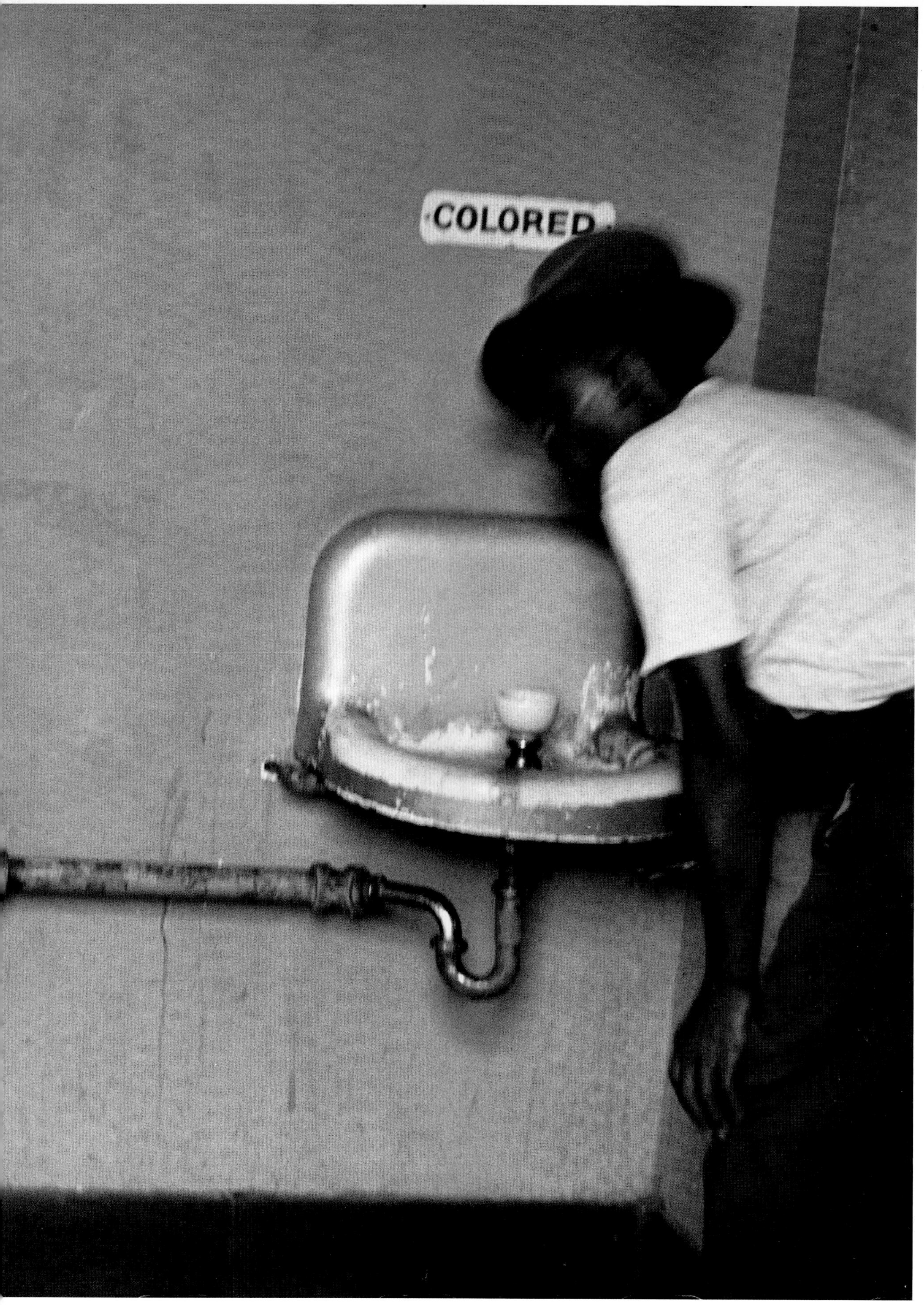
COLORED

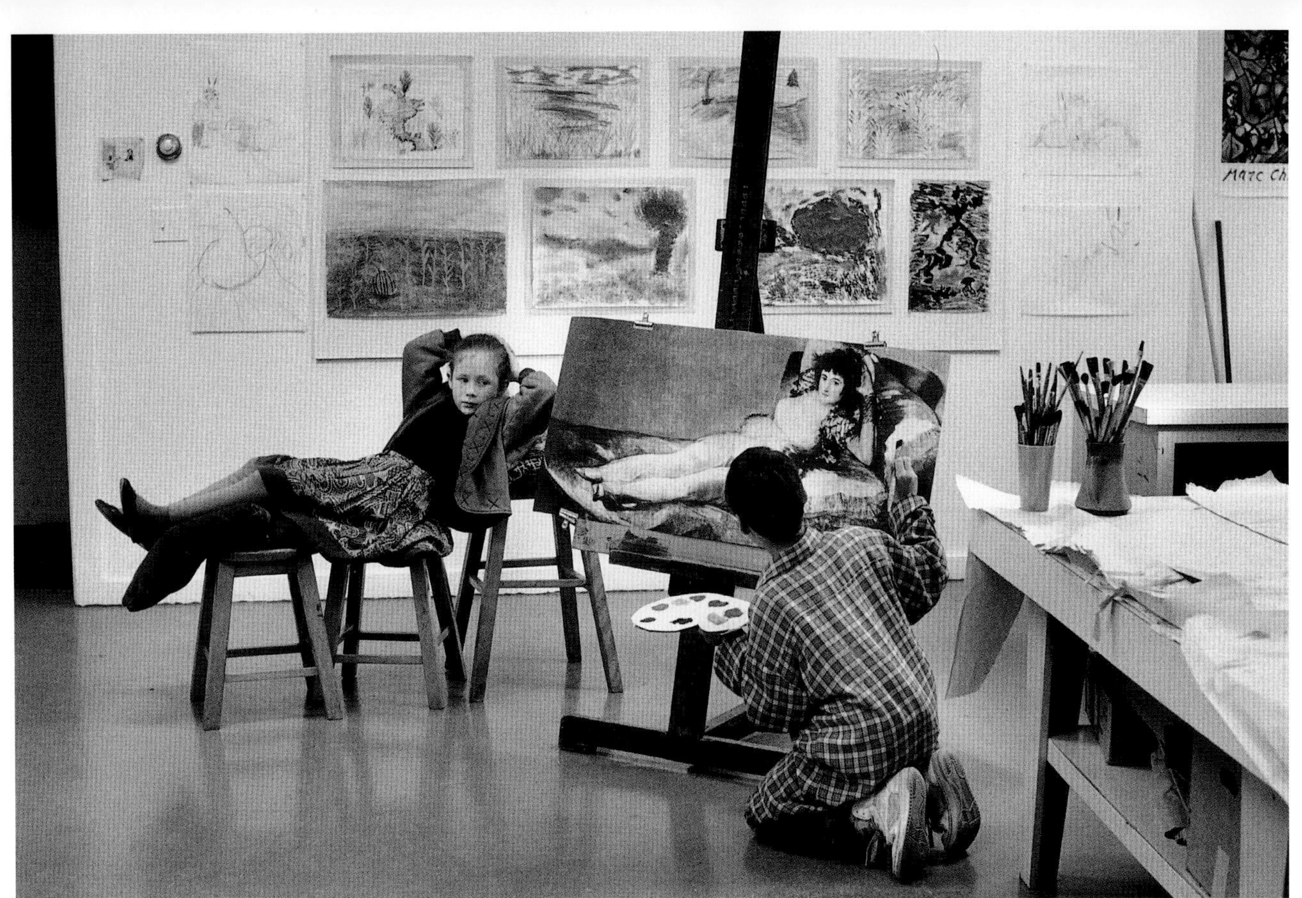

Bridgehampton, New York, 1990

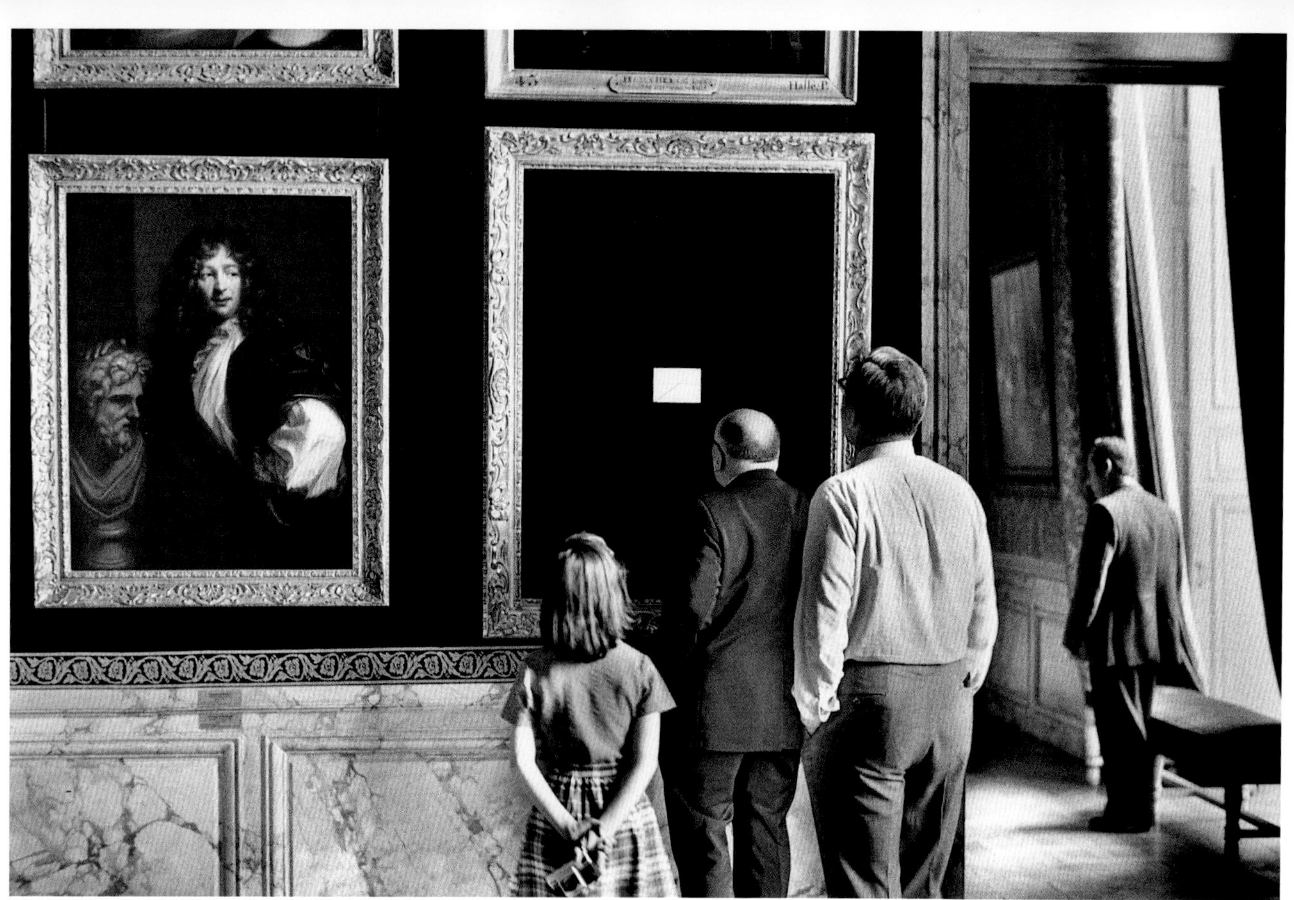

Versailles, France, 1975

Puerto Rico, 1969 **/** *Ohio, 1969*
Newcastle, England, 1969 **/** *Hoboken, New Jersey, 1954*

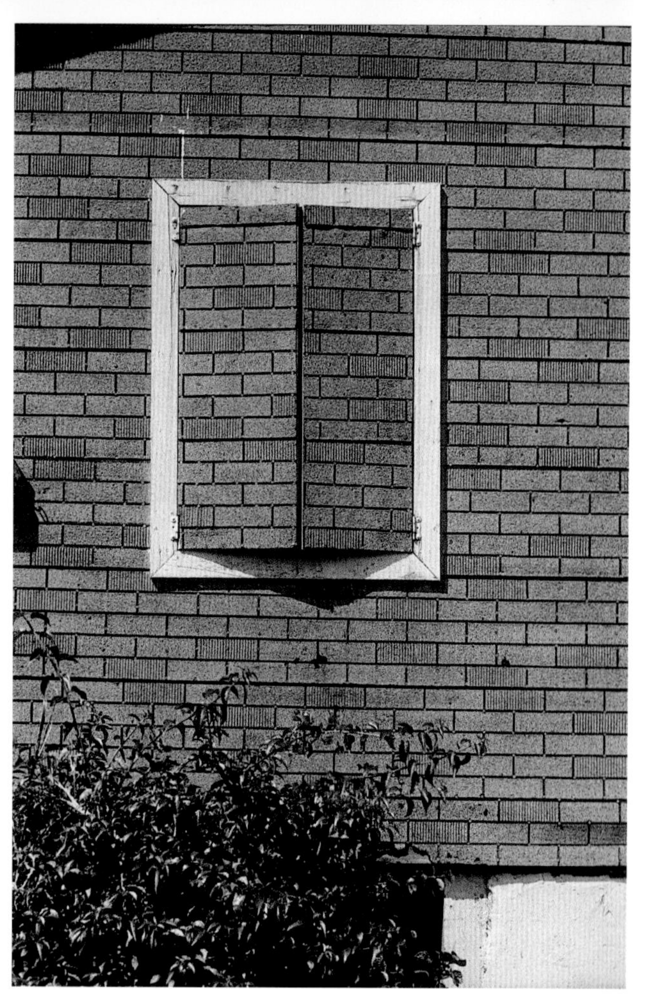

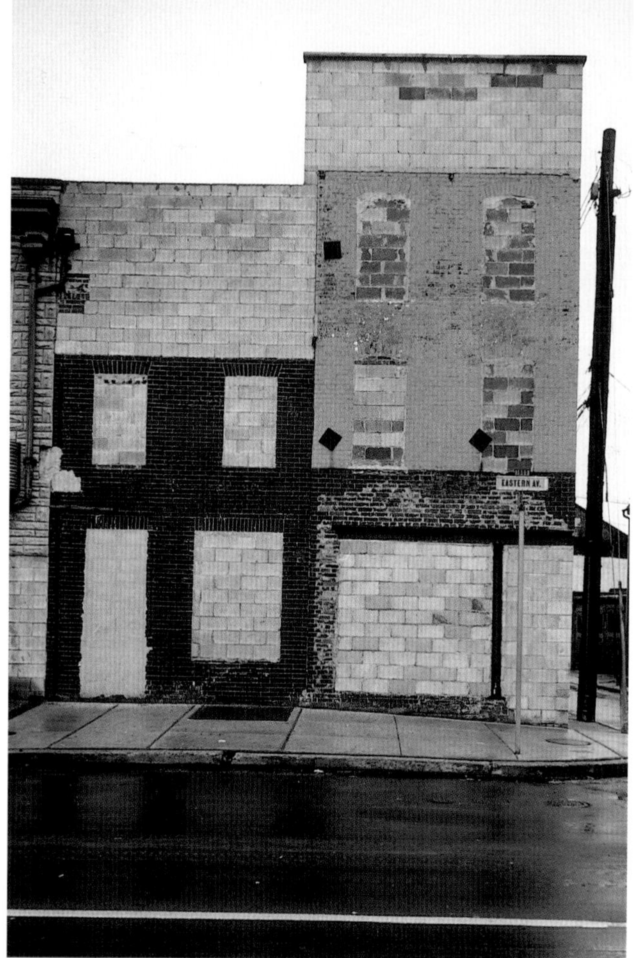
EASTERN AV.

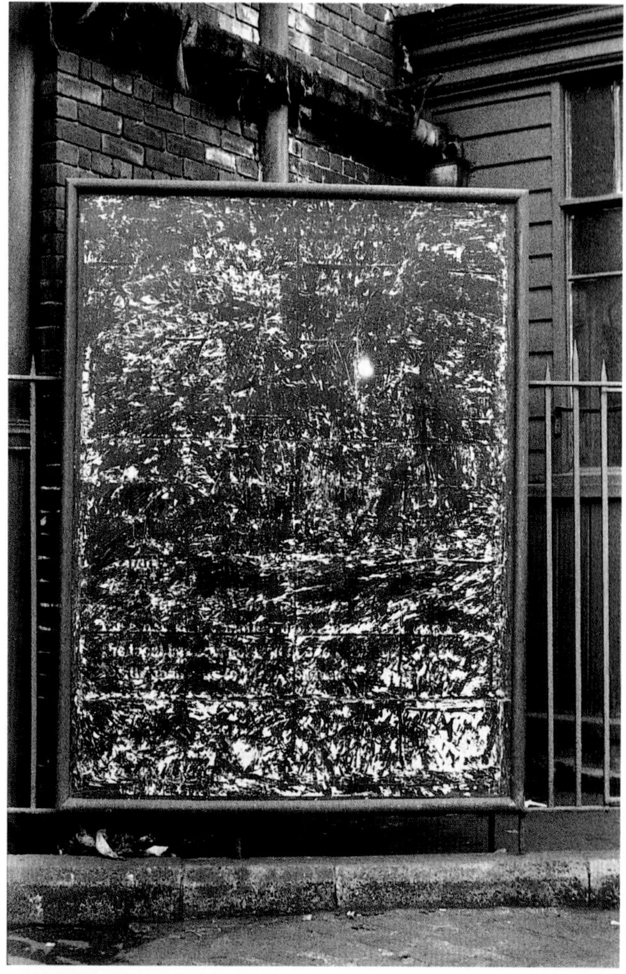

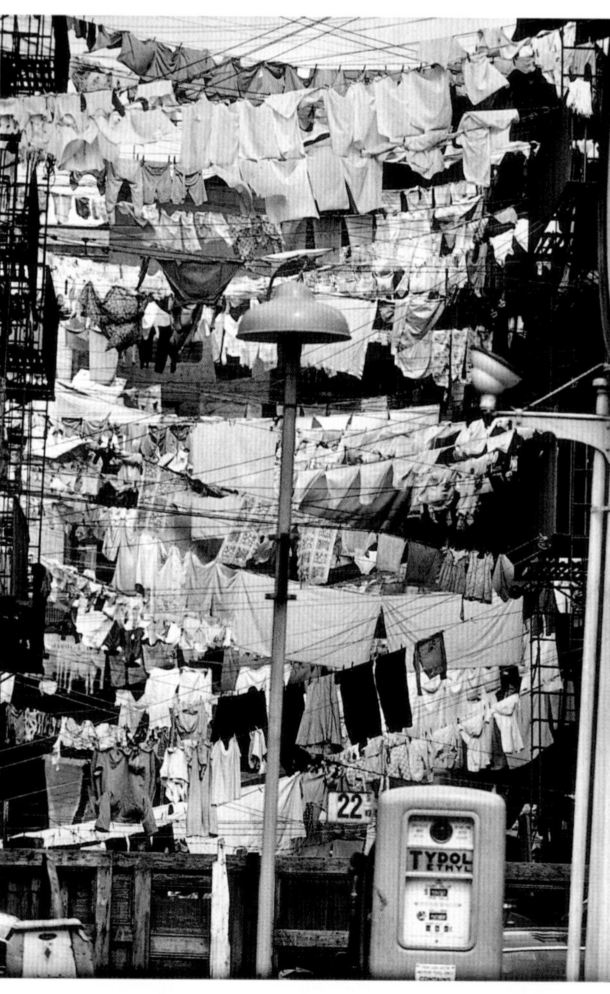
22
TYPOL
ETHYL

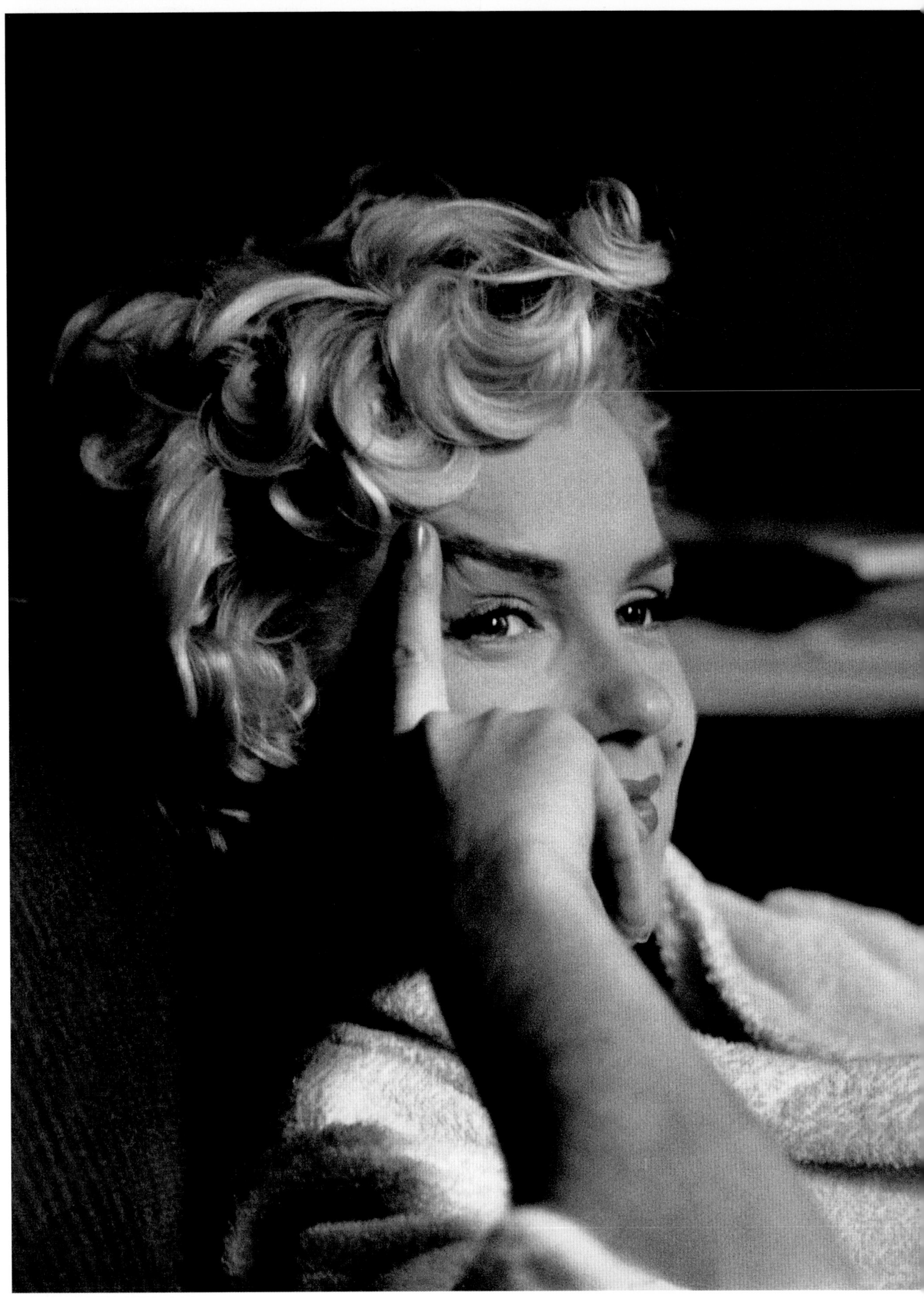

Marilyn Monroe, New York, 1956

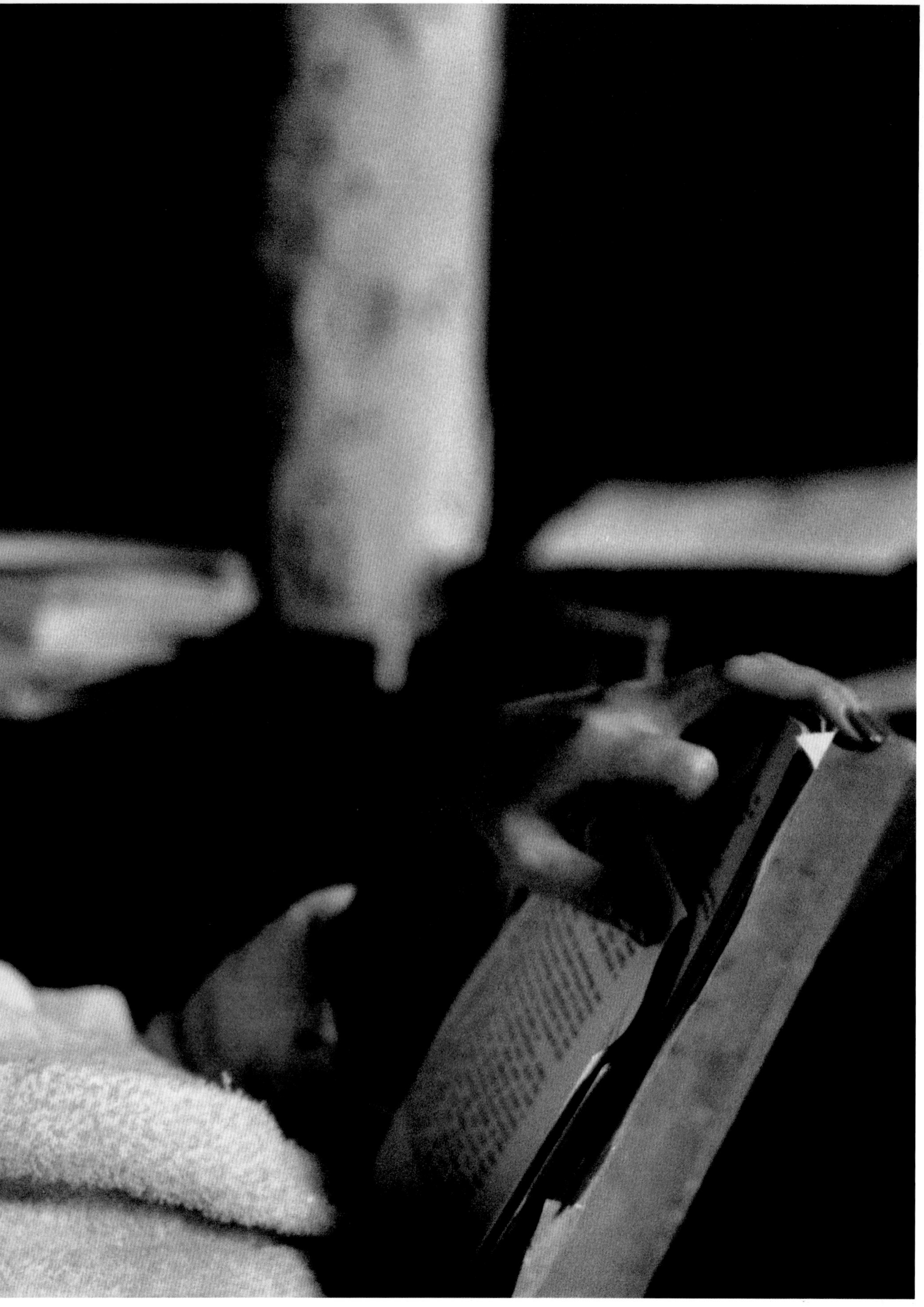

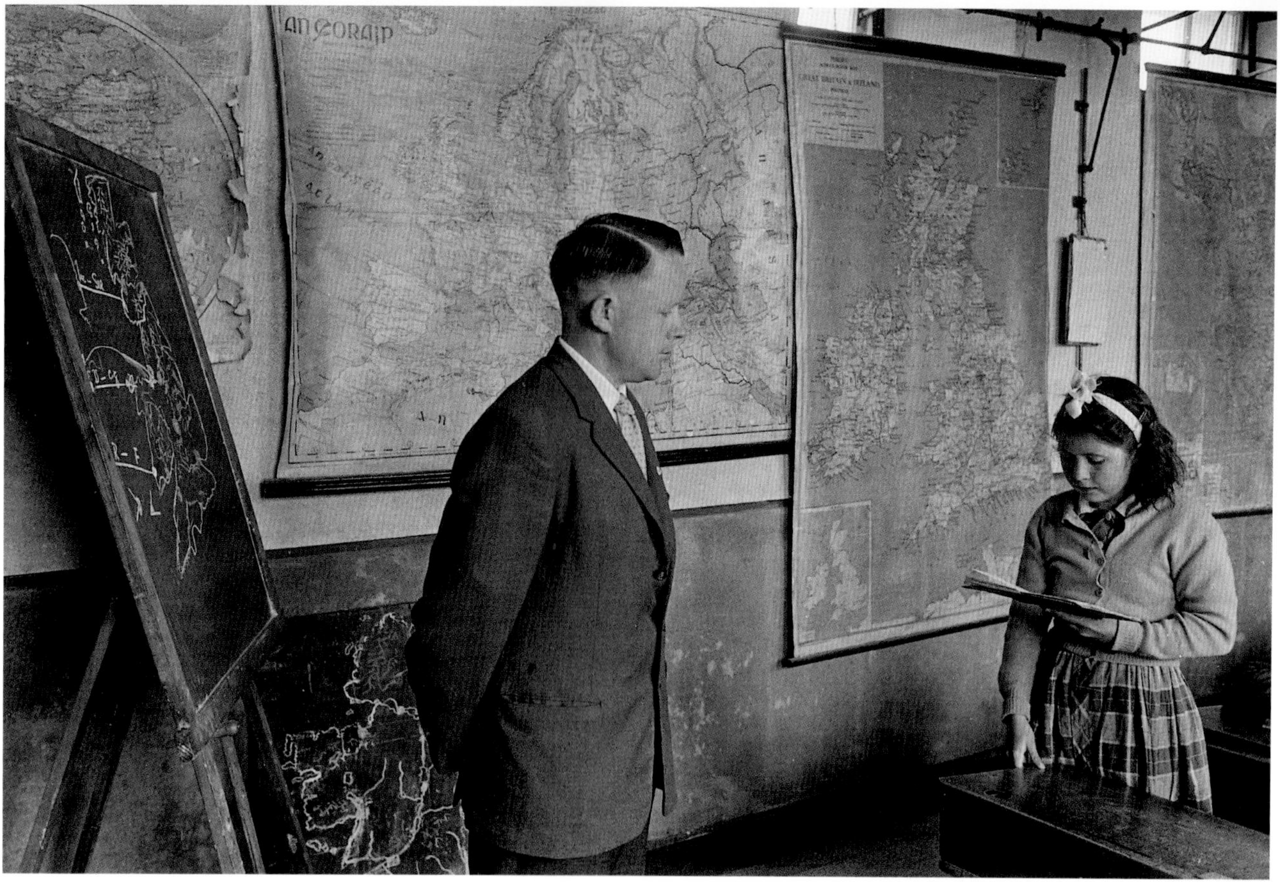

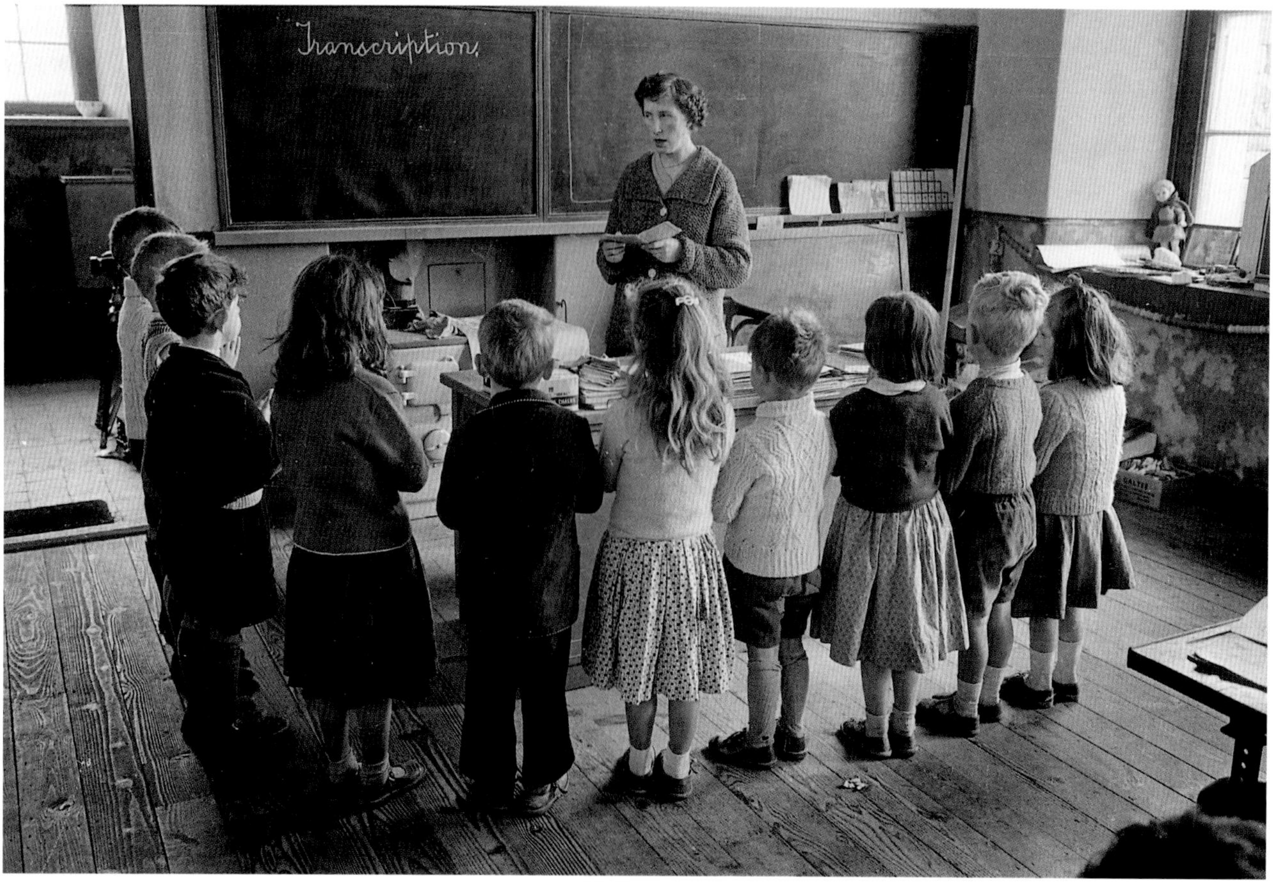

Aran Islands, Ireland, 1962 / Aran Islands, Ireland, 1962

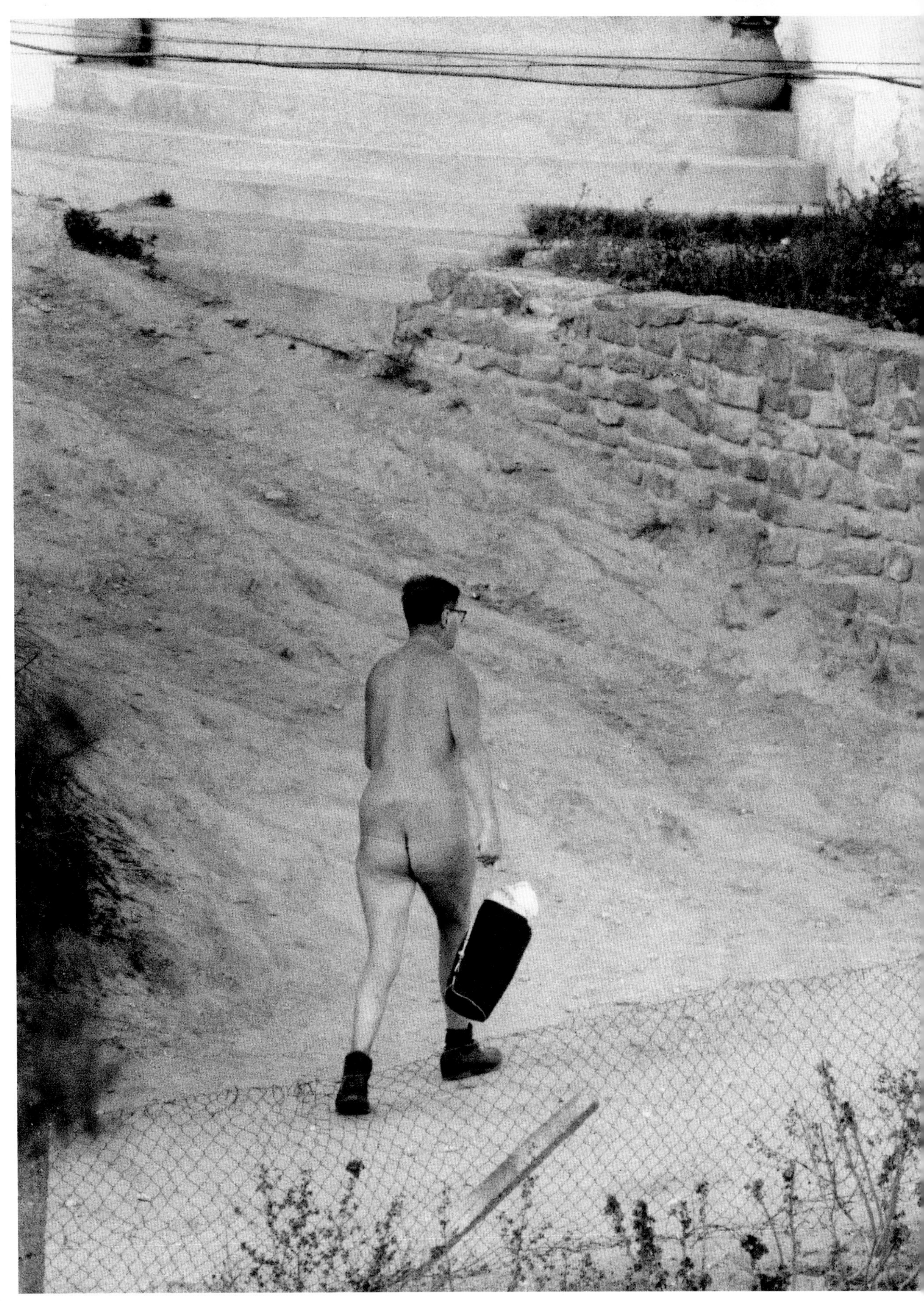

Ile du Levant, France, 1968

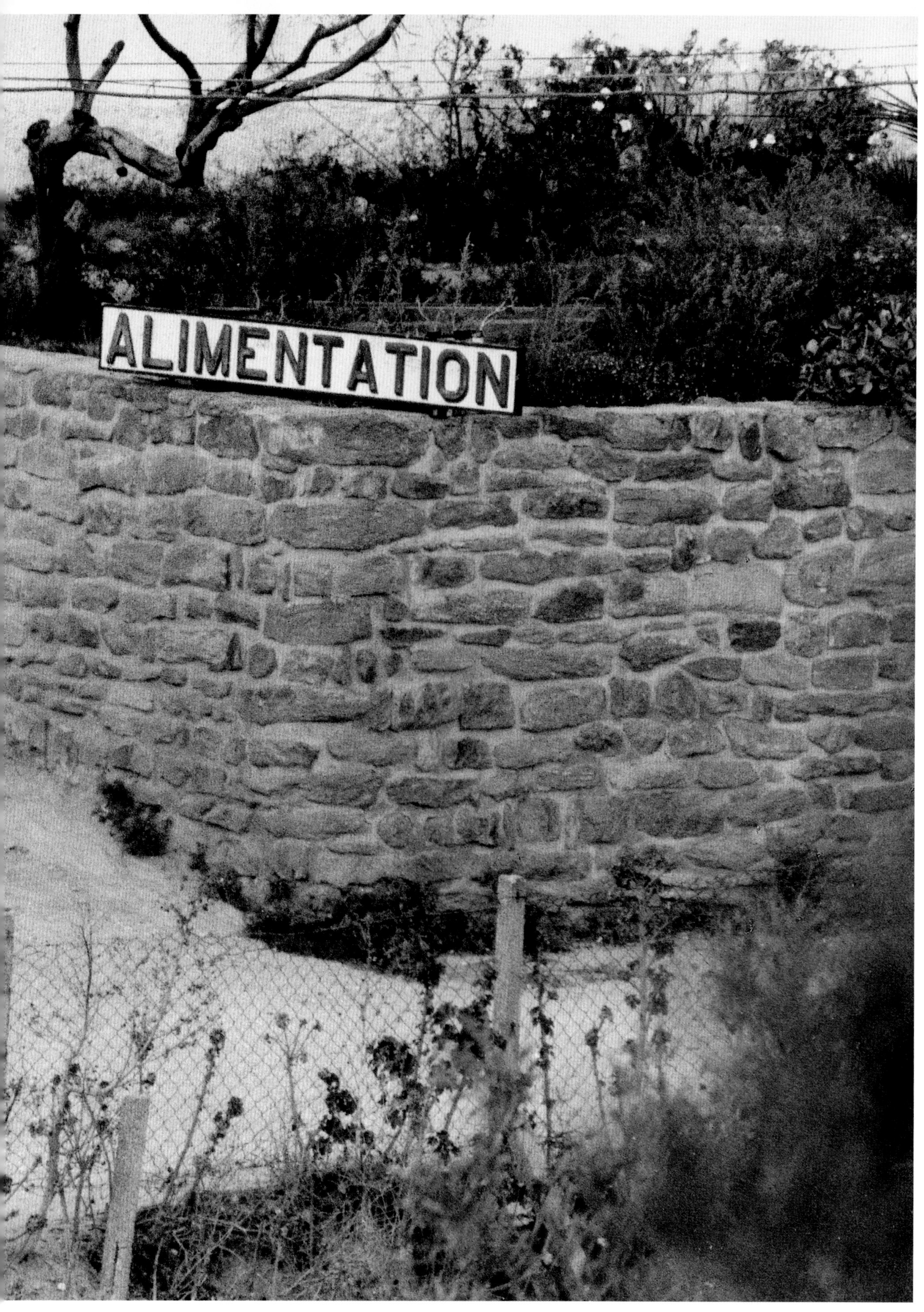

overleaf *Amsterdam, 1950s* / *Tulsa, Oklahoma, 1973*

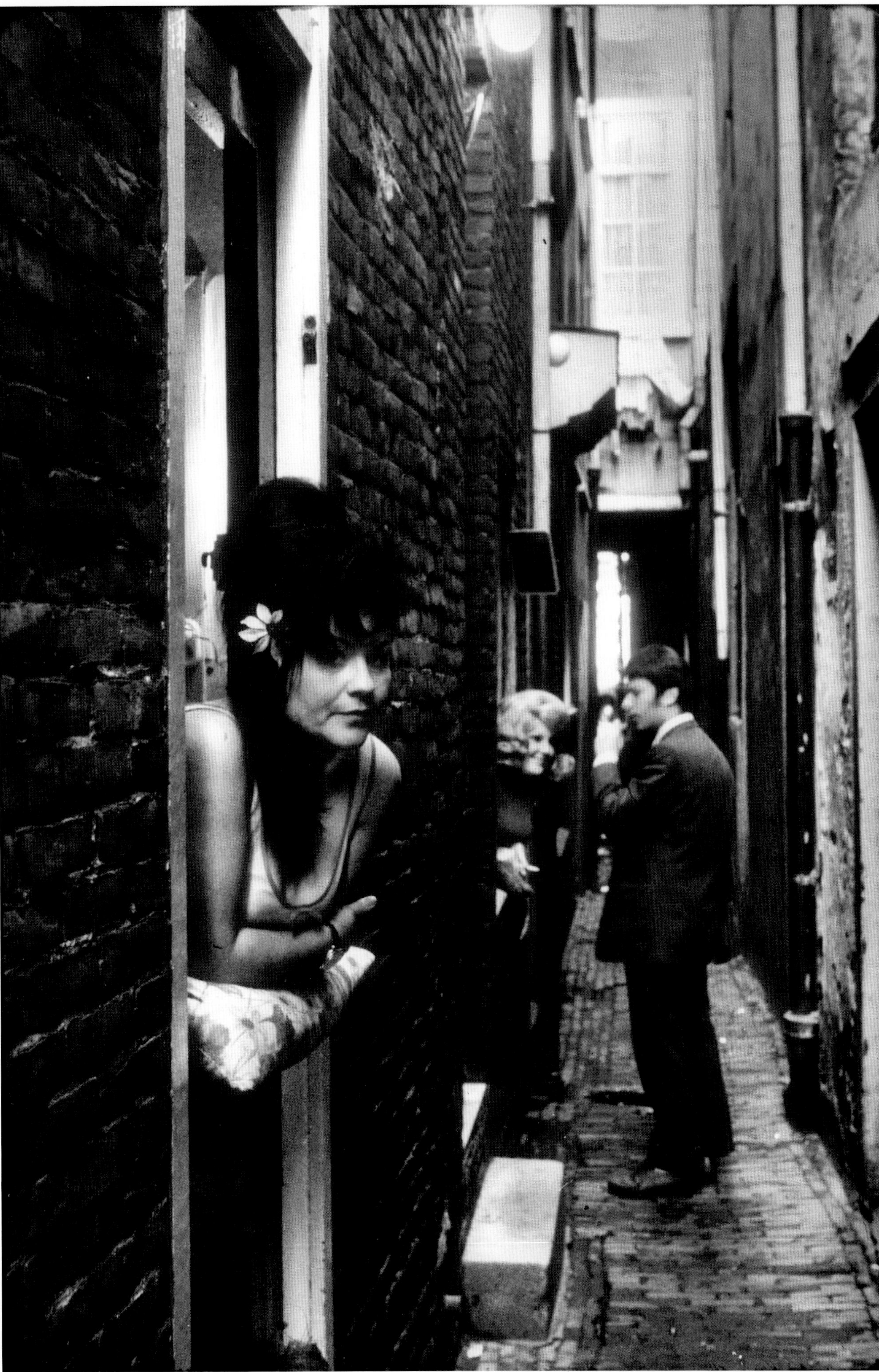

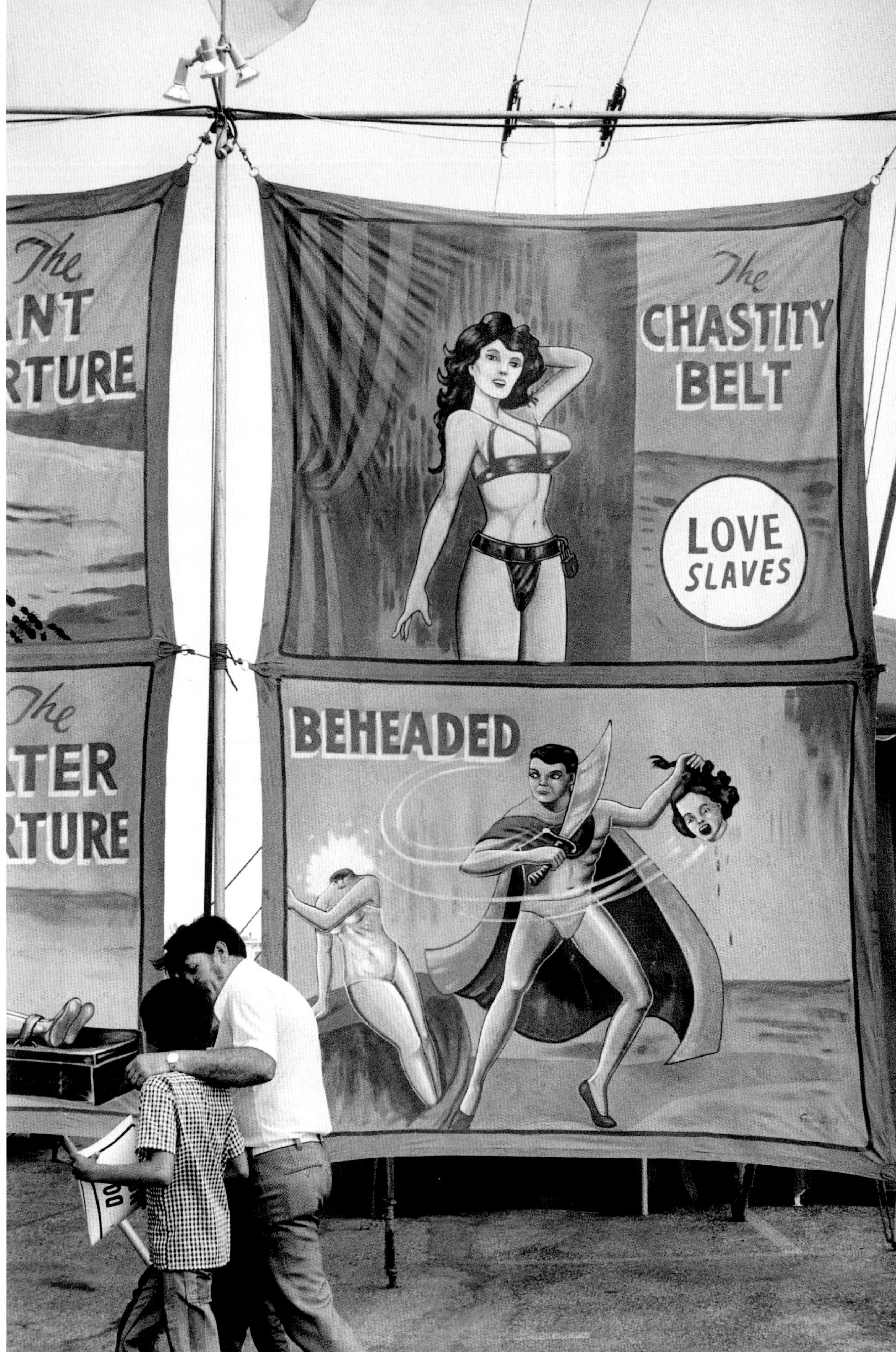
The
The
The
CHASTITY
BELT
LOVE
SLAVES
BEHEADED

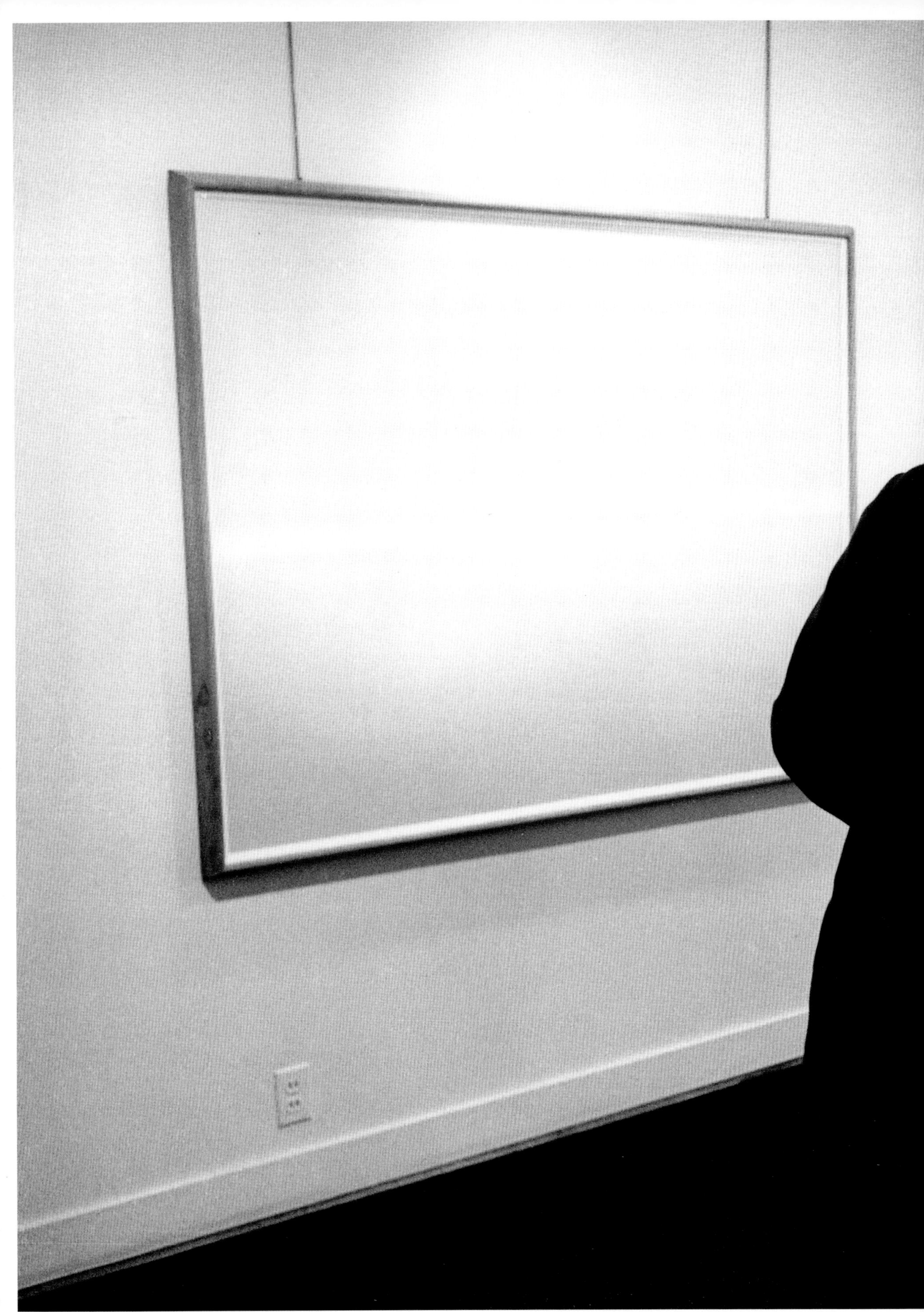

57th Street Gallery, New York, 1963

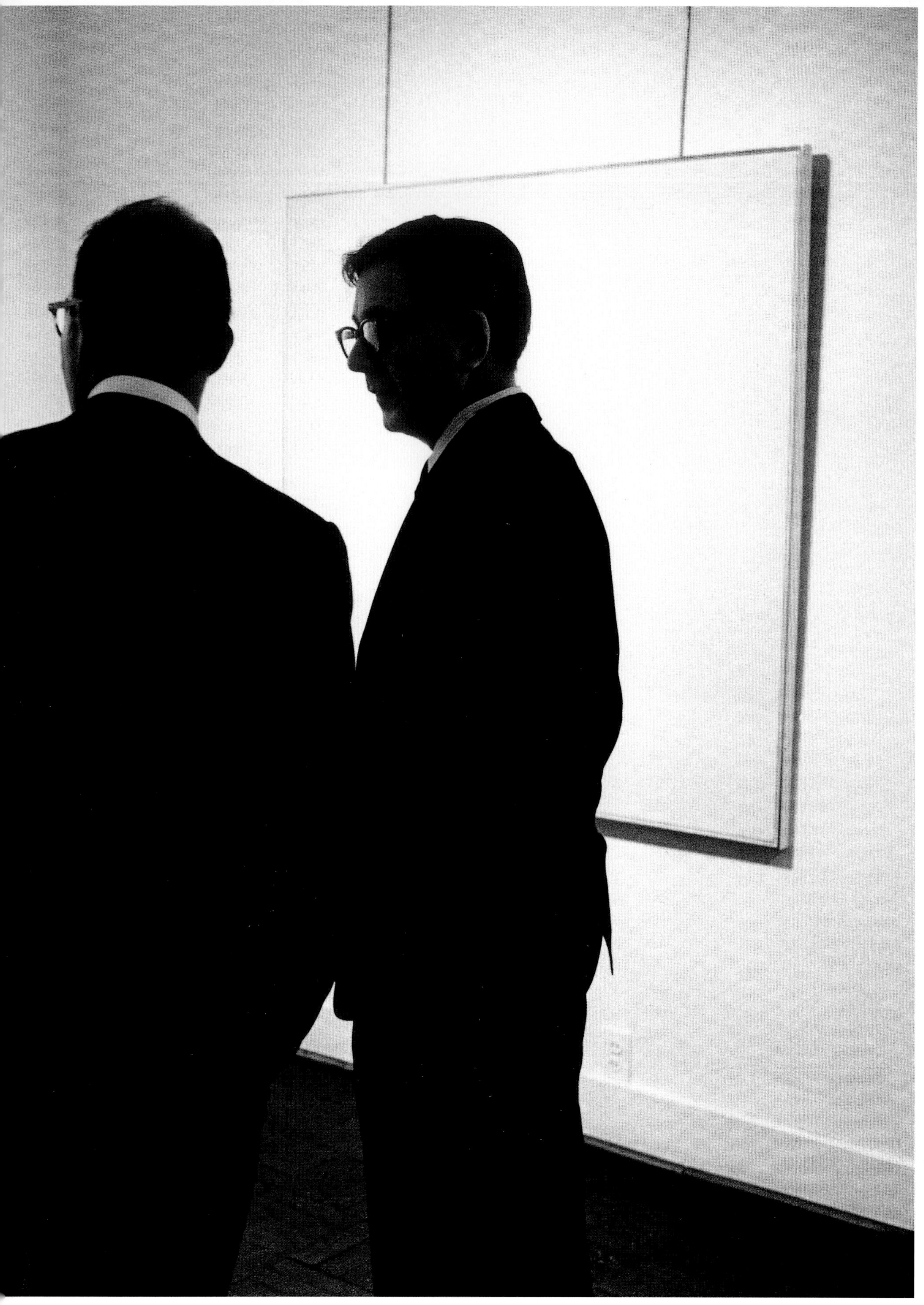

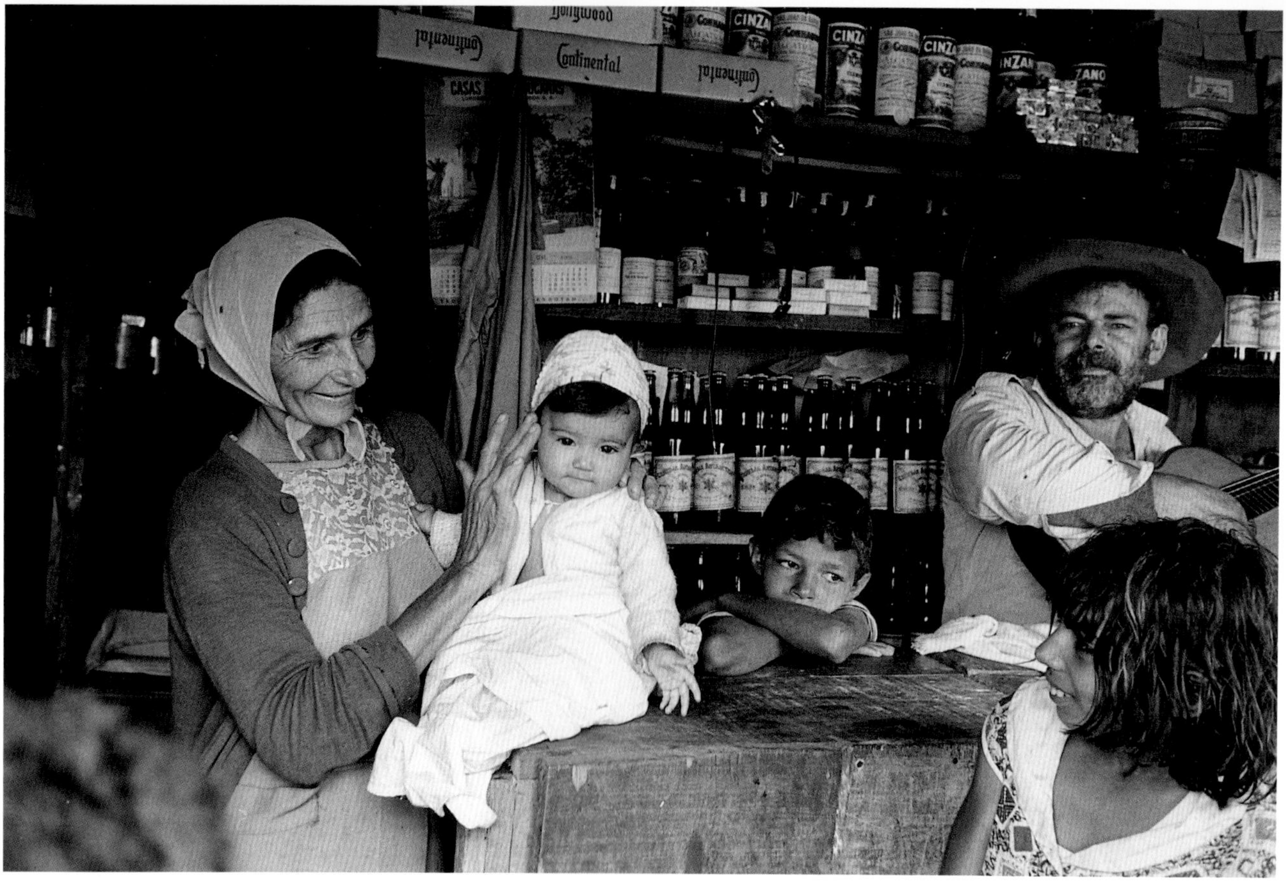

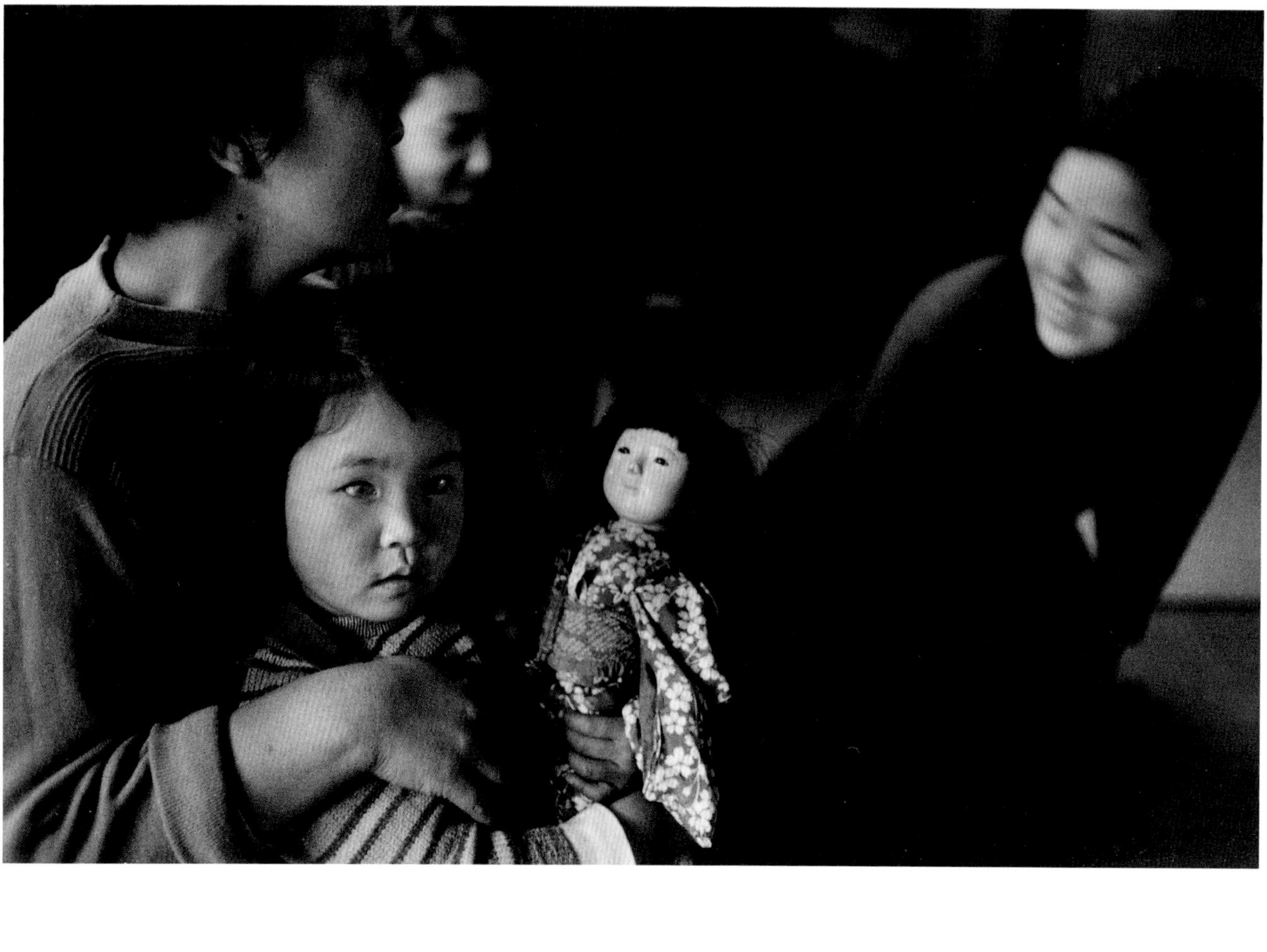

Brasília, Brazil, 1961 / *Hiroshima, 1958*

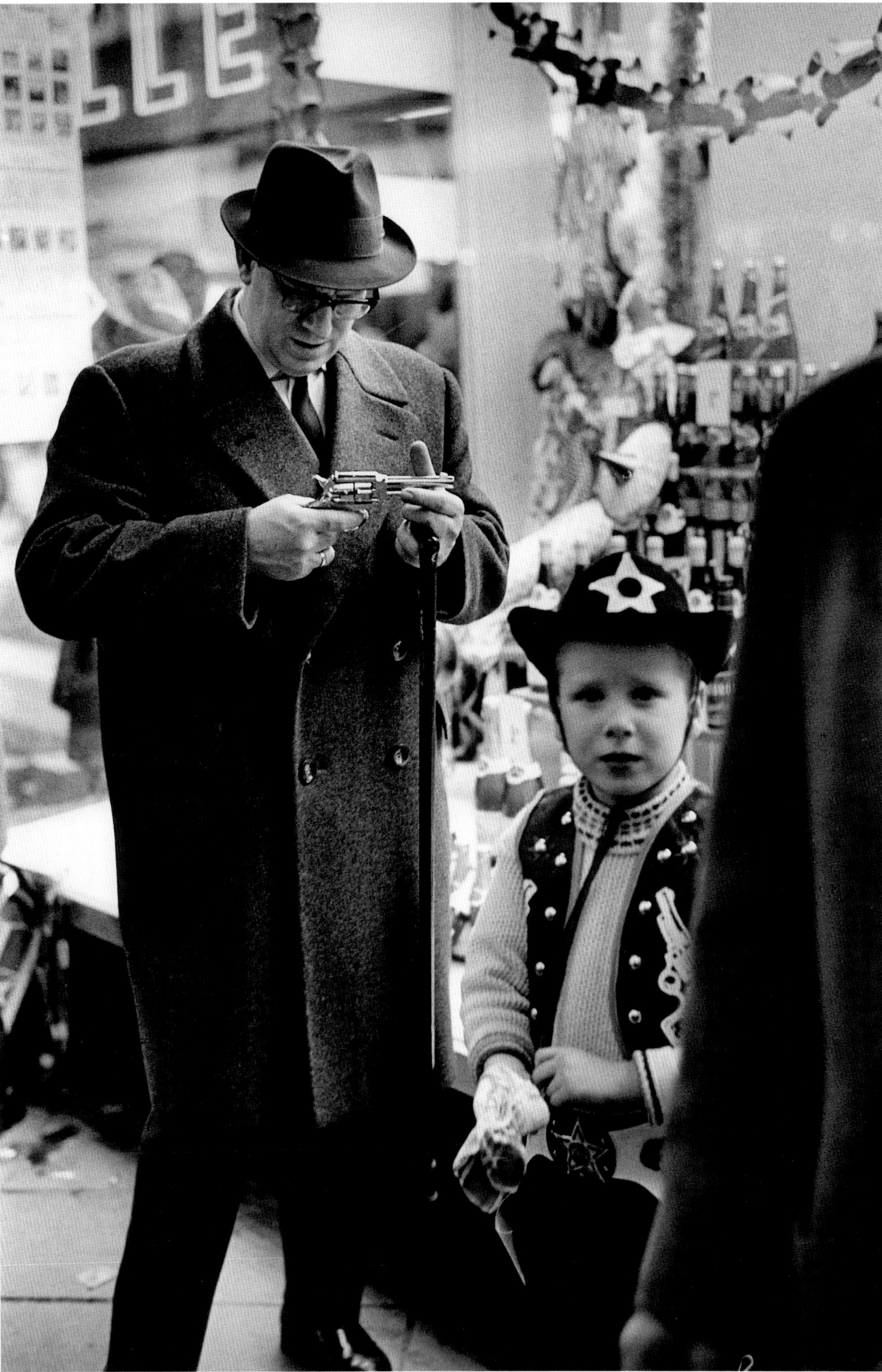

Cologne, Germany, 1967
overleaf *New York, c. 1949* / *New York, 1955*

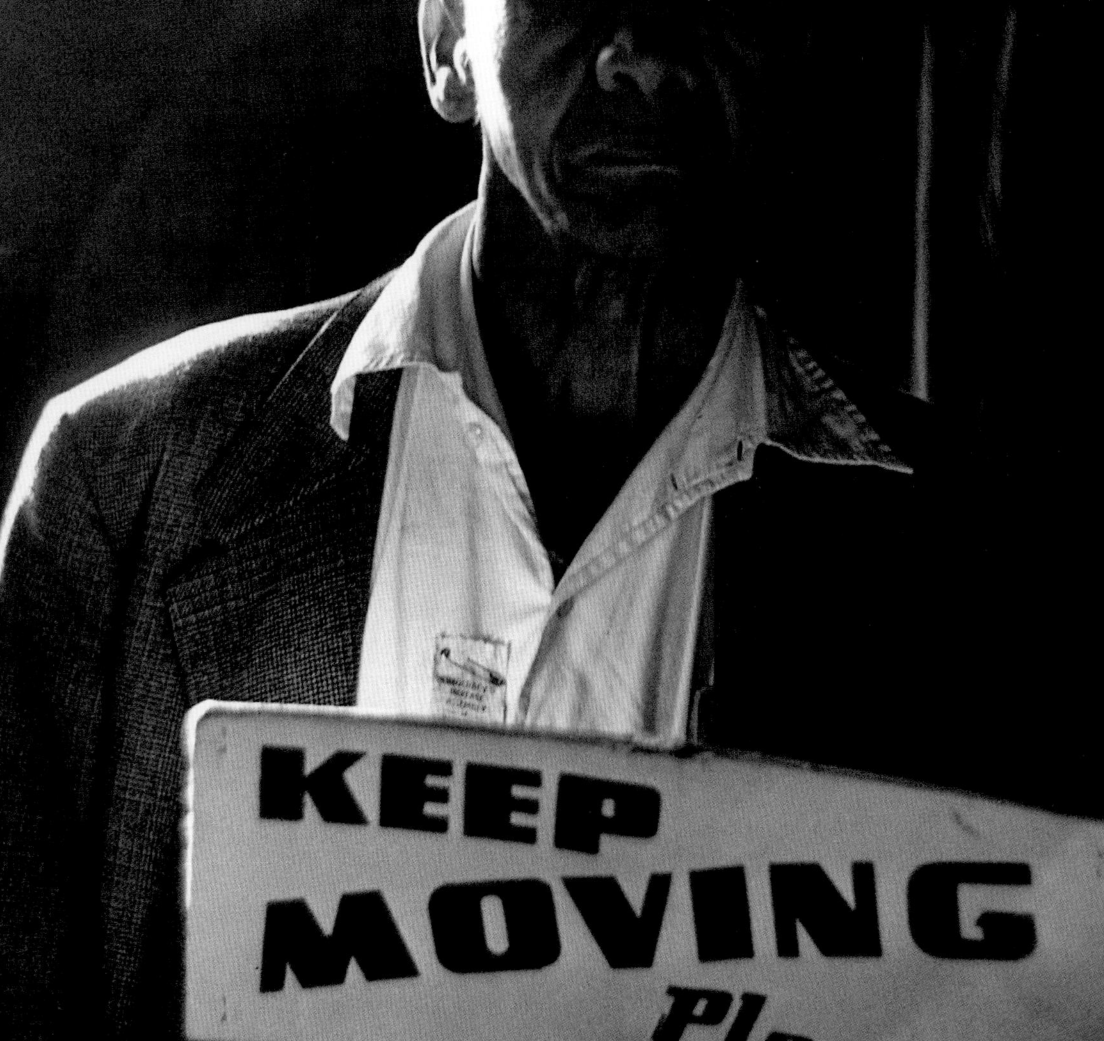
KEEP
MOVING
Please!

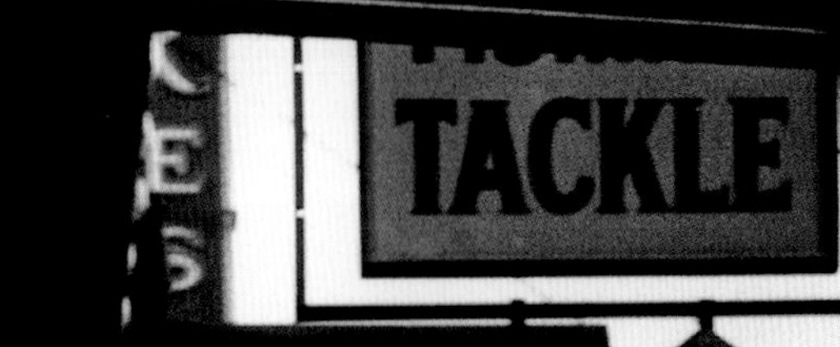
TACKLE
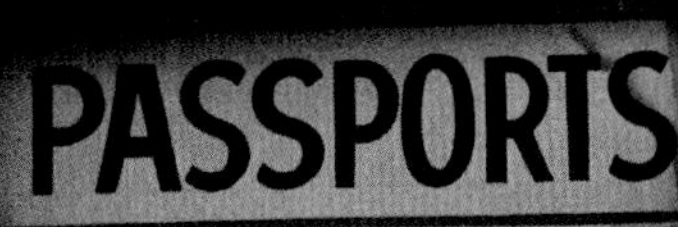
PASSPORTS
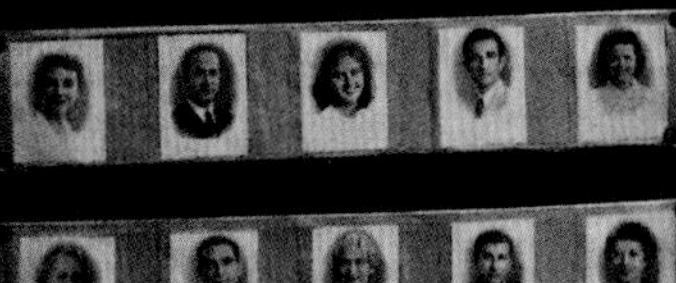

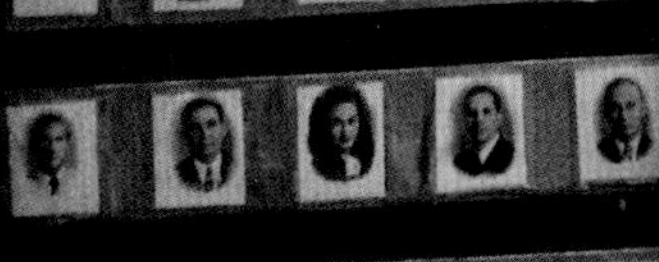
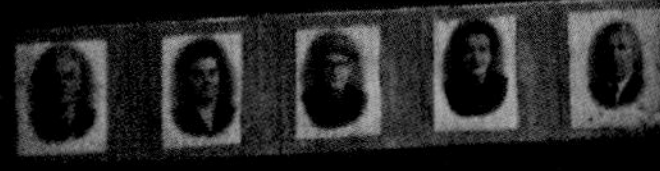

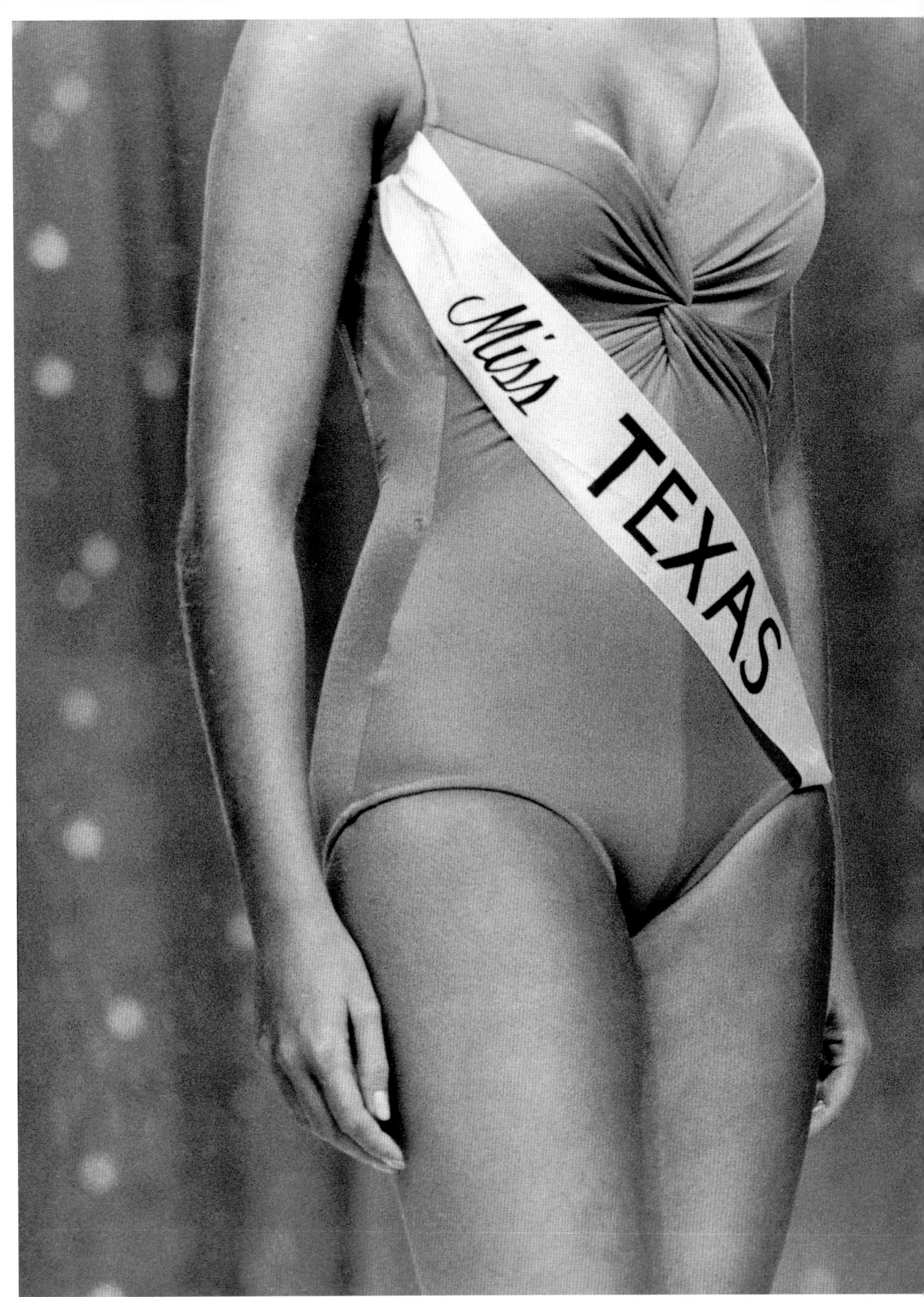

Atlantic City, New Jersey, 1974

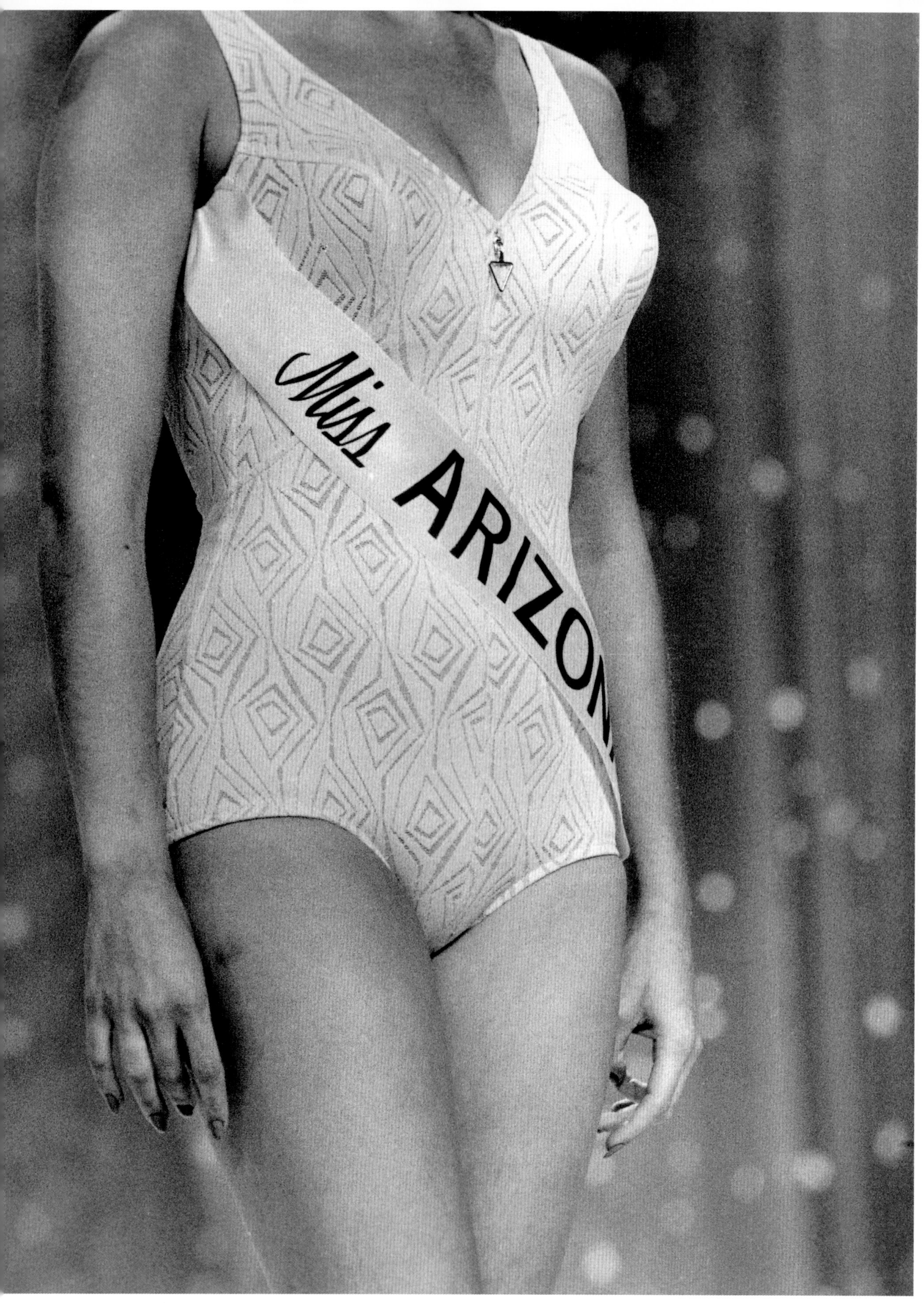

overleaf *Miami Beach, 1962* / *Times Square, New York, 1950*

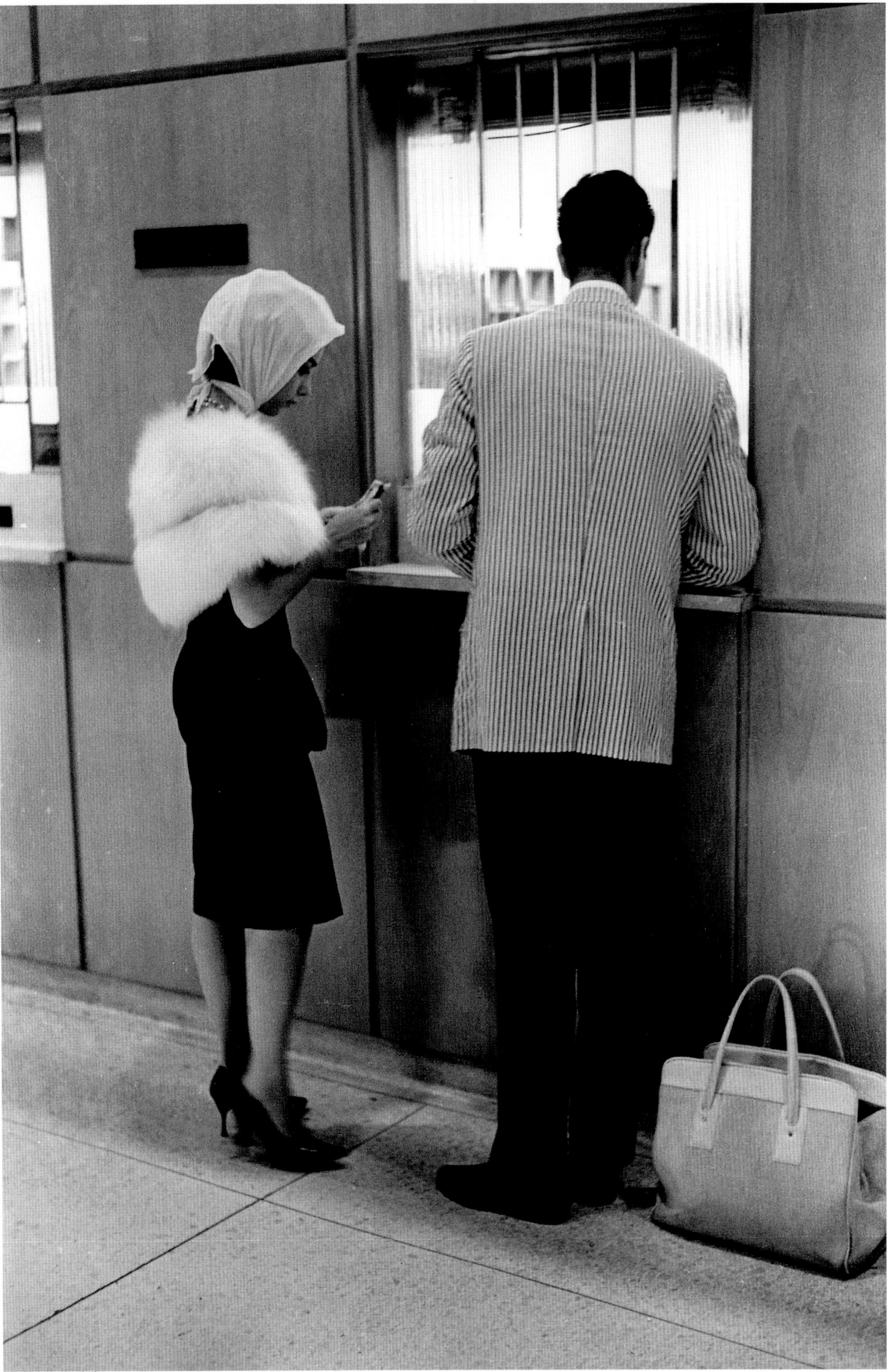

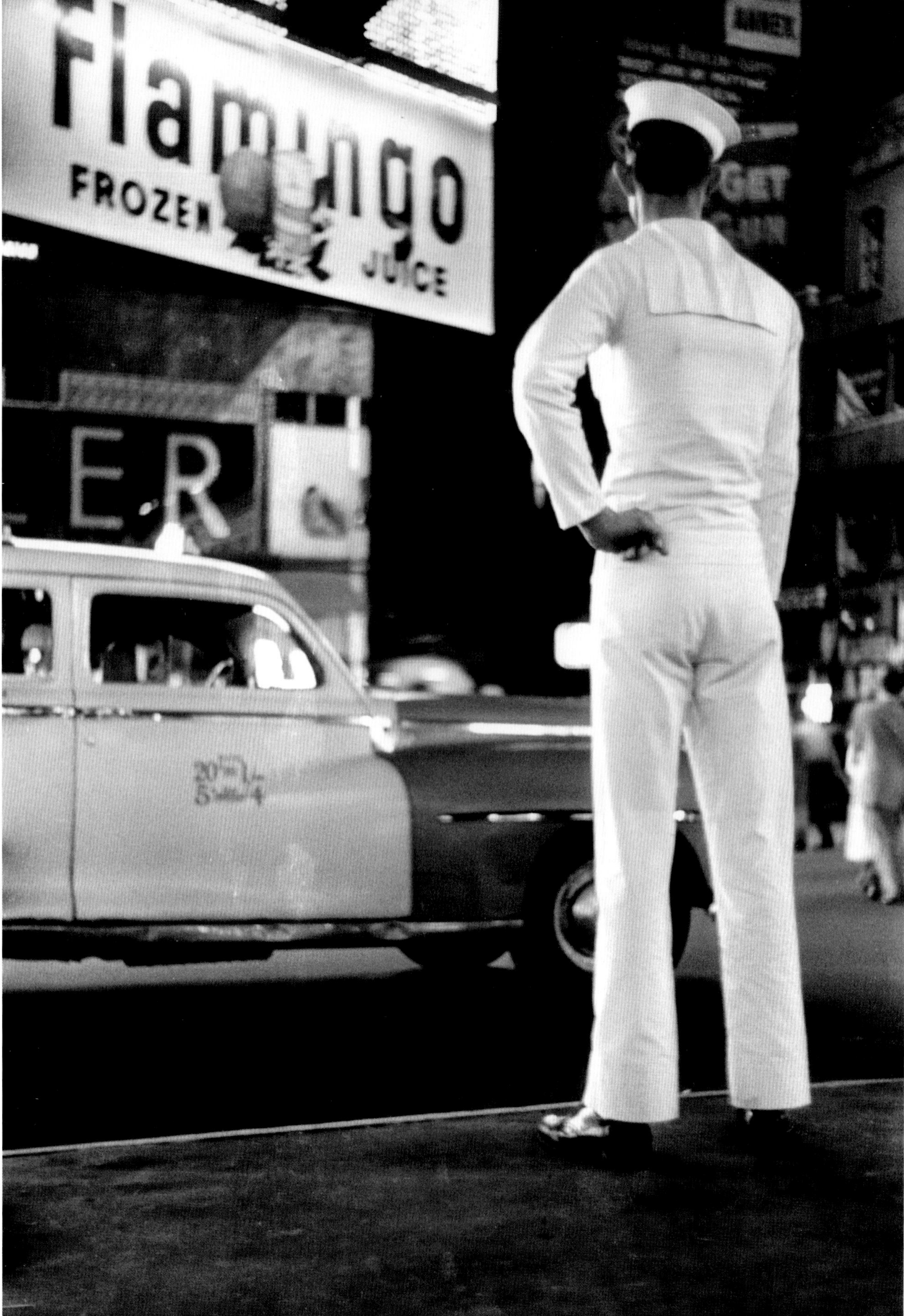
Flamingo
FROZEN
JUICE
ER

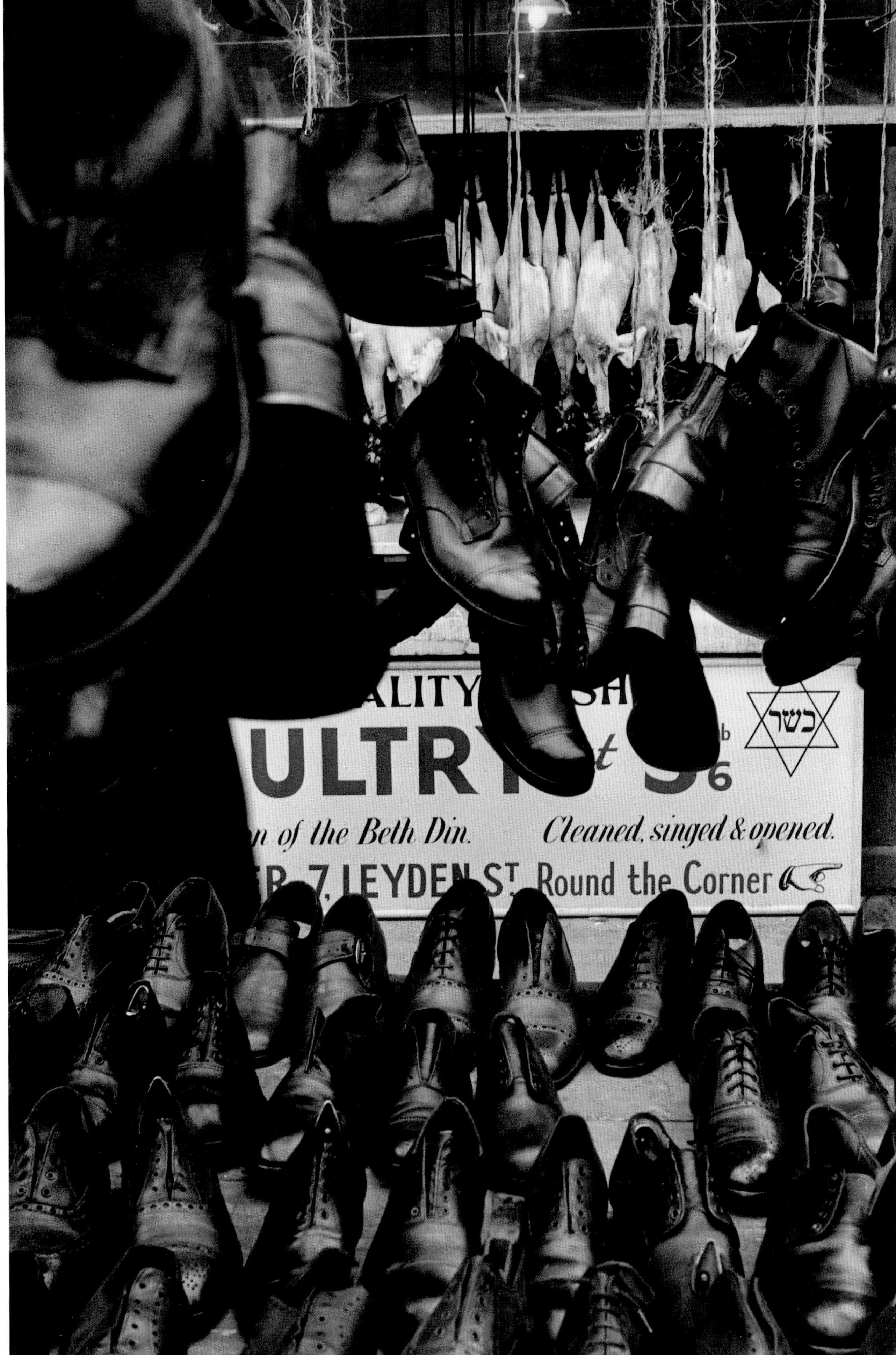

ALITY
SH
ULTRY
6
כשר
n of the Beth Din.
Cleaned, singed & opened.
7, LEYDEN ST
Round the Corner

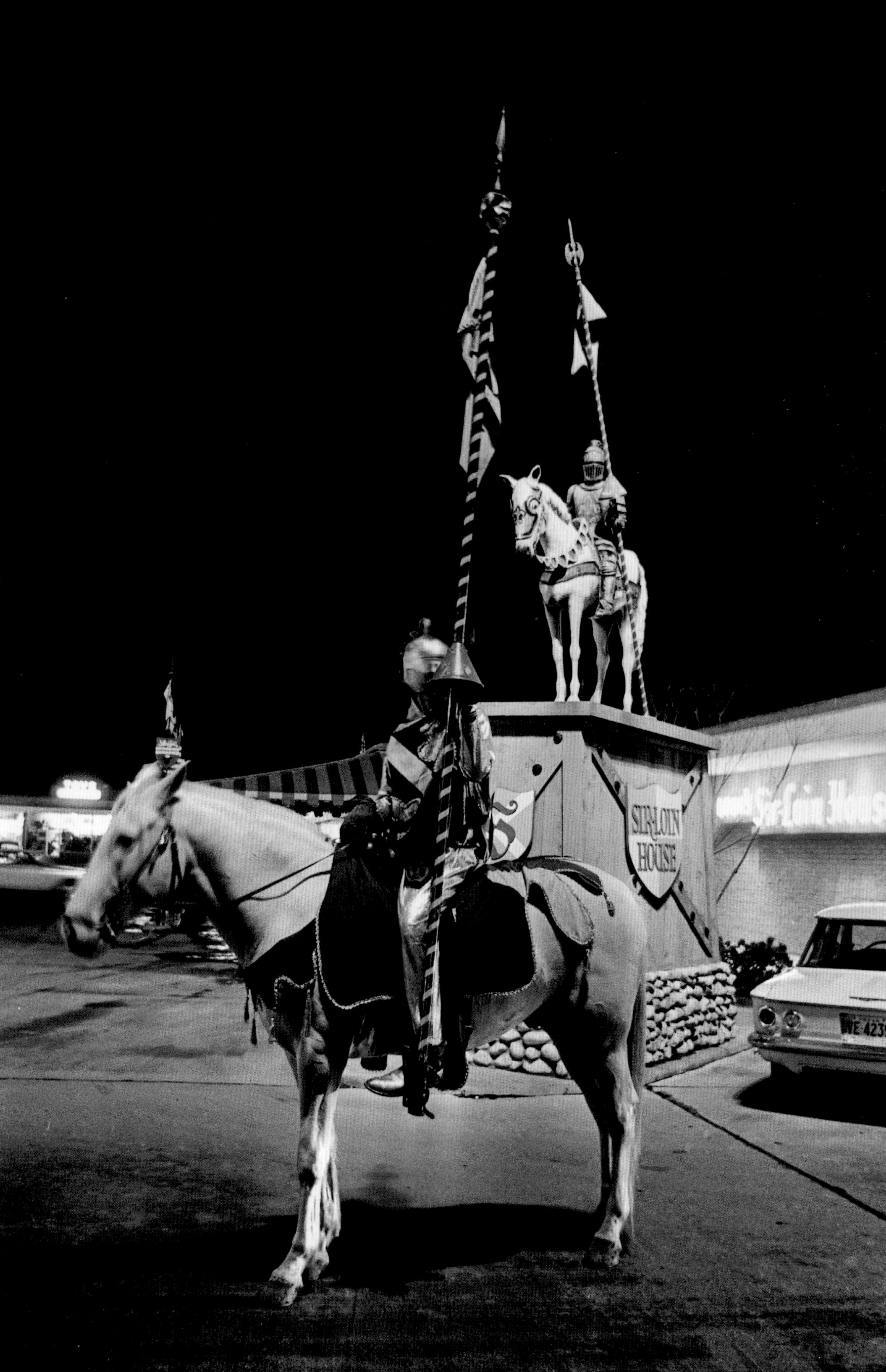
SIR-LOIN
HOUSE

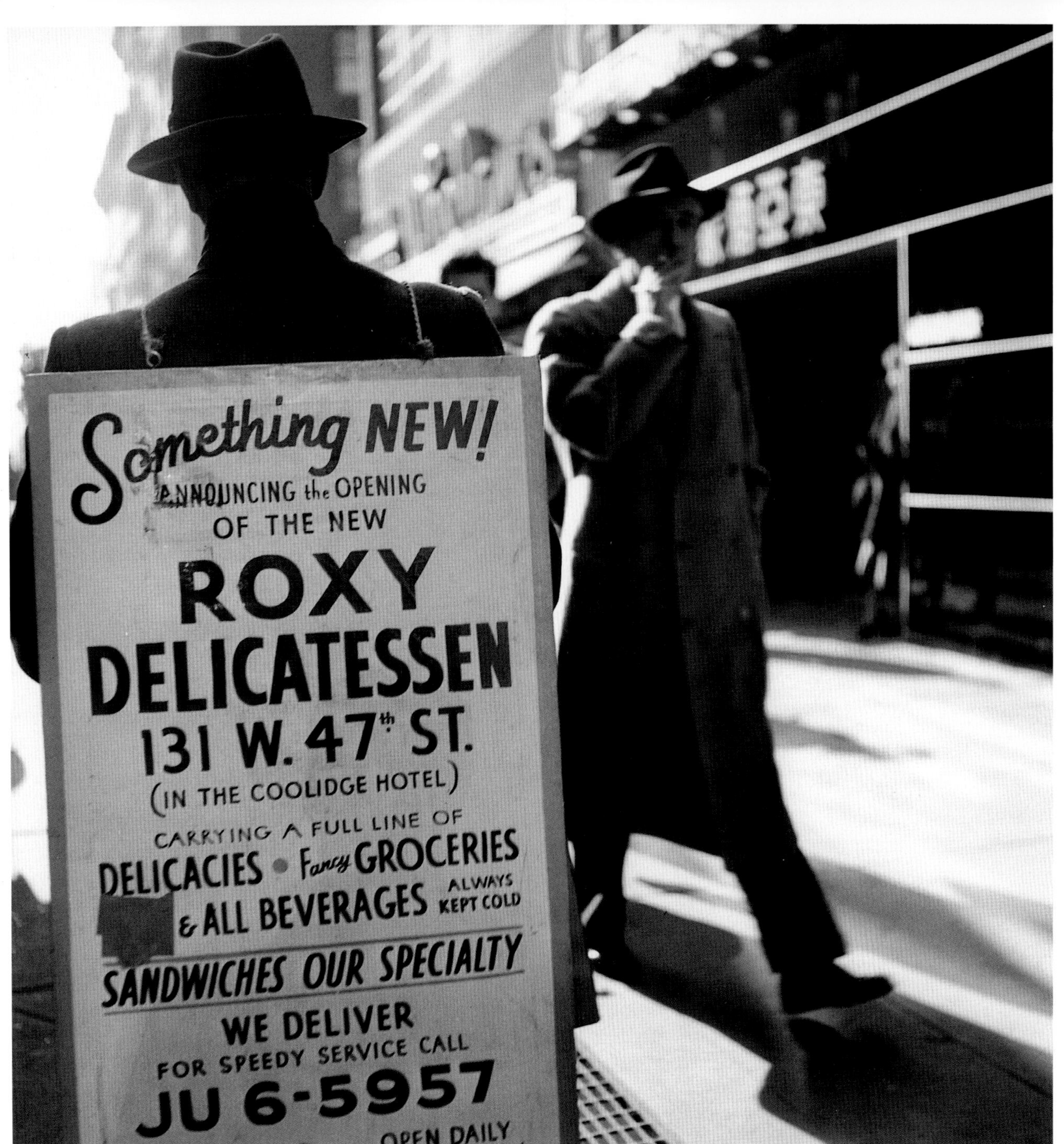

previous page *London, 1951* / *Dallas, 1963*
New York, 1948

Le Soir
et par Correspondance
LUCIEN RIMELS
BACCALAUREATS . EXAMENS DE PASSAGE
Le Soir
par Correspondance
SPORTS
DES BOMBES ATOMIQUES EN EUROPE ?
BRADLEY
l'Humanité
1949
Paris
THEATRE DE LA HUCHETTE
PYLADE
GROS CHAGRINS
UNE DEMANDE EN MARIAGE
AVIS
à la
POPULATION
et TOUTES à 15 heures
du 14 Juillet
CANCAN DE TABARIN
APPRENEZ à
DANSER
PASCAUD
60, RUE ST-ANTOINE
APPRENEZ à
DANSER
PASCAUD
60, RUE ST-ANTOINE

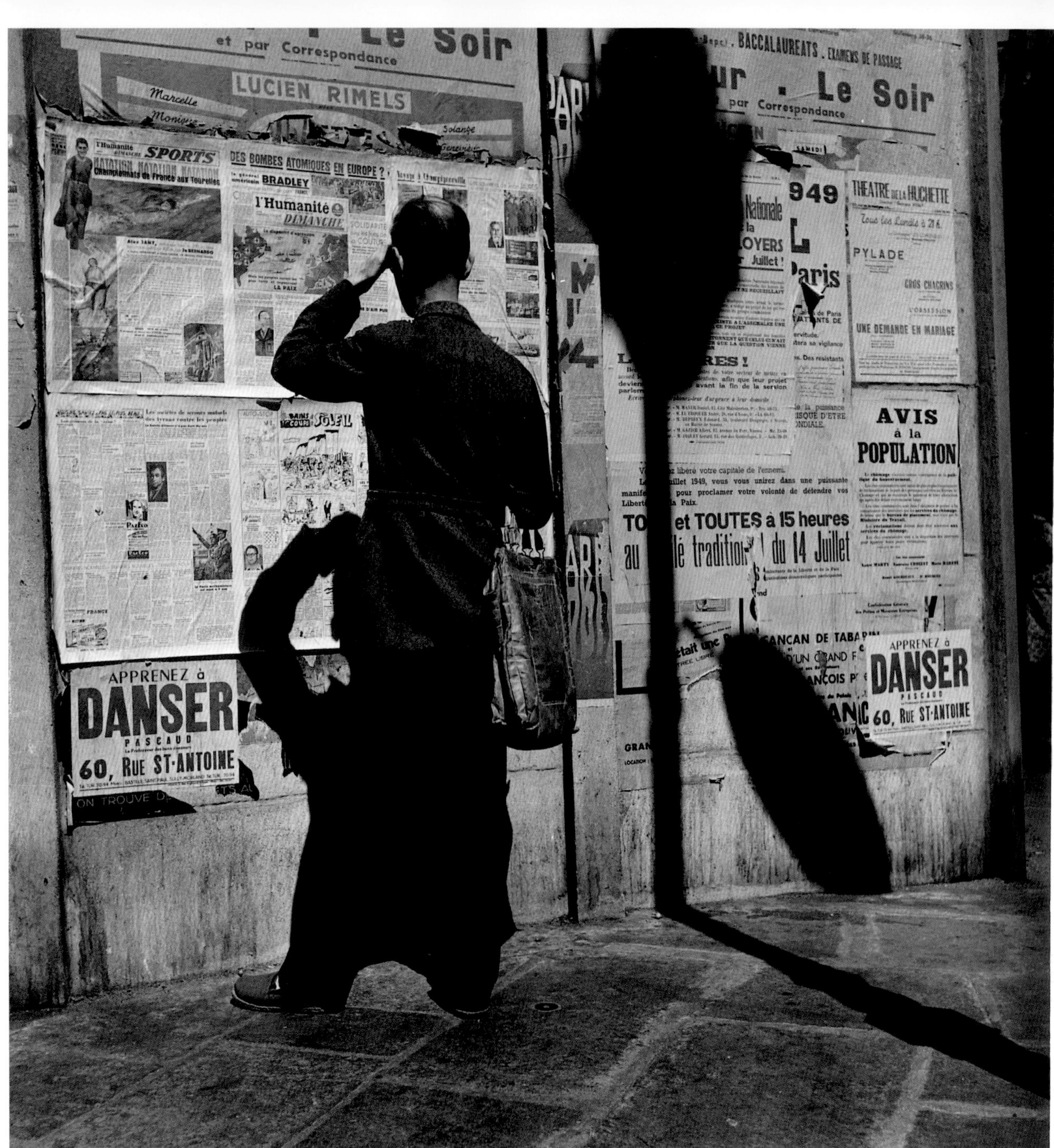

Paris, 1949

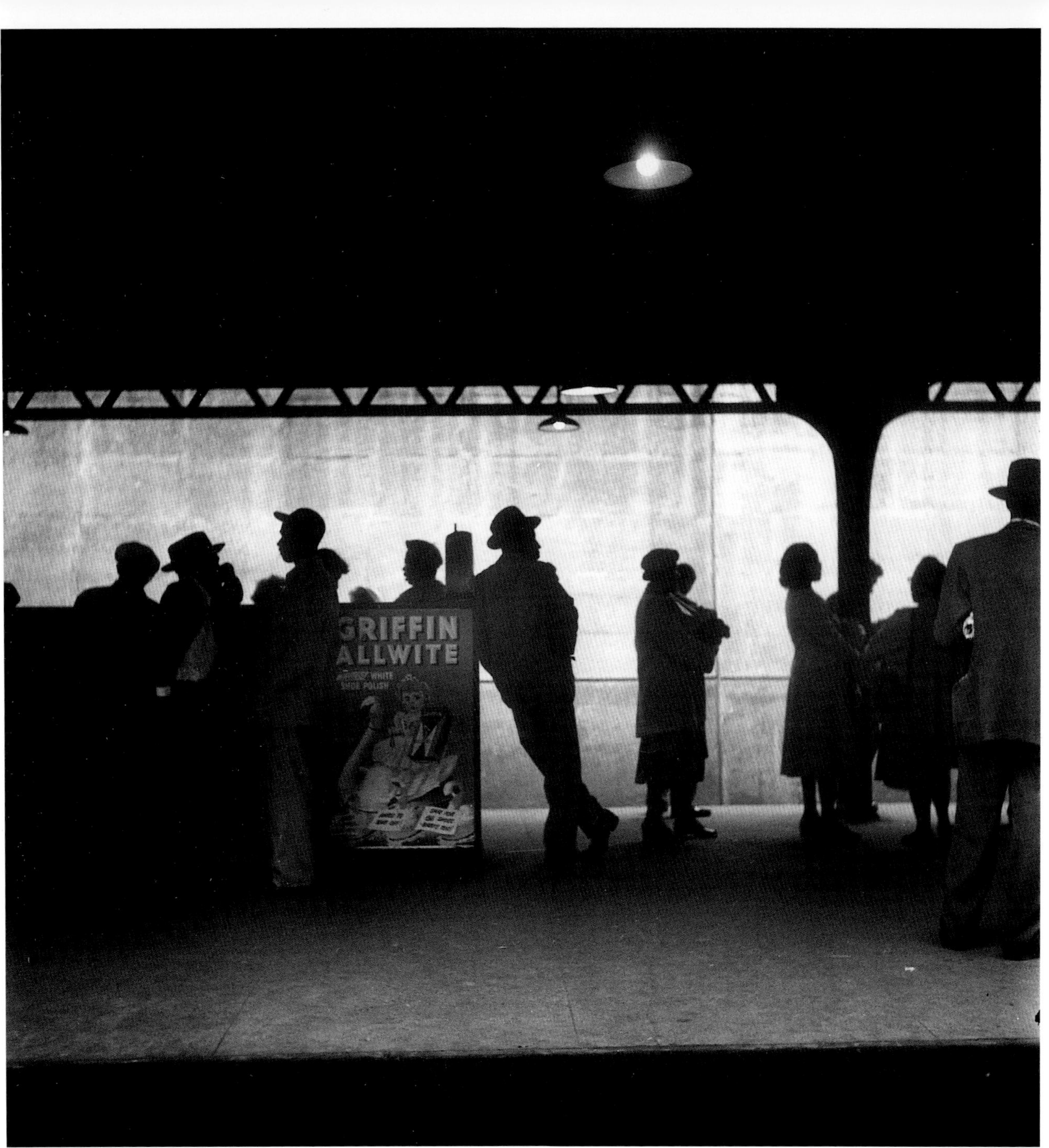

New York, 1948

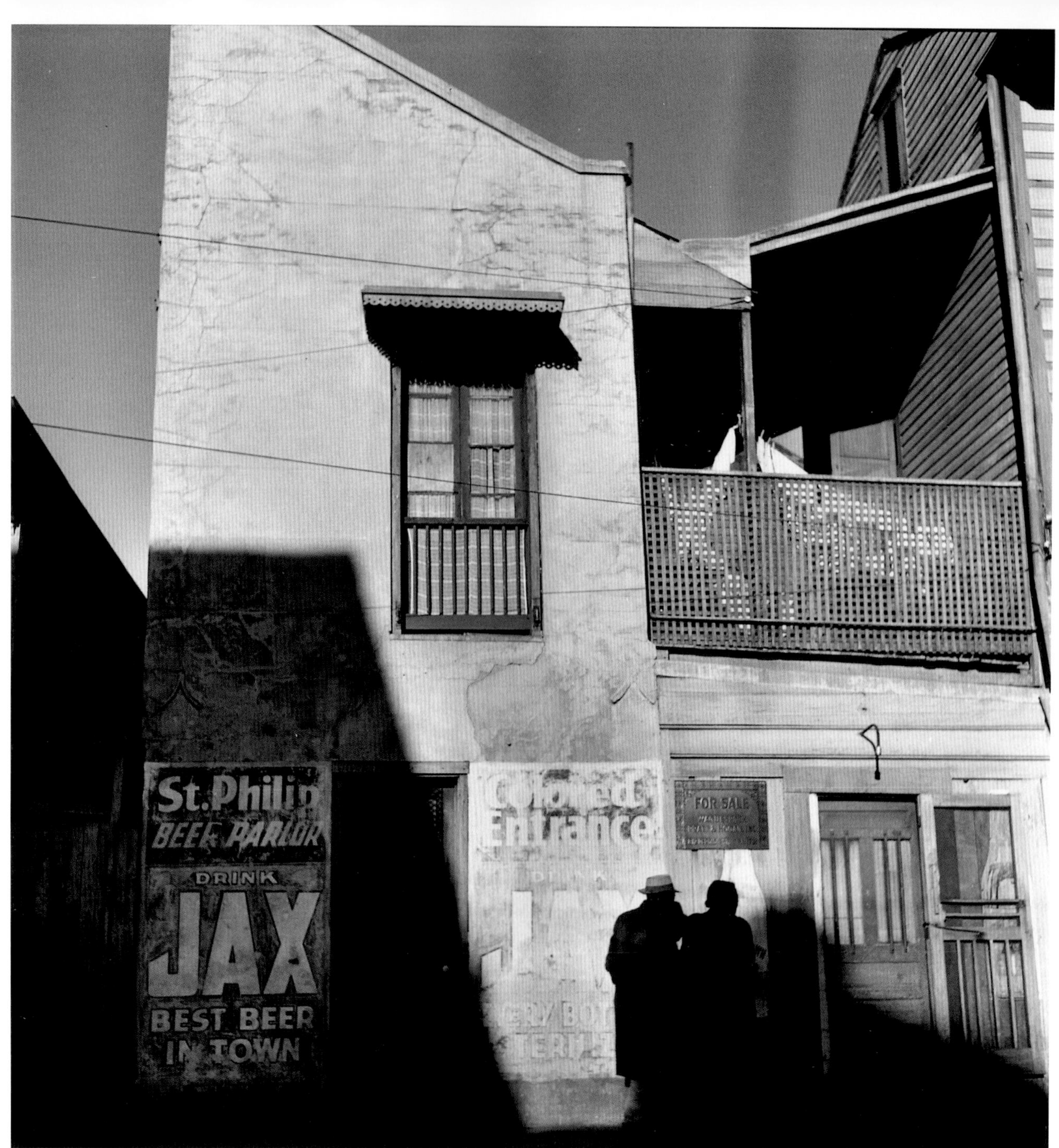

New Orleans, 1949

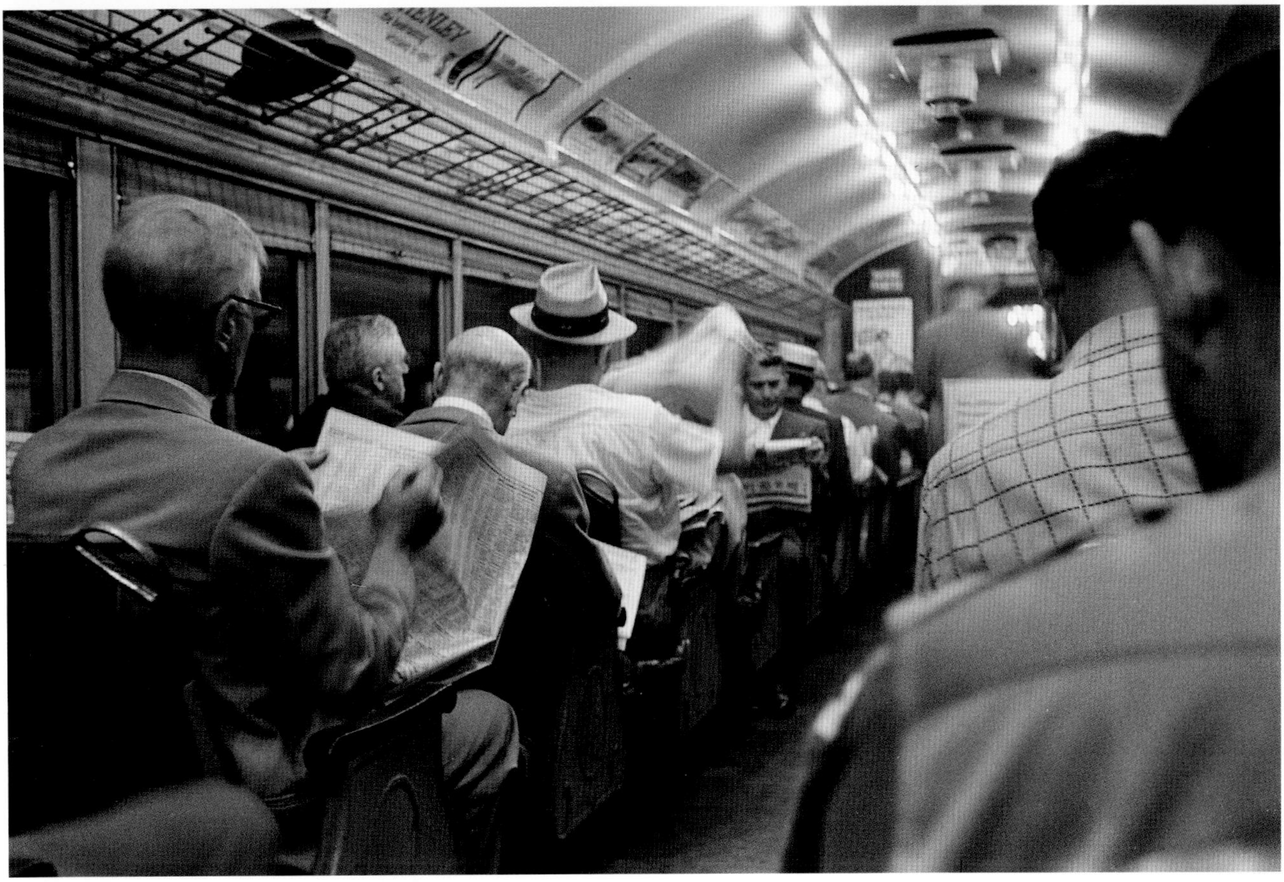

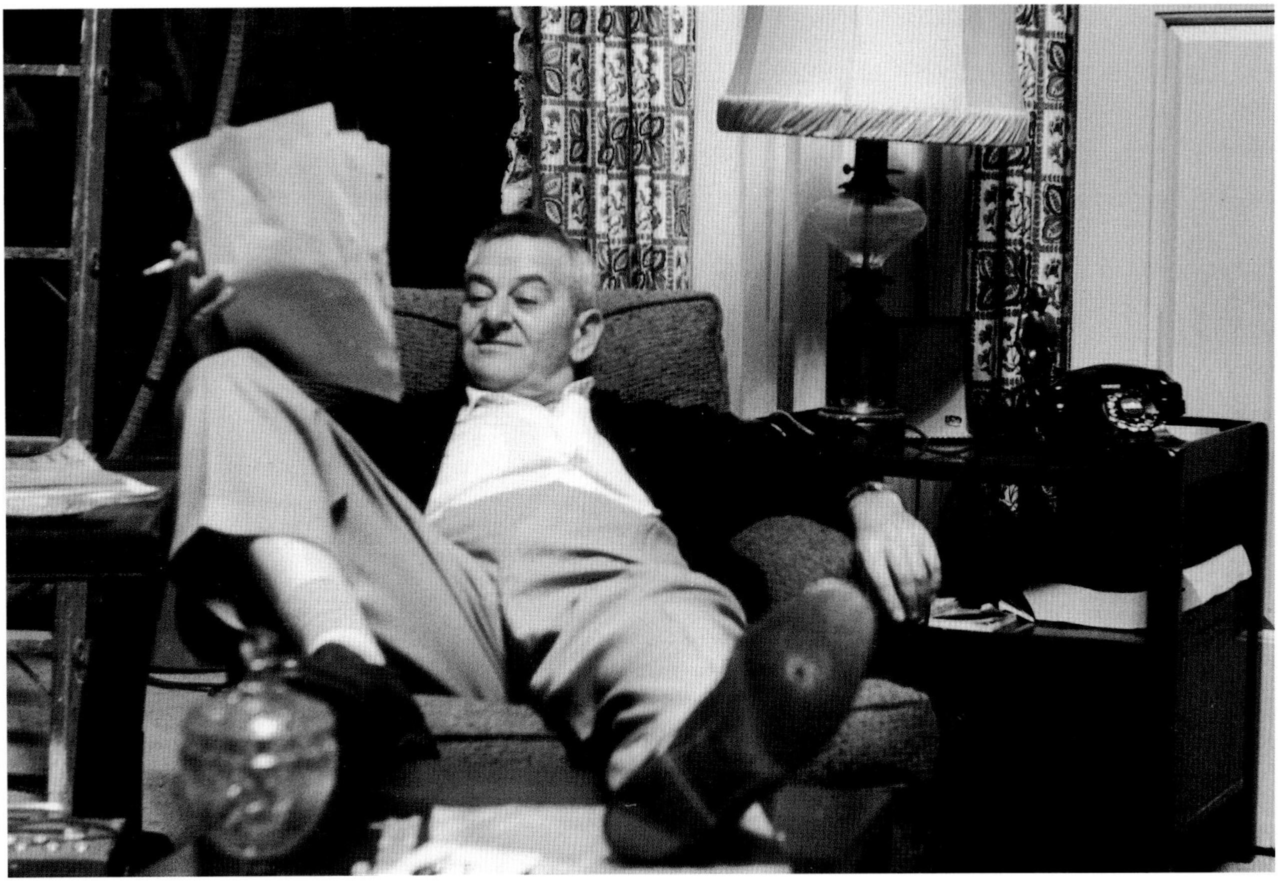

New York, 1955 / *William Wyler, Hollywood, 1956*

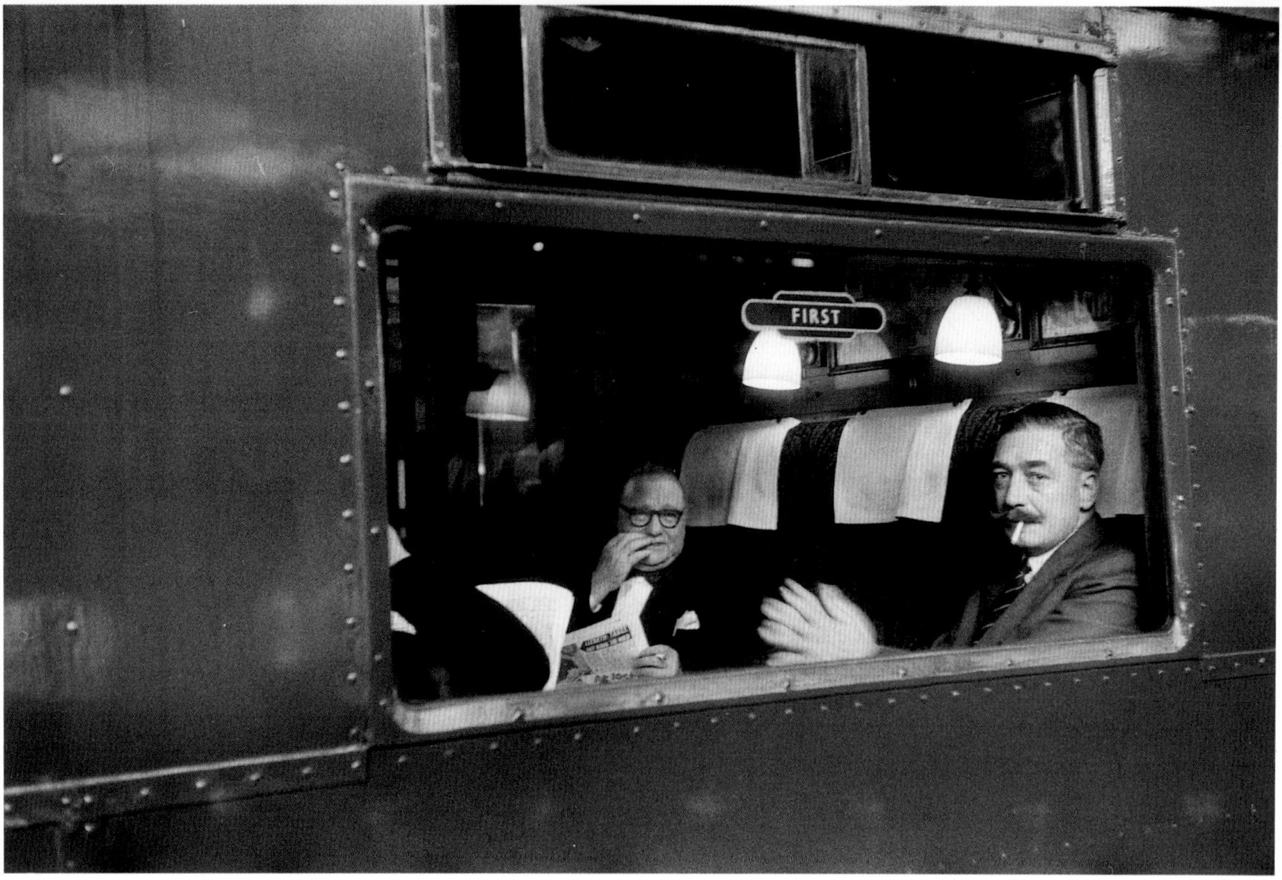

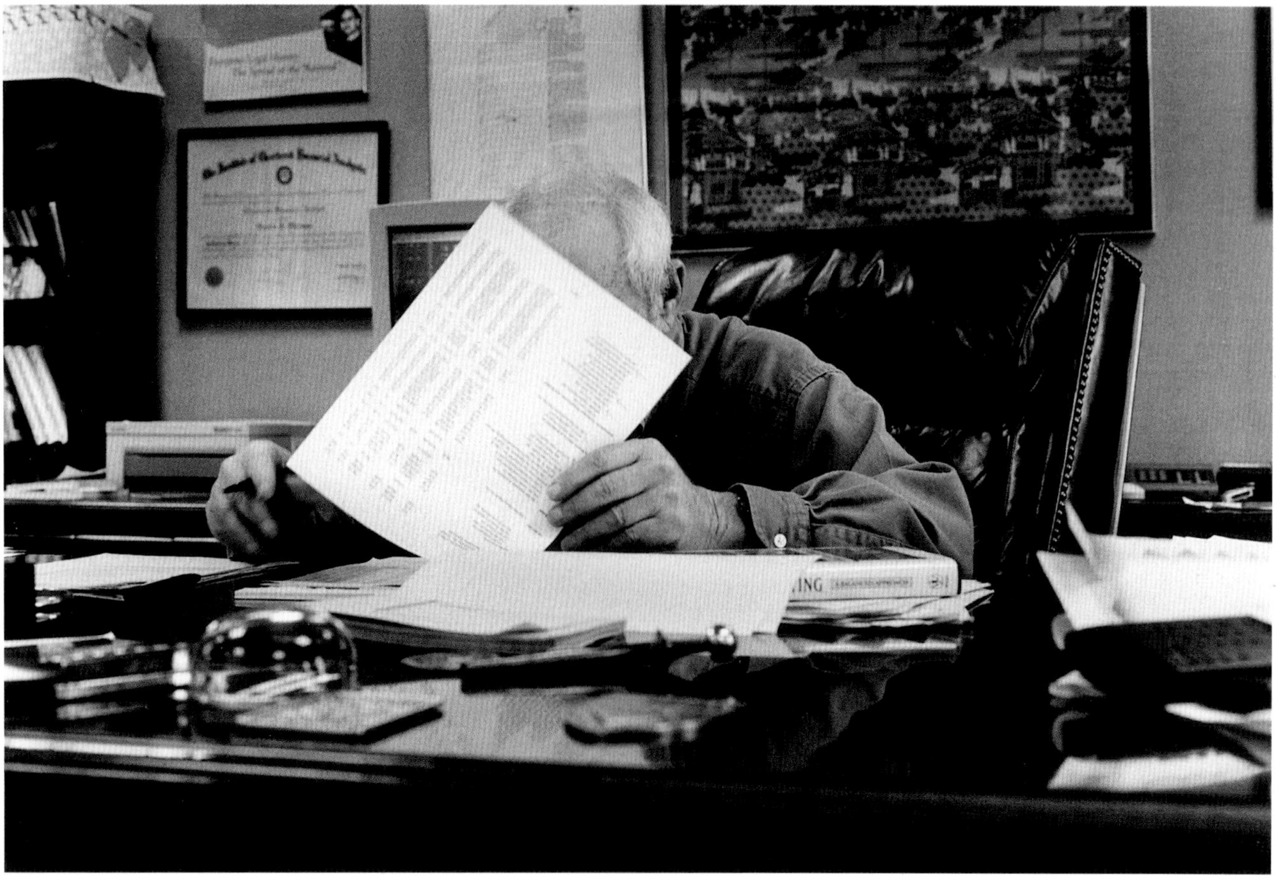

London, 1956 / *New York, 1999*

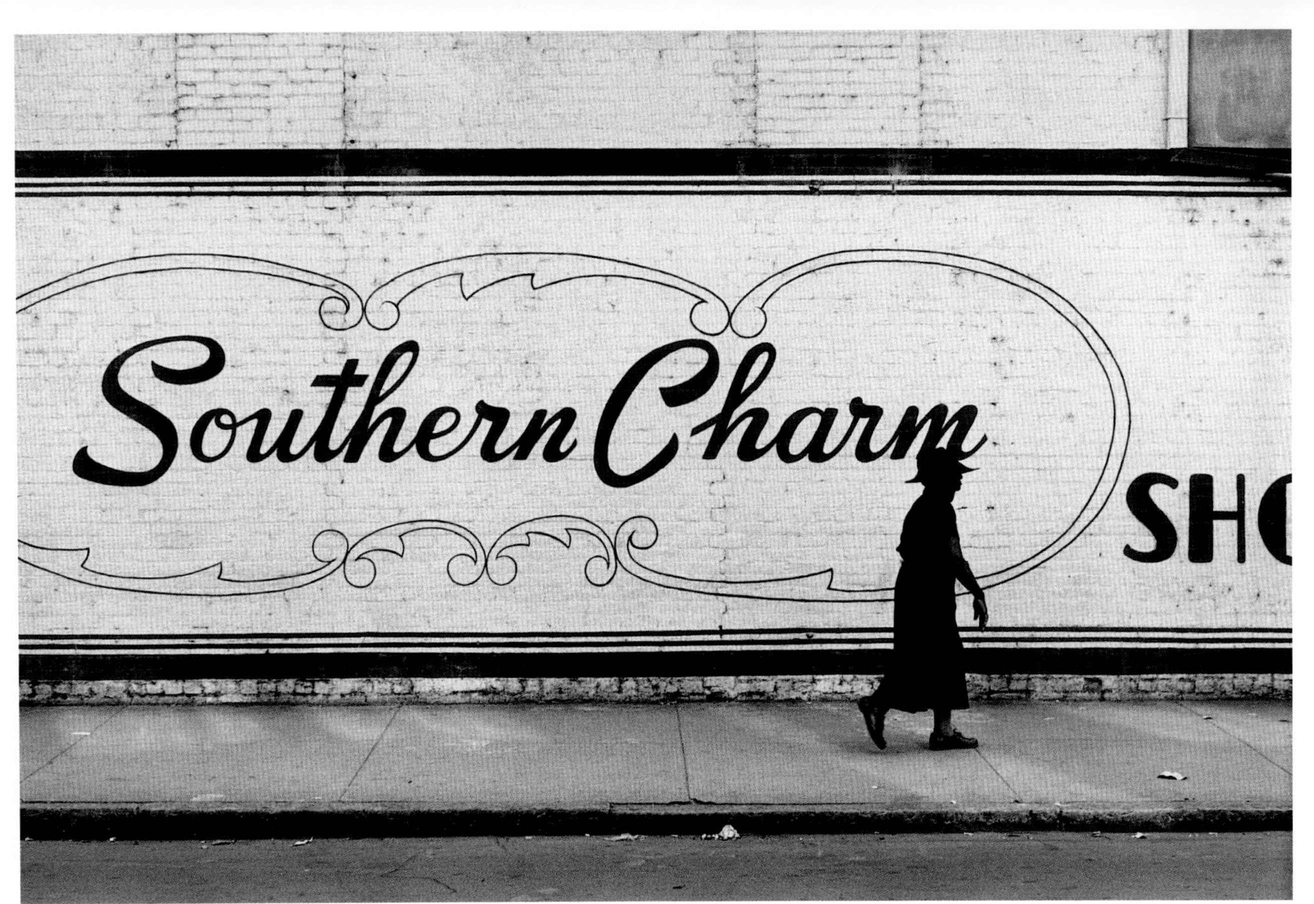

Alabama, 1955

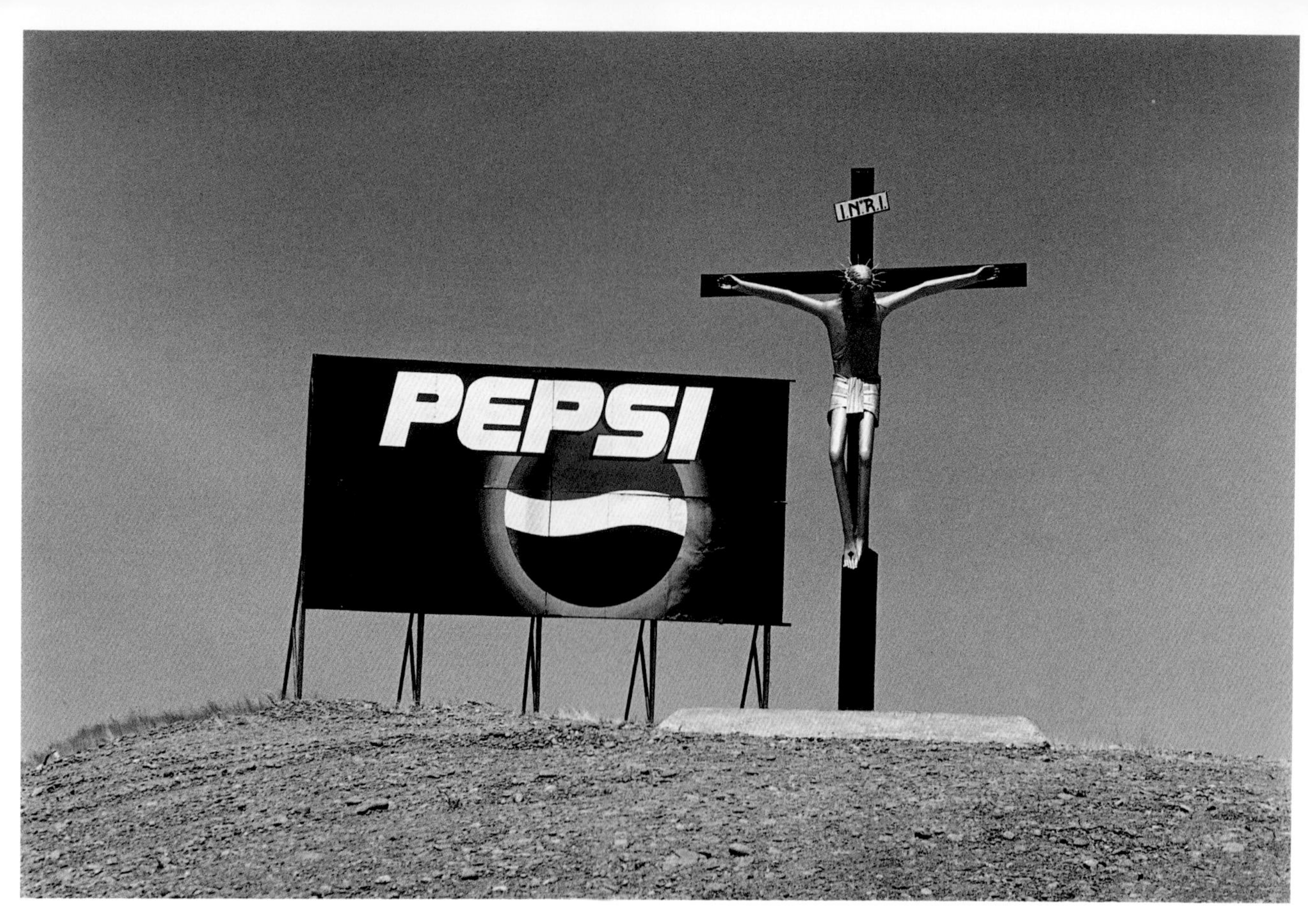

Valdés Peninsula, Argentina, 2001
overleaf, top row left to right: *Bert (Ivan) Meyers, Los Angeles, 1966* / *Hiroshi Hamaya, Oiso, Japan, 1977*
Elizabeth Bowen, New York, 1955 / *Martin Buber, Tel Aviv, 1962*
bottom row left to right: *John Szarkowski, New York, 1988* / *John Kenneth Galbraith, Cambridge, Massachusetts, 1998*
Marcel Ophuls, Paris, 1982 / *Norman Mailer, East Hampton, New York, 1968*

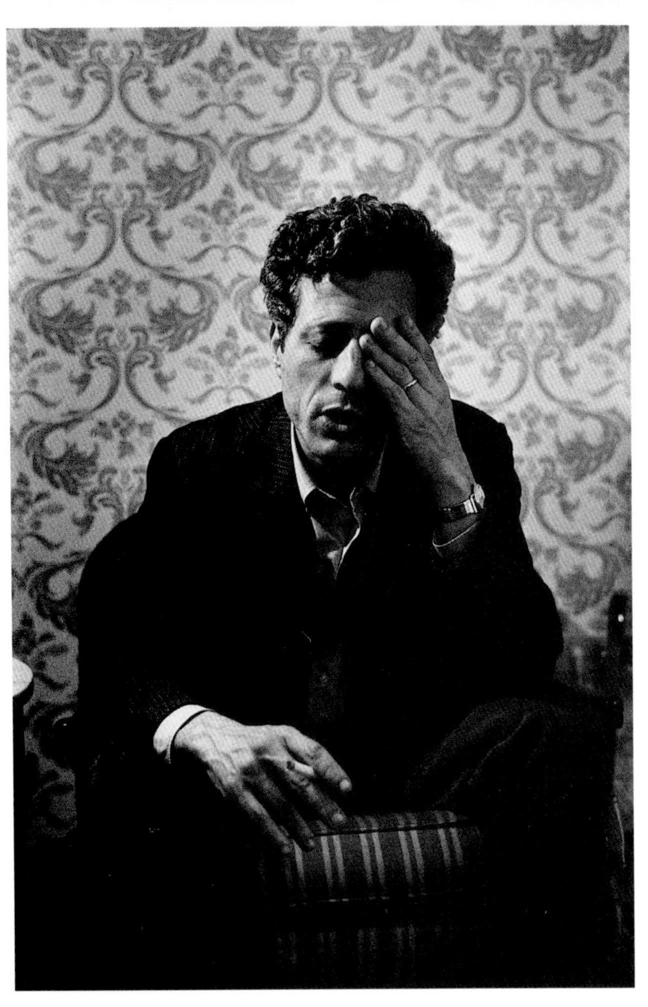

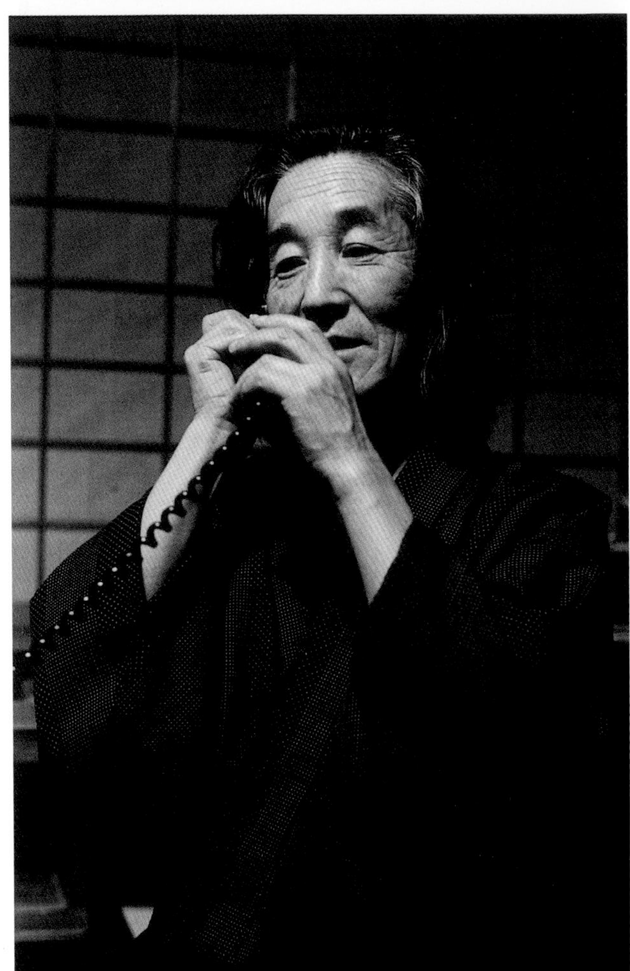

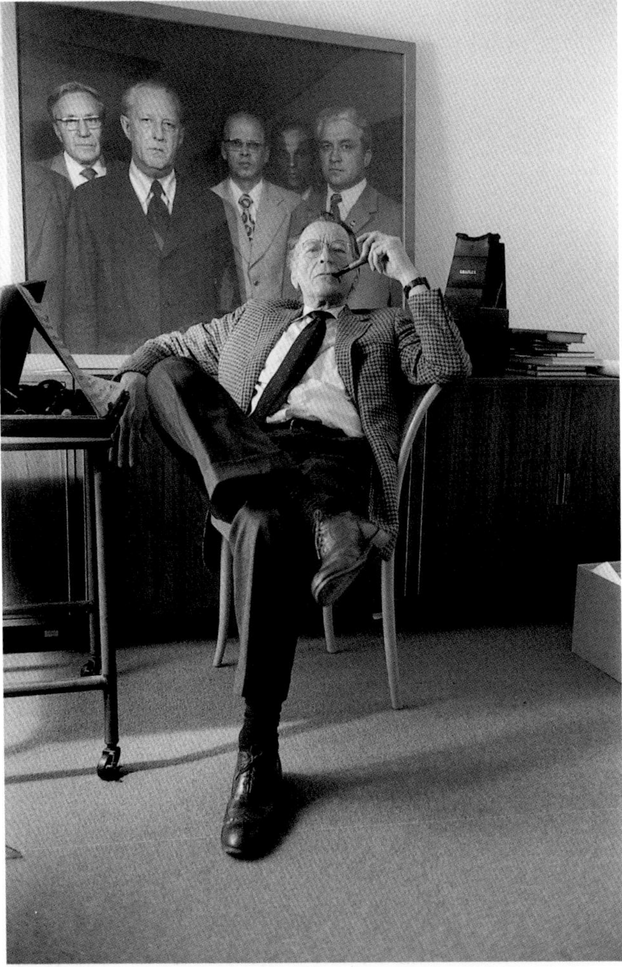

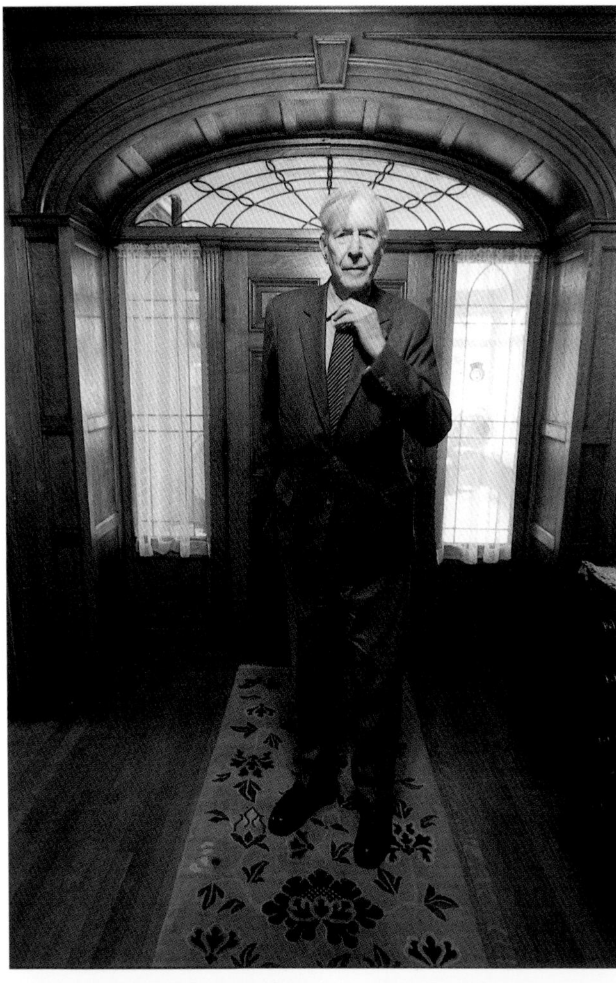

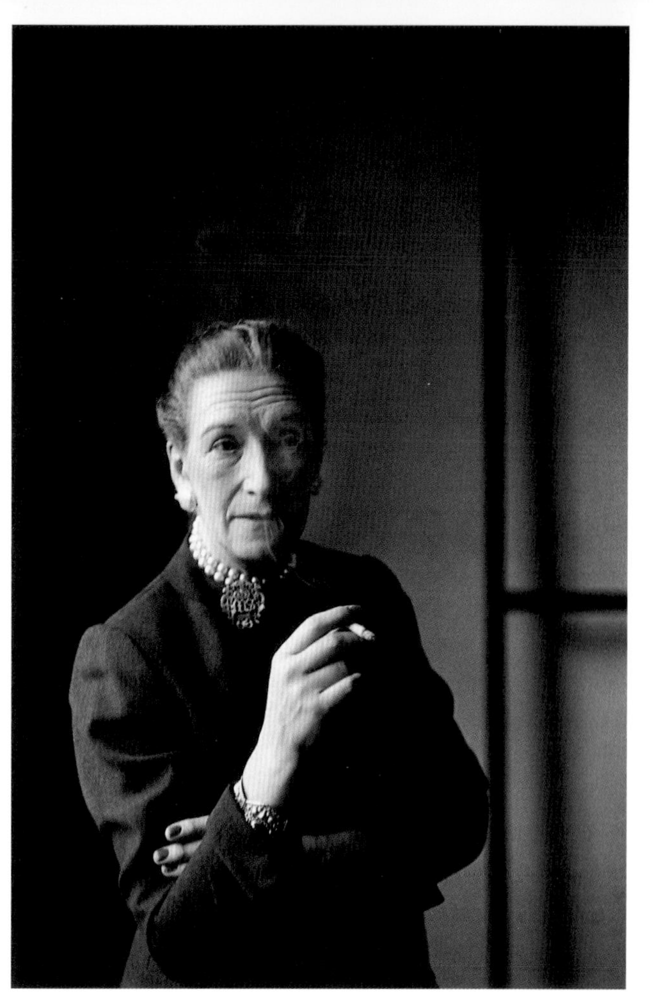

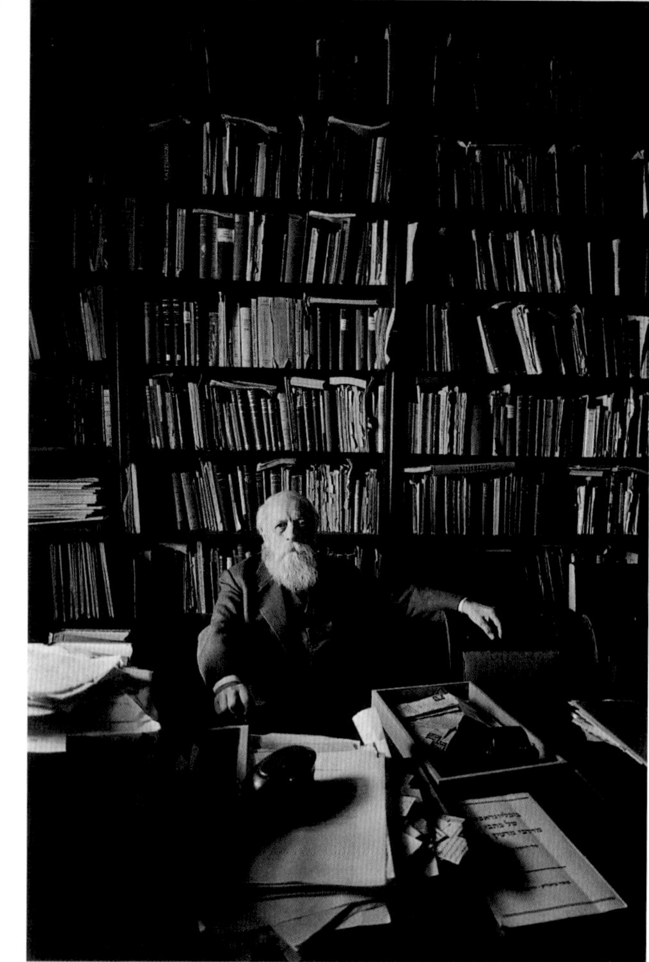

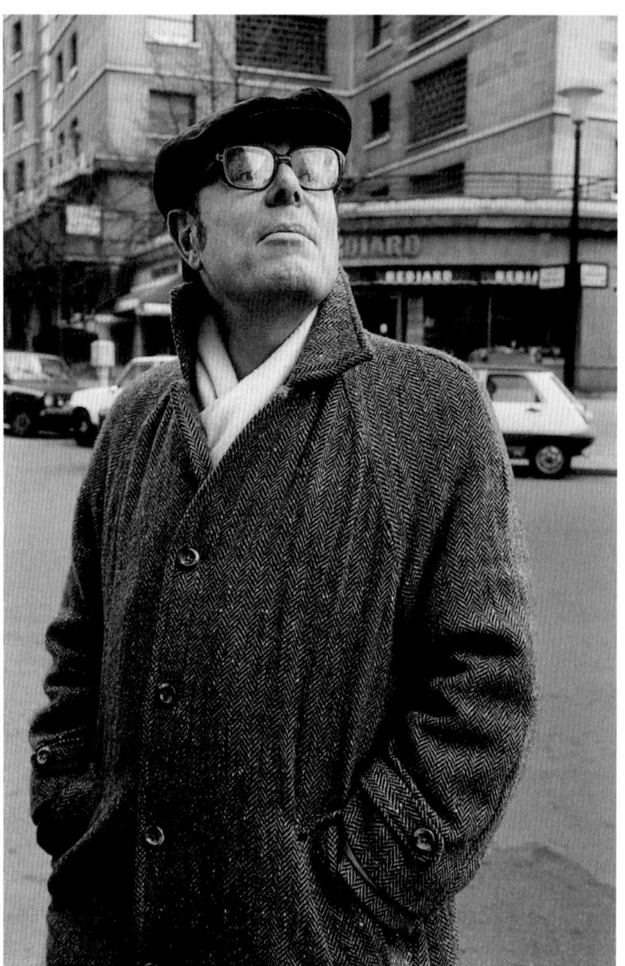

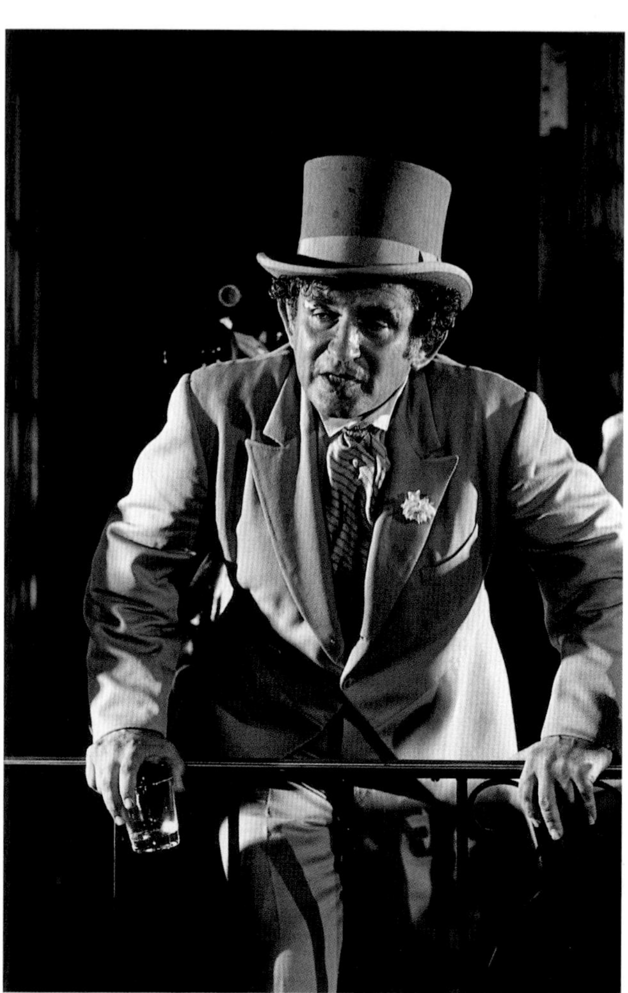

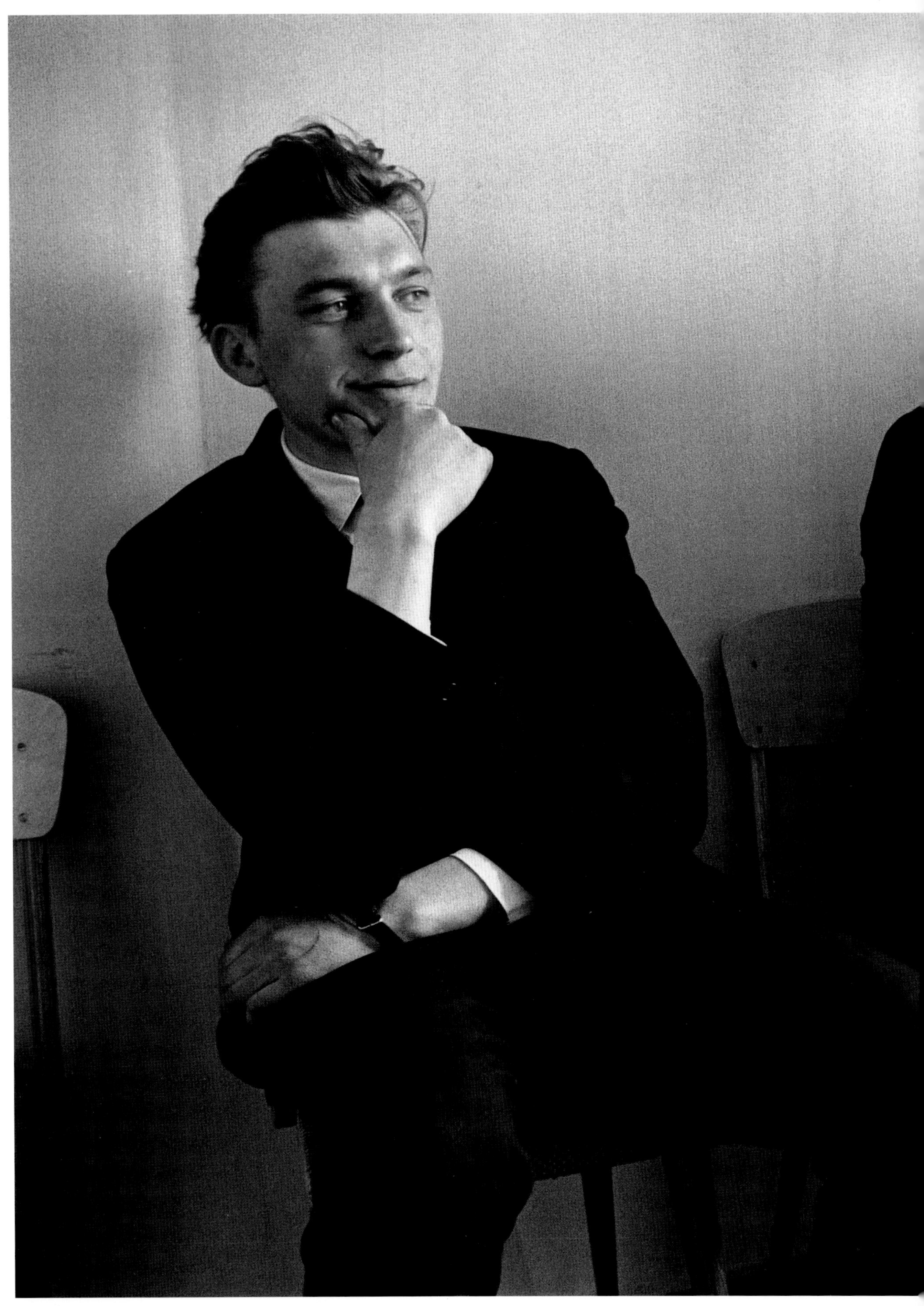

Bratsk, Siberia, 1967

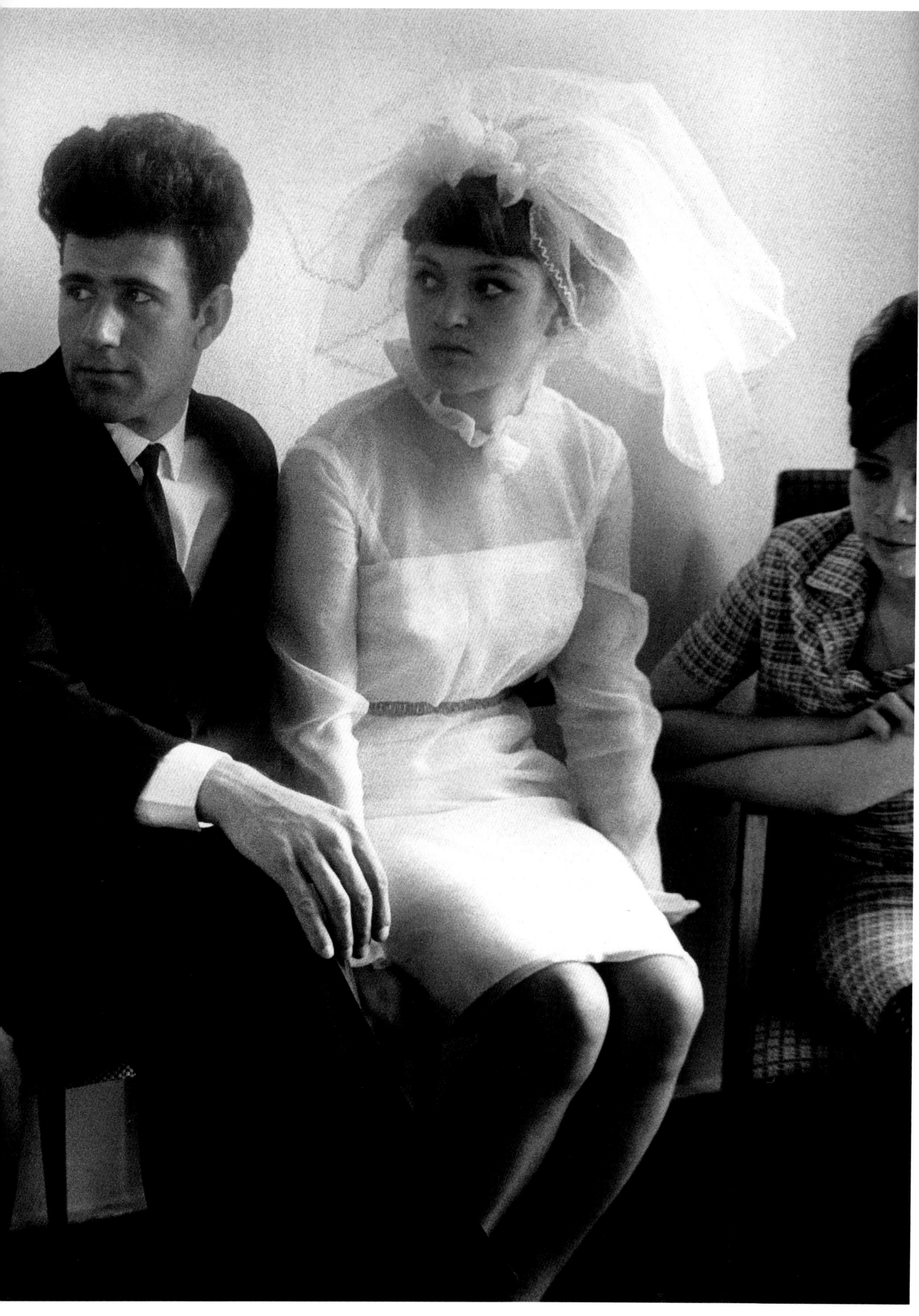

Rest

A man 'rests' beside a coffin in use; automobiles and office buildings and entire neighbourhoods seem forlorn in disuse; intellectuals keep themselves awake on hard chairs, and cots or mattresses roughly support loners or losers near the rim of despair. If resting people and objects at rest seem slightly unsettling here, I think I know why. Rest is not a concept congenial to this photographer.

Elliott began supporting himself in his teens in southern California while still attending Hollywood High School. He did not turn down any kind of freelance photography or darkroom work, having decided after one depressing stint behind a soda fountain that he would never tie himself down to a steady job. After graduating from high school, he staged exhibits of his photographs in Los Angeles and New Orleans, moved to New York City and caught the attention of Edward Steichen and others on the scene there, was hired by Roy Stryker for a project with the Mellon Foundation and shared a national award for a photo essay about Pittsburgh. In 1951 he was drafted into the US Army, not long before his work caught the attention of Robert Capa, who ensured that Elliott was accepted into Magnum as soon as he returned to civilian life.

What is not immediately clear, perhaps, from this summary of a Dick Whittington-like rise is that young Elliott, like today's version, may have looked to the casual observer like an object at rest, observing others in motion from the sidelines, seeming to participate only by eye and by intellect. He thought then, and now, that it is the photographer's task to blend into the woodwork. But that's only part of the story. Beneath the unperturbed surface his mind is racing, and then he makes his snaps, often without being caught at it, and falls back again into apparent rest. It is later, poring over contact sheets and making several tries in the darkroom to produce the most satisfying print possible, that he might be seen working up a sweat. And it is later still, when the books and magazines and posters and TV spots have found their way into the public eye, that we can infer from the multifarious product that he works like a demon possessed. He will never starve.

Here is a lesson for anyone in the arts who does not have a trust fund or an income-producing significant other: Elliott has always split his camera time between 'work' – the assignments from magazines and ad agencies that reliably support the spacious apartment on Manhattan's Central Park West and the house with sapphire pool in the Hamptons – and the 'snaps', the photos that are truest to his vision and might never bring in a cent. He has balanced these two activities perfectly. But he does not rest. Most of these photos are at least ambivalent towards the concept.

Except for my favourite. In my childhood home, with a young father on the road looking for work and a young mother busy with my two younger sisters, one a newborn, there was little money for reading matter. But my mother, sympathetic to a gawky door-to-door salesman who claimed to be working his way through college, subscribed to *Life* magazine and, as a premium, got a copy of Steichen's book, *The Family of Man*. Elliott's photo (p.67), included in that landmark collection, immediately drew me in; it was, in ways I could not articulate, somehow about me and my struggling family. I went frequently into its world; it was both what I had and did not yet have.

But for the photographer, it is his first wife and his first child…He is married for the fourth time now, and there are six children and five grandchildren, but in this photo the contented young mother, the eager infant and the inquisitive kitten are at rest, and so are we. It is only in real life, with its constant hurtling towards the future, that the infant is now nearing middle age and the wife long estranged. My father is now dead and my mother lost in the befuddlement of third-stage Alzheimer's disease, but this photo still takes me back to a moment caught forever, to the simulation of rest. In this simulation, moreover, is the gift of peace to any receptive viewer, an affirmation of rest that is unusual in Elliott's work.

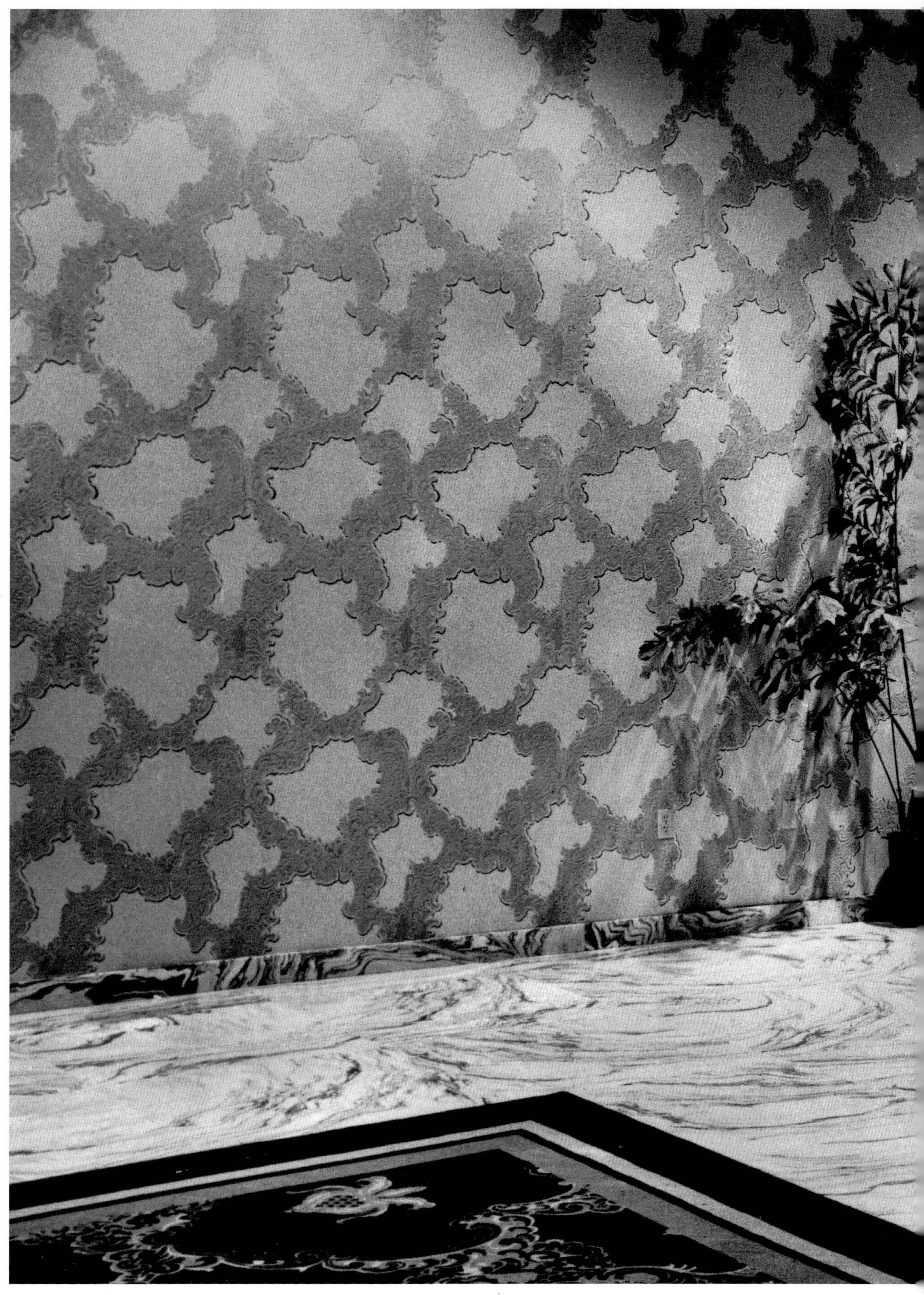

Miami Beach, 1962

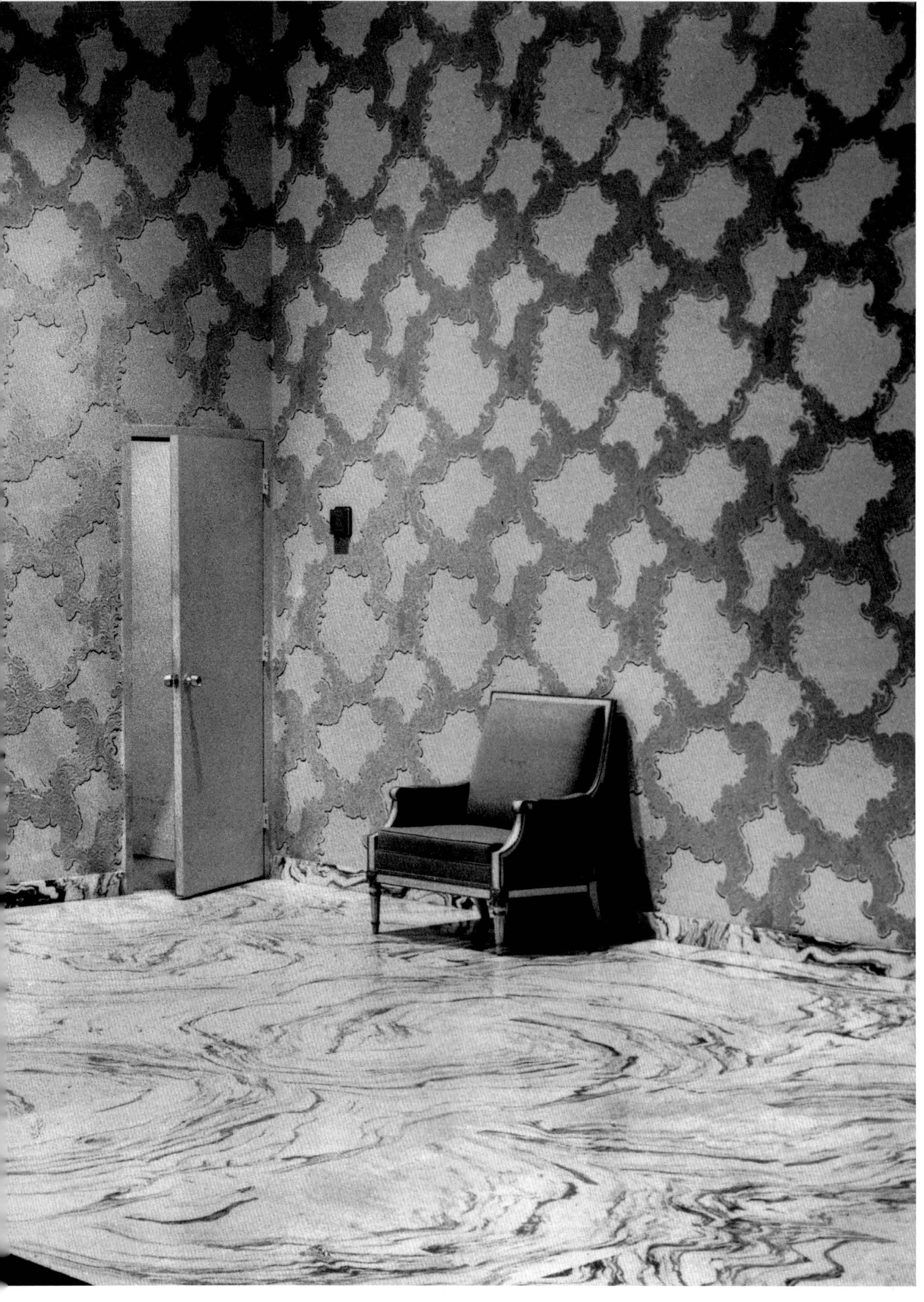

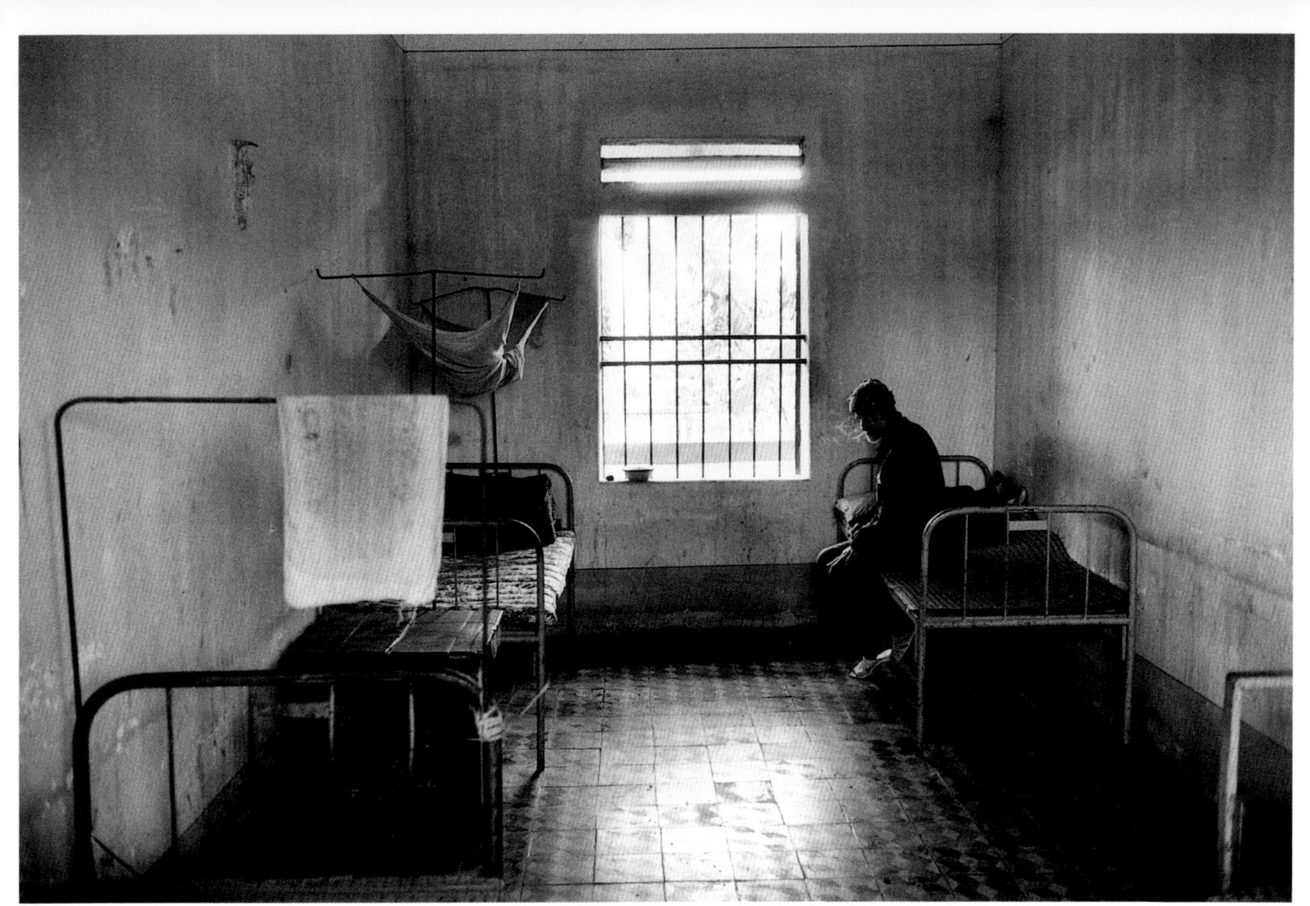

Thai Binh, Vietnam, 1994

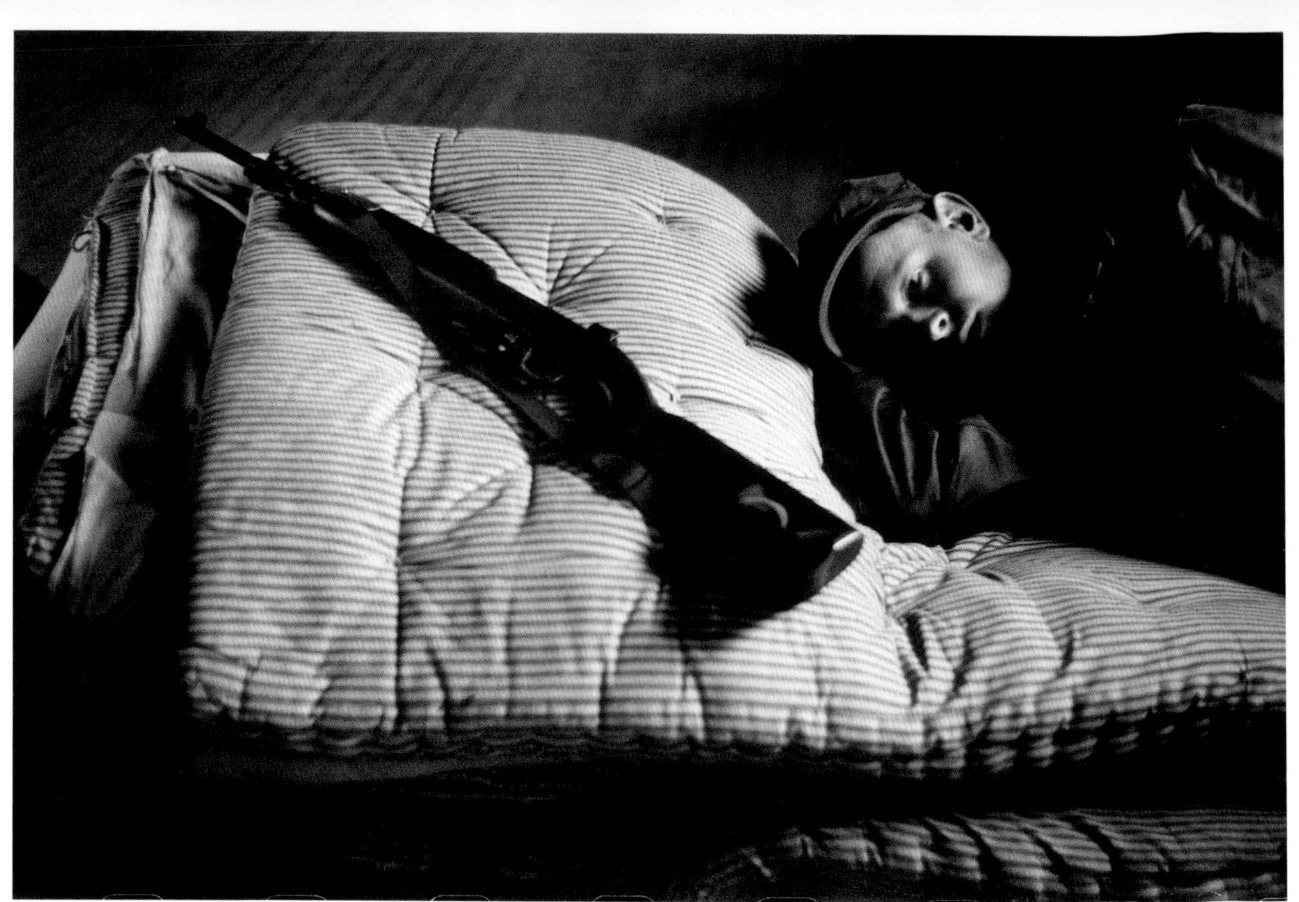

New Jersey, 1951

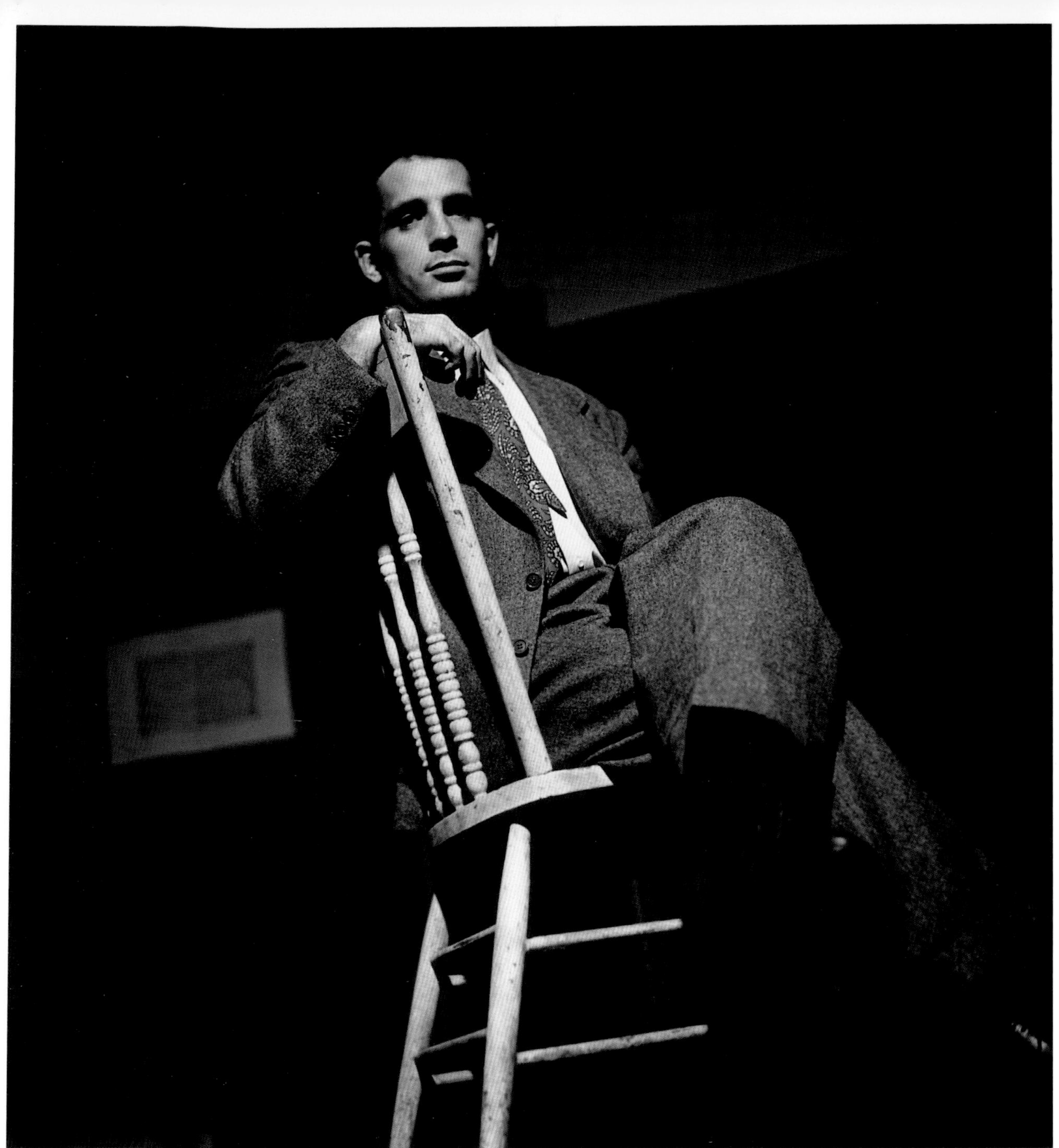

Jack Kerouak, New York, 1953

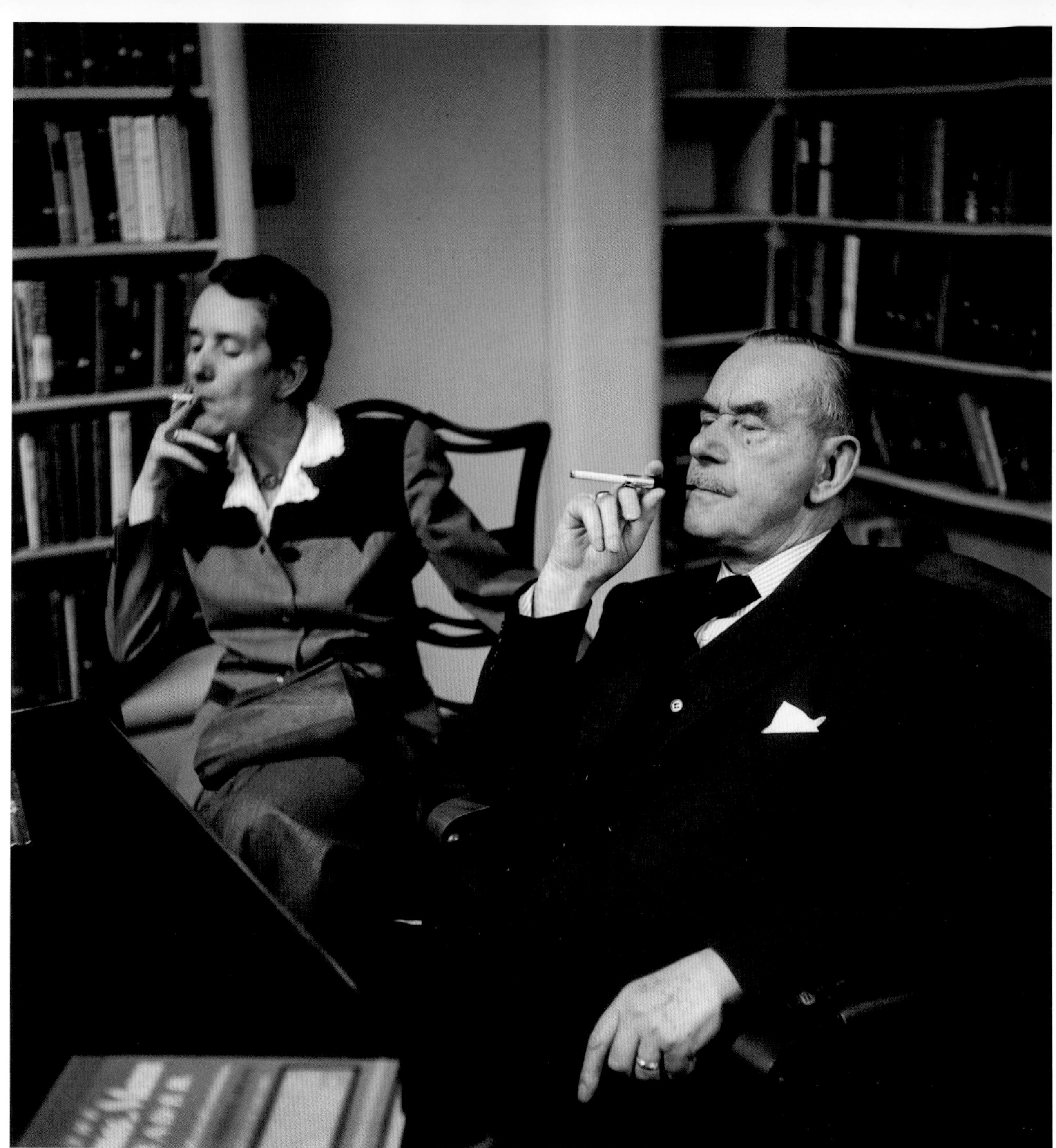

Erika and Thomas Mann, New York, 1950

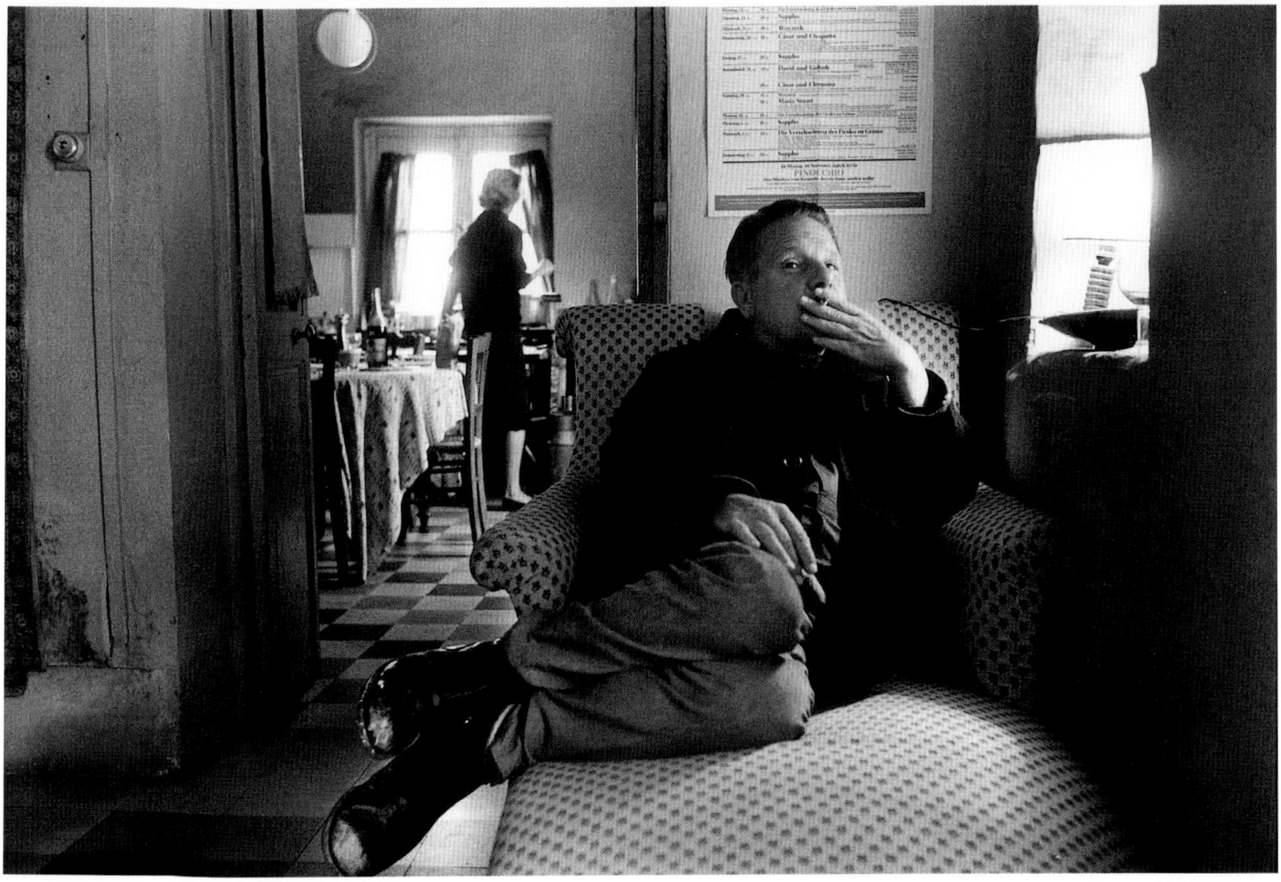

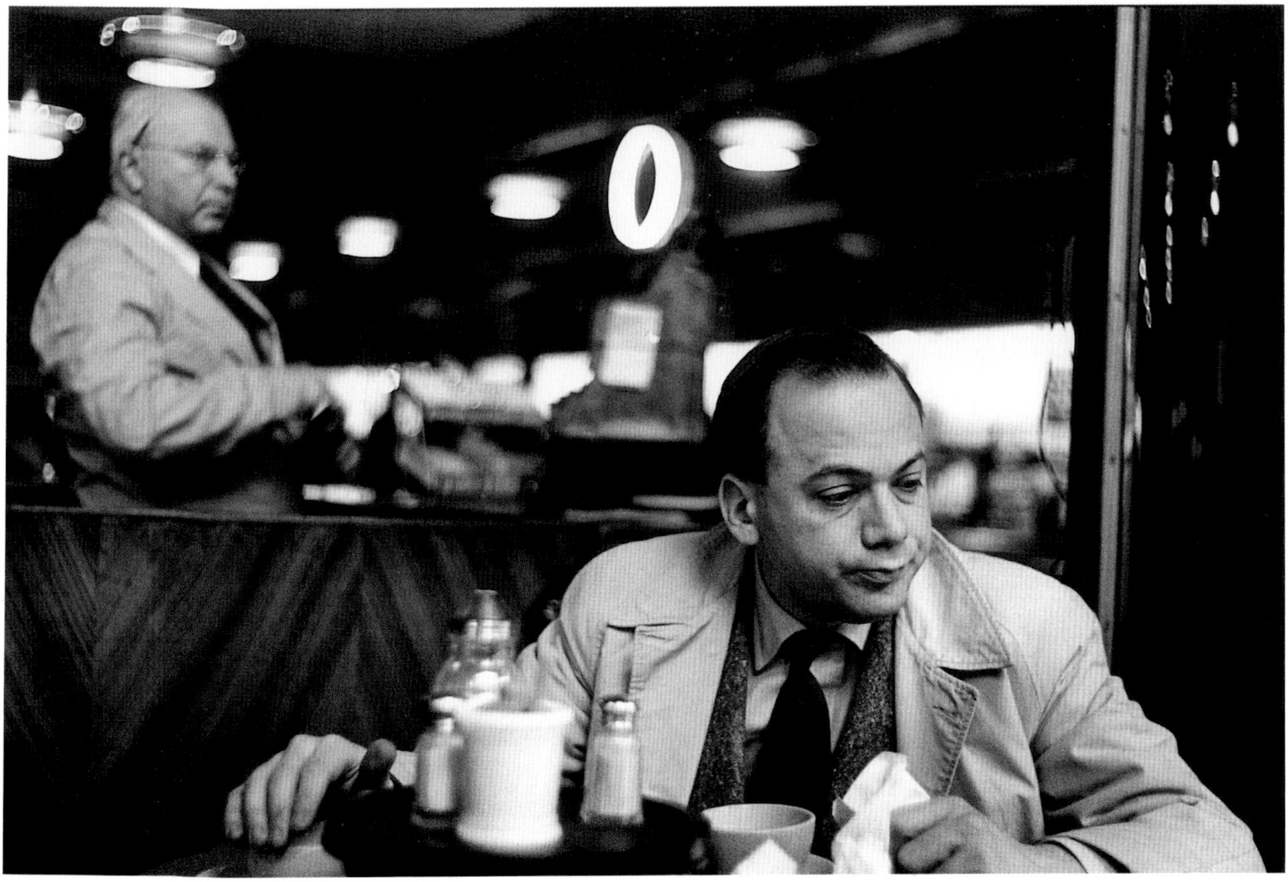

Lawrence Durrell, Provence, France, 1961 / *Louis Faurer, New York, 1950*

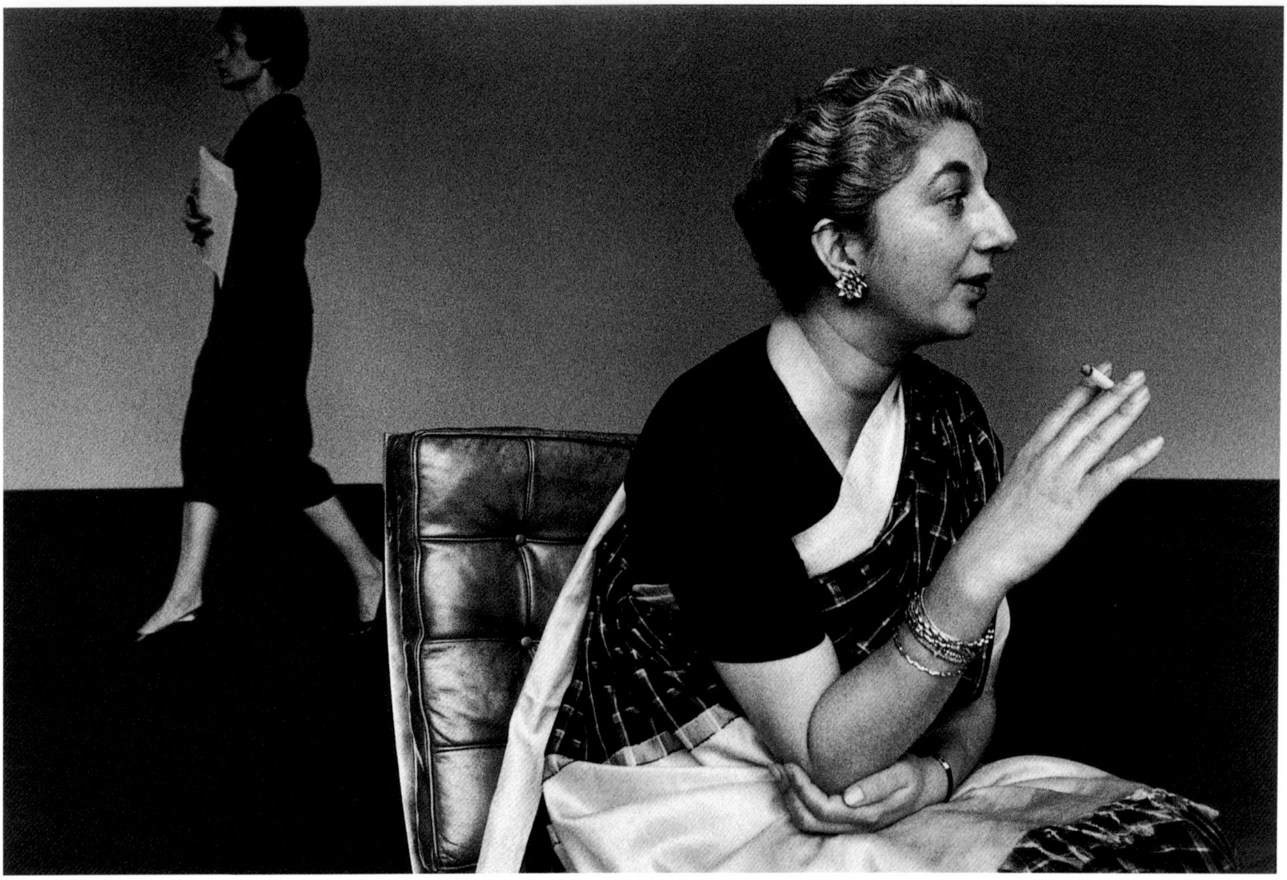

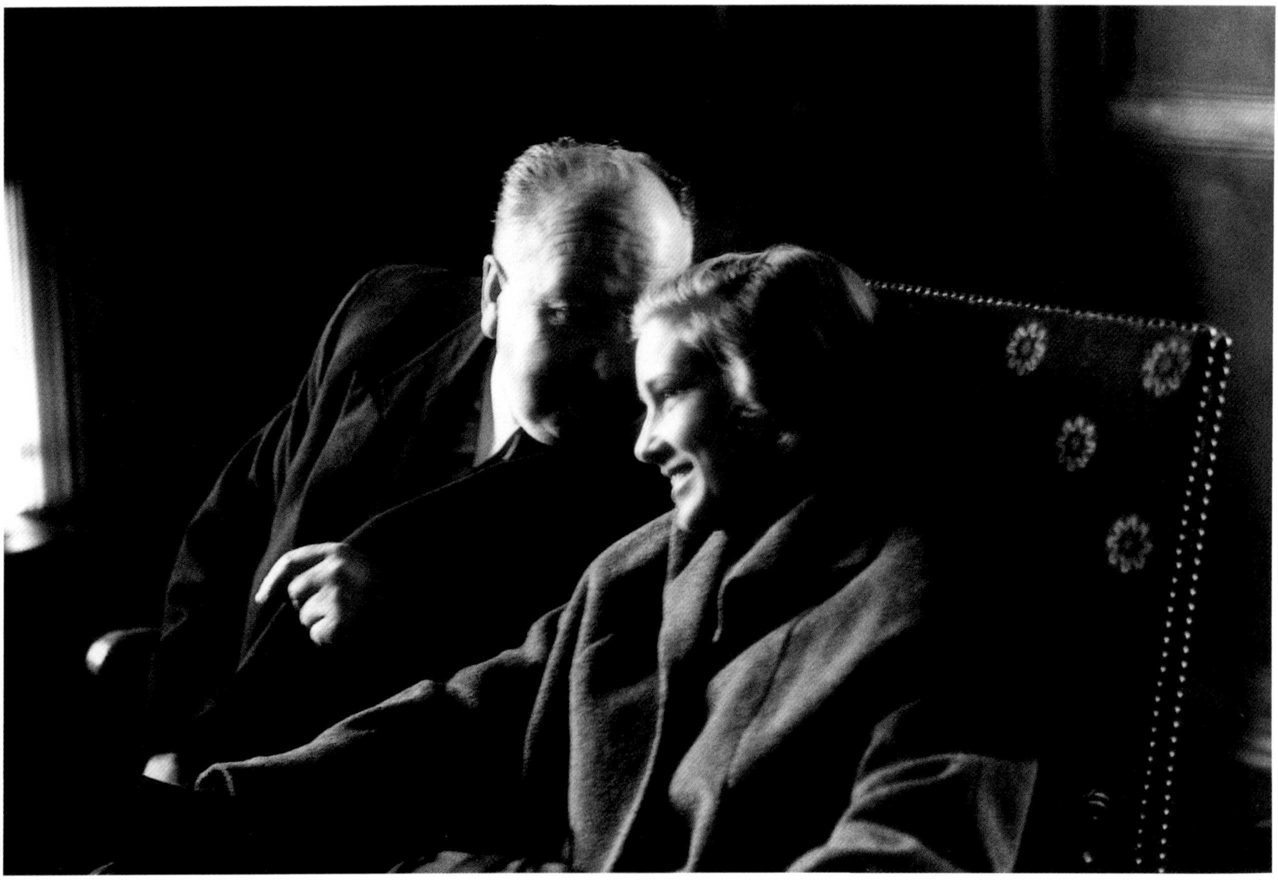

United Nations, New York, 1960 / Alfred Hitchcock and Vera Miles, New York, 1957

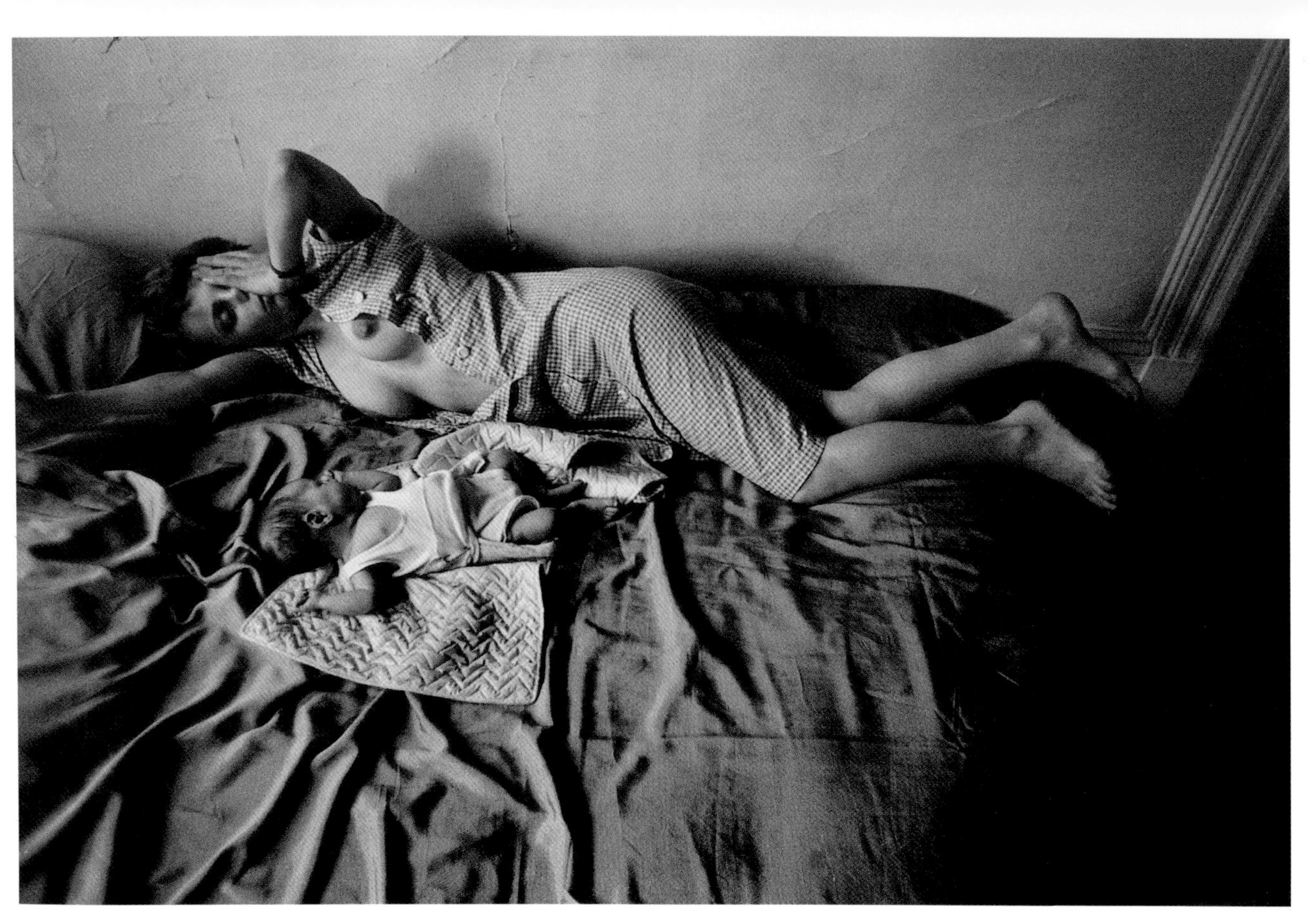

New York, 1953

Rest

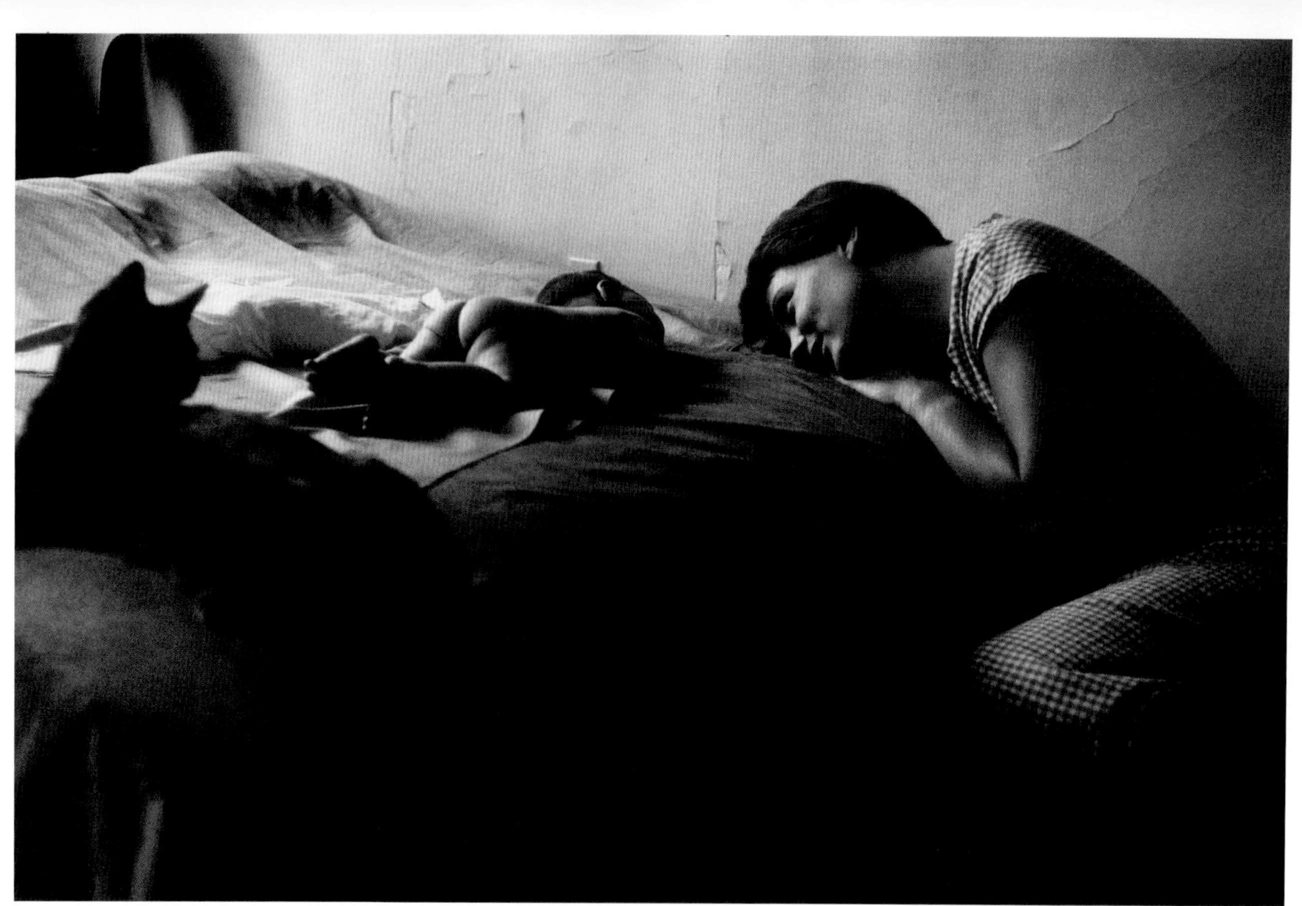

New York, 1953

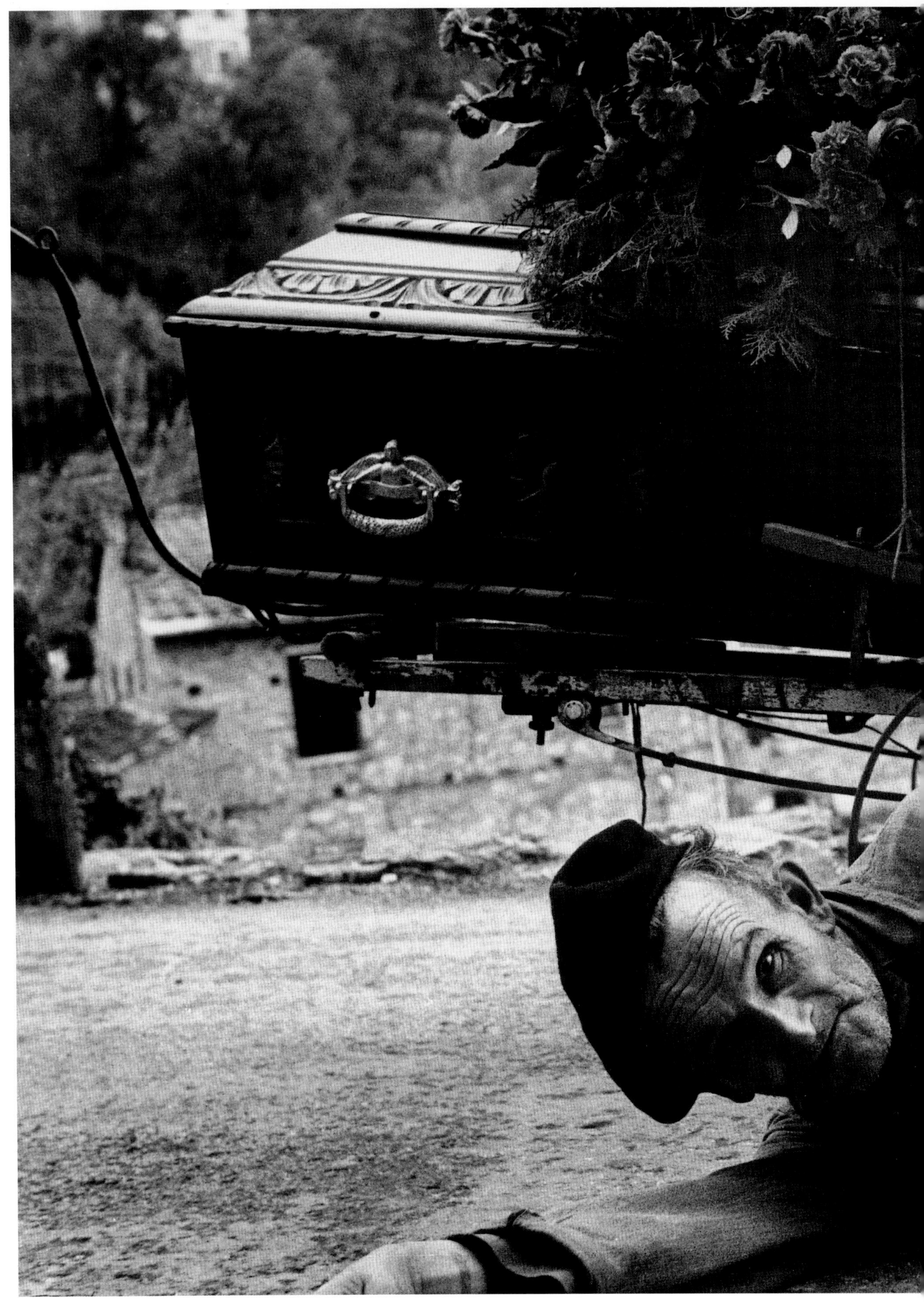

Tuscany, Italy, 1949

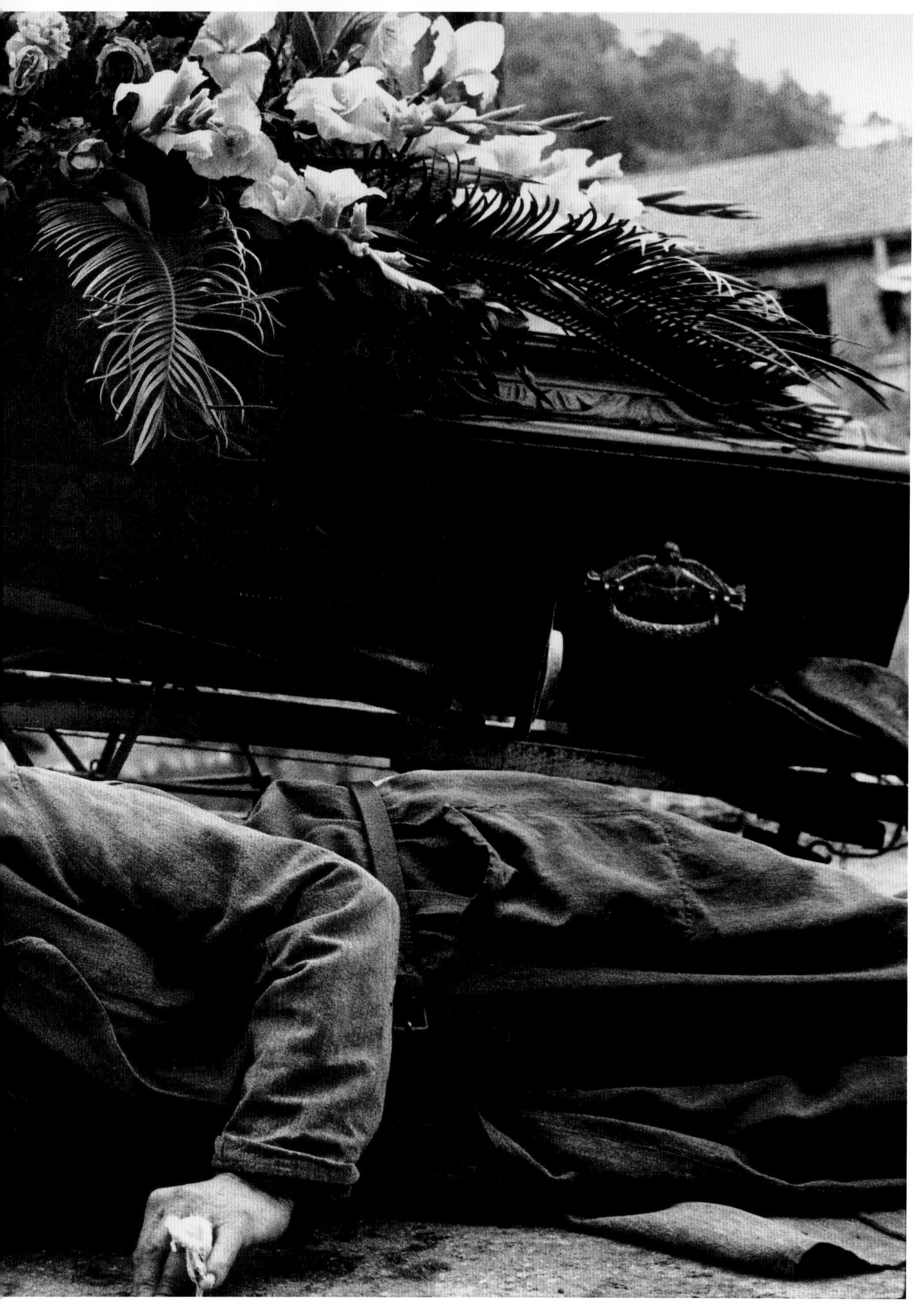

overleaf *New York, 2001* / *London, 1995*

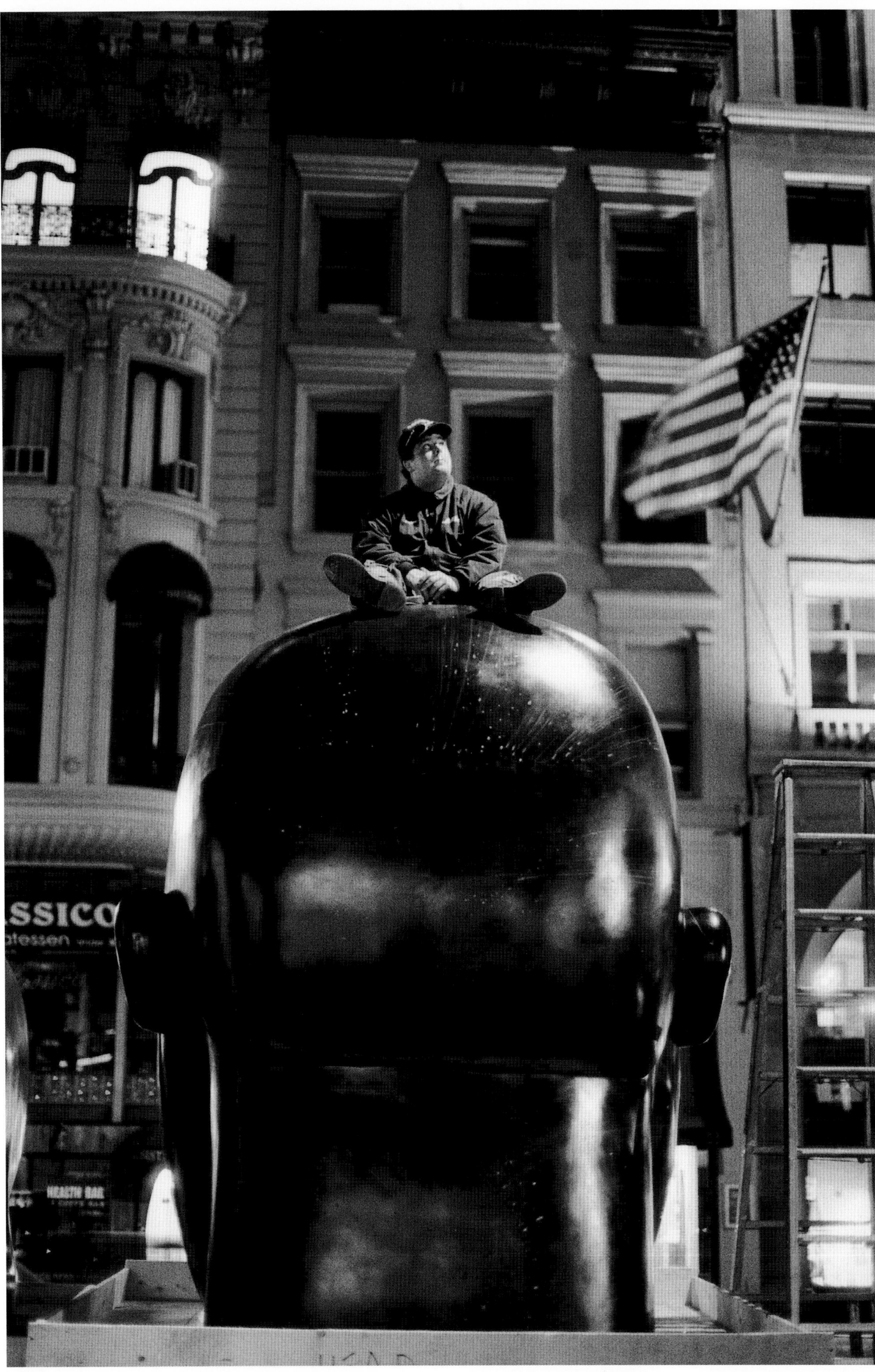

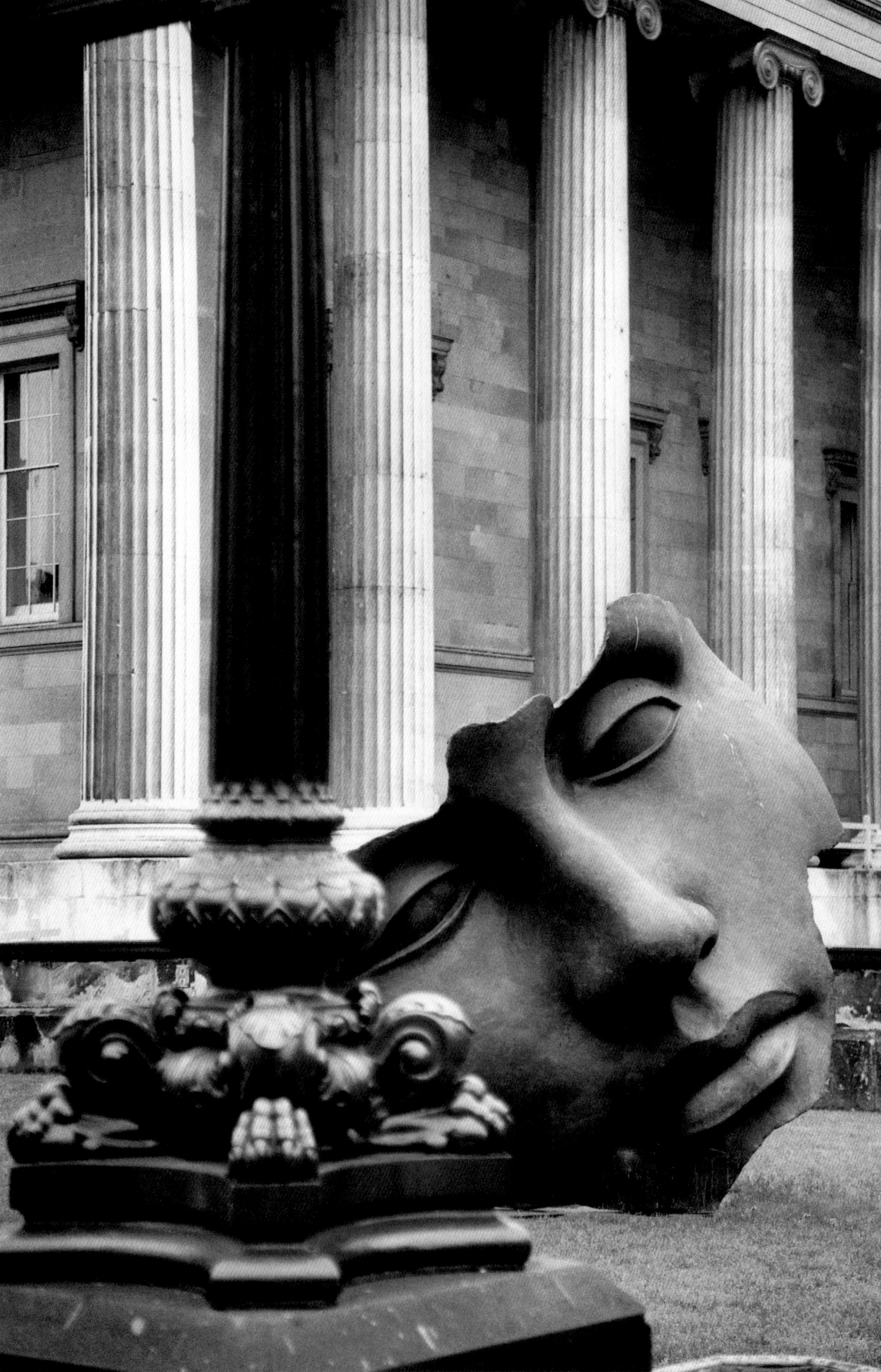

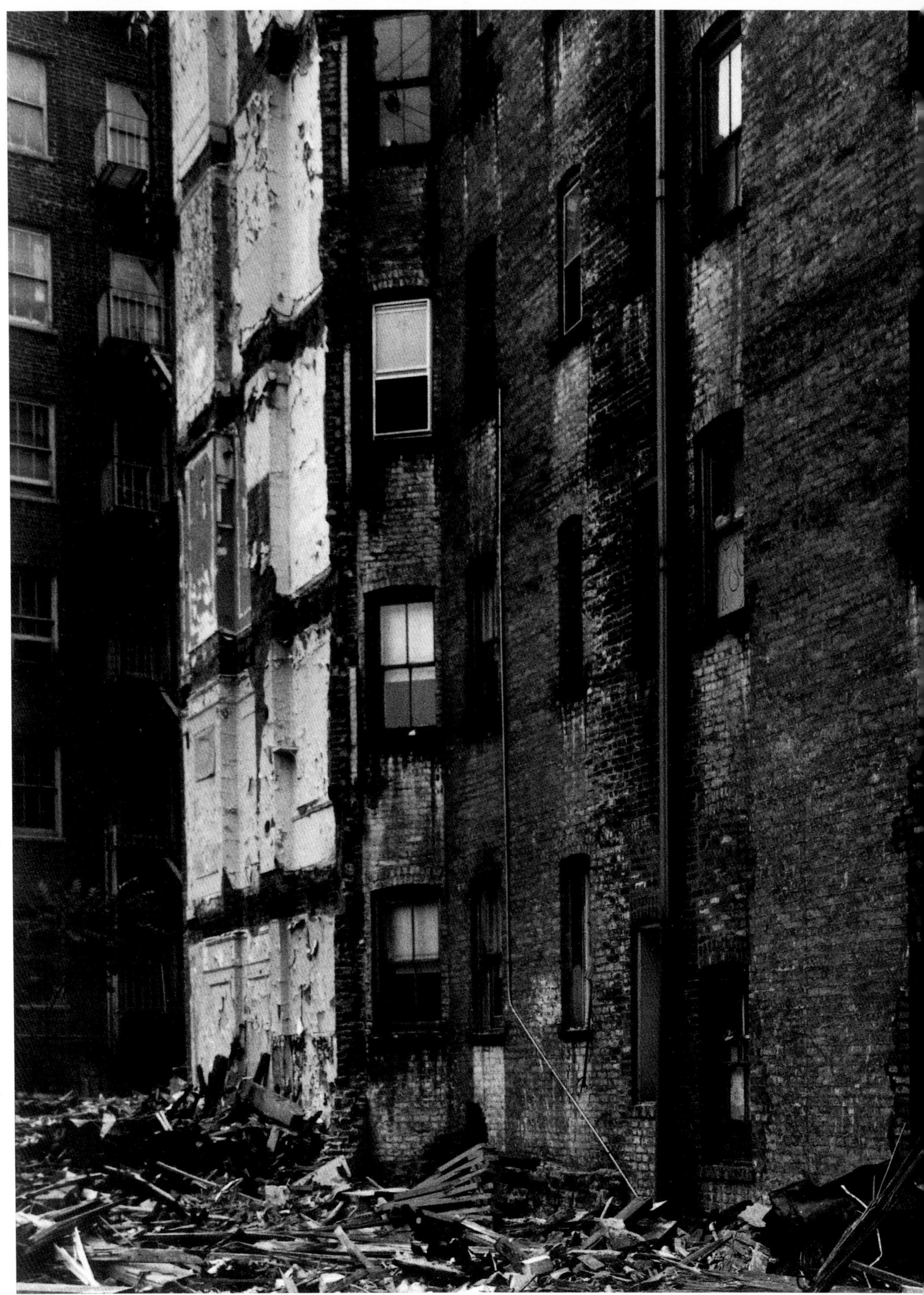

New York, 1974

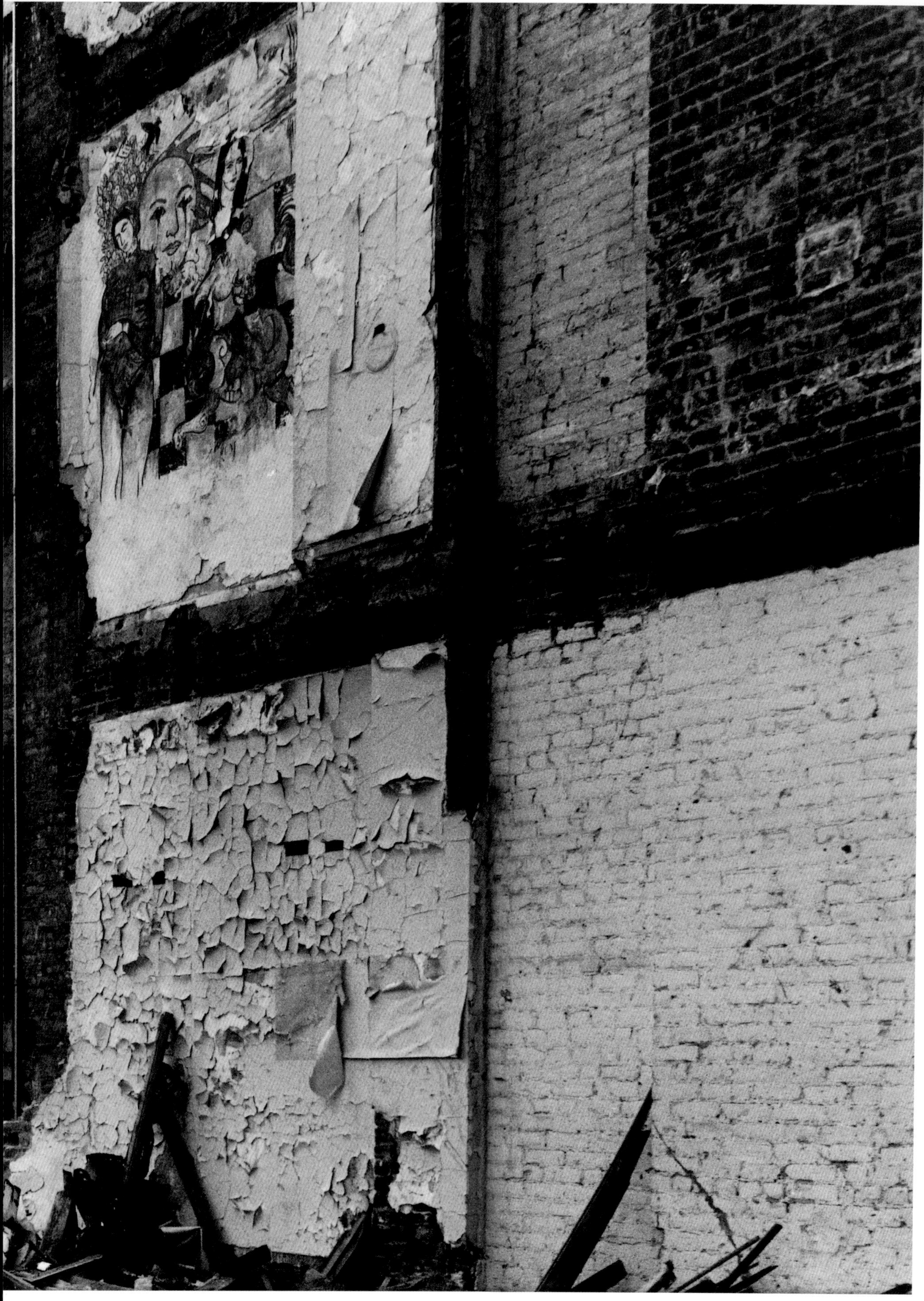

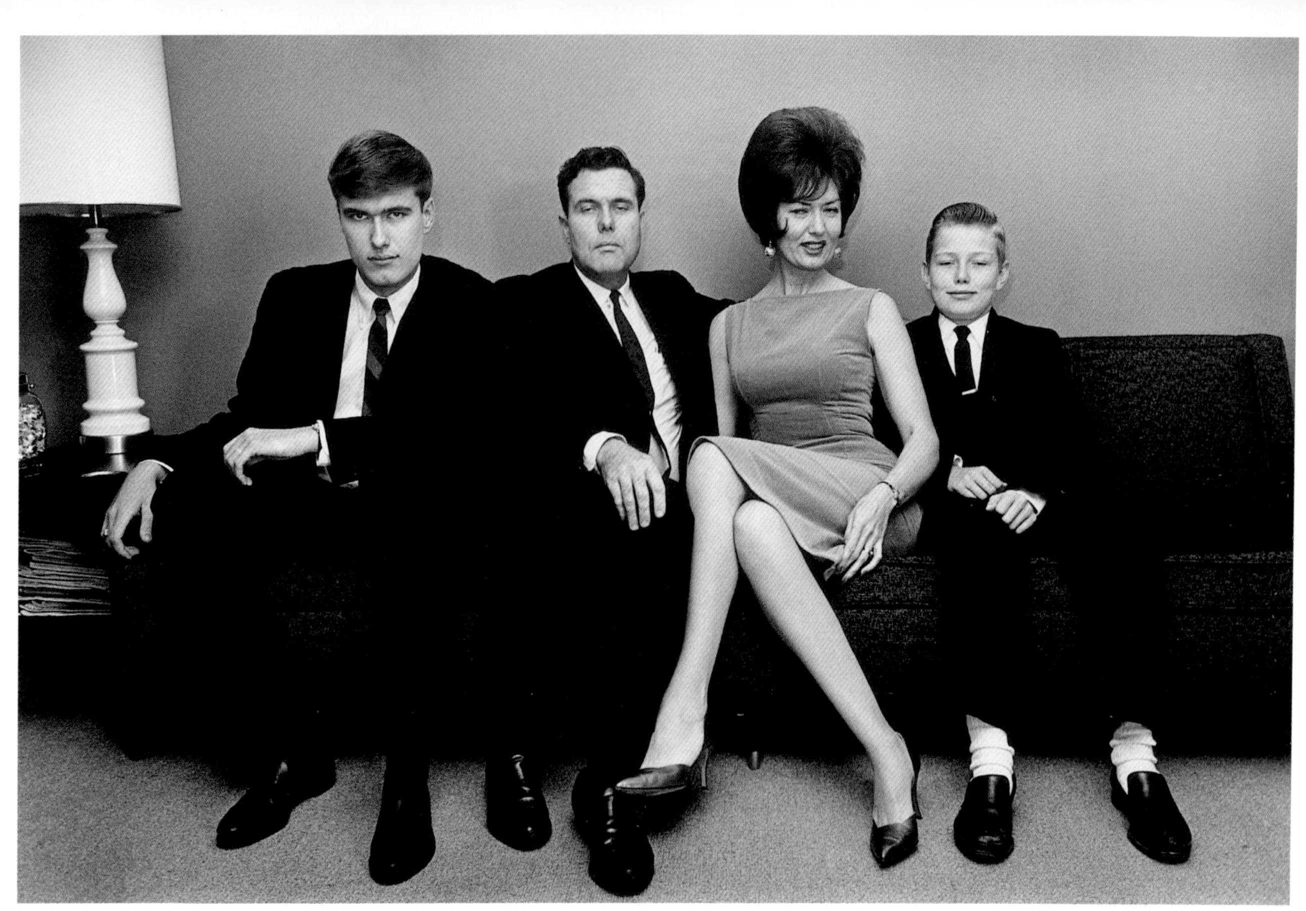

USA, 1962
overleaf *Las Palmas, Canary Islands, 1964* / *Bangkok, 1962*

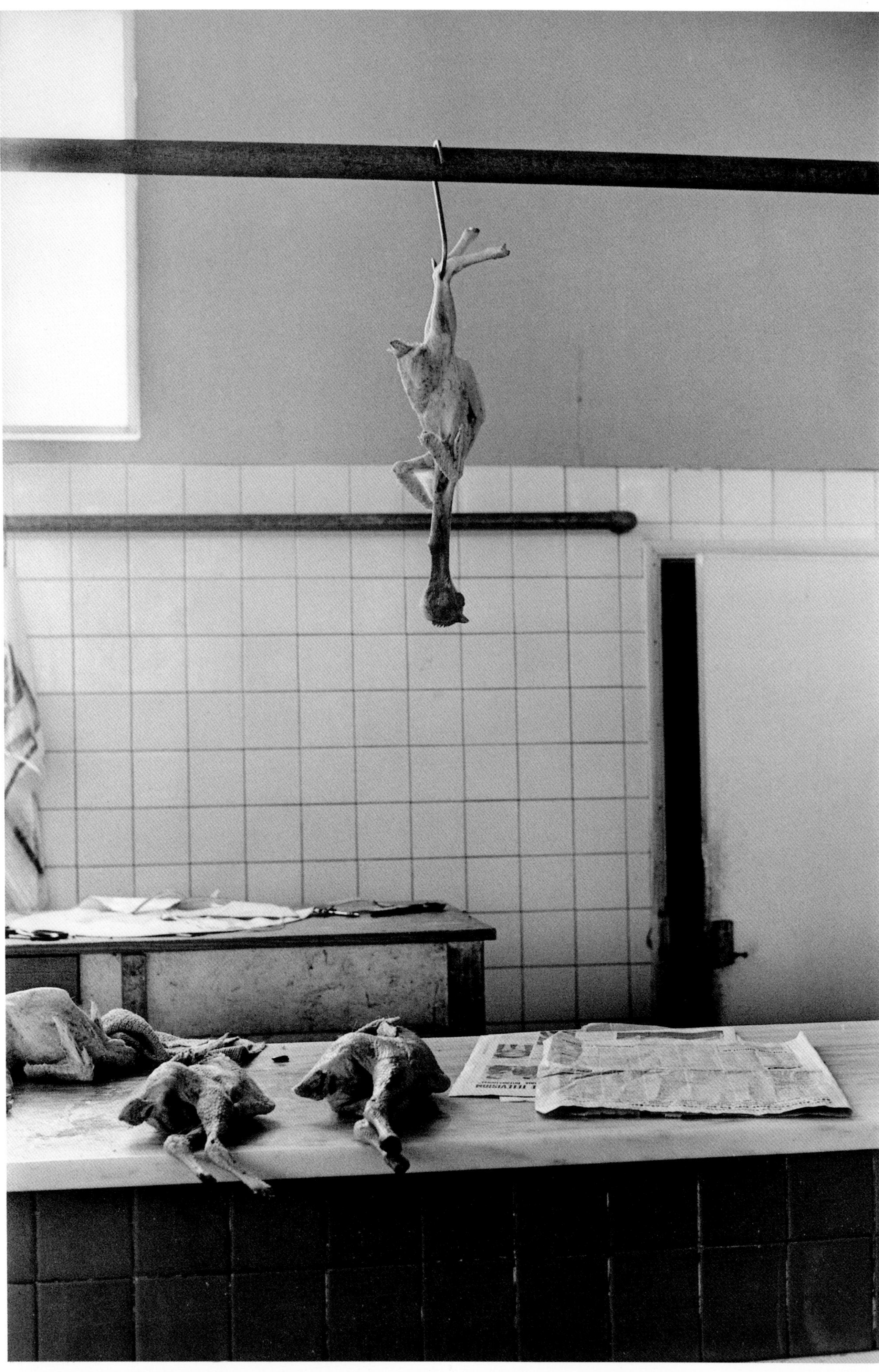

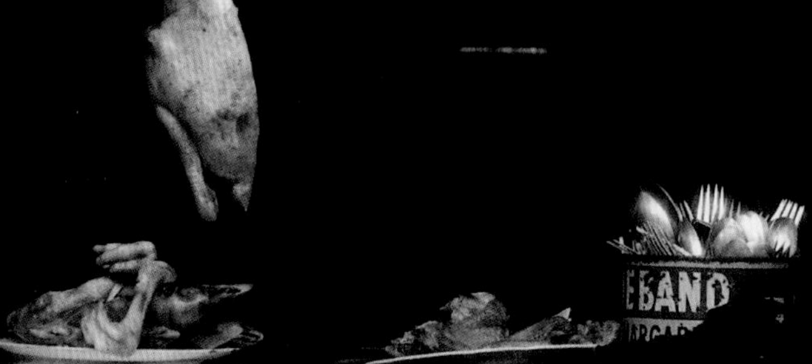
ดื่ม
Coca-Cola

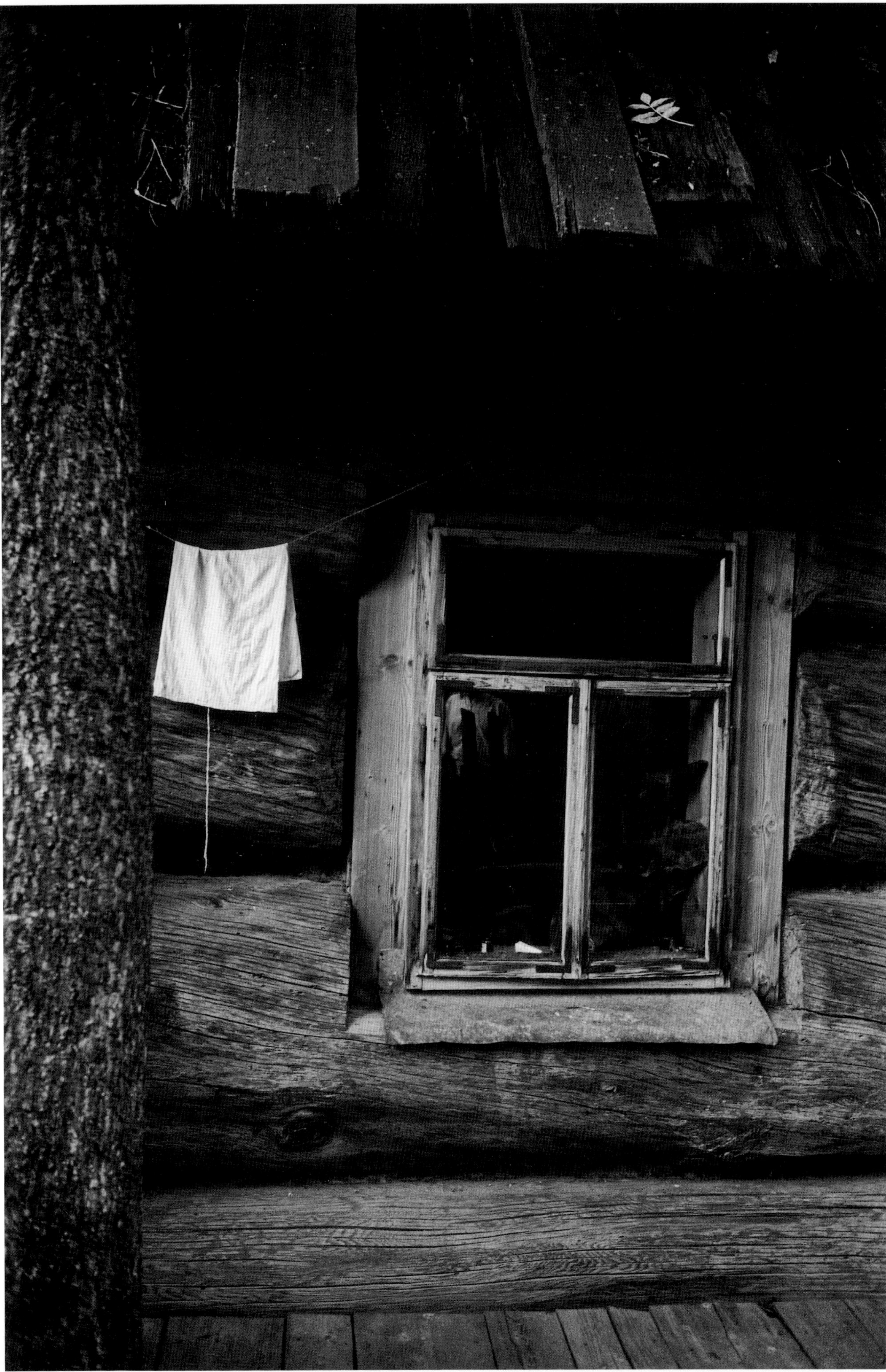

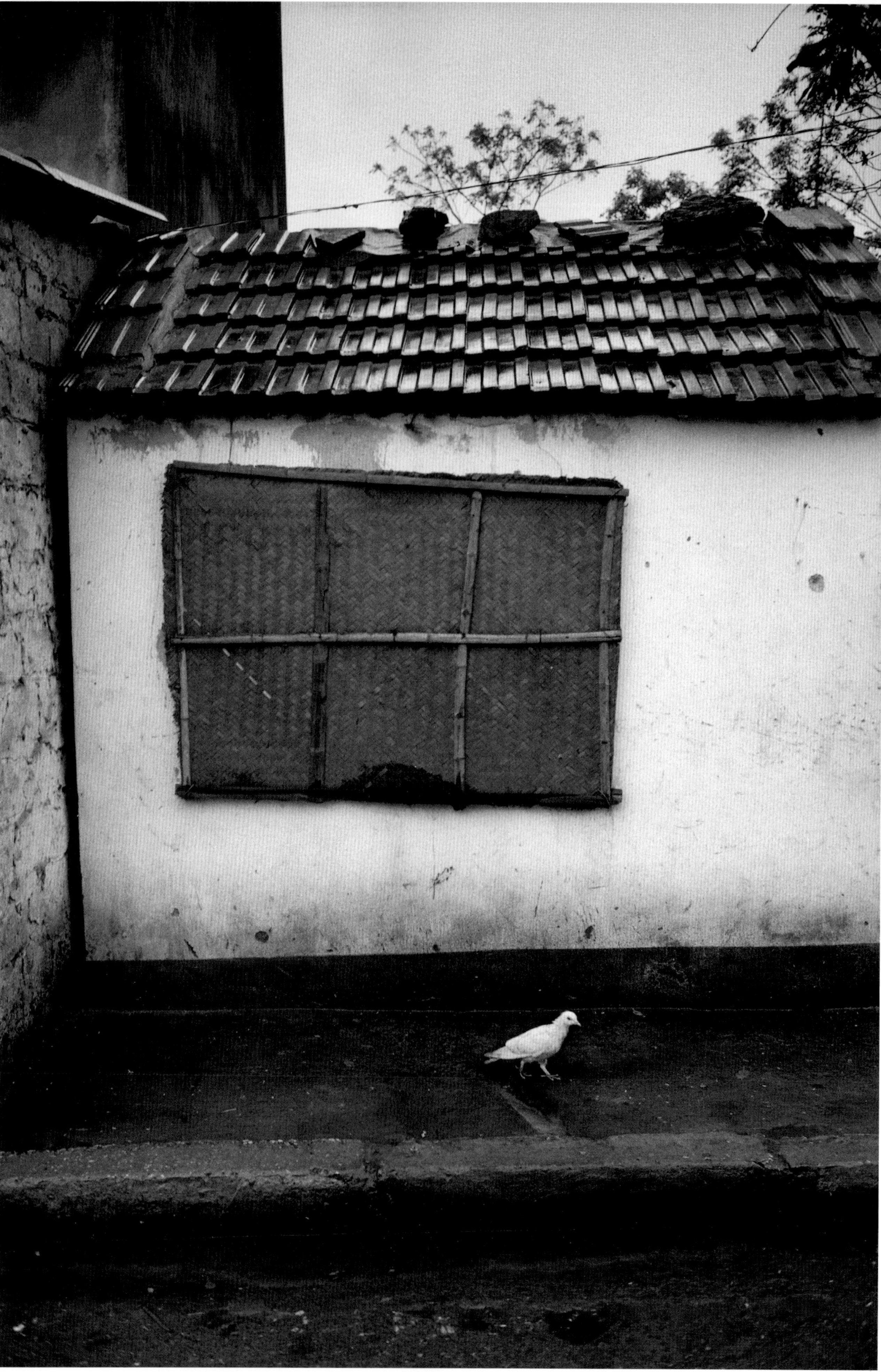

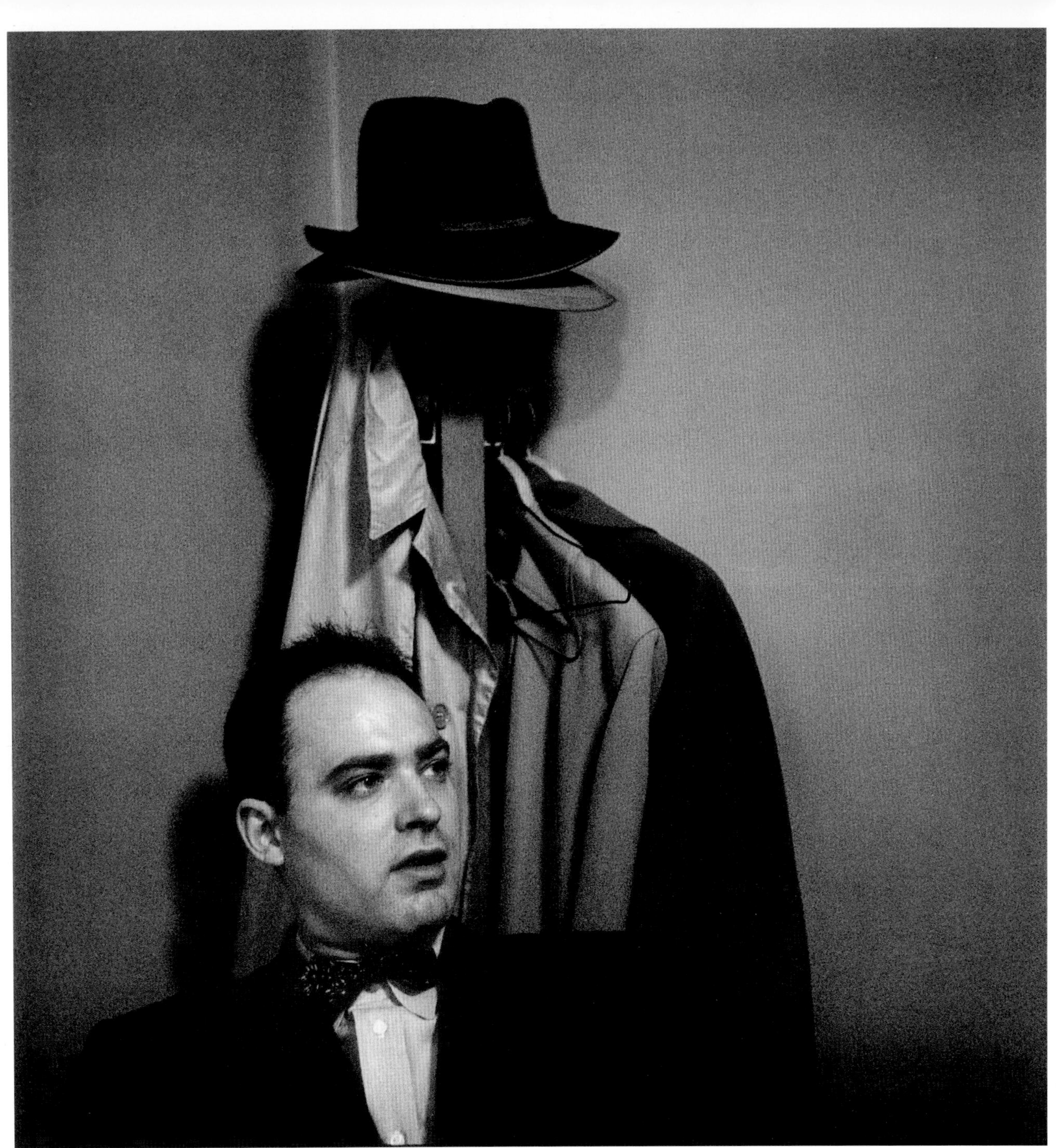

previous page *Poland, 1964* / *Vietnam, 1994*
Harold Corsini, Pittsburgh, Pennsylvania, 1950

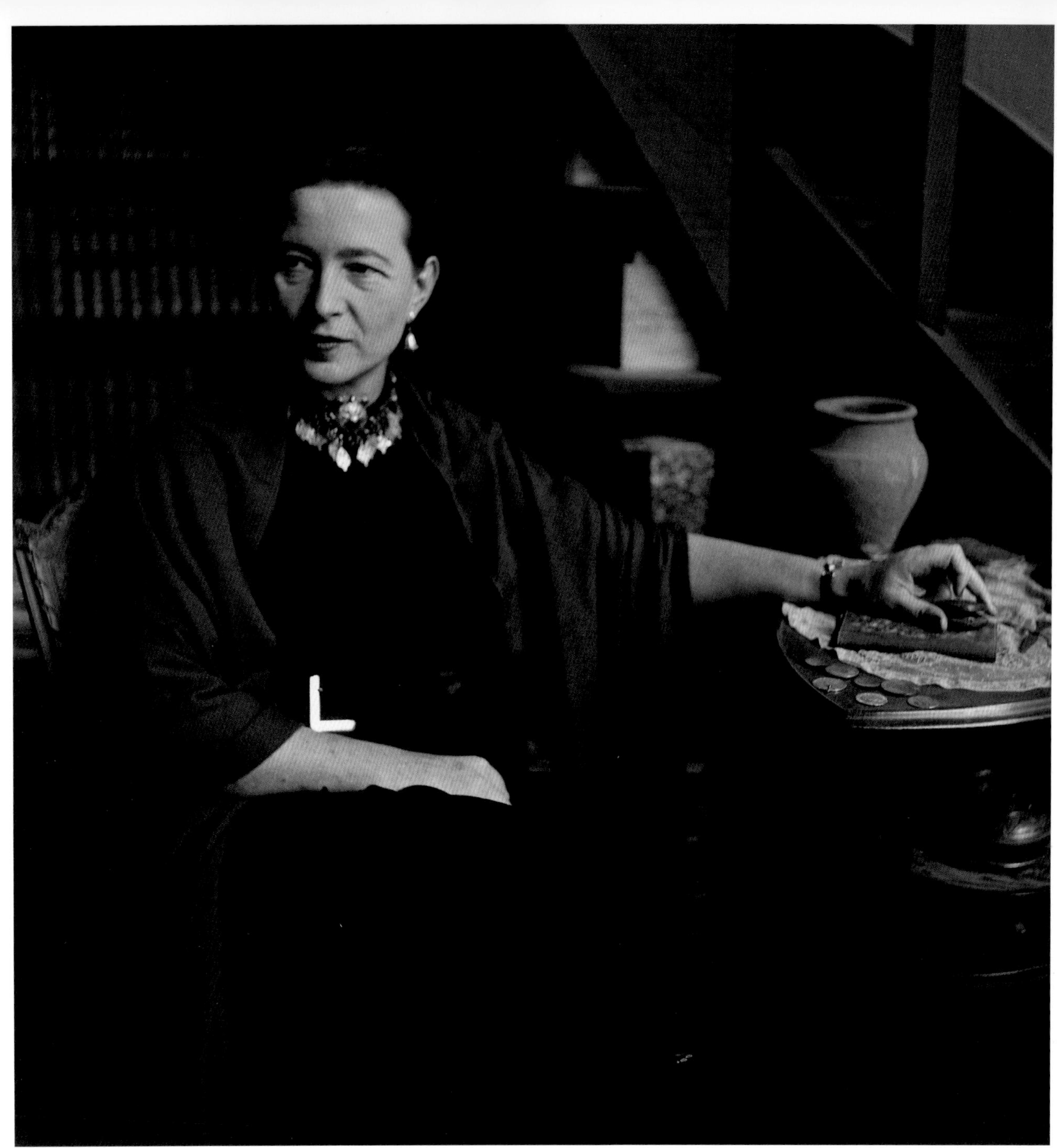

Simone de Beauvoir, Paris, 1949

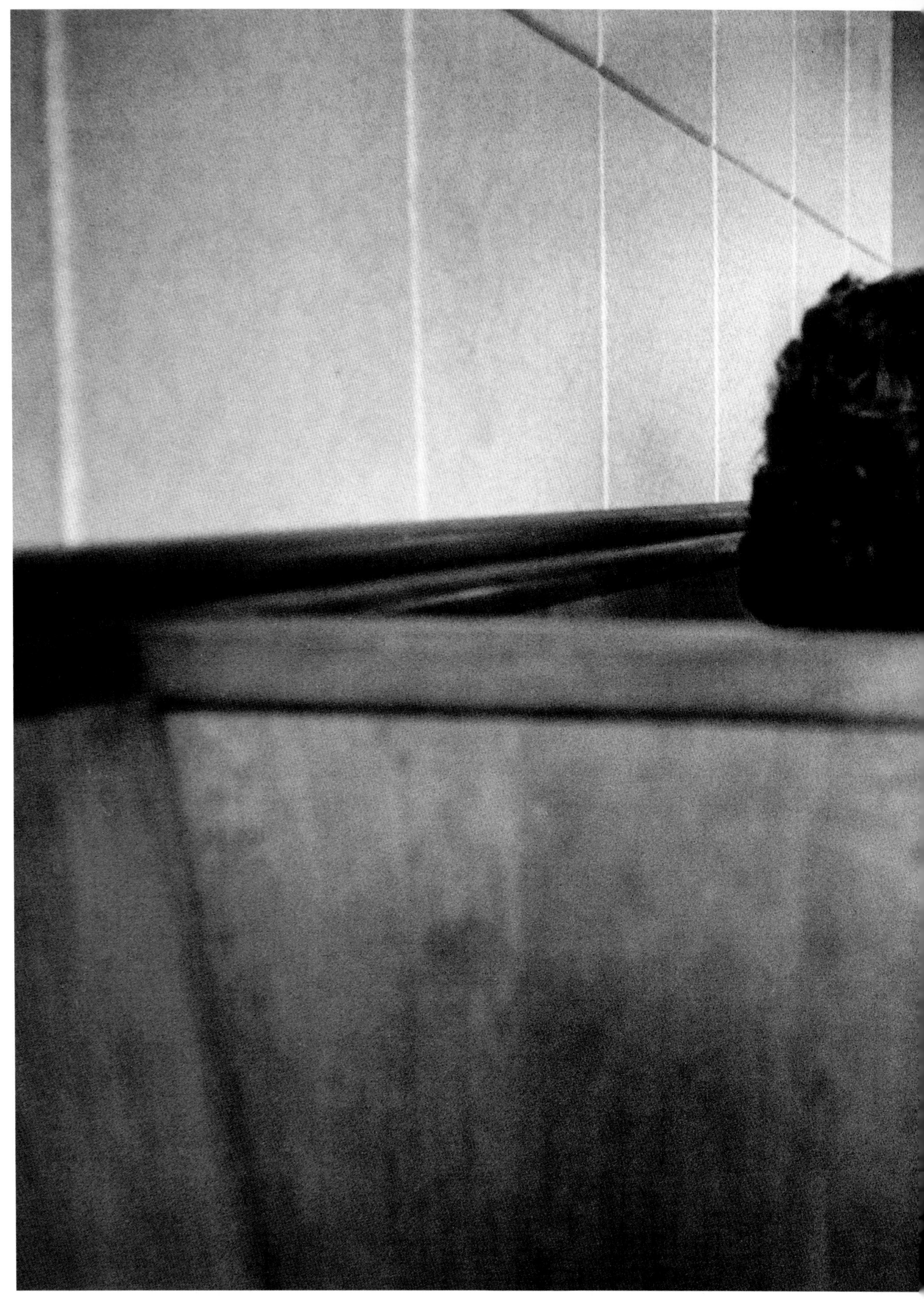

New York, 1953

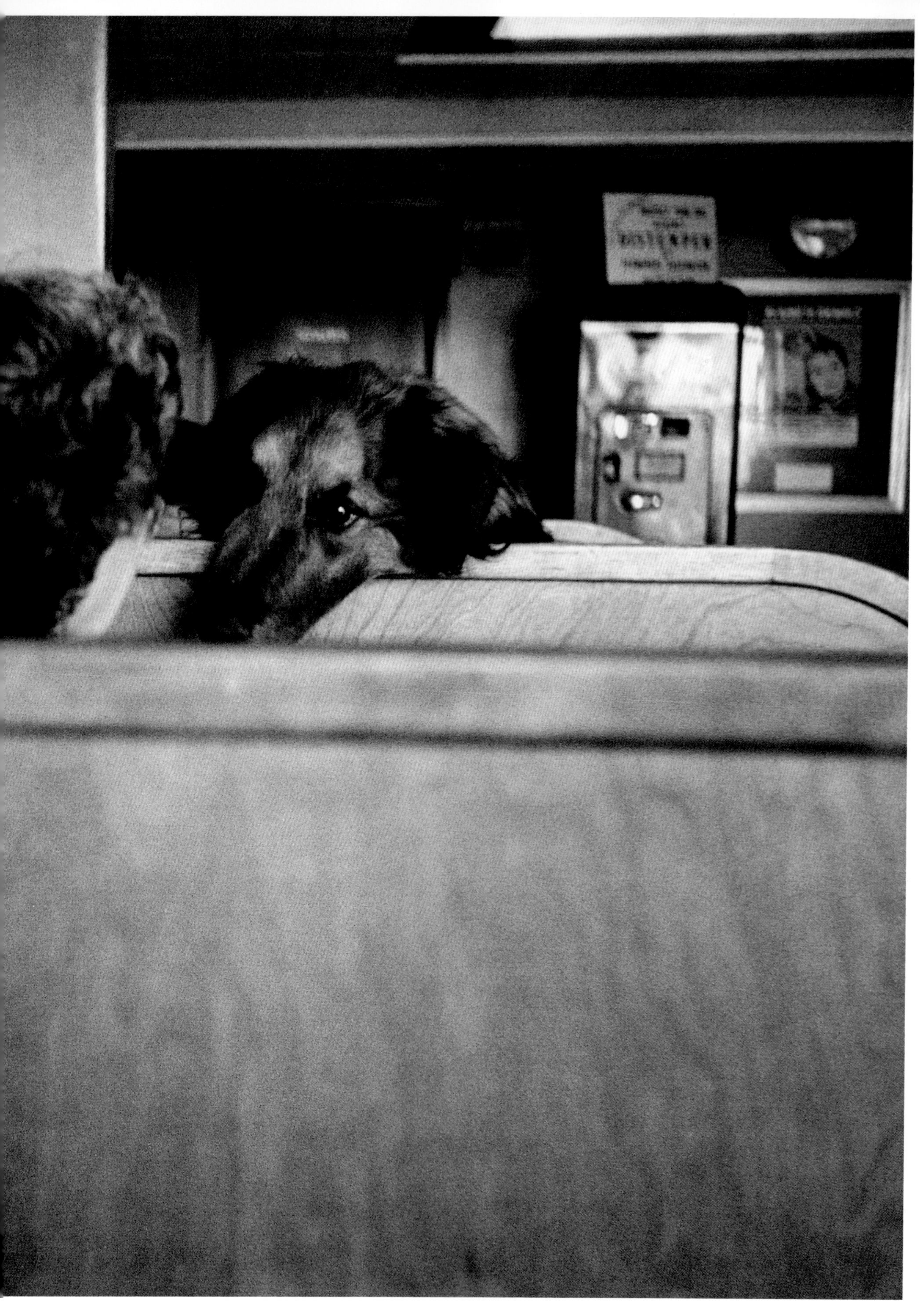

overleaf *Paris, 1969* / *New York, 1978*

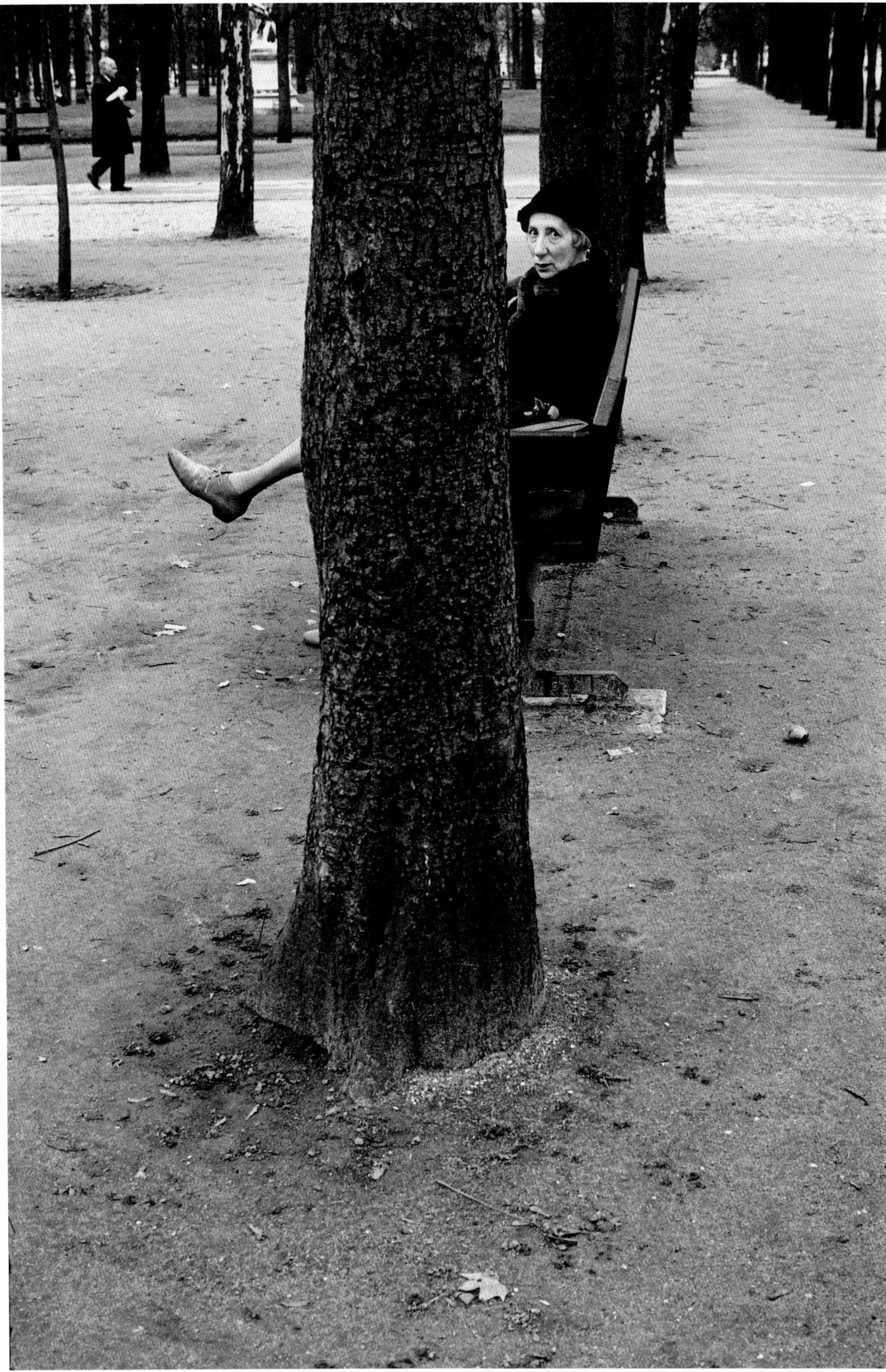

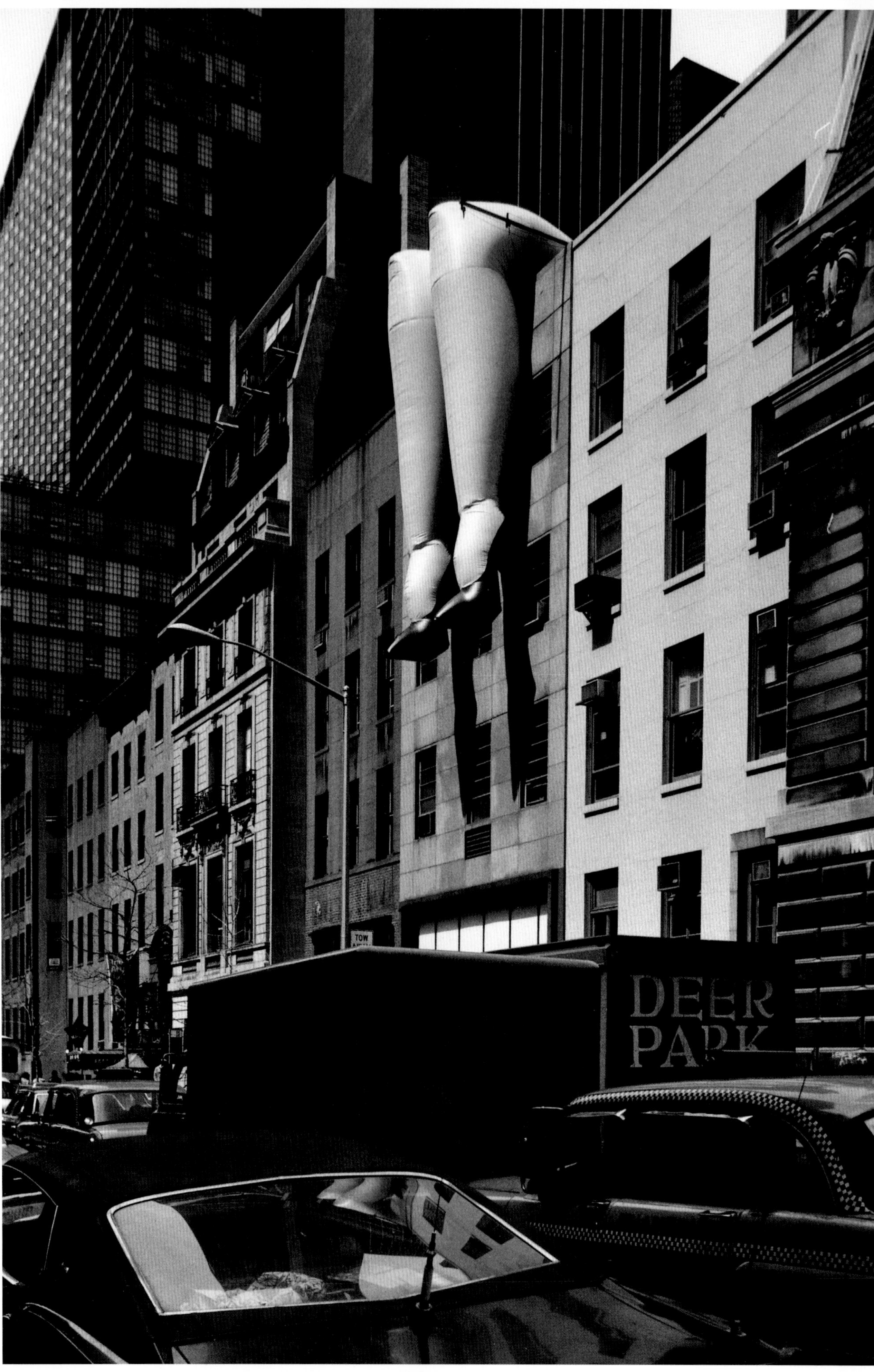
DEER
TOW

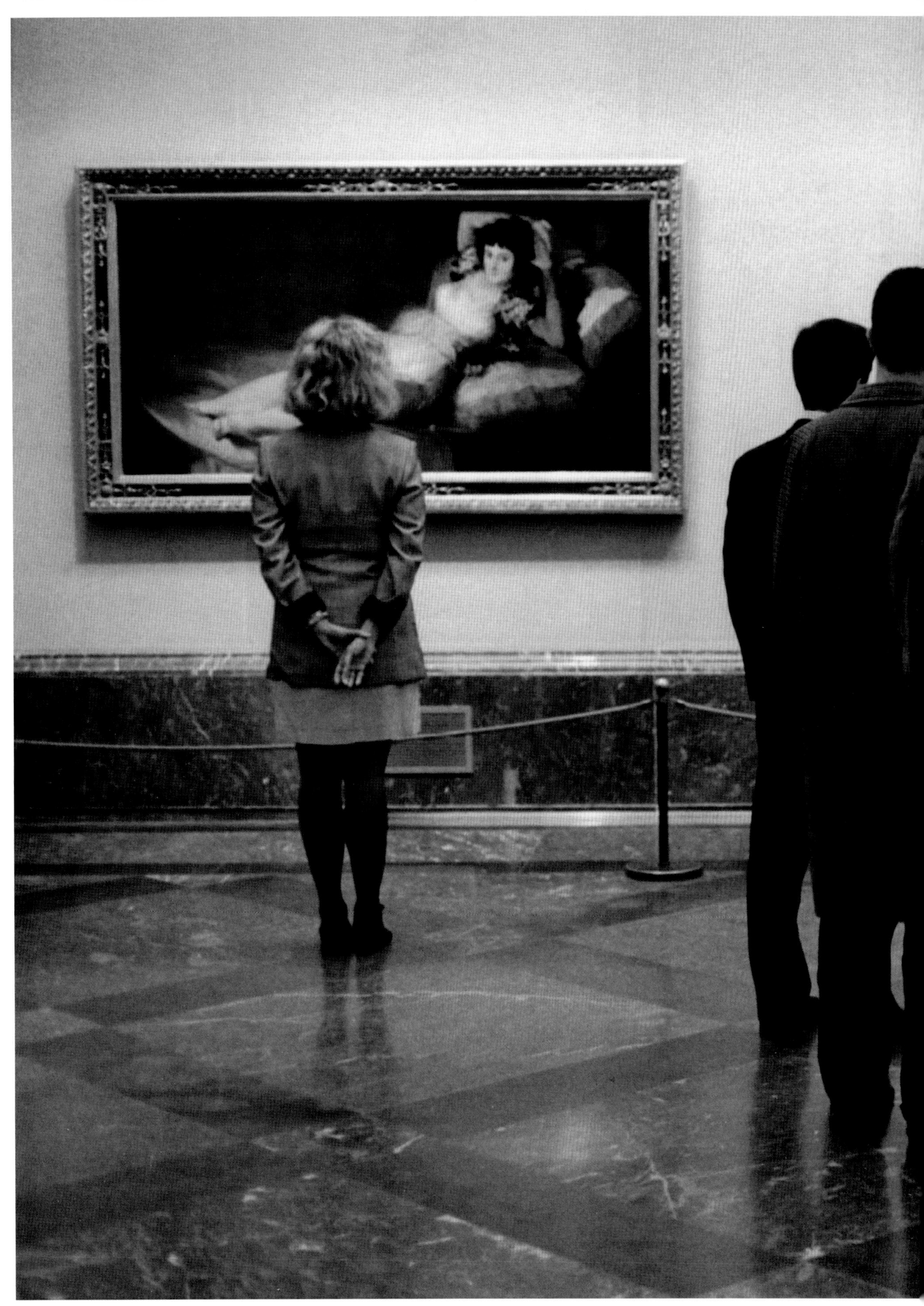

Museo del Prado, Madrid, 1995

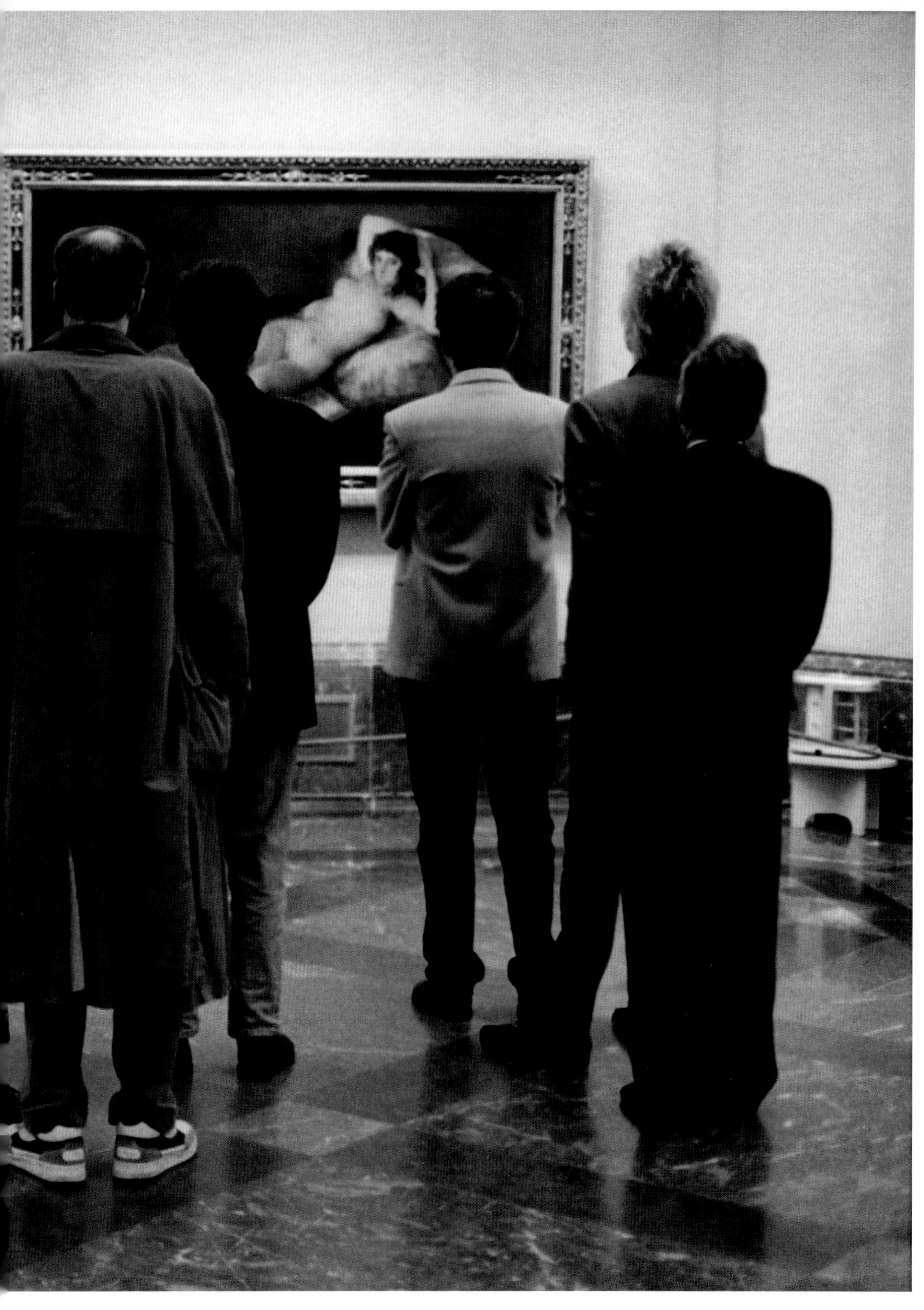

overleaf *Rio de Janeiro, 1961* / *Rome, 1965*

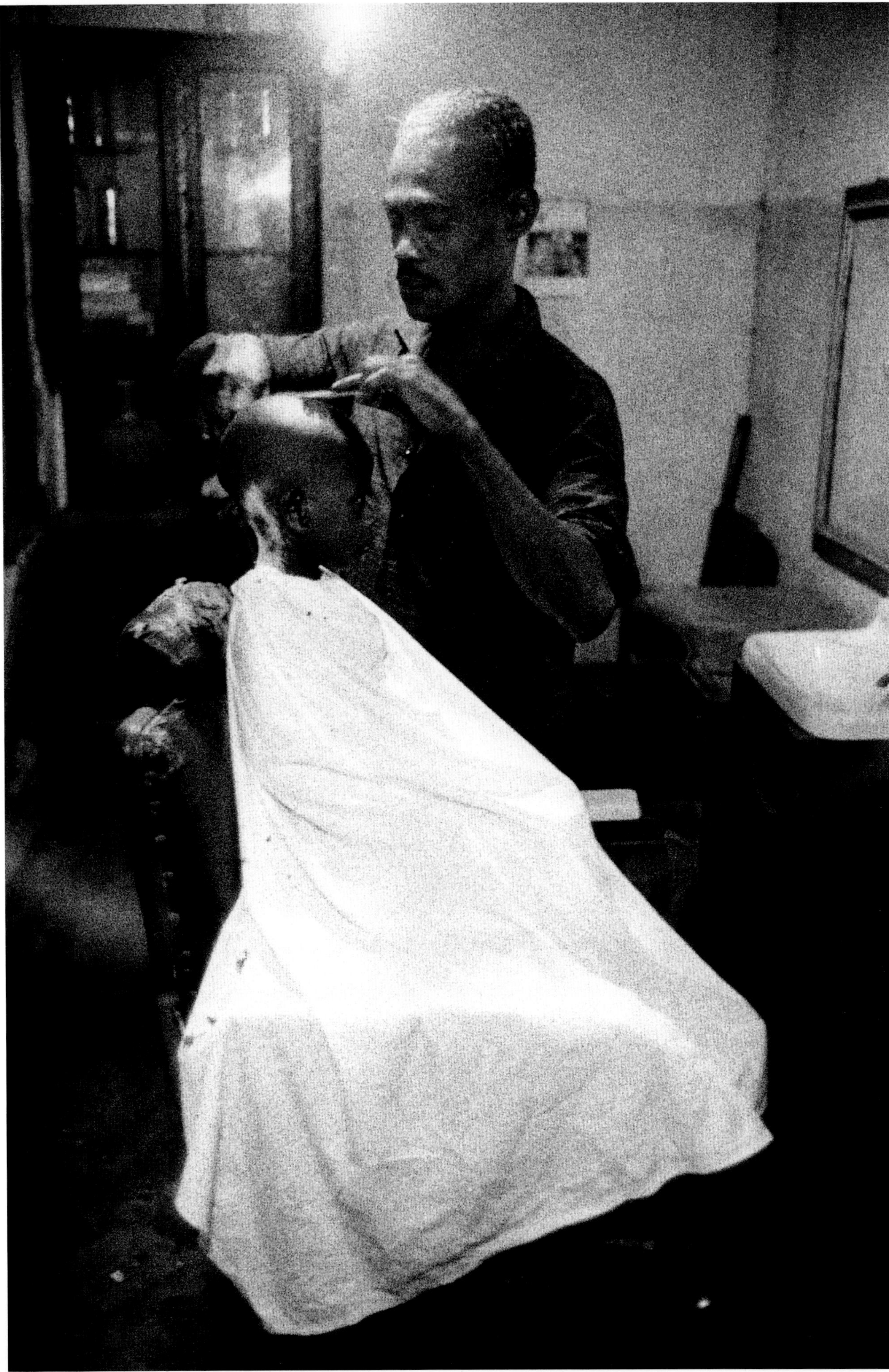

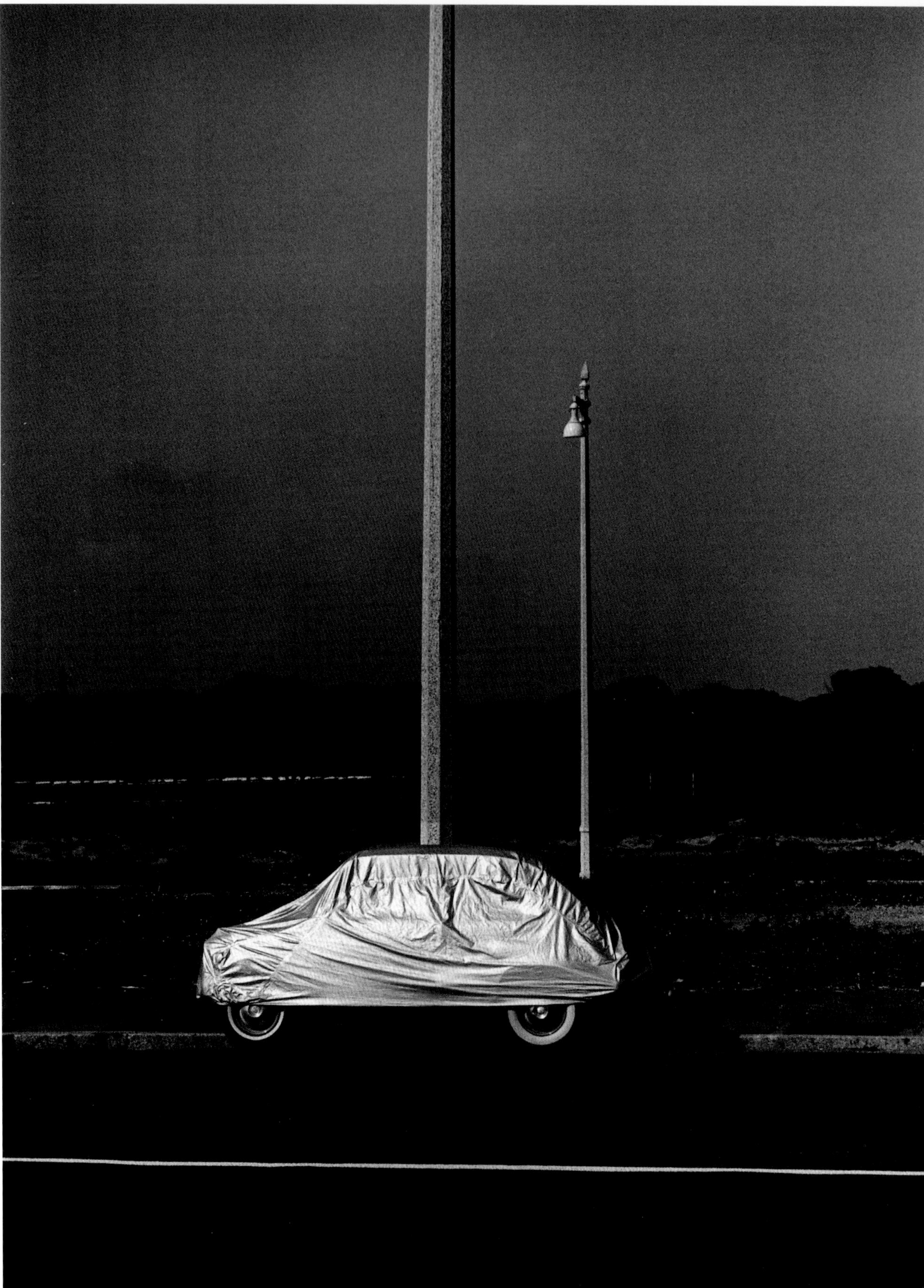

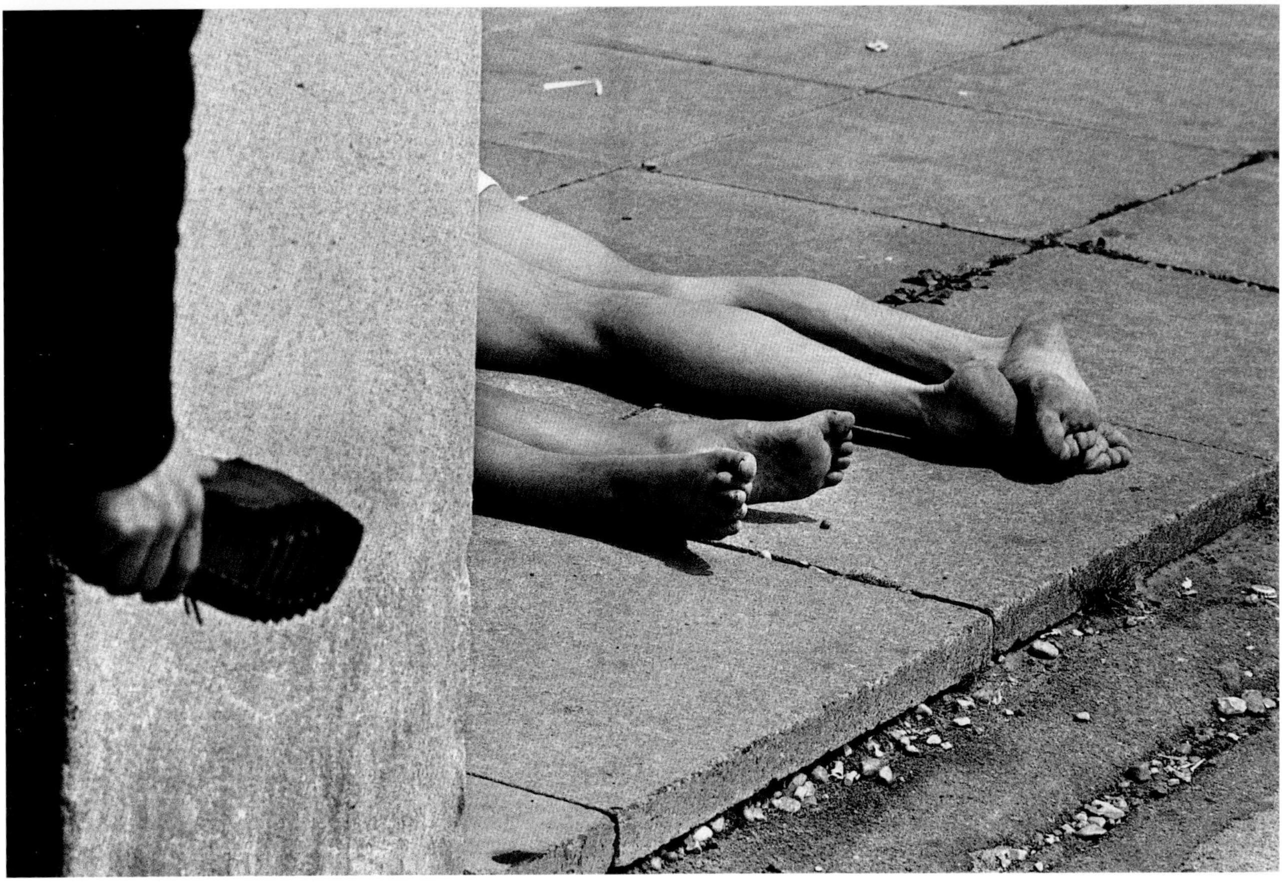

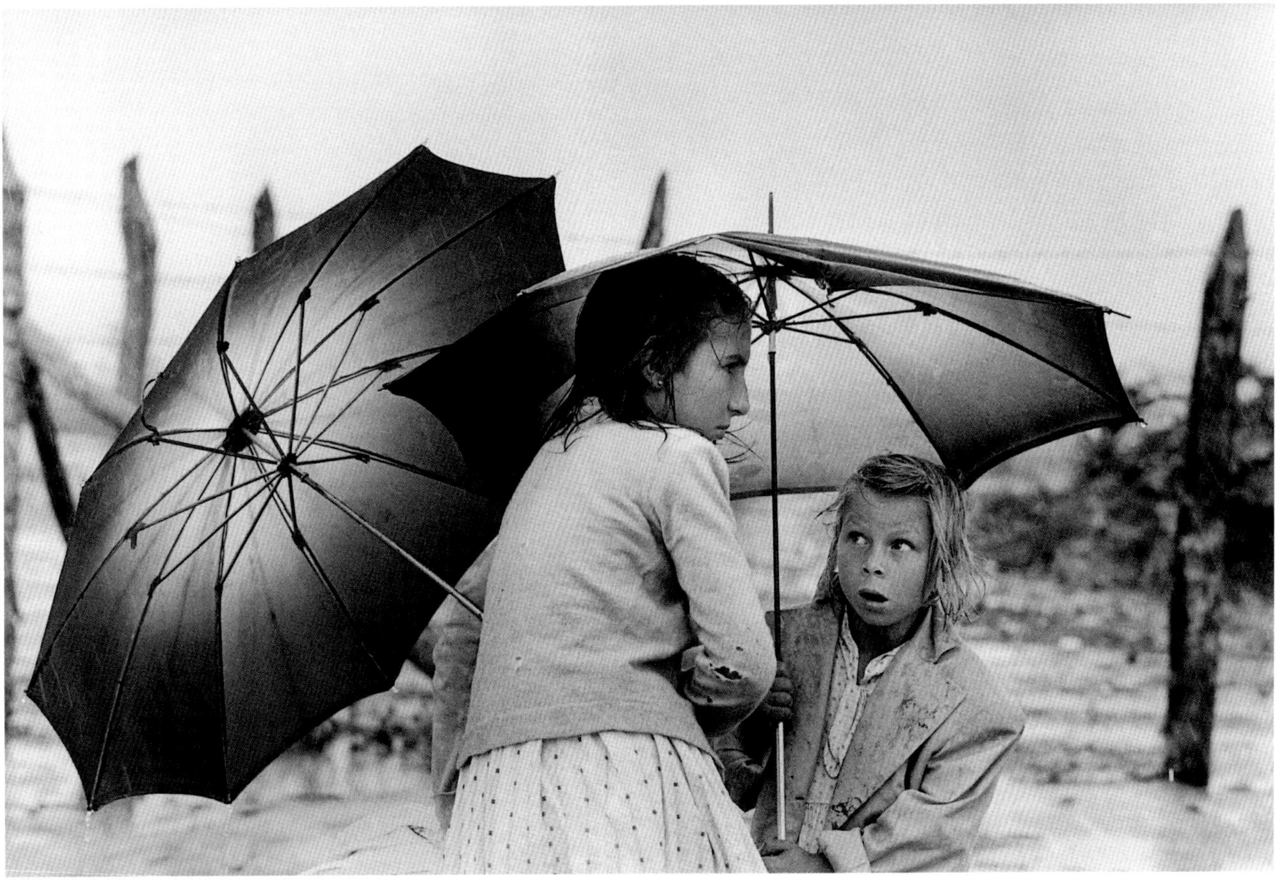

Brighton, England, 1970 / *Brasília, Brazil, 1961*

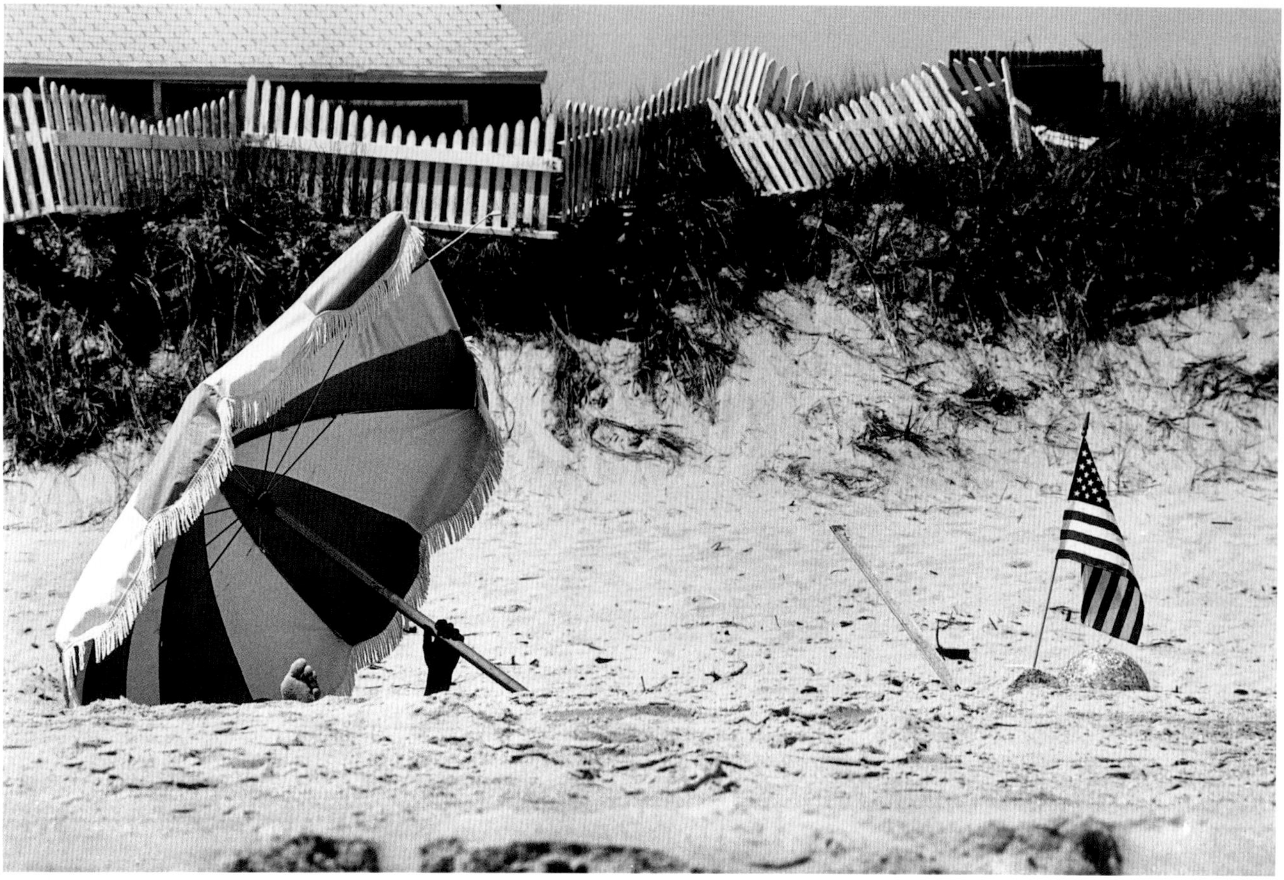

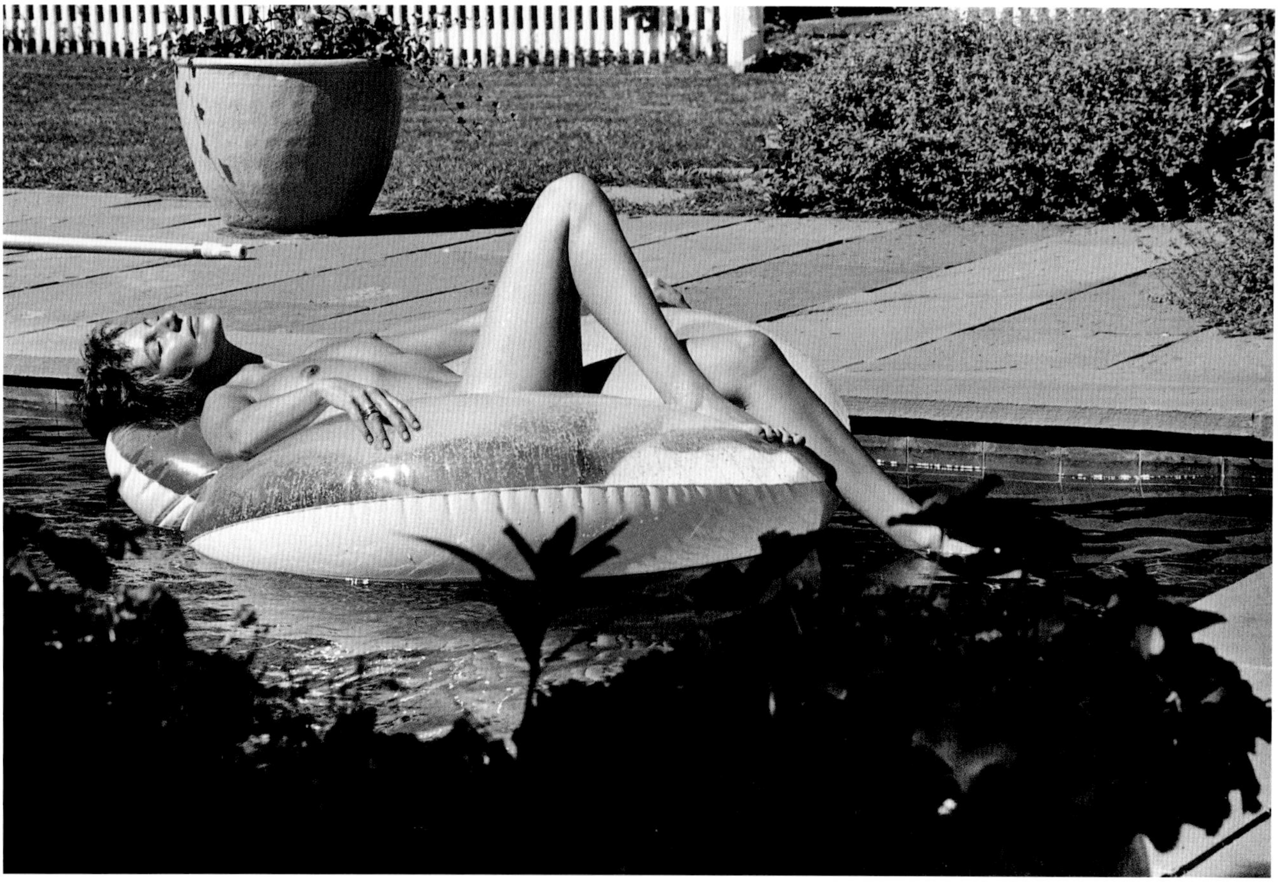

Amagansett, New York, 1969 / *East Hampton, New York, 1998*
overleaf *New Jersey, 1951* / *Coney Island, New York, 1955*

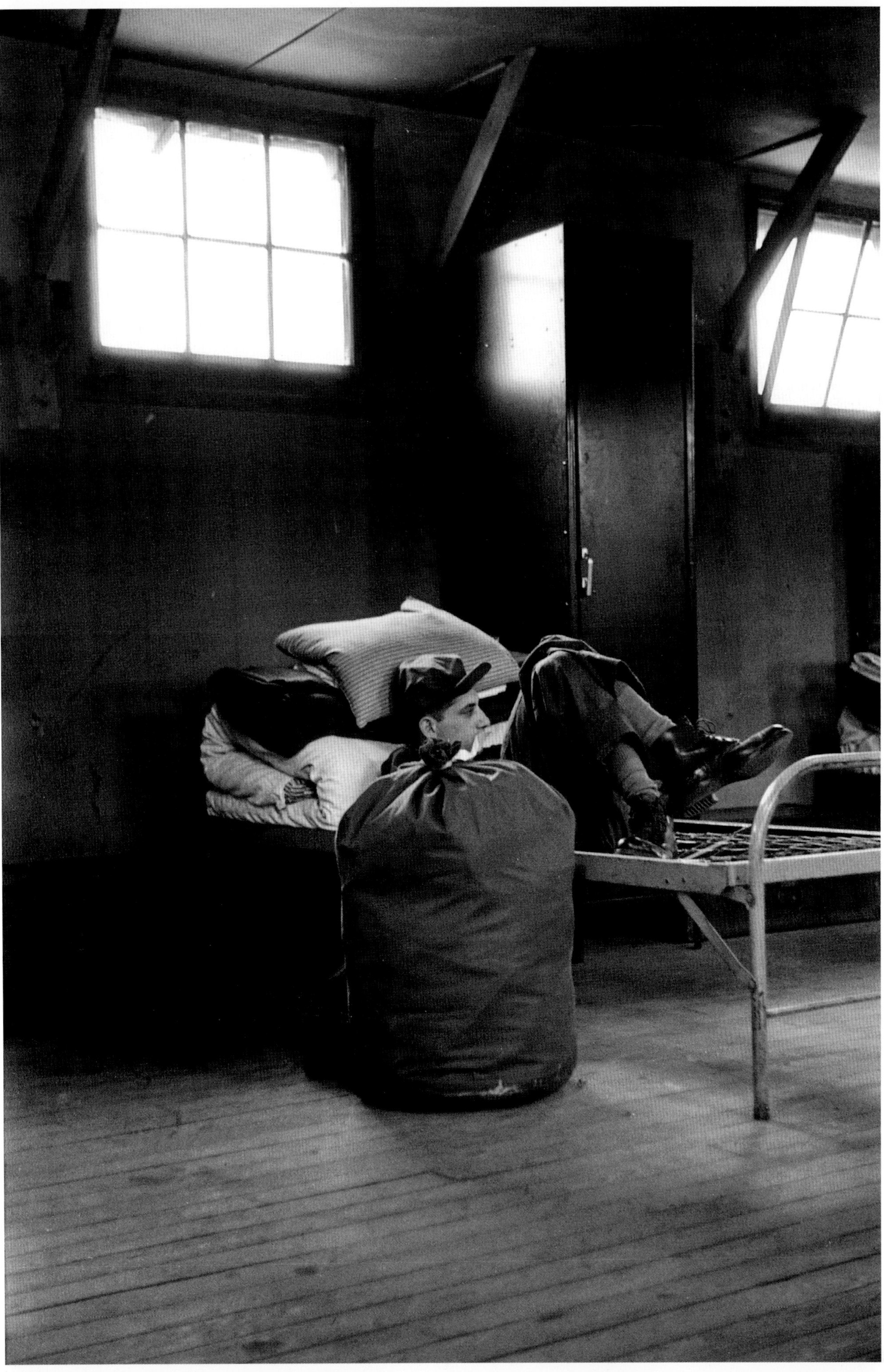

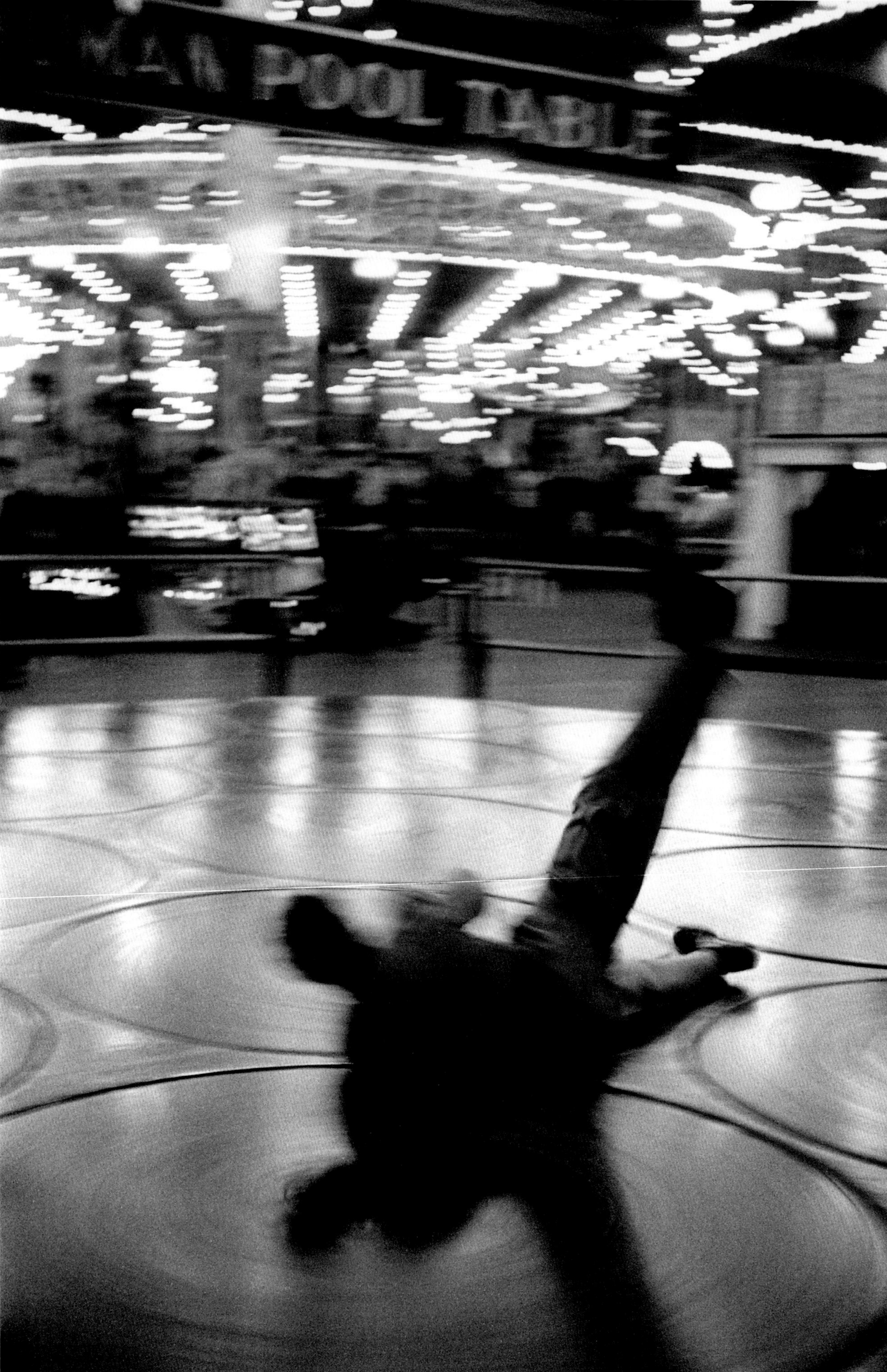
POOL TABLE

Moscow, 1957

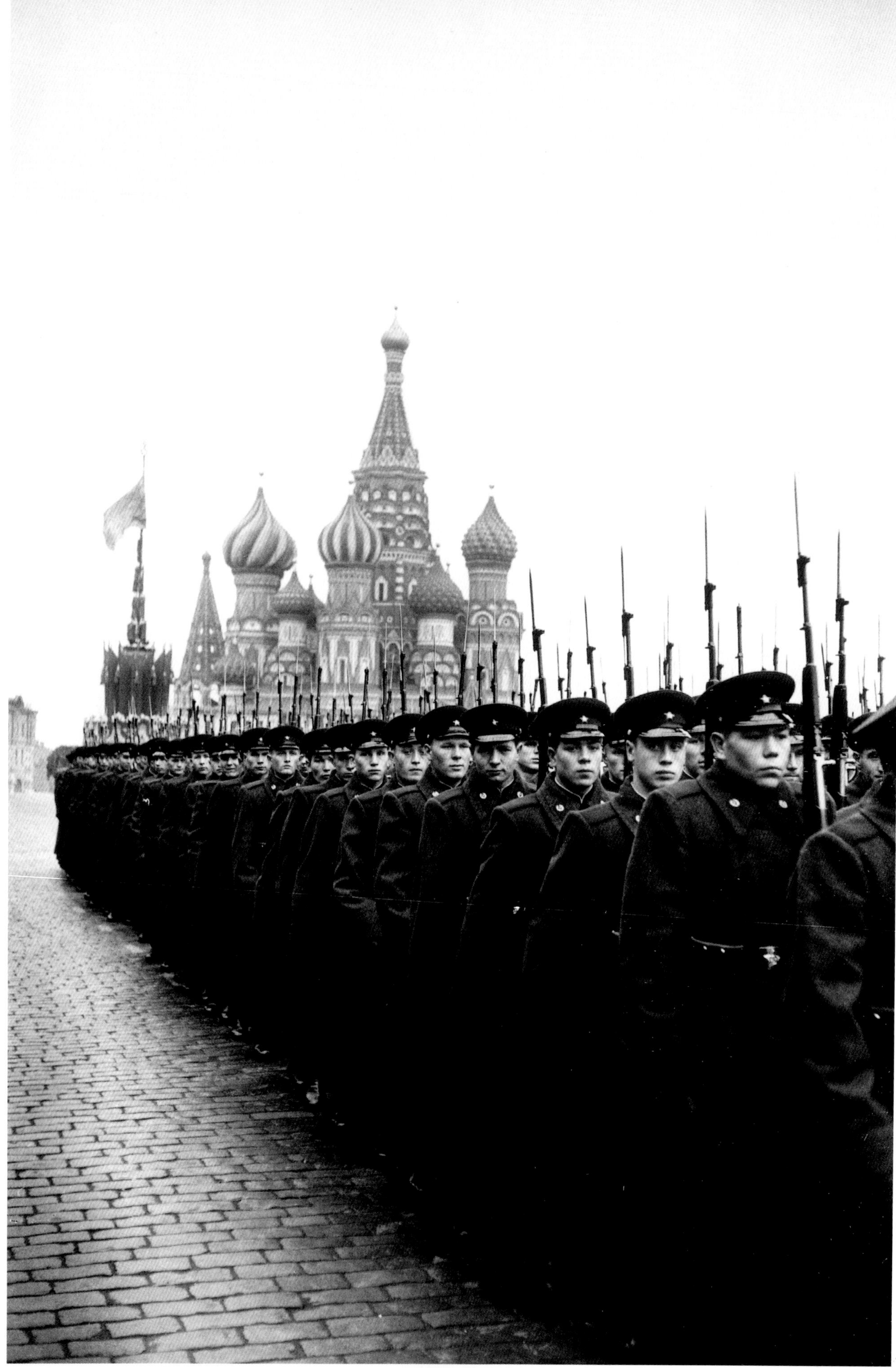

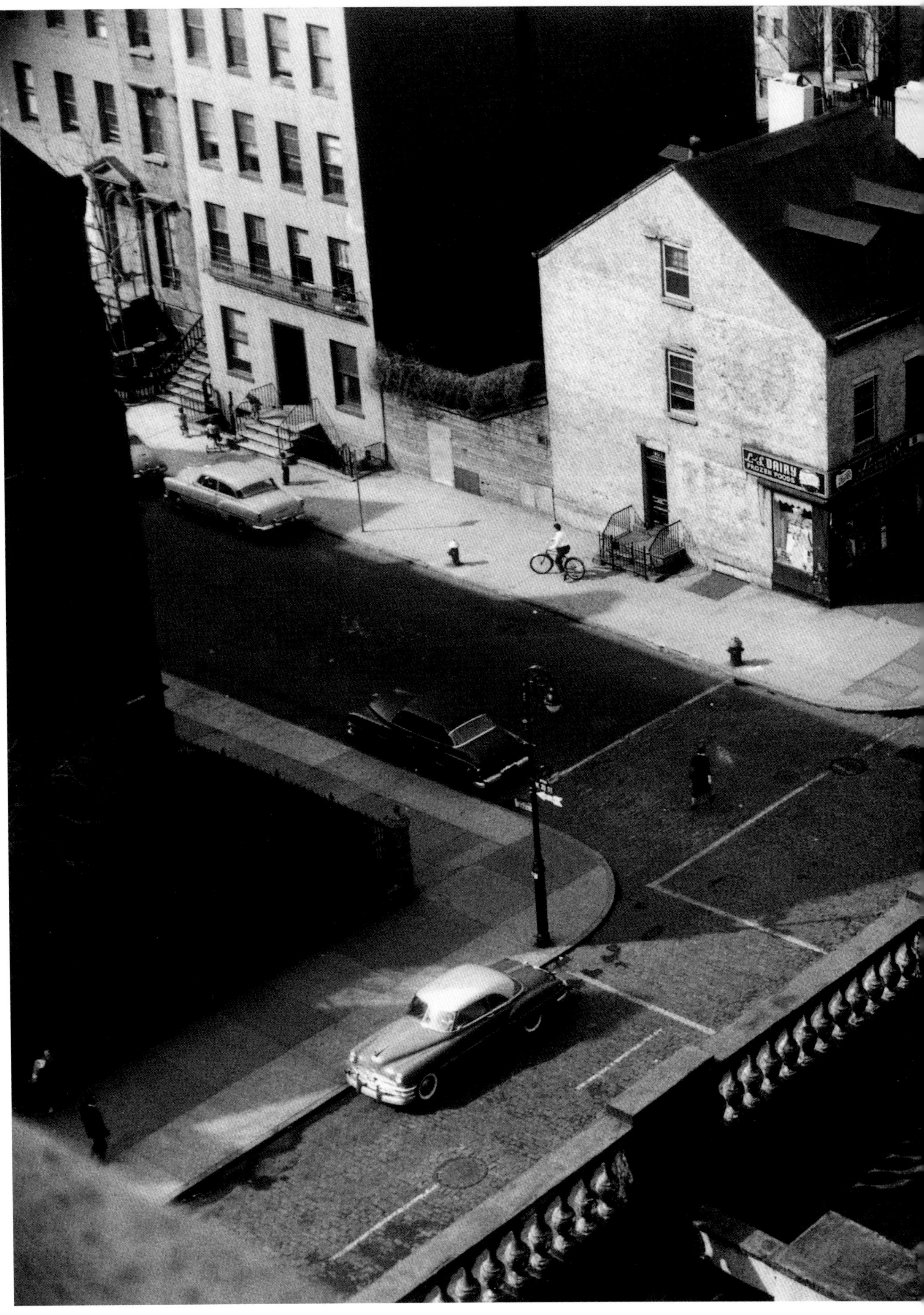

New York, 1954

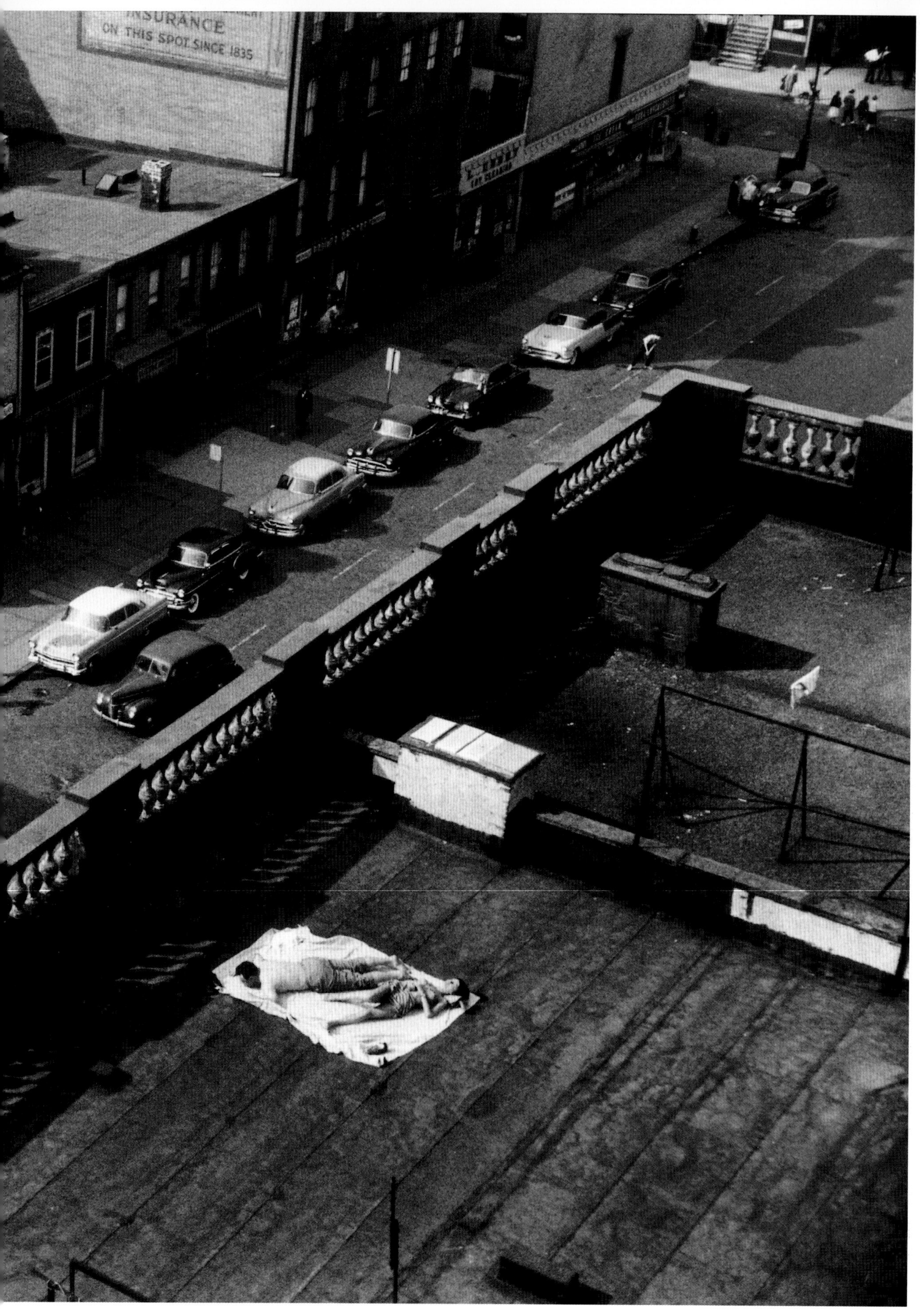

overleaf *Paris, 1964* / *Galina Ulanova, Moscow, 1957*

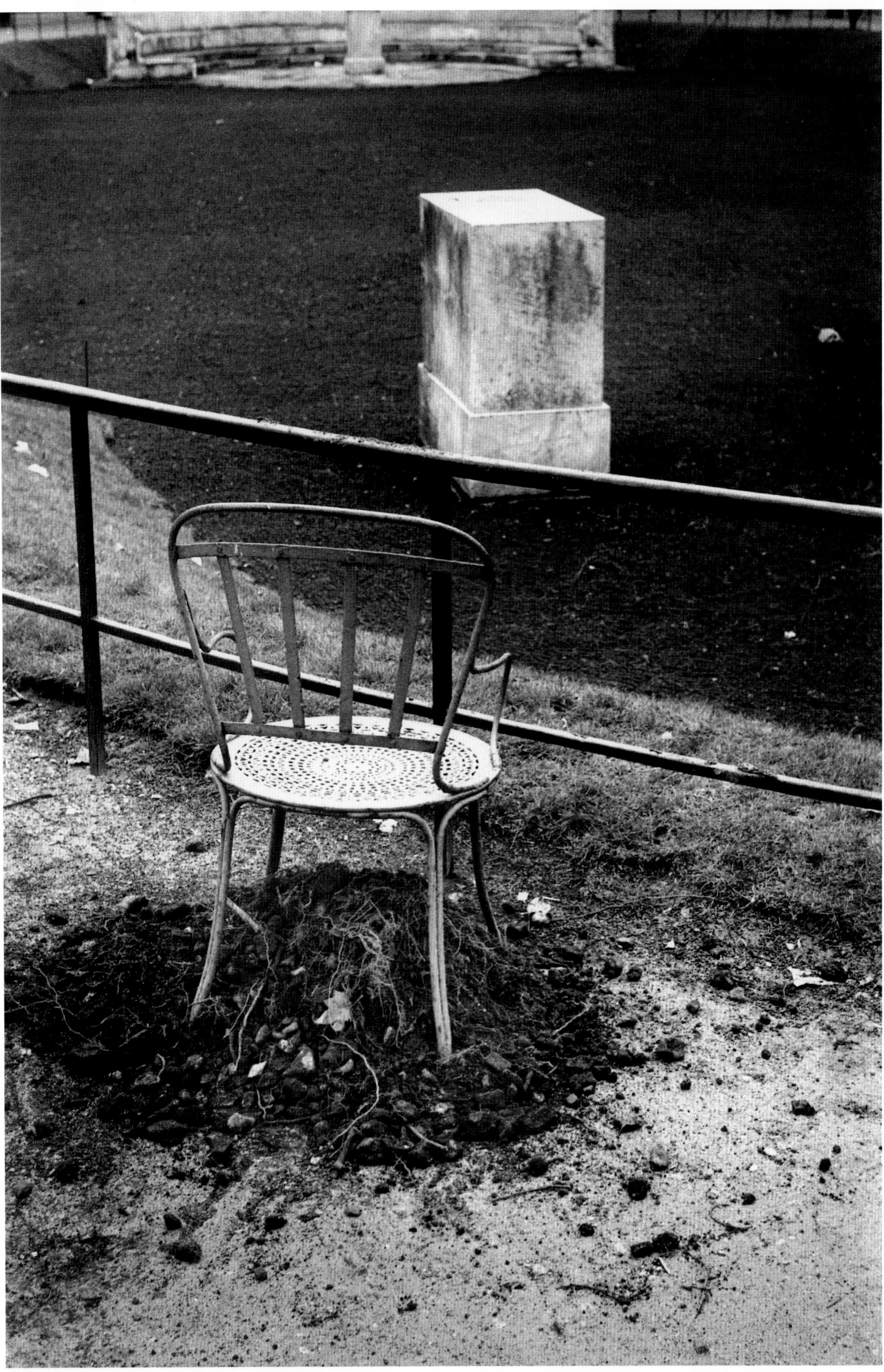

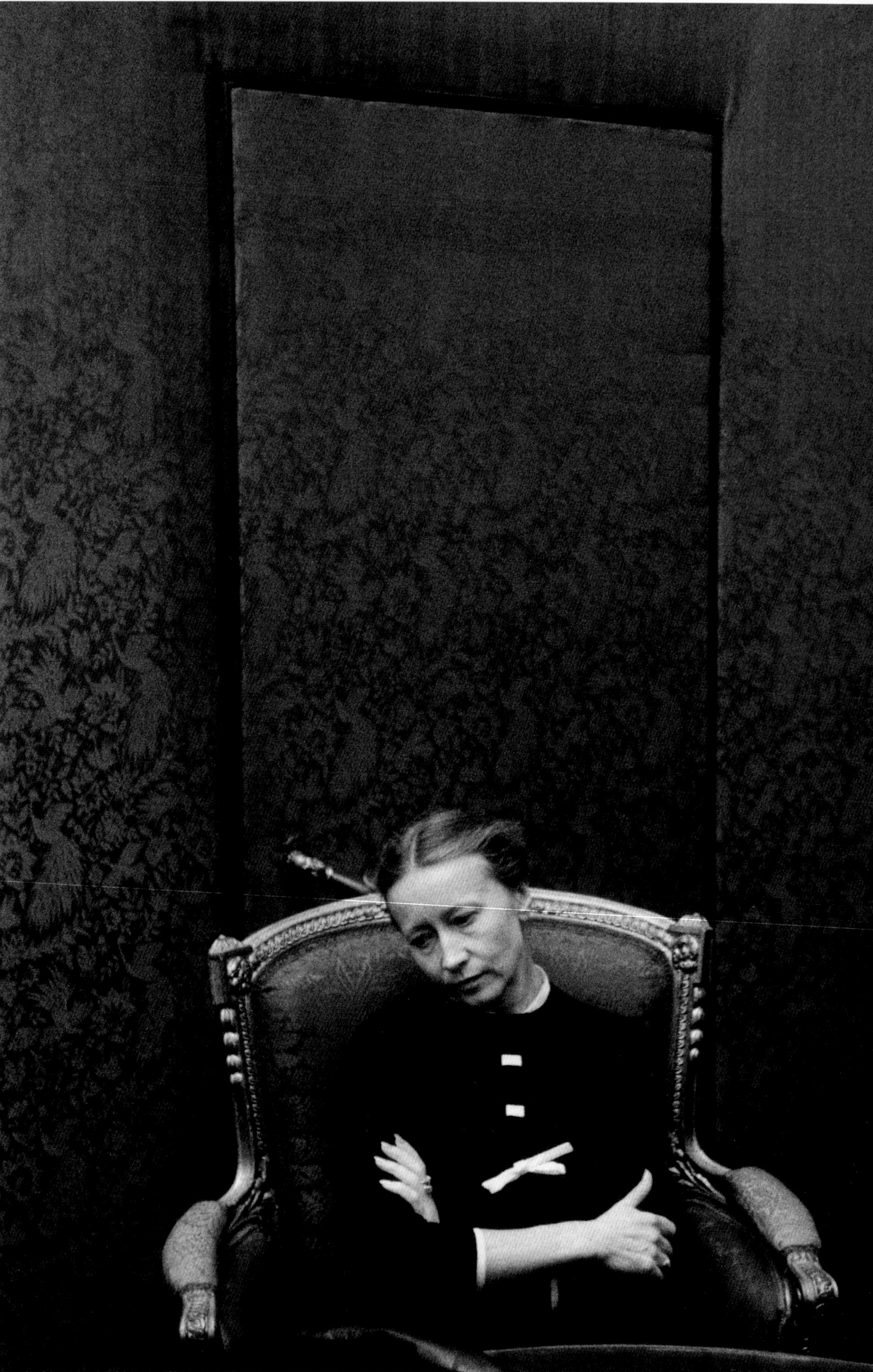

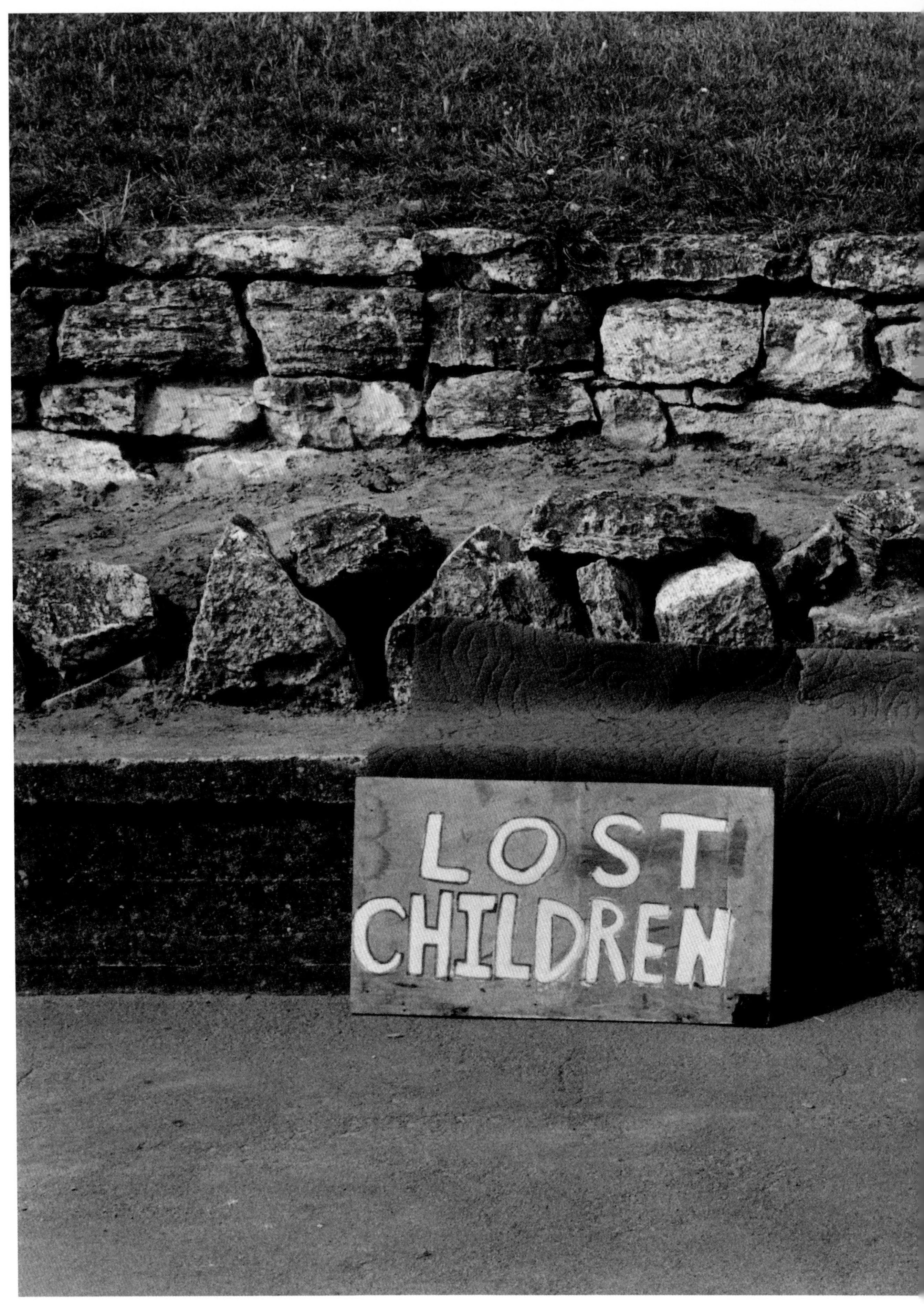

Barry Island, Wales, 1978

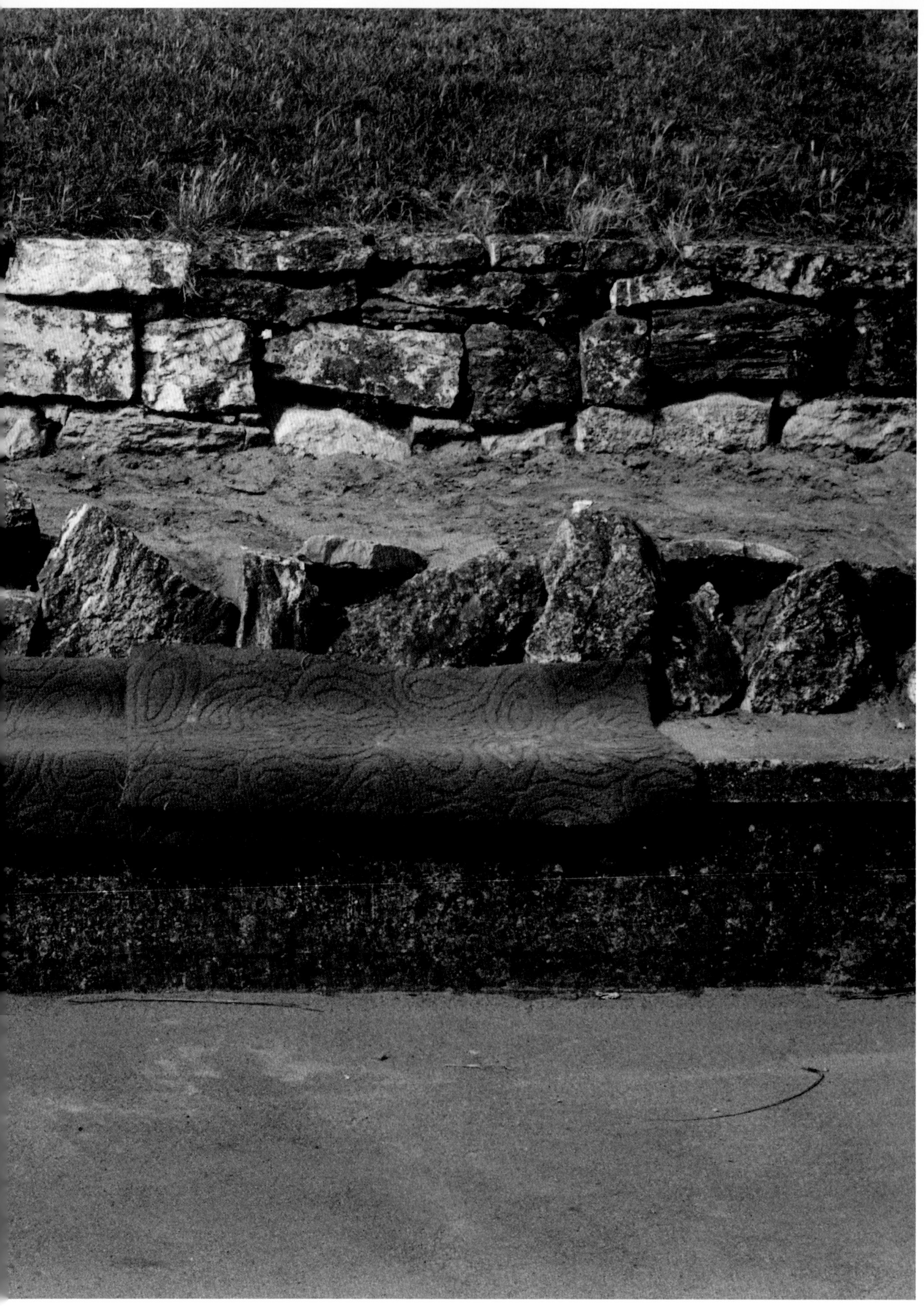

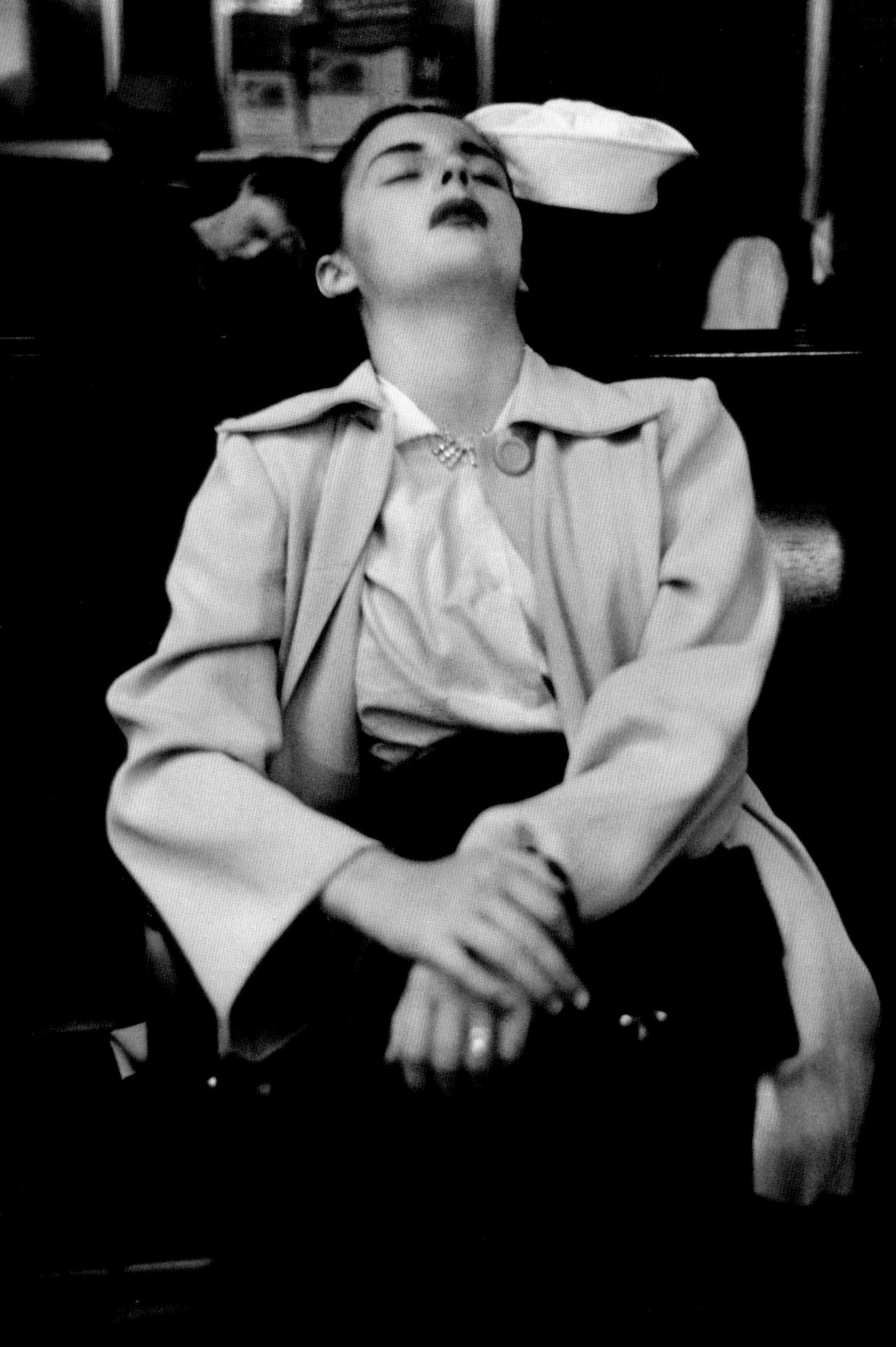

Fernandina Beach, Florida, 1950

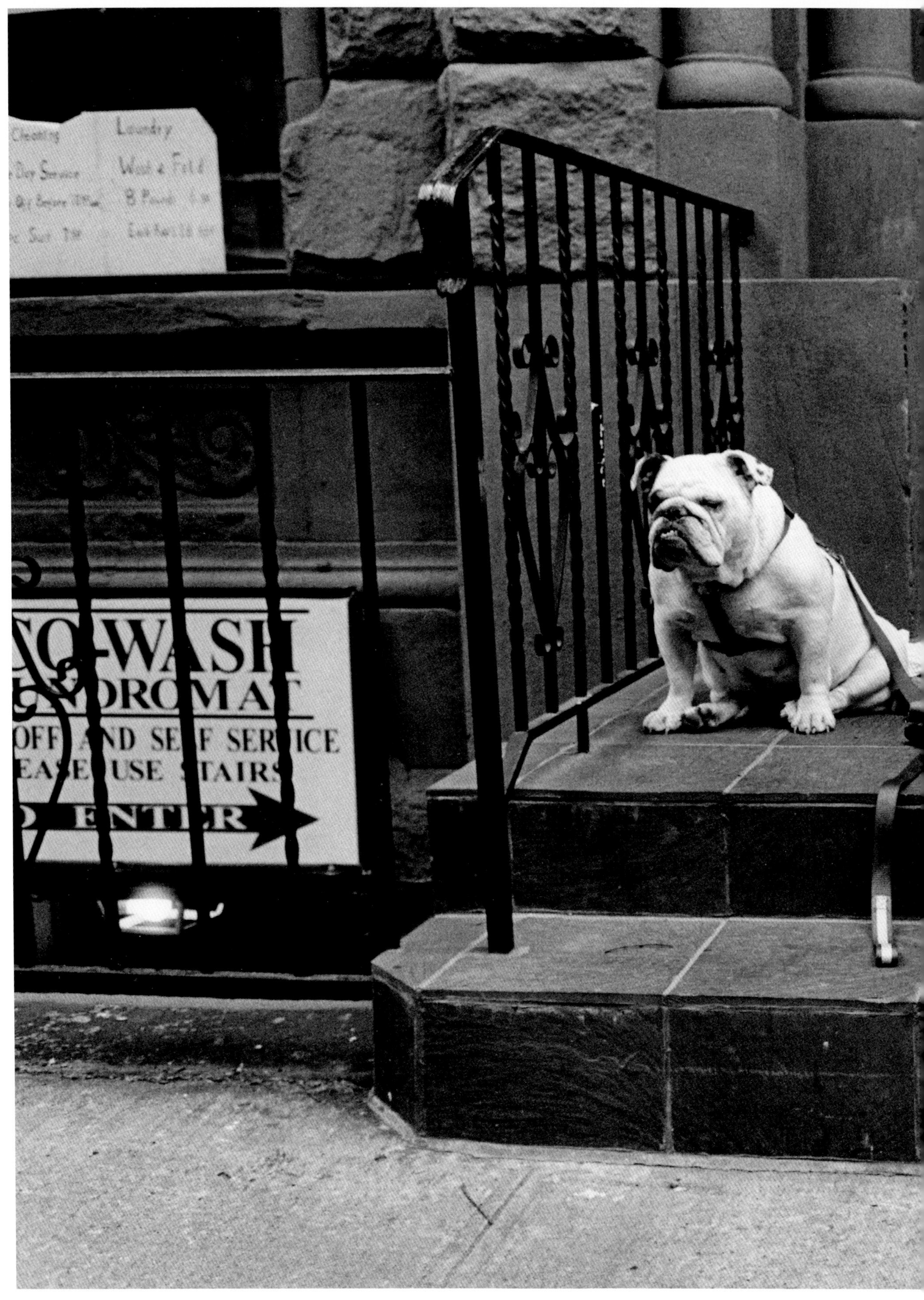

New York, 2000

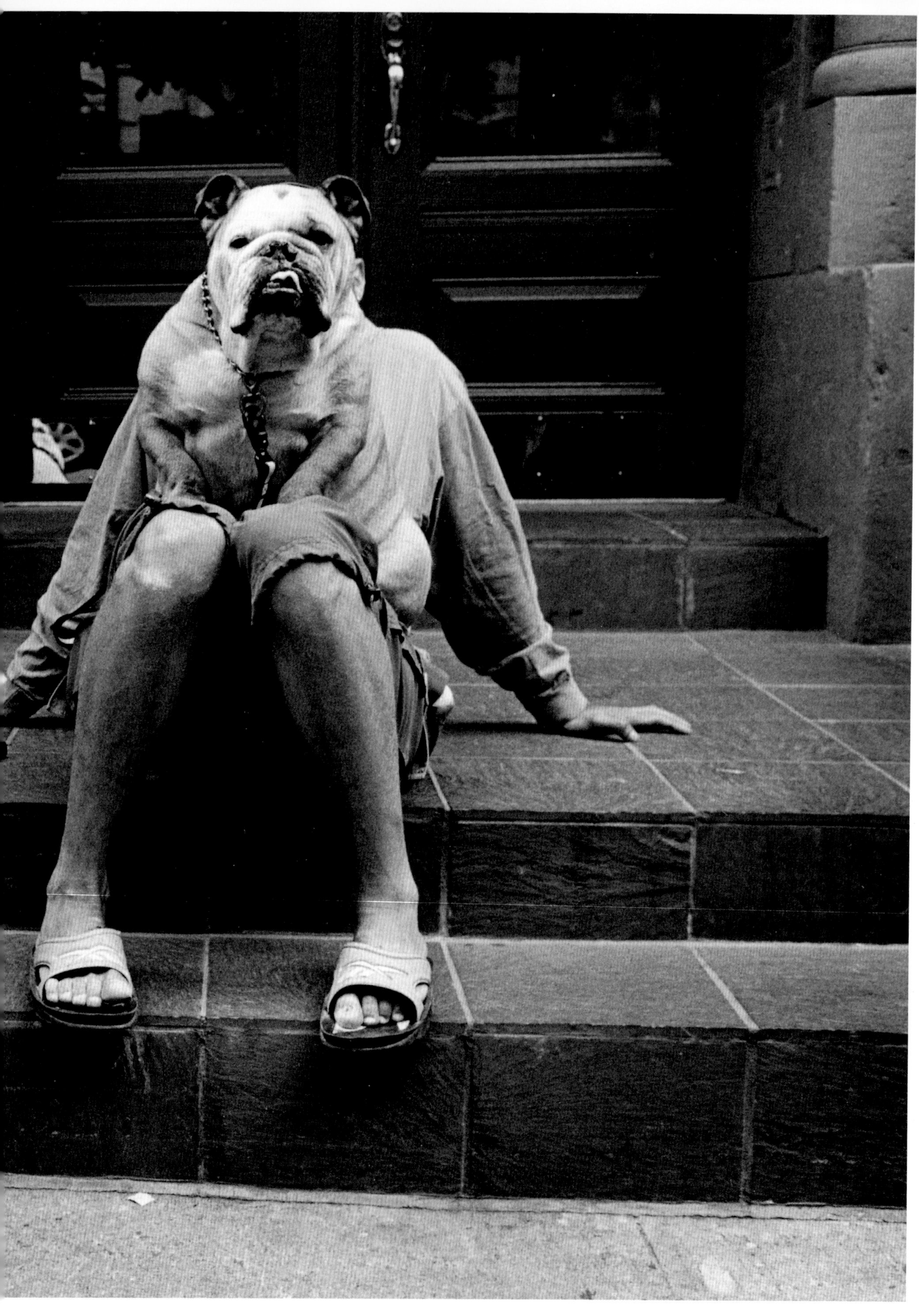

overleaf *Miami Beach, 1968* / *Princeton, New Jersey, 1955*

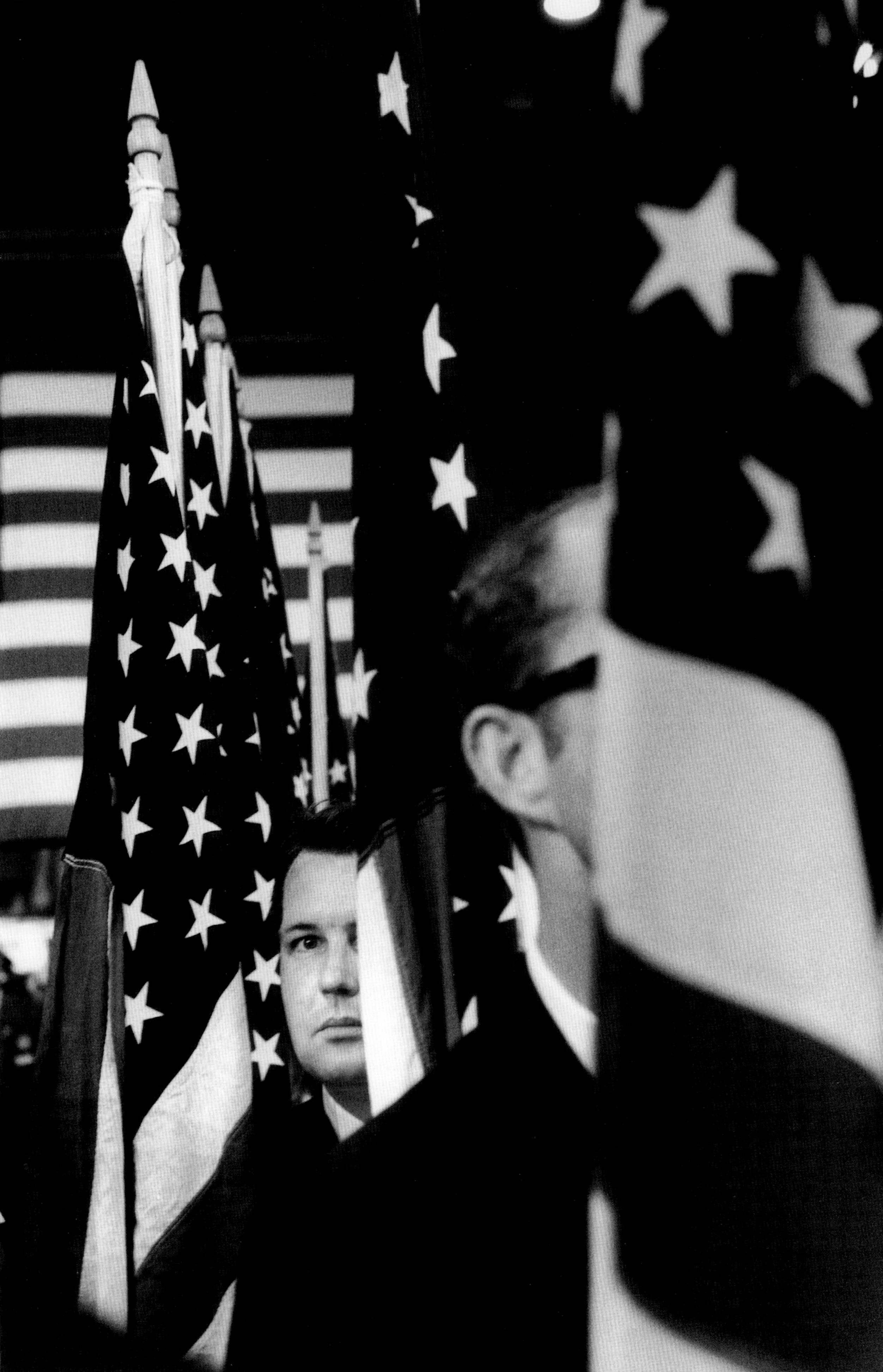

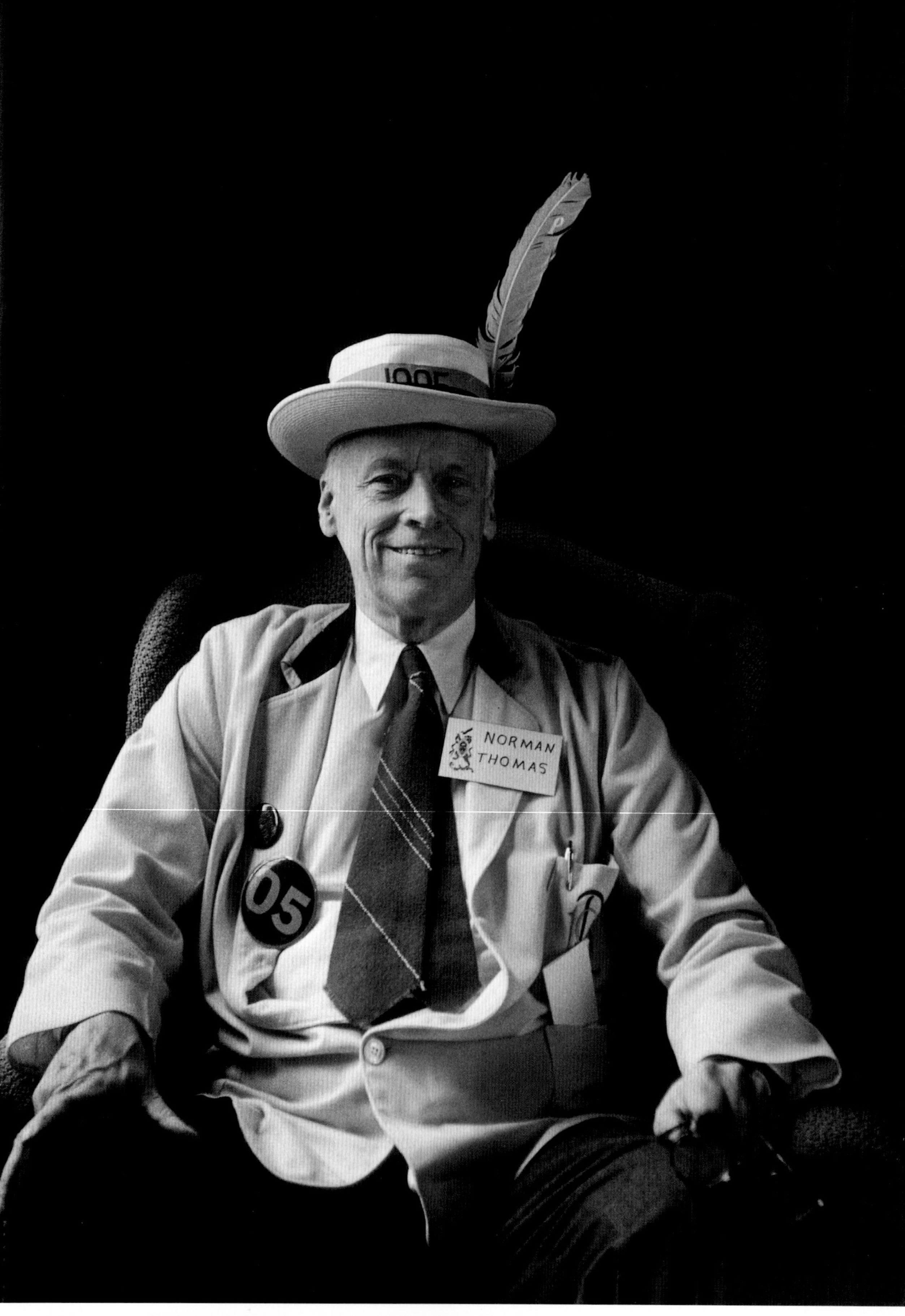
NORMAN
THOMAS
05

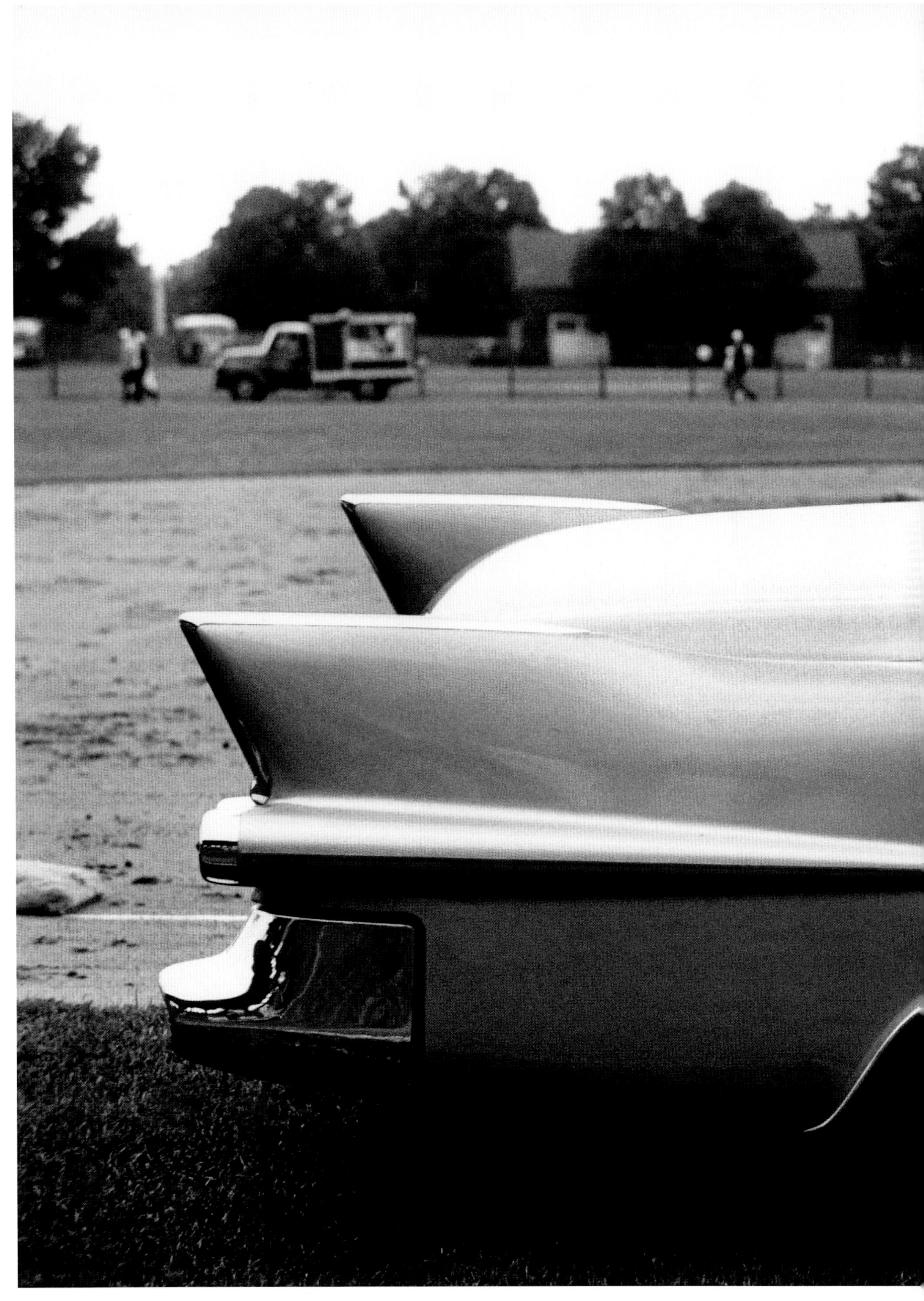

New Haven, Connecticut, 1955

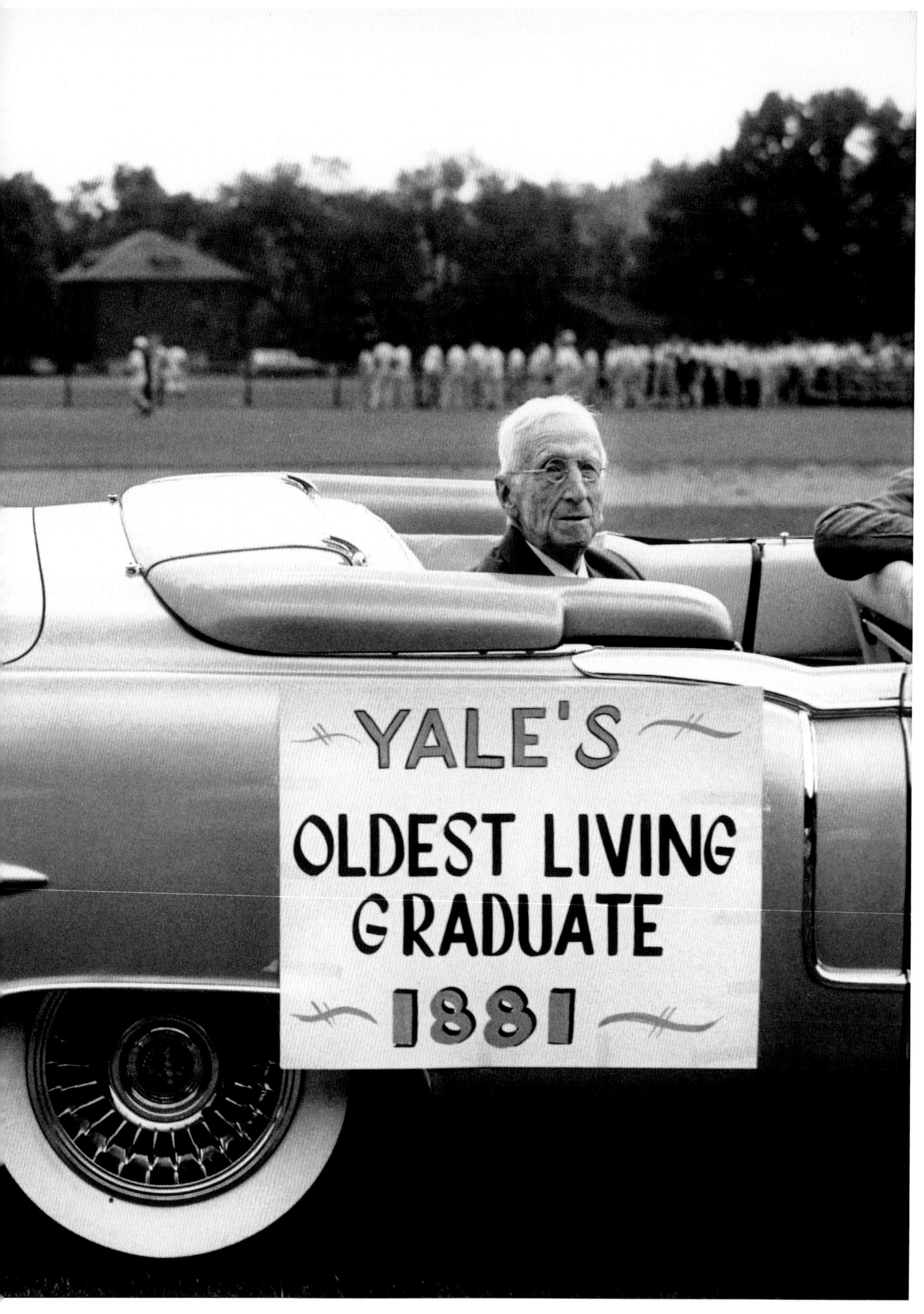

overleaf *Atlantic Ocean, 1951* / *Hungary, 1964*

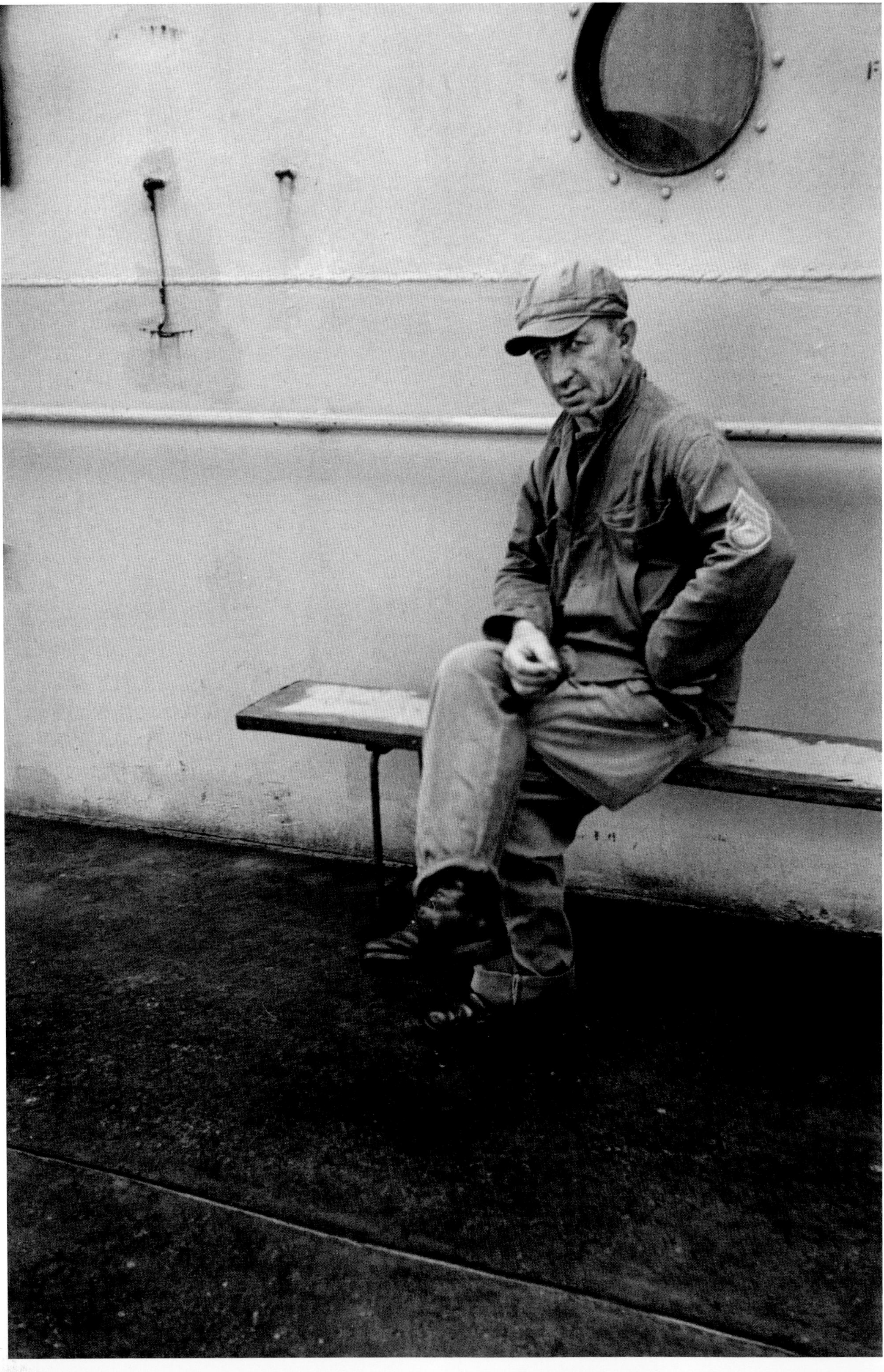

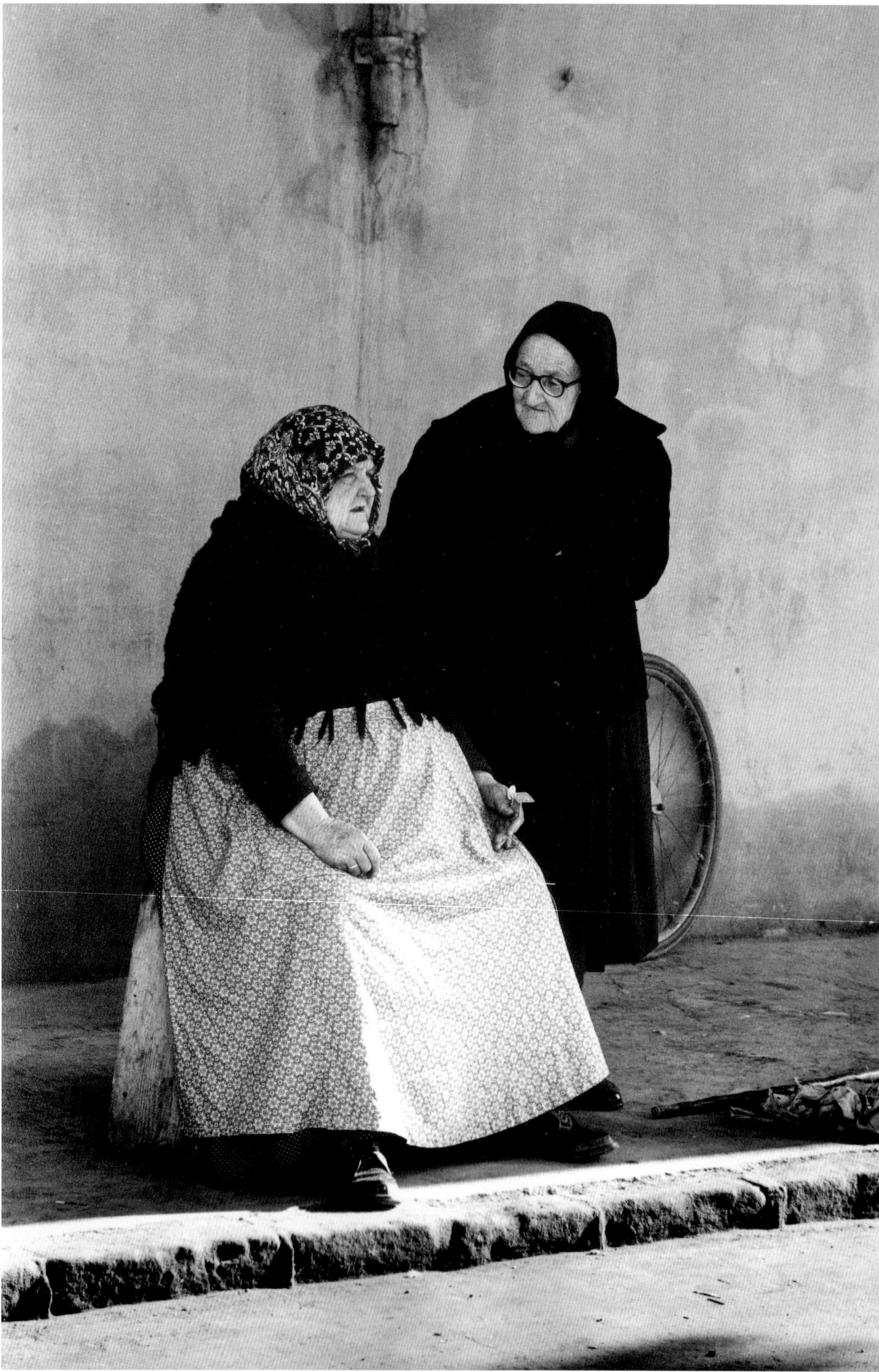

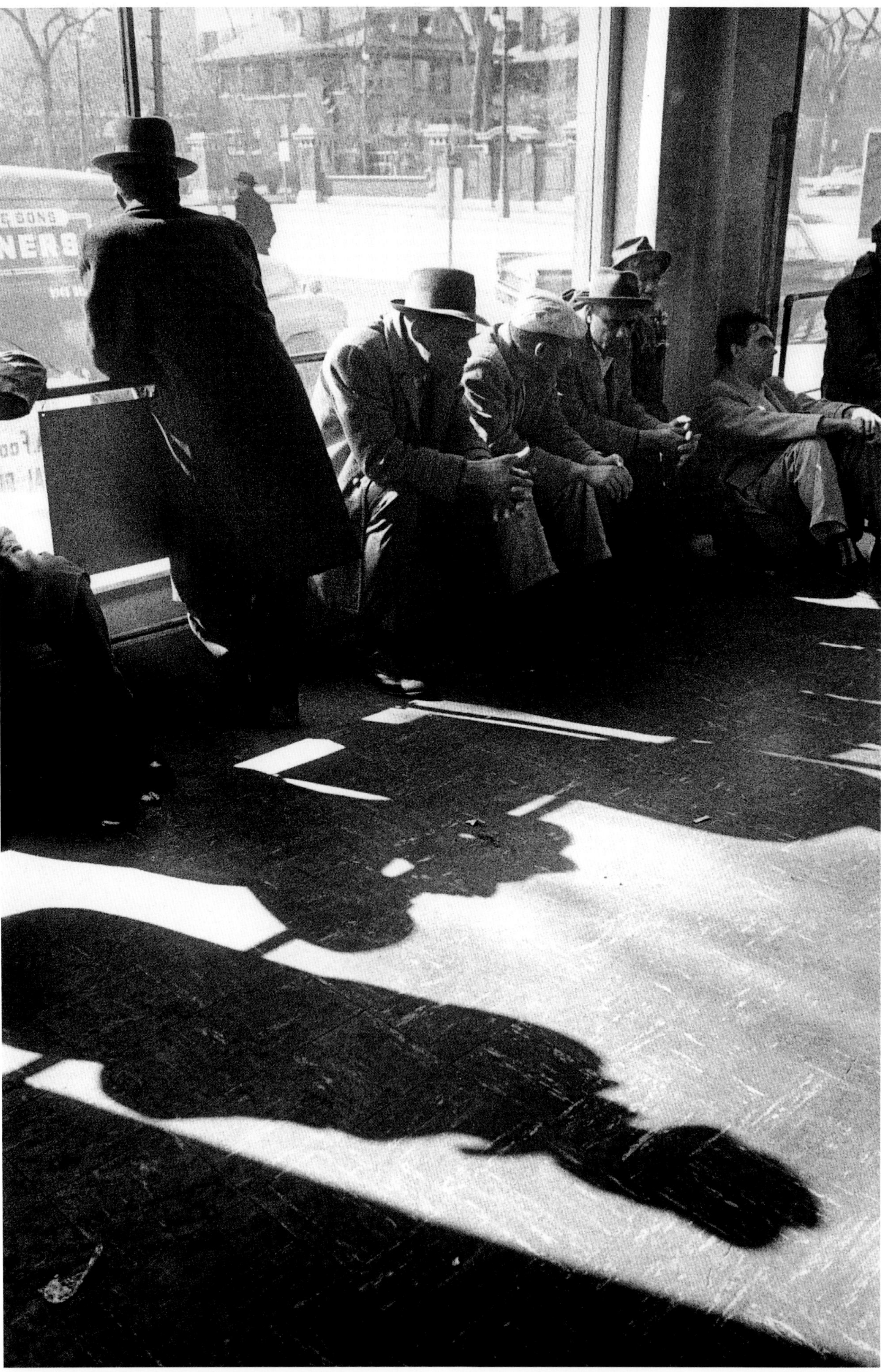

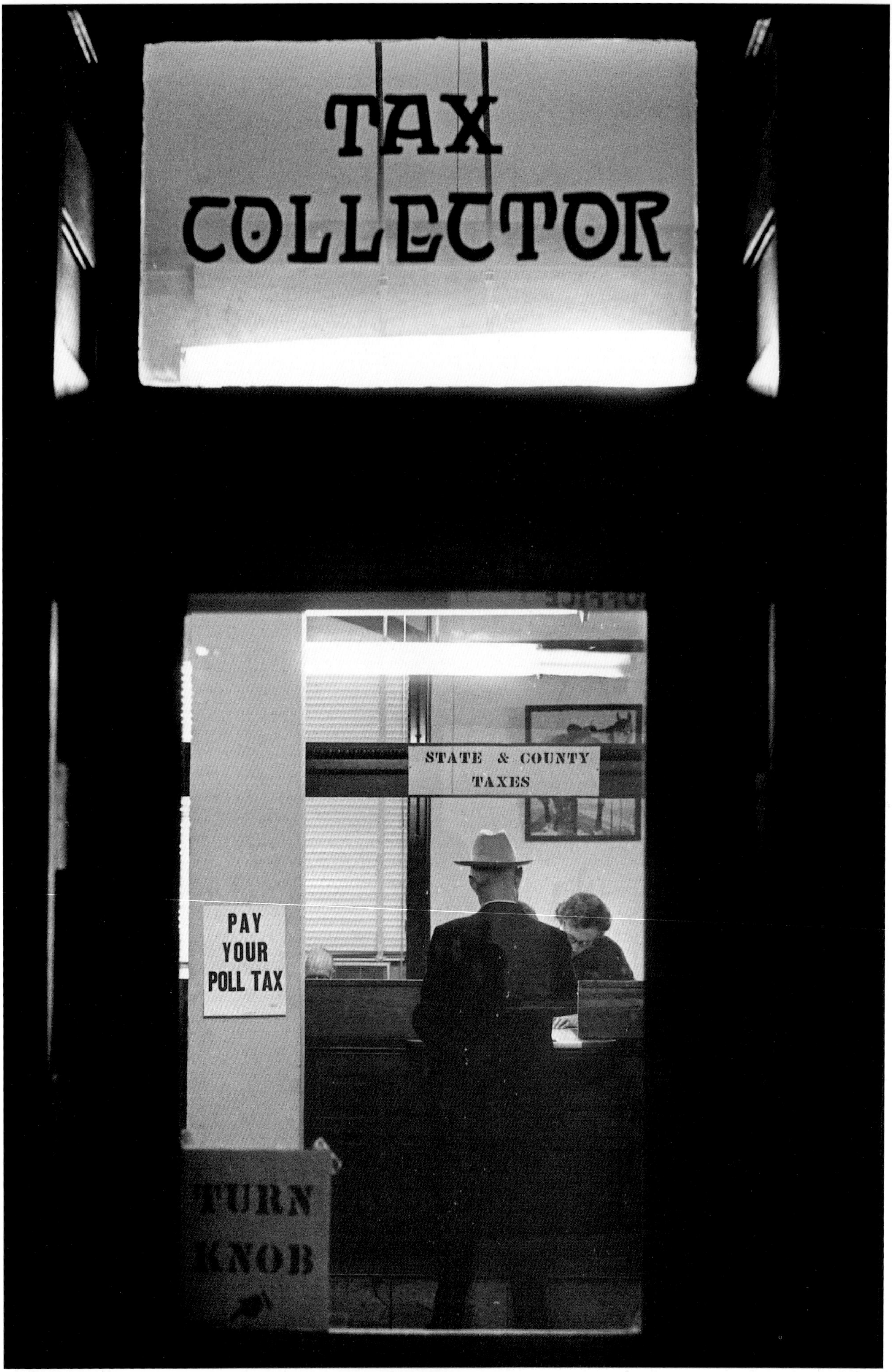

TAX
COLLECTOR
STATE & COUNTY
TAXES
PAY
YOUR
POLL TAX
TURN
KNOB

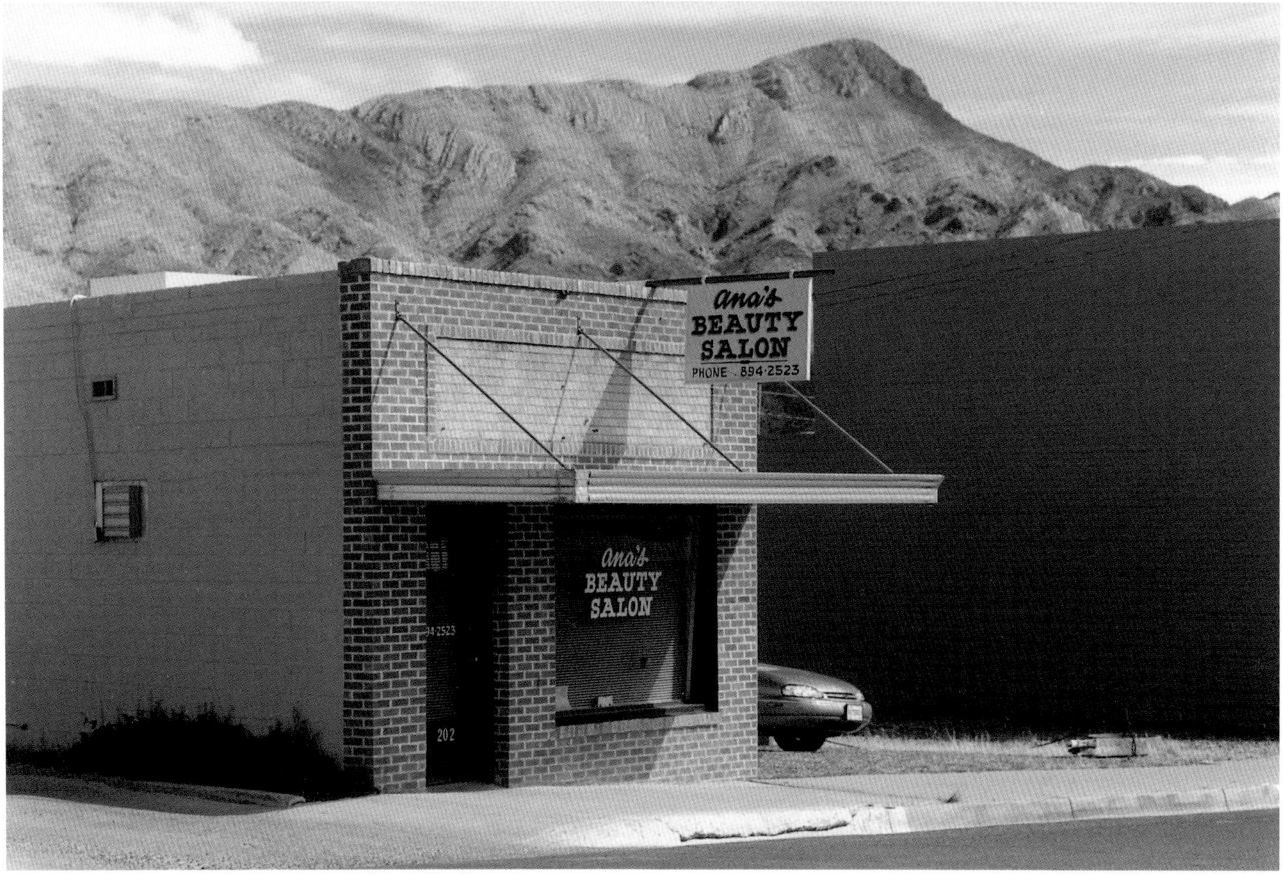

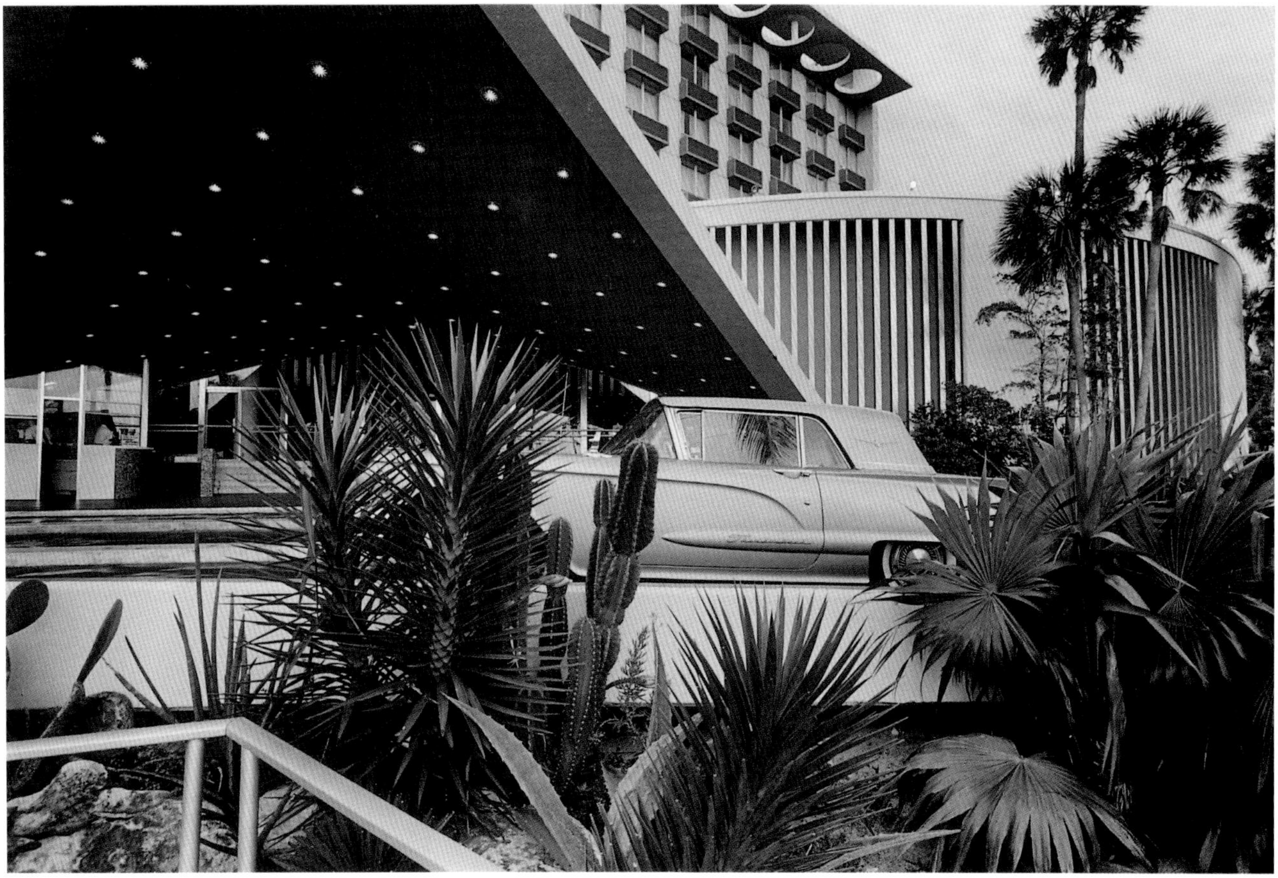

previous page *Detroit, 1961* / *Texas, 1963*
Truth or Consequences, New Mexico, 1998 / *Miami Beach, 1962*

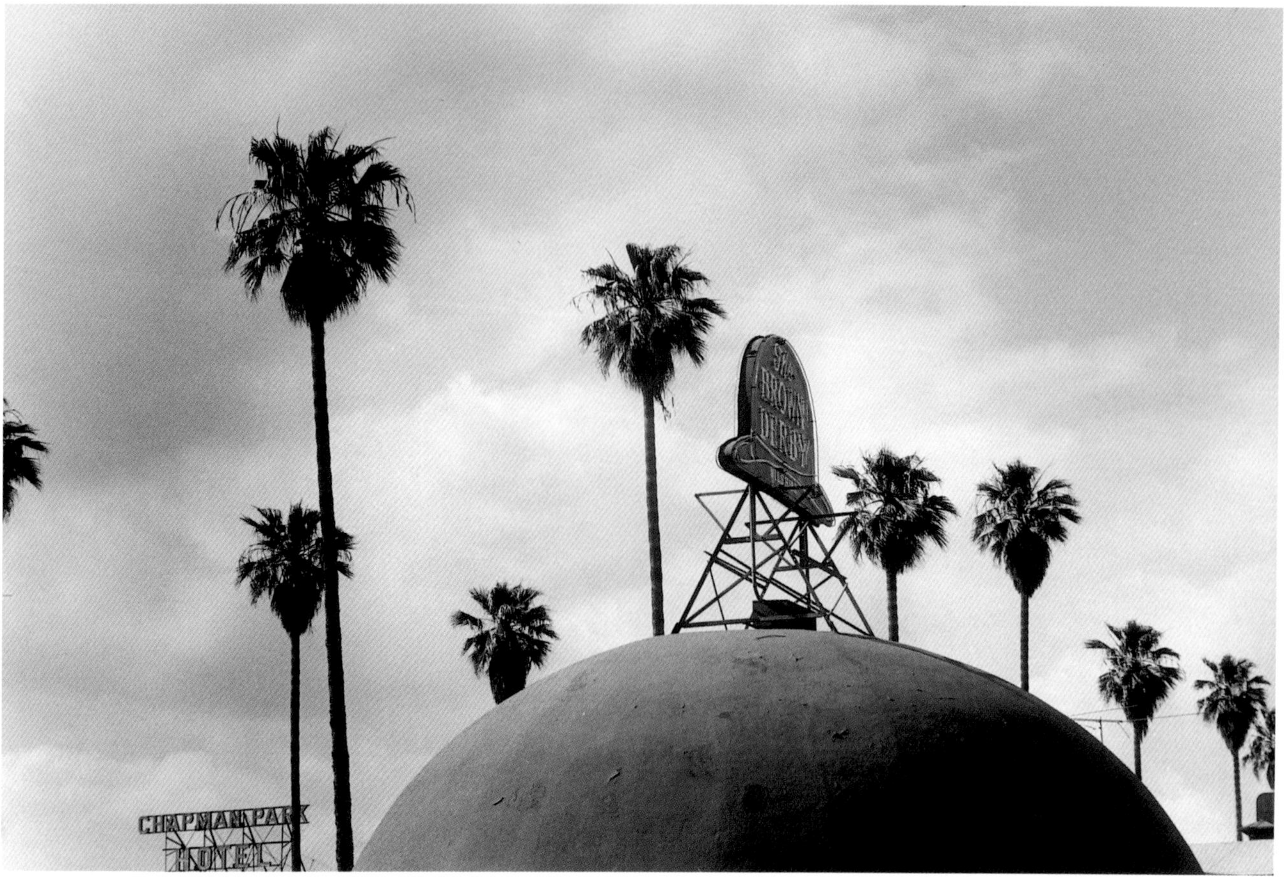

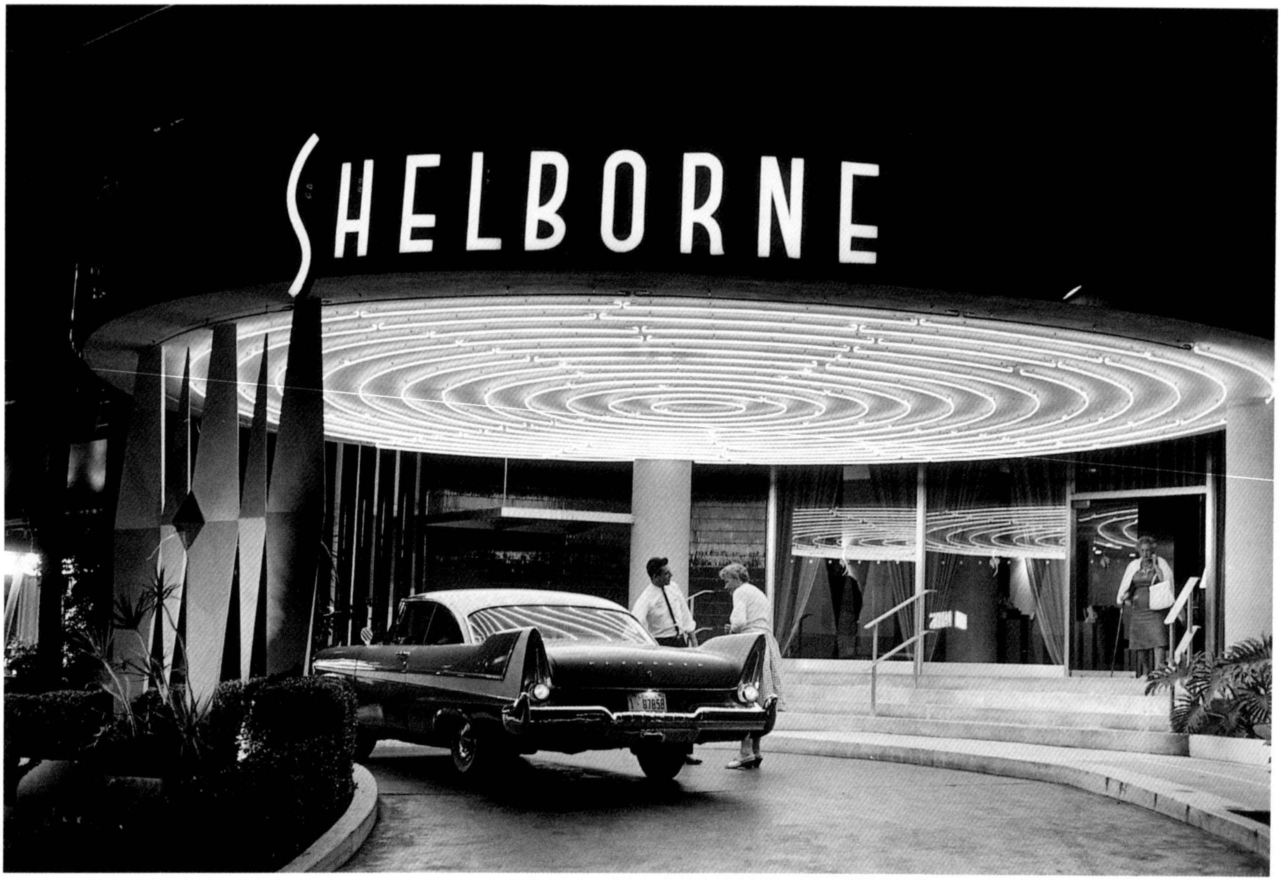

Hollywood, 1956 / *Miami Beach, 1962*

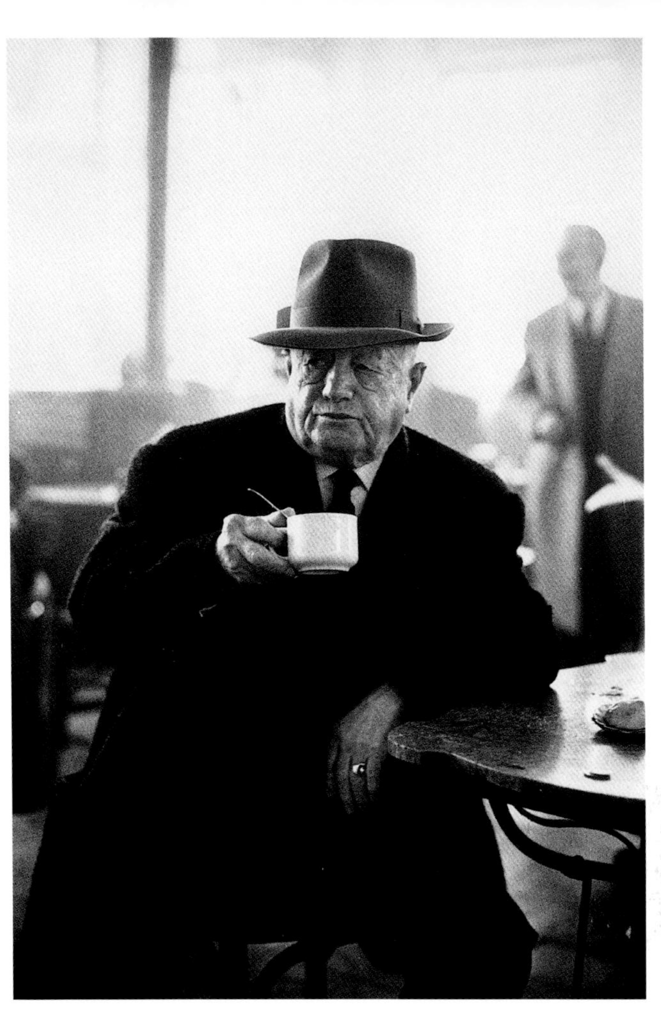

Kalamáta, Greece, 1966

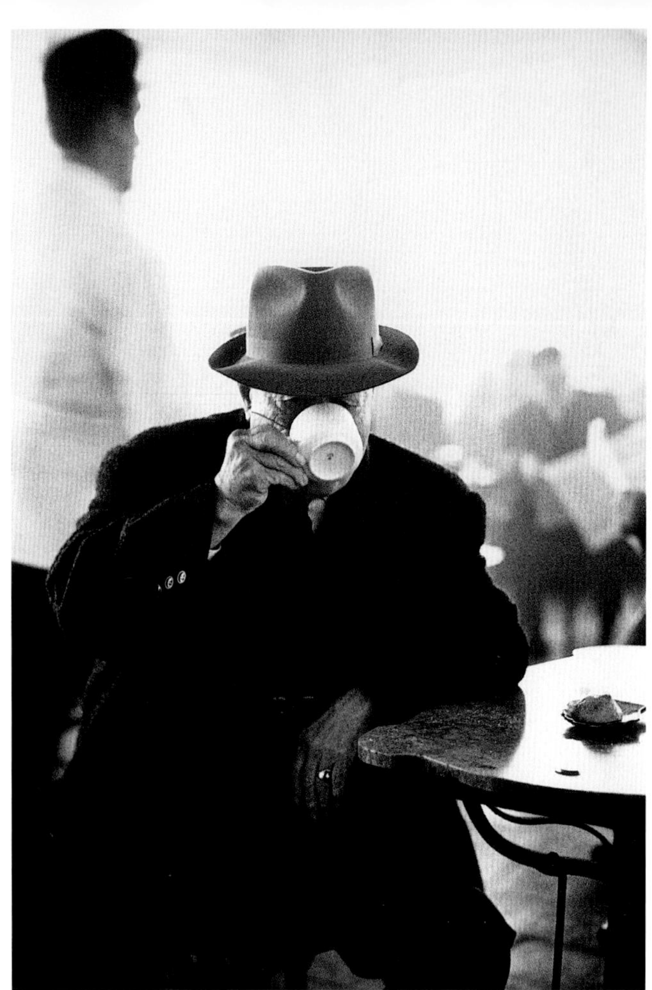

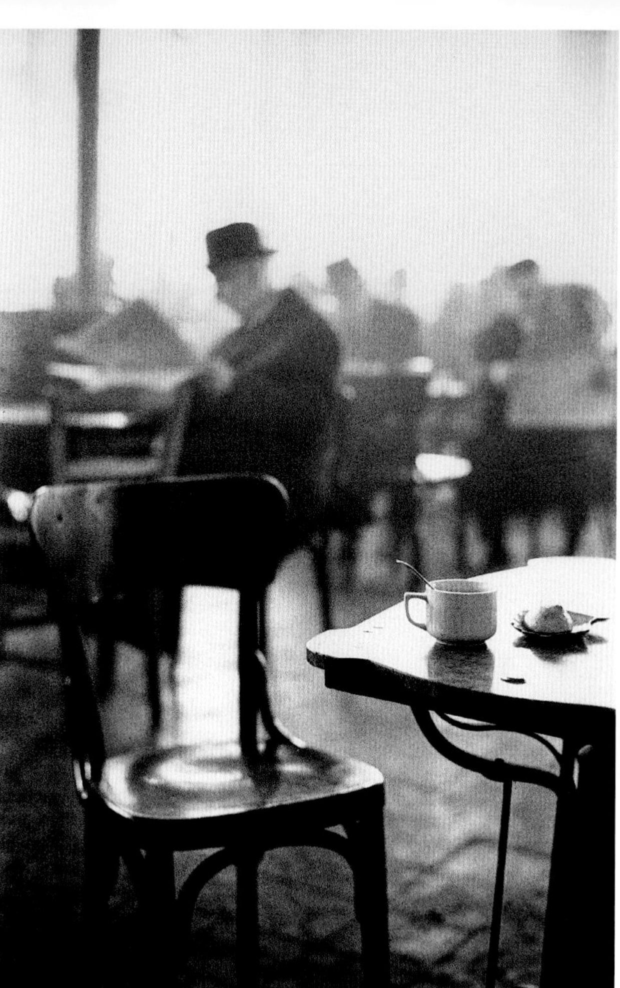

Touch

In this section humans and our animal companions touch each other, themselves or inanimate objects either as an afterthought, or as a way of expressing love, or in the thick of a fight. Some of these photos are born of sentiment, though skirting sentimentality; some are lighthearted spoofs.

The critic and curator John Szarkowski once wrote that '[Erwitt's] subjects seem the patient victims of unspecified misunderstandings…Over their inactivity hangs the premonition of a pratfall.'

Certainly, in all human activity, no action can be more misguided or misunderstood, more likely to lead to embarrassment or disaster or loneliness, than the touch gone awry. Yet we tend to assume otherwise, as sweetly documented here. Sometimes these lovers are touching with shared understanding, at least for the duration of the 'snap', and the child and parent or grand-parent lean towards each other with equal interest. At other times, we know that the touching is false, the duplicity unlikely to last. So simple and direct an action as physical touch, thanks to the nature of humanity's puzzling world, is likely to produce or reveal 'unspecified misunderstandings'.

But I slog close to the kind of talk Elliott despises. What he will agree to here is that love between parents and children, between humans and their pets and, above all, between adult lovers is the principal joy available to us in life.

When his marriages fail, he is devastated. He makes no secret of that. If a child is angry with him for a season, he is miserable. It takes no psychologist to see that Elliott, a boy raised without siblings and forced to move often into alien circumstances, might be seen to idealize the kind of family life that others of us take for granted or flee from at the first opportunity. Friends, too, are cherished and aided, worried about and forgiven. His affirmation of family and friendship grows outward into the larger community, both in his life and his work. It is essential to him that no snap, however humorous or sceptical, ridicules the subjects caught unawares. He and we smile along with the people not at them, because we recognize that the premonition of a pratfall is our own natural state of living, too. The humour is shared, not barbed. We see ourselves in these snaps as we otherwise cannot. We are not being asked to gasp at grotesques.

This is the morality that underpins these photos, and it is the morality of Elliott's own conduct. I was astonished recently when an editor told me that she was 'too intimidated' to fax or call him about a photo that had gone missing. She had never met him, but the fame, the success, the awards and the numerous books projected, for her, some cartoon image of world-weary sophistication and arrogance, a celebrity too important to be bothered by the little people.

Nothing could be further from the truth. Elliott is a loyal friend without pretension, a man happier in the company of children and dogs than at openings or awards banquets. To learn about his latest triumph you generally have to use hammer and tongs. The medals mean nothing when a friend is stricken with melanoma or saddled with debt.

Such emotional touching is not necessarily physical, nor are some of the touches snapped in this chapter: Mammalian gazes touch through the air at the speed of light, conveying or receiving or exchanging wonder, amusement, intensity, satisfaction or surprise. Objects also touch or wind up together in odd parallels. Sometimes they were moving past each other, creating ambiguous brief interludes that Elliott caught and turned into mind games. A gull and an airliner conjoin, as do a lanky shorebird and an outdoor tap. Meaning? No, being. Just touching…or almost. Simply aligned in time. The objects are of course unaware of the rhythms of the composition – no less or more so than the people. While these various subjects engage in the act of touching, you will also feel strongly, for it is there, that the photographer, too, is touching these bits and pieces of the animate and inanimate world, eager to connect somehow, if such a thing is possible.

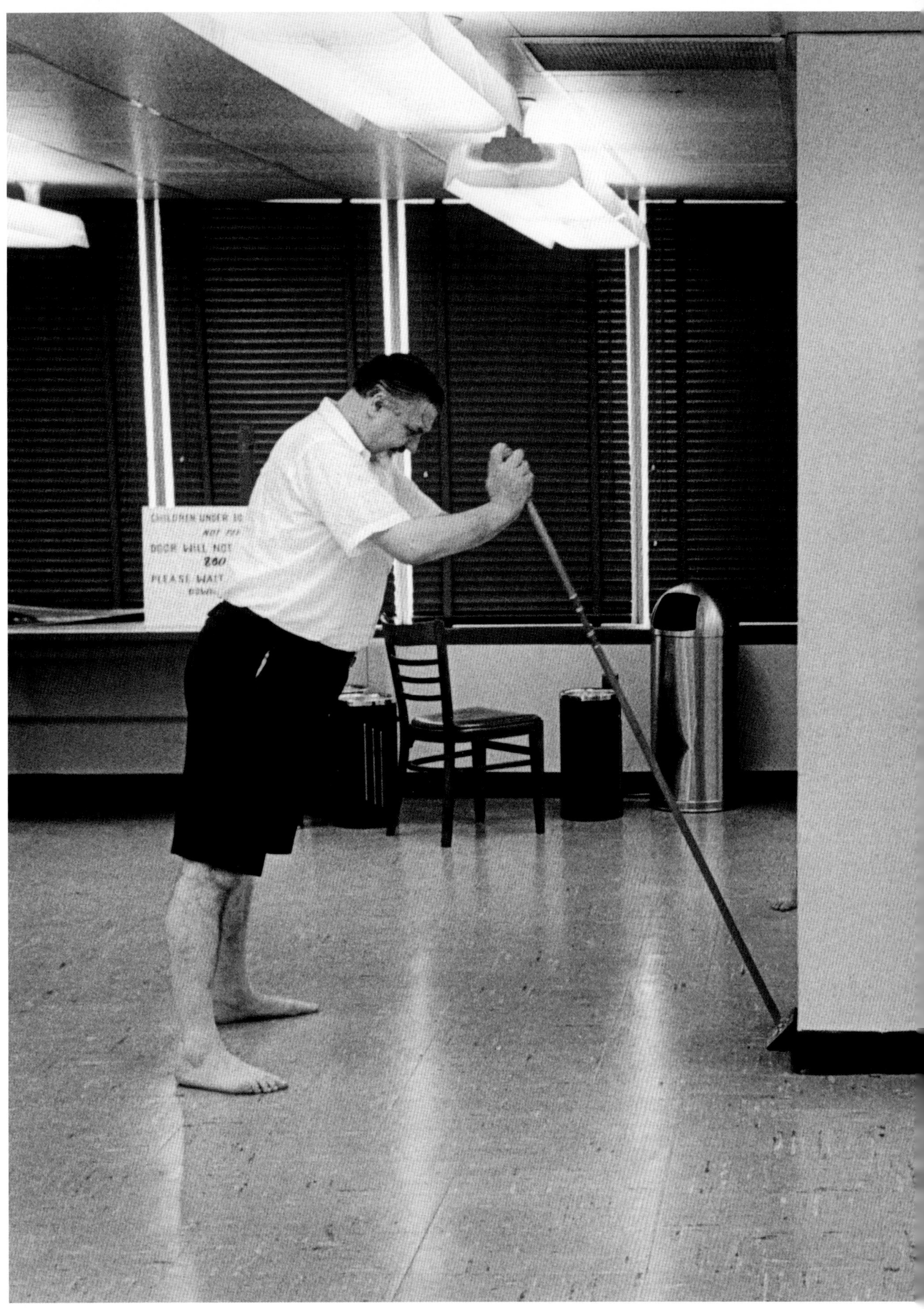

New York, 1964

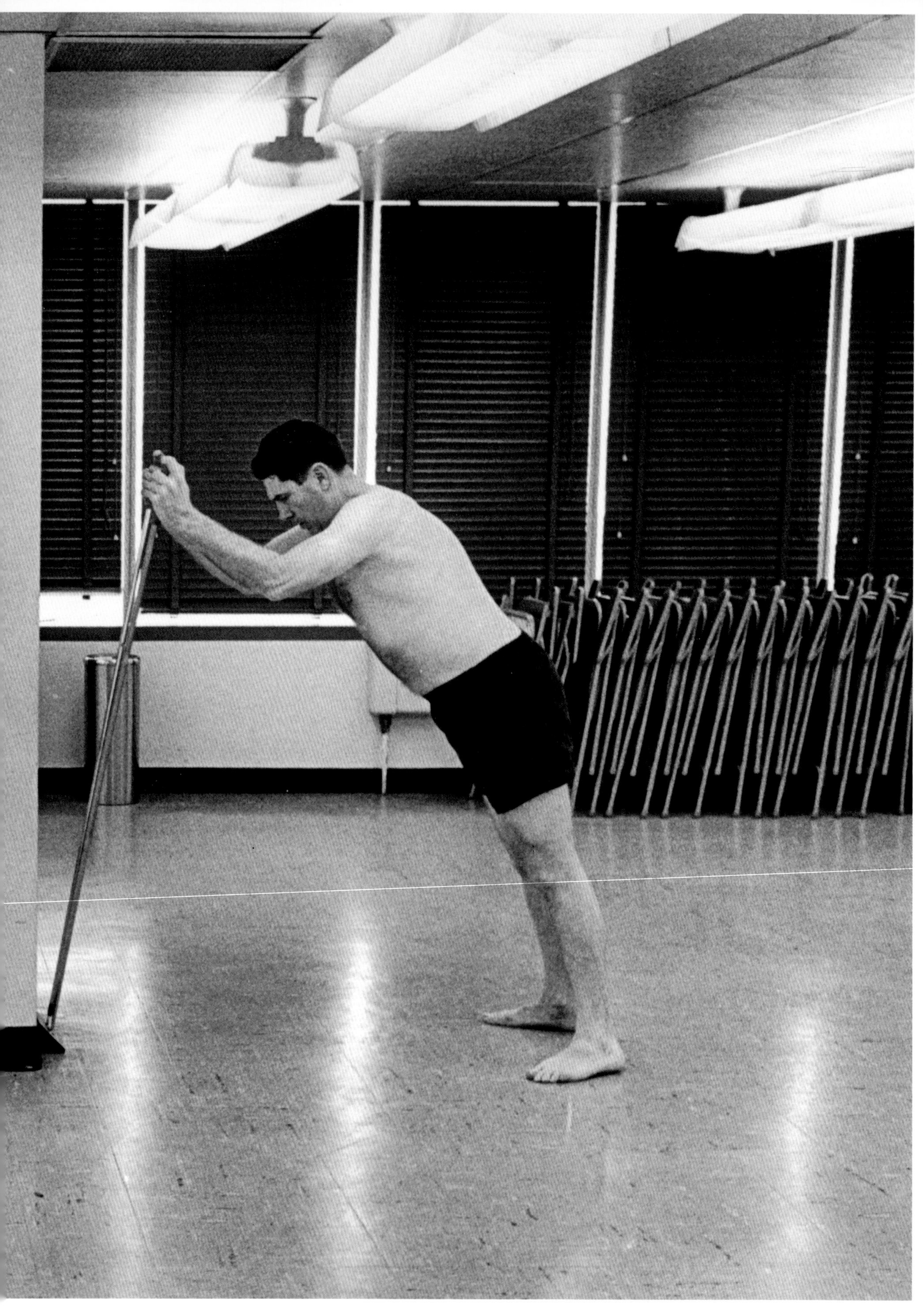

overleaf *Louisiana, 1954* / *San Francisco, 1955*

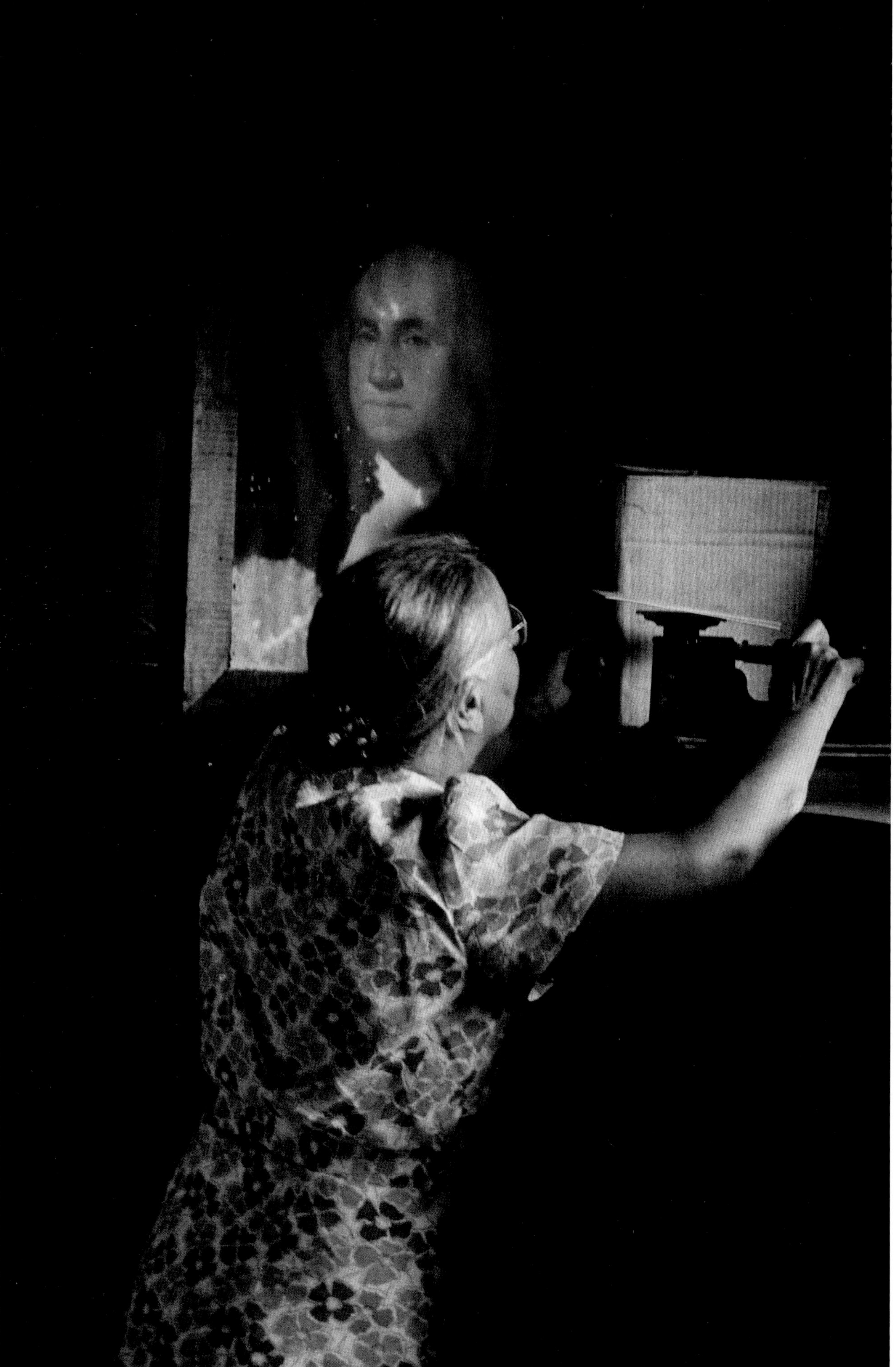

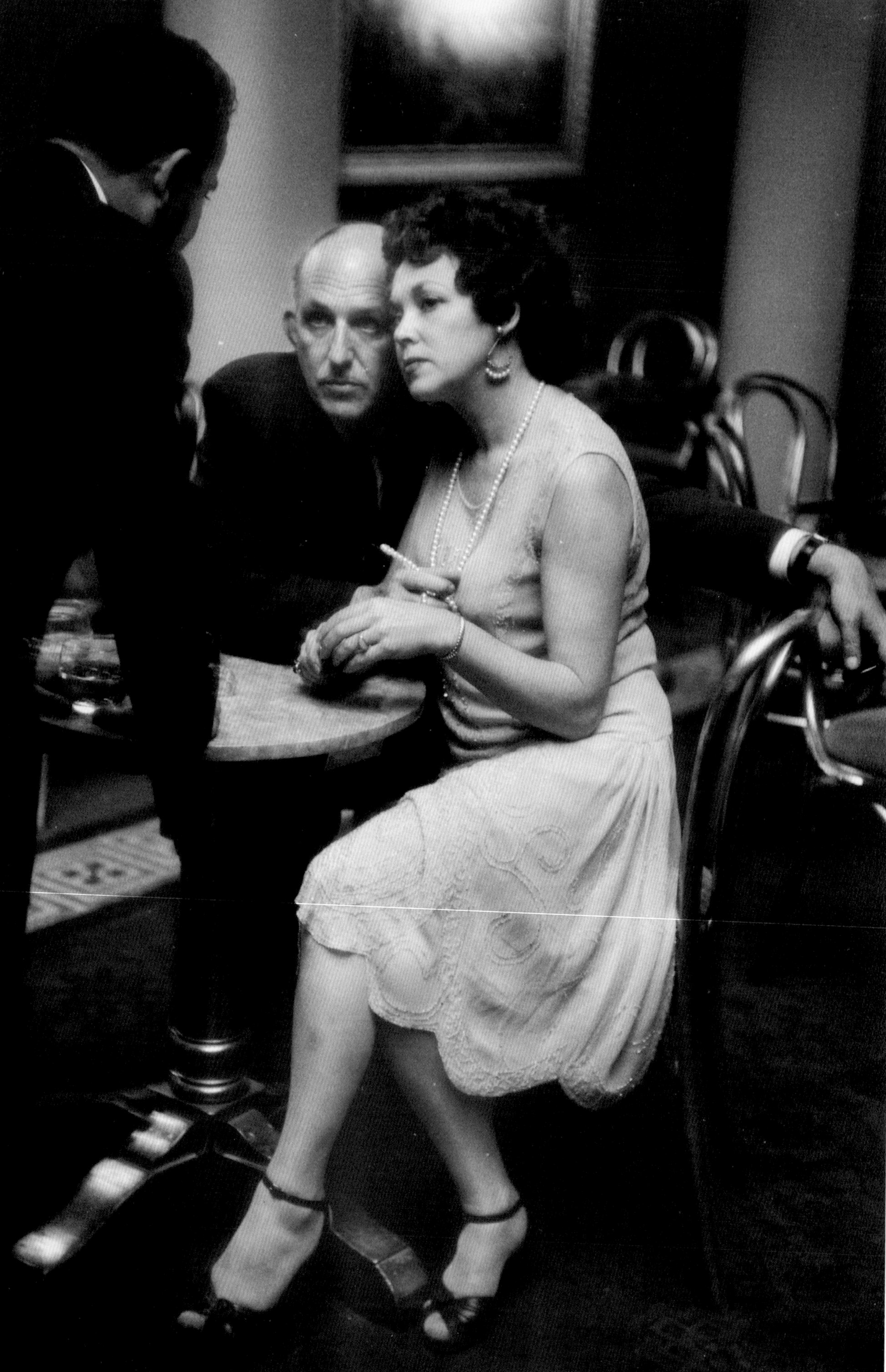

Kraków, Poland, 1964
overleaf, top row left to right: *Elie Wiesel, New York, 1973 / Arthur Rothstein, New York, 1977*
Pablo Casals, San Juan, Puerto Rico, 1957 / Roald Dahl, New York, 1953
bottom row left to right: *Edward R. Murrow, New York, 1961 / Frank O'Connor, Brooklyn, 1954*
Randall Jarell, New York, 1954 / C. P. Snow, London, 1952

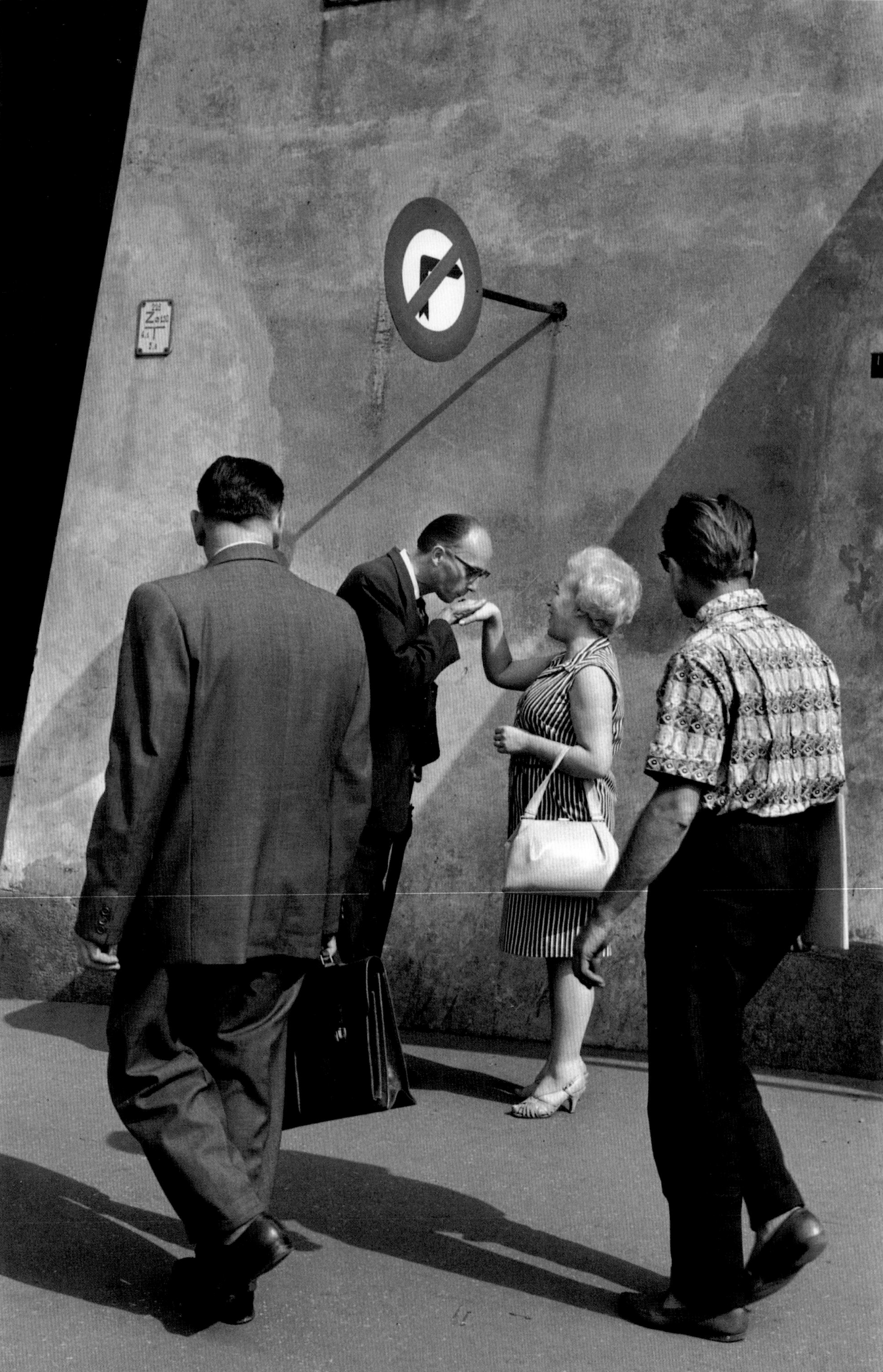

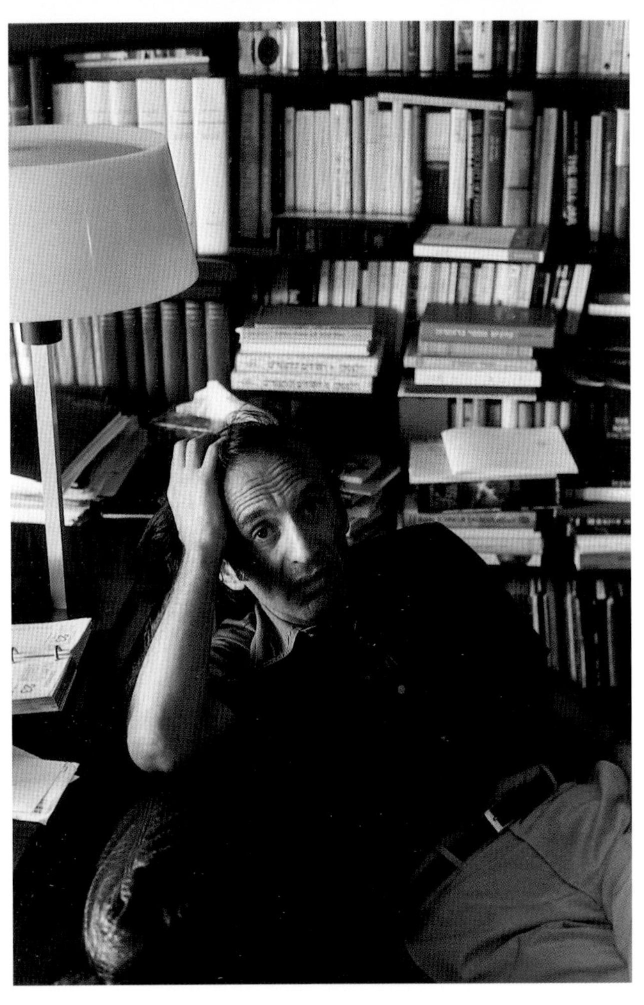
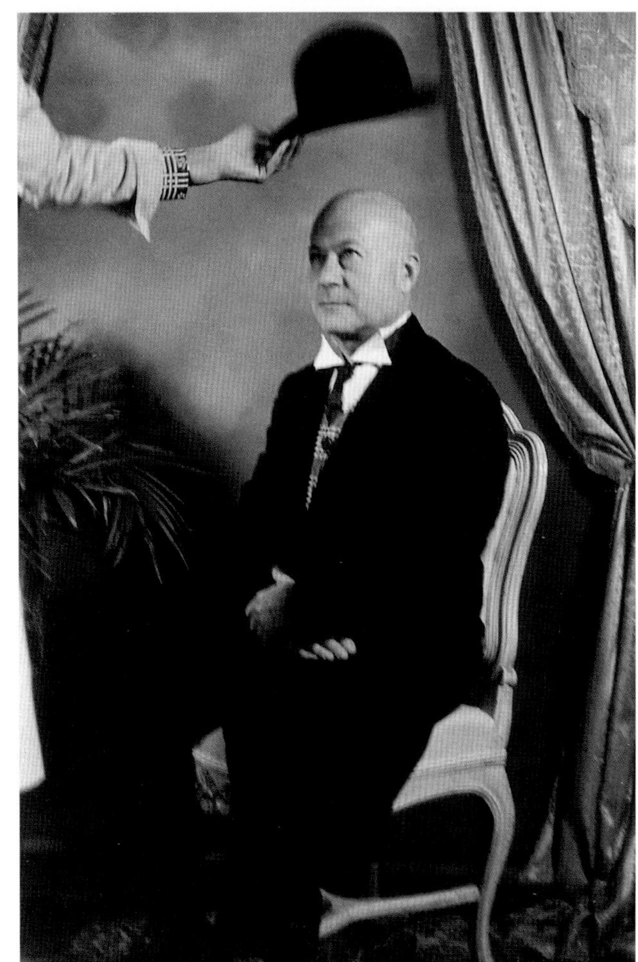
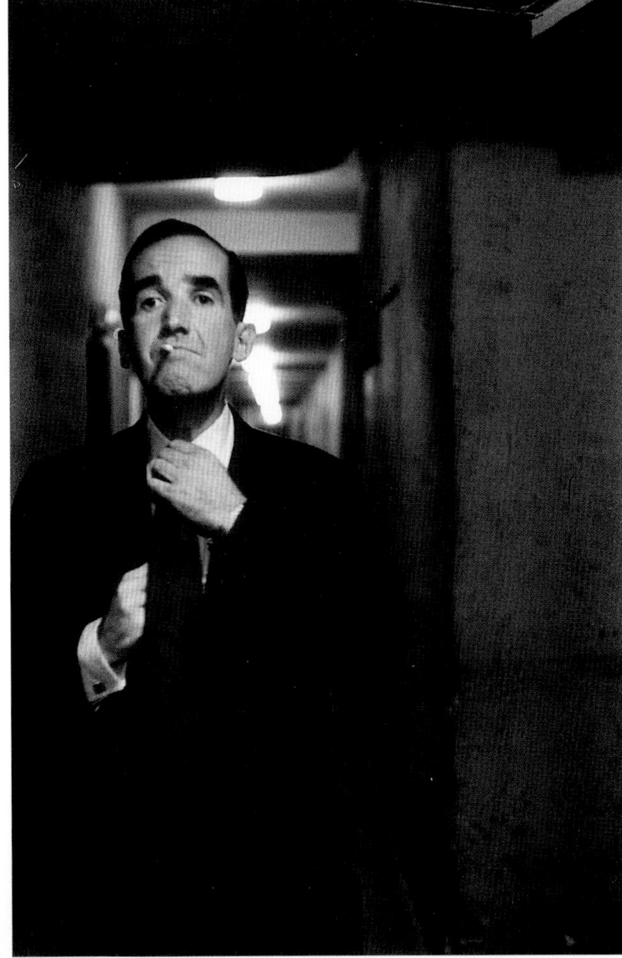
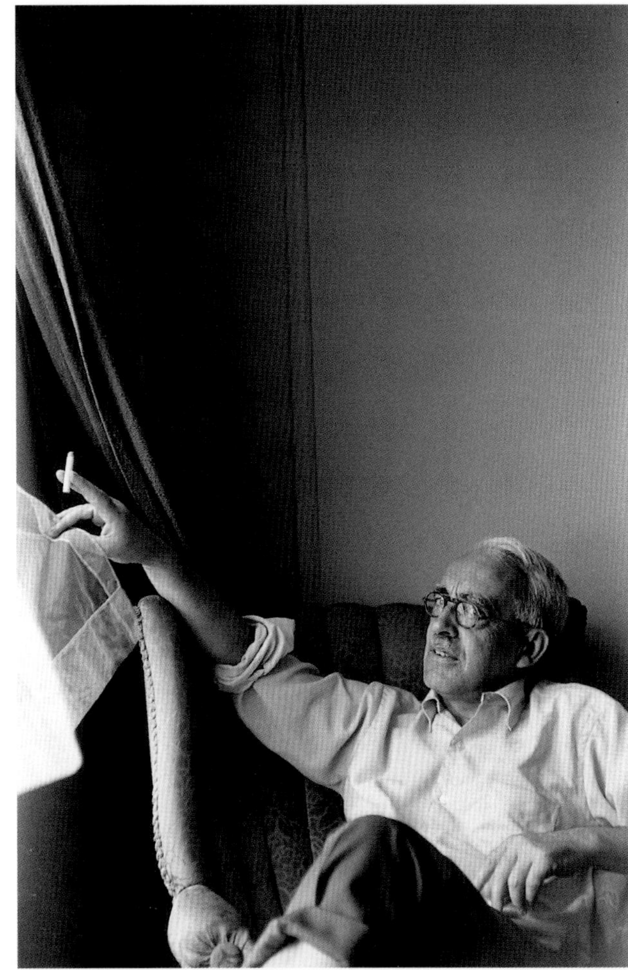

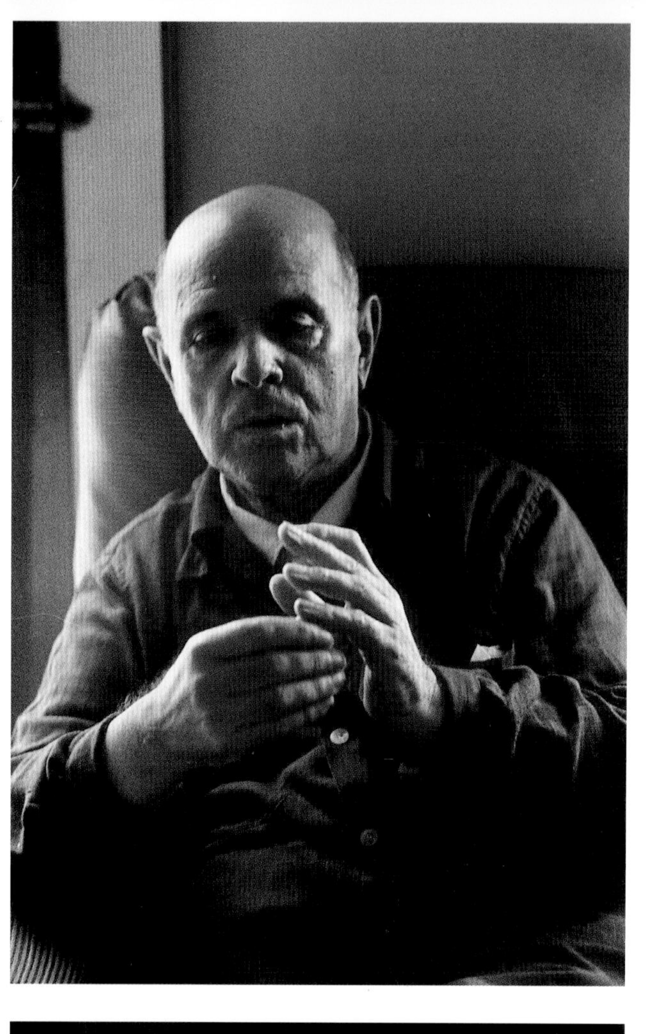
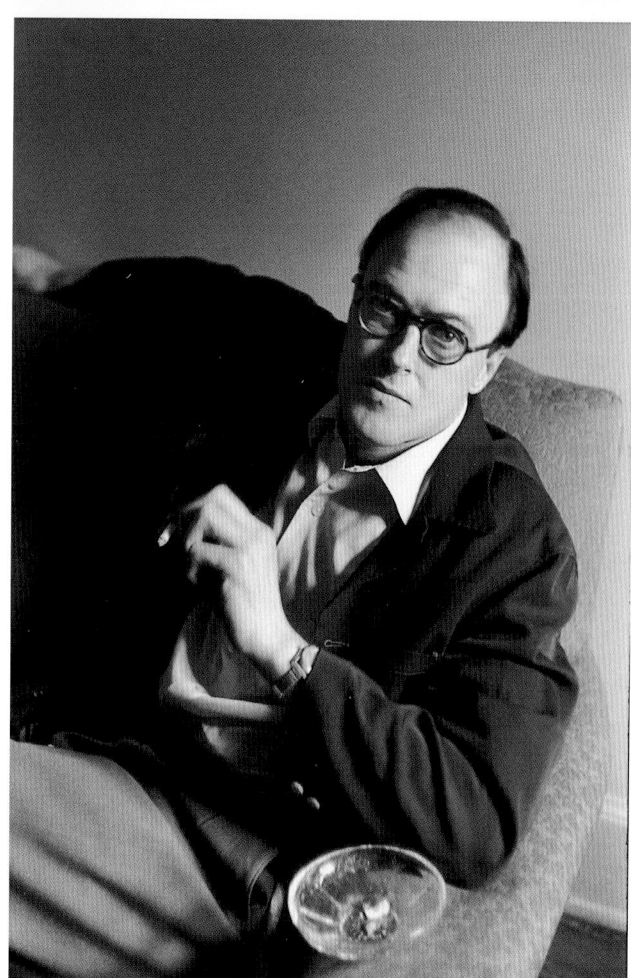
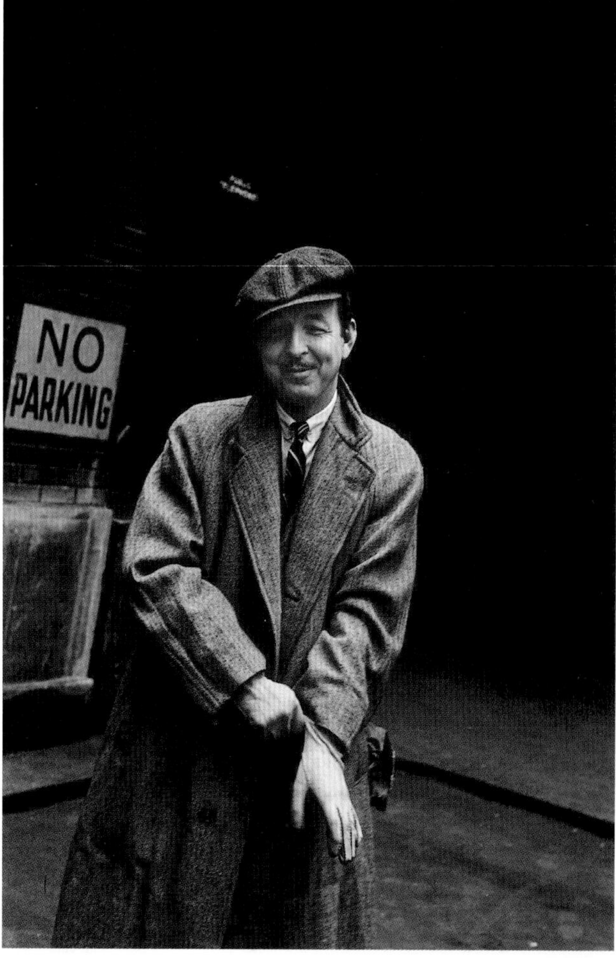
NO
PARKING
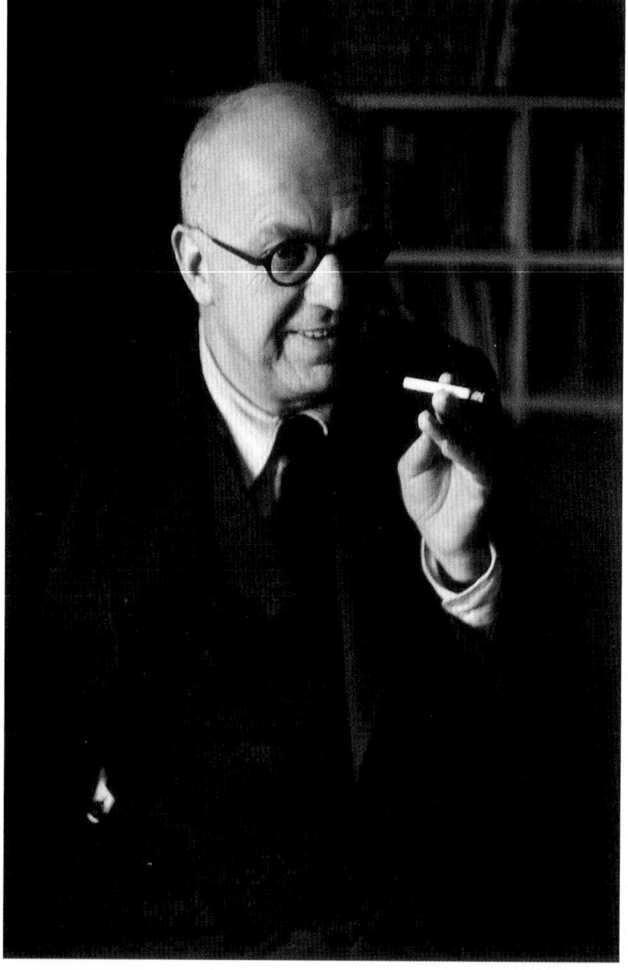

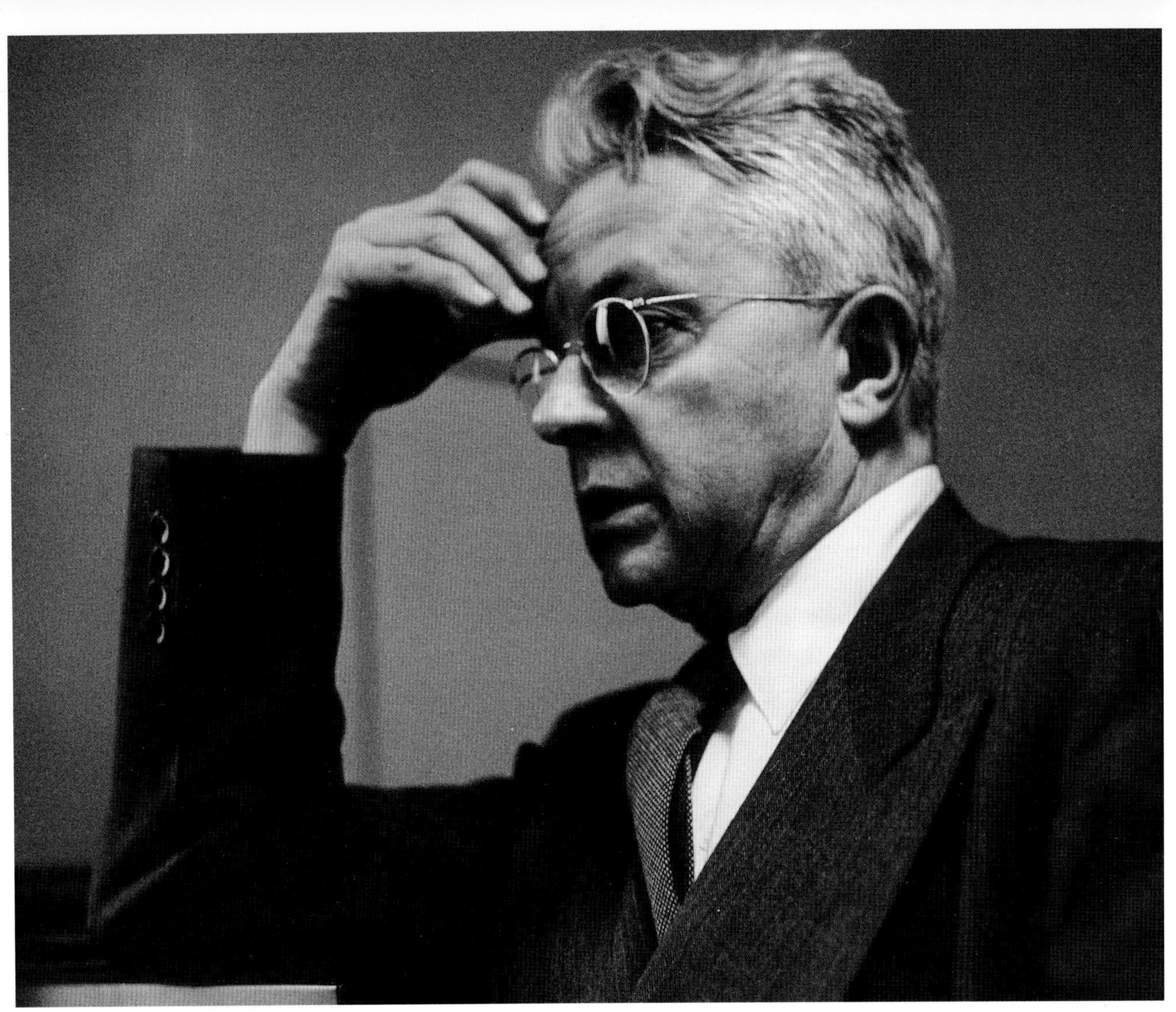

Roy Stryker, Pittsburgh, Pennsylvania, 1950

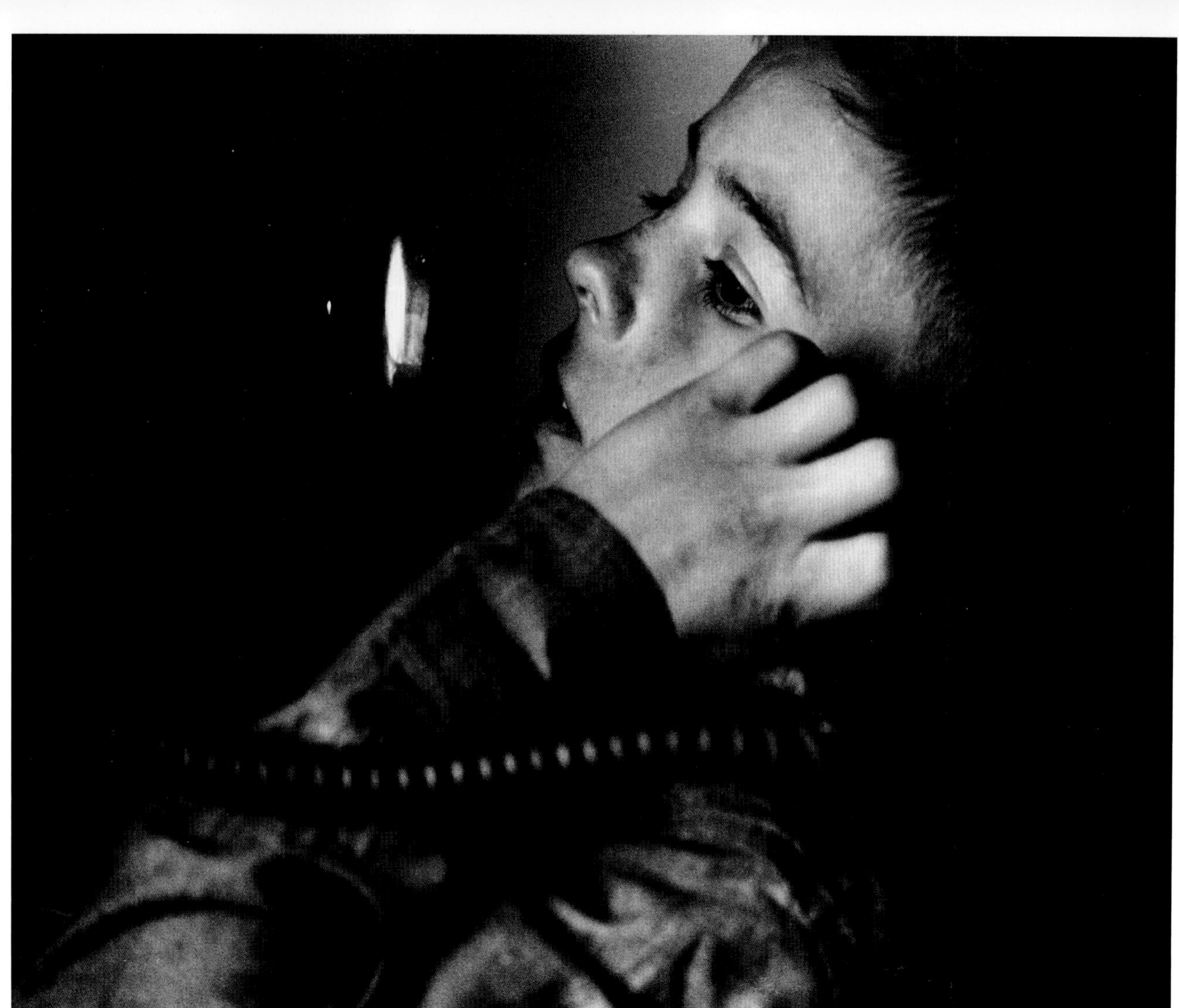

Wyoming, 1954

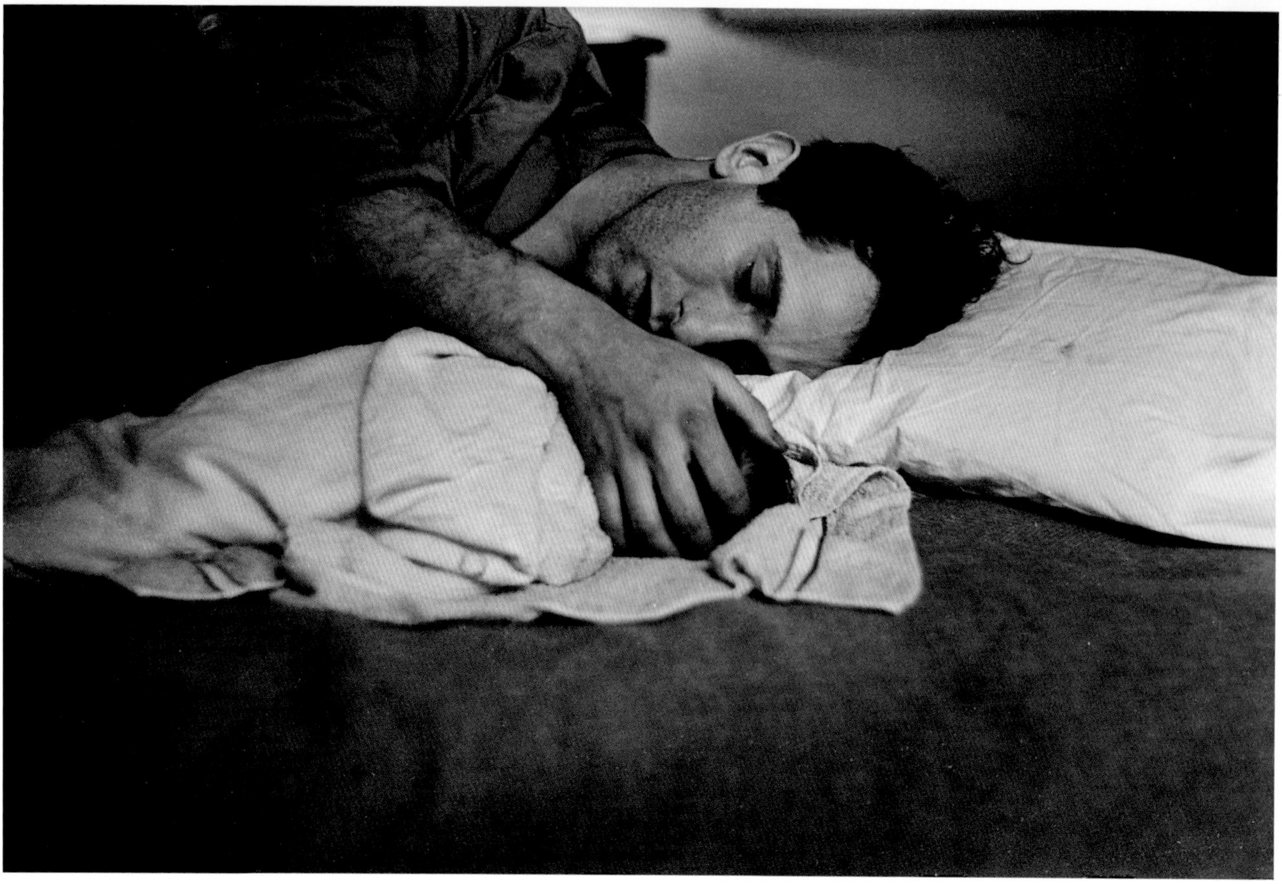

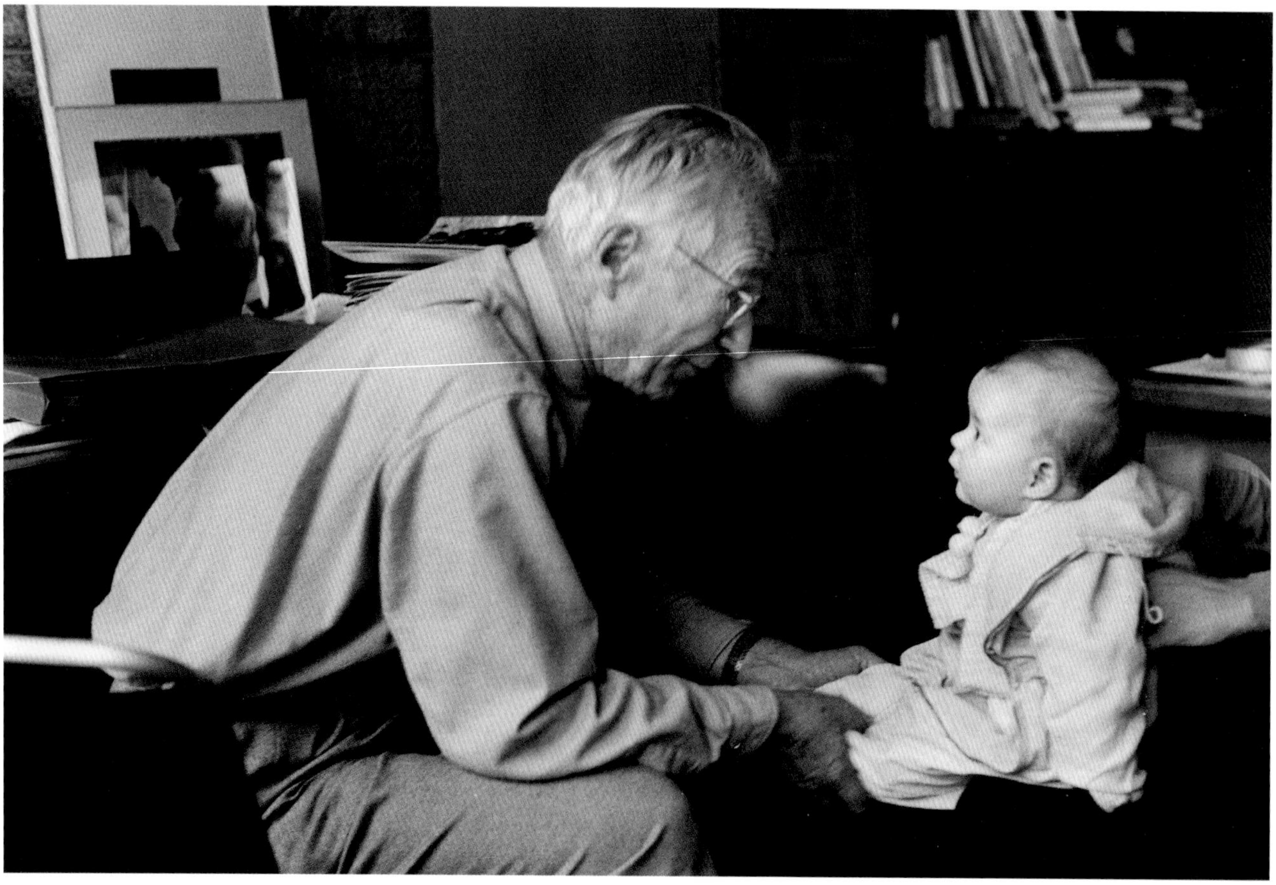

Robert Frank and son, New York, 1951 / *Edward Steichen and Ellen Erwitt, New York, 1953*

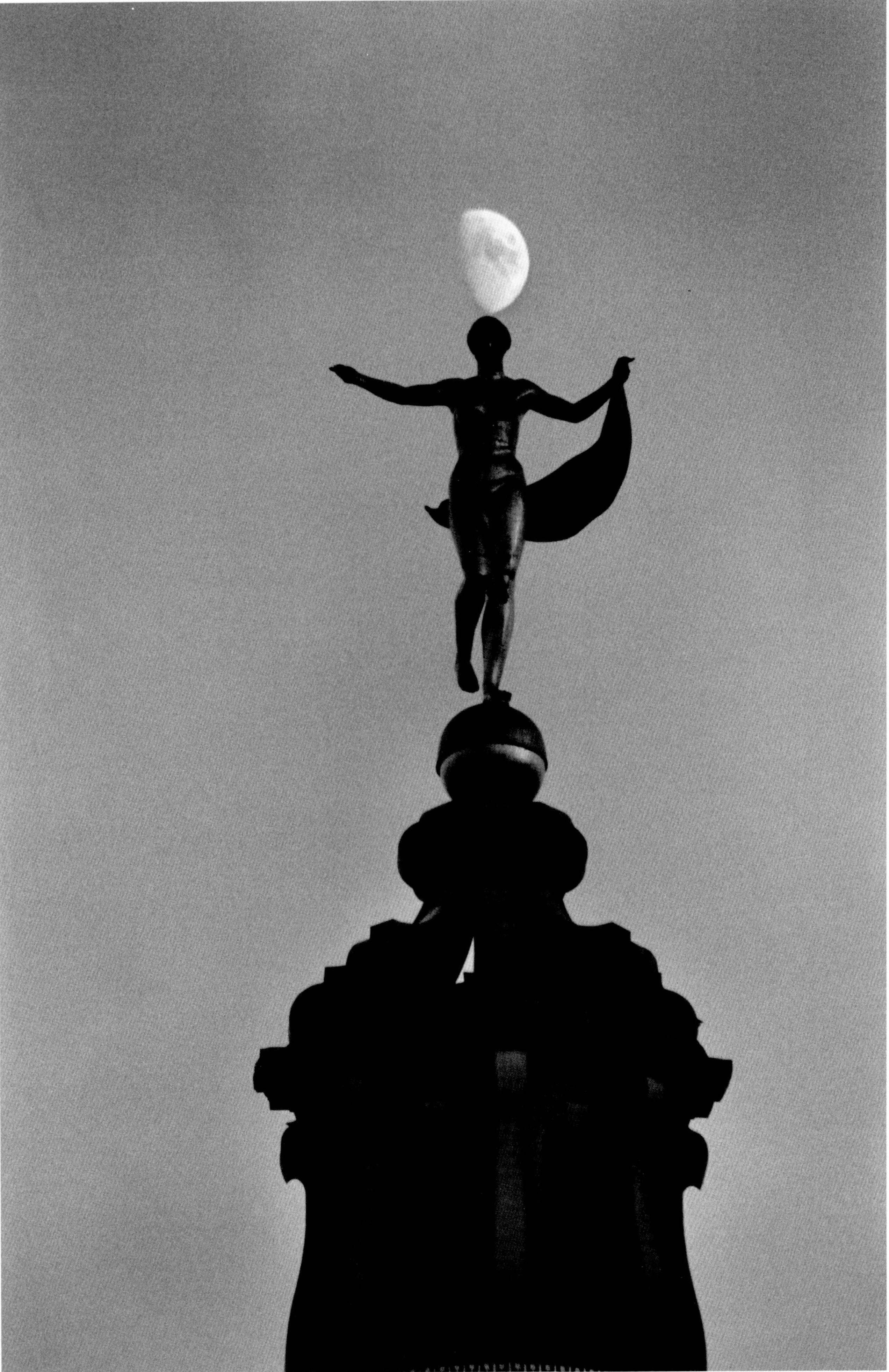

Schloss Charlottenburg, Berlin, 1995

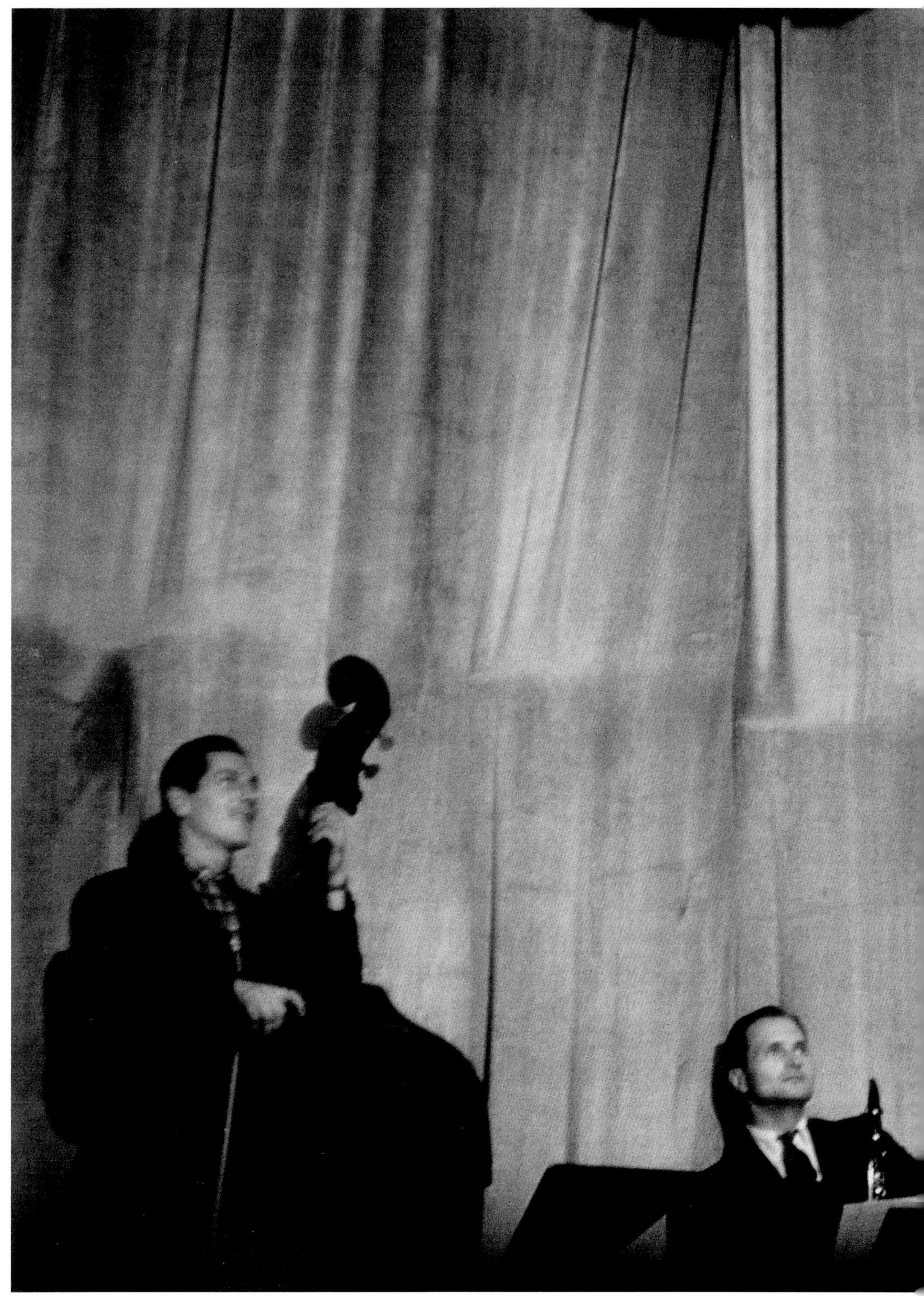

Paris, 1952

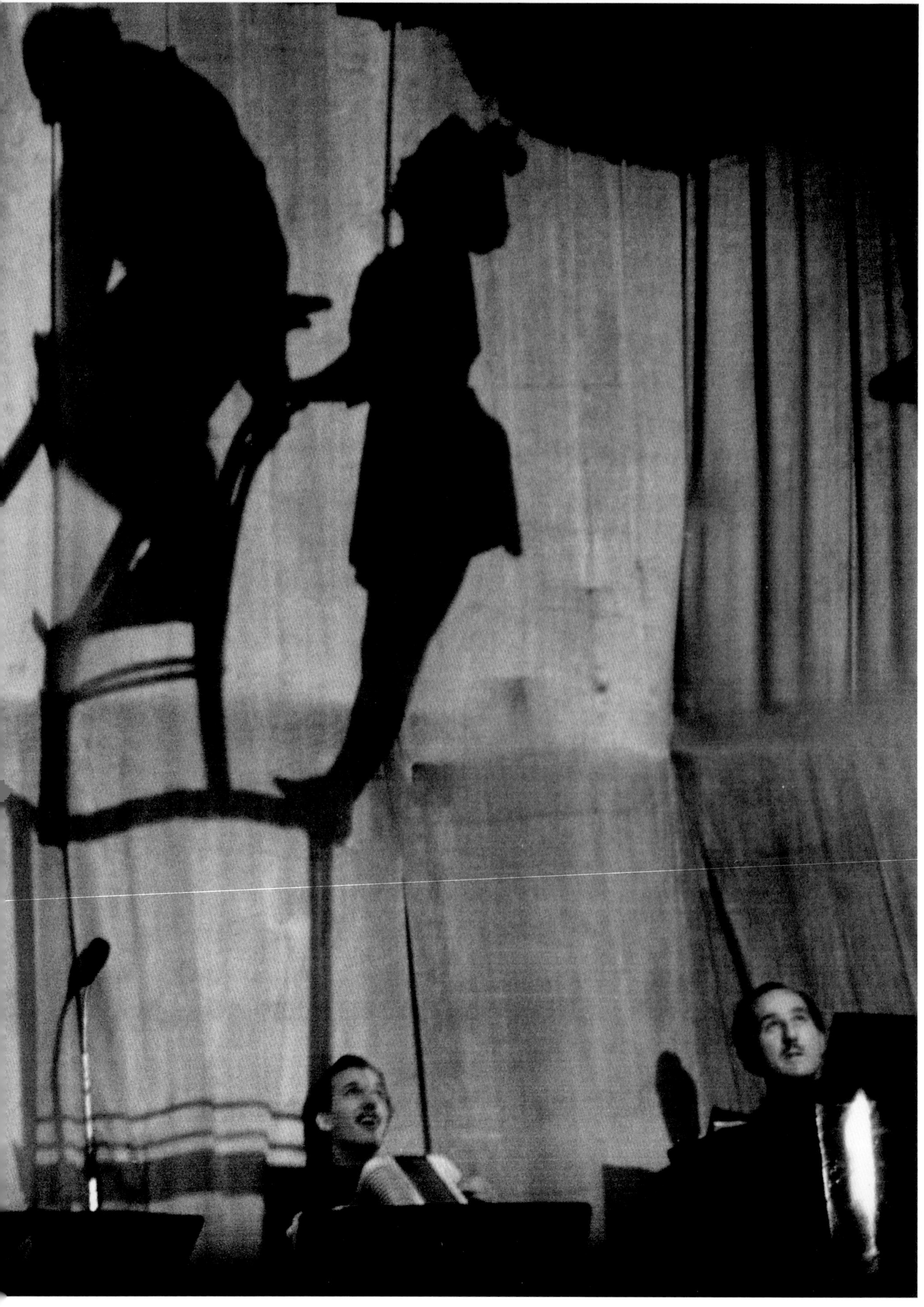

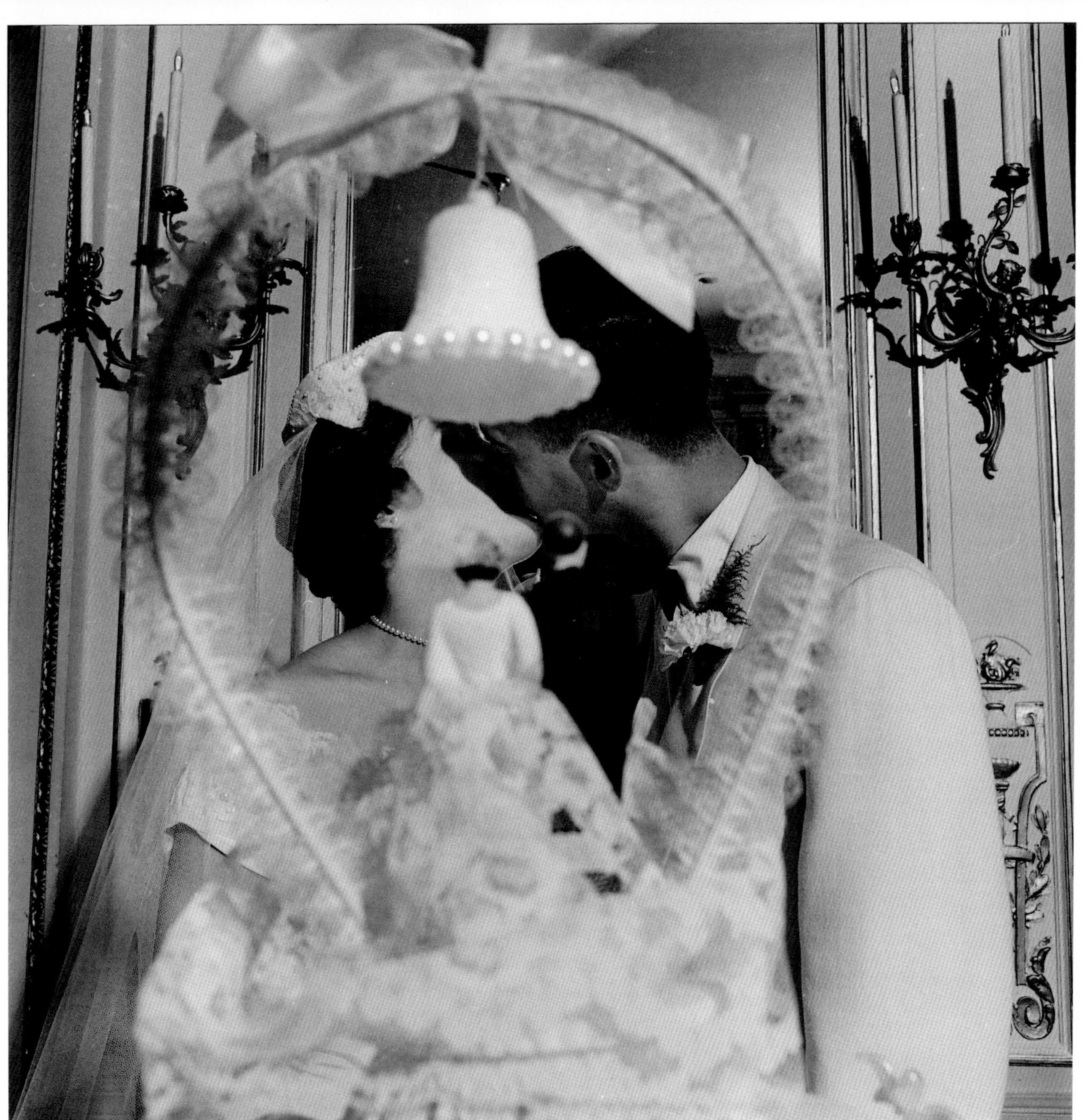

New York, 1962

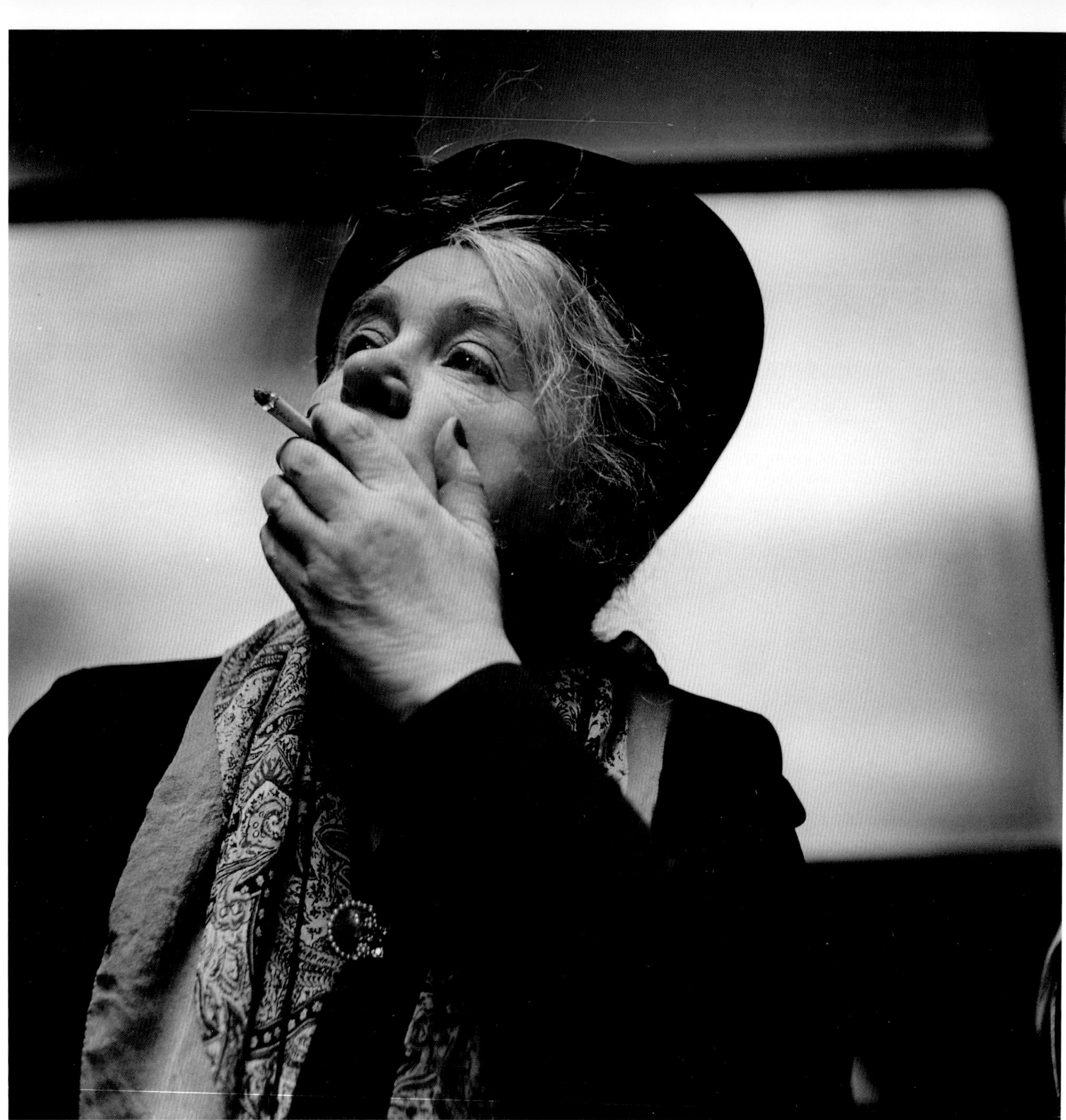

New York, 1950

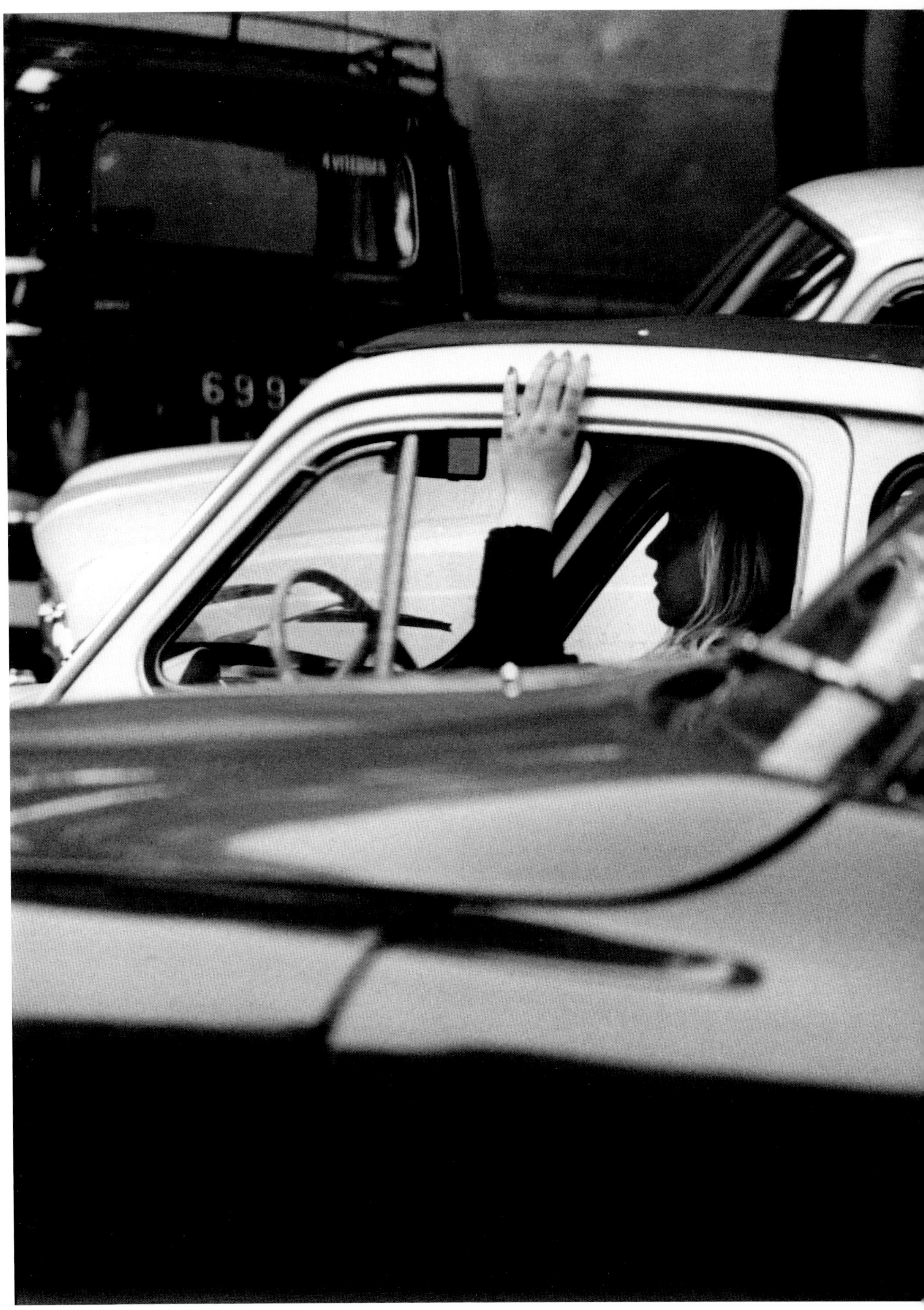

Paris, 1968

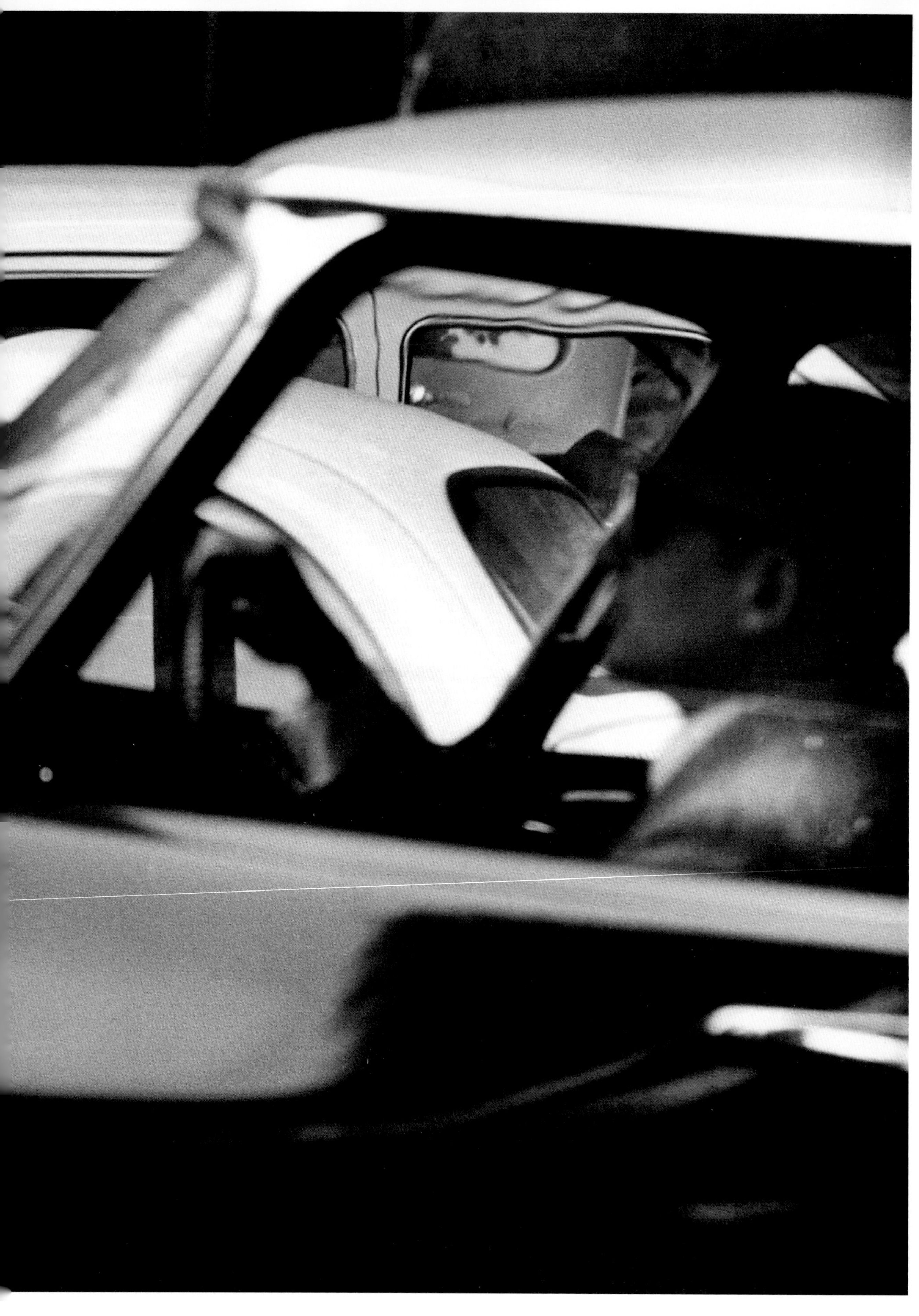

overleaf *Baton Rouge, Louisiana, 1976* / *Des Moines, Iowa, 1954*

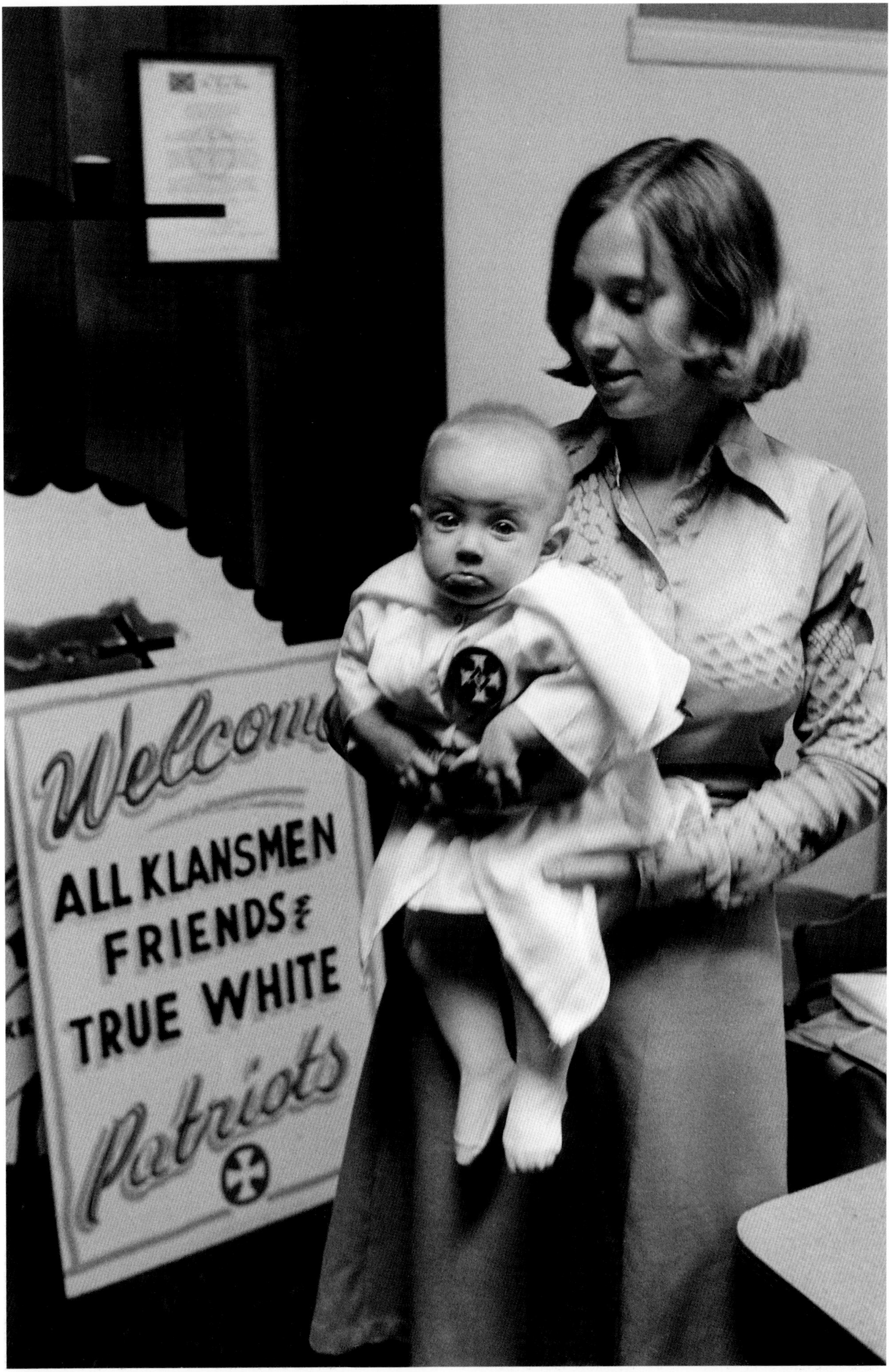

Welcom
ALL KLANSMEN
FRIENDS &
TRUE WHITE
Patriots

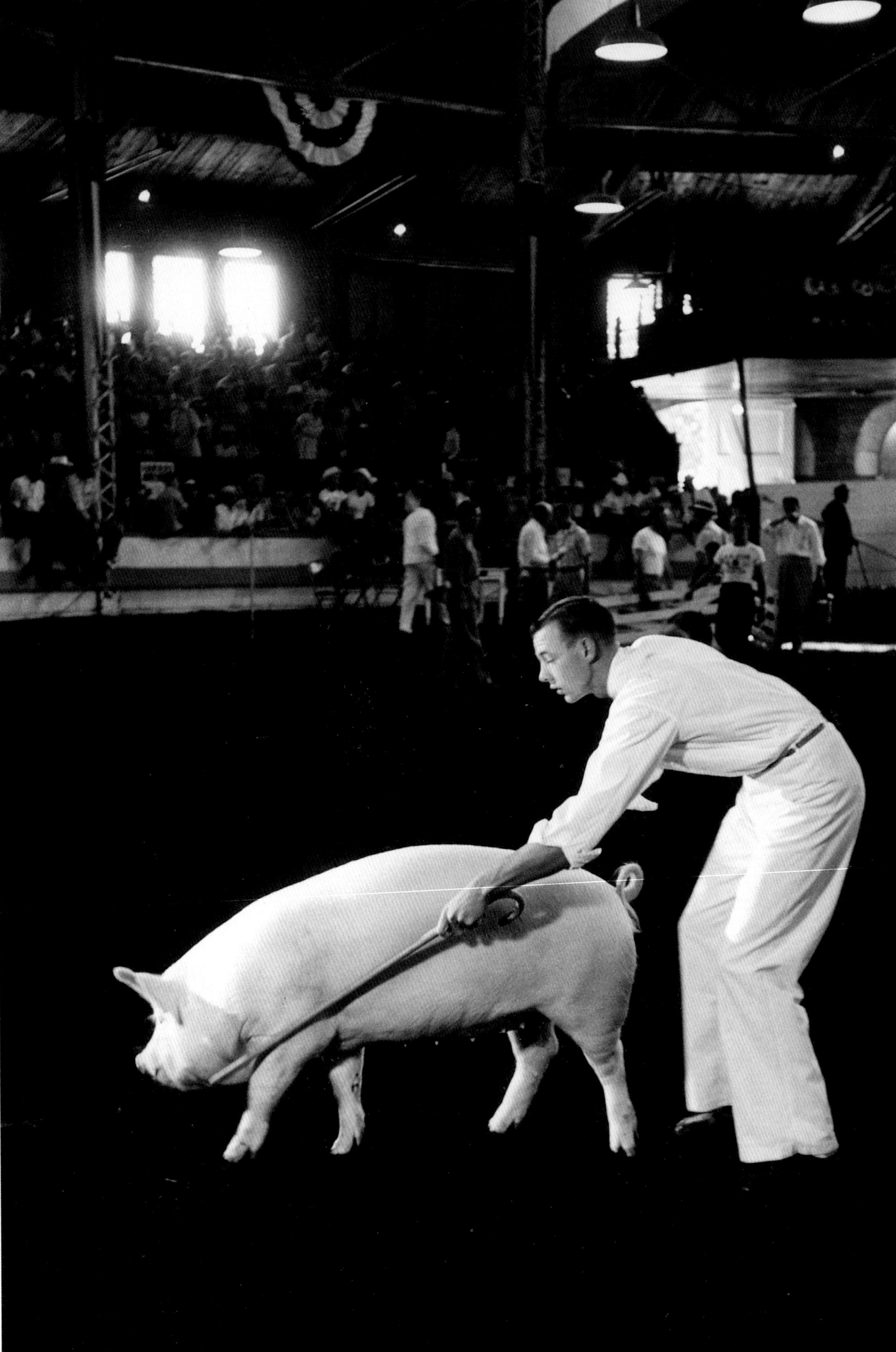

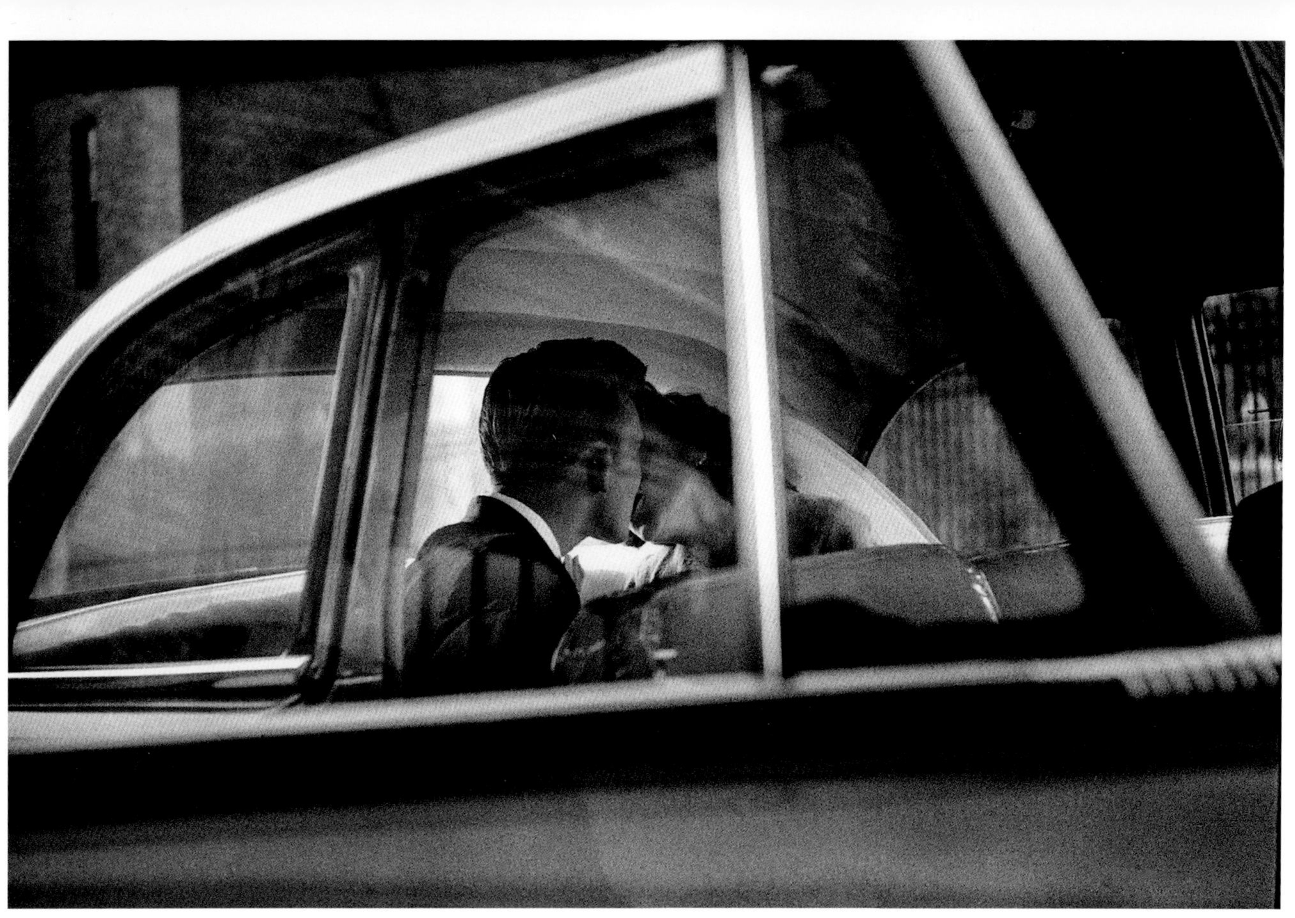

New York, 1955

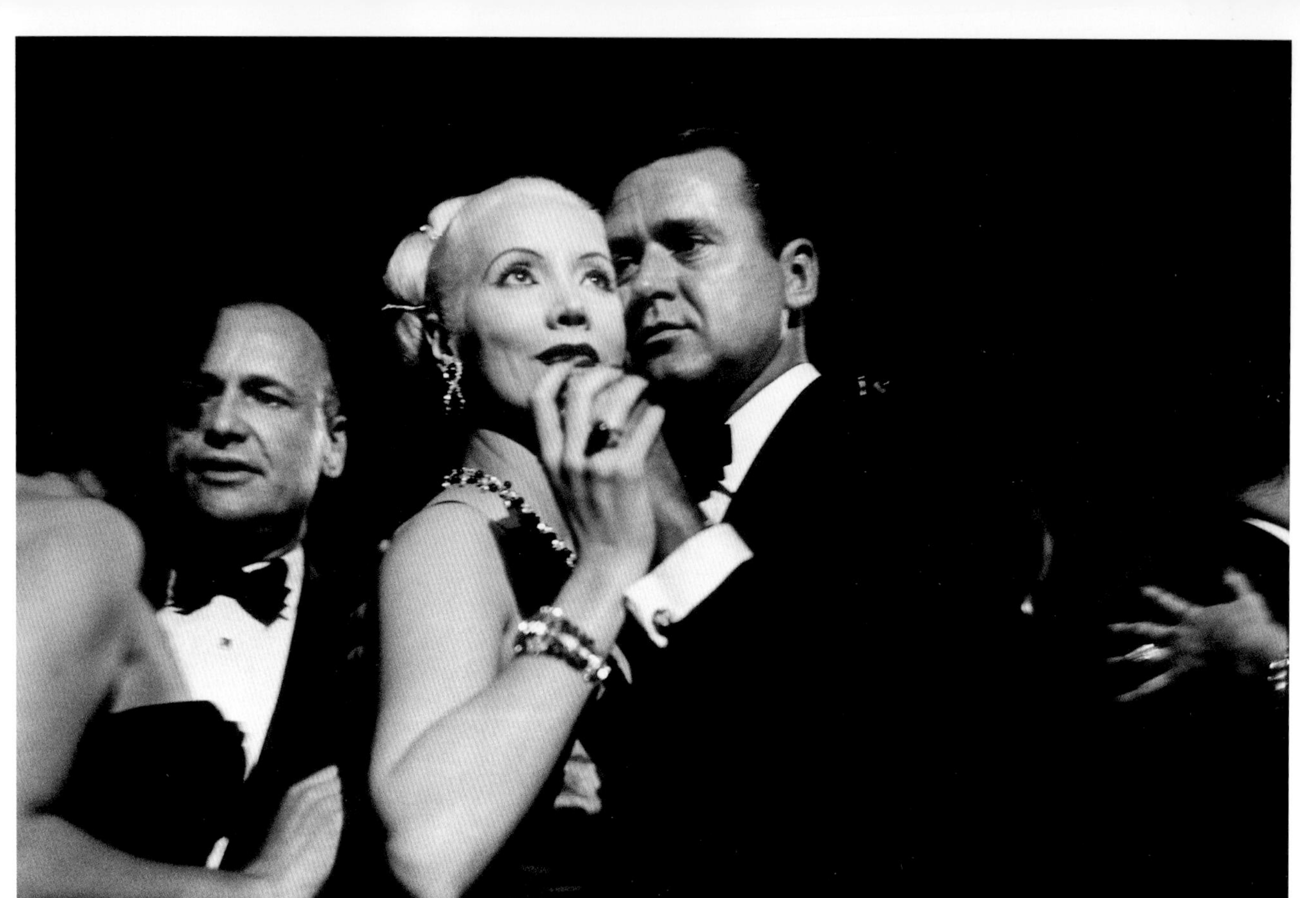

New York, 1959

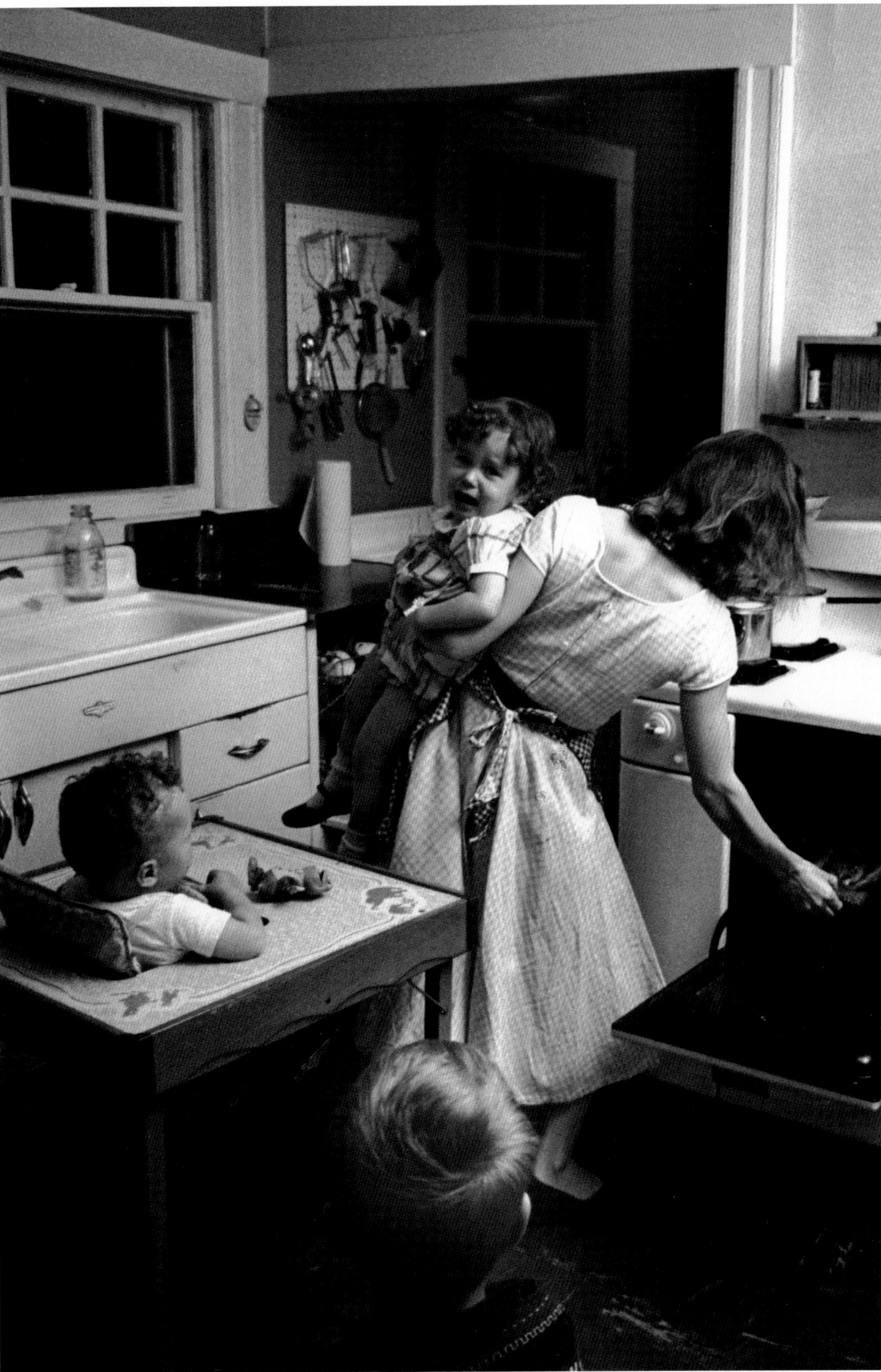

New Rochelle, New York, 1955
overleaf *St Tropez, France, 1981* / *Leningrad, 1988*

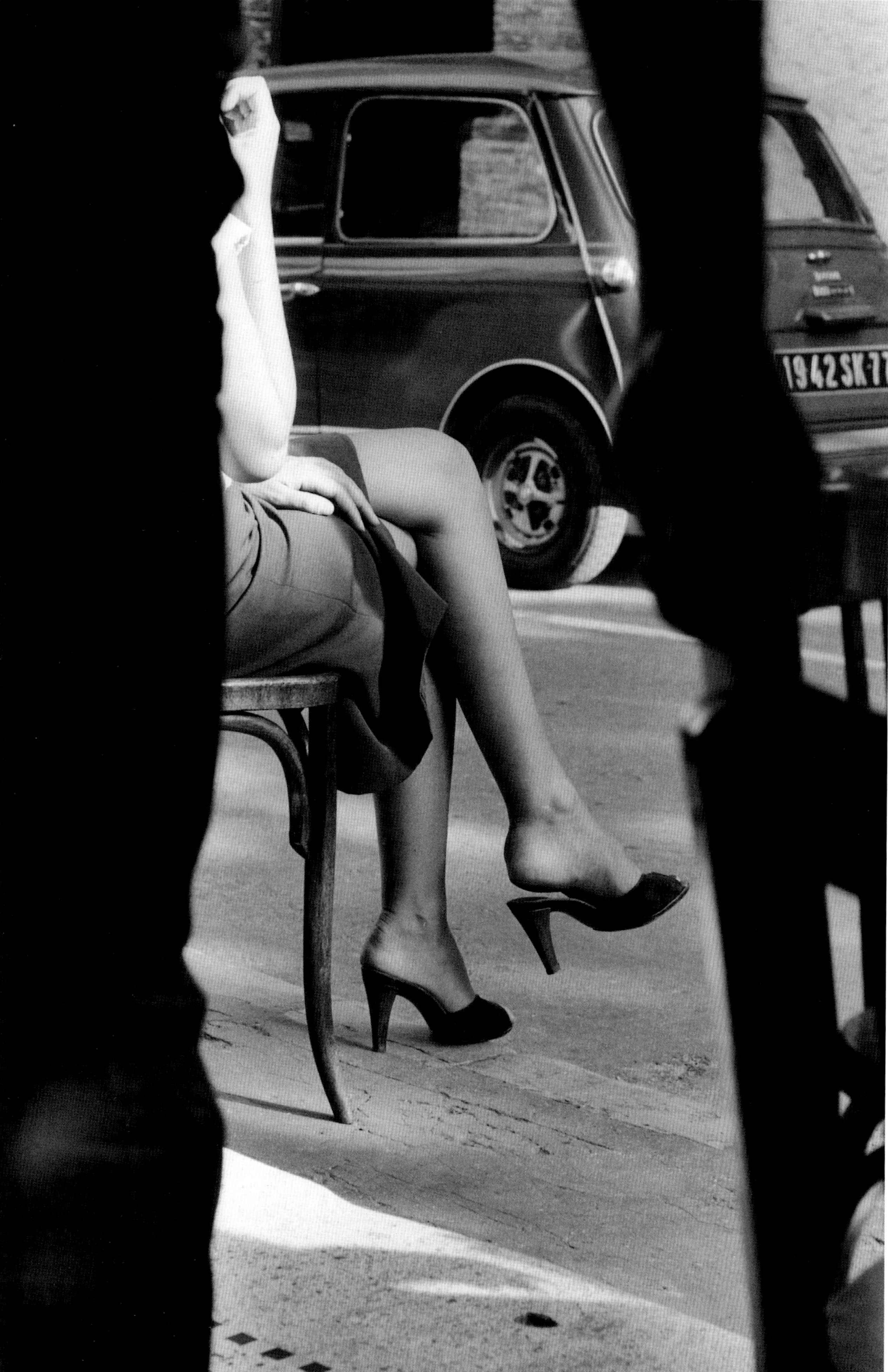
1942 SK-7

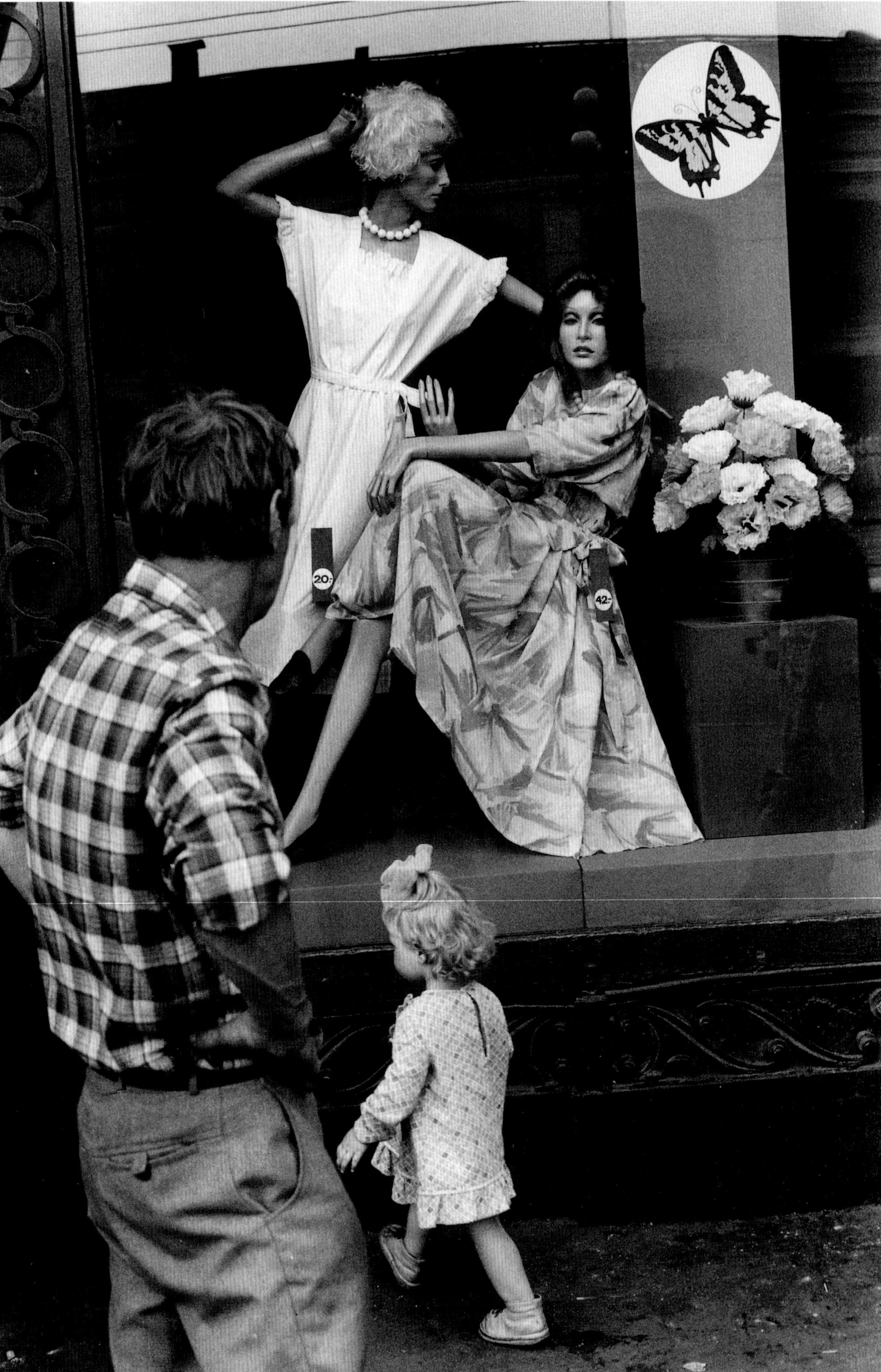
20:-
42:-

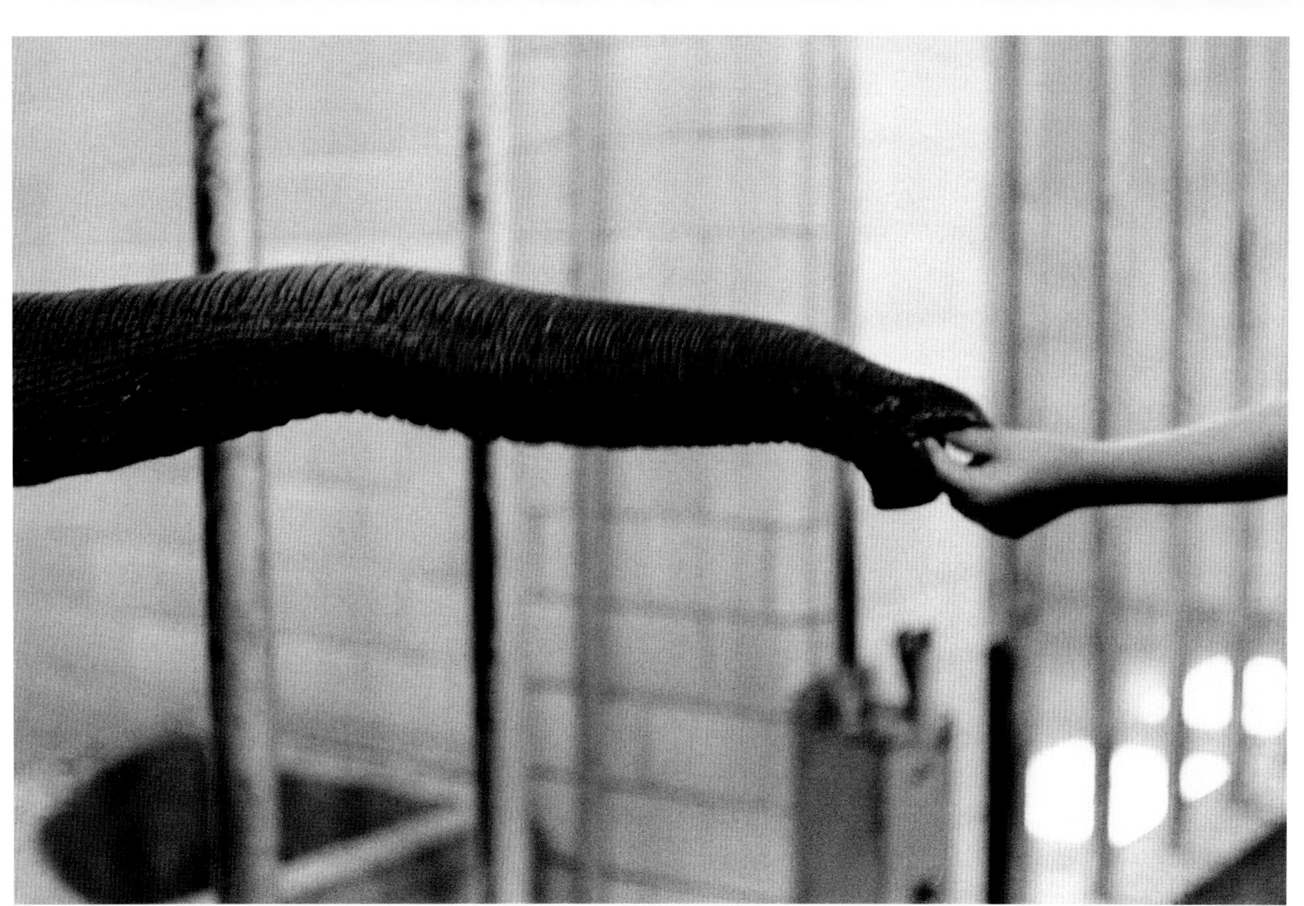

Central Park Zoo, New York, 1953

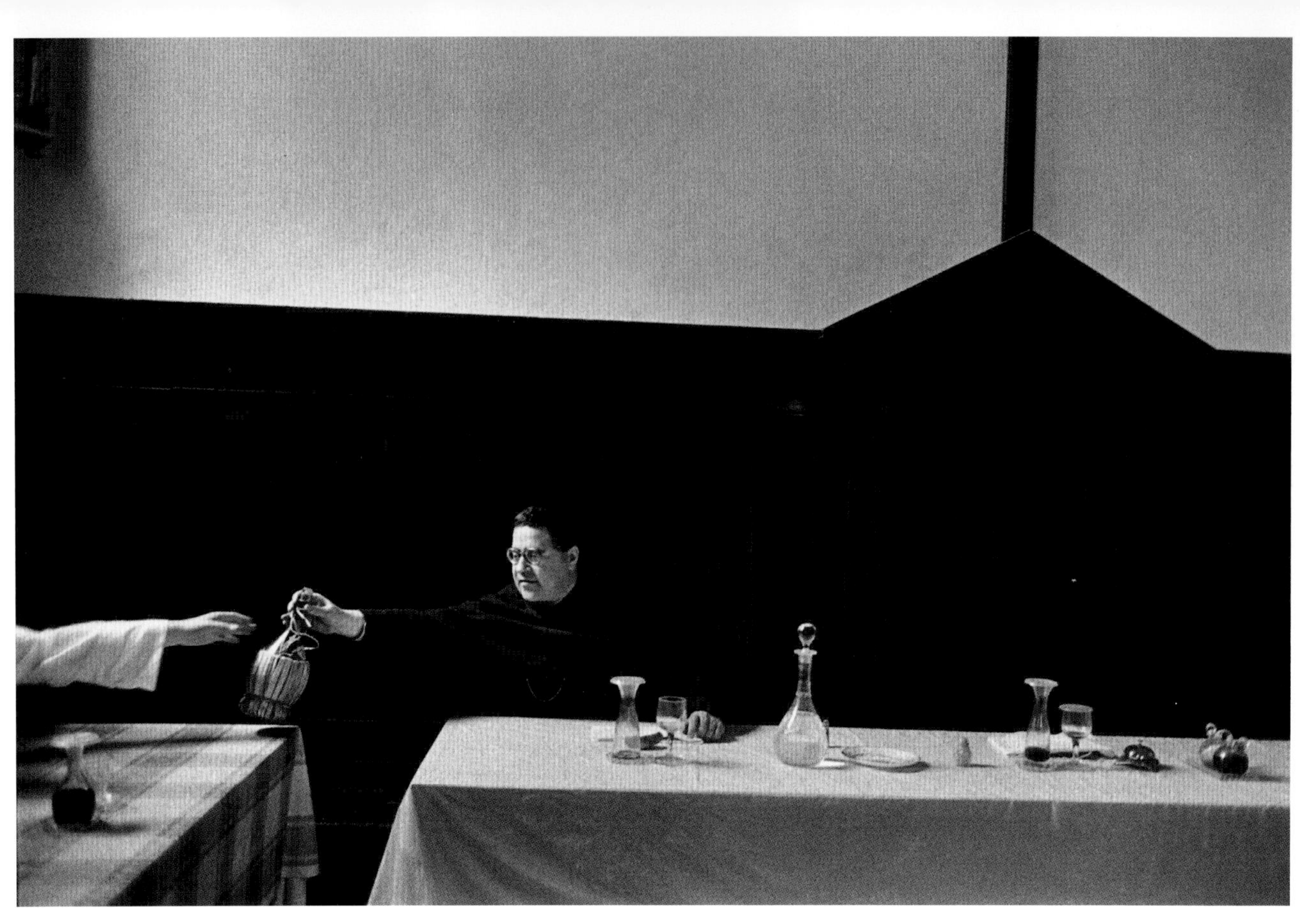

San Gimignano, Italy, 1959
overleaf *New York, 1953* / *Kyoto, Japan, 1977*

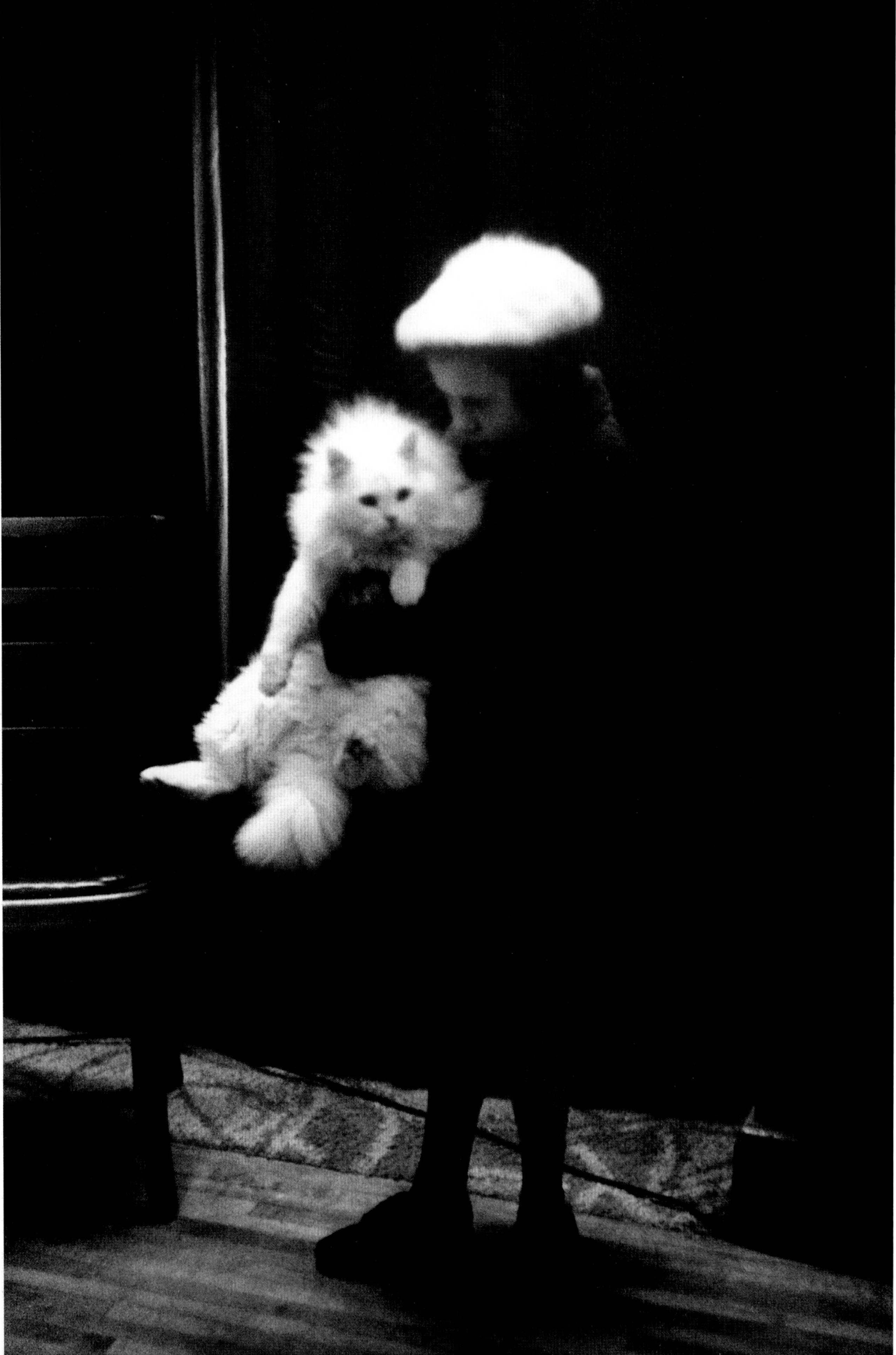

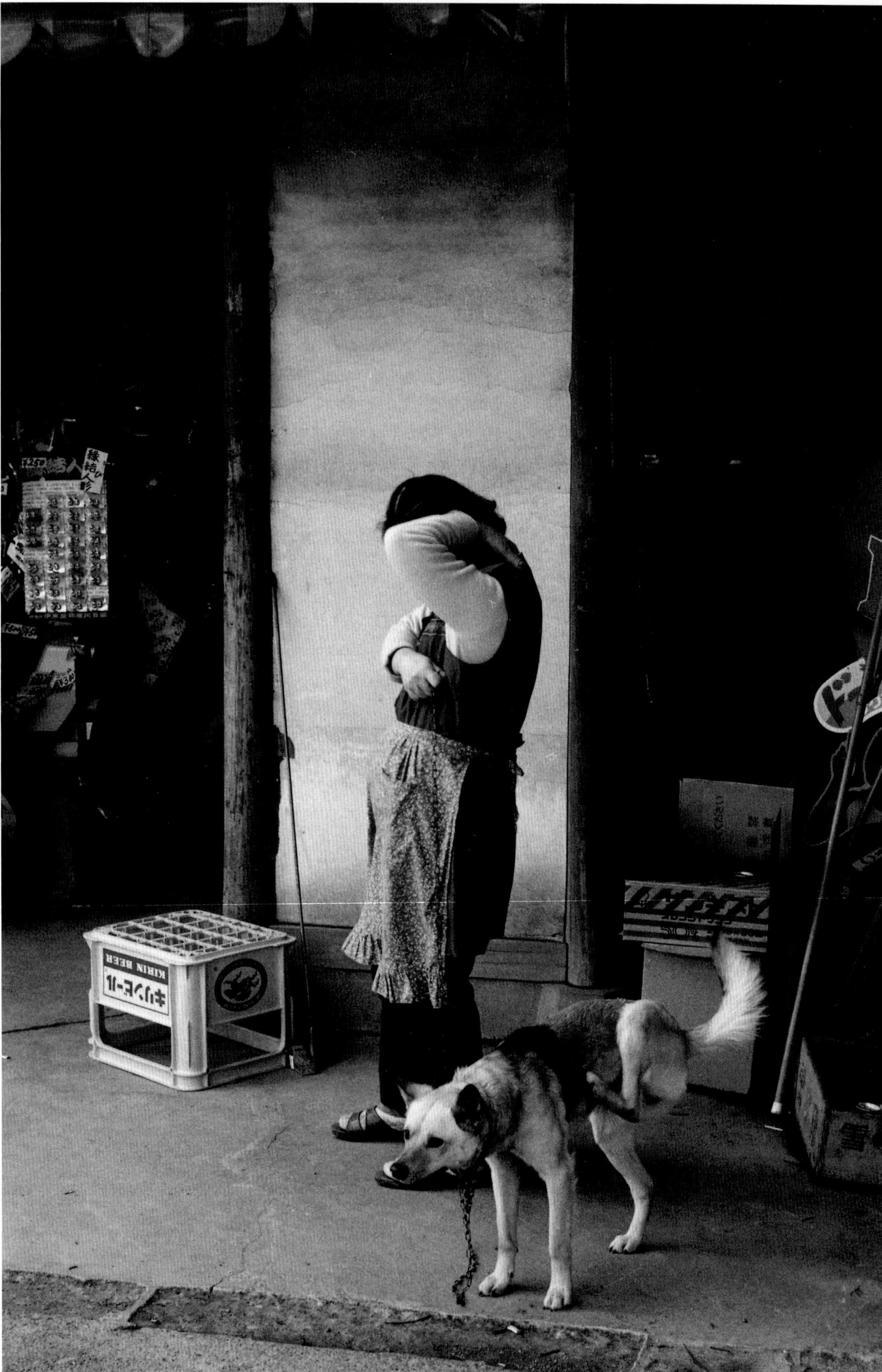
KIRIN BEER
キリンビール

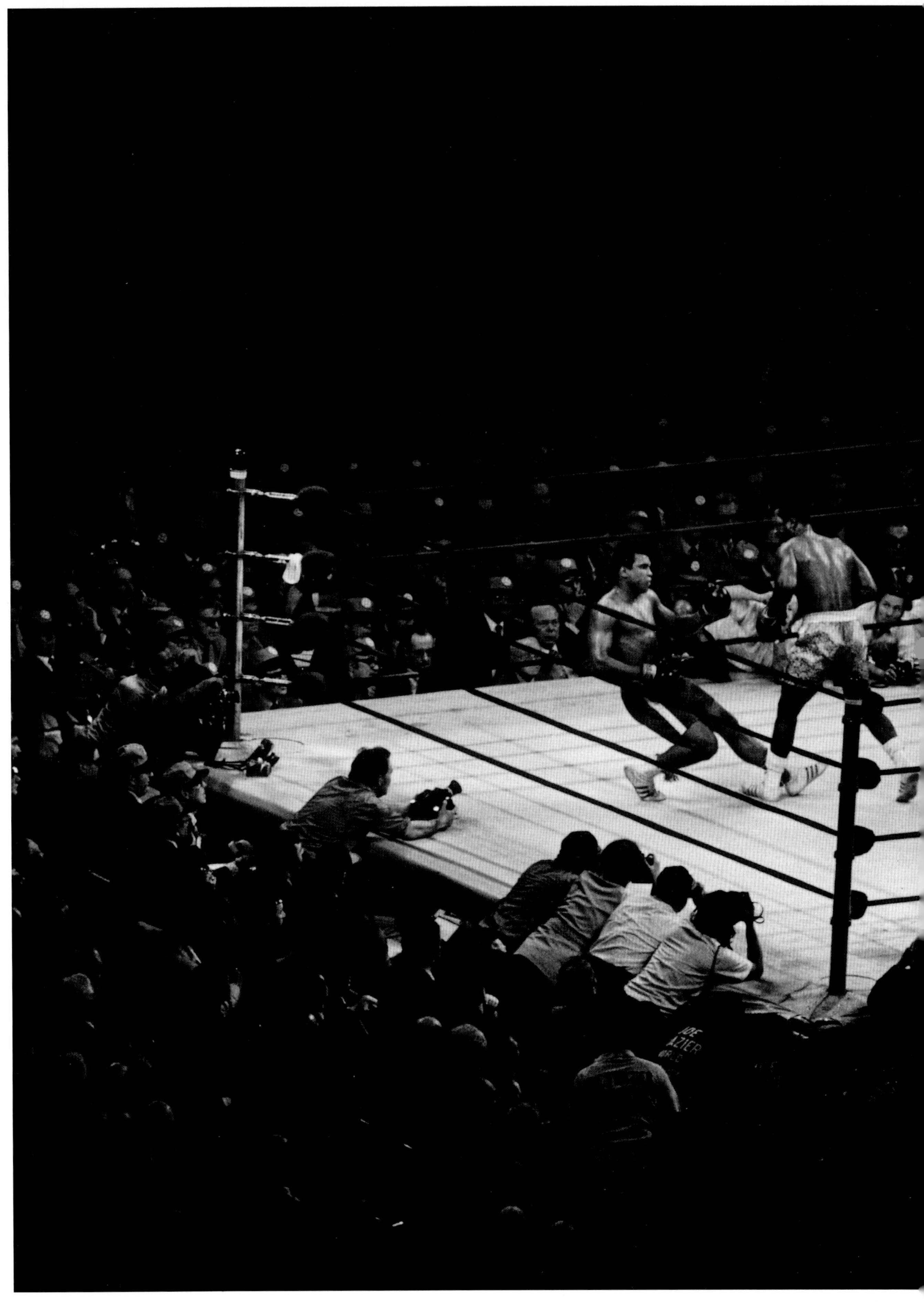

Joe Frazier and Muhammad Ali, New York, 1971

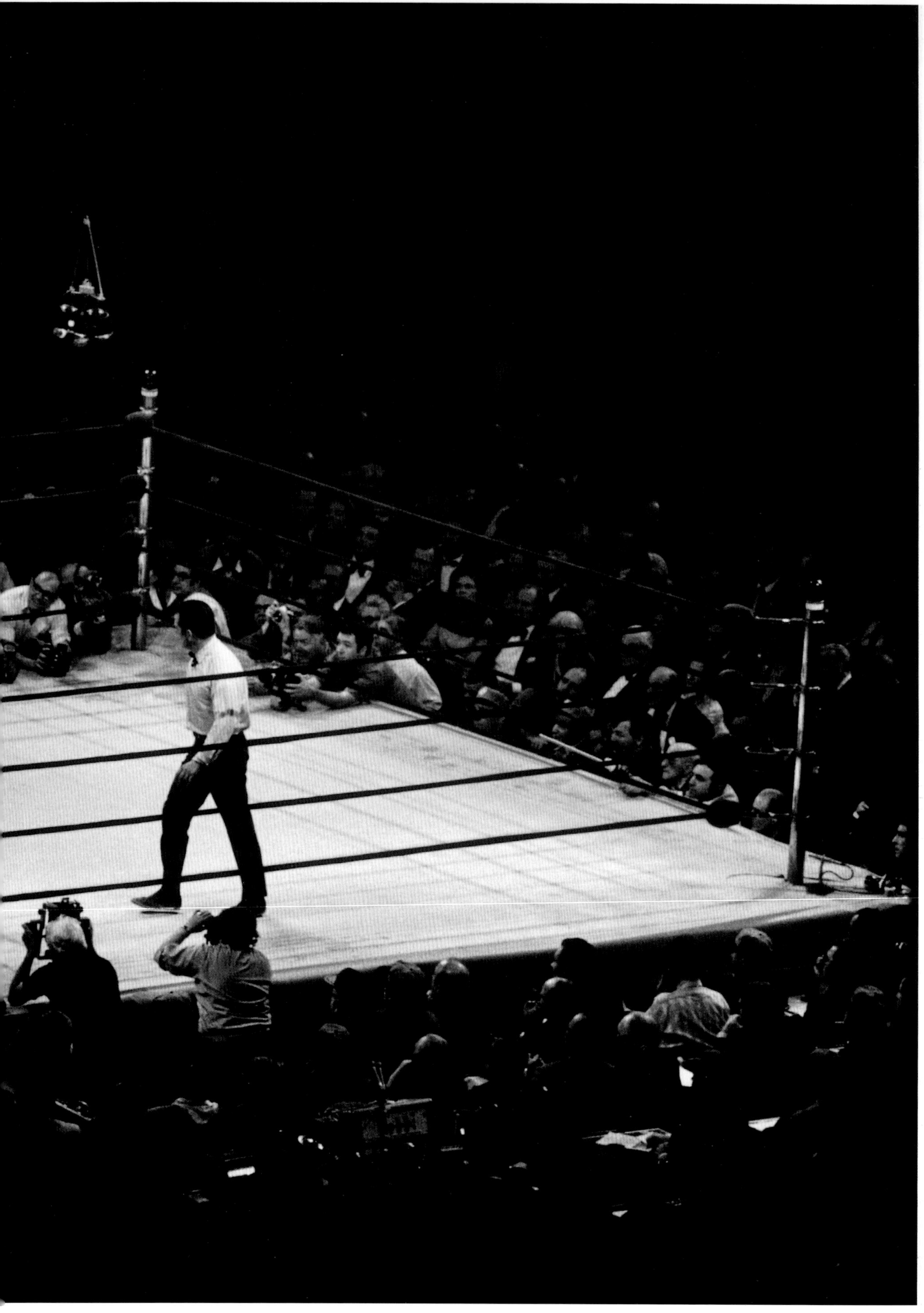

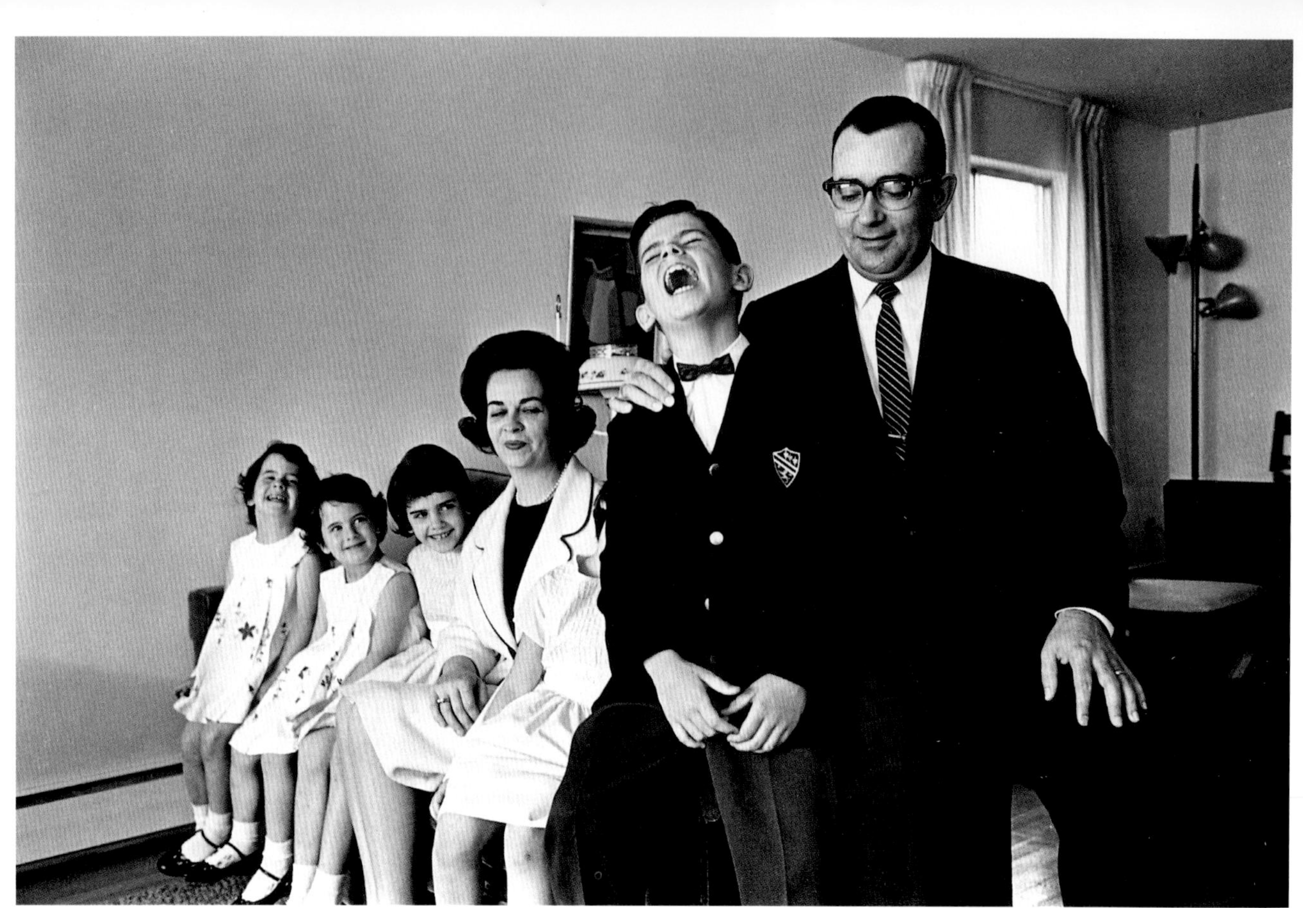

USA, 1963

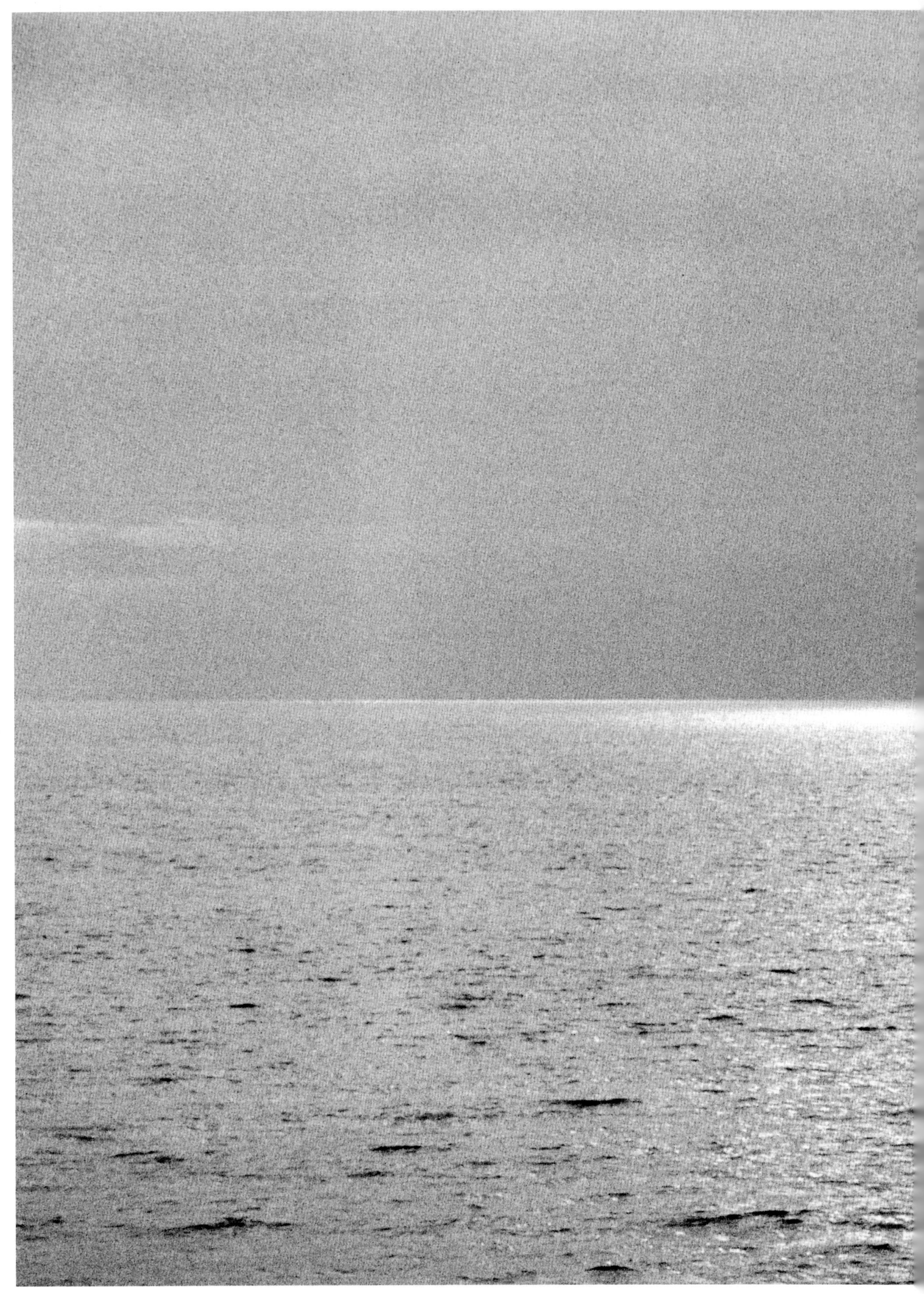

East Hampton, New York, 1978

overleaf *New Orleans, 1953* / *New Orleans, 1953*

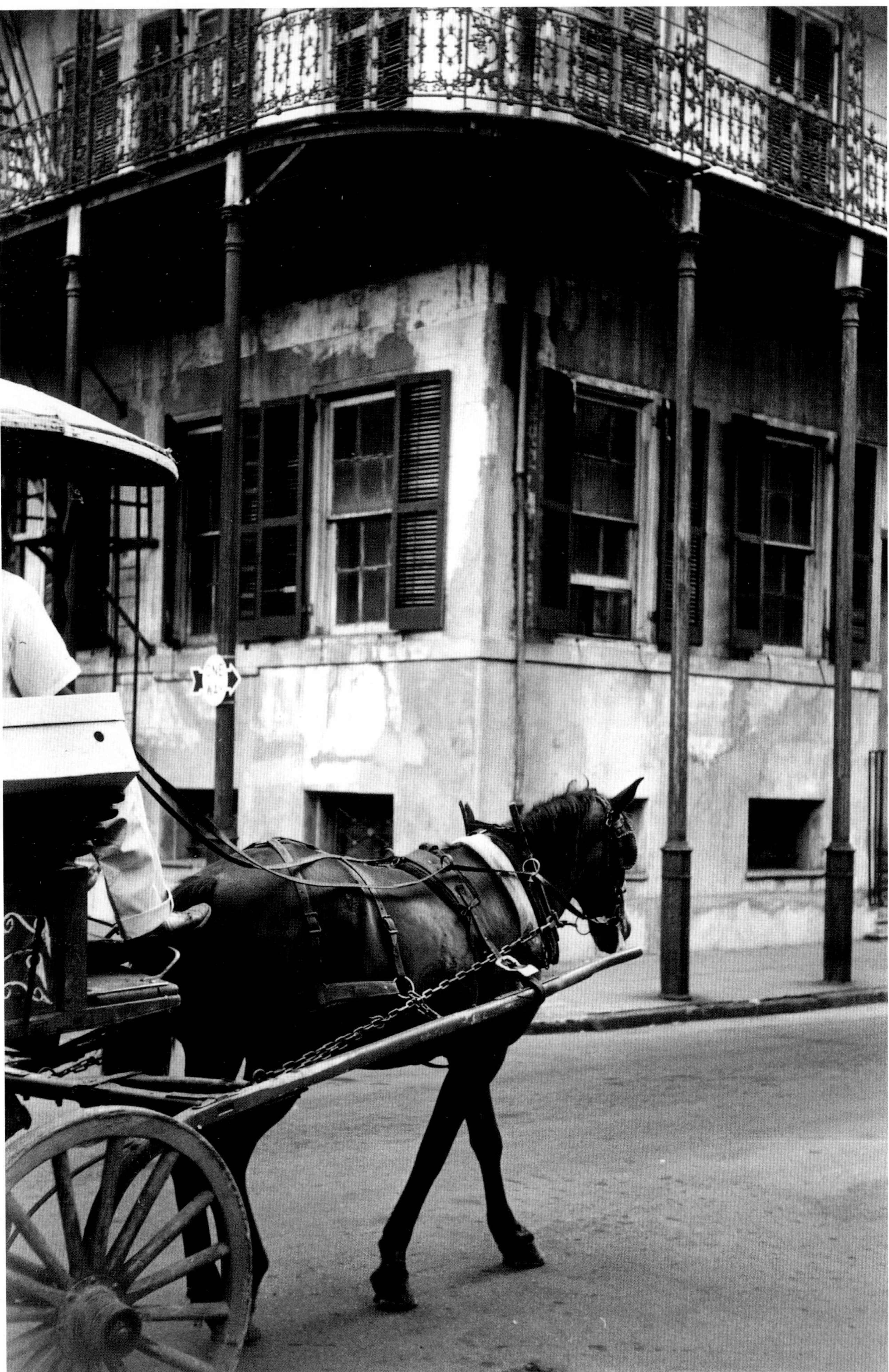

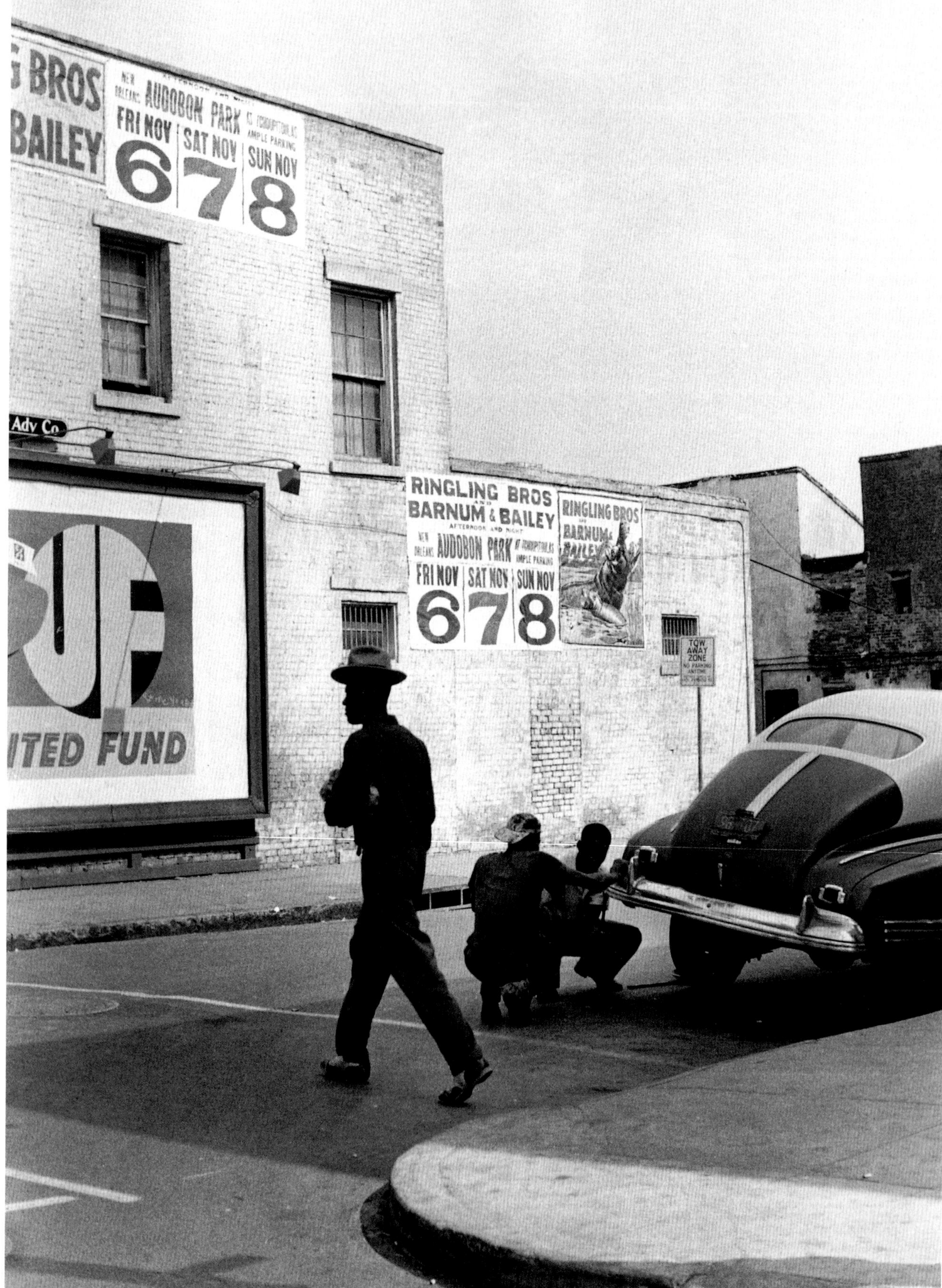
G BROS
BAILEY
NEW ORLEANS
AUDOBON PARK
FRI NOV 6
SAT NOV 7
SUN NOV 8
Adv Co
ITED FUND
RINGLING BROS AND BARNUM & BAILEY
AFTERNOON AND NIGHT
NEW ORLEANS AUDOBON PARK
AMPLE PARKING
FRI NOV 6
SAT NOV 7
SUN NOV 8
RINGLING BROS AND BARNUM & BAILEY
TOW AWAY ZONE

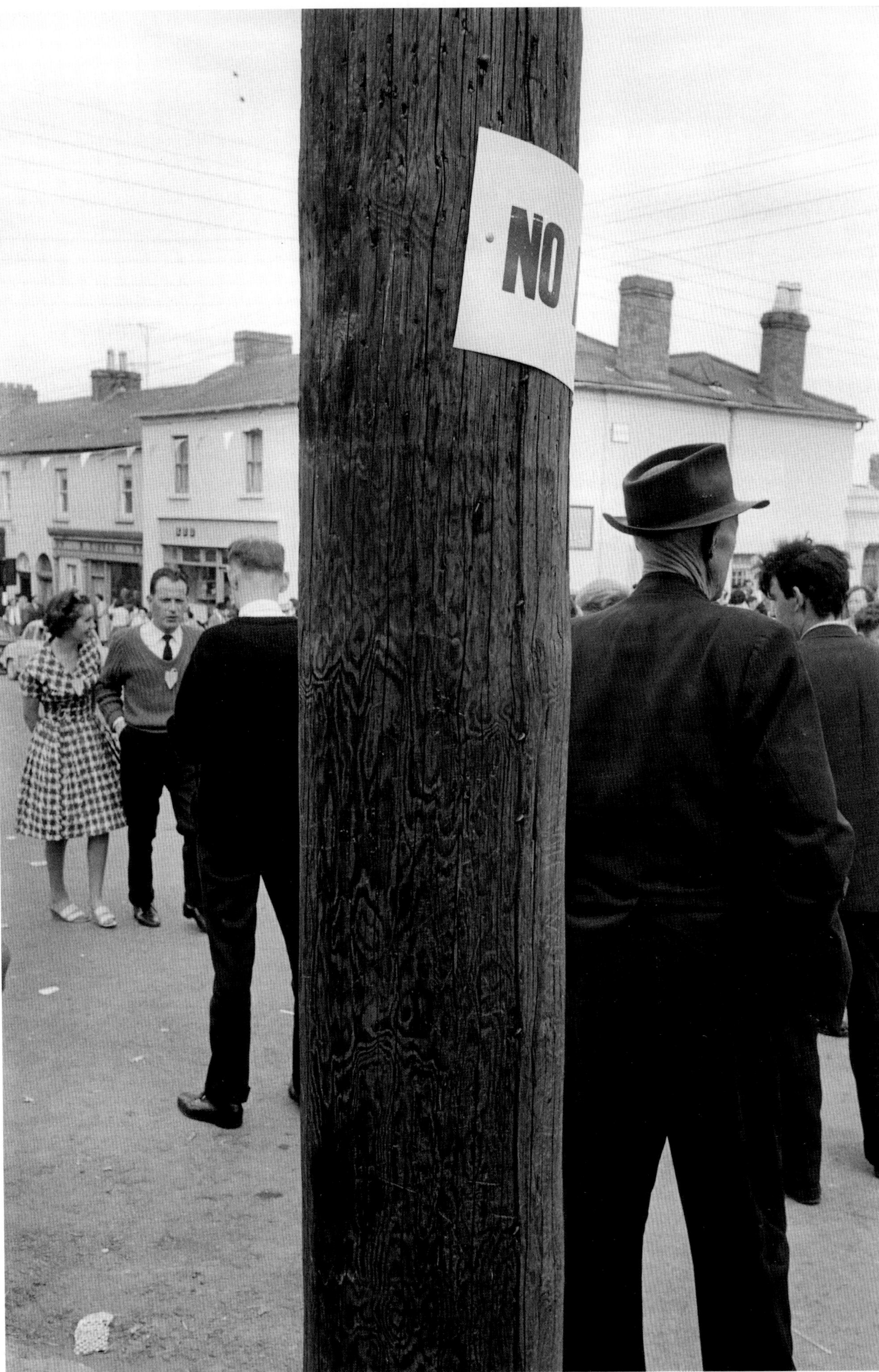
NO

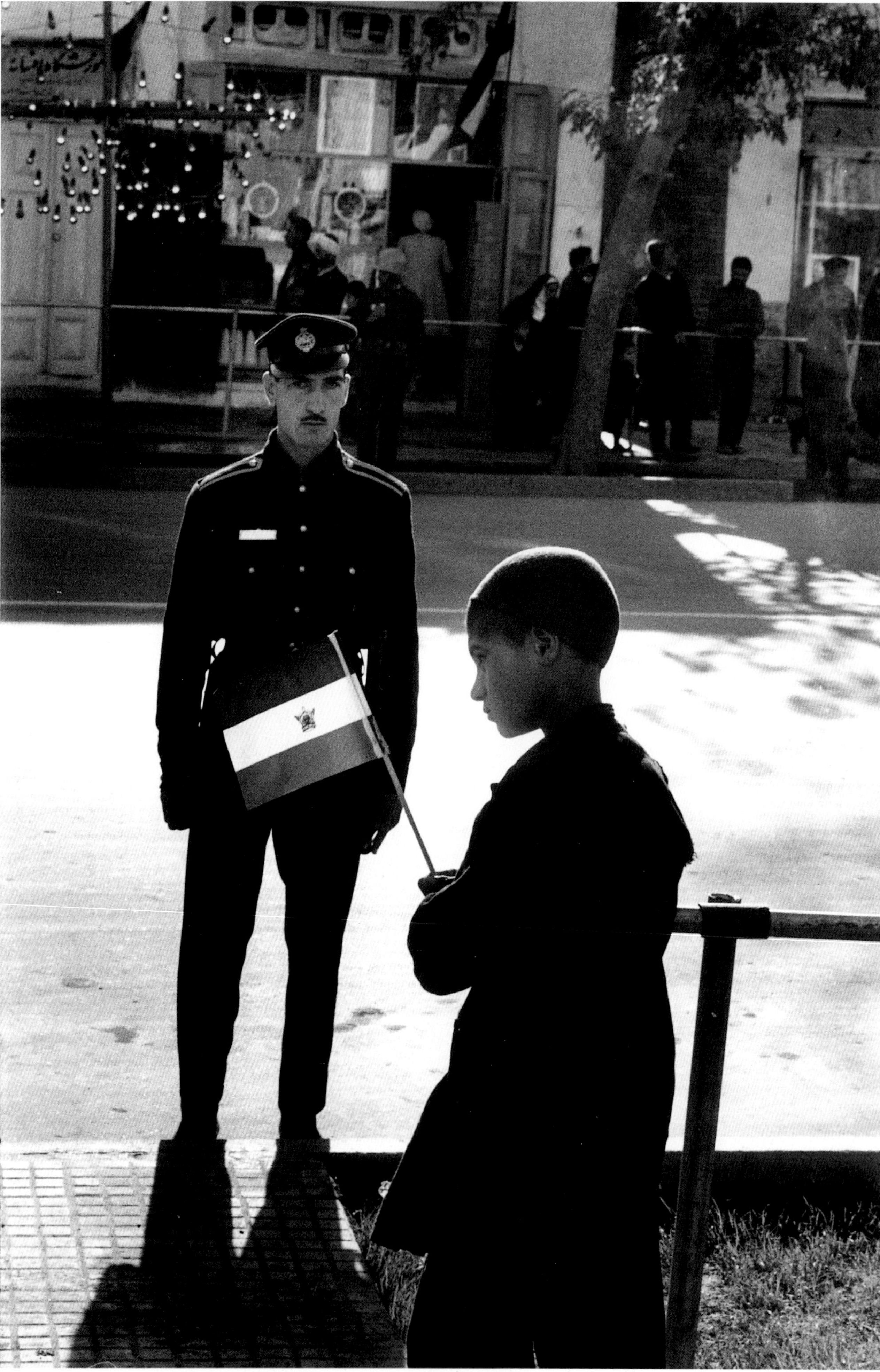

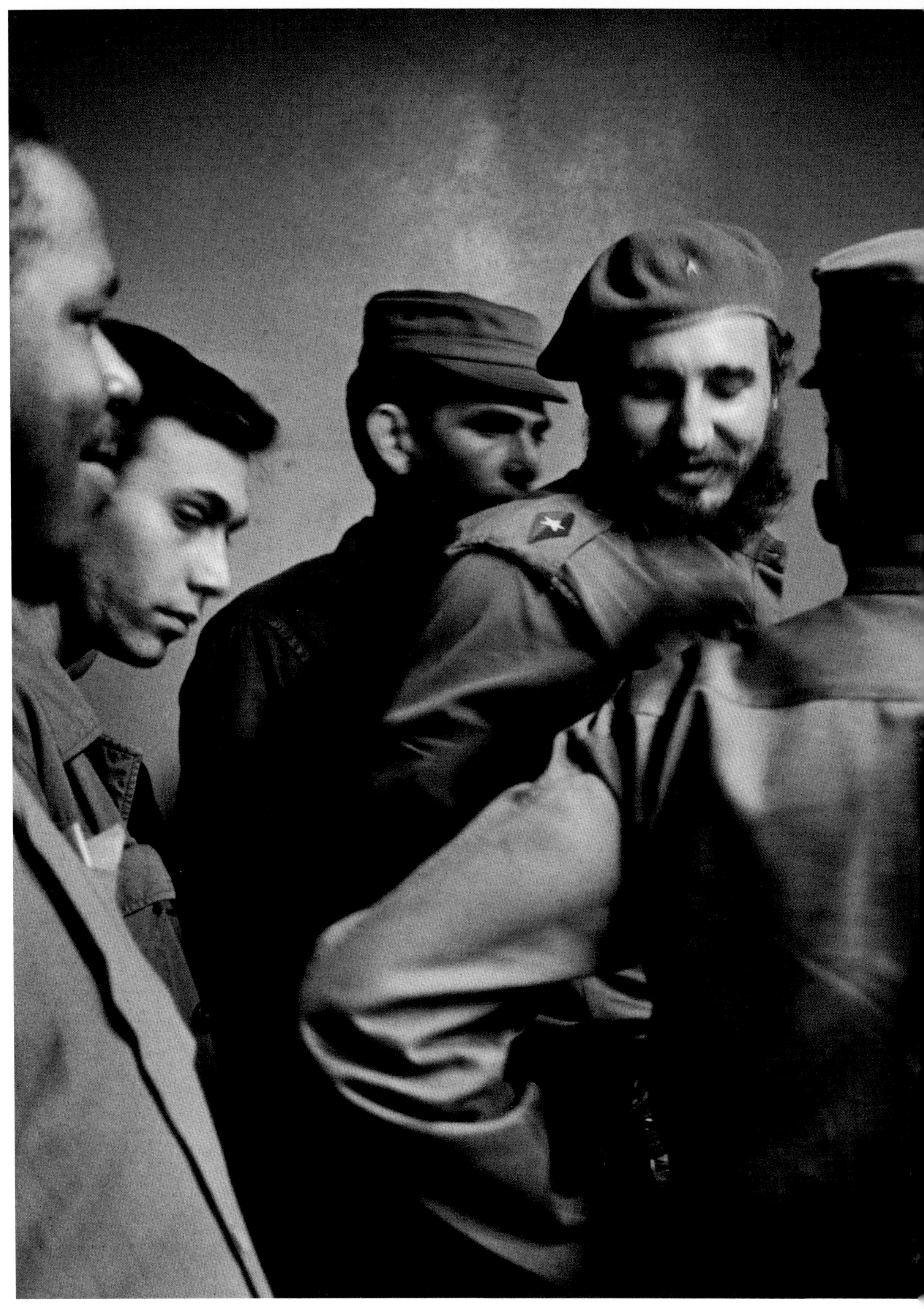

previous page *Ireland, 1962* / *Tehran, Iran, 1967*

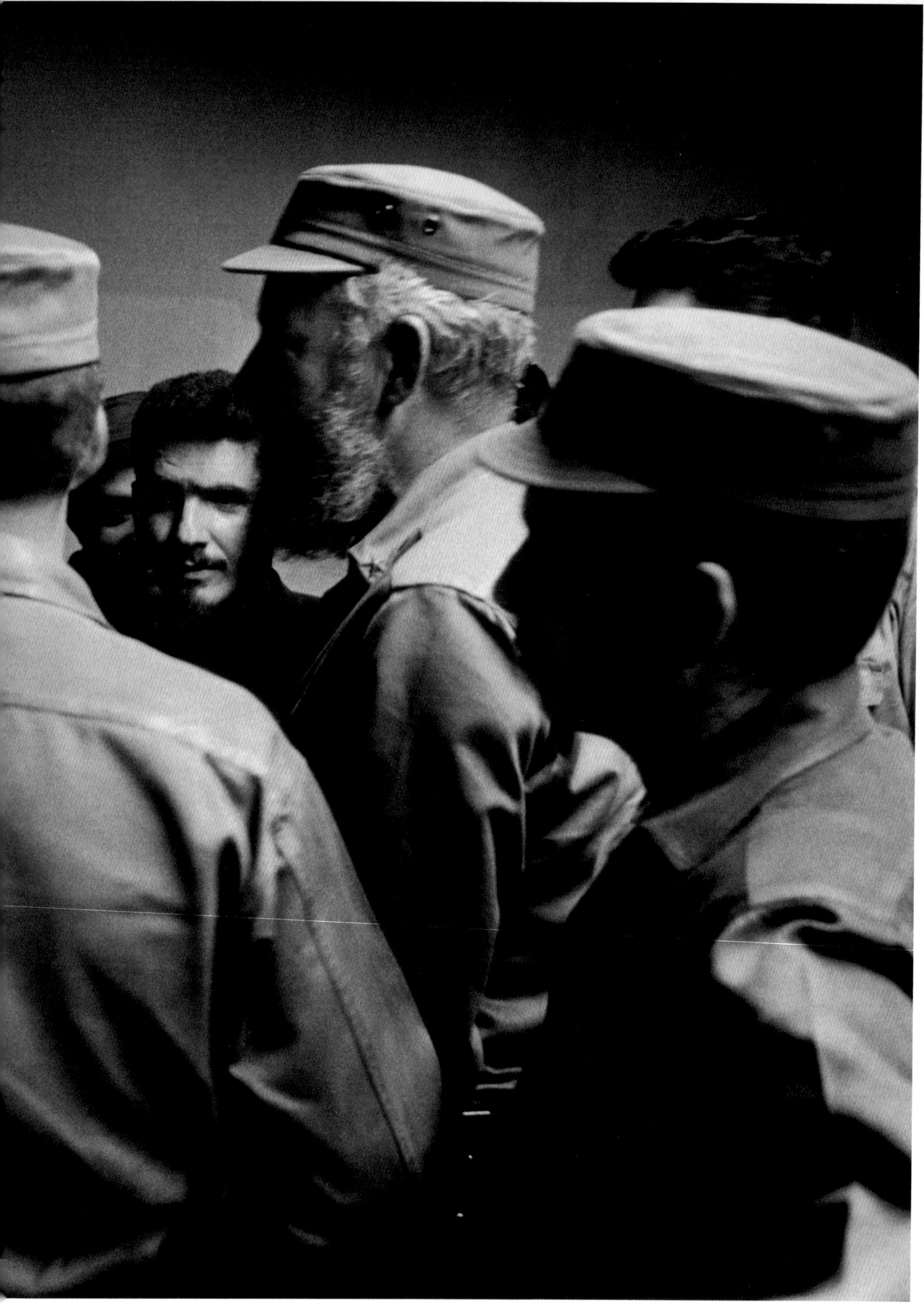

Havana, Cuba, 1964

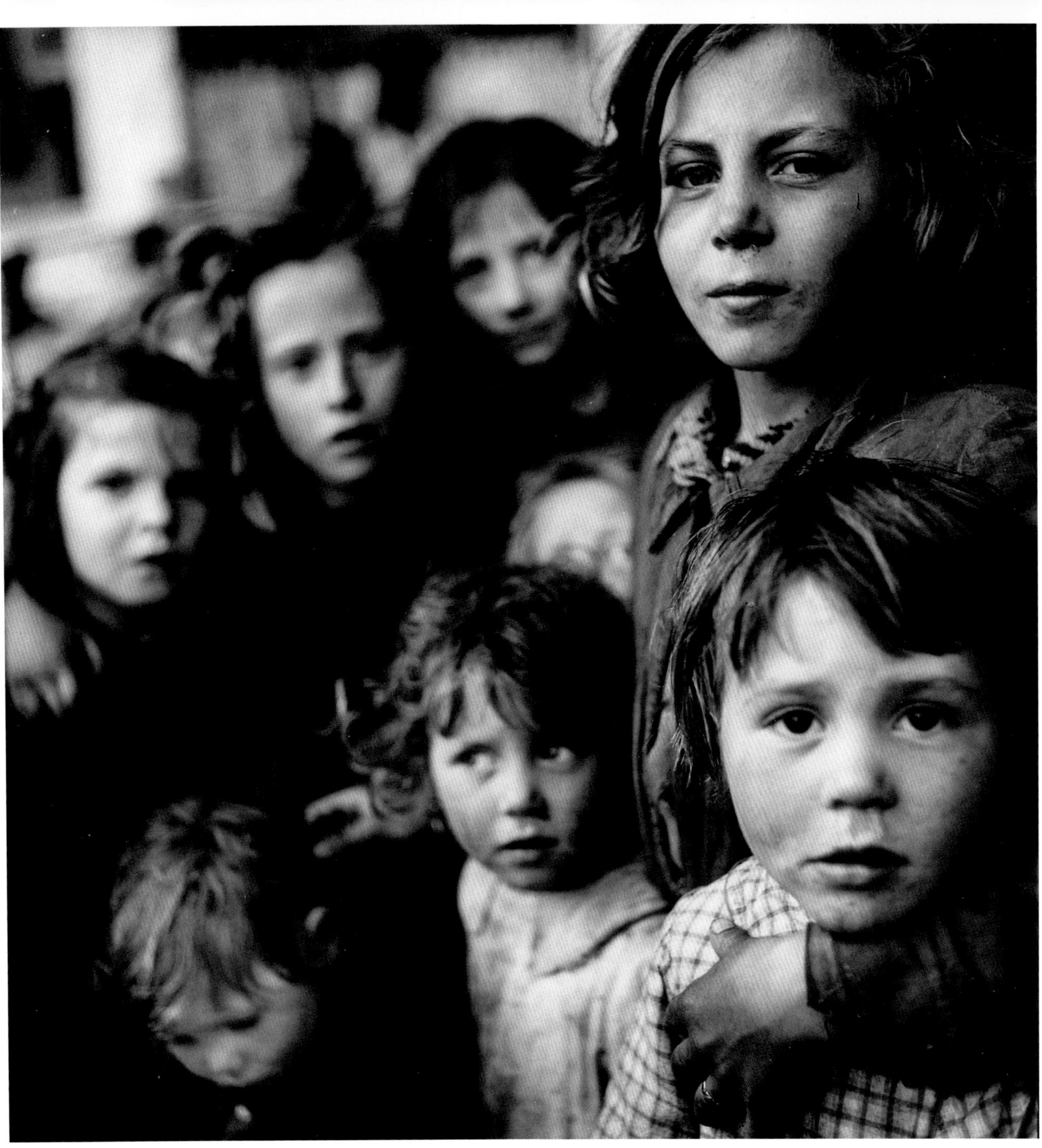

Venice, 1949

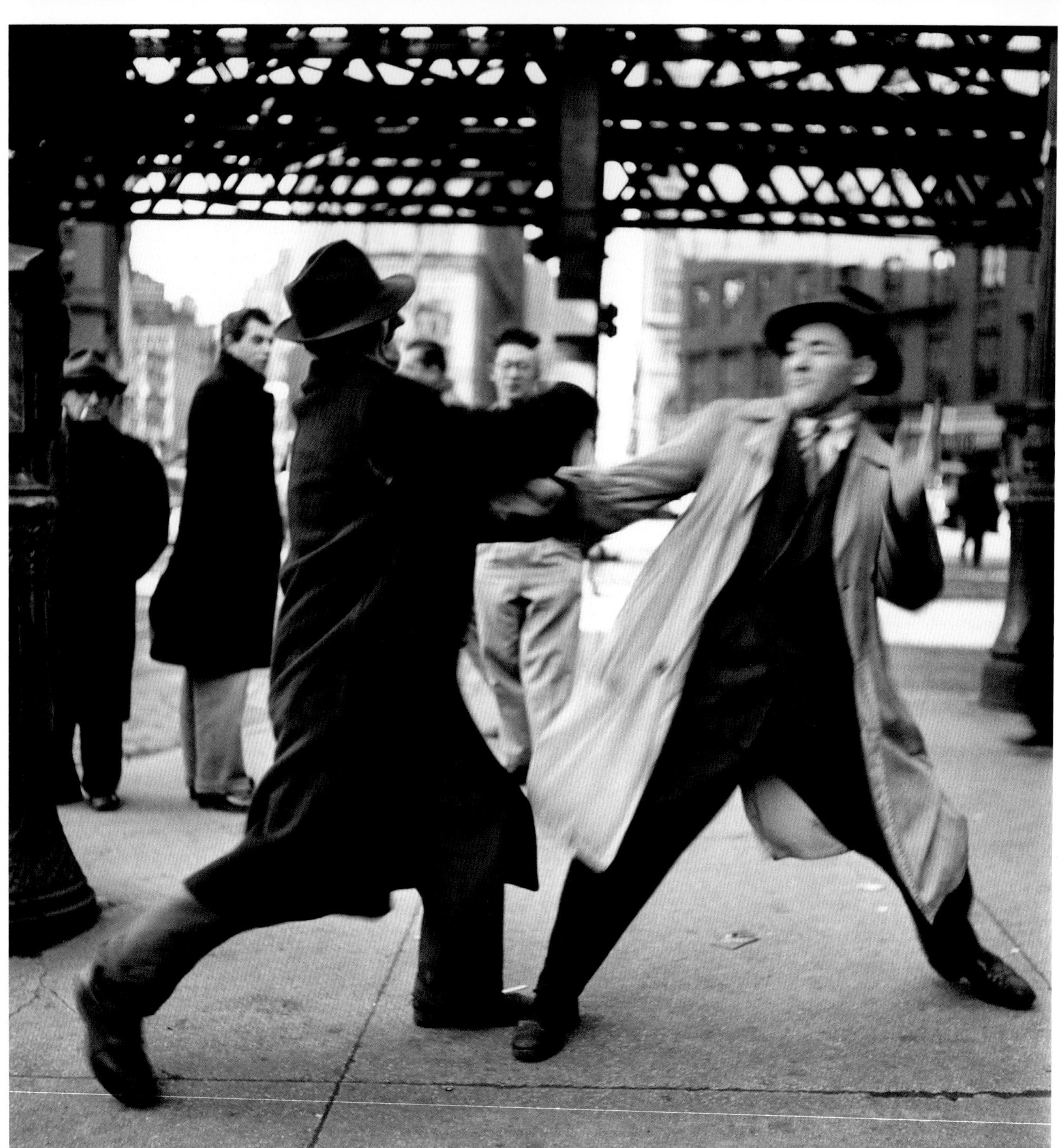

New York, 1950

Valencia, Spain, 1952
overleaf *Paris, 1949* / *New York, 1953*

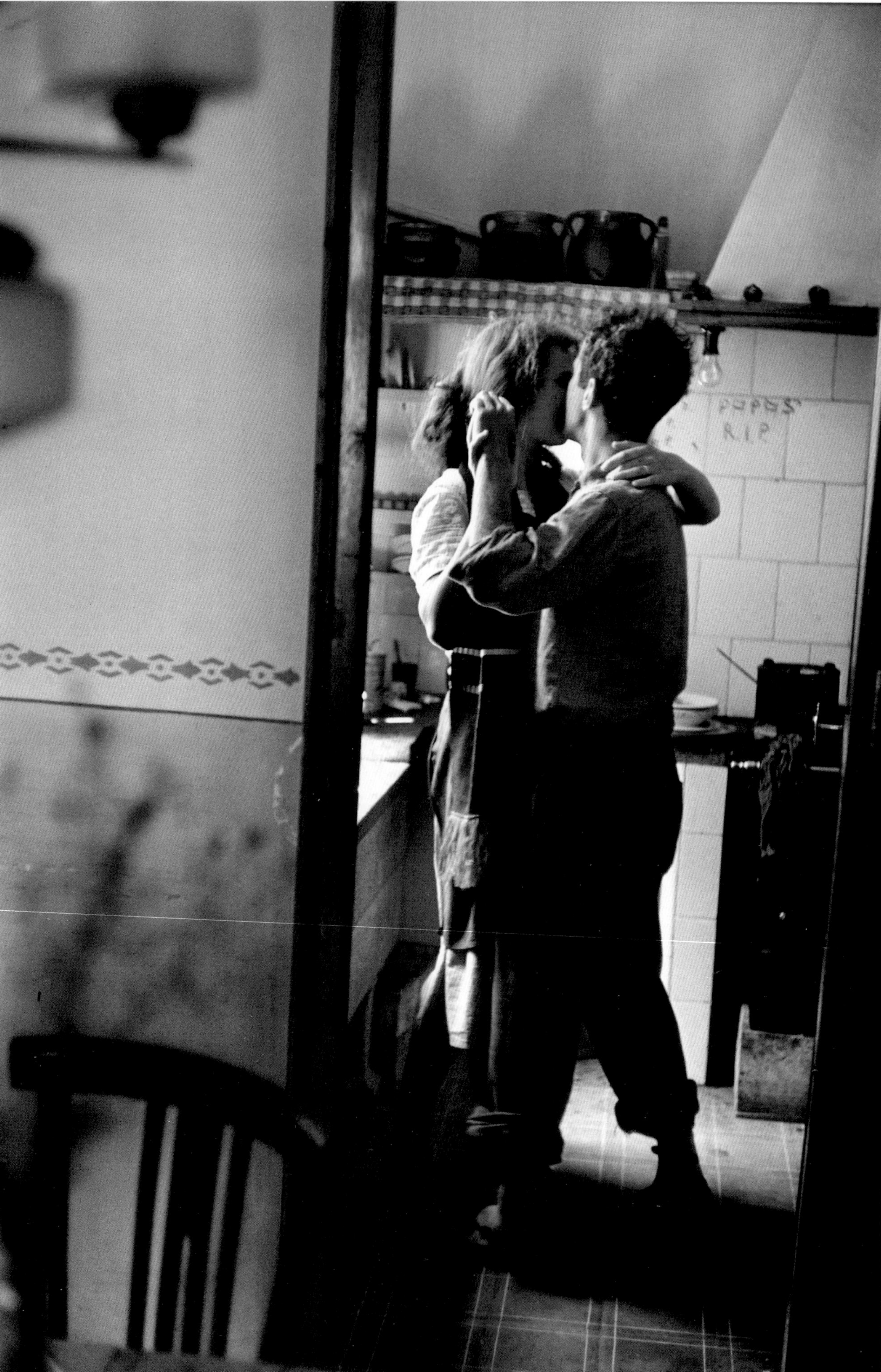
R.I.P

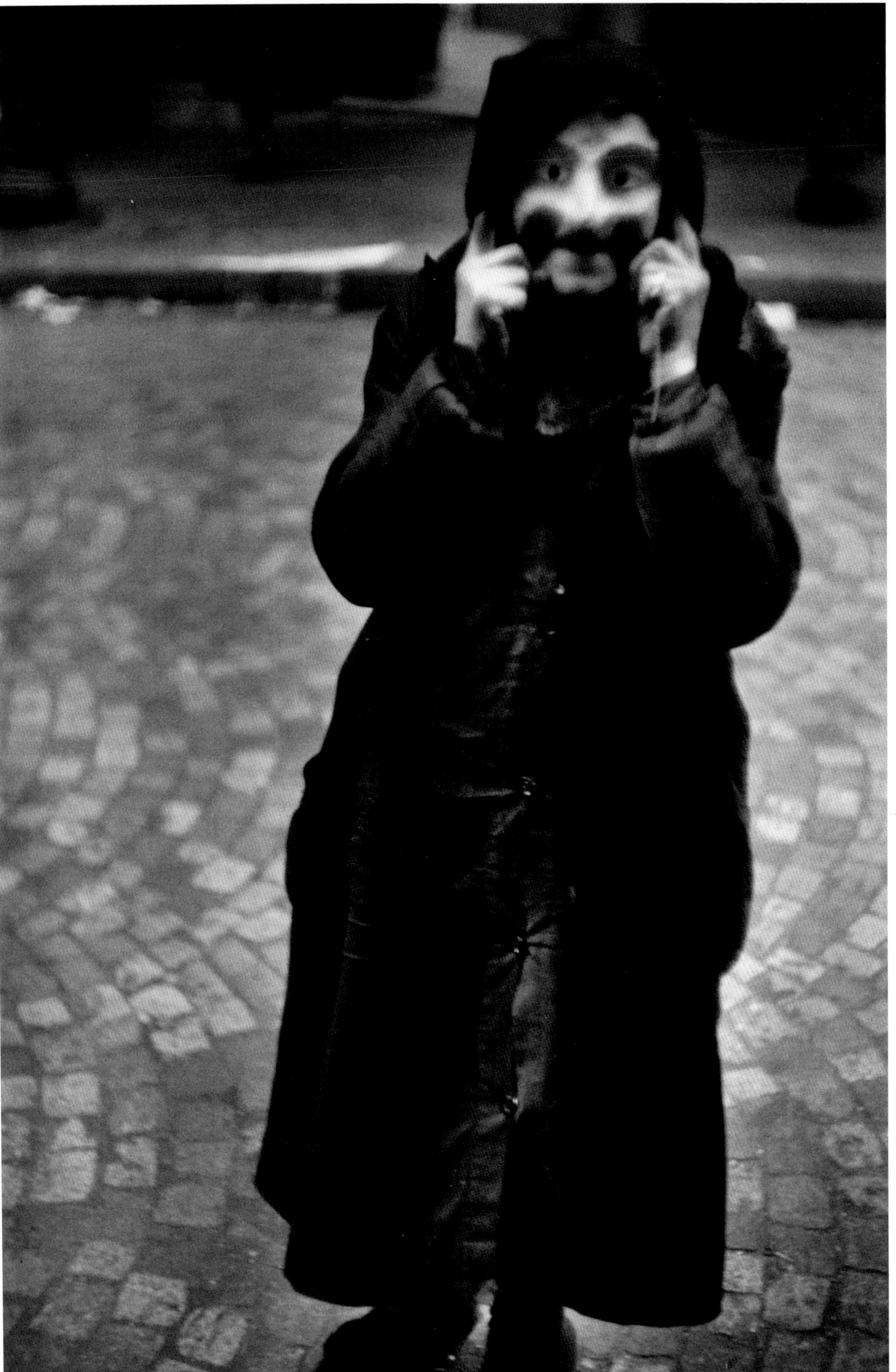

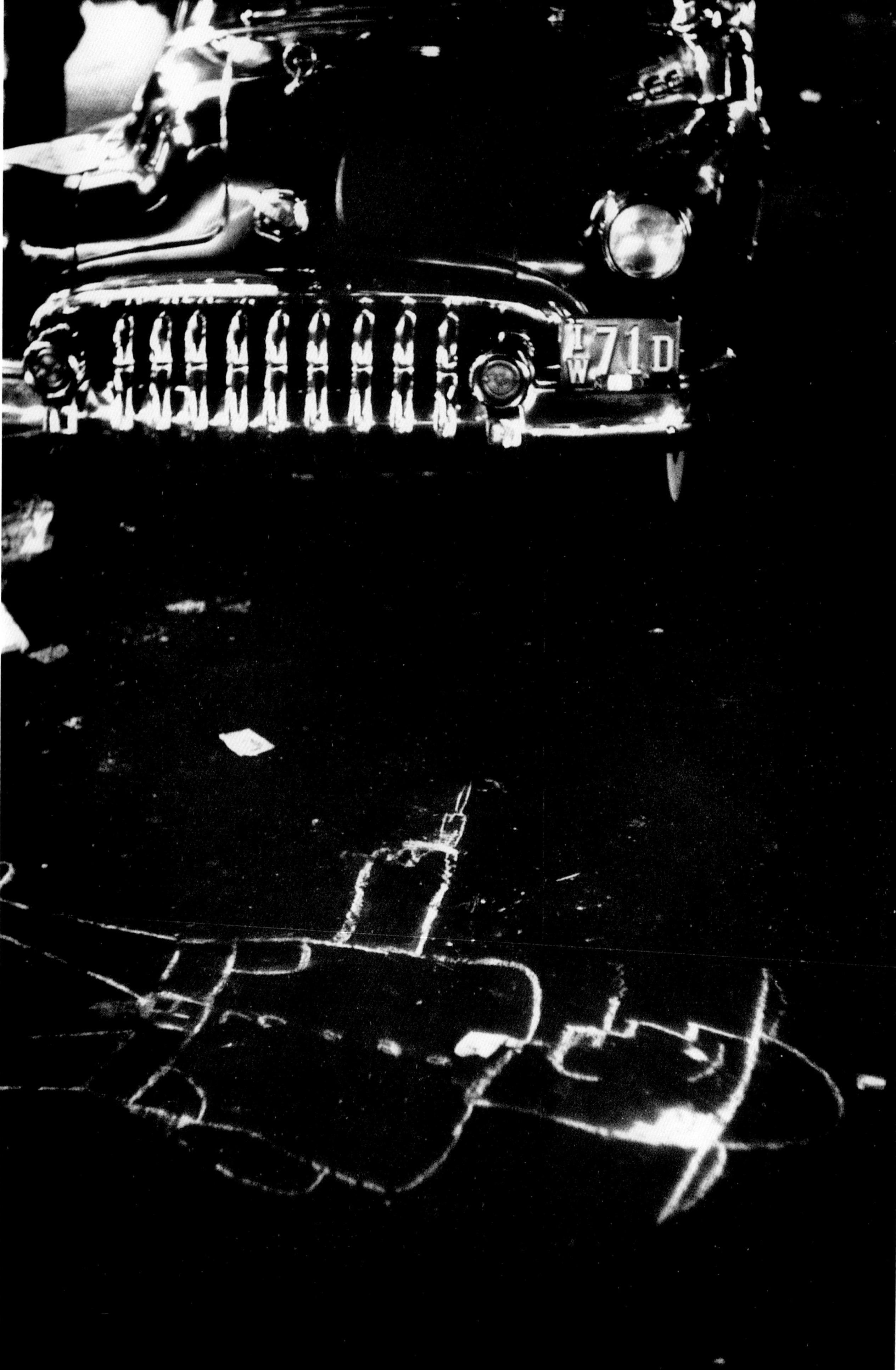
W 71D

Stand

The very 'essence of Elliott's art,' the witty novelist Wilfrid Sheed wrote nearly a quarter of a century ago, is 'to be tender without crying, funny without laughing, intelligent without thinking'.

These phrases, as Sheed would probably agree, apply also to the photographer's style of ambling through life – always the slight detachment and bemusement, always the intense awareness of everything going on, inevitably the summing up of someone as true or phoney.

A particular pleasure of friendship with Elliott is the quick exchange of glances, nothing said aloud, when someone notably preposterous (and not always a publisher or advertising exec) acts or babbles in character. That glance is the same reflex that creates the snaps. His sense of the imminent absurd never goes on 'idle'. But while he may wait for the humorous conjunction in his photos, which are rarely thought out ahead of time, he does not wait for humour in life.

Almost no one has written about Elliott without mentioning the wacky objects that greet visitors to either of his homes. In Easthampton life-size statues of Japanese policemen stand as sentinels near the front entrance. Visible outside to the left, in the centre of the large flowering garden is a ten-foot-tall three-dimensional replica of the Statue of Liberty. In the foyer between elevator and front door of his New York apartment, the prodigious moose head garlanded with shiny red tinsel may stand out under the strip of tinny theatrical lighting, or perhaps the chime that works like a panic lock, or two more of the stolid Japanese policemen, or the candelabrum topped with a bile-yellow tennis ball, or the sign reading 'Danger de Mort', or some other object. In both places, the statues stand as if with secret purpose; you will see their like, and their human reflections, throughout the following section of snaps.

The apartment presents an improbable but seamless blend of his wife Pia's contemporary American and European art, Art Deco furniture and portable foldaway pool table with her husband's eclectic mix of photo books, framed photographs, toys and remarkable art objects, including a large Cambodian puppet and a Japanese fertility idol with a formidably symbolic nose. The gimcrackery mocks the fine art; everything is levelled or raised to the pursuit of having a good laugh; visitors usually become as unaffected as children, whatever their sober adult intent in the first place.

This sense of fun obviously led to Elliott's choices of the many different stances seen in this section of photos. Lamps, palm trees, chimneys stand with no less presence, perhaps, than people making phone calls, dancers ready to perform, horses waiting for the next assignment or families posing for the private posterity of their photo albums.

Elliott himself is less patient with standing around, however. Once he paid me and a couple of friends to be non-union extras in a print ad for a major investment house. Our role was to pretend to sleep in the seats of a mock-up airliner. As the shoot continued, I began to notice – my eyes still closed – something very odd. Each time the art director walked over to make a change in the setup, Elliott would lower his voice just slightly. Finally, he had the man whispering whenever he approached, as if not wanting to wake us from our doze. I cracked up, of course.

Why spend time arranging this gag in the middle of a job? The answer is seen again and again in the snaps, I think. Elliott wants to find humour in almost every situation, and he will add it himself if life fails to provide. As Sheed also wrote; 'Genuinely funny photos can be taken only by someone who lives in a funny world.' Like the people in the photos, by the way, the art director had no idea he'd been snapped.

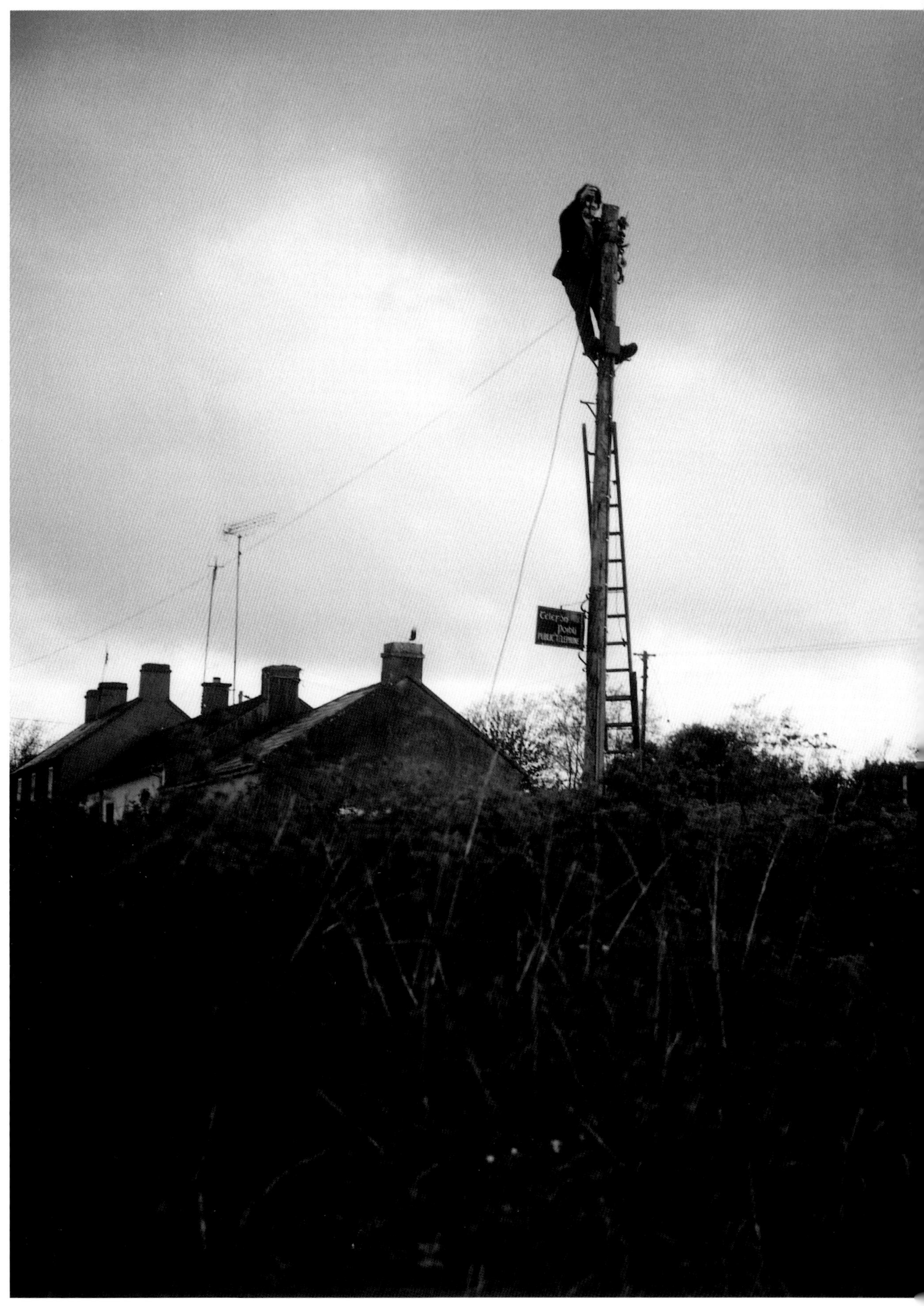

Ballycotton, Ireland, 1982

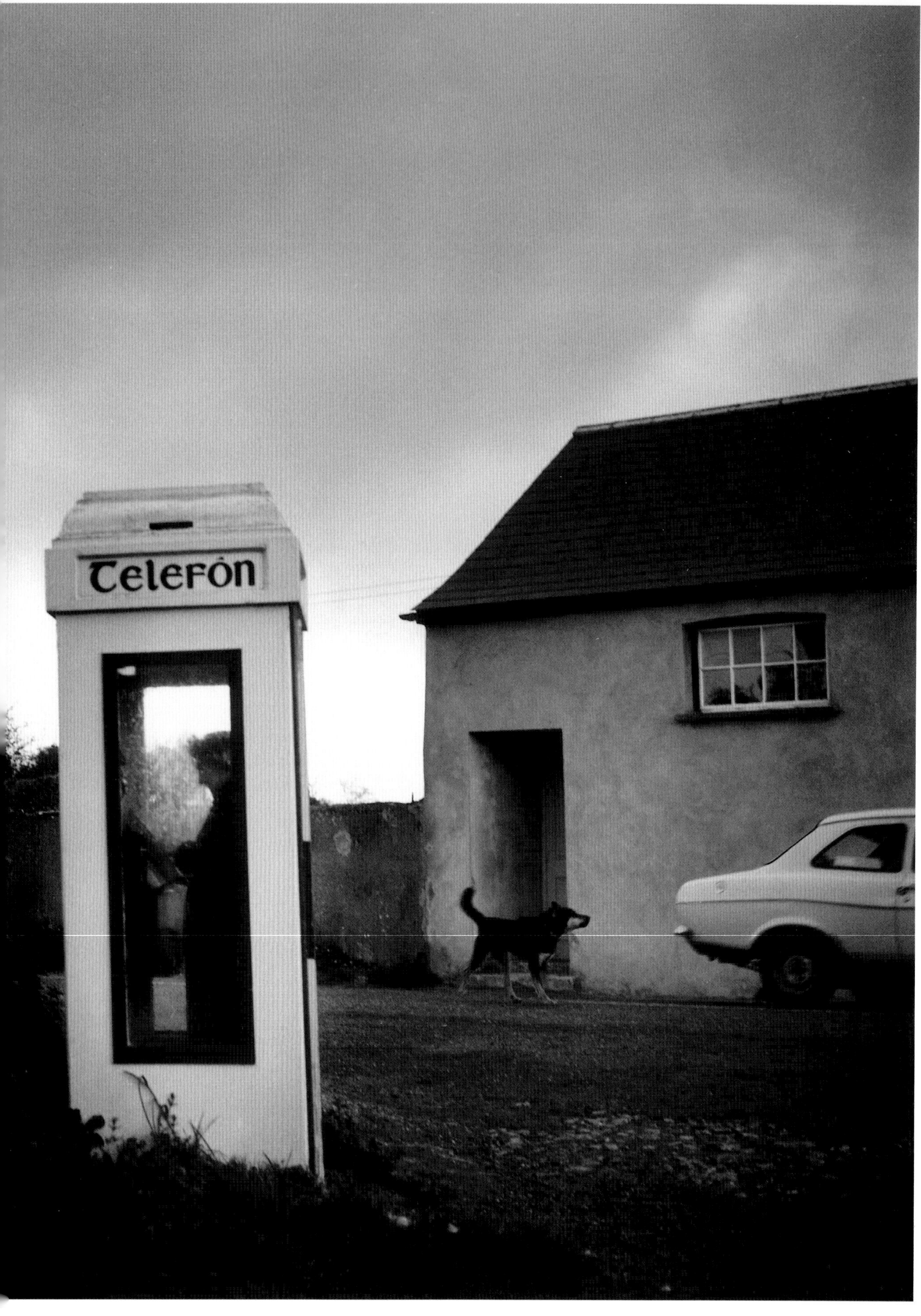
Telefón

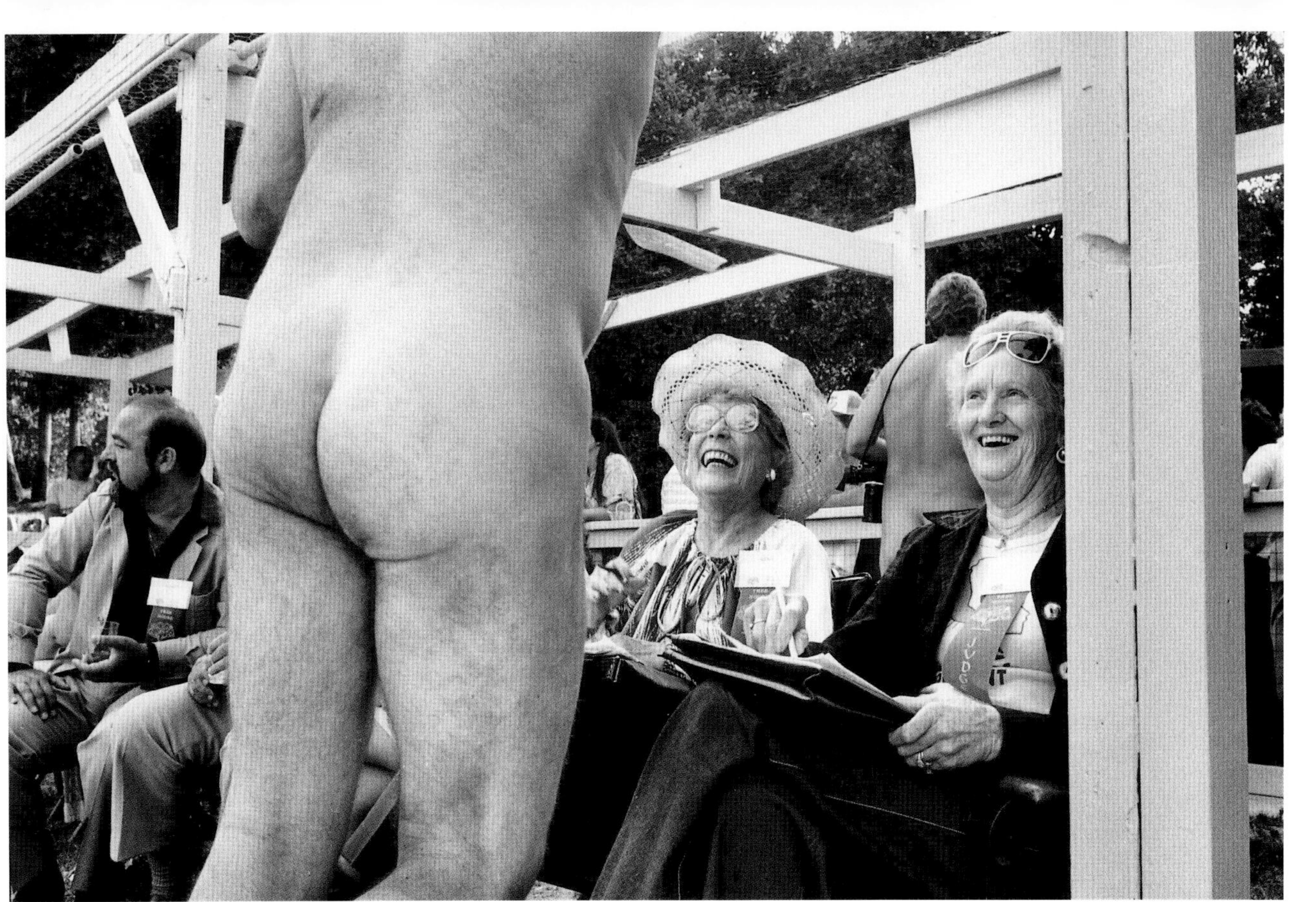

Bakersfield, California, 1983

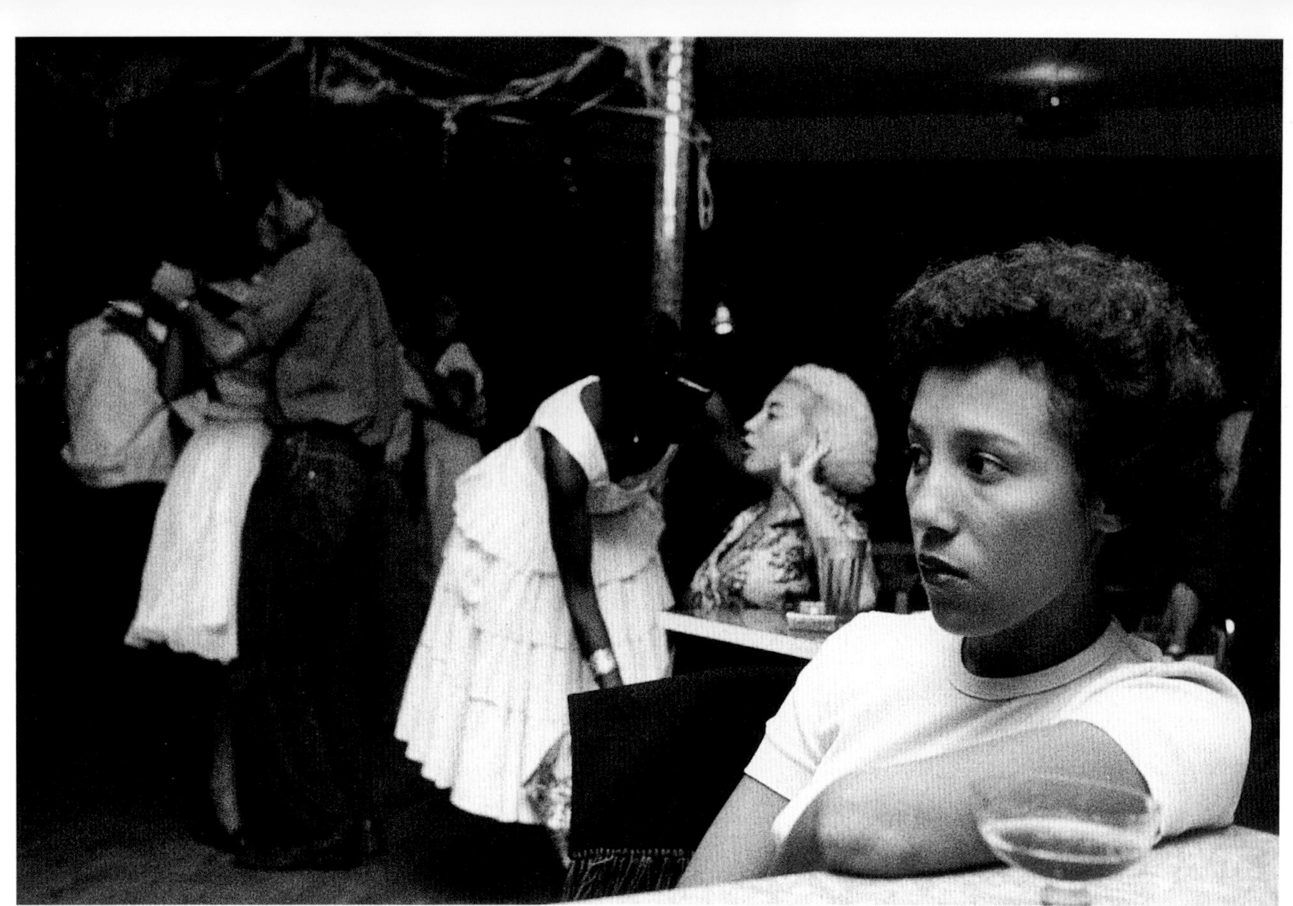

Brasília, Brazil, 1961

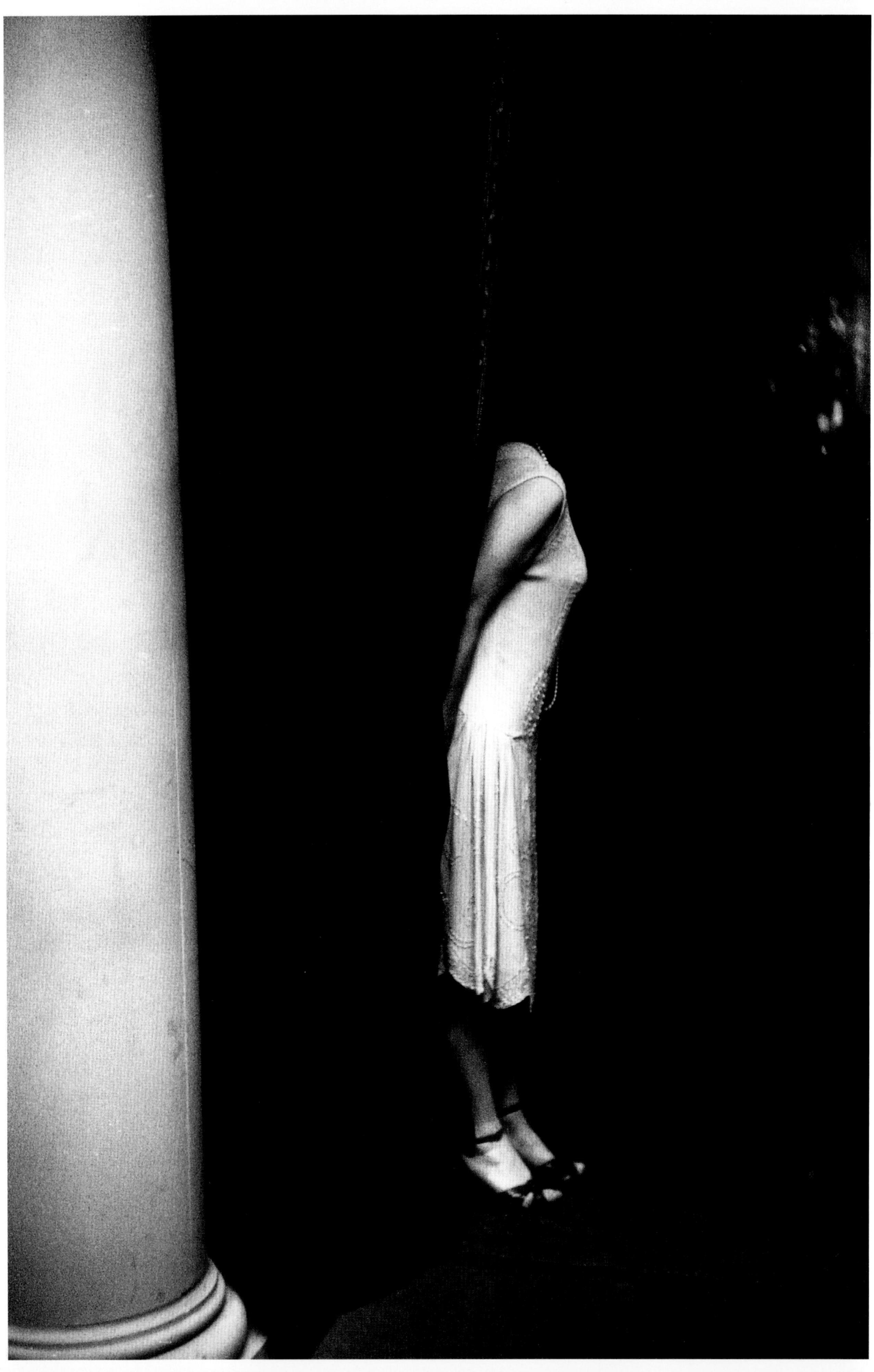

San Francisco, 1955

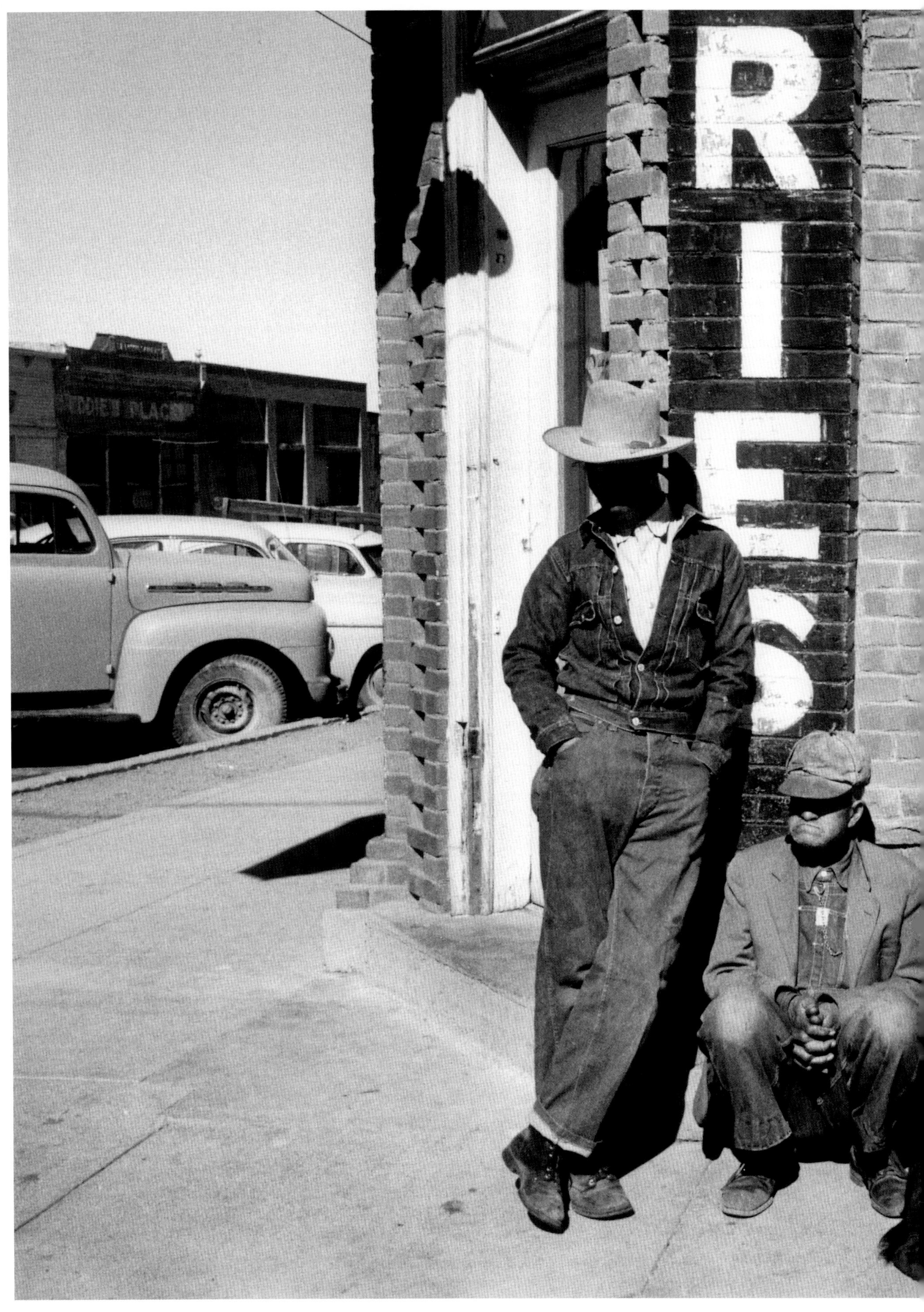

Idaho, 1954

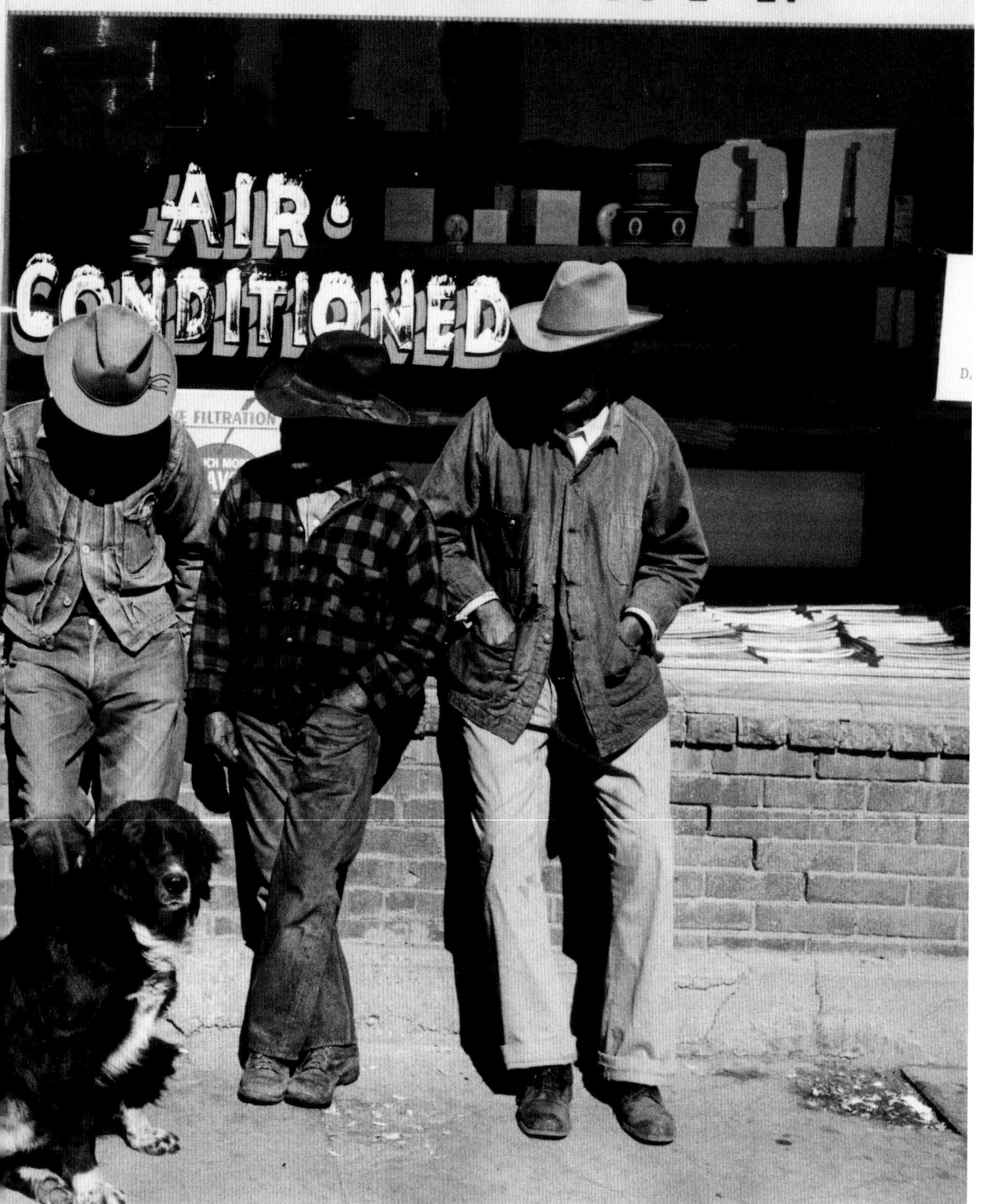

overleaf *Hollywood, 1992* / *Las Vegas, 1957*

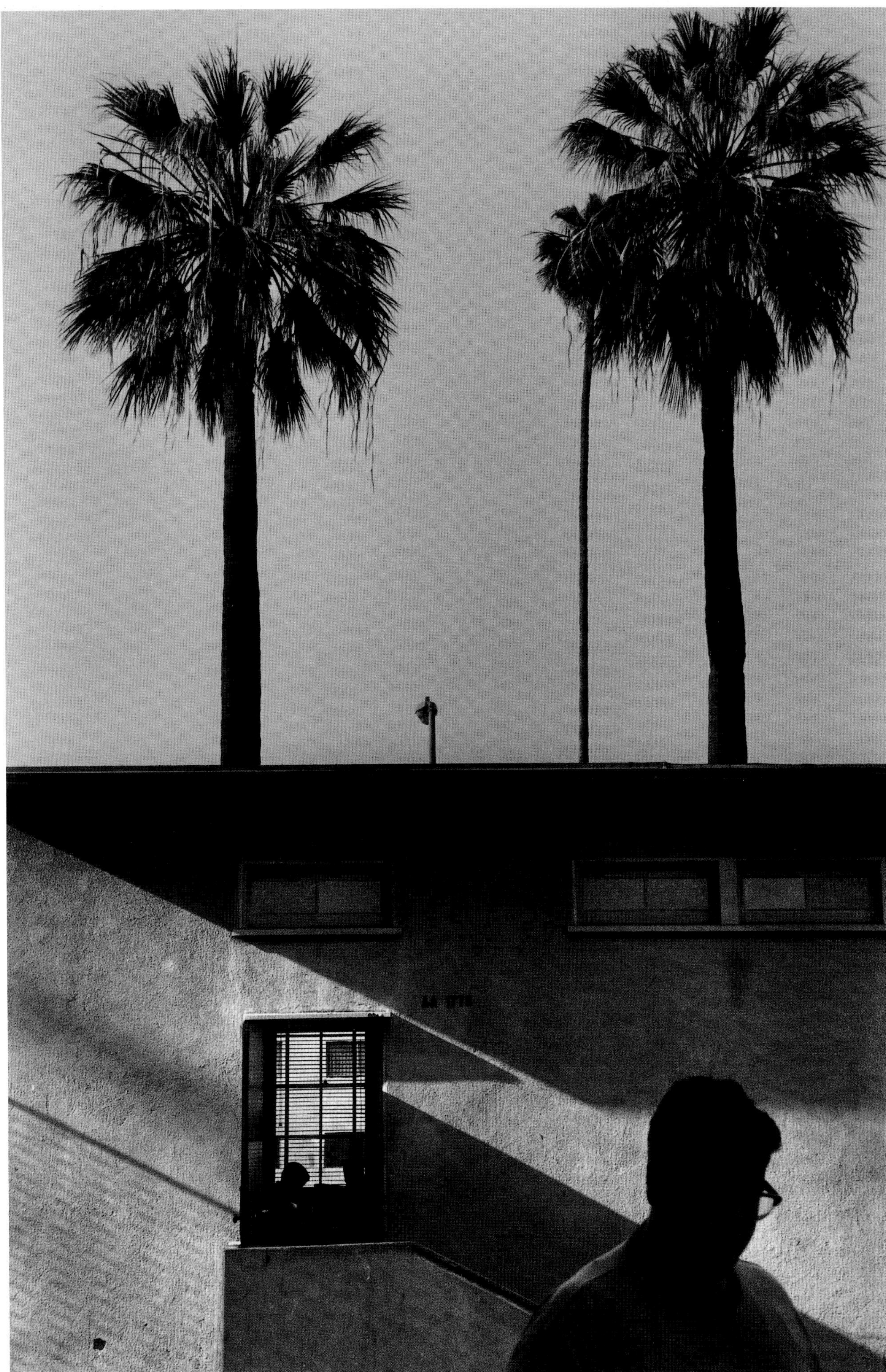

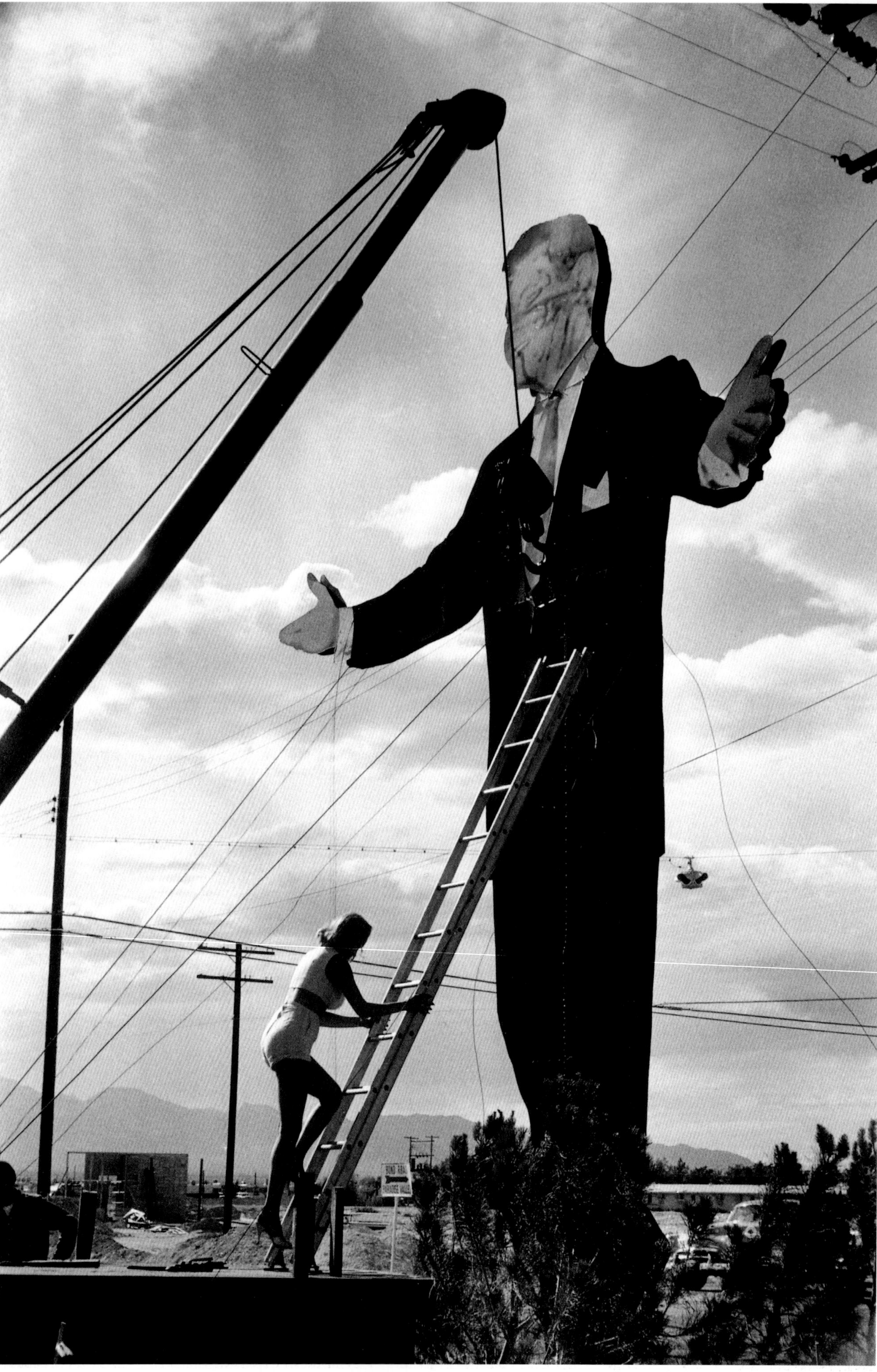

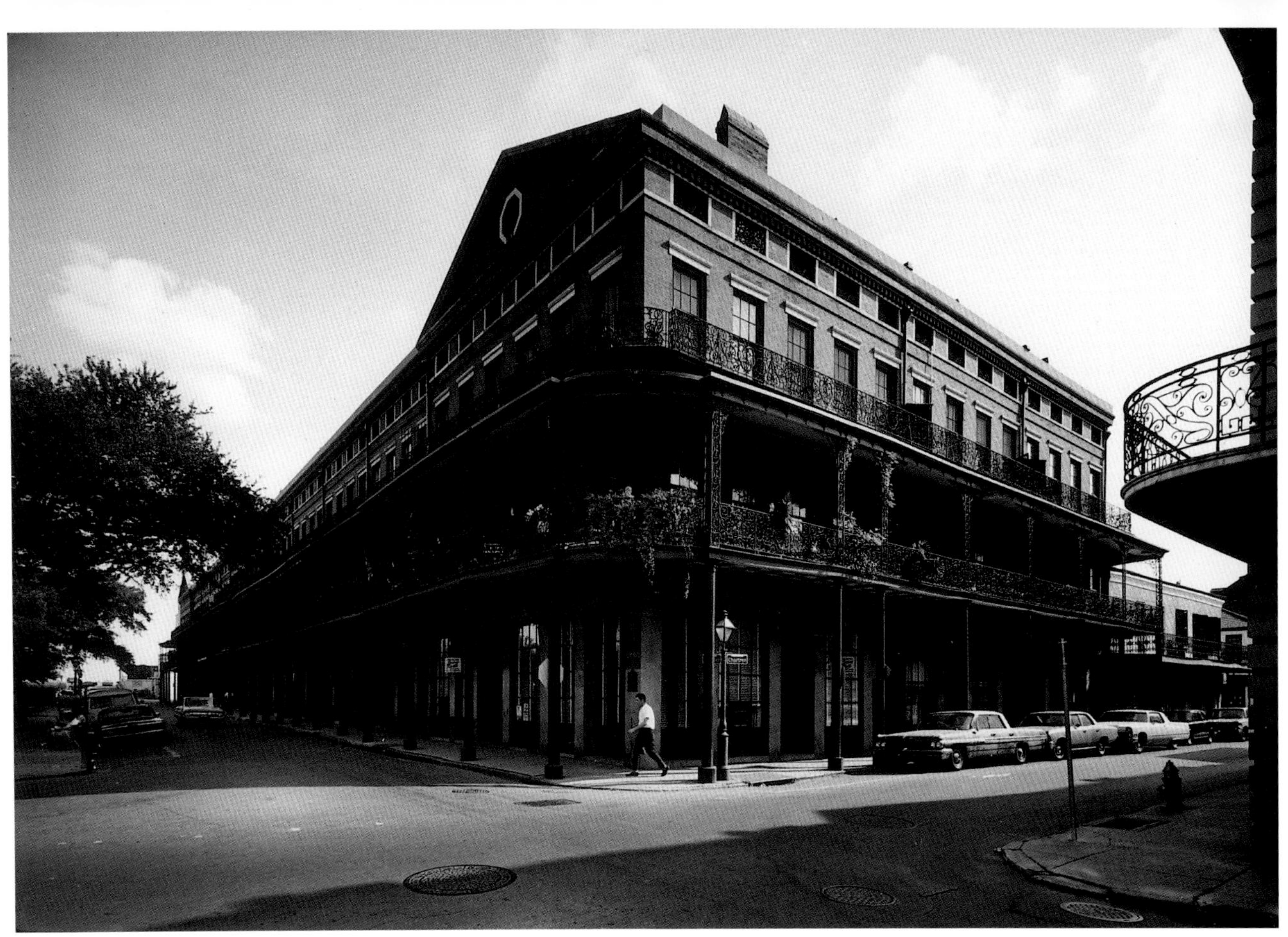

New Orleans, 1969

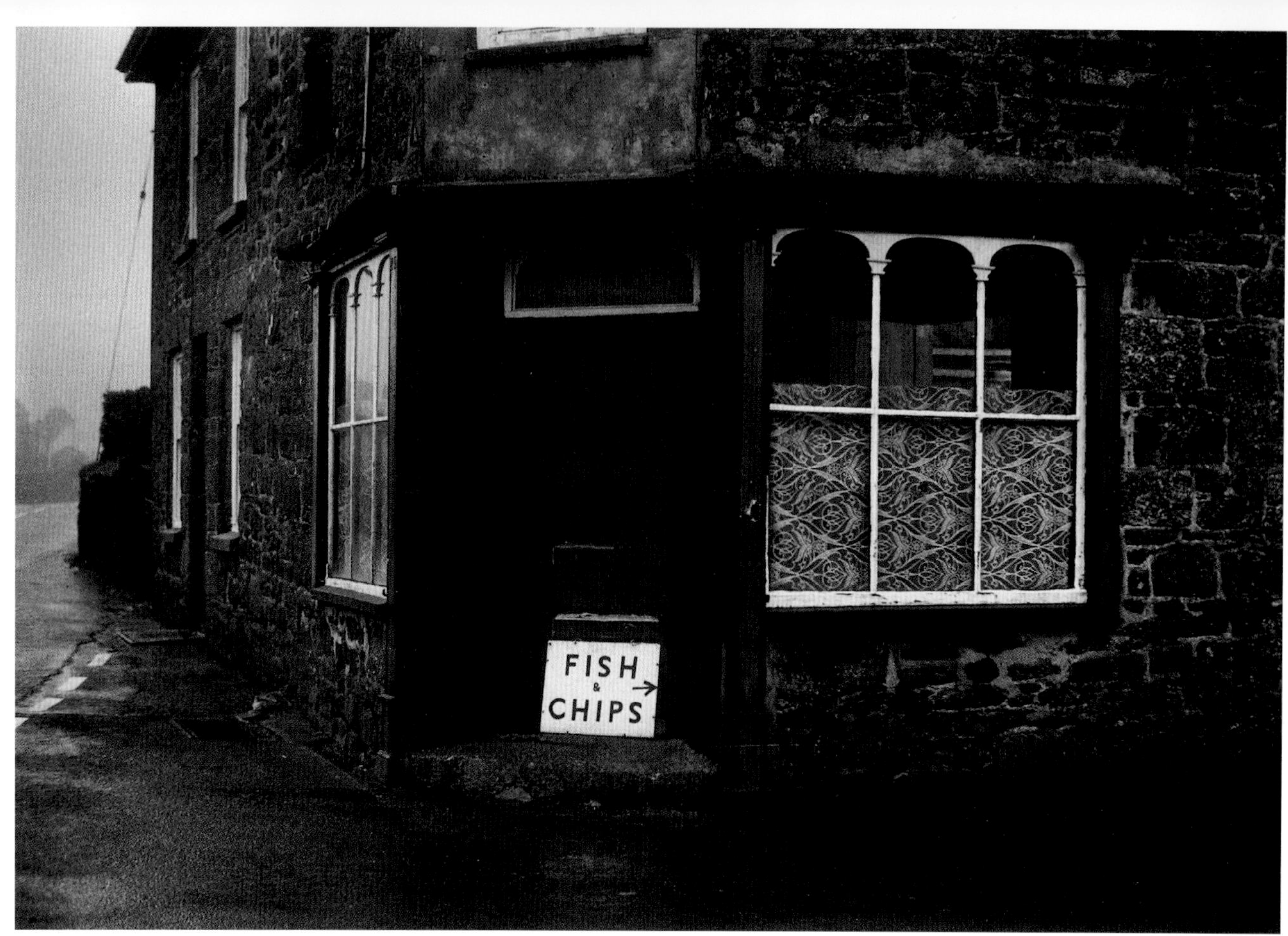

Land's End, Cornwall, England, 1971

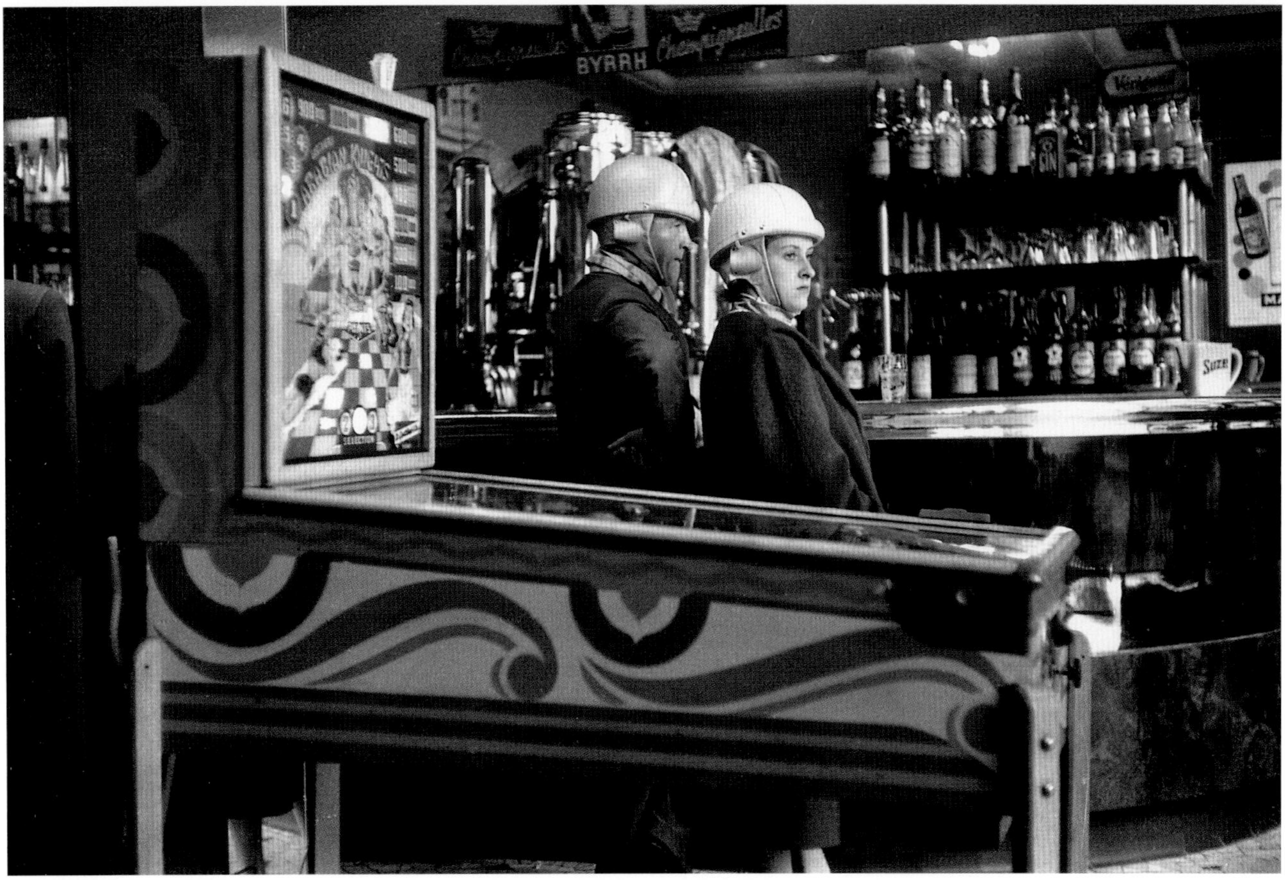

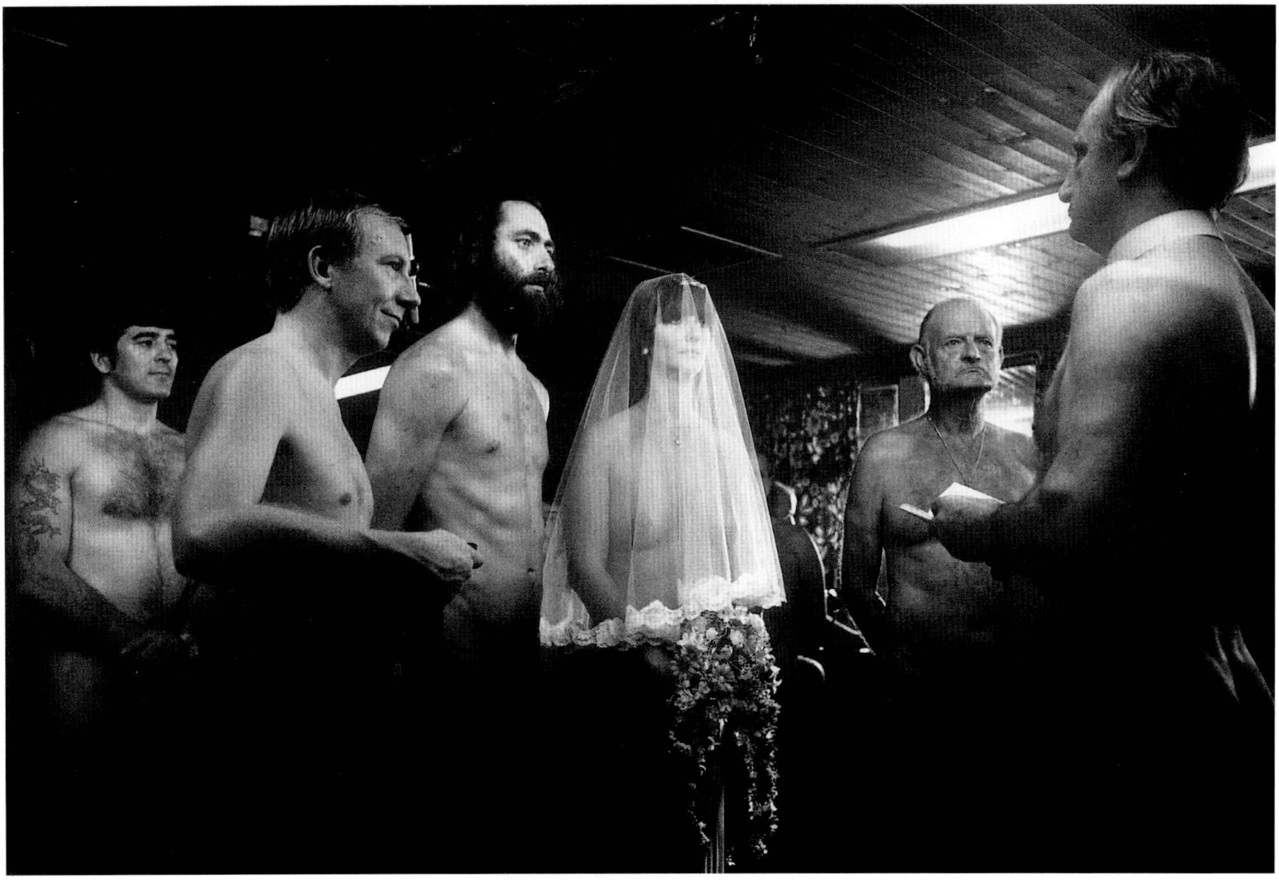

Paris, 1952 / *Kent, England, 1984*

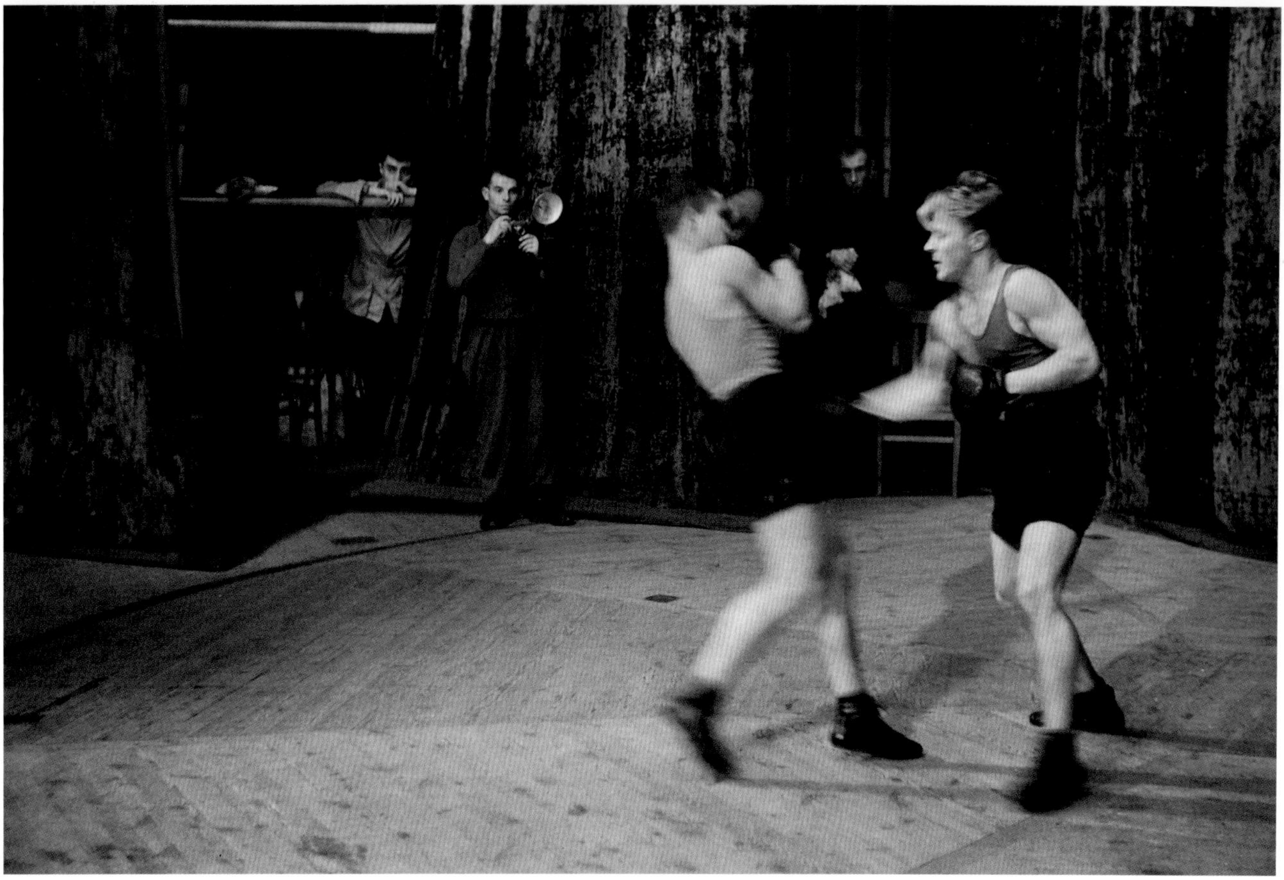

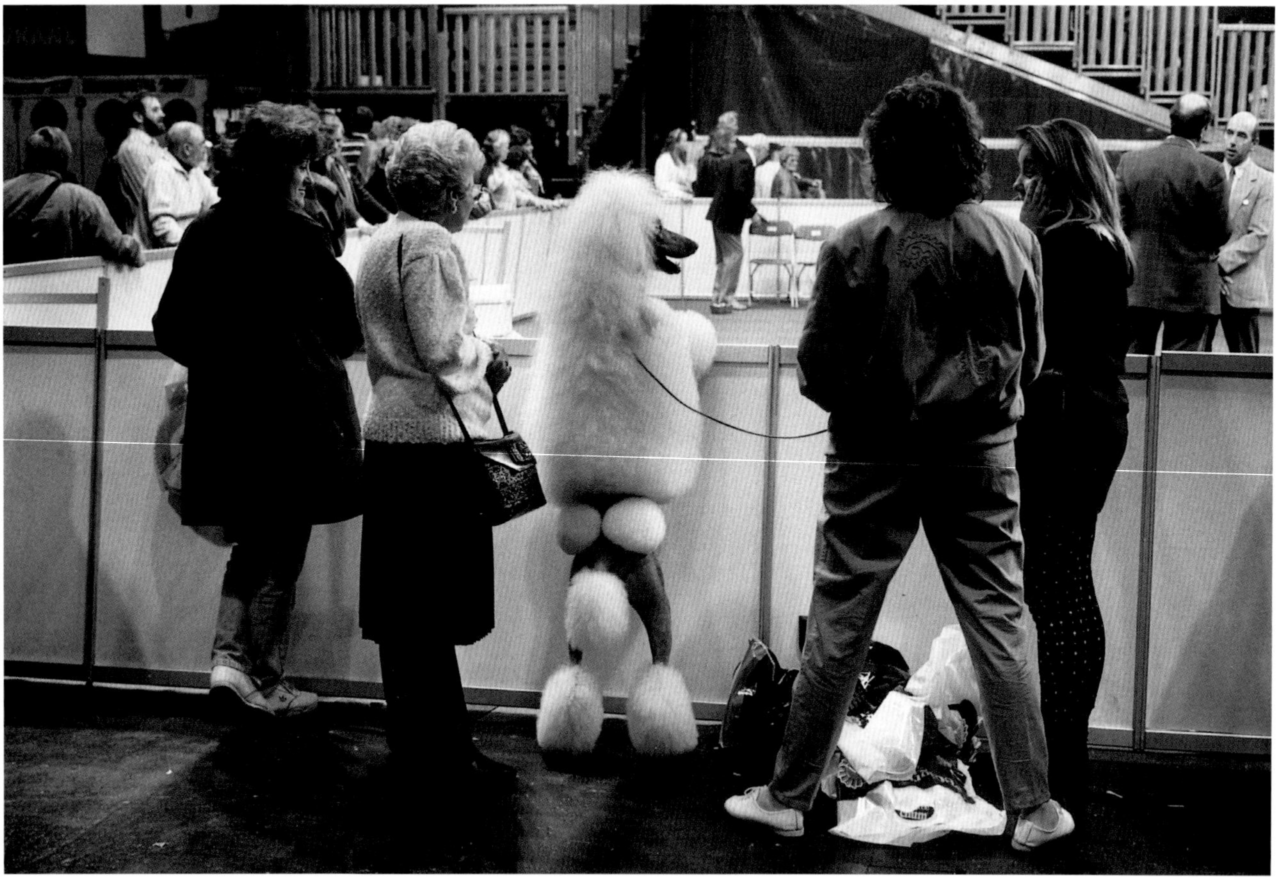

Kiev, 1957 / *Birmingham, England, 1991*
overleaf *Hollywood, 1956* / *Lahore, Pakistan, 1958*

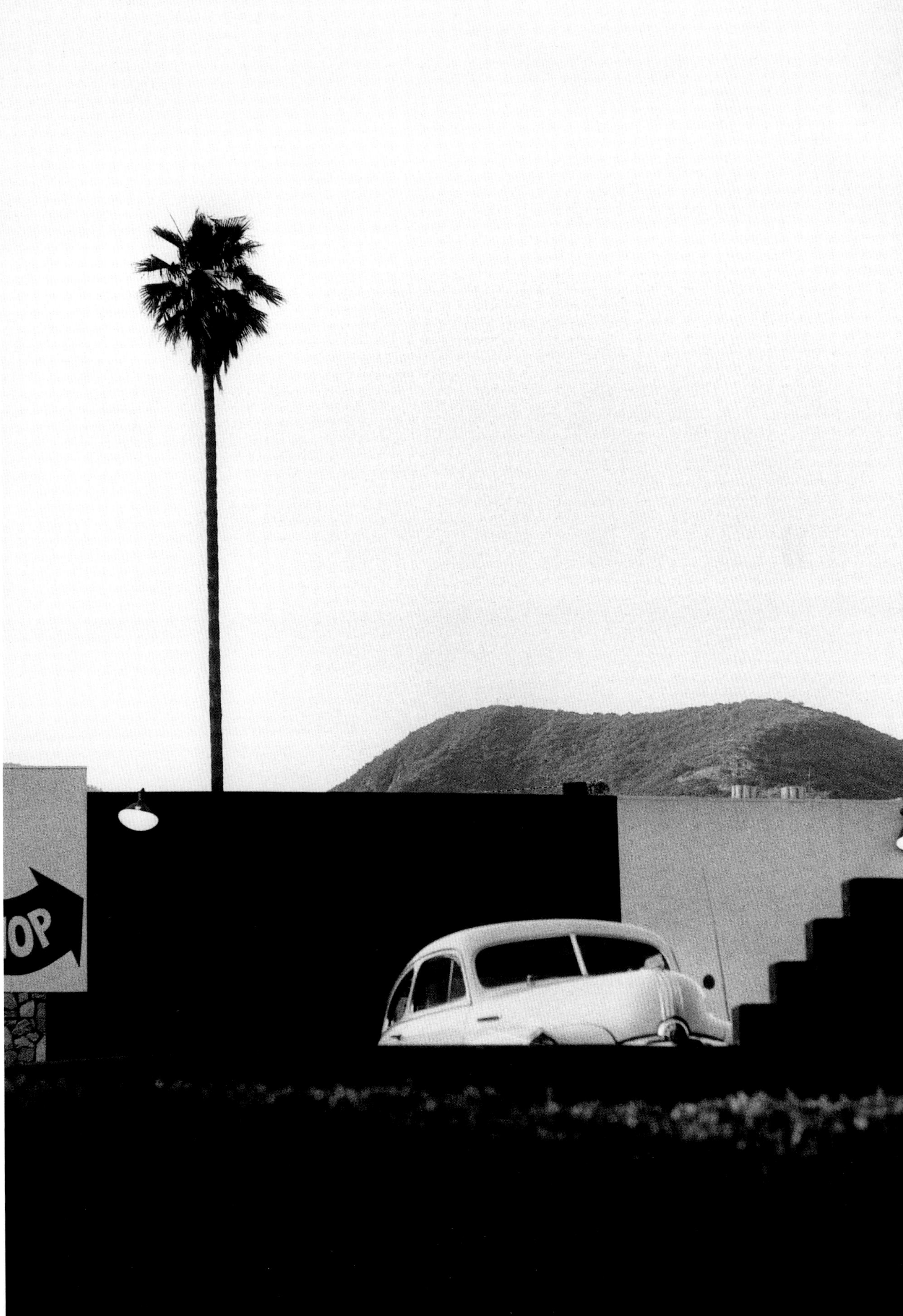
OP

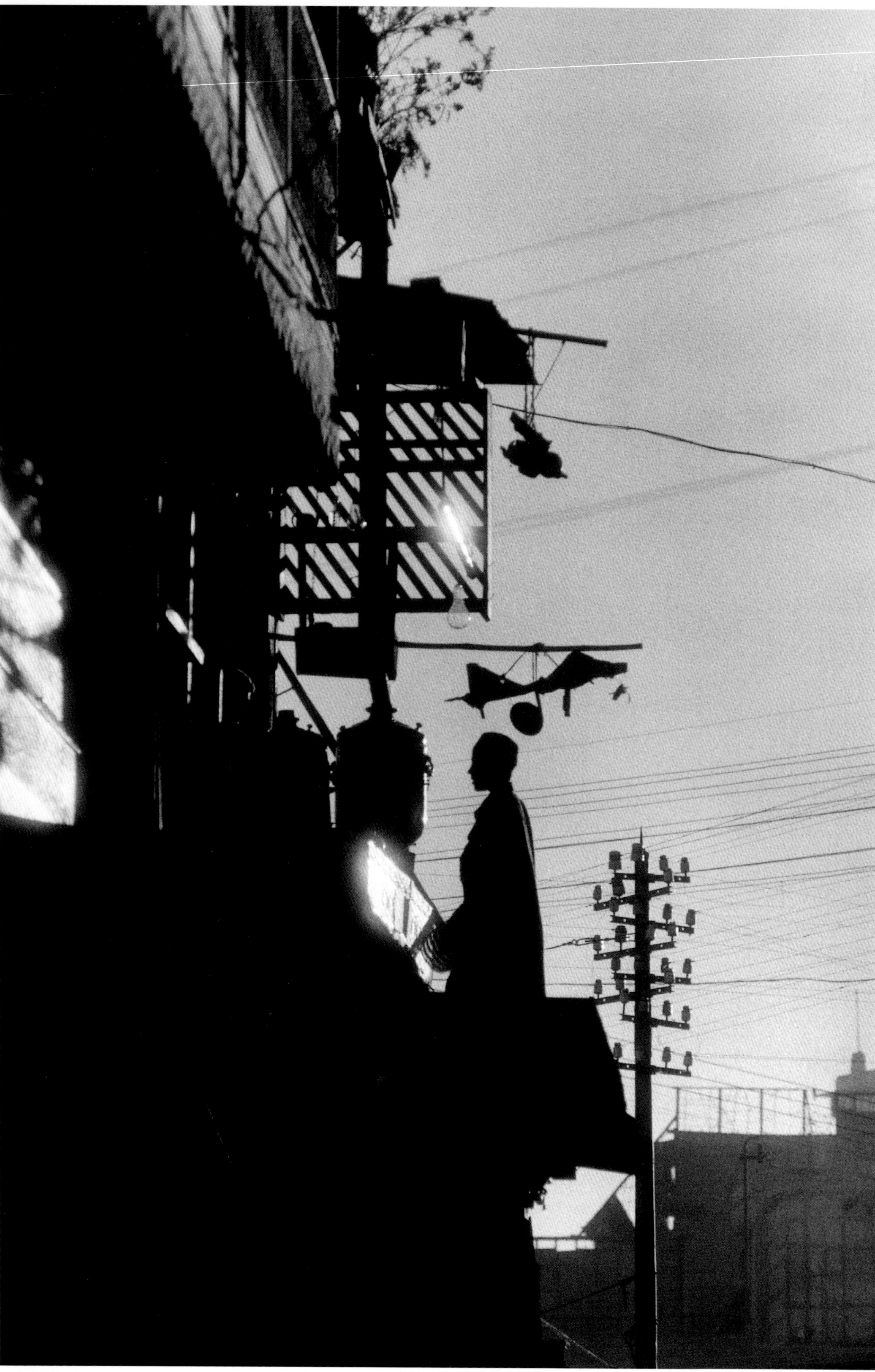

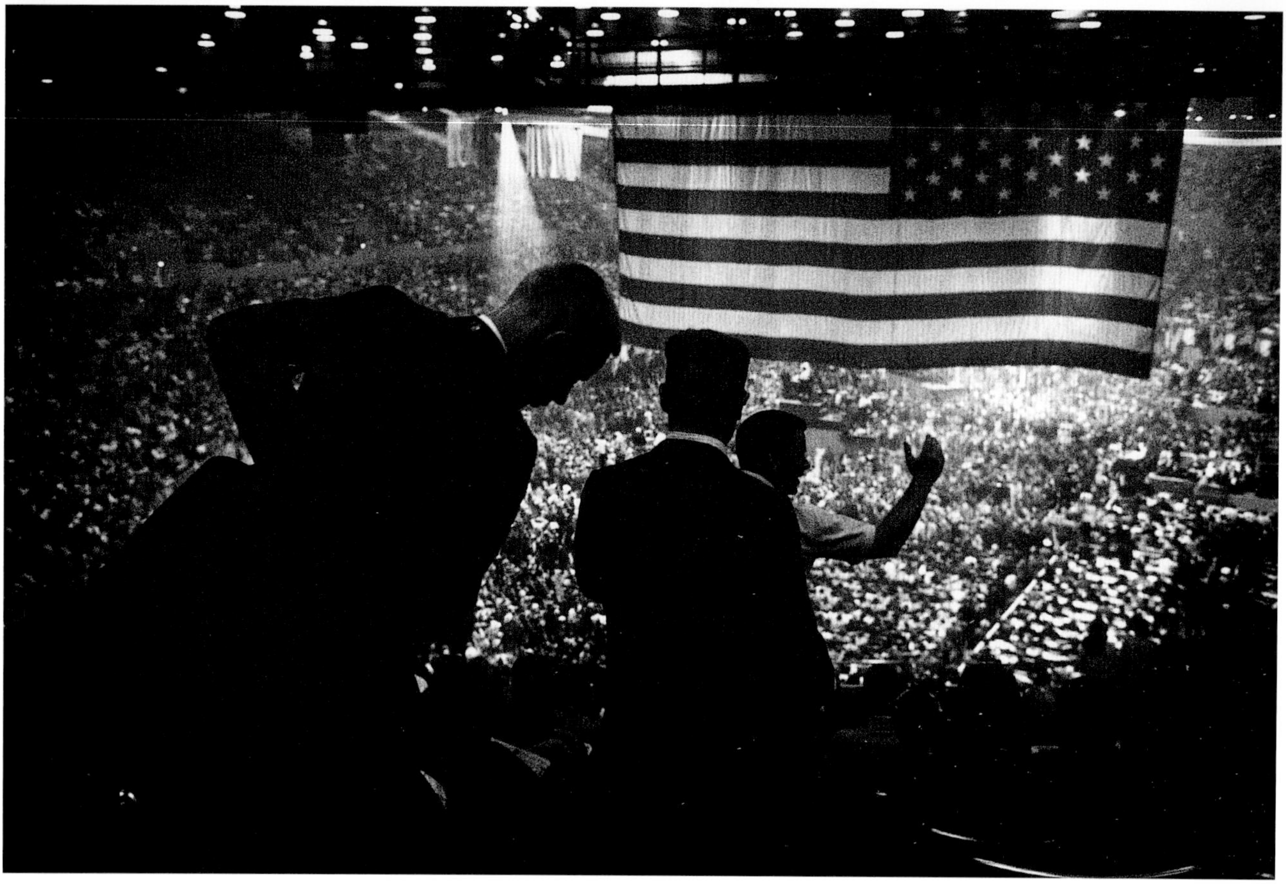

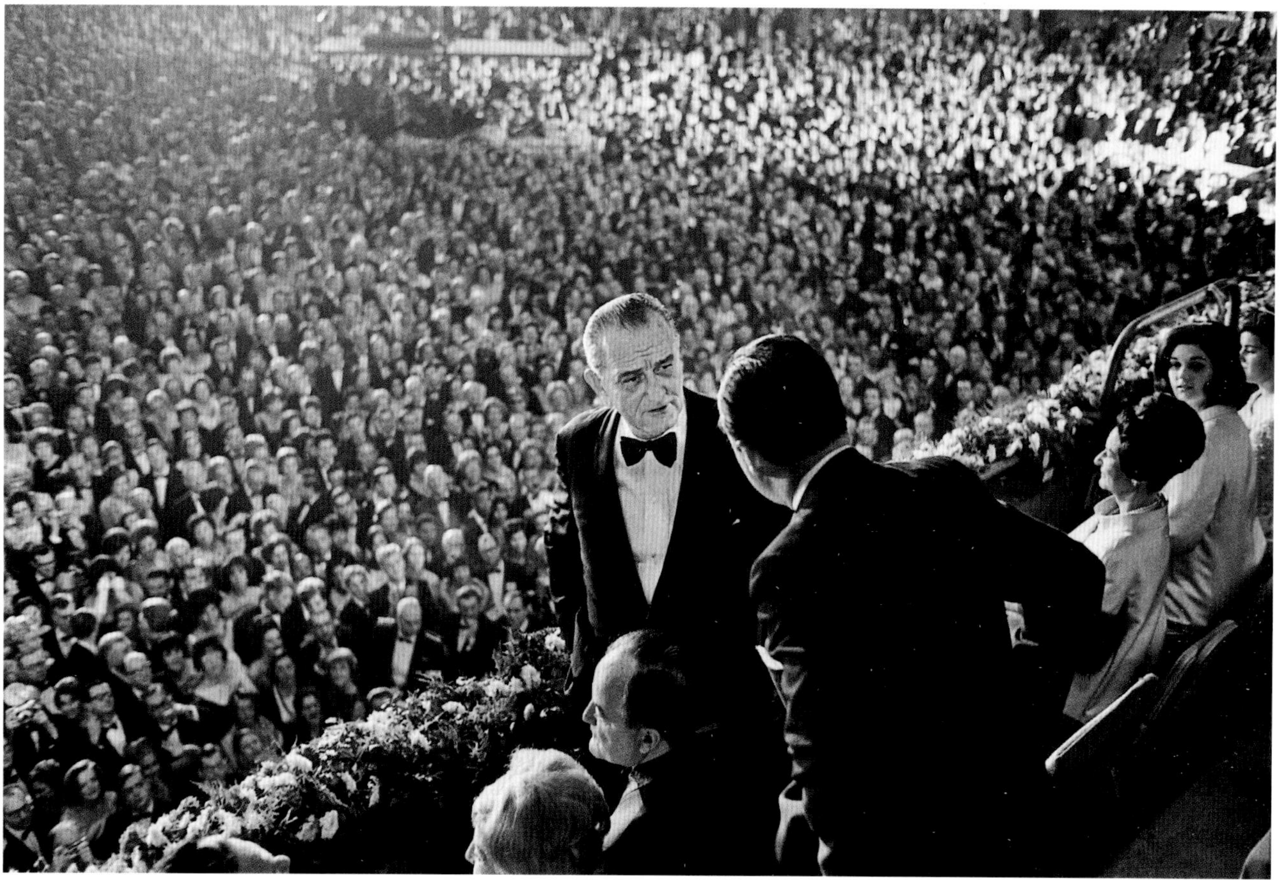

Los Angeles, 1960 / *Lyndon B. Johnson, Washington, DC, 1965*
overleaf *Eric Ambler, London, 1952* / *William Carlos Williams, Paterson, New Jersey, 1955*

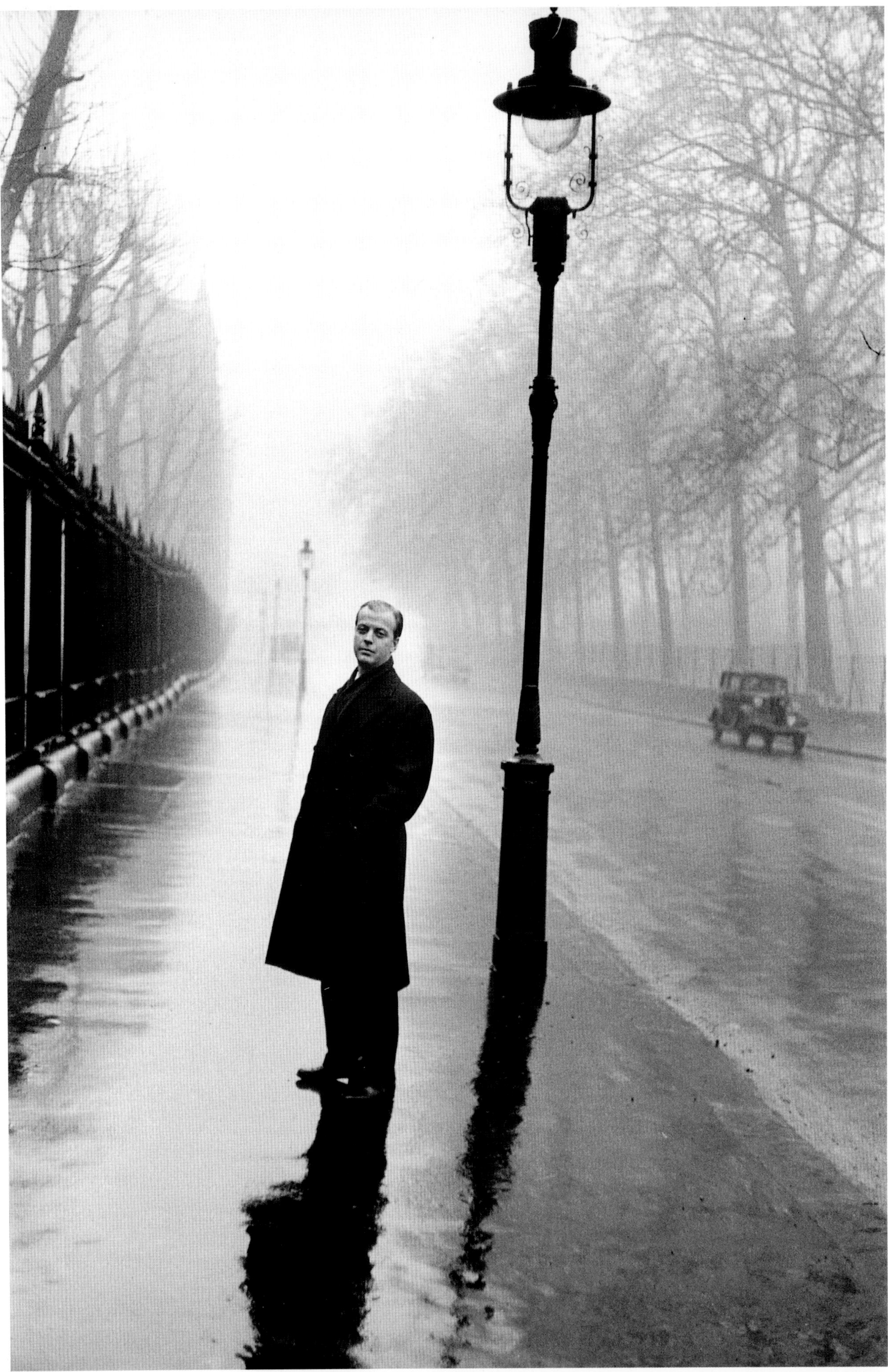

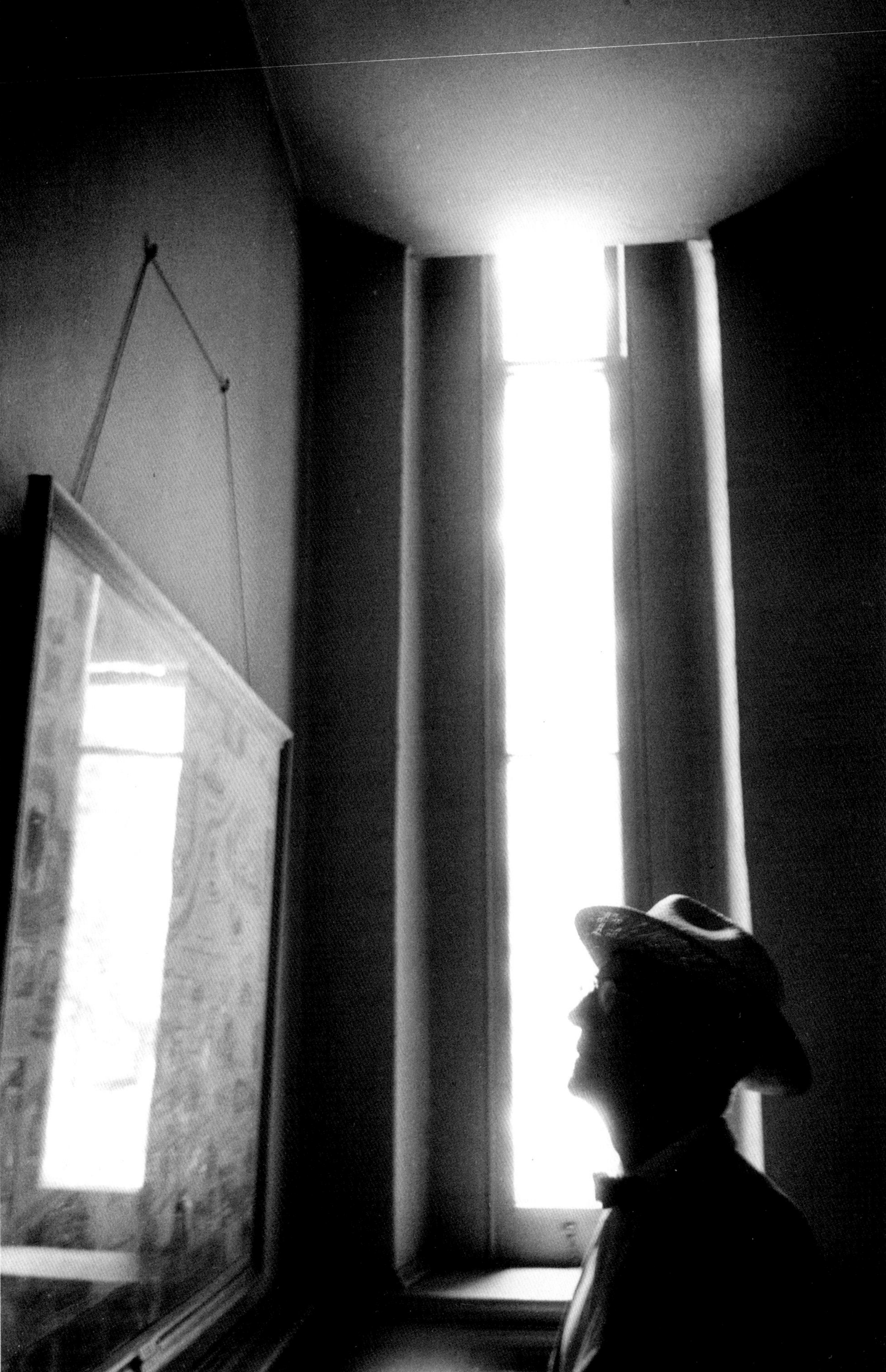

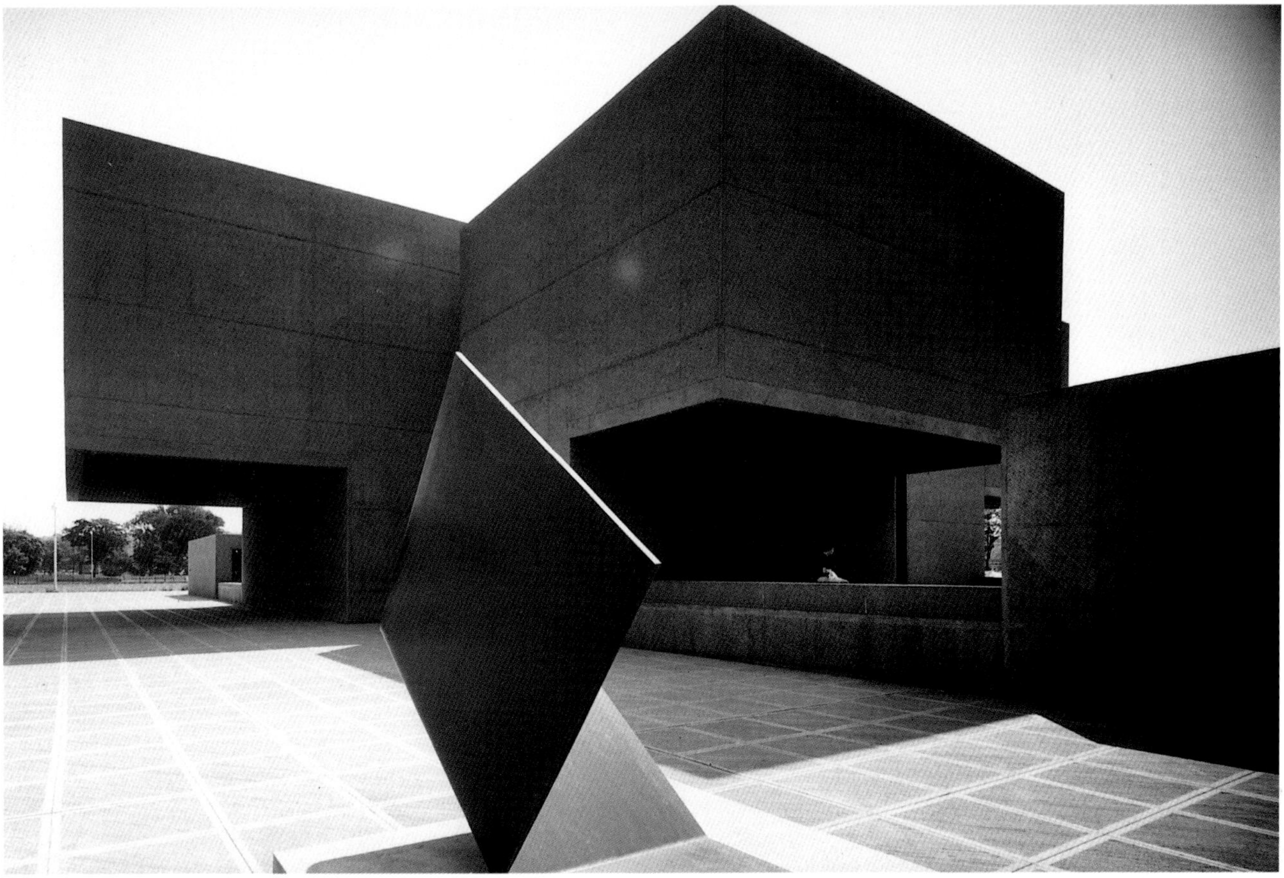

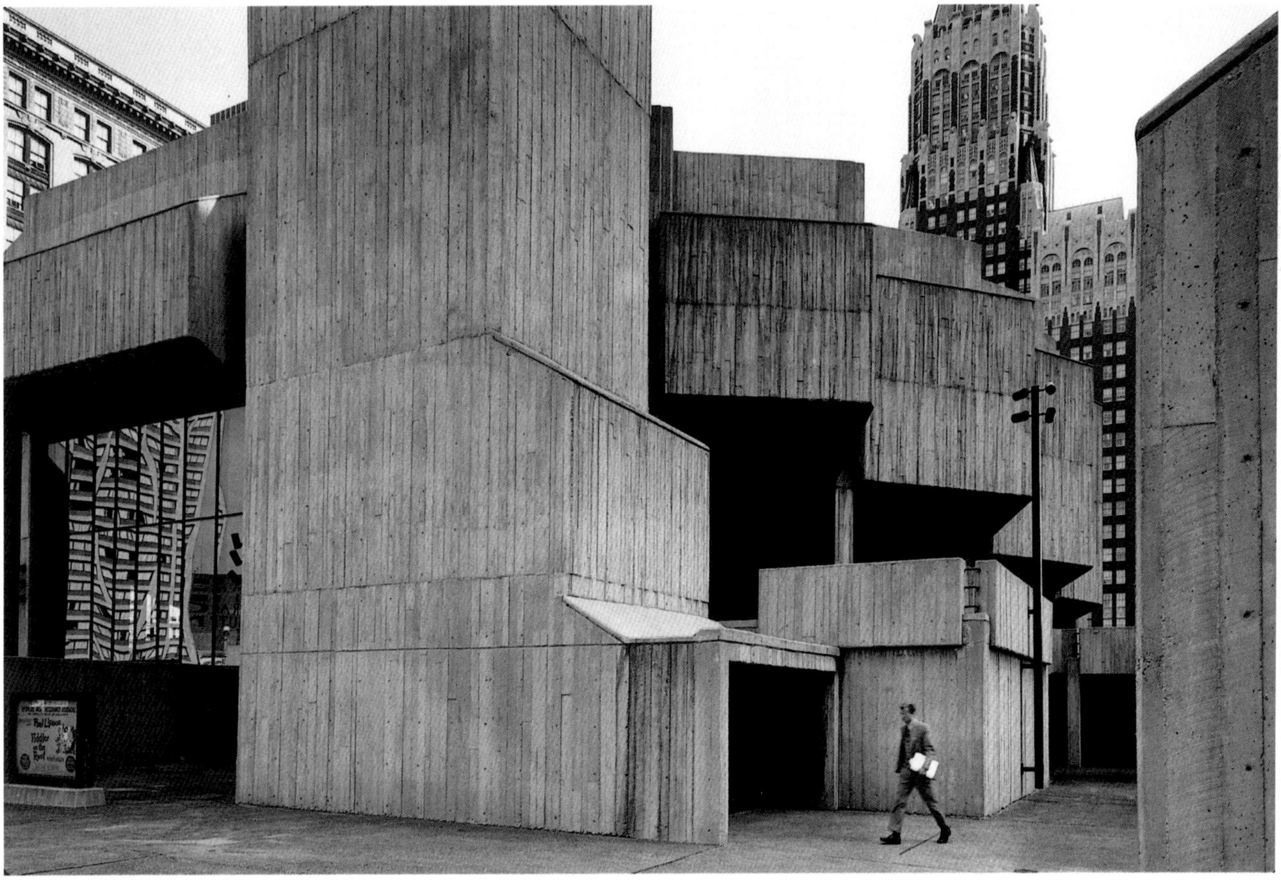

Syracuse University, Syracuse, New York, 1969 **/** *Baltimore, Maryland, 1969*

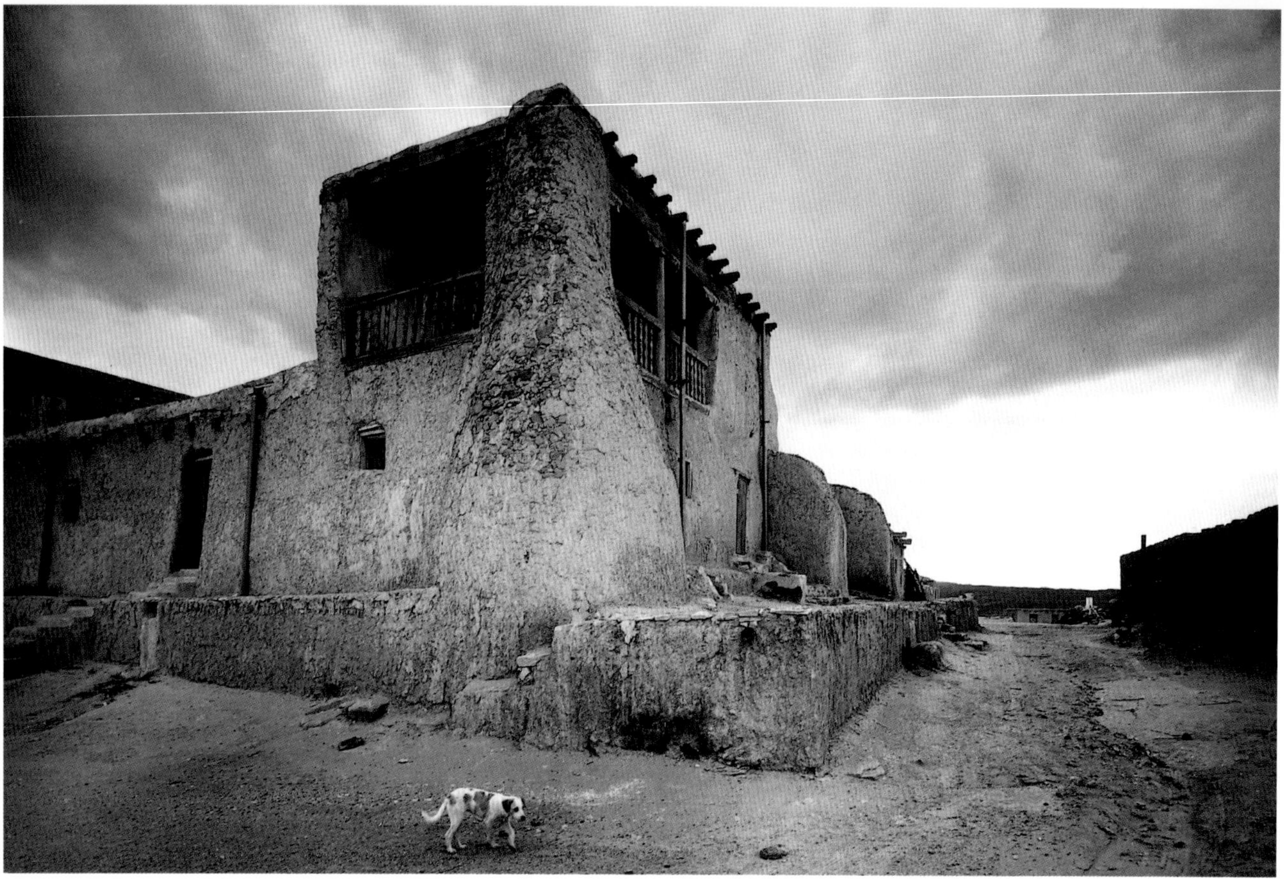

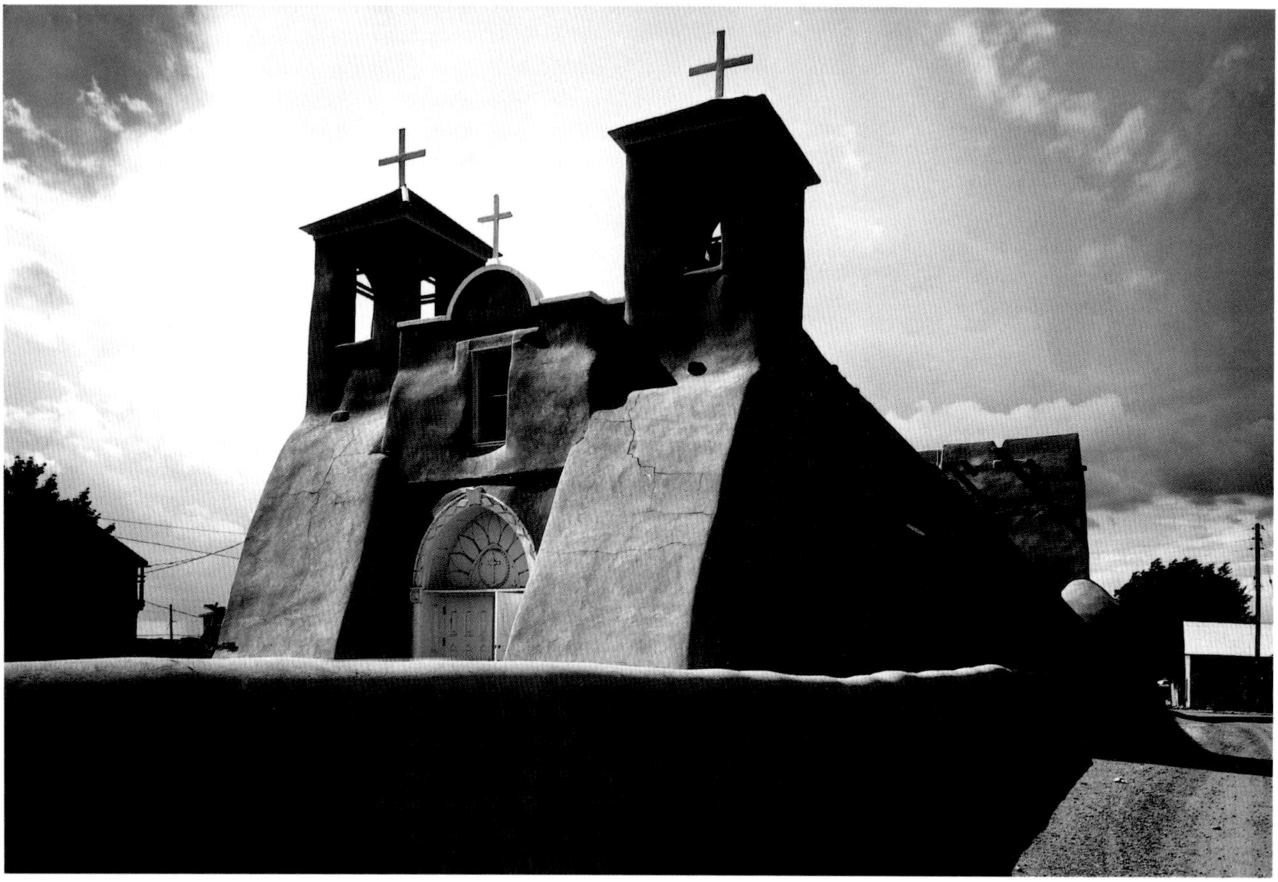

Acoma, New Mexico, 1969 / *Taos, New Mexico, 1969*

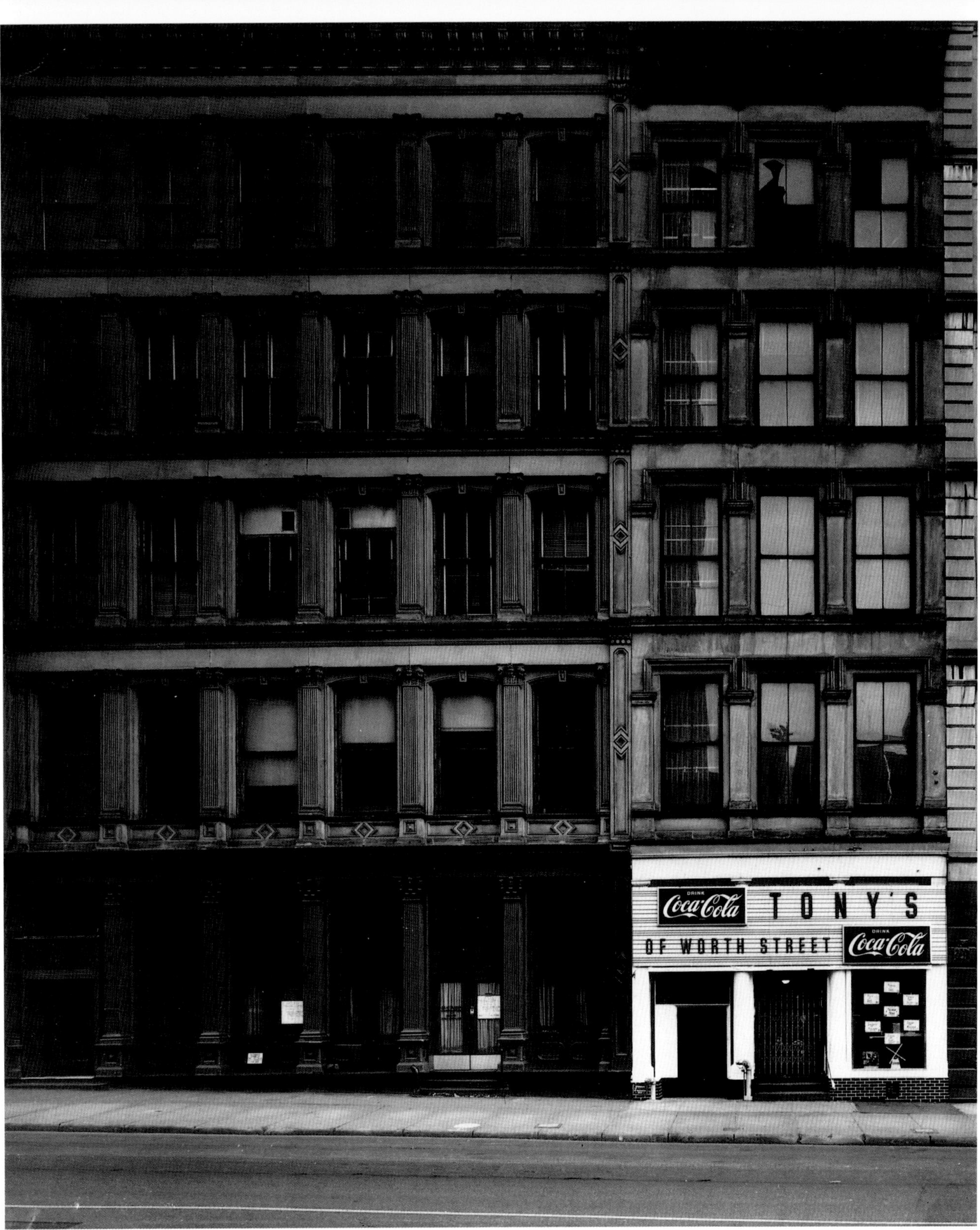

New York, 1969

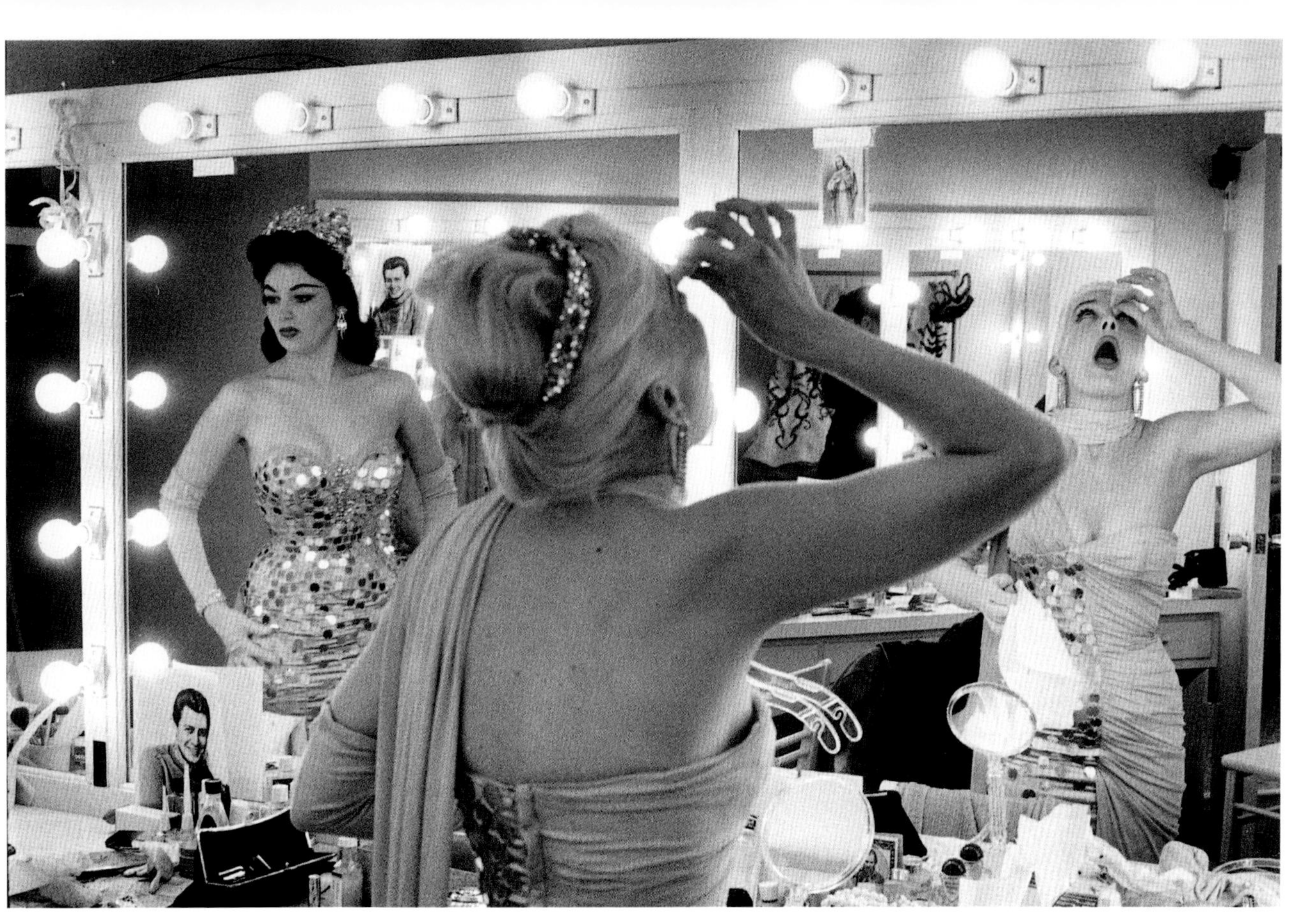

Las Vegas, 1957

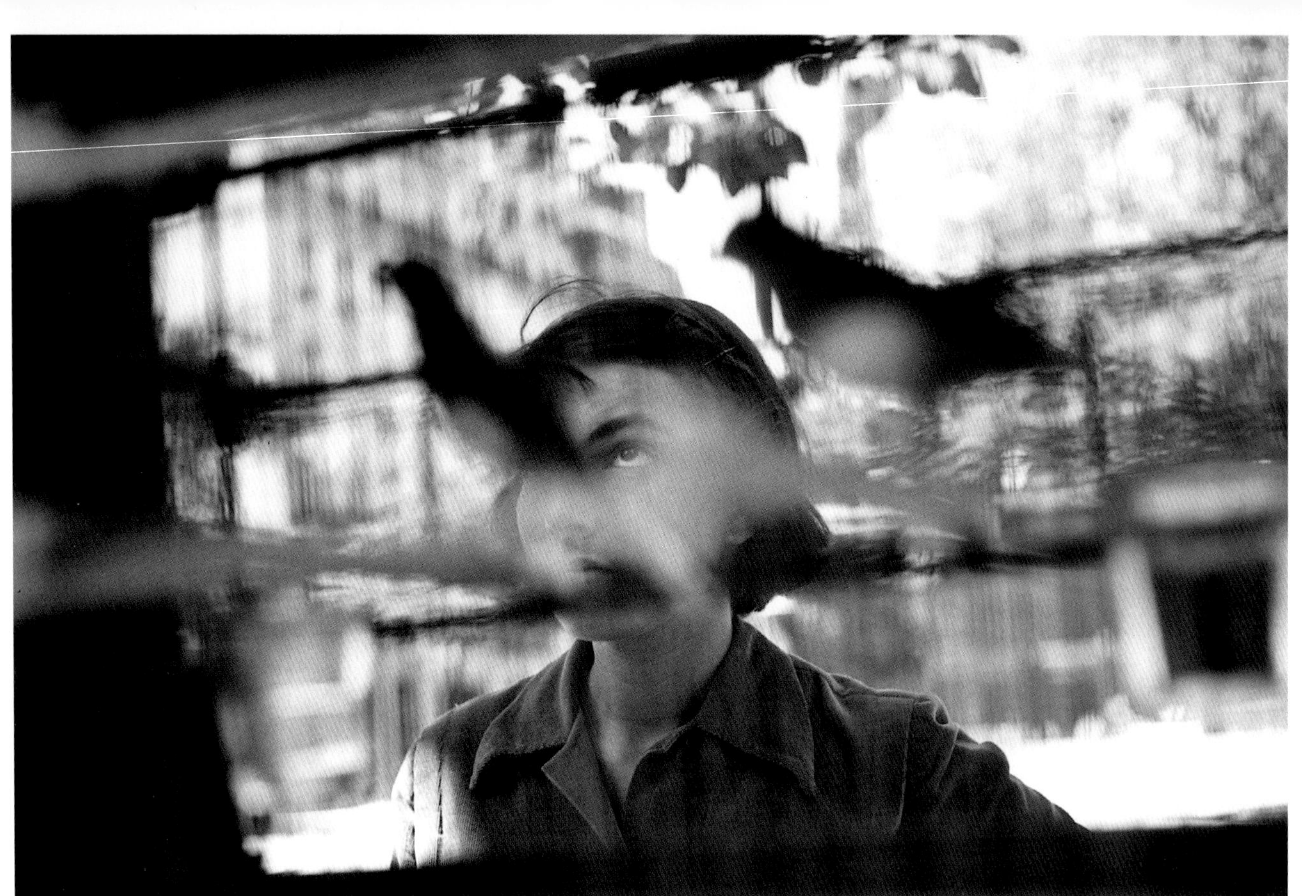

Paris, 1949

Coney Island, New York, 1975

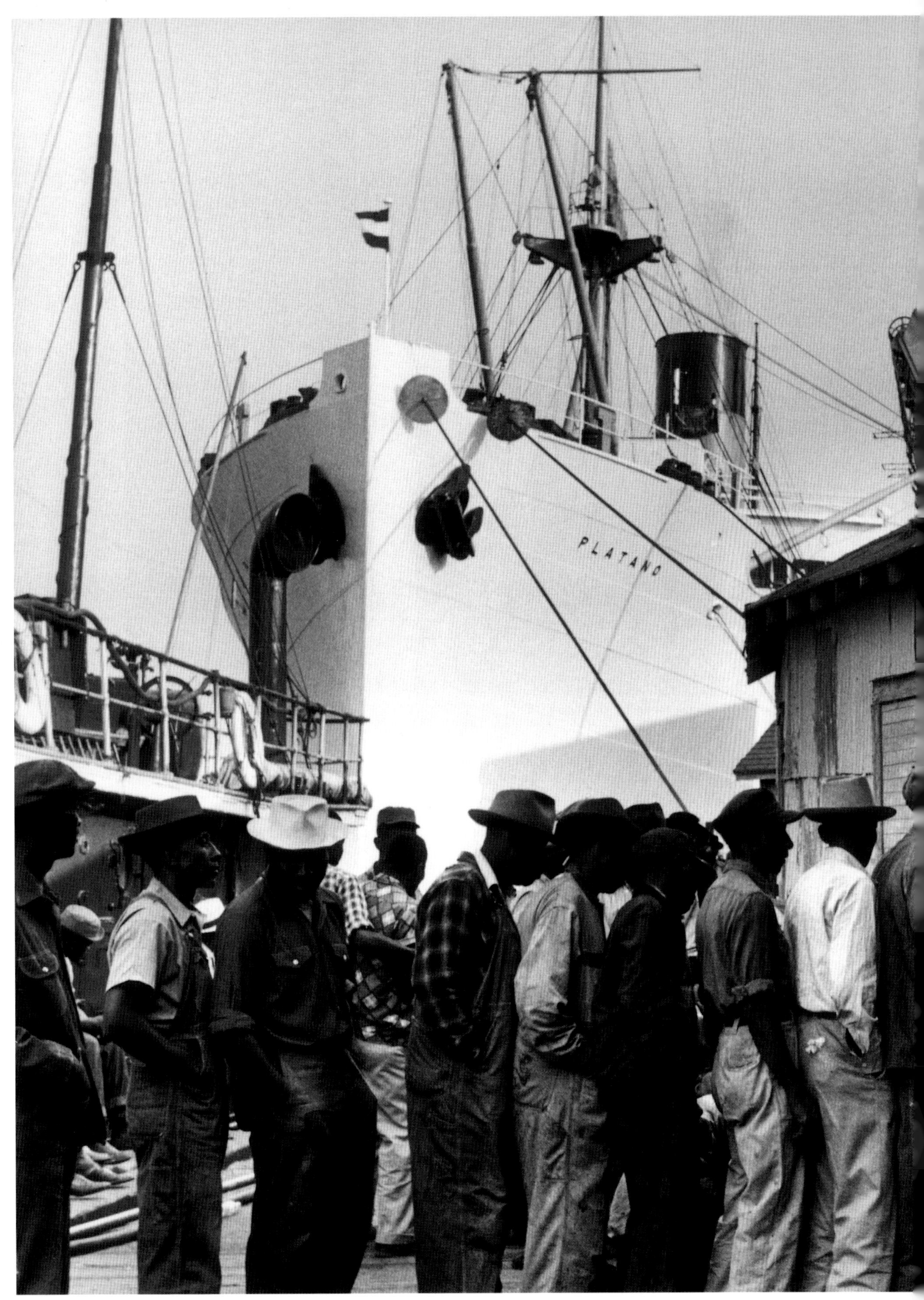

Hoboken, New Jersey, 1954

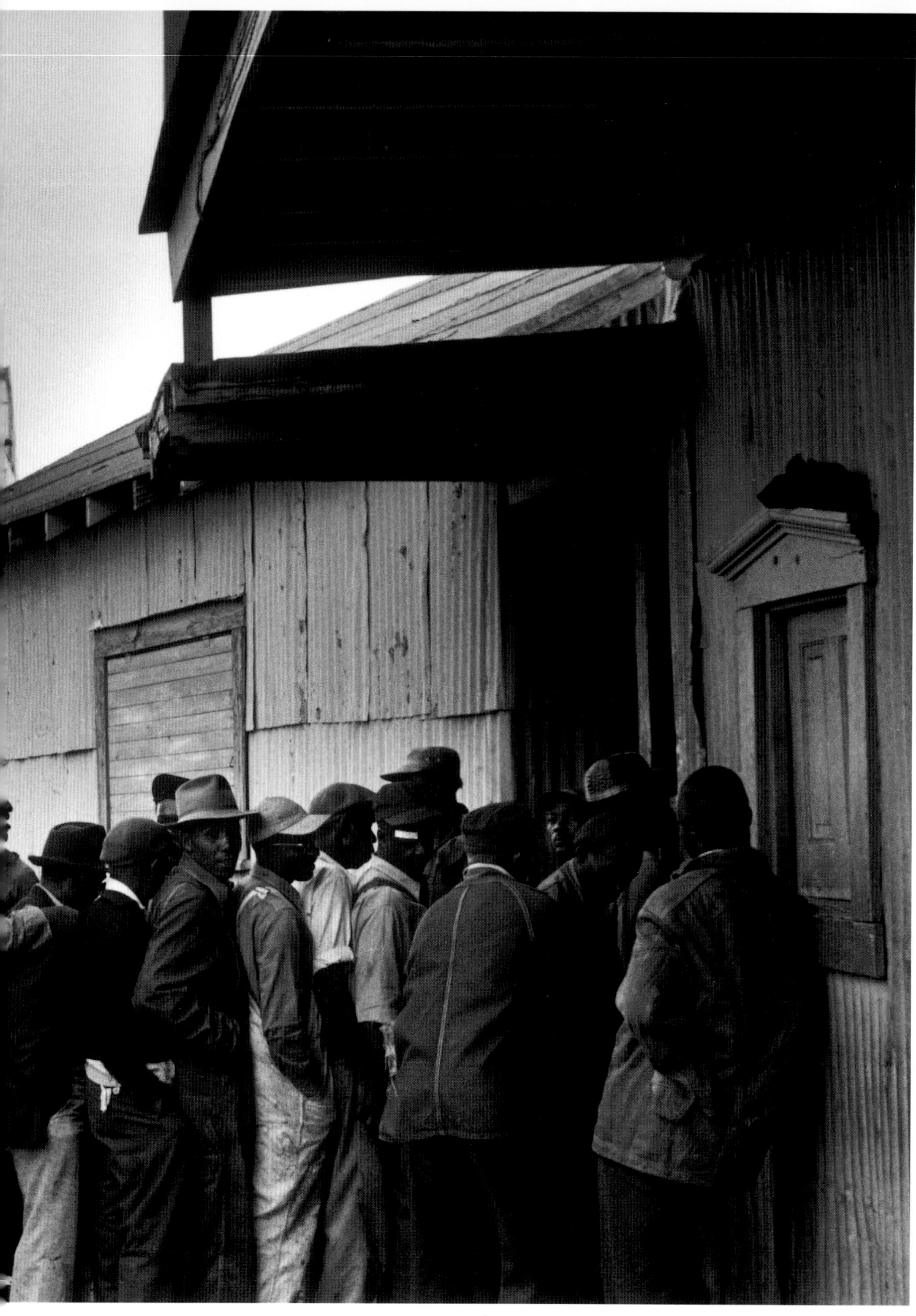

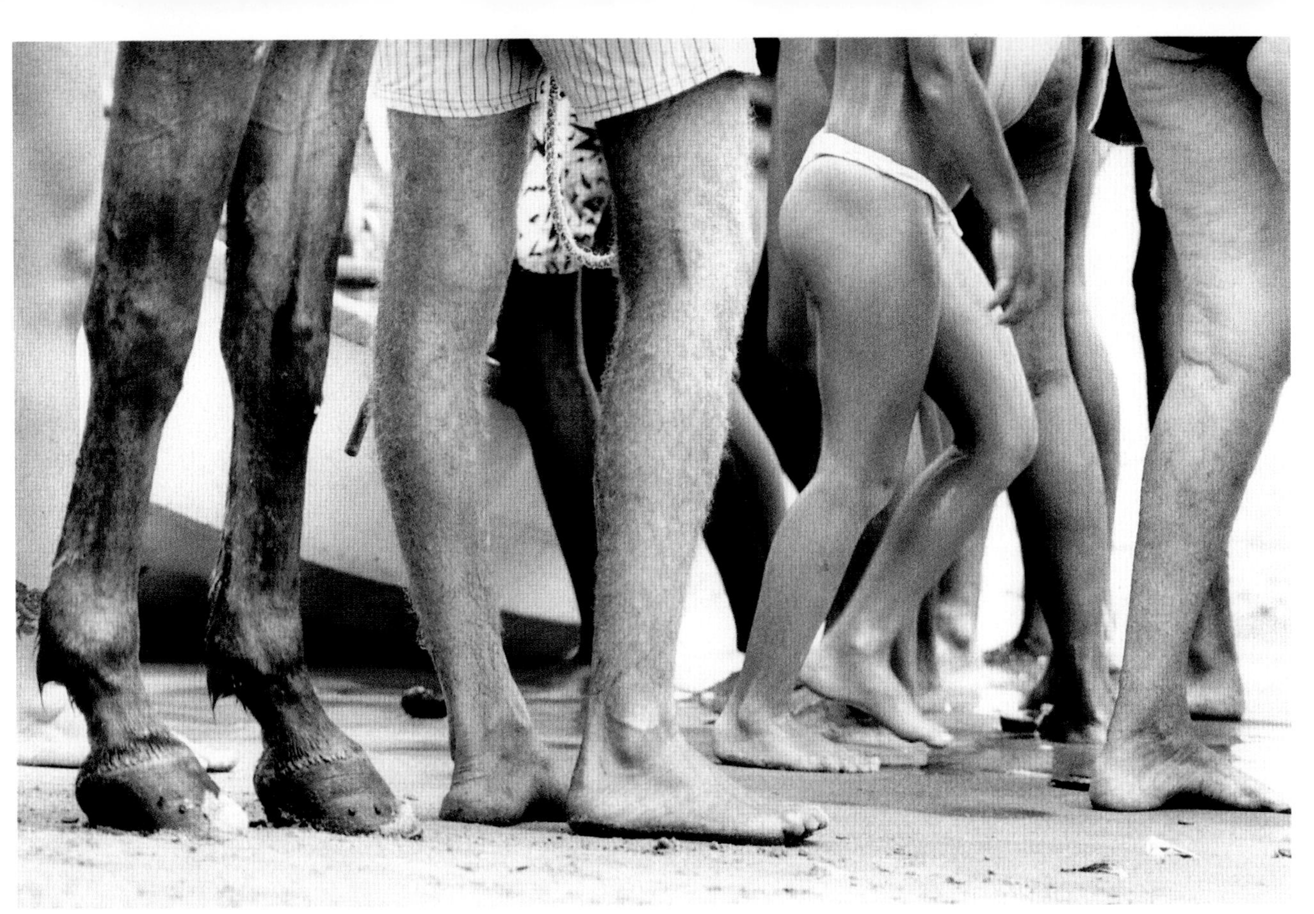

Buzios, Brazil, 1990

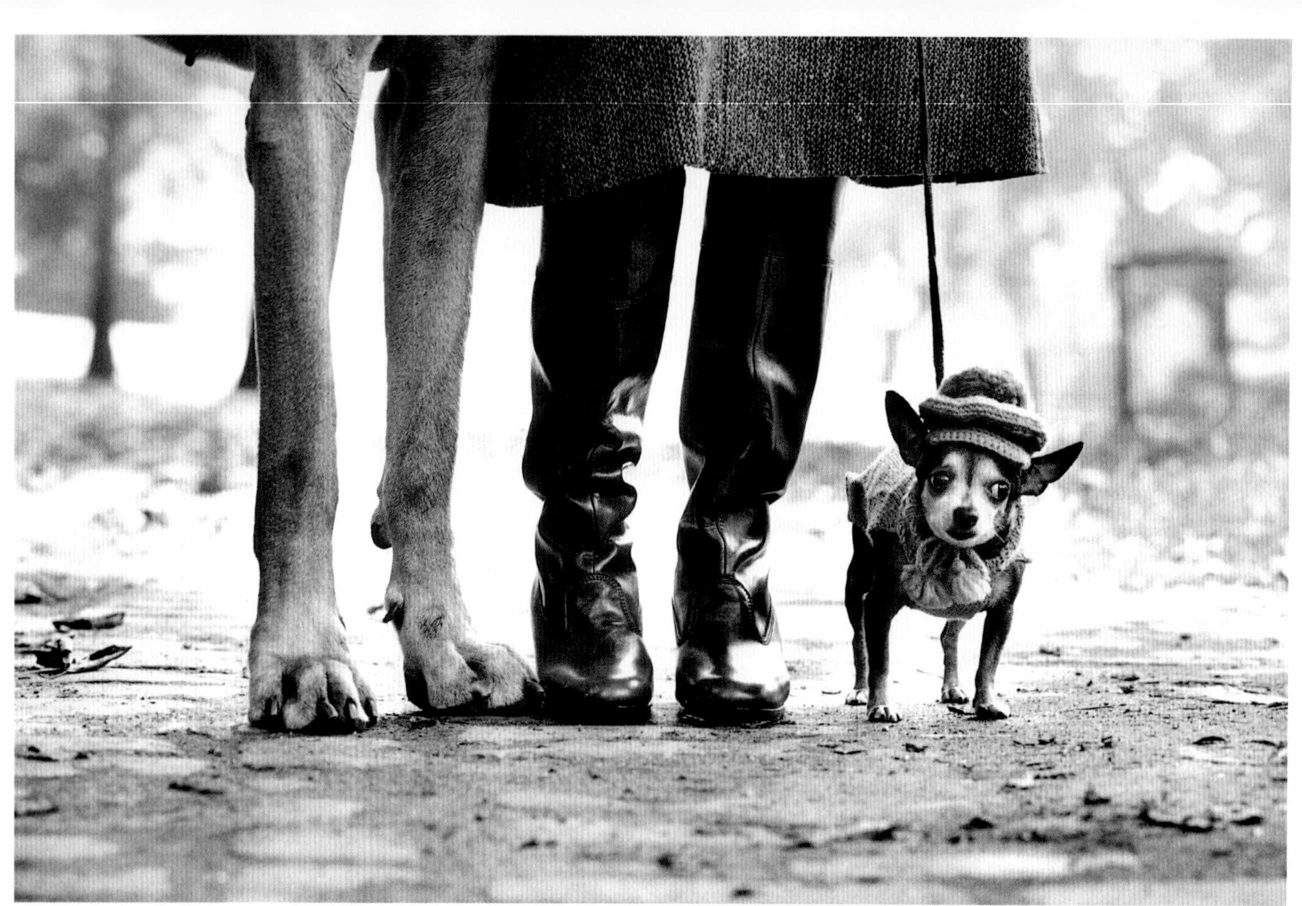

New York, 1974

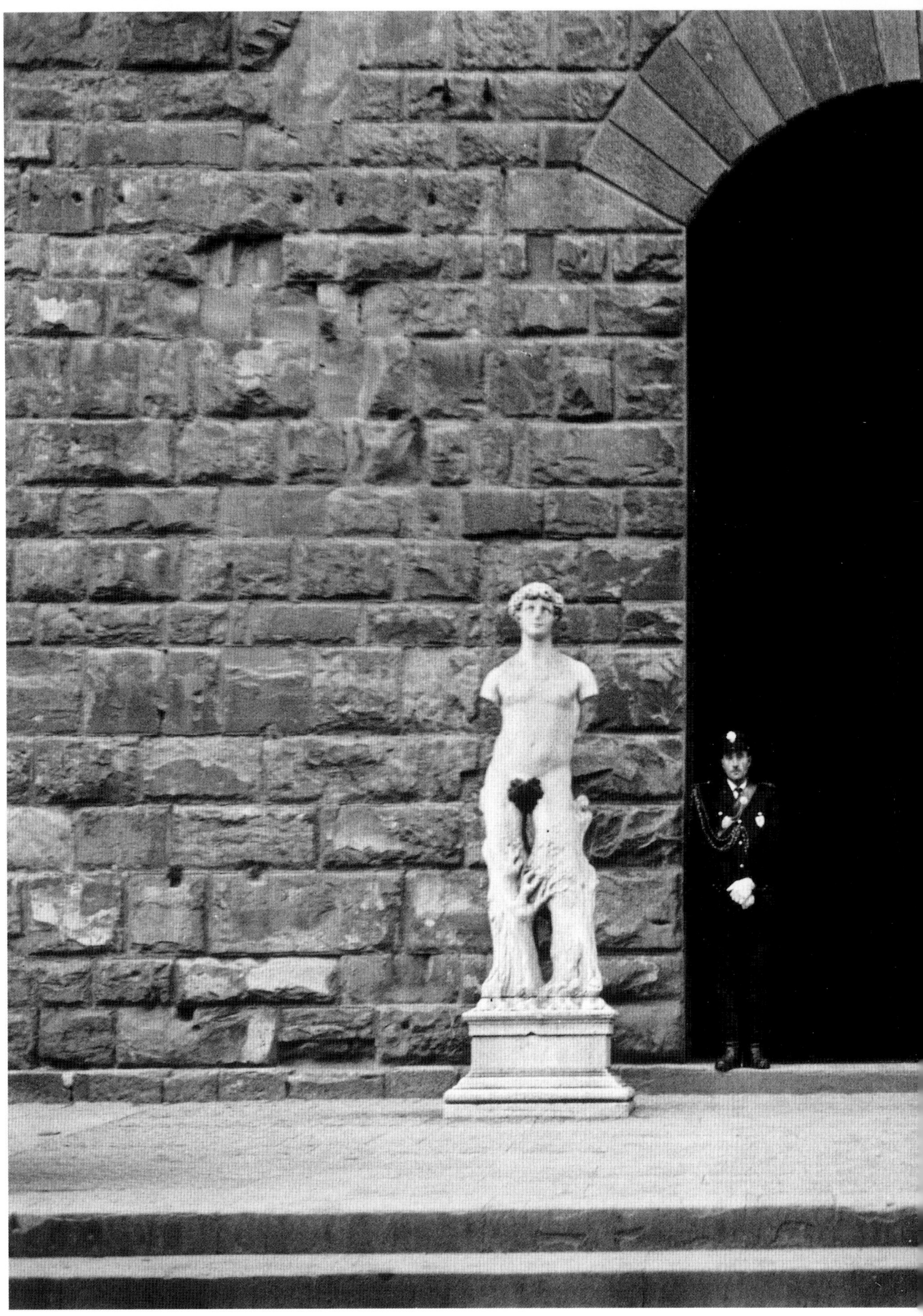

Florence, 1949

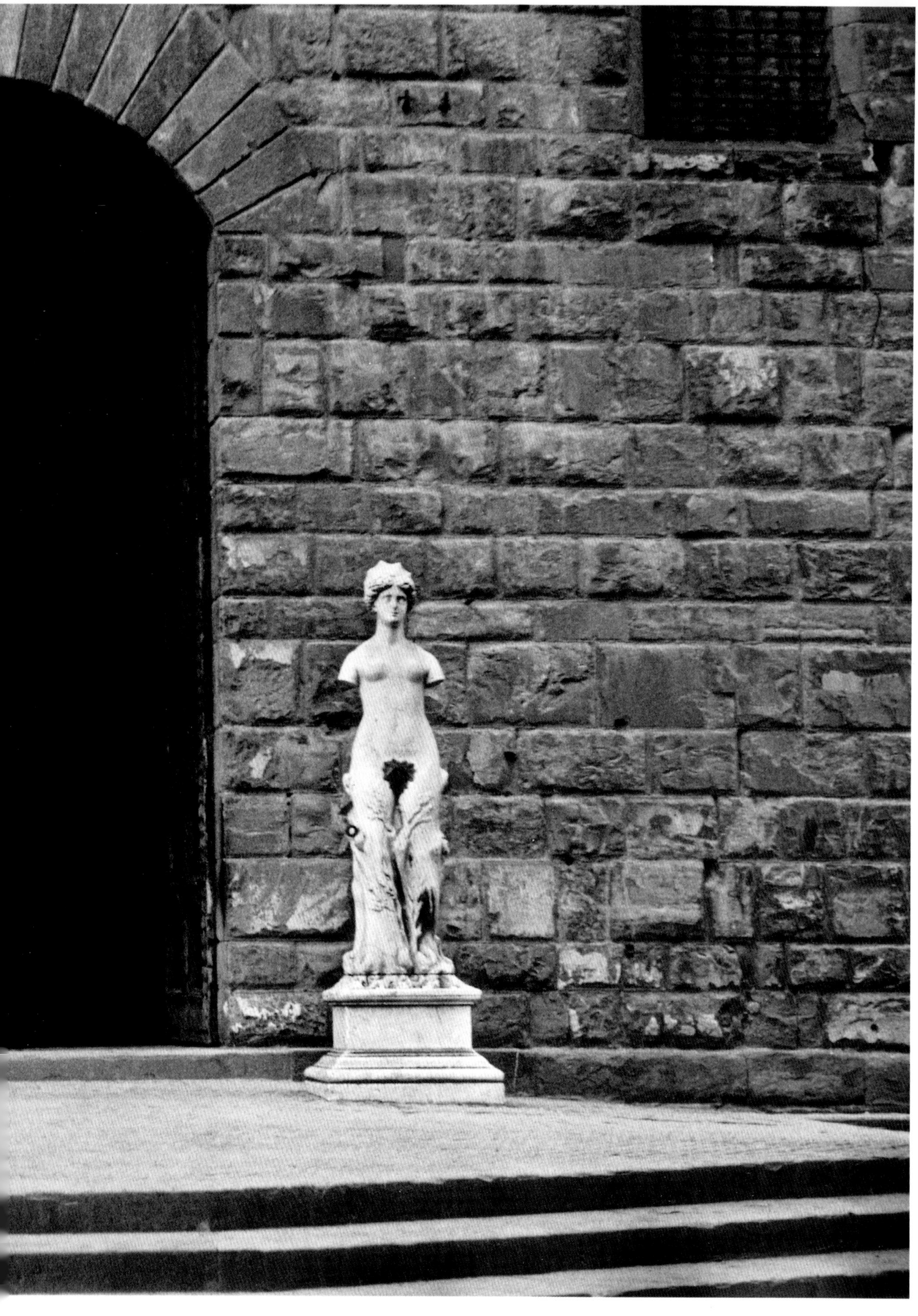

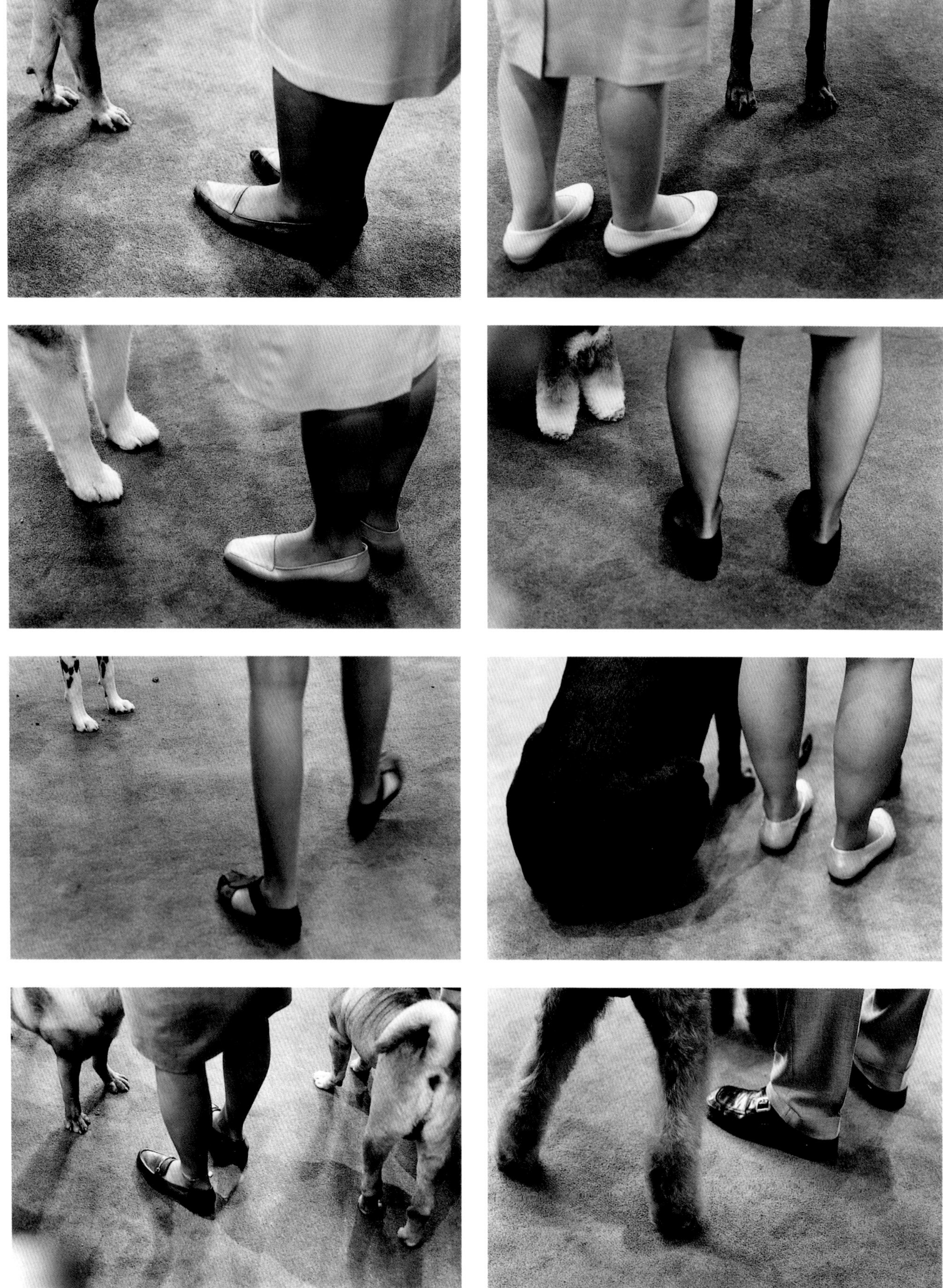

New York, 1999

Cologne, Germany, 1967
overleaf *Brasília, Brazil, 1961* / *Las Vegas, 1998*

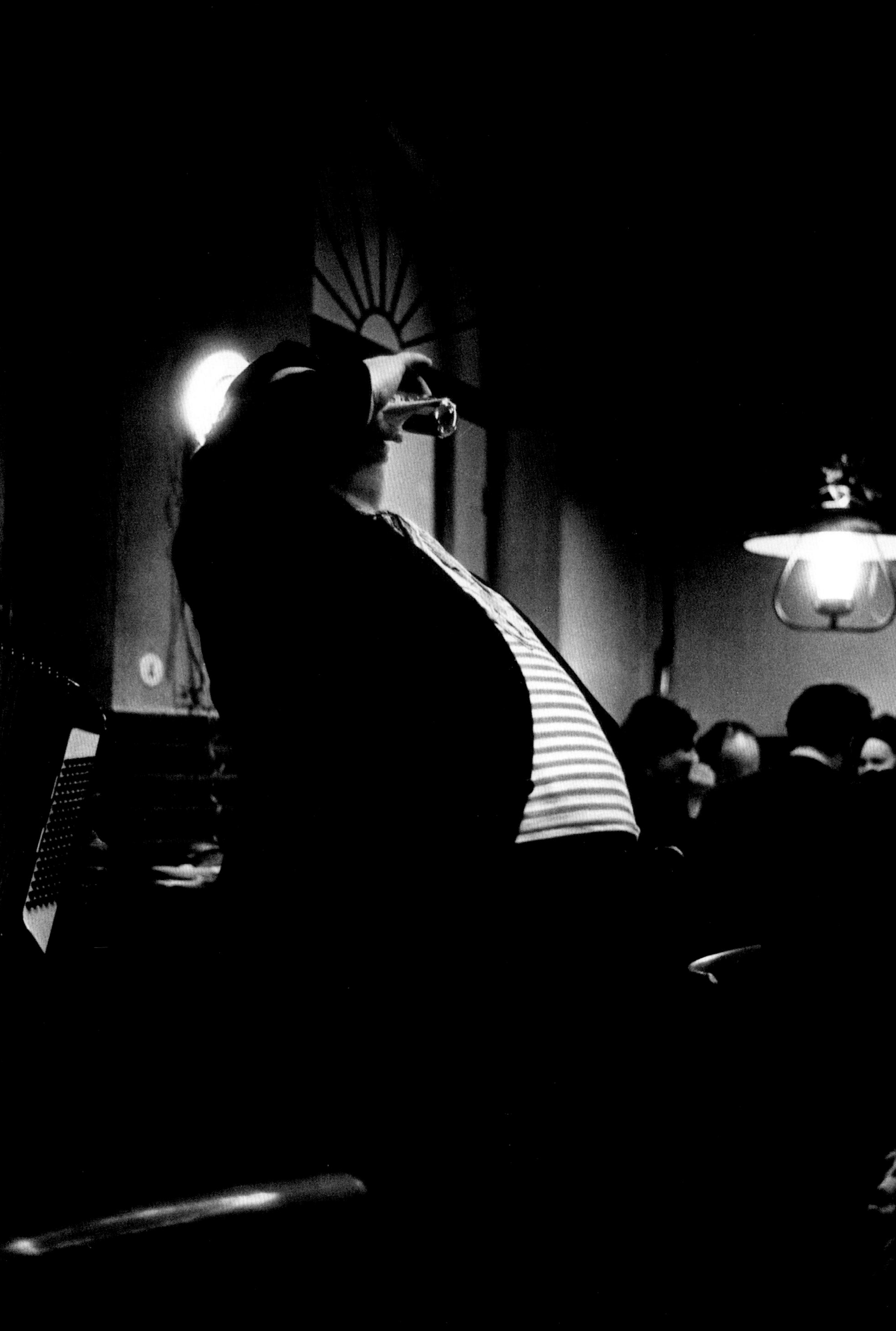

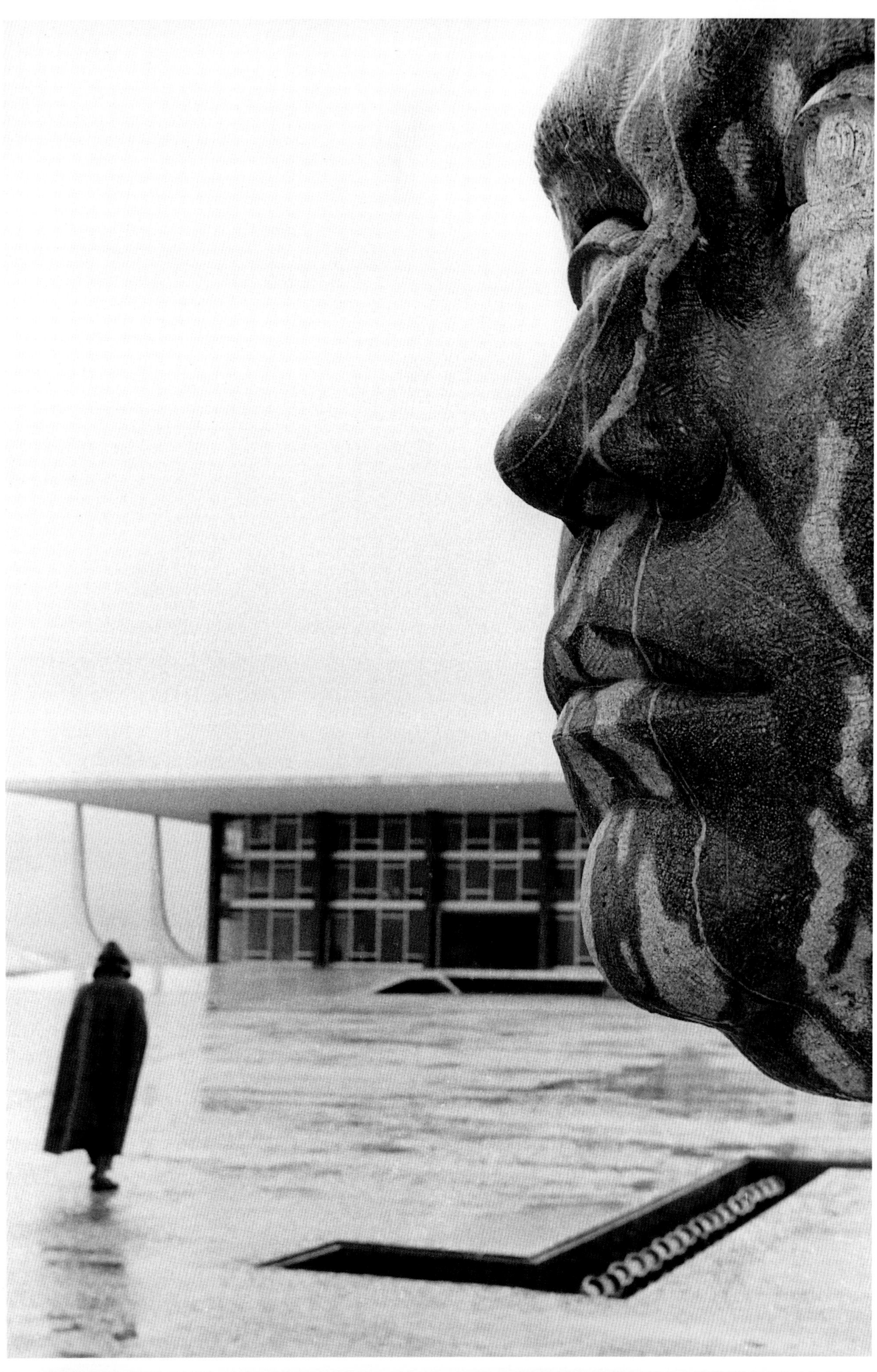

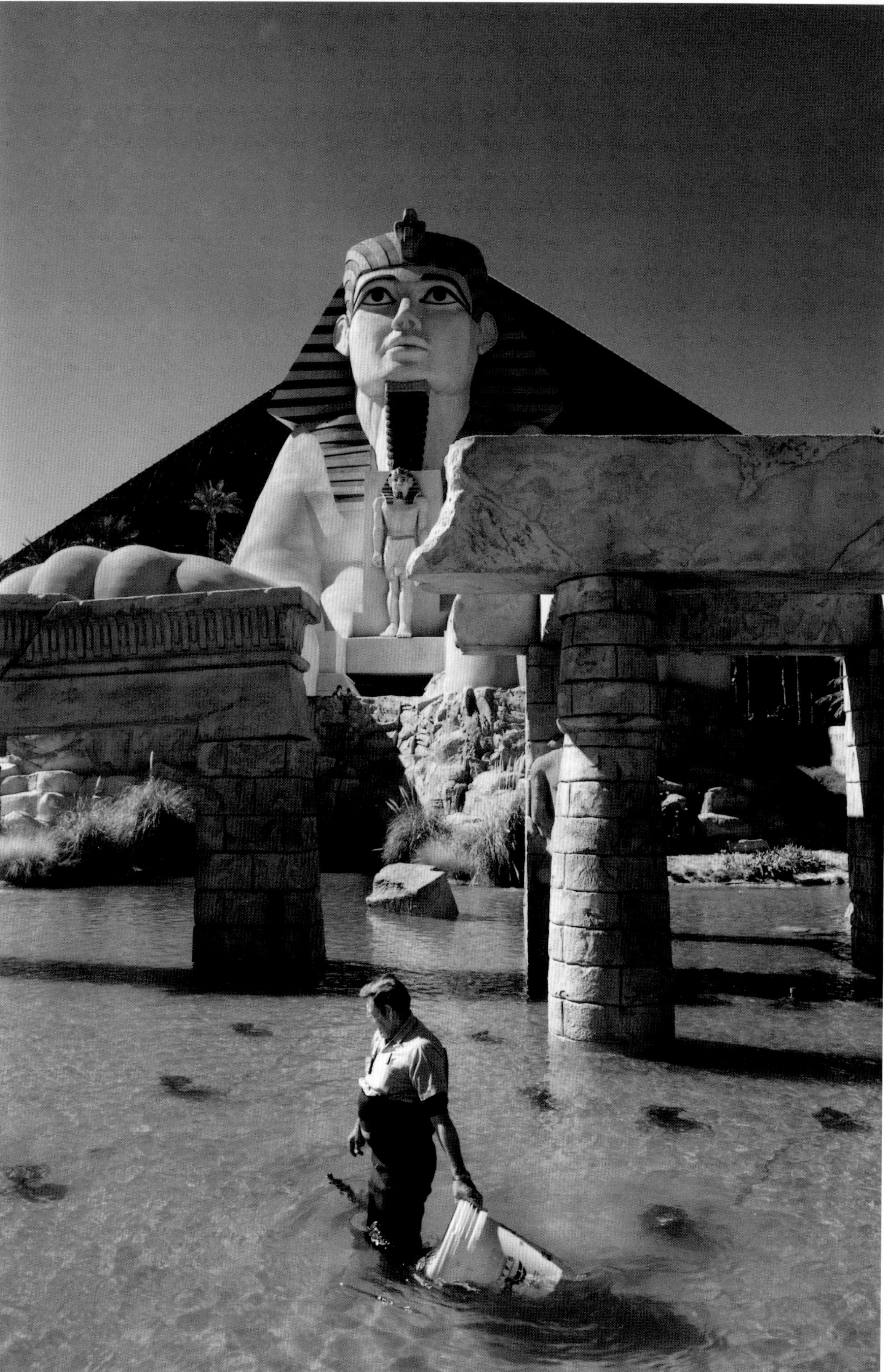

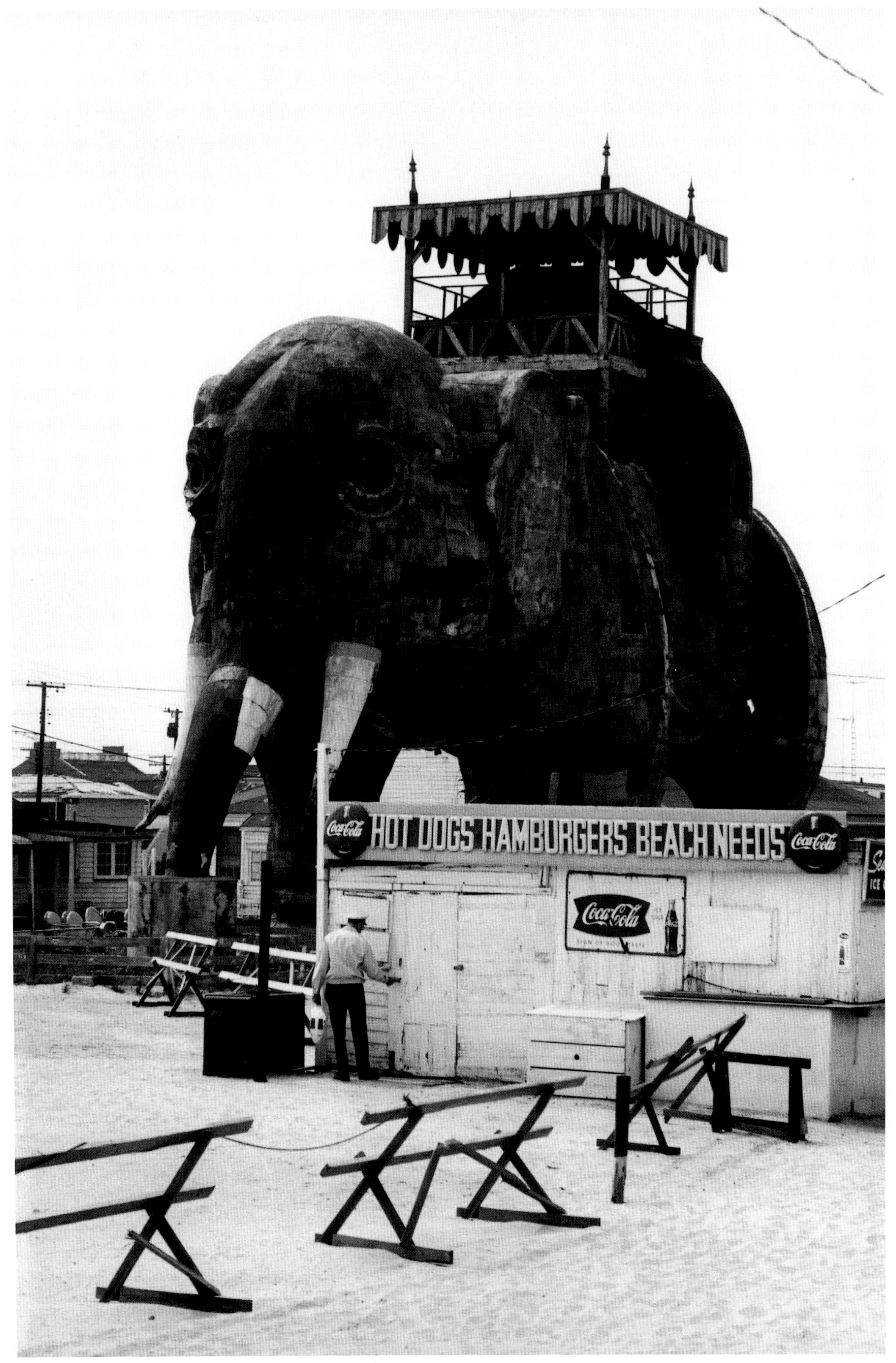
Coca-Cola
HOT DOGS HAMBURGERS BEACH NEEDS
Coca-Cola
Coca-Cola

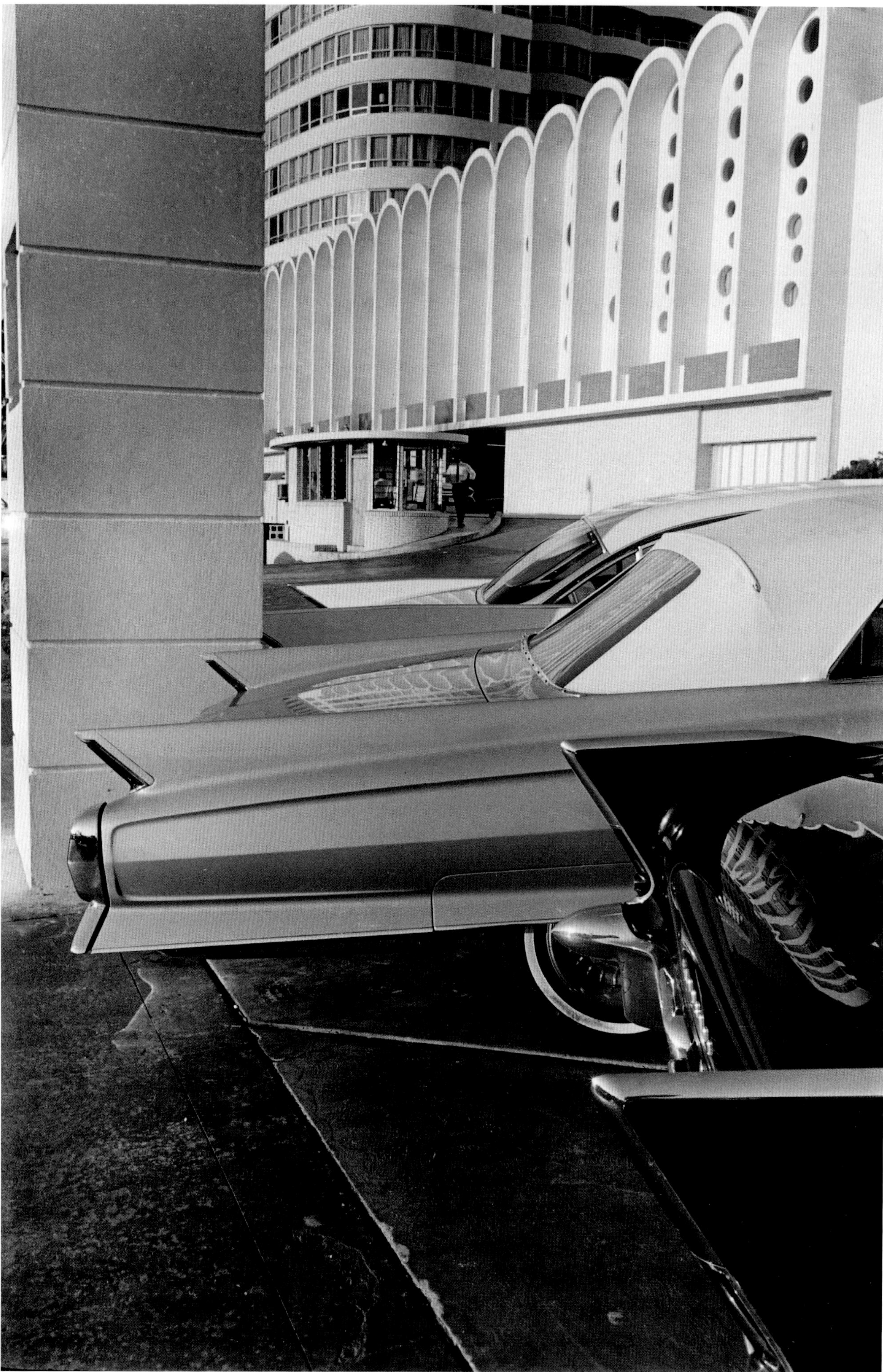

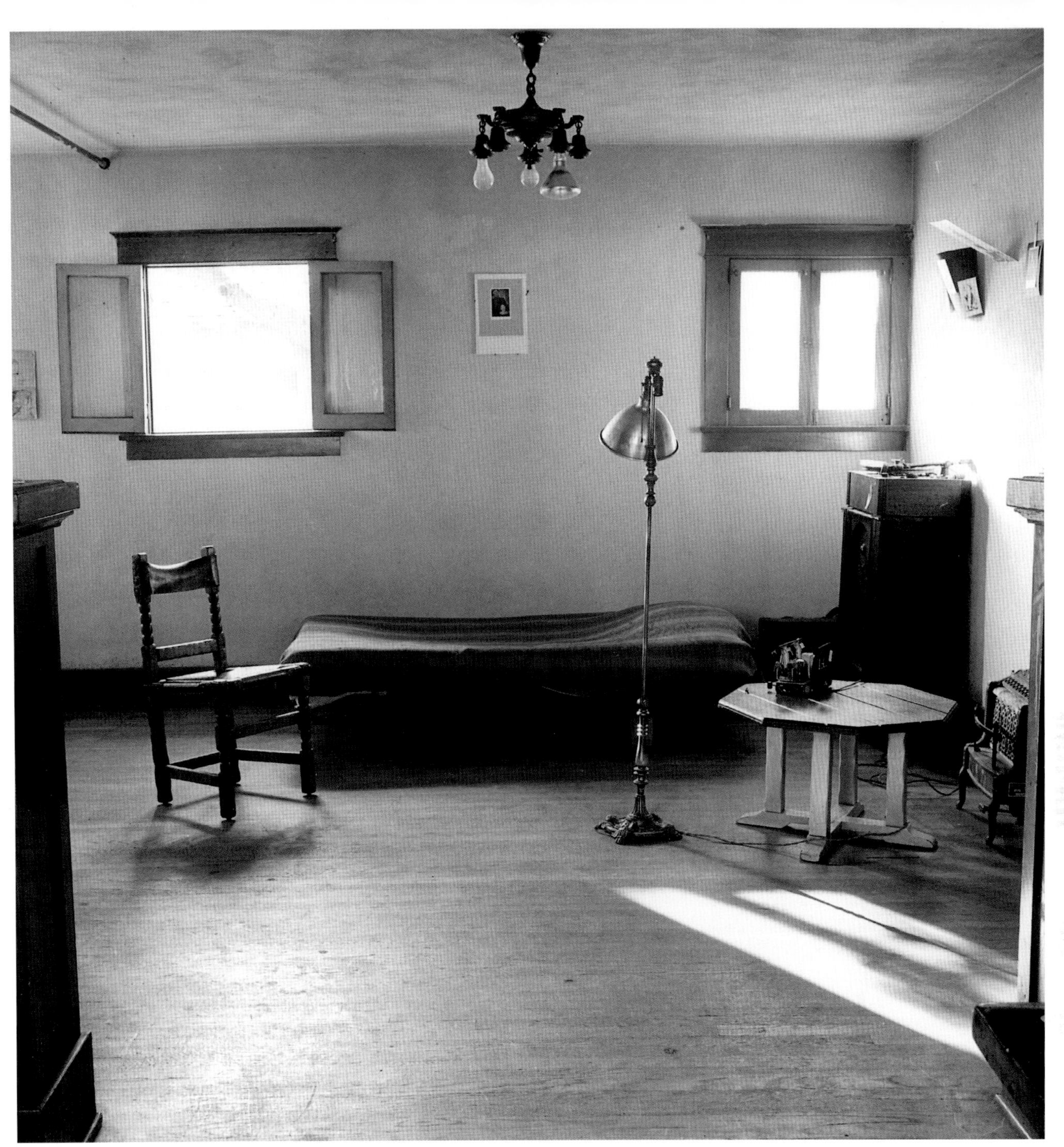

previous page *New Jersey, 1969* / *Miami Beach, 1962*
Hollywood, 1946

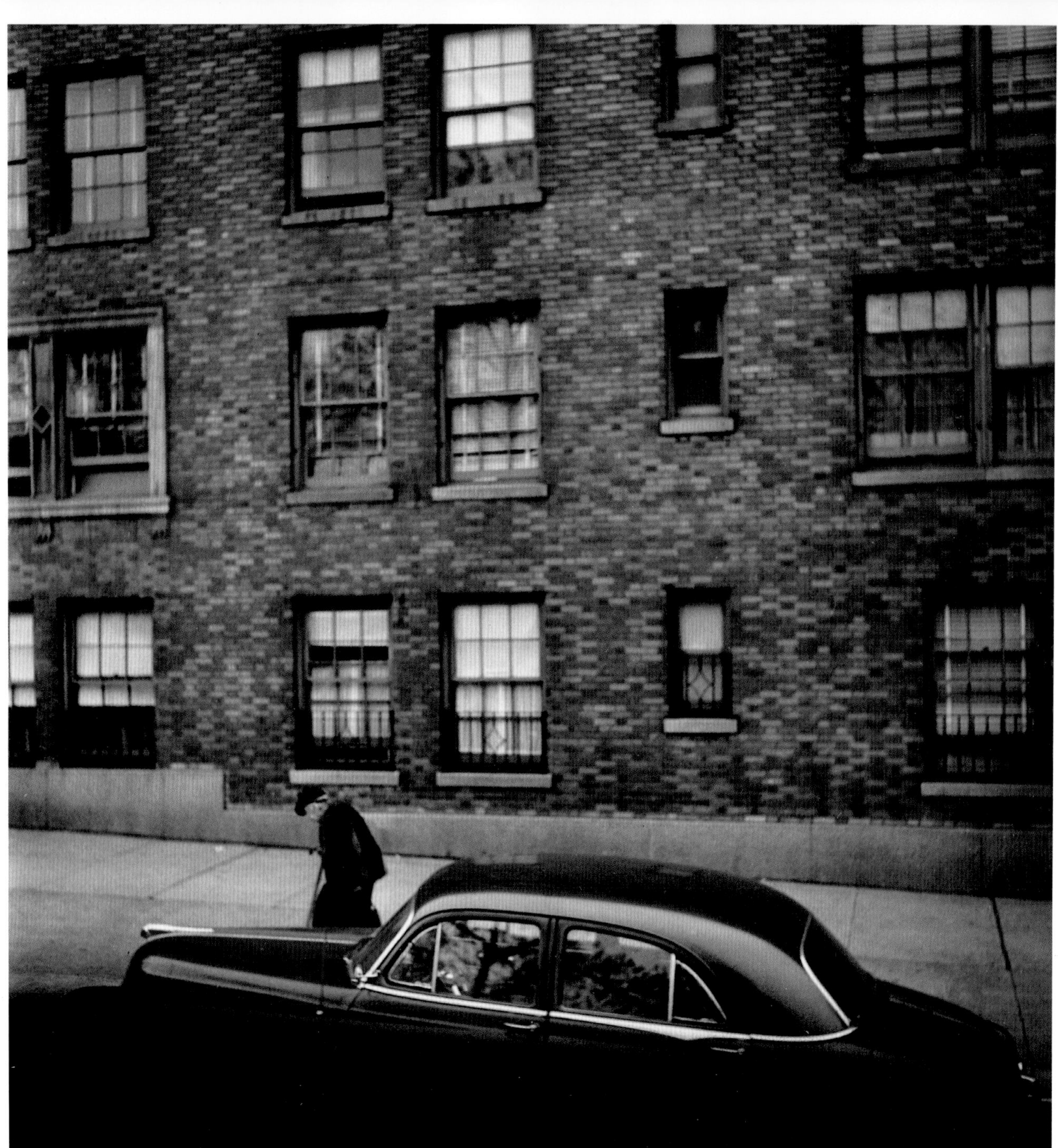

New York, 1949

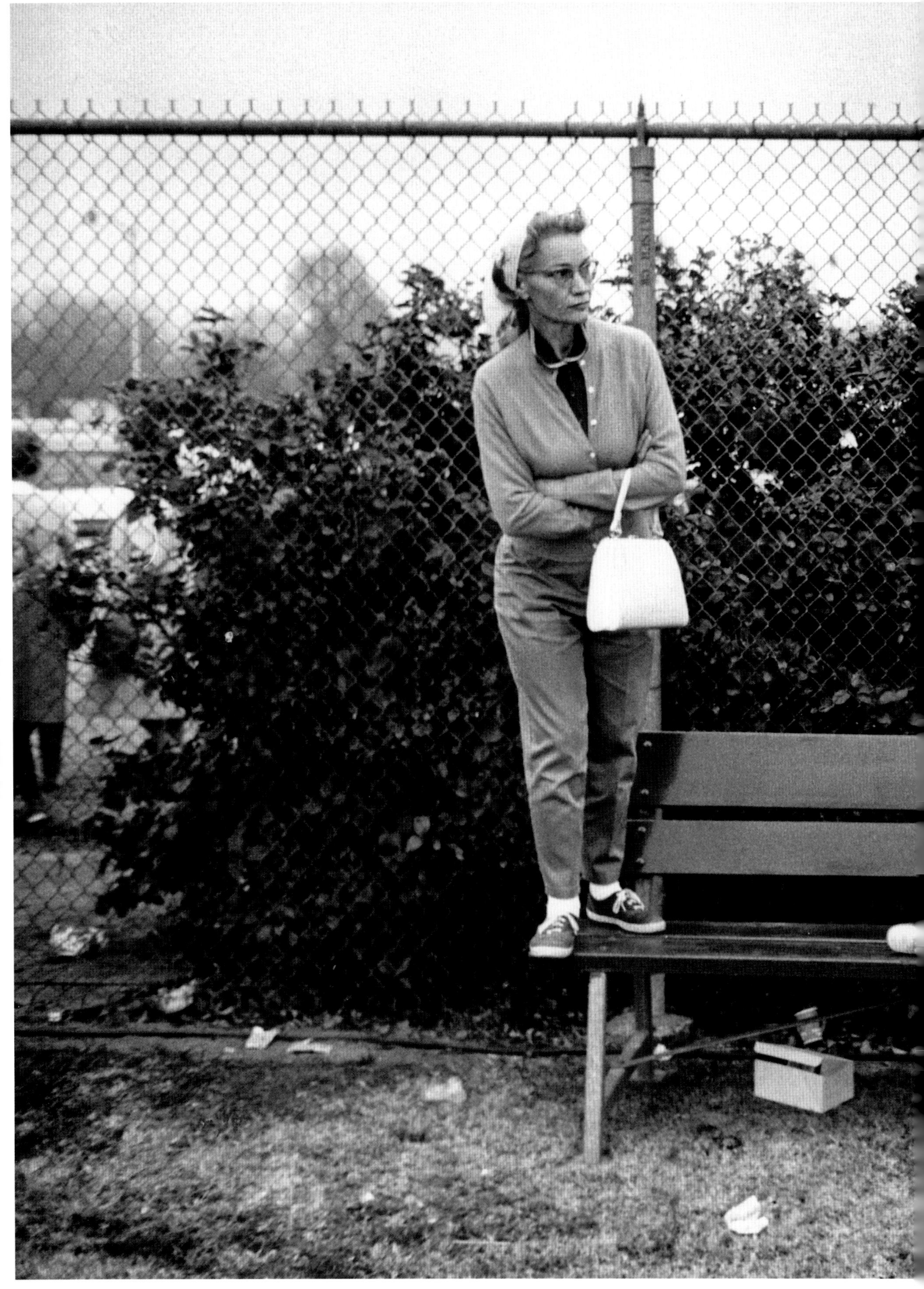

Pasadena, California, 1963

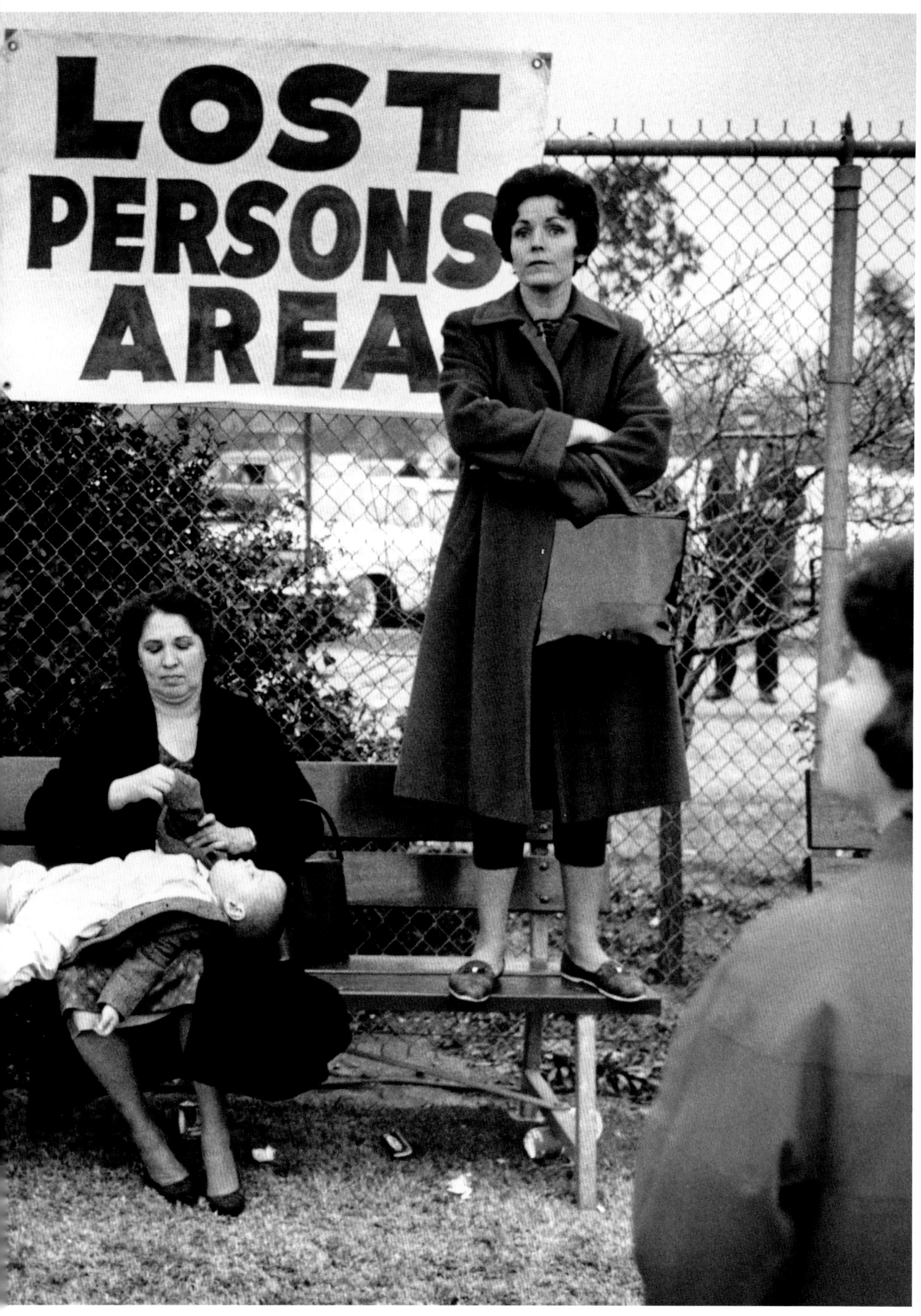
LOST
PERSONS
AREA

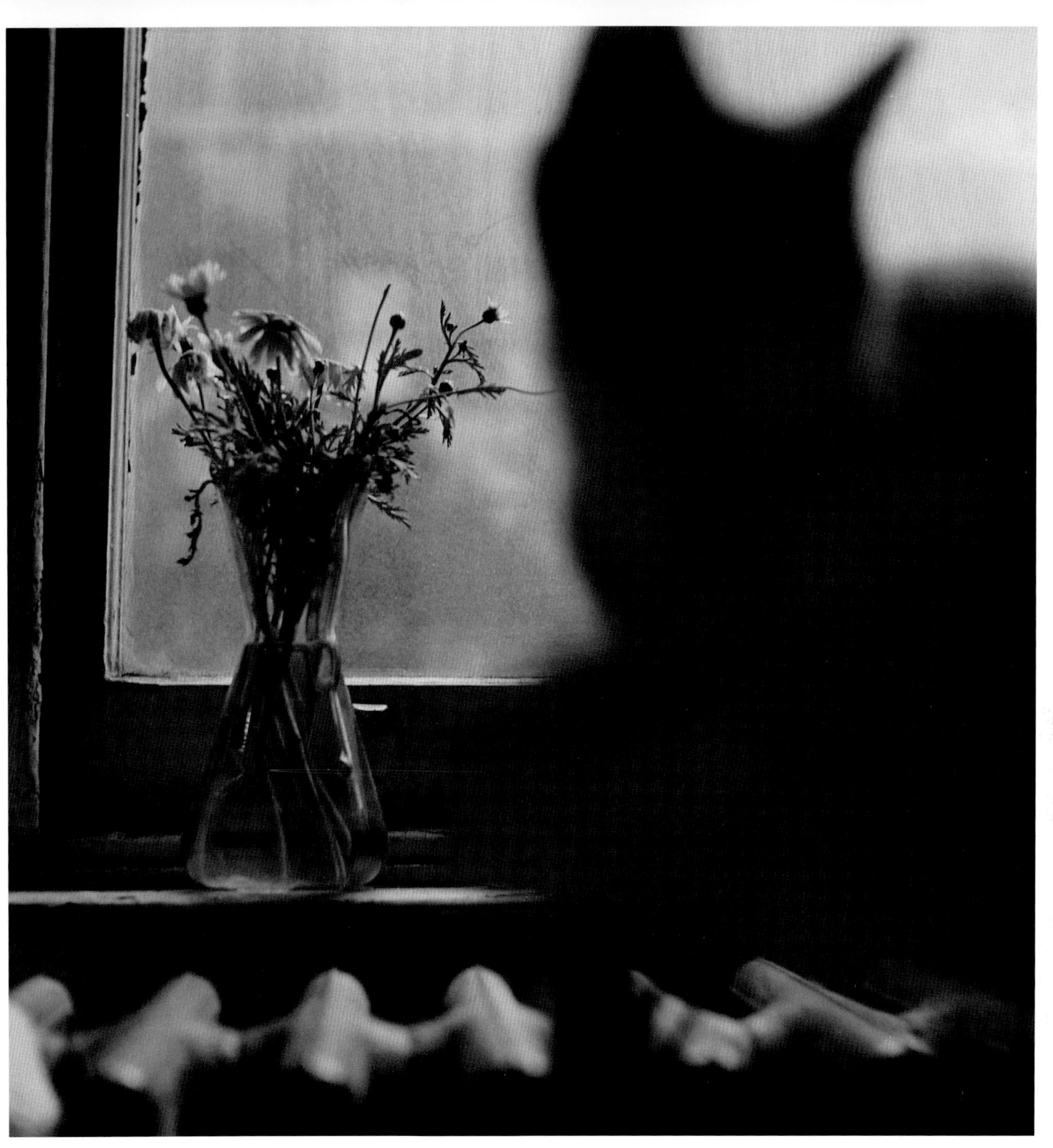

New York, 1950

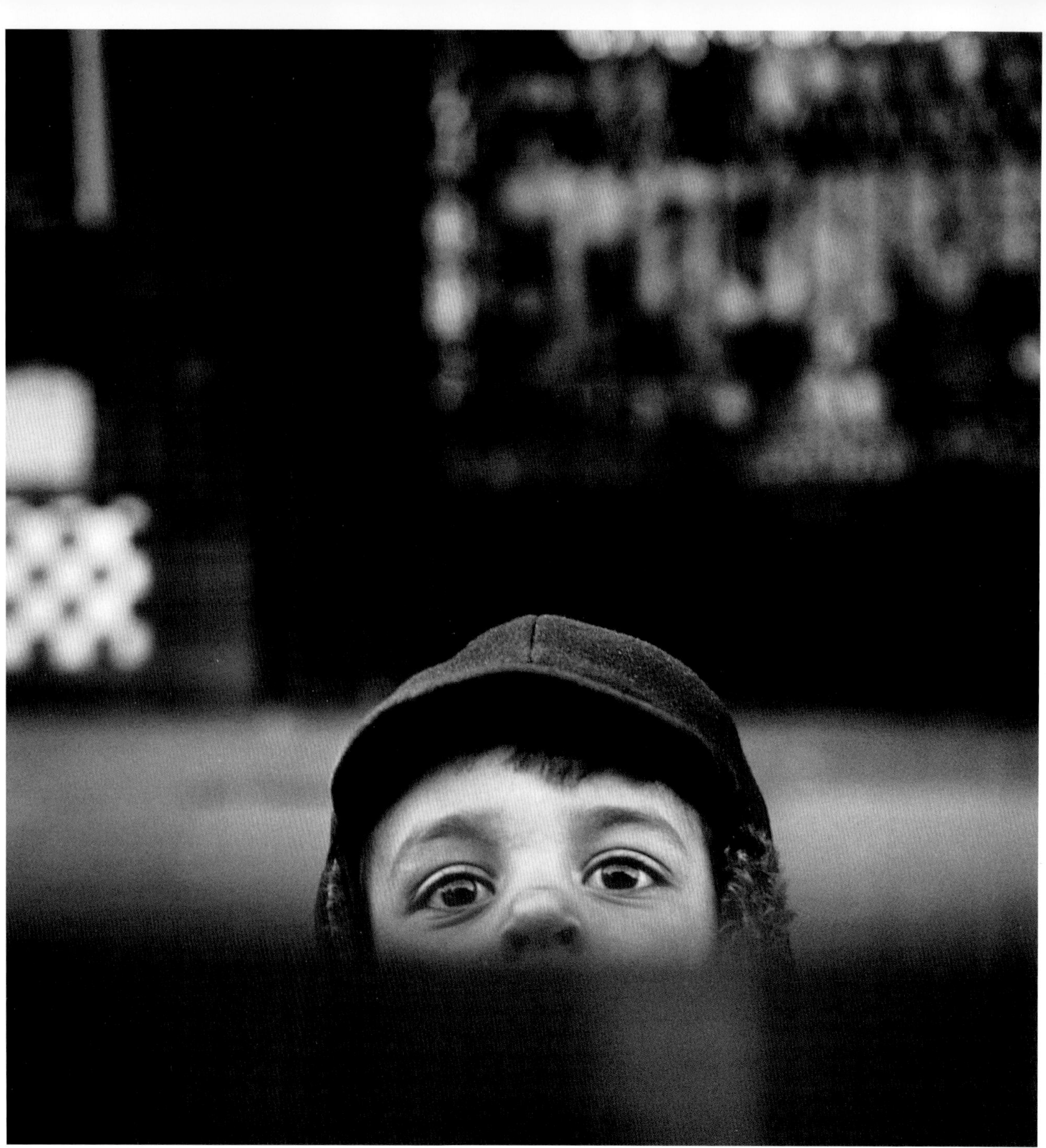

New York, 1951

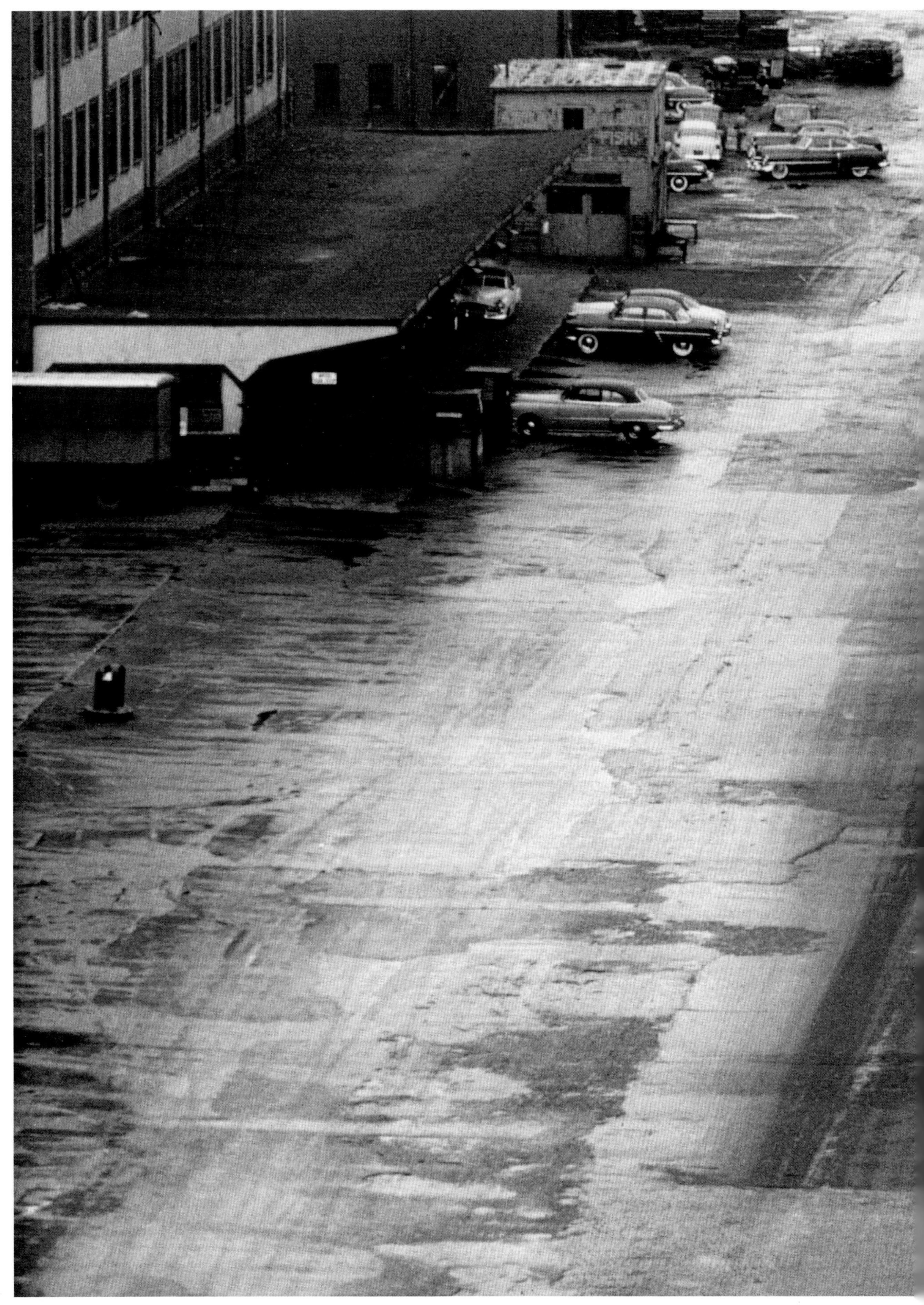

New York, 1953

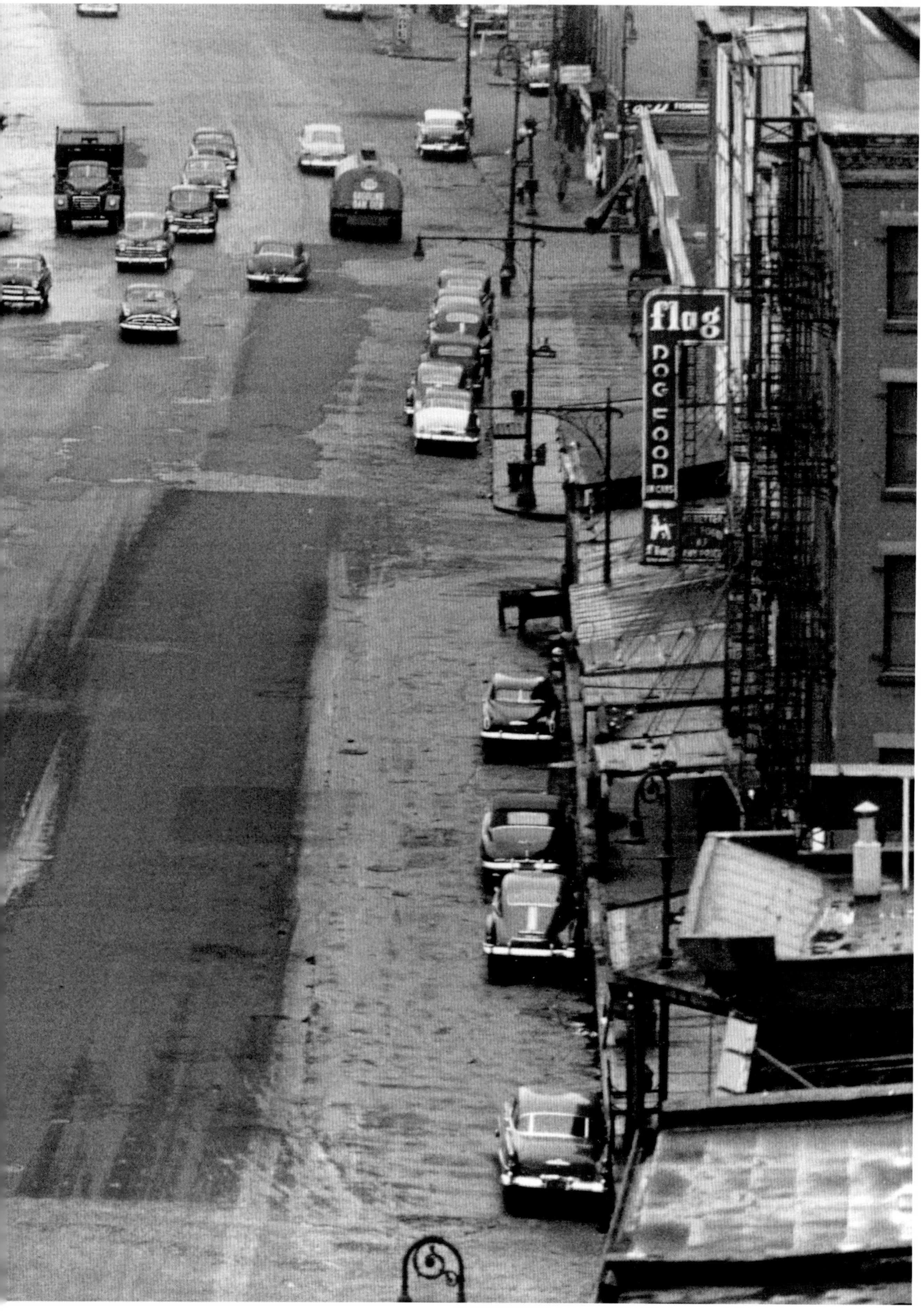
flag
DOG FOOD

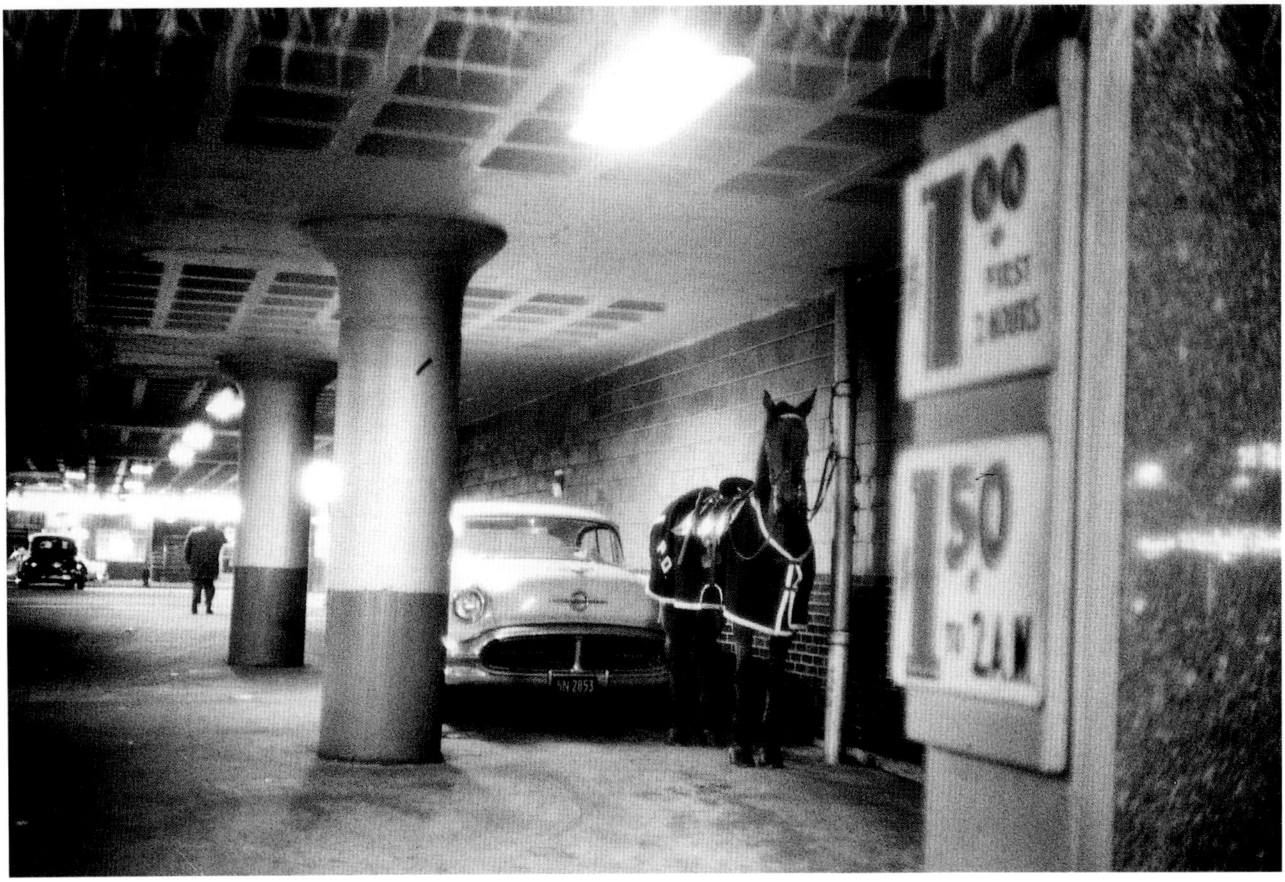

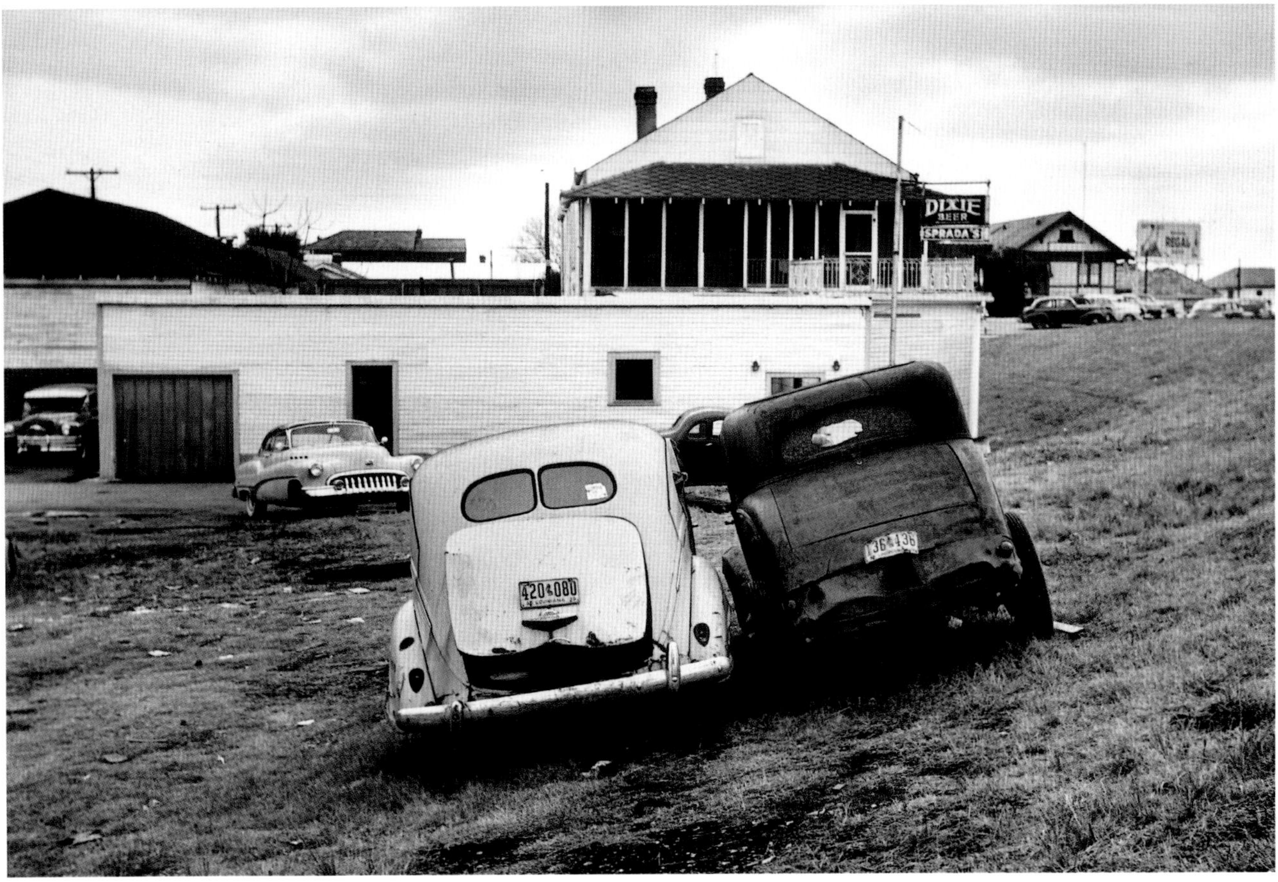

New York, 1955 / *New Orleans, 1950*

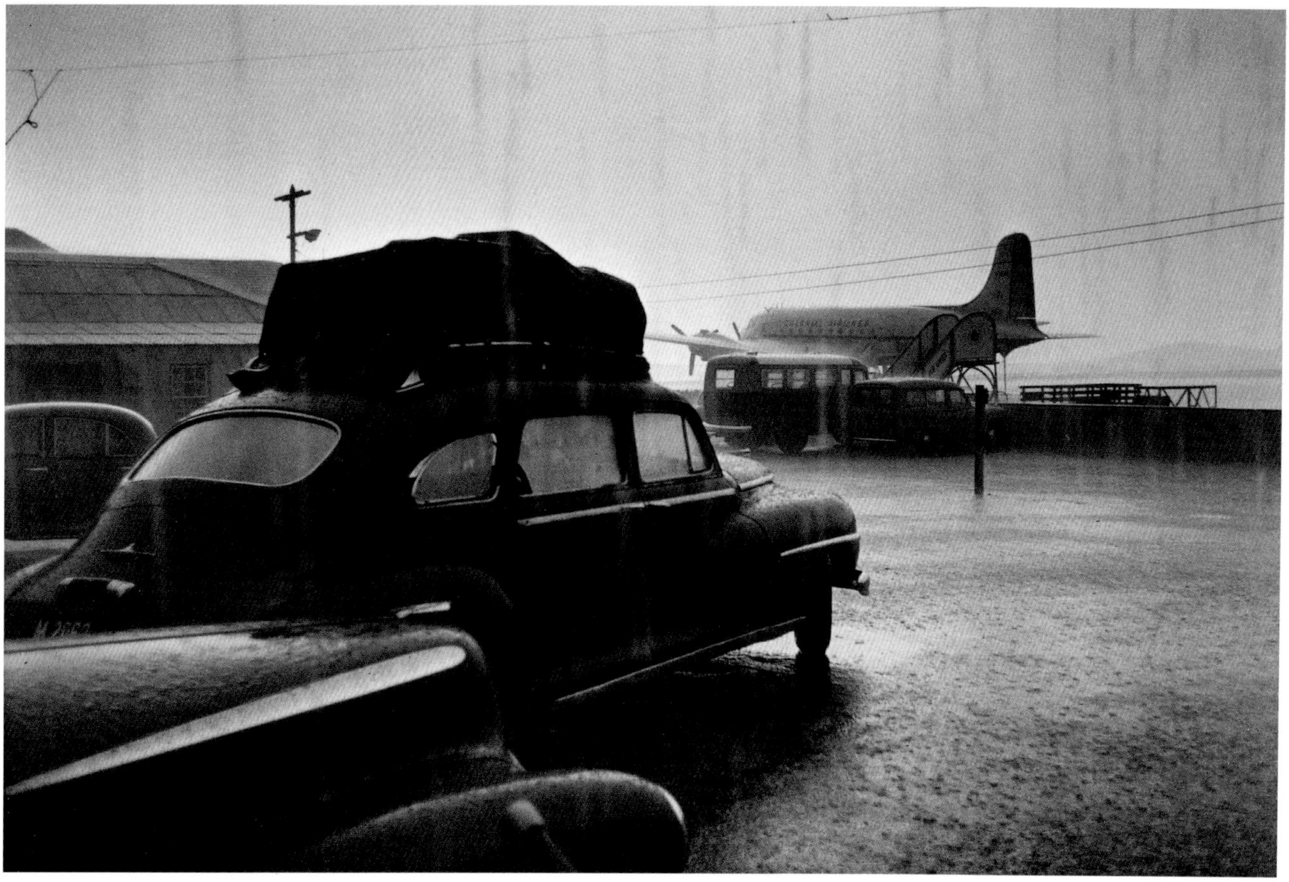

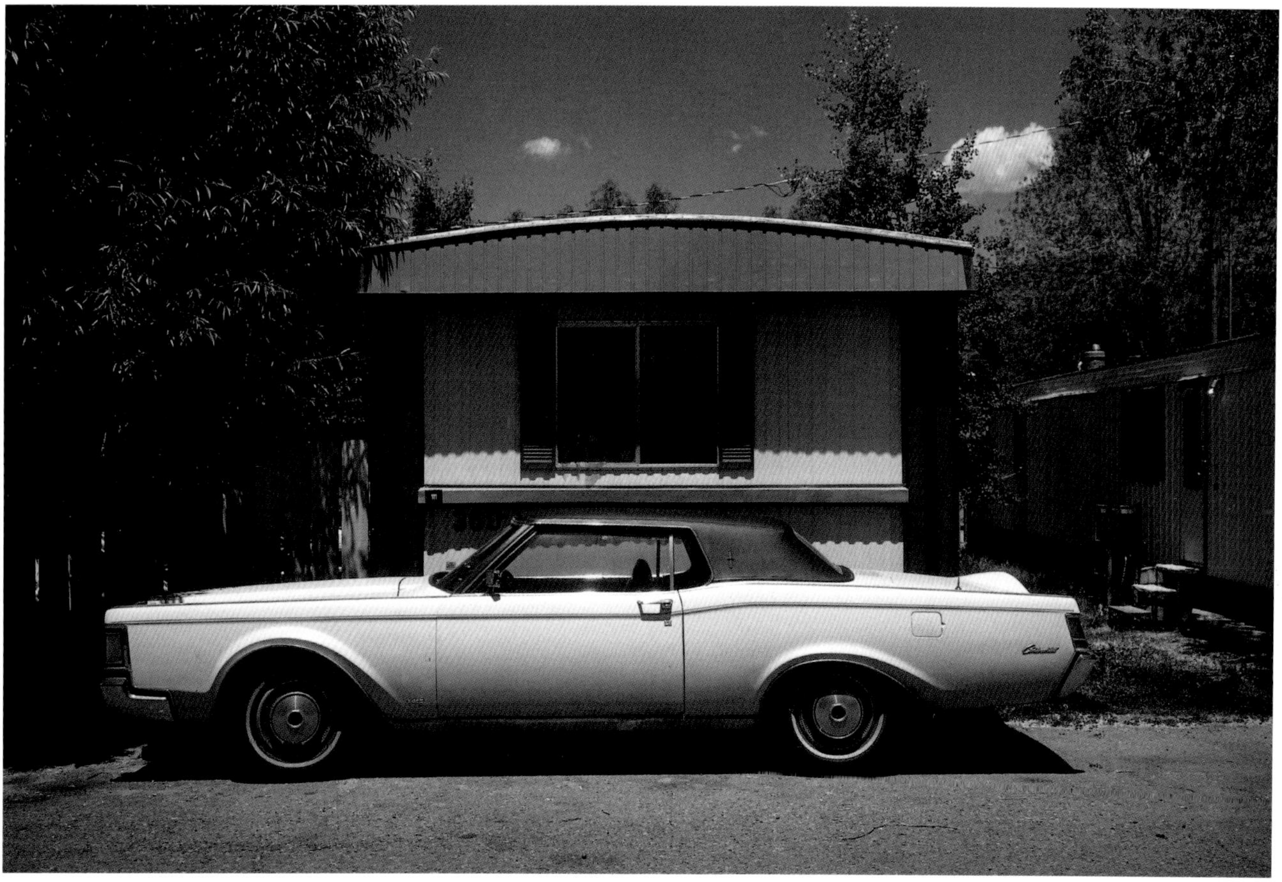

Bermuda, 1953 / Twin Lakes, Colorado, 1992

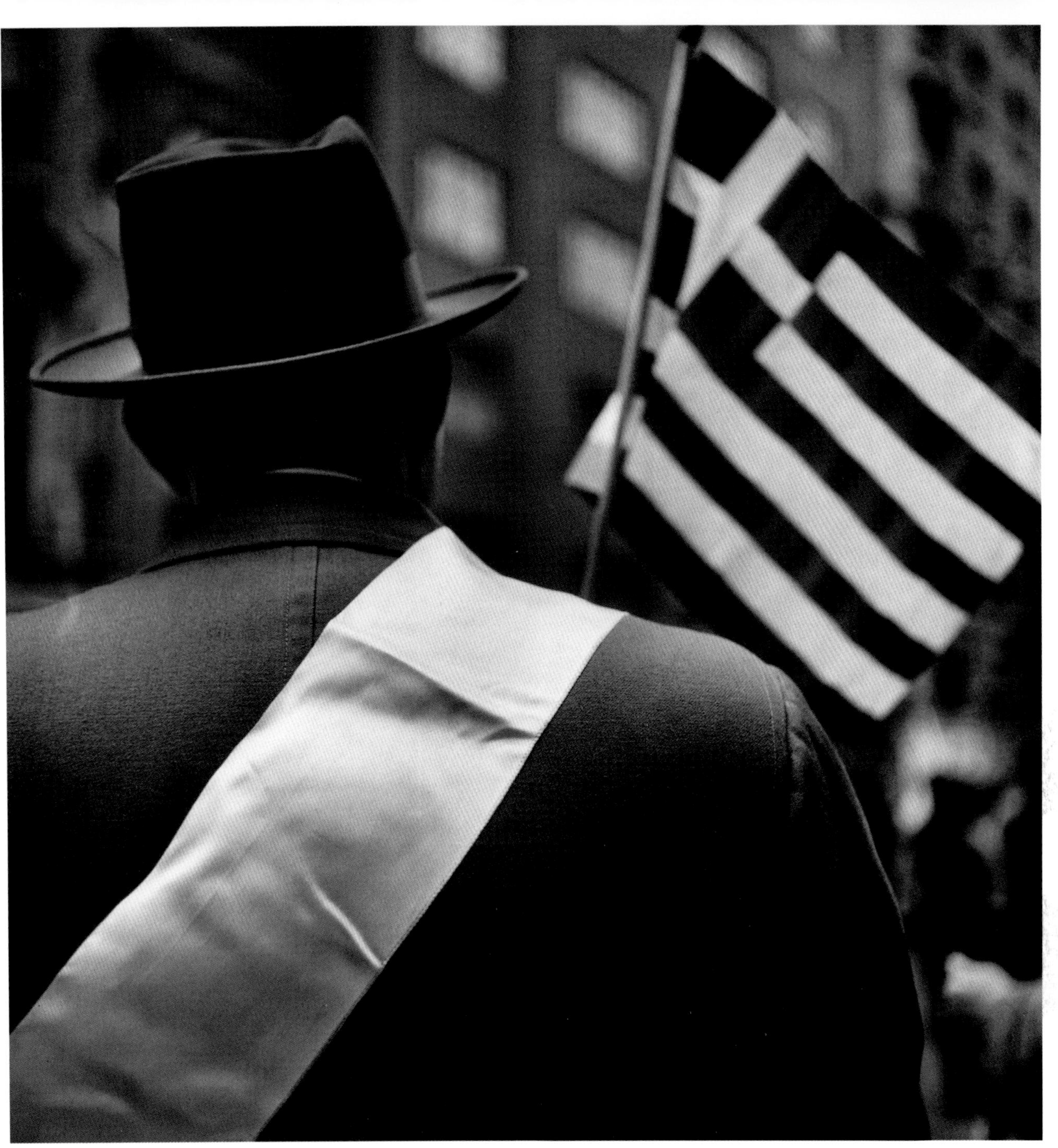

New York, 1950

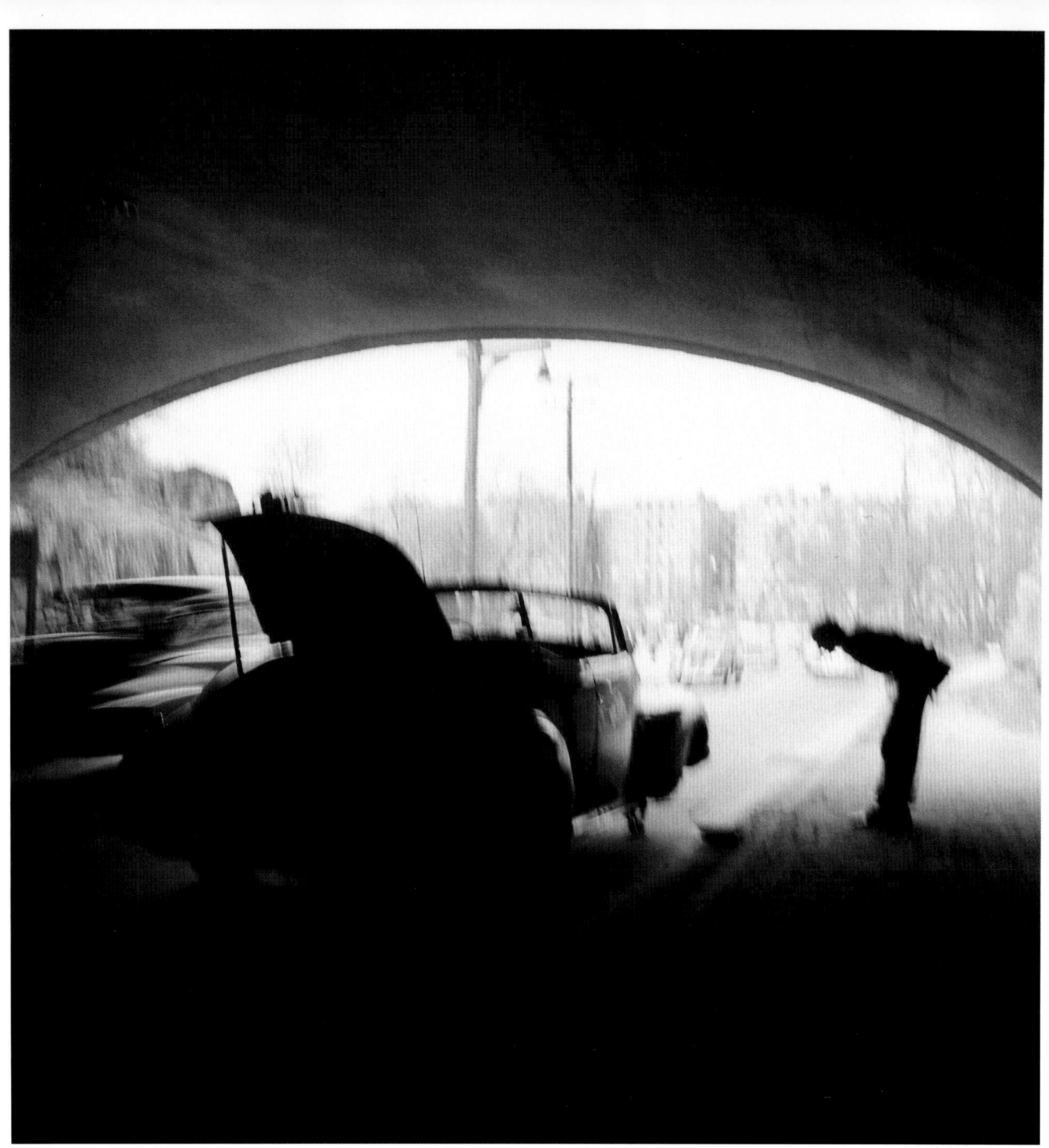

New York, 1949

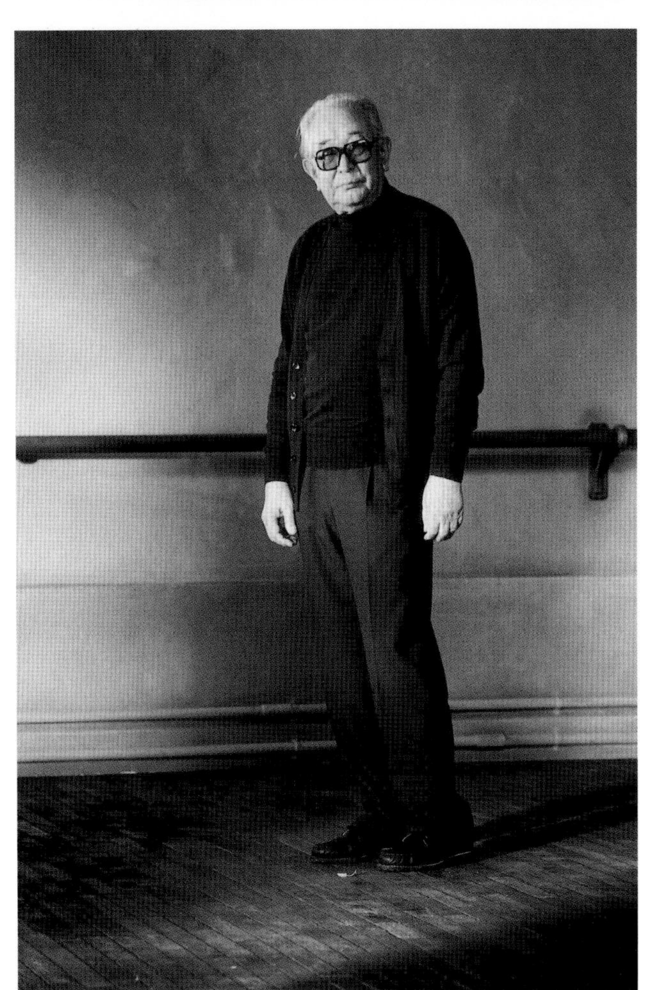

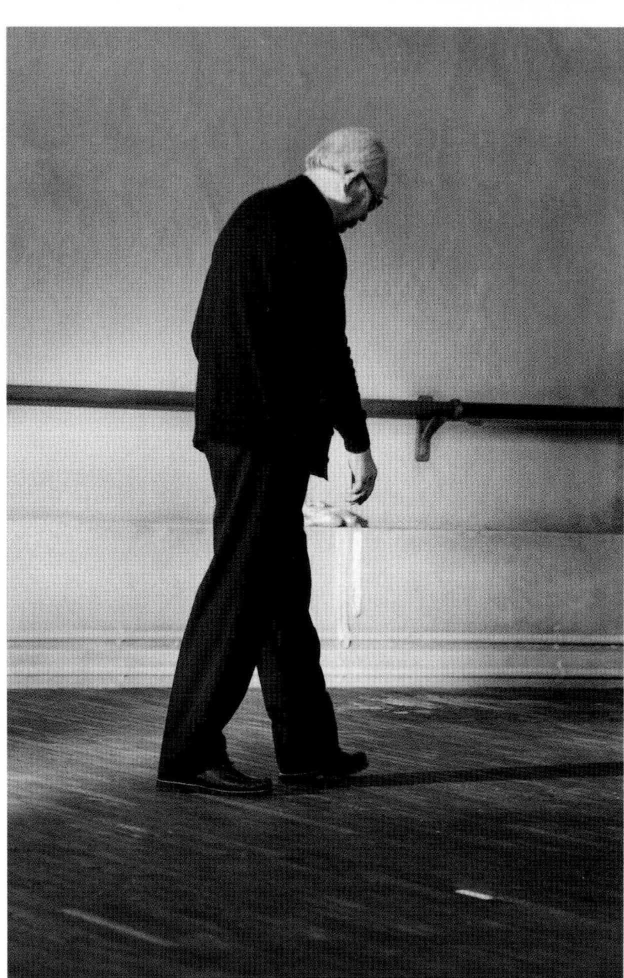

Akira Kurosawa, Tokyo, 1989

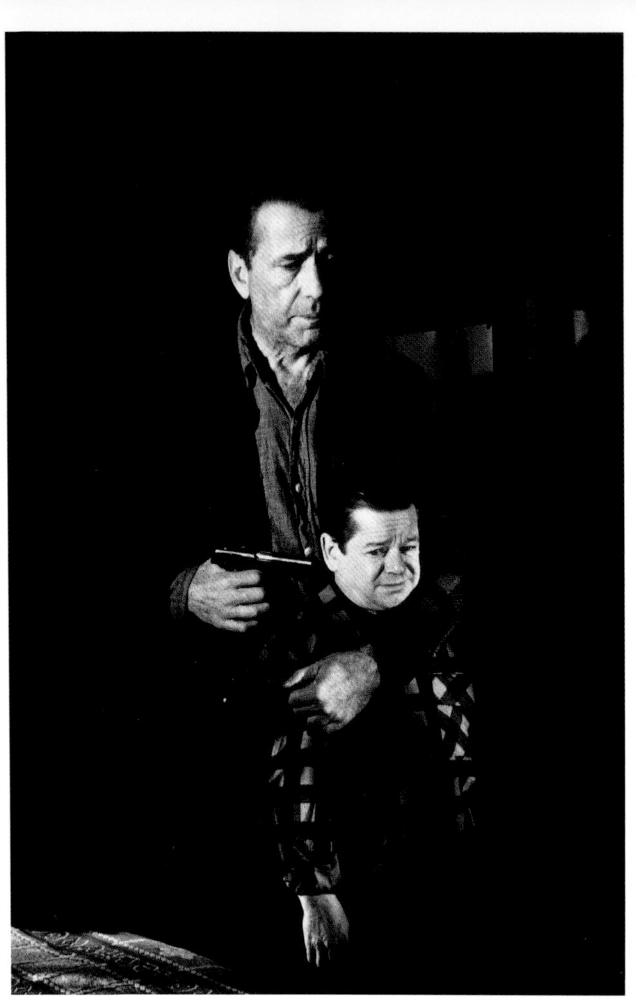

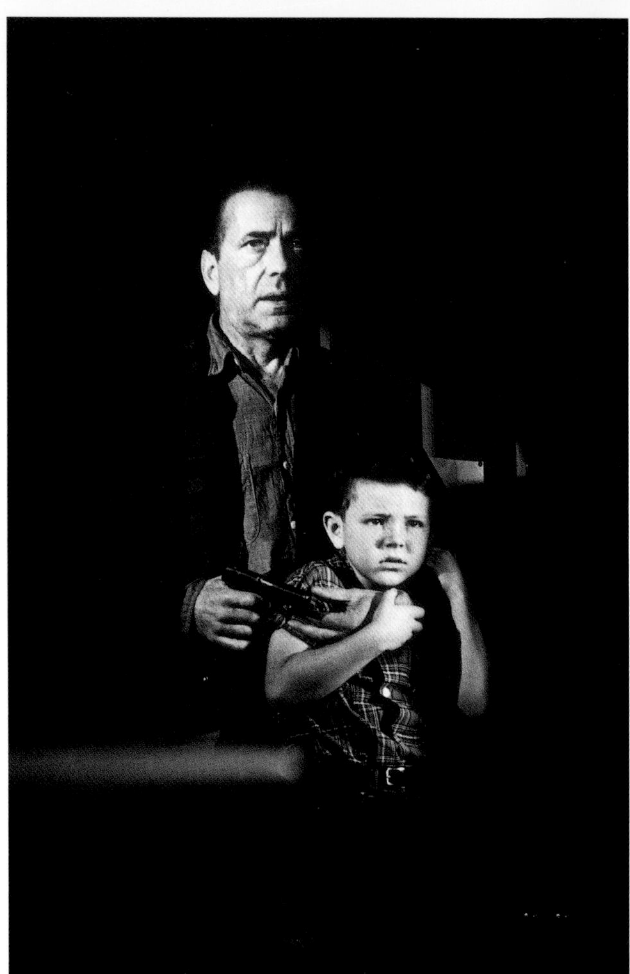

Humphrey Bogart, Hollywood, 1956

overleaf *Fernandina Beach, Florida, 1950* / *Barcelona, 1951*

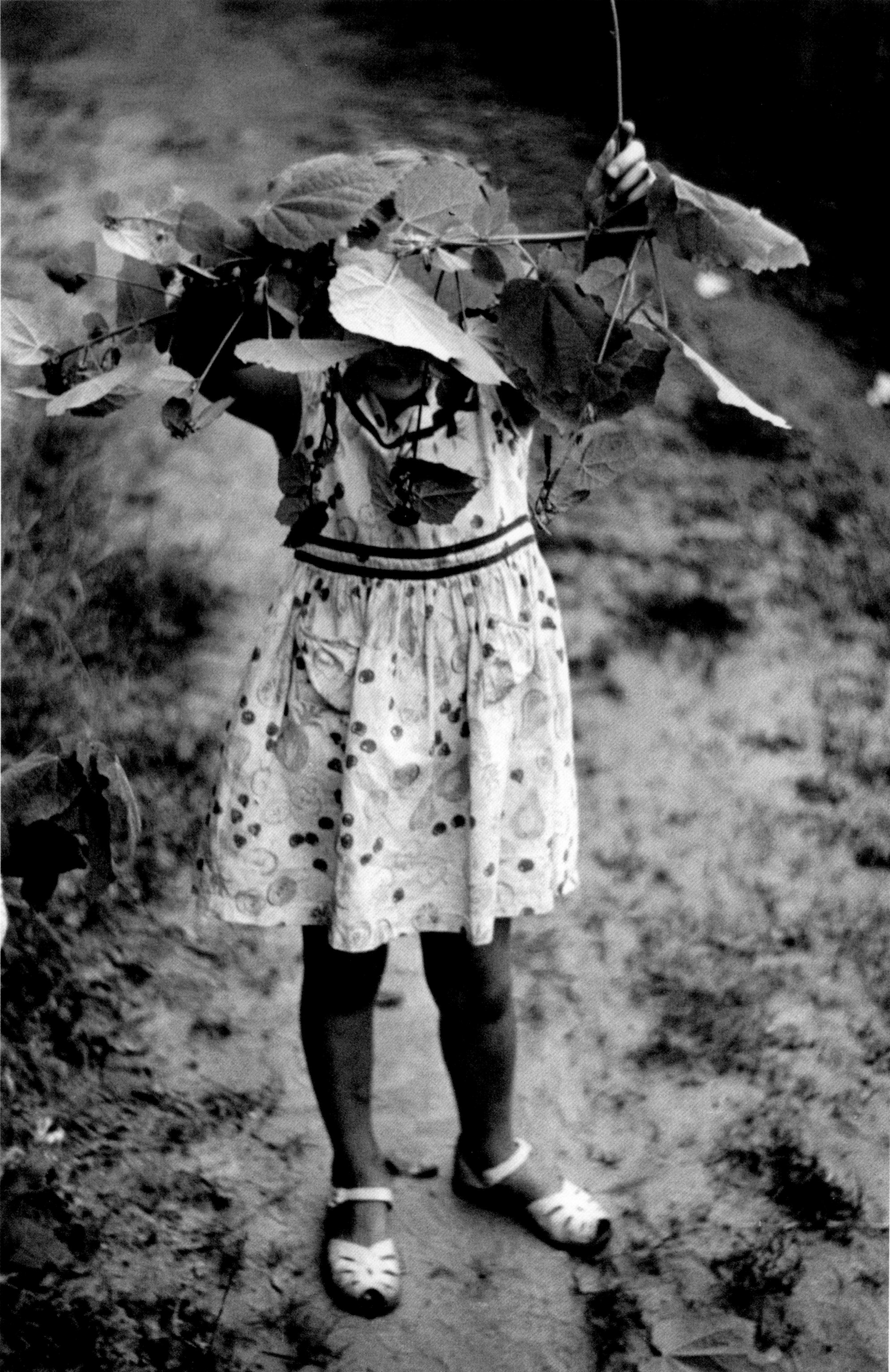

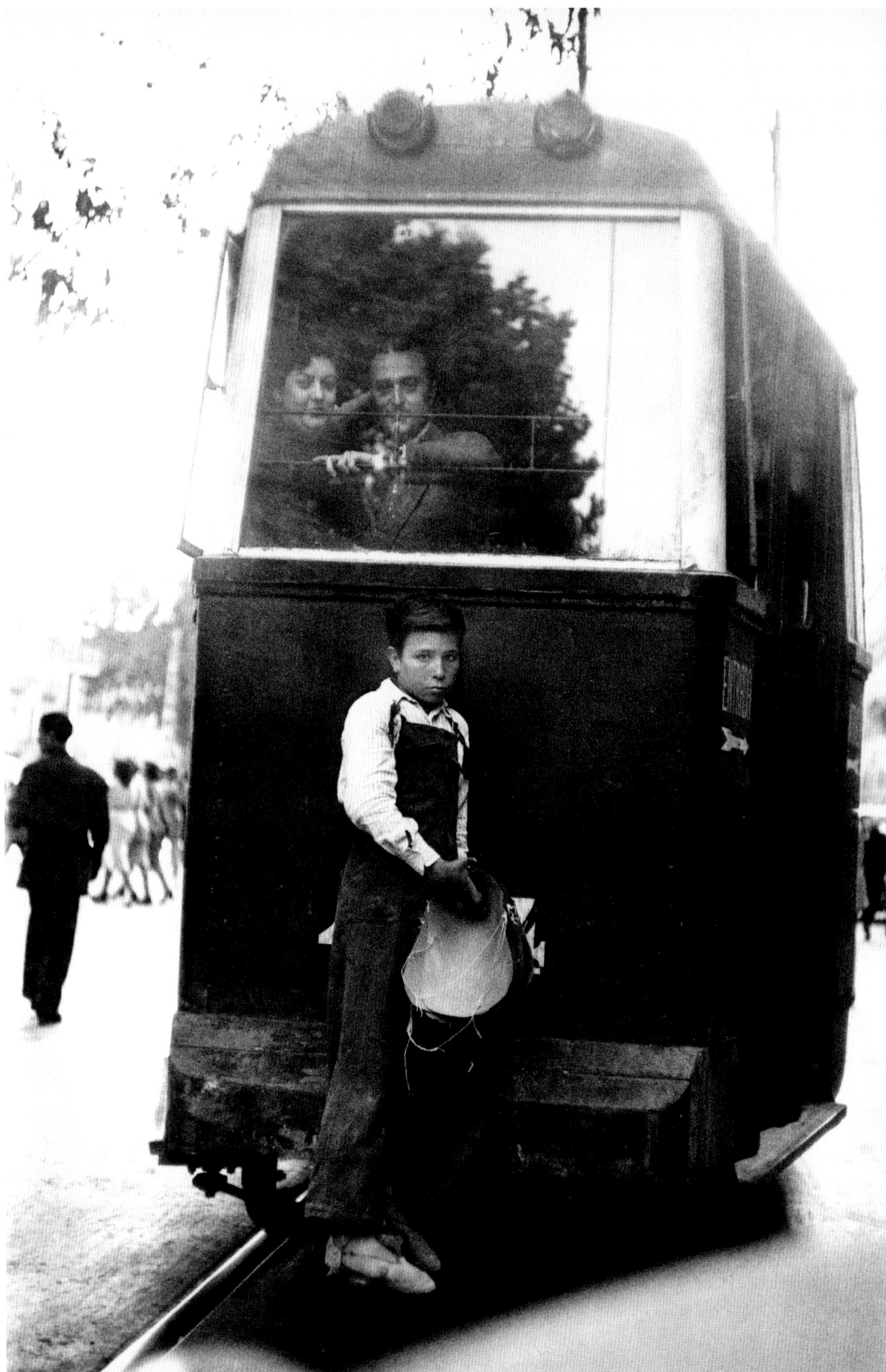

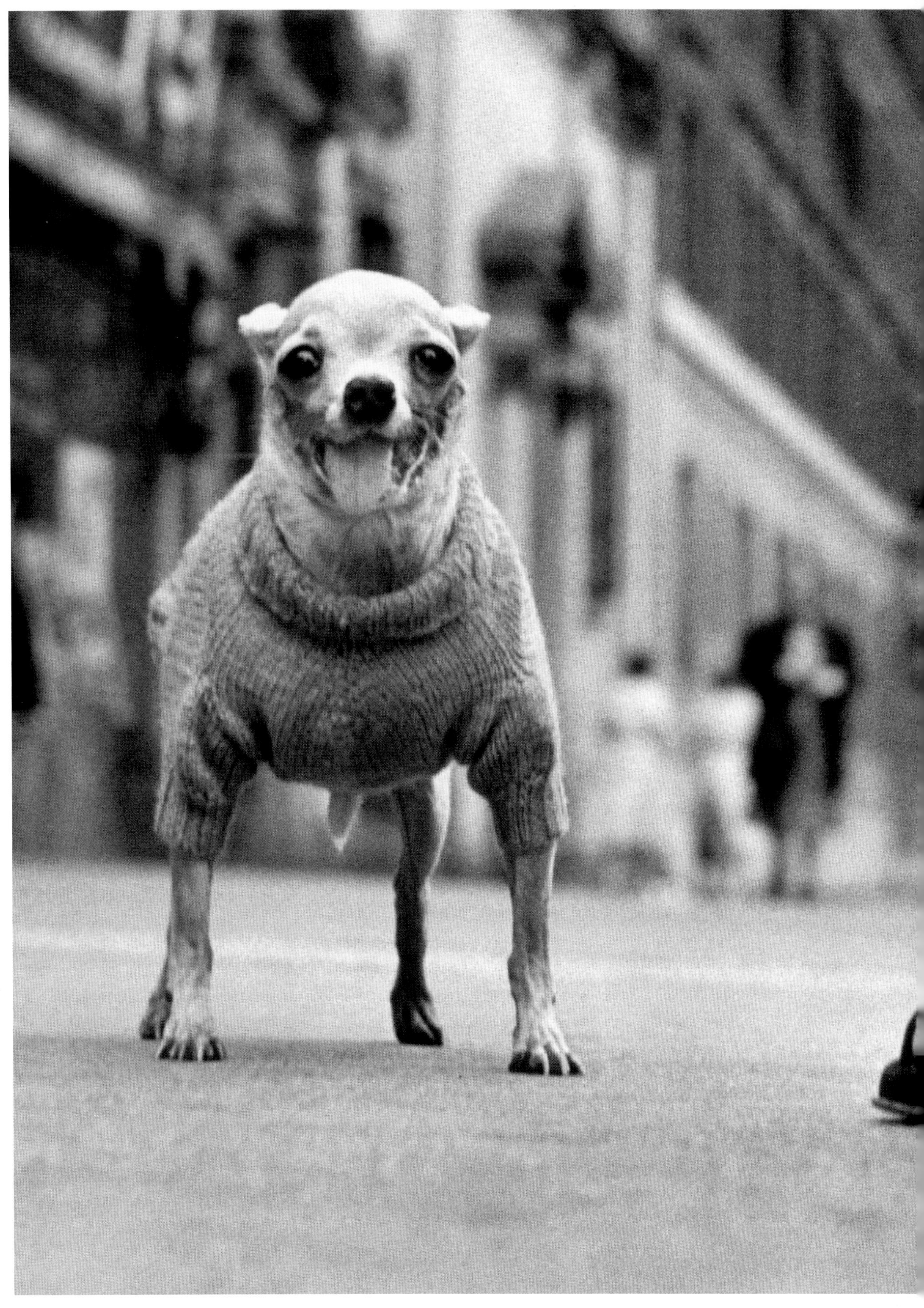

New York, 1946

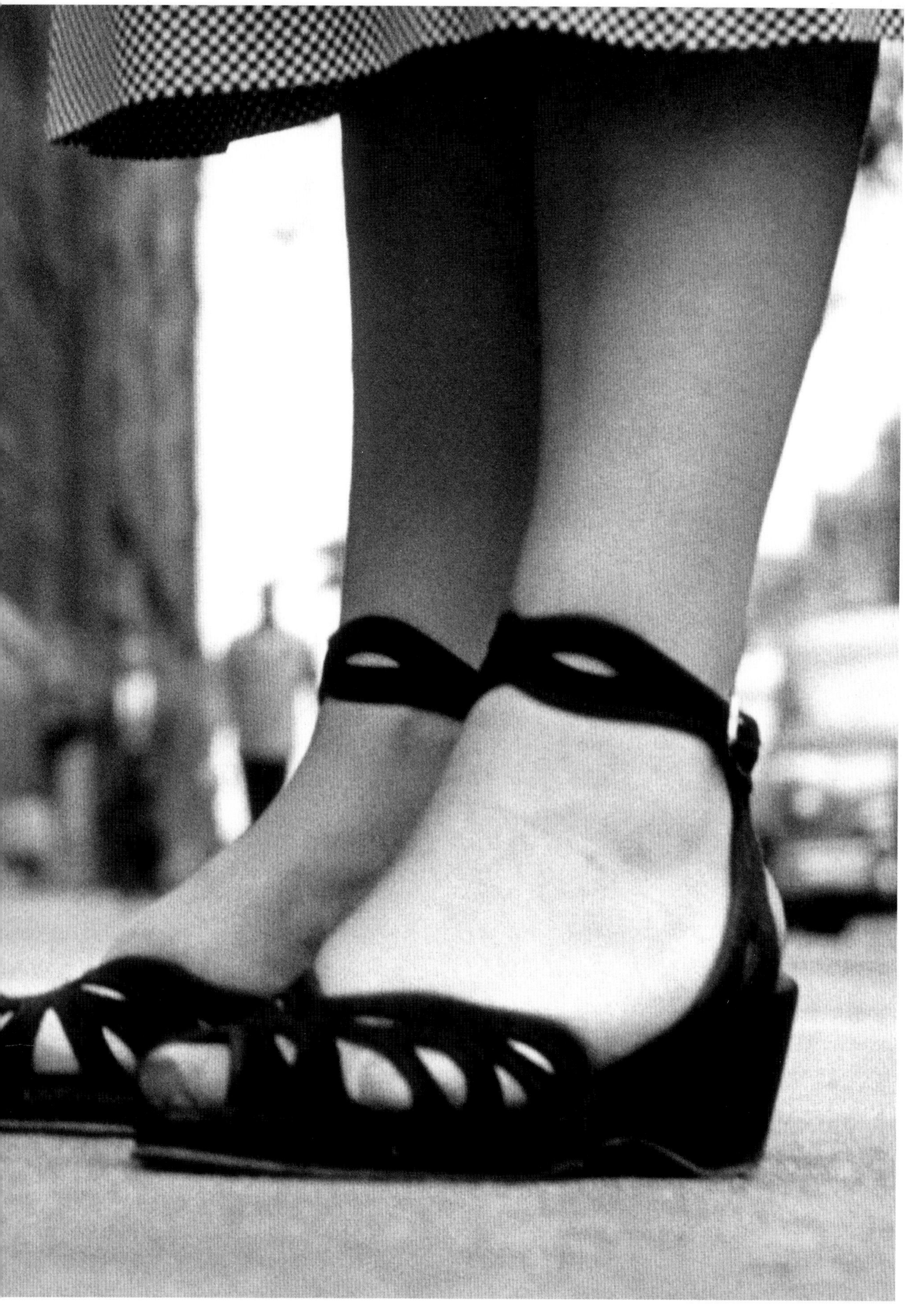

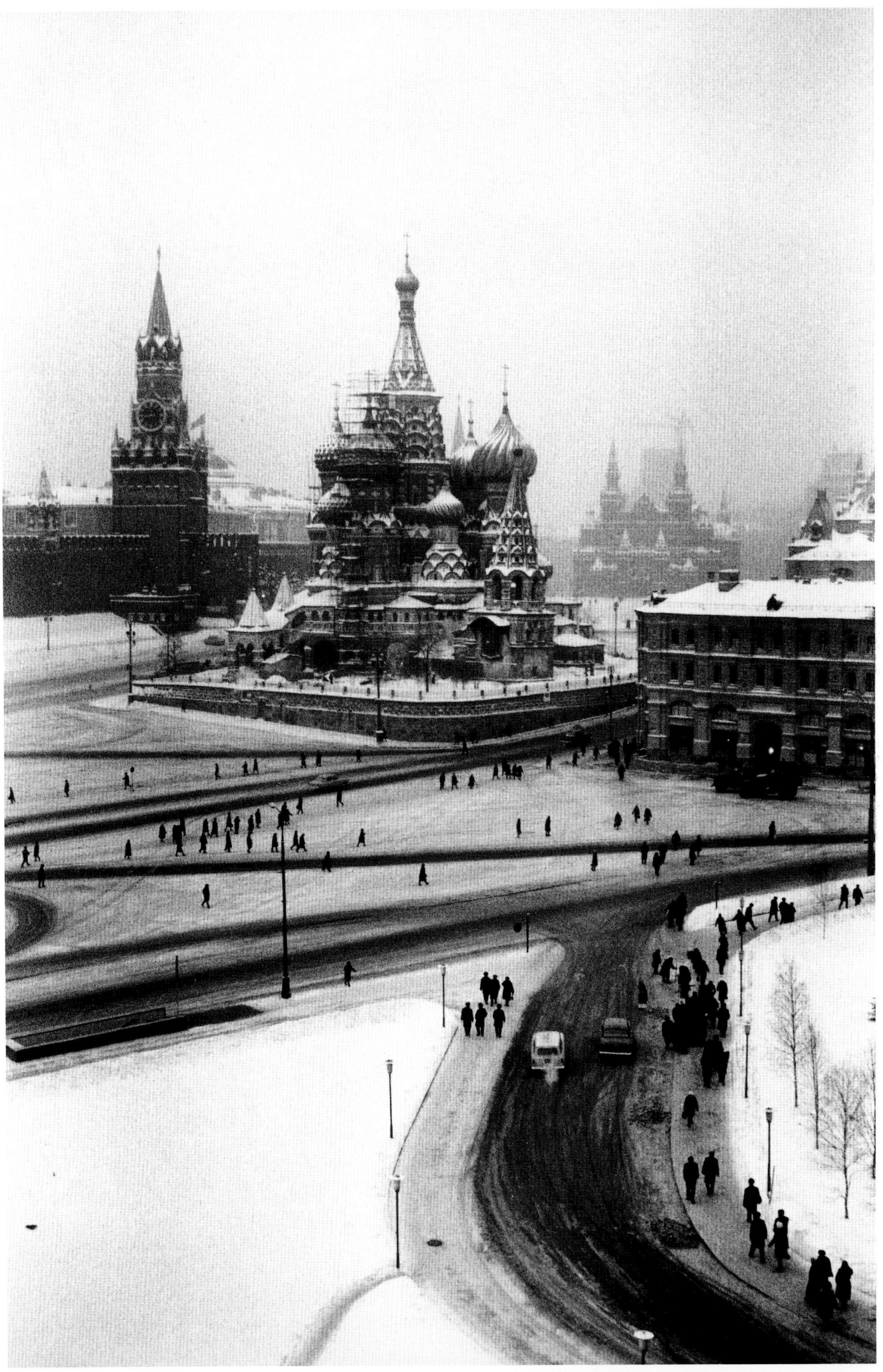

Moscow, 1968

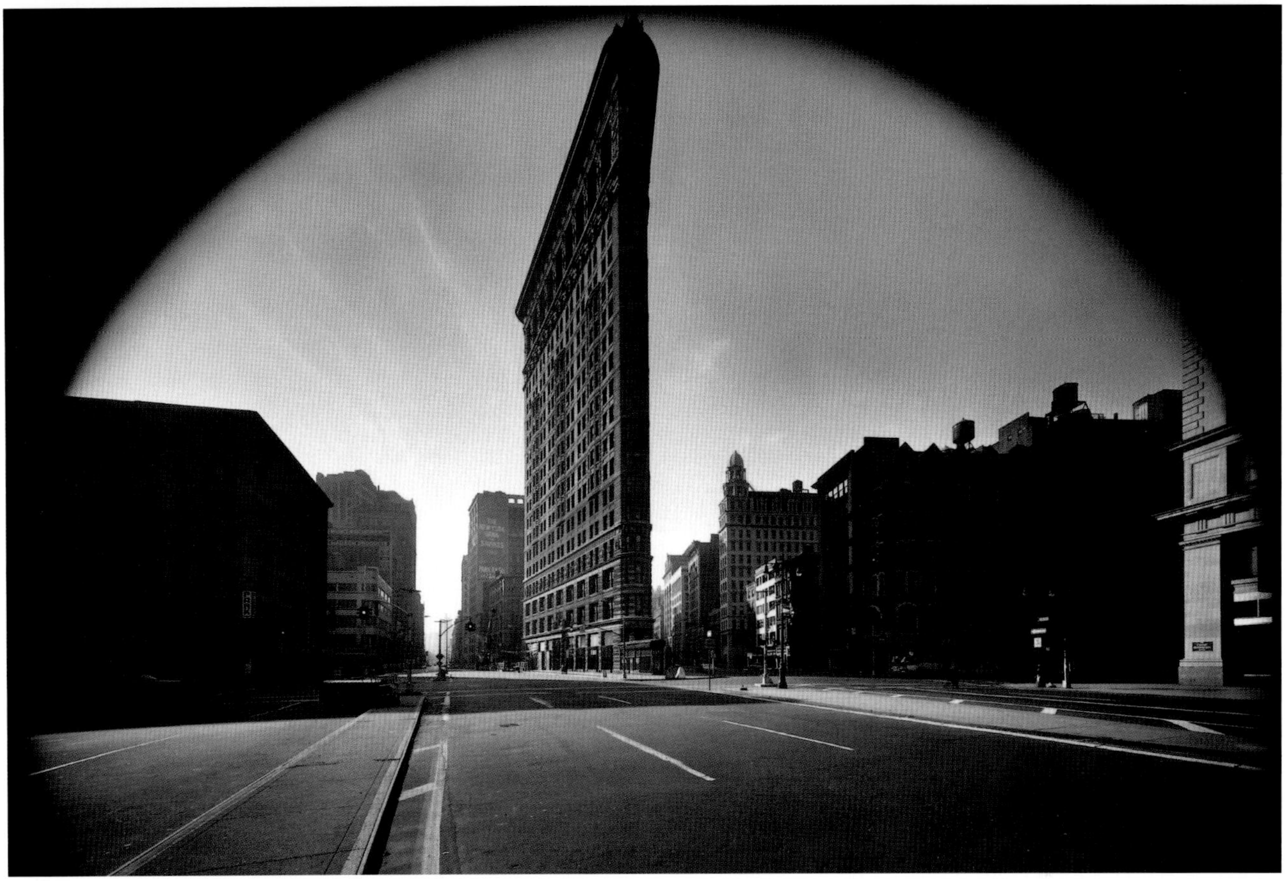

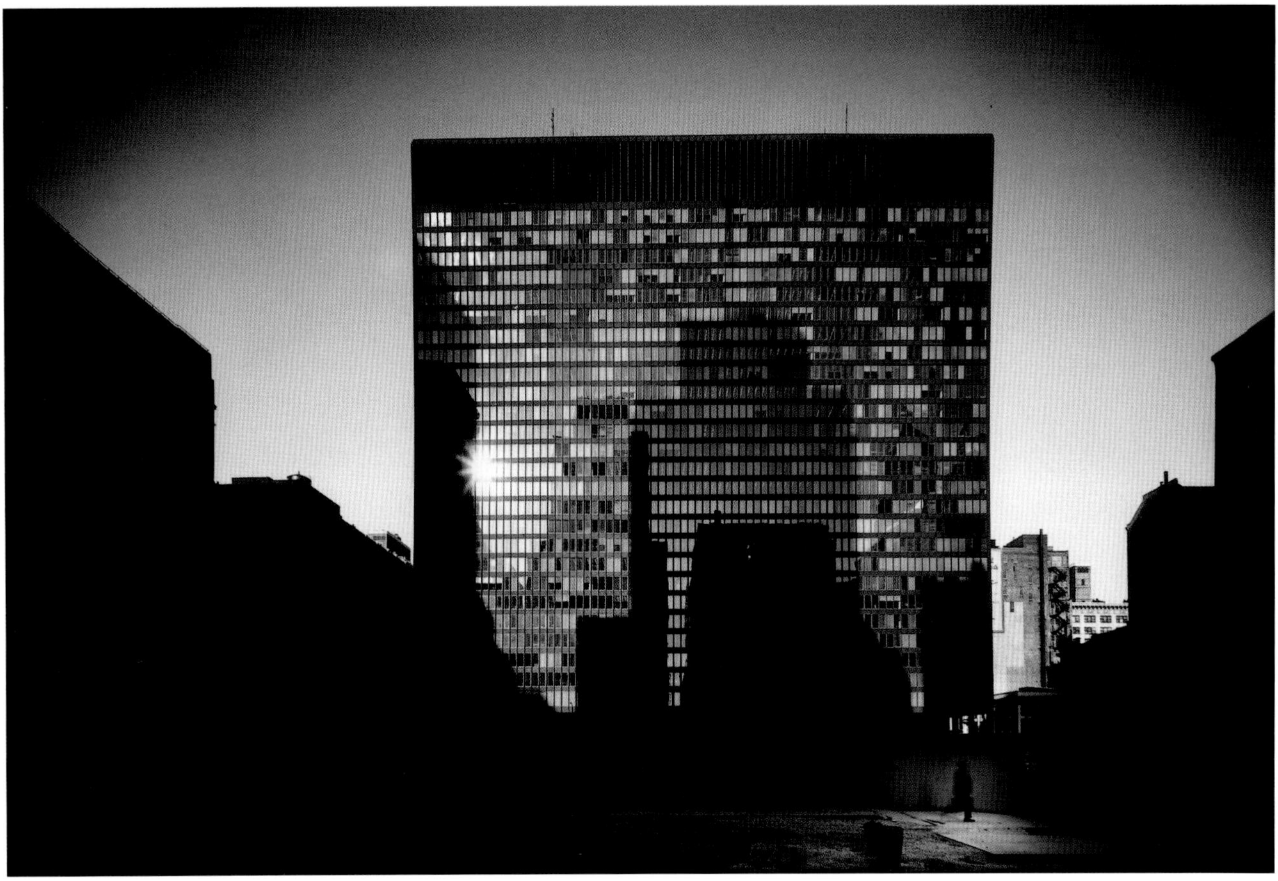

New York, 1969 / *Chicago, 1969*

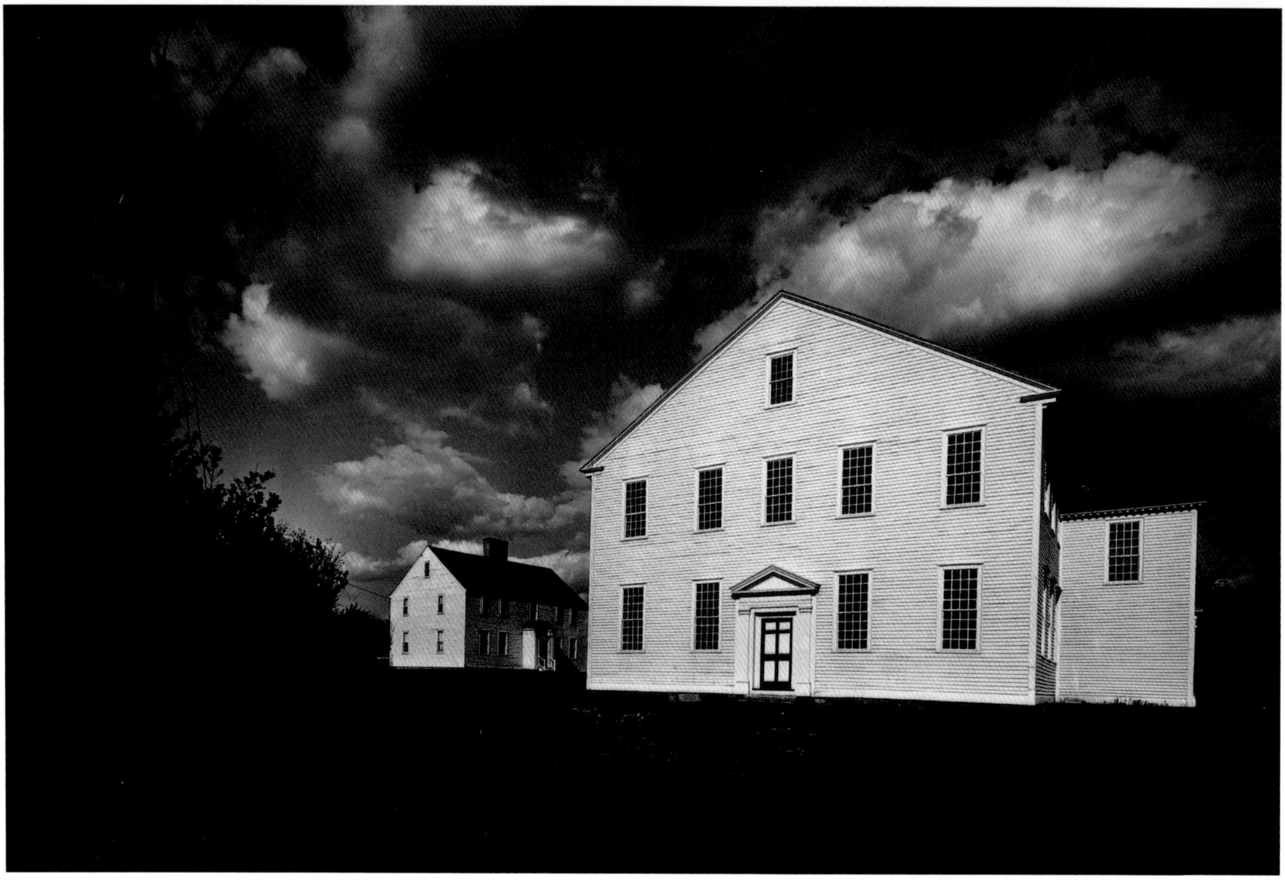

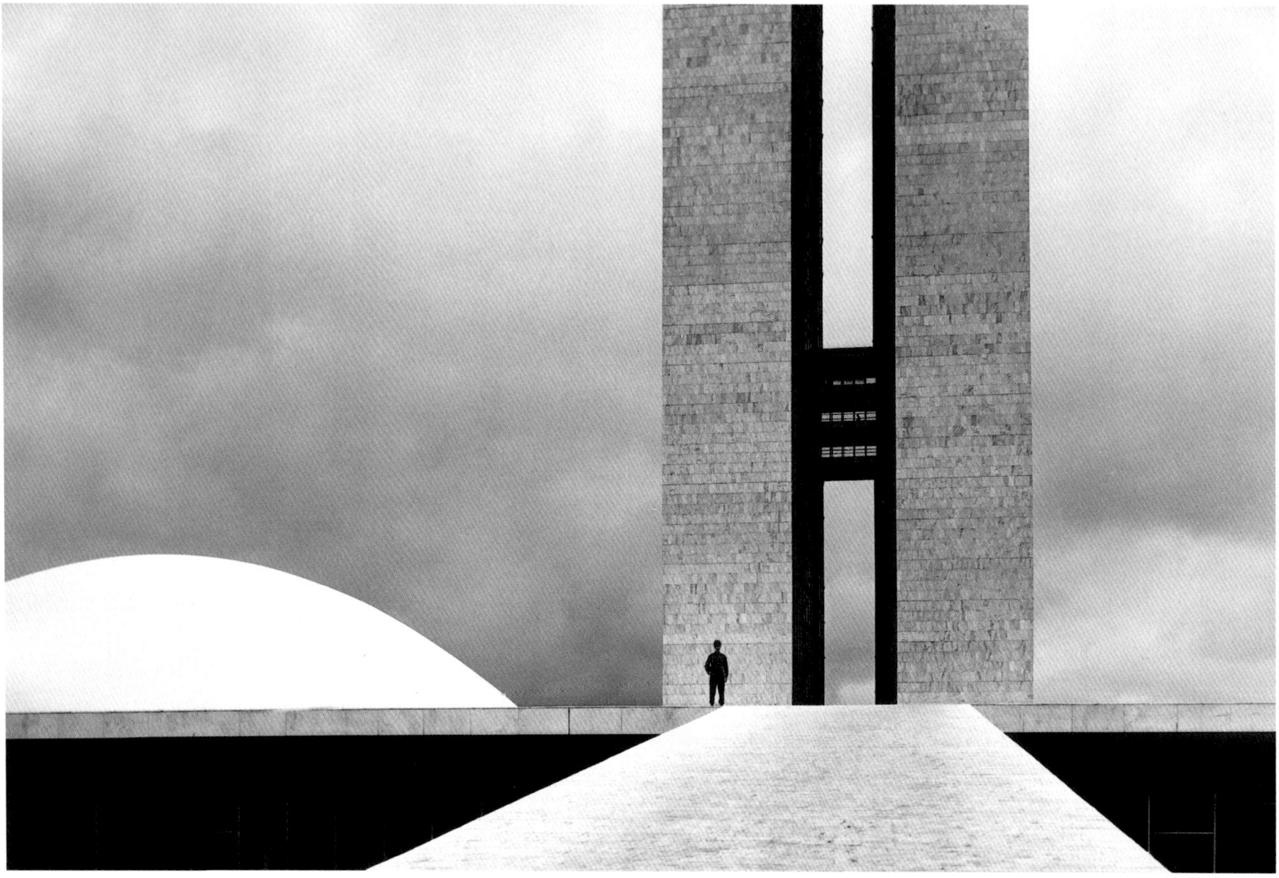

Amesbury, Massachusetts, 1969 / *Brasília, Brazil, 1961*

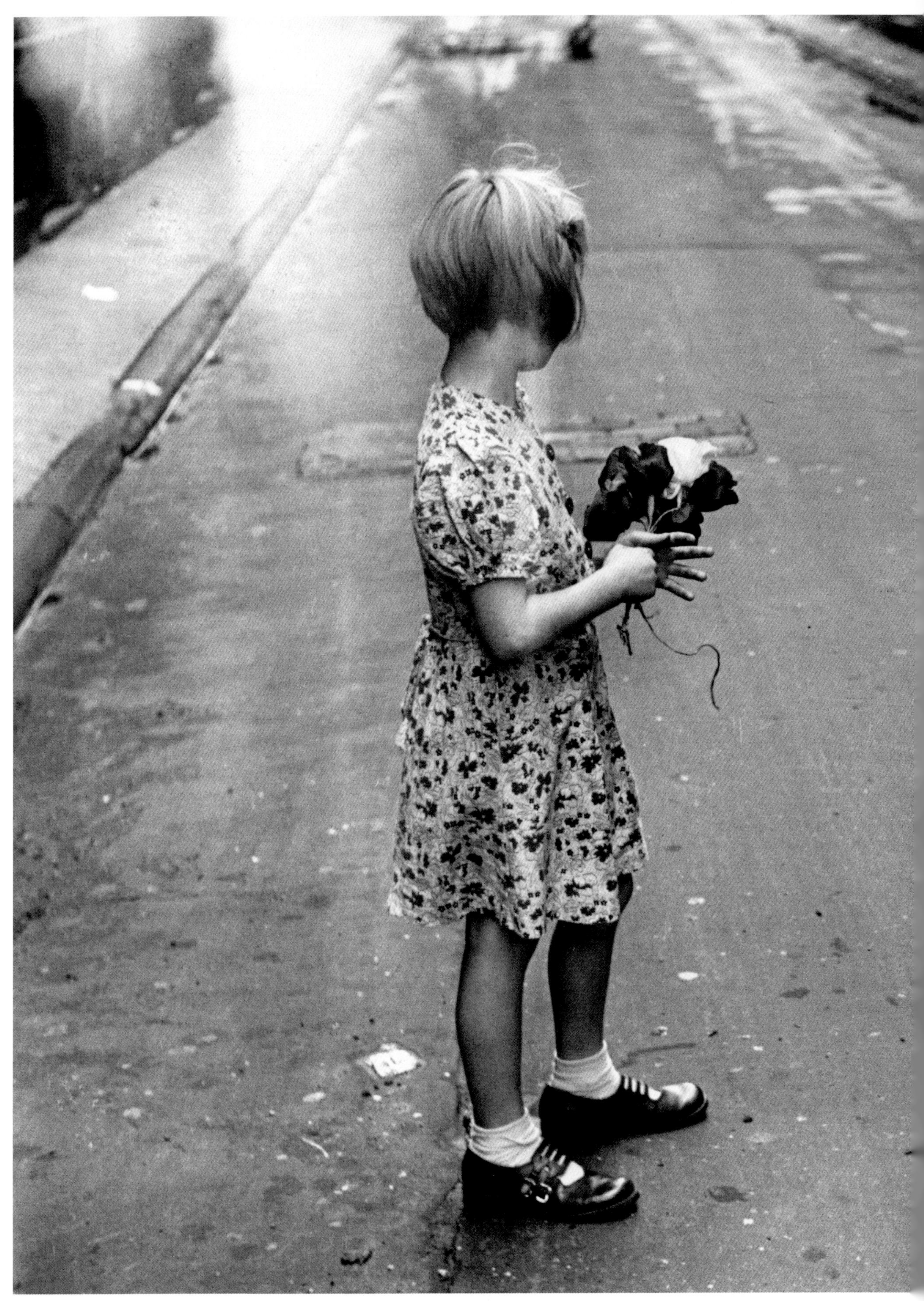

Pittsburgh, Pennsylvania, 1950

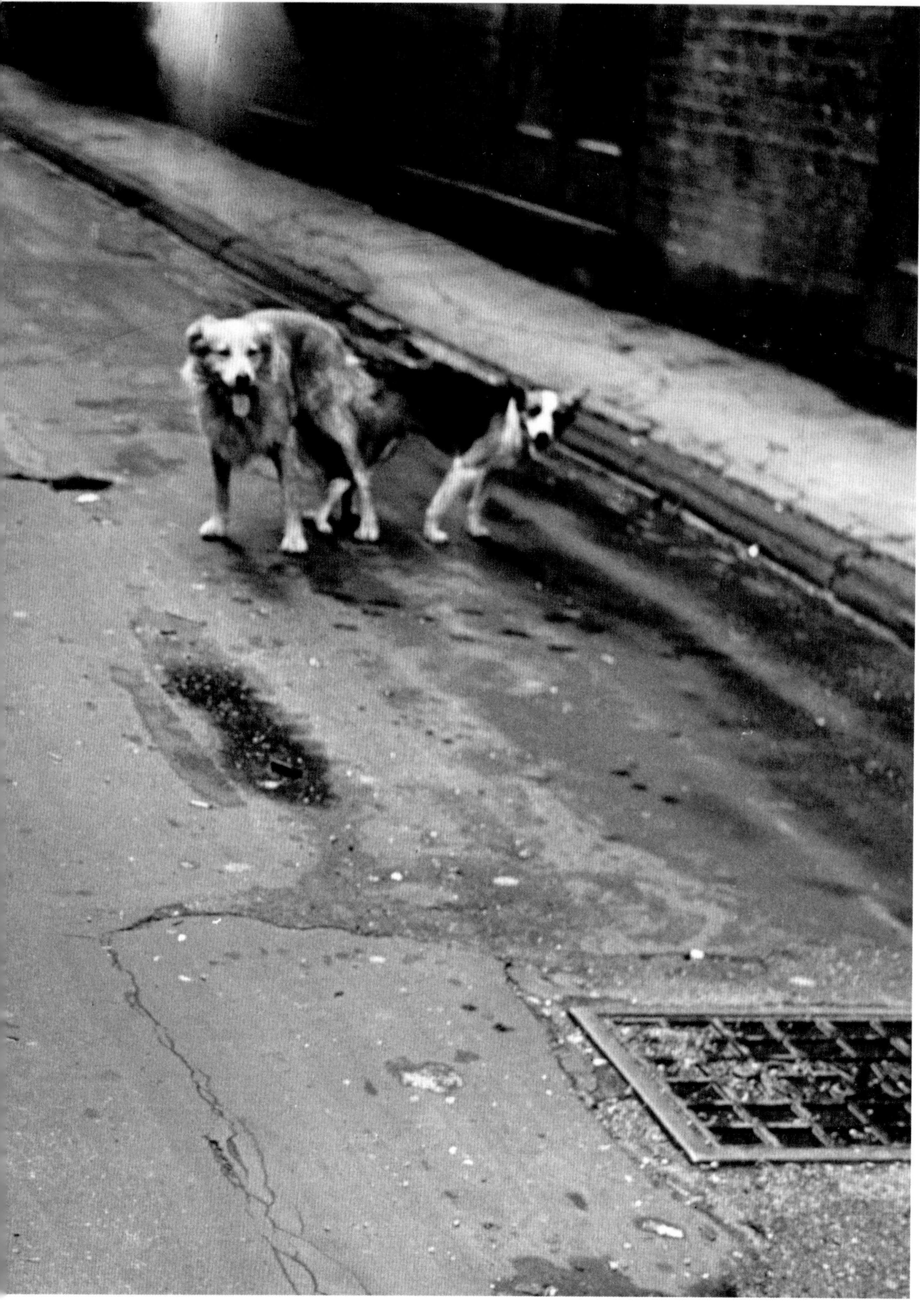

Corning, New York, 1976
overleaf *Corning, New York, 1976*

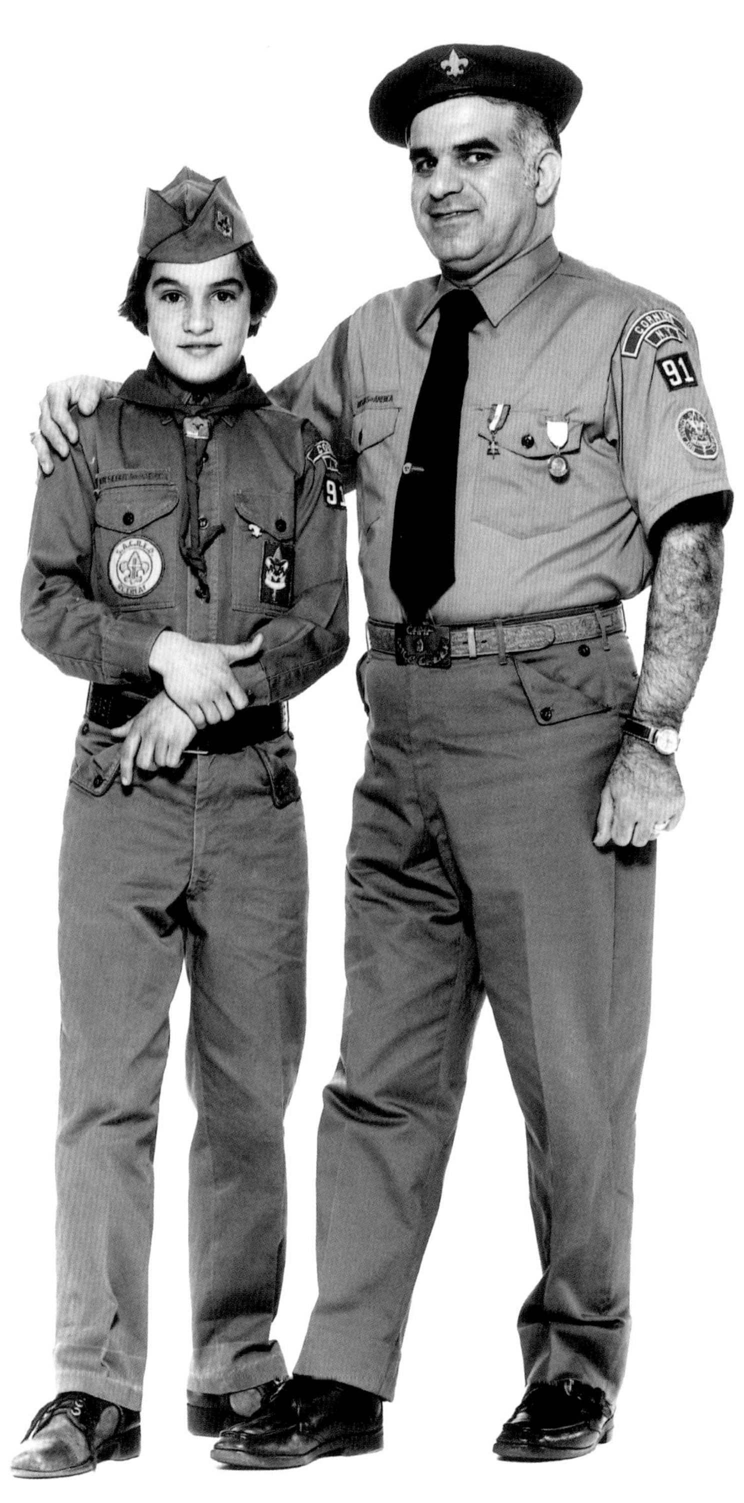
91

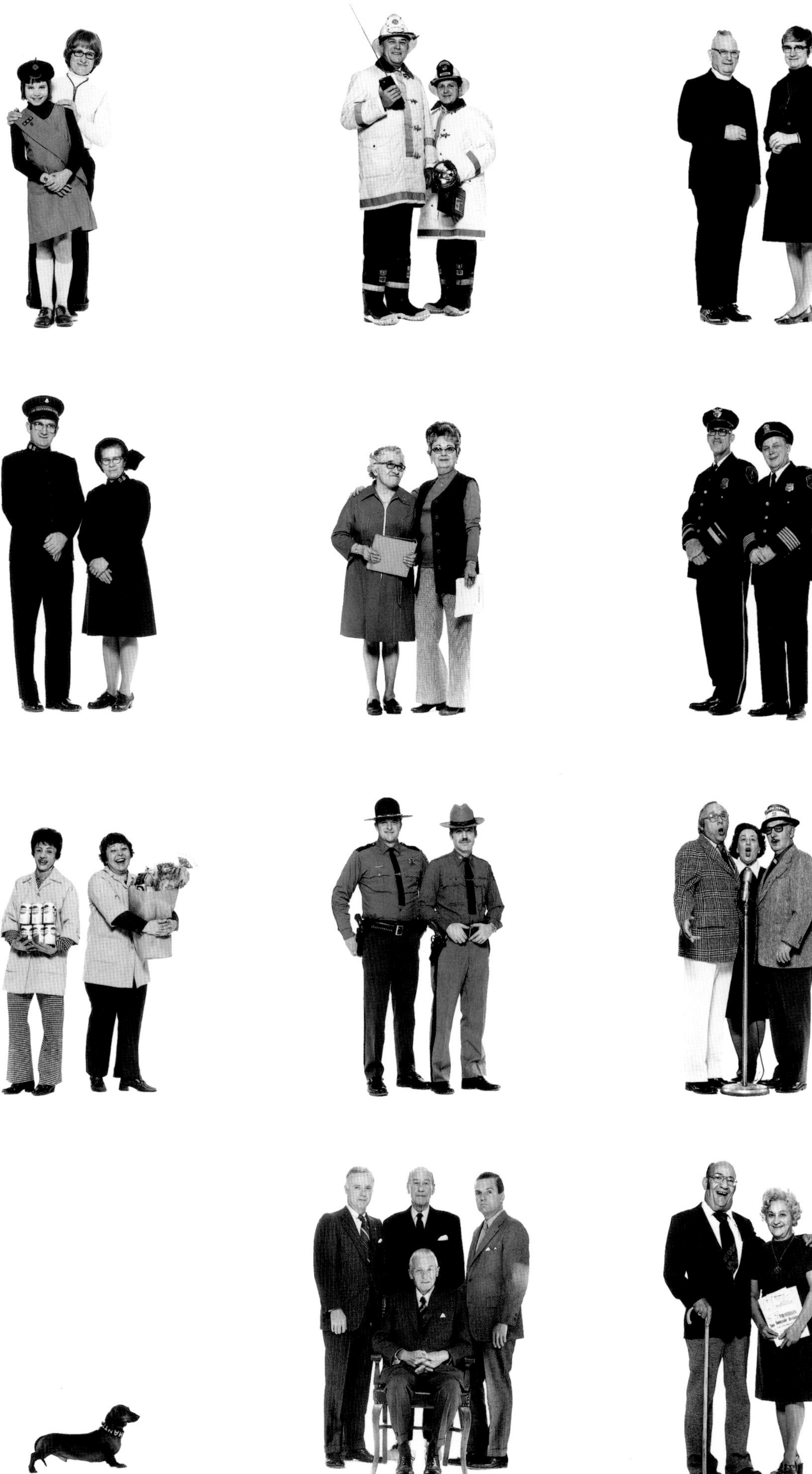

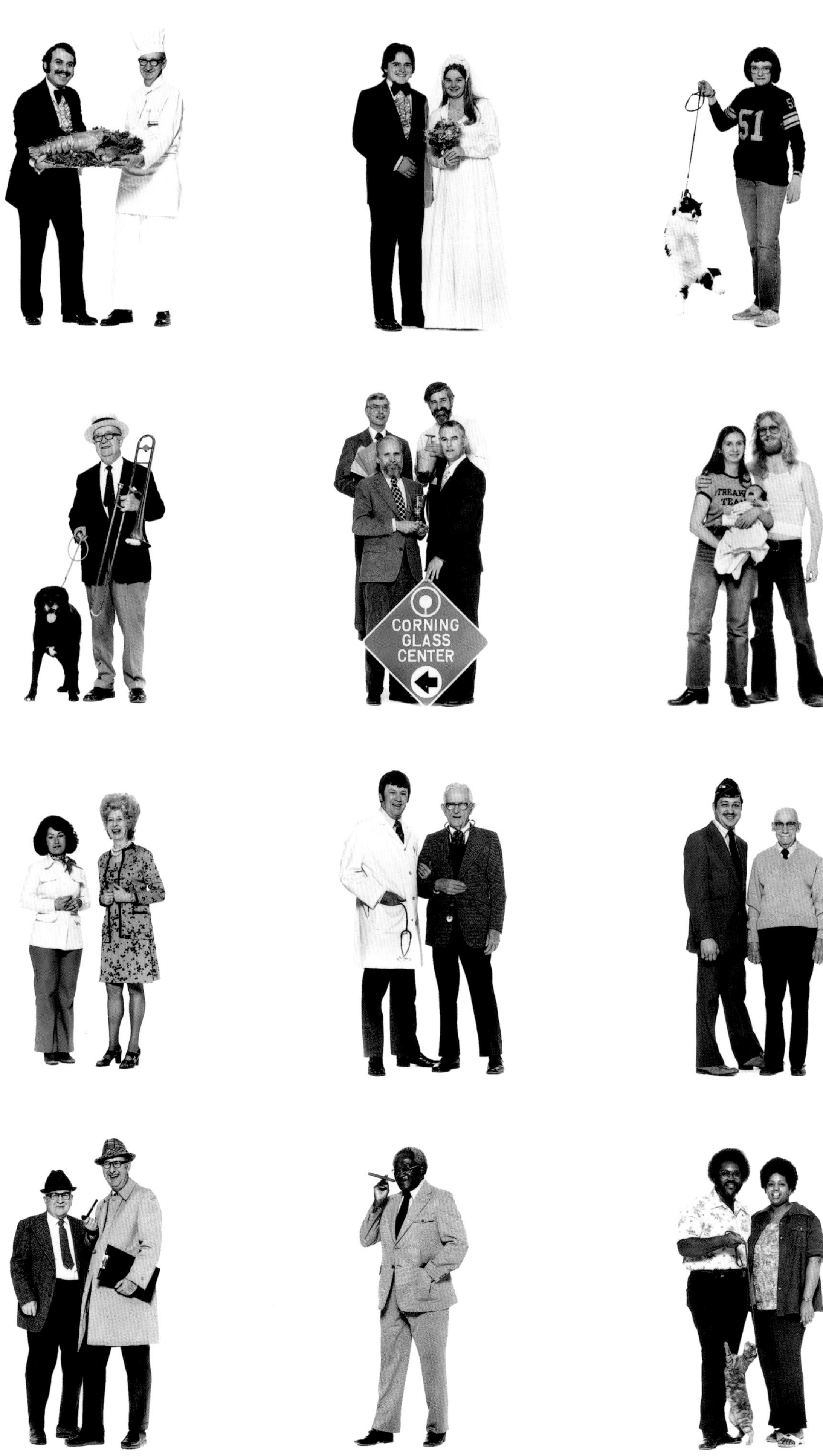
51
CORNING
GLASS
CENTER

Tell

Except for the sporadic bark, the abrupt chorus of geese, perhaps a neigh, the only voices in the telling here are human. Is it the real world, or only Elliott's, that is characterized by telling within genders – women enjoying together a secret or an engagement ring, men smirking or preening or acting as if they know the male secrets of an infinite clan?

As seen here, humans tell not only in words but with glances, by means of gestures and in writing. They tell it all to the world with uniforms, flags, signs and significant gear. Adam's first task in Eden was to name the other animals; his progeny have not shut up since.

According to one contemporary linguist, the average person in the world – no matter what the cultural background, age, economic status, educational level, ethnicity or religion – spends sixty per cent of daily conversation in 'gossip'. This could be an ancient survival strategy, he theorizes; *Homo sapiens* may have lasted our 100,000 years or so because we constantly find out and mull over how others are succeeding, what the prevailing mores and dangers within the tribe might be on any given day. Gossip keeps us one step ahead.

If there is any truth to that, it makes all the more sense that women tend to gossip with women, men with men. We are separate battalions; when we pair off, we are wise to keep our supply lines open.

In the matter of women, Elliott is as distinctive in his snaps as in much else. As a successful commercial photographer, he has lensed, as they say, many a comely lass, scantily or not at all clad, on tropical beaches while the rest of us hunker down in blizzards. (It is very difficult to like him in mid-February.)

Once when we were lunching at a rather dreary 'exclusive' club on 43rd Street in Manhattan, such a woman strode across the room to our table, shouting for all the ageing preppies to hear, 'It's Elliott Erwitt, the world's best man!'

He did not blush.

Elliott's appeal to that other sex will have to be explained by the many women who have reported it, but it must have something to do with the wit, honesty and respect that he shows the female and her form in his snaps. There is much gentle ribbing of the body, the overdone make-up, trendy fashions and awkward poses, but there is never exploitation or carnality.

Elliott's women are people. And the interplay with overweening or bug-eyed men in some photos is never a fair contest; the men are always more clueless than the women.

There are some very well-constructed ladies scattered throughout *Snaps*, but not one of these shots would survive an editorial meeting at *Maxim* or *Playboy*. Nude or topless and lathered in suntan oil, scampering in the surf or dancing in a nightclub, Elliott's women are not seen smouldering with lust or promising ecstasy. They laugh, skip, flirt, saunter. They are seizing the day. There's not a victim among them.

And they are stronger even than institutions. On p.256, a priest of Mother Church listens gravely at the left to a presumed penitent's confession. This is serious business. But to the right, where one woman gossips cheerfully with another, is a glimpse of the real telling of life. It is her story we want to hear.

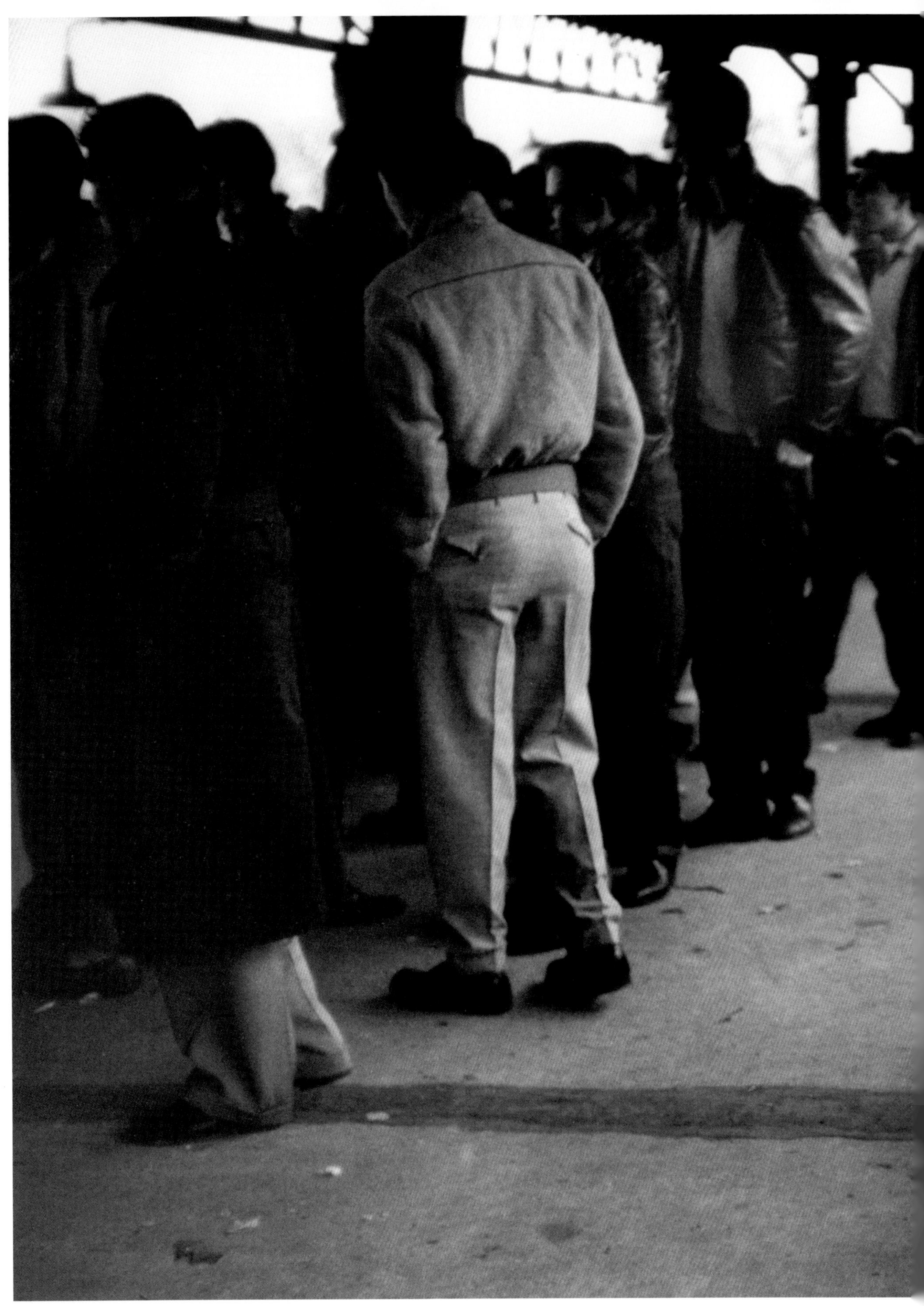

USA, 1956

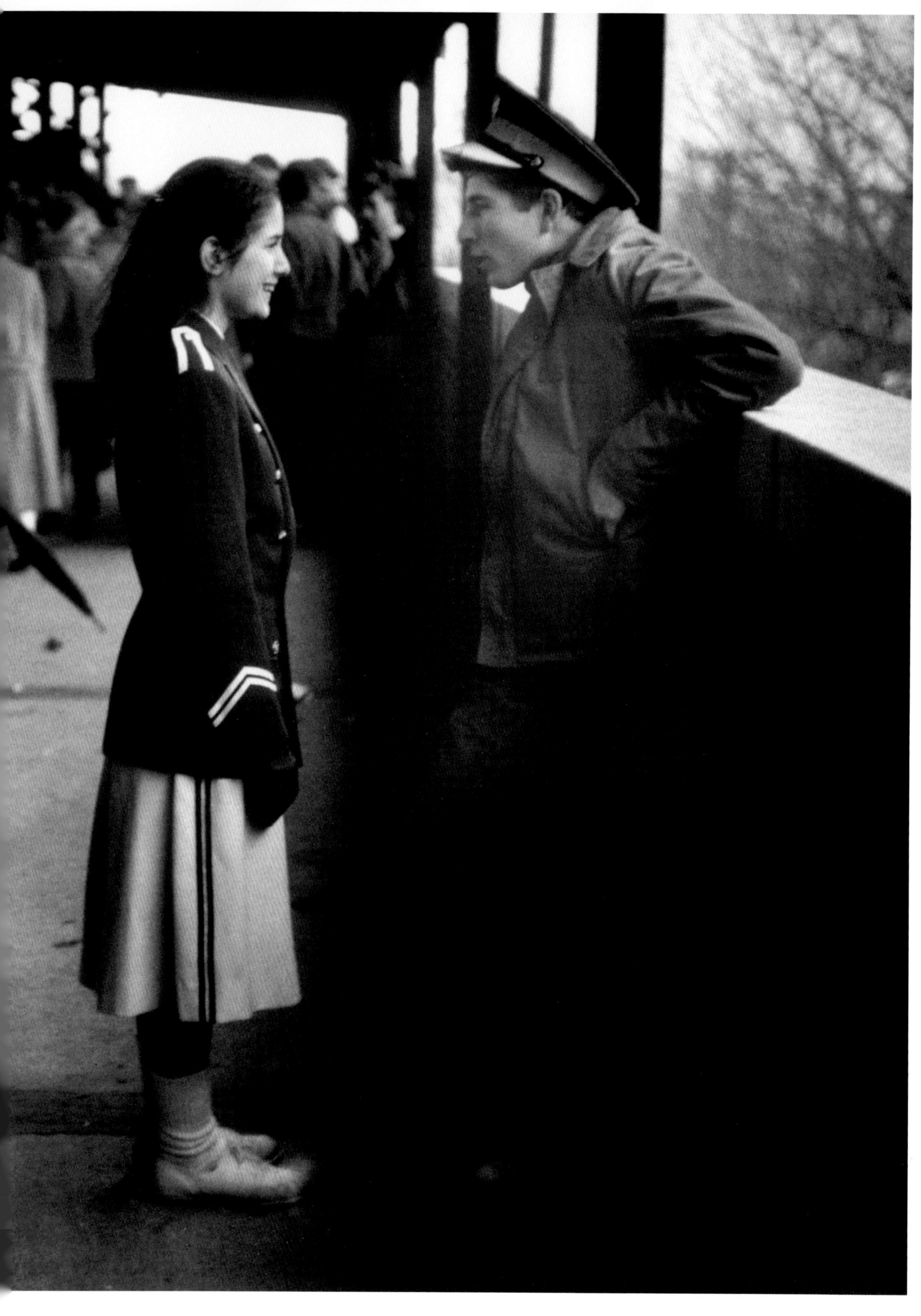

overleaf *New York, 1955* / *Kent, England, 1984*

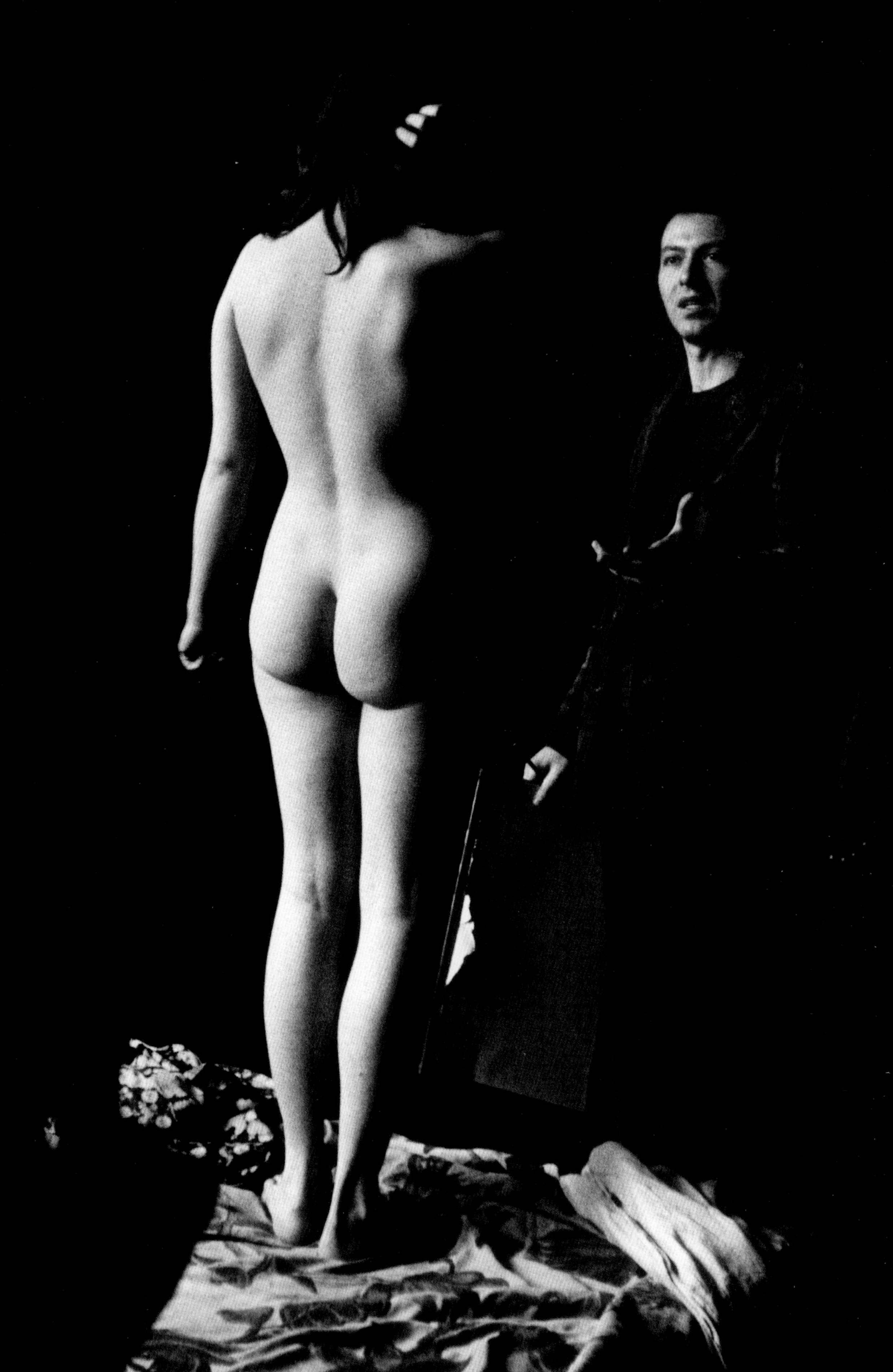

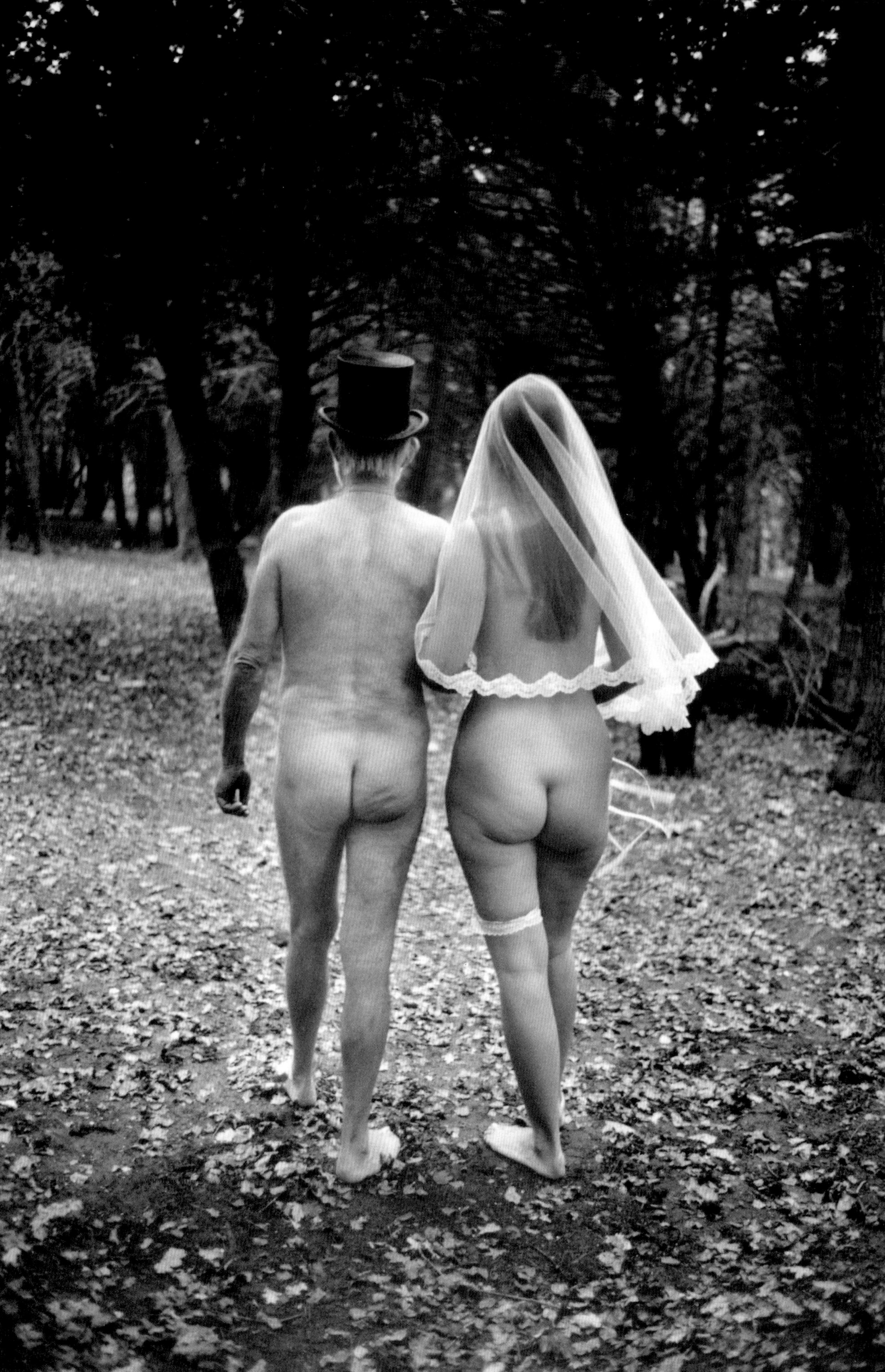

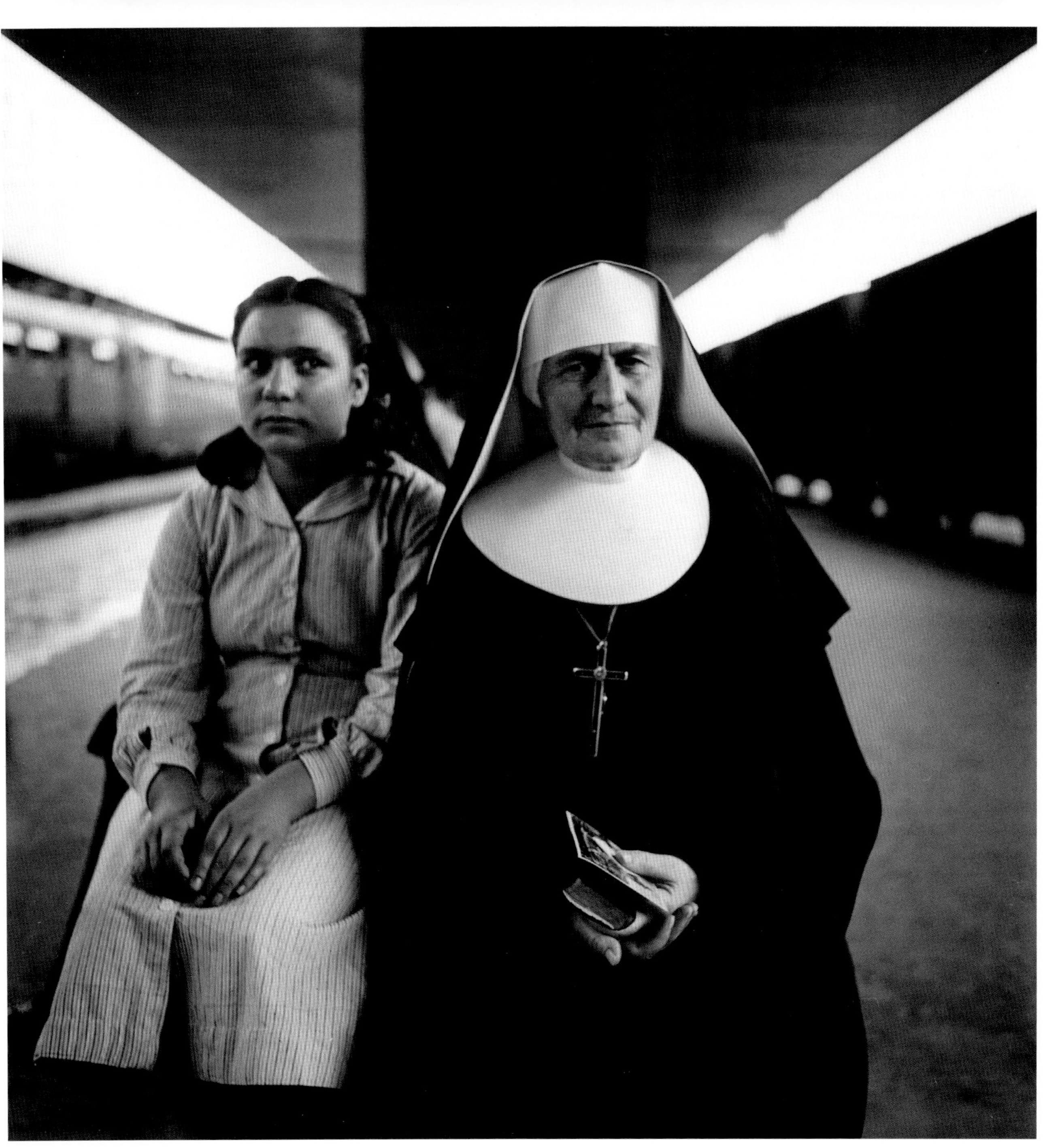

Florence, 1949

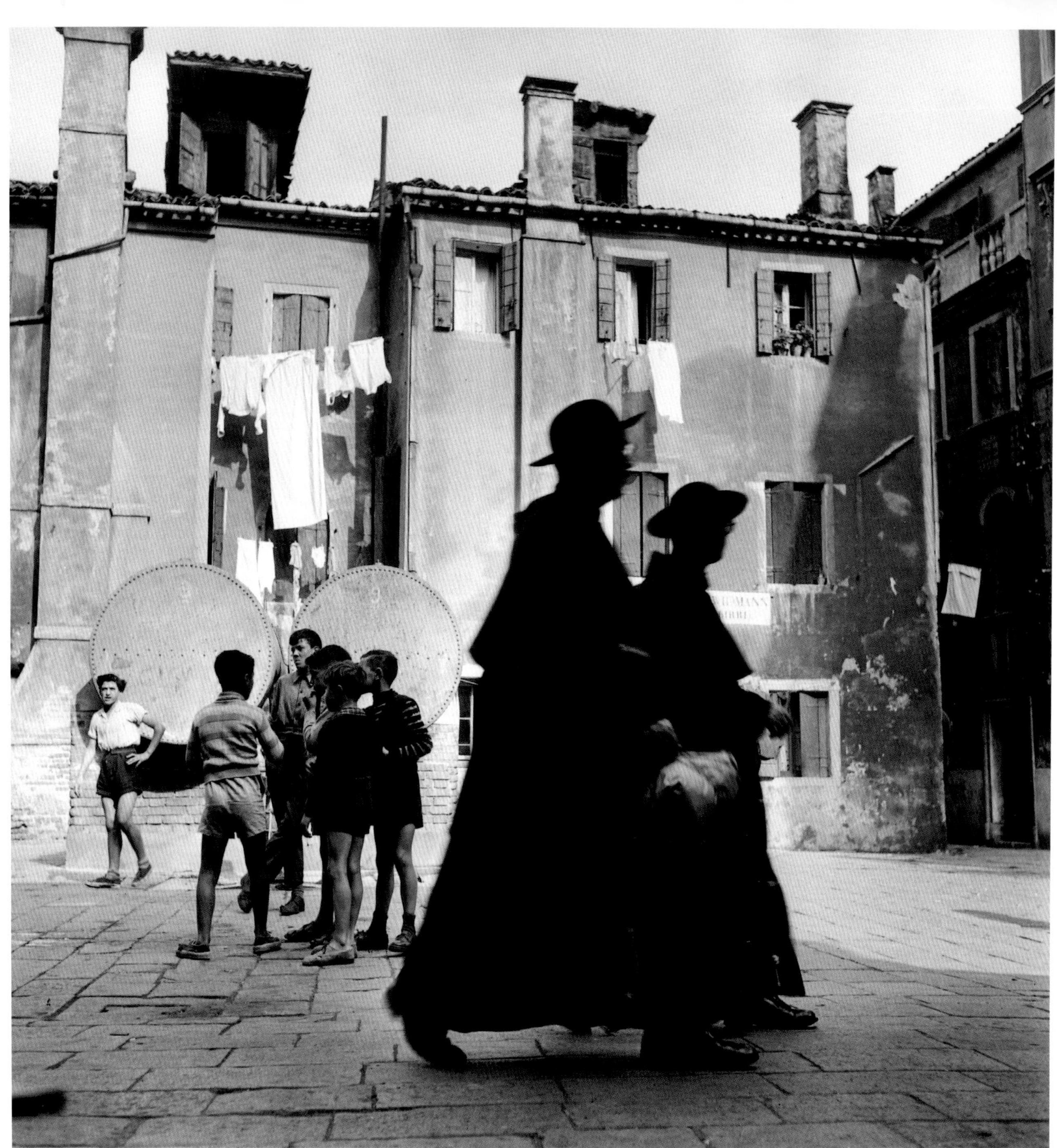

Venice, 1949

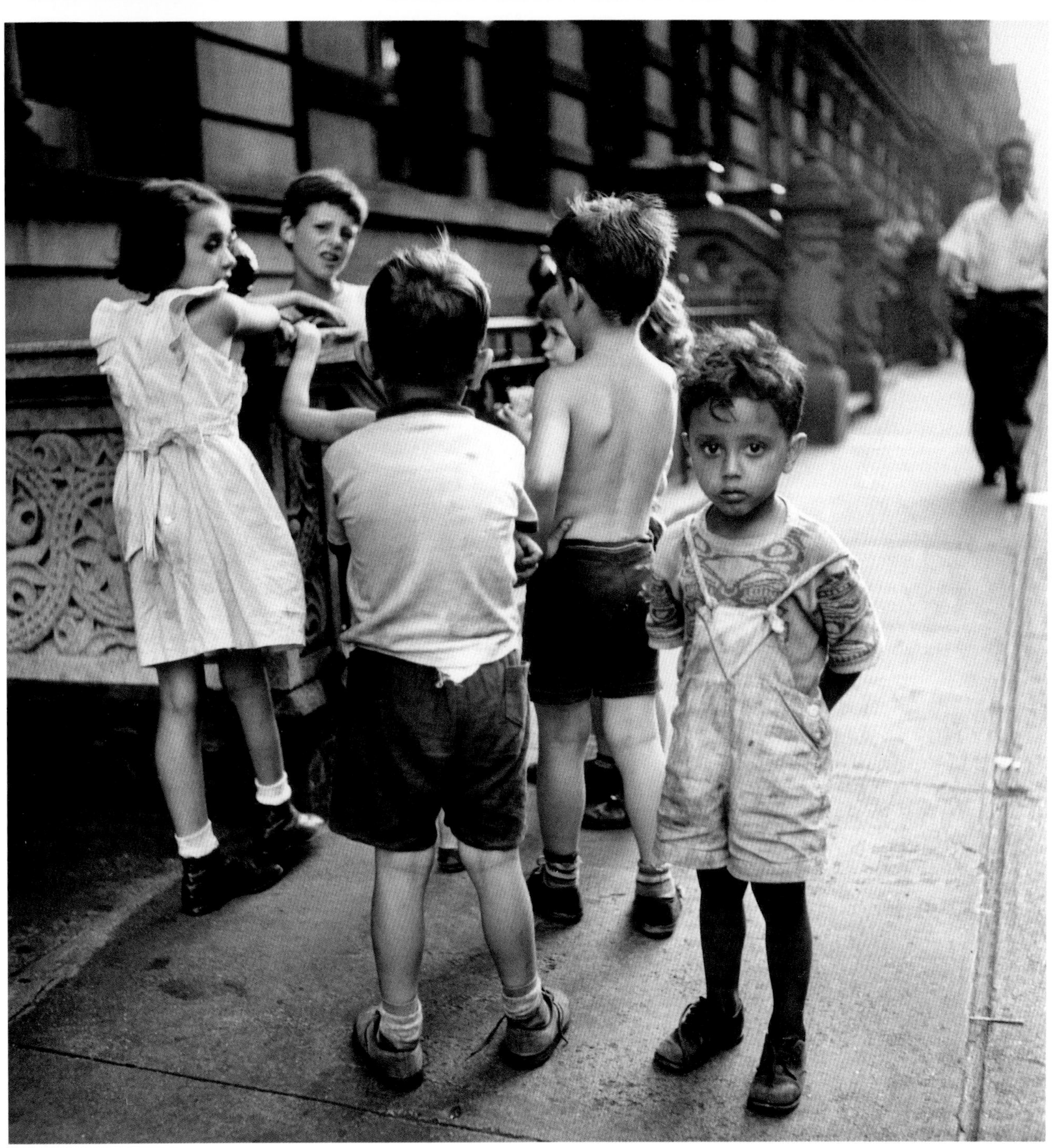

New York, 1946

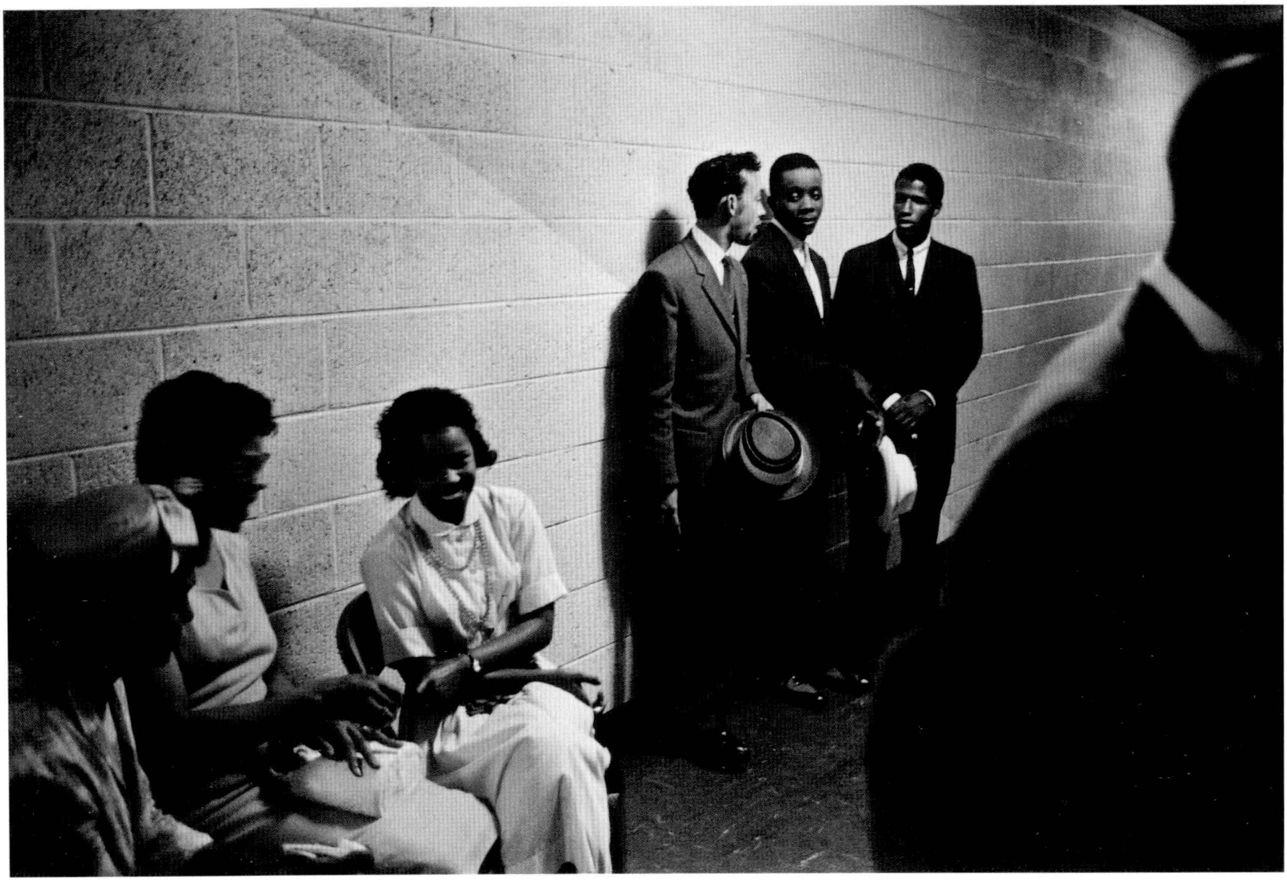

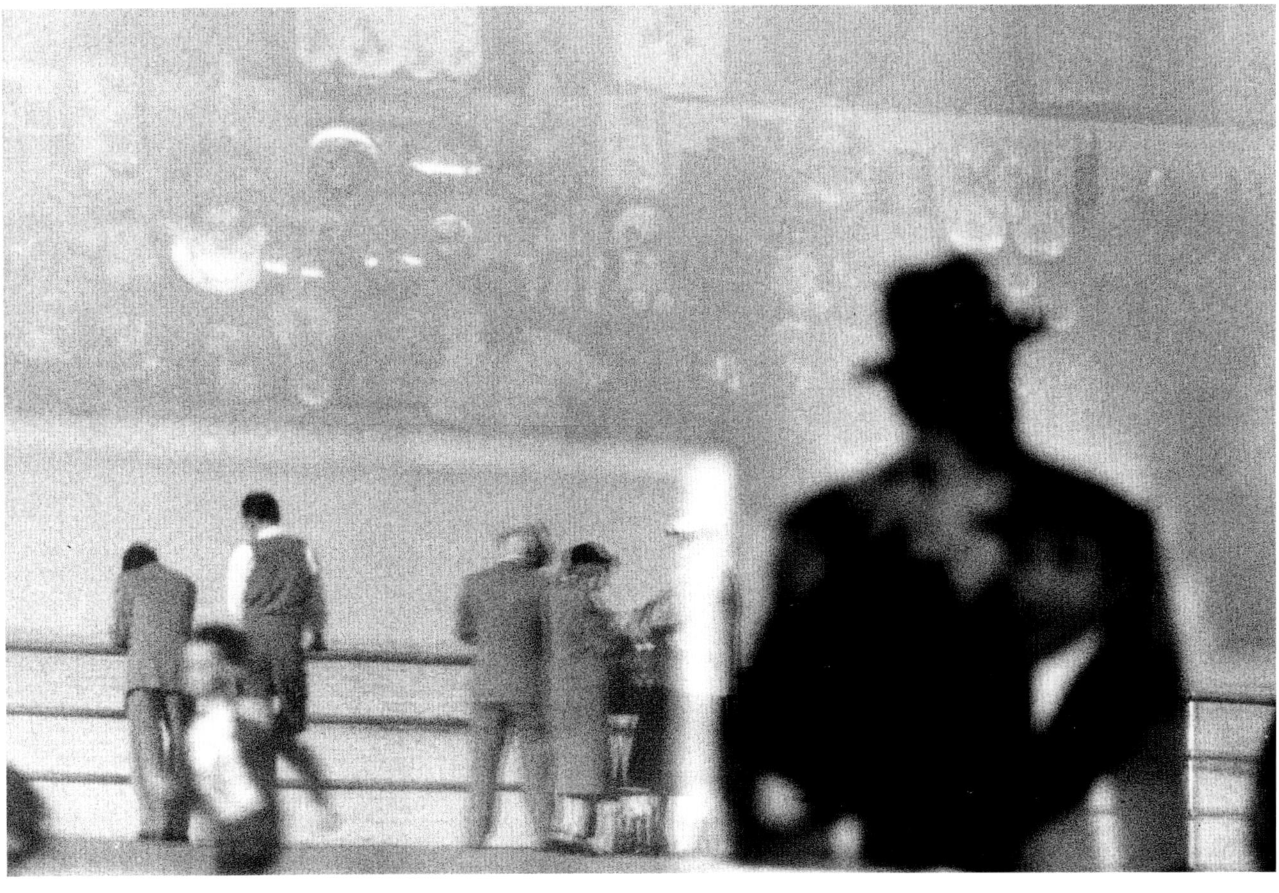

Detroit, 1959 / *New York, 1954*

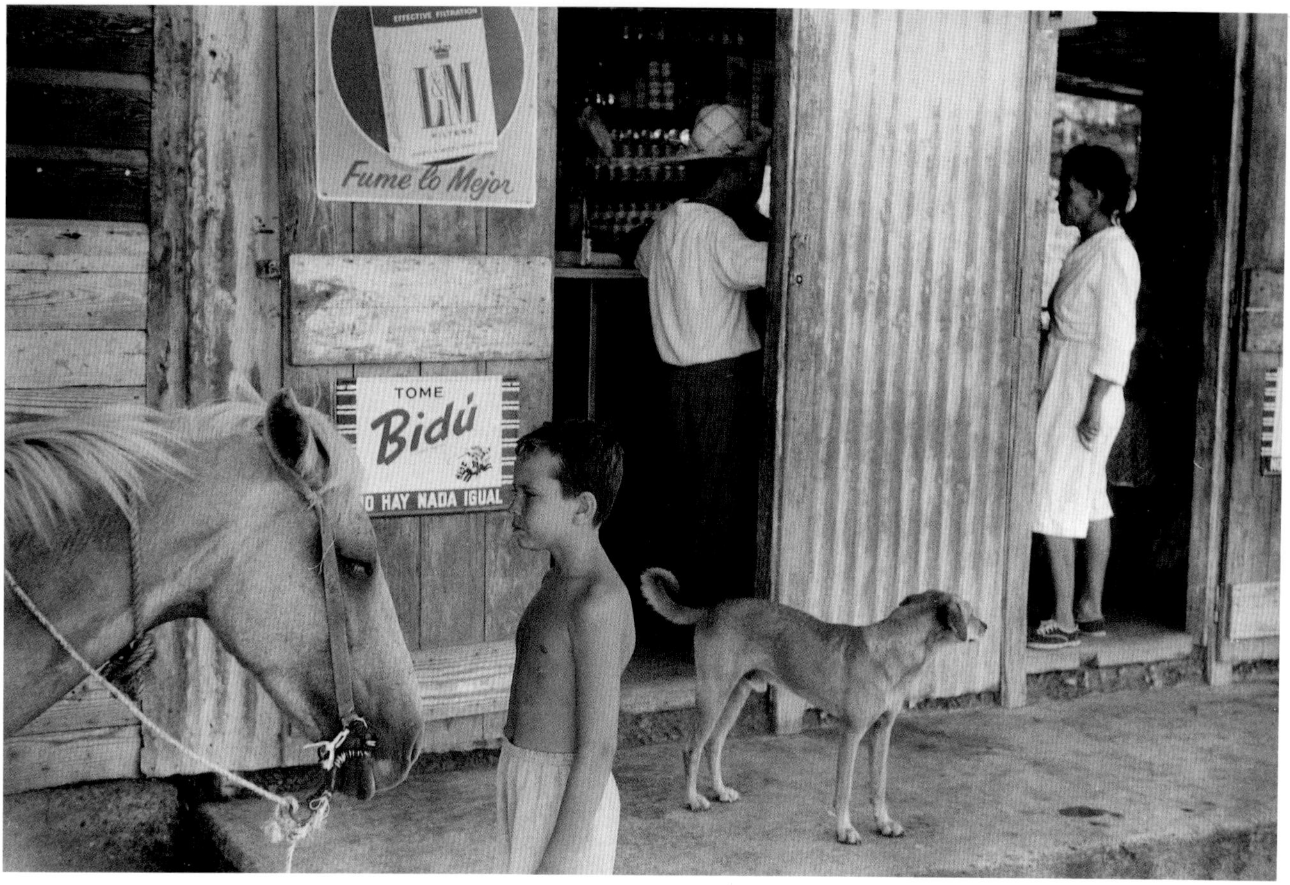

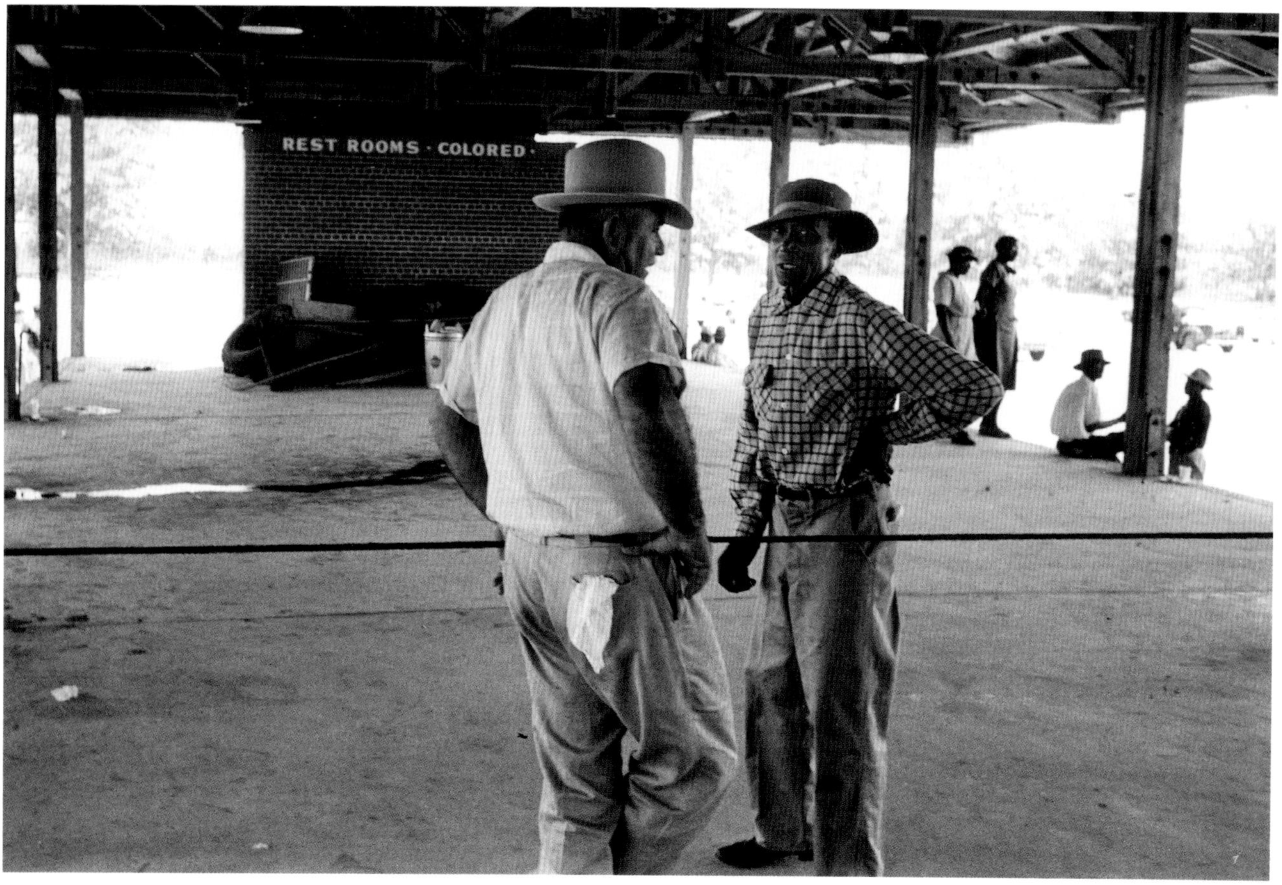

Puerto Rico, 1957 / *Georgia, USA, 1954*

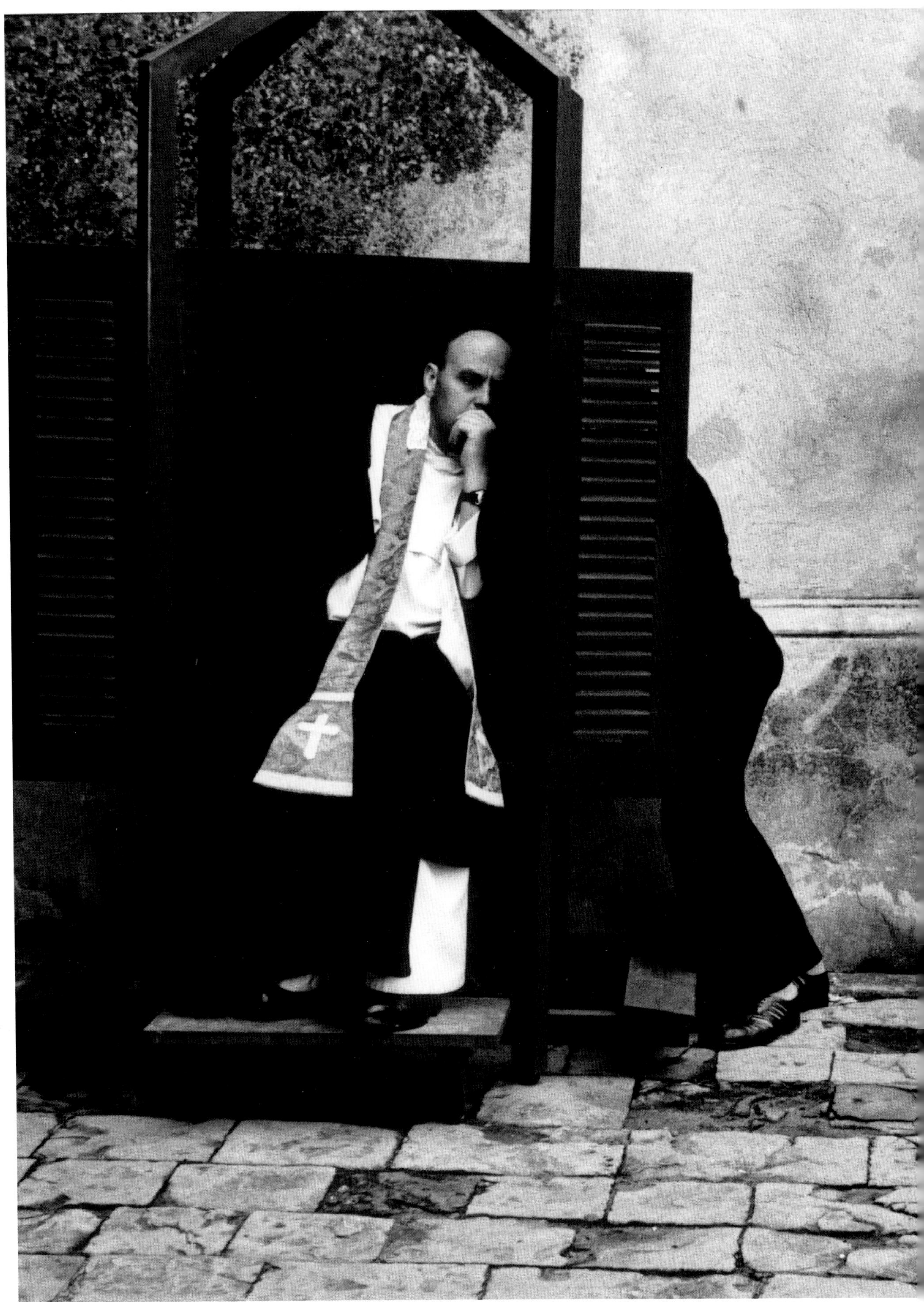

Czestochowa, Poland, 1964

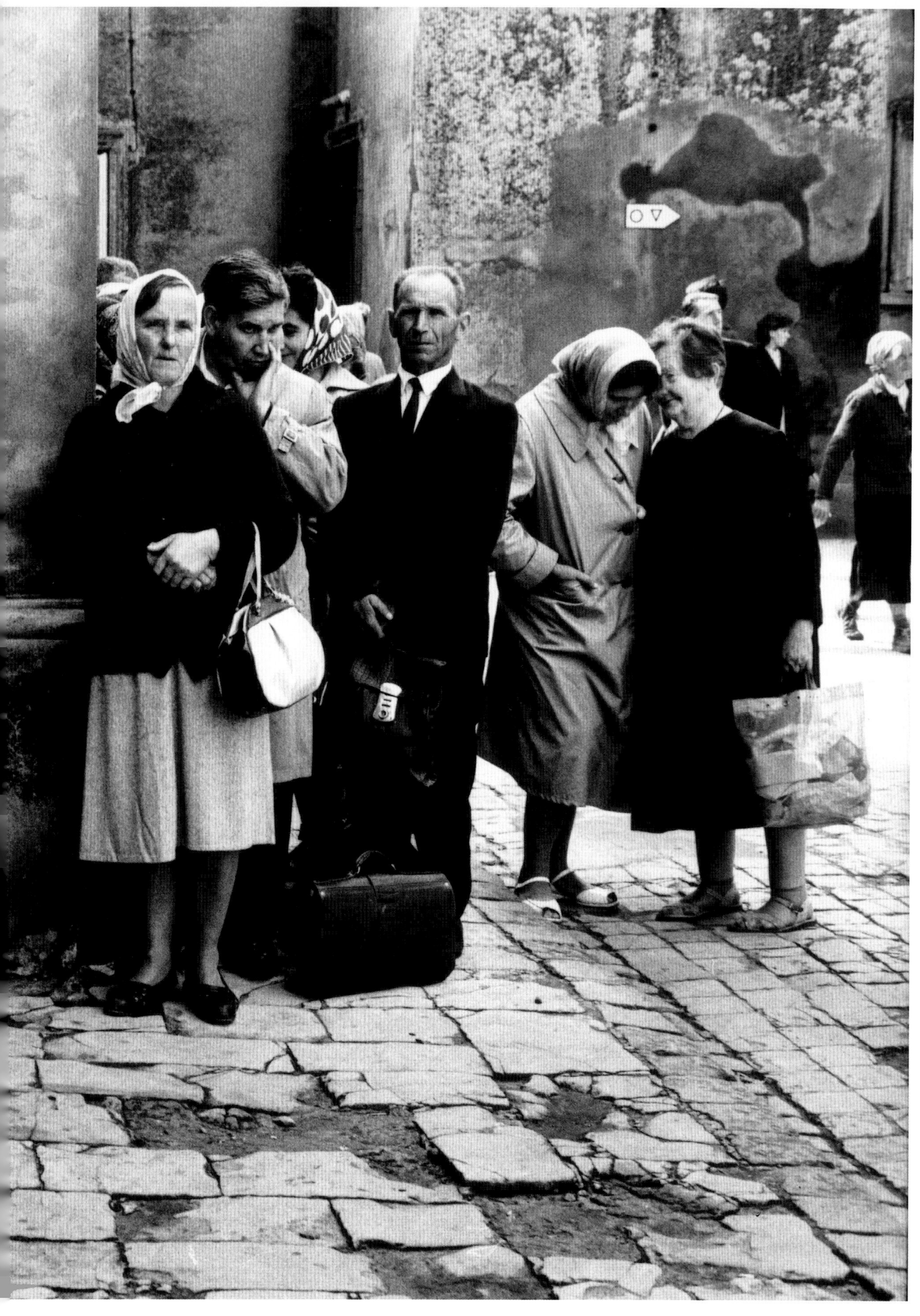

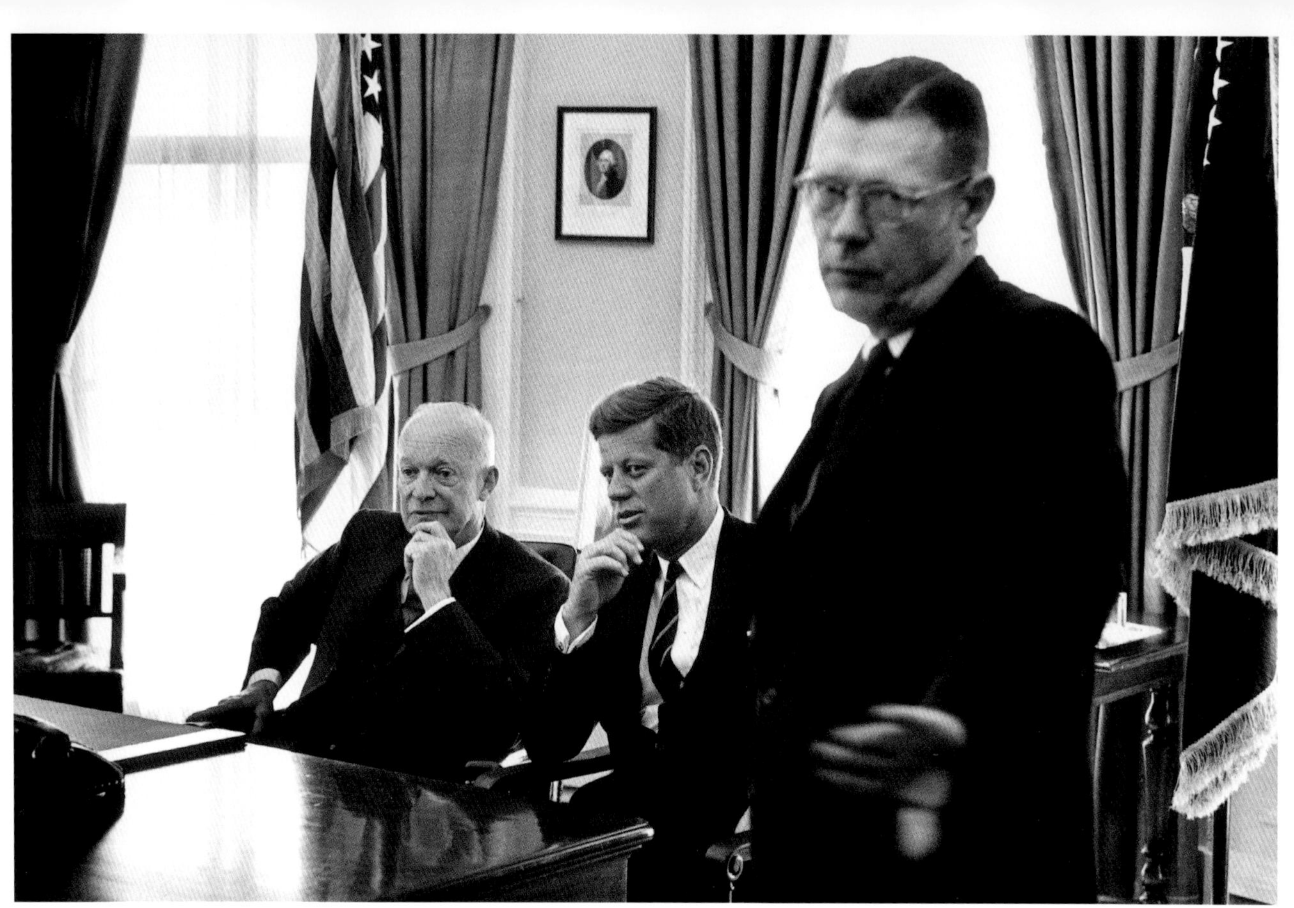

Dwight D. Eisenhower, John F. Kennedy and Jim Hagerty, Washington, DC, 1960
overleaf *Nevada, 1954* / *Wyoming, 1954*

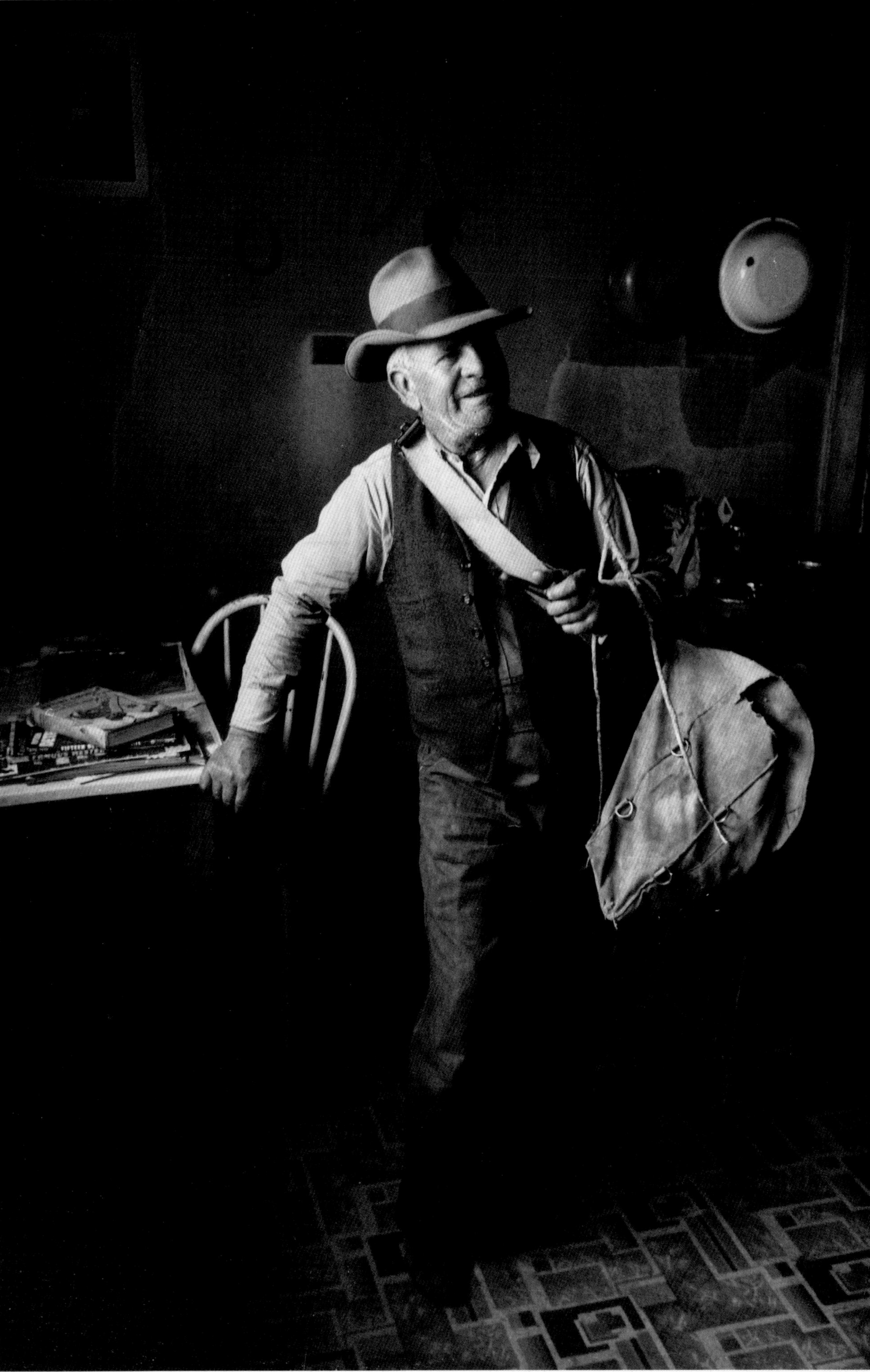

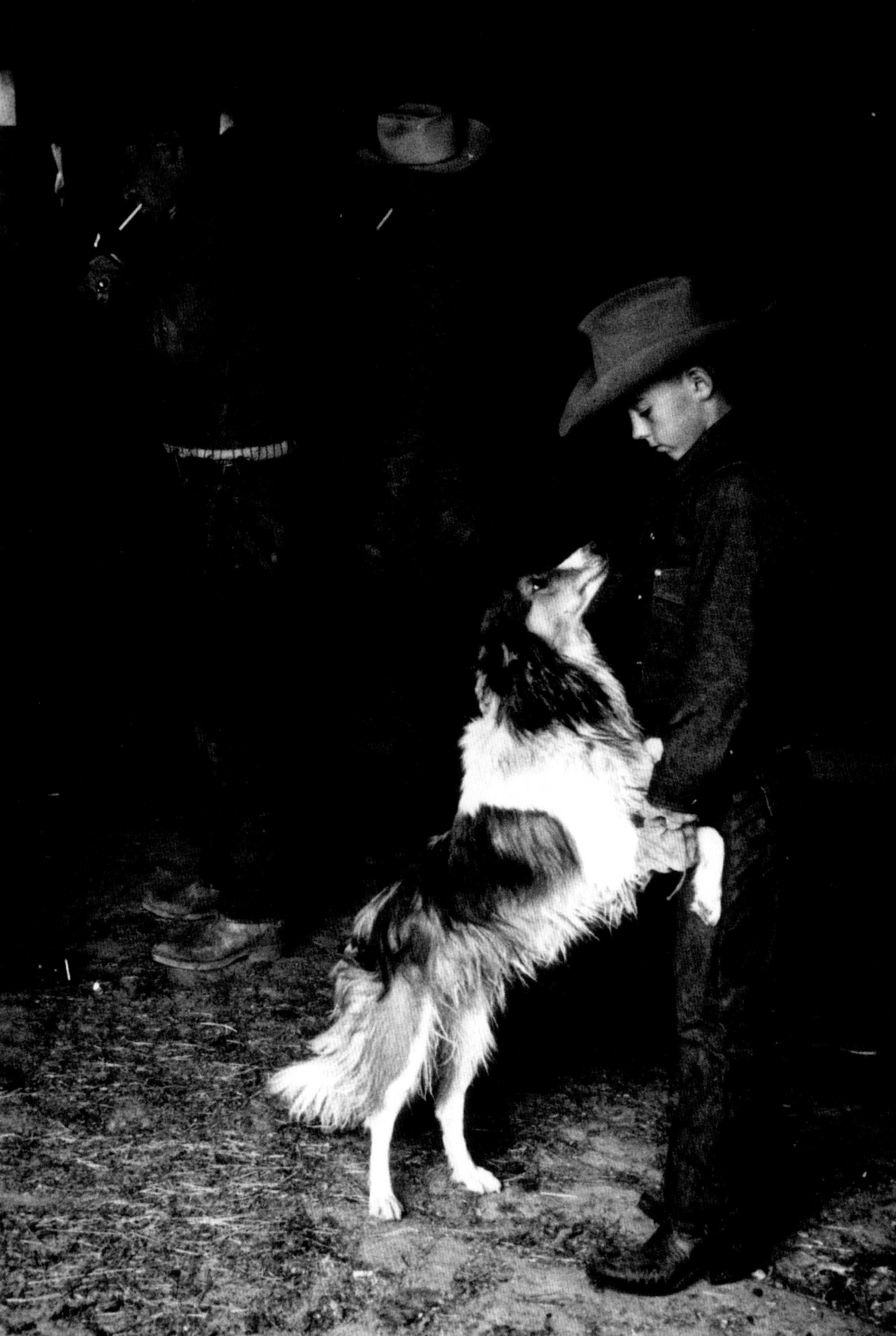

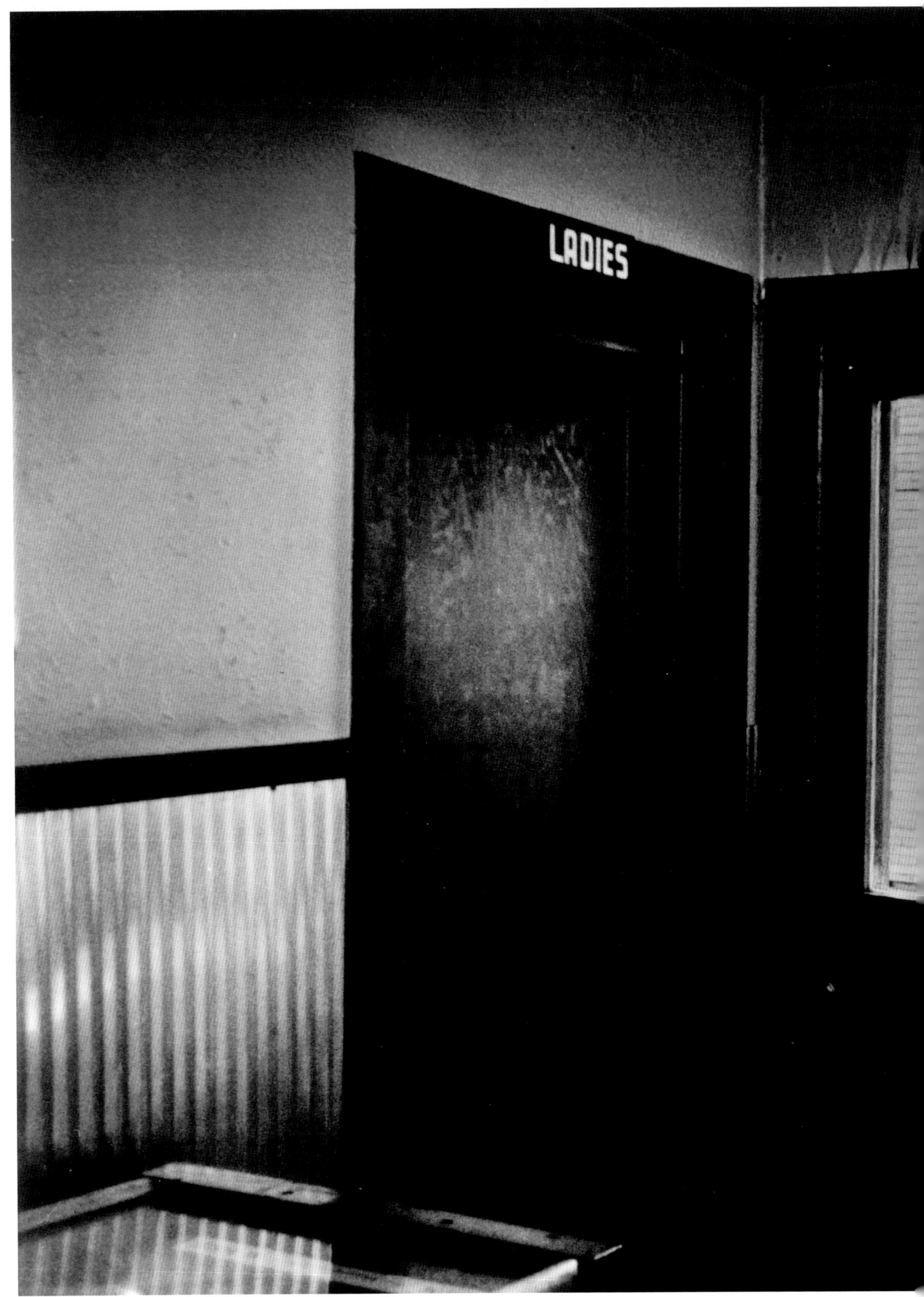

Western United States, 1954

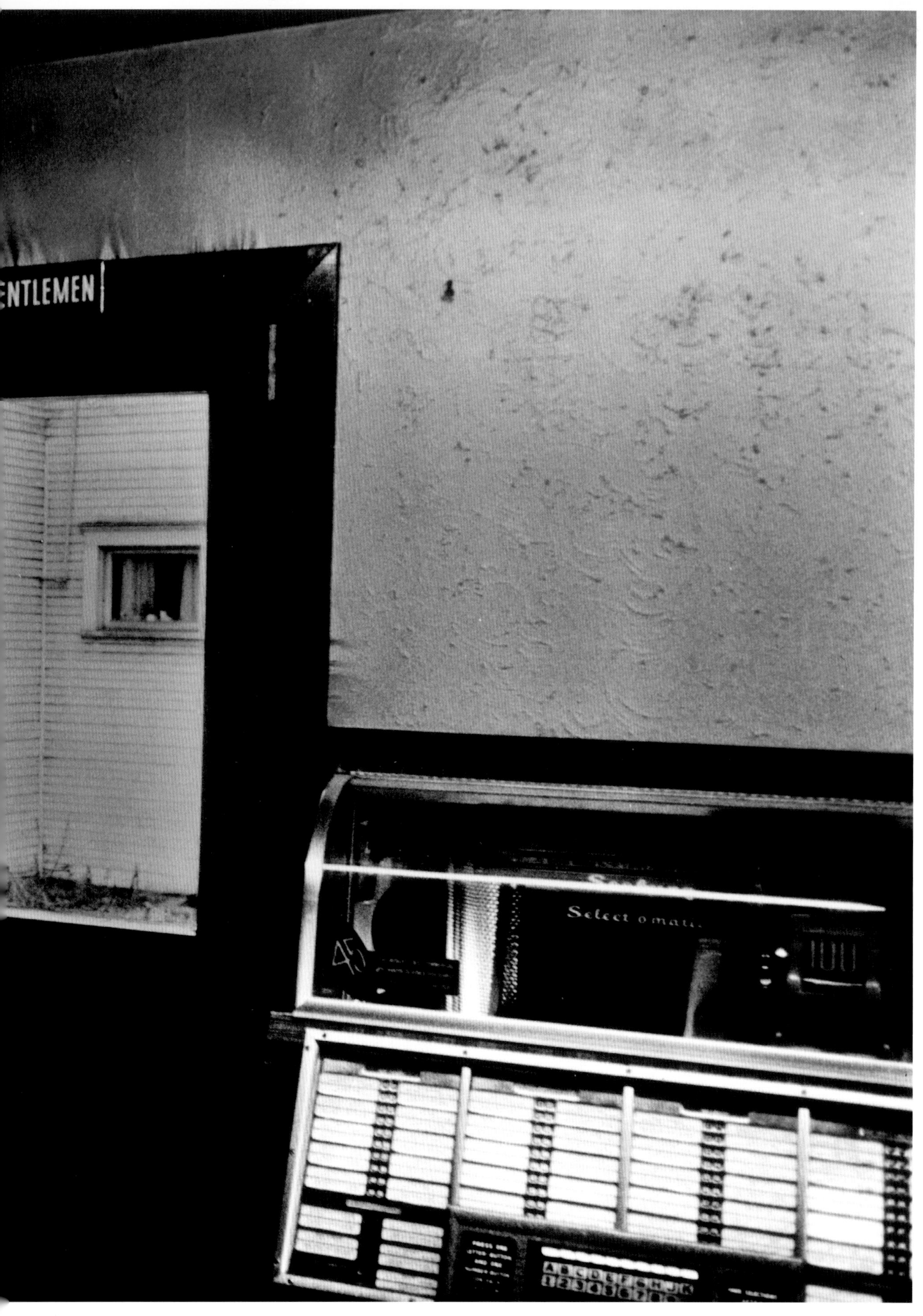
Select o matic

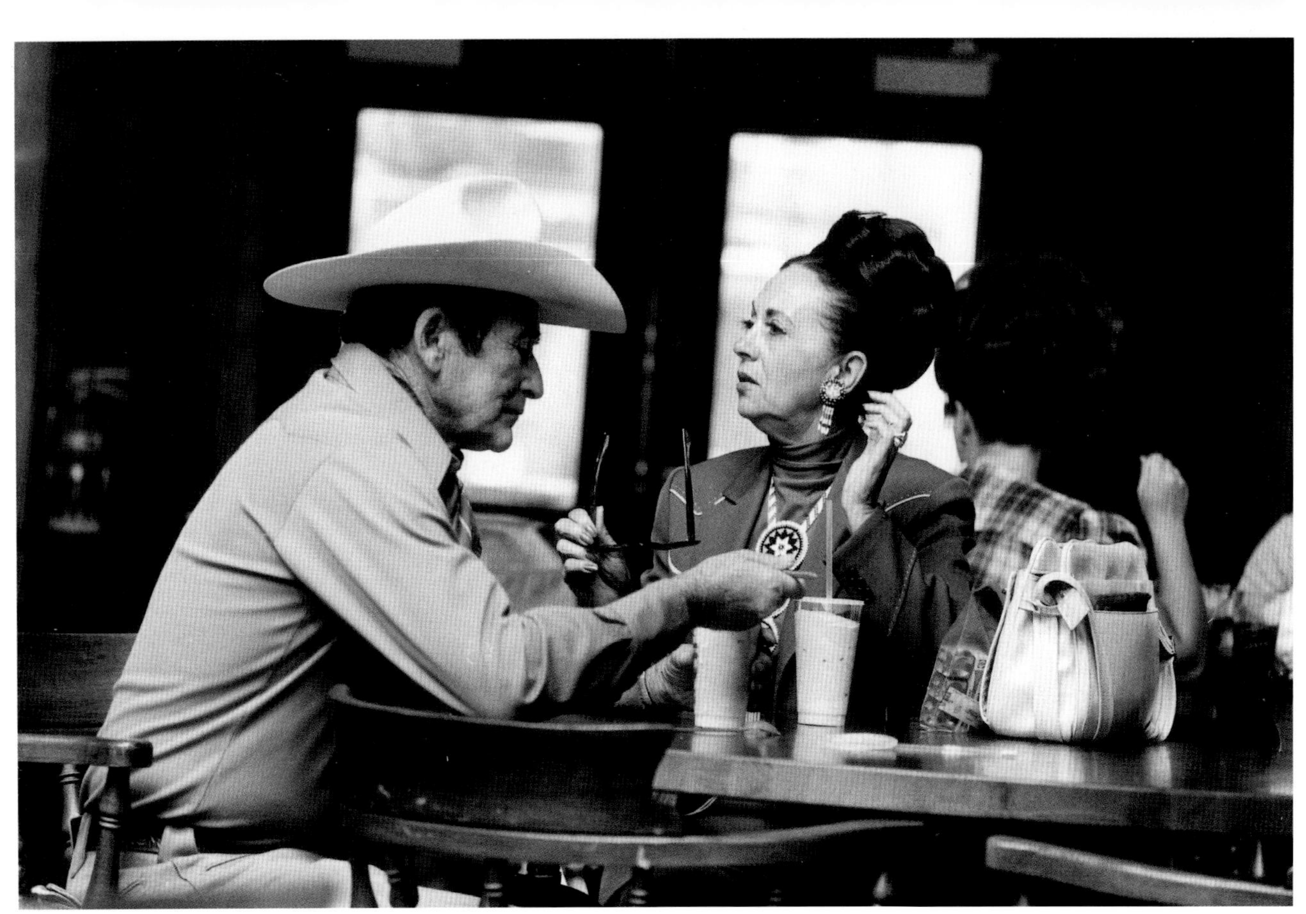

Atlantic City, New Jersey, 1974

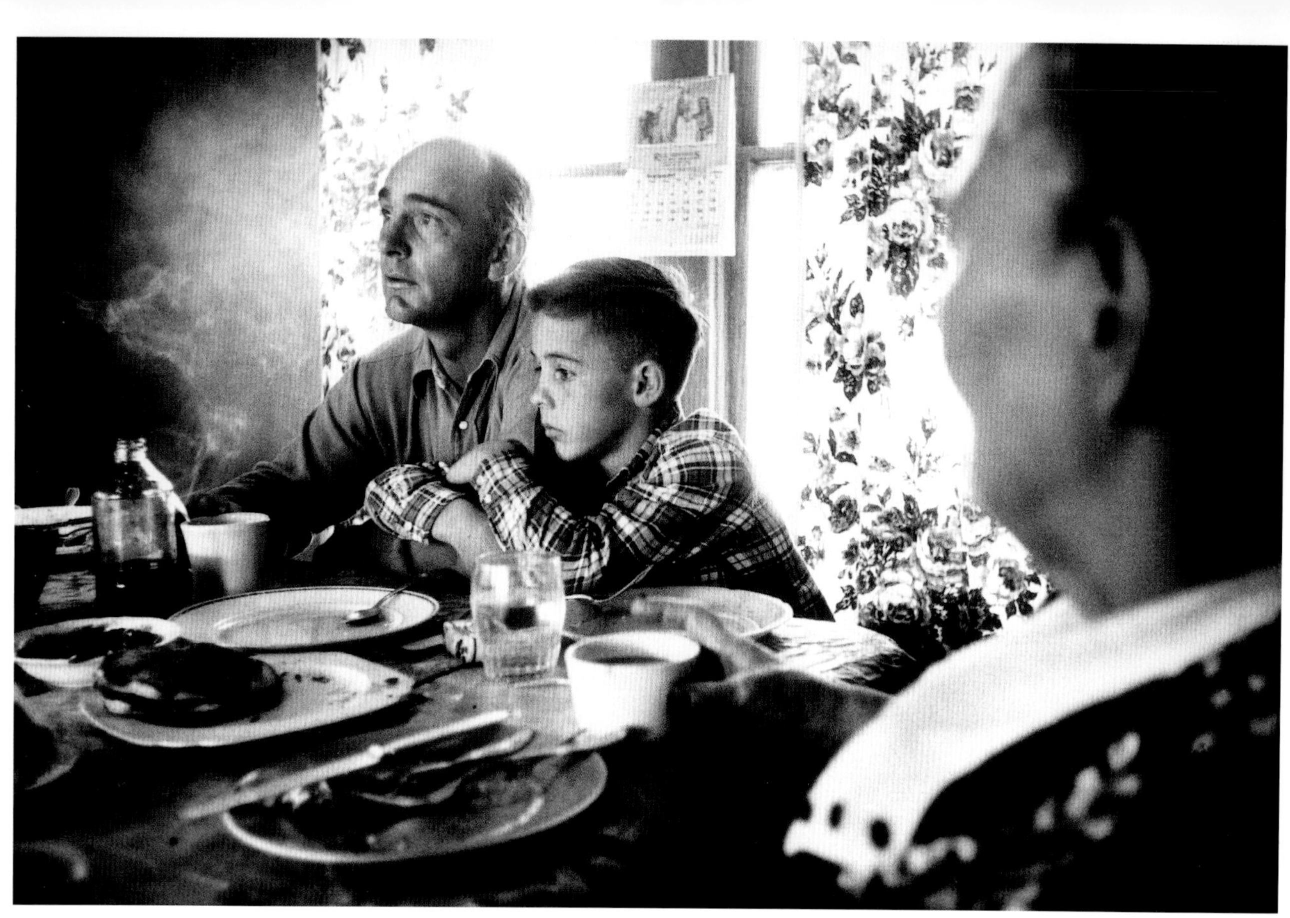

Wyoming, 1954

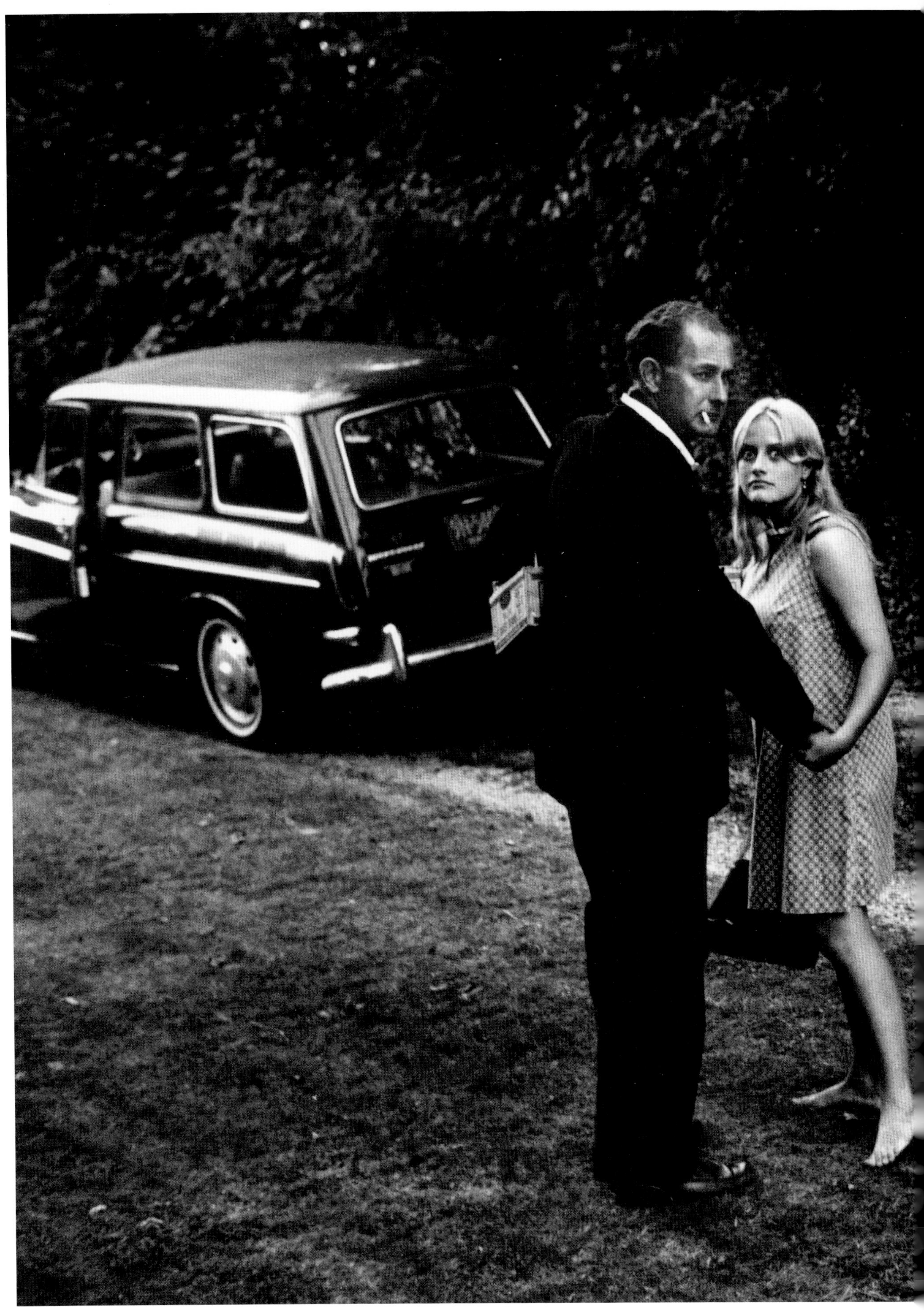

East Hampton, New York, 1966

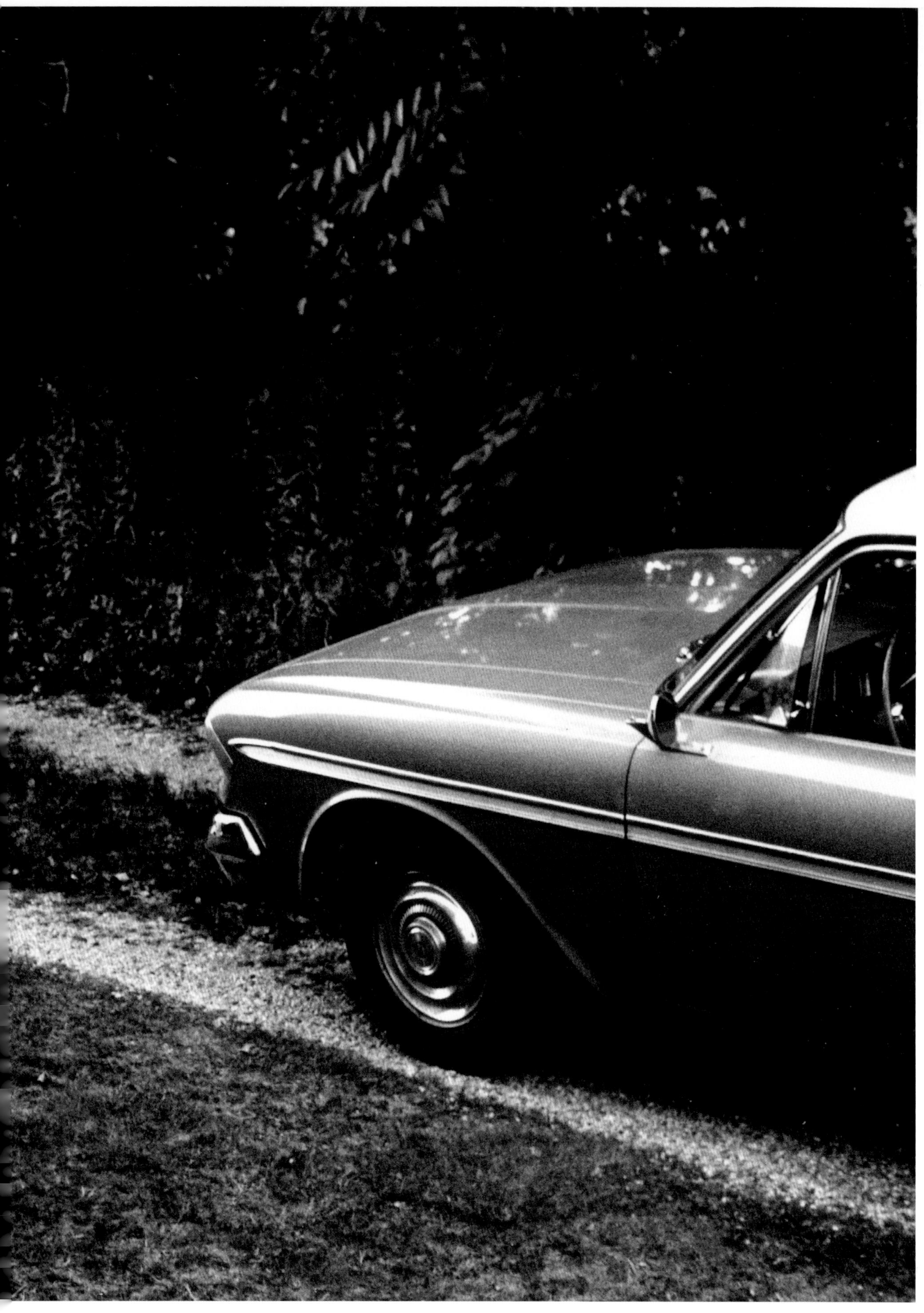

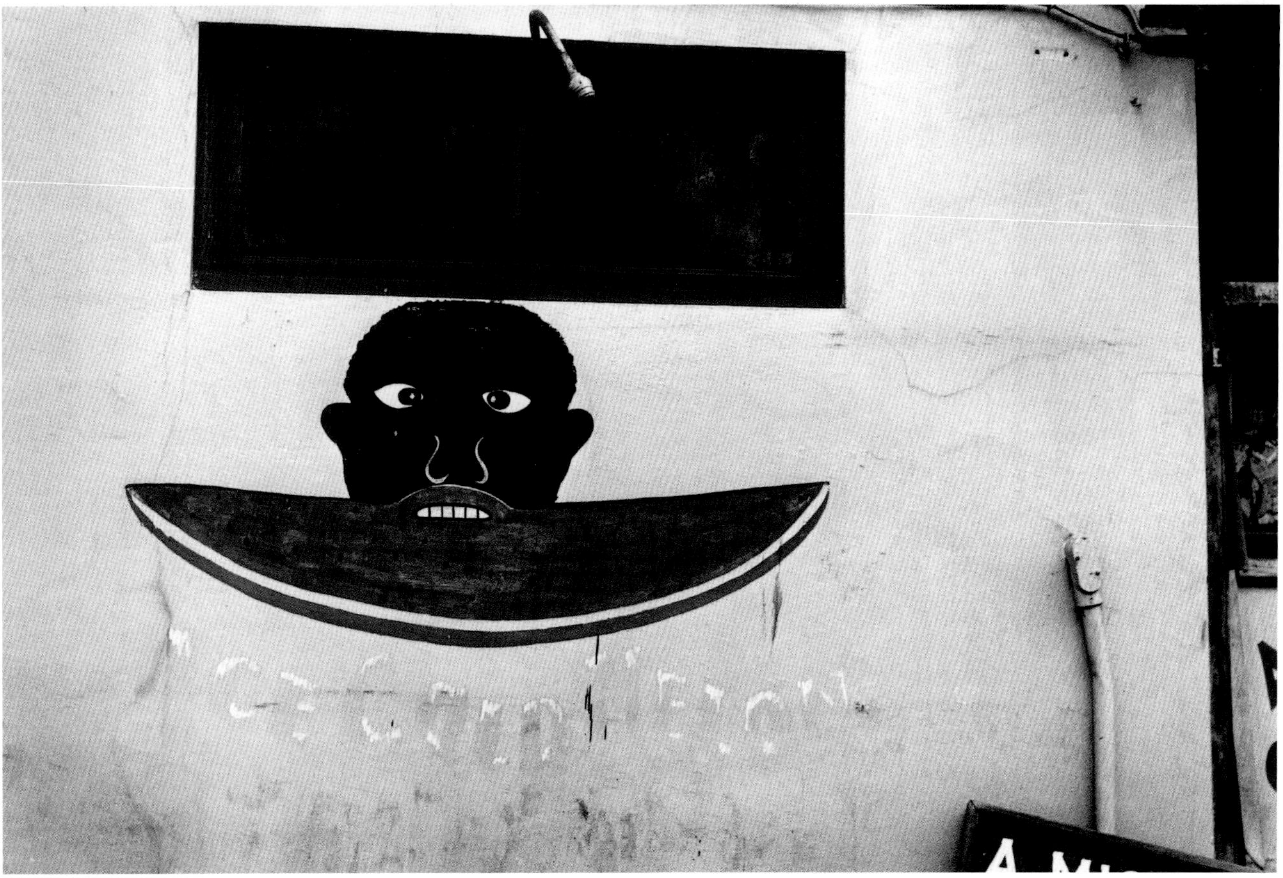

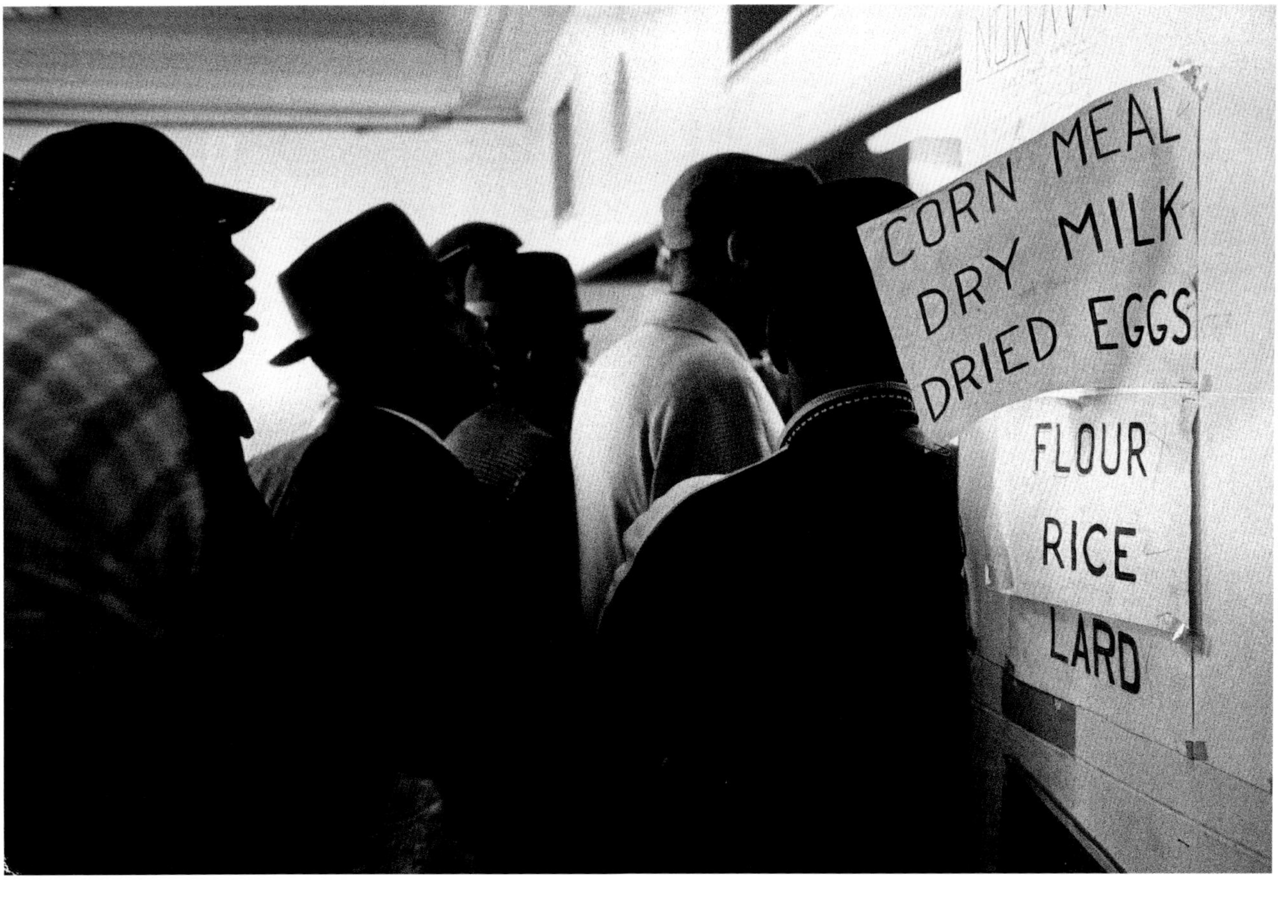

New Orleans, 1949 / Detroit, 1968

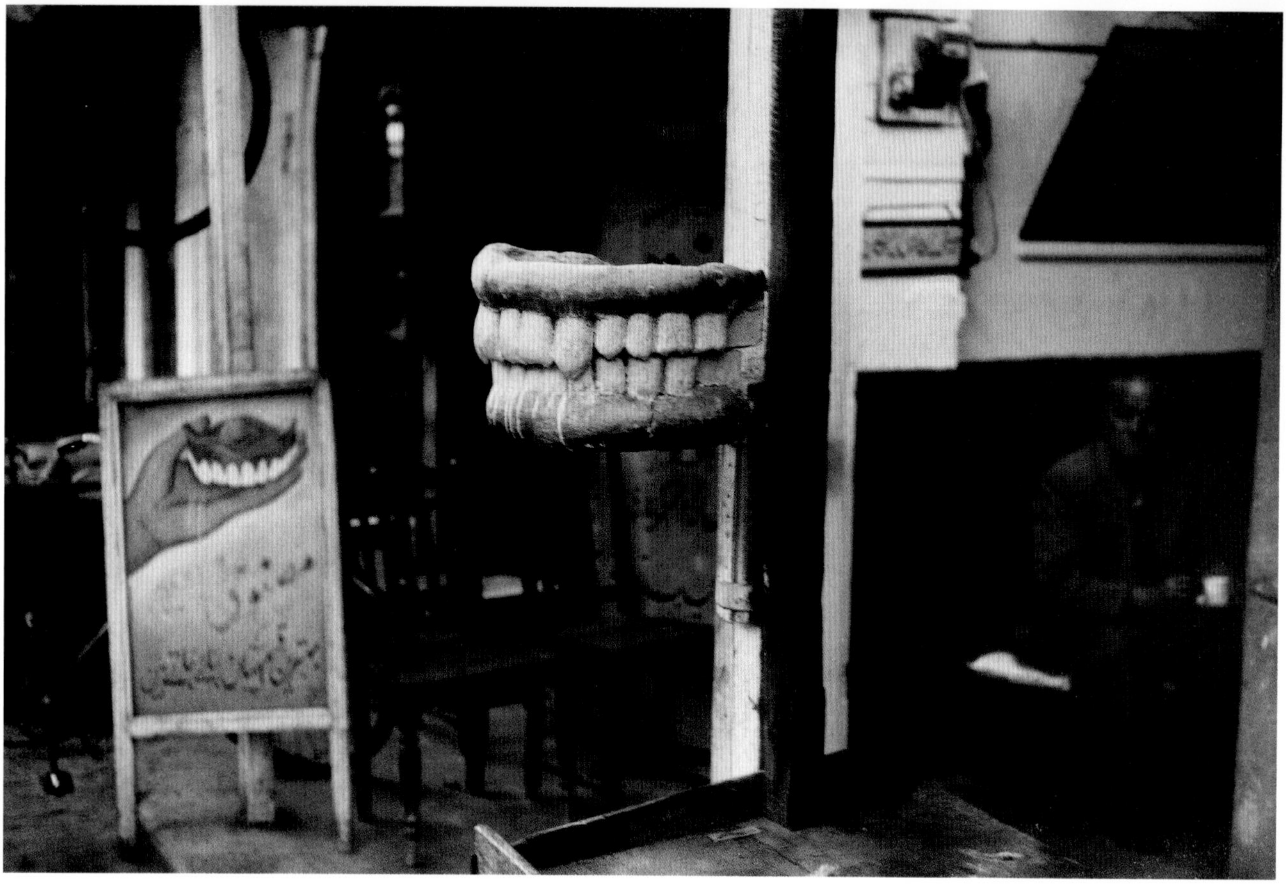

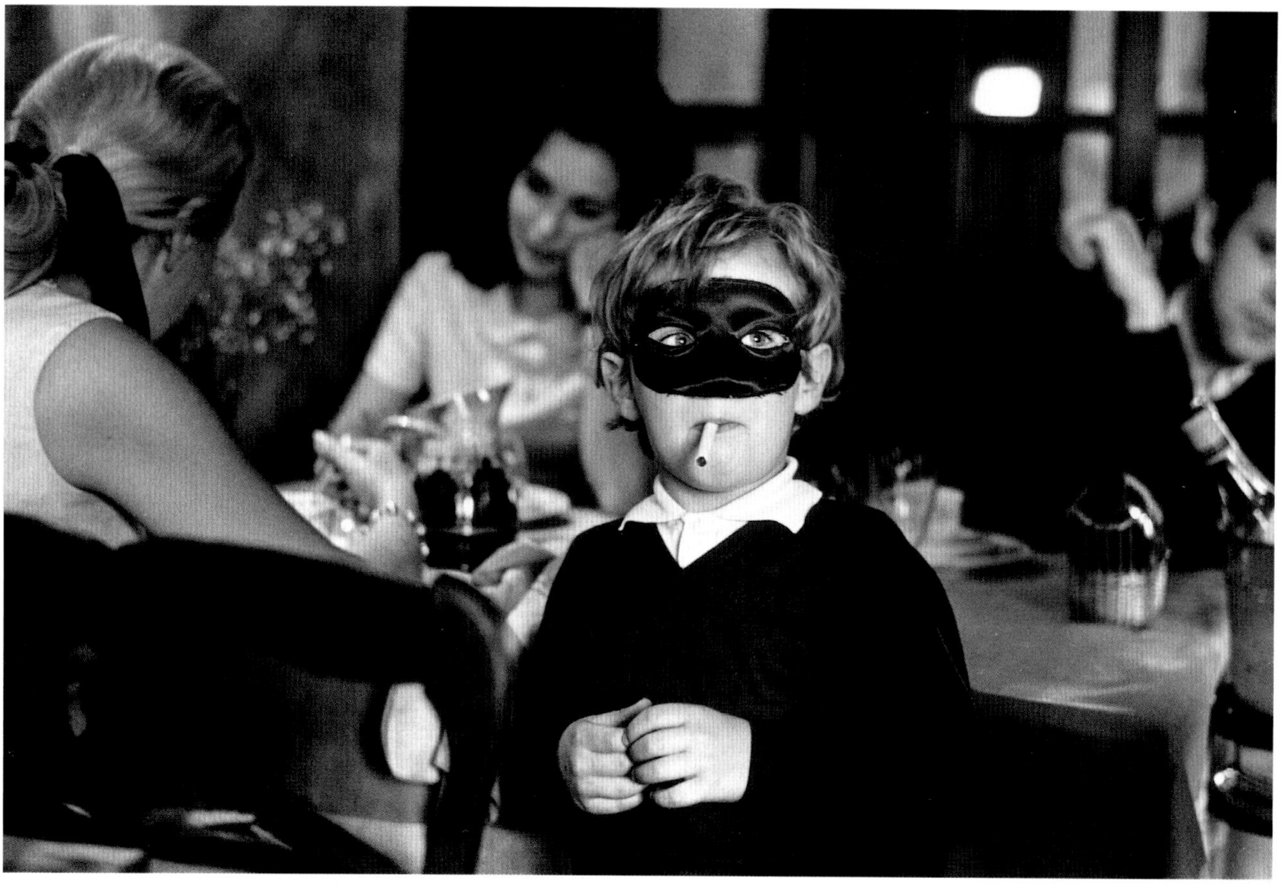

Lahore, Pakistan, 1958 / *Honfleur, France, 1968*

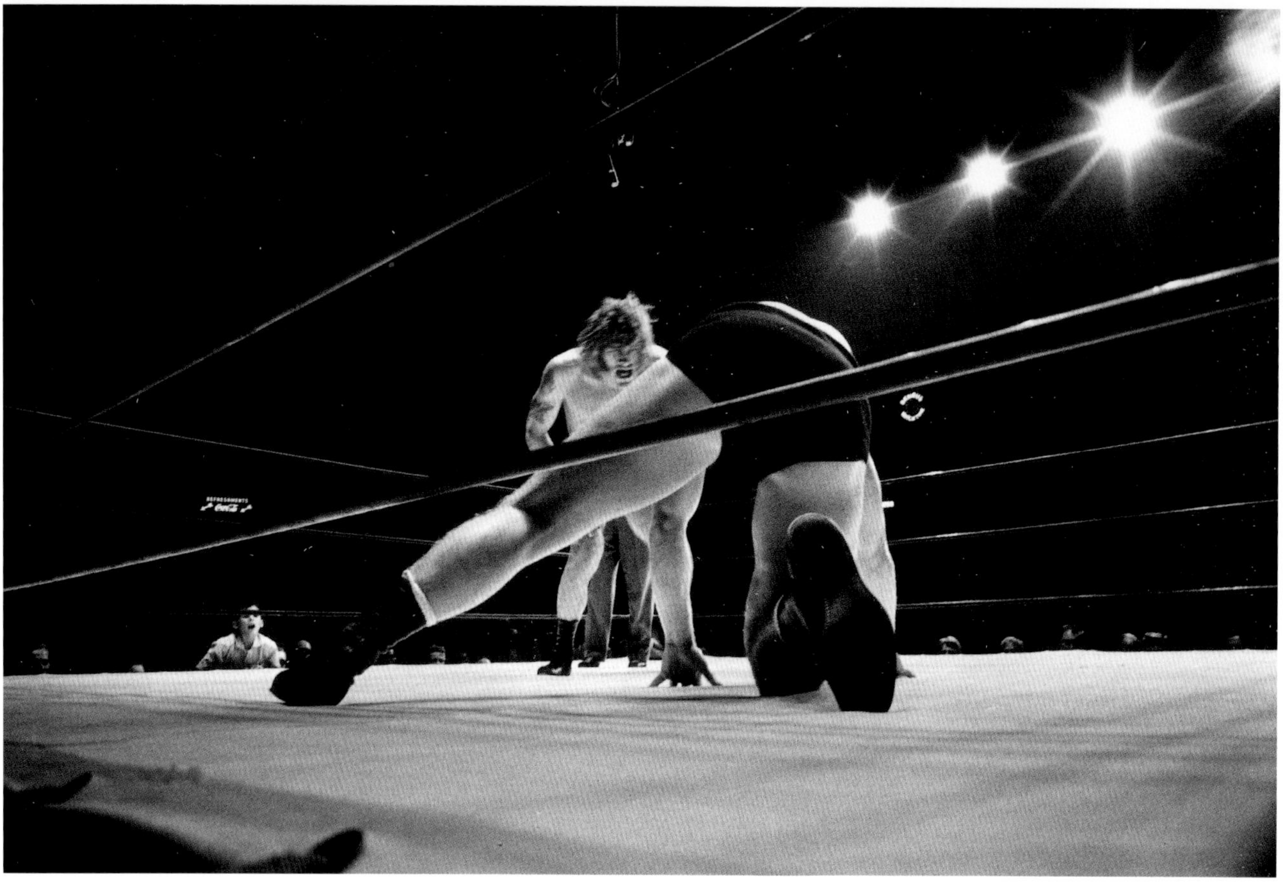

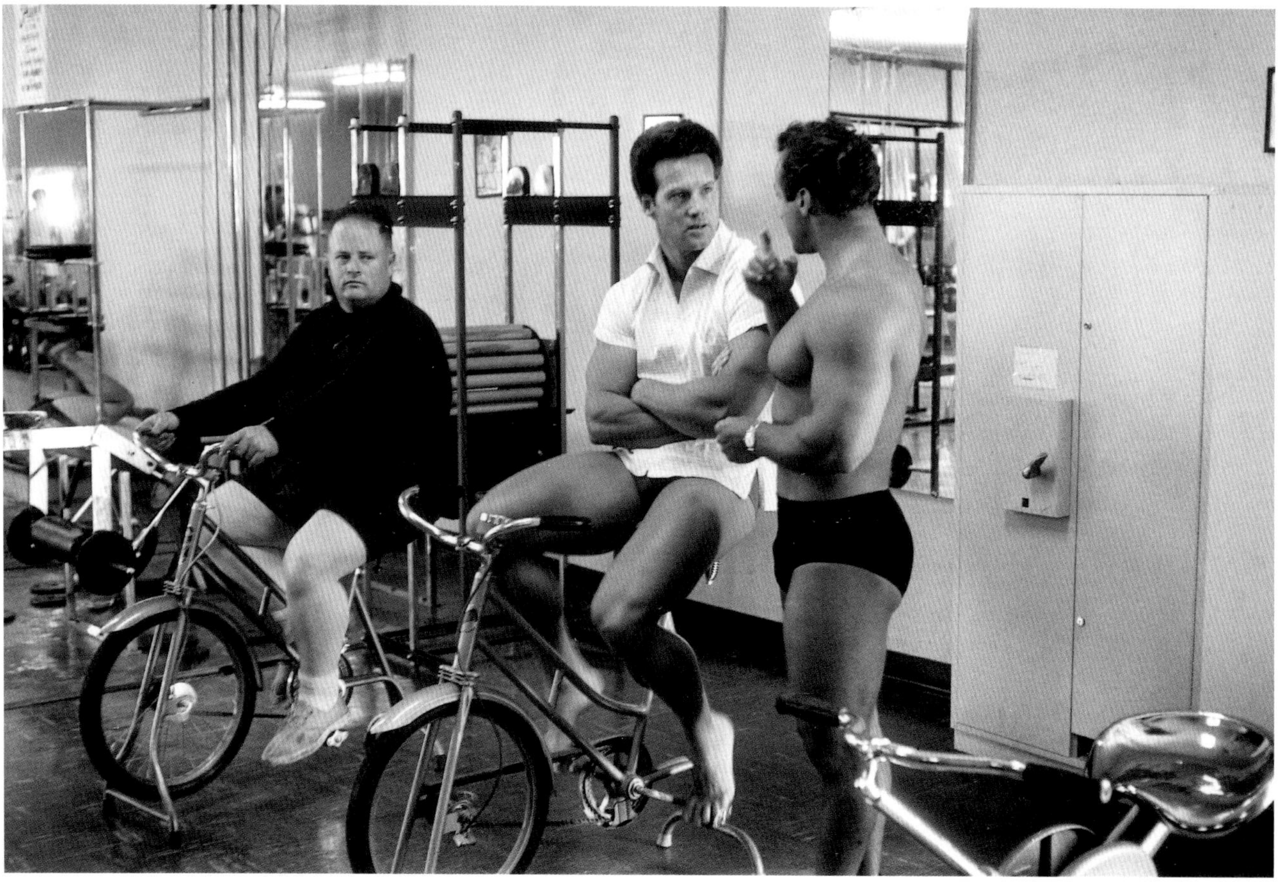

Los Angeles, 1957 / *Los Angeles, 1957*

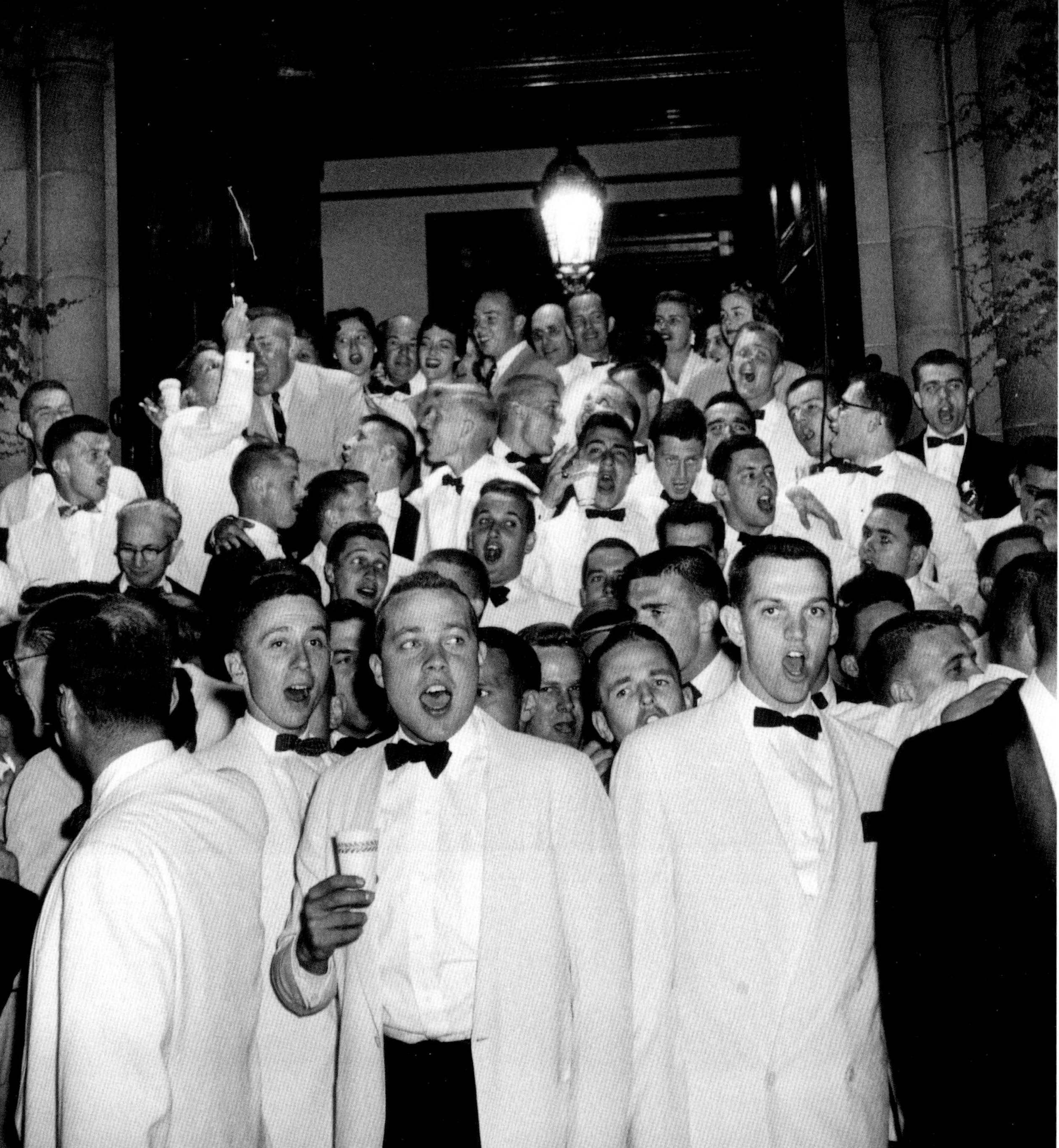
1955

Providence, Rhode Island, 1955

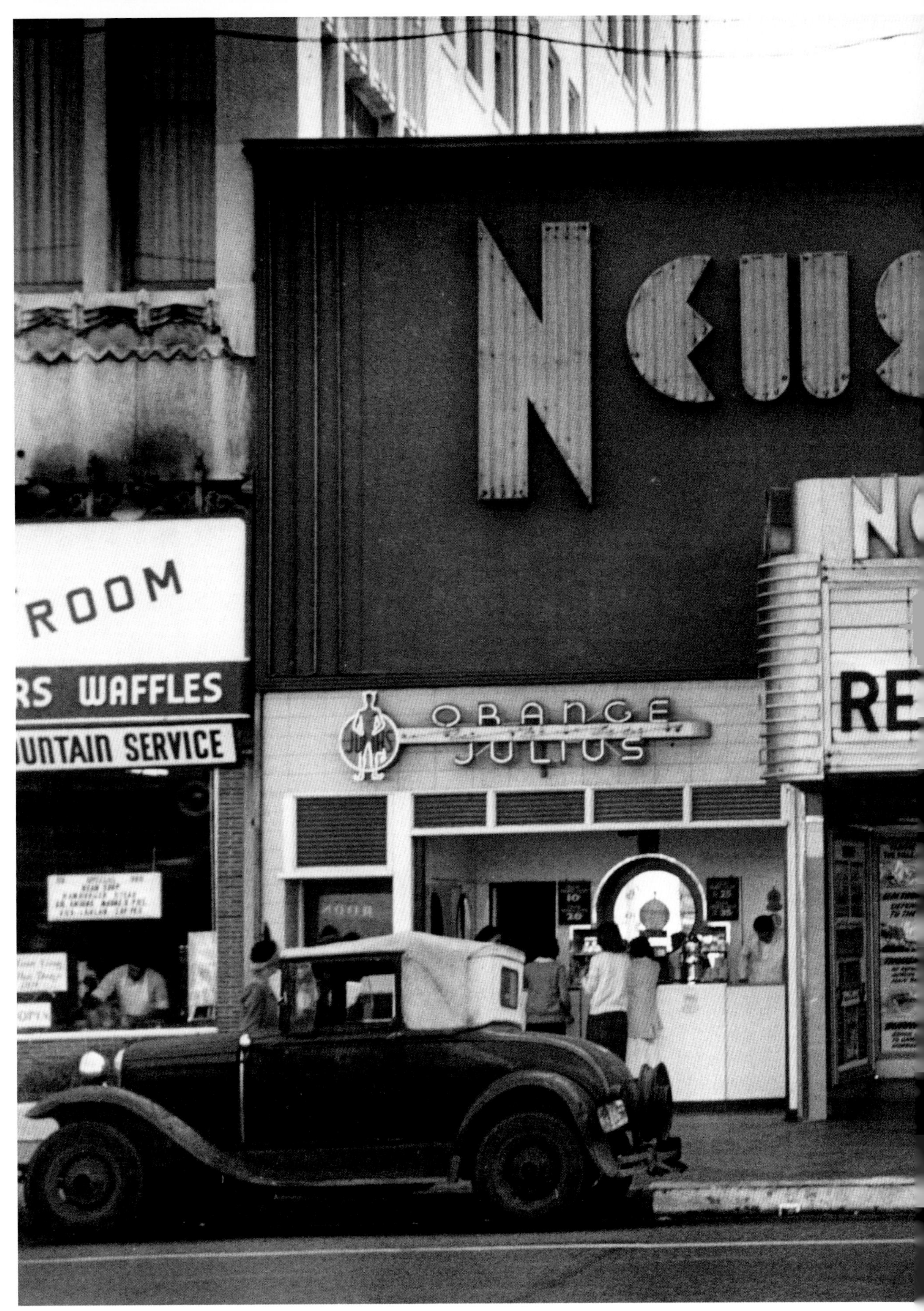

New York, 1951

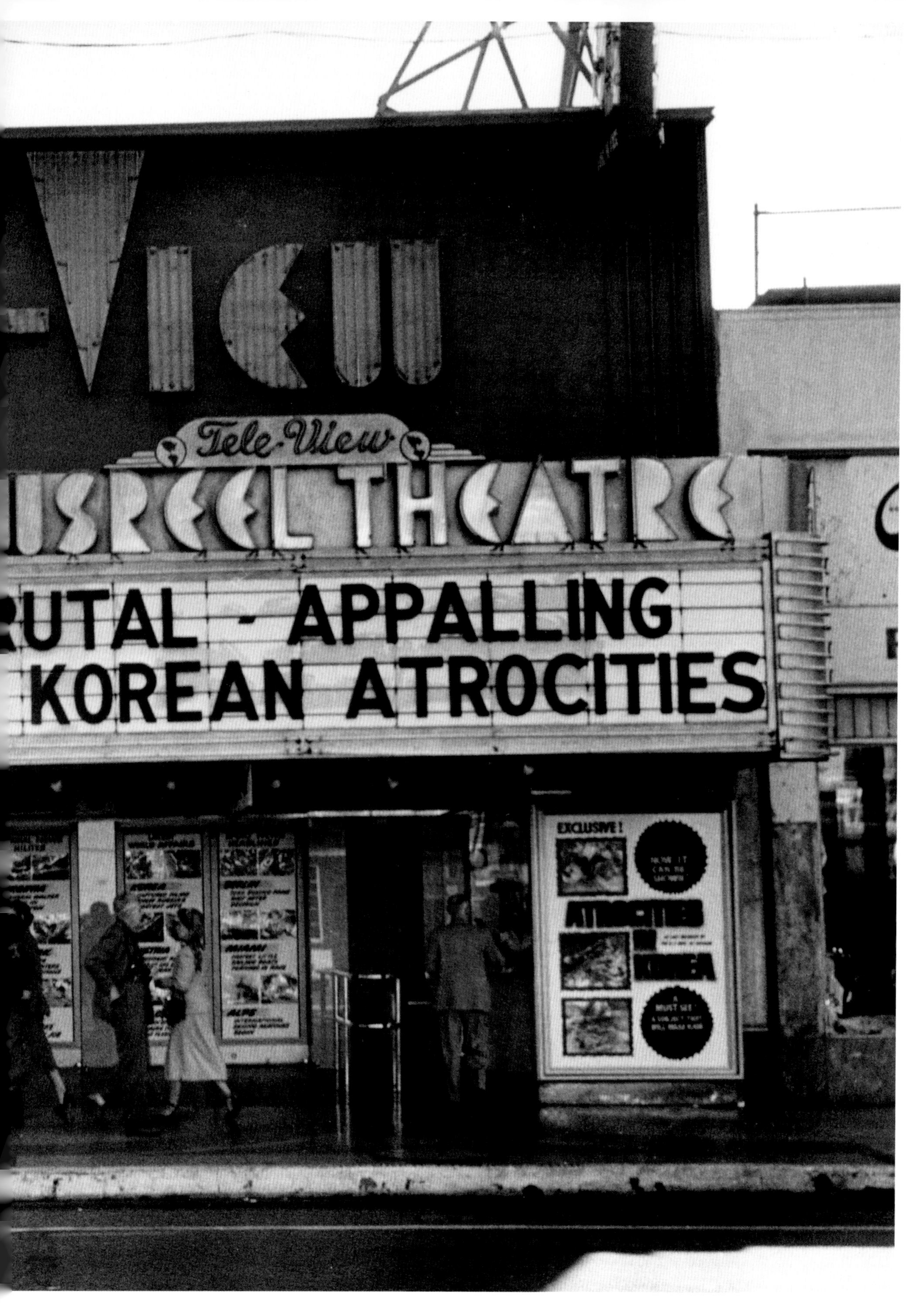

overleaf *Hyde Park, London, 1978* / *New York, 1973*

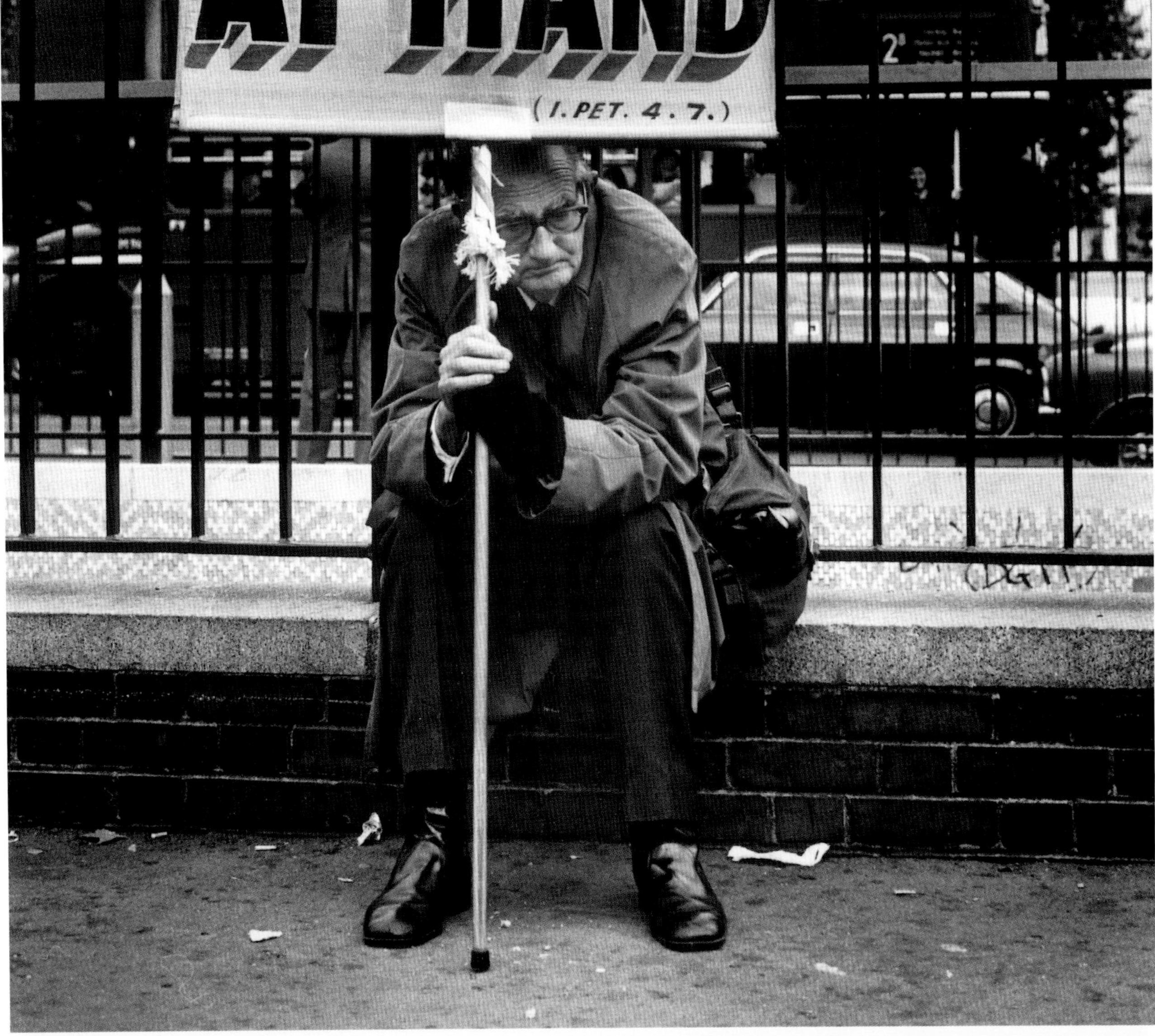
THE
END
IS
AT HAND
(I. PET. 4.7.)
30

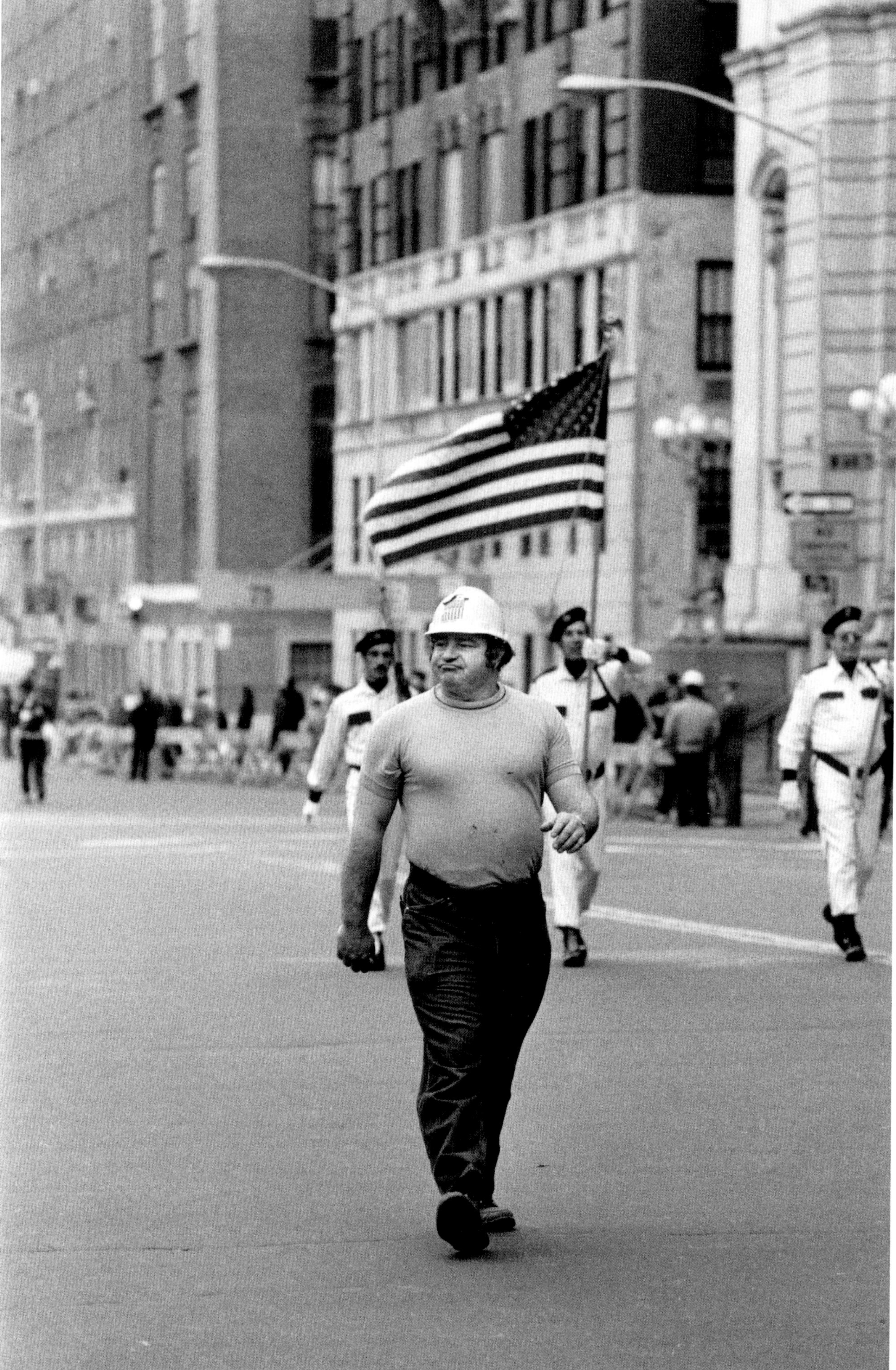

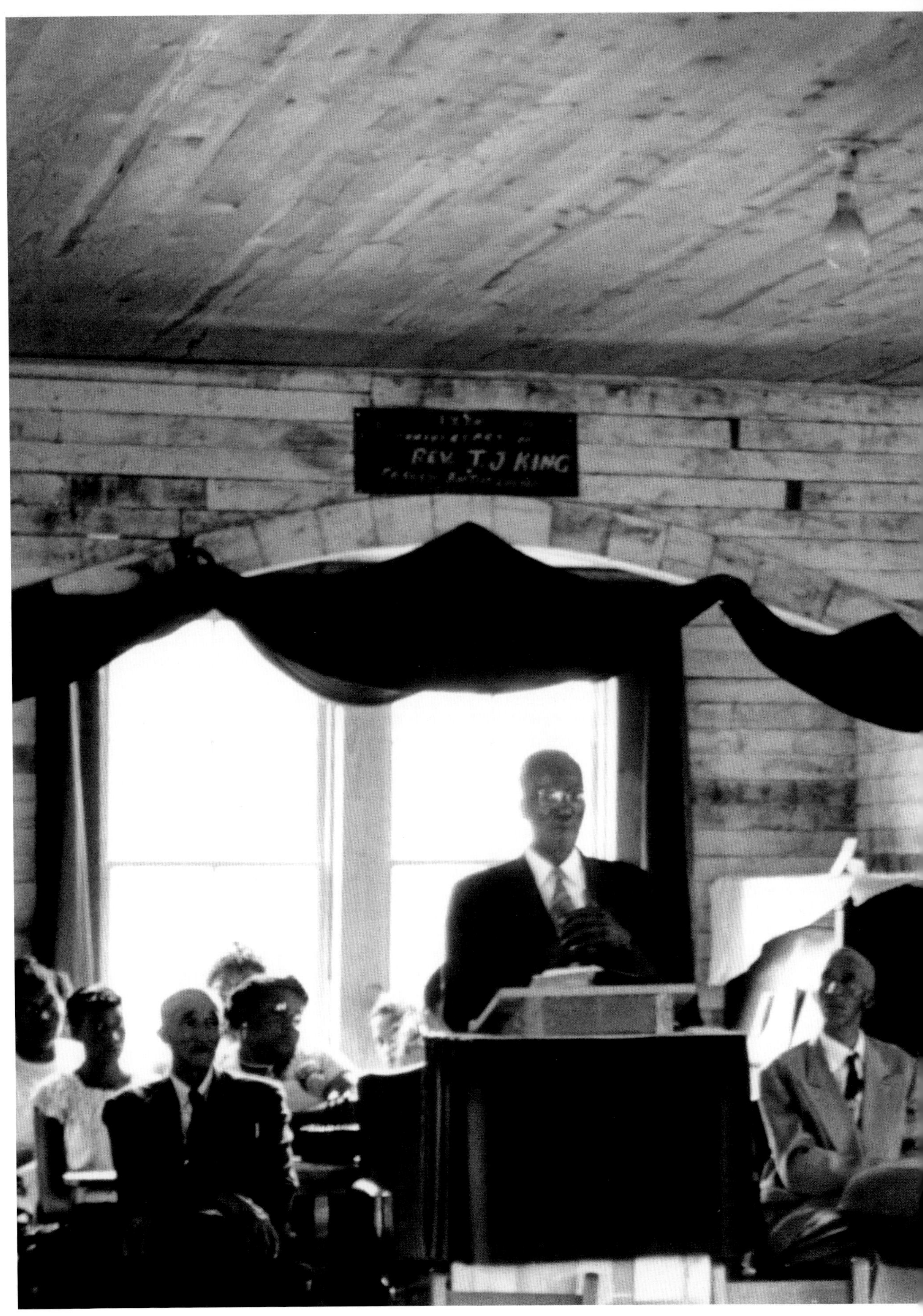

Arkadelphia, Alabama, 1954

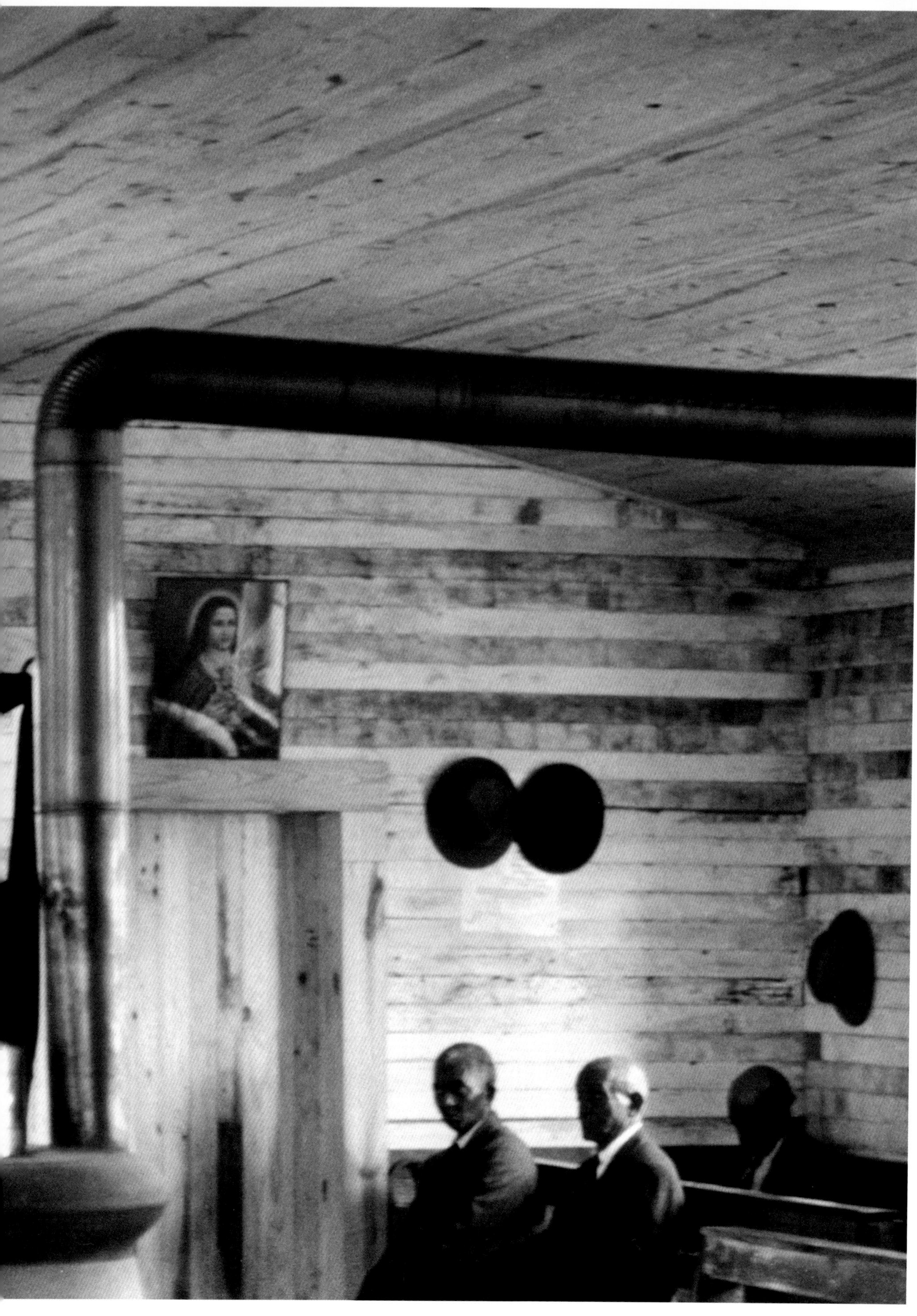

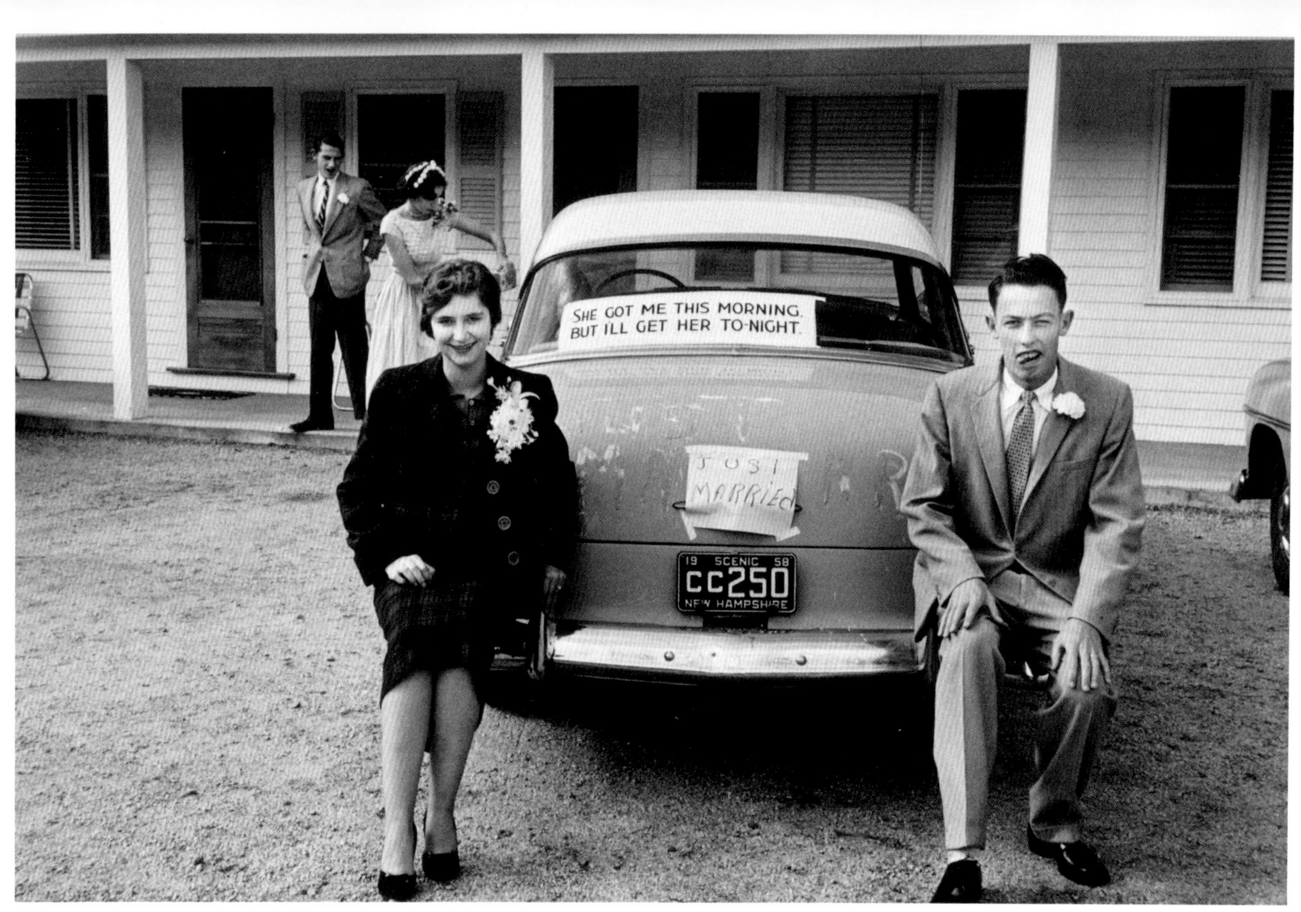

New Hampshire, 1958

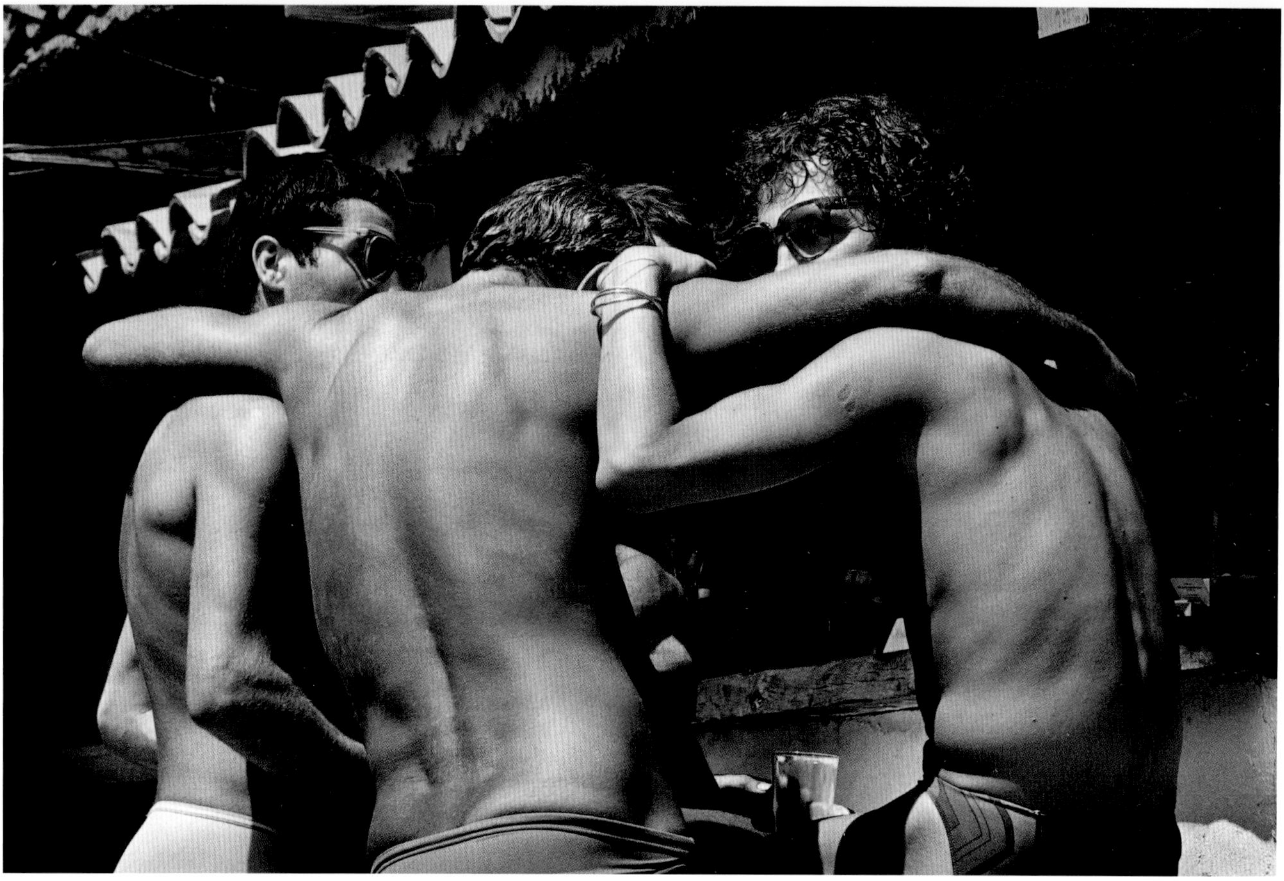

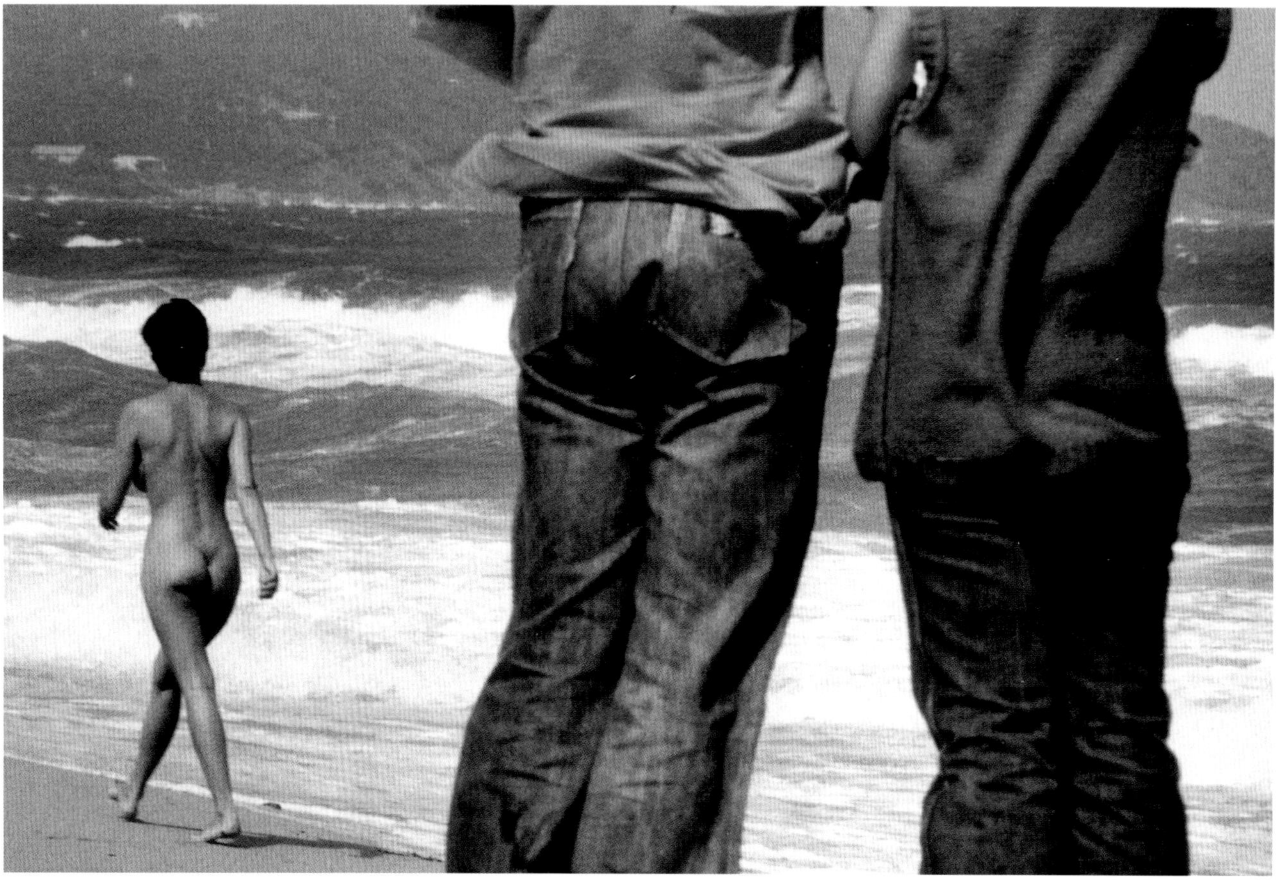

St Tropez, France, 1978 / *St Tropez, France, 1979*
overleaf *Arkansas, 1954* / *County Cork, Ireland, 1962*

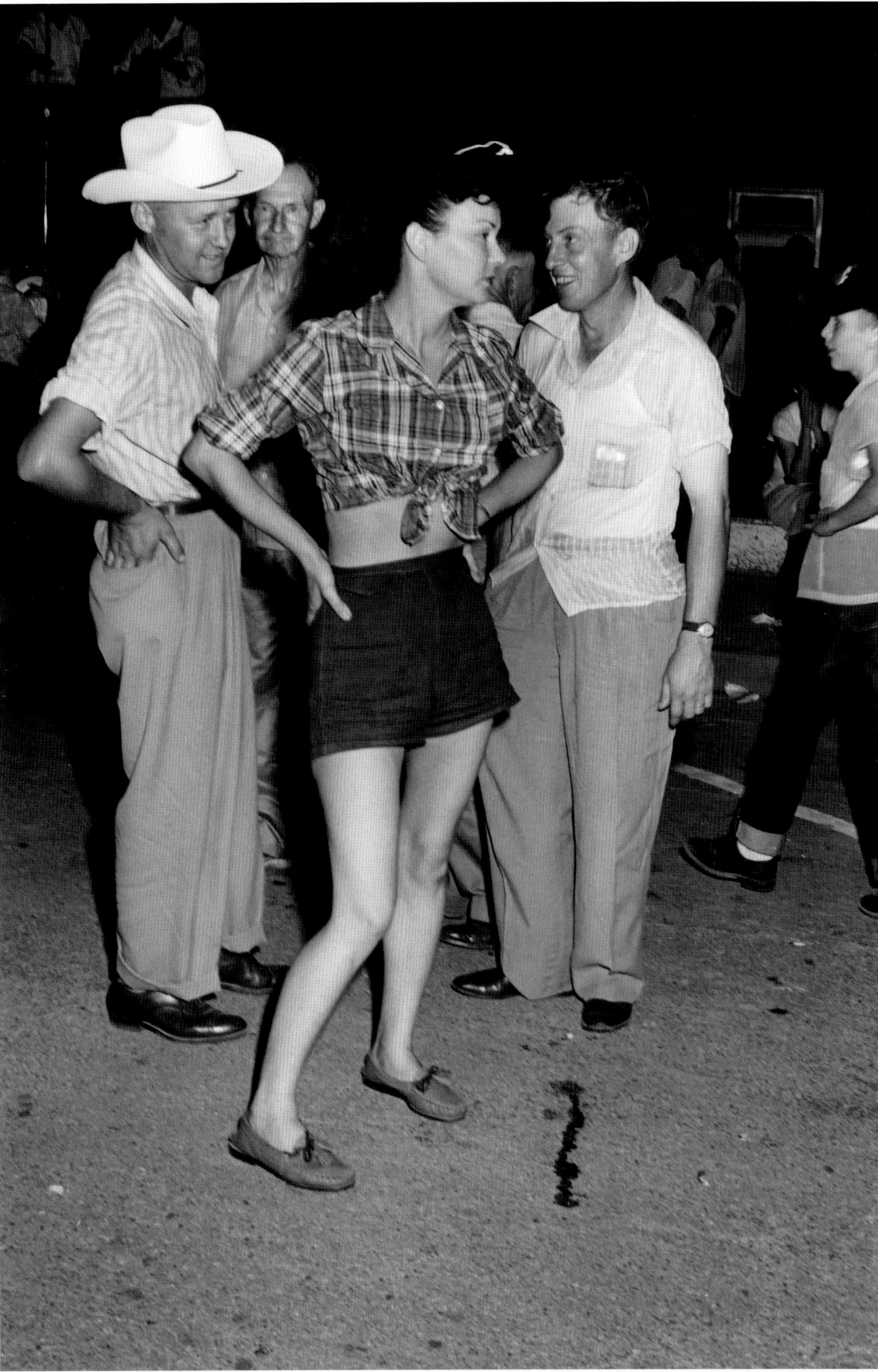

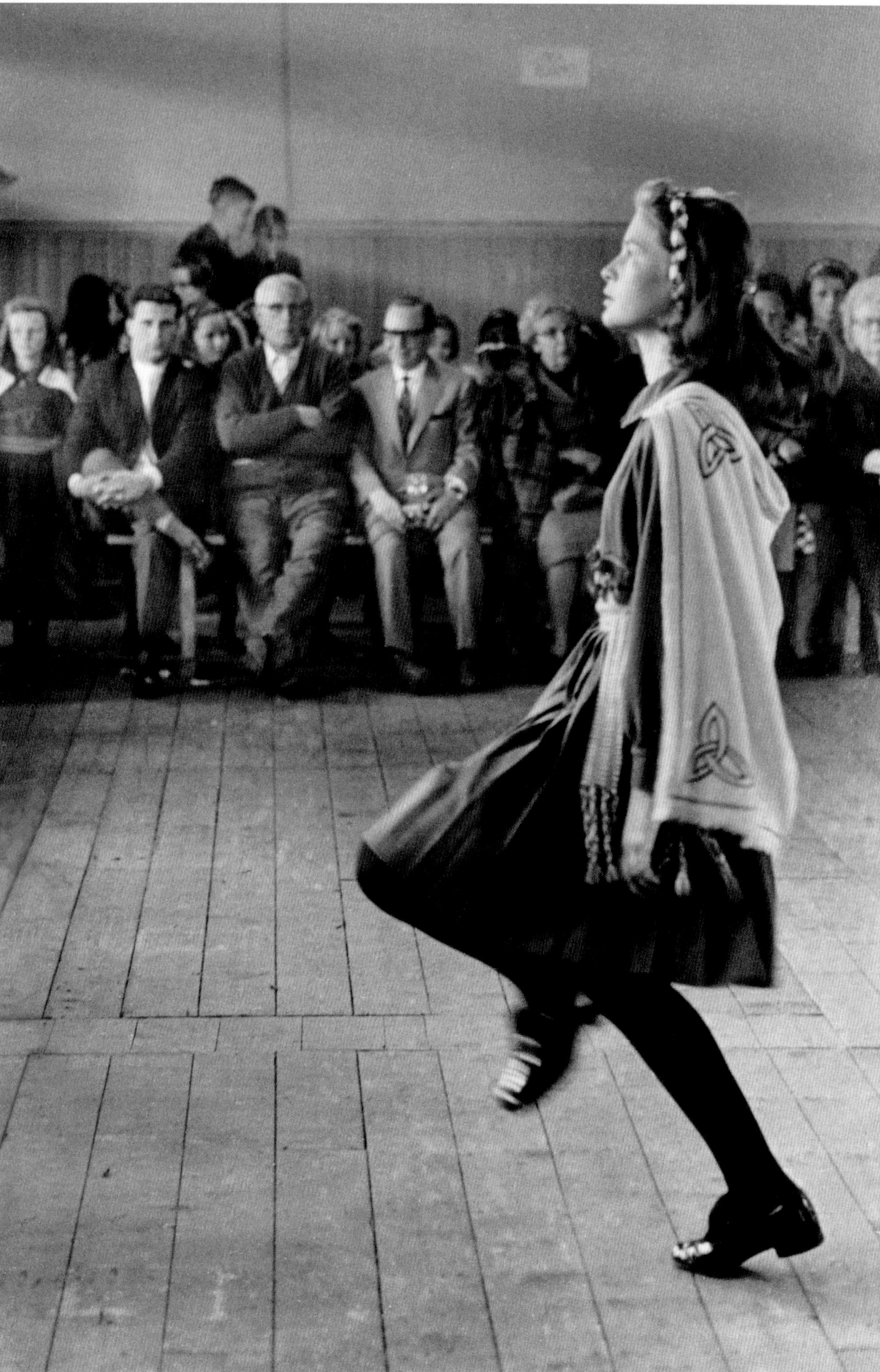

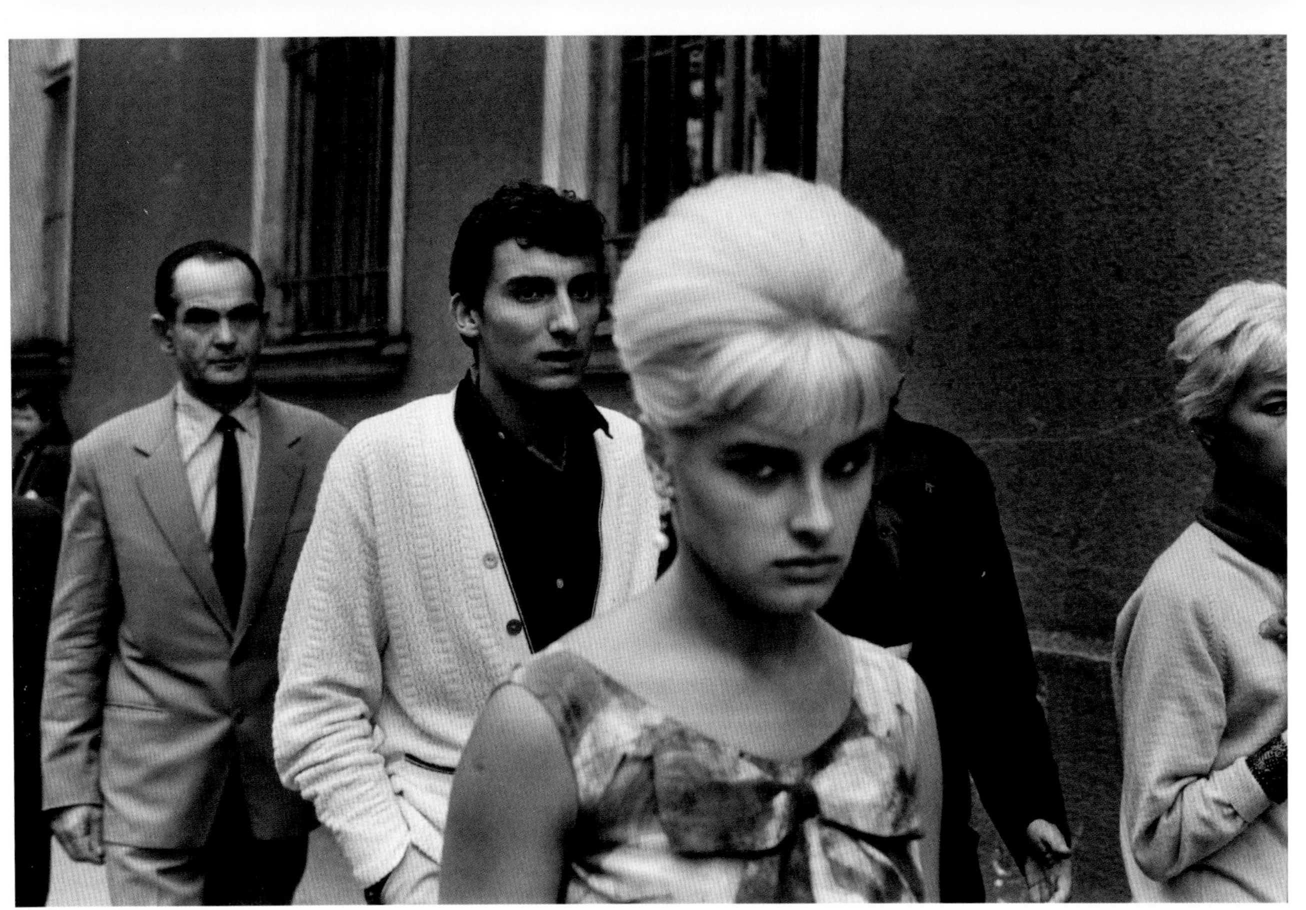

Warsaw, Poland, 1964

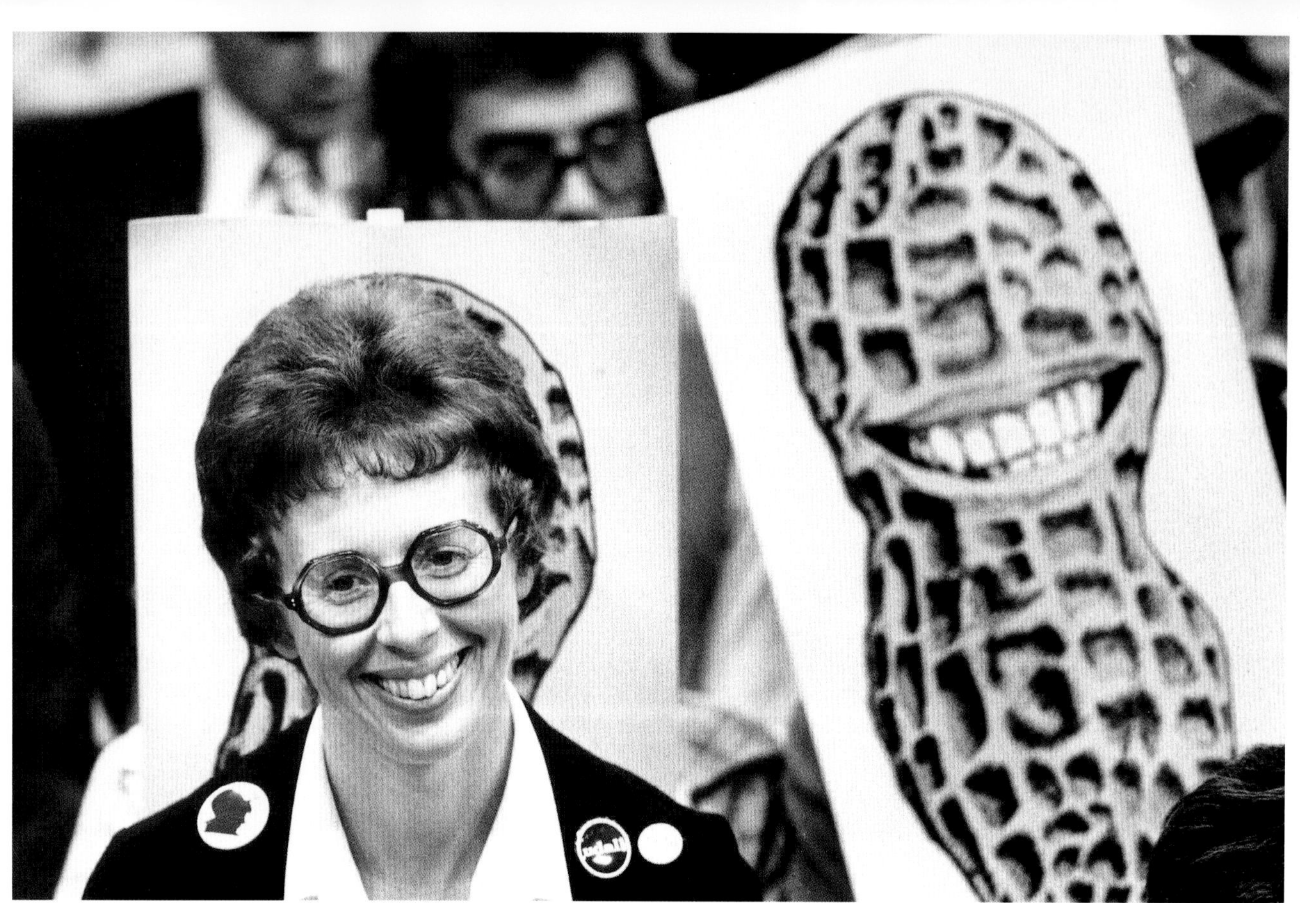

New York, 1976

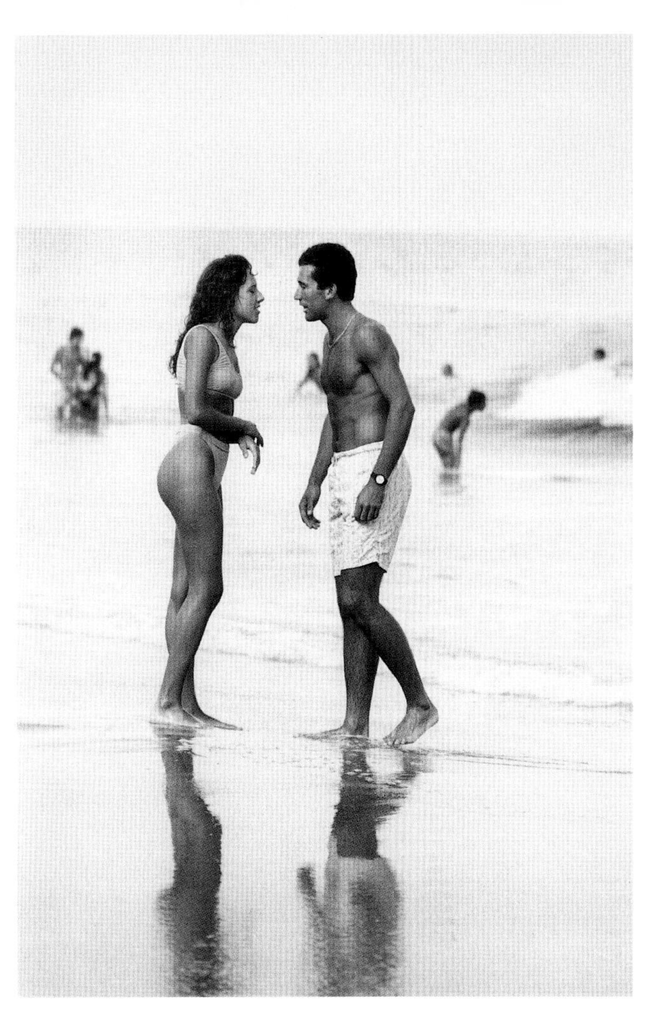

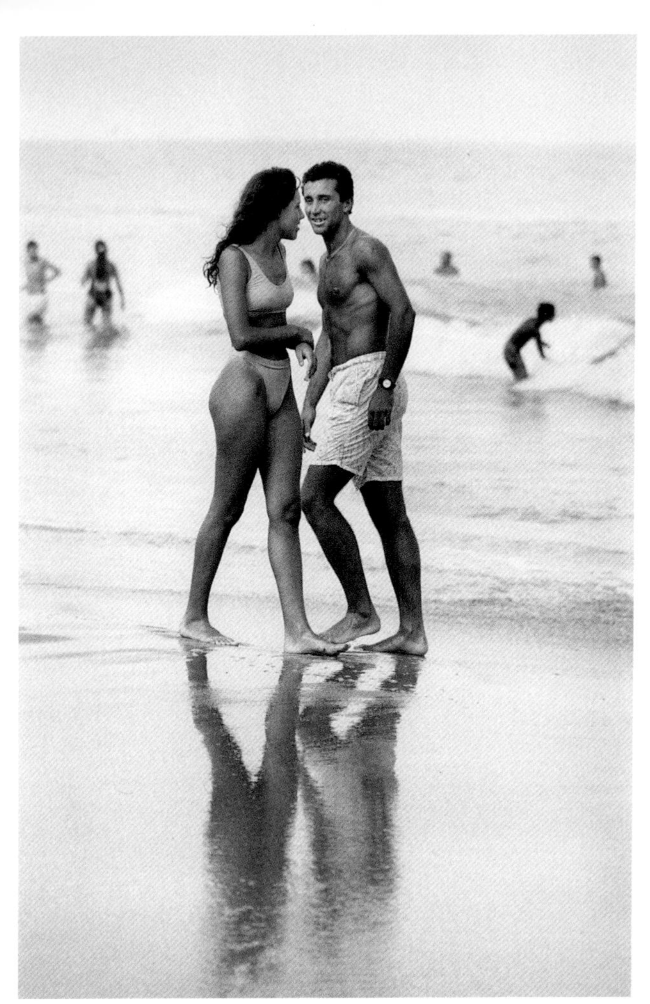

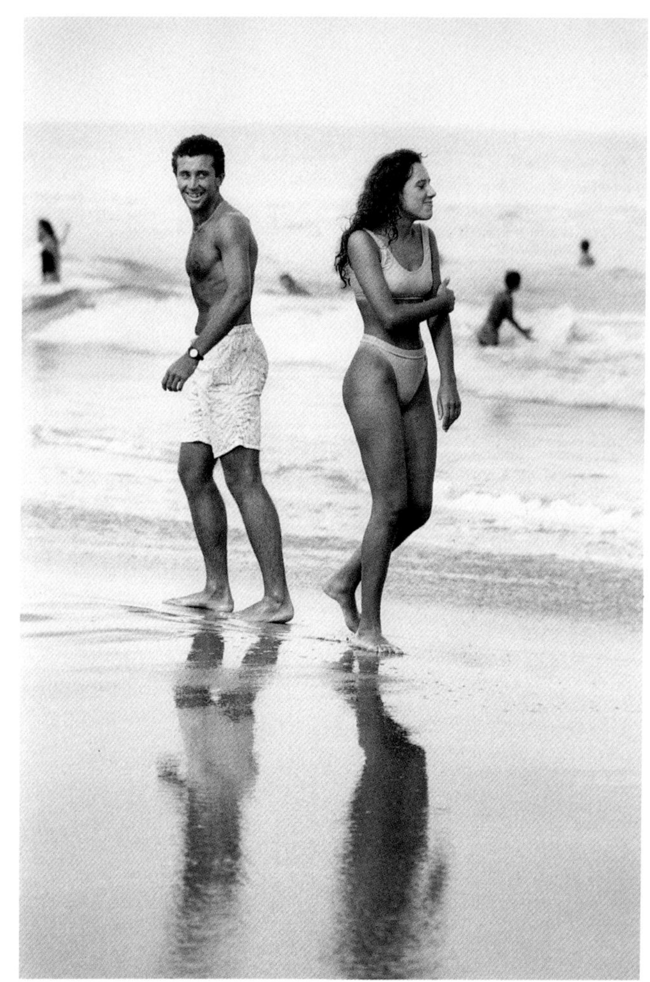

Buzios, Brazil, 1990

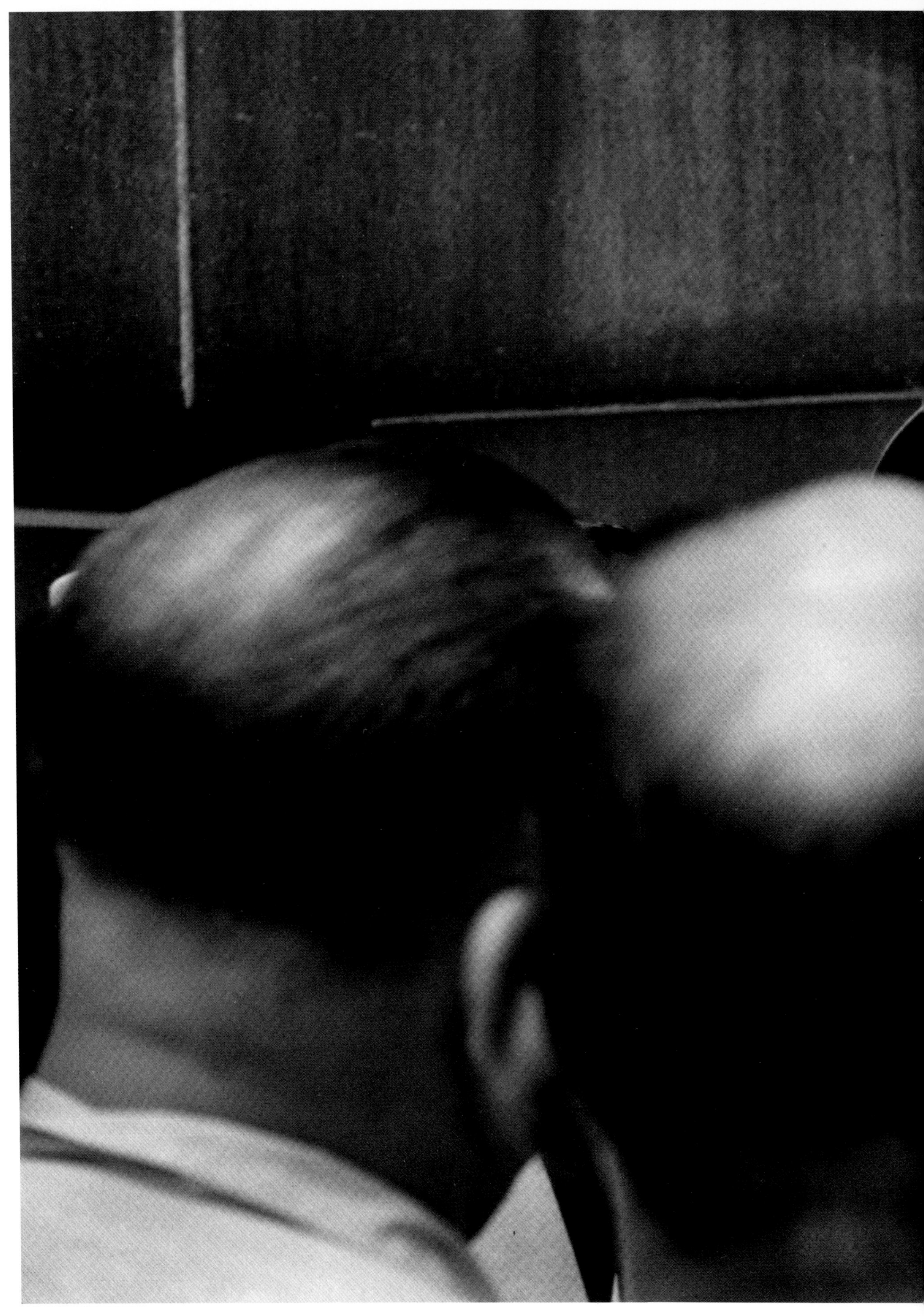

New York, 1955

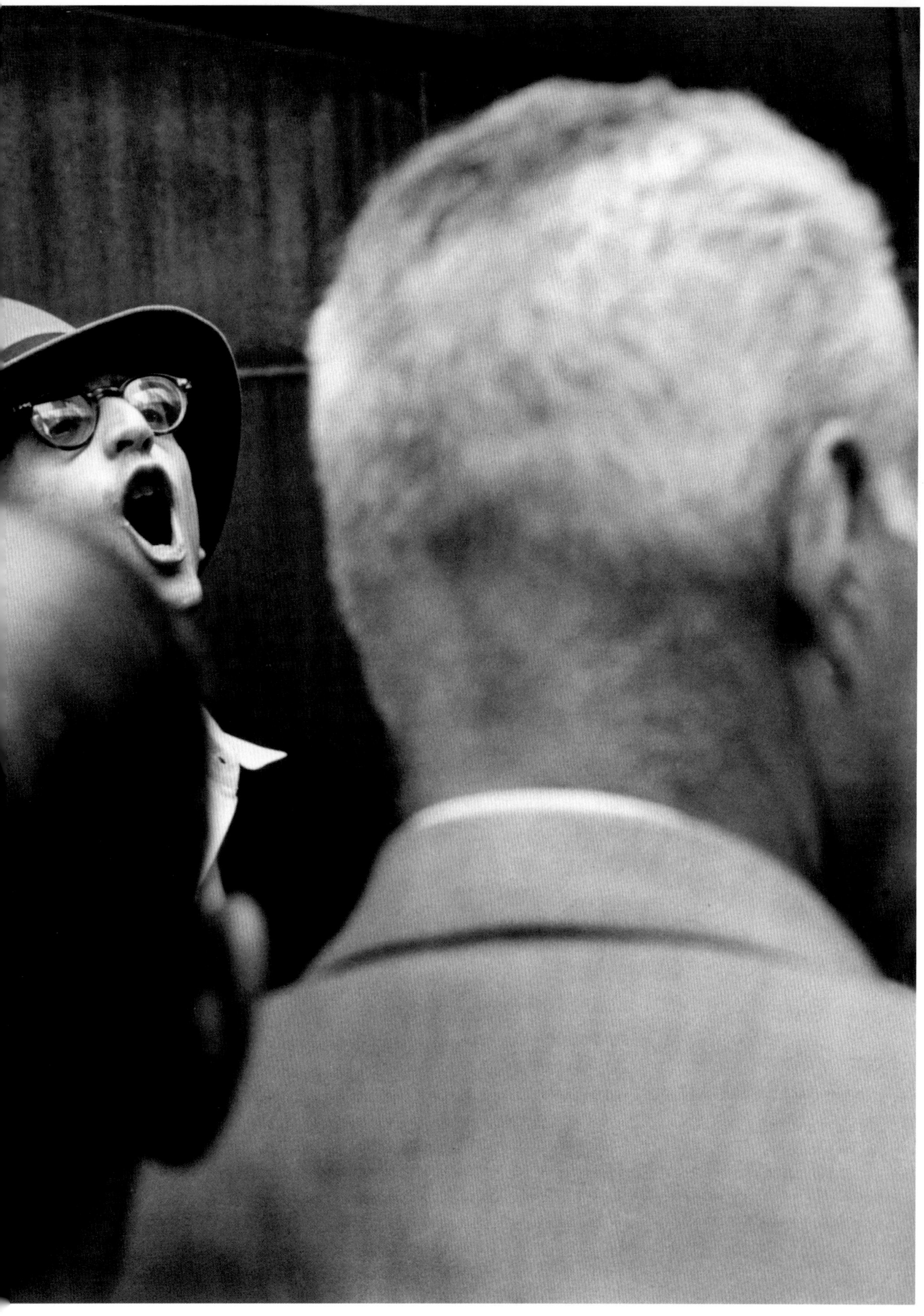

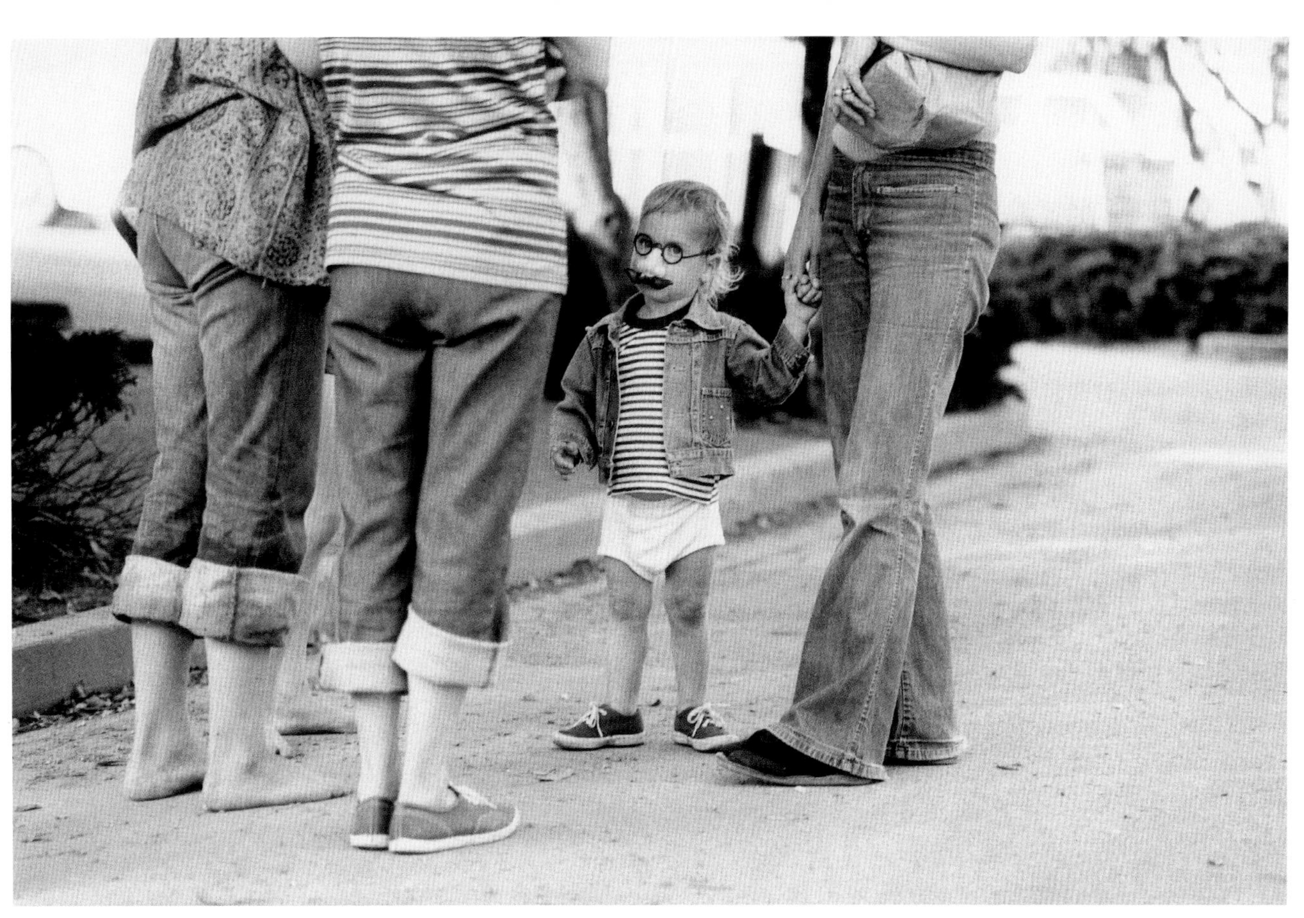

Stinson Beach, California, 1973

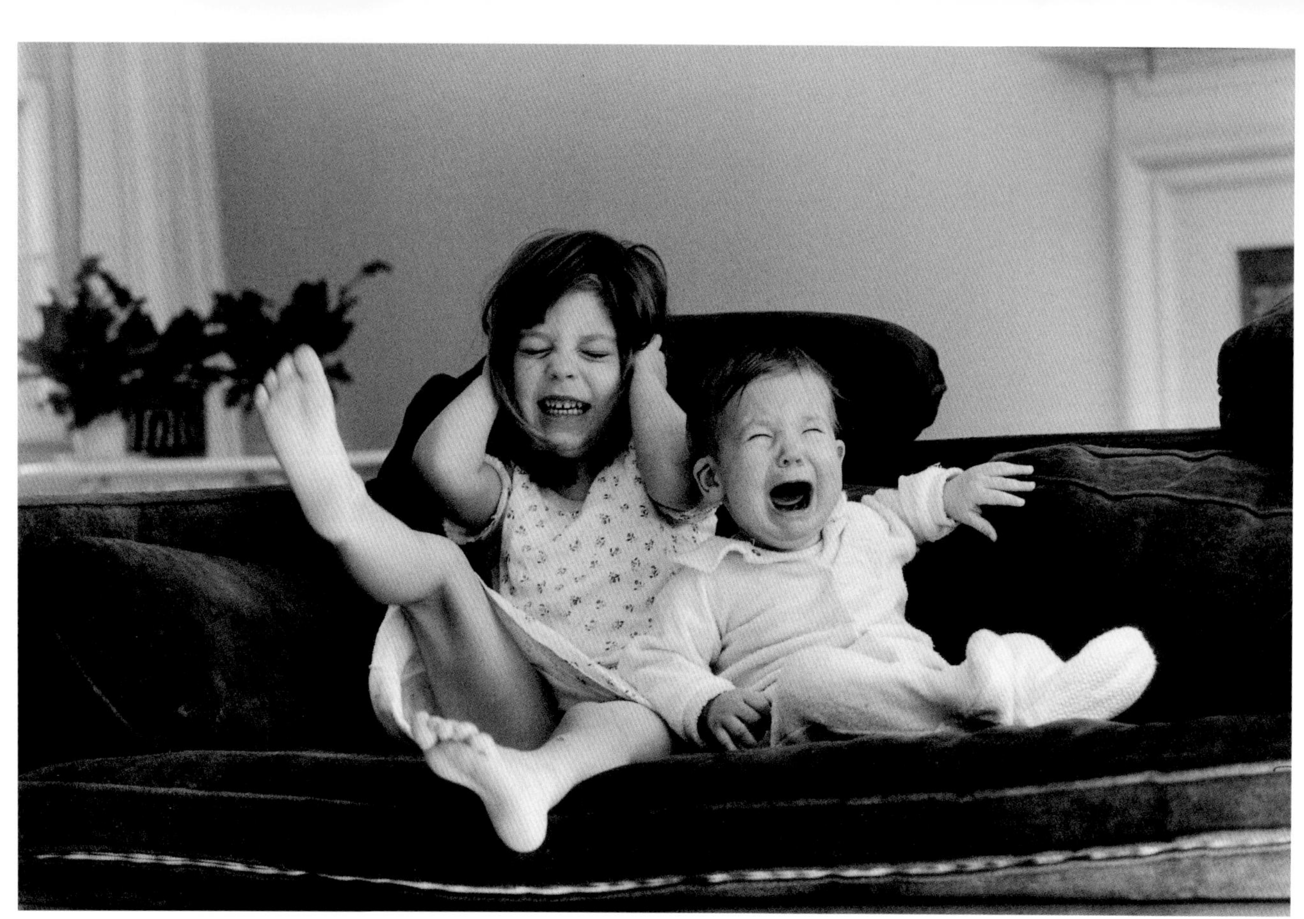

East Hampton, New York, 1981

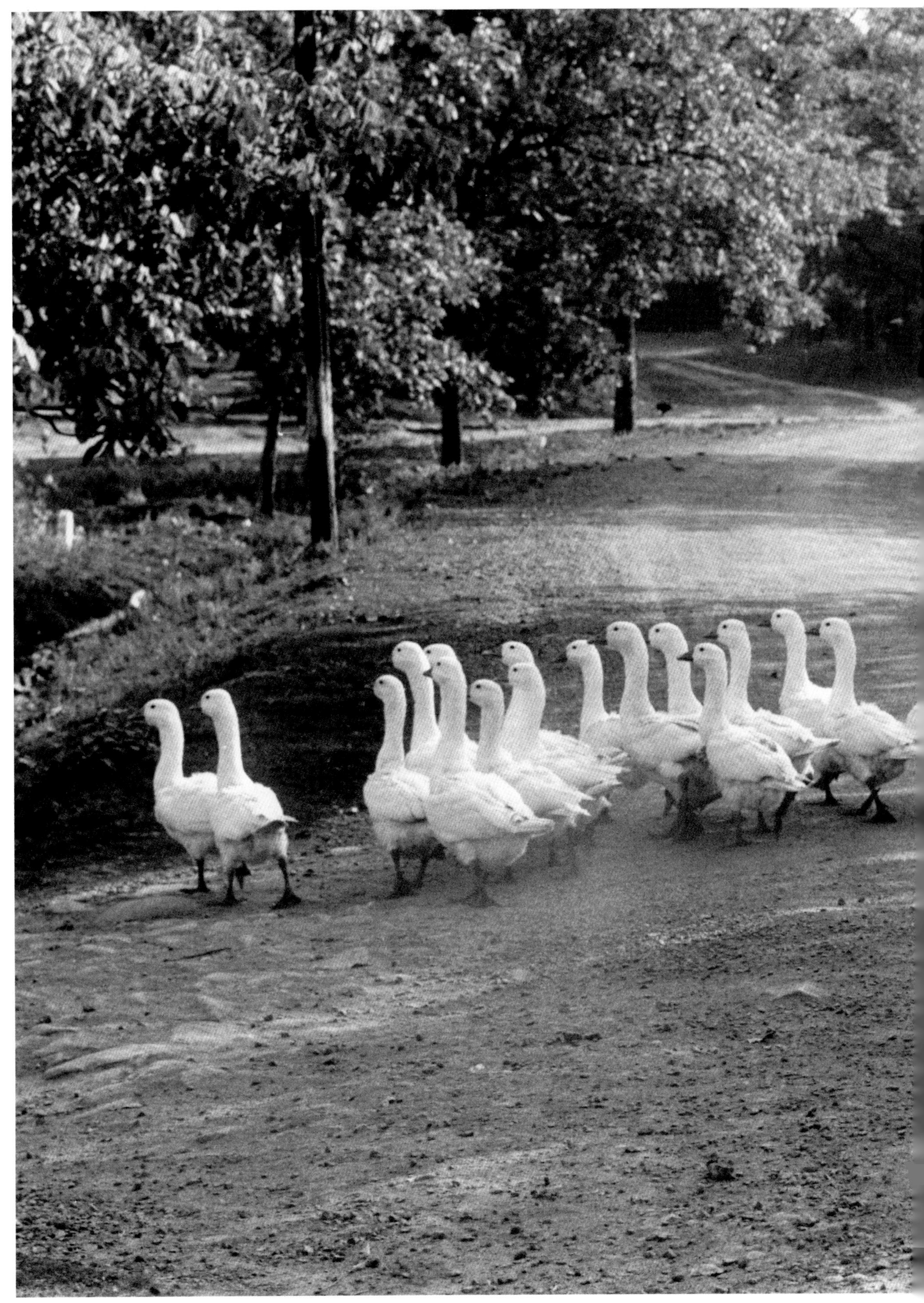

Hungary, 1964

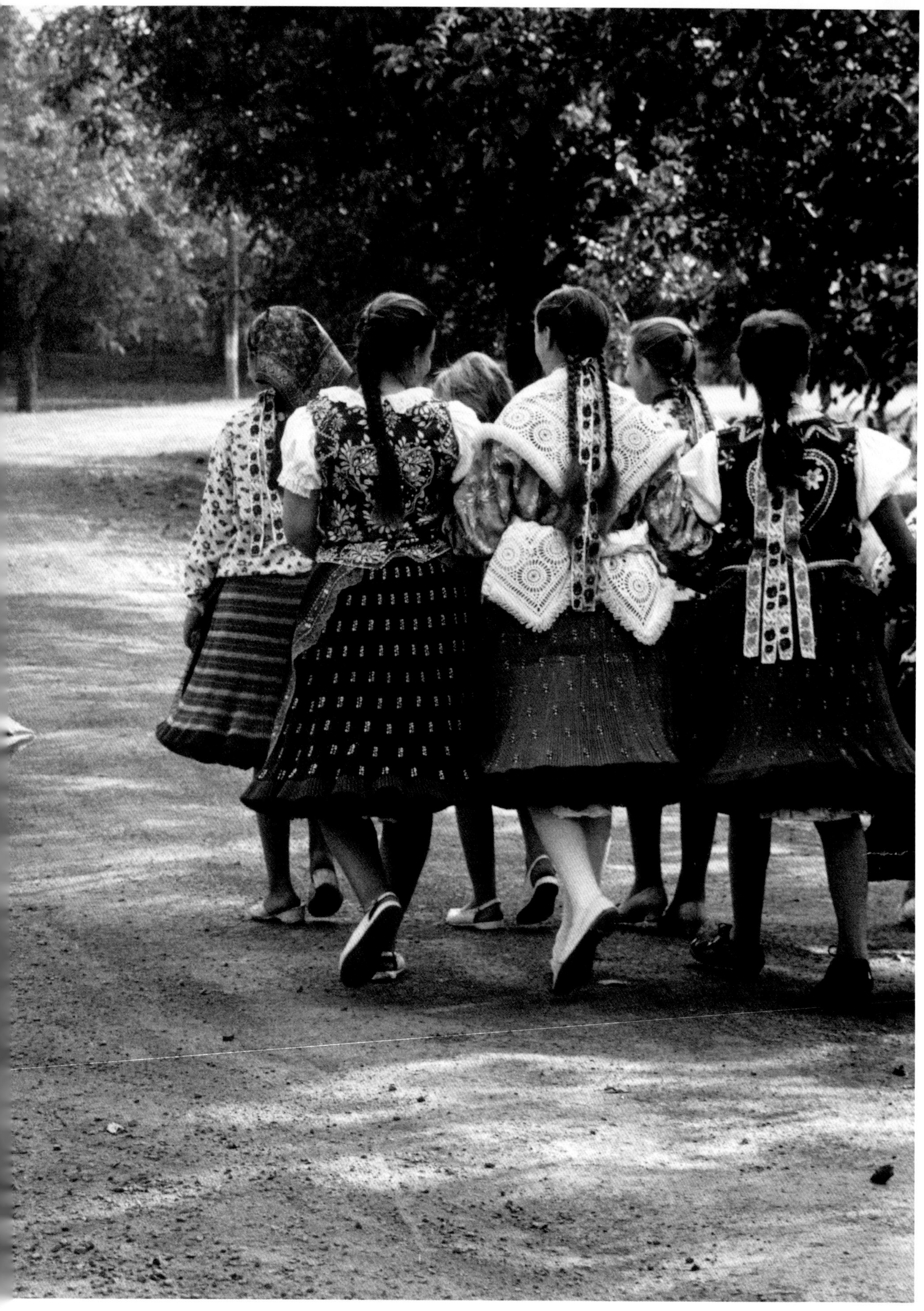

Point

Pointing is often an aggressive act, sometimes condescending and virtually always intrusive. The finger invades our space, questions our capacity to find out things for ourselves, directs us when we like to think we can very capably direct ourselves. There are many reasons why our elders warned us it was rude to point.

It is no surprise to find Richard Nixon here pointing at Nikita Khrushchev, in a renowned snap (p.307), and he is in the company of arrows, cannon, a penis, pistols, missiles and animal horns. A church steeple and pairs of female breasts do not move all that far from the more obvious signages of power.

The joke in many of these snaps is that the power is impotent or a poor imitation of the real thing. Pointing is pretty much a ridiculous posture in Elliott's world. The people who point can be hilariously self-deceived, and he will skewer them (since they are hardly defenceless) as wickedly as Molière.

Elliott's work has often put him in contact with men and women who are famous or powerful for a while. Few of them have seen him as more than a shadowy functionary, which is just the way he likes it. The exceptions, like John F. Kennedy and Marilyn Monroe, knew exactly how important his little Leica could be to their careers; they played to his lens and co-operated fully. Others, like Harry Truman and Lyndon Johnson, simply went about their business, trusting him to catch what they believed to be a truth in no need of varnishing.

Throughout *Snaps* you will see other celebrities as you have never seen them – an impossibly boyish Castro on the cusp of world fame, a Grace Kelly luminous at the engagement party before the wedding that will make her a princess, Marilyn Monroe laughing so happily that she might have this one time in her life forgotten that a camera was in the room.

Elliott, like most of the rest of us, has been fascinated by some of these people, while greatly contributing to their legends. But he is clearly not intimidated. When he could not get Khrushchev's attention (mind you, this was in the thick of the so-called Cold War), he pulled out a bicycle horn and honked it. The Premier of all the Russias whipped around to face him, and Elliott got his snap. For the adventure of it, Elliott passed Pia off as his photographer's assistant for an Oval Office shoot with Bill Clinton. The ploy worked, although this particular leader of the free world may have sensed something in the air. With a sardonic grin, he glanced over at Elliott and said, 'Who's that guy who lets a lady carry that heavy stuff?'

Elliott's most treasured memory of photographing someone authentically great involved Pablo Casals. Elderly and frail, the cellist could not summon up the strength to bow a solo Bach suite to completion while Elliott took pictures. He rested, holding his instrument, until the photo session was done. Casals apologized for his weakness and shambled over to a piano. Then one of the twentieth century's most significant musicians finished the piece in his parlour, so that his visitor would hear the masterpiece entire.

As for the greatness of political figures, Elliott, who despises all pretension and most Republicans, was never able to take a dignified photo of Nixon. And his pairing of Charles de Gaulle with his good friend Murray Sayle dressed as a comic-opera Samurai (p.323) speaks for itself.

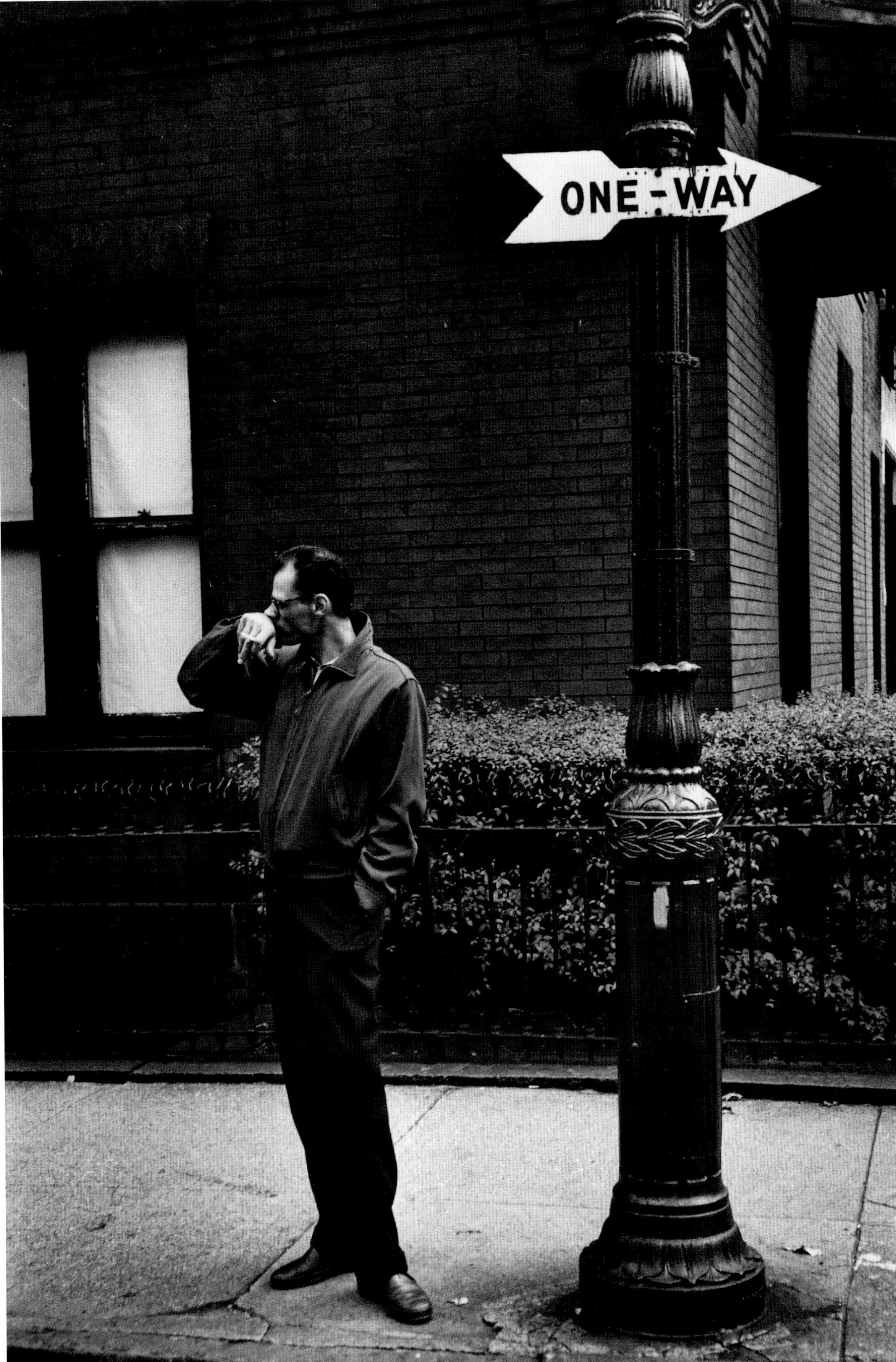
ONE-WAY

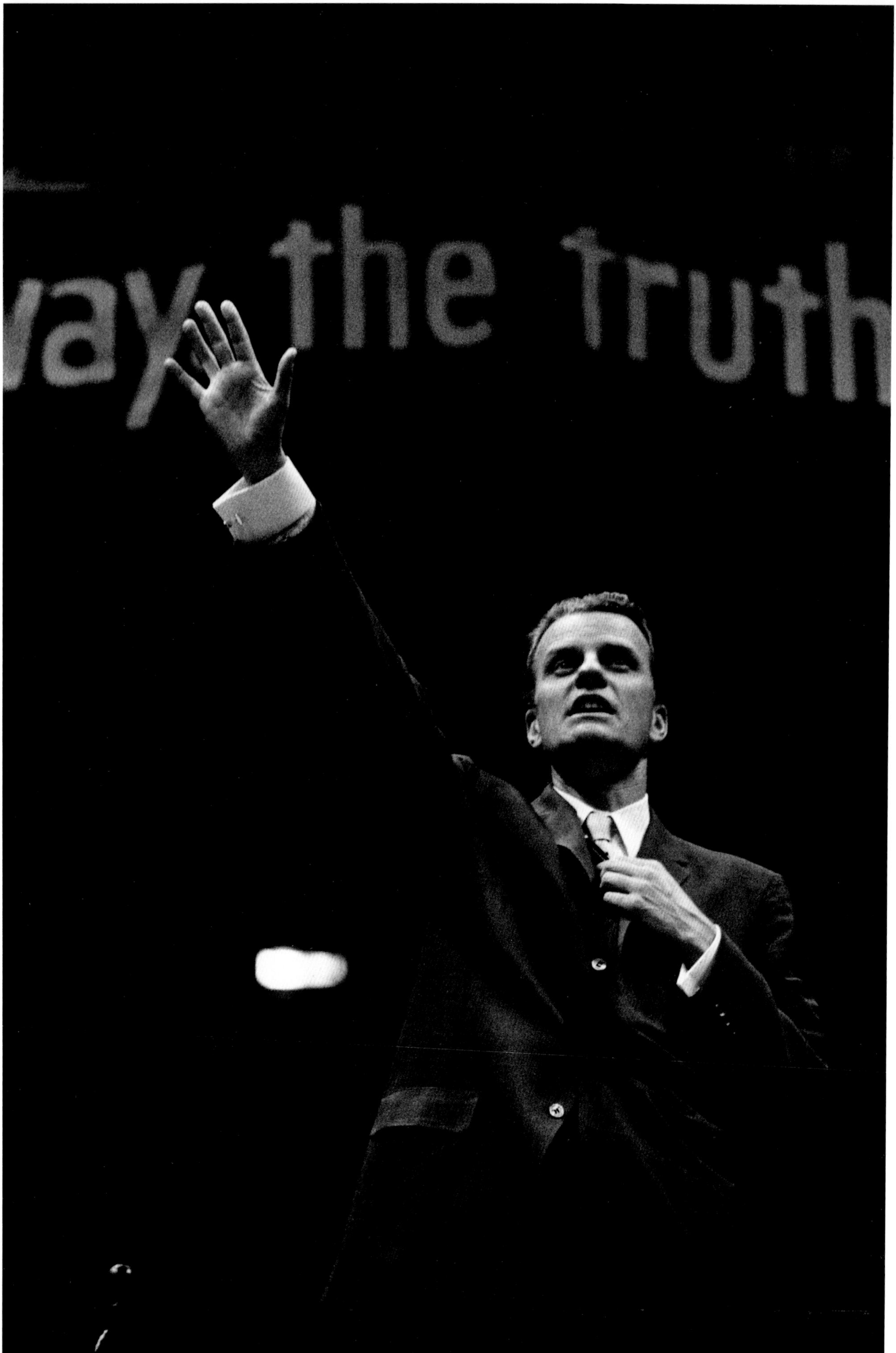

way the truth

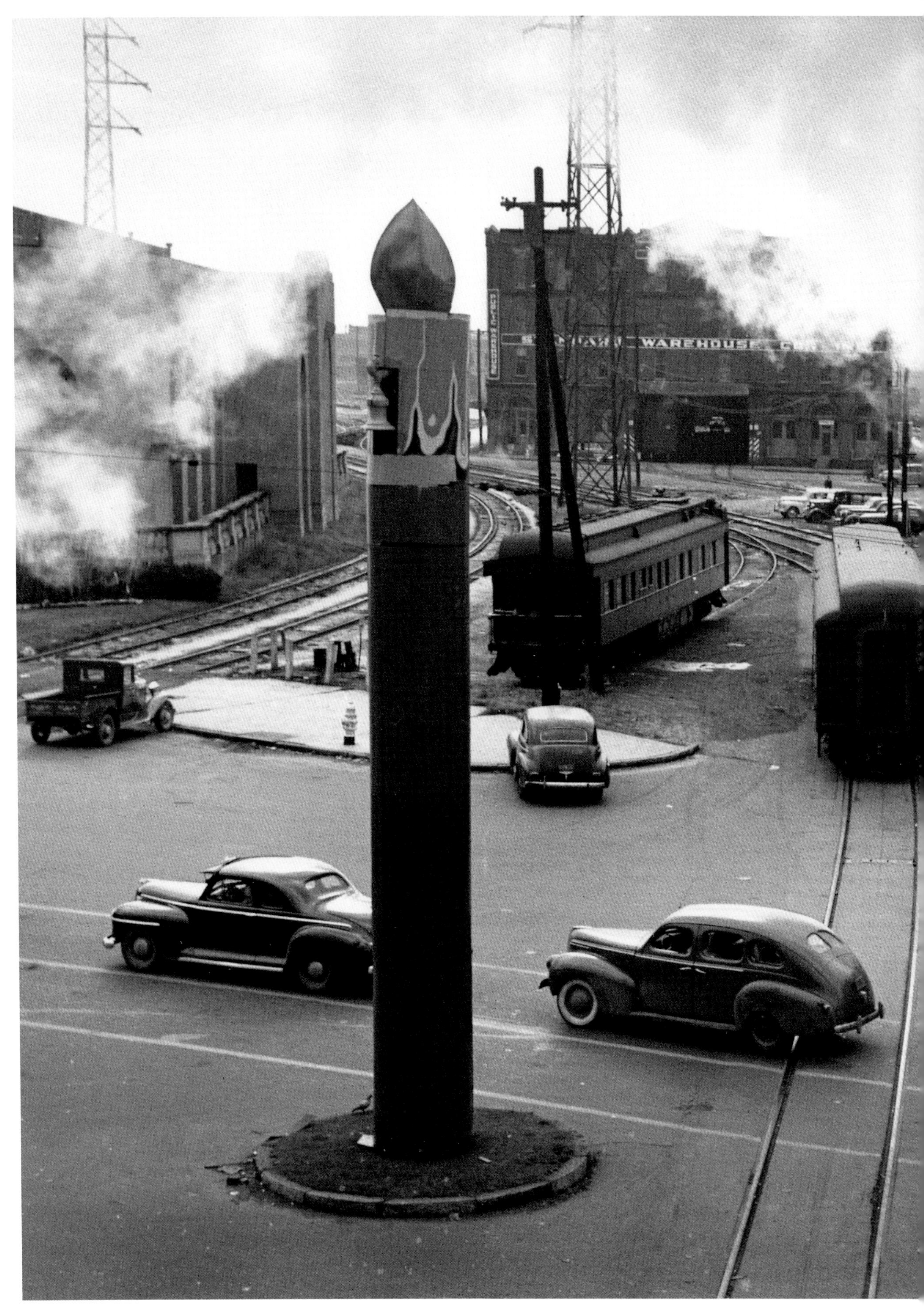

previous page *Arthur Miller, Brooklyn, New York, 1954* / *Billy Graham, New York, 1957*

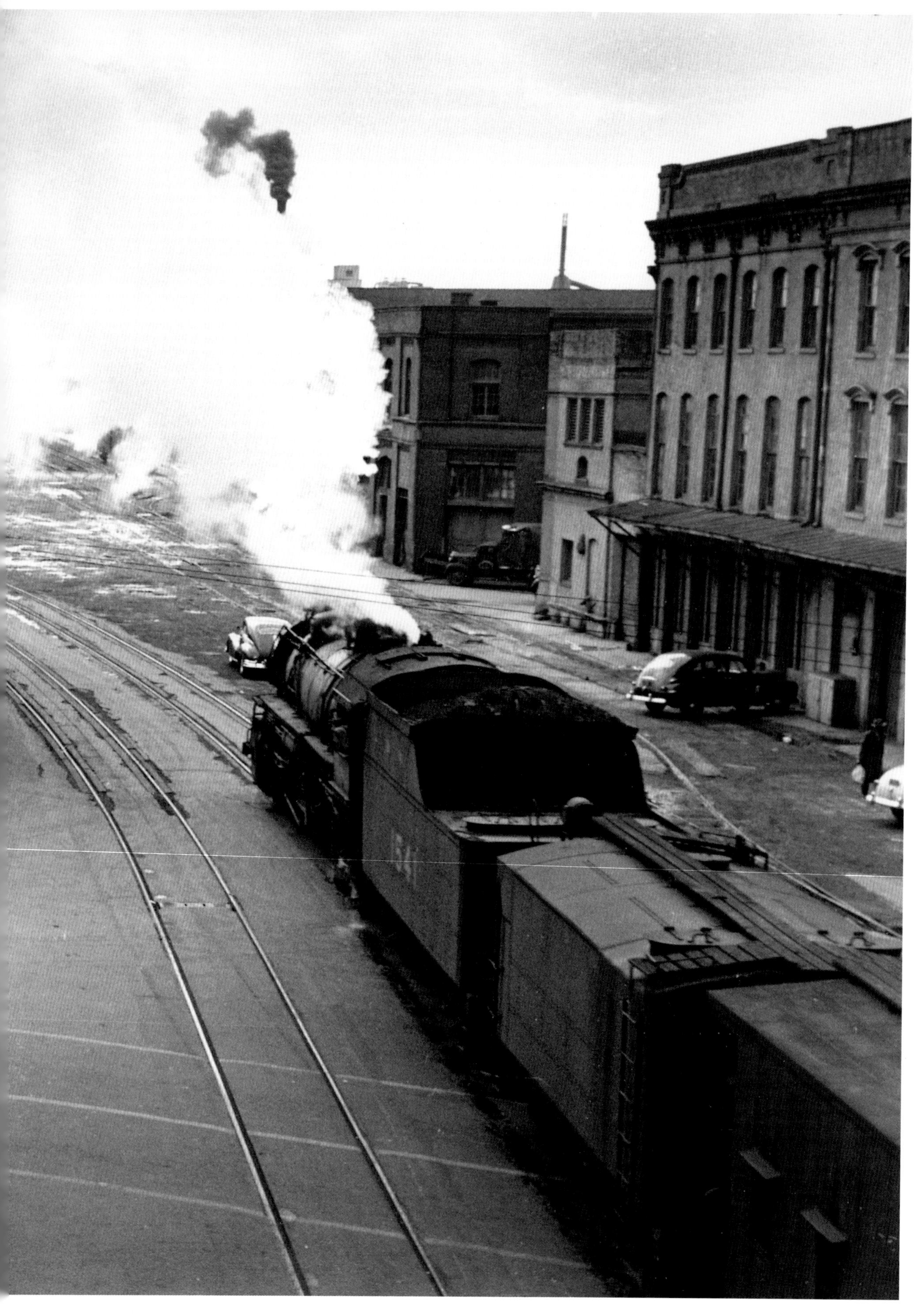

New Orleans, 1949

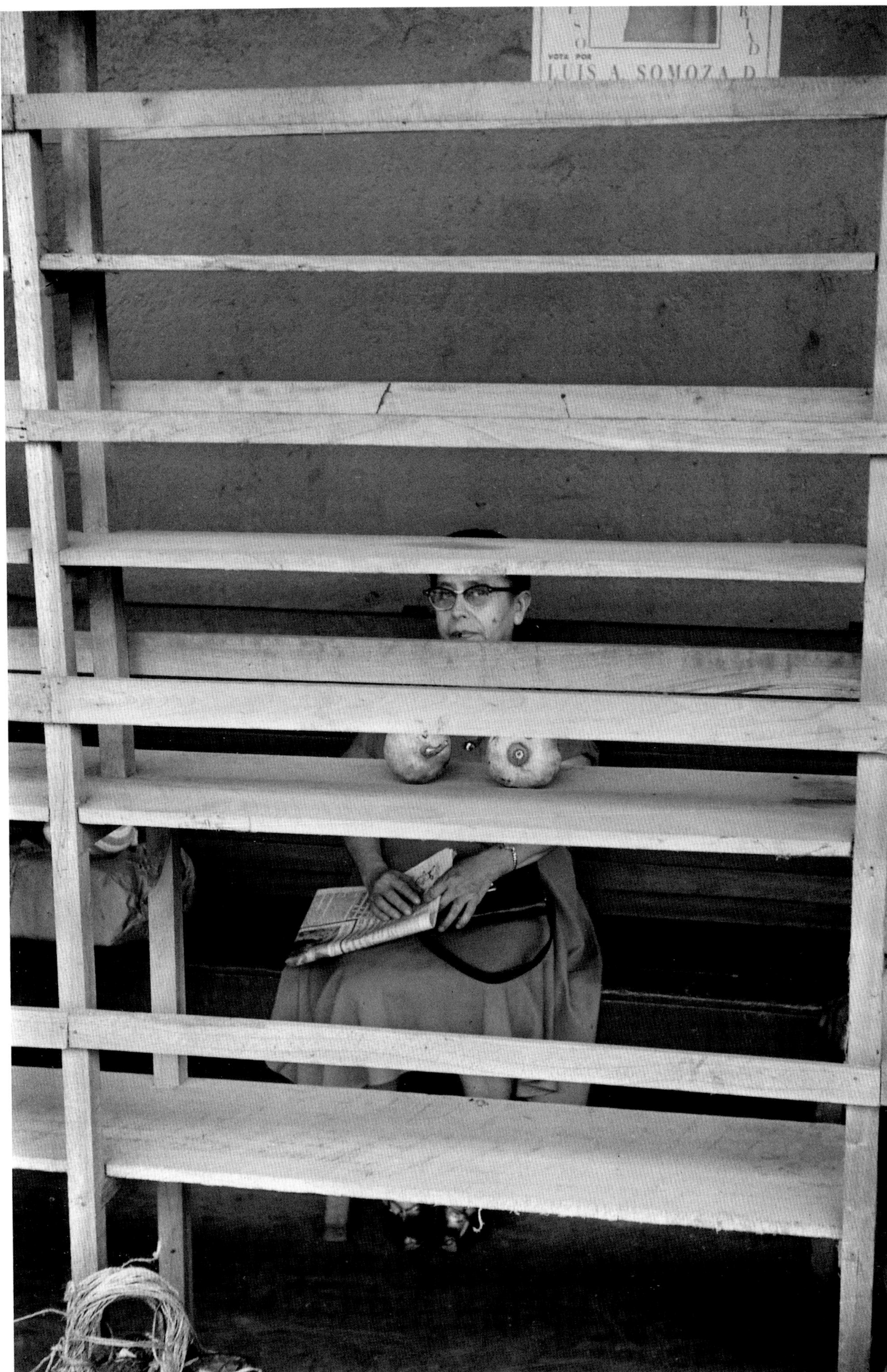
VOTA POR
LUIS A. SOMOZA D.

Managua, Nicaragua, 1957

clockwise from left *Paul Rudolph, New Haven, Connecticut, 1965* / *Michelangelo Antonioni, Rome, 1965*
Richard Leakey, New York, 1963 / *Nelson Algren, New York, 1950*

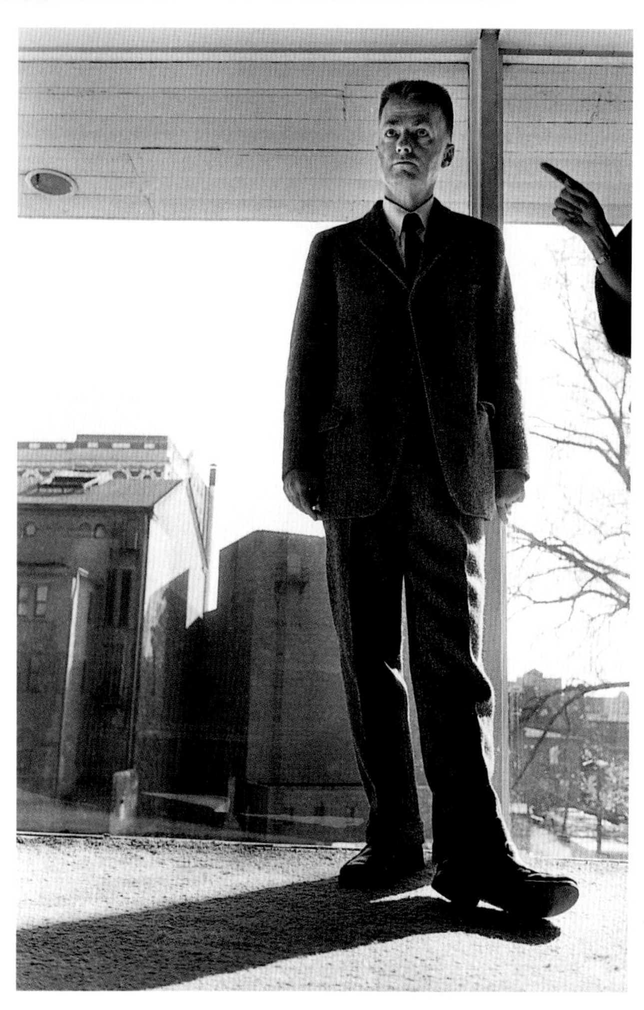
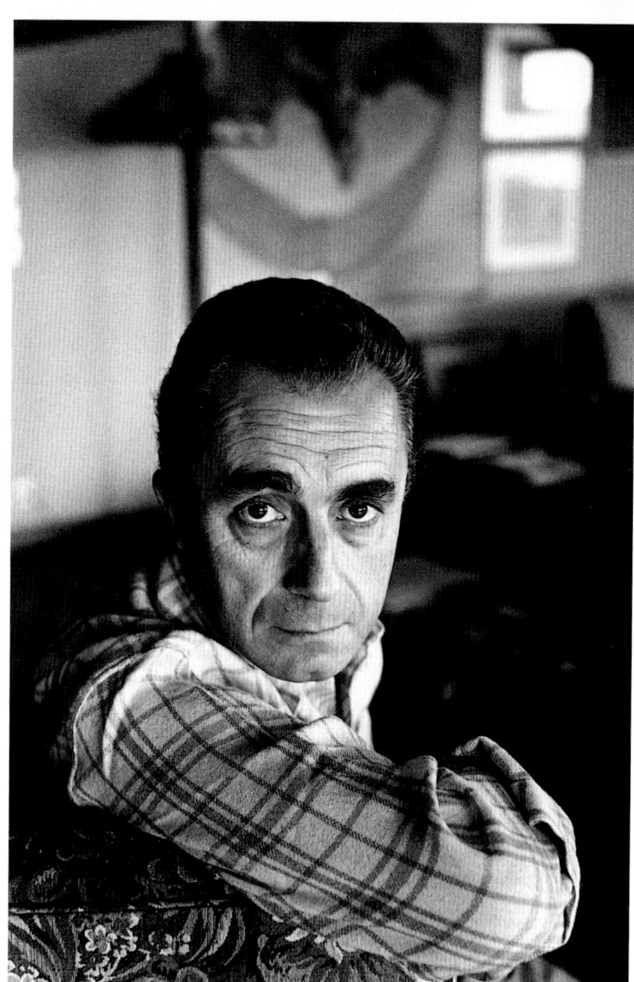
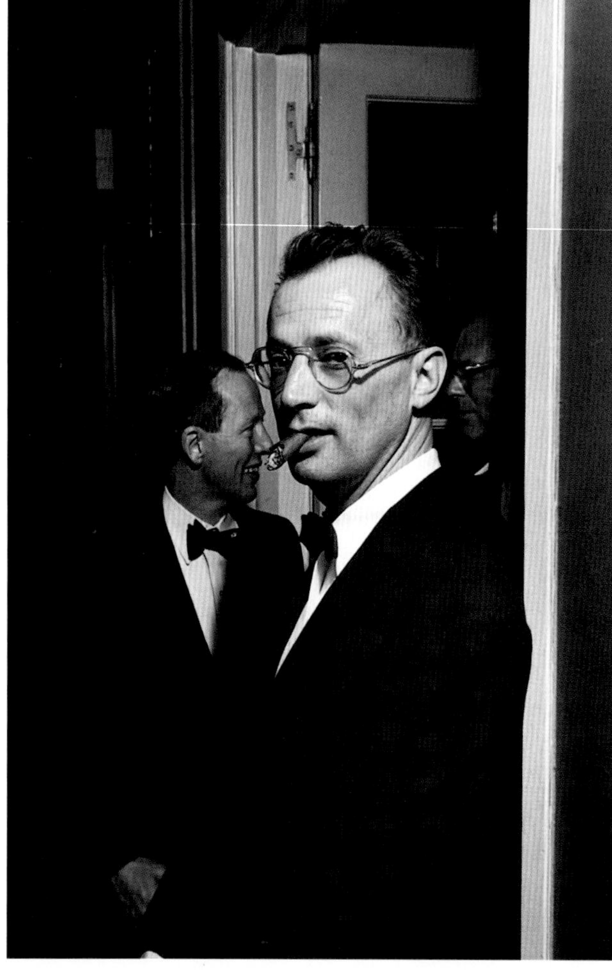
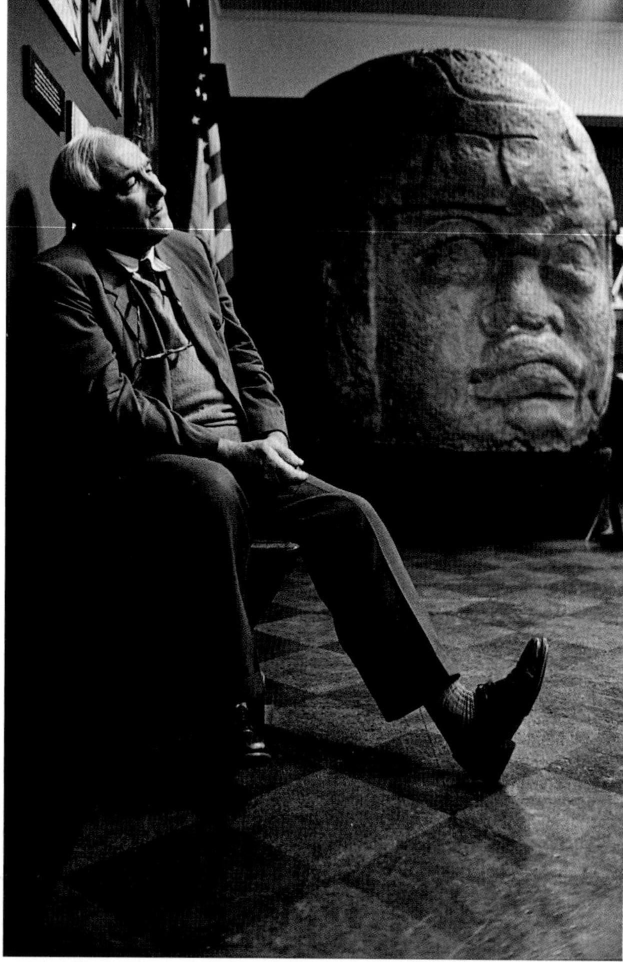

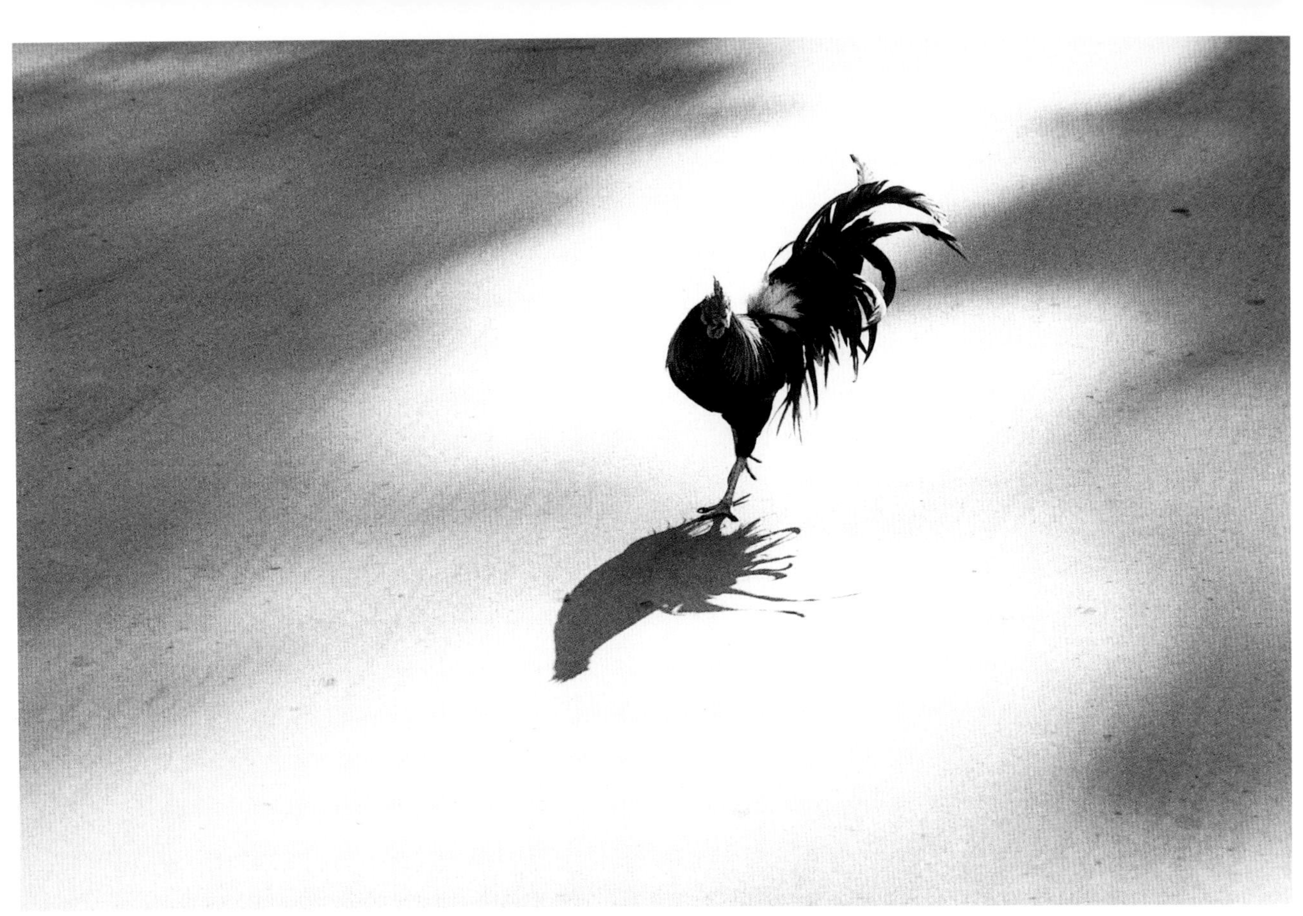

San Diego, California, 1973

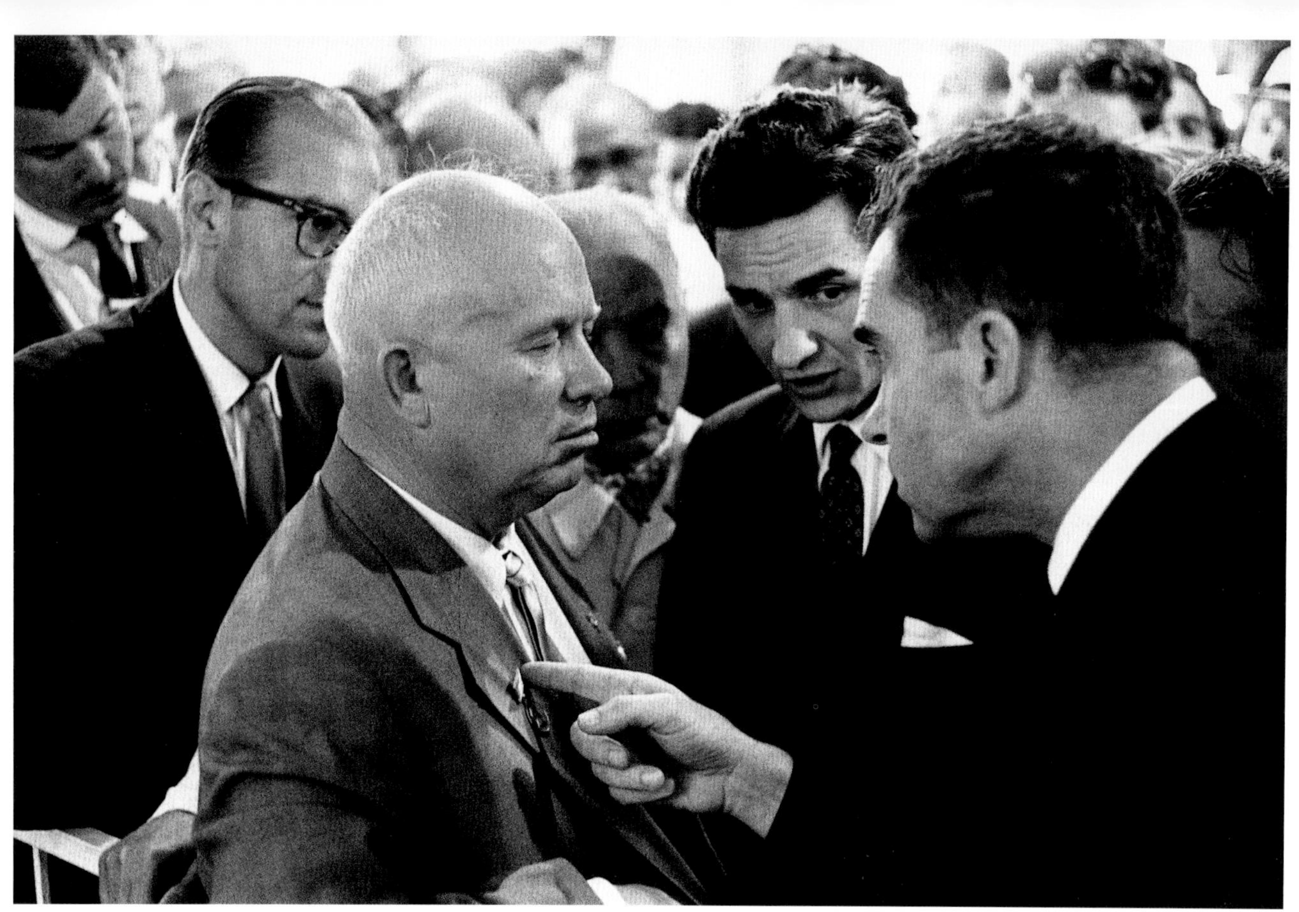

Nikita Khrushchev and Richard Nixon, Moscow, 1959

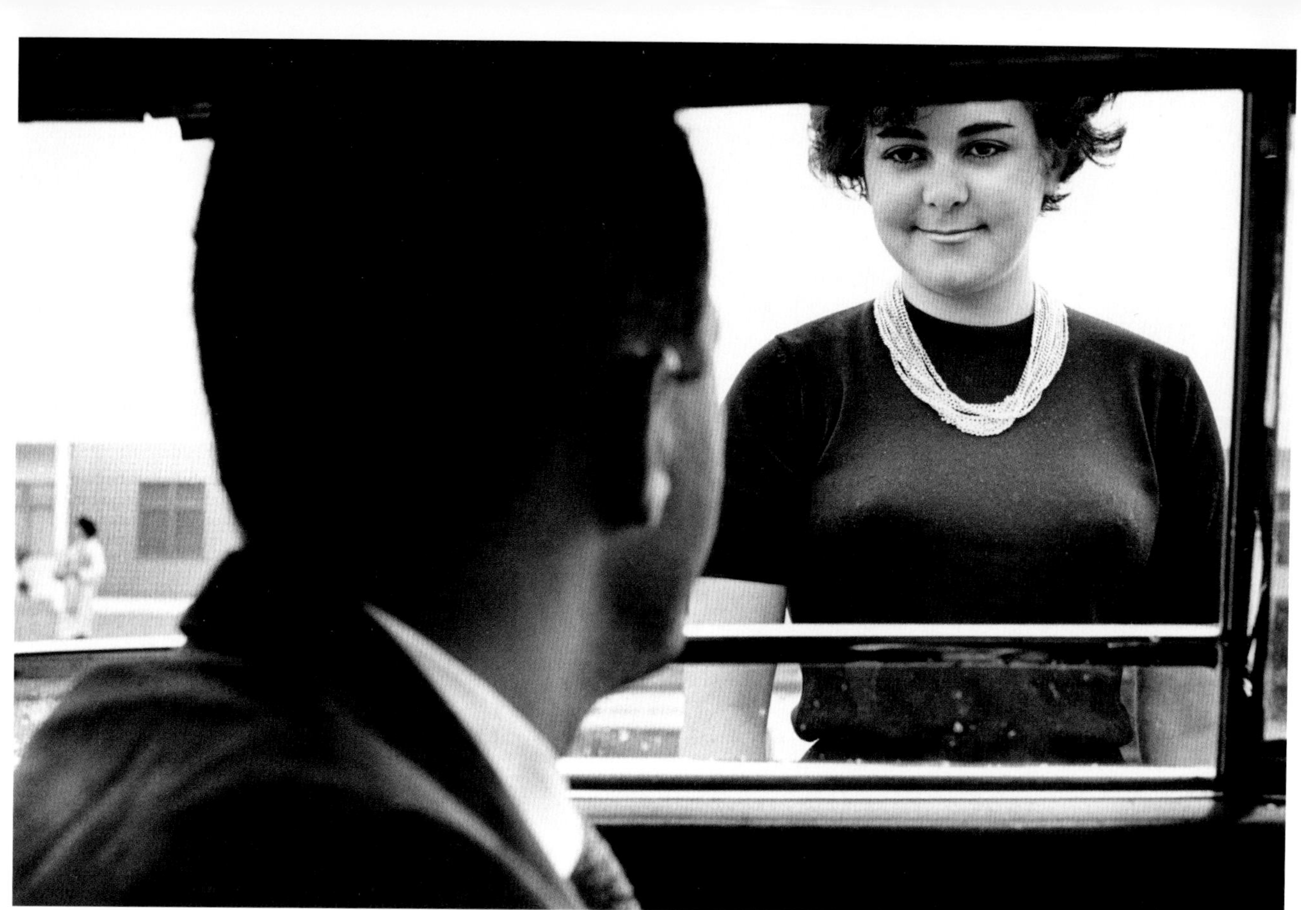

Brasília, Brazil, 1961
overleaf *Shanghai, 1978* / *Amboise, France, 1972*

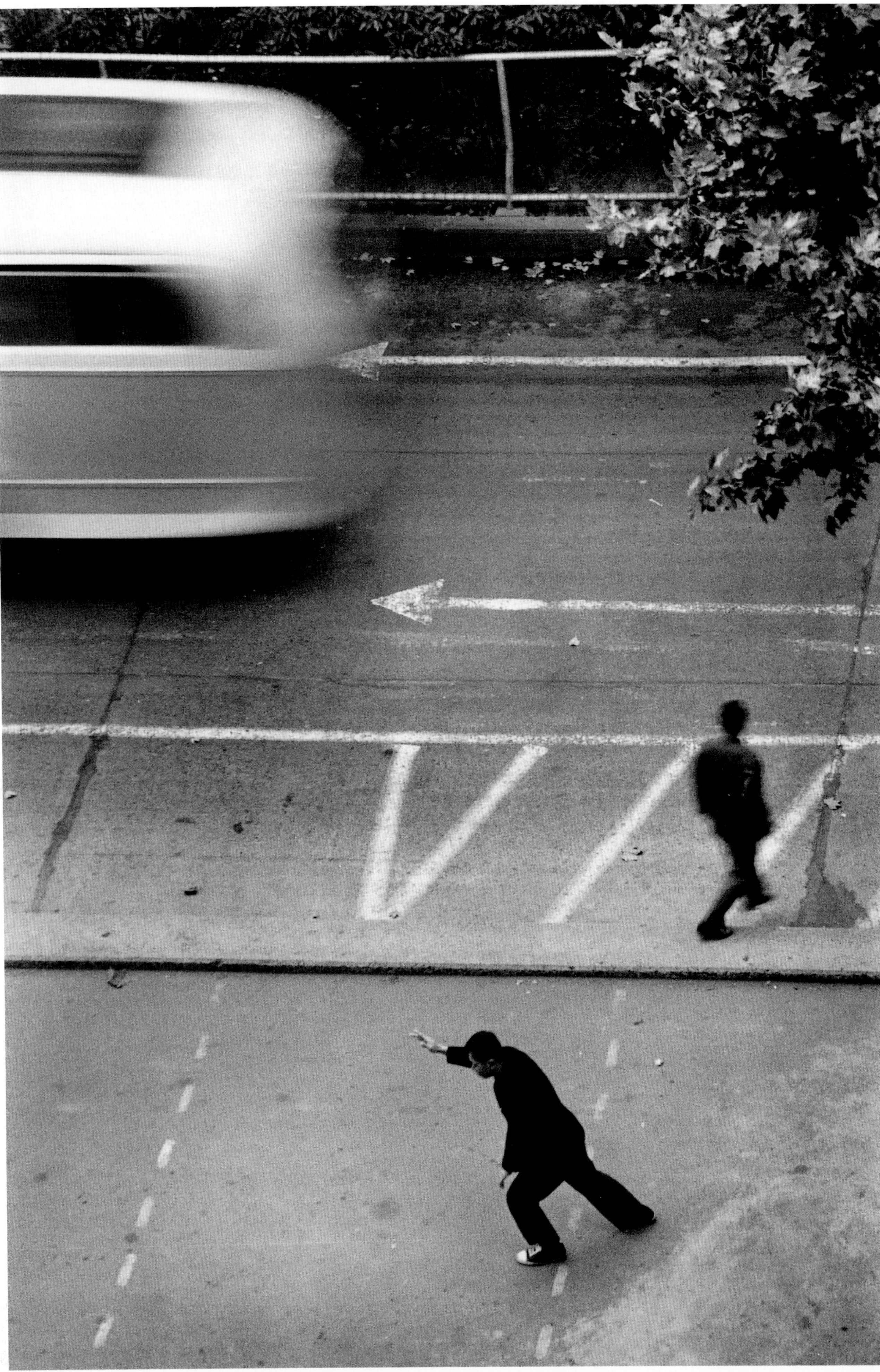

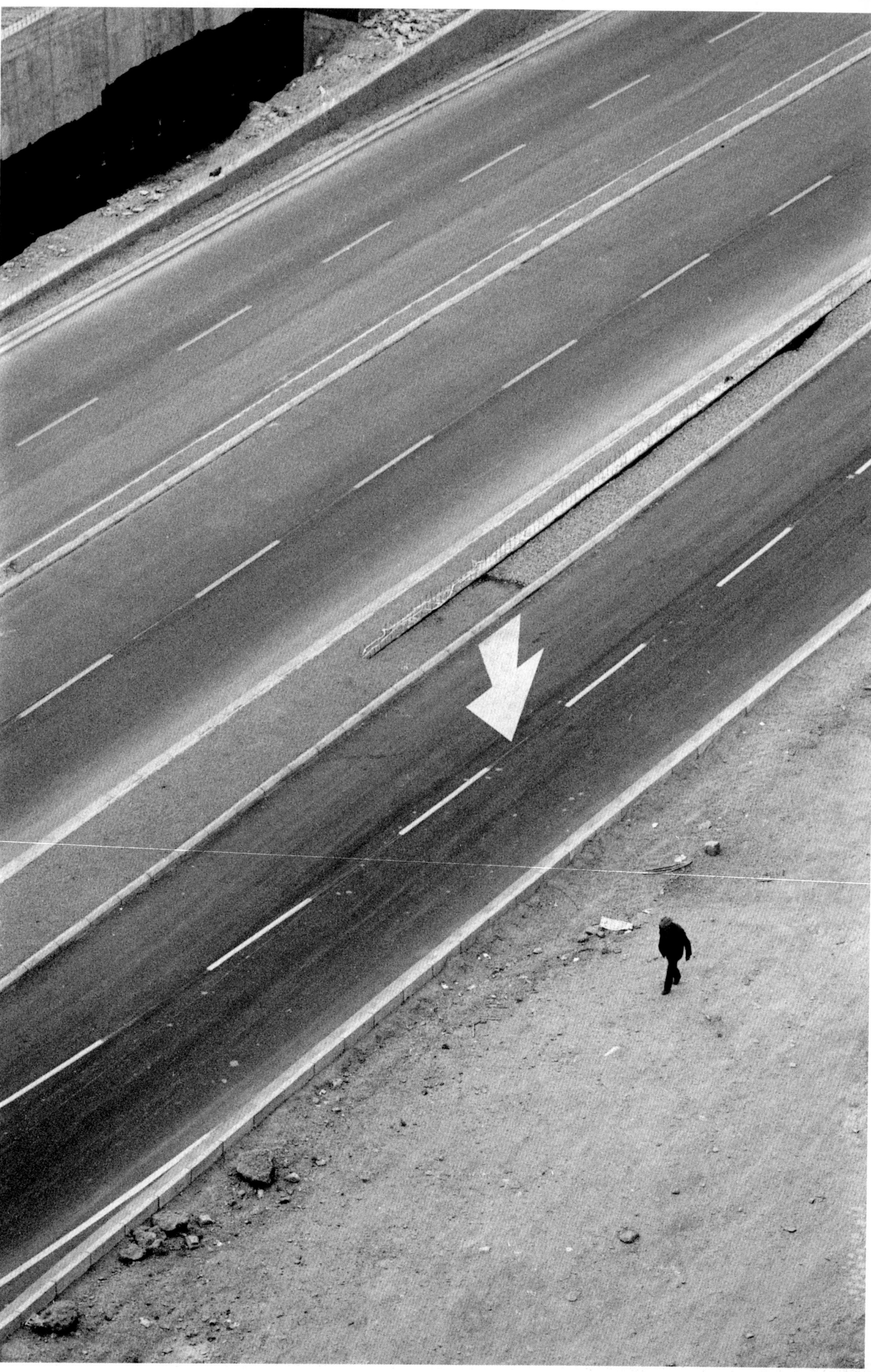

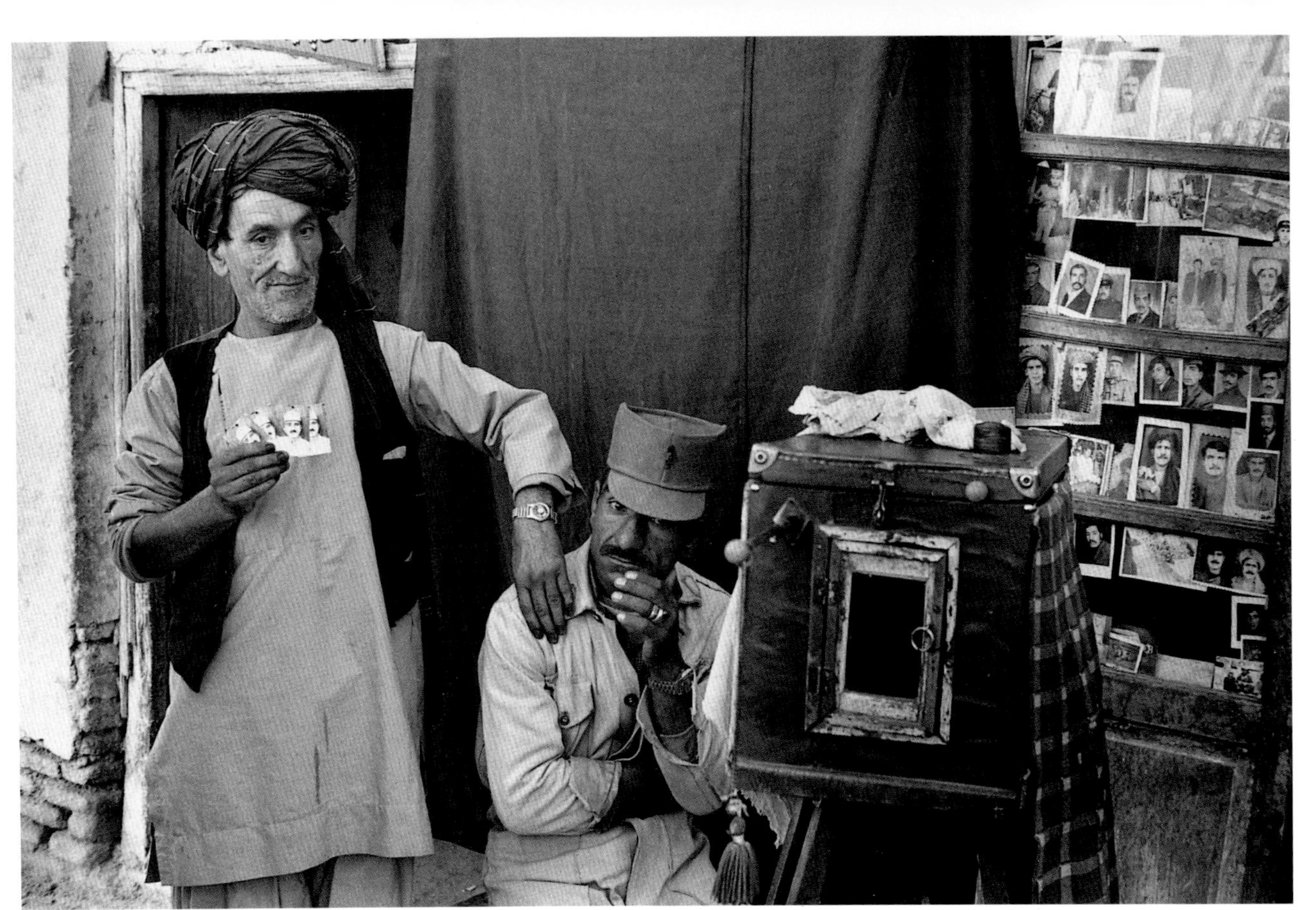

Herát, Afghanistan, 1977

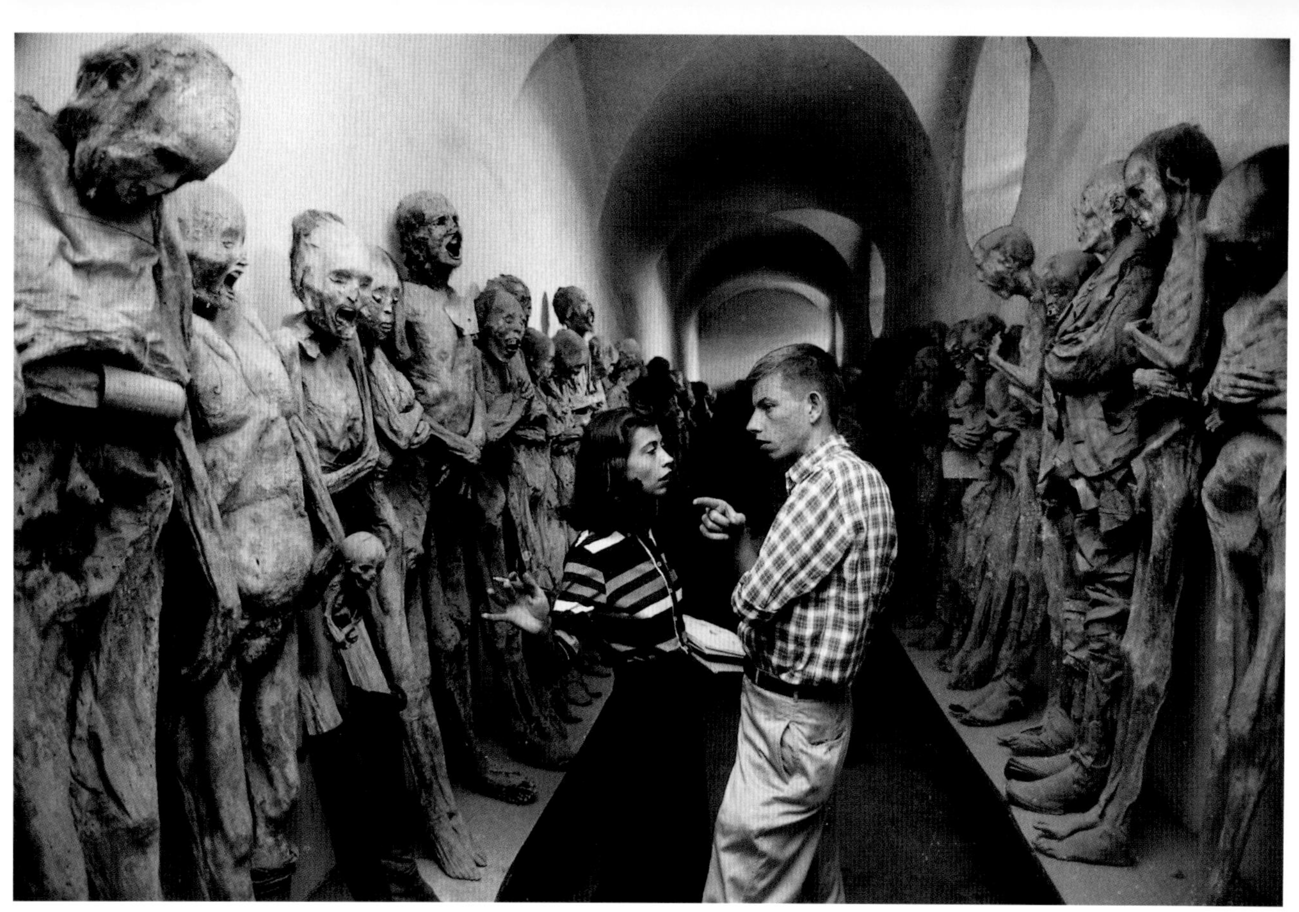

Guanajuato, Mexico, 1957

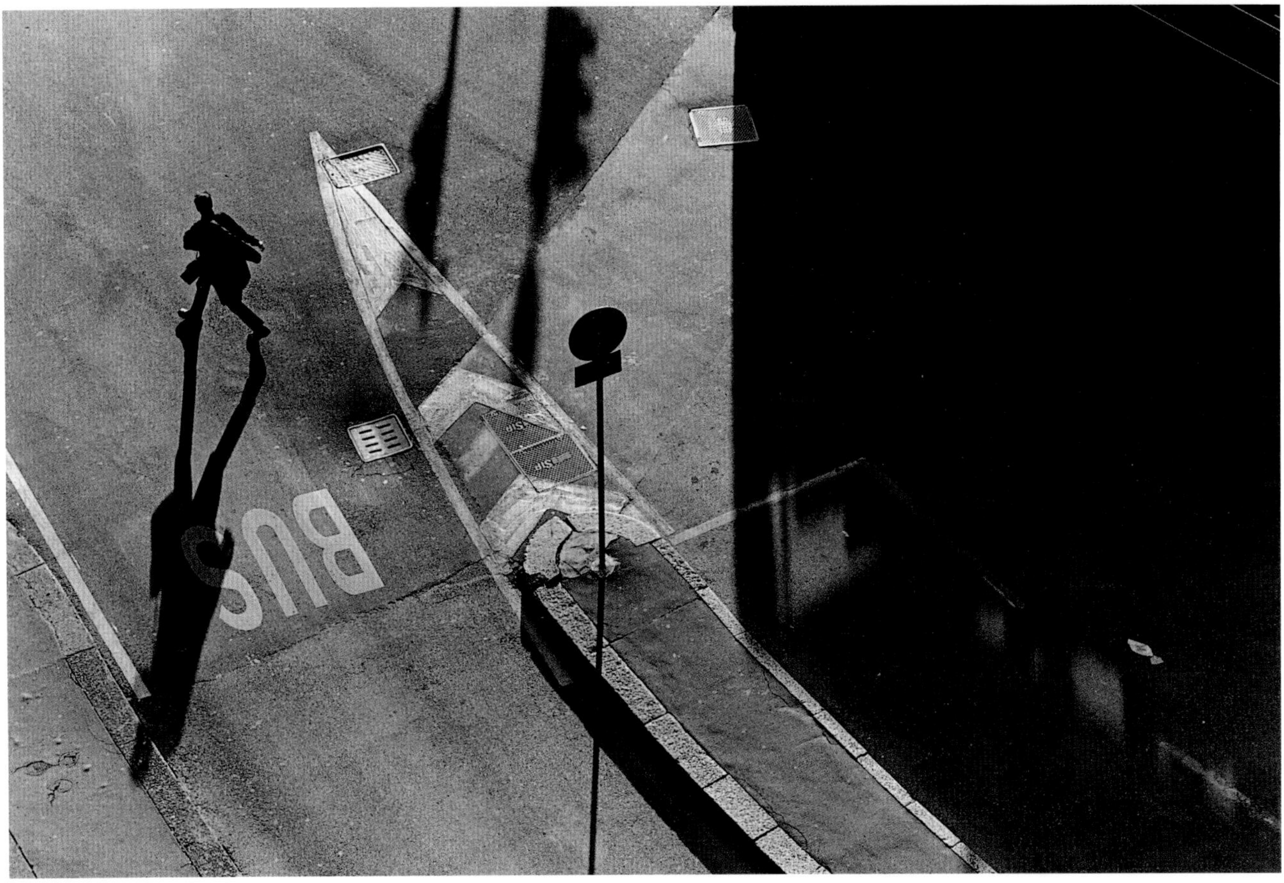

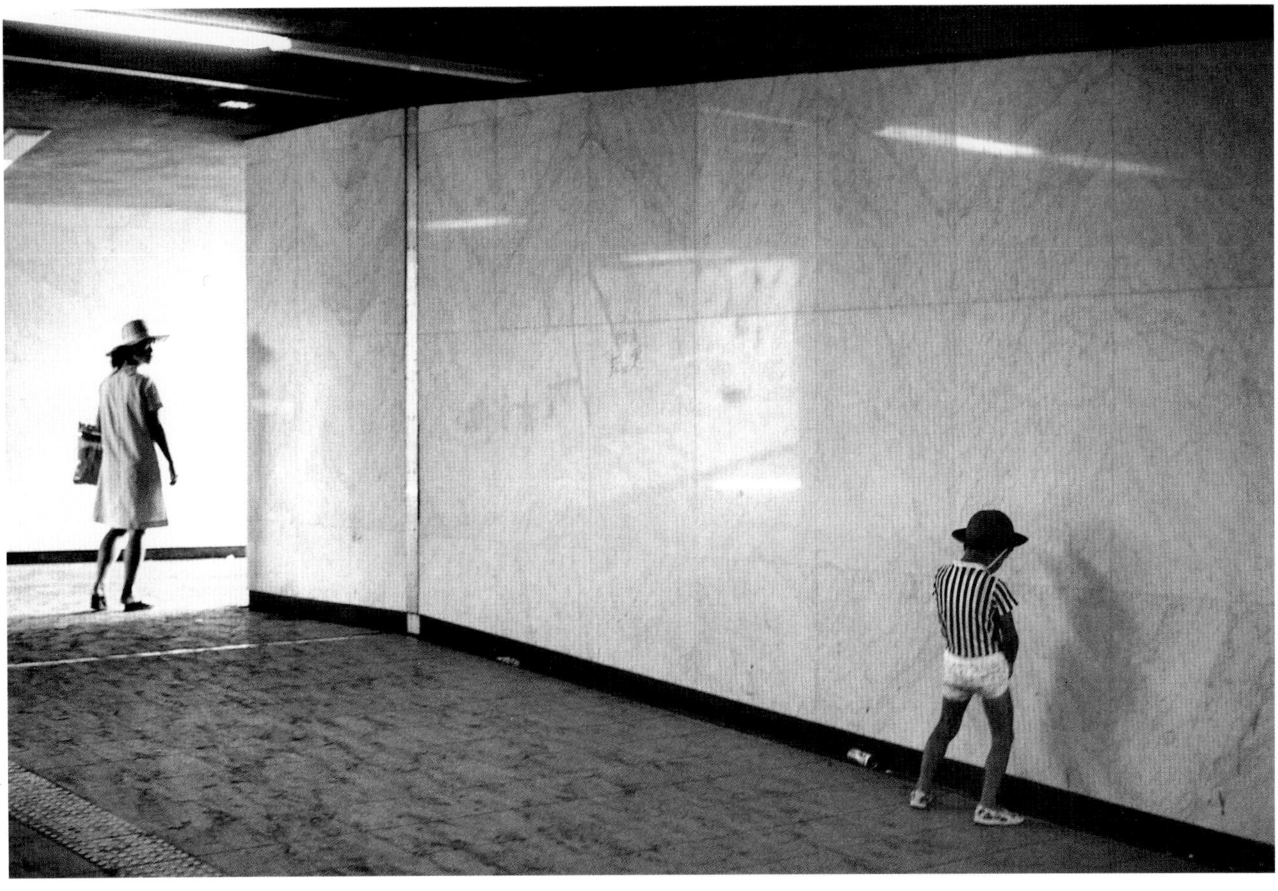

Milan, 2000 / *Chigasaki, Japan, 1977*

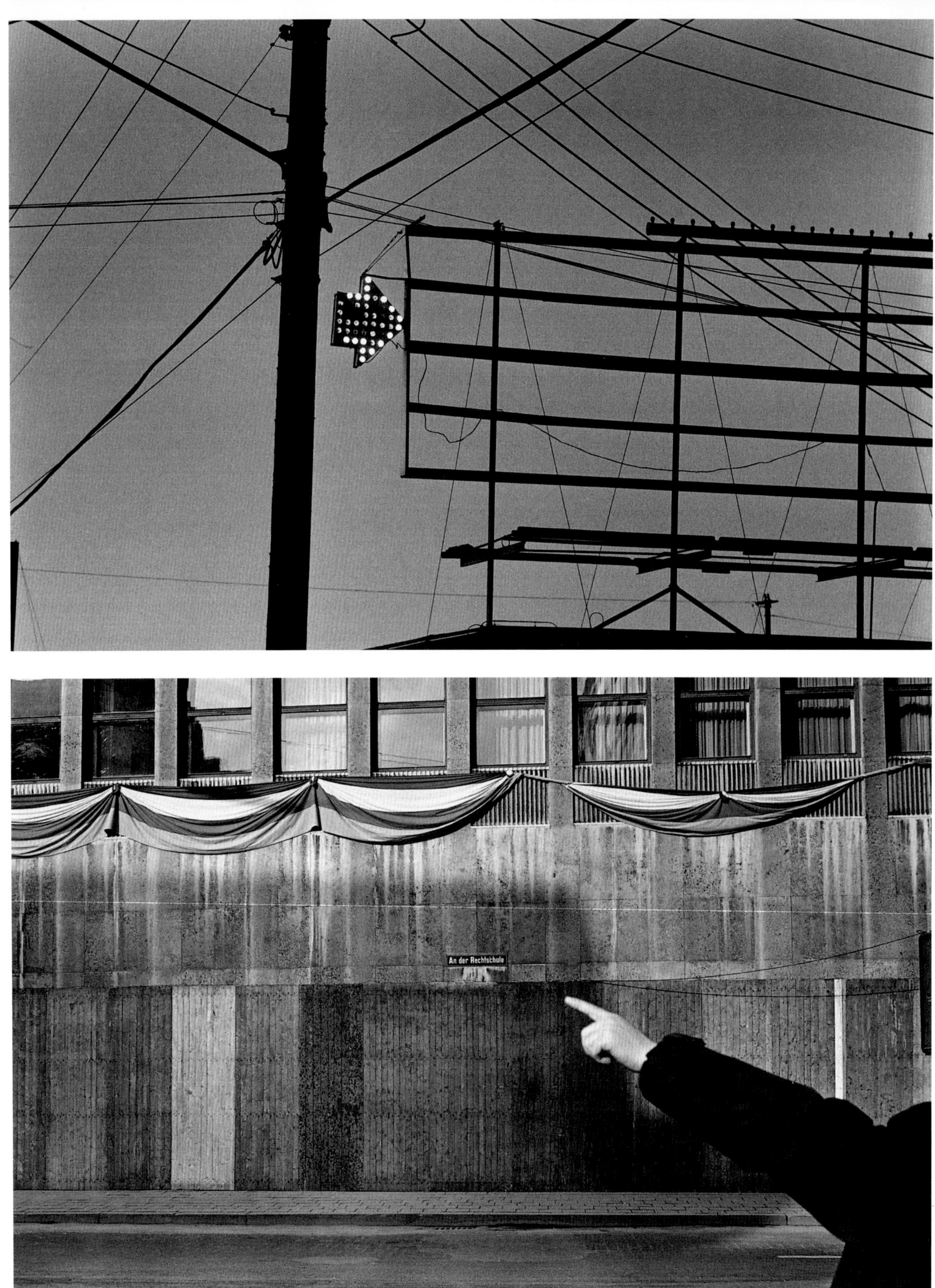

Los Angeles, 1974 / *Cologne, Germany, 1967*
overleaf *Amsterdam, 1968* / *Coney Island, New York, 1955*

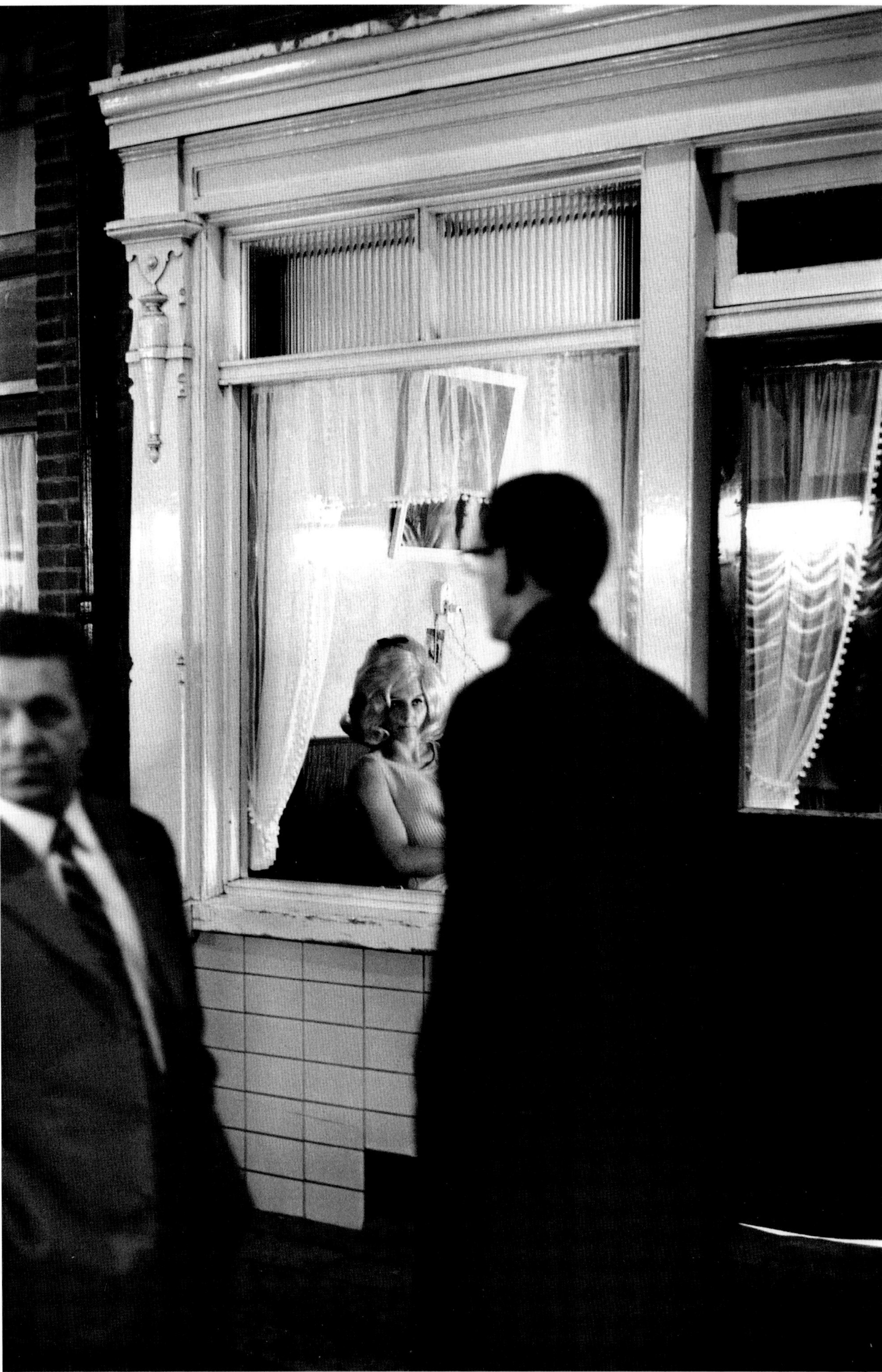

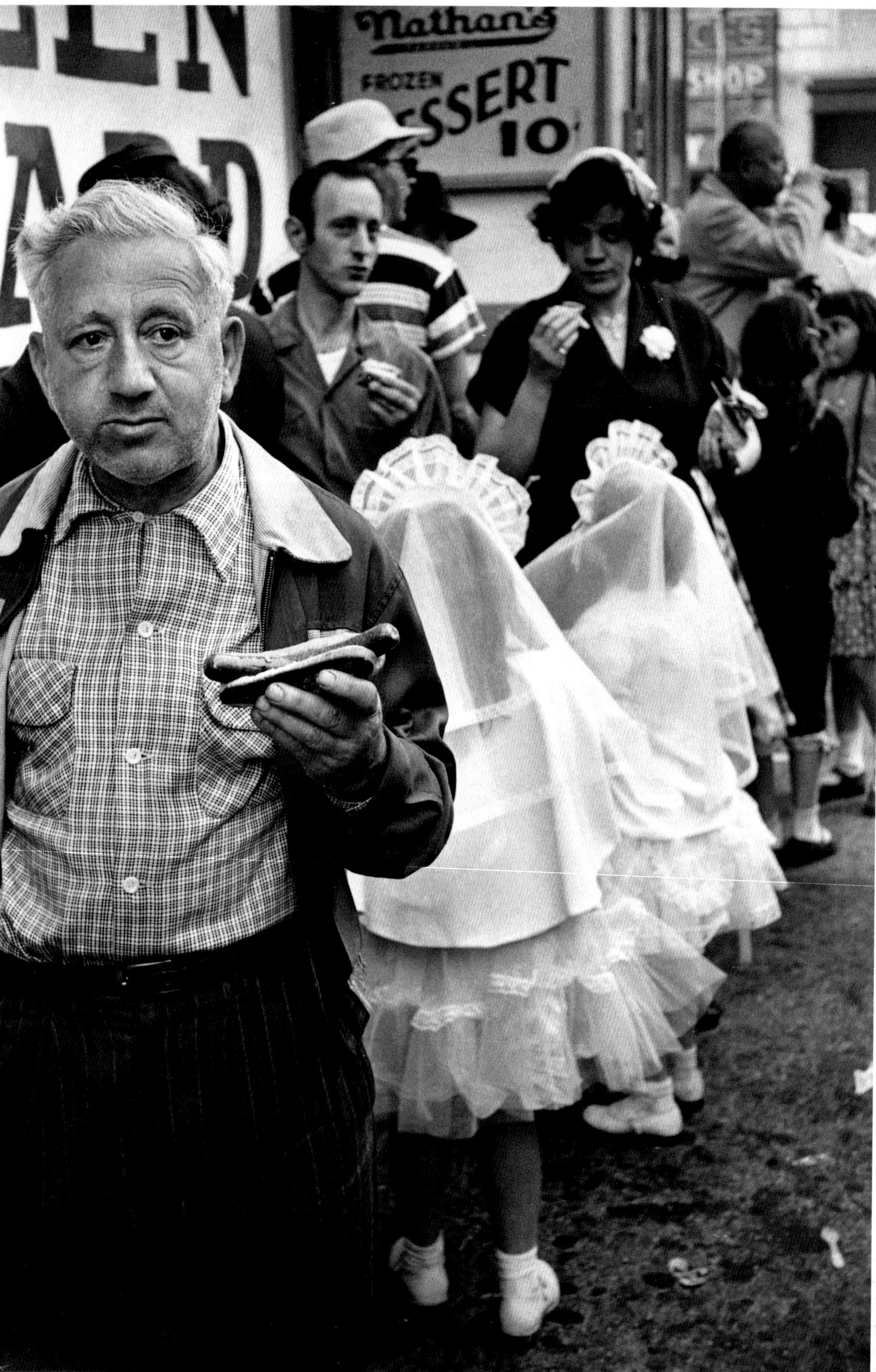
Nathan's
FROZEN
ESSERT
10
SHOP

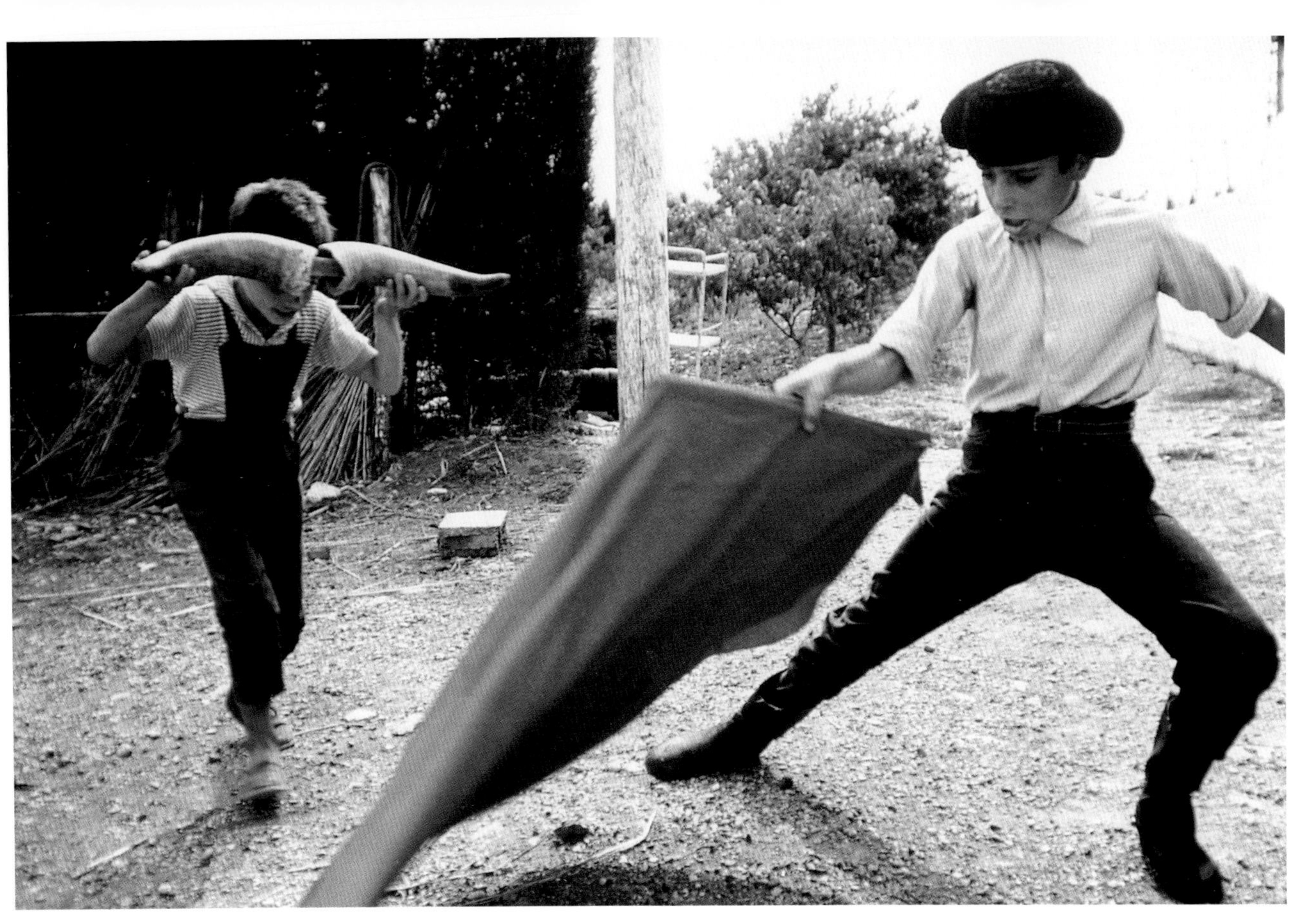

Southern Spain, 1969

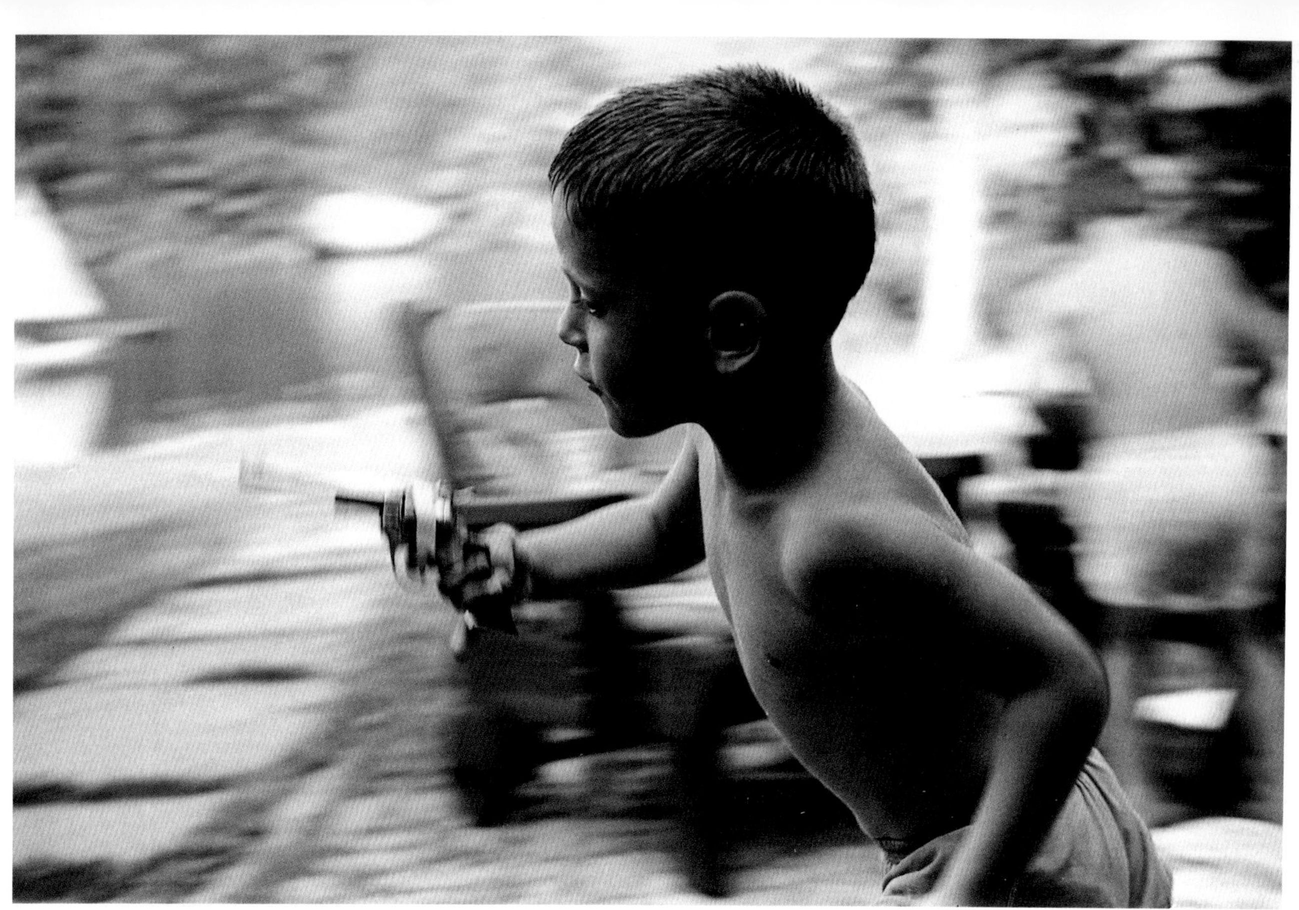

Armonk, New York, 1959

Henry Kissinger, Las Vegas, Nevada, 1986
overleaf, top row left to right: *Alger Hiss, New York, 1956 / Richard Nixon, Washington, DC, 1955*
Society lady, Brighton, England, 1956 / George Balanchine and Igor Stravinsky, 1965
bottom row left to right: *Nikita Khrushchev, Moscow, 1959 / Nikita Khrushchev, Moscow, 1959*
Charles de Gaulle, Moscow, 1966 / Murray Sayle, Kyoto, Japan, 1985

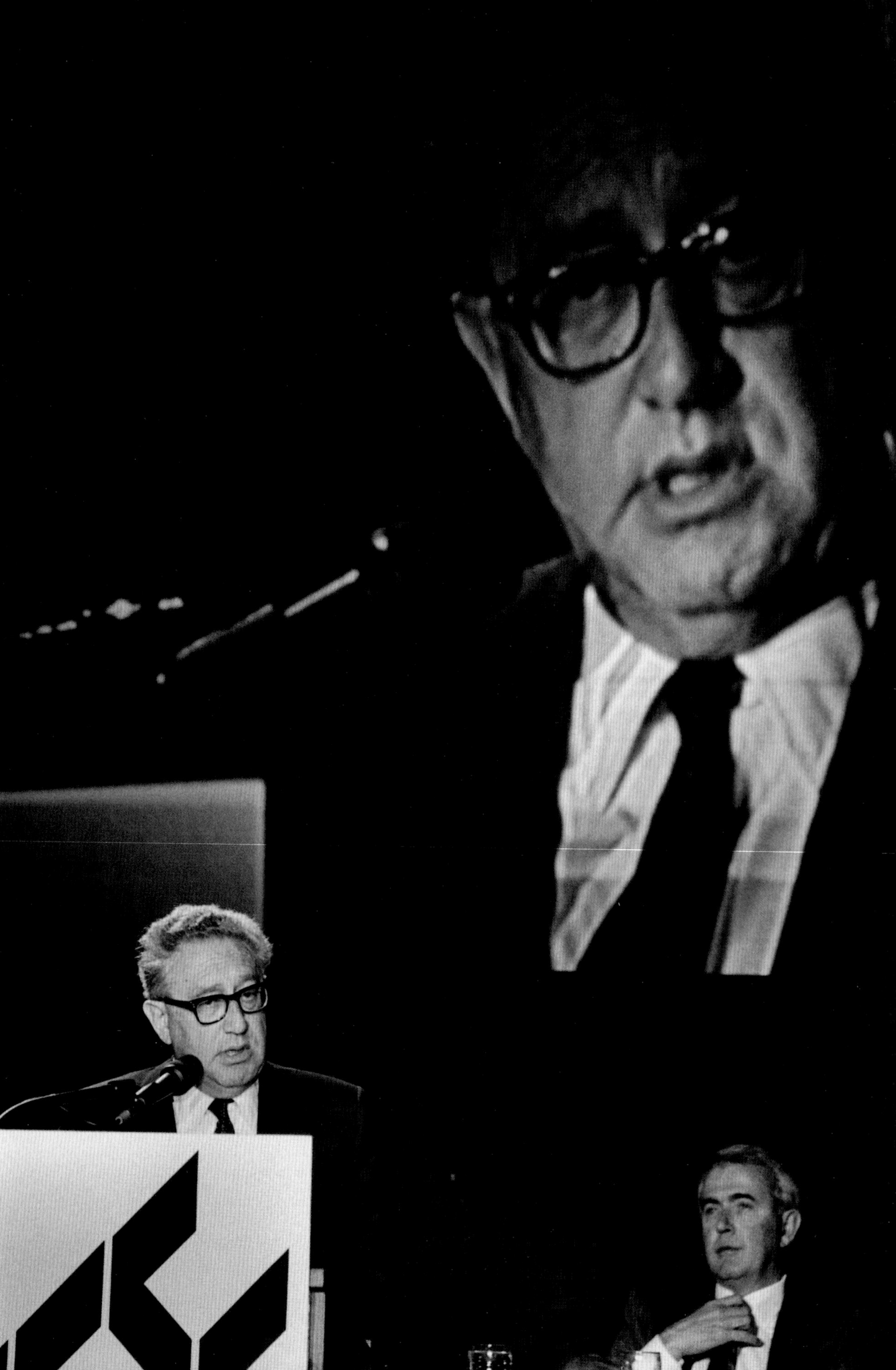

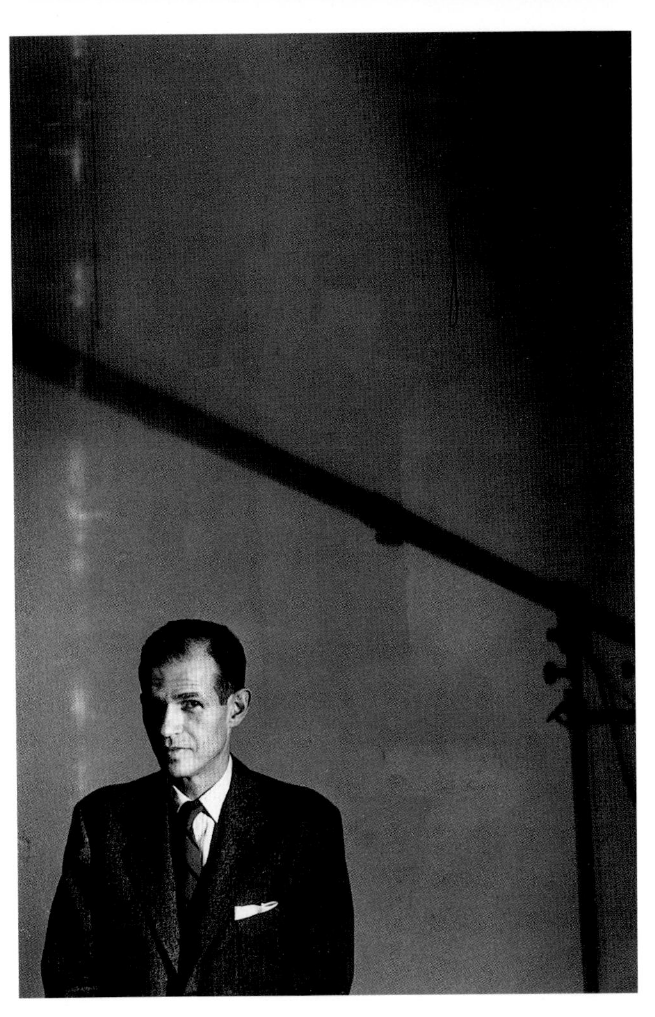
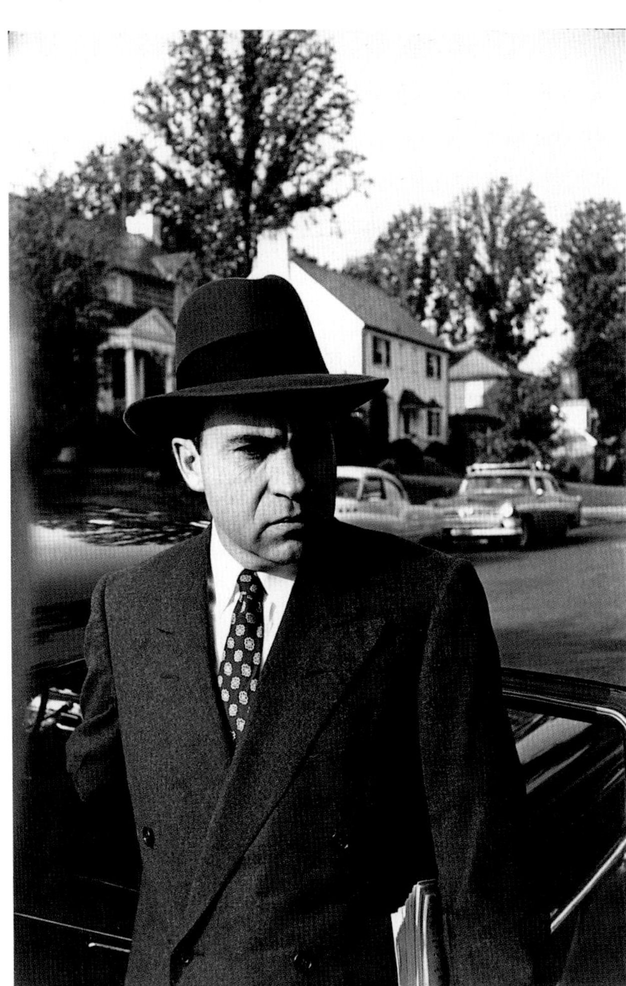
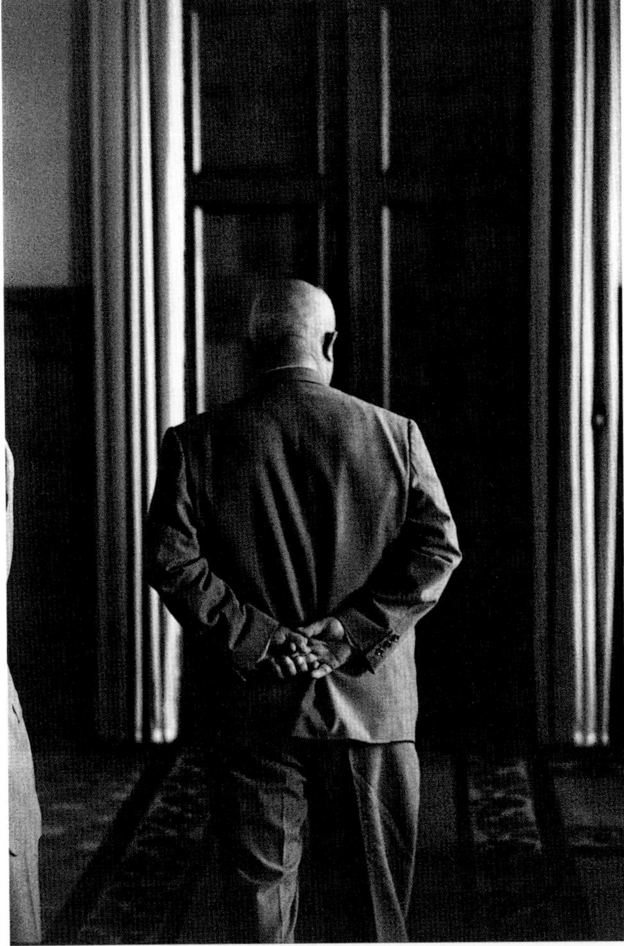
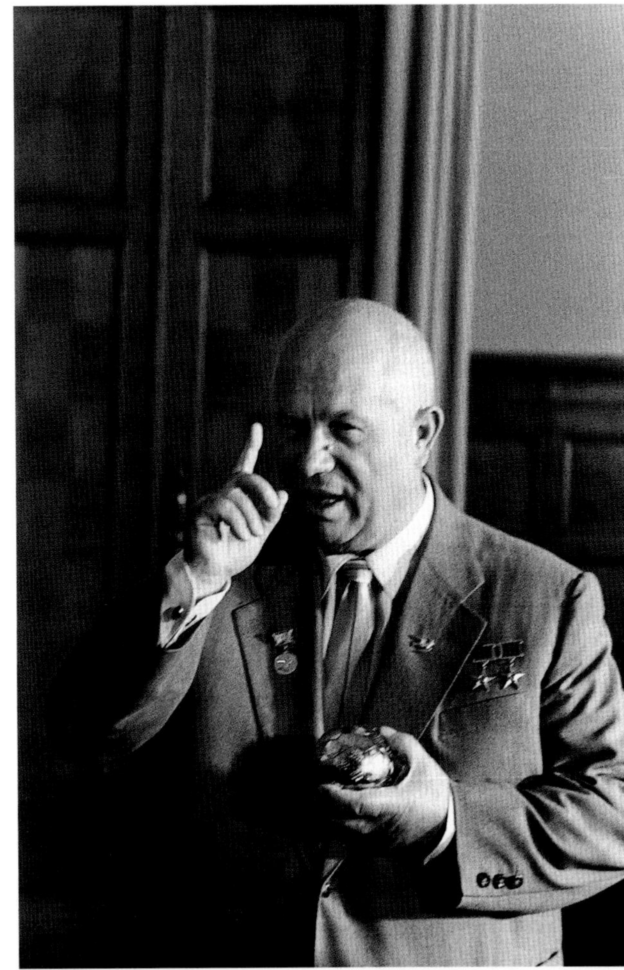

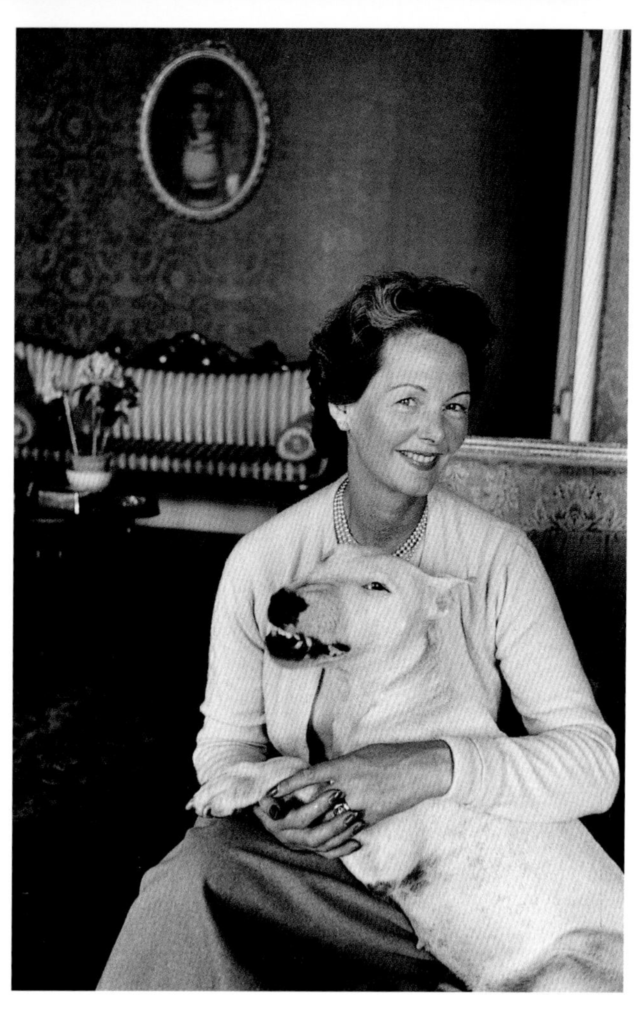

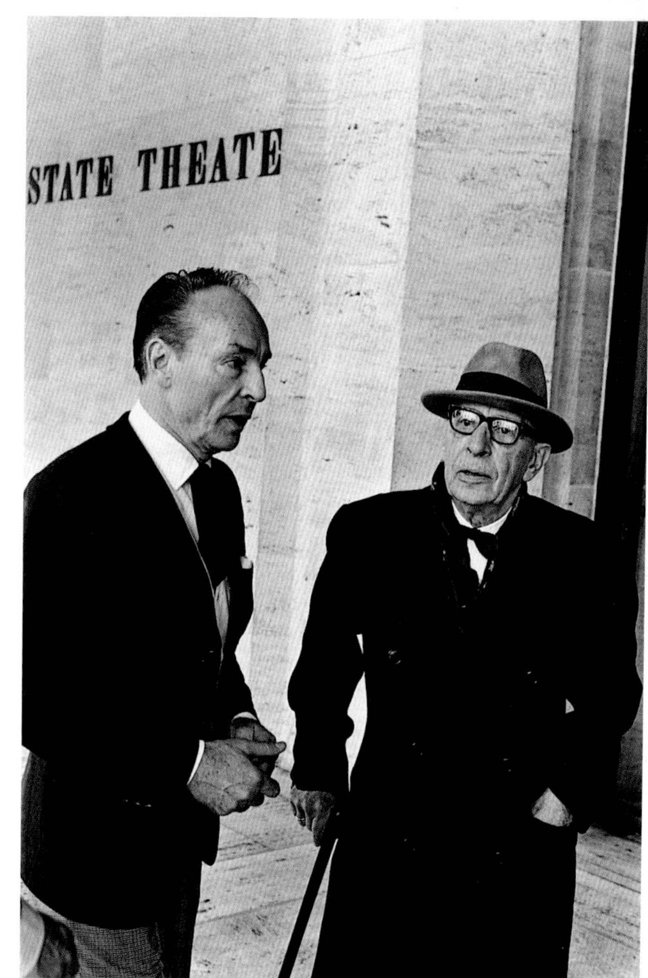
STATE THEATE

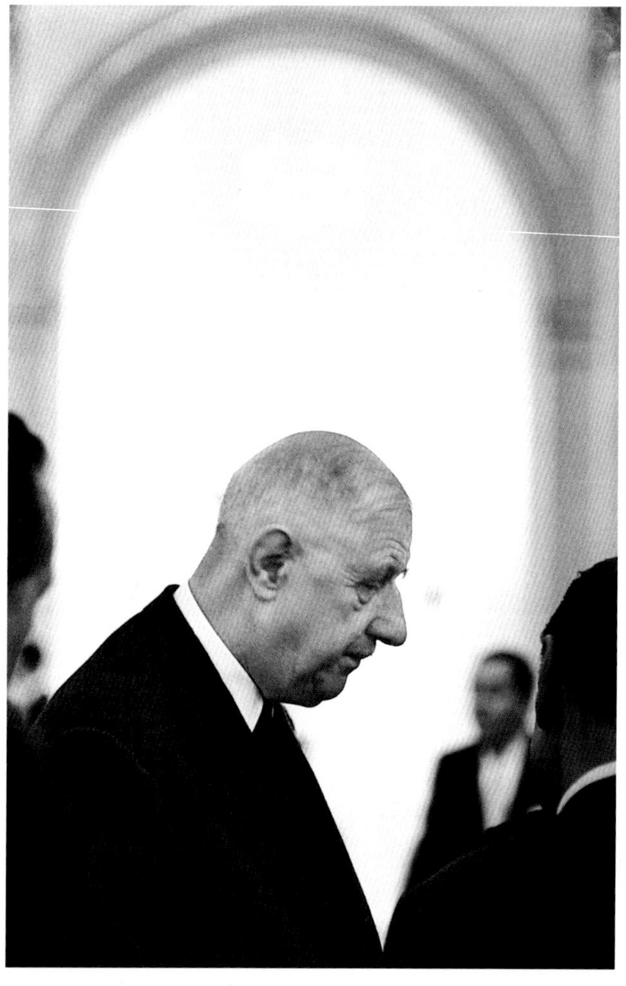

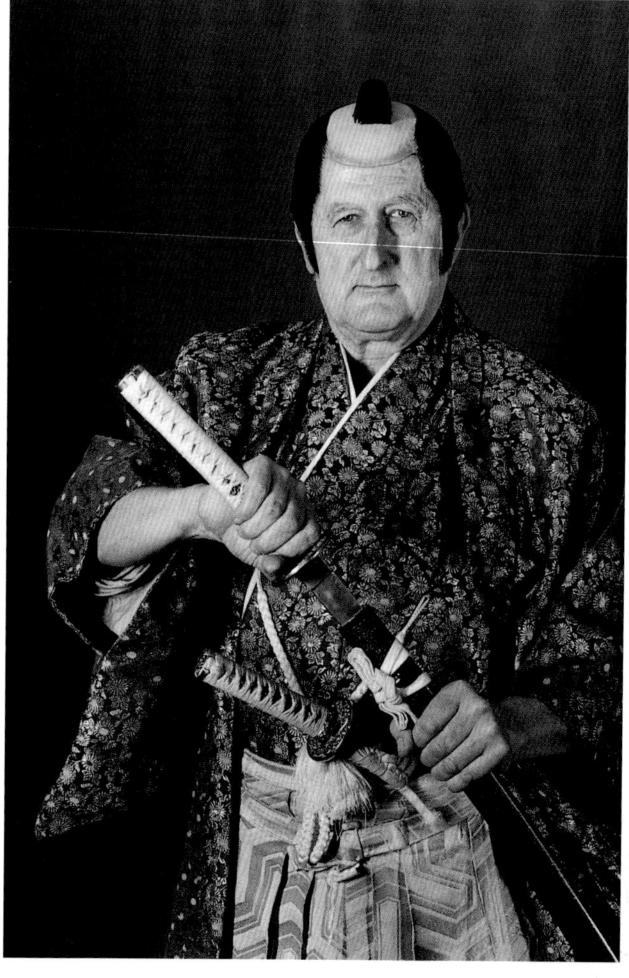

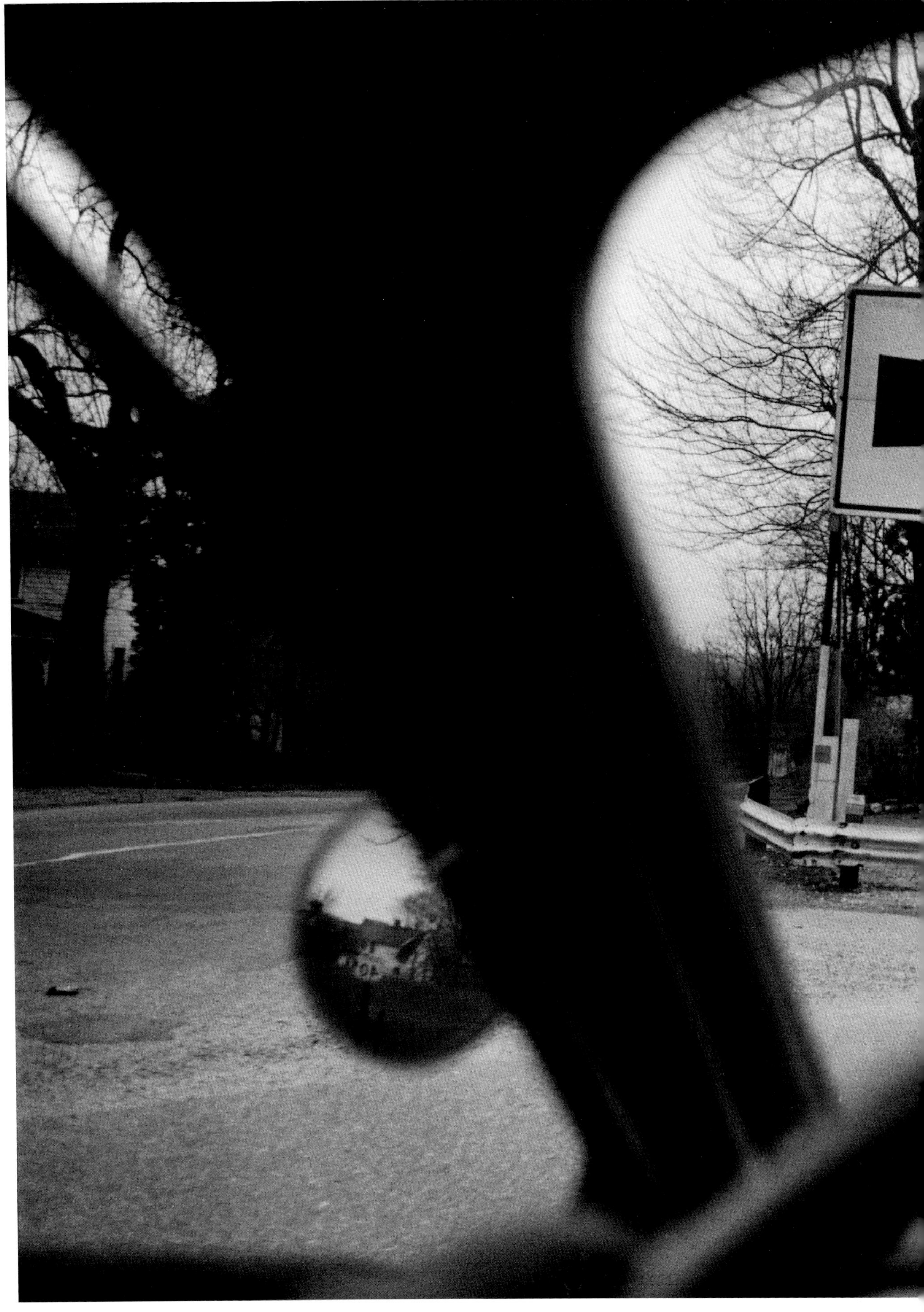

Idaho, 1954

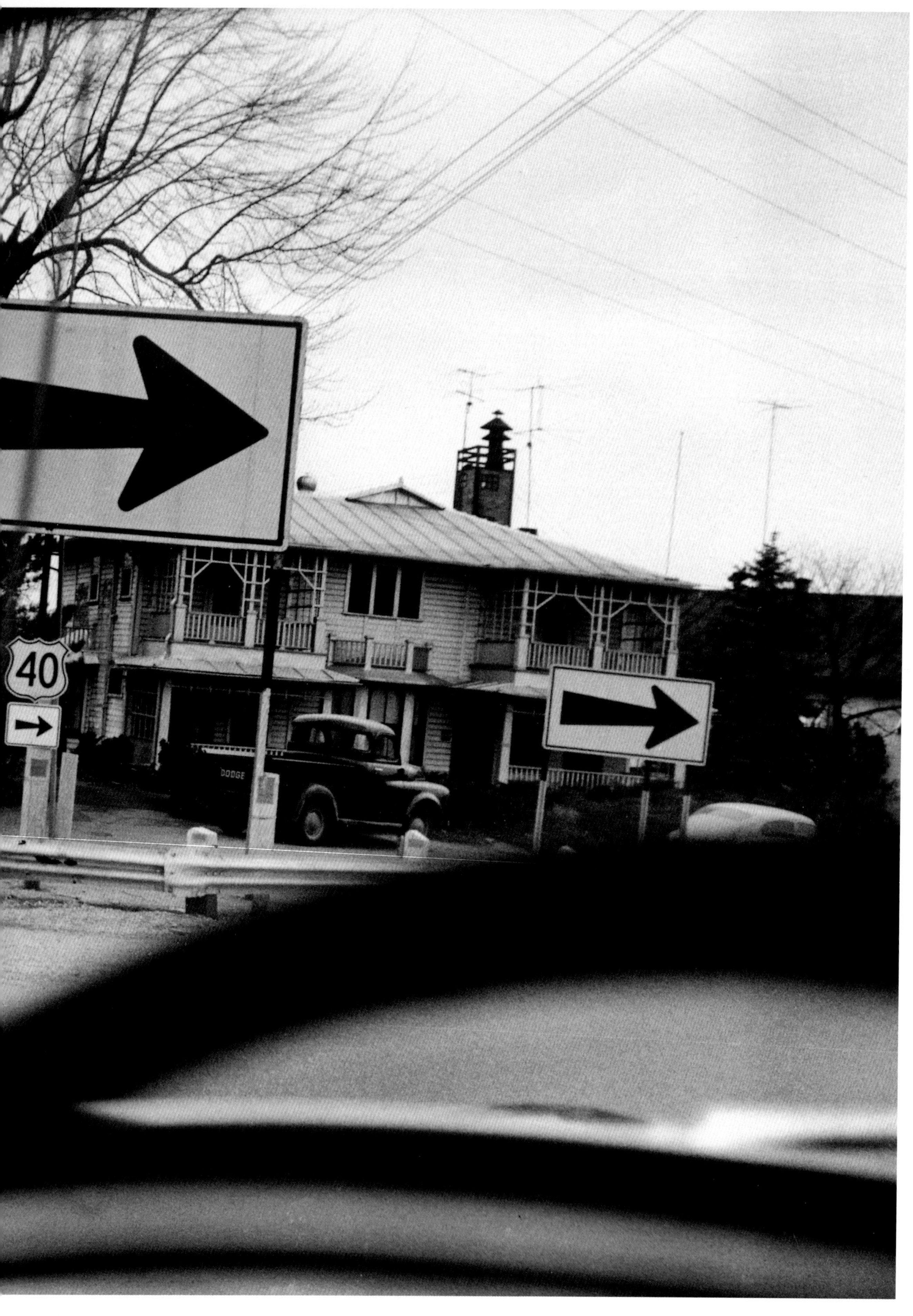

overleaf *Athens, 1976* / *Florida Keys, 1968*

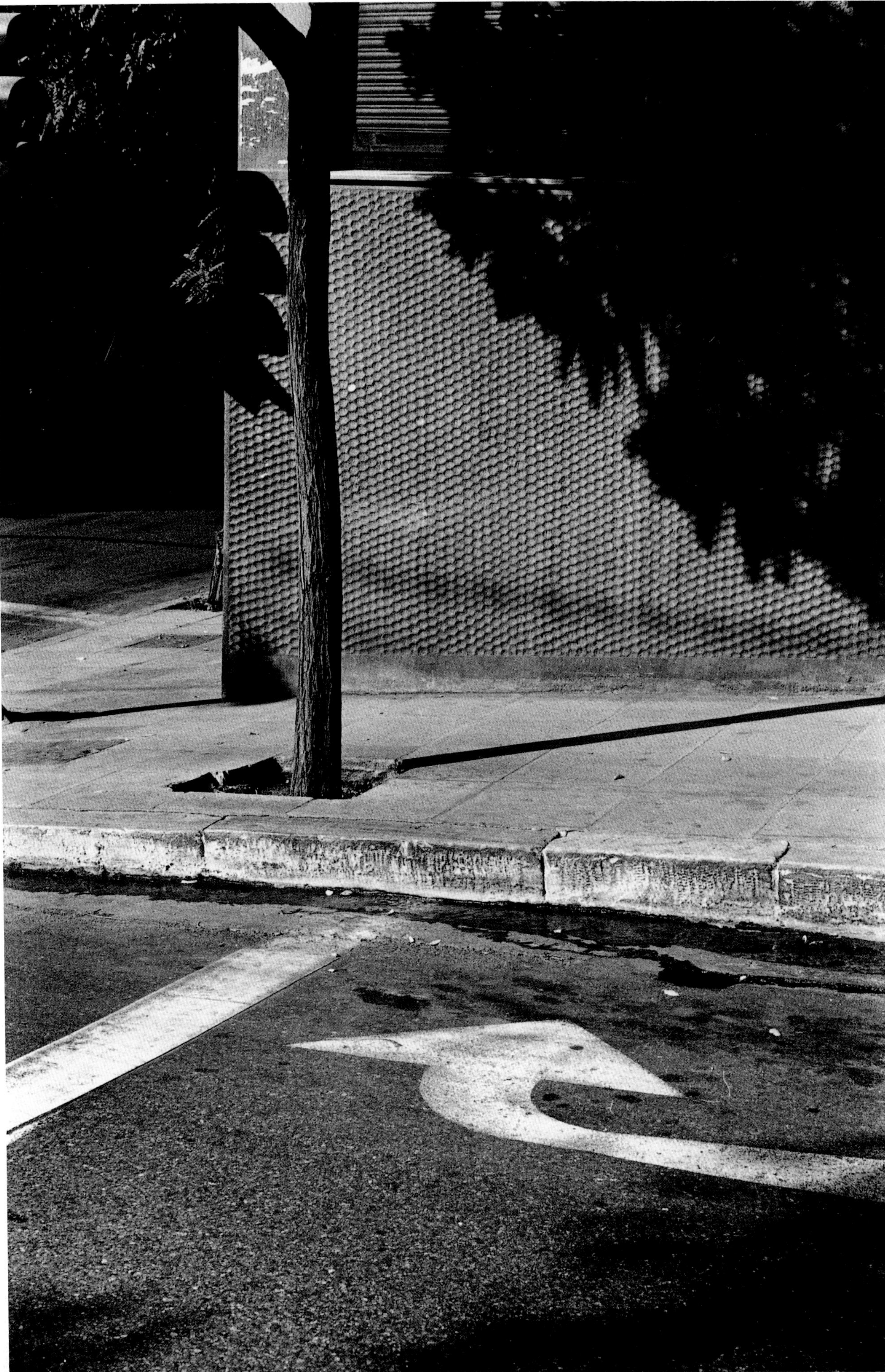

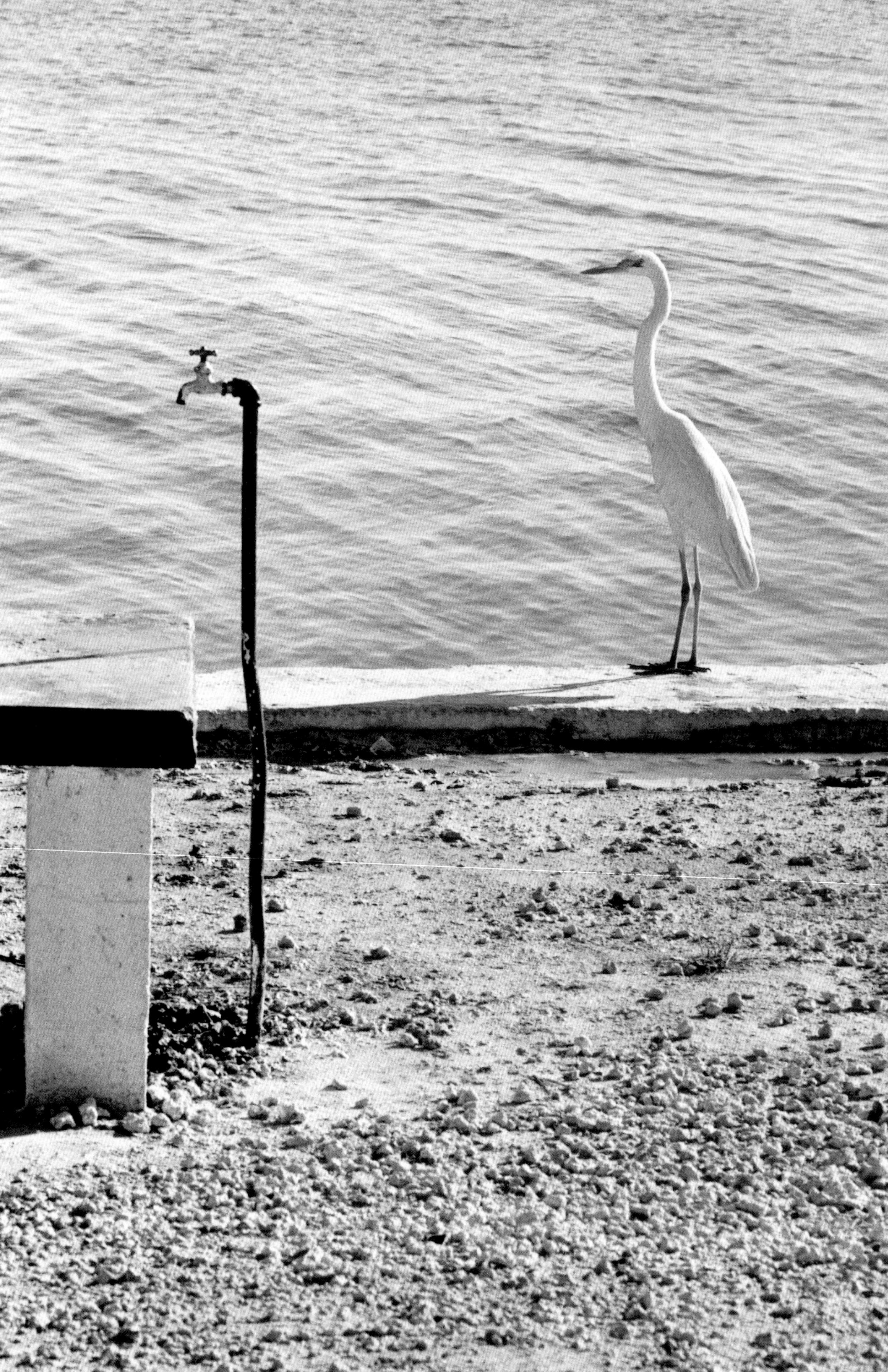

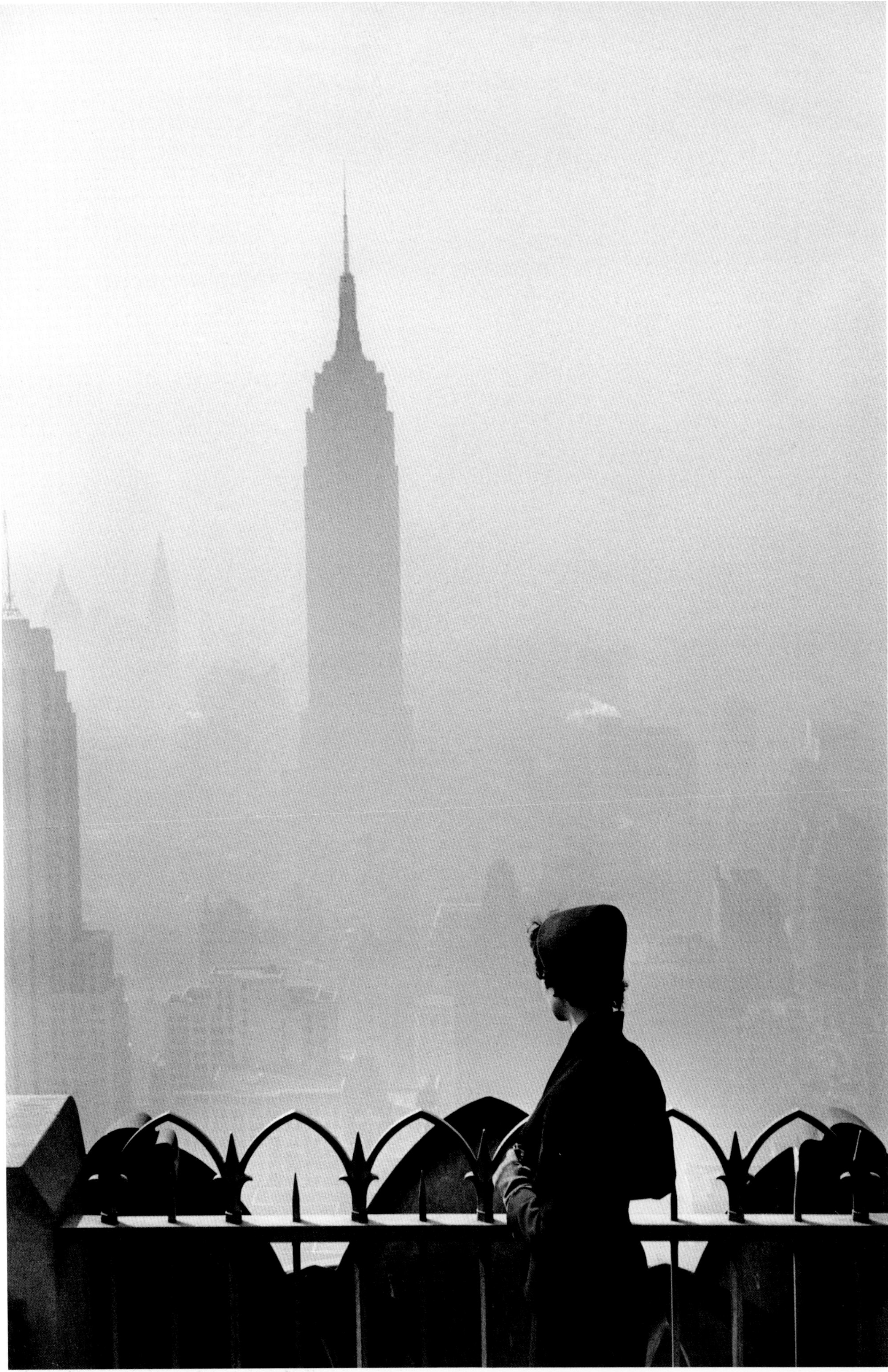

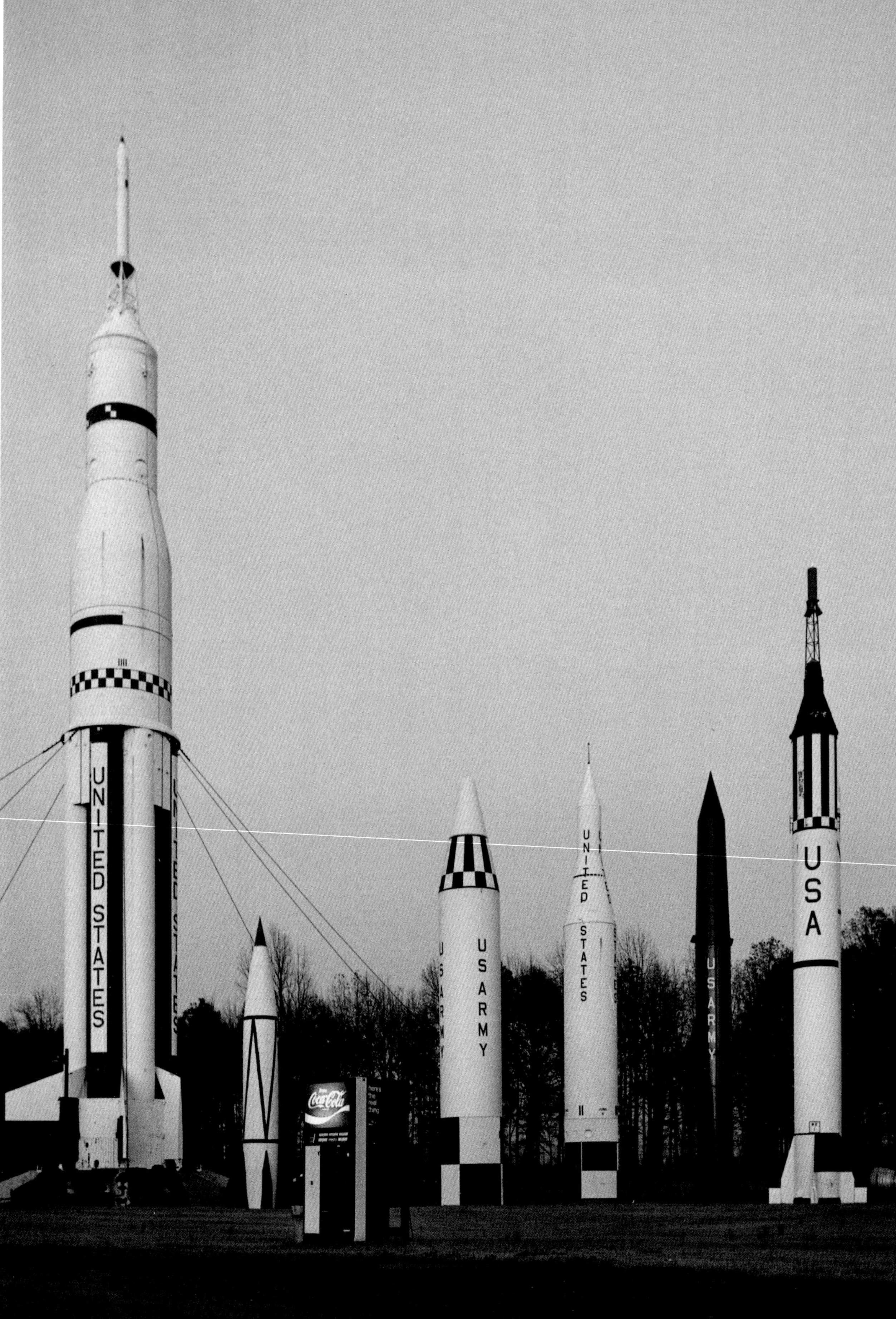
UNITED STATES
UNITED STATES
US ARMY
UNITED STATES
US ARMY
USA
Coca-Cola

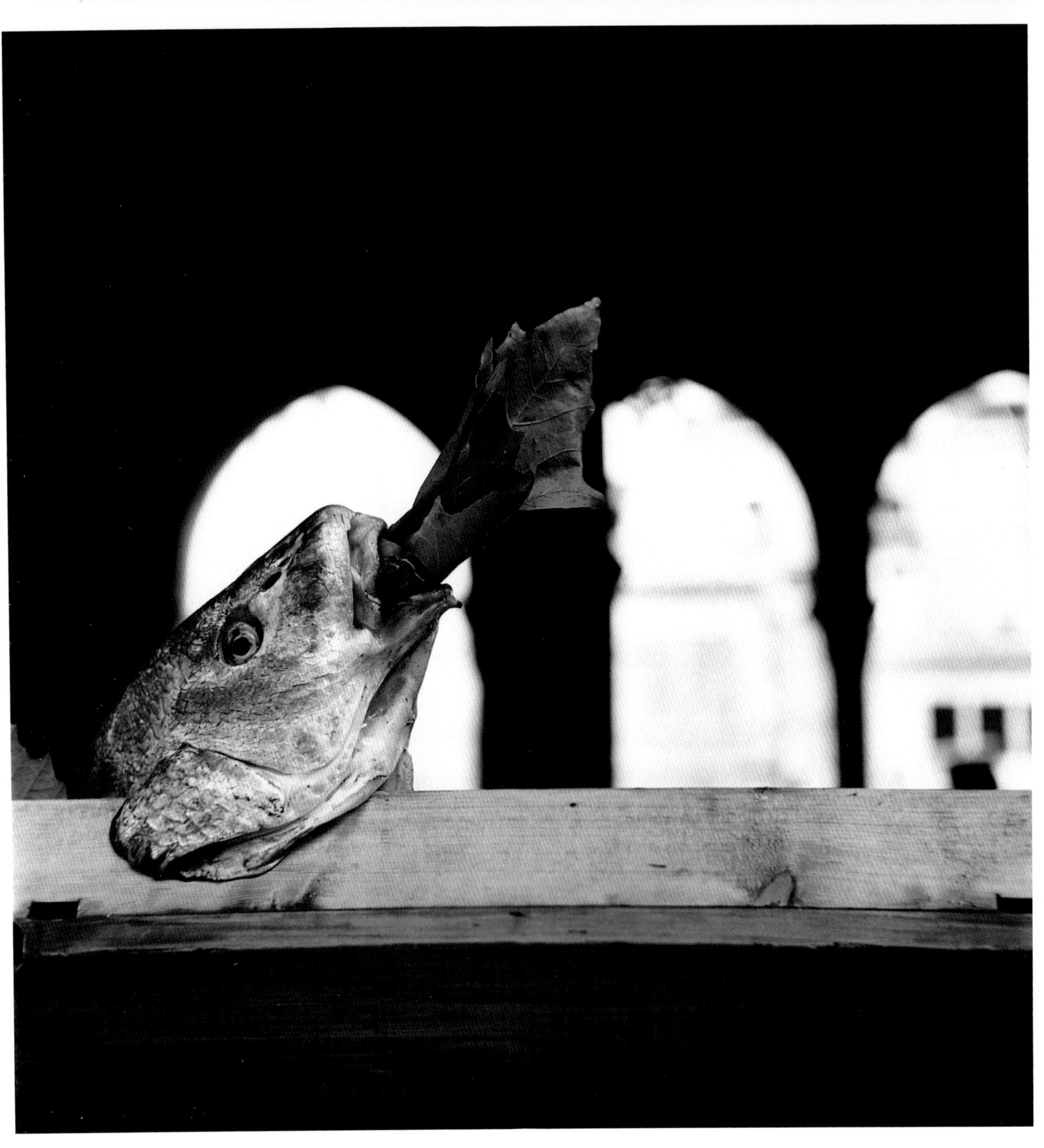

previous page *New York, 1955* / *Air and Space Museum, Huntsville, Alabama, 1974*
Venice, 1949

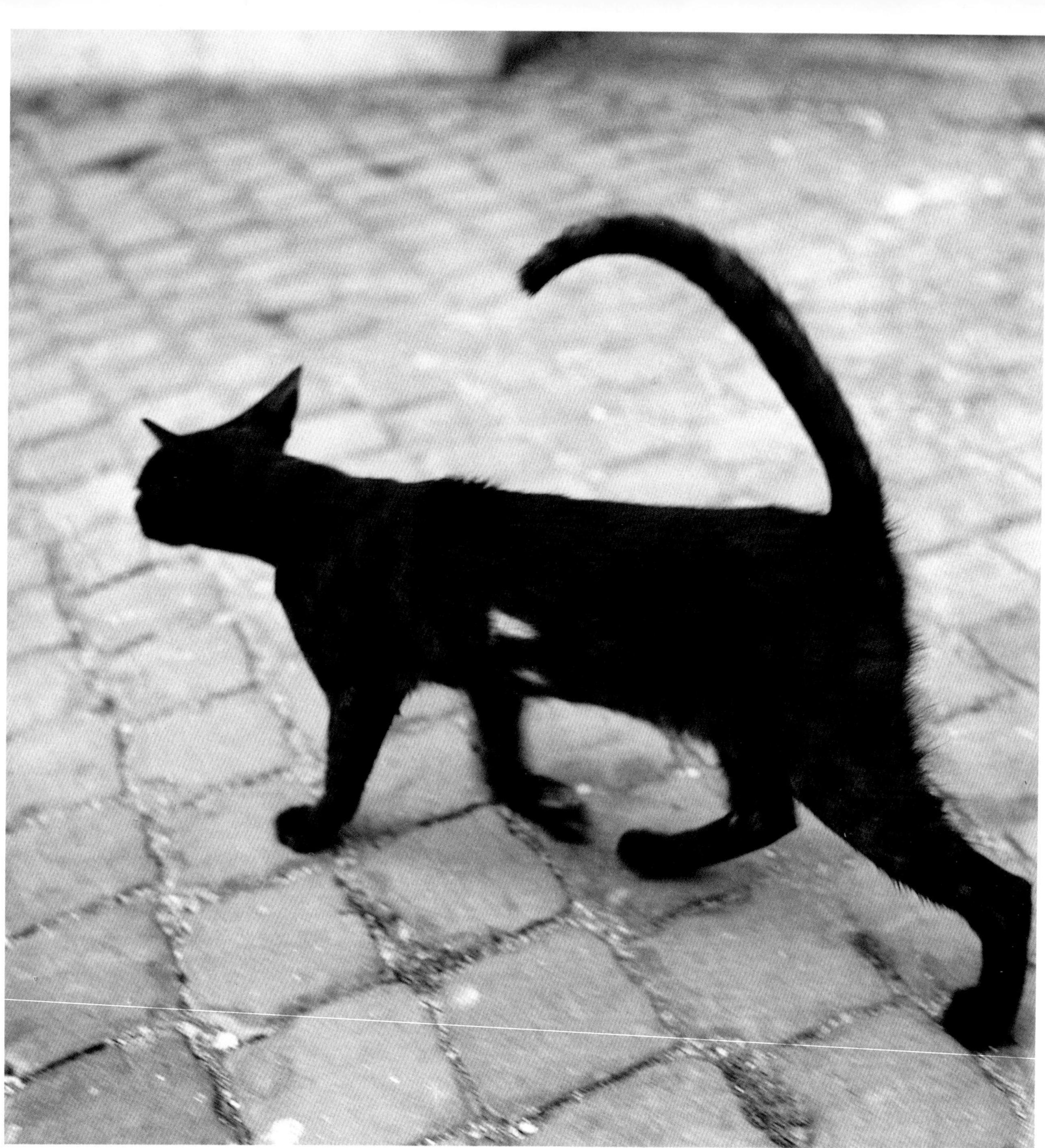

Rome, 1952

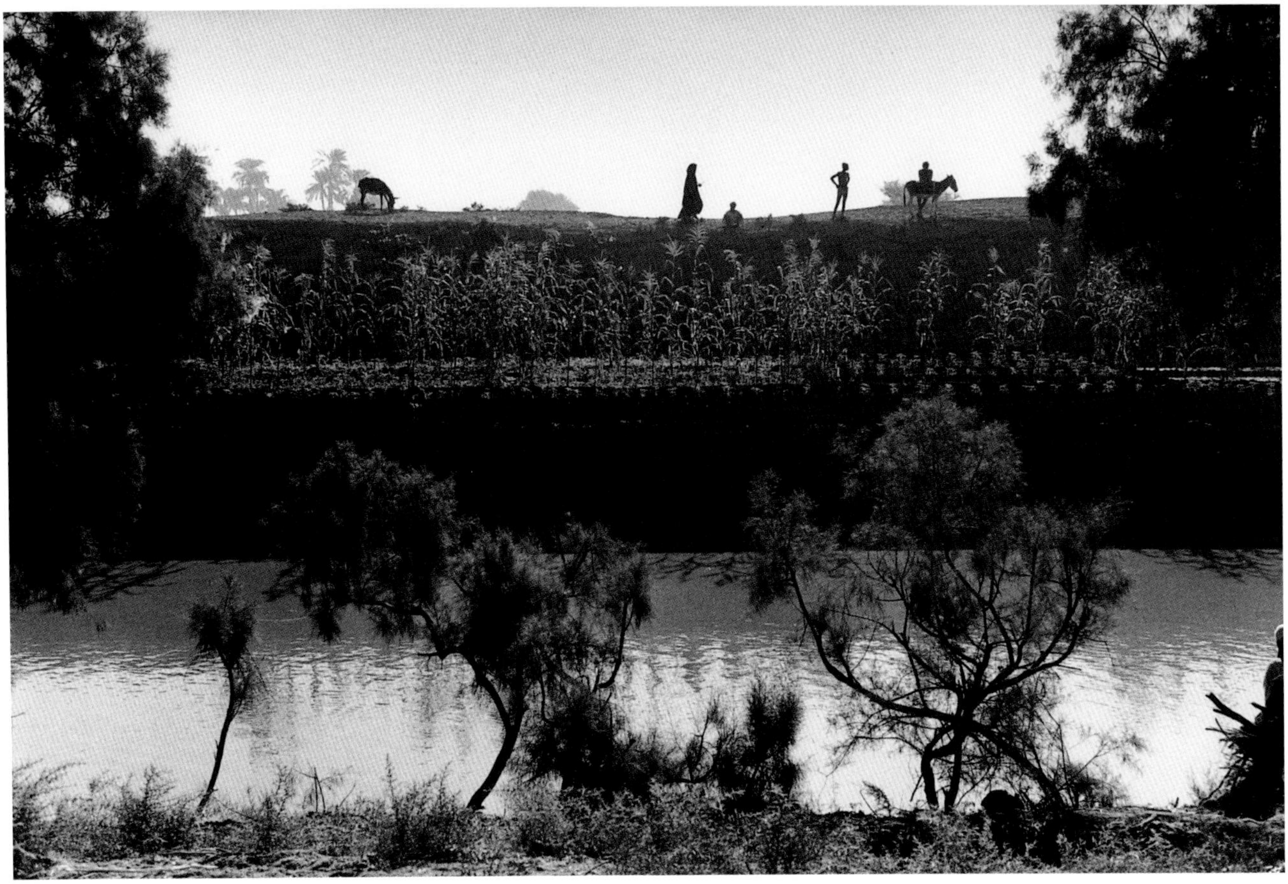

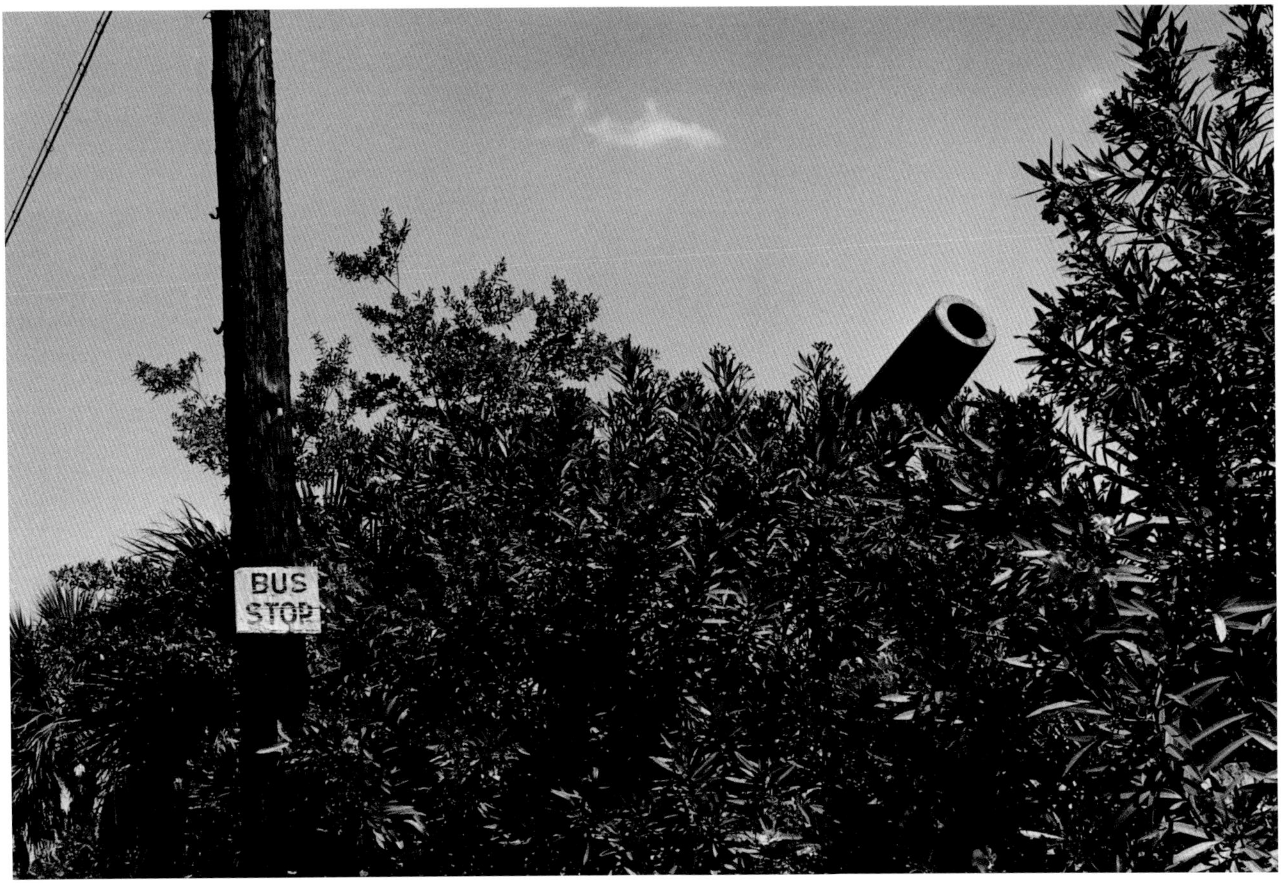

Luxor, Egypt, 1958 / *Fort Dix, New Jersey, 1951*

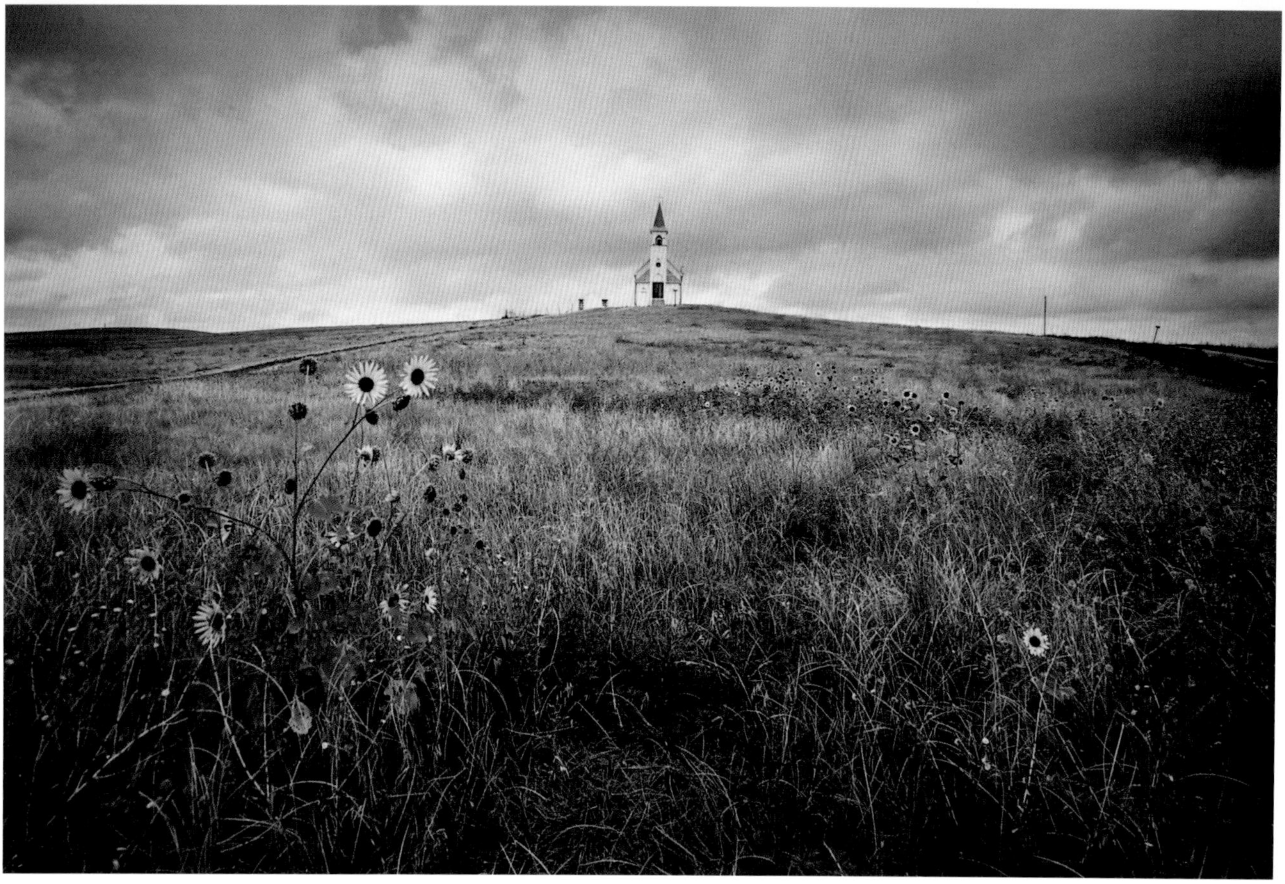

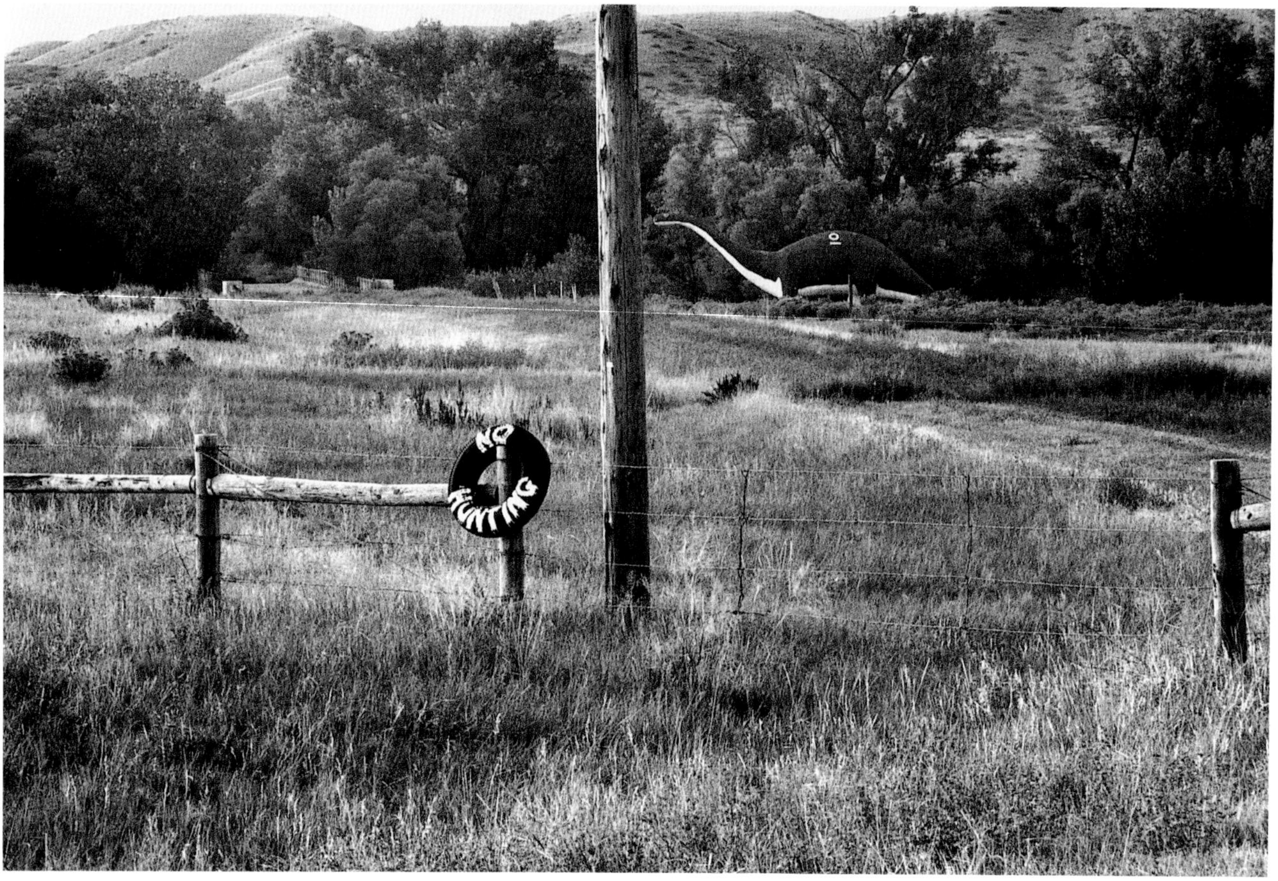

Wounded Knee, South Dakota, 1969 / *North Dakota, 1969*

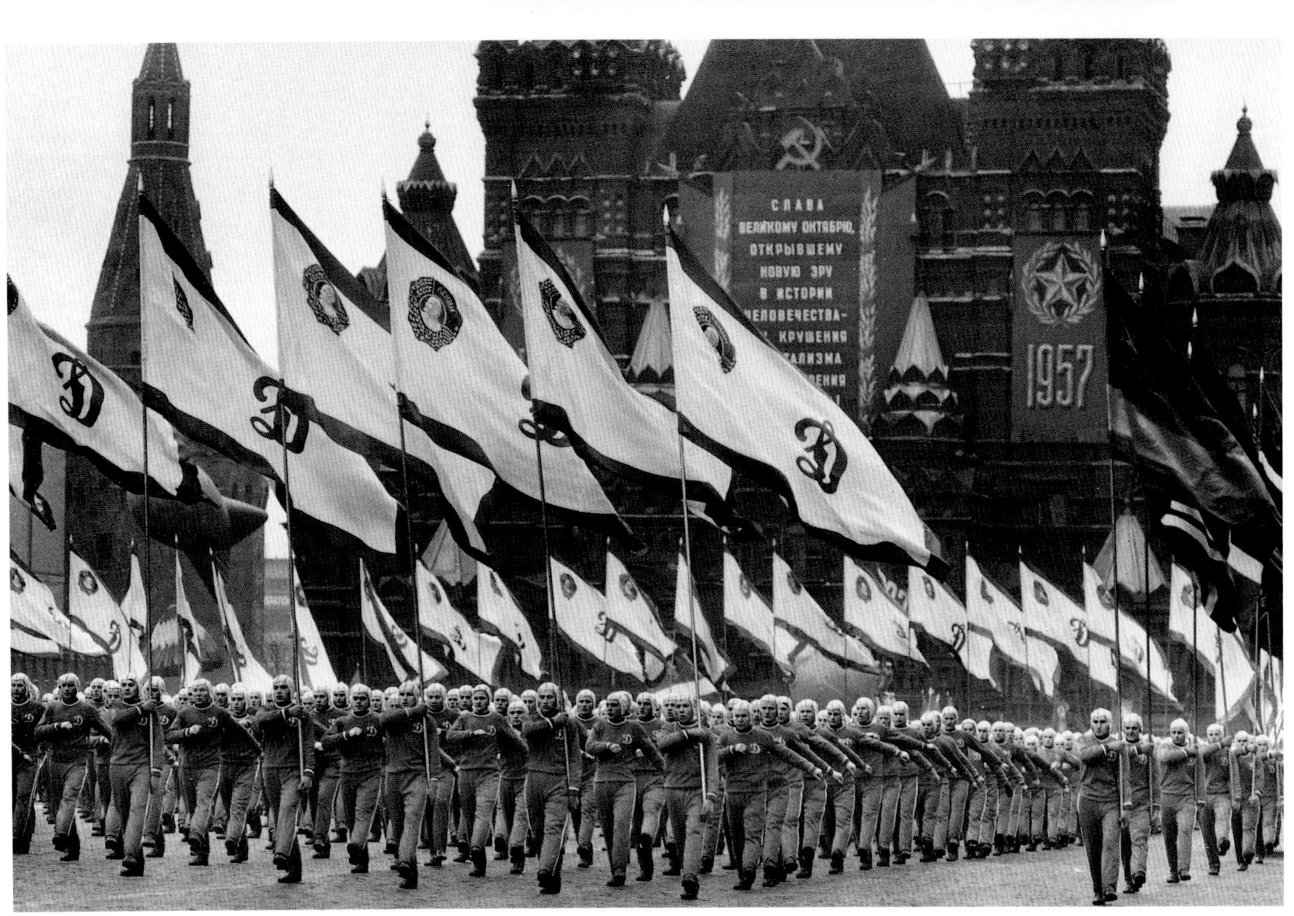
СЛАВА
ВЕЛИКОМУ ОКТЯБРЮ,
ОТКРЫВШЕМУ
НОВУЮ ЭРУ
В ИСТОРИИ
ЕЛОВЕЧЕСТВА-
КРУШЕНИЯ
АЛИЗМА
ЕНИЯ
1957

Moscow, 1957

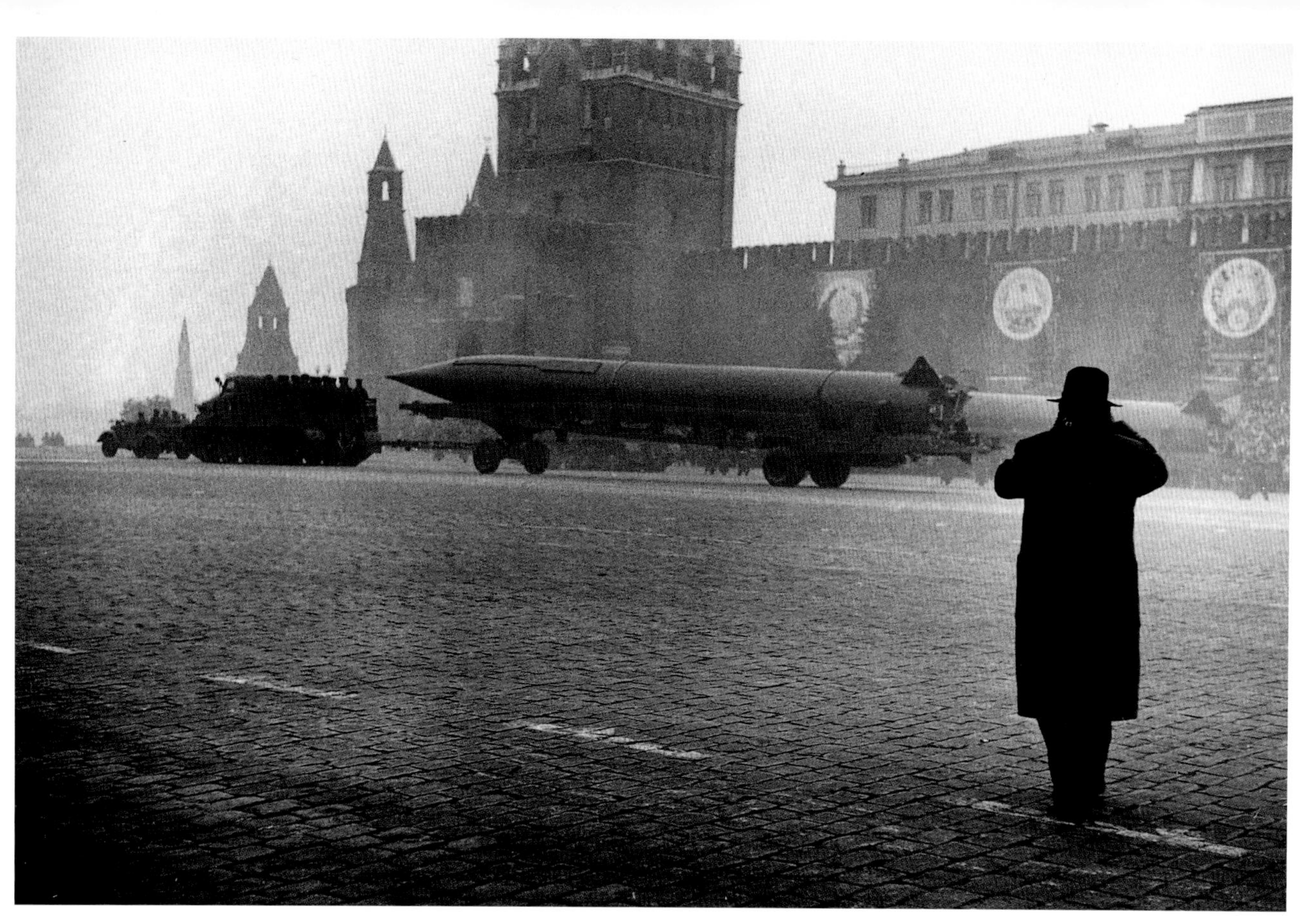

Moscow, 1957

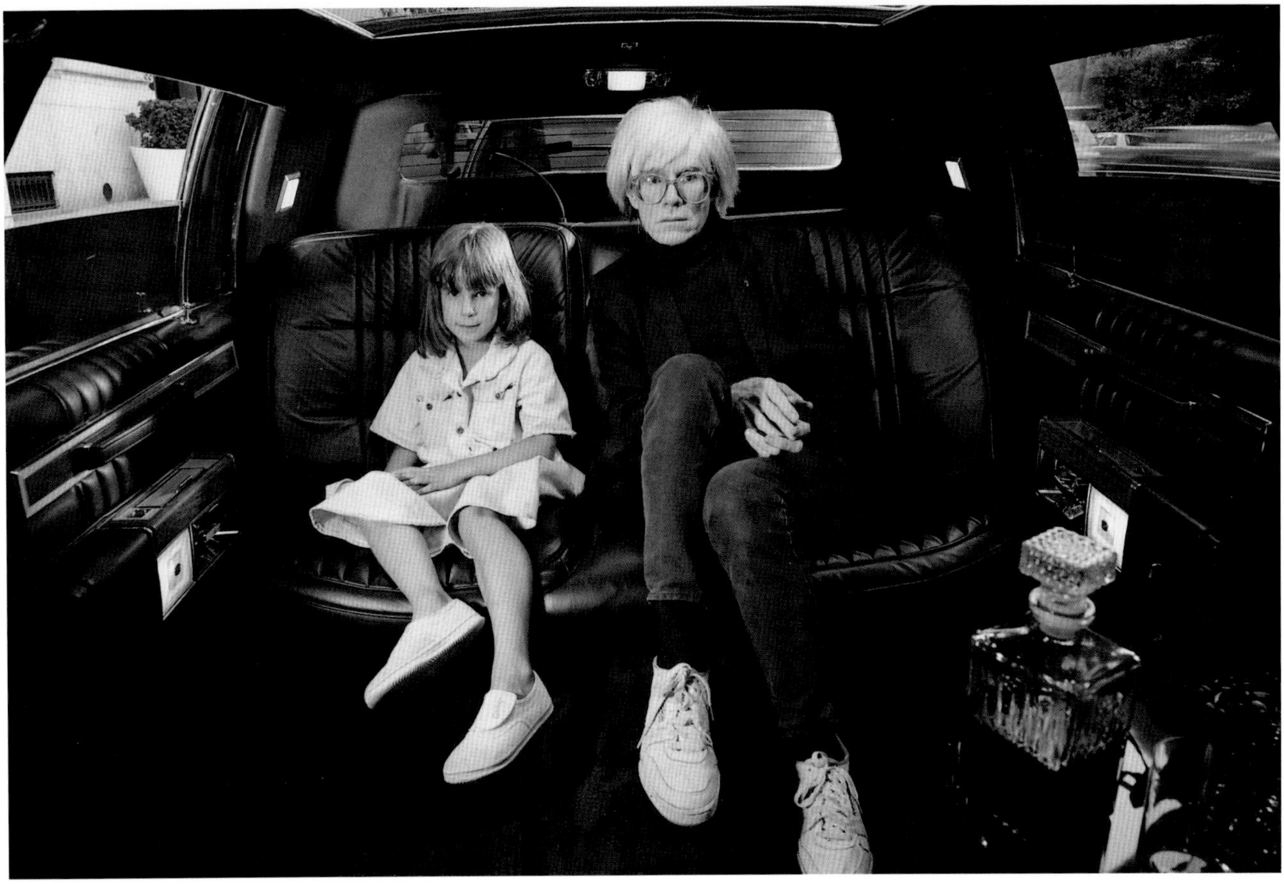

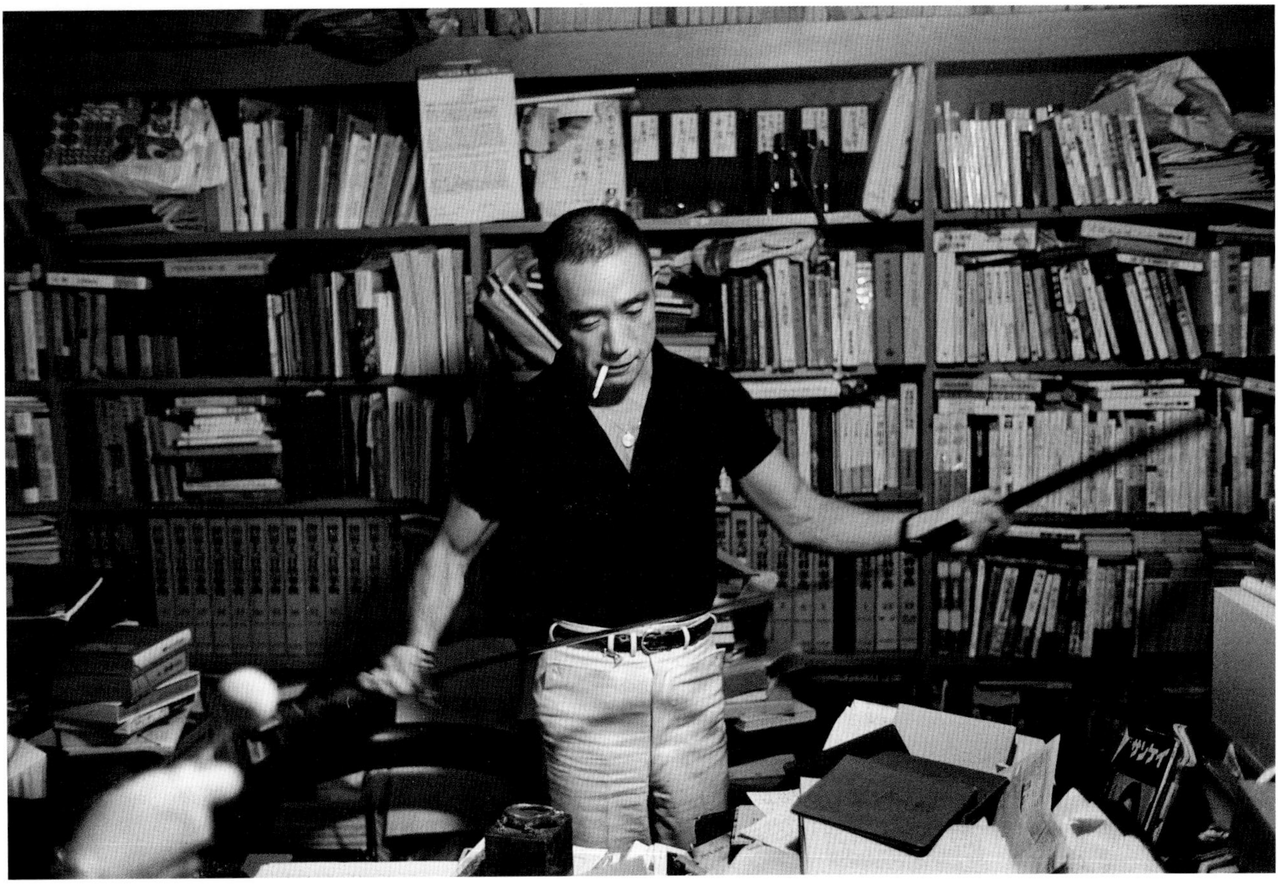

Andy Warhol, New York, 1986 / *Yukio Mishima, Tokyo, 1970*

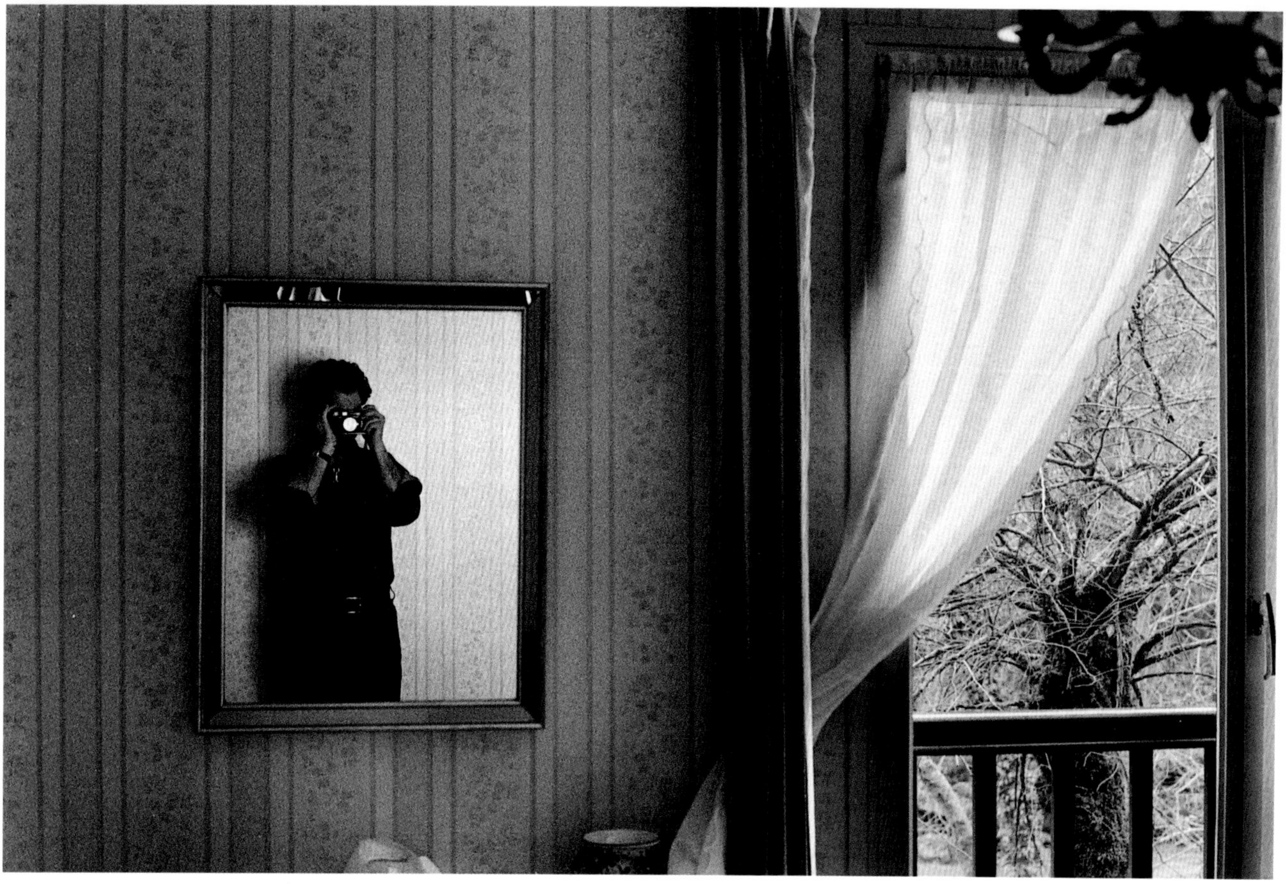

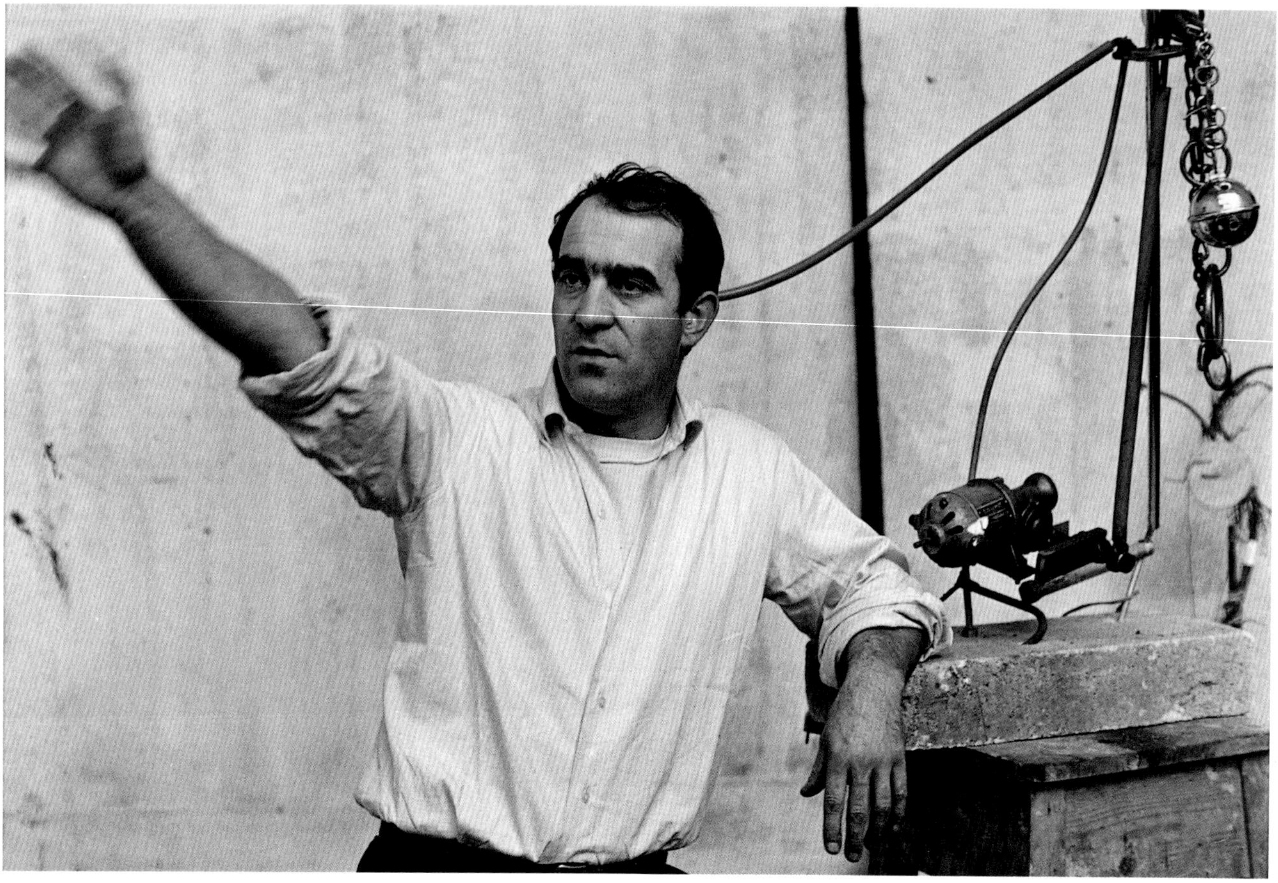

Orléans, France, 1974 / *Yves Tinguely, Paris, 1961*

Look

If the photographer cannot sharply see, he cannot memorably record. If the photographer cannot see what no one else sees, he is no artist. Even with today's rapid-fire cameras, even when professional photographers are ranged tightly together behind a rope a prescribed distance from celebrity or event, 'No one will take the same photo', says Elliott, 'as anyone else.'

The photographer looks at the scene, but he is looking with eyes that have seen many scenes before, and with a prepared mind. For all of Elliott's devotion to chance, he meets each snap at least halfway. As his old friend Sam Holmes wrote once, 'Sometimes Elliott's pictures are conceptions imposed upon reality by his ingenious mind.'

So, the looking is not unfiltered. Elliott snaps what he sees, and that is a combination of intent and opportunity. If, as the cliché has it, the eyes are windows to the soul, the snaps are windows to the photographer's convictions and emotions.

It is natural that Elliott would be fascinated by the very nature of looking, and he has snapped people looking at each other or at the camera, dogs looking at the camera and, to turn the point around, the select group of Magnum photographers, whose paychecks come from looking, refusing to look (p.380), perhaps because they're off the clock.

The eye is so complex a mechanism that it is the principal evidence cited by creationists or by theorists of intentional design to argue against evolutionary theory. By comparison, the combination of camera lens and film is very rudimentary, indeed. The photographer winnows out a multitude of possibilities before leaving the studio.

Loungers at the beach, dogs at play, uniformed marchers on parade, abandoned buildings – before finding Marlowe's infinite riches in a little room, the photographer has to define the little room. For Elliott, as can be seen throughout *Snaps*, a favourite subject is the dog. He is frequently quoted to the effect that he regards this species as human. The humour of this remark may lie in its implied antithesis. Often, the canine expression seems to be, 'I'm trying, but I'm not in control.' That plaint can be heard around the edges of more than one snap of human activity here. The human subjects look, but perhaps for what cannot be seen.

Taken for granted, though it should not be, is the easy relationship so many lookers here have established with the lens. Is the subject looking through the lens at Elliott? Does she only pretend to 'look', while imagining what she will look like when the photograph is developed and printed? Do any of these people or dogs imagine one of us looking back at them, a homunculus in the camera body?

Probably not. Why, then, is the illusion of visual contact so striking? We believe that we are being seen when we know that no contact was intended. Looking becomes very suspect, thanks to the mechanical intervention of the camera. The person looking at a reflection in a roundel of glass seems to be intimately available, seems to be throwing open the windows of the soul, but it is all film speed and mirrors.

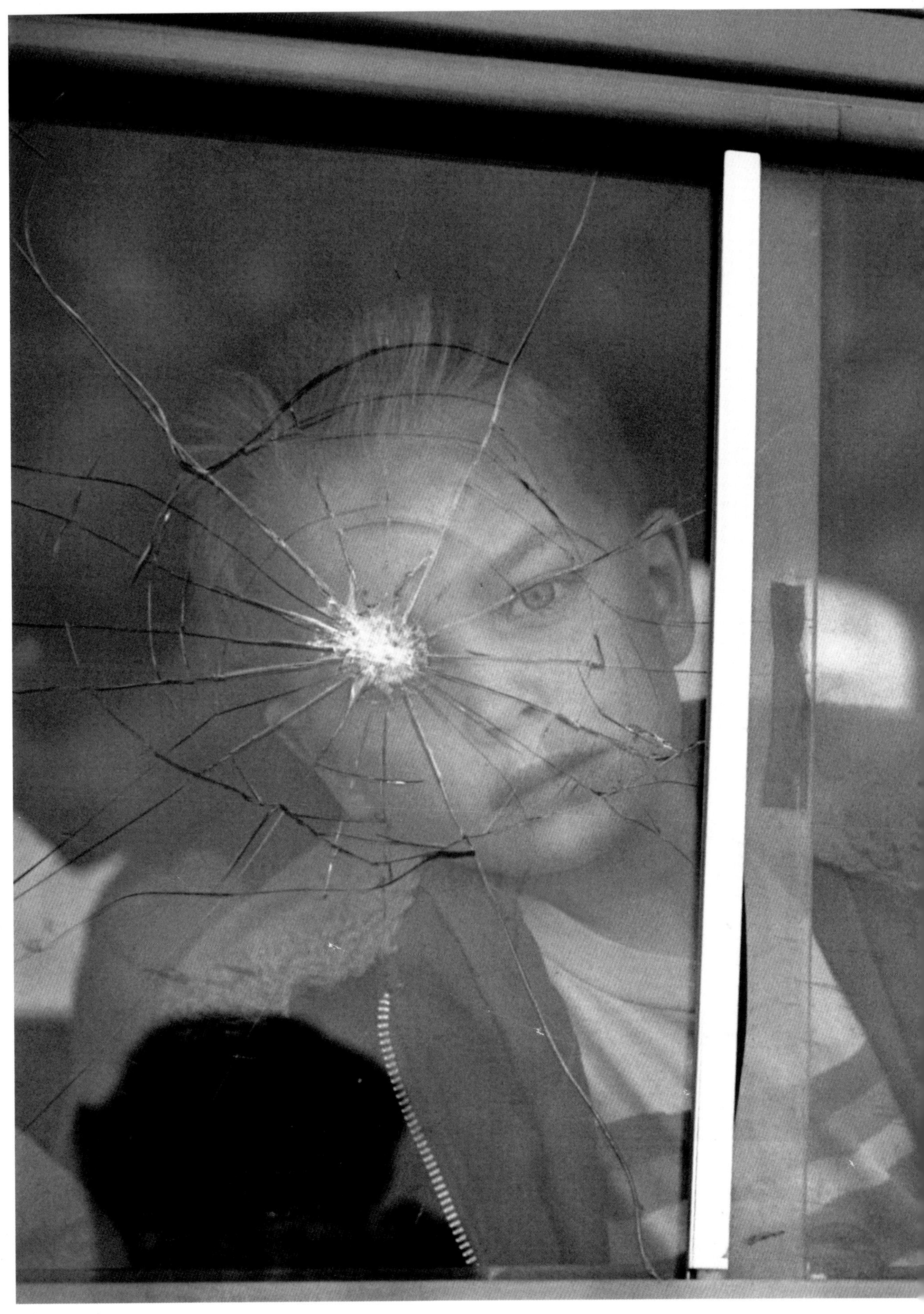

Colorado, 1955

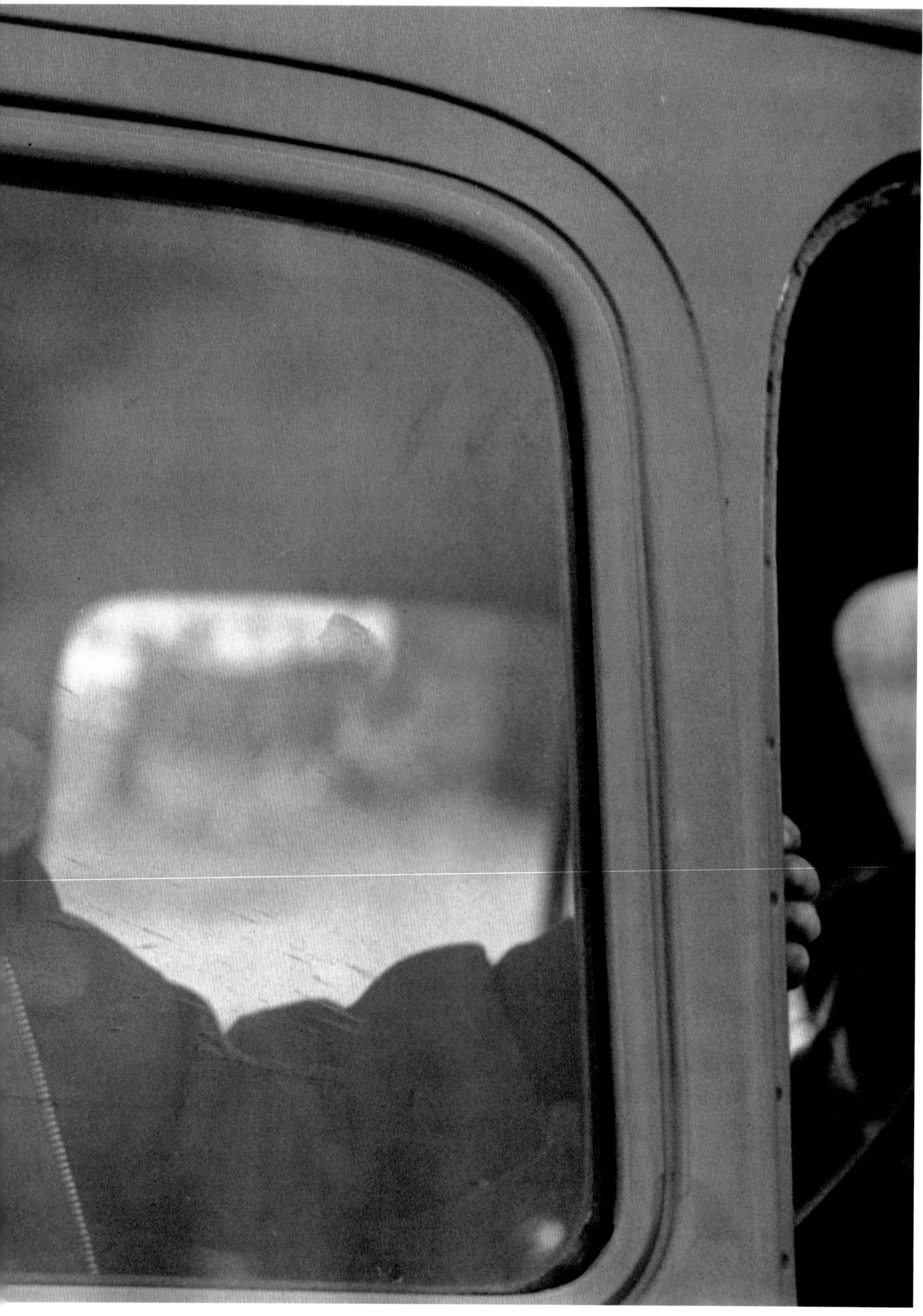

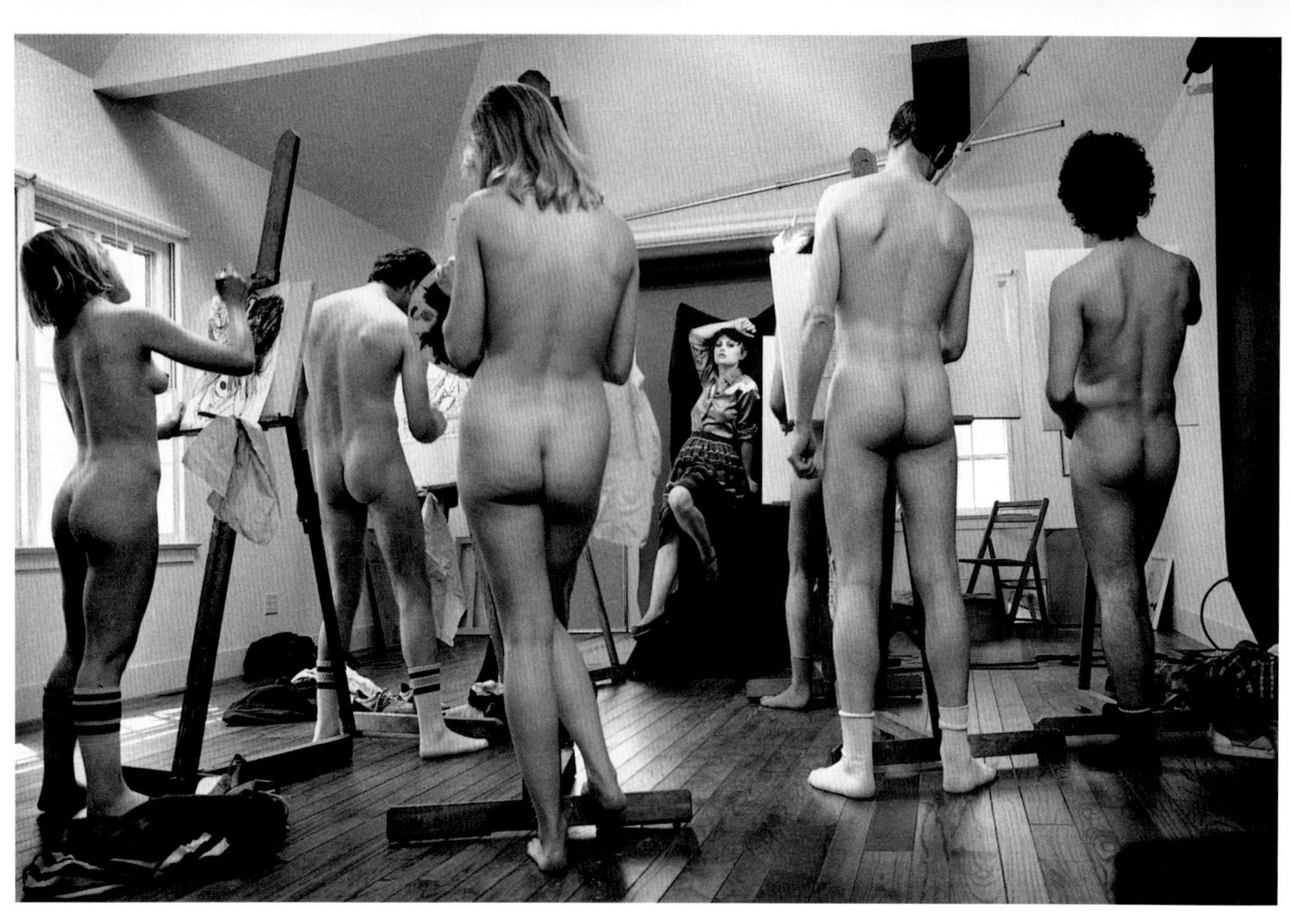

East Hampton, New York, 1983

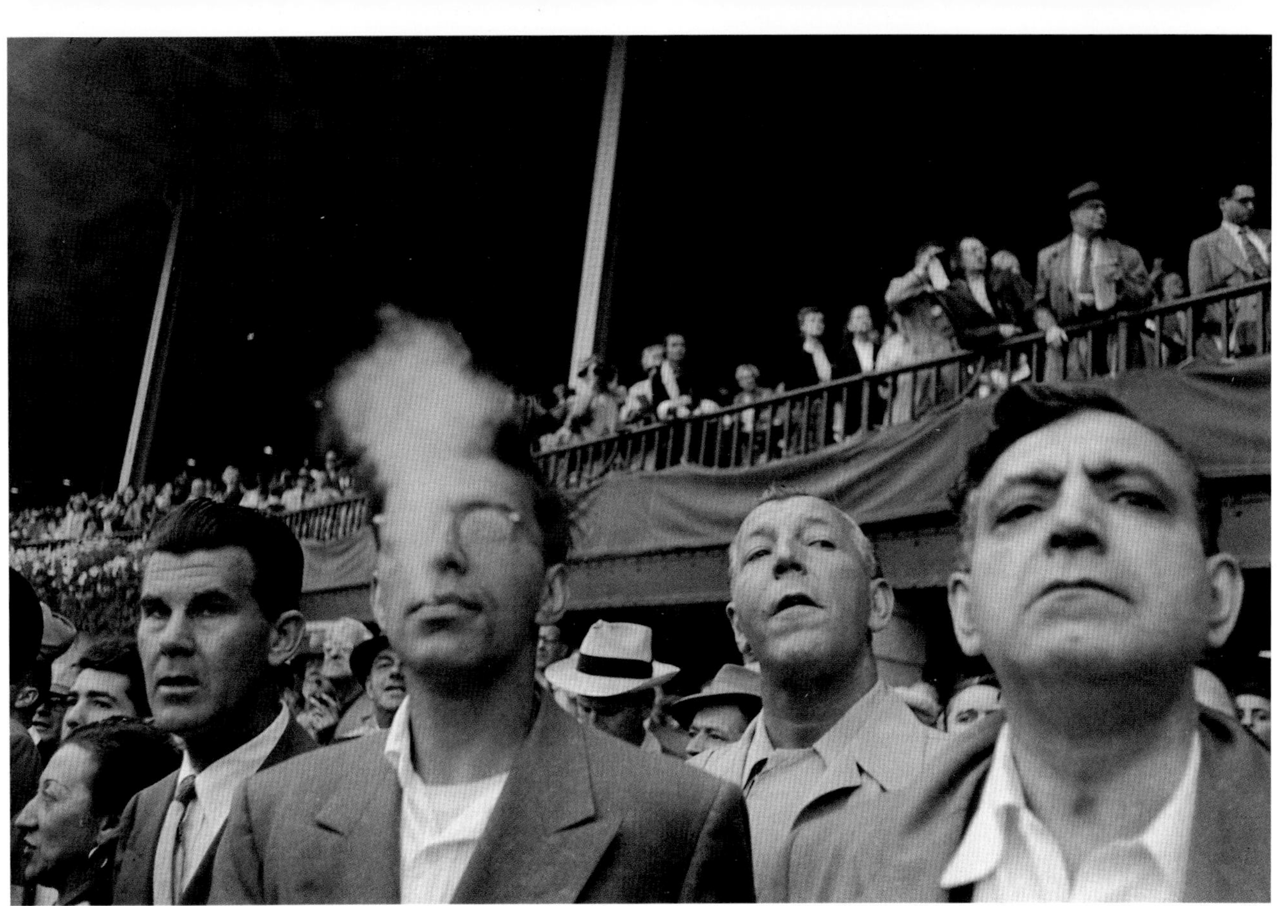

Belmont Park, New York, 1953

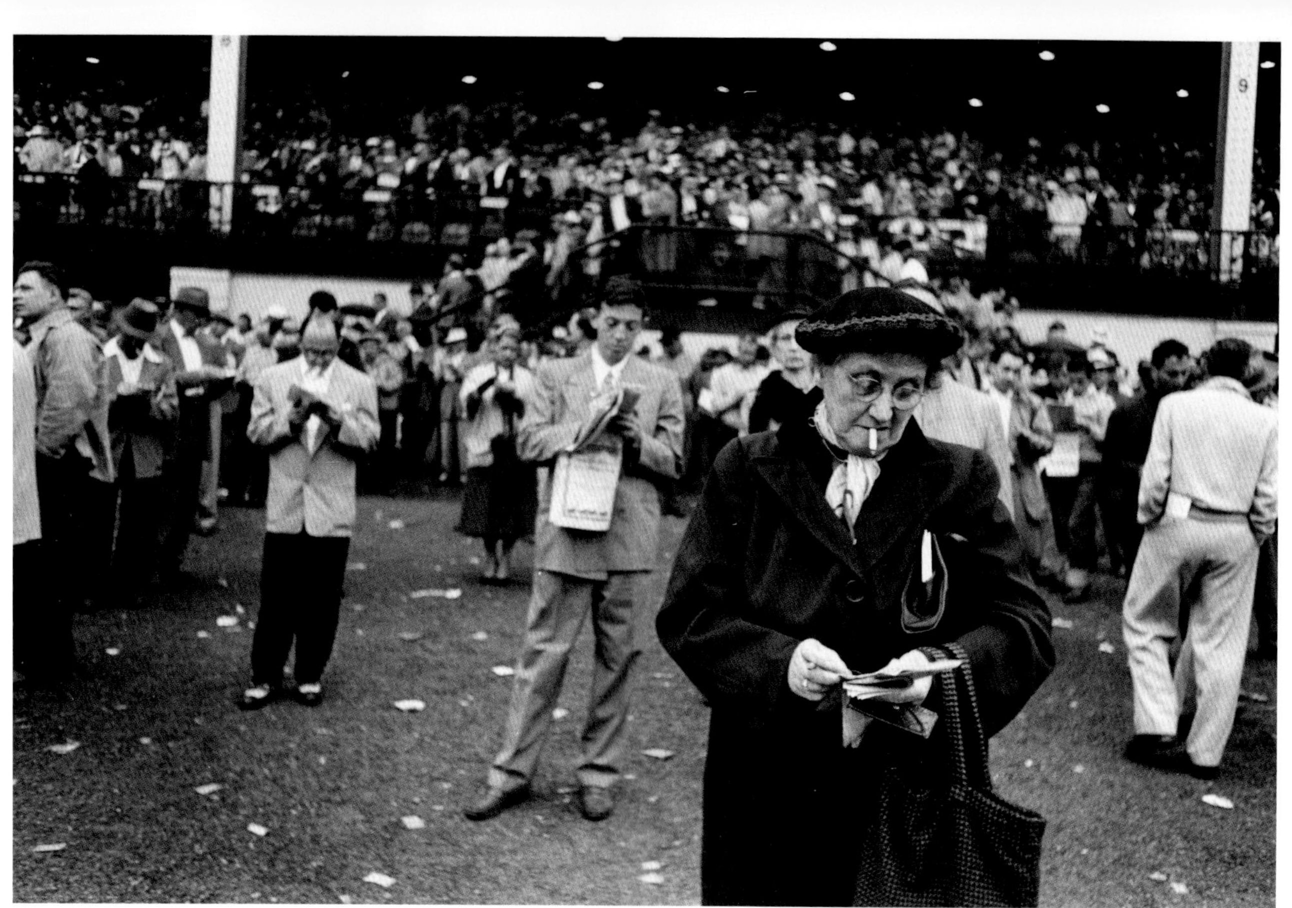

Belmont Park, New York, 1953

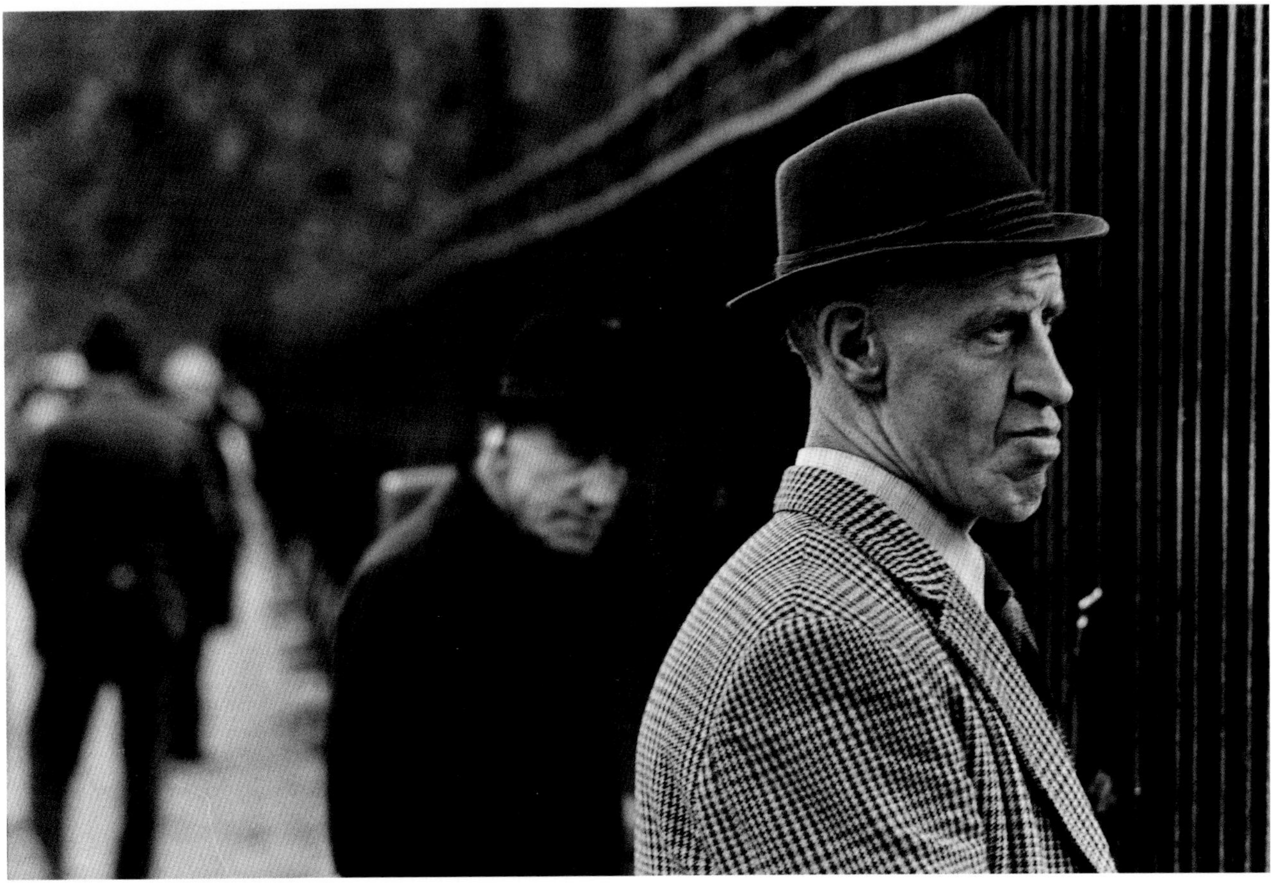

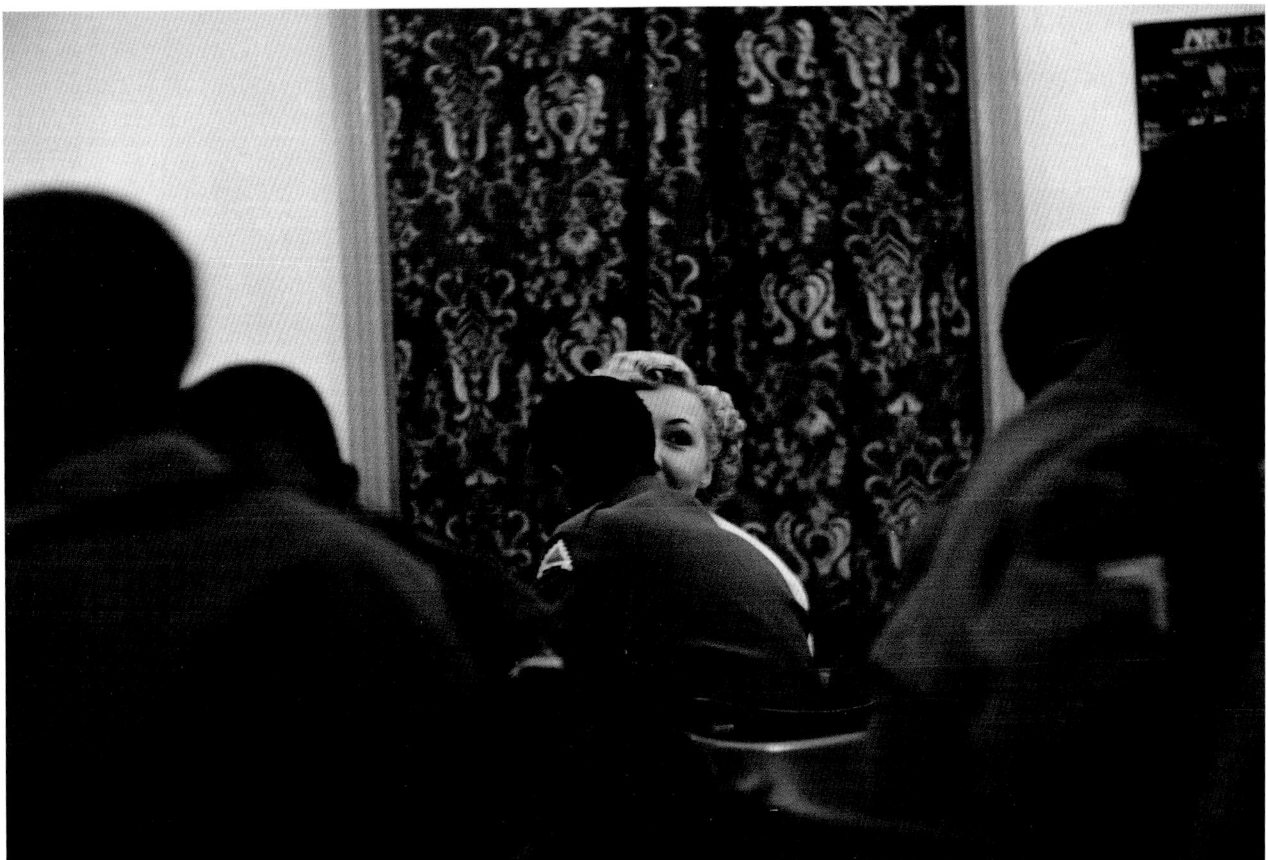

London, 1978 / *Bremerhaven, Germany, 1951*

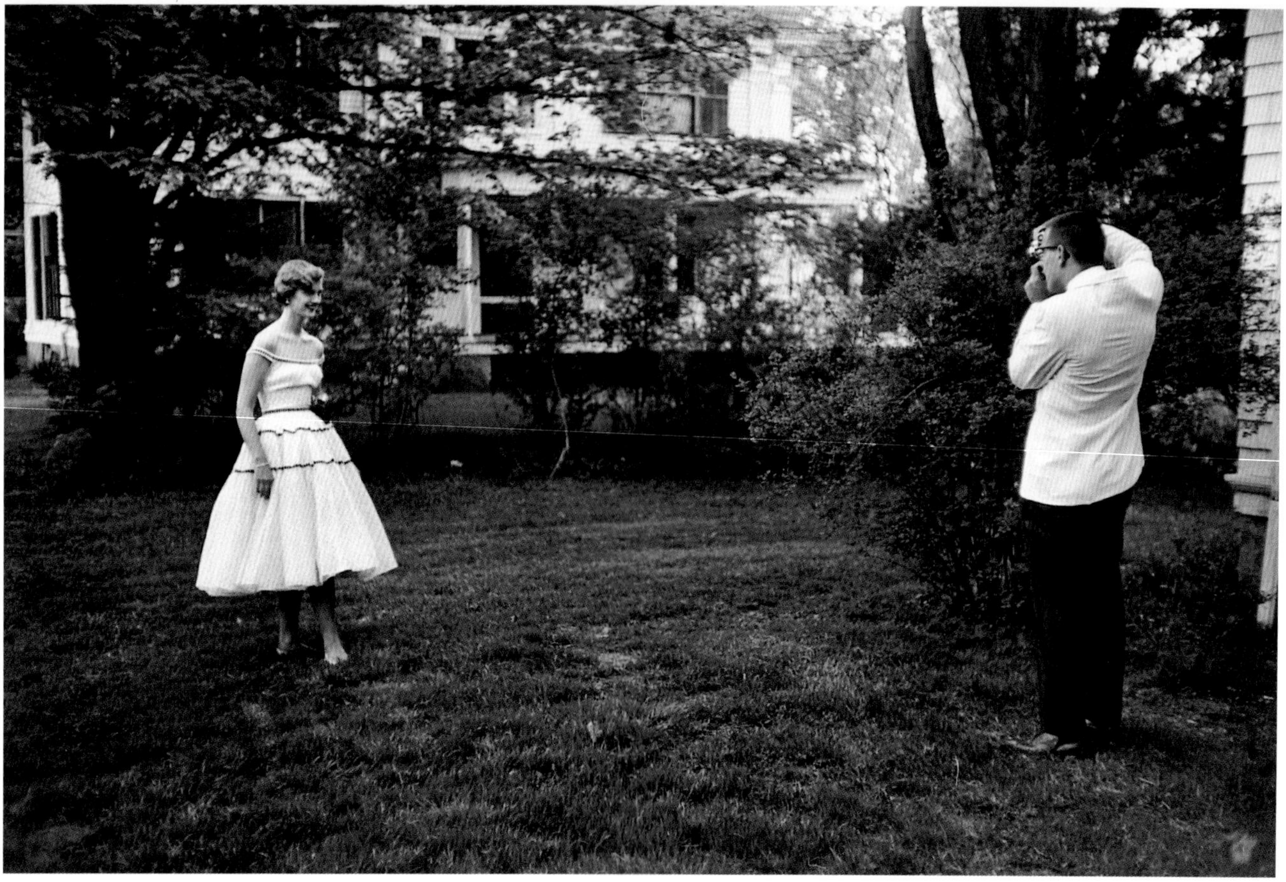

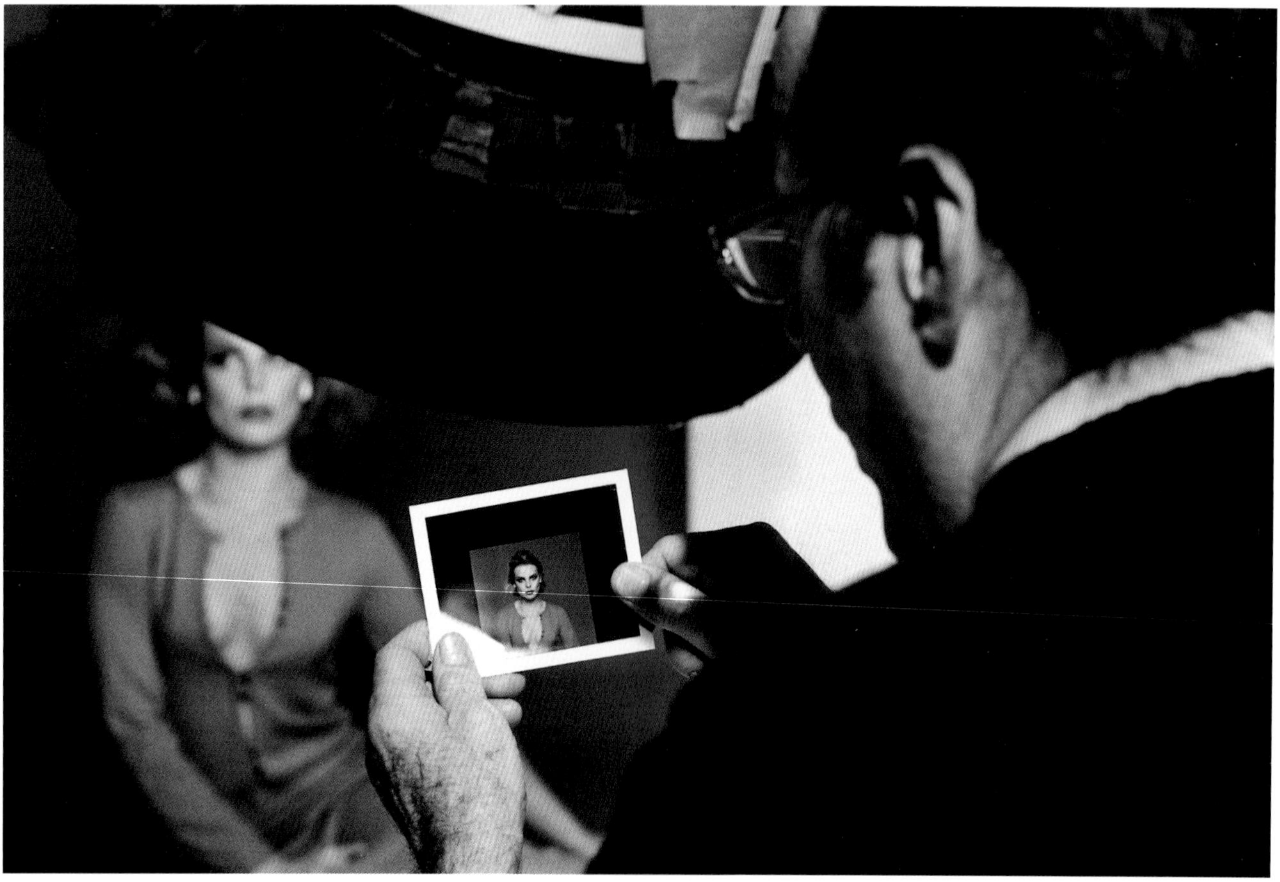

New Rochelle, New York, 1955 / New York, 1977

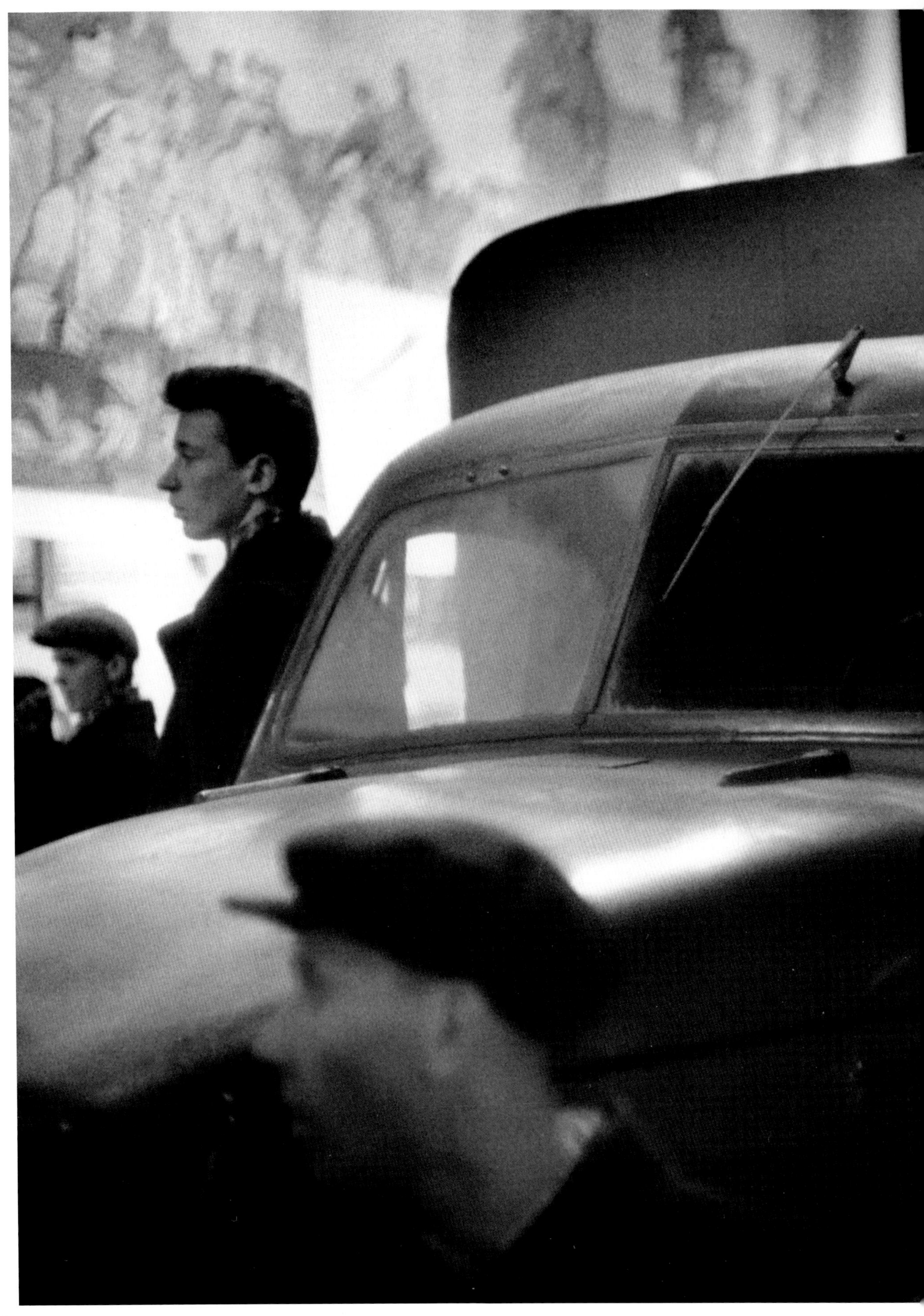

Moscow, 1957

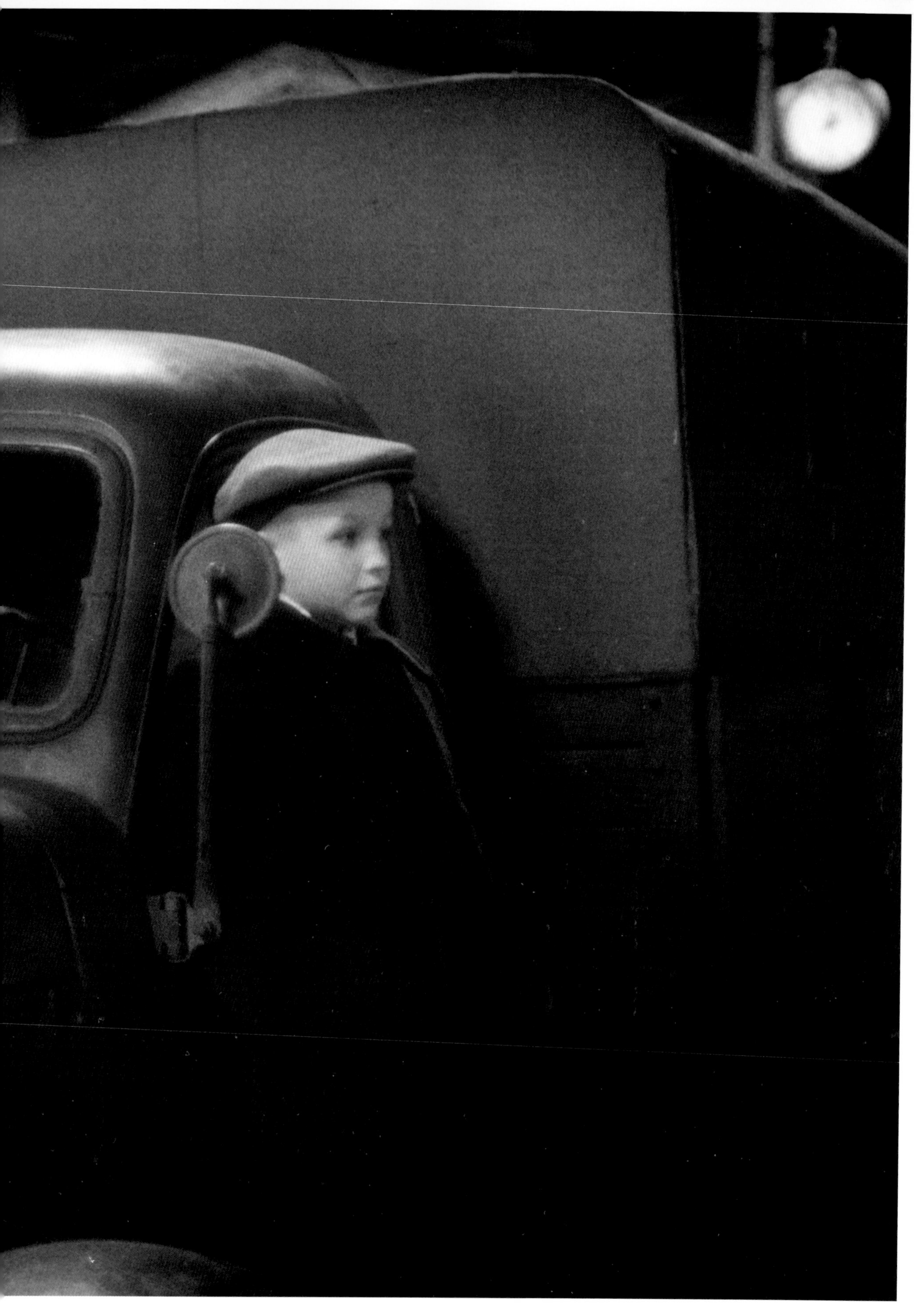

overleaf *London, 1952* / *New York, 1953*

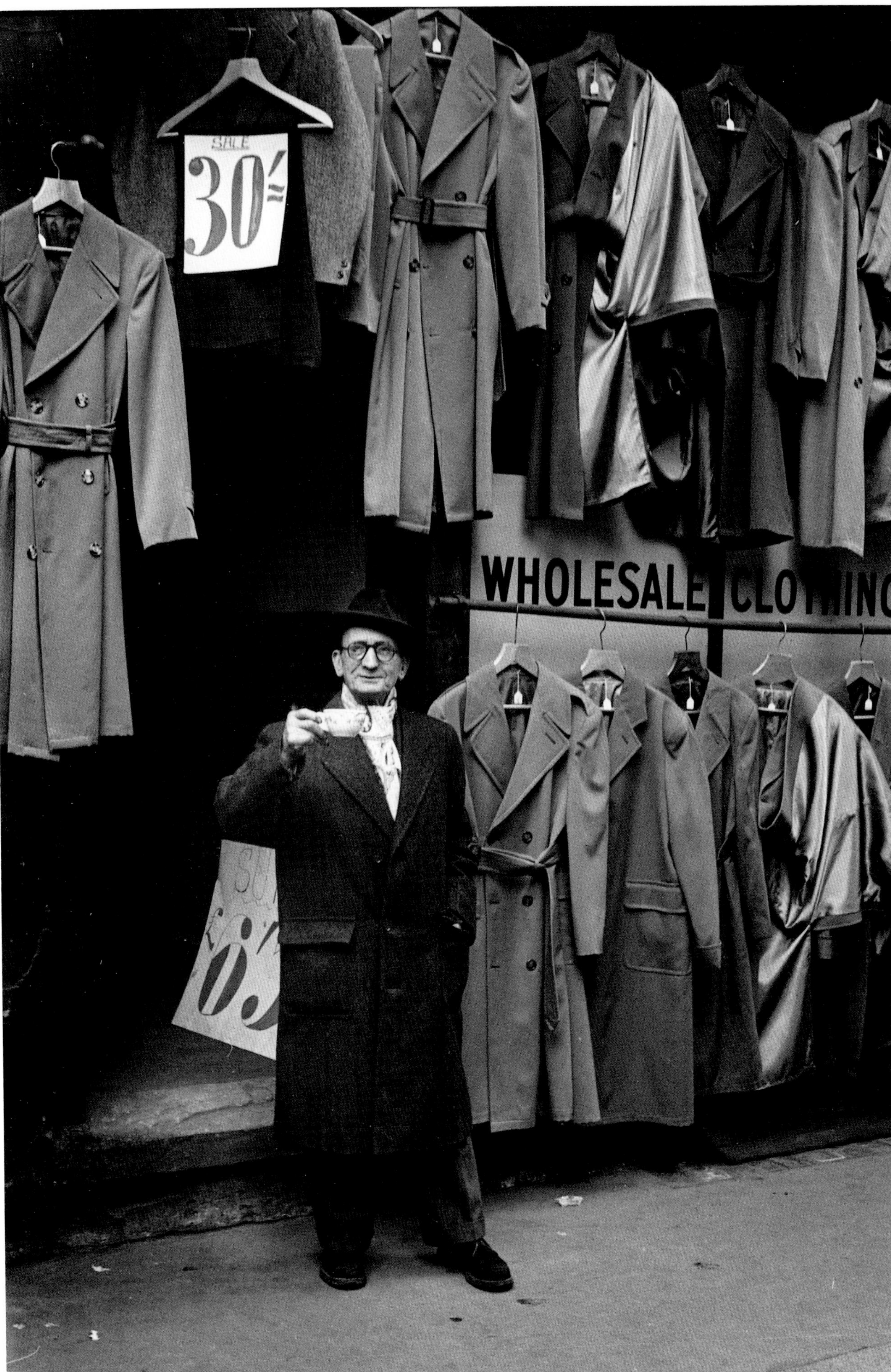
SALE
30/-
WHOLESALE CLOTHING

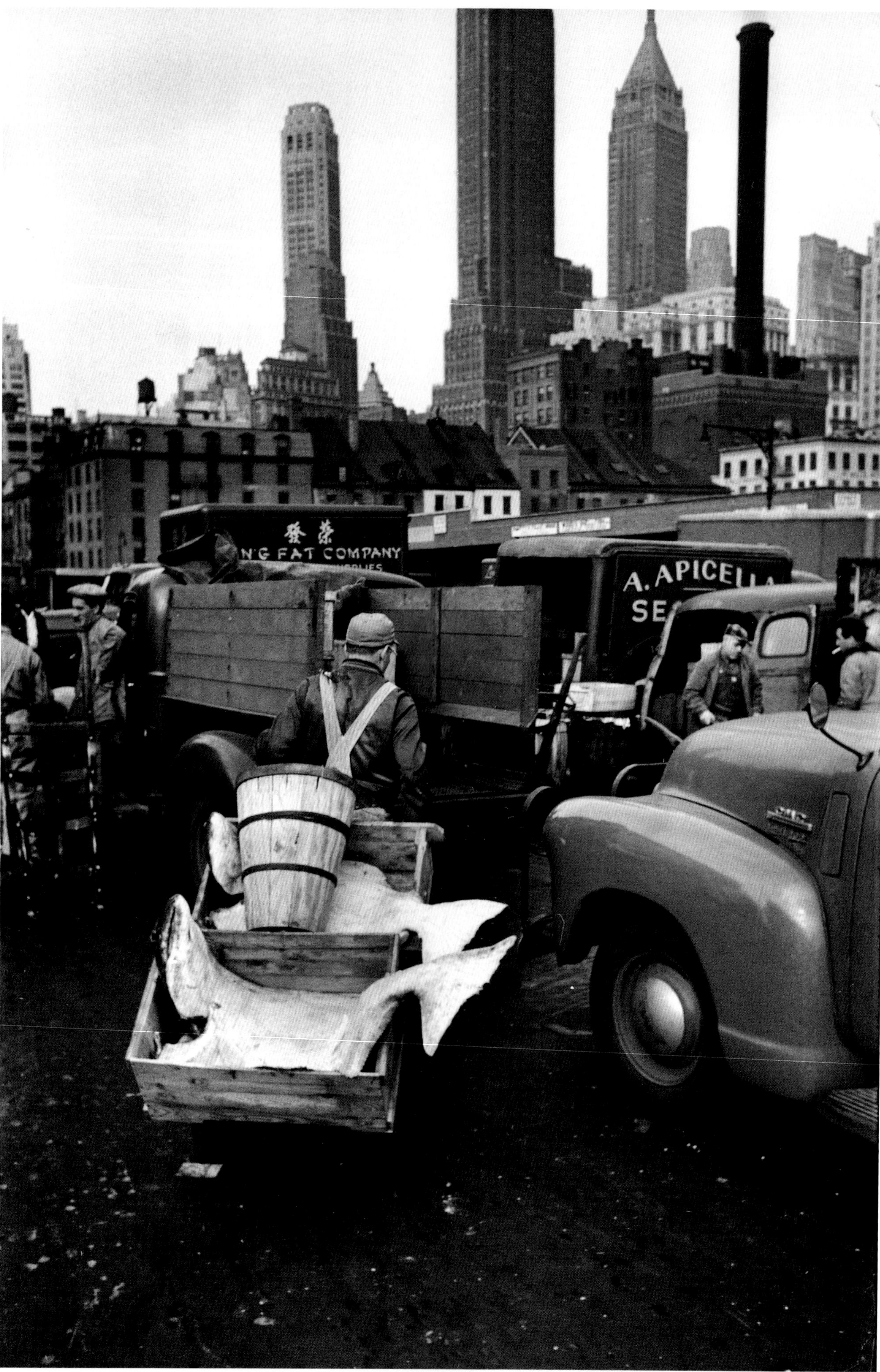
N'G FAT COMPANY
A. APICELLA
SE

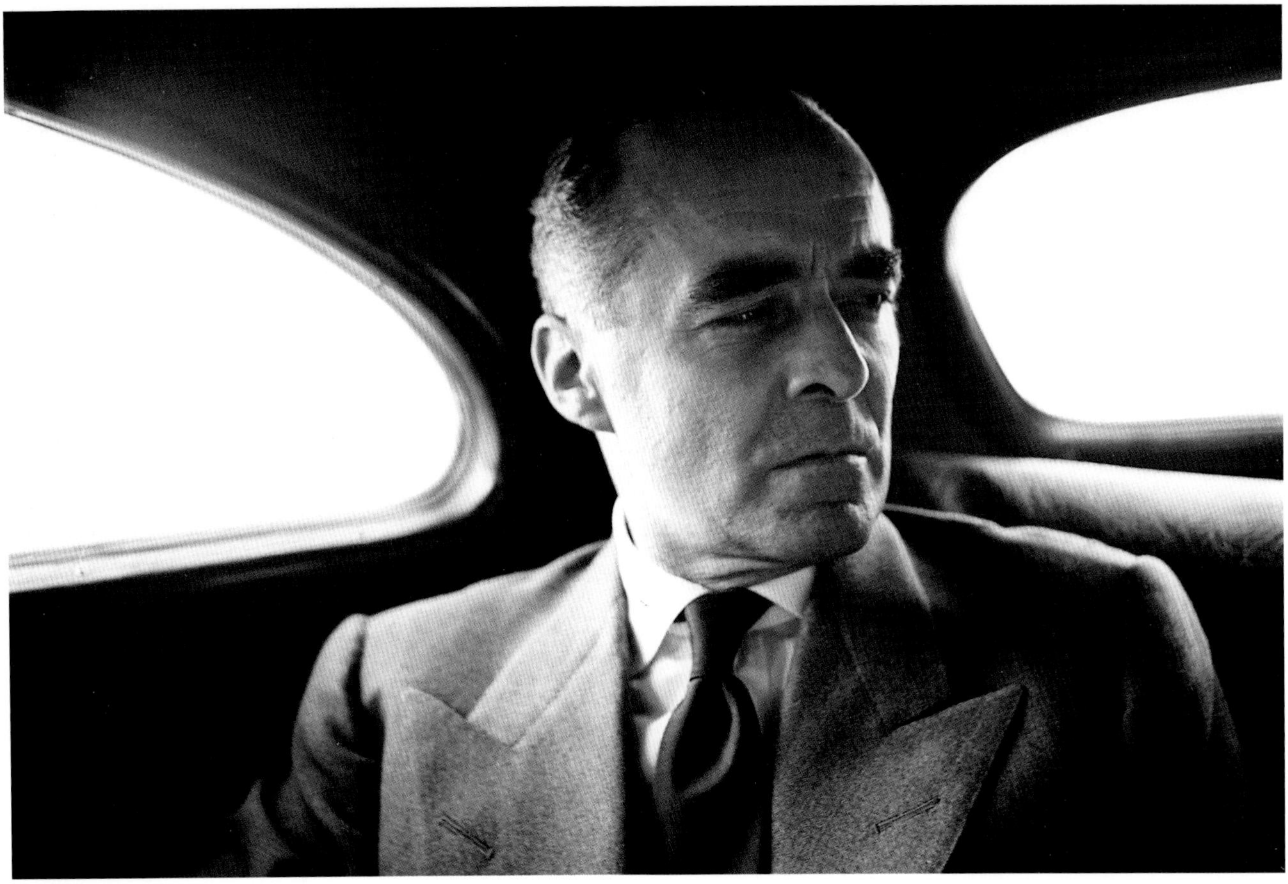

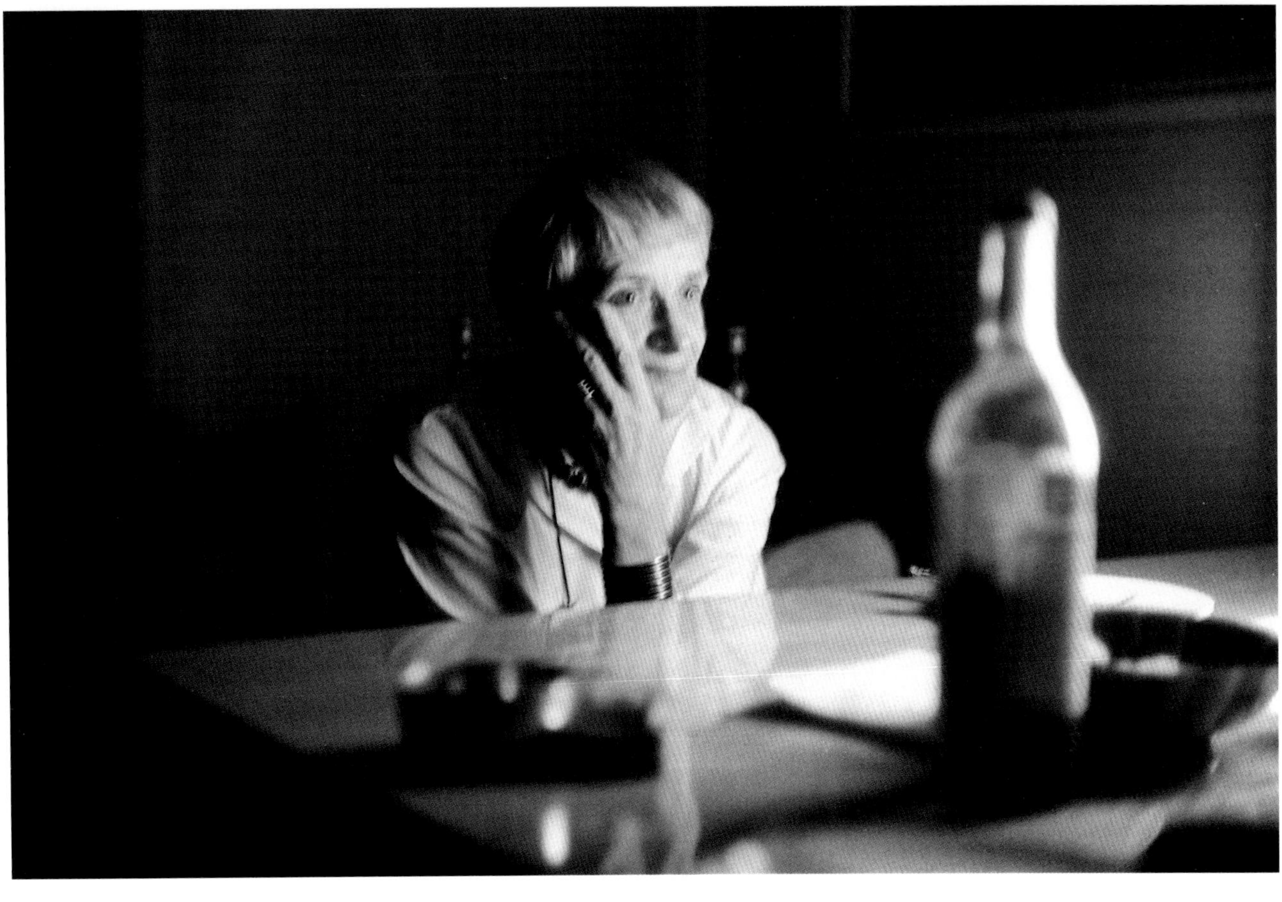

Richard Llewellyn, New York, 1949 / *Dorothea Lange, Berkeley, California, 1955*

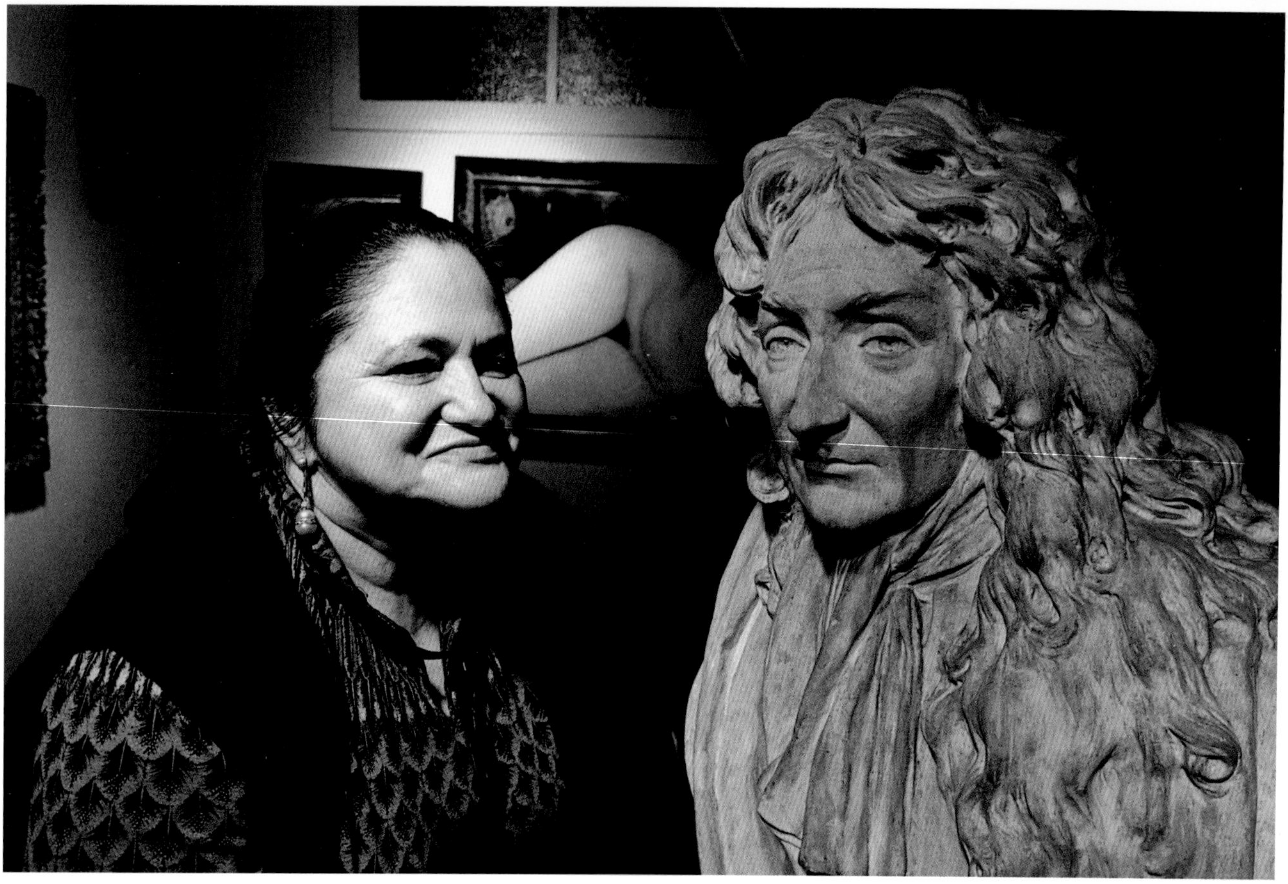

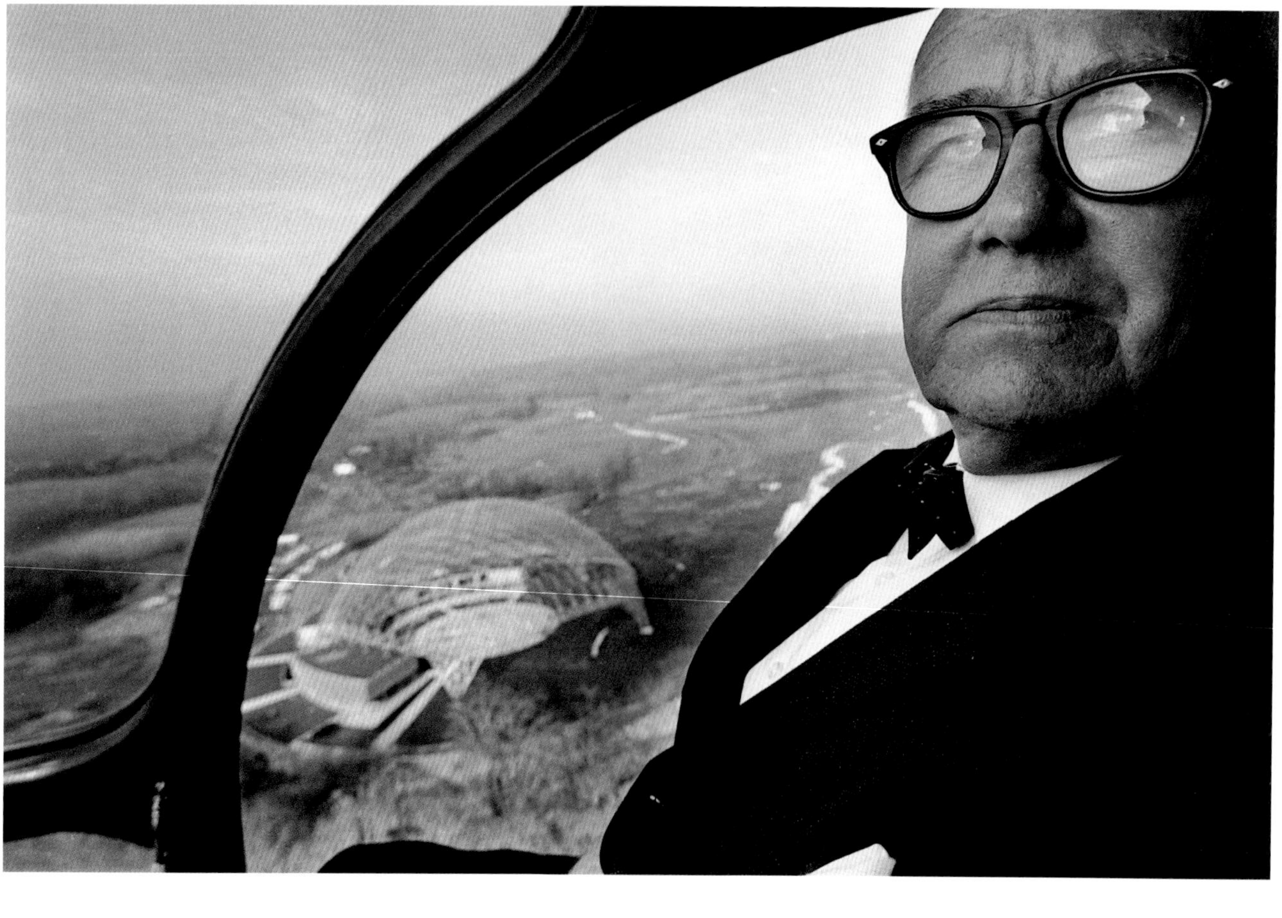

Dina Vierny, Paris, 1982 / *Buckminster Fuller, Ohio, 1959*

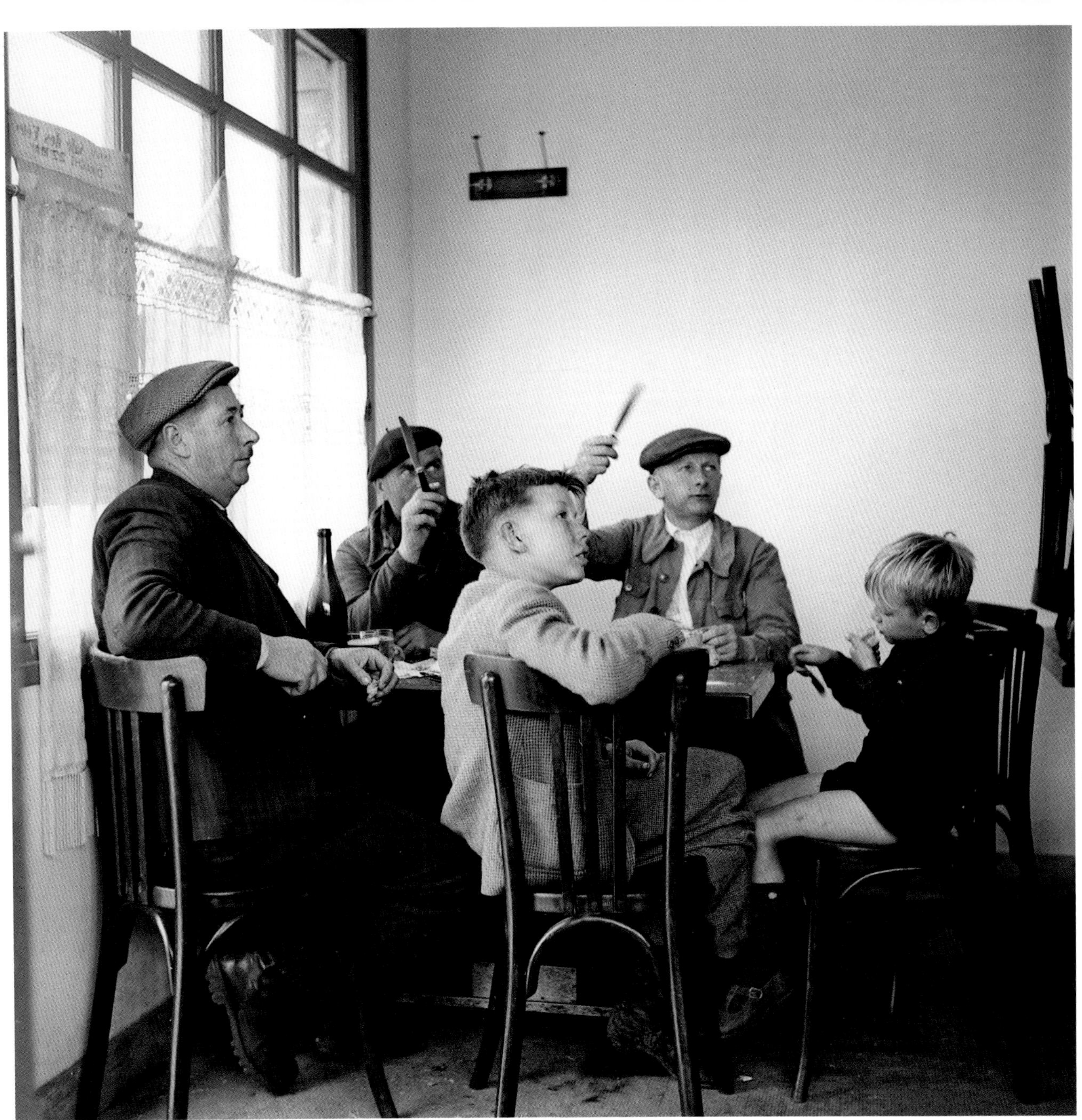

Loire Valley, France, 1952

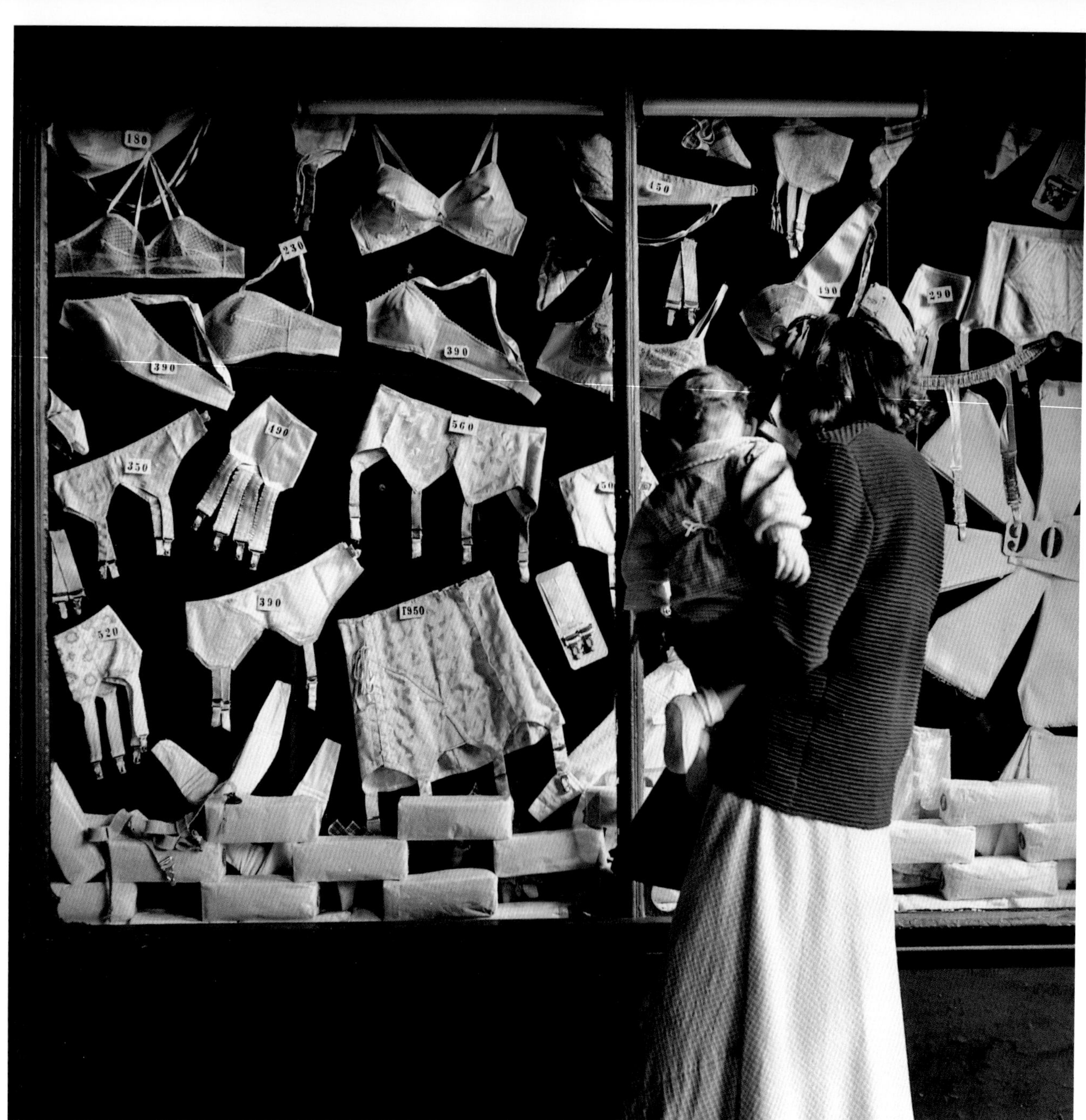

Venice, 1949

overleaf *Hotel rooms in France and England, '68, '78, '81, '69, '75*

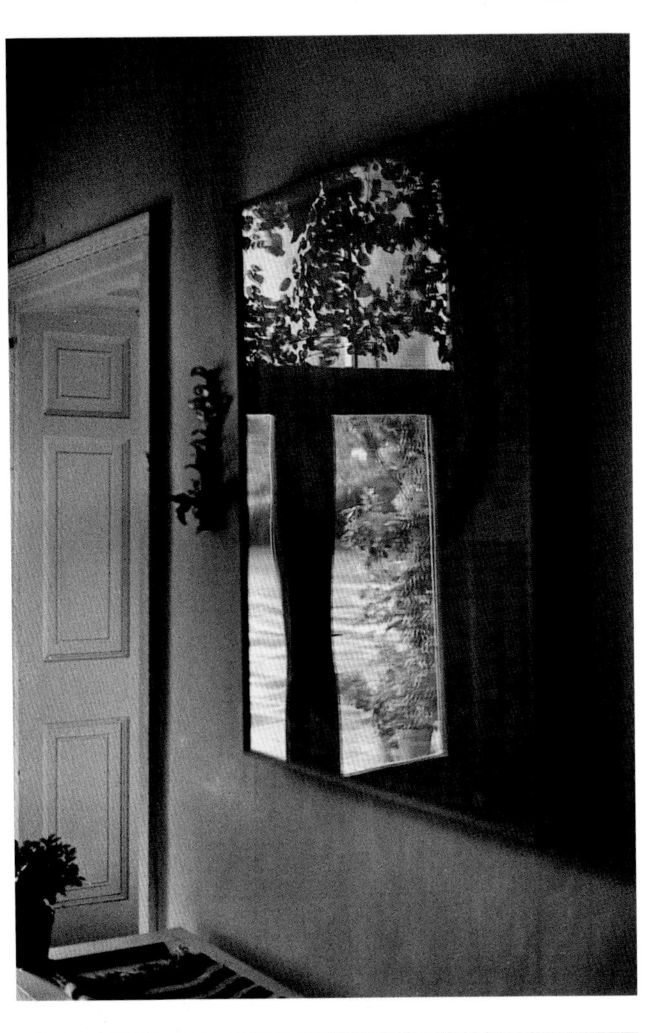
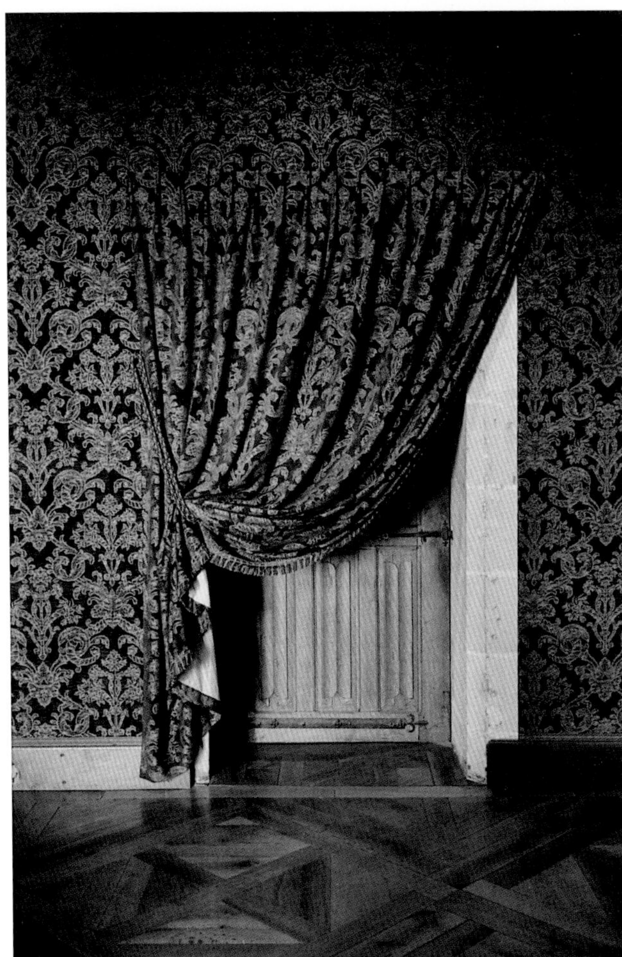
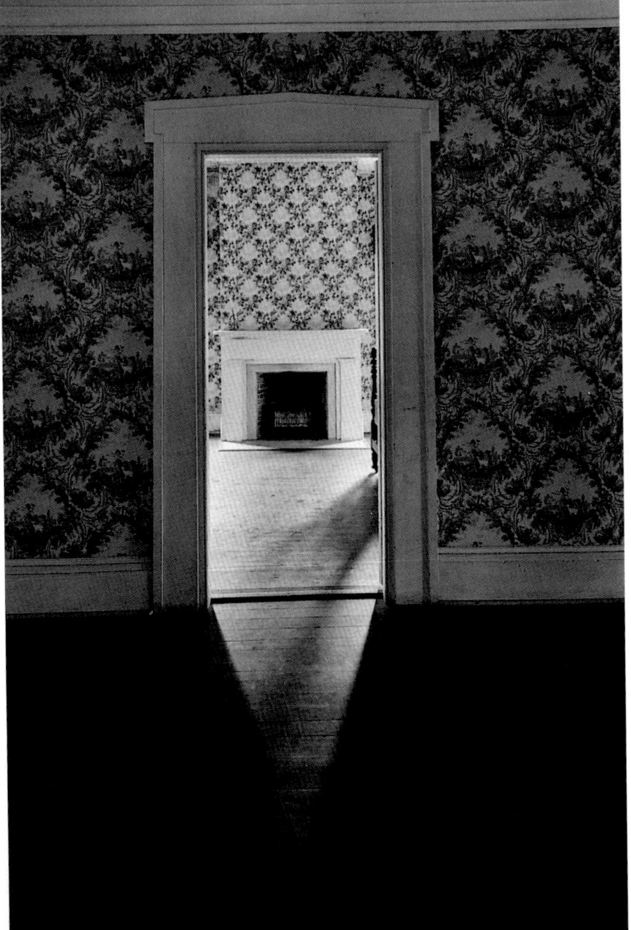
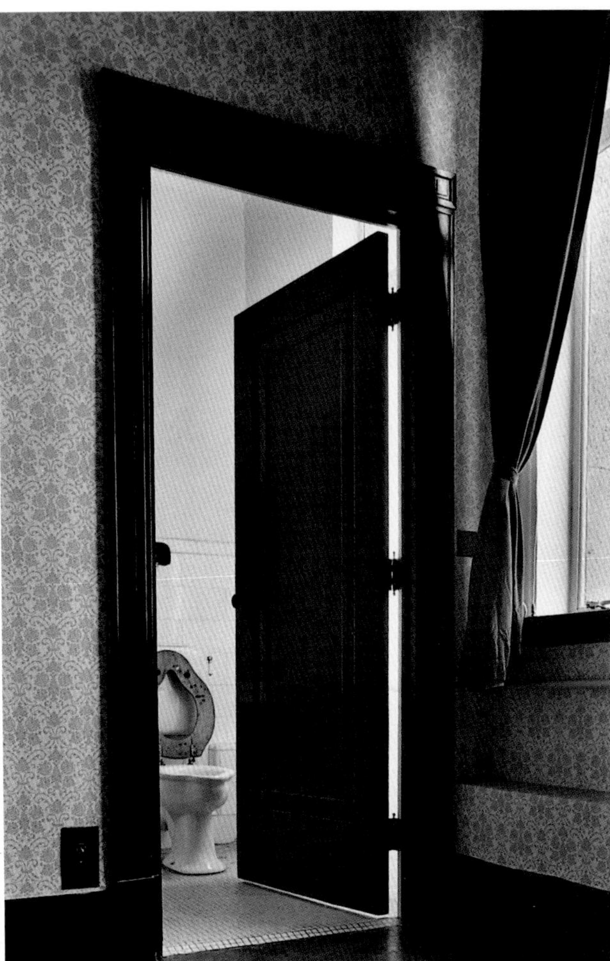

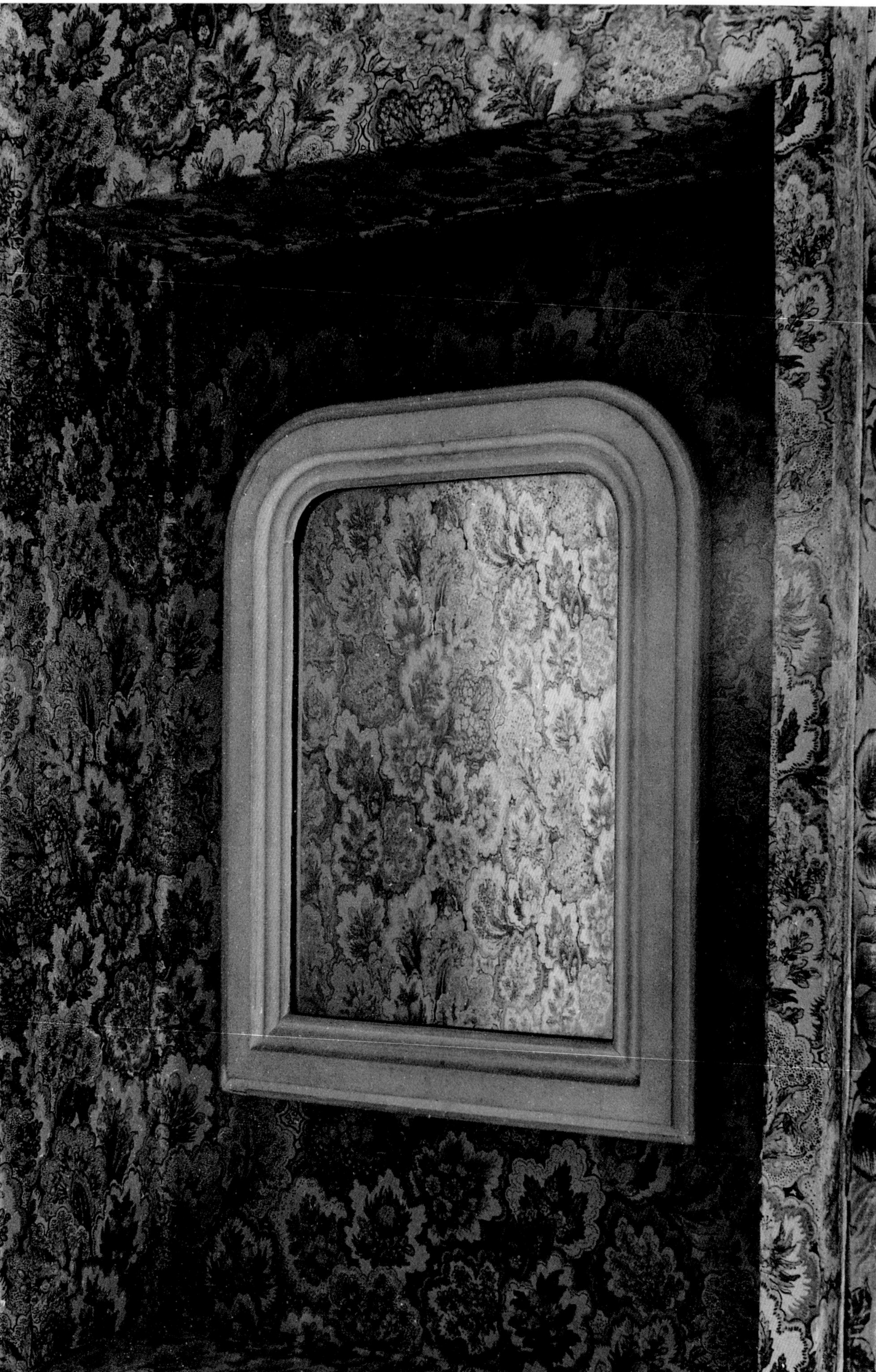

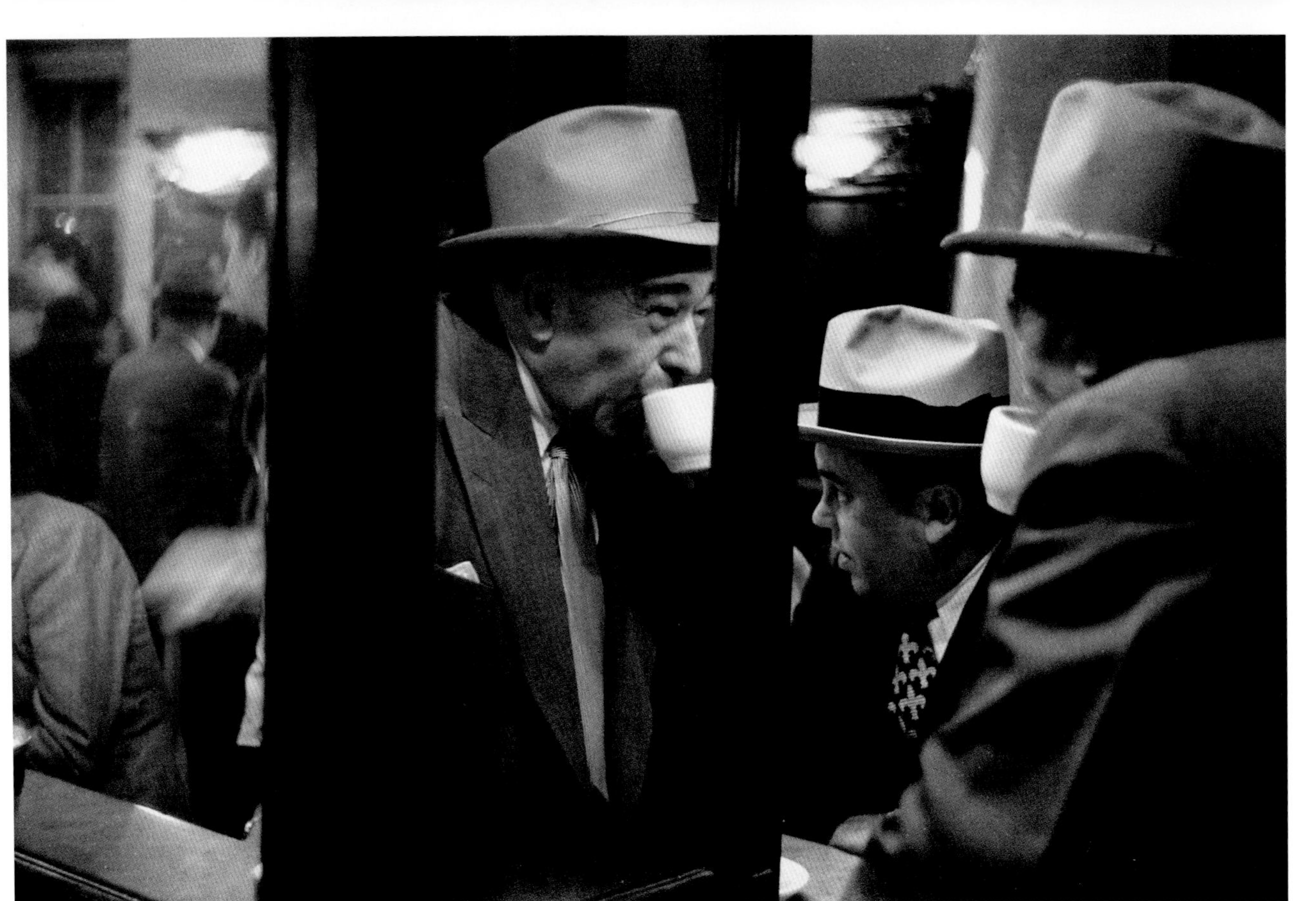

New Orleans, 1949

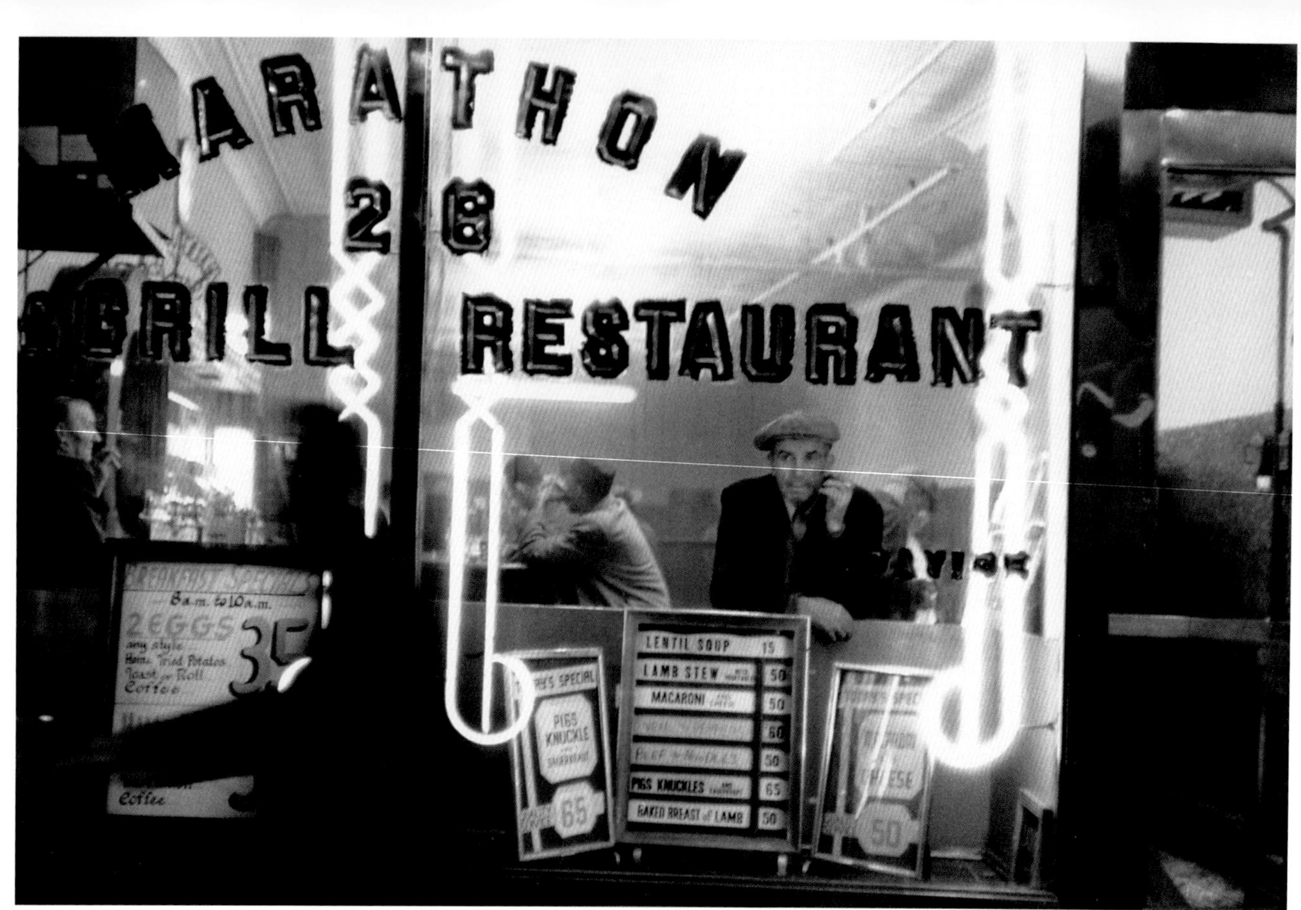

New York, 1956

Paris, 1958

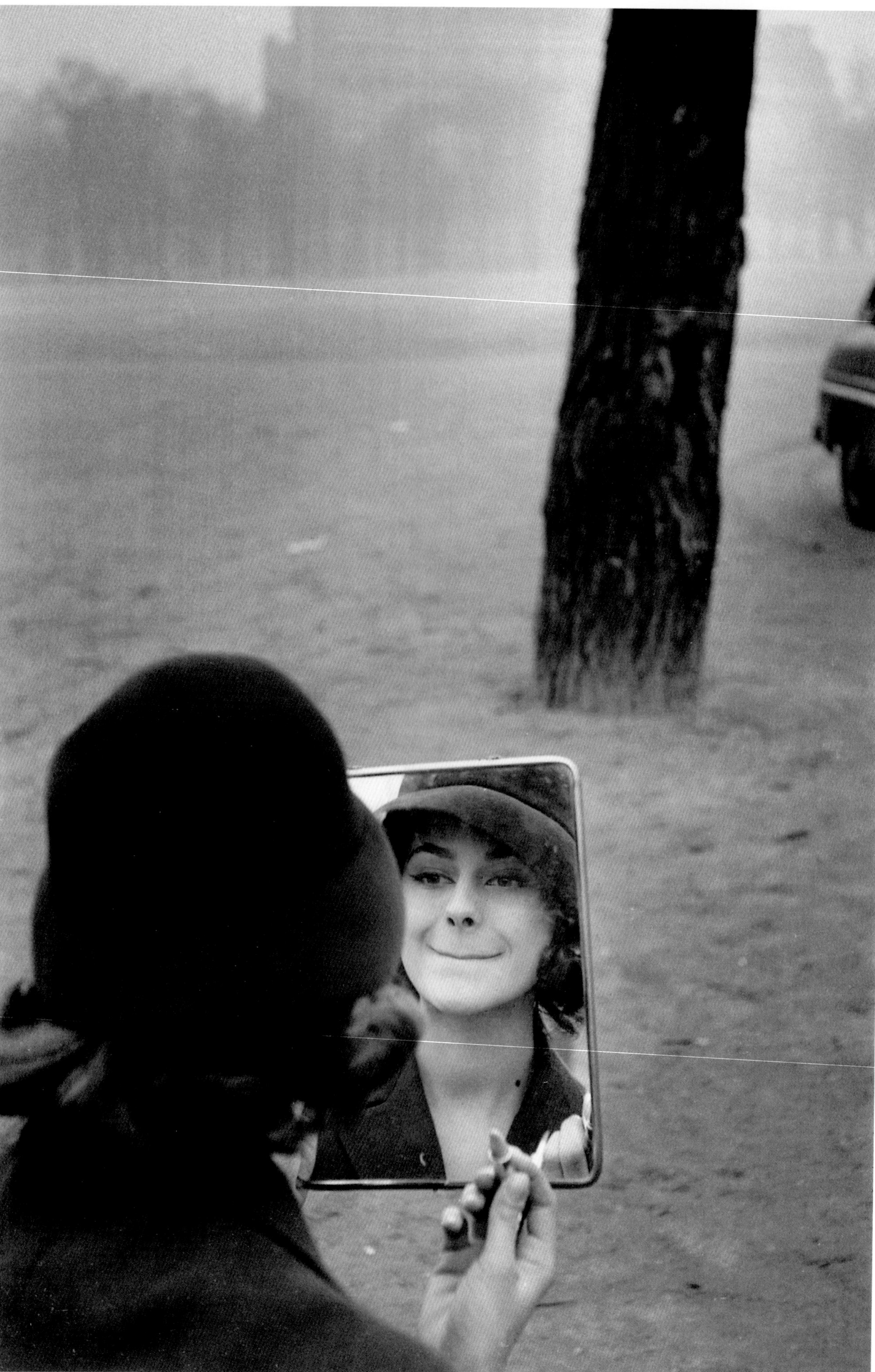

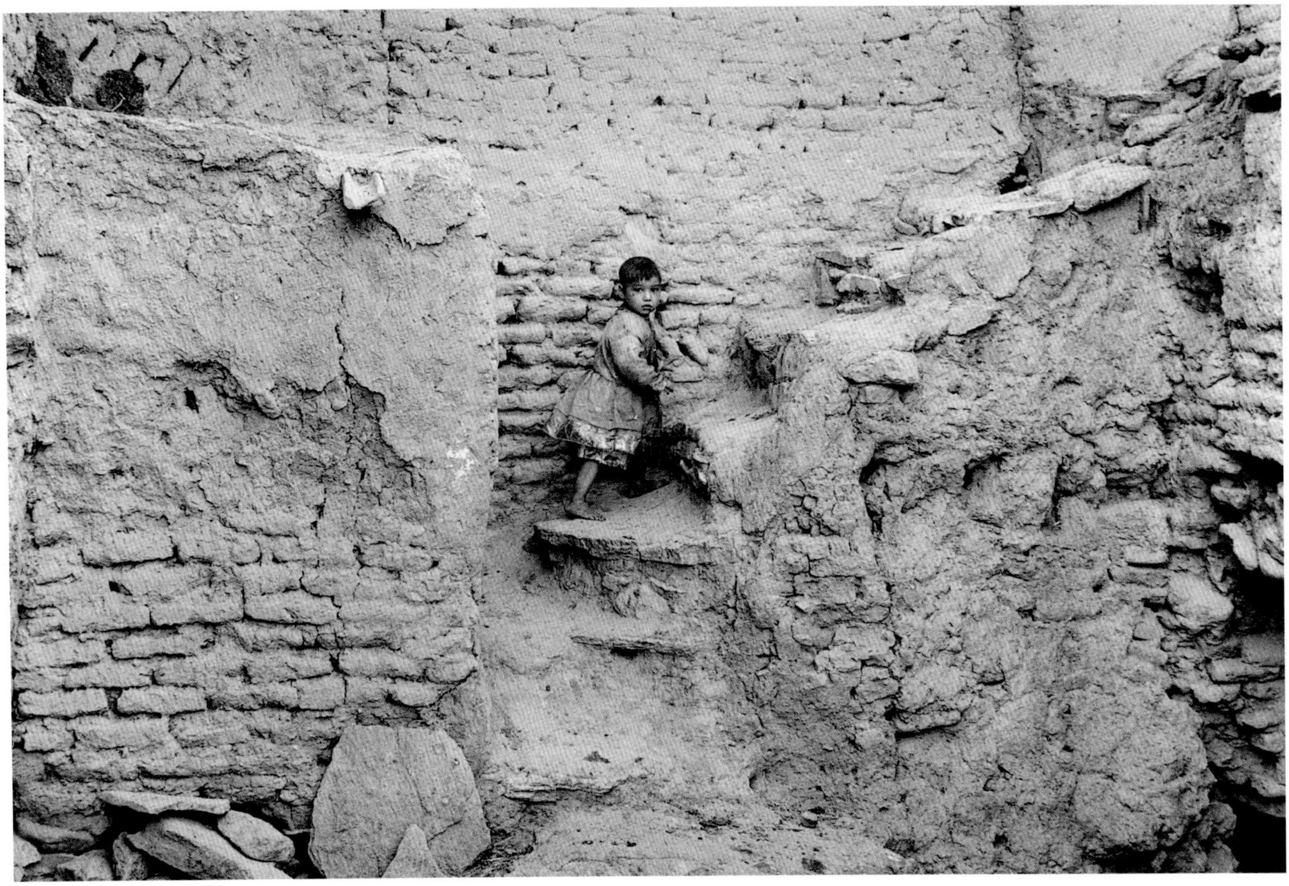

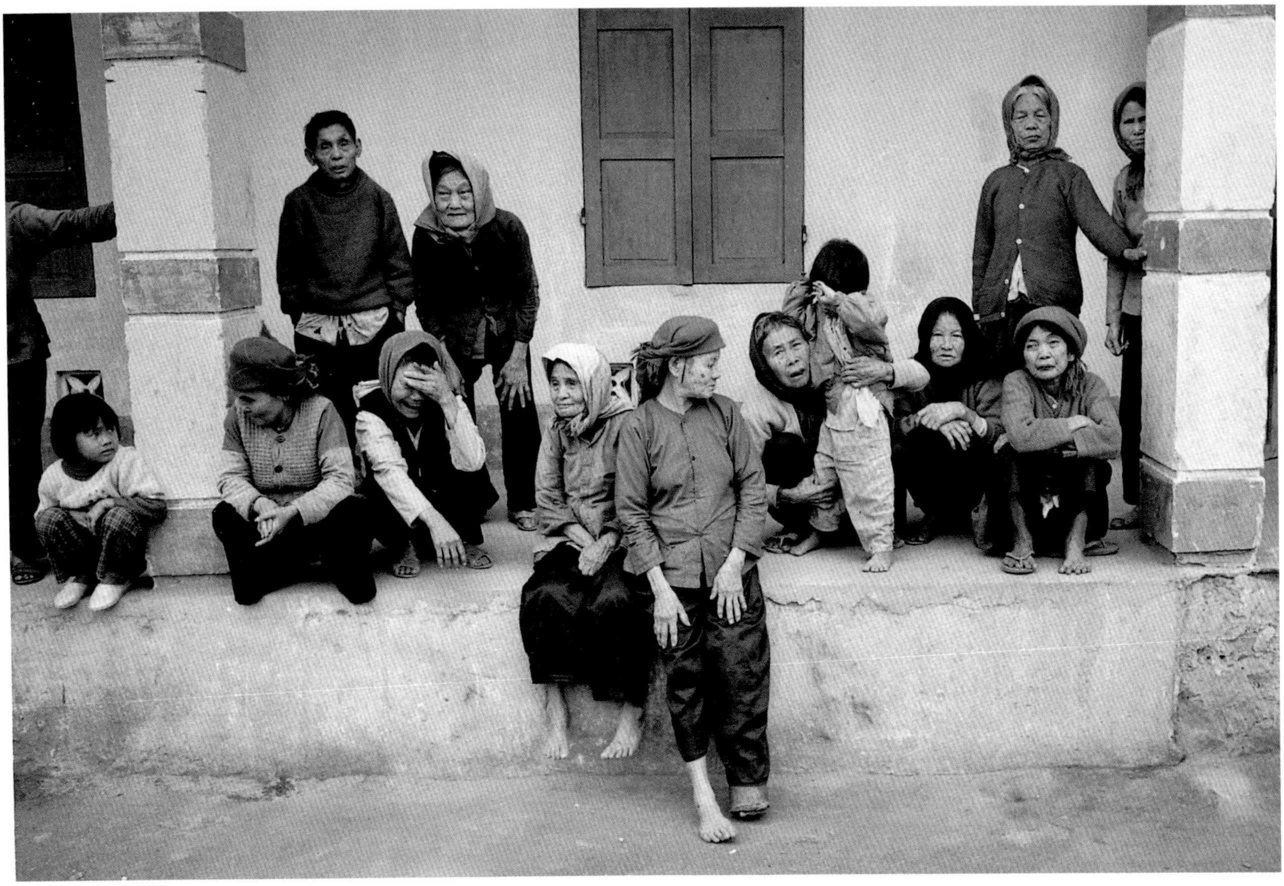

Herát, Afghanistan, 1977 / *Ninh Binh, Vietnam, 1994*

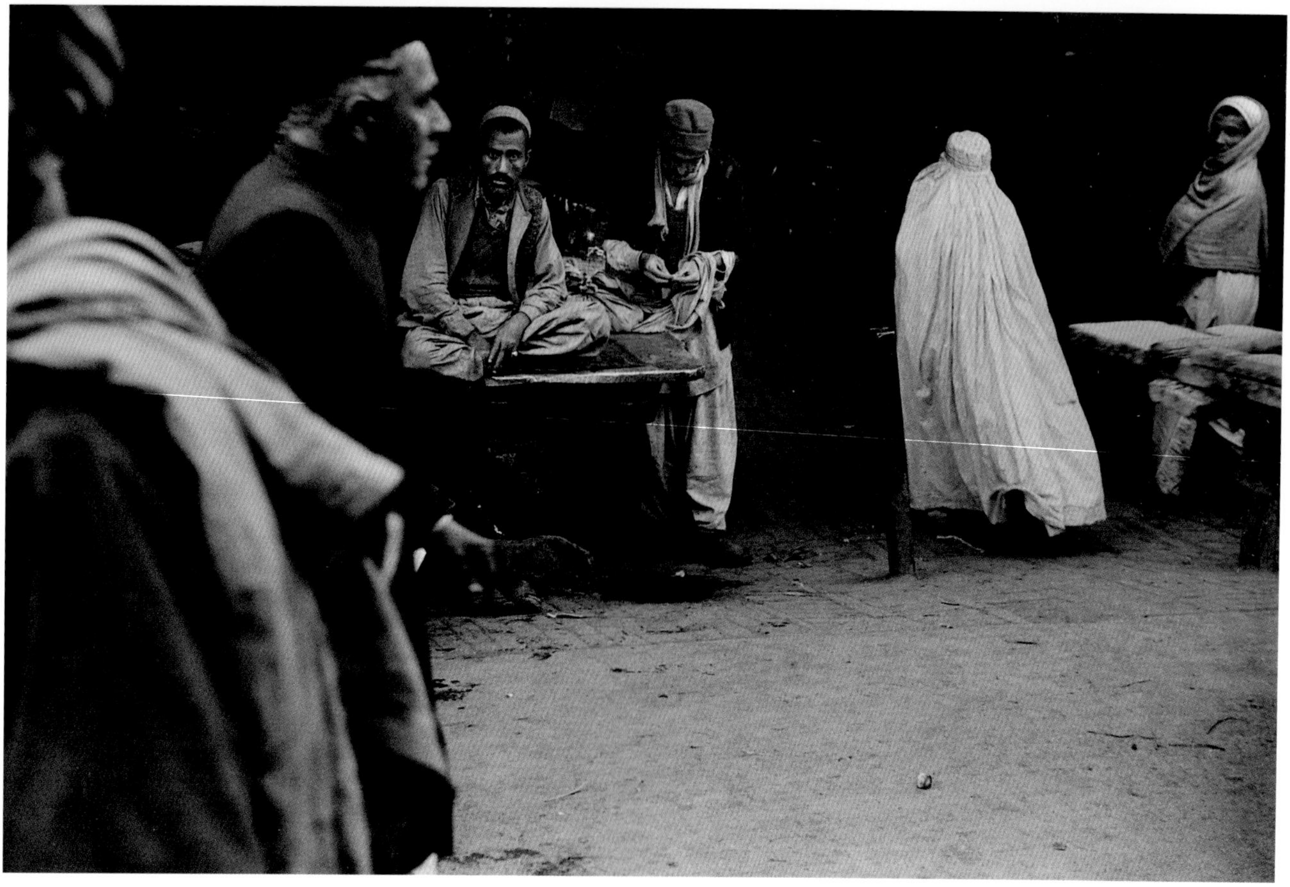

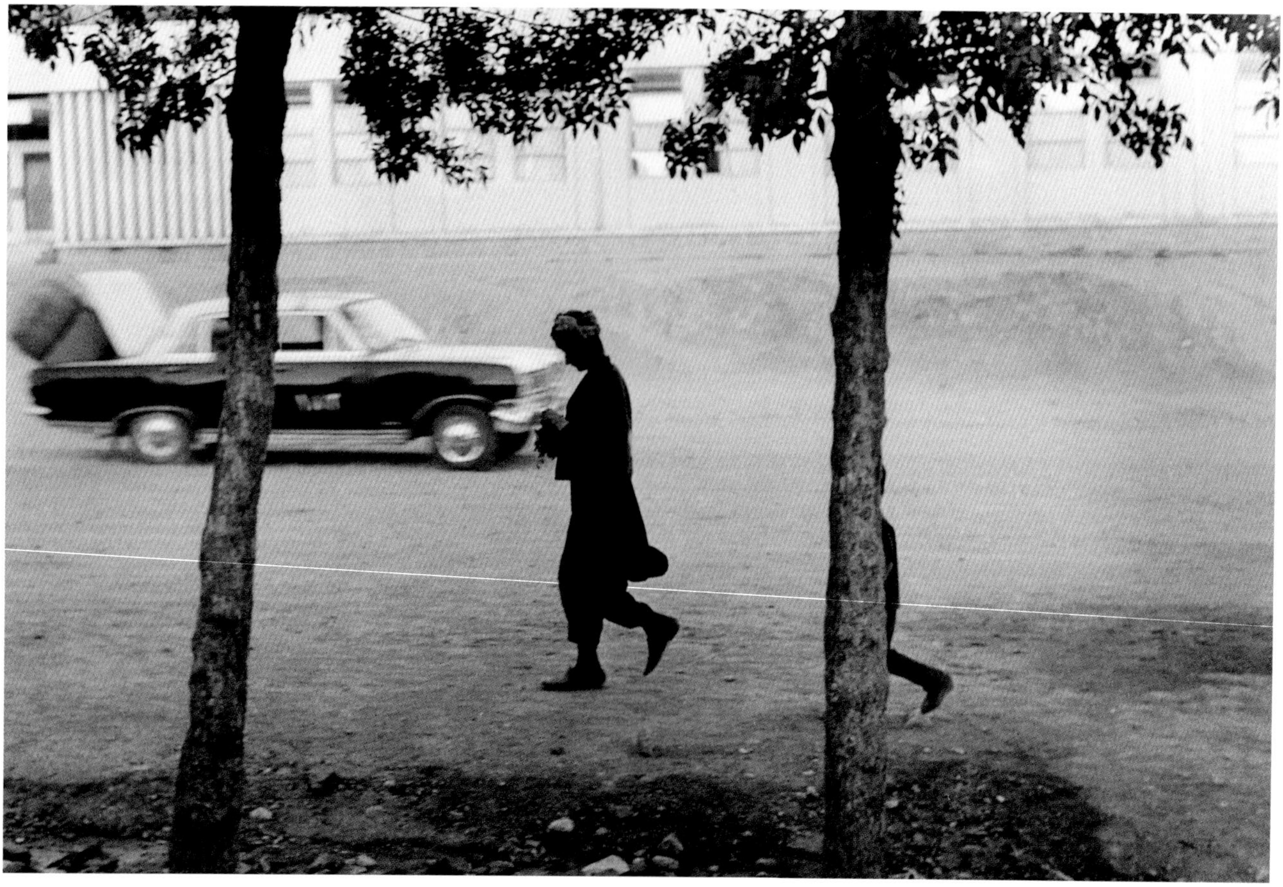

Lahore, Pakistan, 1960 / *Herát, Afghanistan, 1977*

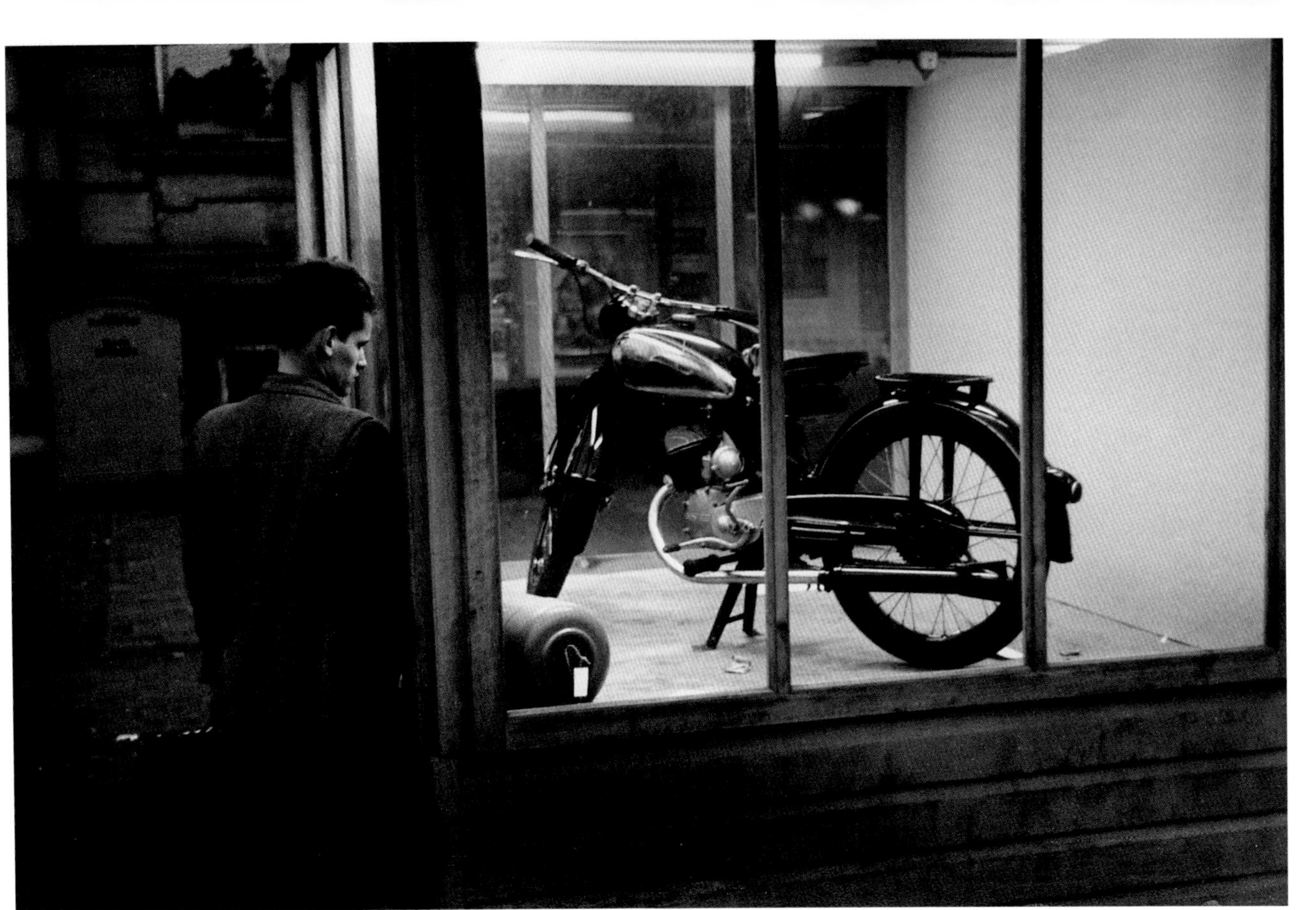

Karlsruhe, Germany, 1951

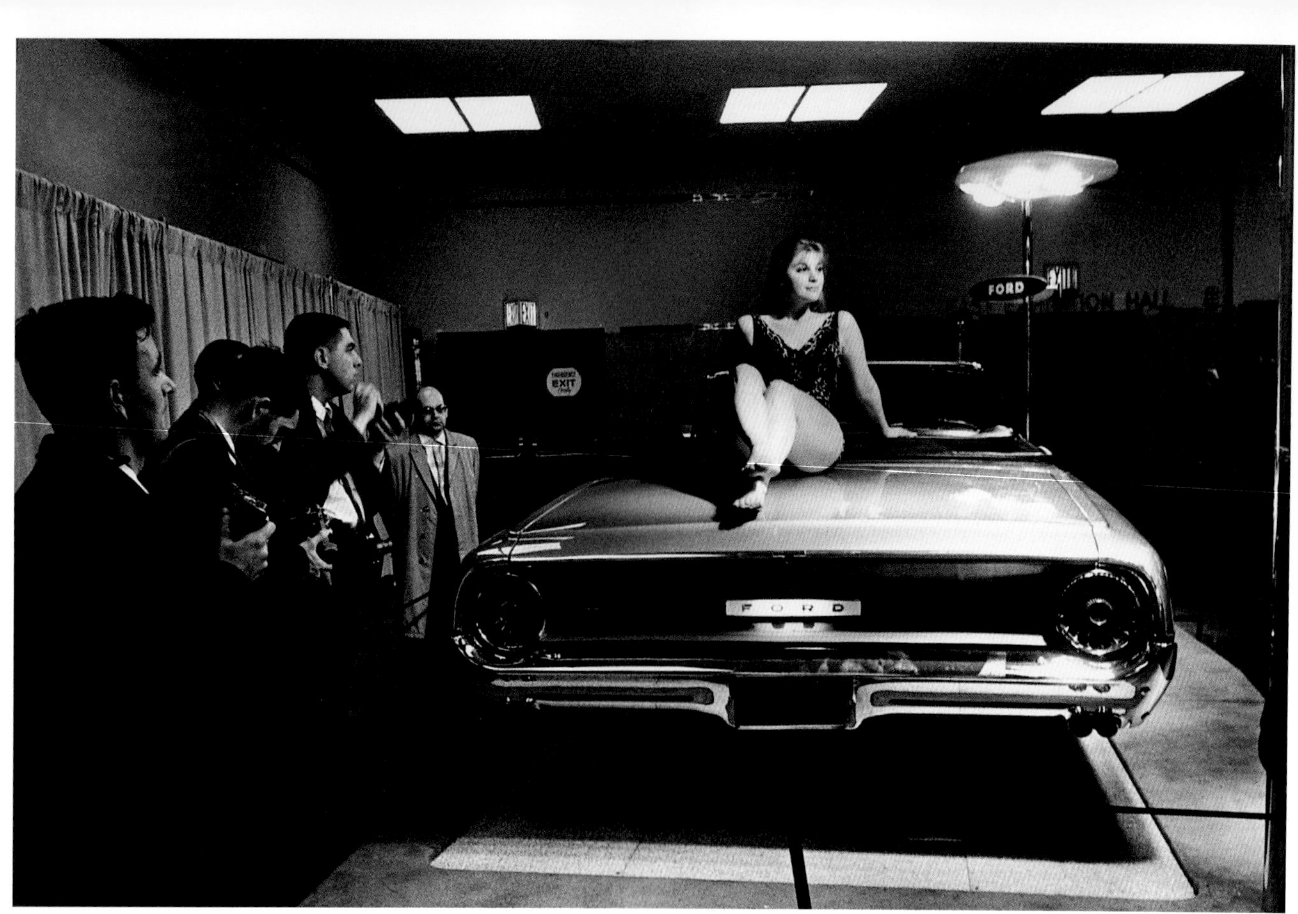

New York, 1964

overleaf *France, 1999* / *New York, 1999*

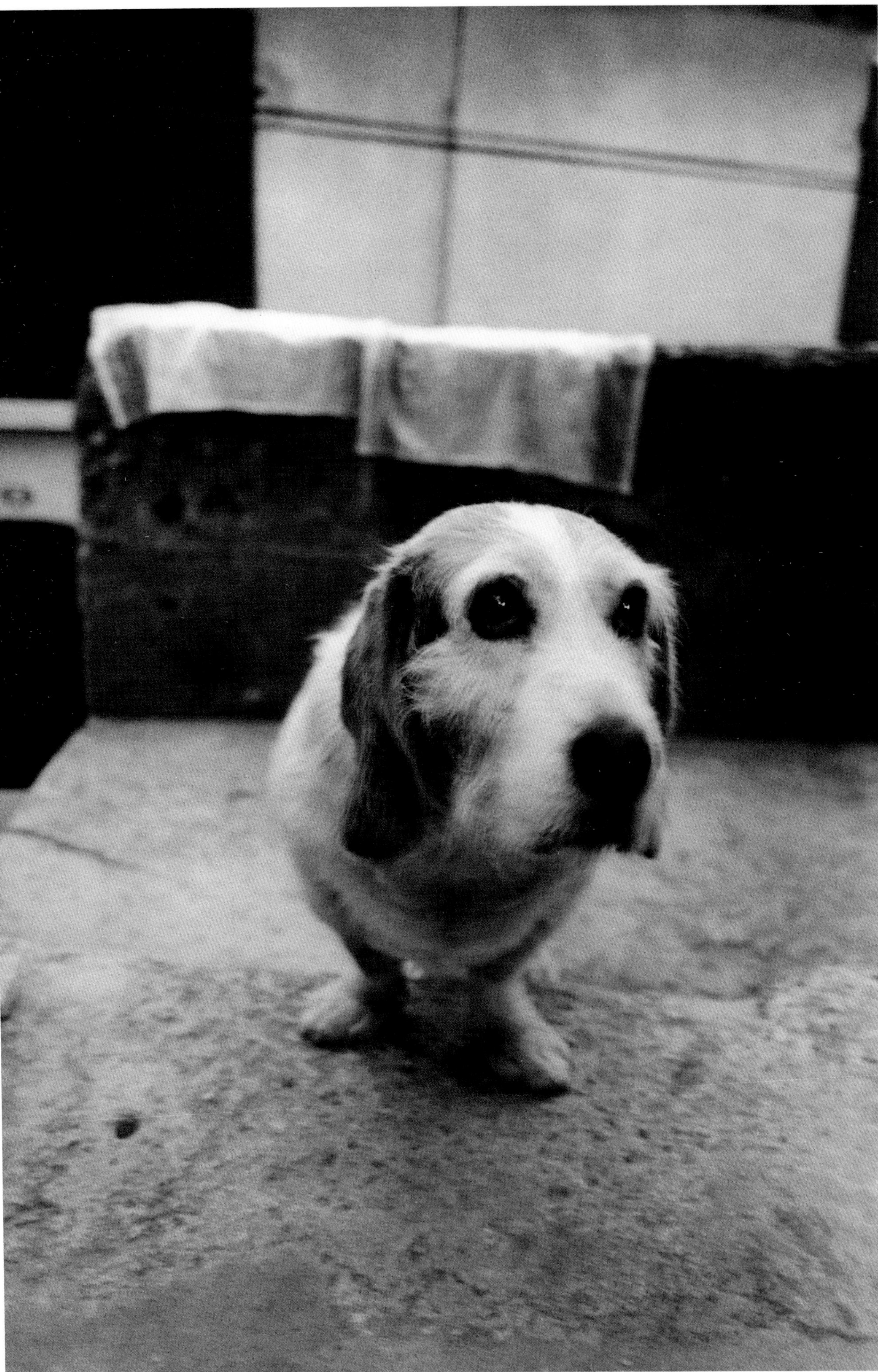

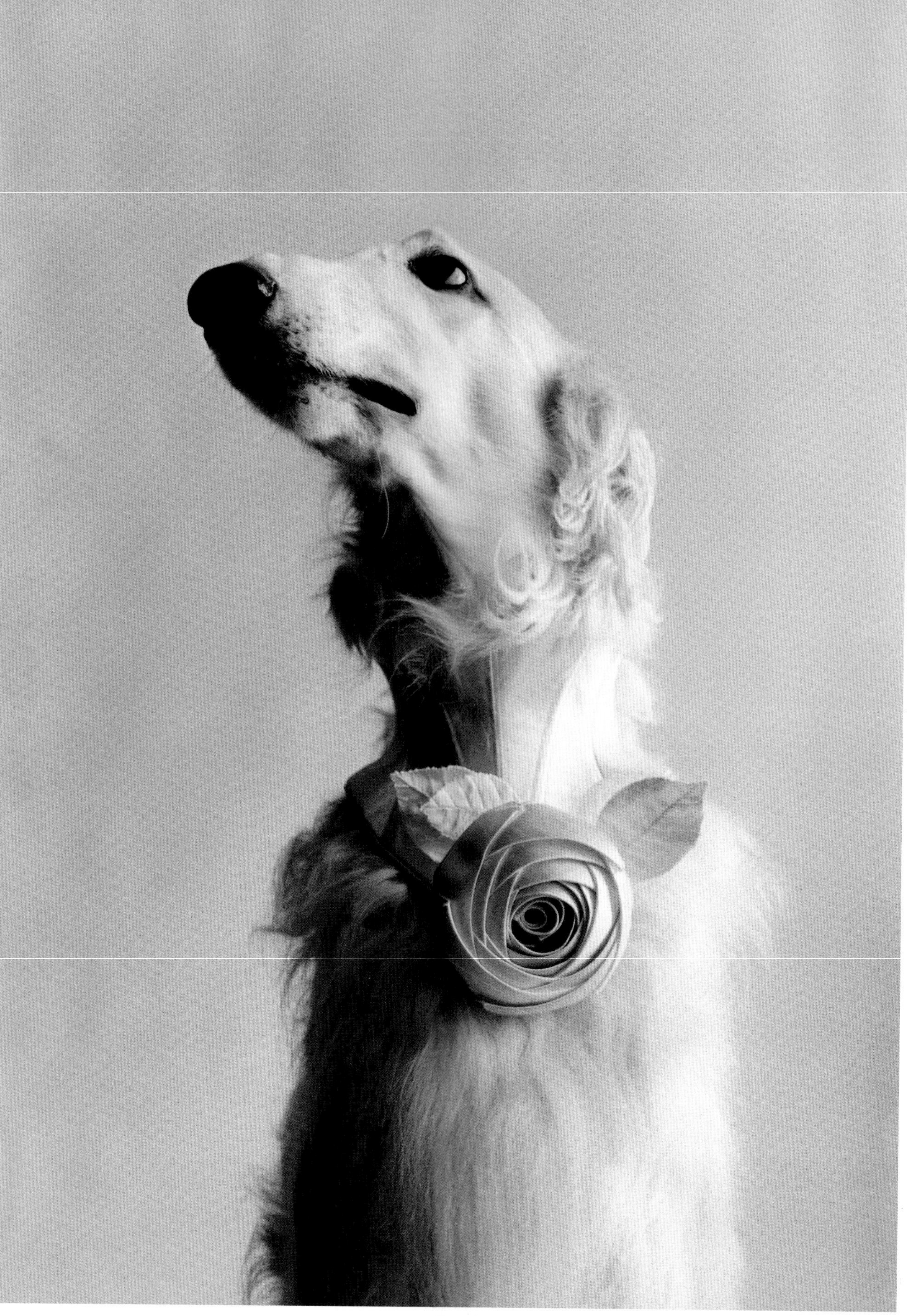

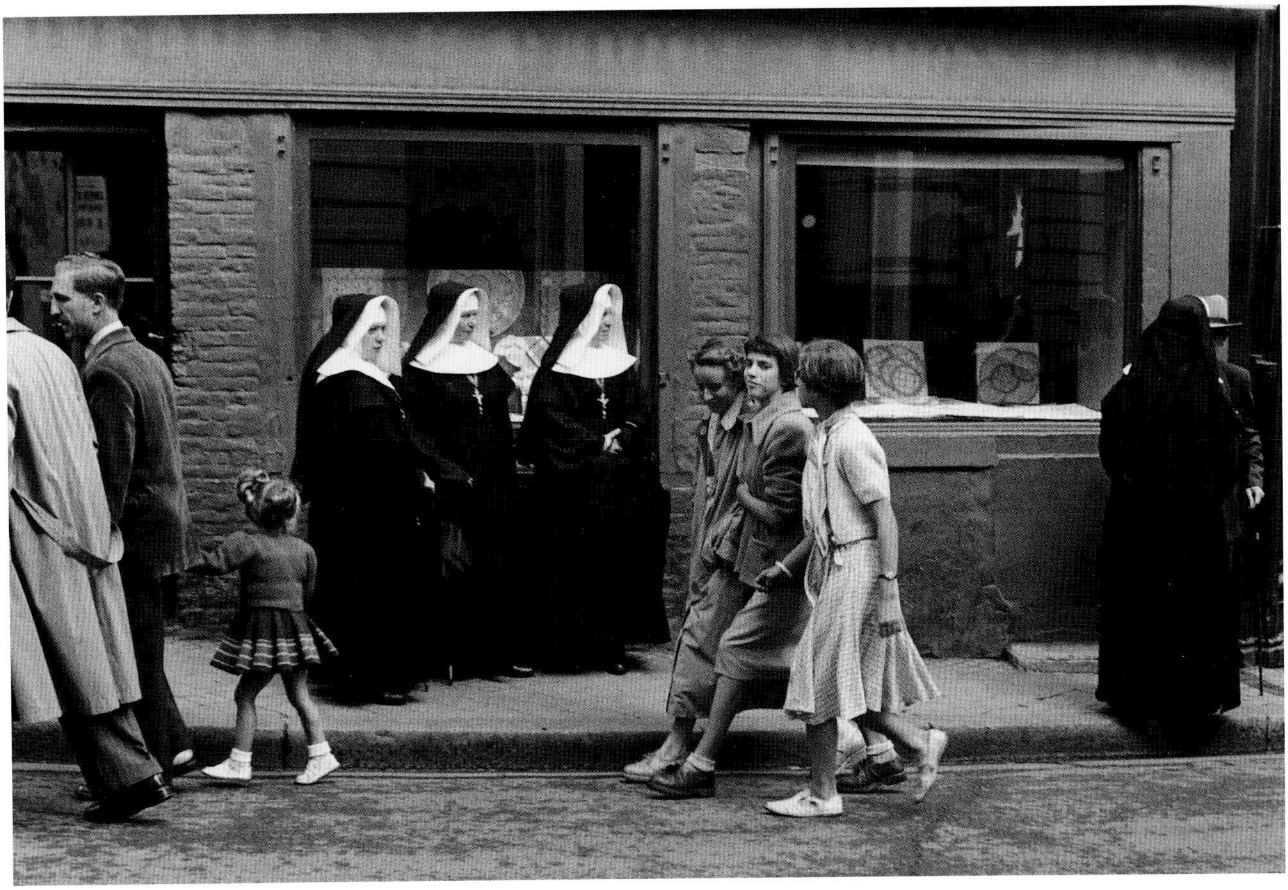

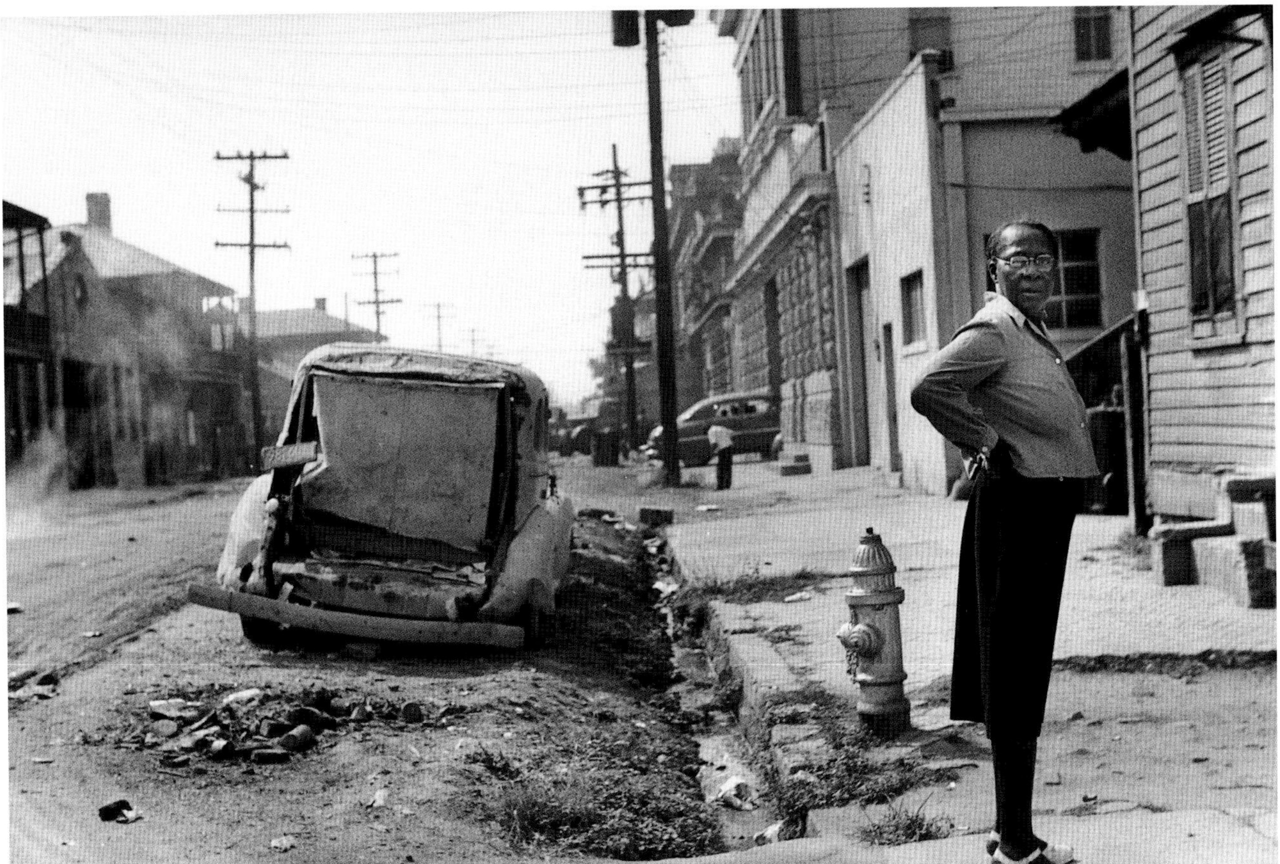

Verdun, France, 1951 / *New Orleans, 1950*

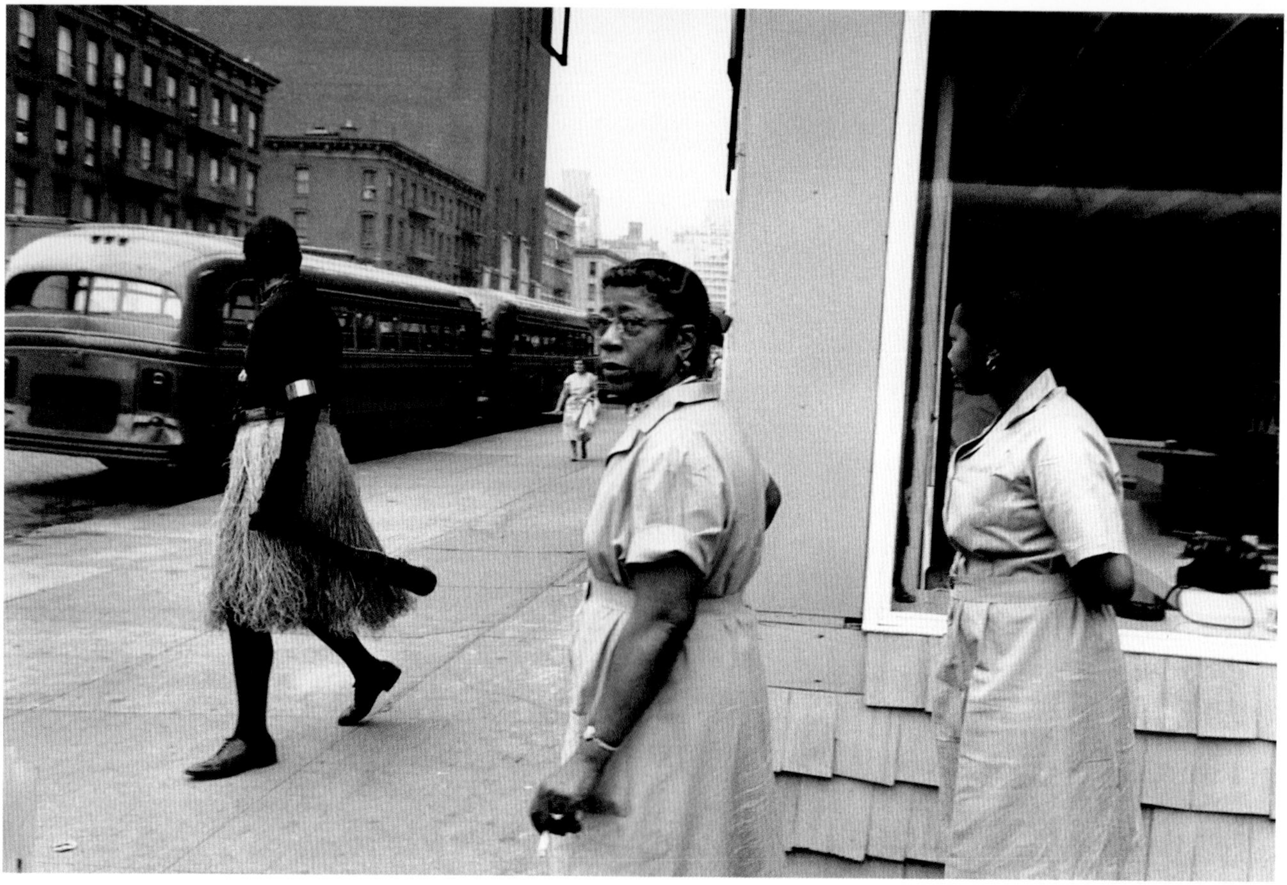

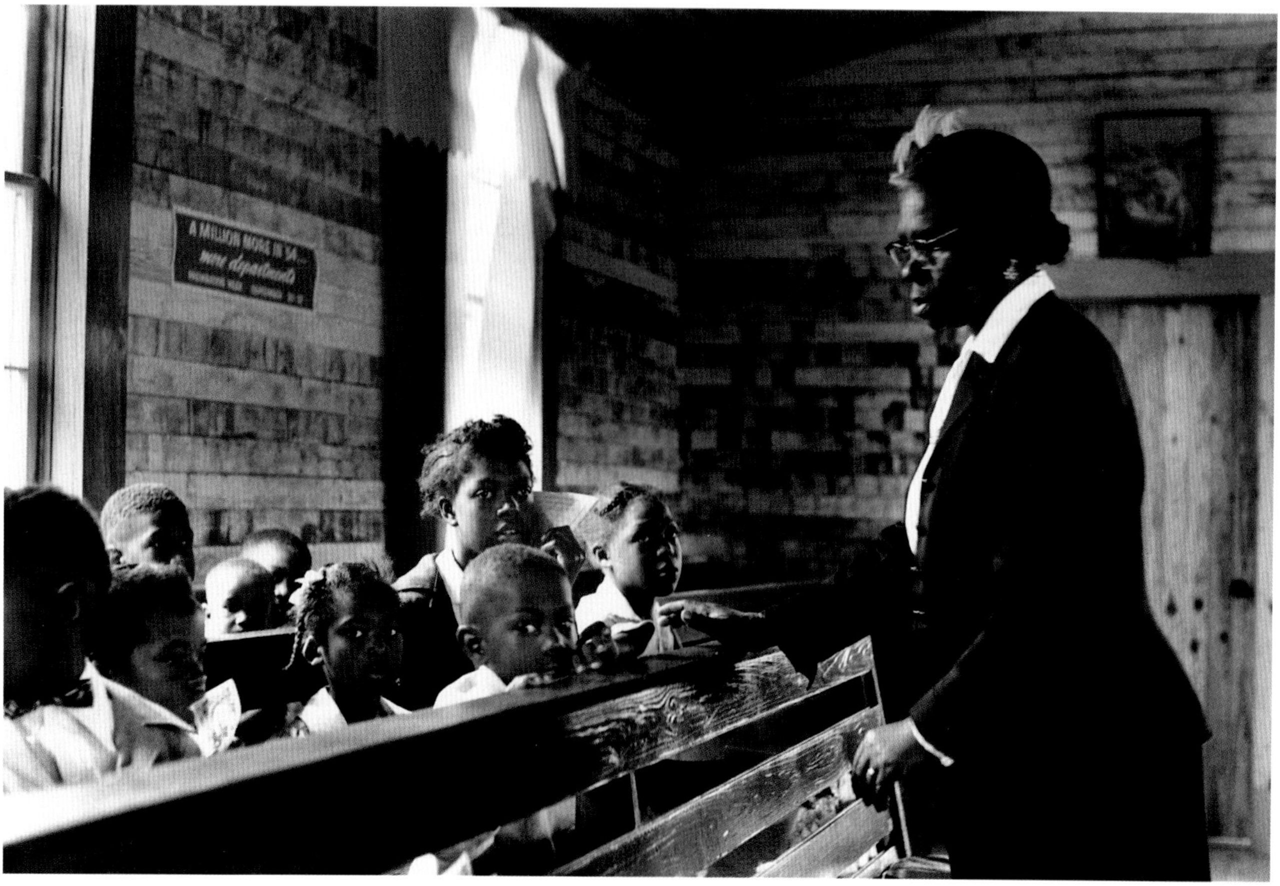

New York, 1953 / *Arkadelphia, Alabama, 1954*

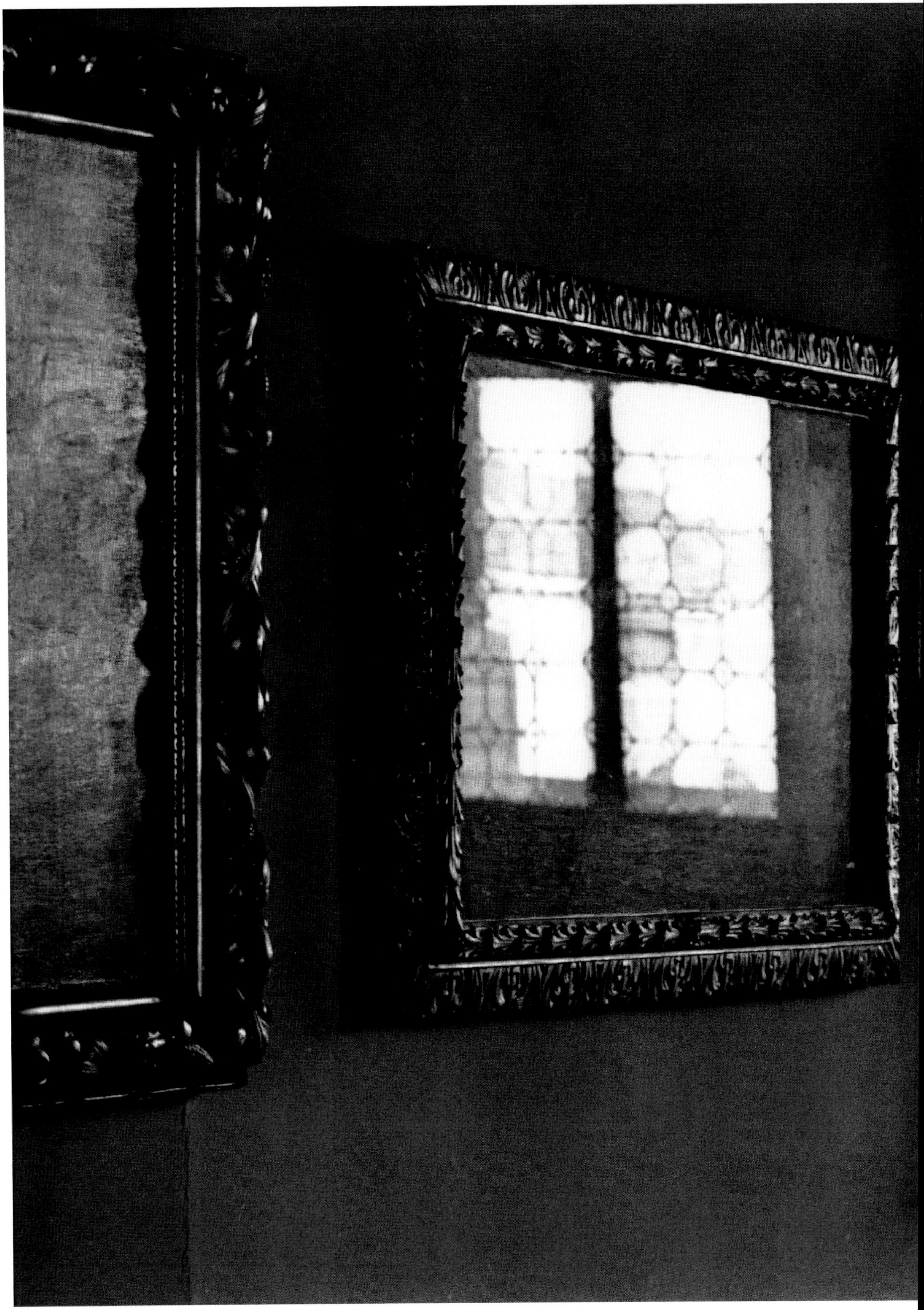

Venice, 1965

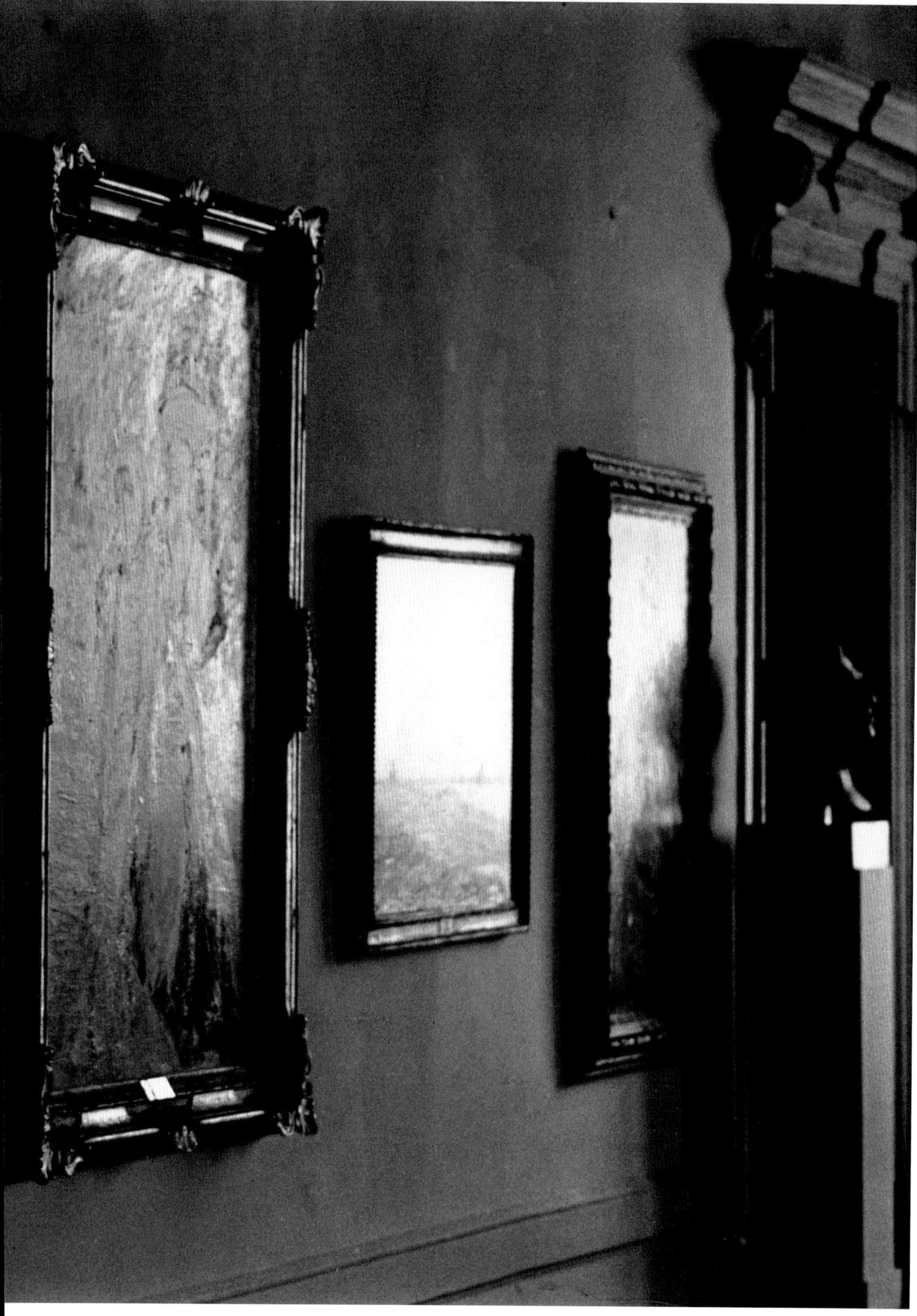

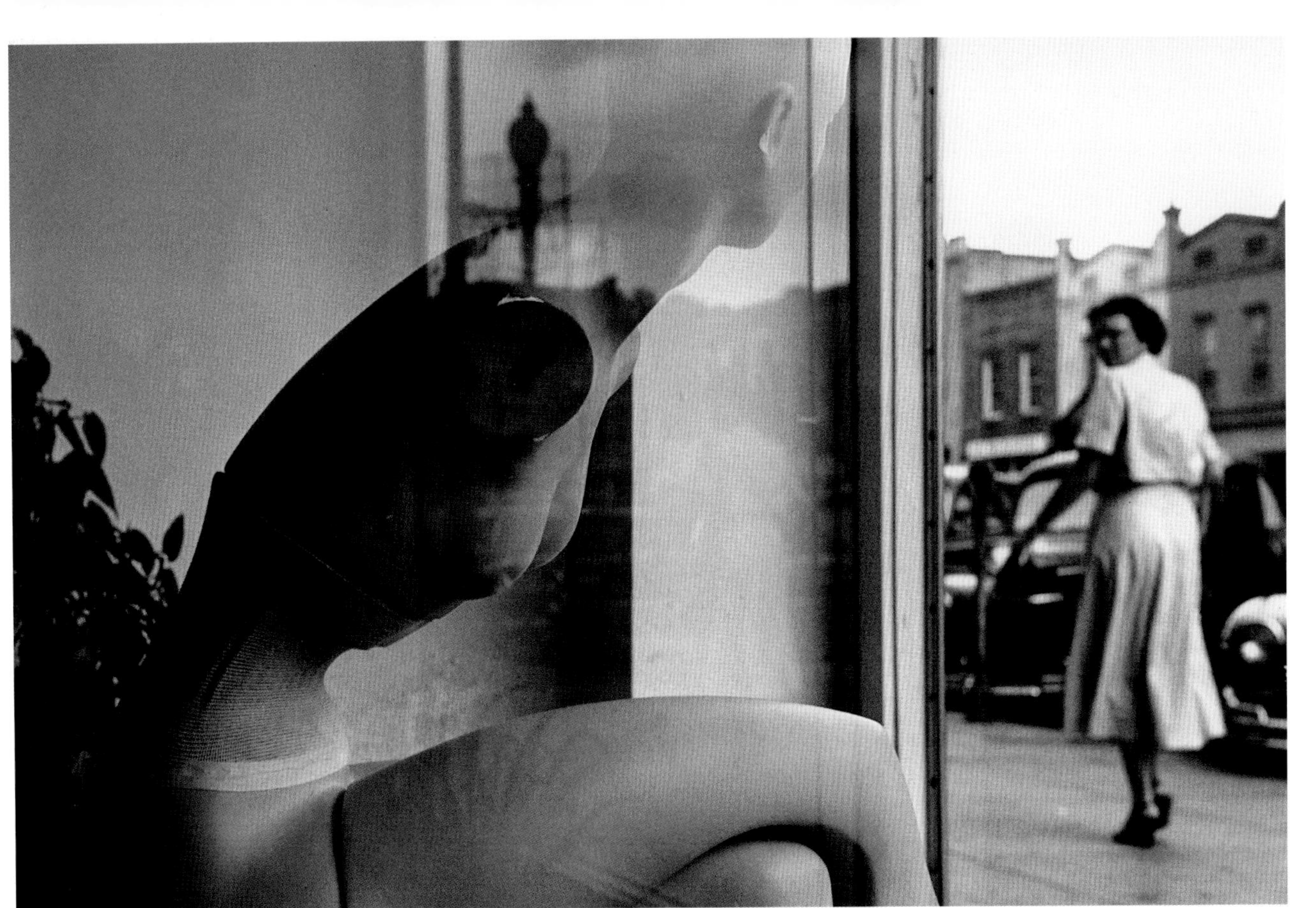

Wilmington, North Carolina, 1950

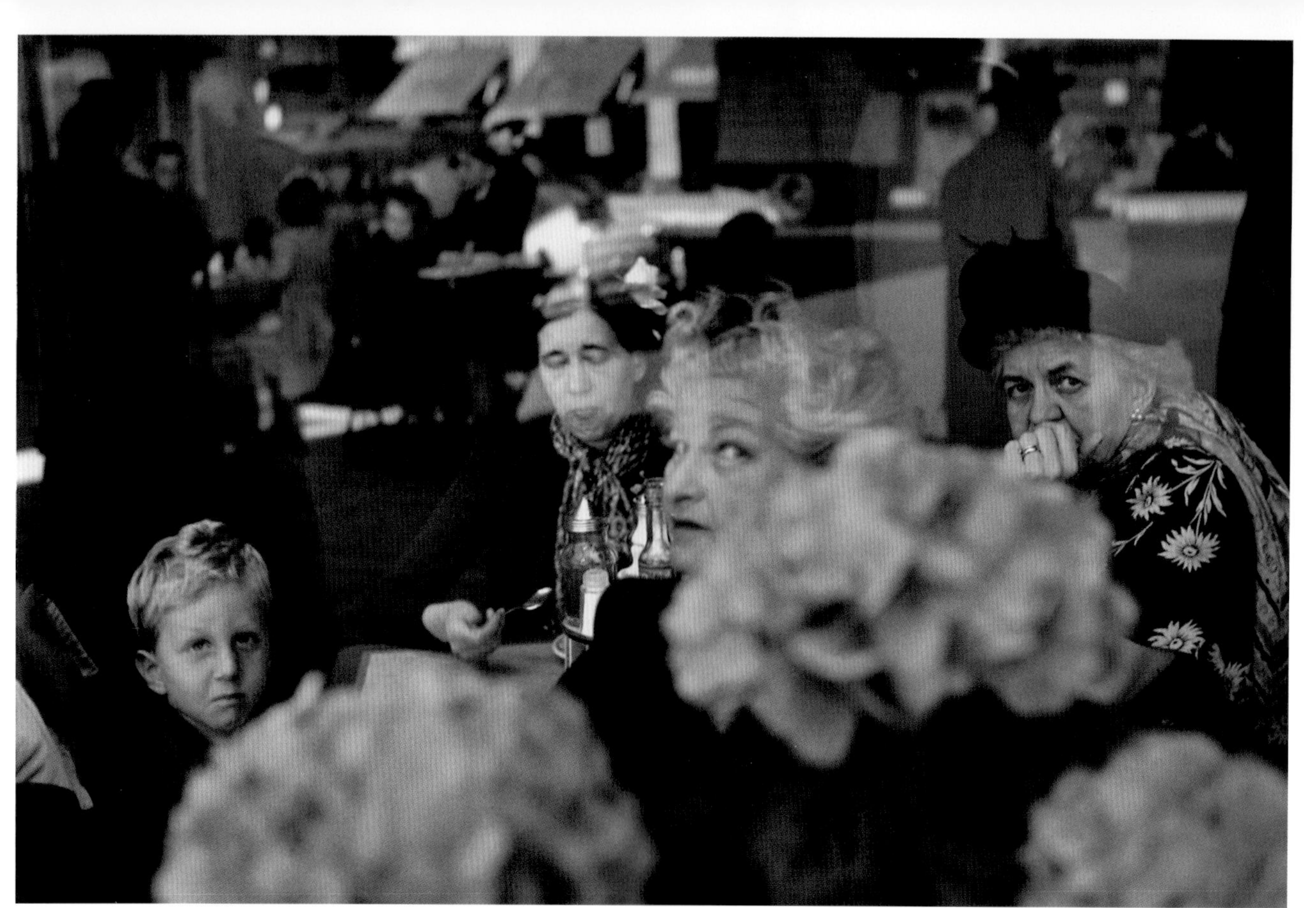

New York, 1950

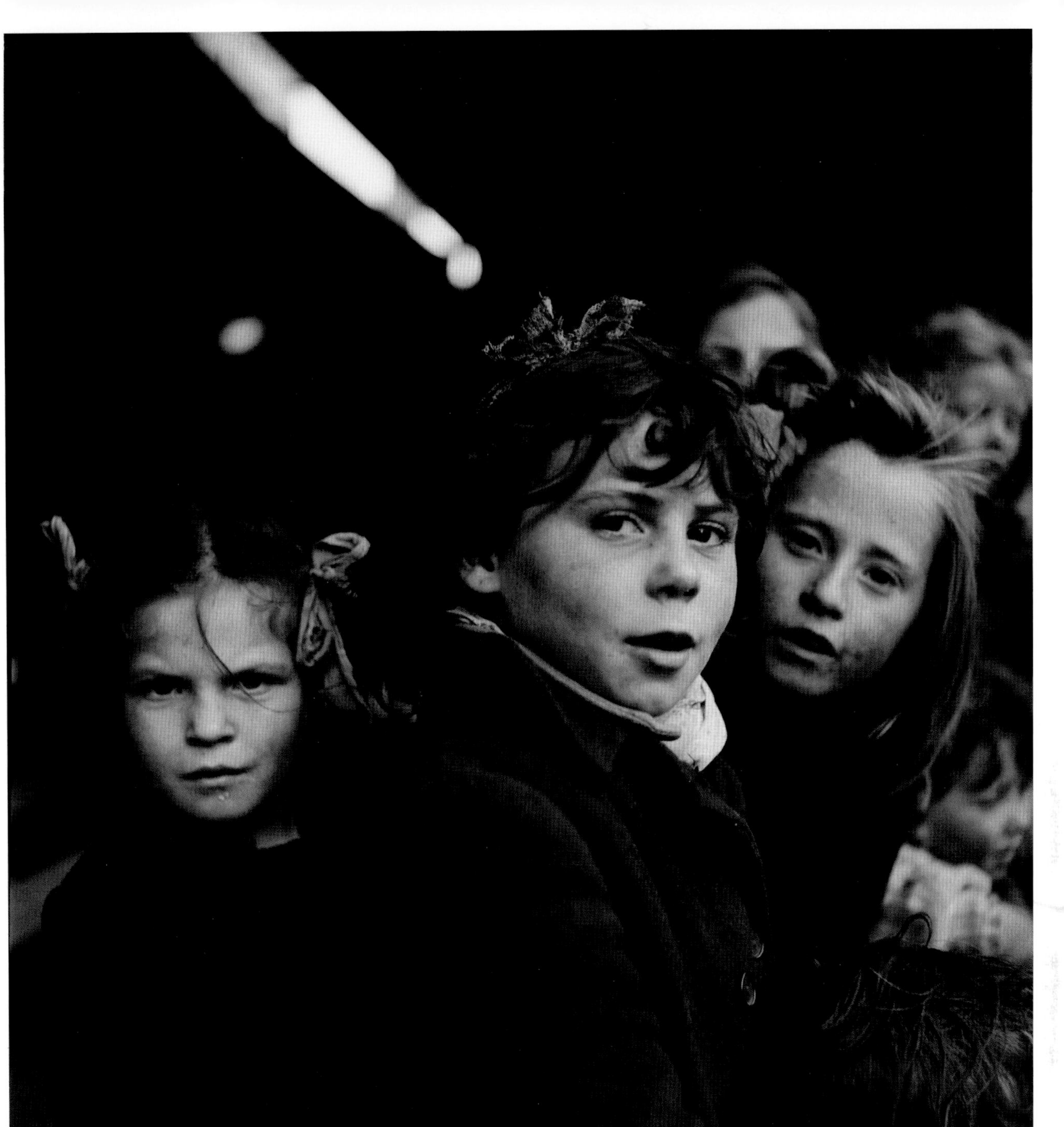

Venice, 1949

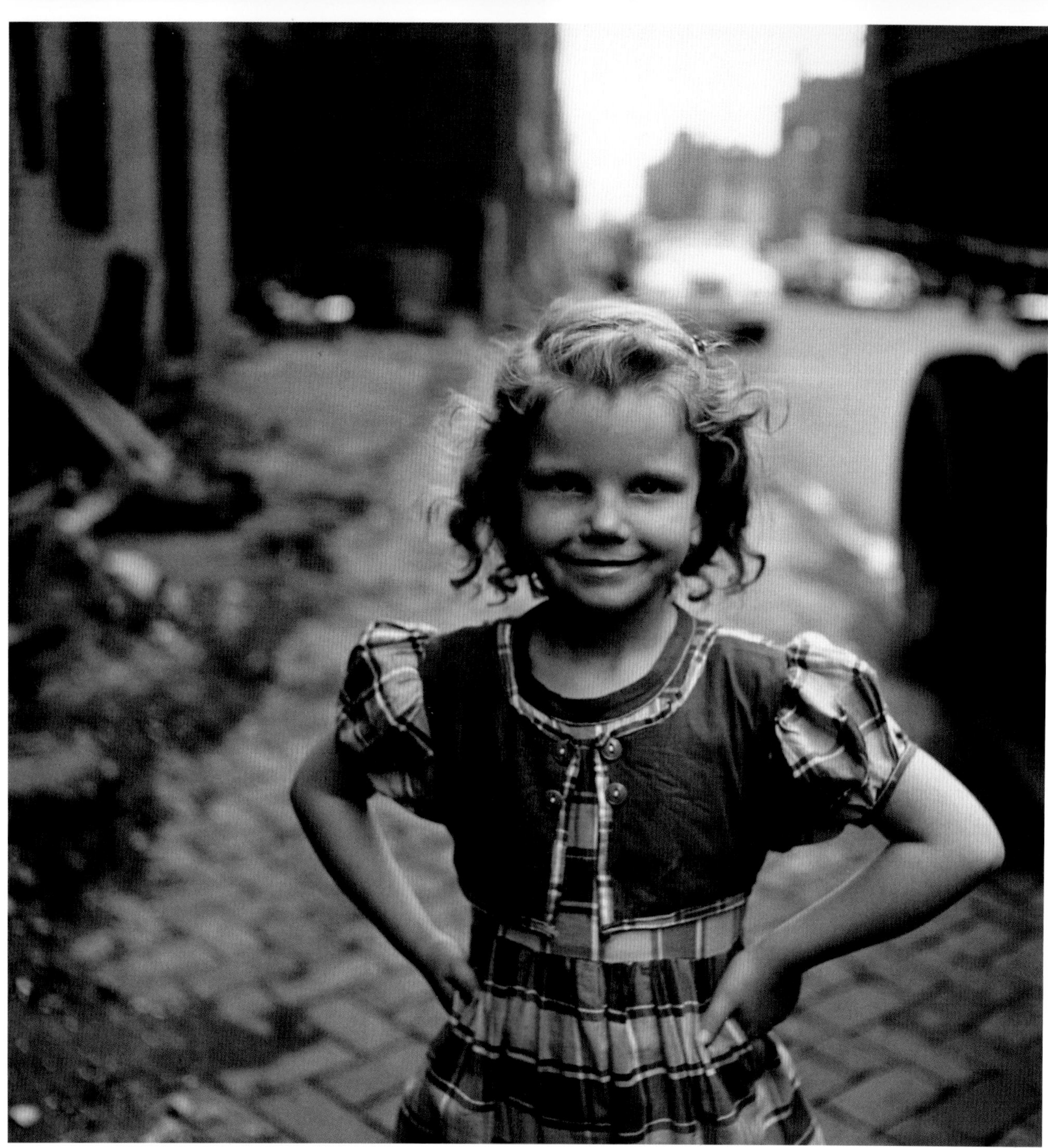

Pittsburgh, Pennsylvania, 1951

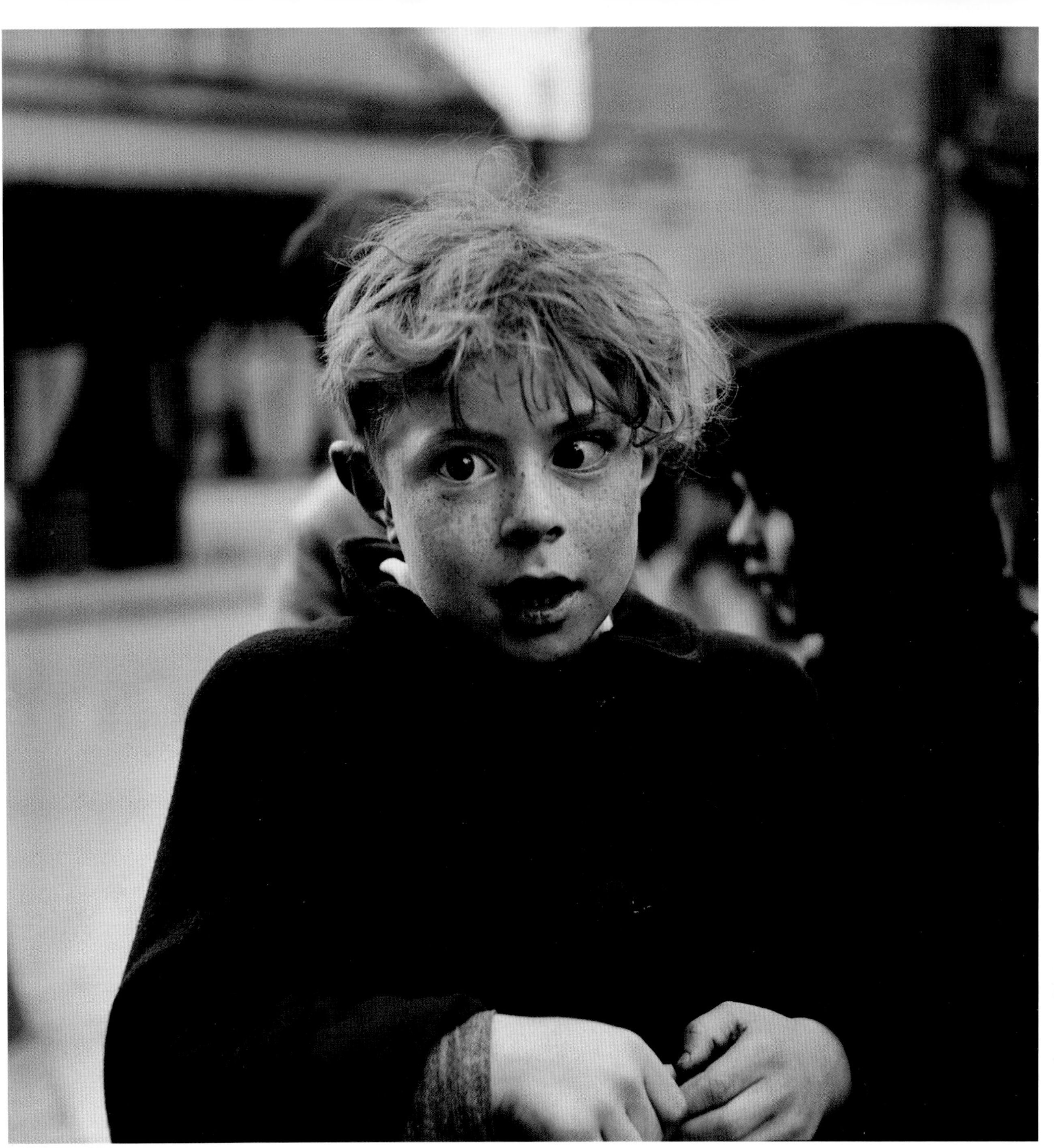

Trieste, Italy, 1952

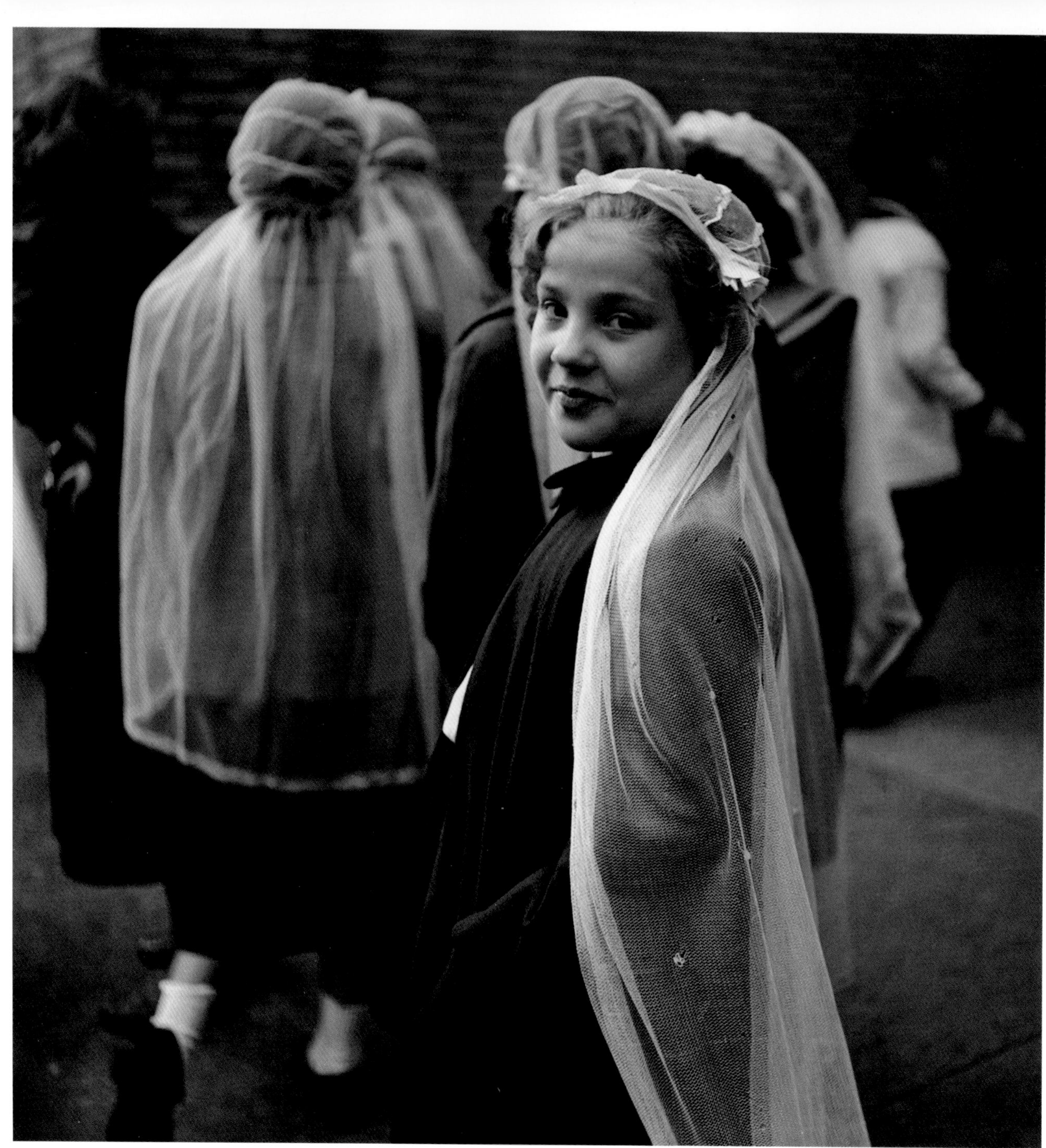

New York, 1949

overleaf *Japan, 1977* / *New Orleans, 1954*

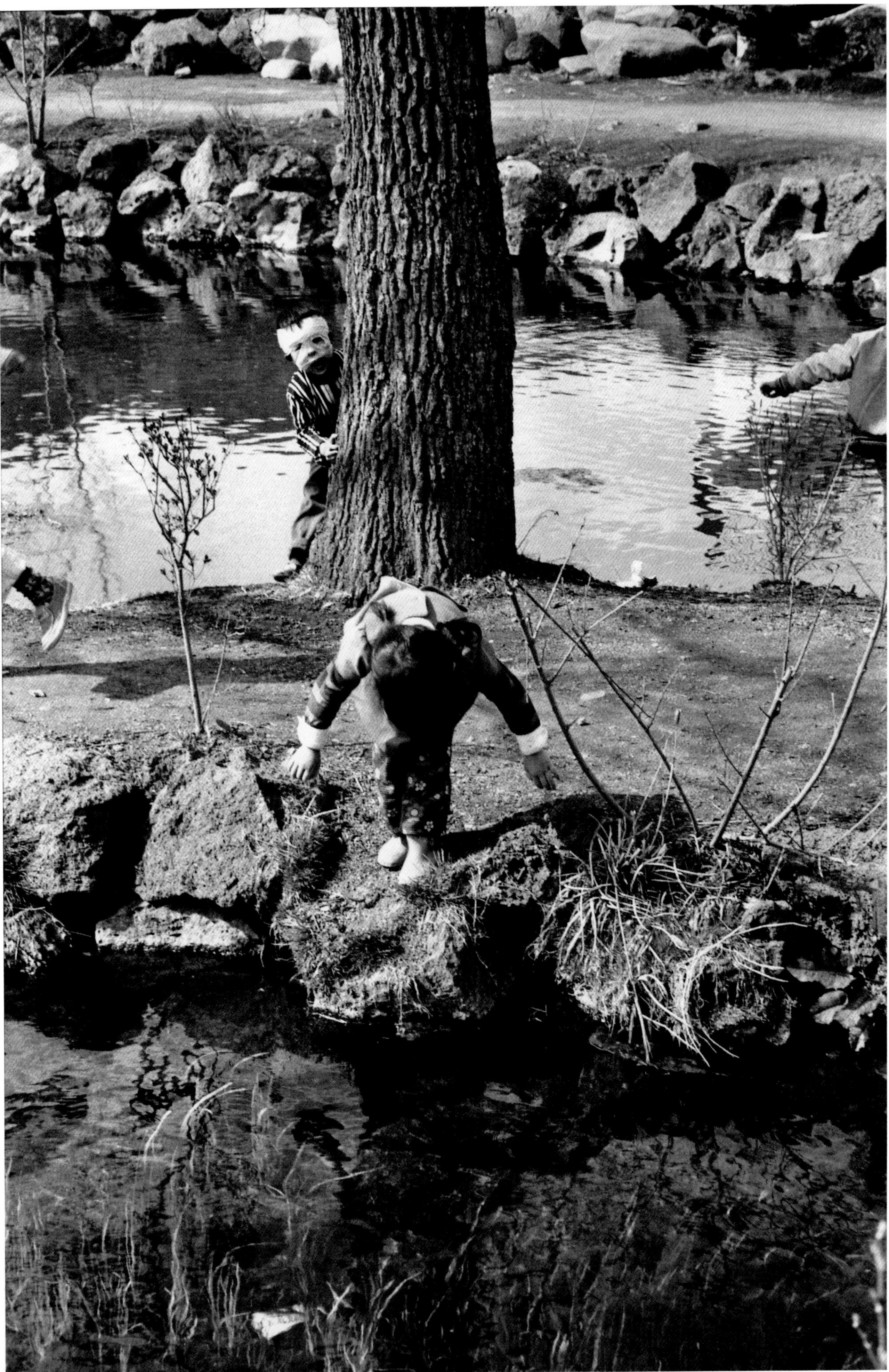

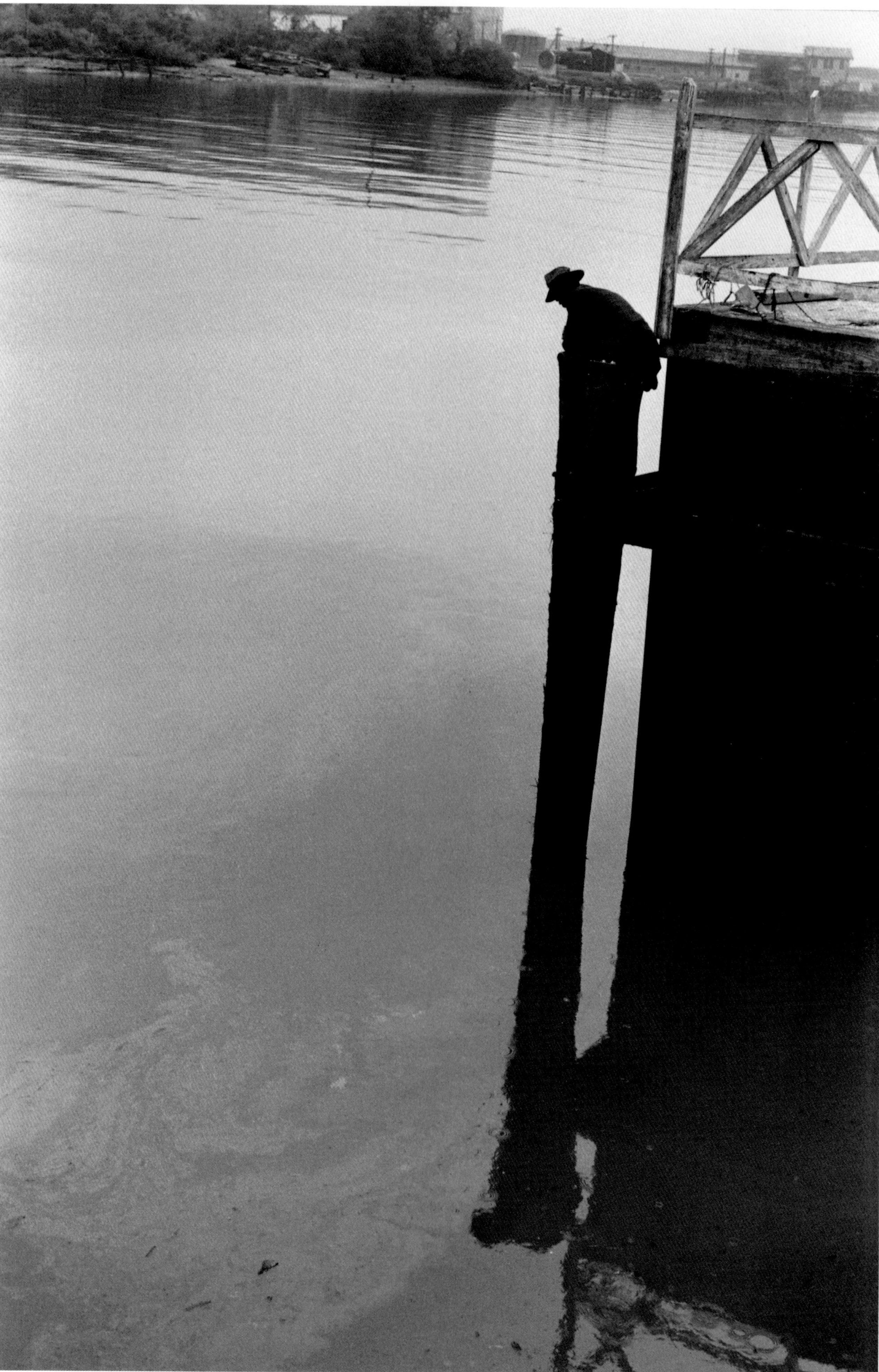

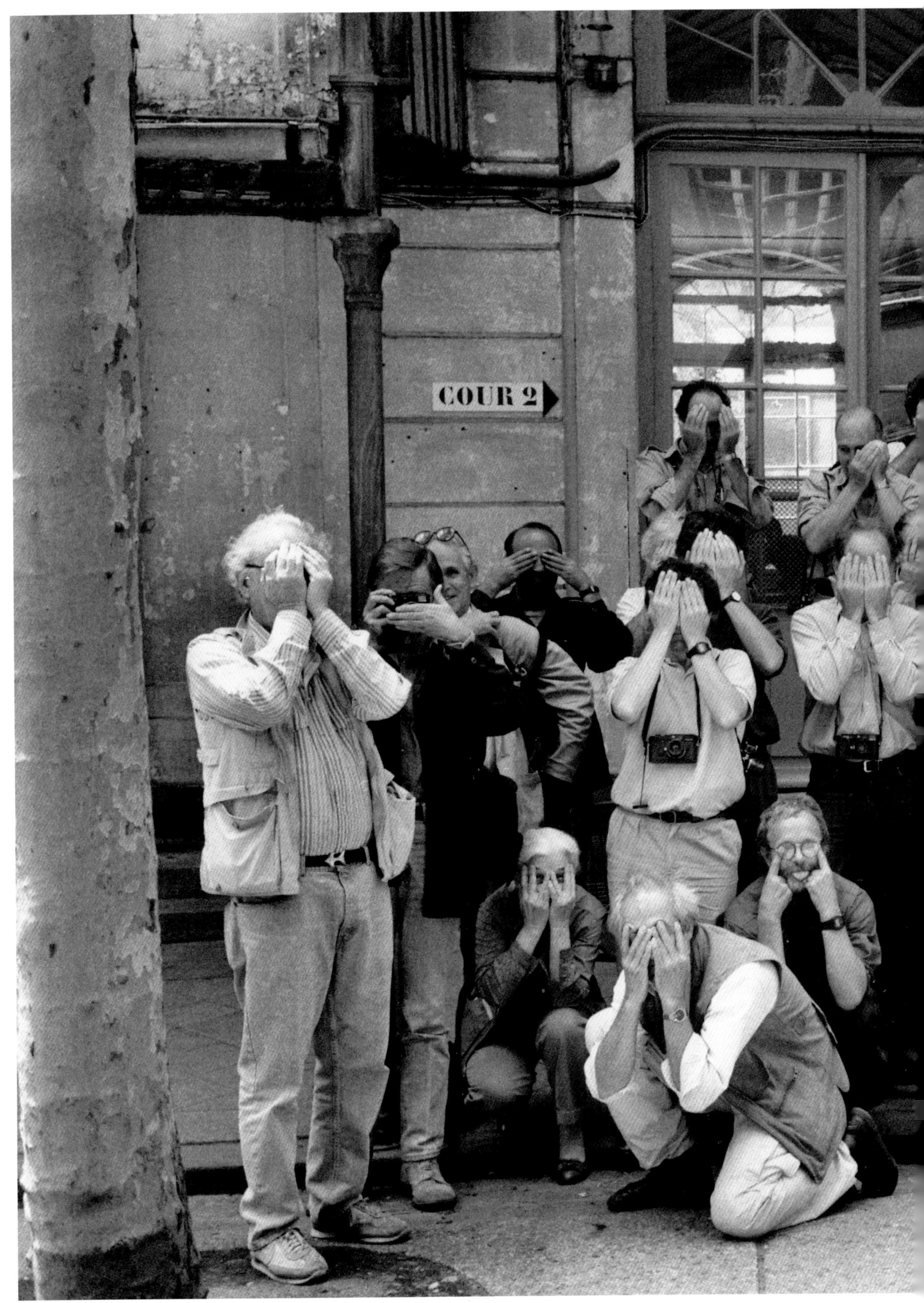

Magnum photographers, Paris, 1988

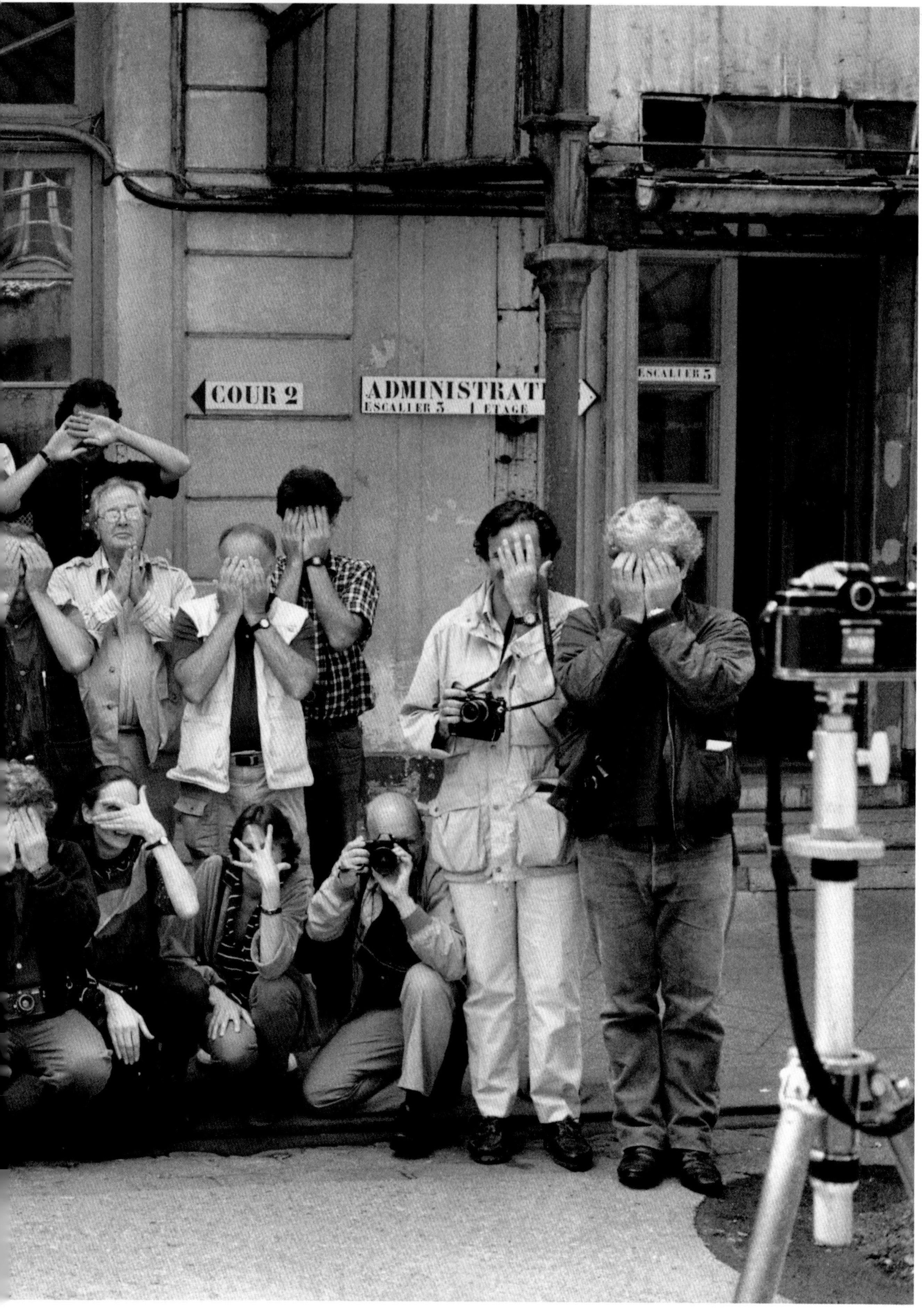
COUR 2
ADMINISTRAT
ESCALIER 5 1 ETAGE
ESCALIER 5

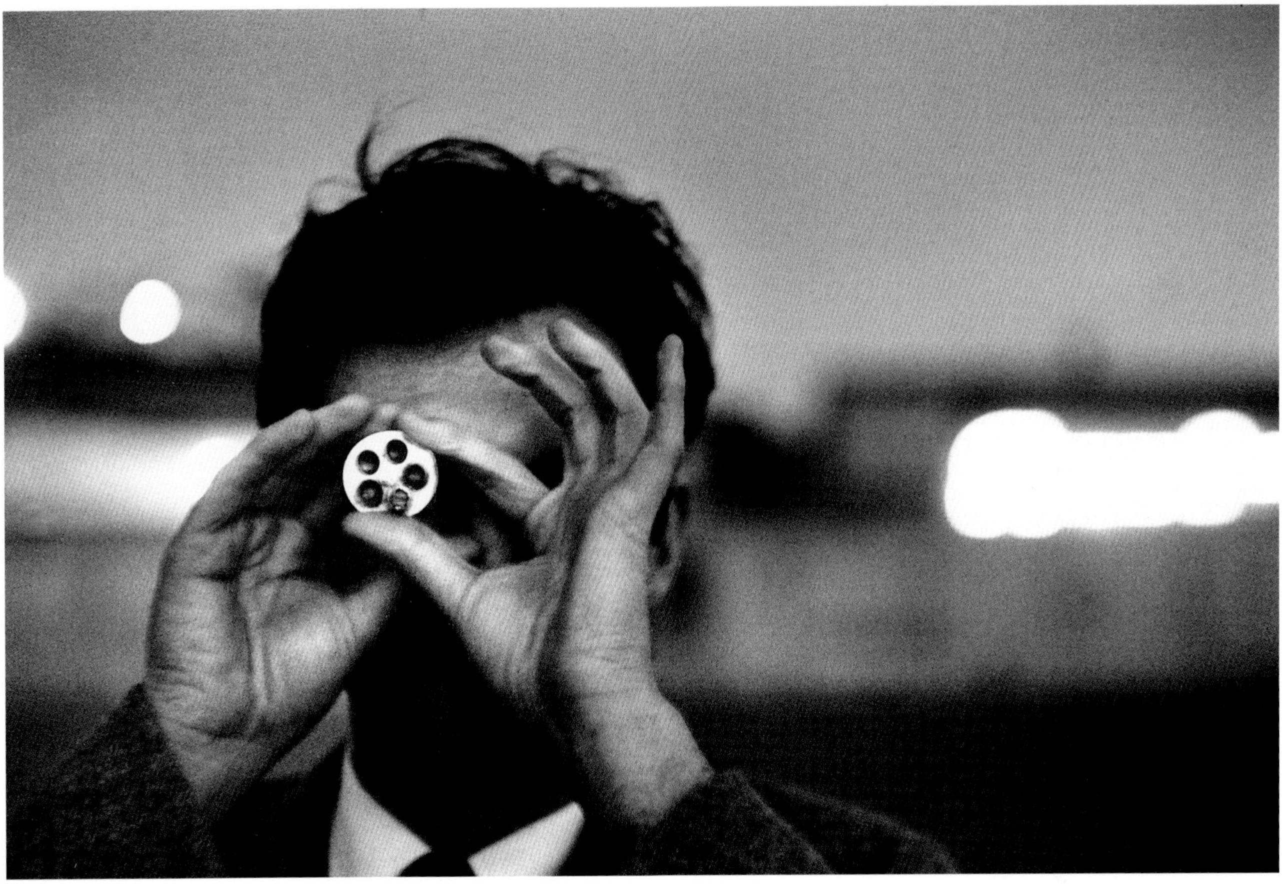

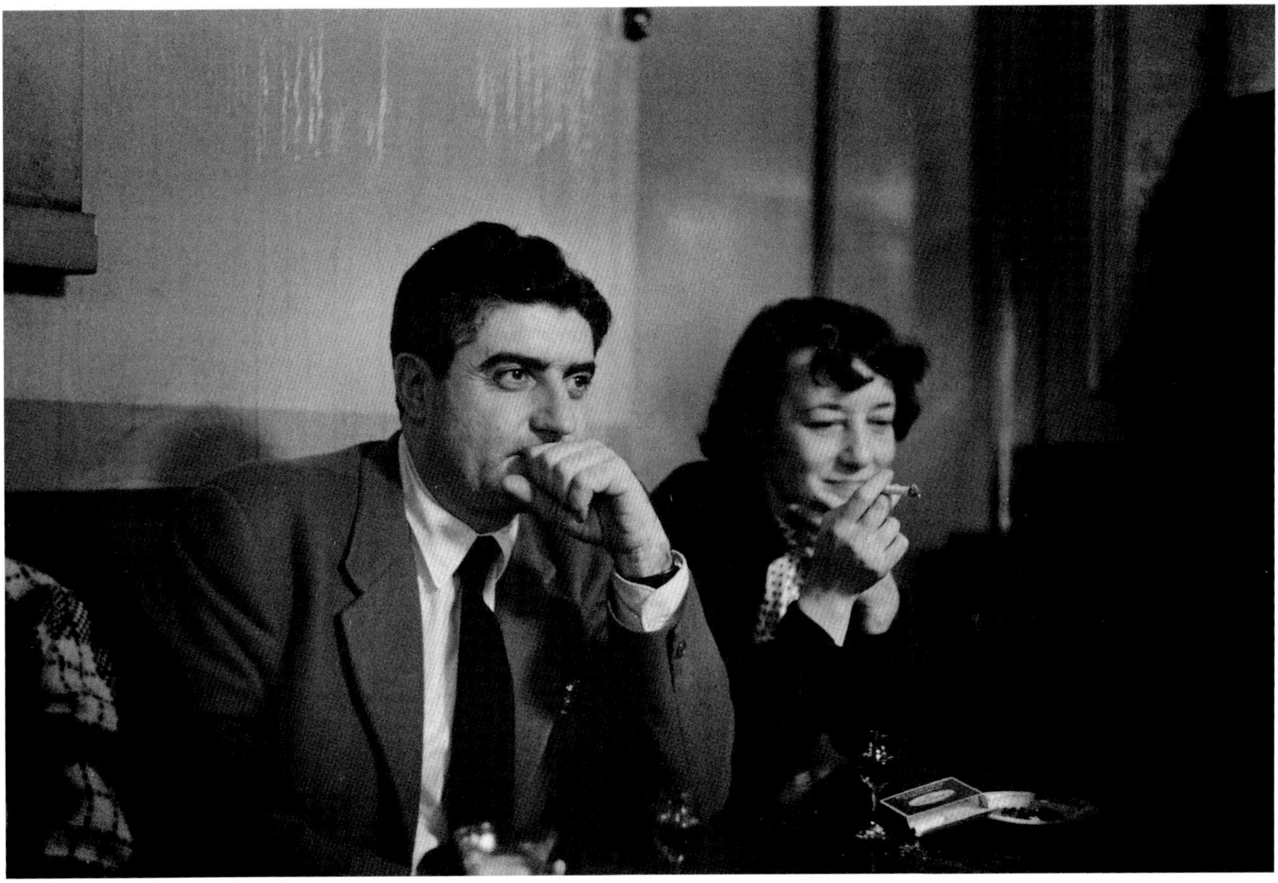

Ernst Haas, San Francisco, 1955 / *Cornell and Edie Capa, Paris, 1960*

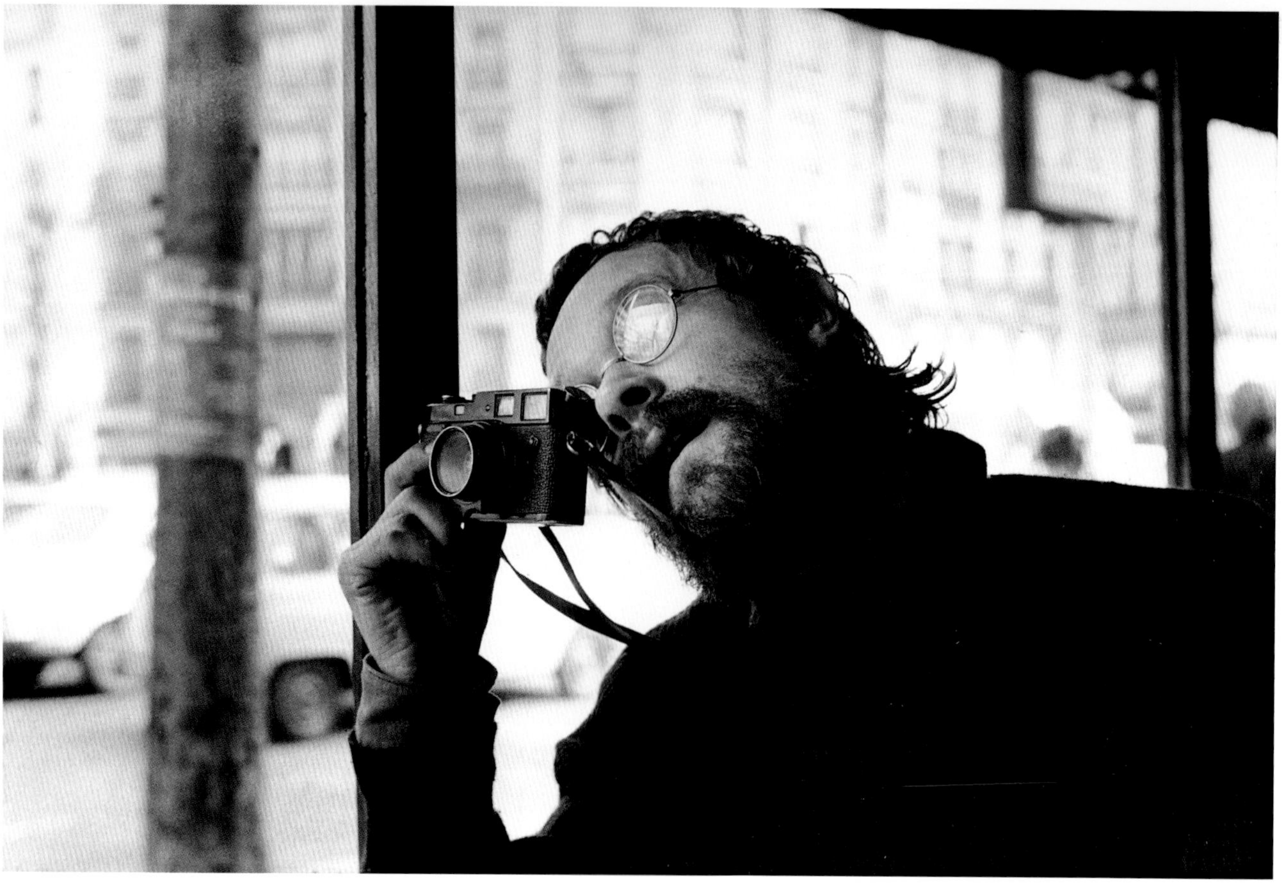

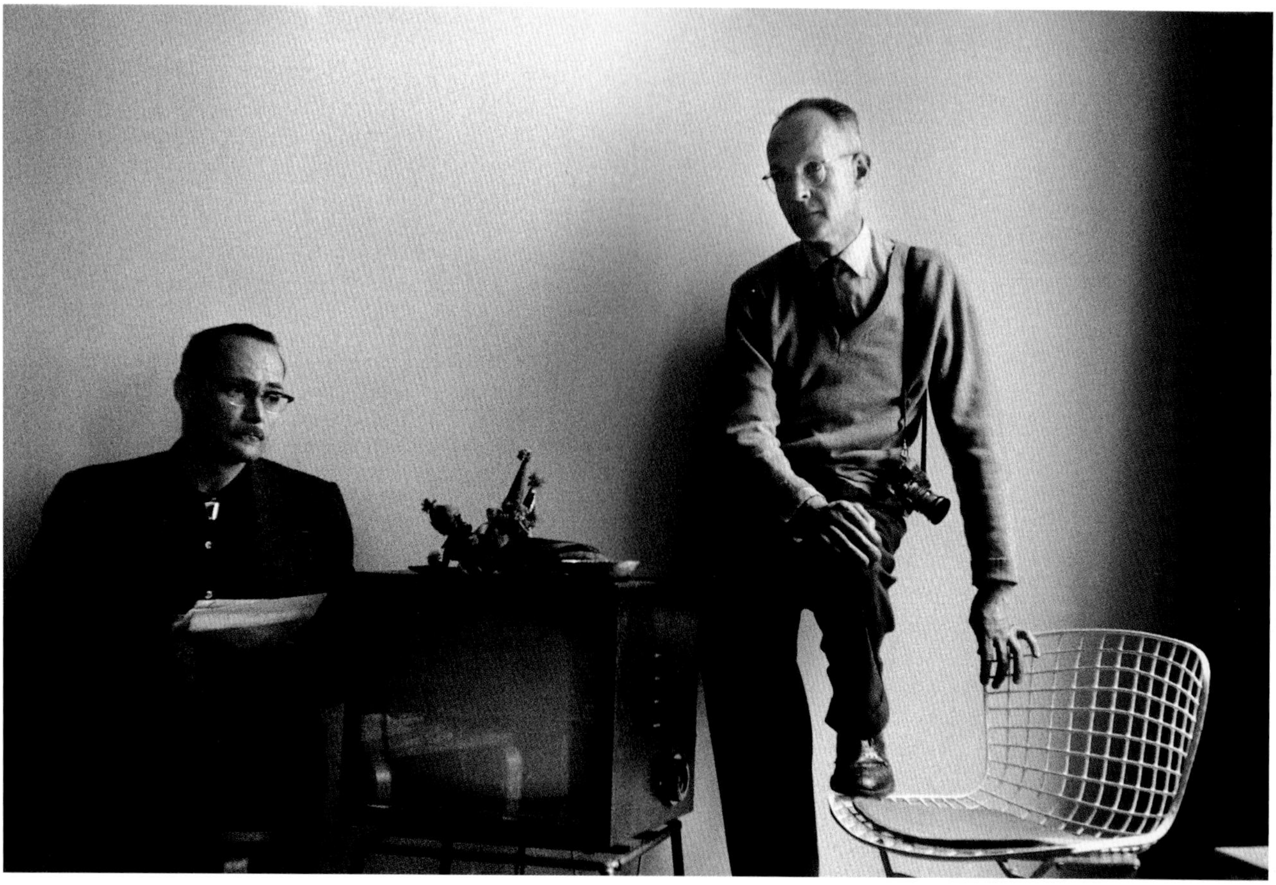

Josef Koudelka, Paris, 1974 / *W. Eugene Smith and Henri Cartier-Bresson, New York, 1955*

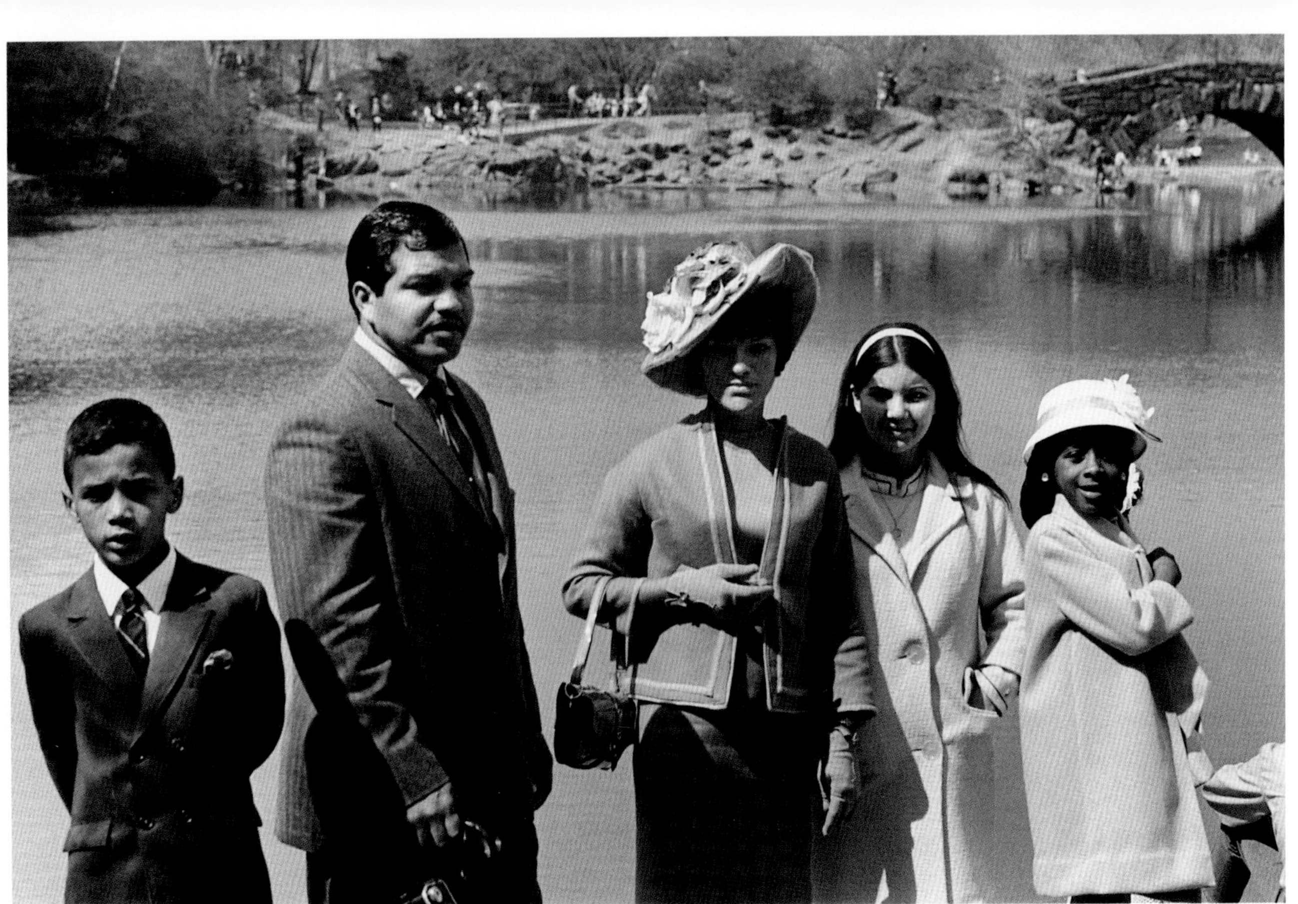

New York, 1968

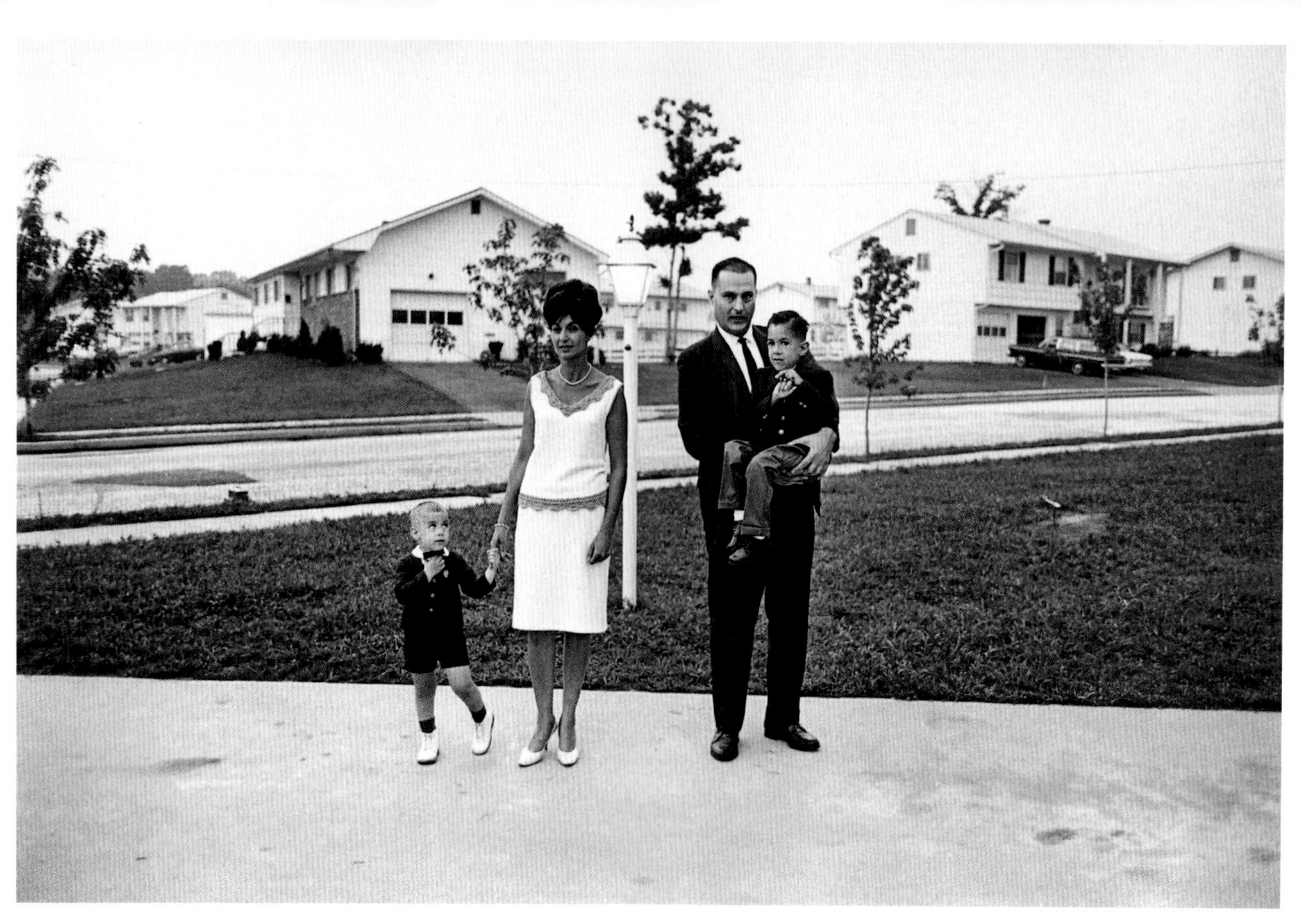

Ohio, 1965

overleaf *Buenos Aires, 1972* / *Cologne, Germany, 1967*

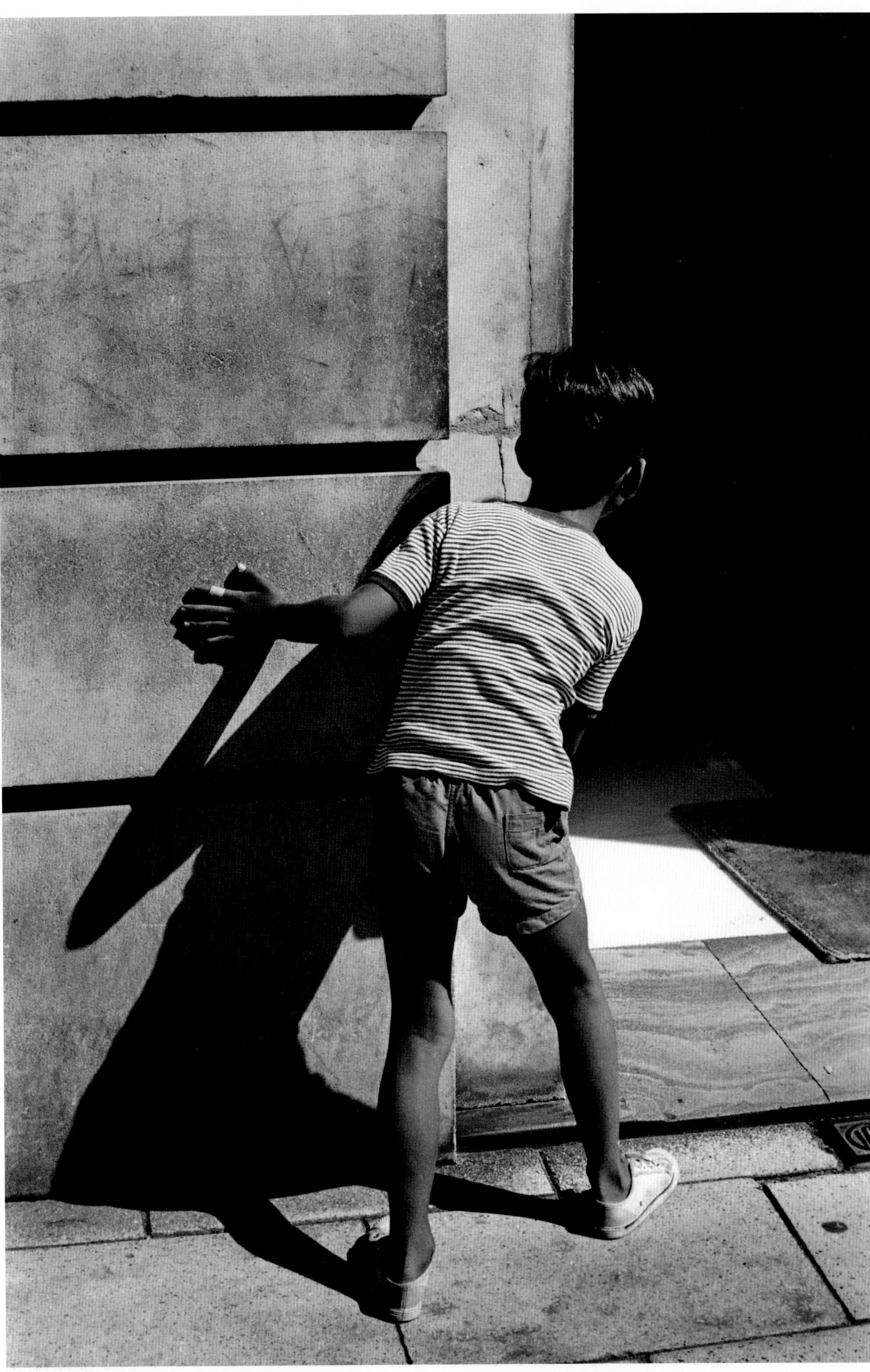

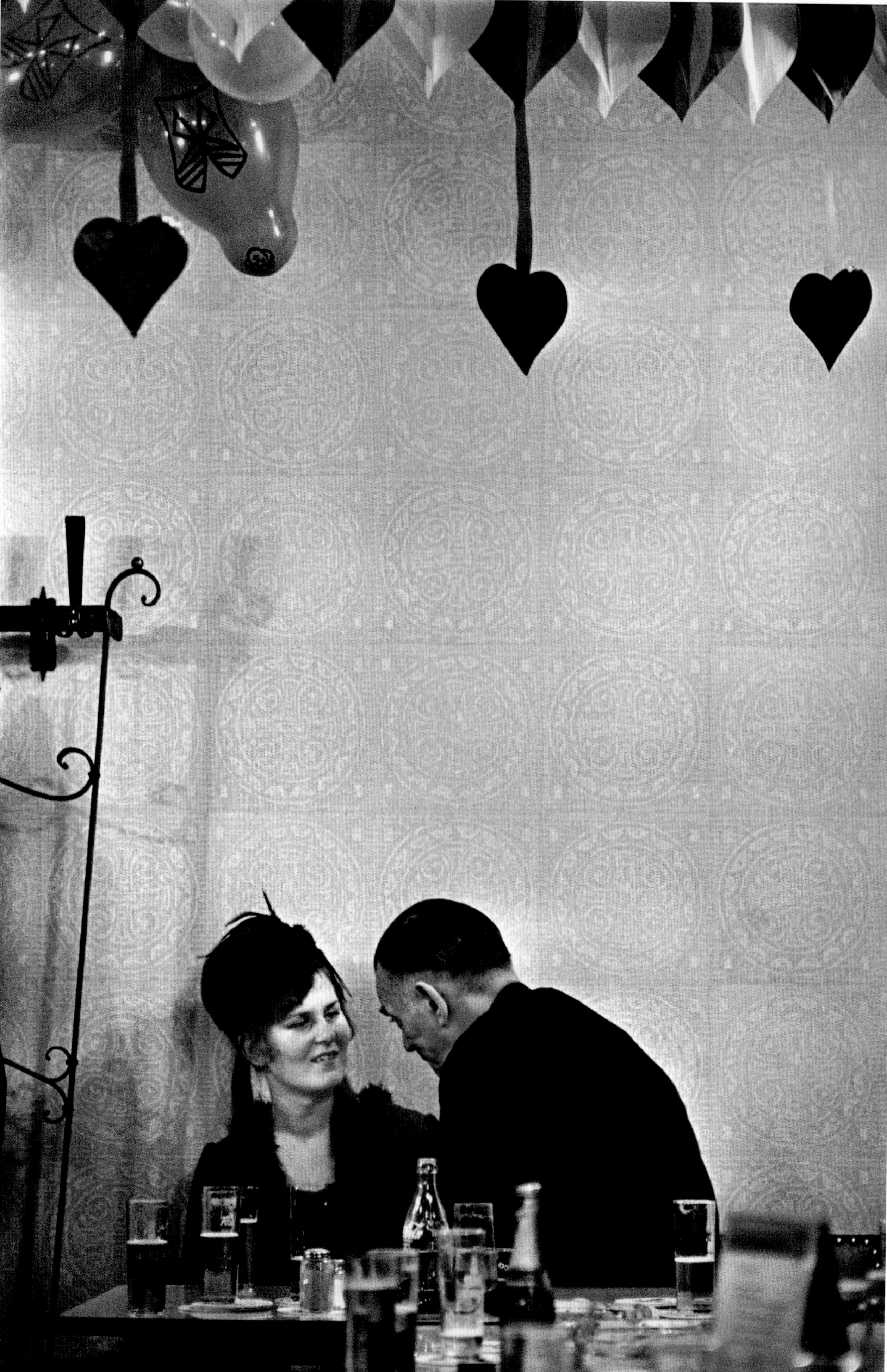

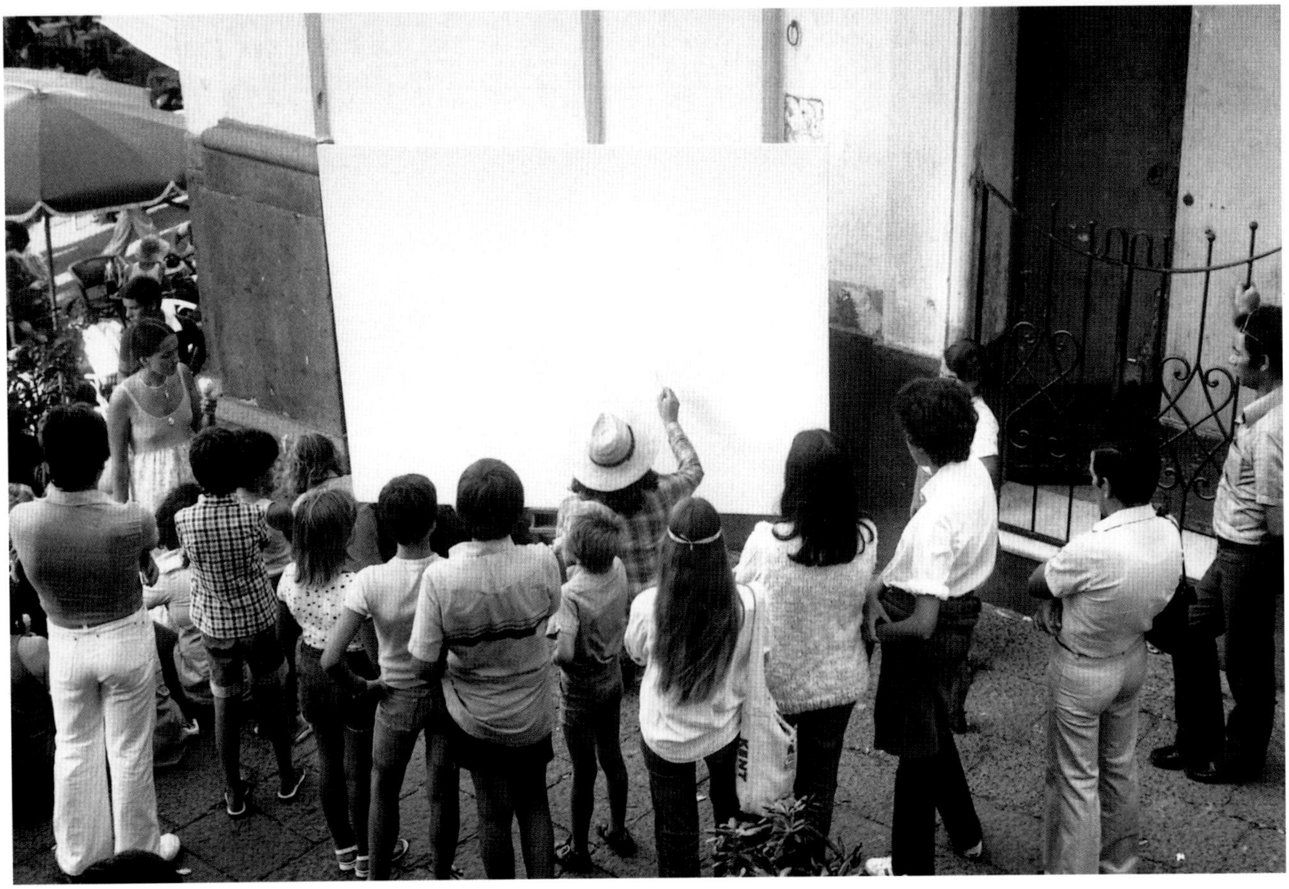

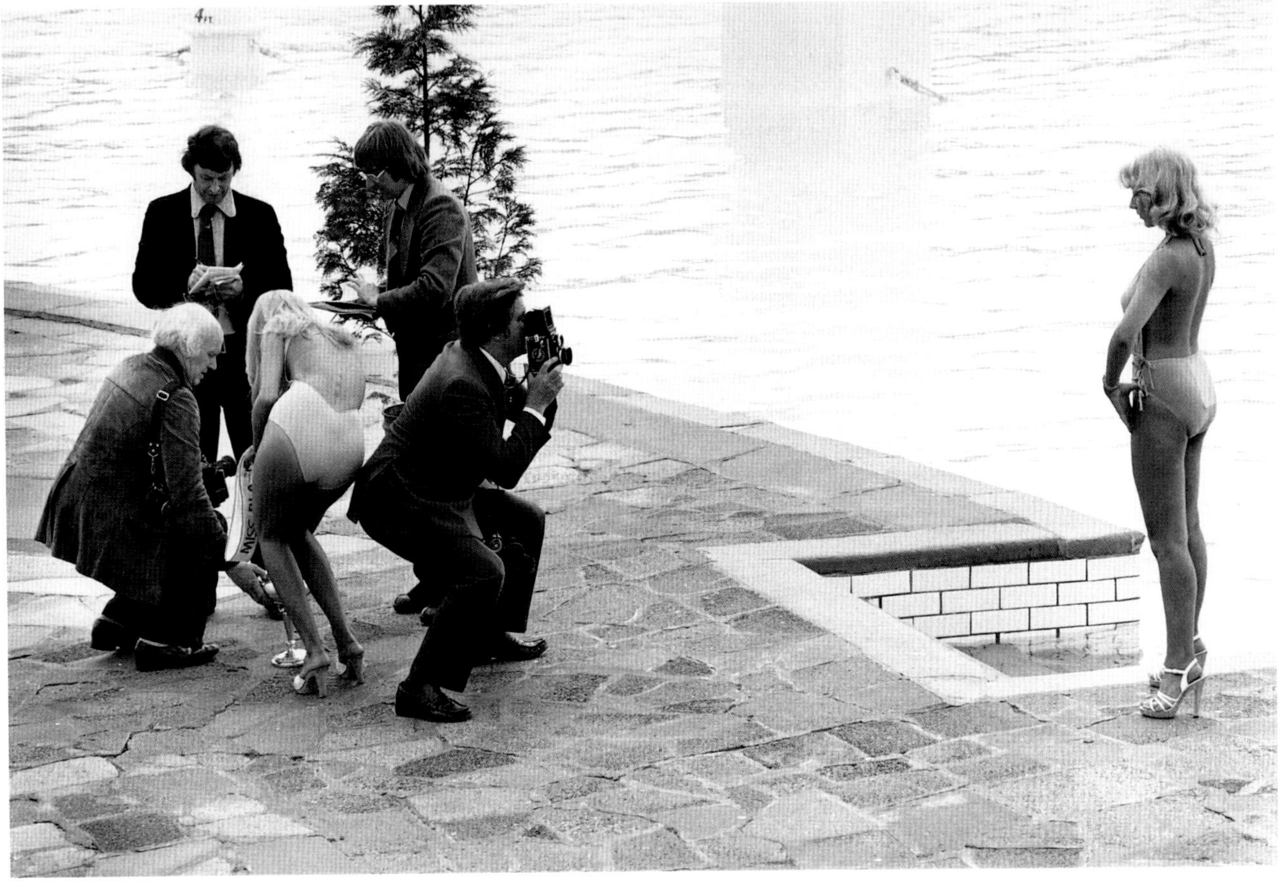

Capri, Italy, 1977 / *Blackpool, England, 1978*

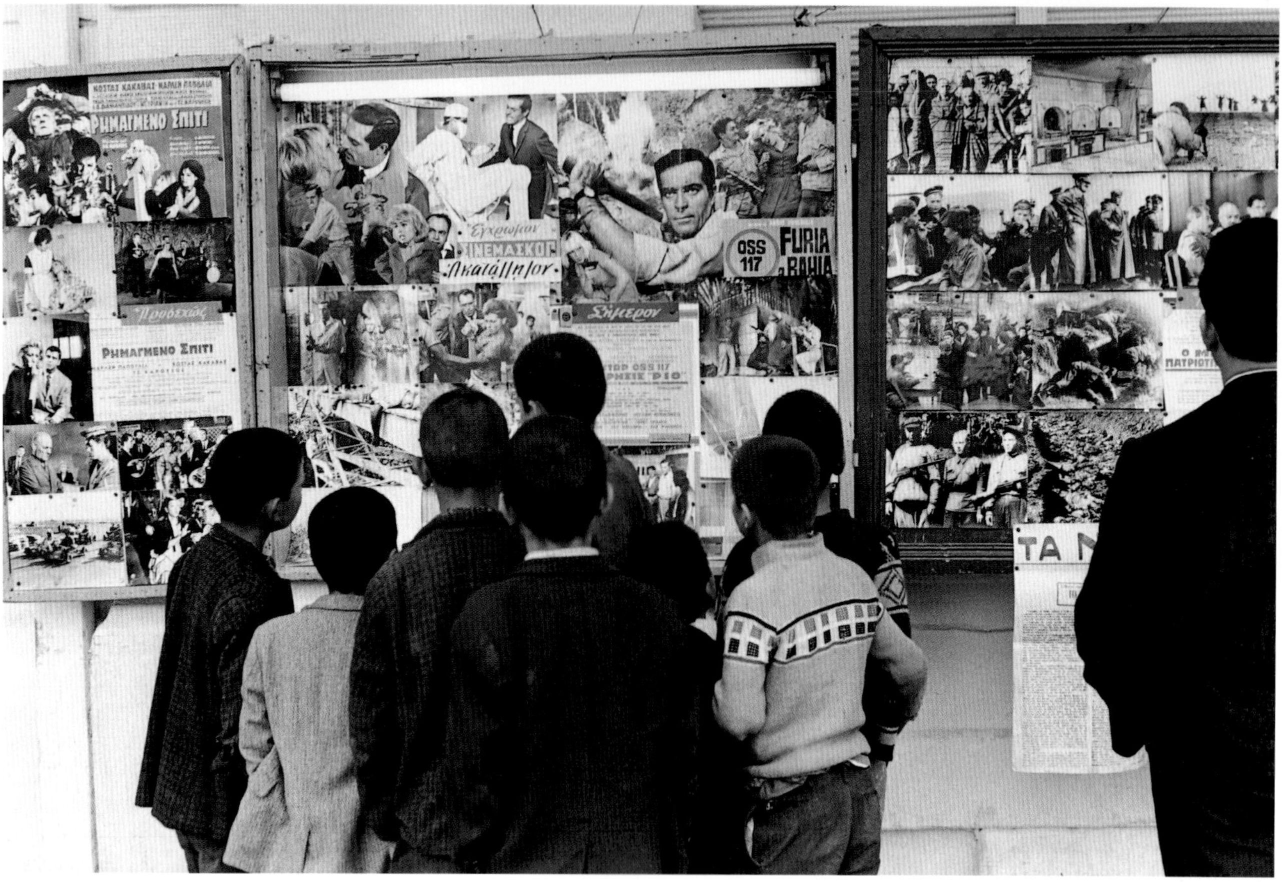

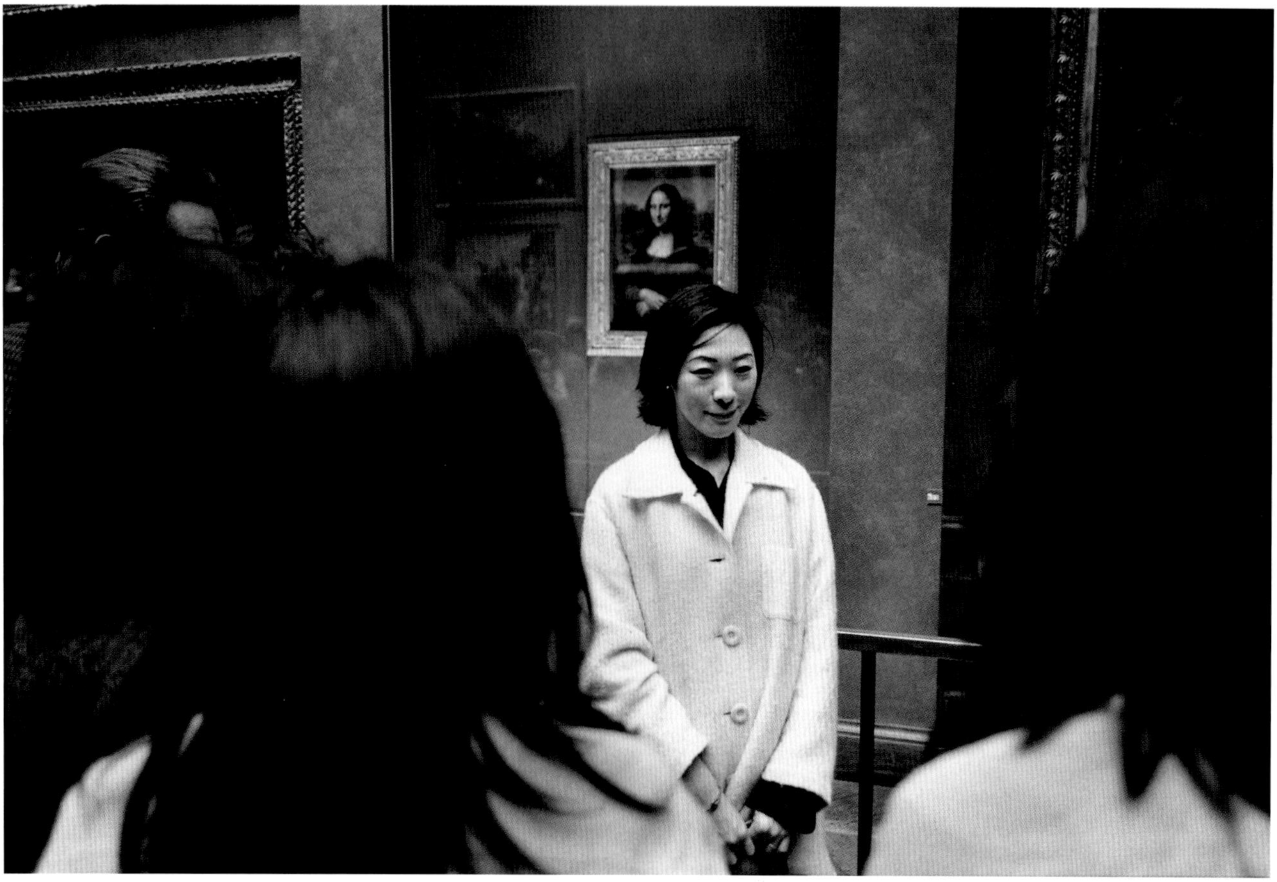

Greece, 1963 / *Paris, 1997*

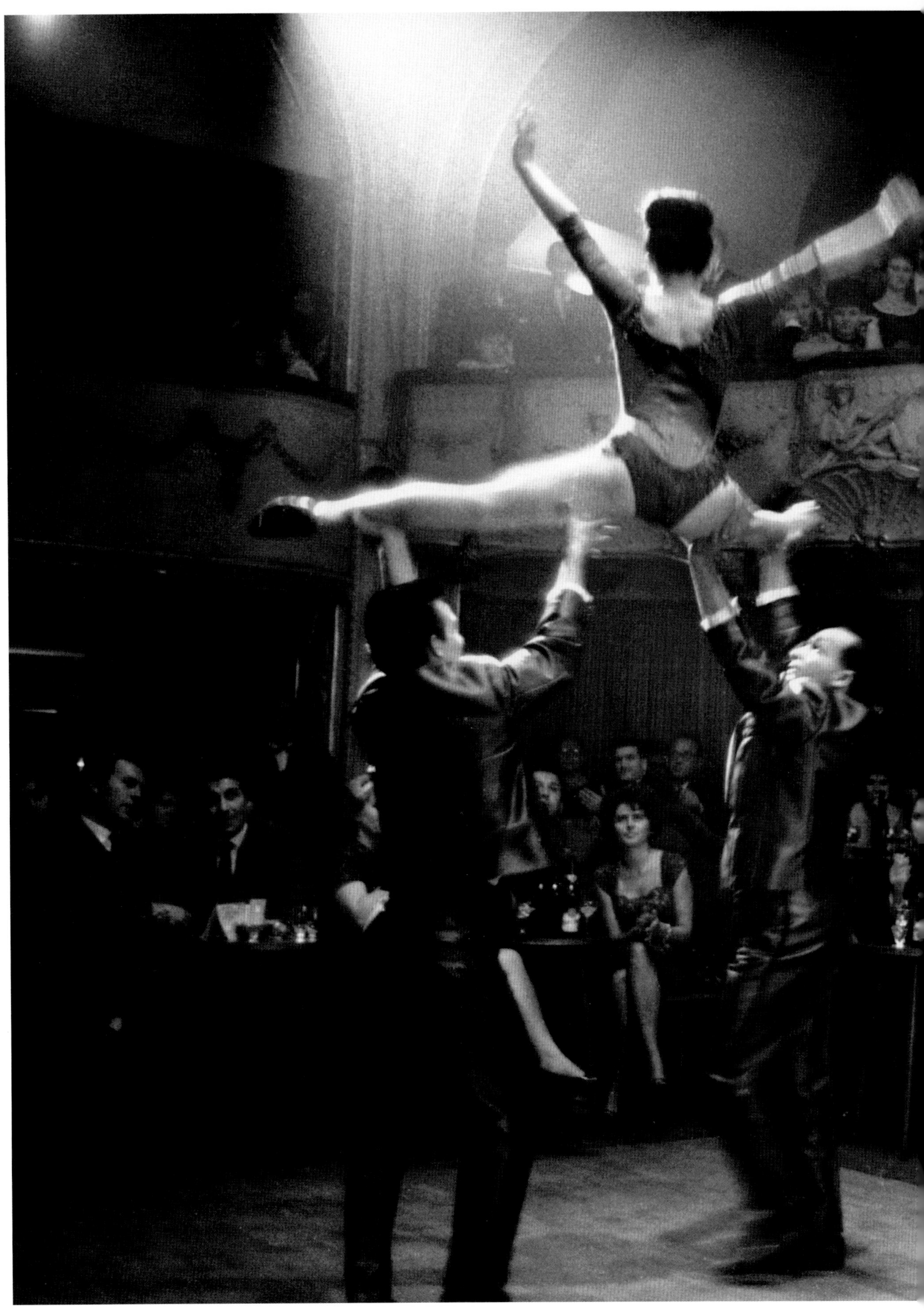

Budapest, Hungary, 1964

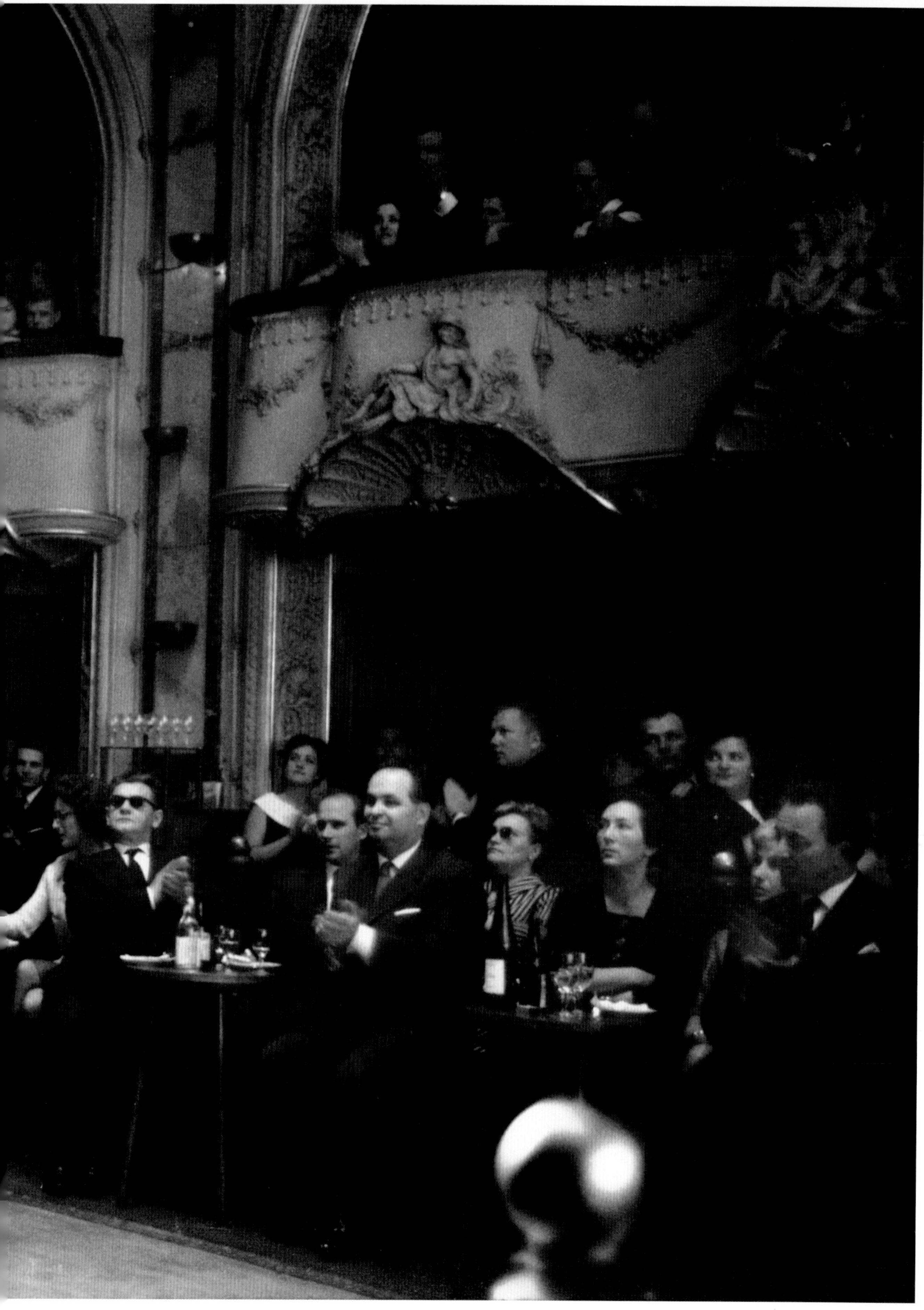

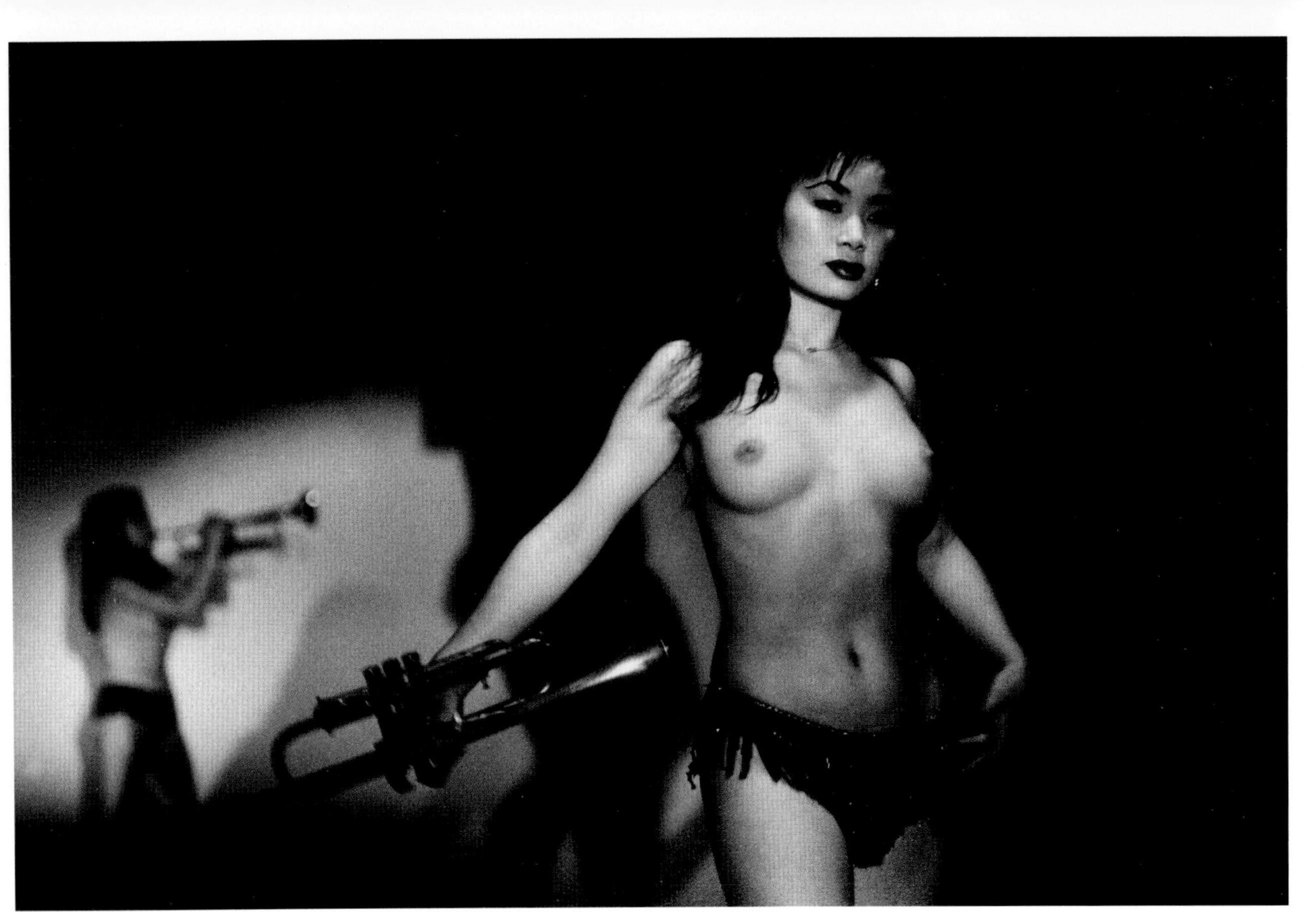

Tokyo, 1960

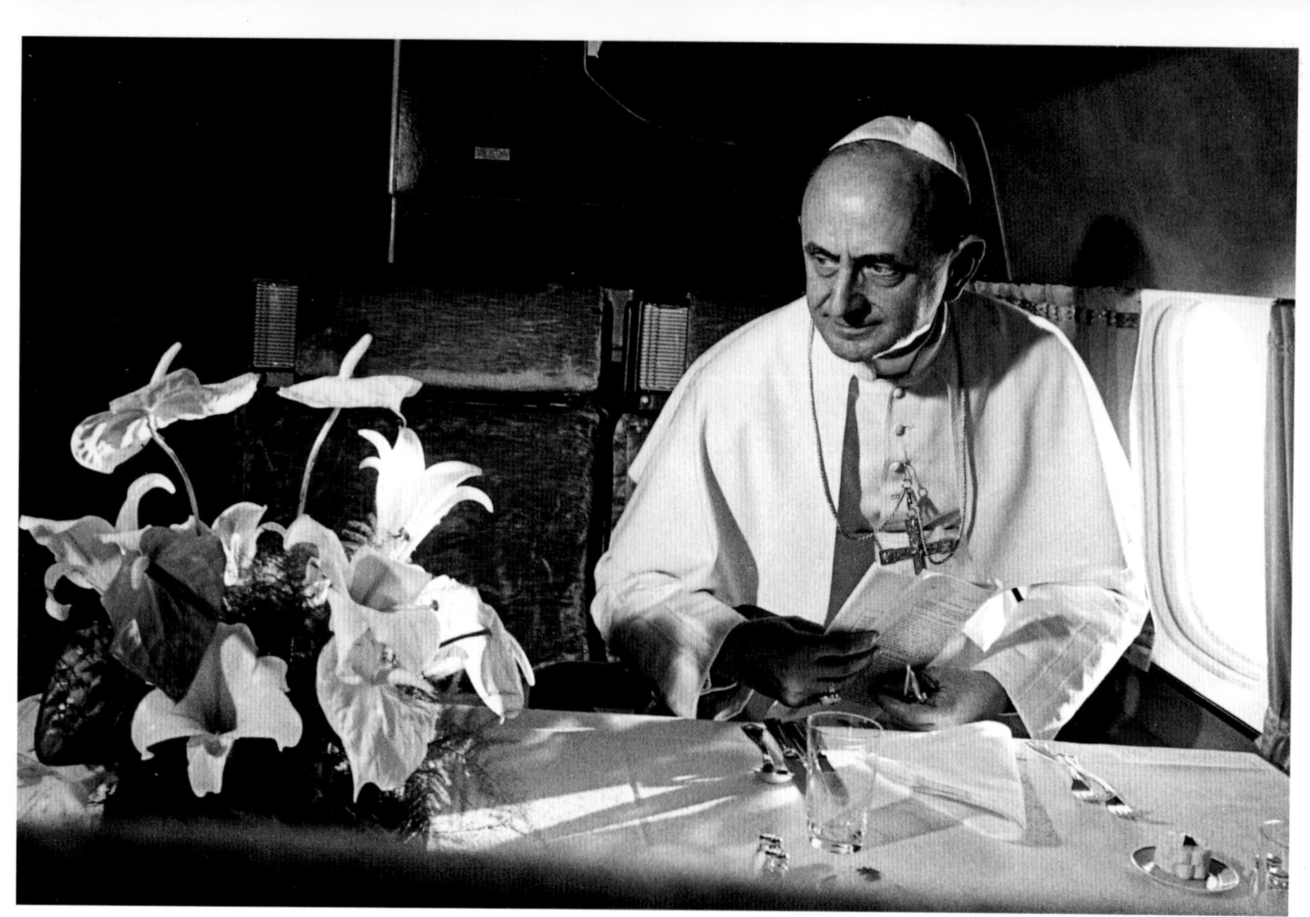

Pope Paul VI on a plane, 1965

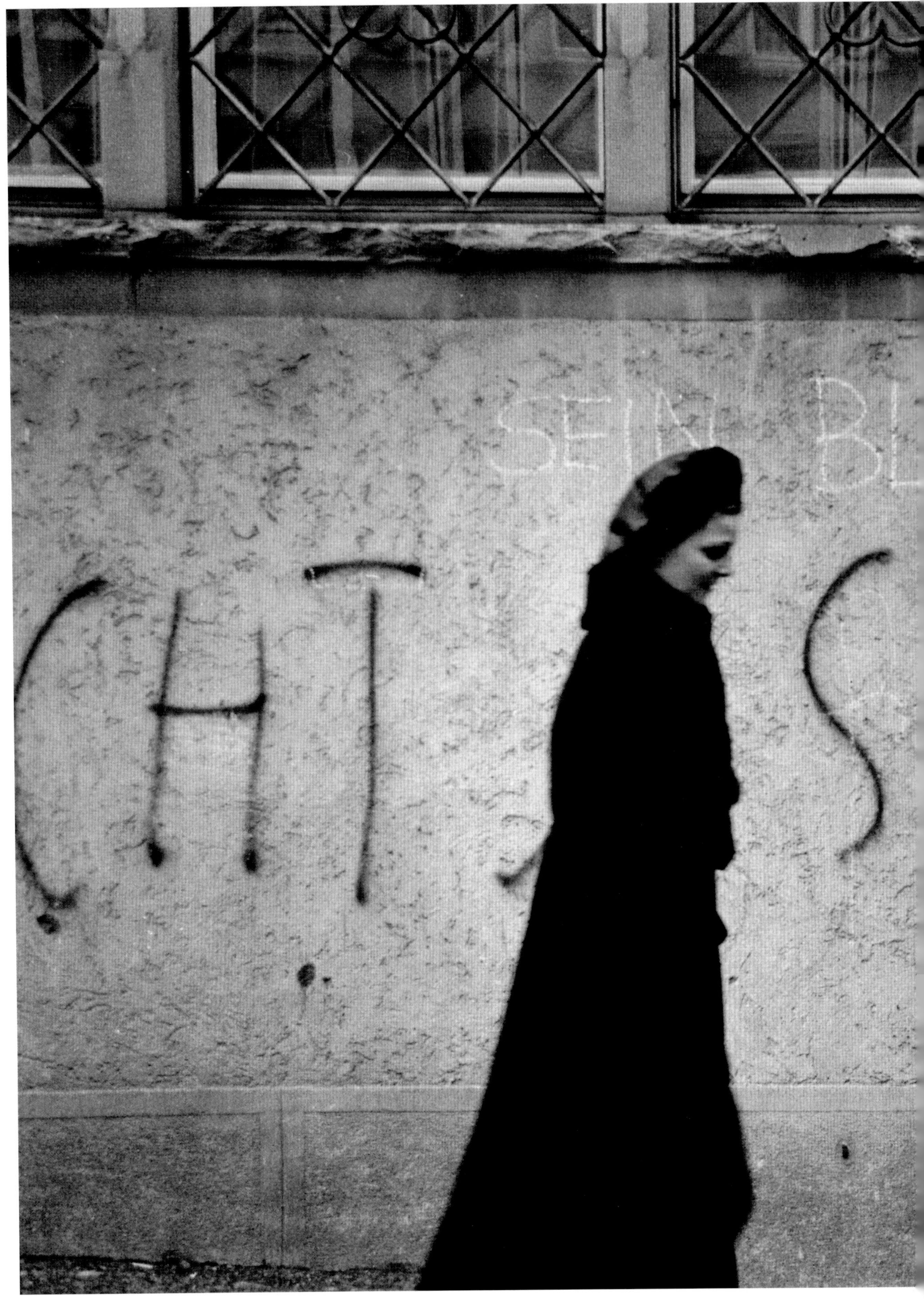

Zürich, 1992

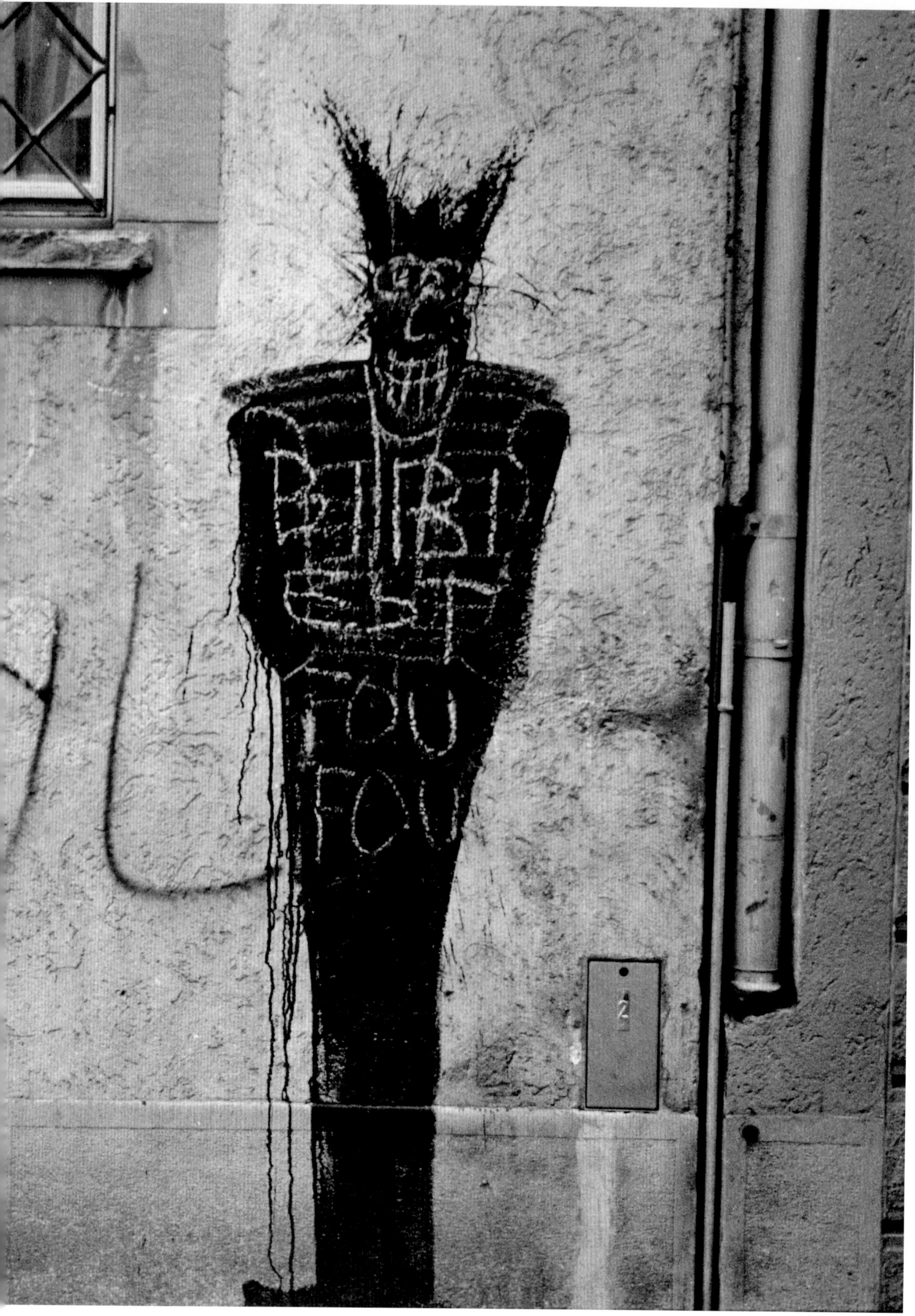

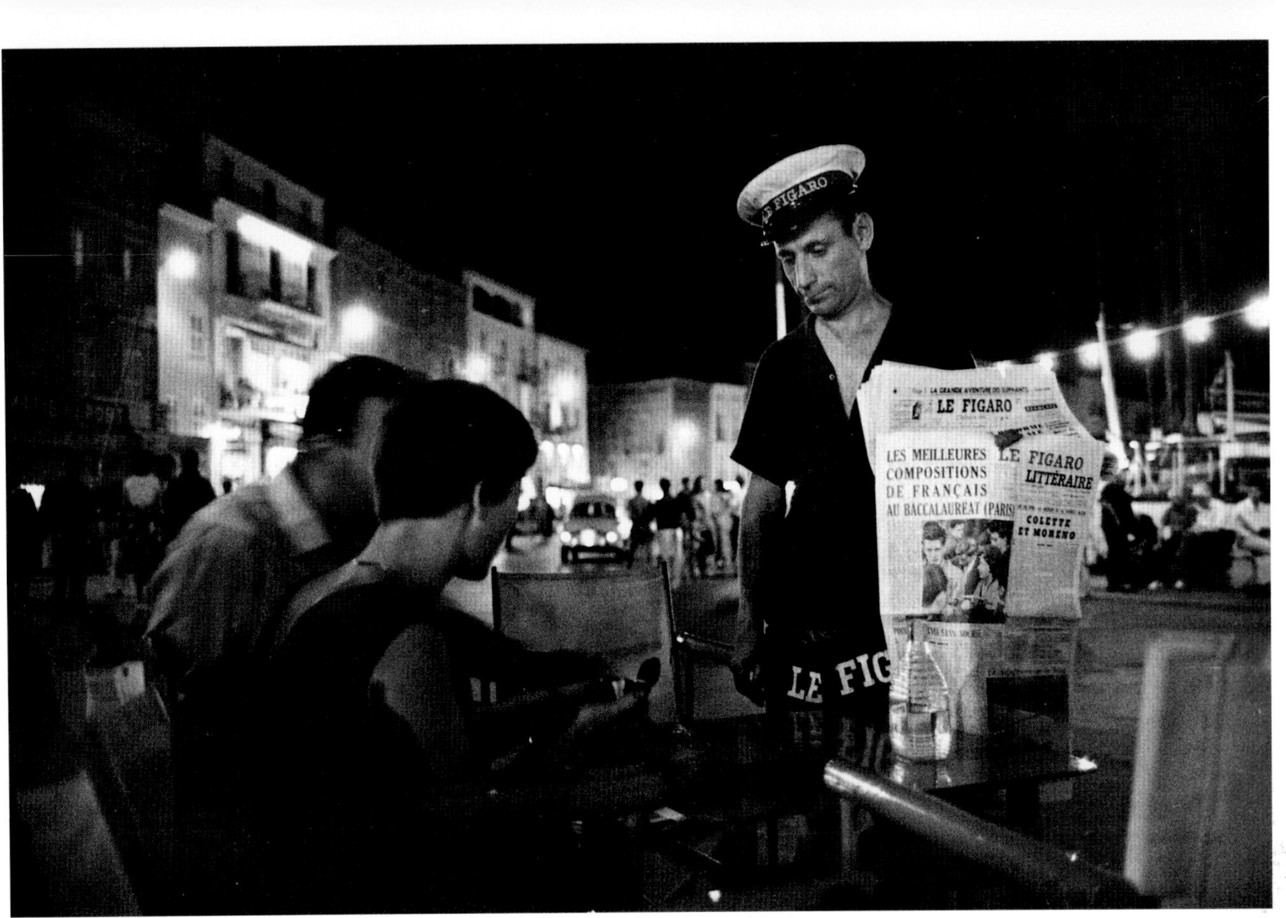

St Tropez, France, 1959

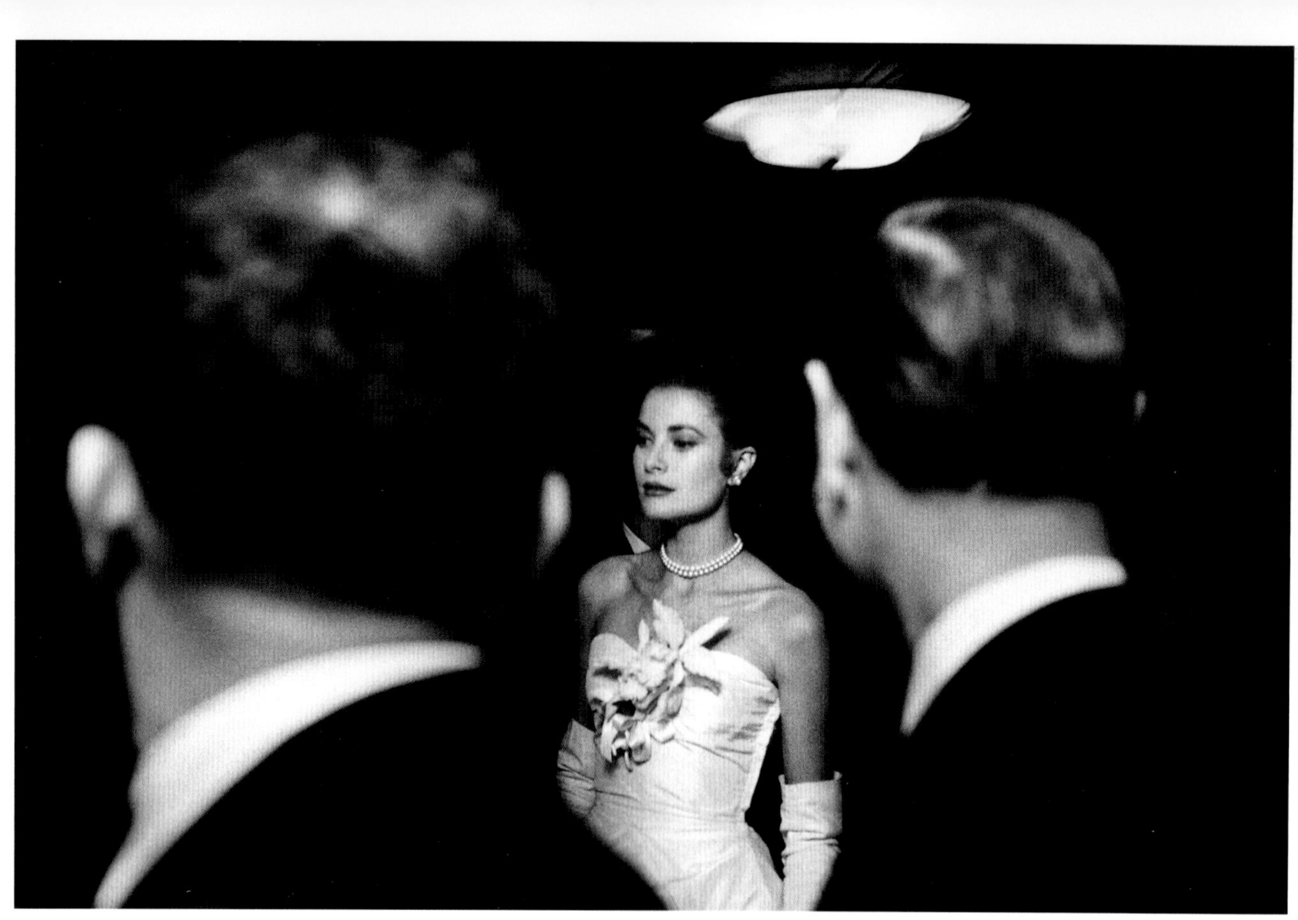

Grace Kelly, New York, 1955
overleaf *Brasília, Brazil, 1961* / *Los Angeles, 1959*

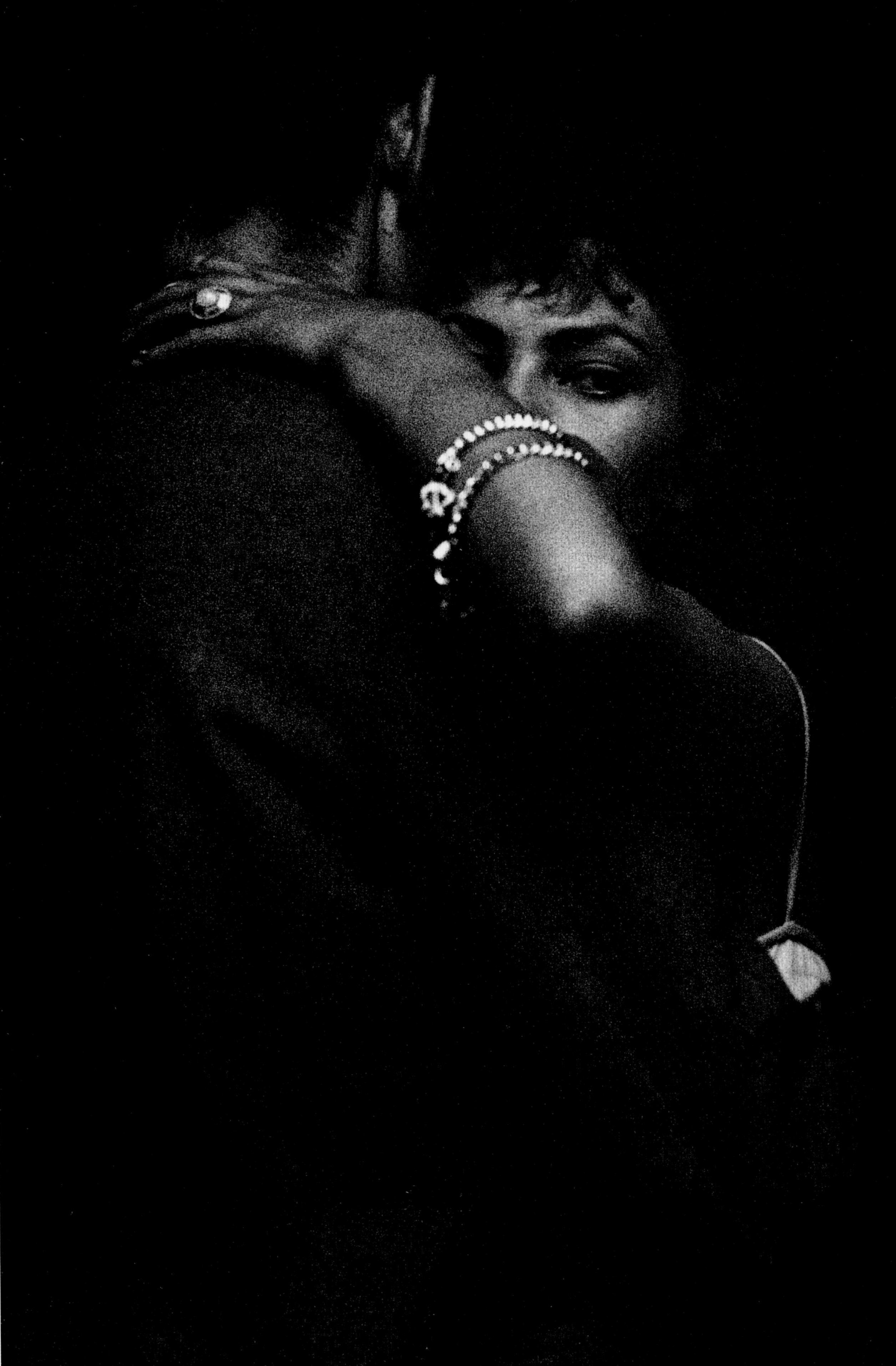

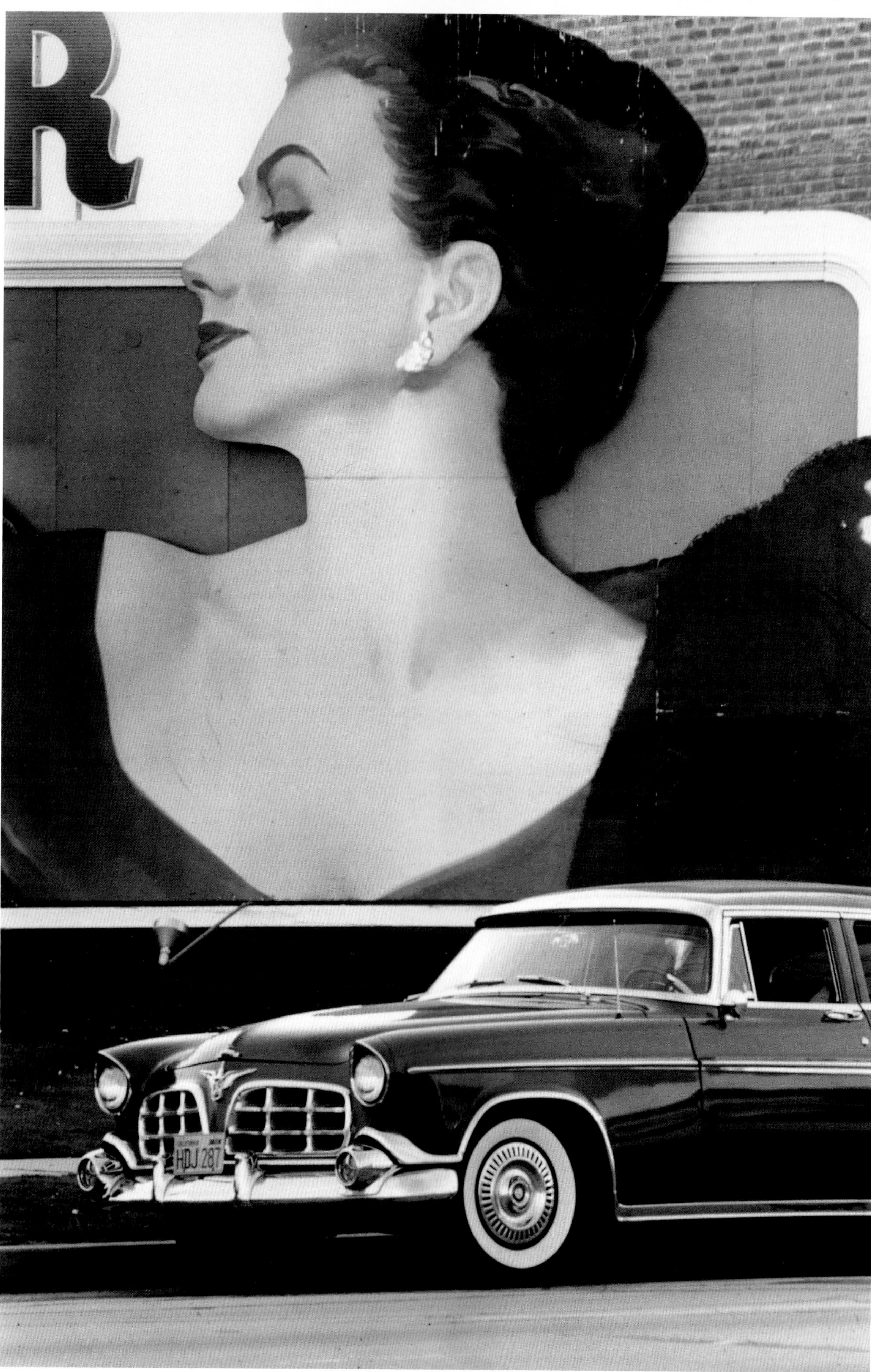
R
HDJ 287

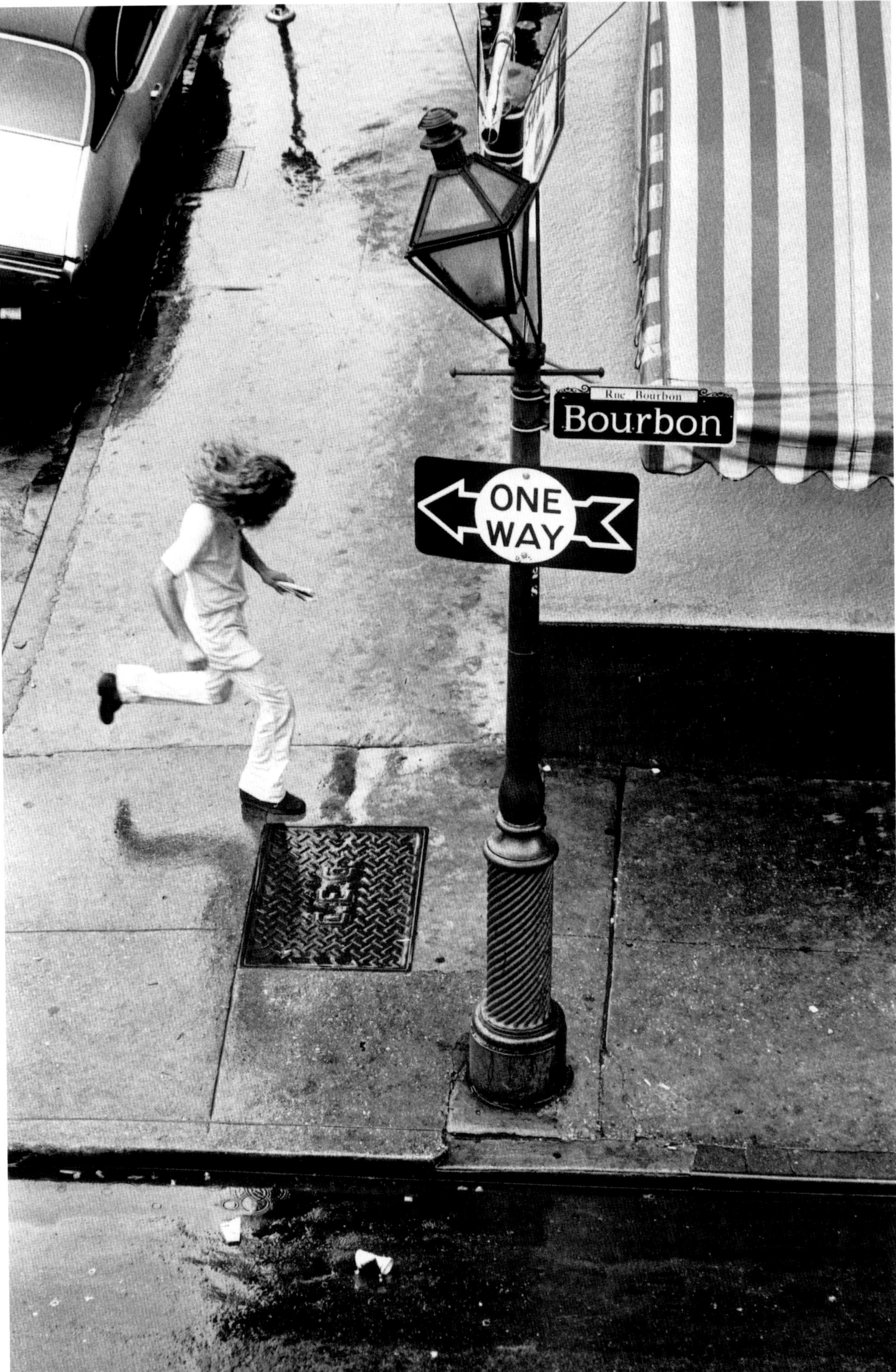
Rue Bourbon
Bourbon
ONE
WAY

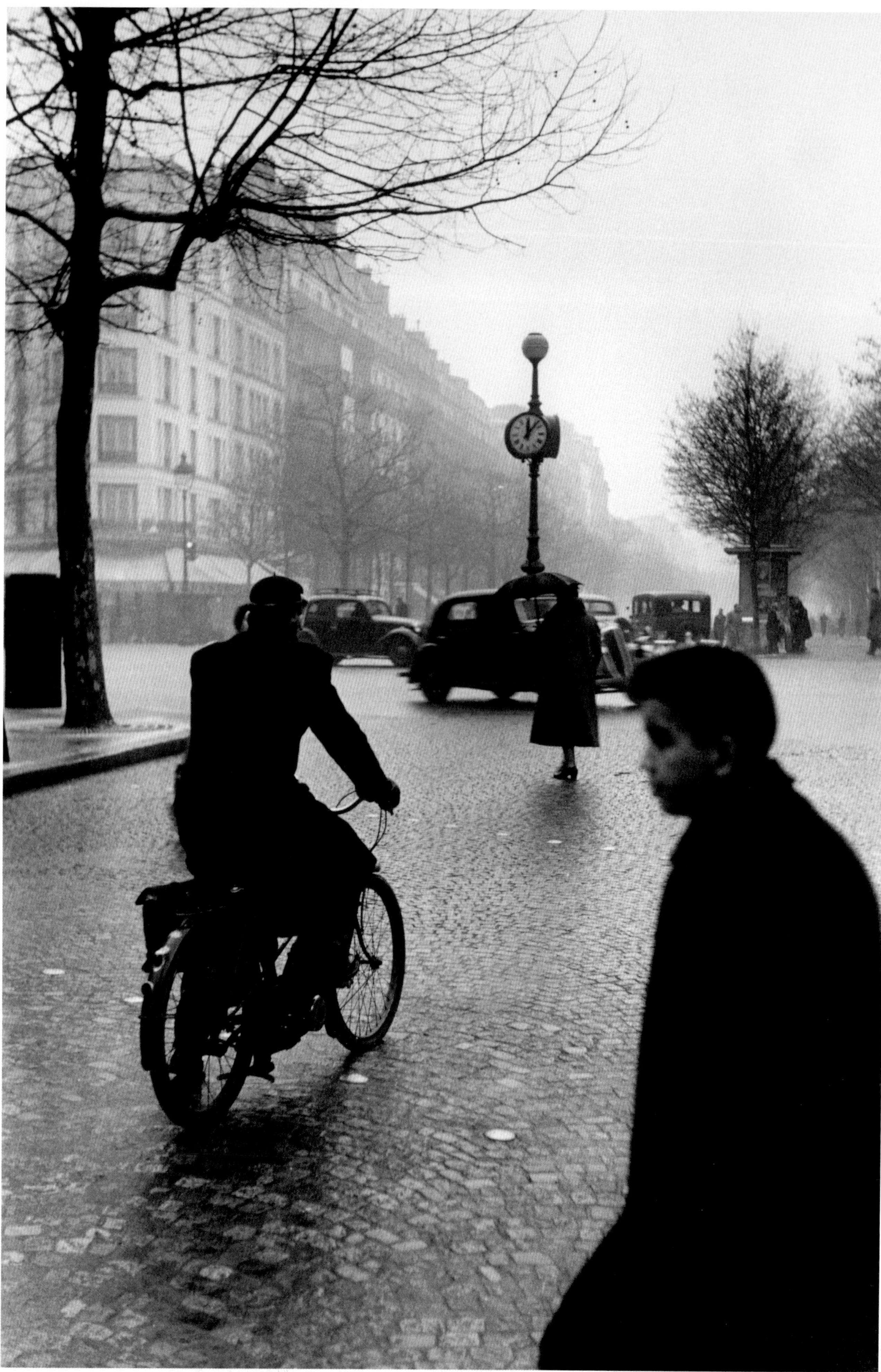

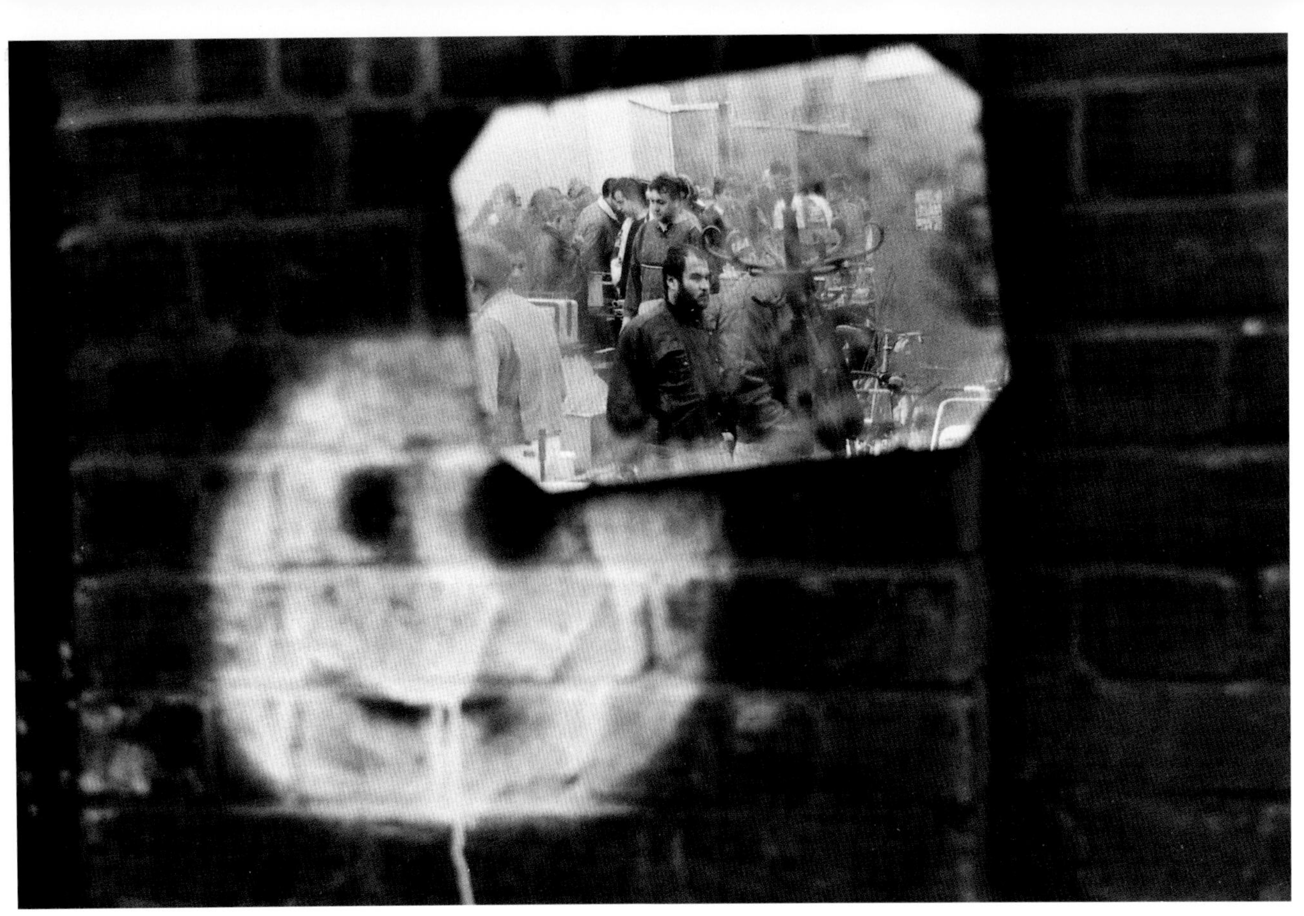

previous page *New Orleans, 1970* / *Paris, 1952*
London, 1994

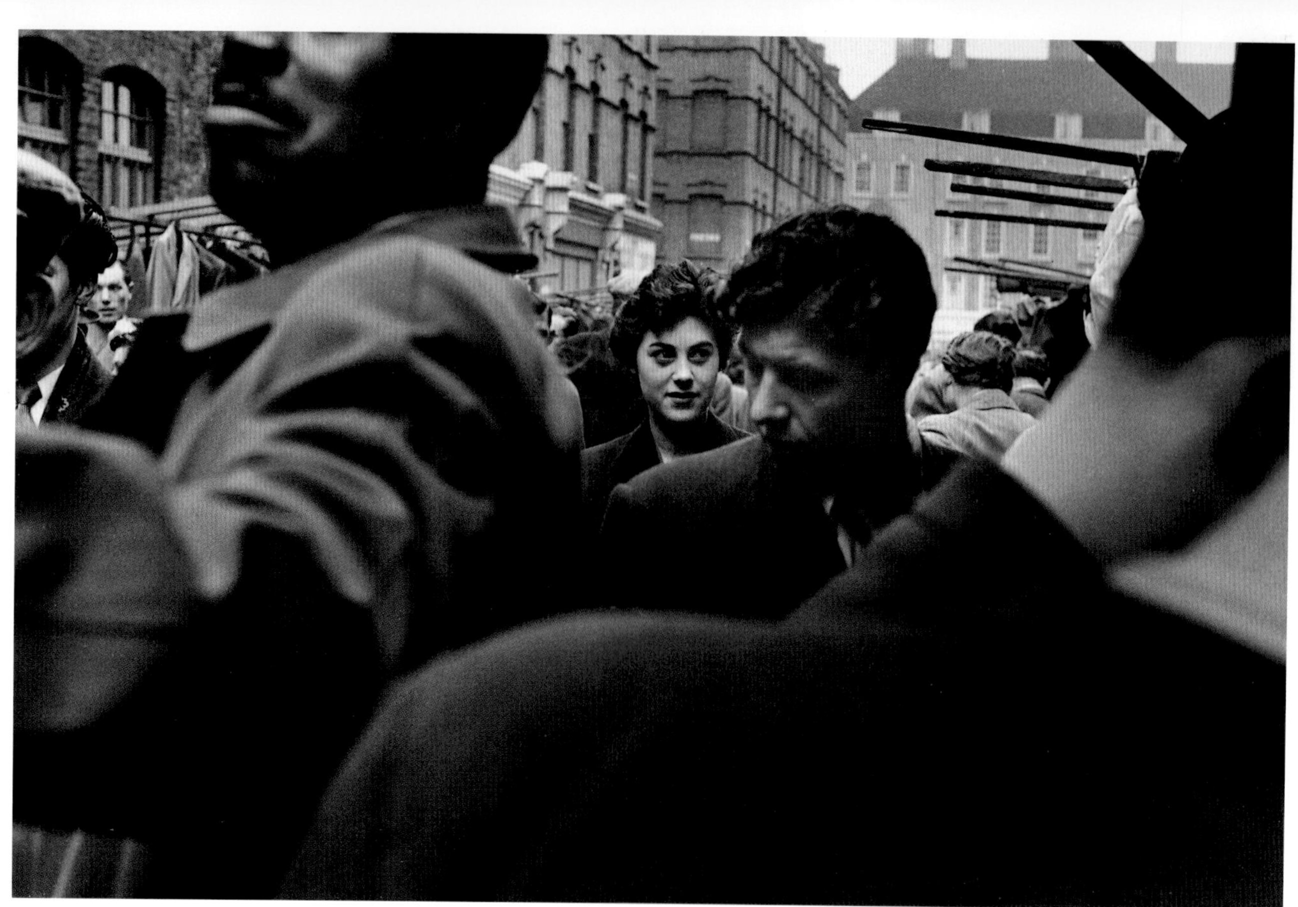

London, 1952

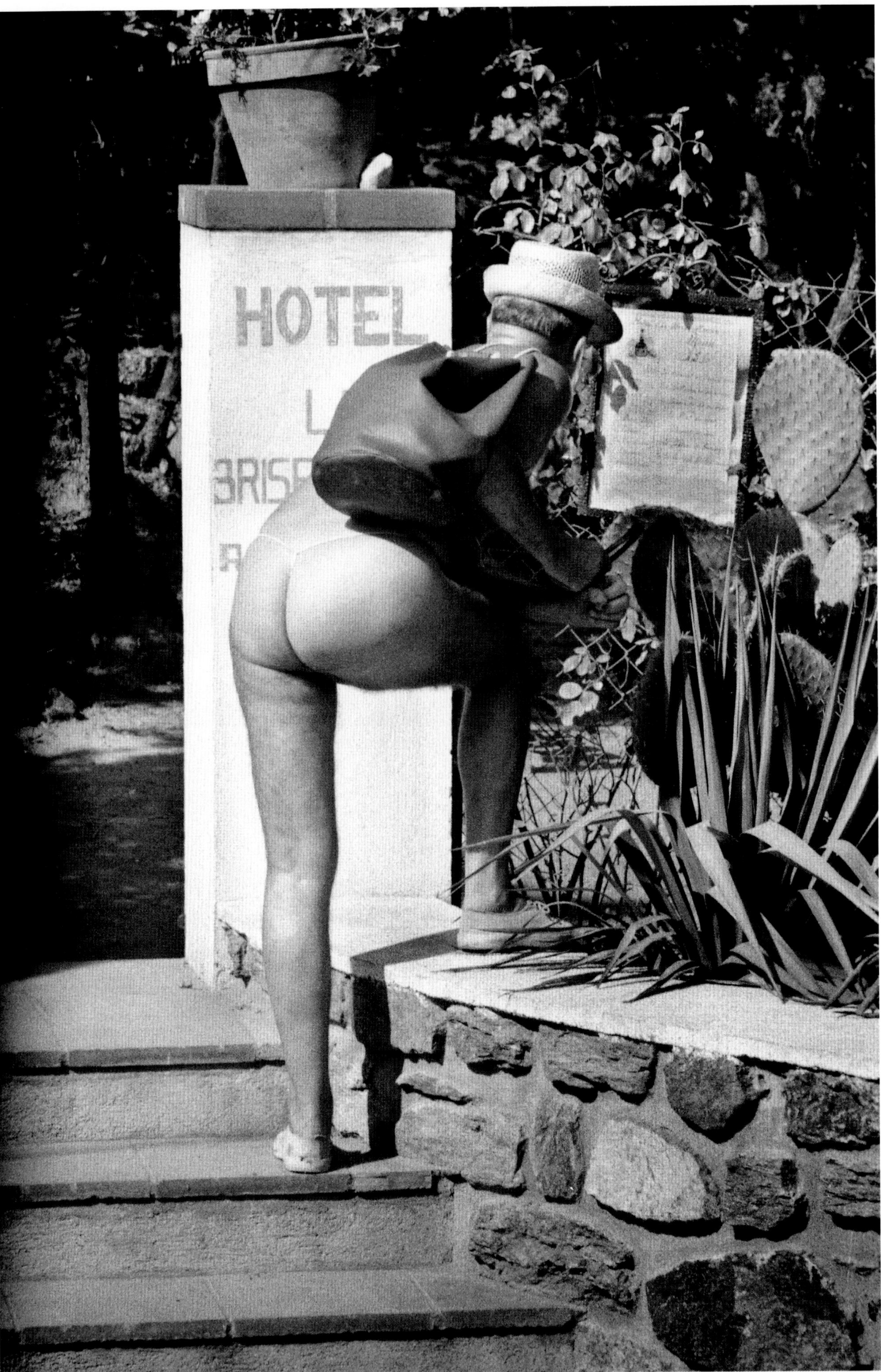
HOTEL

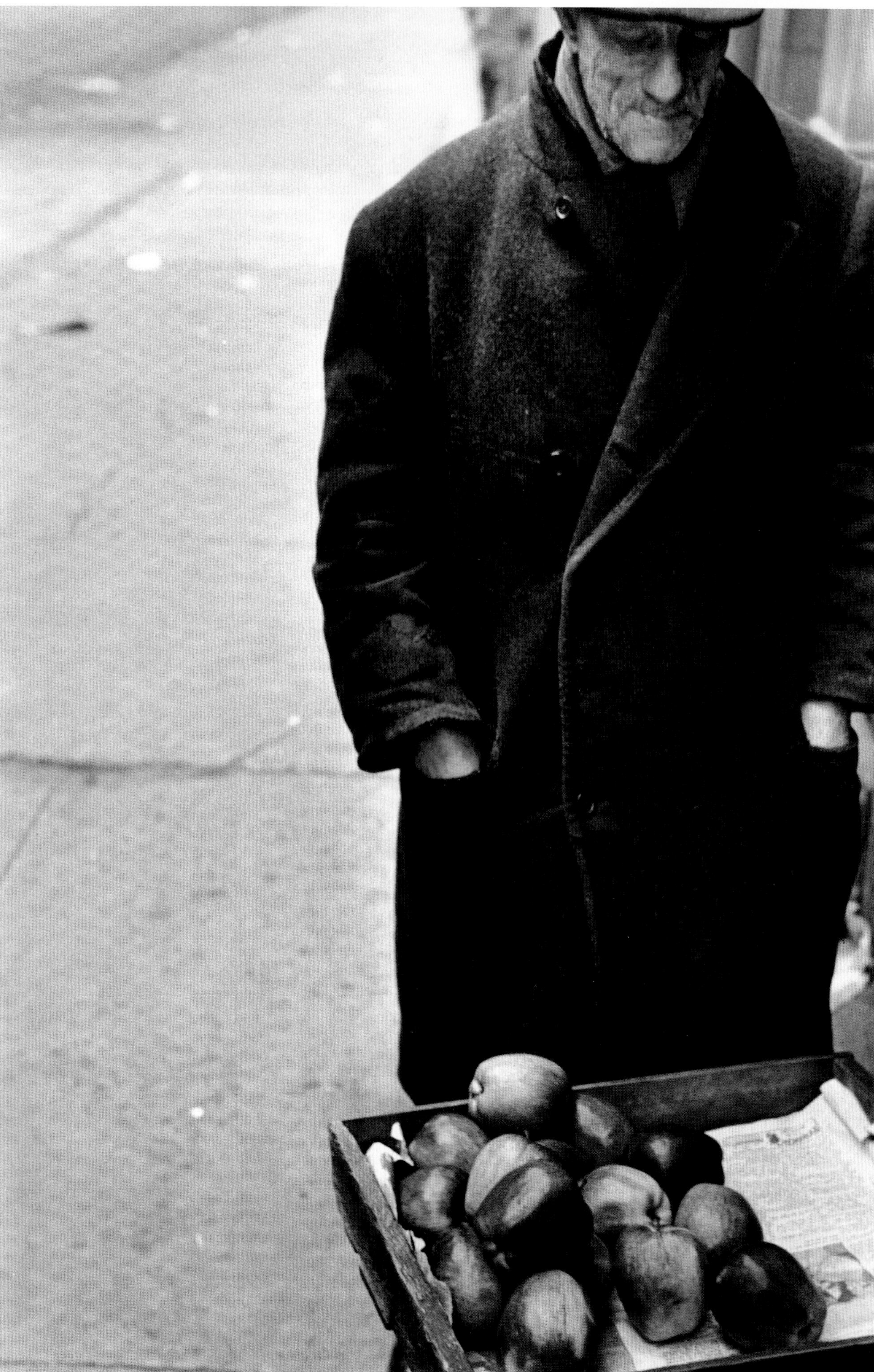

previous page *Ile du Levant, France, 1968* / *New York, 1951*
Che Guevara, Havana, Cuba, 1964

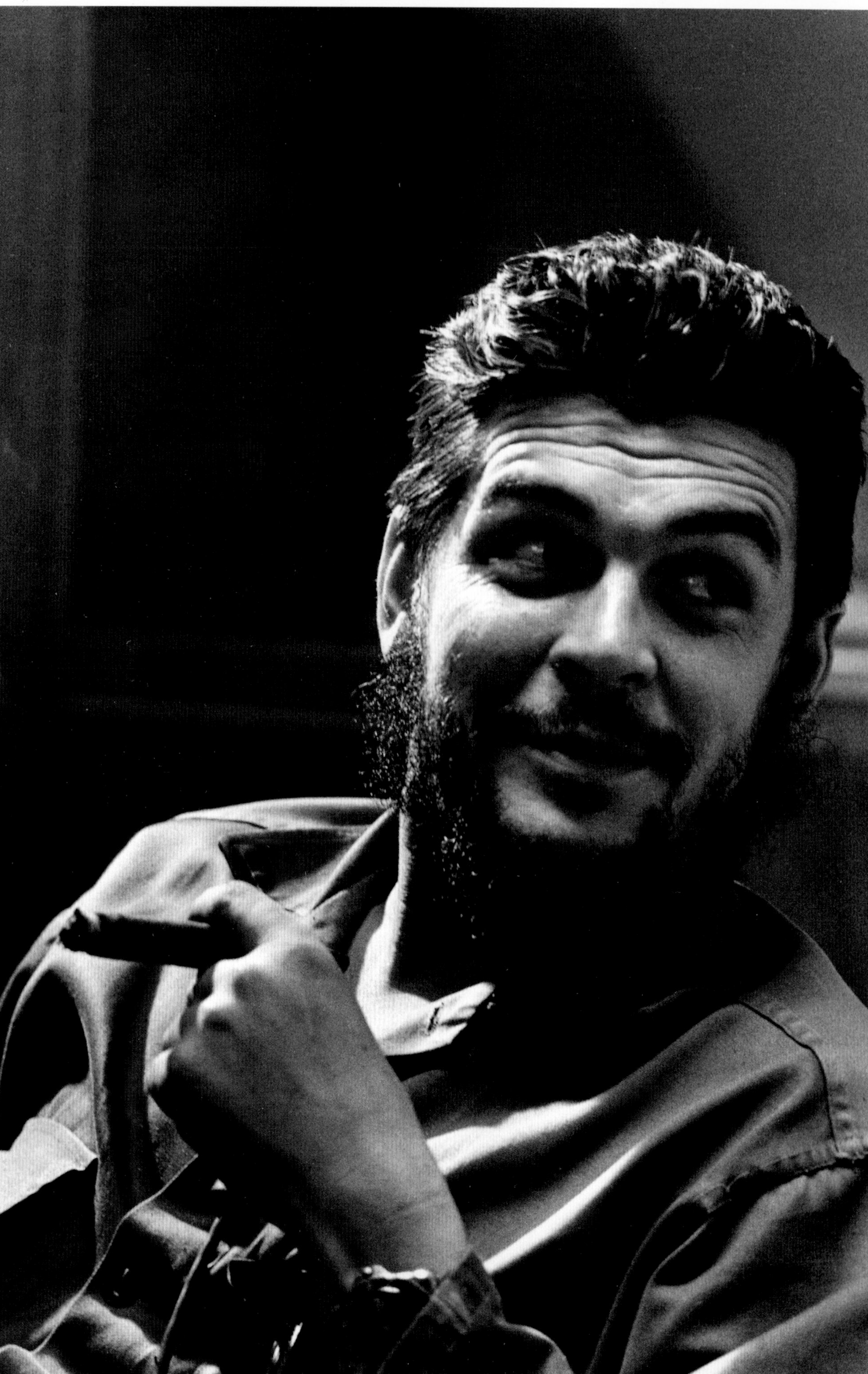

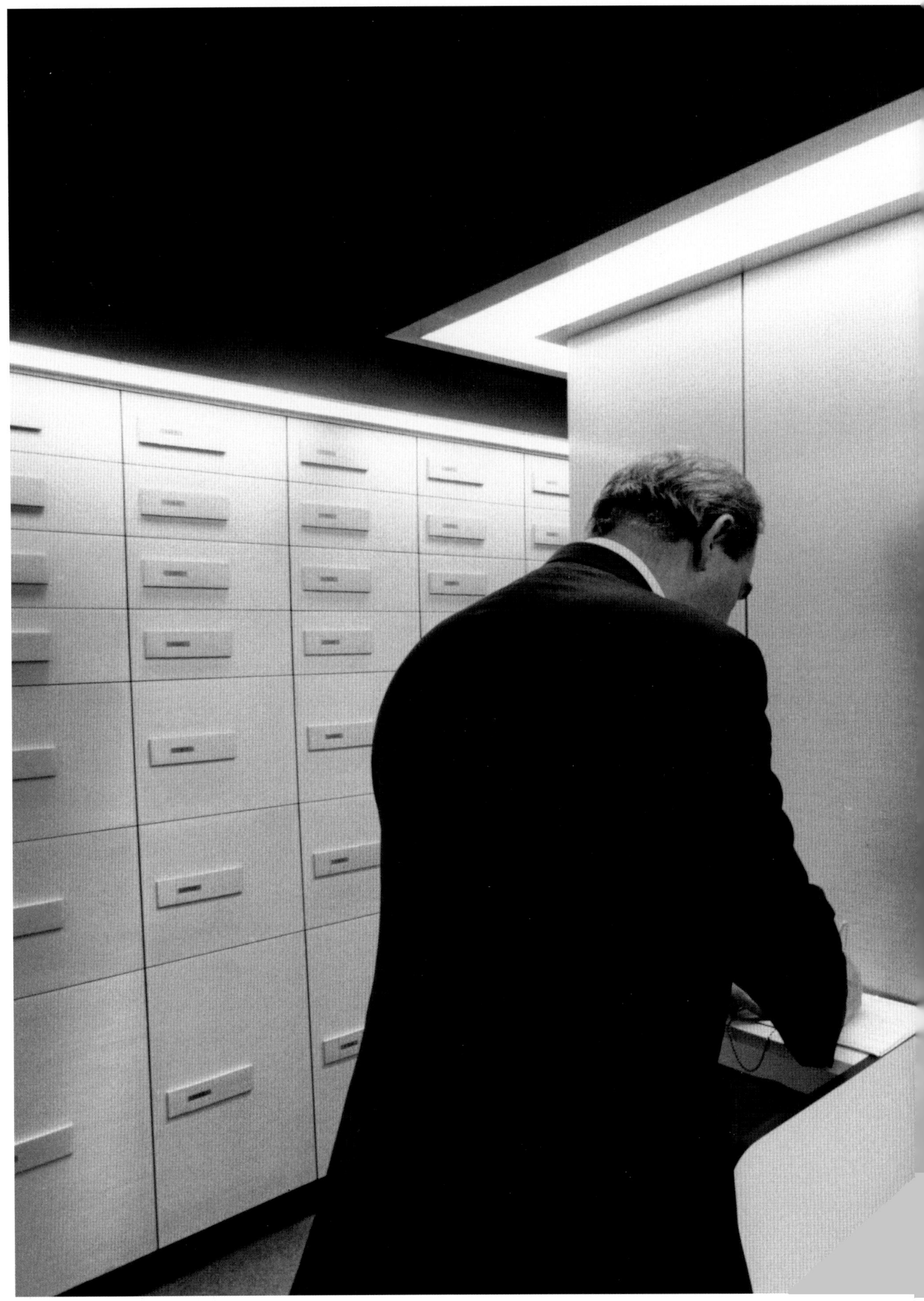

Paris, 1997

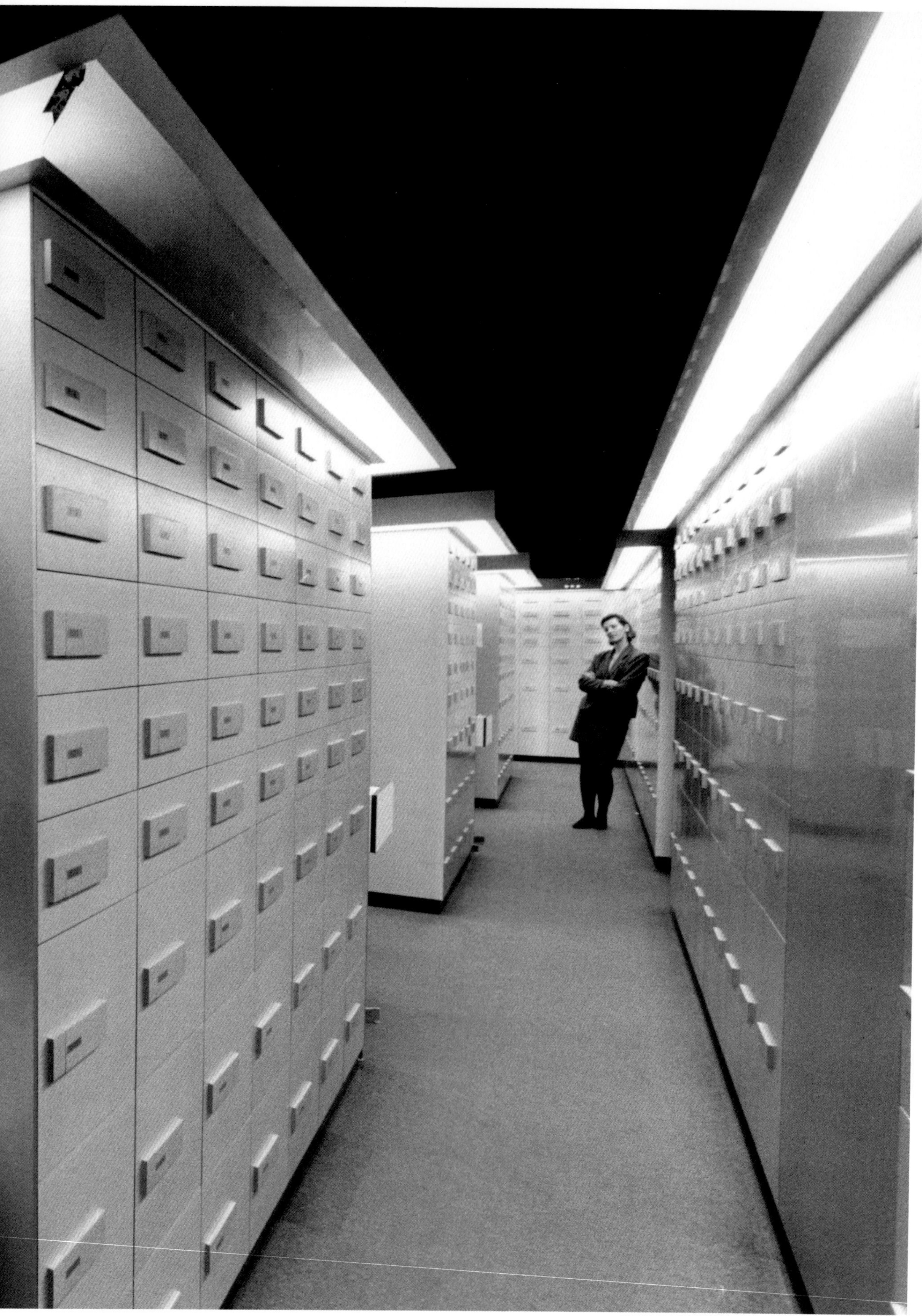

Motel room, Texas, 1962

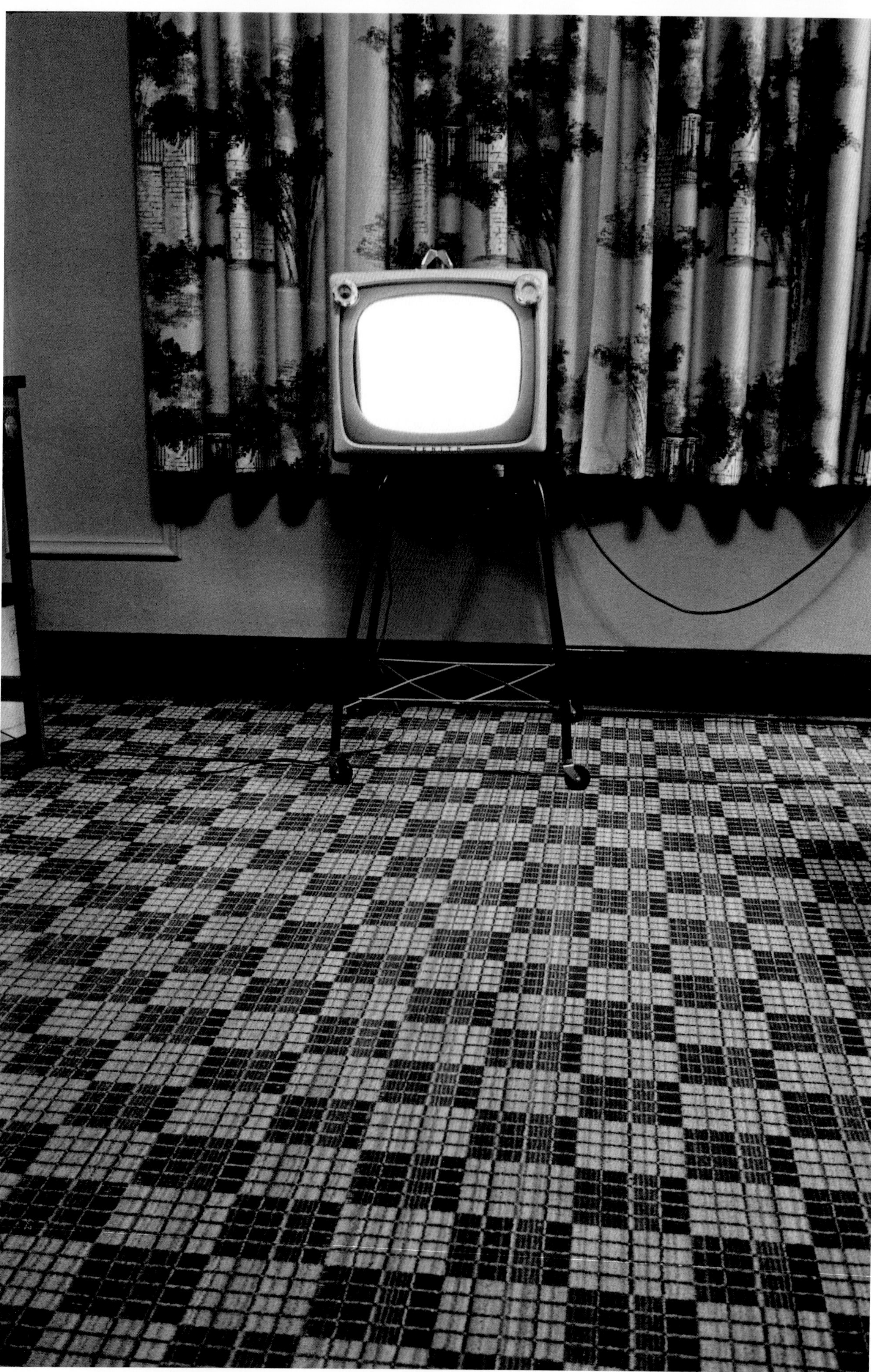

Move

The movements pictured here – flying, dancing, driving, walking, riding, or crossing over into the beyond – are stilled for all time, while implying the actions of past and present. We think we know the arc of most of these movements, the directions from which they came and towards which they incline. We are not always right, unless we look closely.

It is in such snaps of frozen action, when the camera records what the human eye can scarcely glimpse, that Elliott, who characteristically pretends that his technique is no huge matter, relies on his mastery of composition. Not only has he snapped the moment; he has simultaneously chosen the arrangement of objects within the frame so that the story is told clearly.

This skill, basic to Elliott's work since his early twenties, is less and less noticed in our era of manipulated images, digitalization and computer modifications. But the corollary to his rule that snaps generally be unposed is that the image be printed just as it appears in the viewfinder. He almost never crops his photos. What you see is what he got.

Why put such rigorous restrictions on the work? What would be lost or sullied if a stray foot in one corner was cropped in the darkroom or a power line across the top scissored out?

Igor Stravinsky, another original of Russian background, was thought to set down arbitrary, restrictive rules of composition, but he argued that there is greater creative freedom within rigorous limitations. Elliott's visual compositions benefit from a similar conviction that boundaries are not obstacles but opportunities. If there is a foot dangling in one corner, we will find that it is essential to the narrative of the snap. The power line will echo another object or comment upon it or in some other way prove indispensable to the composition.

The really daunting aspect of all this is that it may take us several minutes to understand how the composition works its magic, but Elliott had to grasp it in a millisecond. That's what his rules require.

Movement is time, and vice versa, yet for all the movement in his photos, they are timeless not just because they are lasting, but also because they could have been taken at almost any moment in his career. His vision has not been changed by a rapidly altering world.

In these photos people and animals move as they moved long before the invention of the camera. If they are aware of the implications of new discoveries in quantum physics, the mapping of the human genome or the Hubble telescope's estimates of the age of the universe, you would not know it from their actions here. The humans stroll or waltz just as birds fly, little dogs jump on a leash and curtains rustle in the breeze. These are the ancient movements of life without regard to wars and pestilence.

As the critic Ralph Hattersley put it in a review of Elliott's photos some years ago, 'He made the human comedy easier to bear.' We view the snaps from whatever individual recognition we have of a complex, tumultuous, contentious planet, but in these stilled moments of daily life Elliott brings us back to essentials, to the joy of moving our limbs without much thought of meaning and effect.

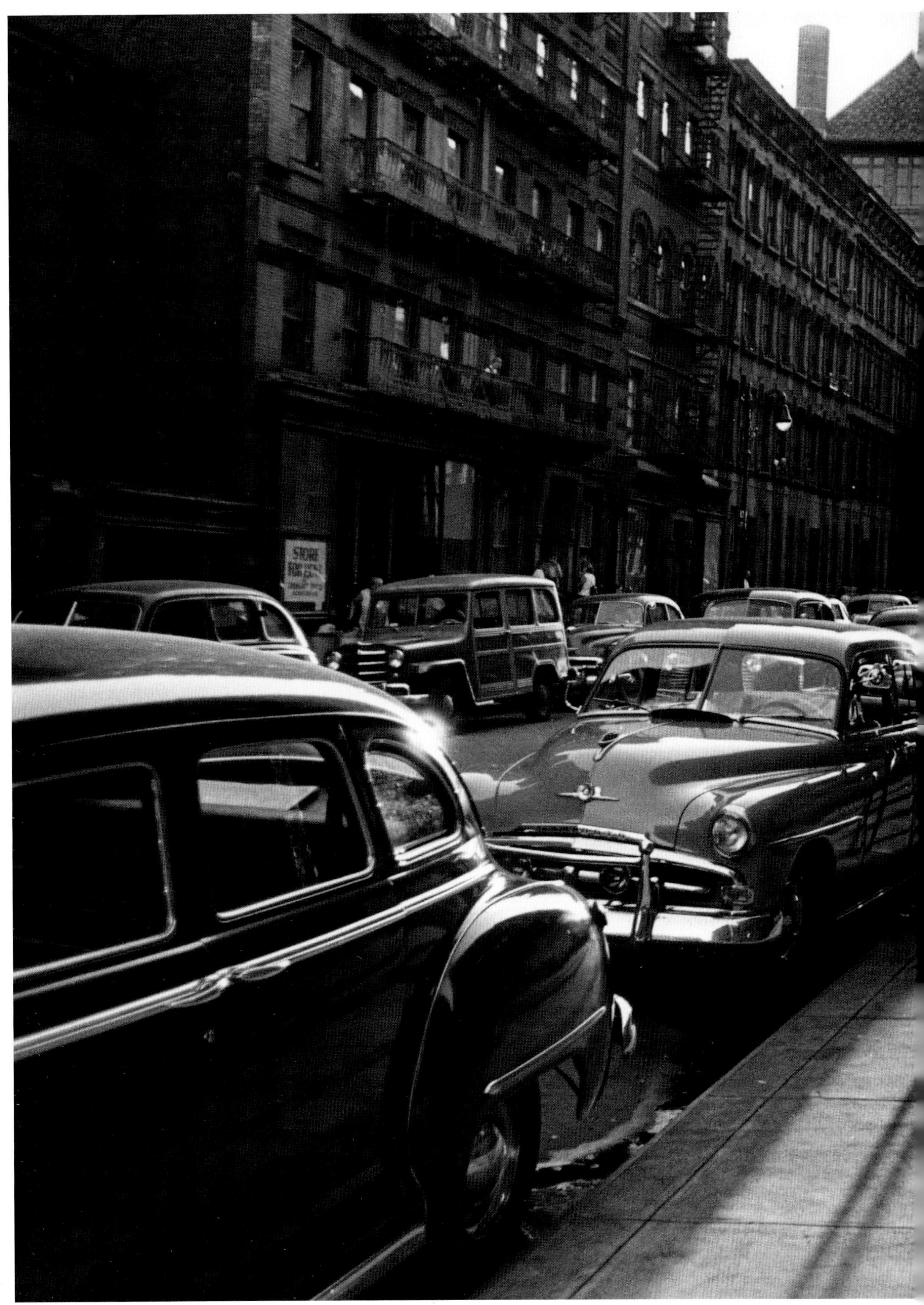

New York, 1953

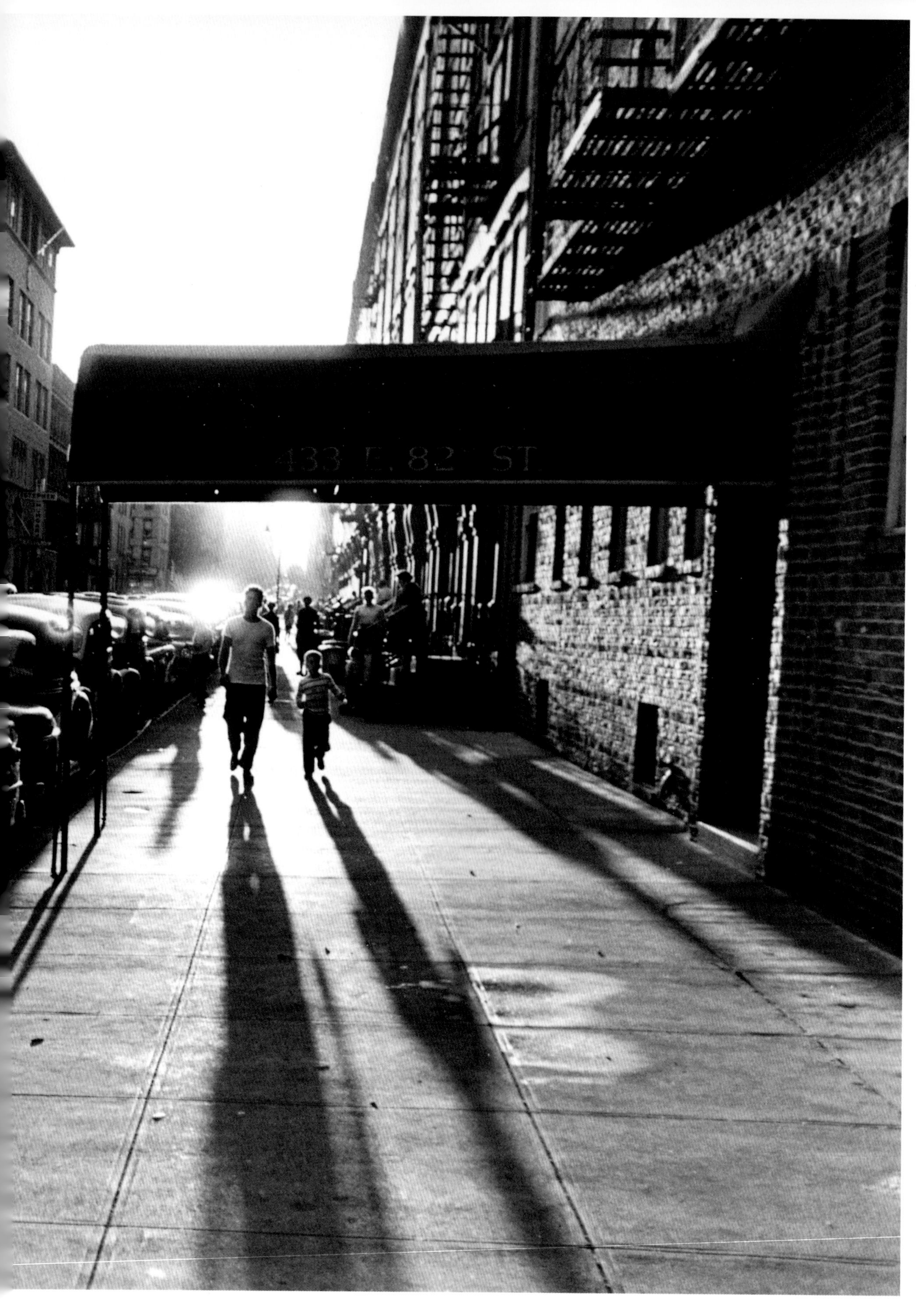

overleaf *Newport, Rhode Island, 1954* / *Chicago, 1962*

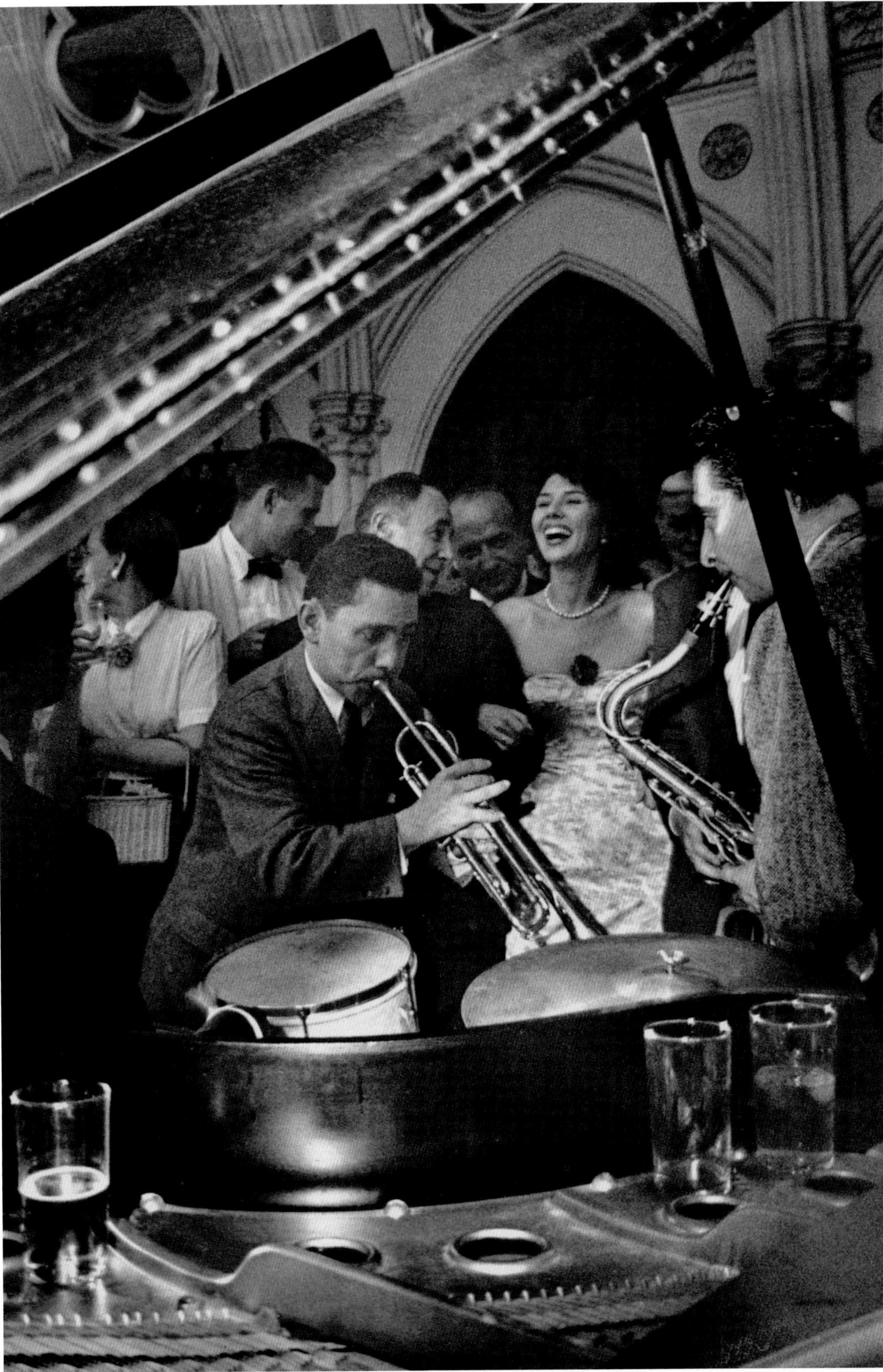

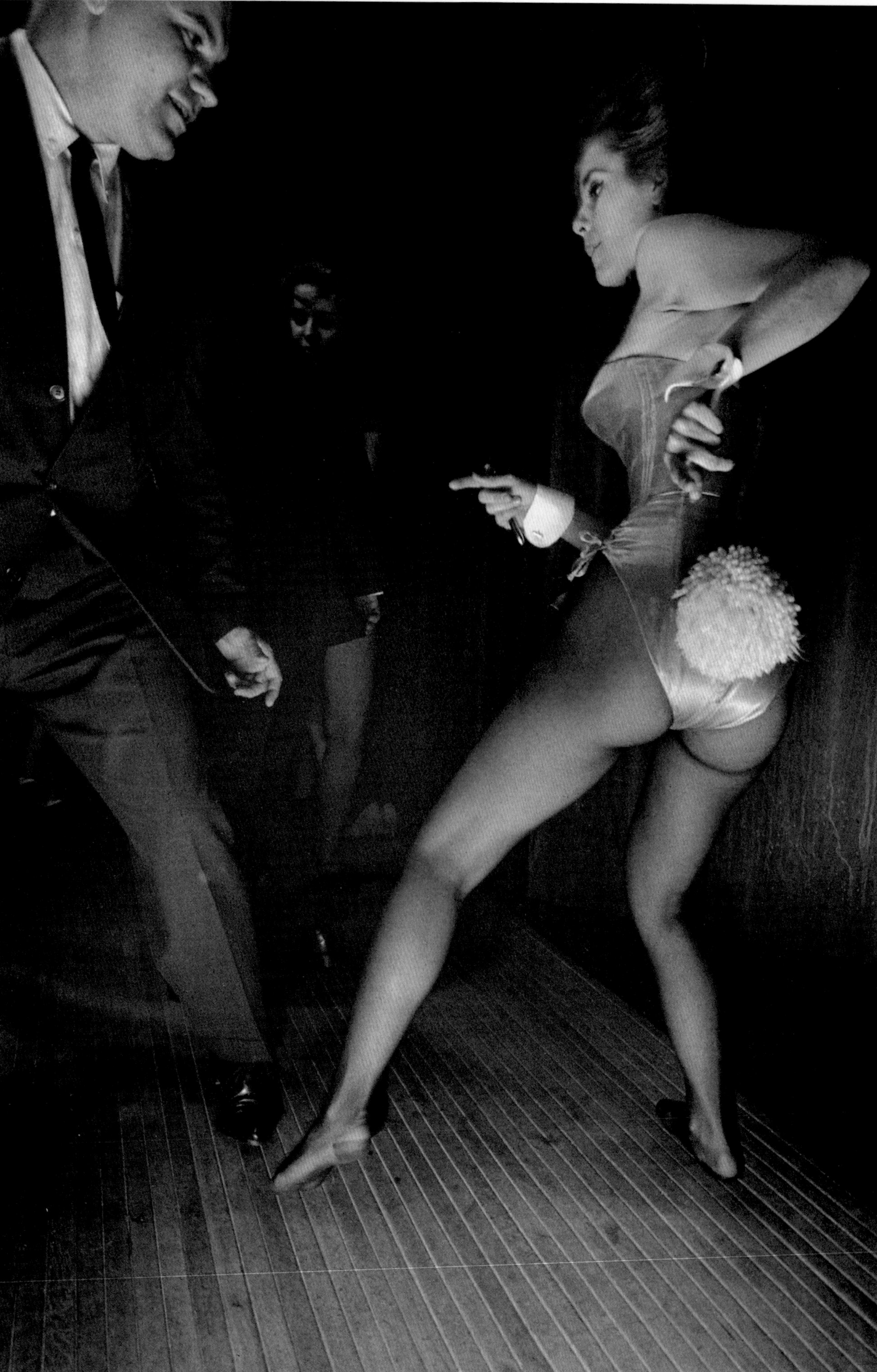

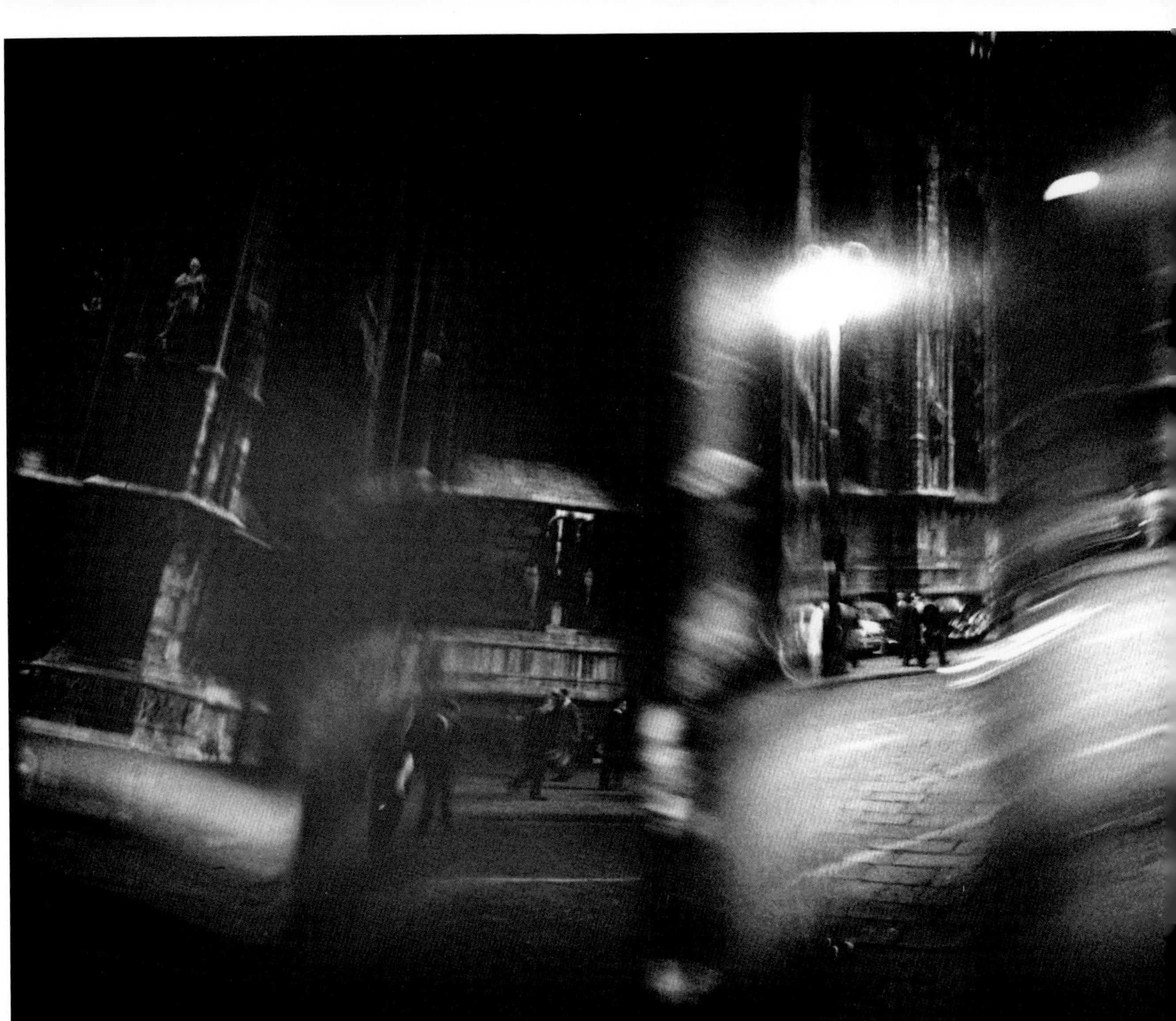

Milan, 1960

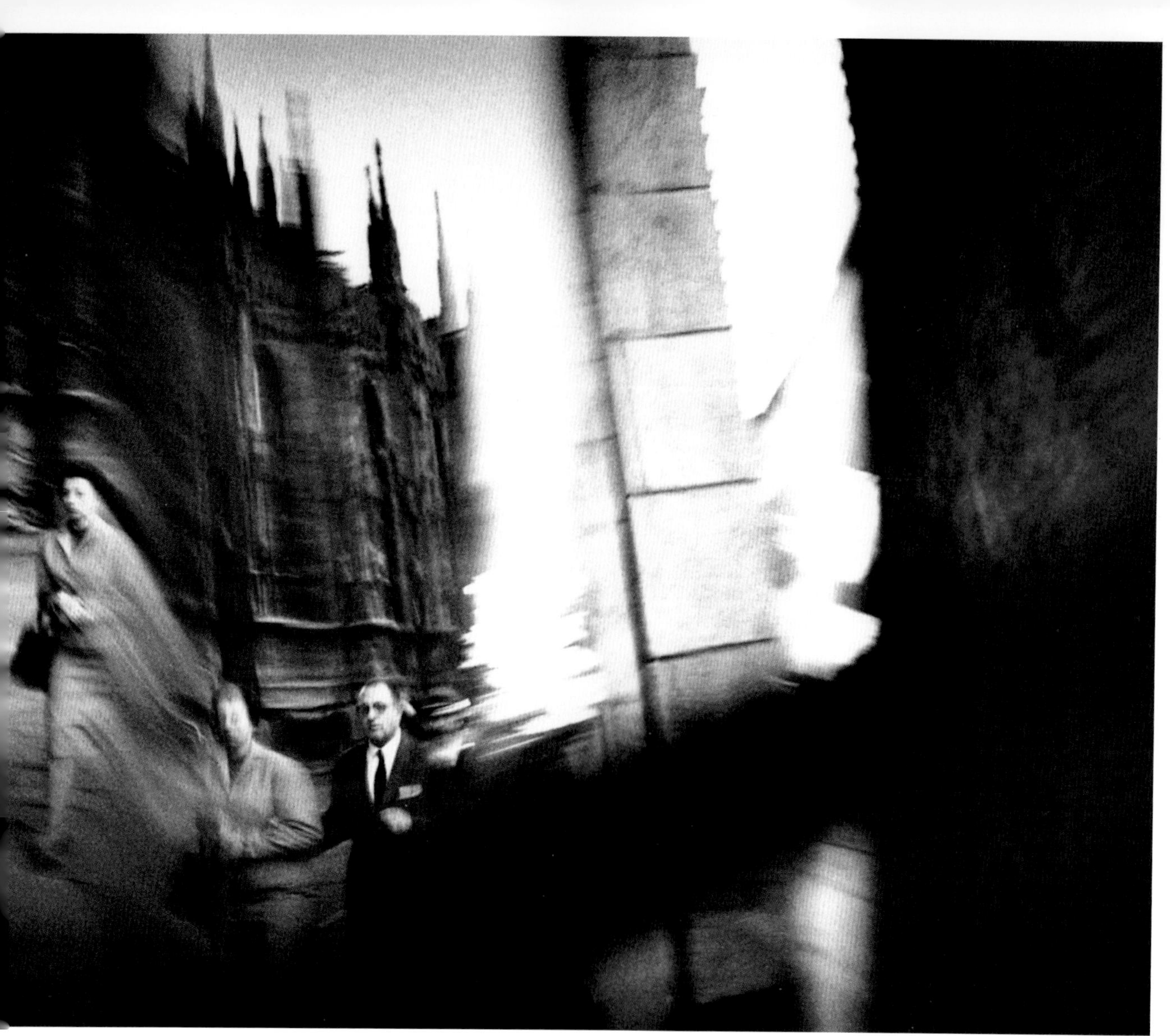

overleaf *London, 1952* / *Kathmandu, Nepal, 1983*

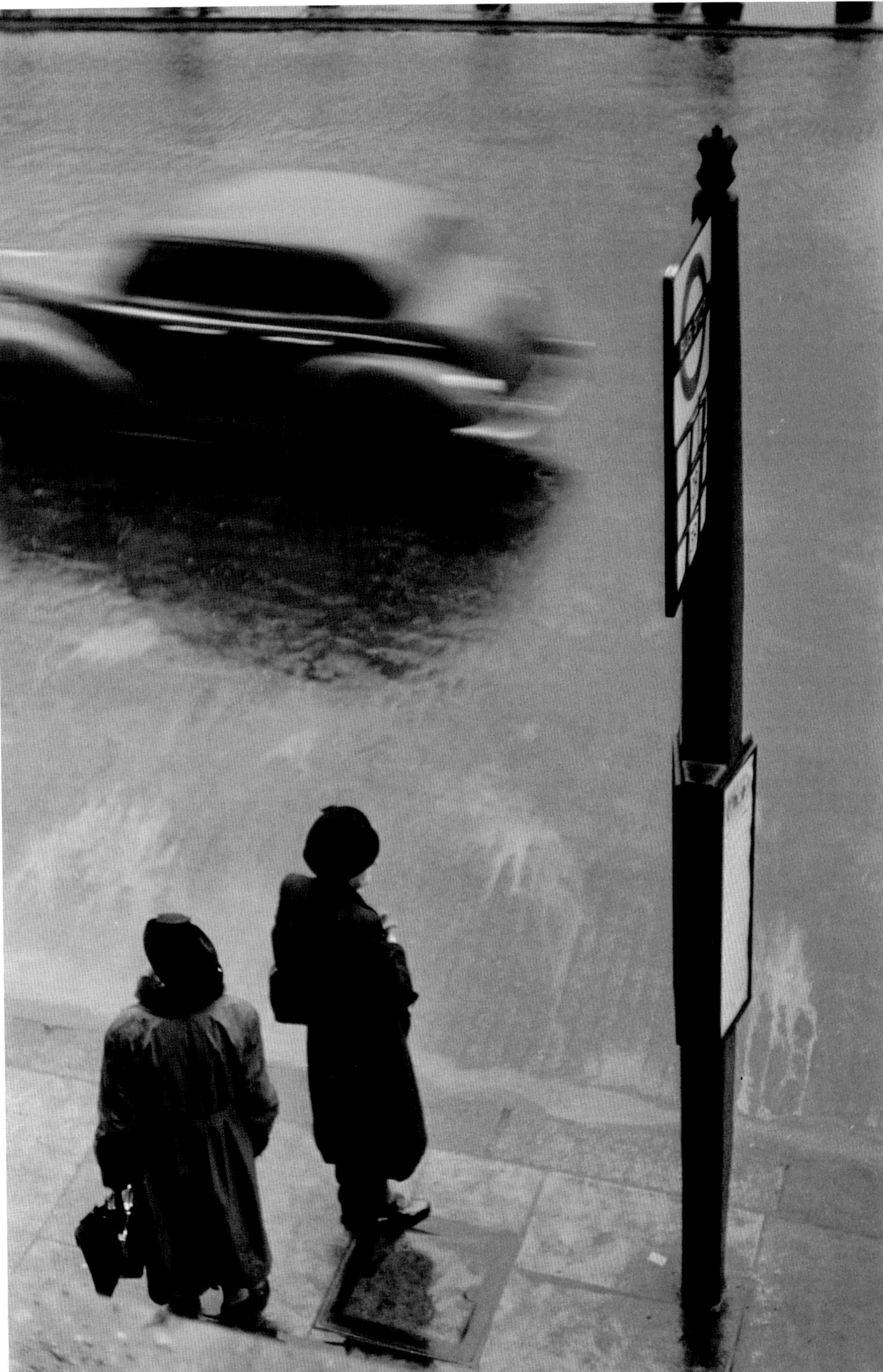

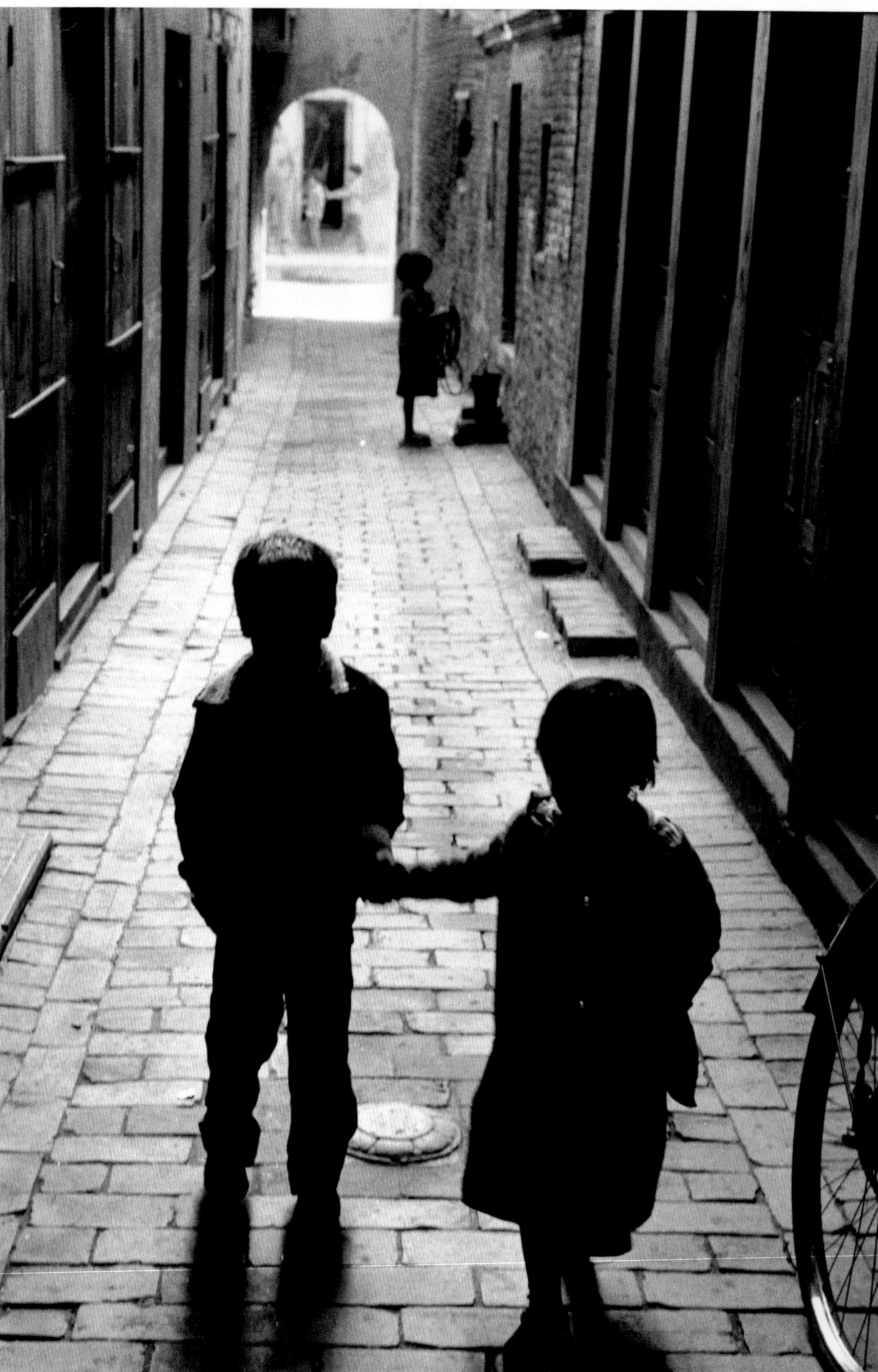

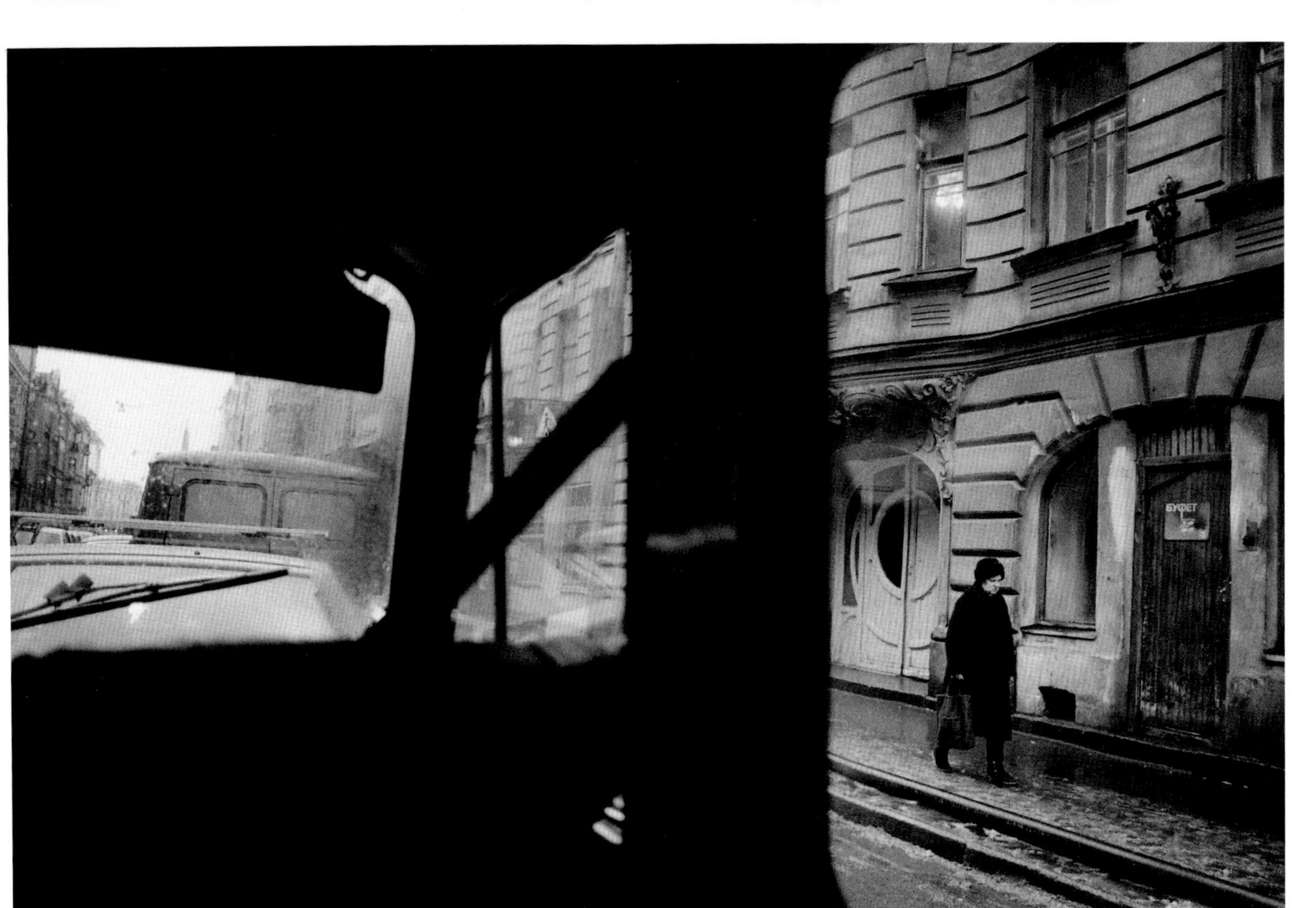

Leningrad, 1989

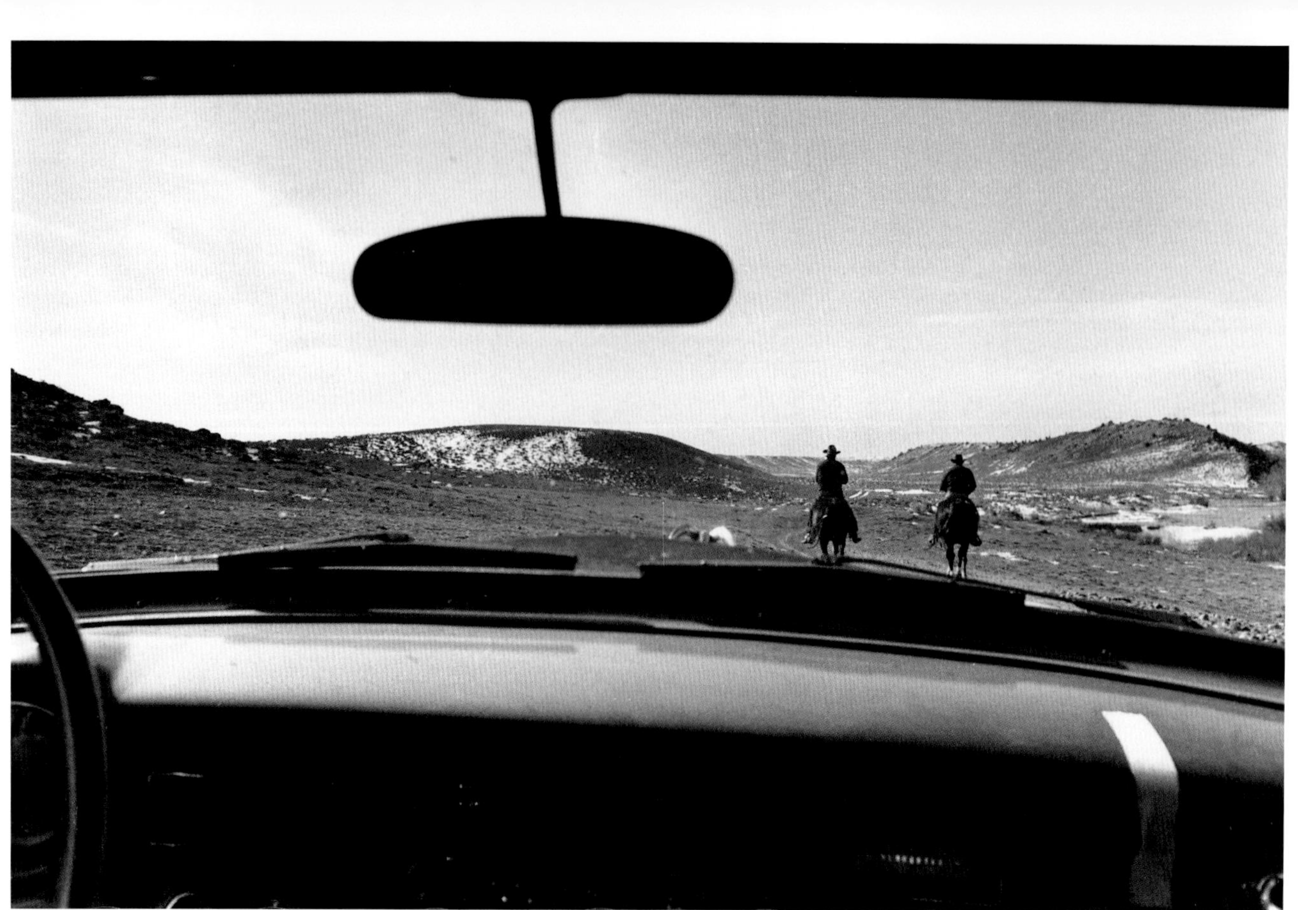

Wyoming, 1953

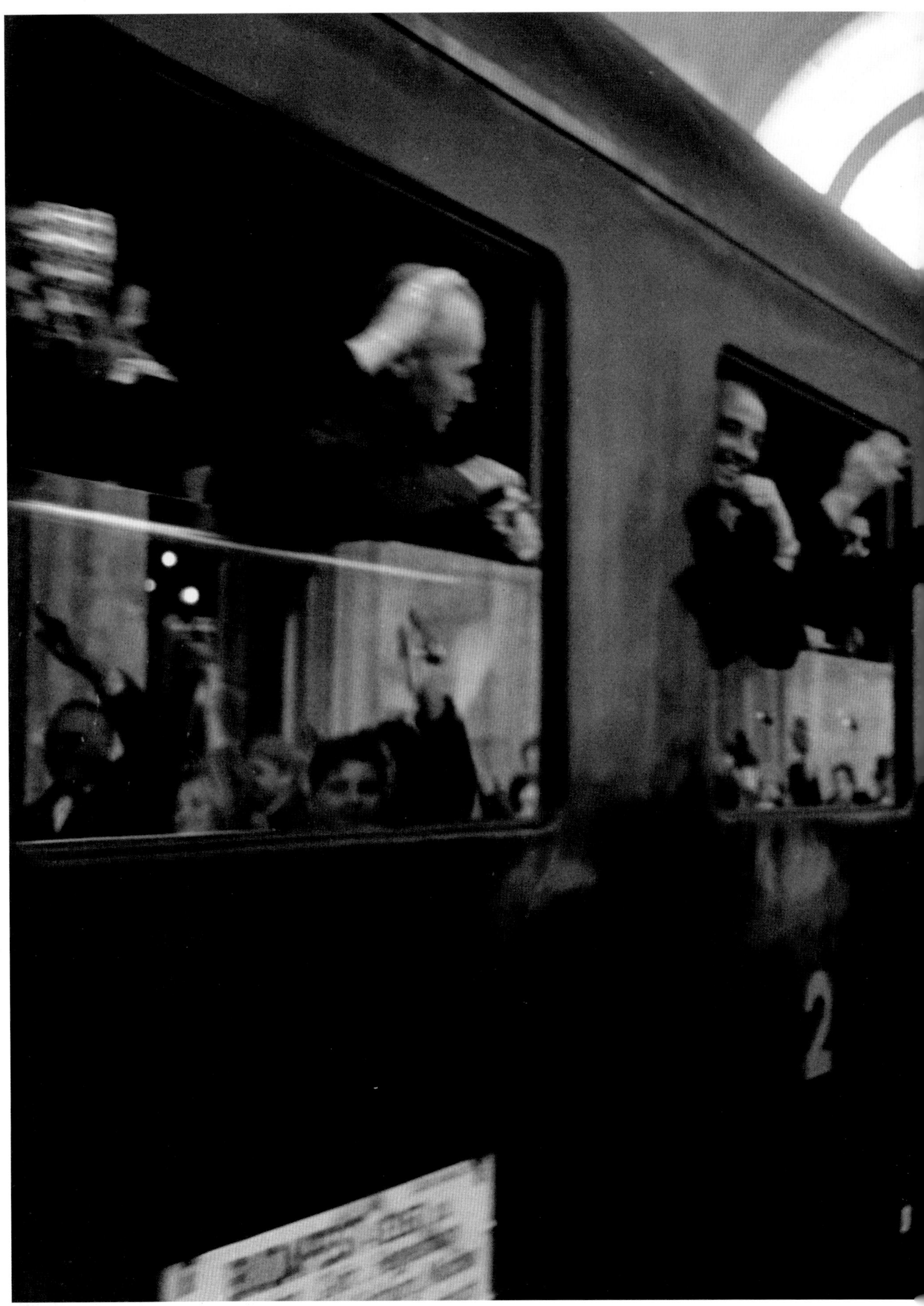

Budapest, Hungary, 1964

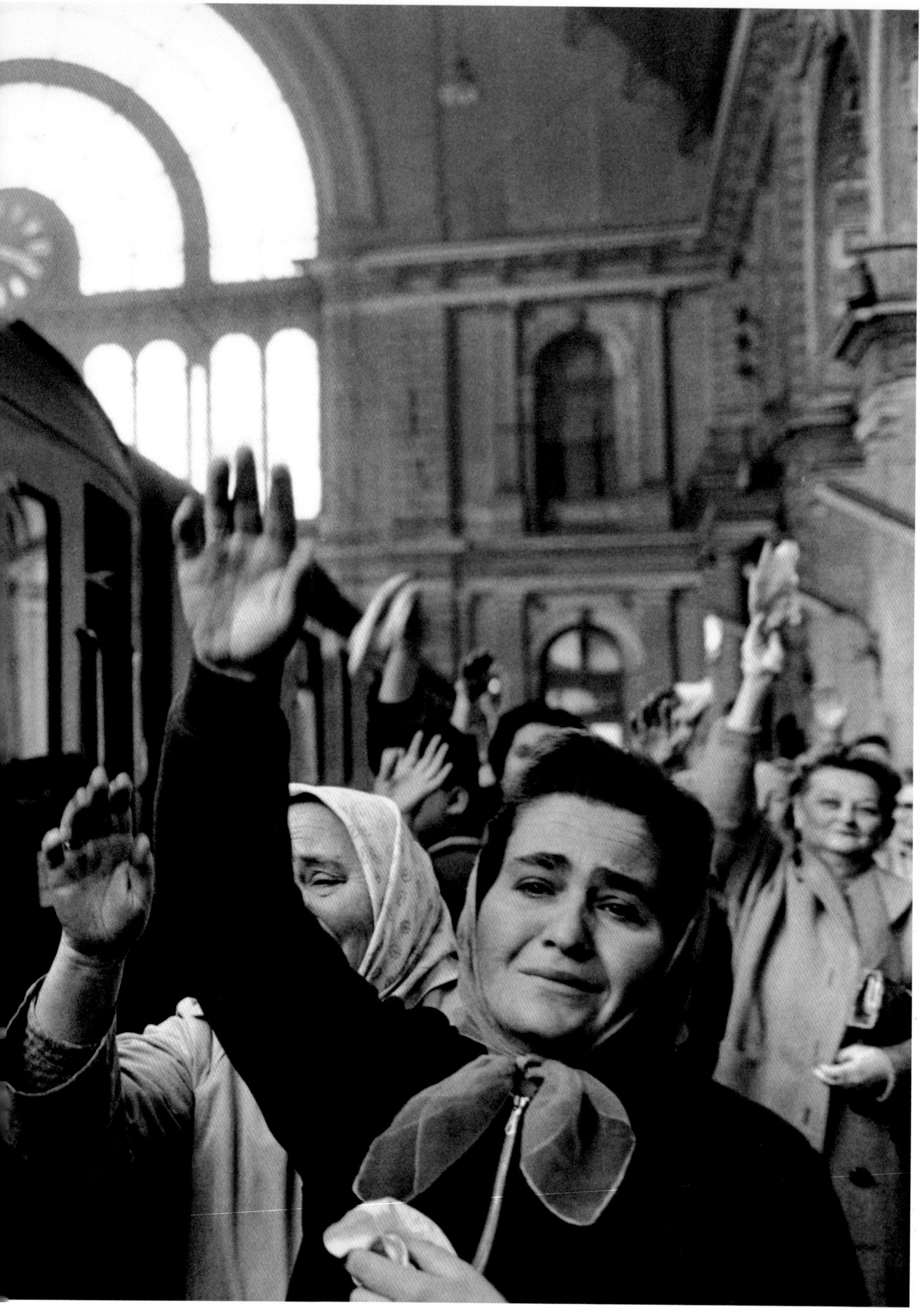

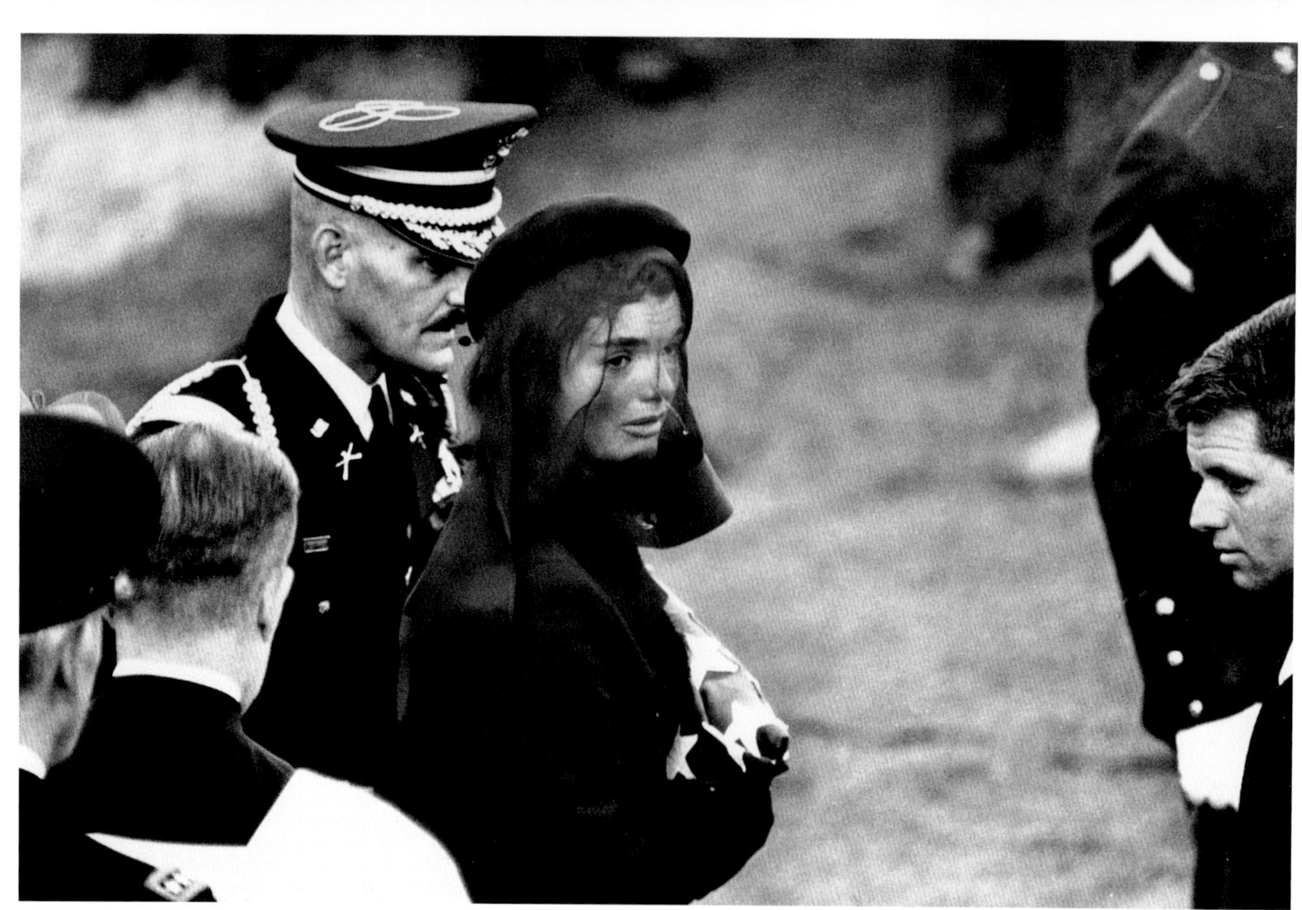

Jackie Kennedy, Arlington, Virginia, 1963

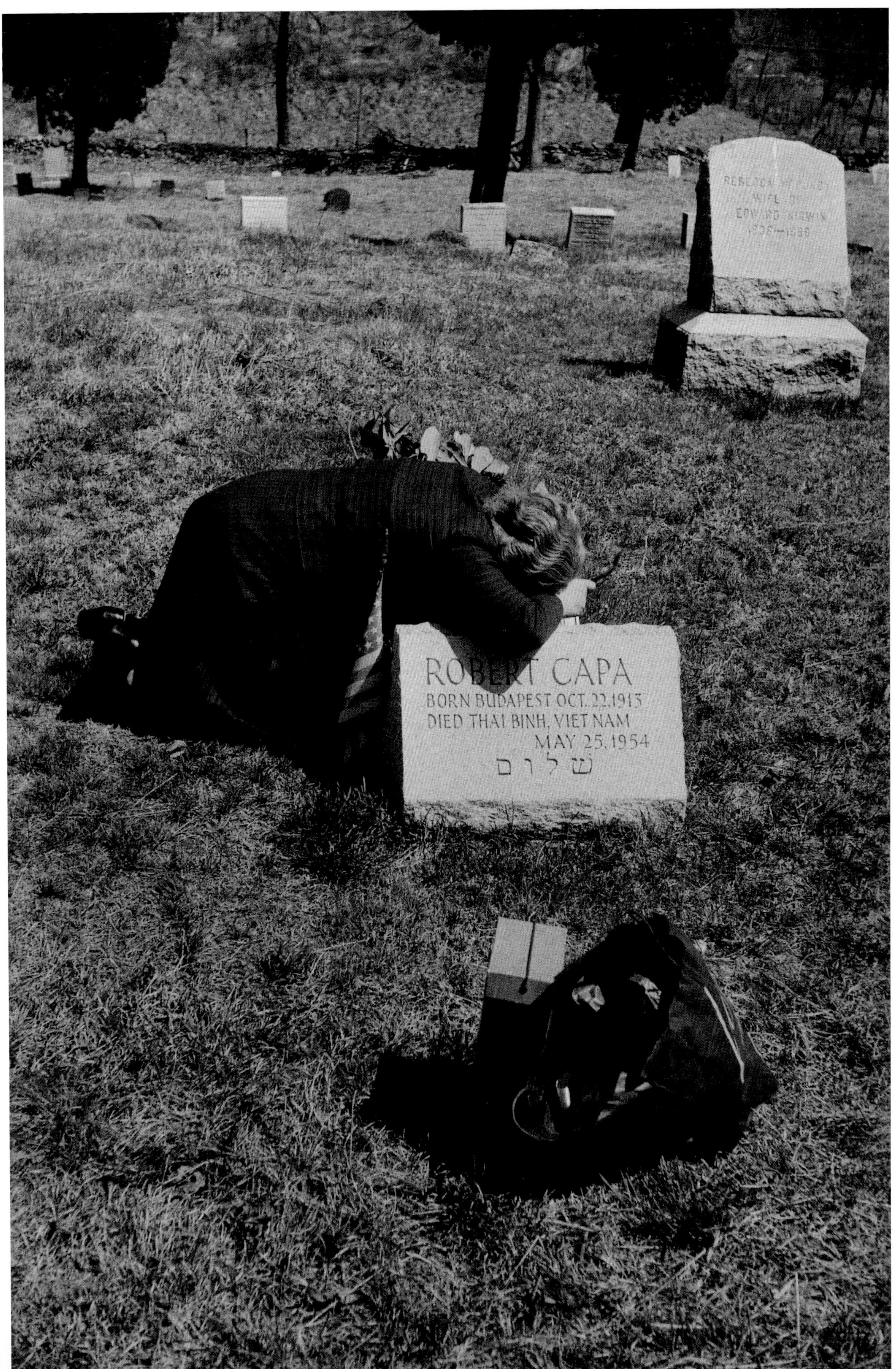
ROBERT CAPA
BORN BUDAPEST OCT. 22.1913
DIED THAI BINH, VIETNAM
MAY 25.1954
שלום

Robert Capa's mother, Julia, Armonk, New York, 1954

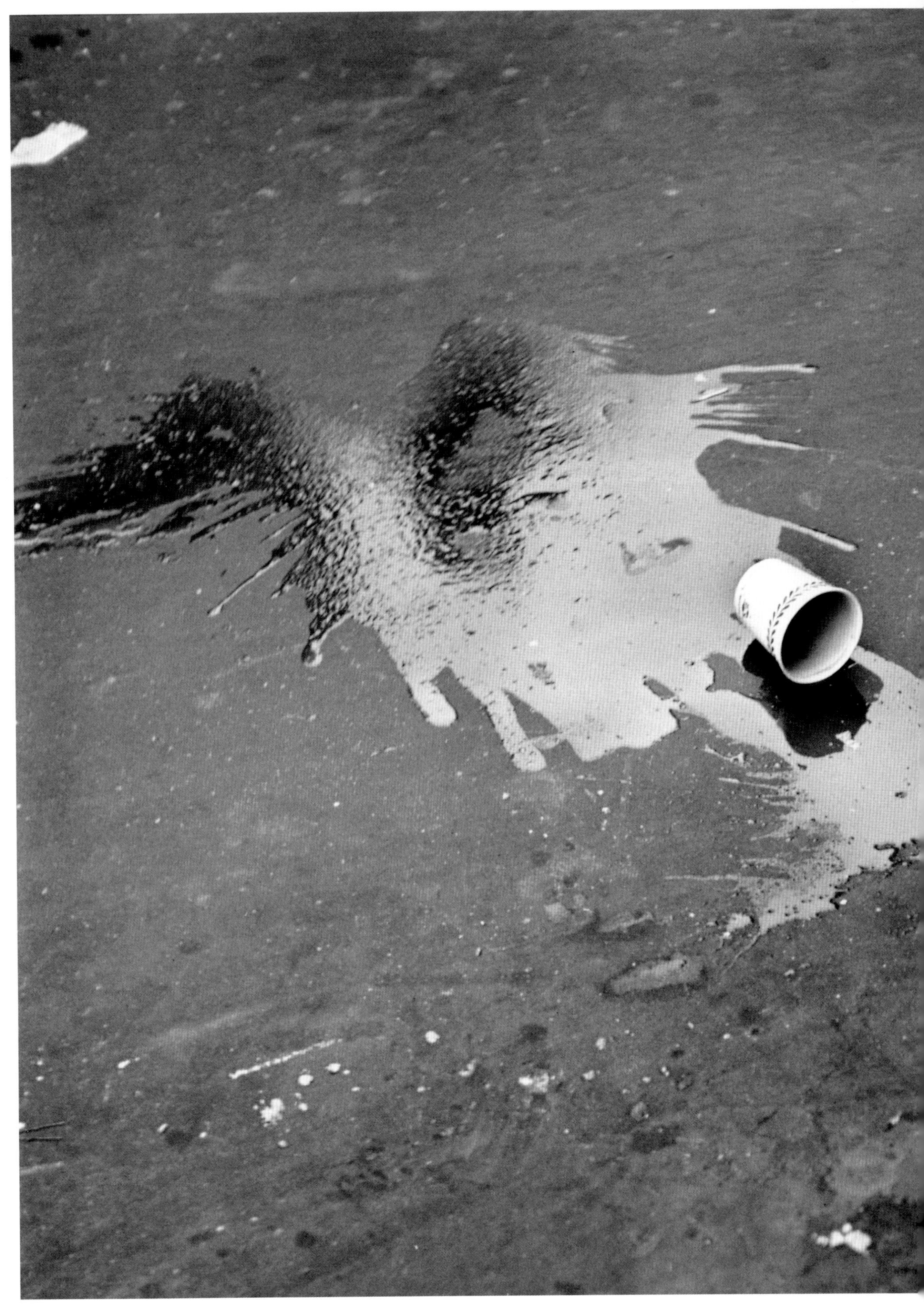

New York, c.1950

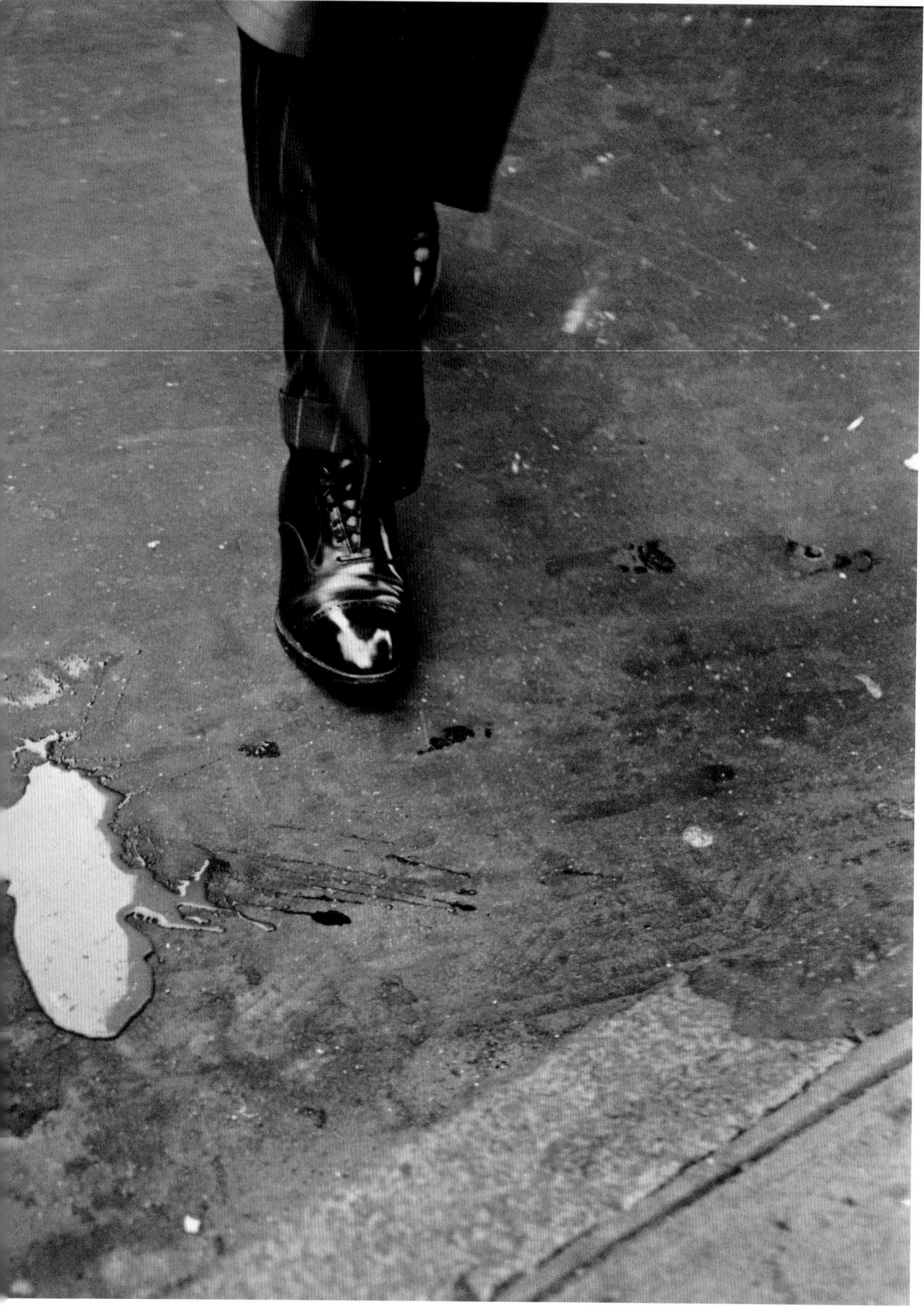

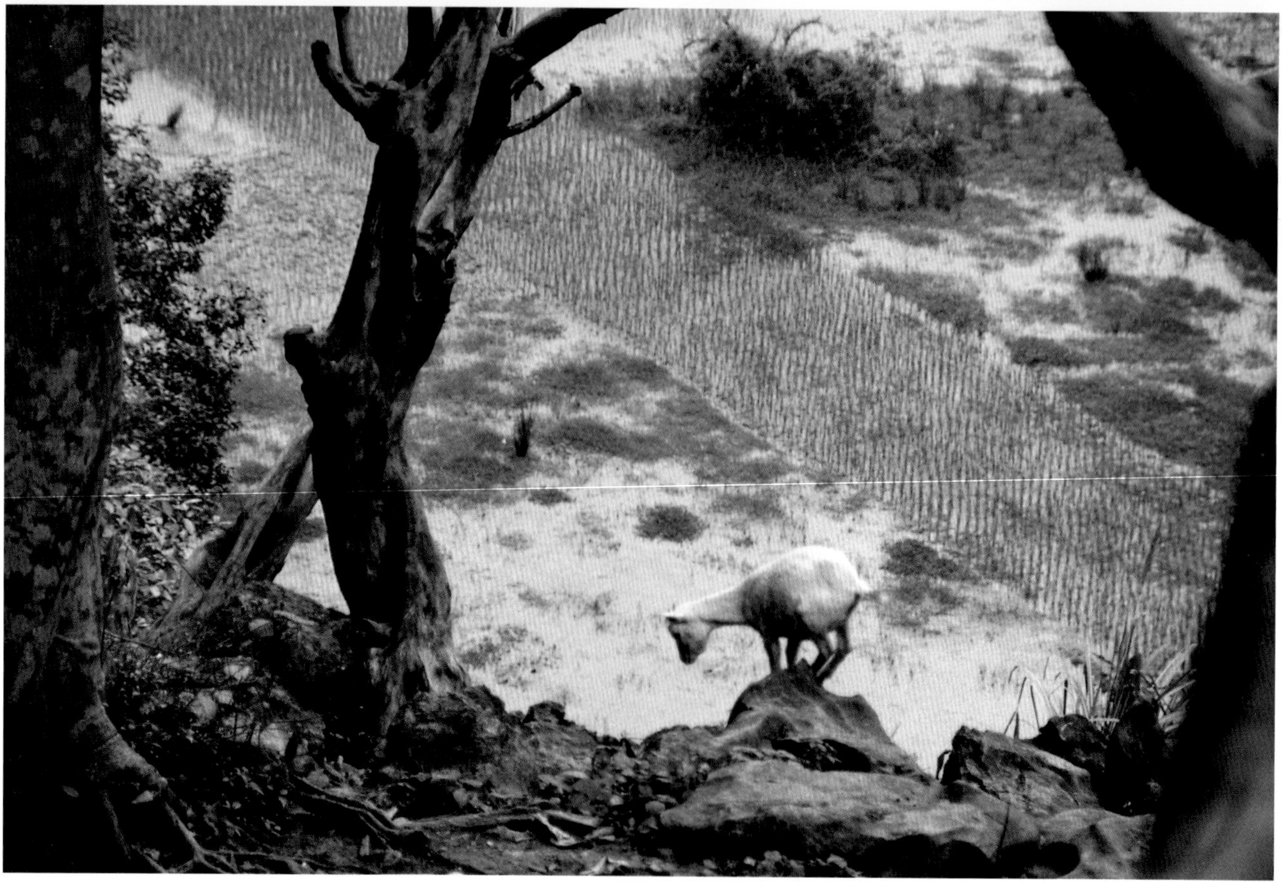

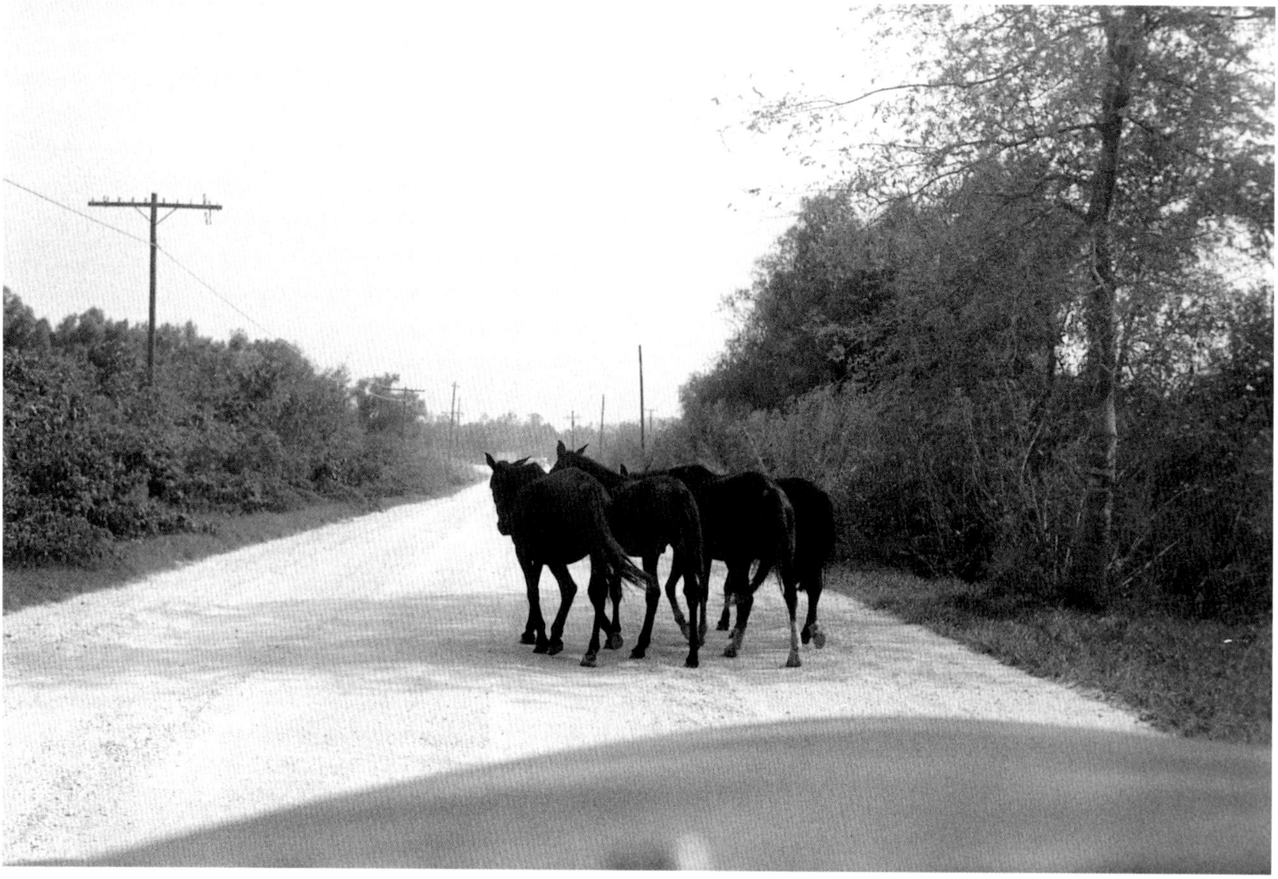

Vietnam, 1994 / *Mississippi Delta, 1950*
overleaf *Paris, 1989*

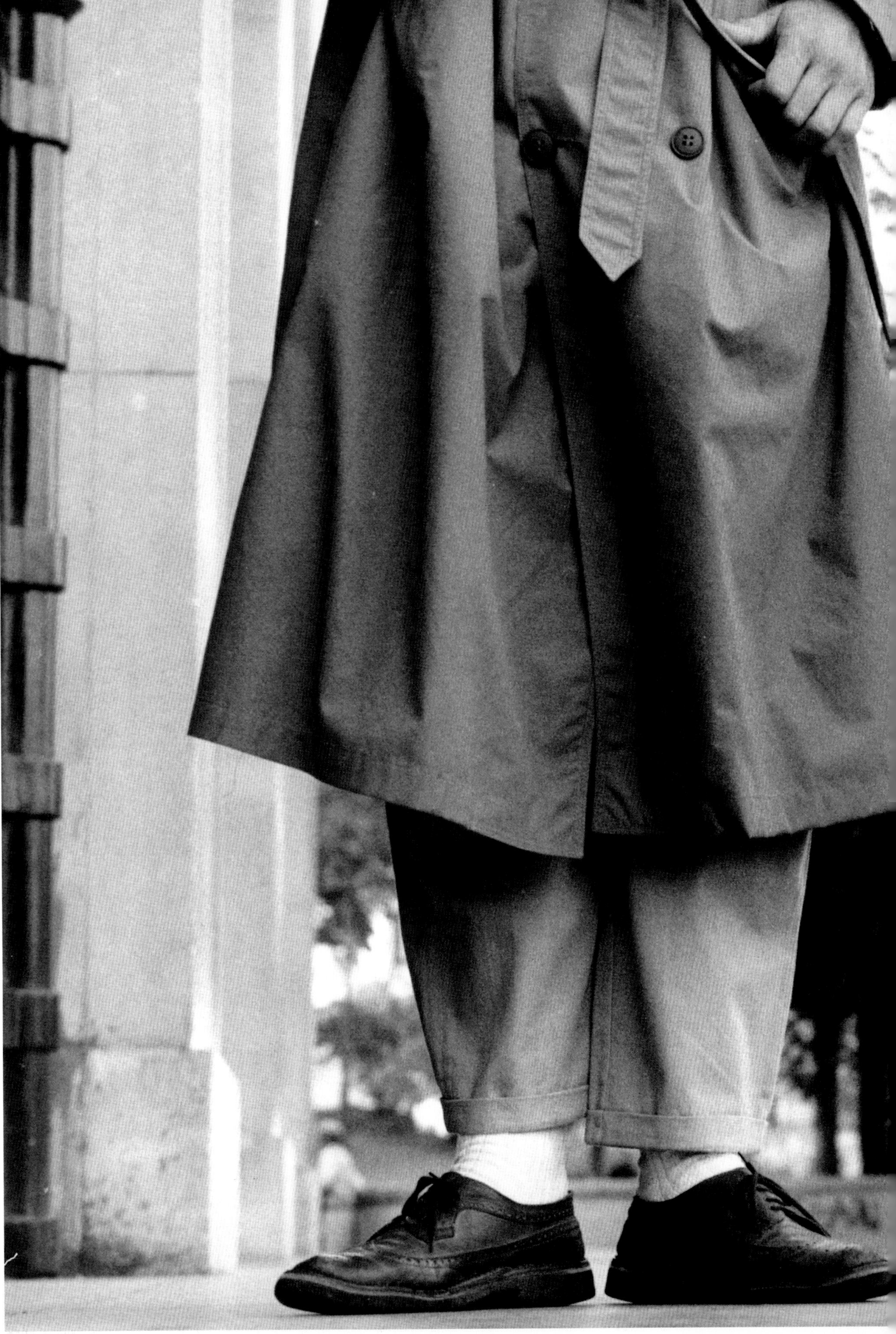

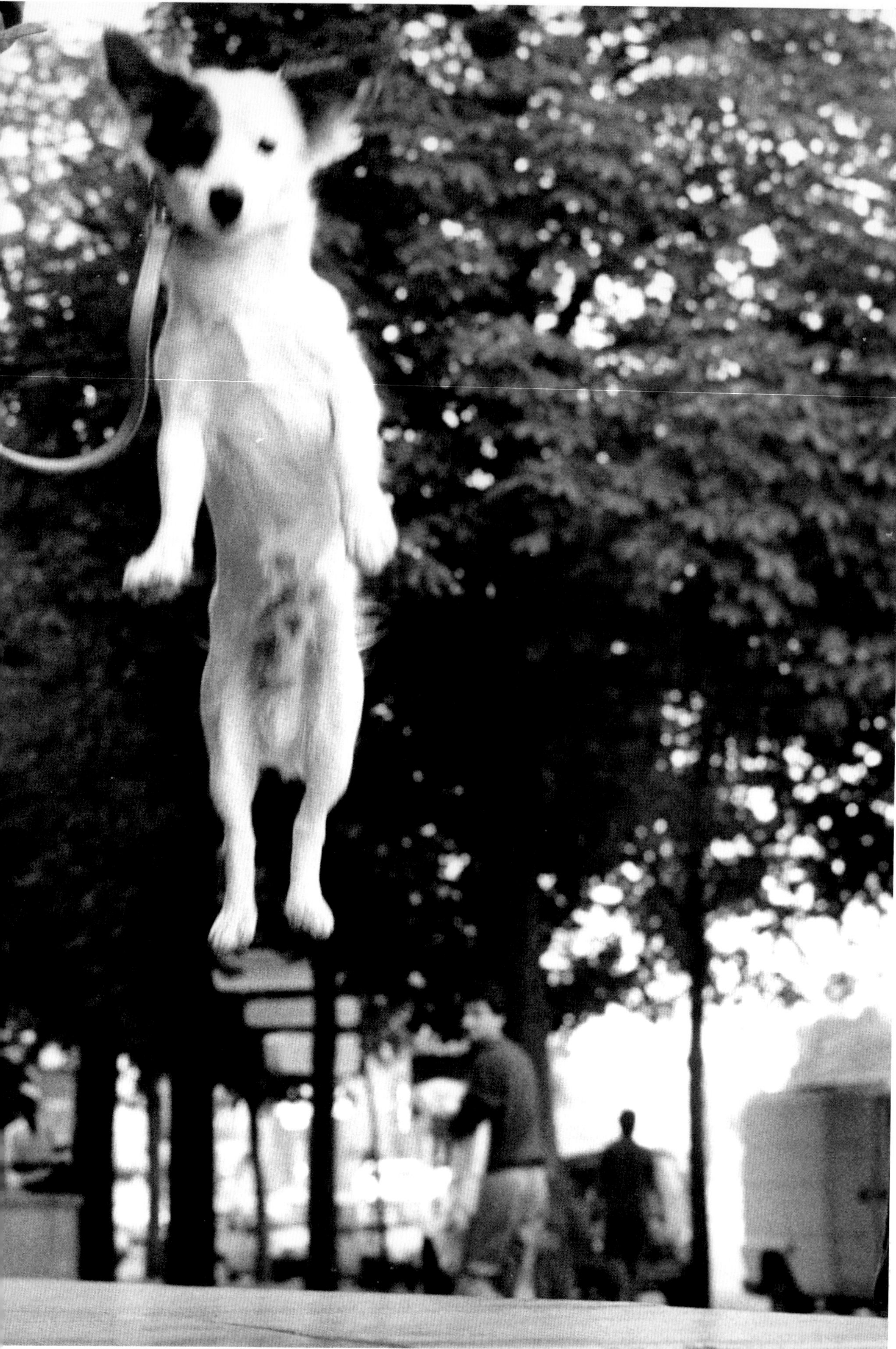

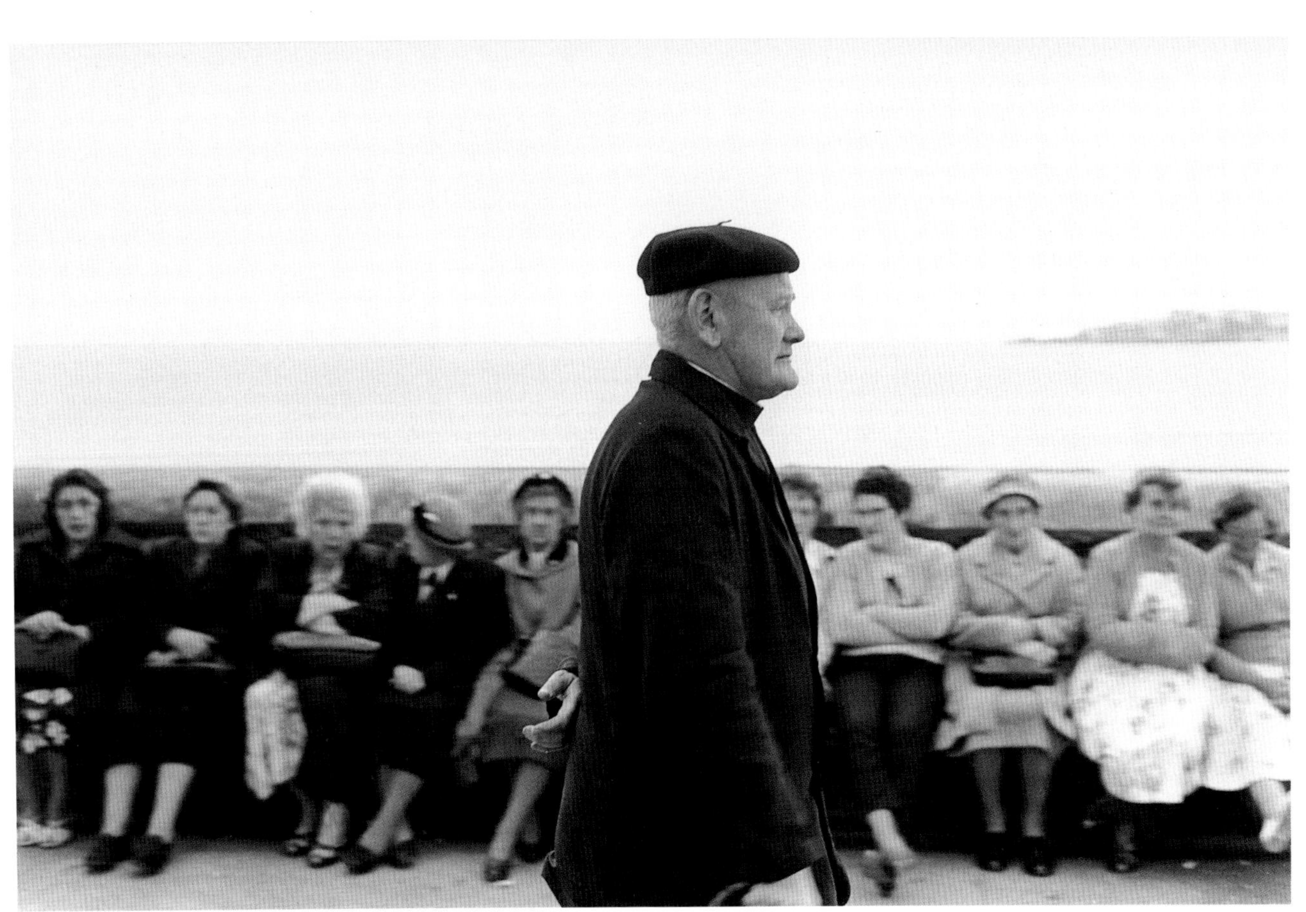

Blackpool, England, 1964

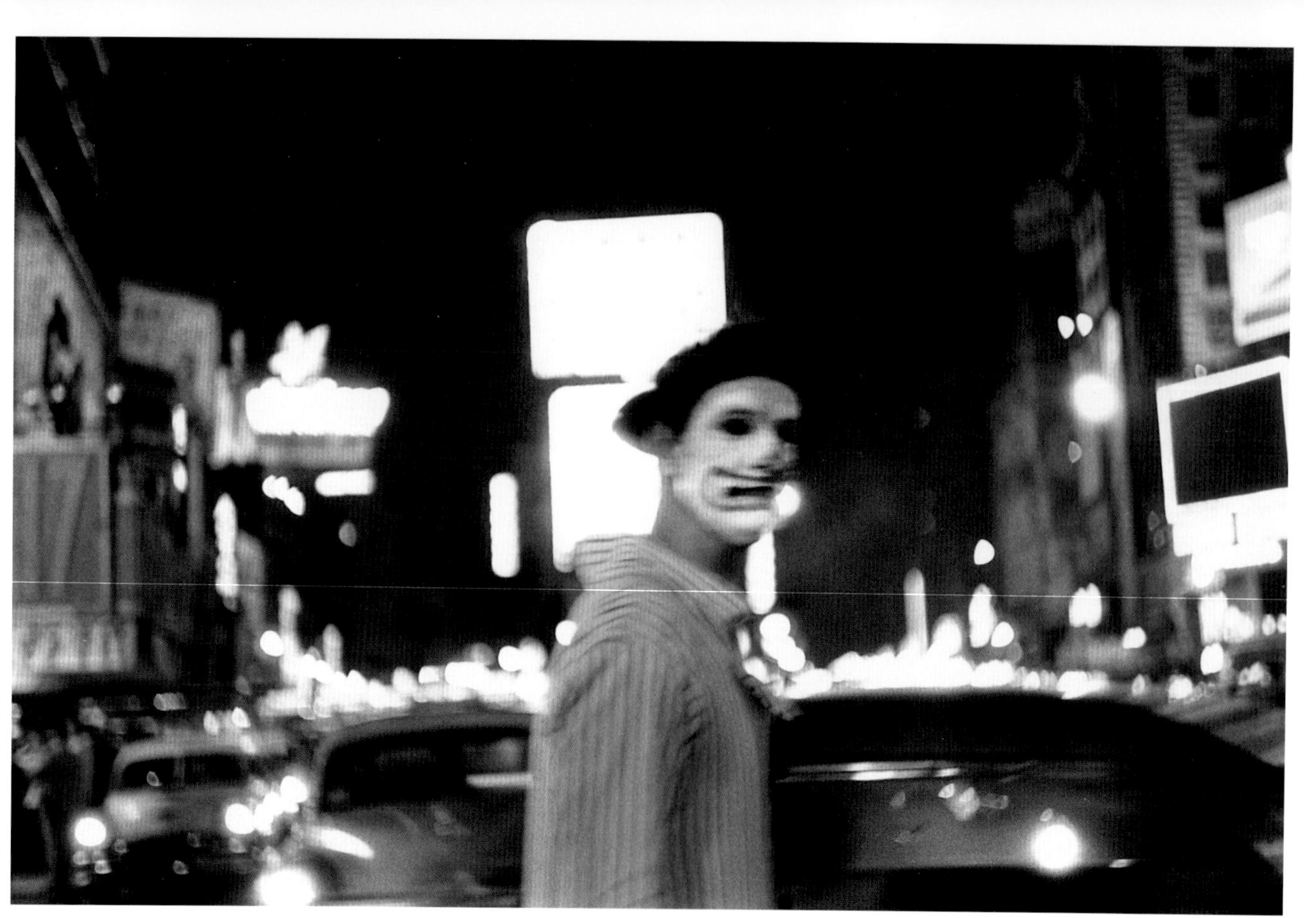

Times Square, New York, 1953

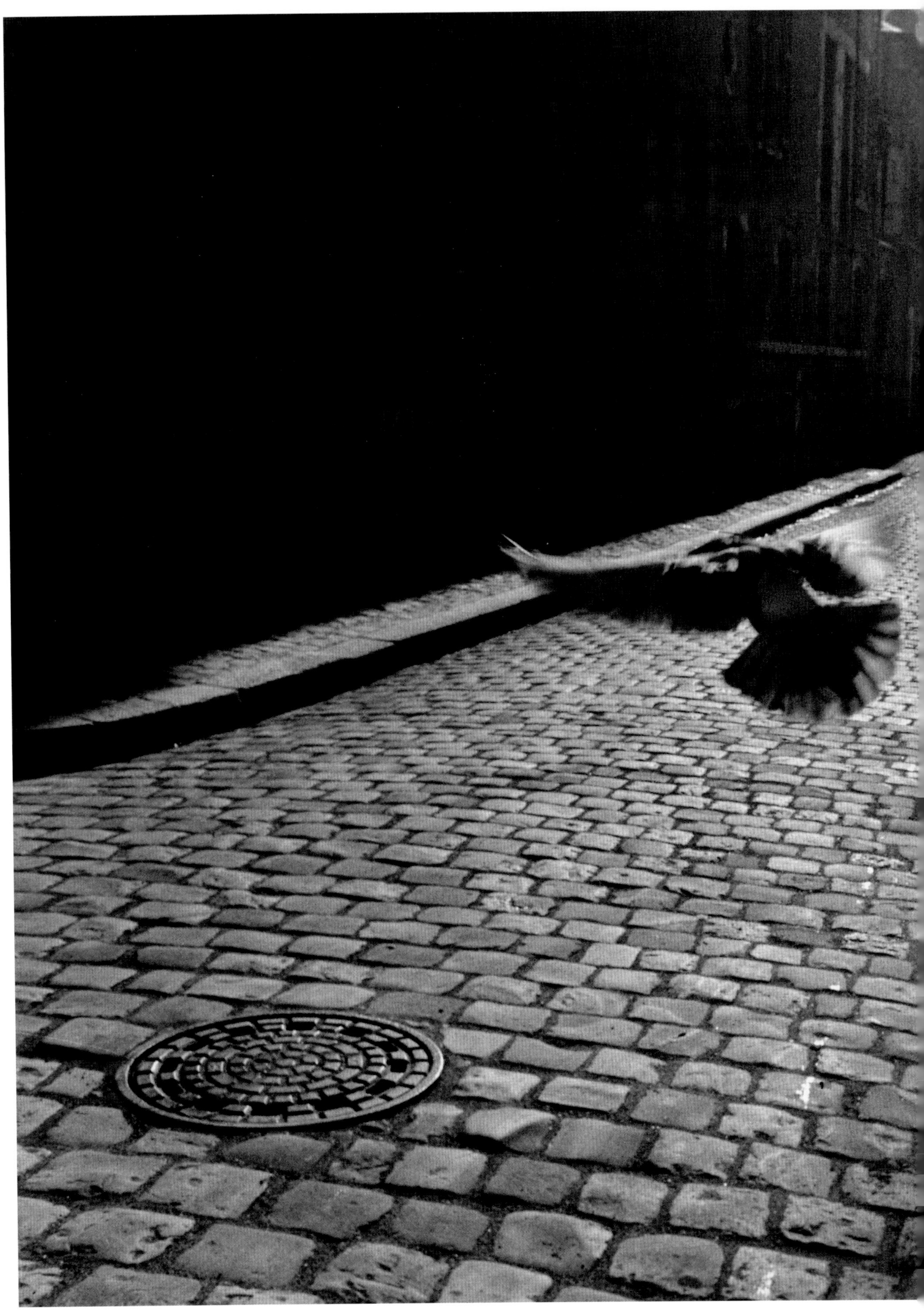

Orléans, France, 1952

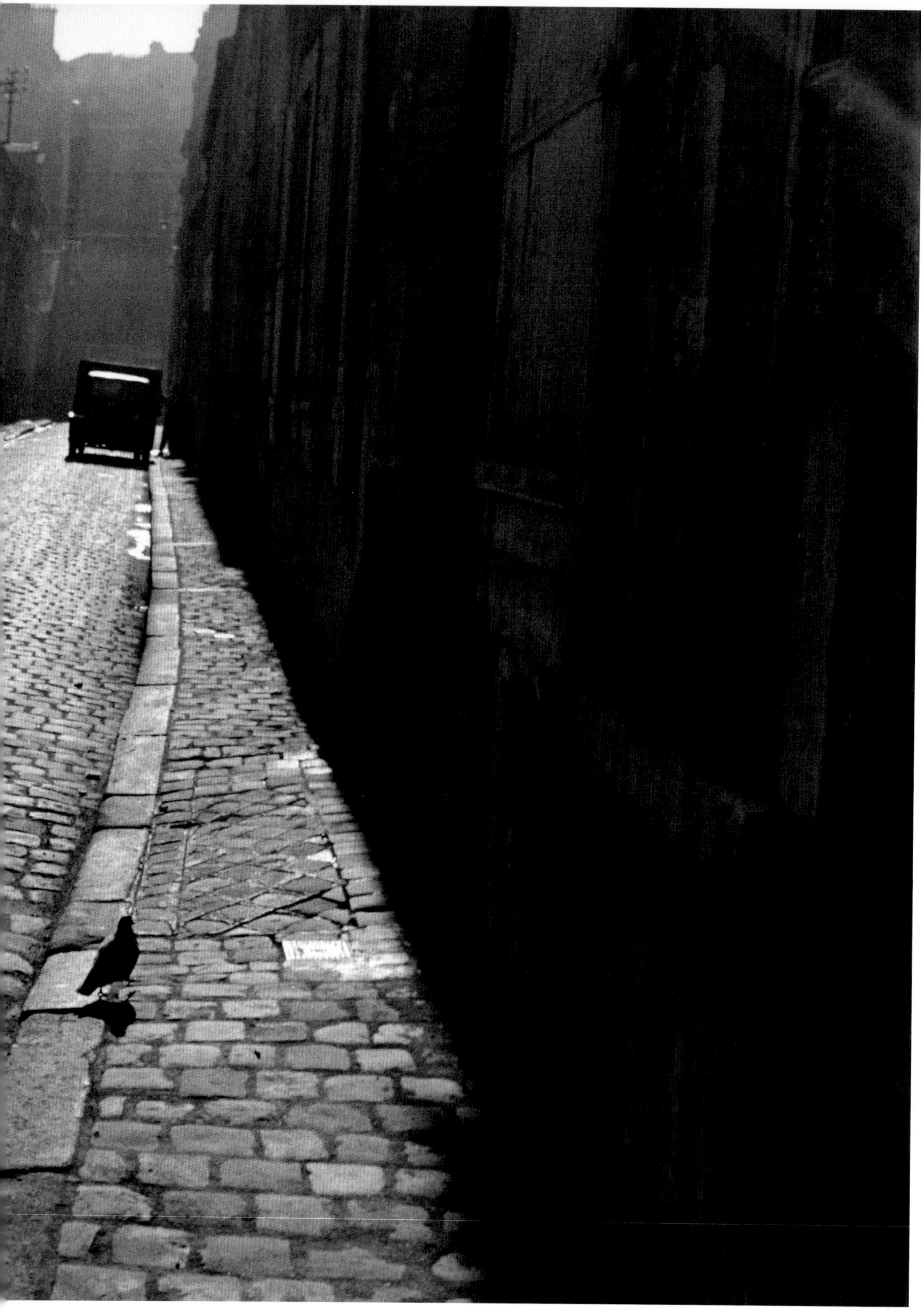

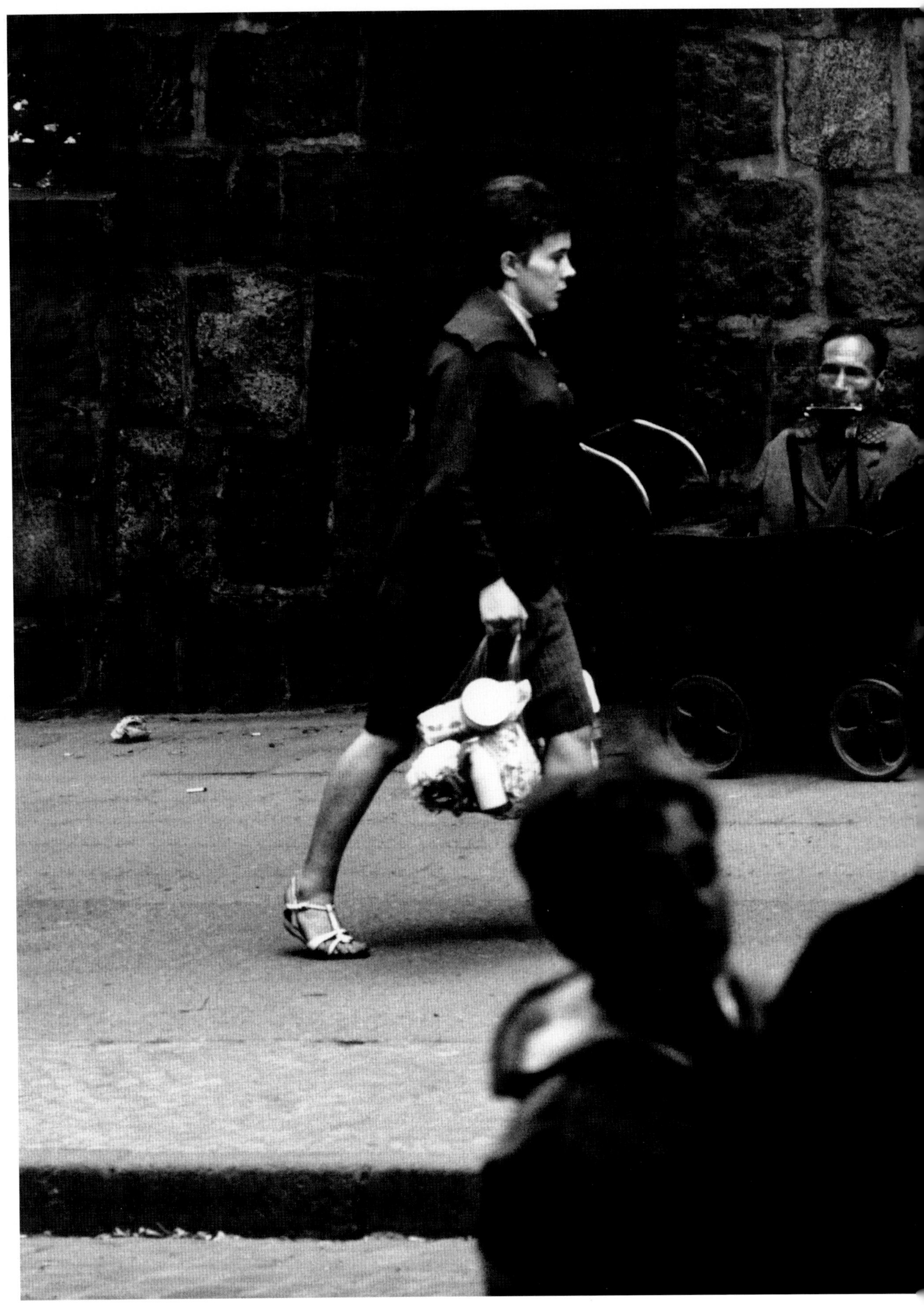

Gdansk, Poland, 1964

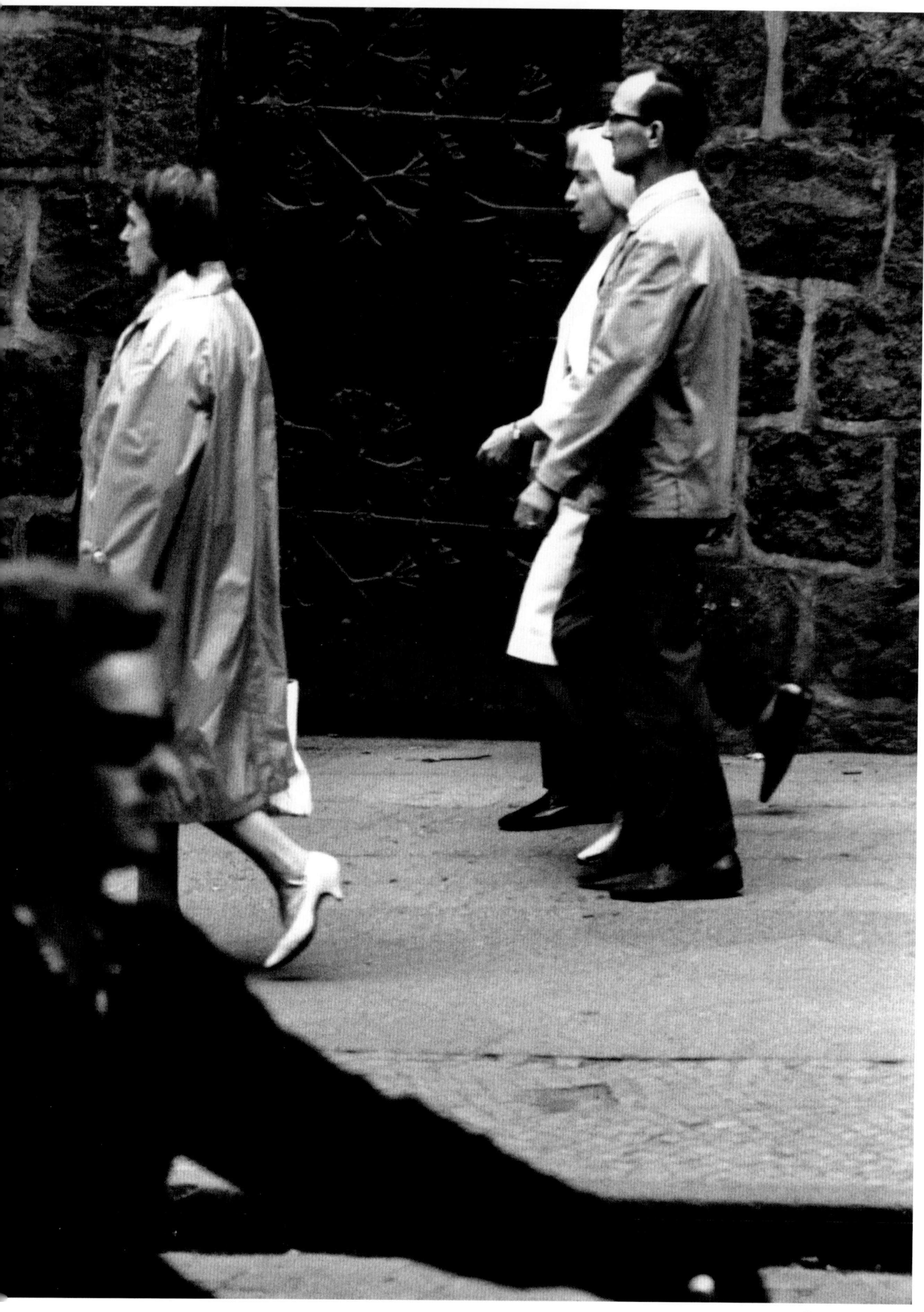

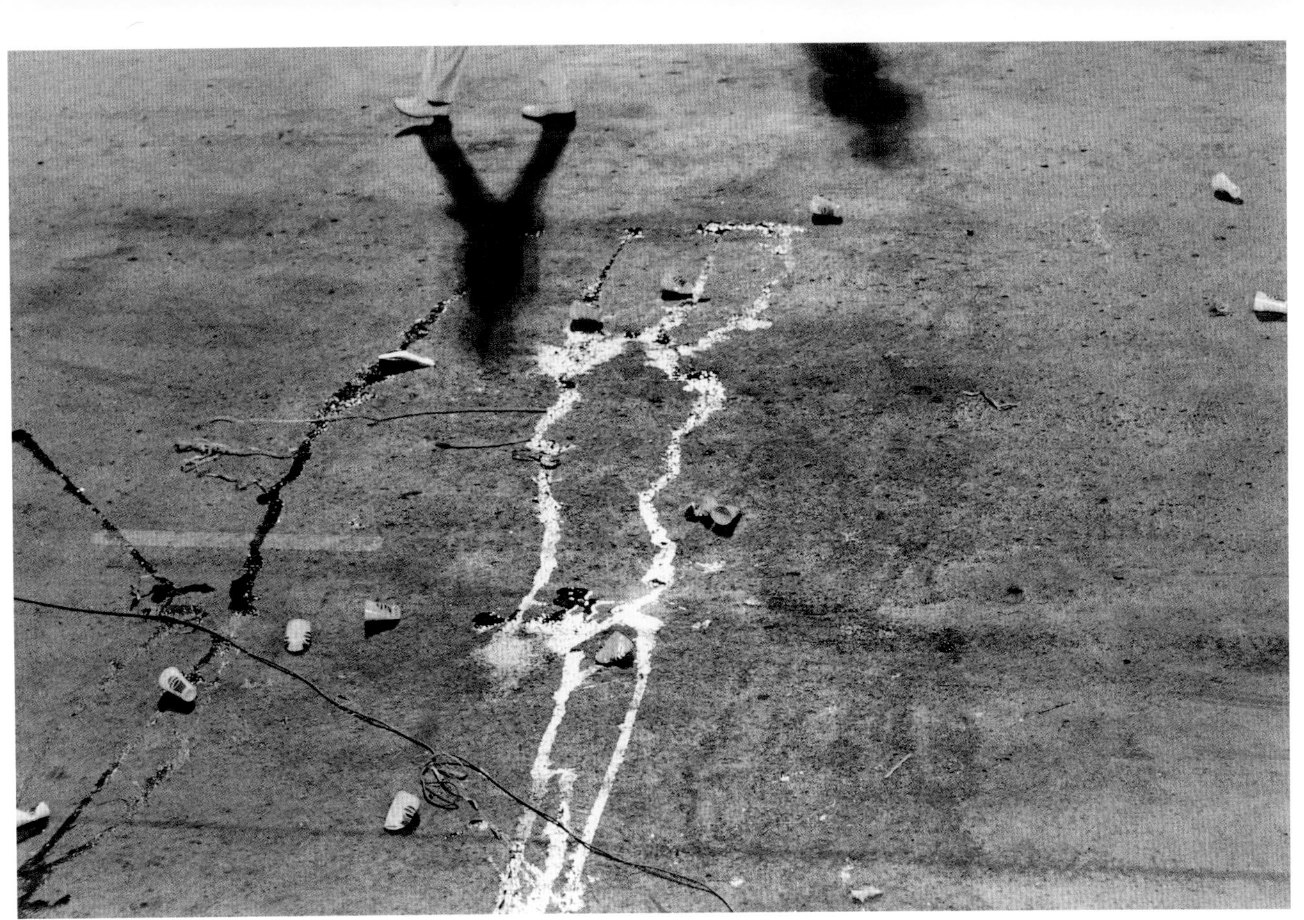

Rio de Janeiro, 1986

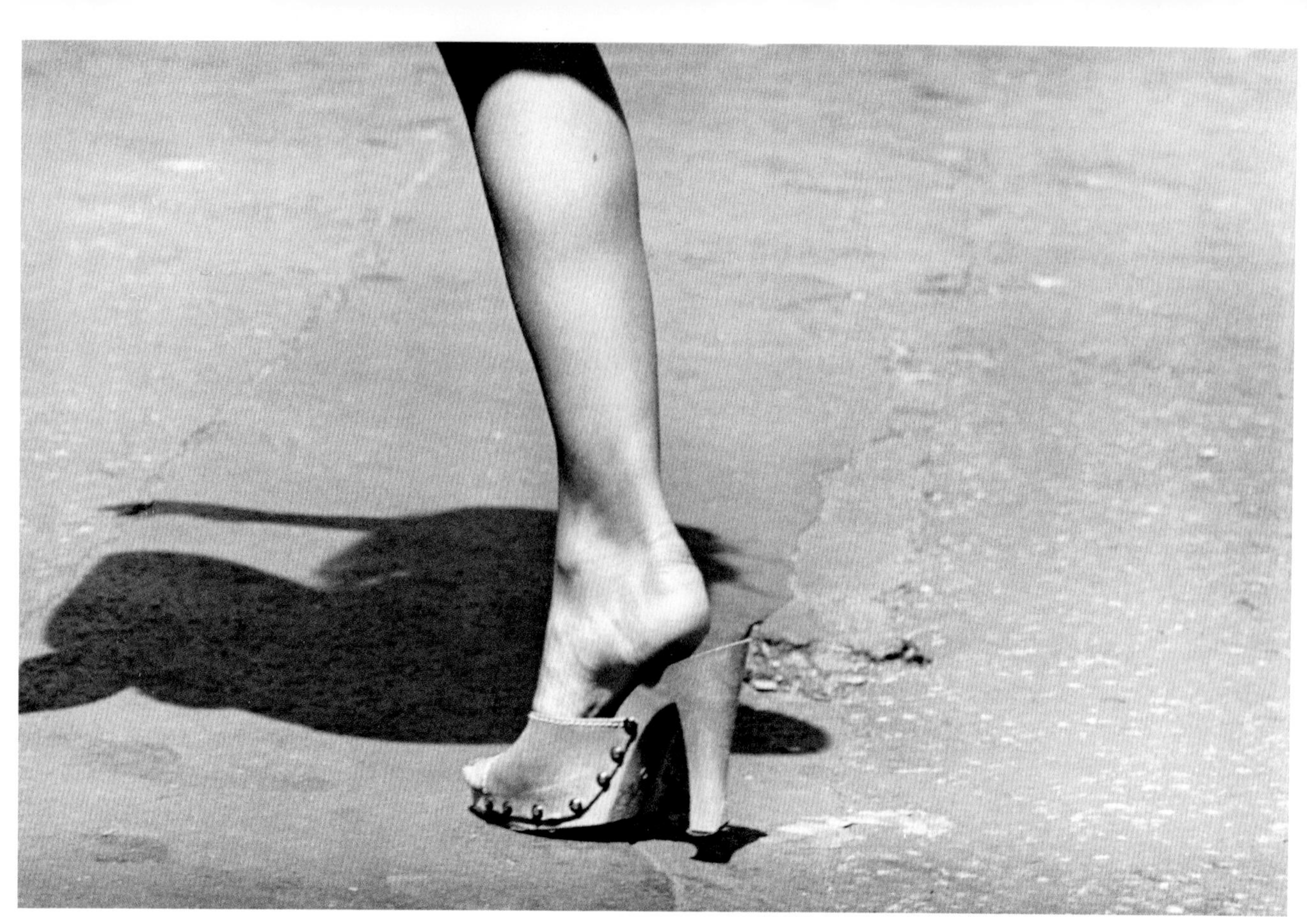

St Tropez, France, 1978

Salvador da Bahia, Brazil, 1963

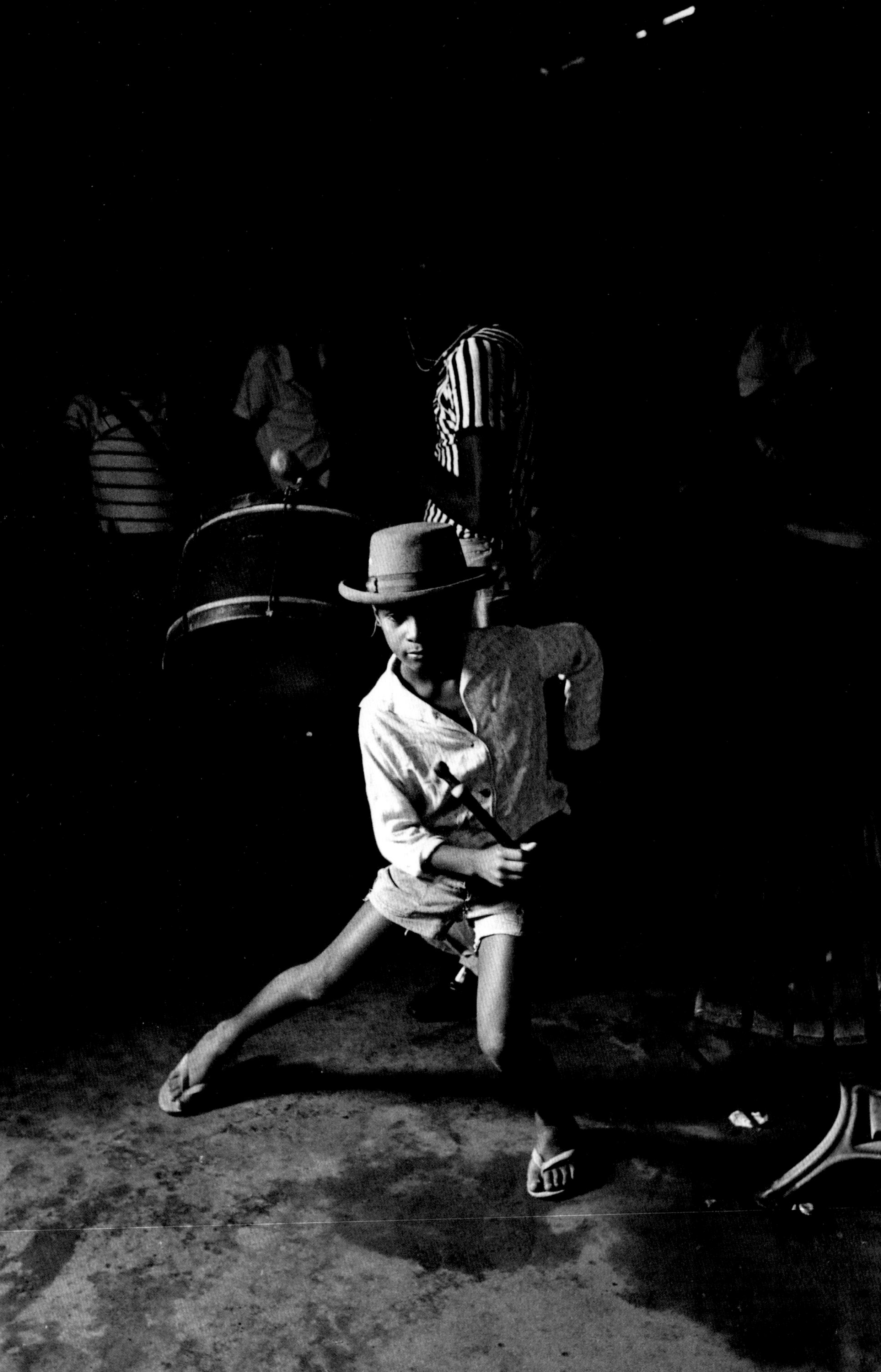

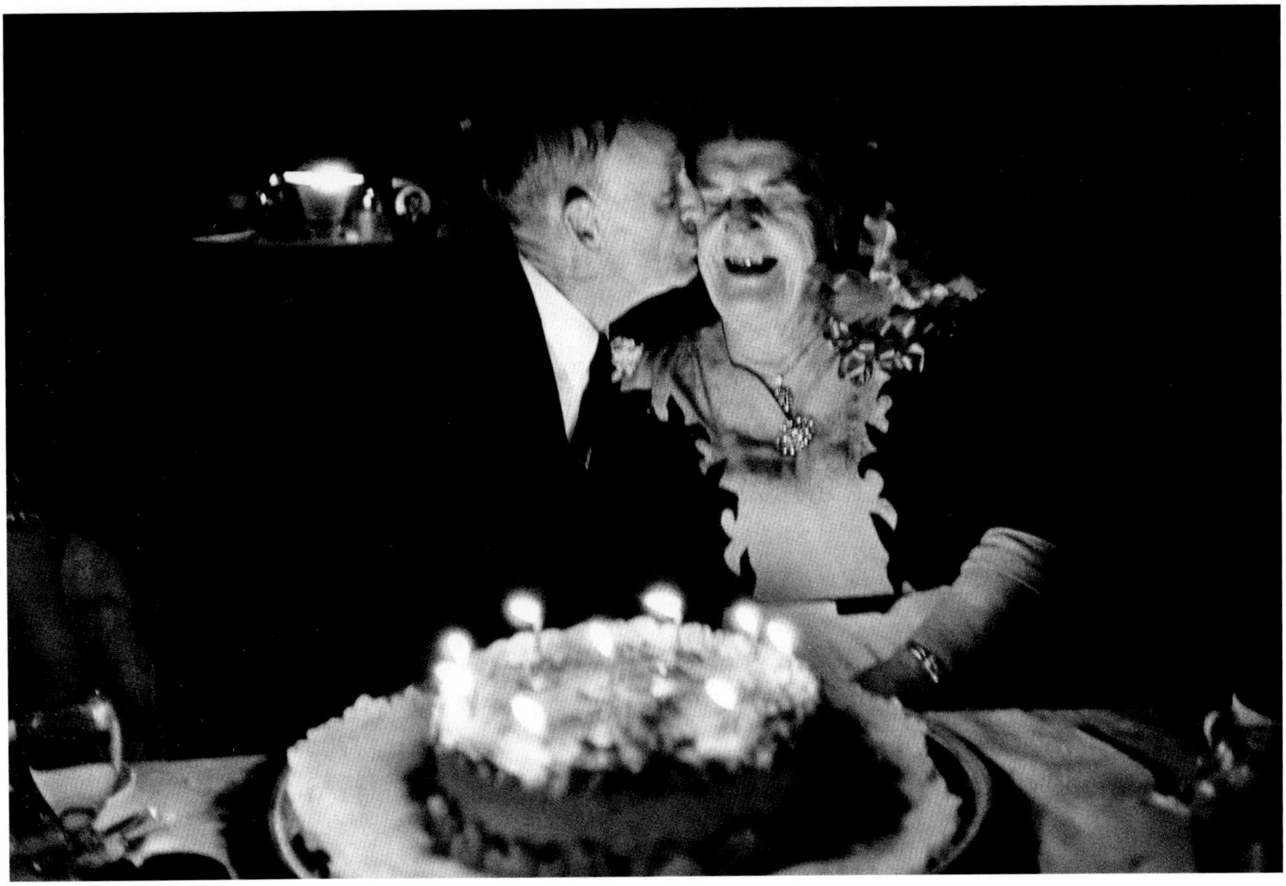

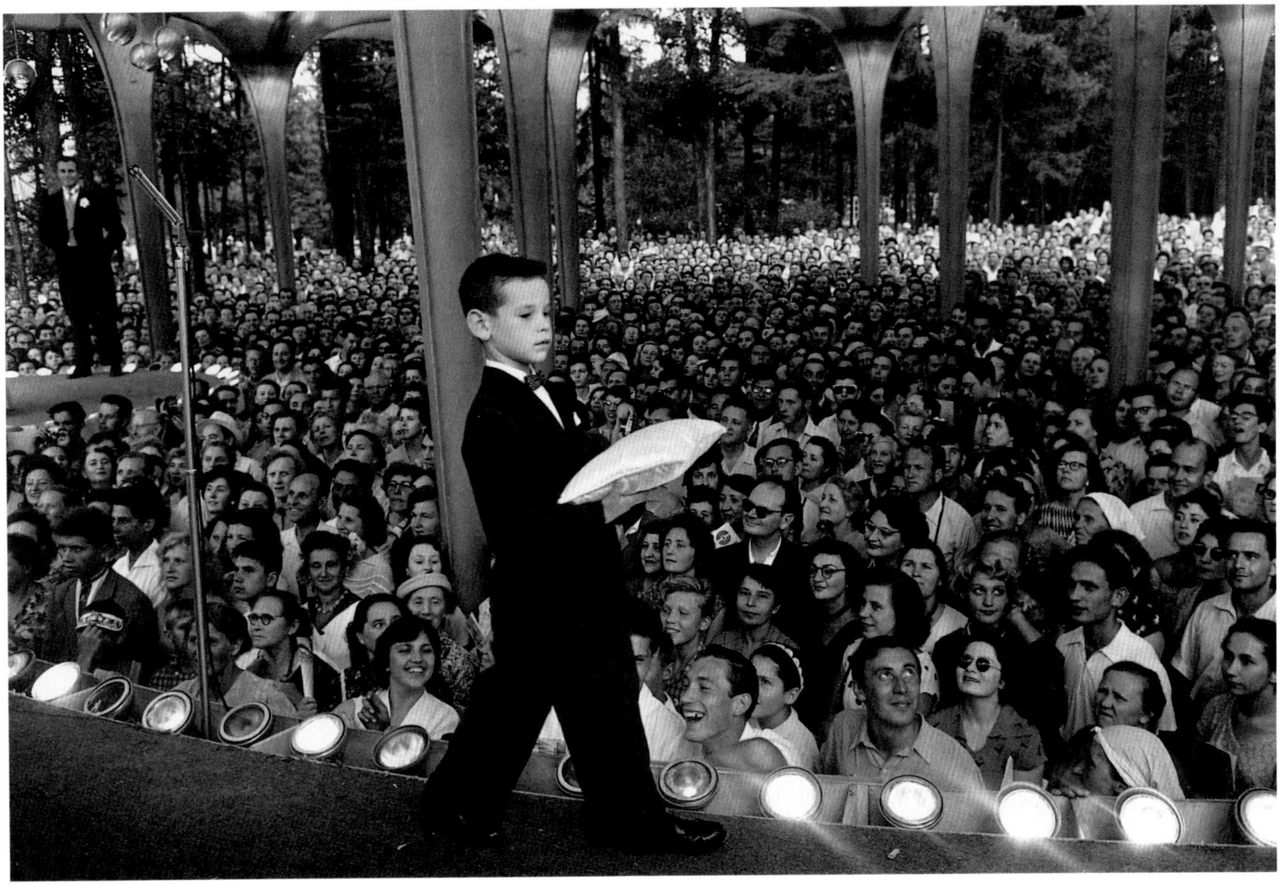

New York, 1955 / *Moscow, 1959*

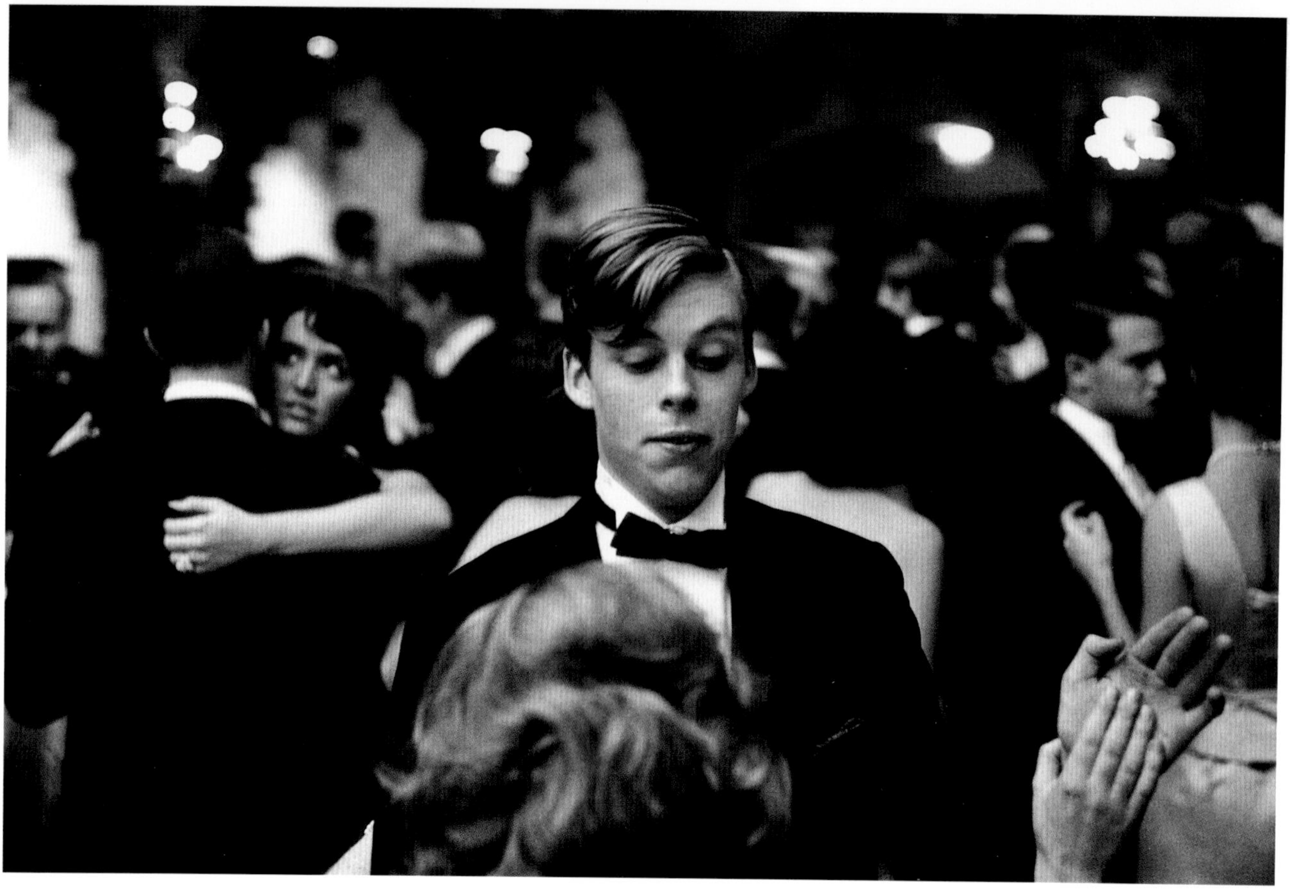

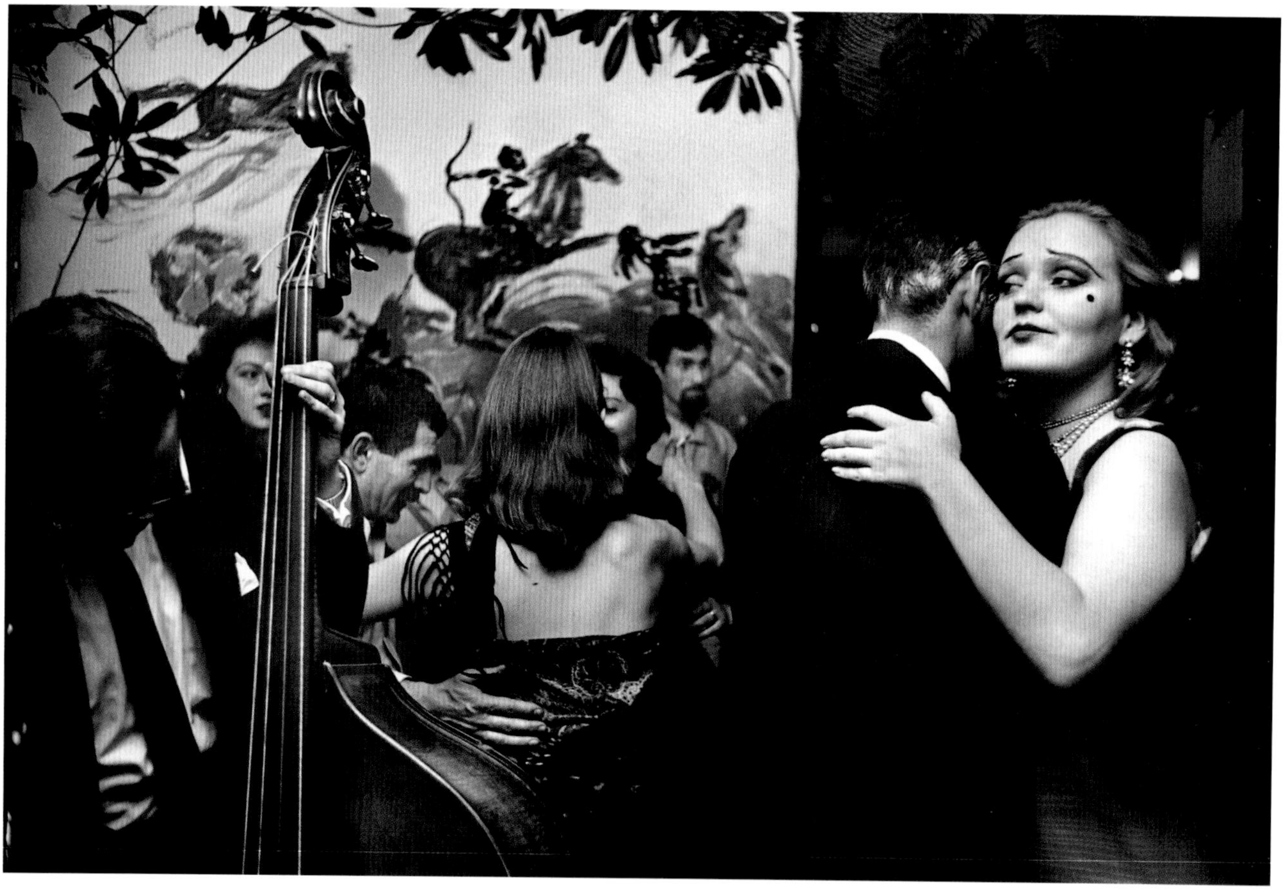

New York, 1962 / *New York, 1945*

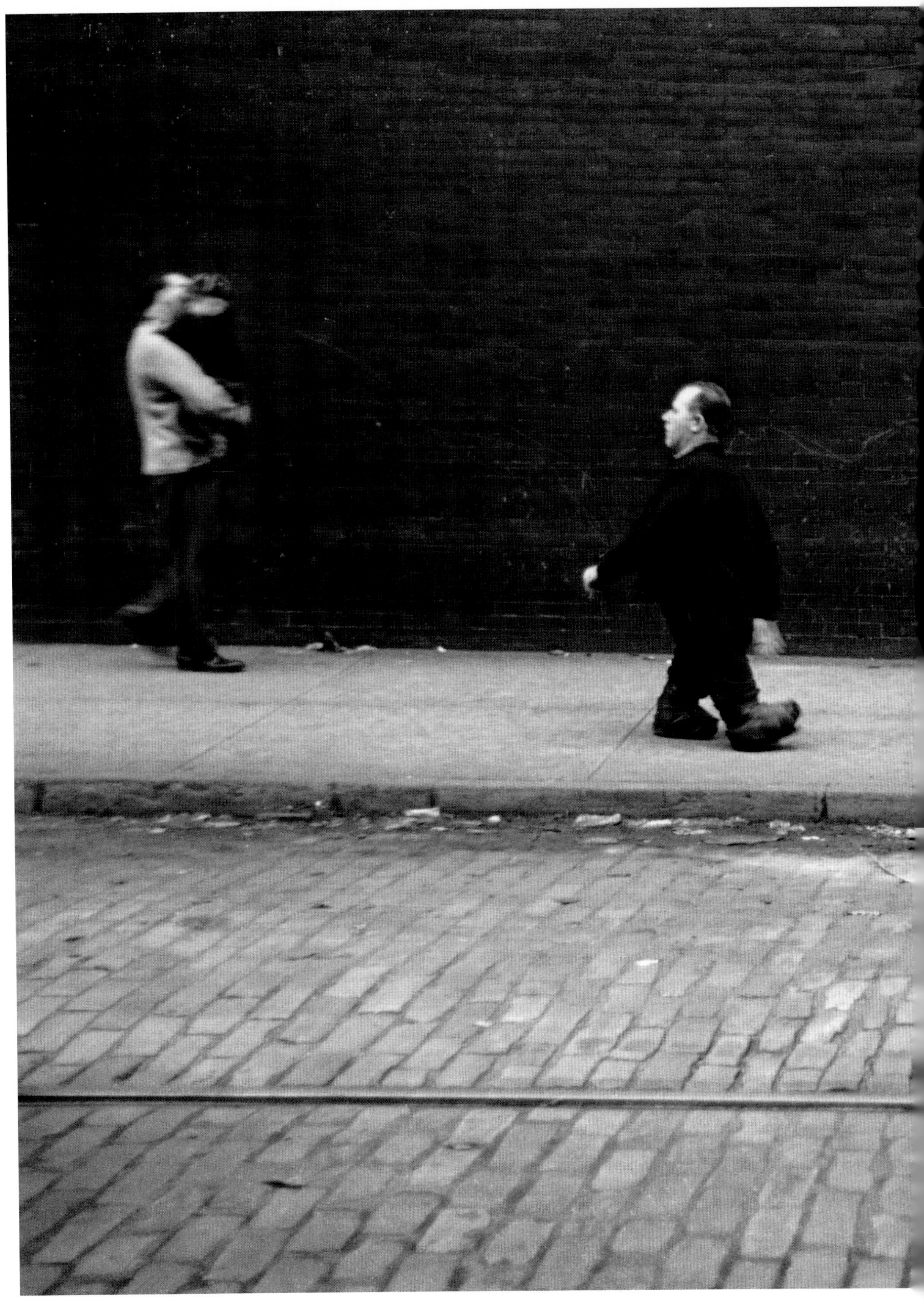

Pittsburgh, Pennsylvania, 1950

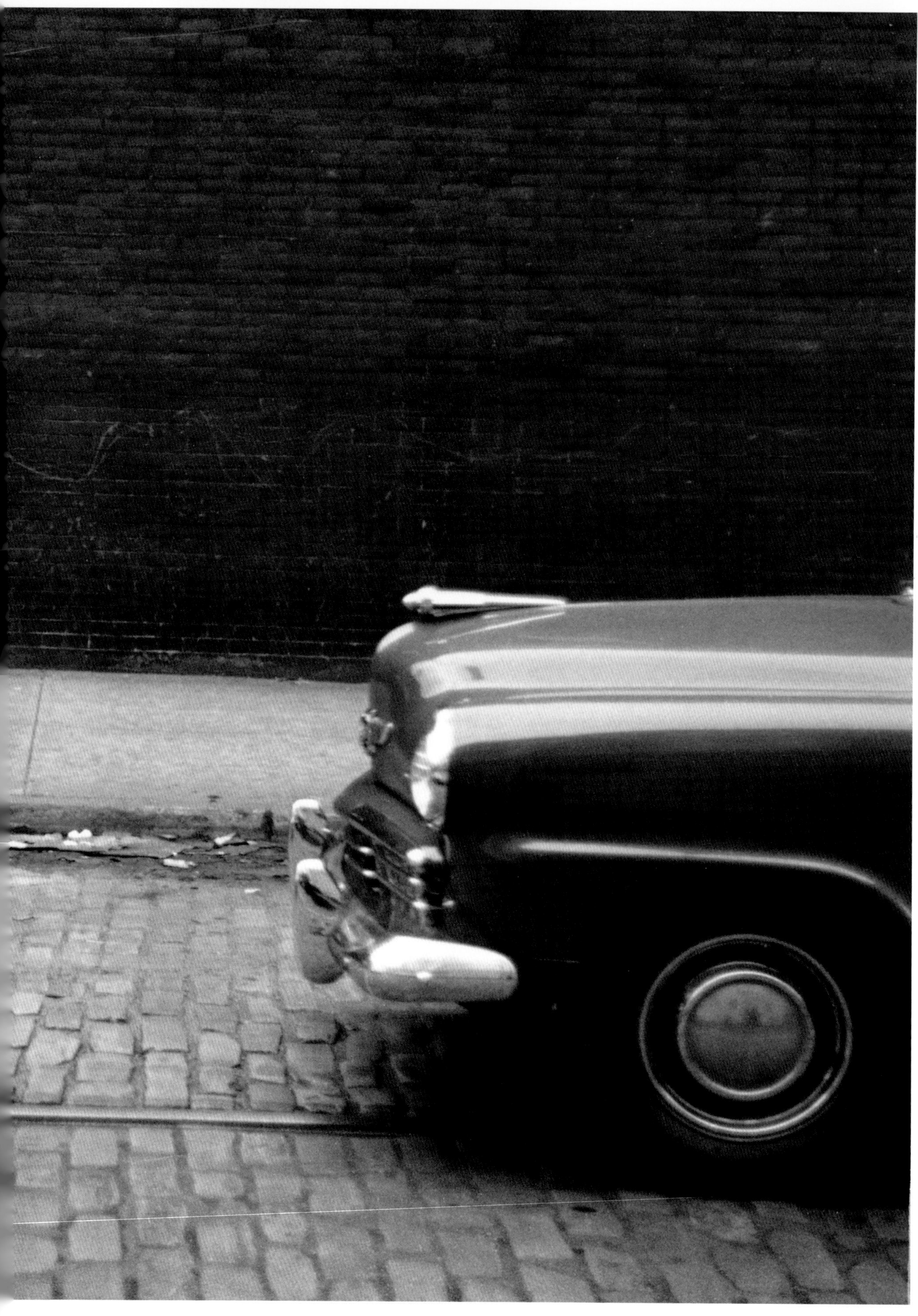

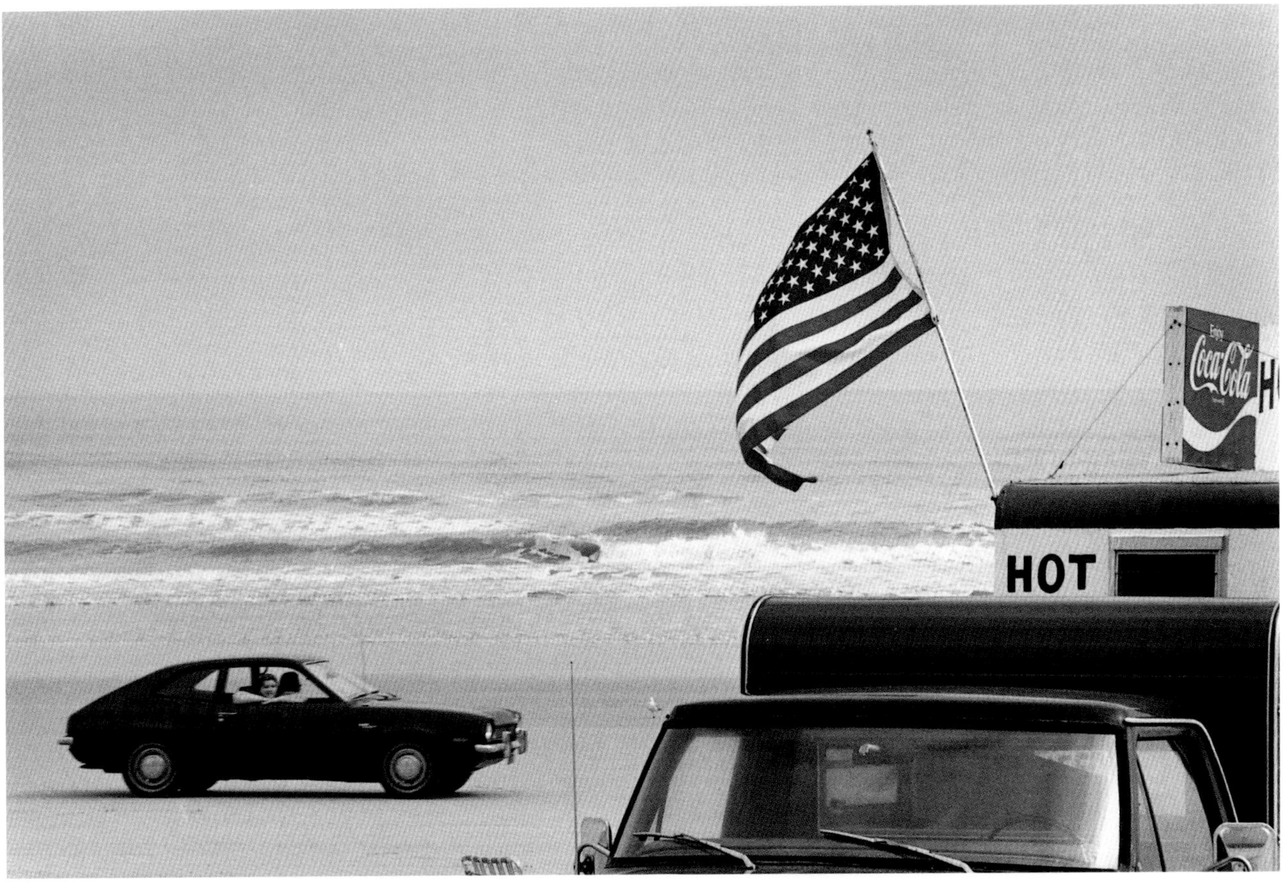

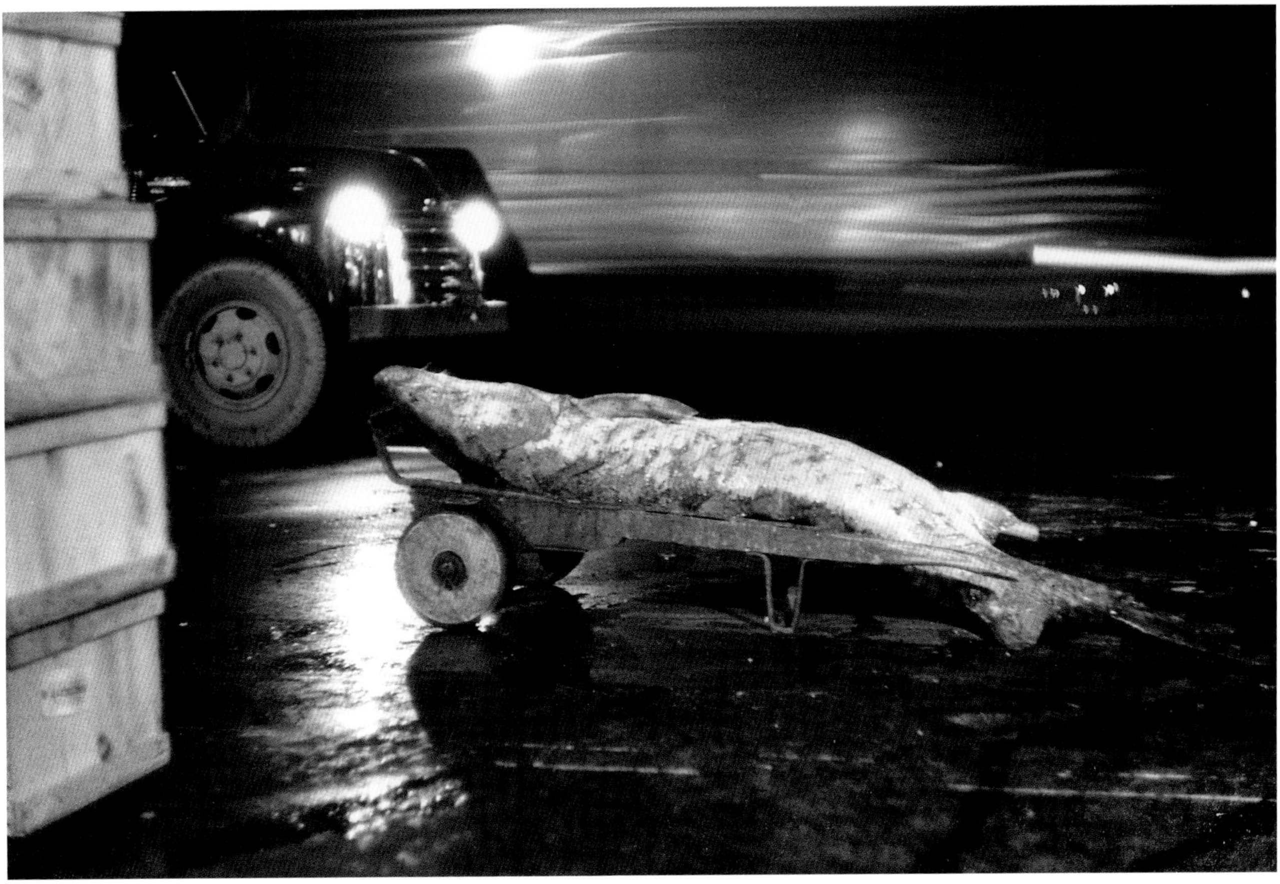

Daytona Beach, Florida, 1975 / *New York, 1953*

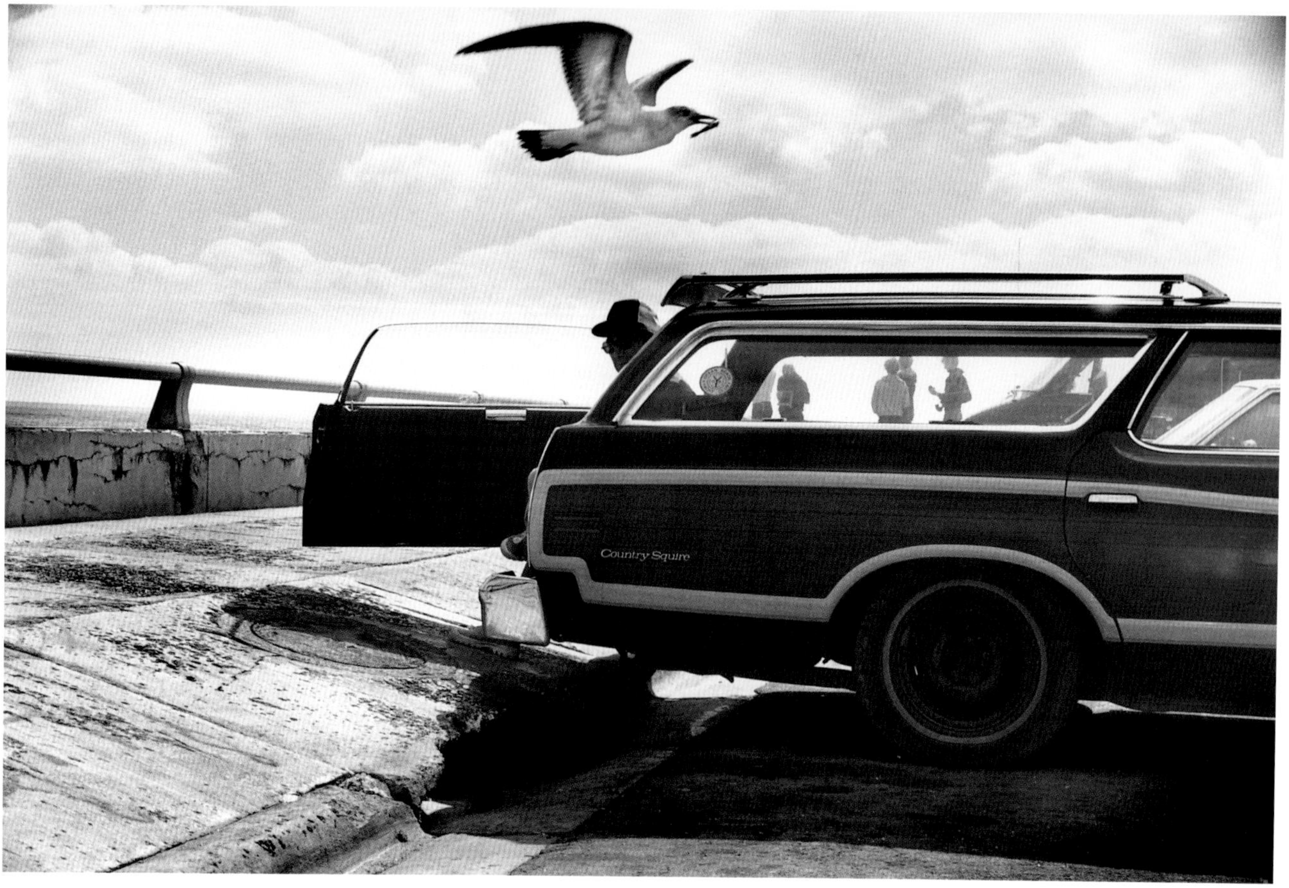

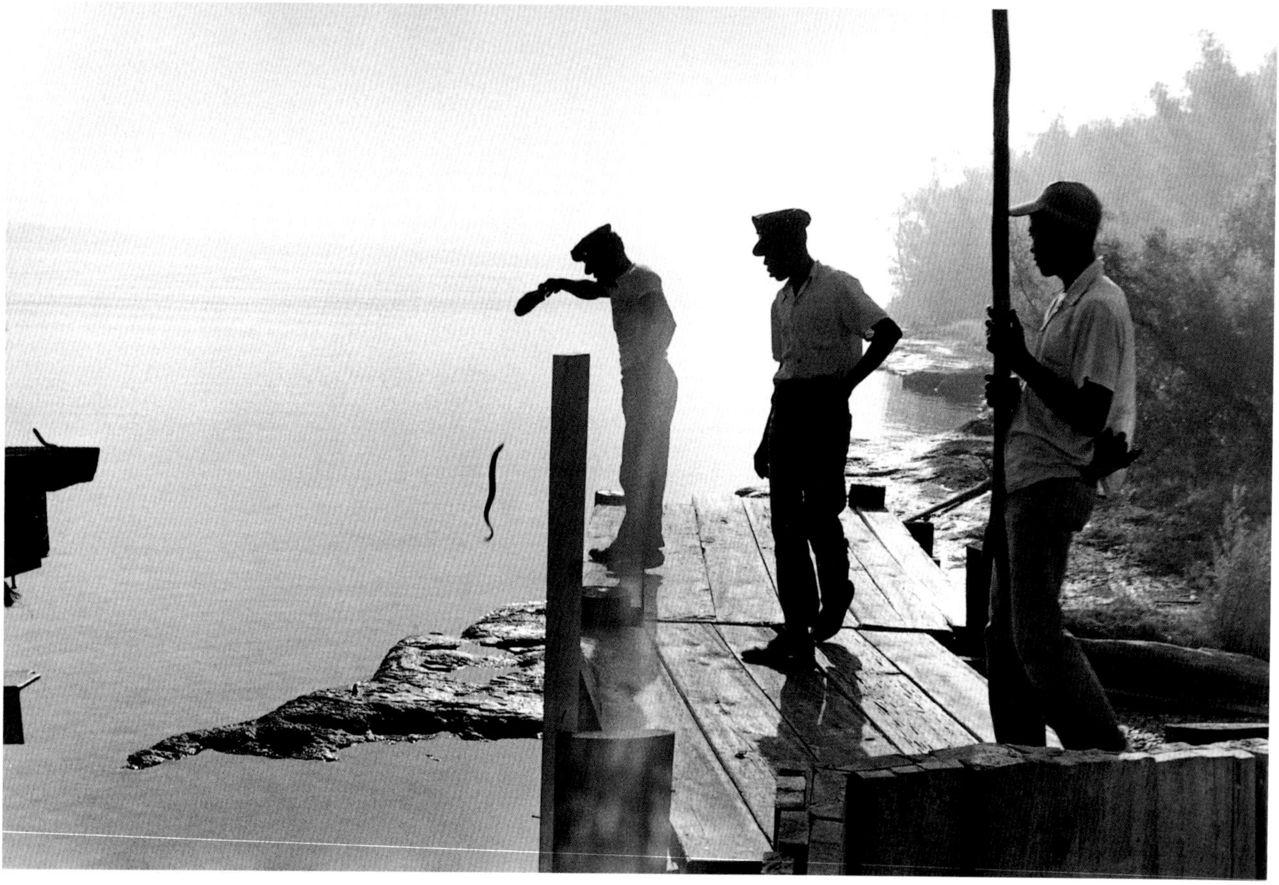

Key West, Florida, 1980 / Mississippi Delta, 1950

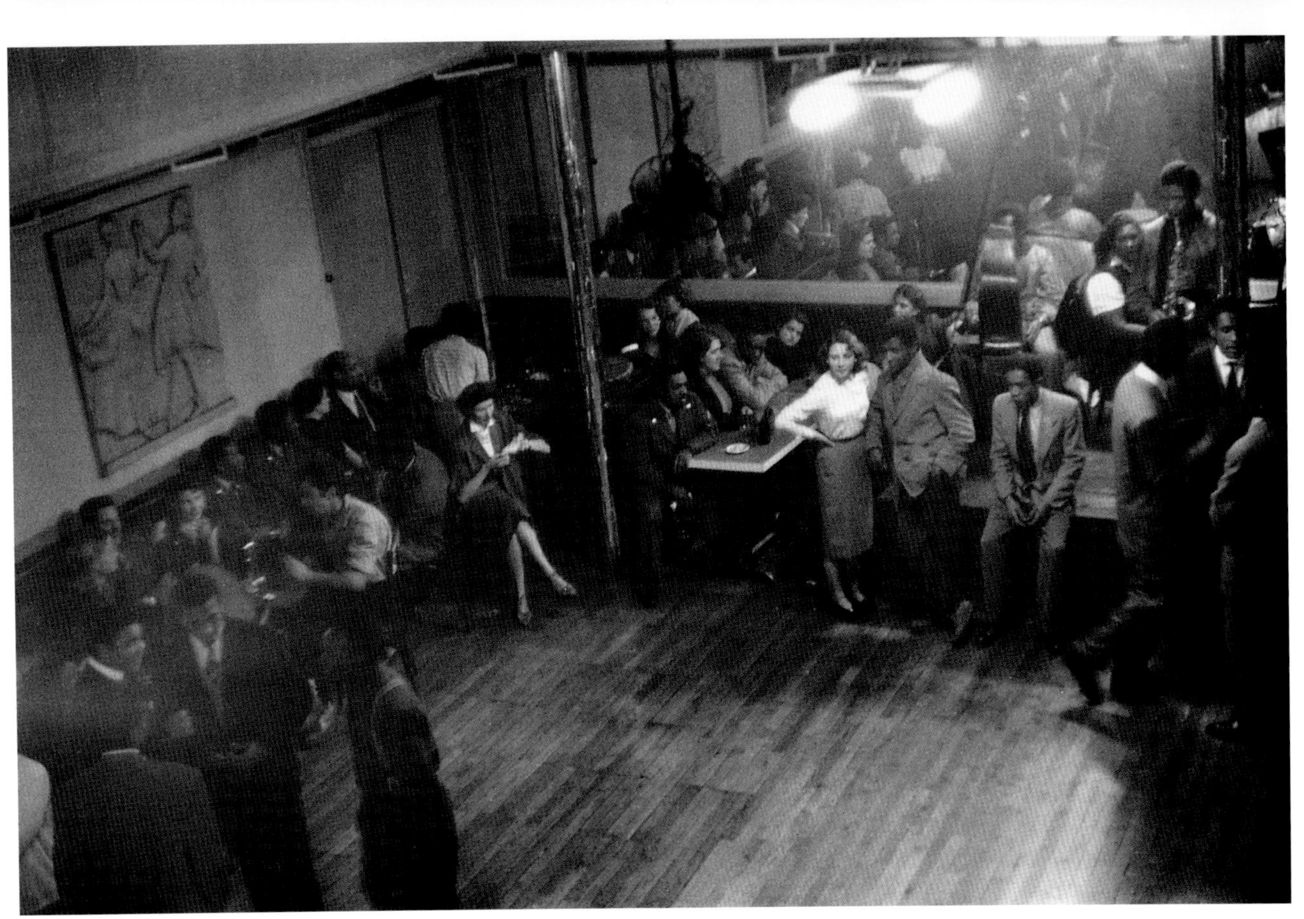

Bal Nègre, Paris, 1952

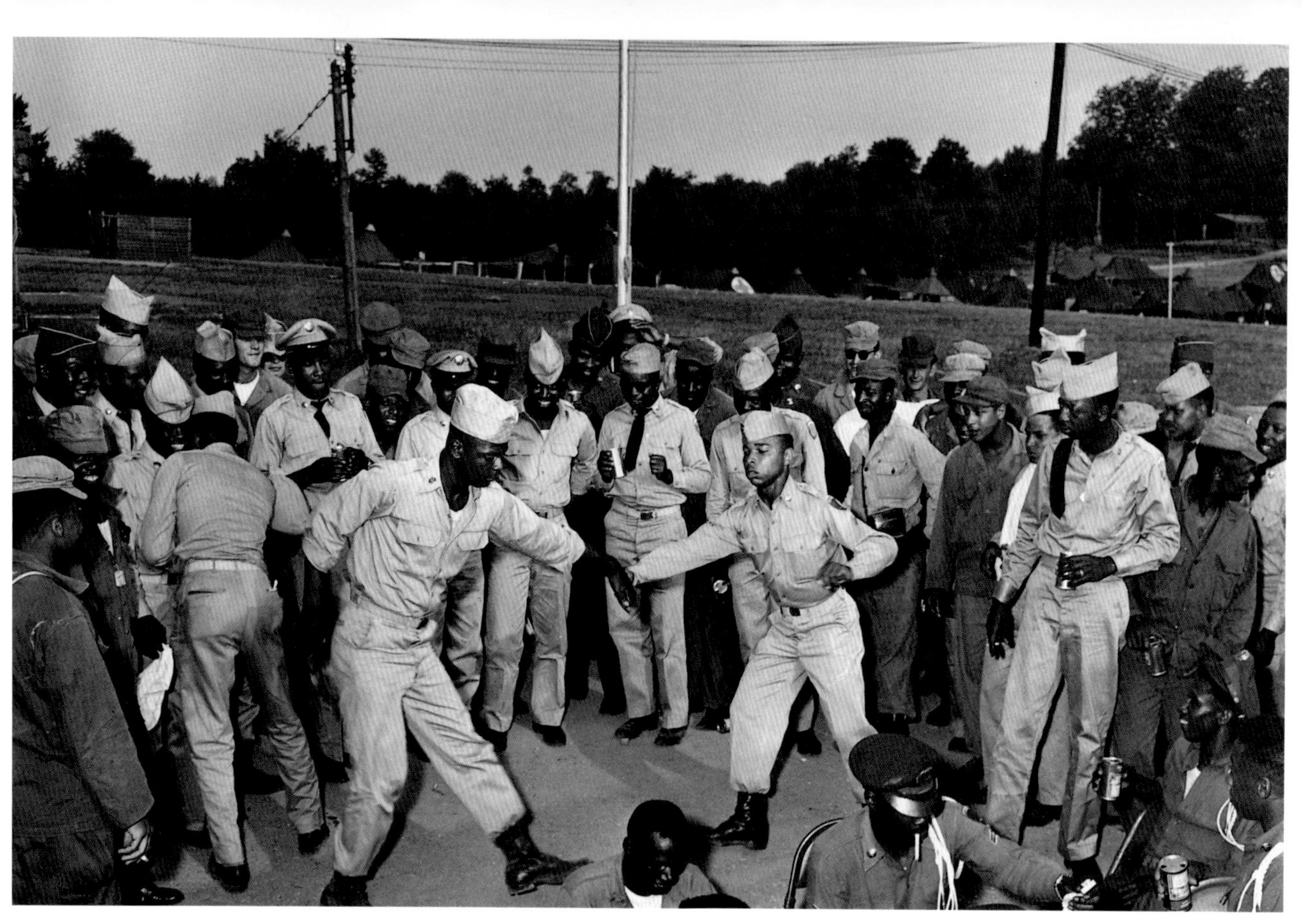

Bremerhaven, Germany, 1951

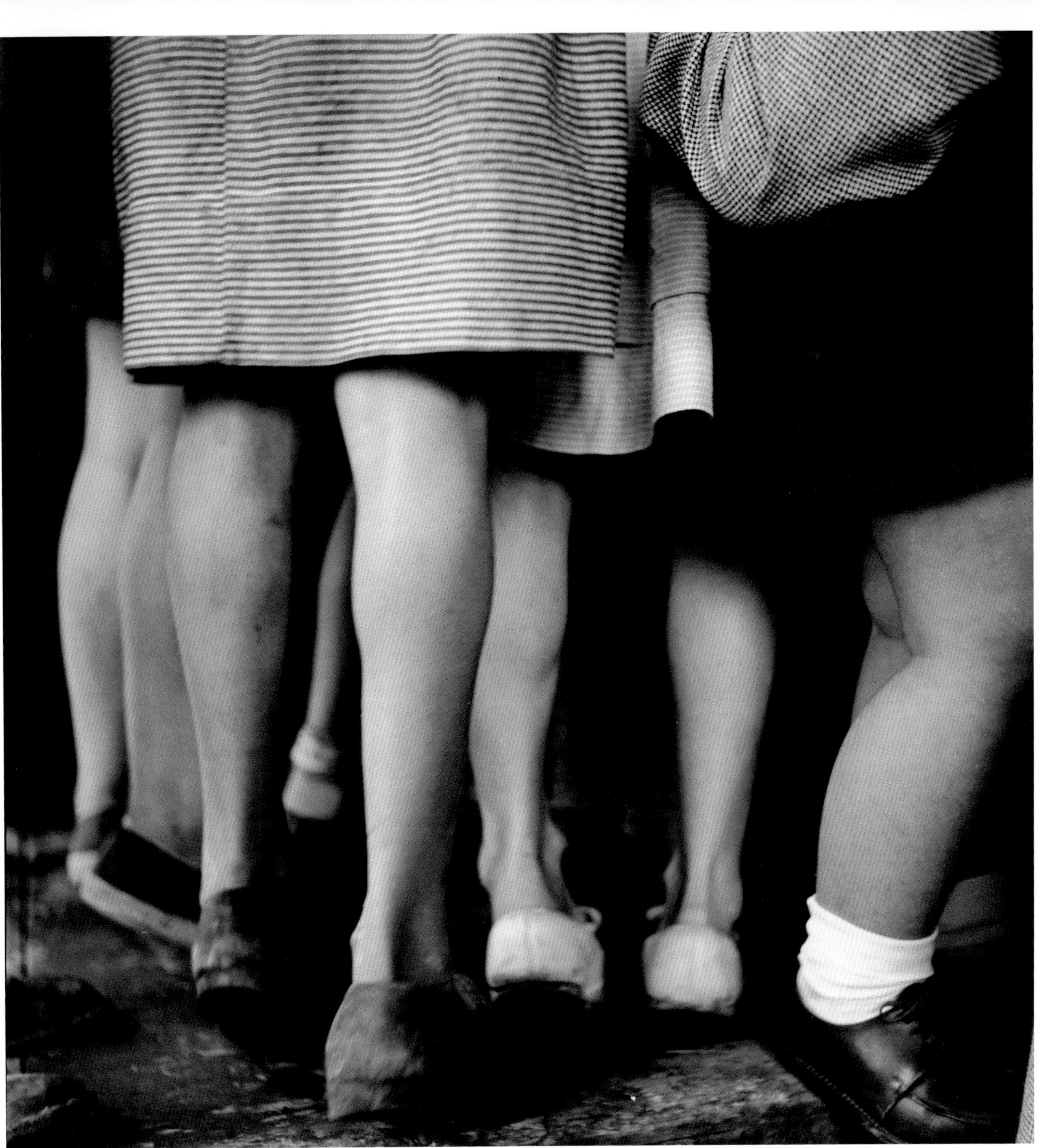

Florence, 1949

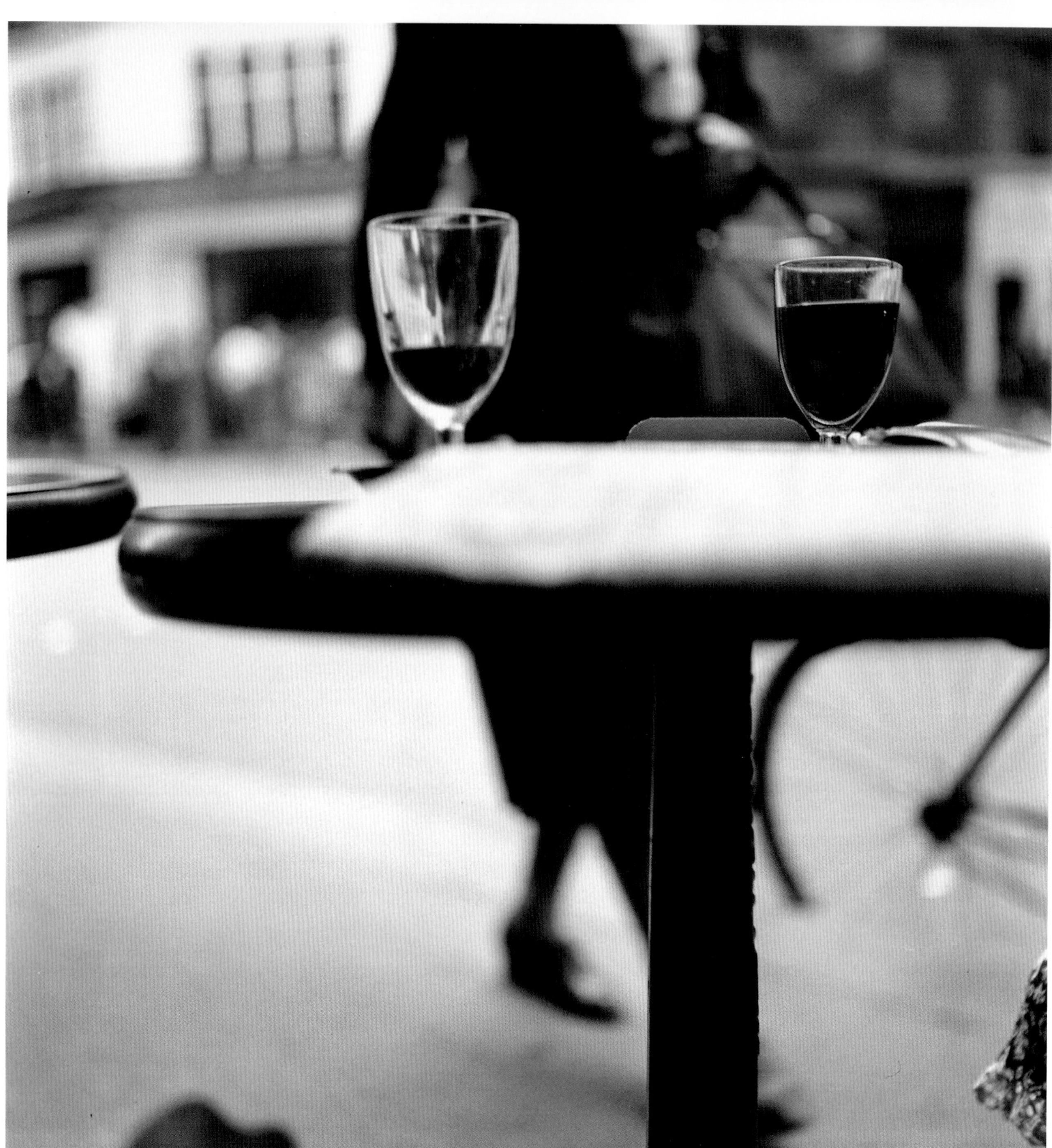

Paris, 1952

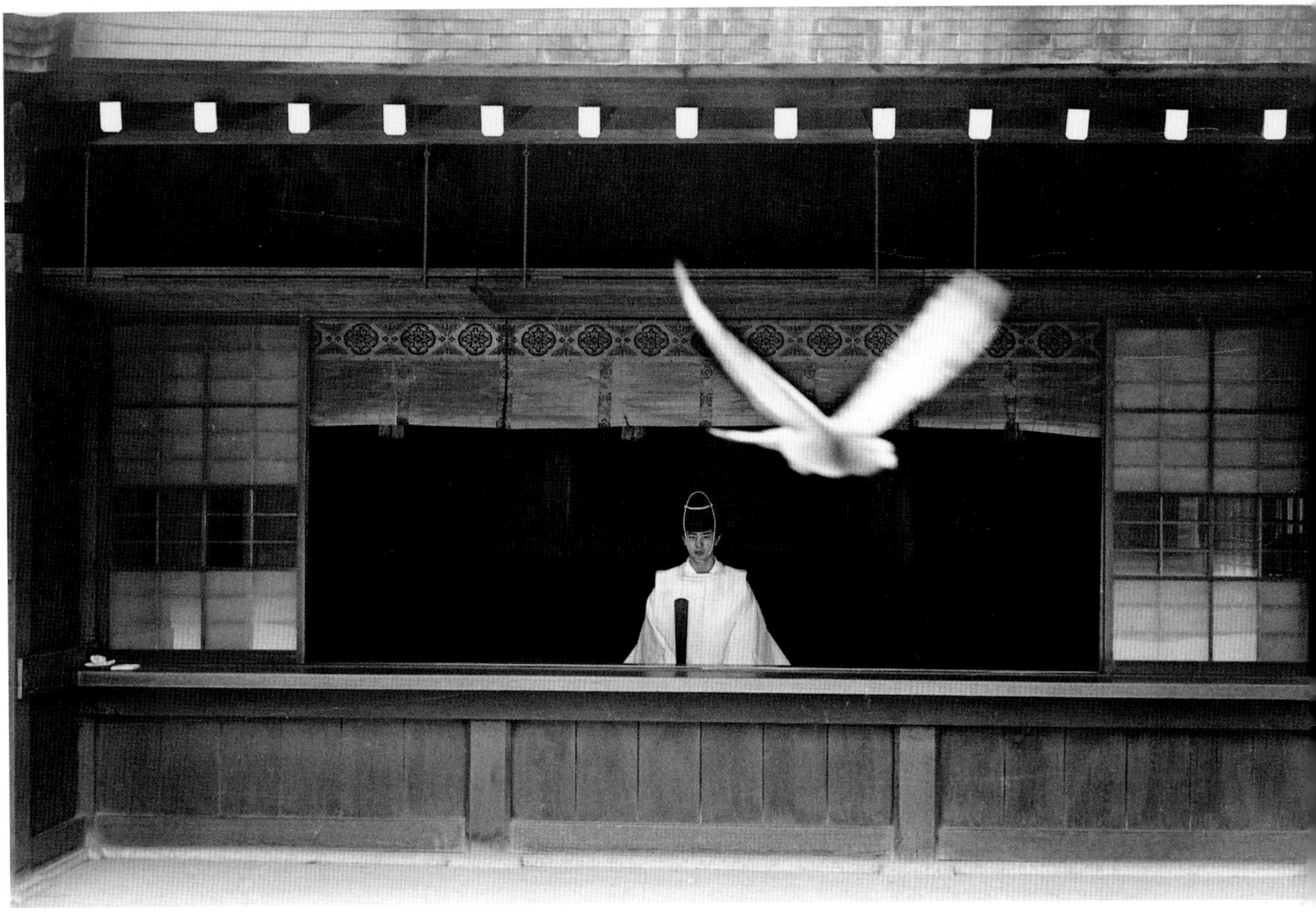

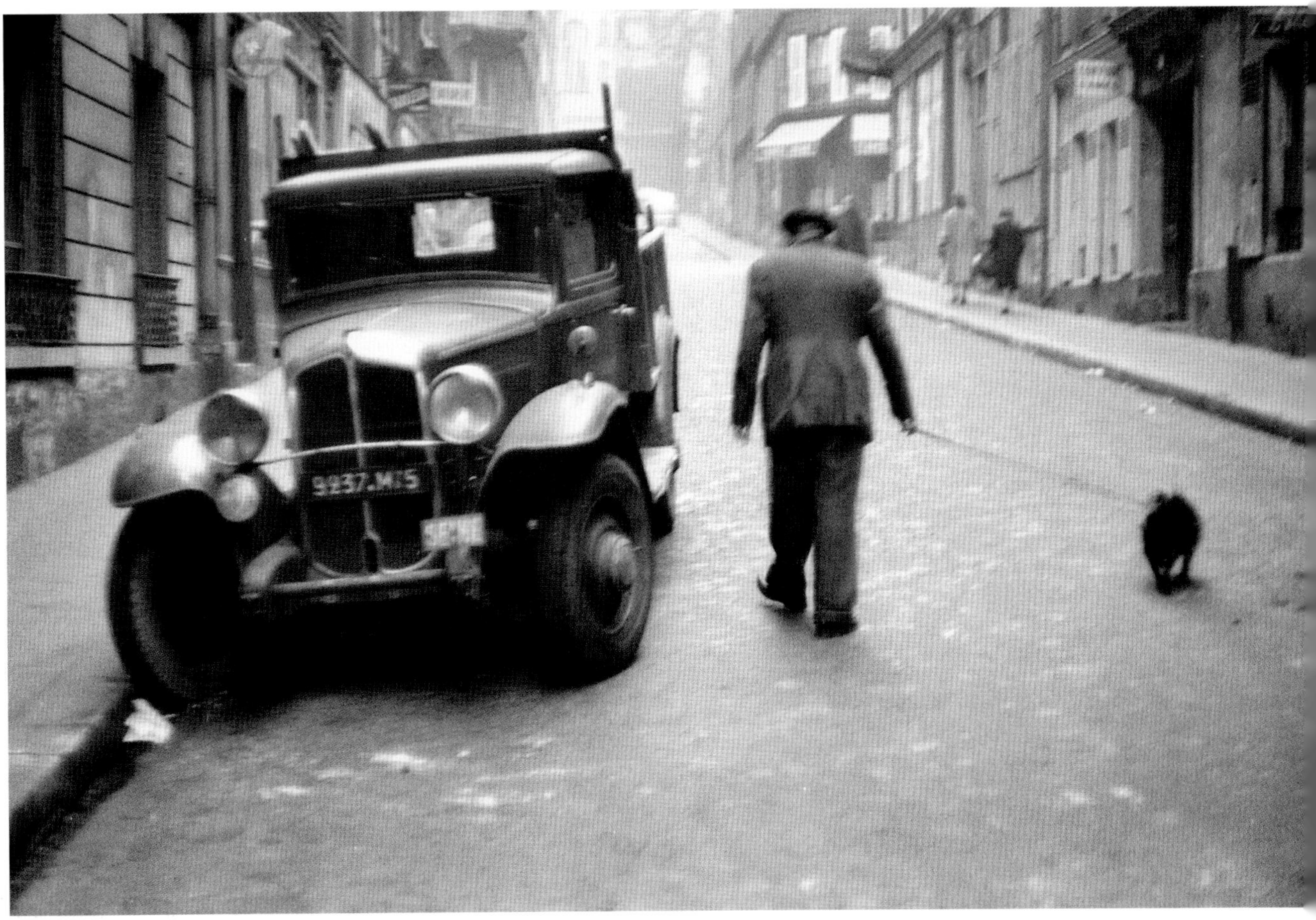

Tokyo, 1970 / *Paris, 1952*

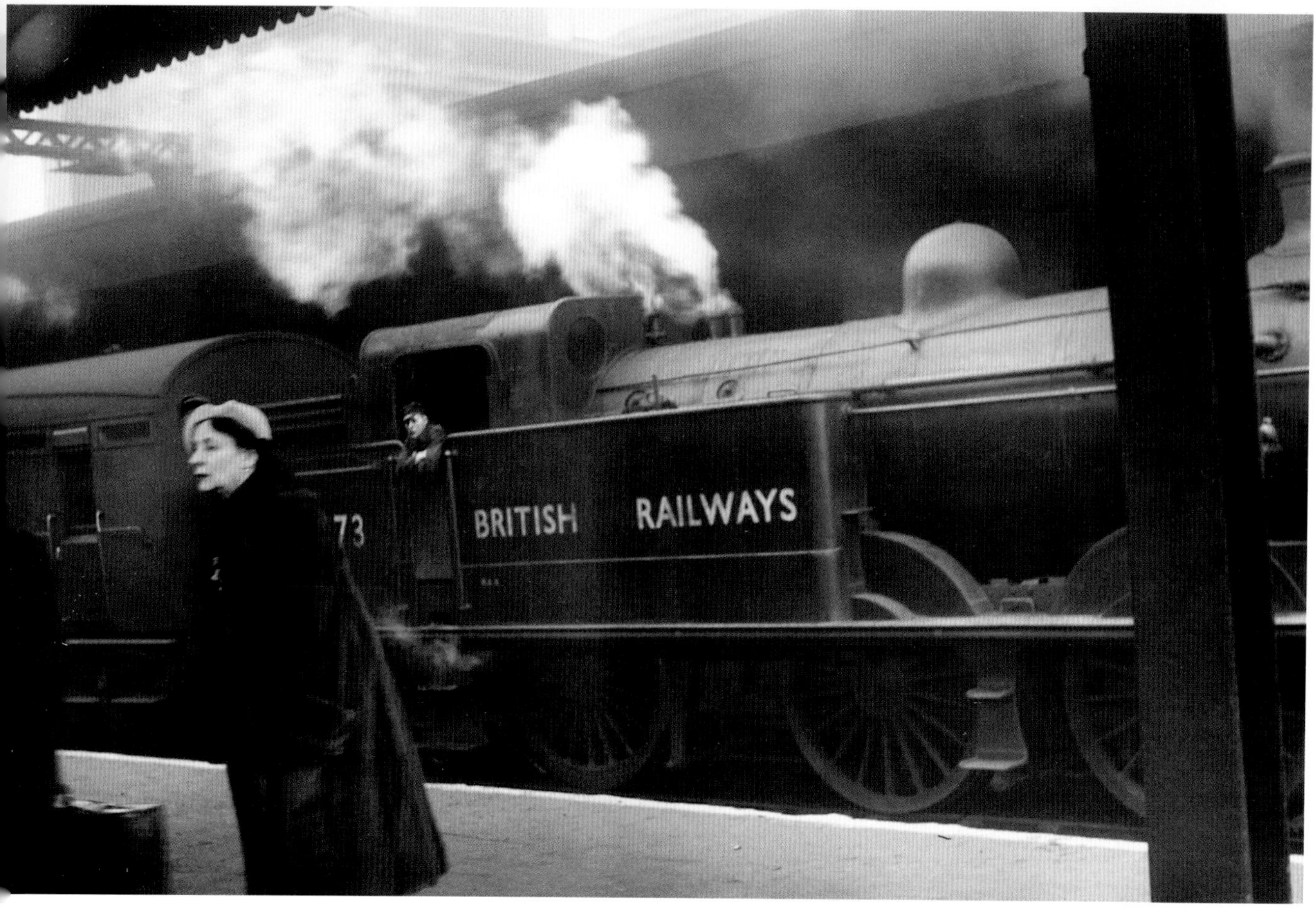

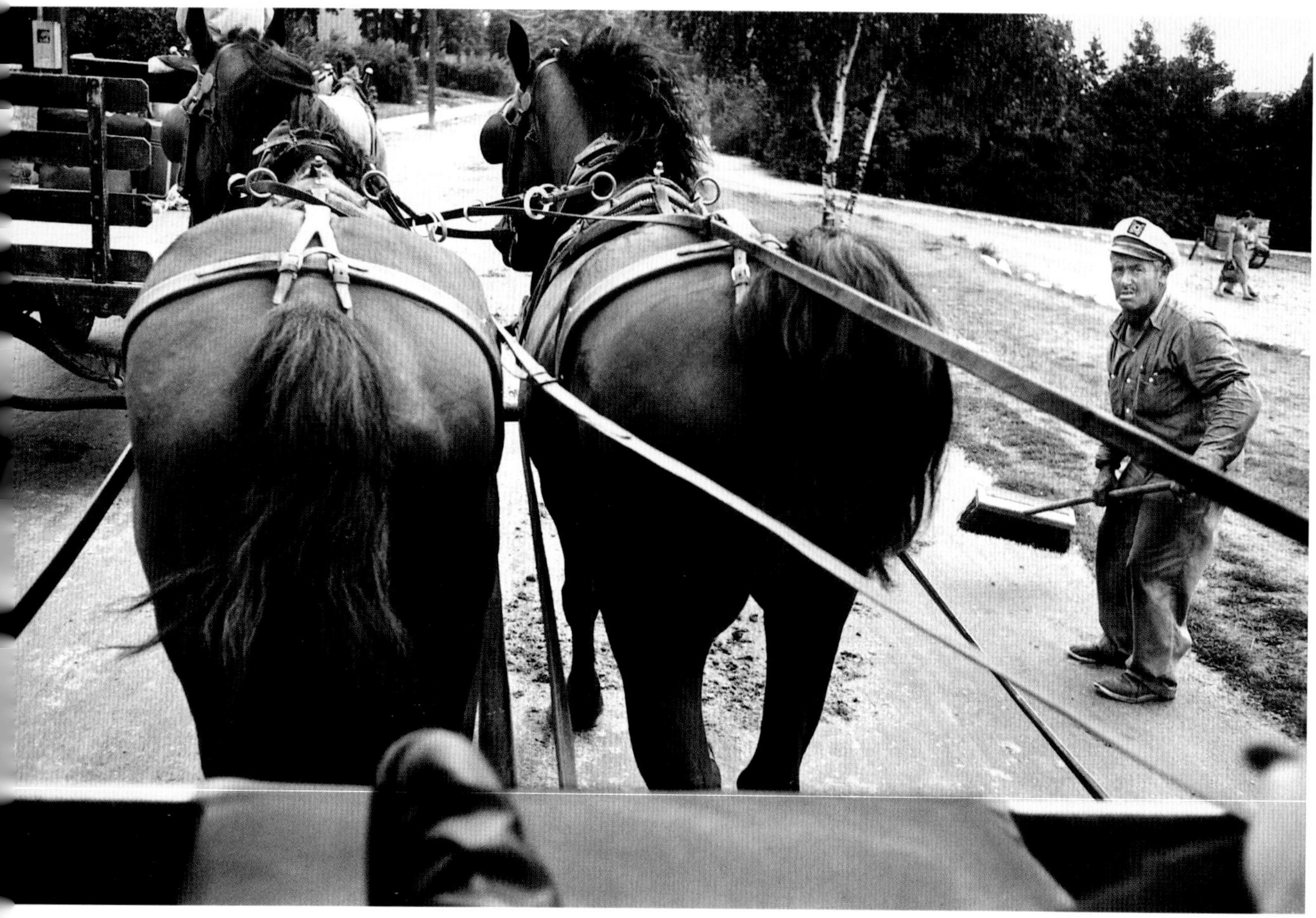

London, 1952 / Mackinac, Michigan, 1954

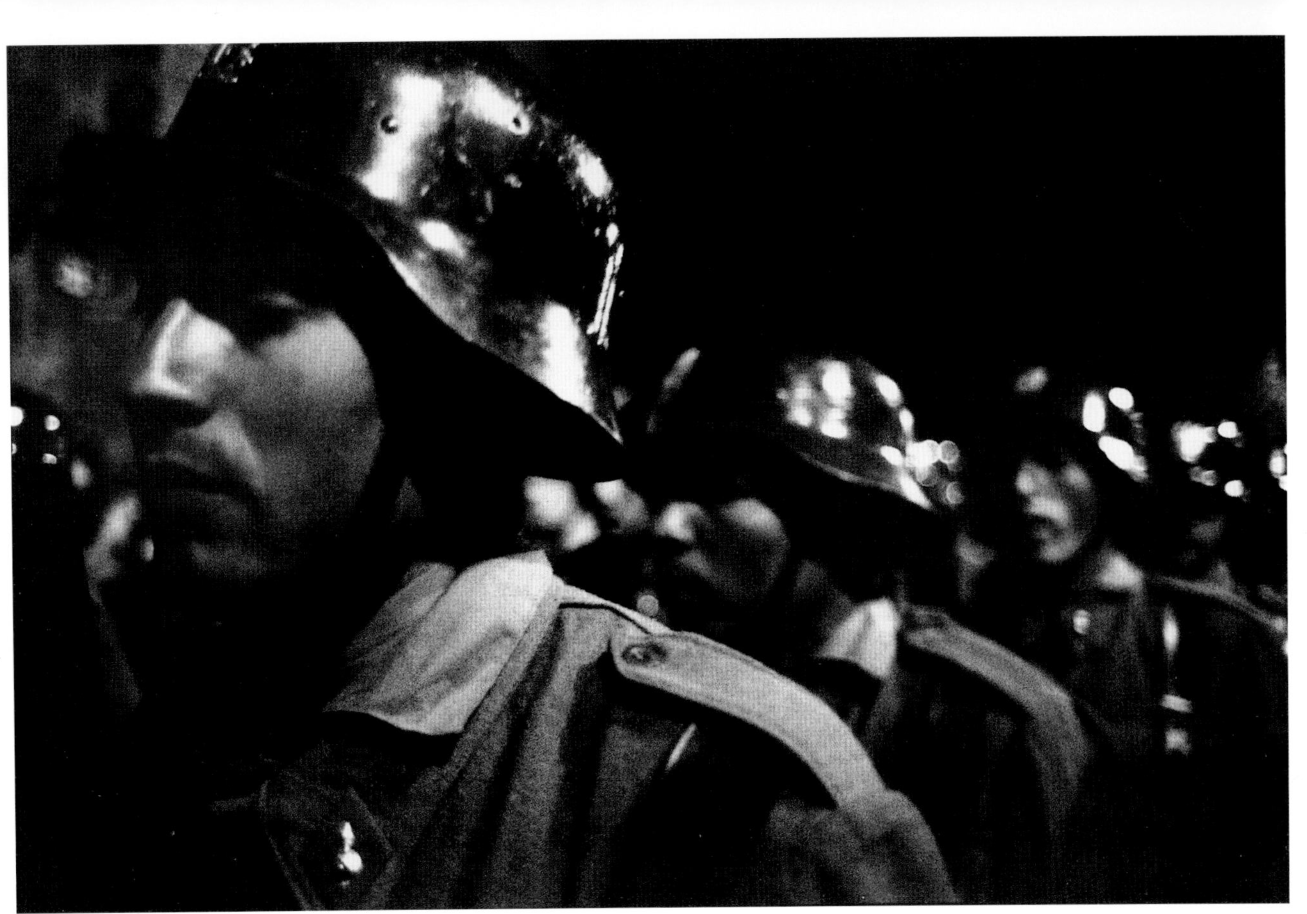

Seville, Spain, 1952

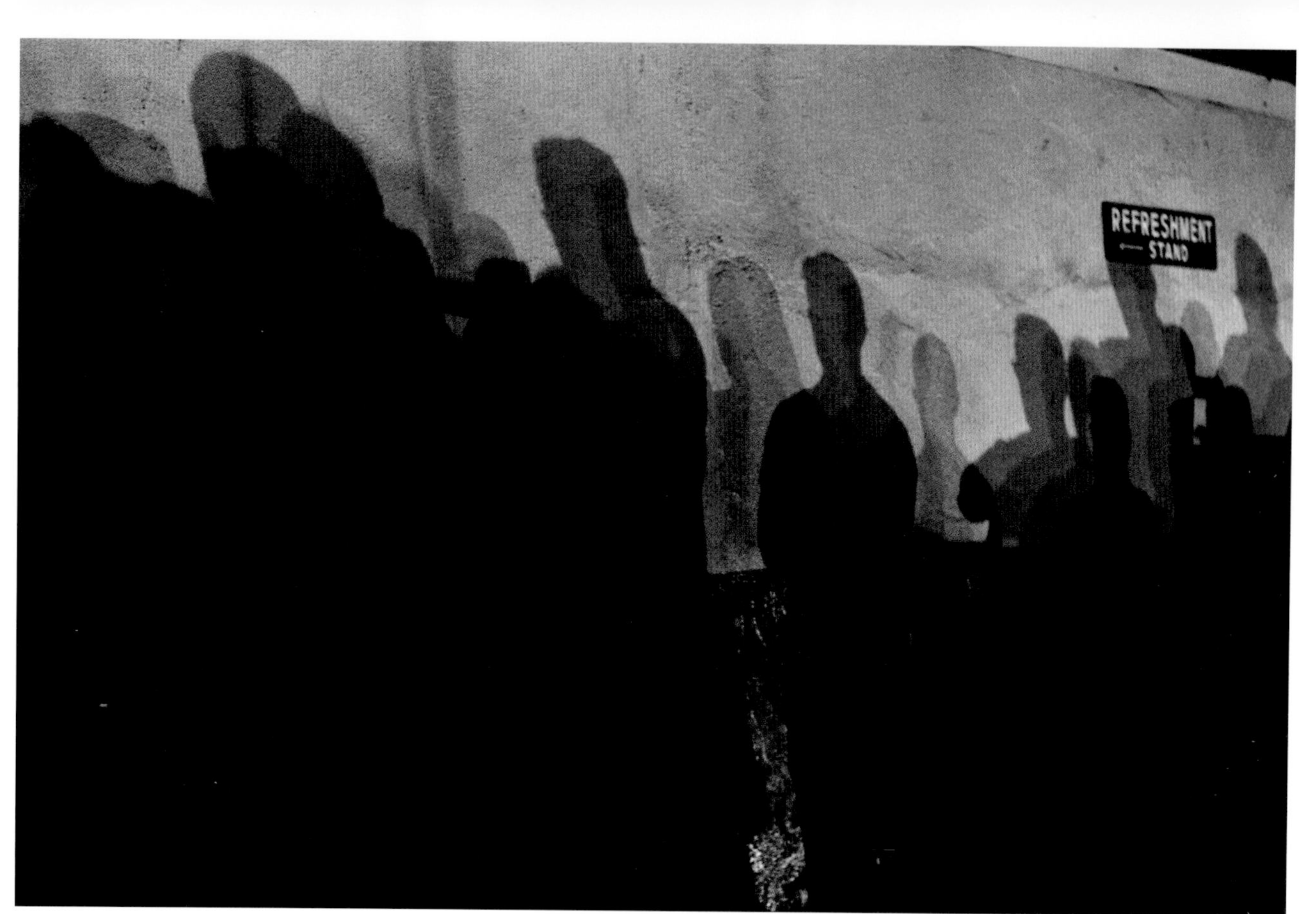

New York, 1957

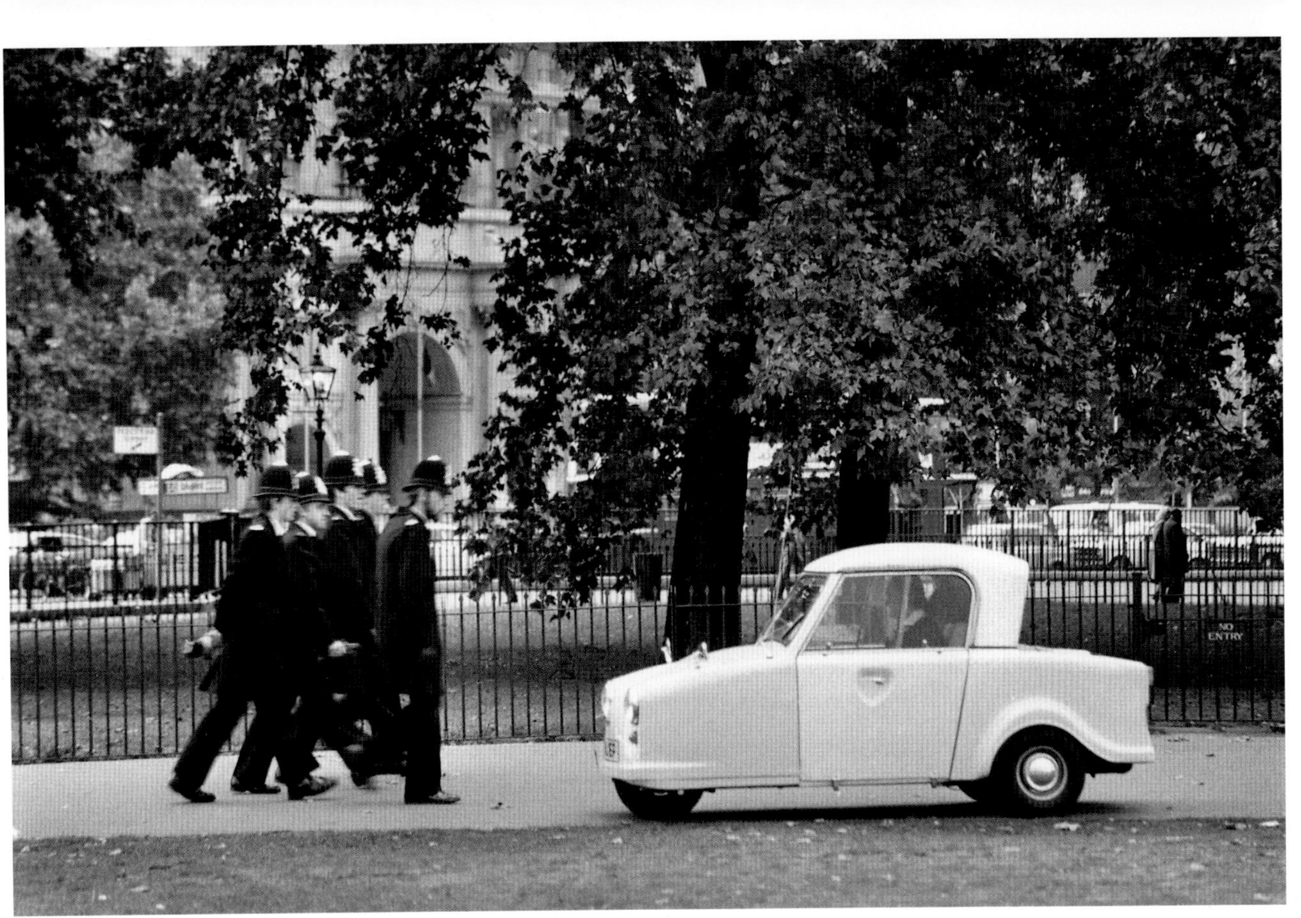

London, 1978

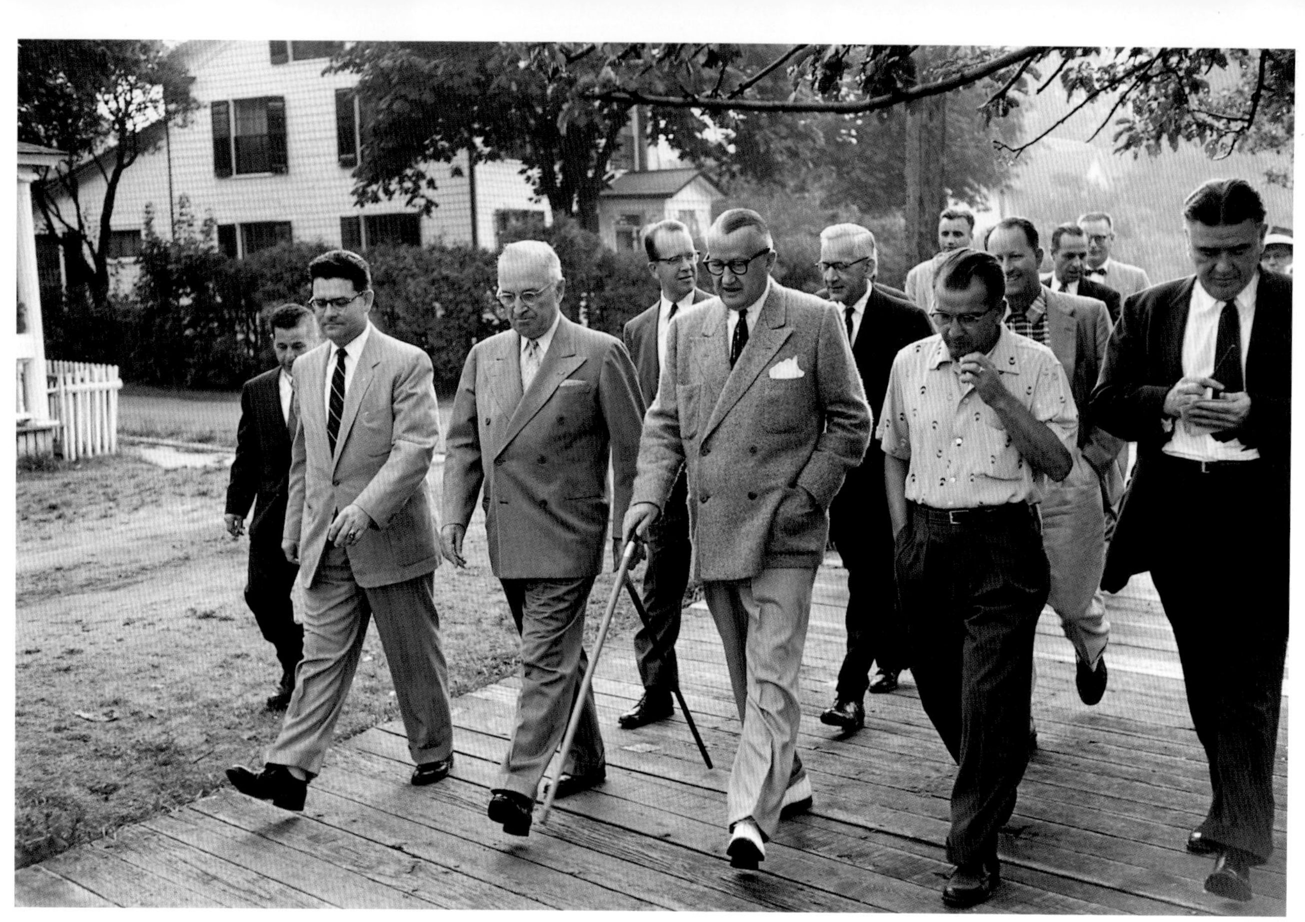

Harry S. Truman, Mackinac, Michigan, 1954
overleaf *Shanghai, 1978* / *Ballycotton, Ireland, 1968*

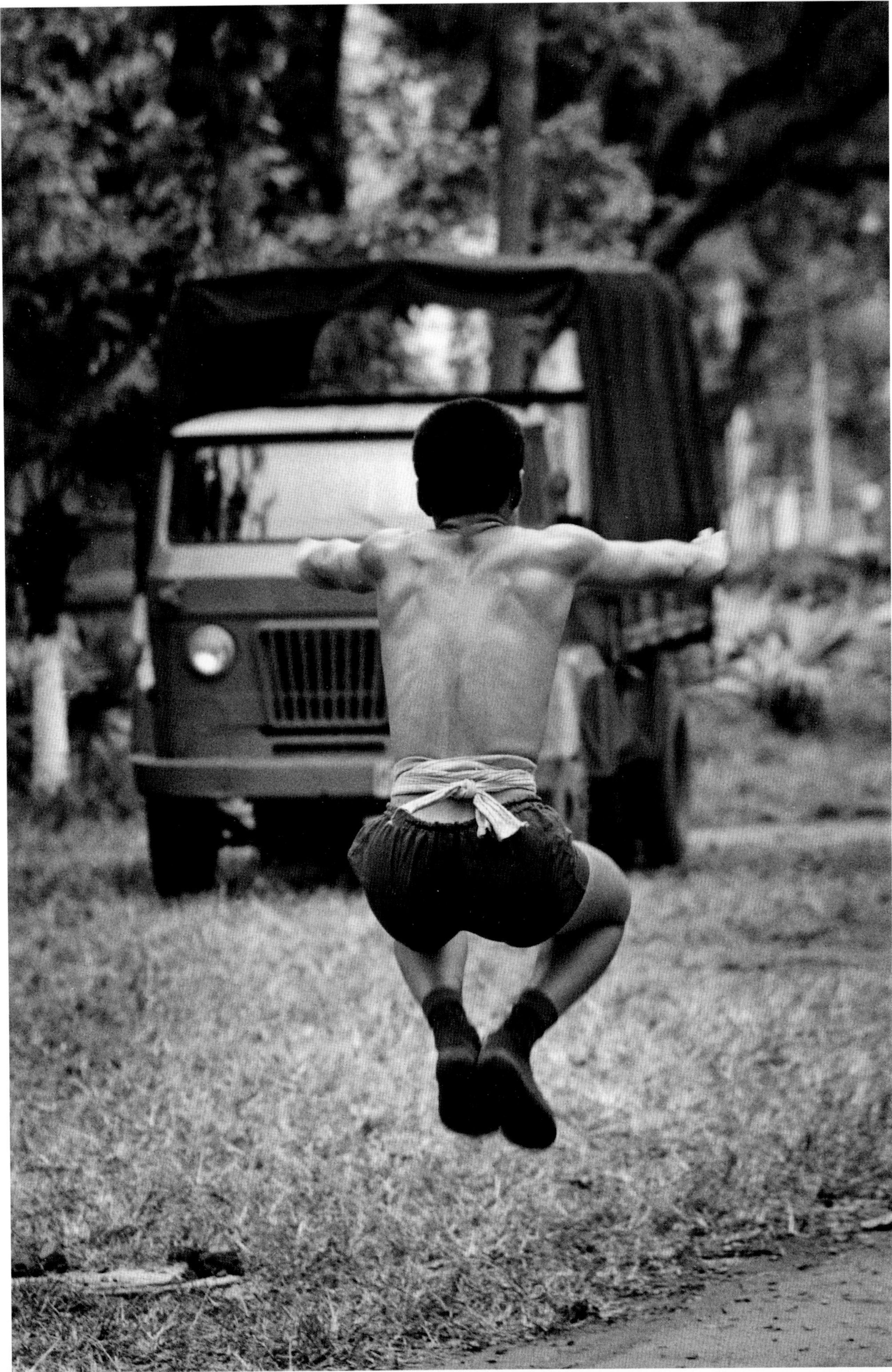

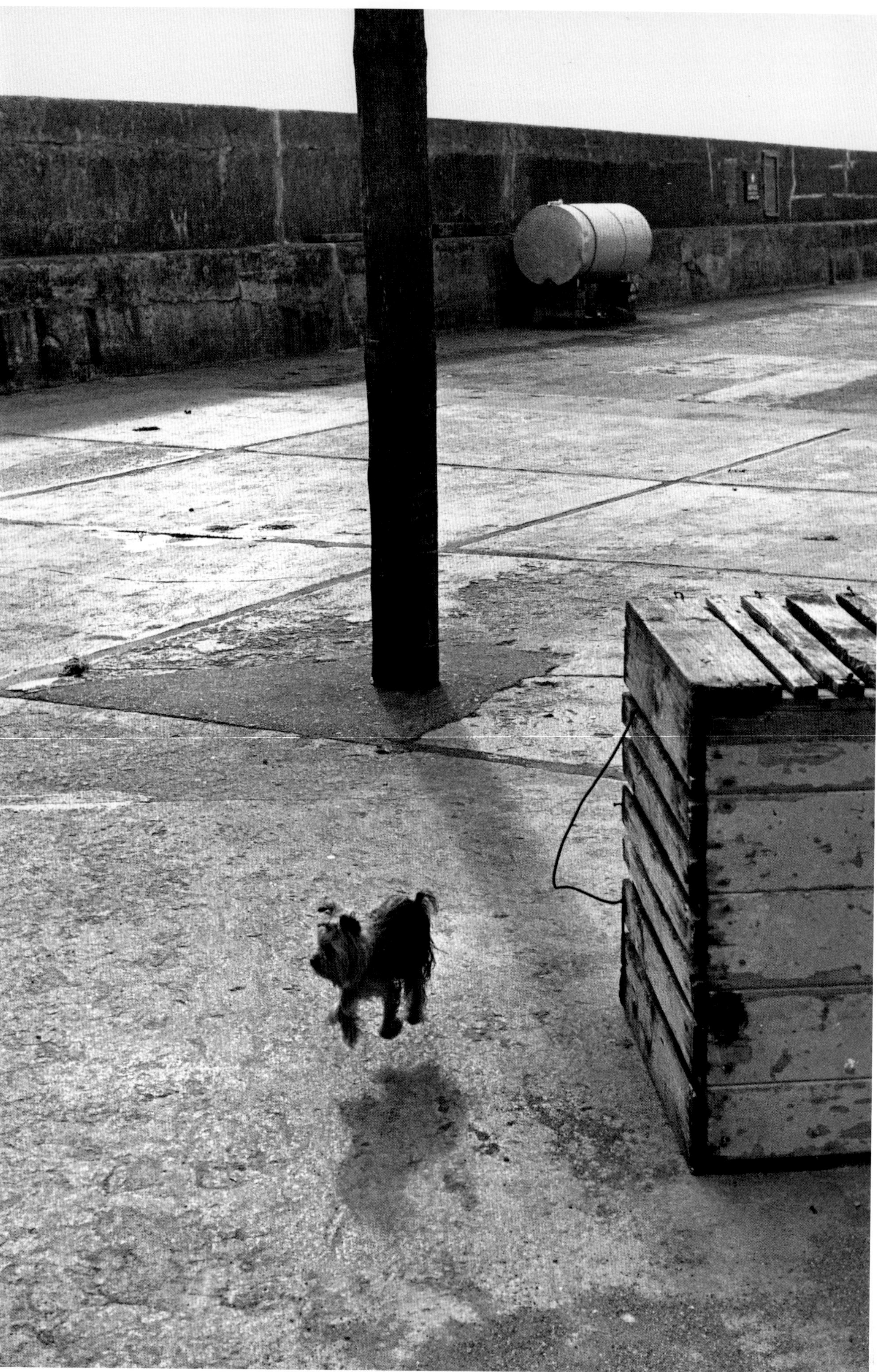

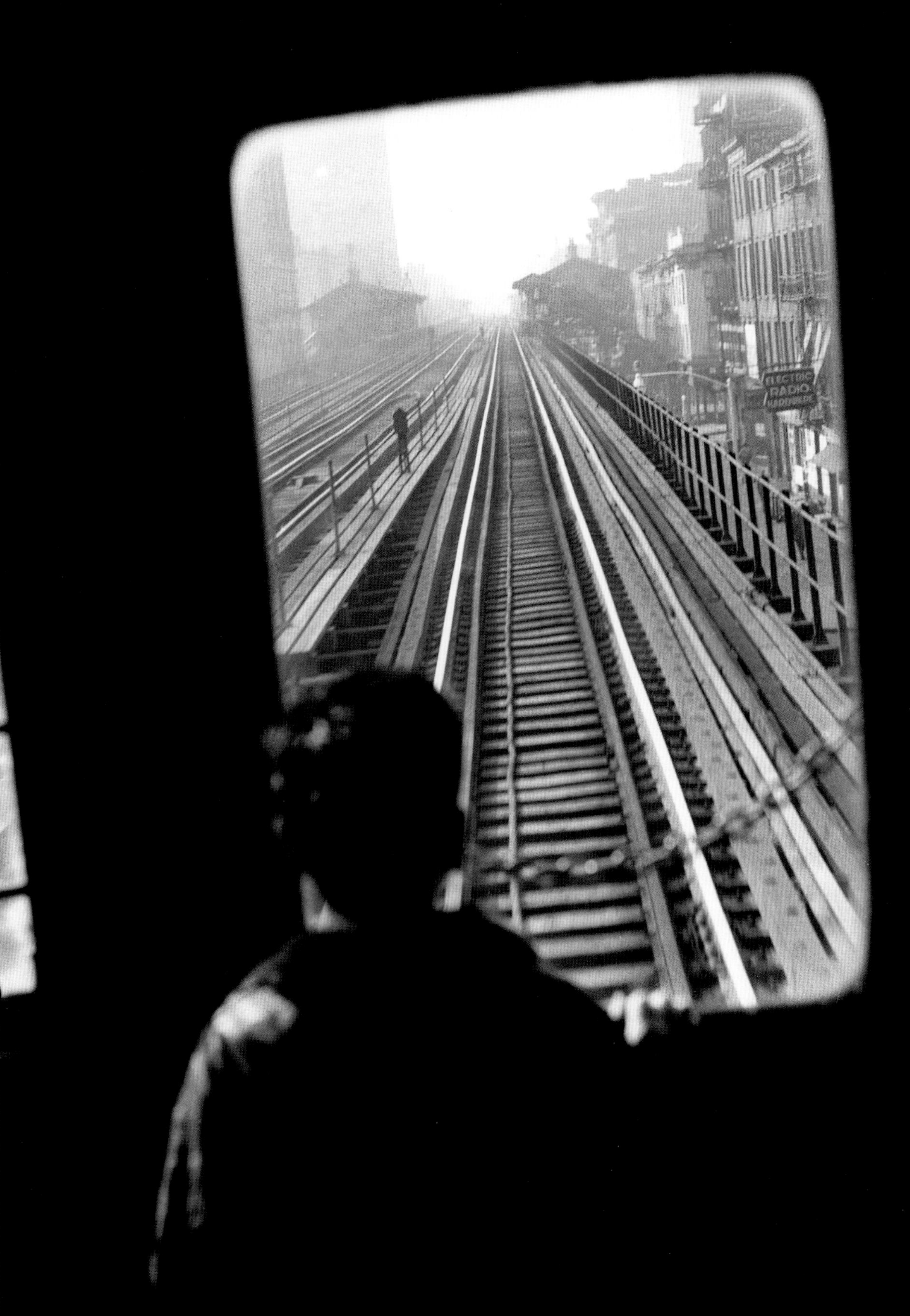
ELECTRIC
RADIO

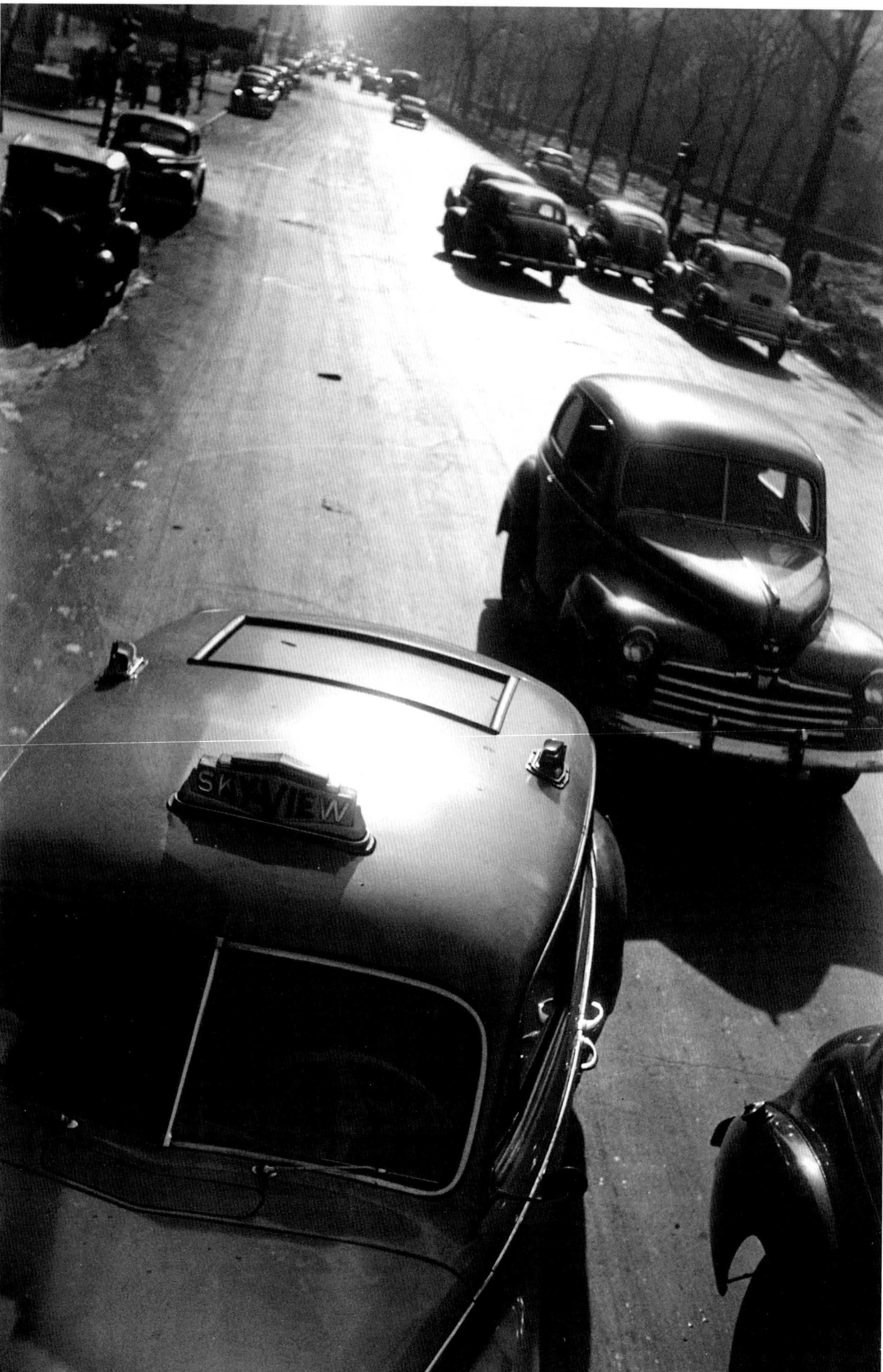

previous page *Third Avenue El., New York, 1955* / *Fifth Avenue, New York, c.1947*

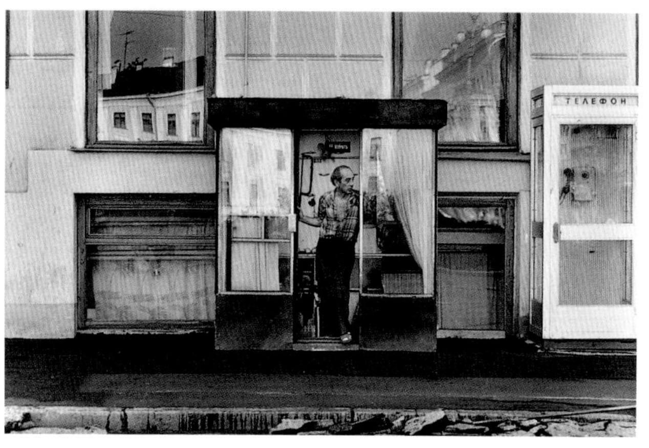

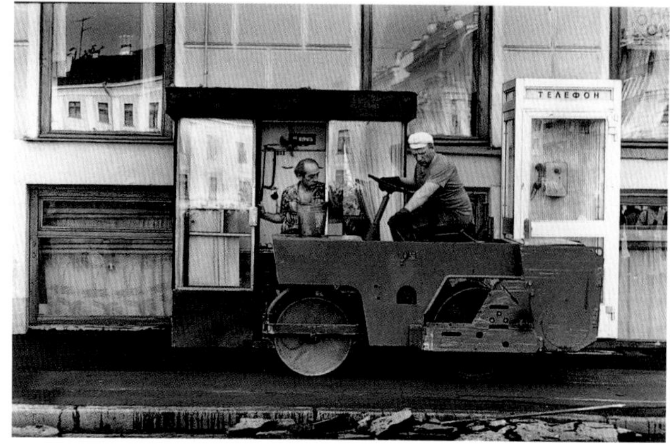

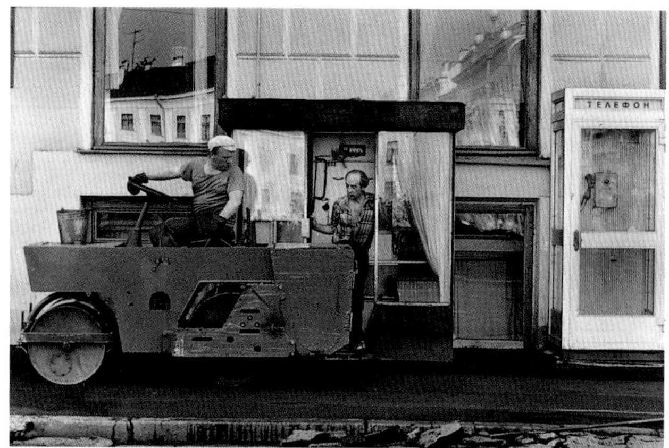

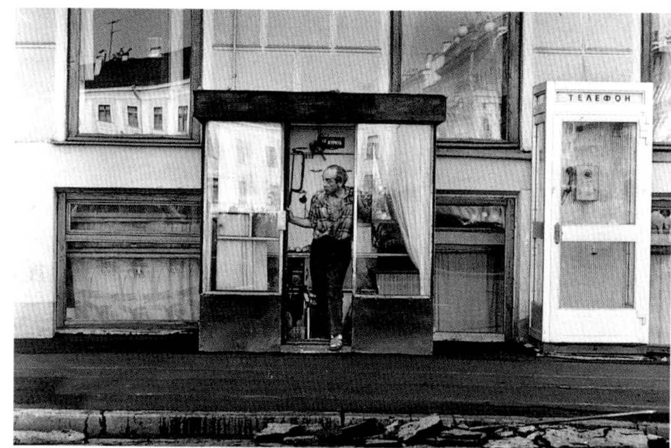

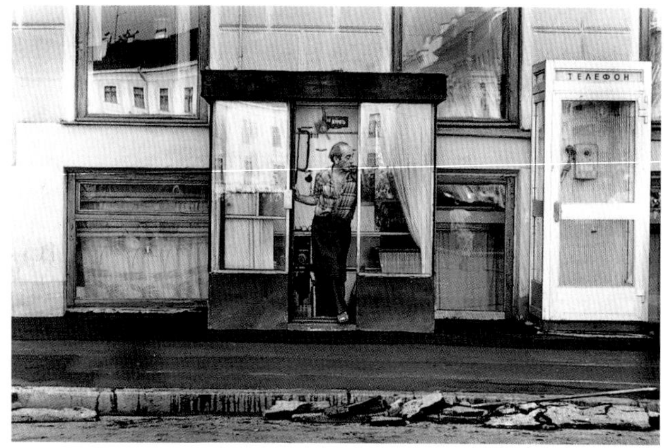

Leningrad, 1988

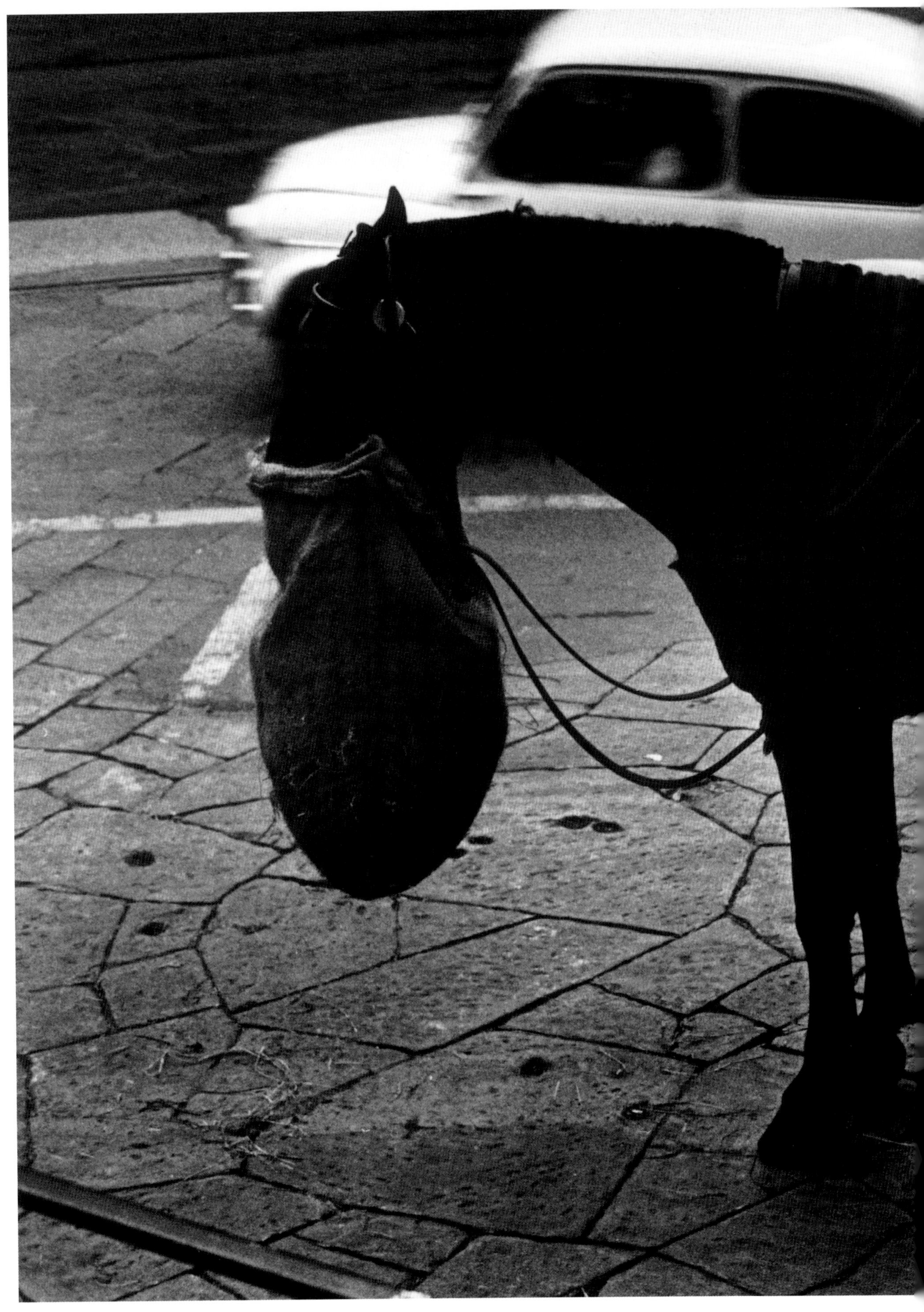

Florence, 1965

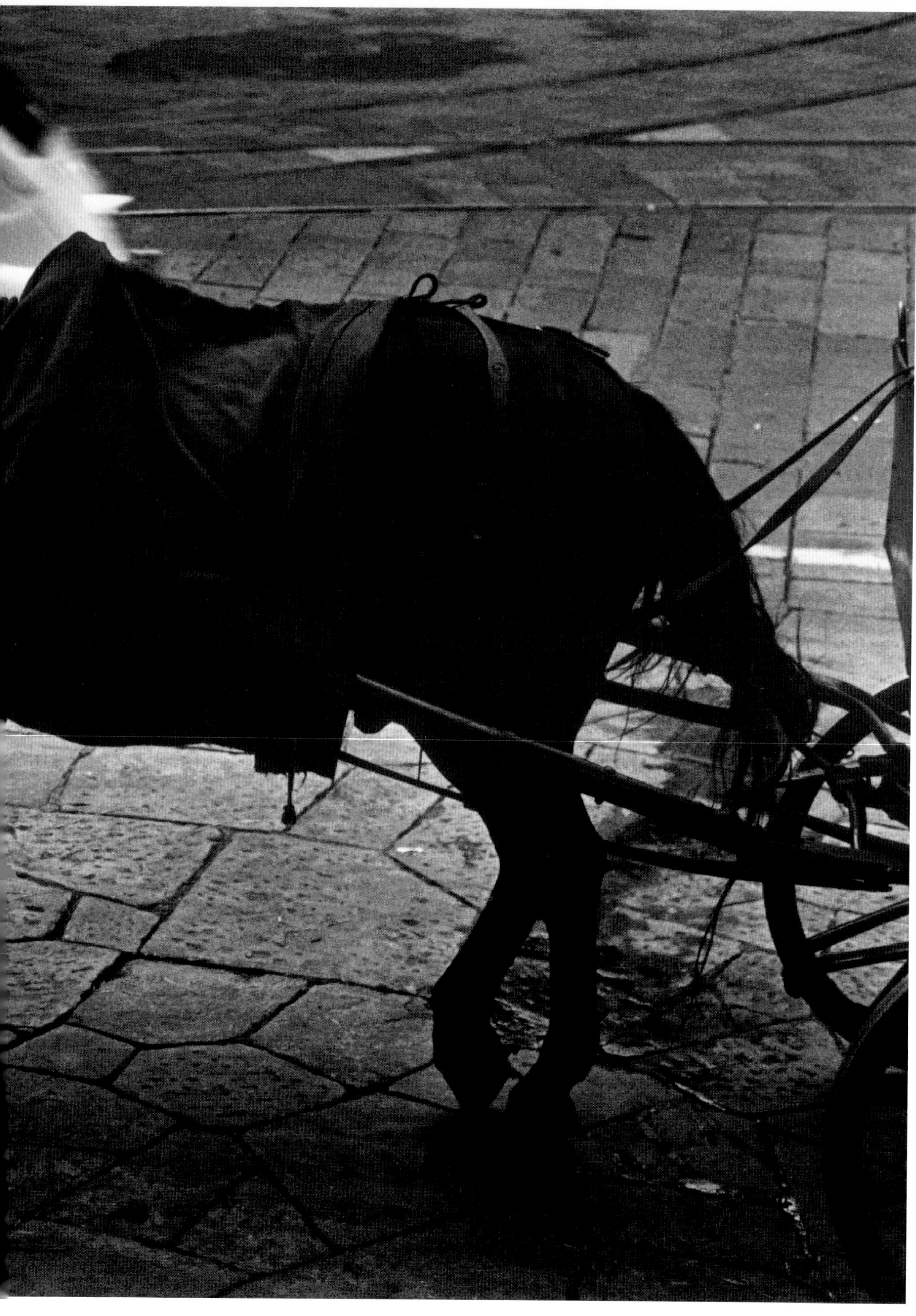

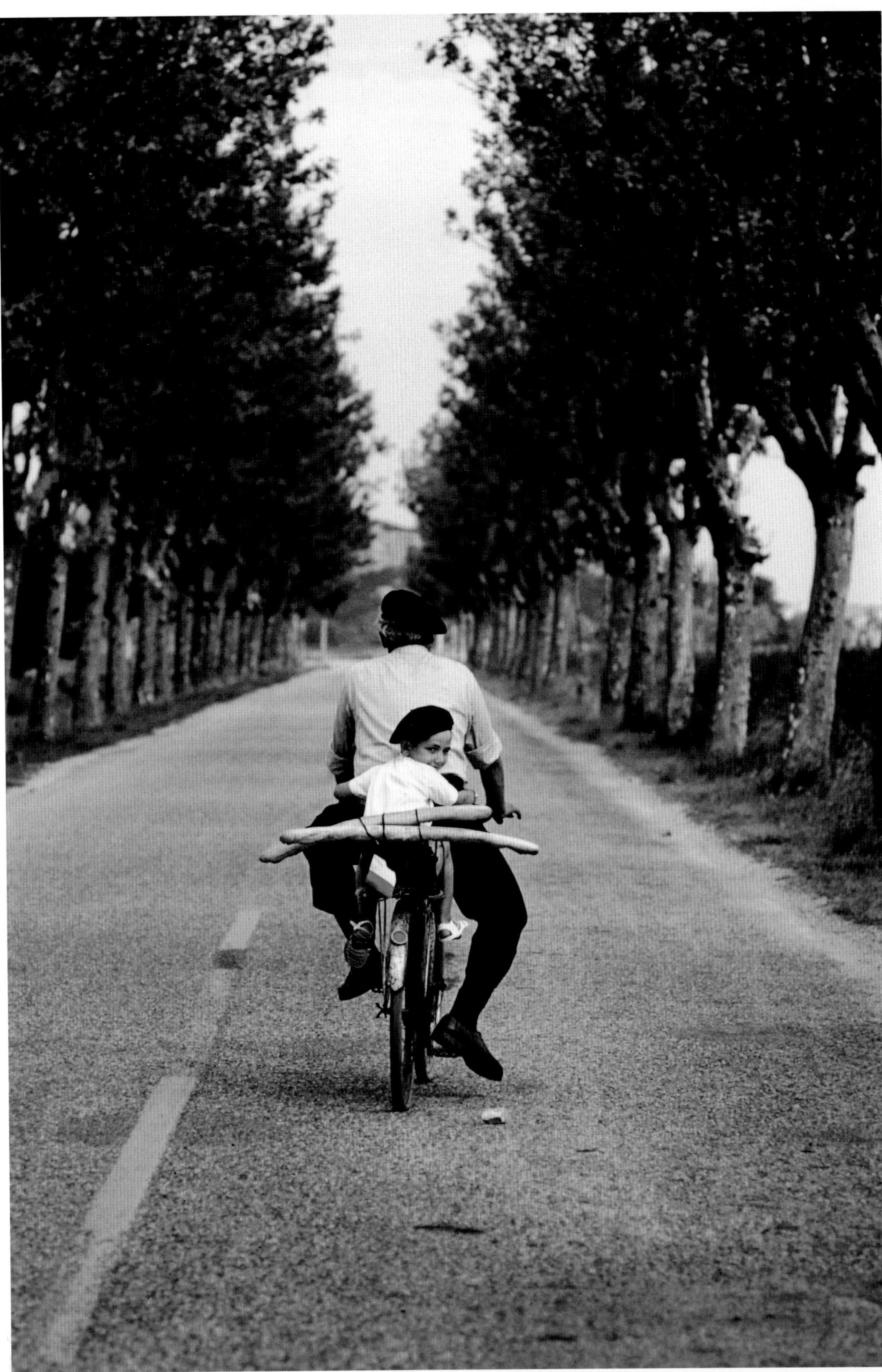

Provence, France, 1955

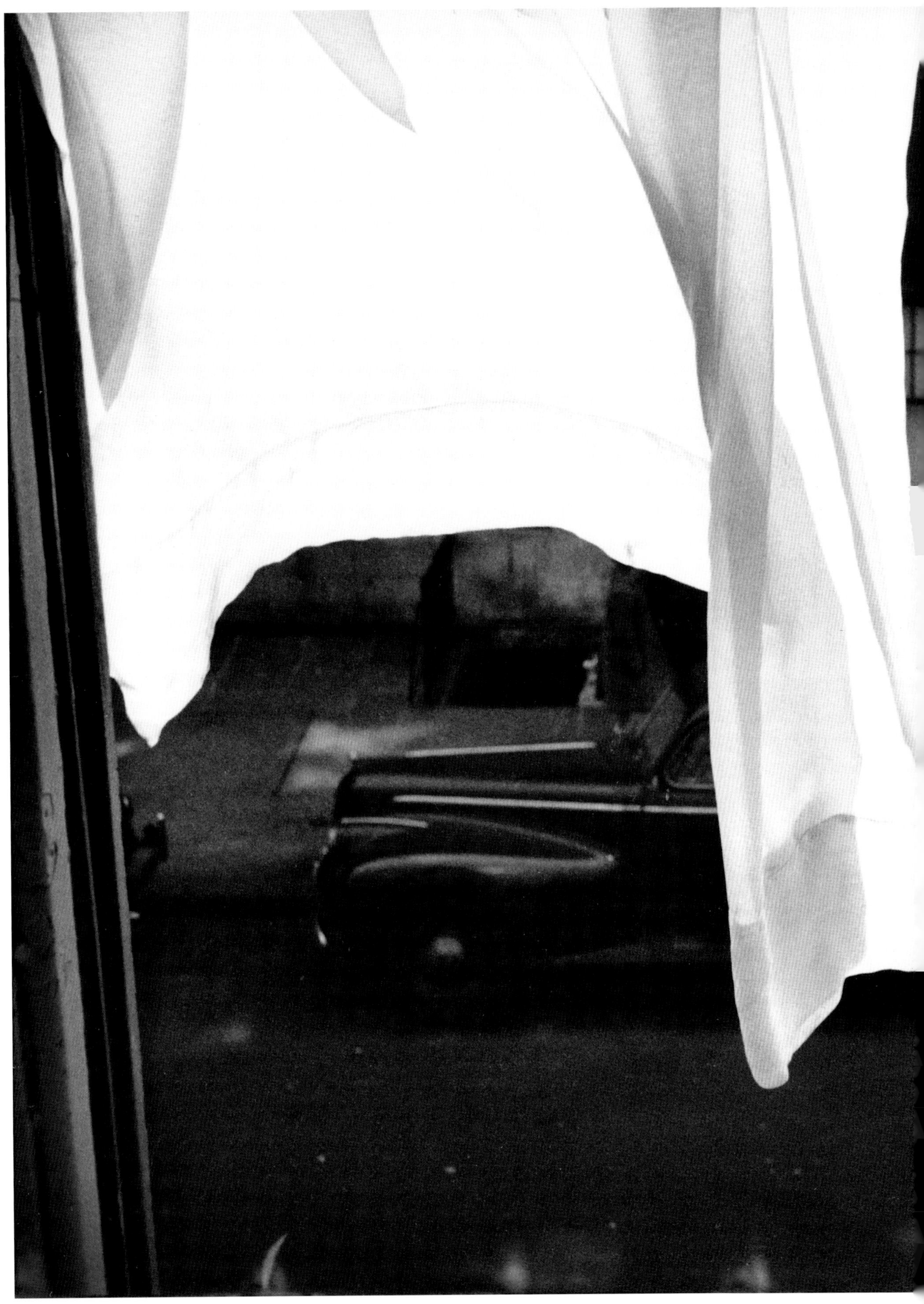

New York, 1954

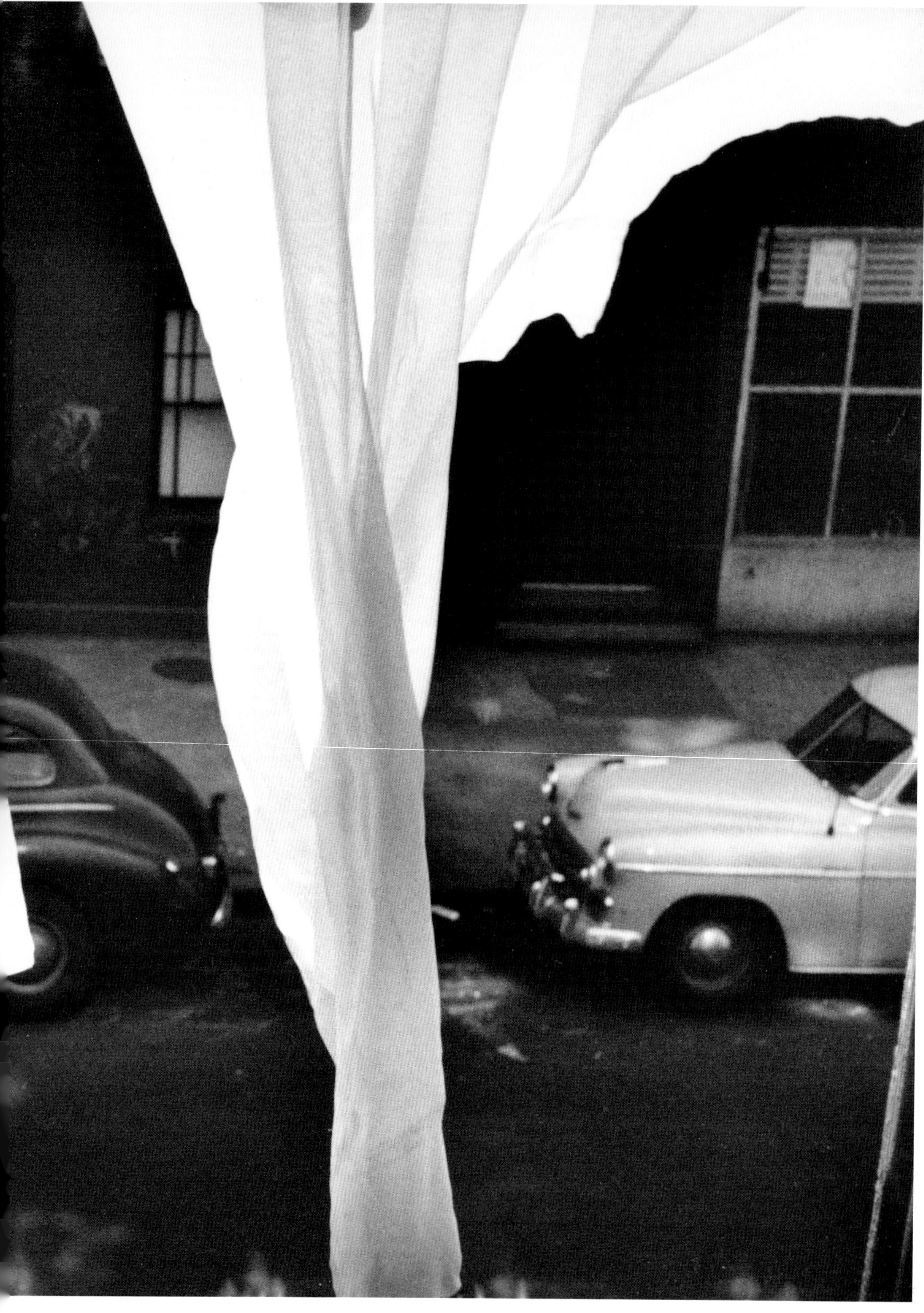

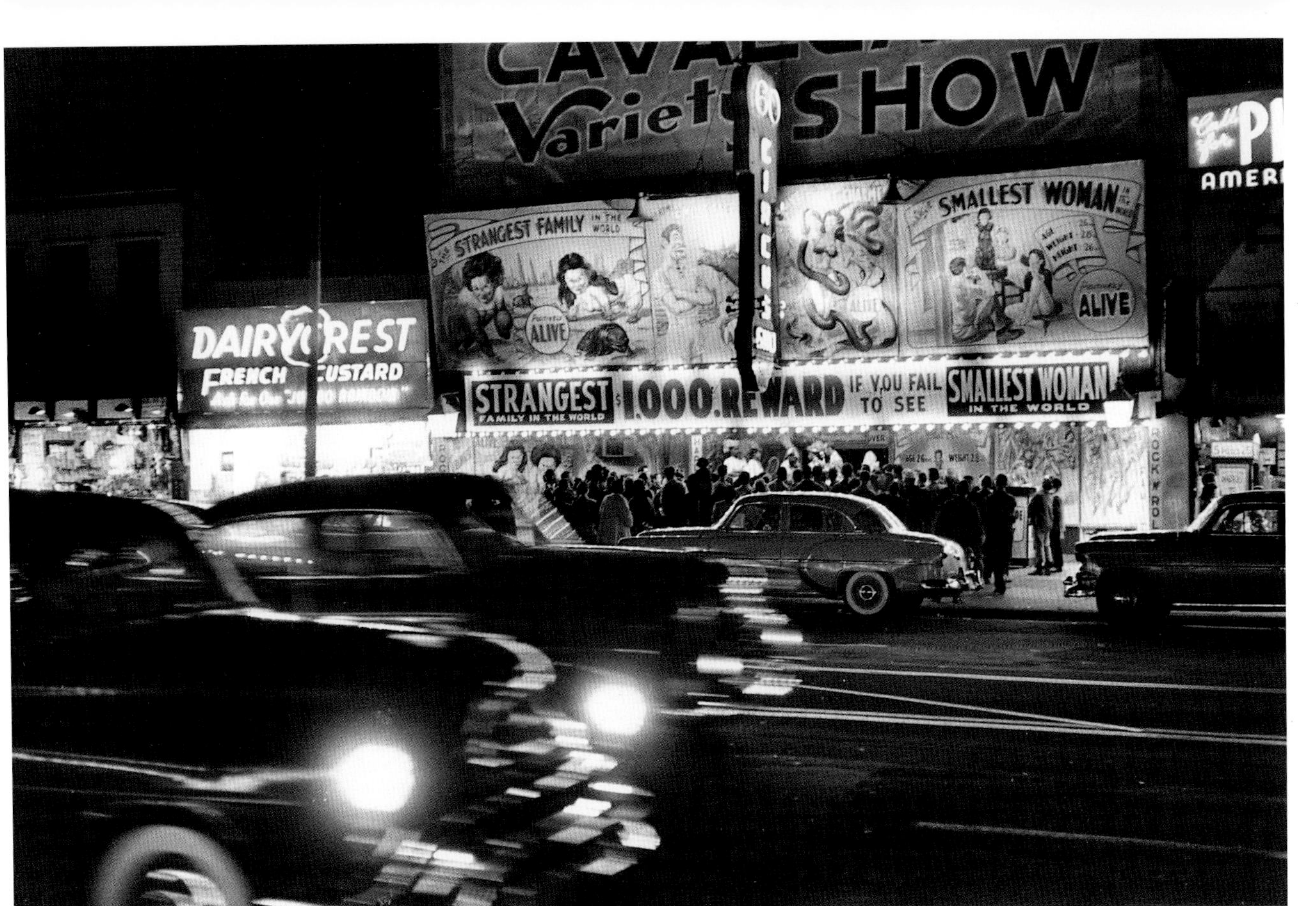

New York, 1954

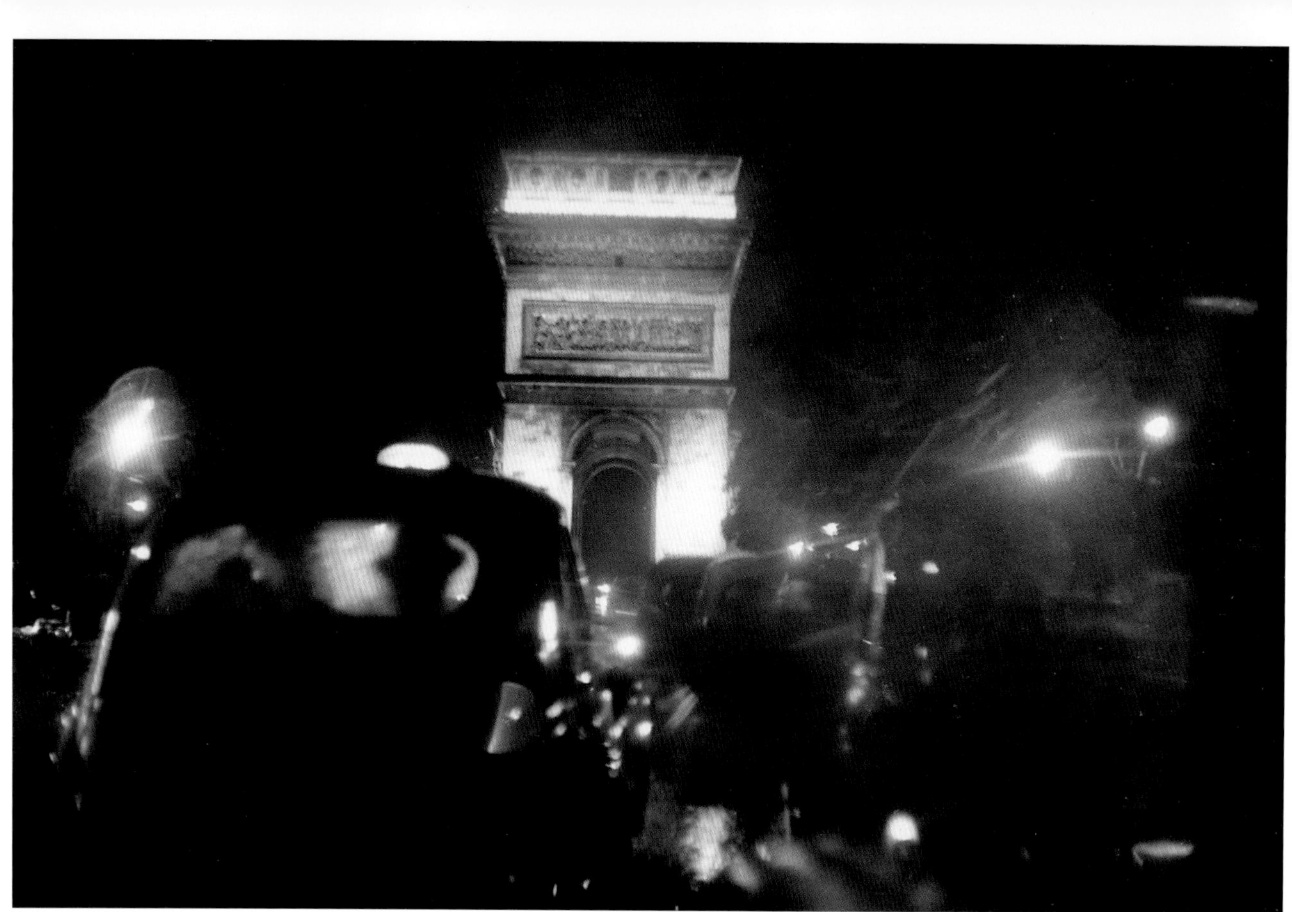

Paris, 1956

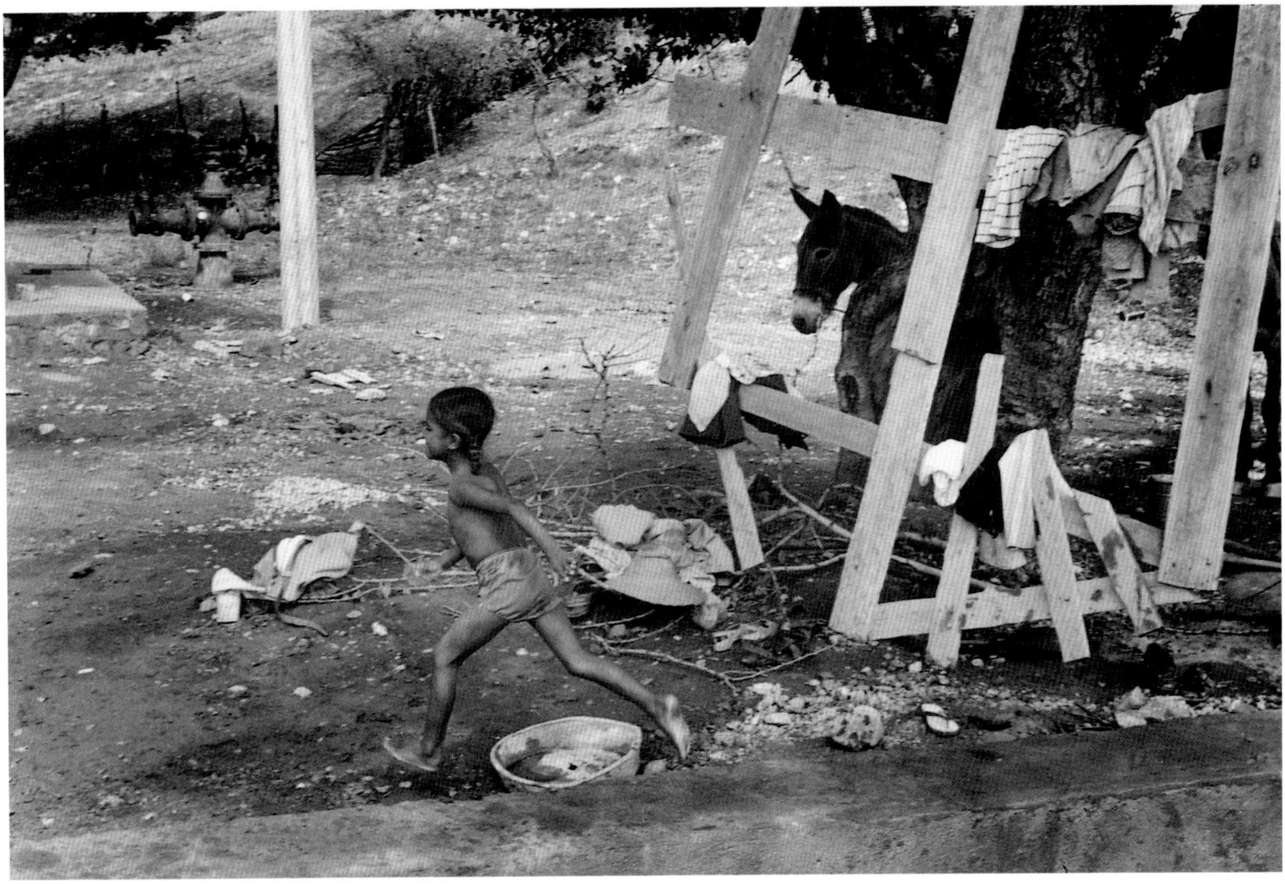

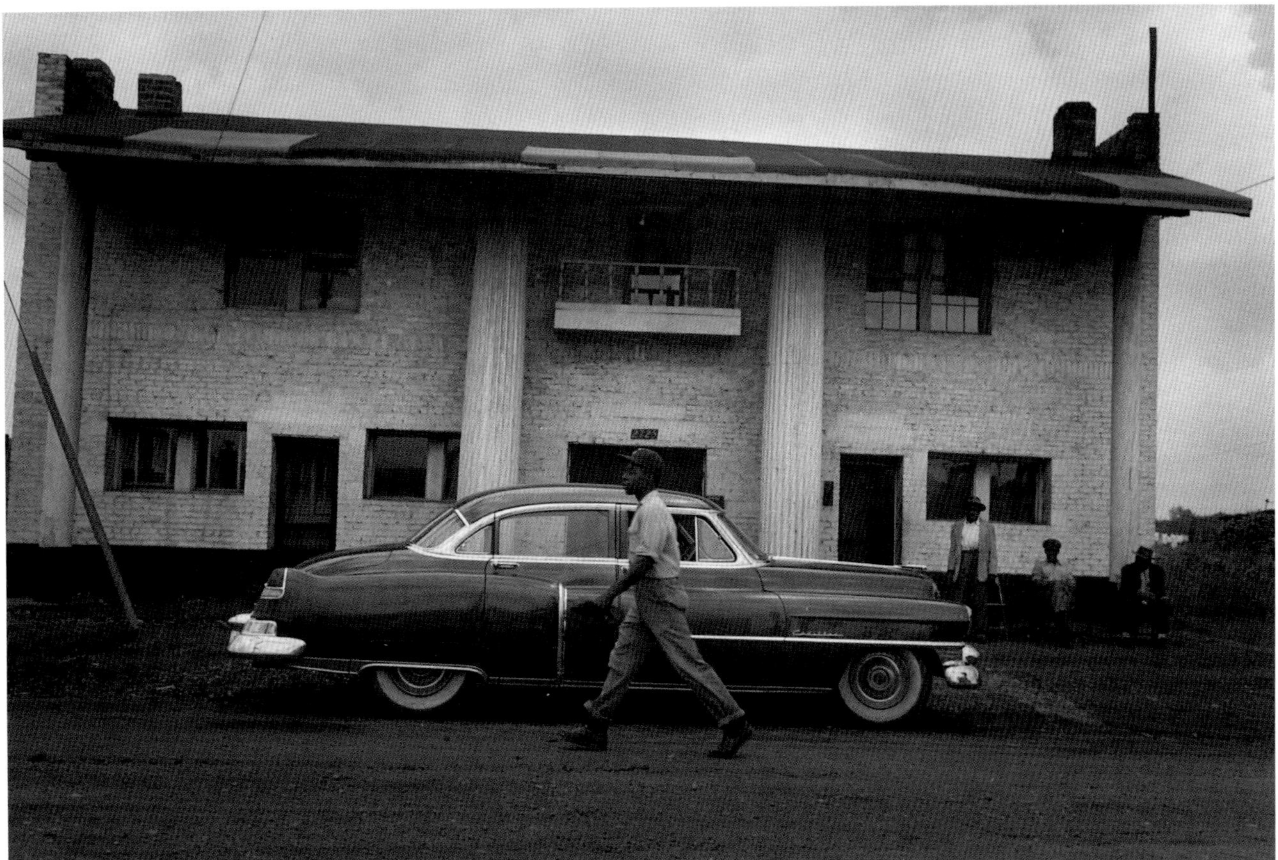

Mexico, 1976 / *Mississippi, 1954*

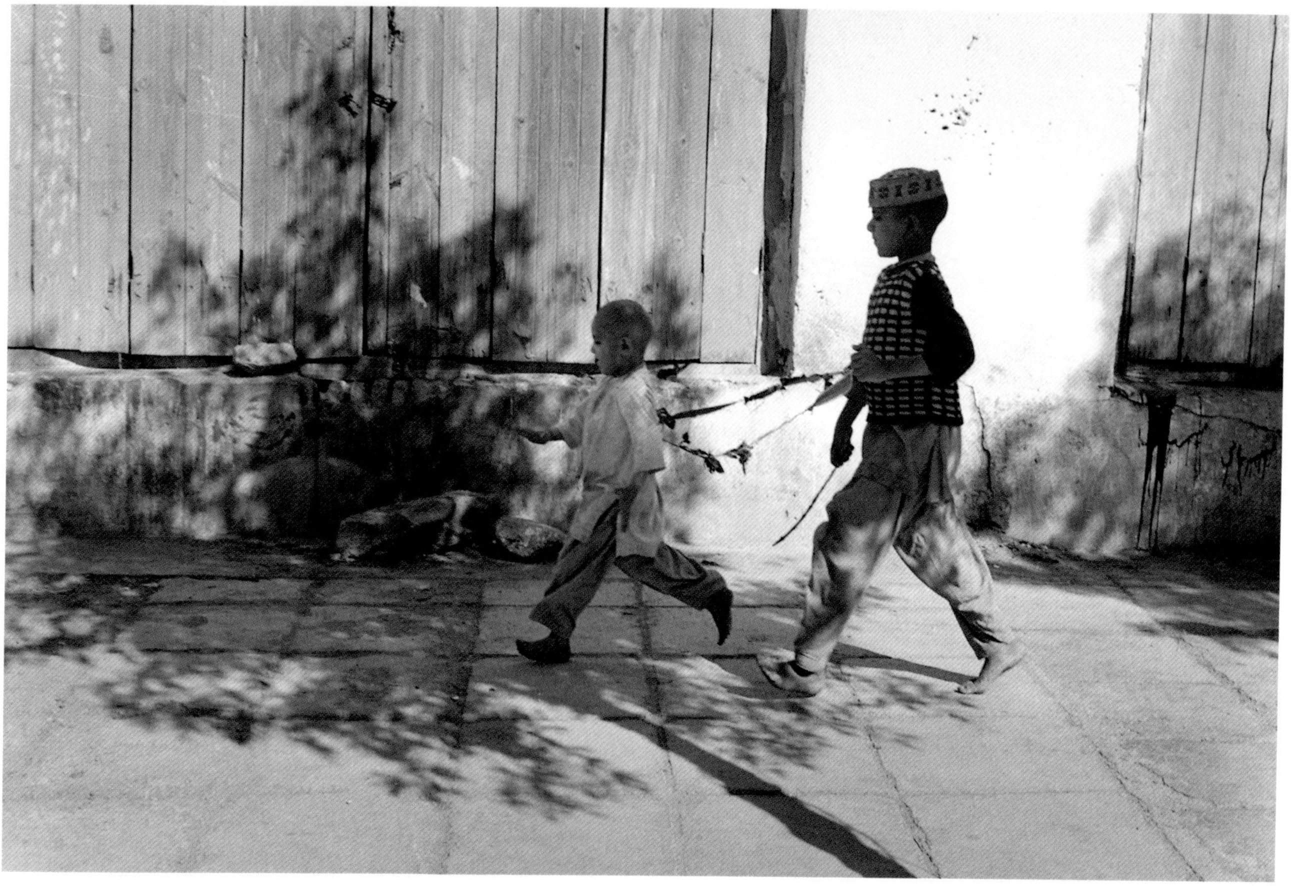

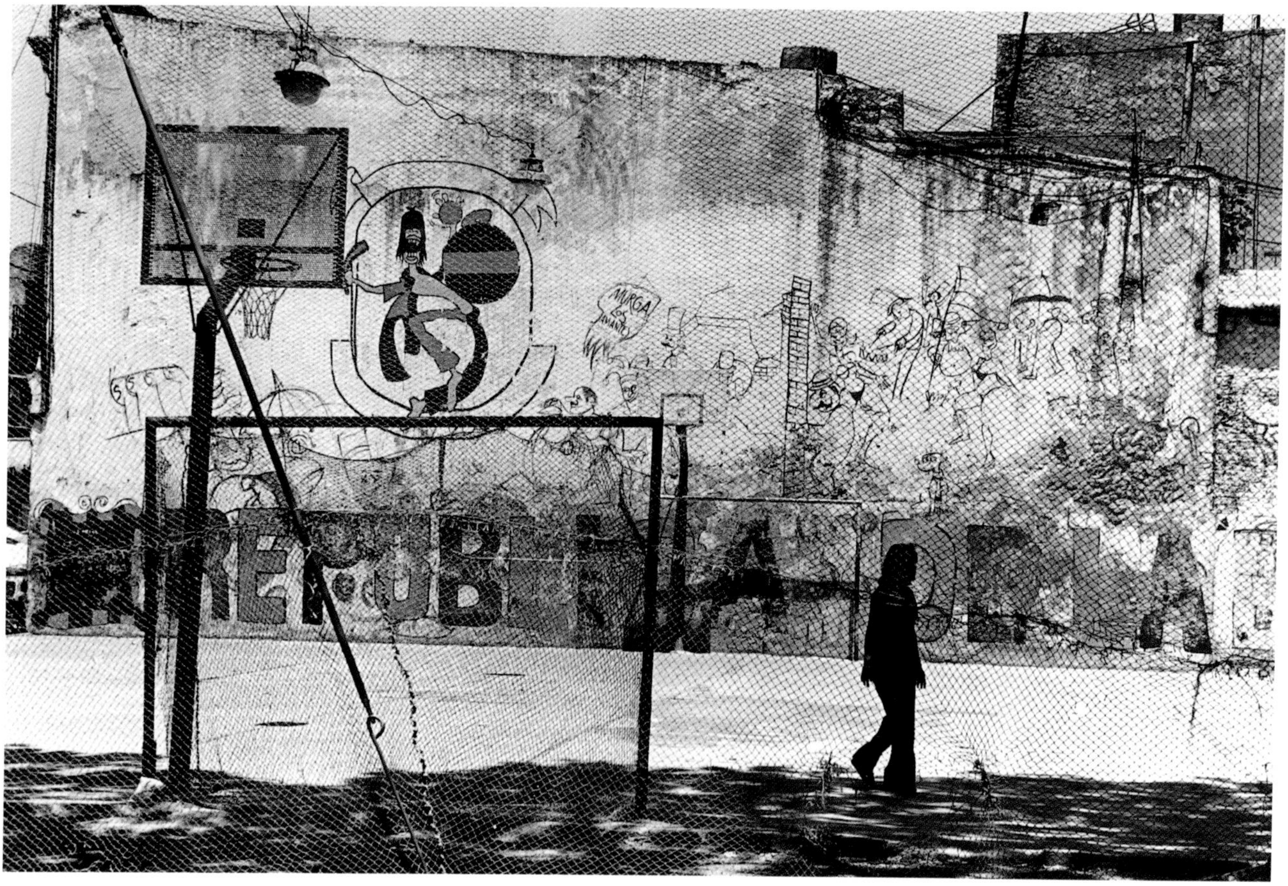

Herát, Afghanistan, 1977 / *Buenos Aires, 2001*

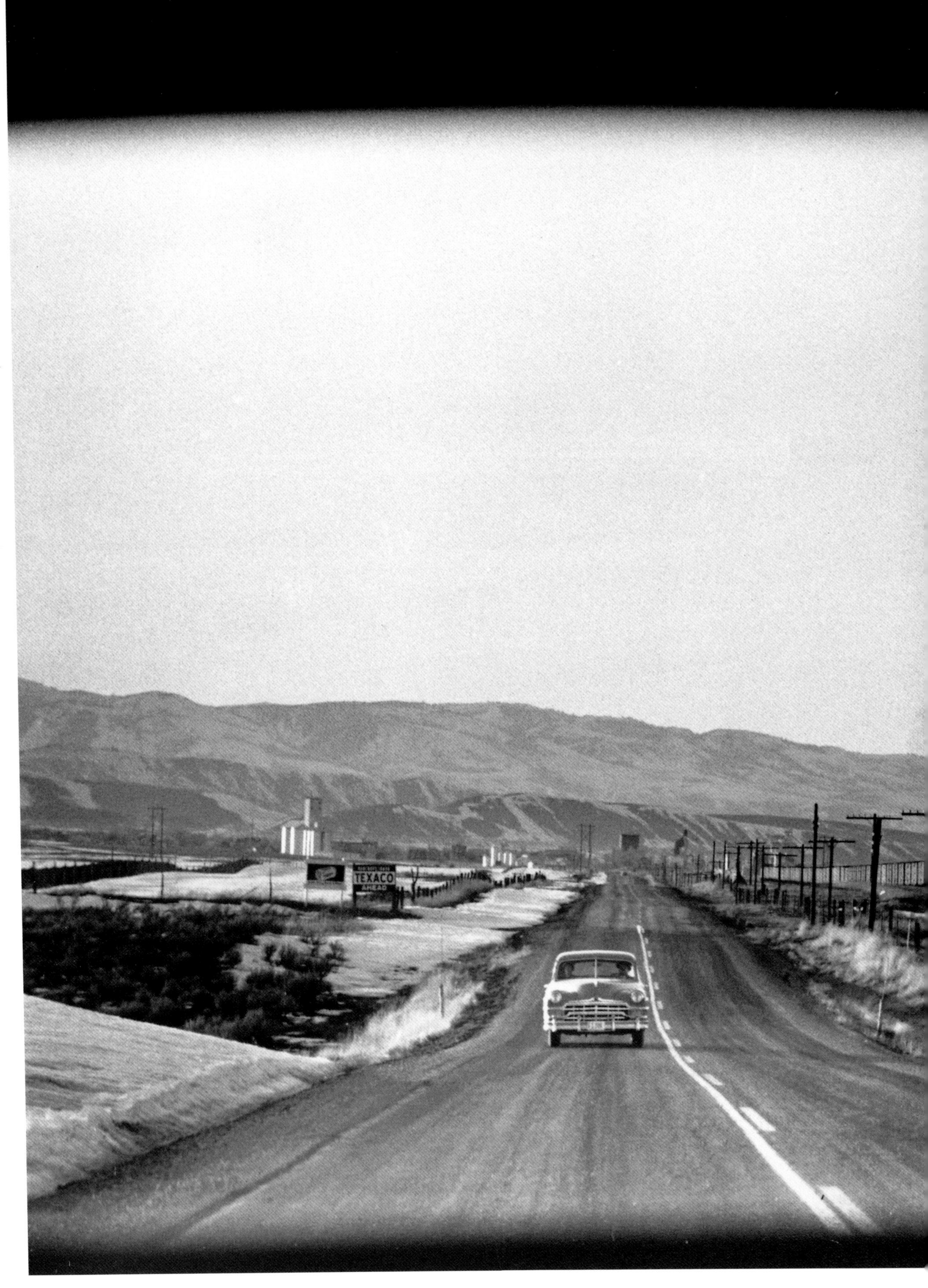

Wyoming, 1954

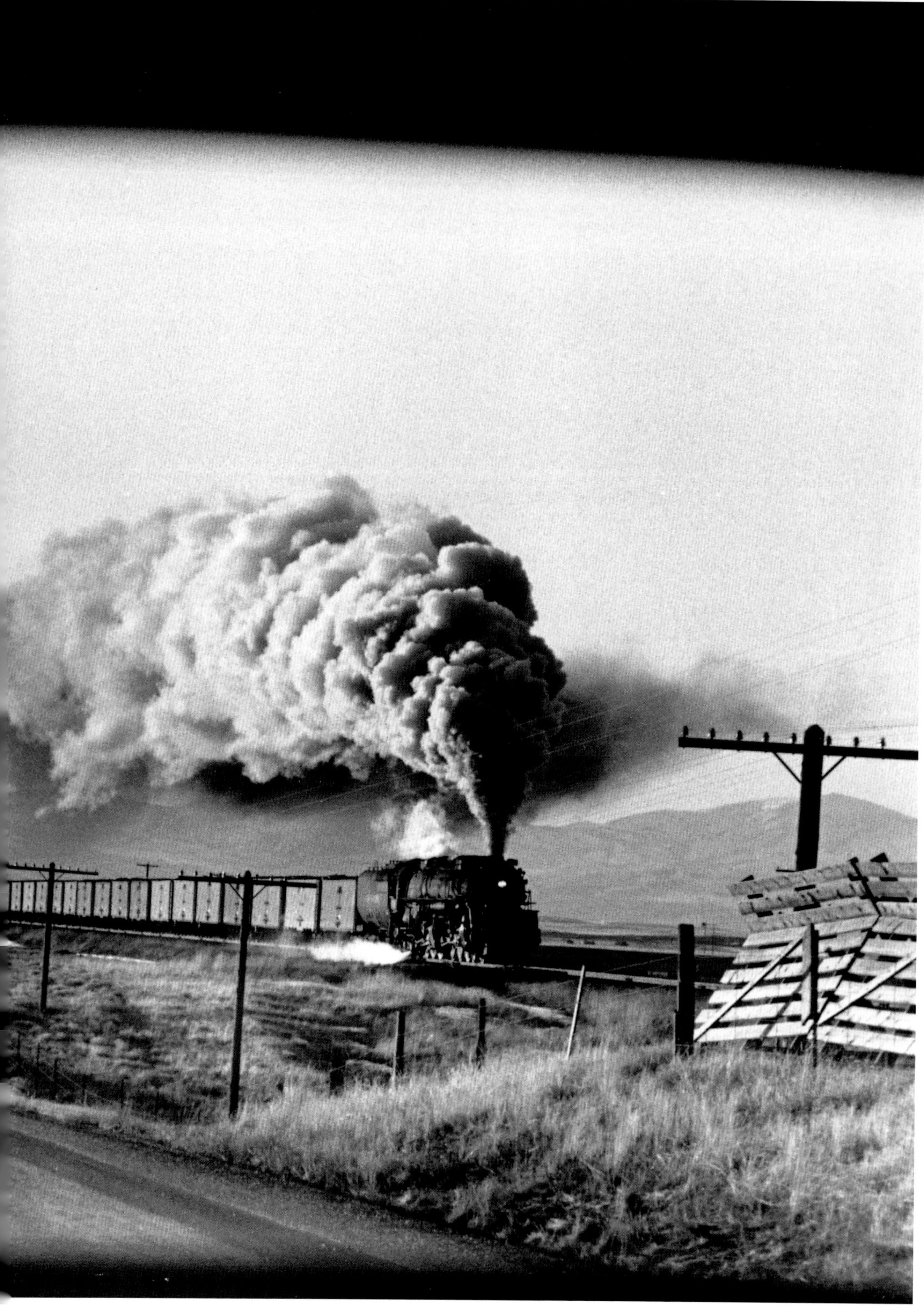

Play

The circus, sports, movies, costumed revels, music, gambling, dancing, making love, singing, acting, fishing – this last section brings together many of Elliott's liveliest snaps of organized play. The ironic undertone, I suppose, is the need itself to come up with such activities. Why do adults play? Why do we seek so many different kinds of entertainment? Is the grim-faced gambler enjoying herself – or the straining athlete?

Probably, Elliott is simply bewildered by all of this nonessential activity. Certainly, his eyes glaze over when Pia's son and I discuss the sterling virtues and periodic travails of the valiant New York Yankees. If he has ever hurled a ball, it would have been to amuse a pet dog. Perhaps it is enough for him to watch others in such organized pursuits, but only briefly, for his own impromptu play permeates virtually every moment of his personal and working life.

As if letting himself out of school, he ends the book with a playful, posed picture of his youngest child, Amy (p.542). She is so much his daughter she was able to find amusement in working as an aide in Al Gore's 2000 campaign for president. And like all of his children and grandchildren, she has been periodically subjected over the years to her father's gag gifts.

A man who does not plunder his assets to buy clothes – brown corduroys, dark jackets, scuffed shoes keep him well in the background – Elliott will splurge on items that cost a fair amount of money but perform no seriously useful function. For example, there is the eight-inch-tall standing telephone in the shape of a penguin that flaps its carmine beak in sync with the person blathering on the other end of the line. It is especially diverting for chats with a lawyer.

Call Elliott two days before Easter Sunday, and he will say, 'Have a good Friday.' (This behaviour cannot be modified.)

Call him anytime and he will answer, 'Speaking', before you say a word. (To be fair, he is speaking, so what's so confusing?)

It has not all been play. In the late 1980s, as Elliott was nearing sixty, the magazine work had dried up, young advertising execs did not know his images, and there were no major exhibitions of new photos. He thought it was all over. He had seen more than one important photographer slide into oblivion. Then his world turned around because his friend Lee Jones, head of editorial projects at the Magnum office in New York, and an editor, James Mairs, put together the retrospective exhibition and book, *Personal Exposures*. Since then, phone, fax and e-mail have been humming, and Elliott is not always home four weeks in a row.

'Live long enough', he shrugs now, 'and you will be famous.'

Not quite. If Elliott is better known now than ever before in his life, I would guess that is because the work accumulates but does not radically change. In each new snap there is the abiding sensibility that is at once charming, a bit unsettling and seriously perplexed about it all.

A mutual acquaintance dumbfounded me recently by asking, 'Isn't Elliott ready to retire? What more could he want?' For Elliott to stop making snaps, and stop perpetrating awful puns in otherwise polite conversation, would be like a bird not flying, a dog not barking, a child not racing towards the outstretched arms of a grandparent. I mean that. He snaps because he is. When he makes self-portraits, a camera or its analog, a mask, is often in the picture. Without the incessant framing of instants caught for meaning, he would not be Elliott.

You will make him happiest if you visit an exhibition, look at a snap hanging on the wall, walk away, stop, then return to reconsider whether or not you actually saw what you think you saw. He may be hiding behind a pillar, watching. Having you make that double-take is his proudest achievement. And by now, I suspect, you have done it often as you've paged through *Snaps*.

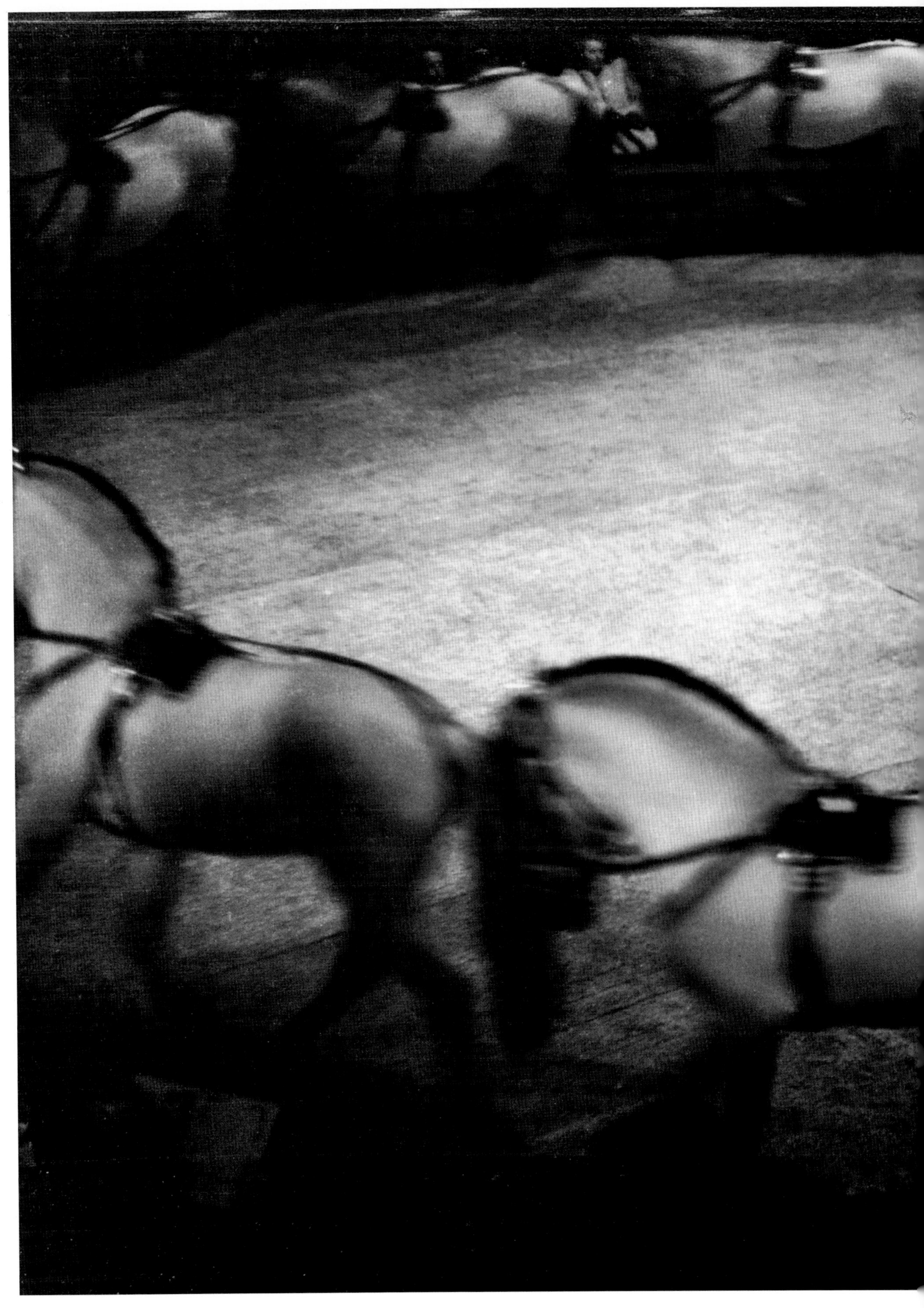

Paris, 1951

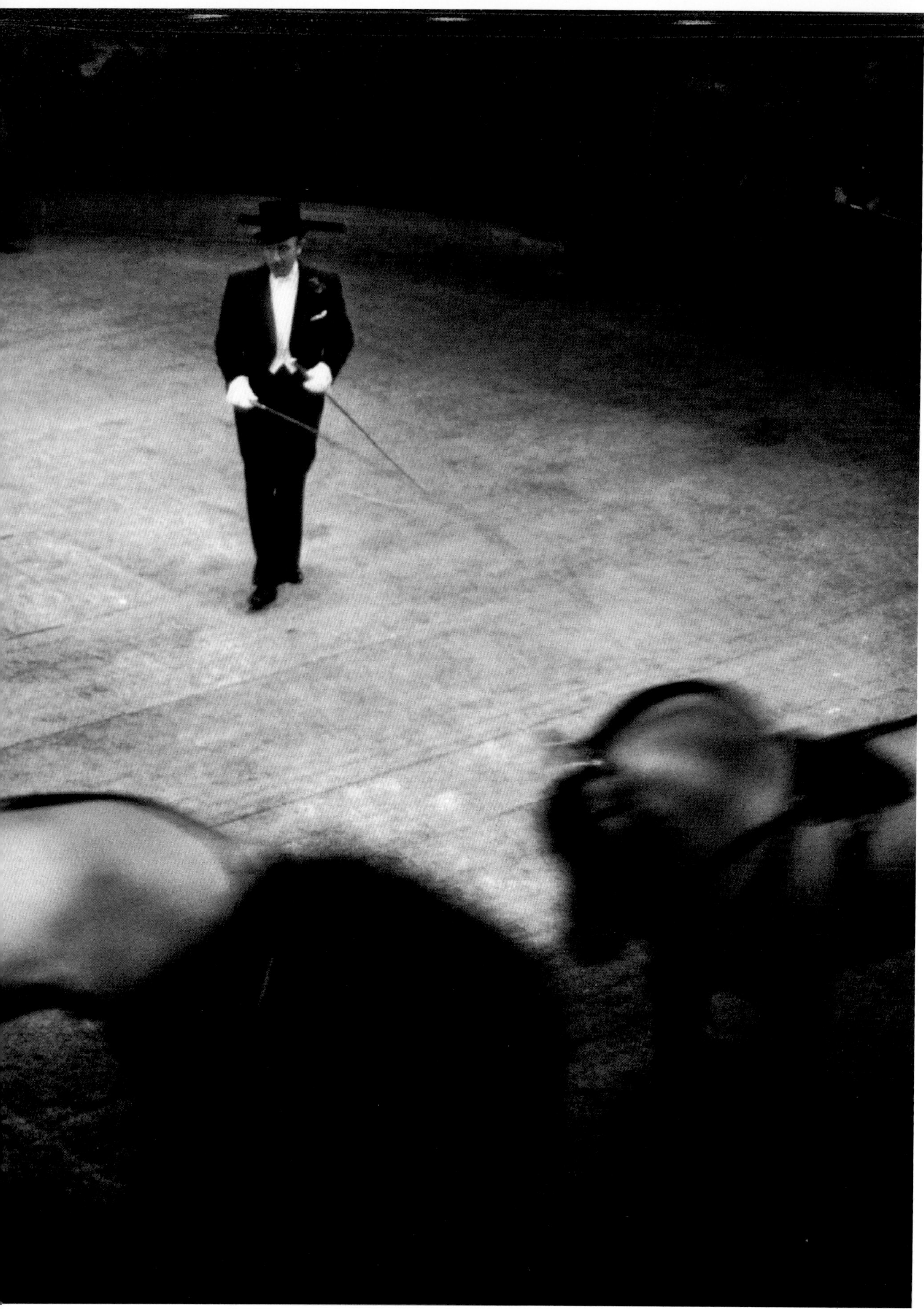

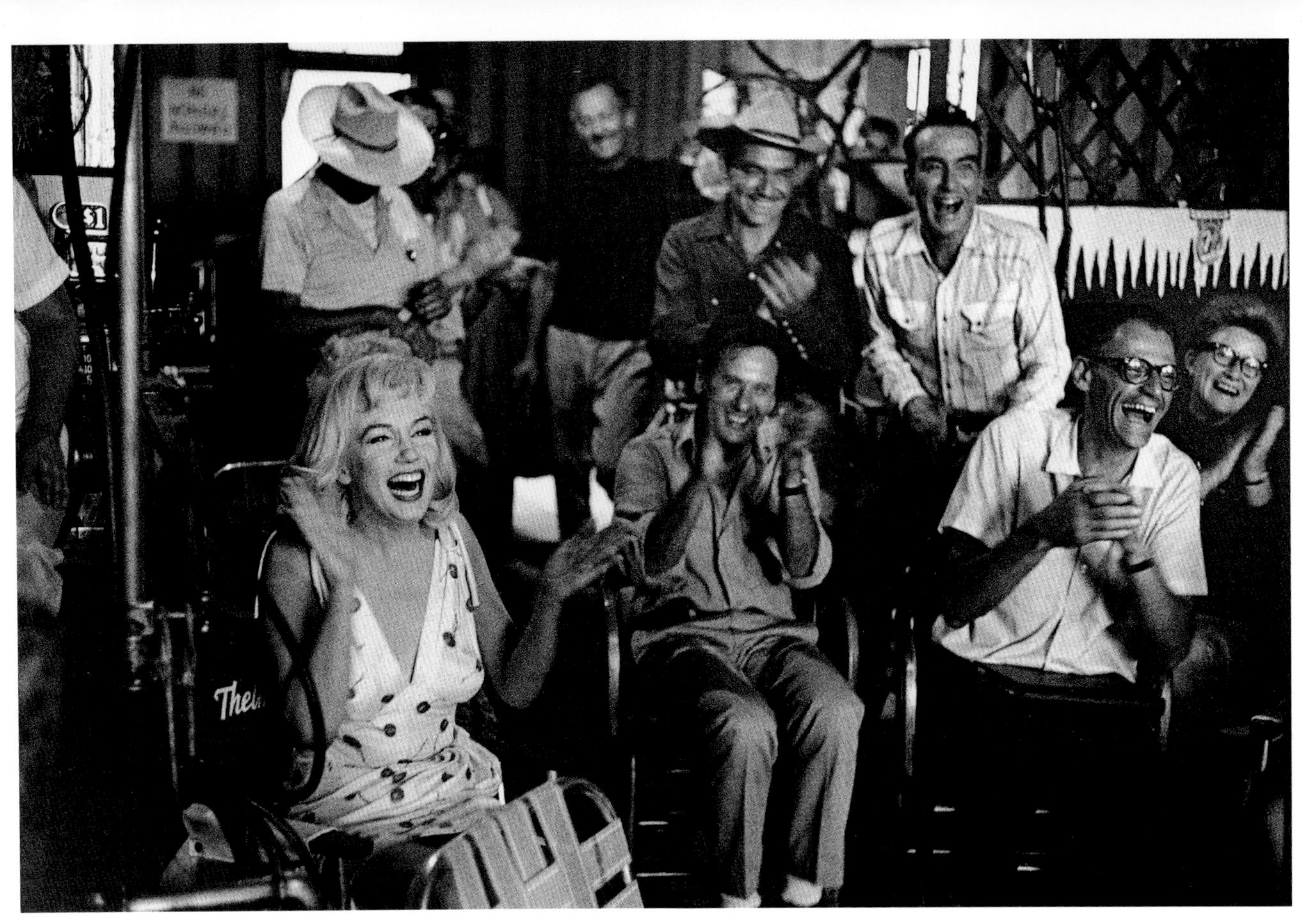

On the set of 'The Misfits', Reno, Nevada, 1960

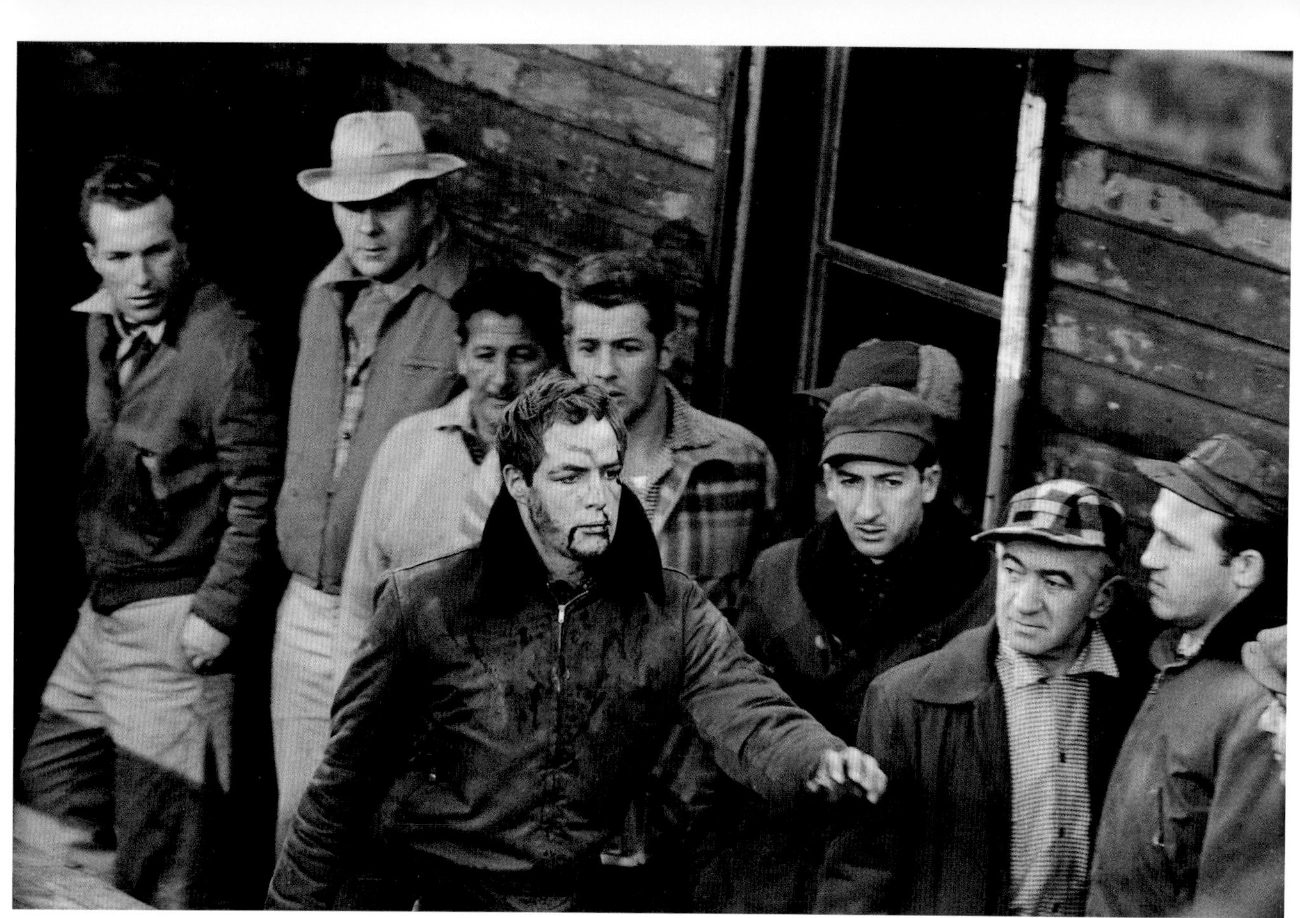

Marlon Brando in 'On the Waterfront', Hoboken, New Jersey, 1954

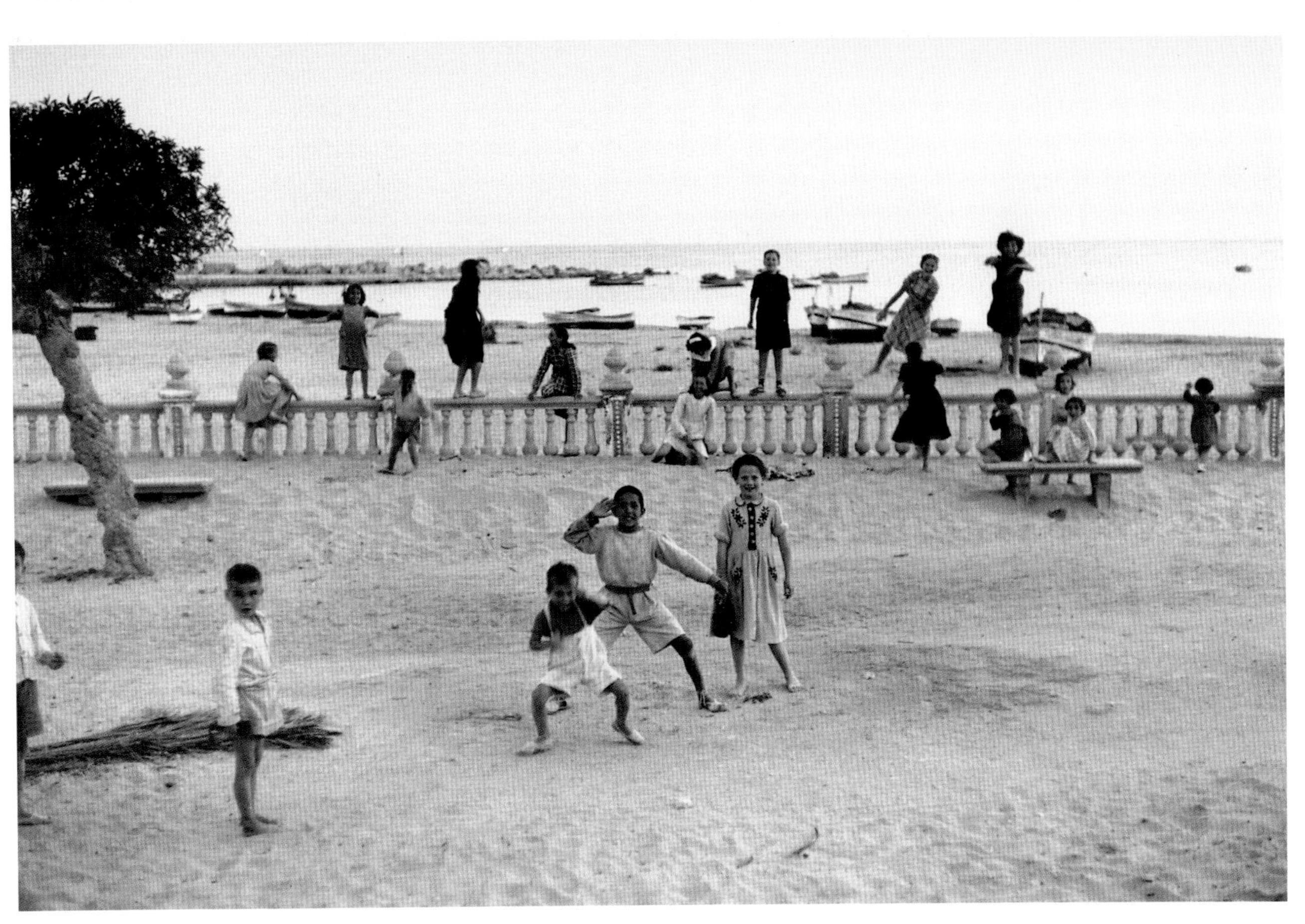

Valencia, Spain, 1952

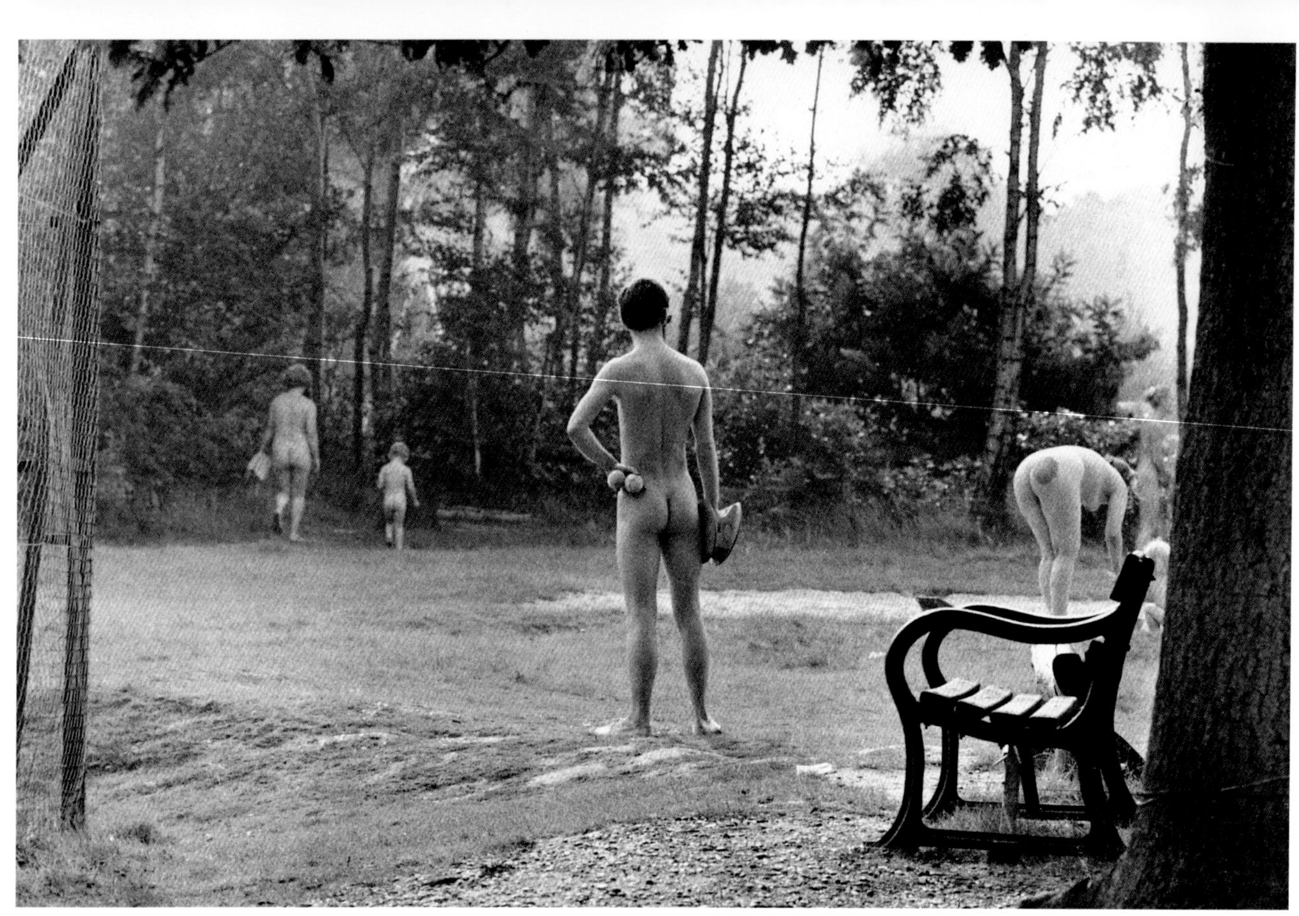

Kent, England, 1968

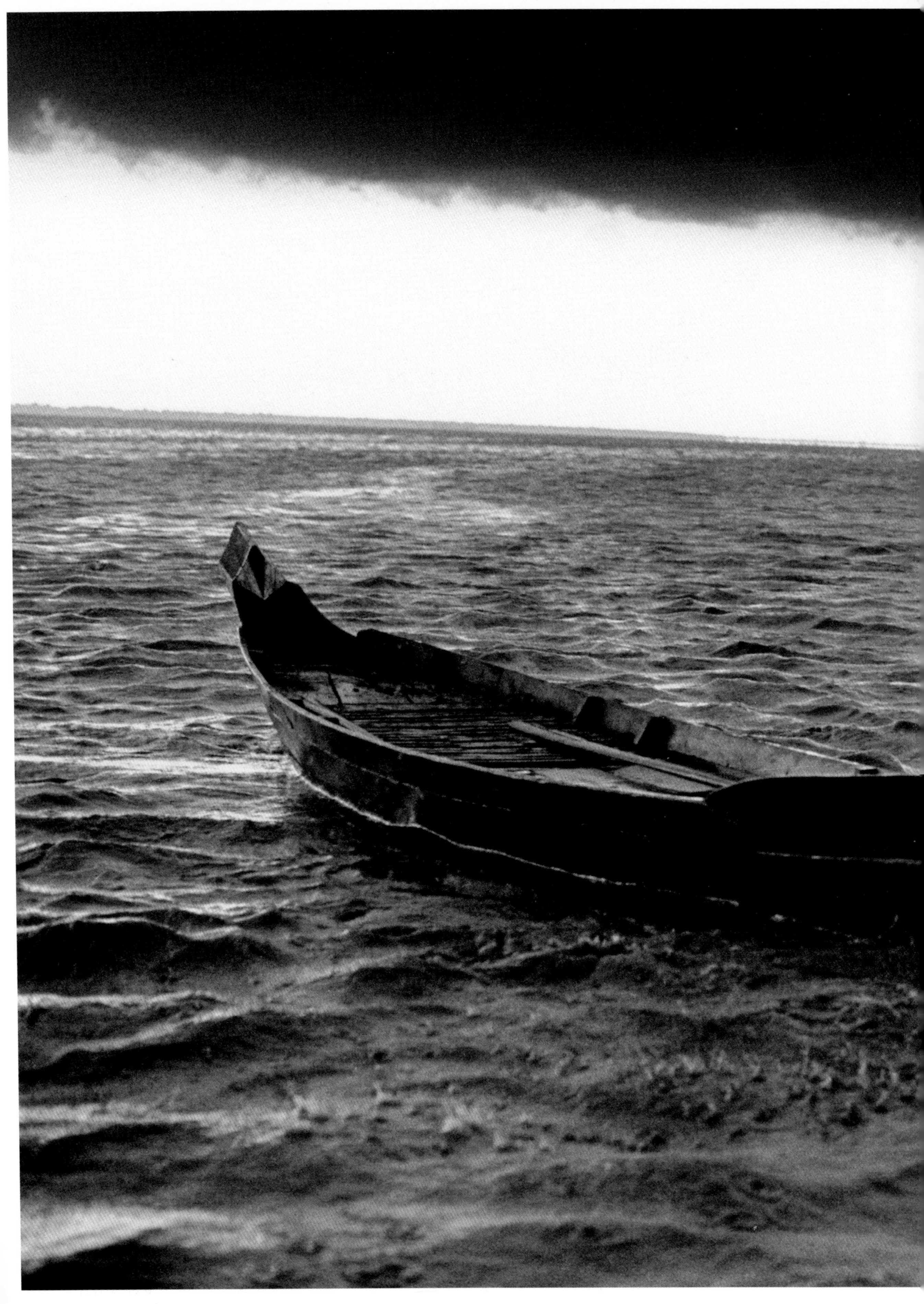

Cambodia, 1998

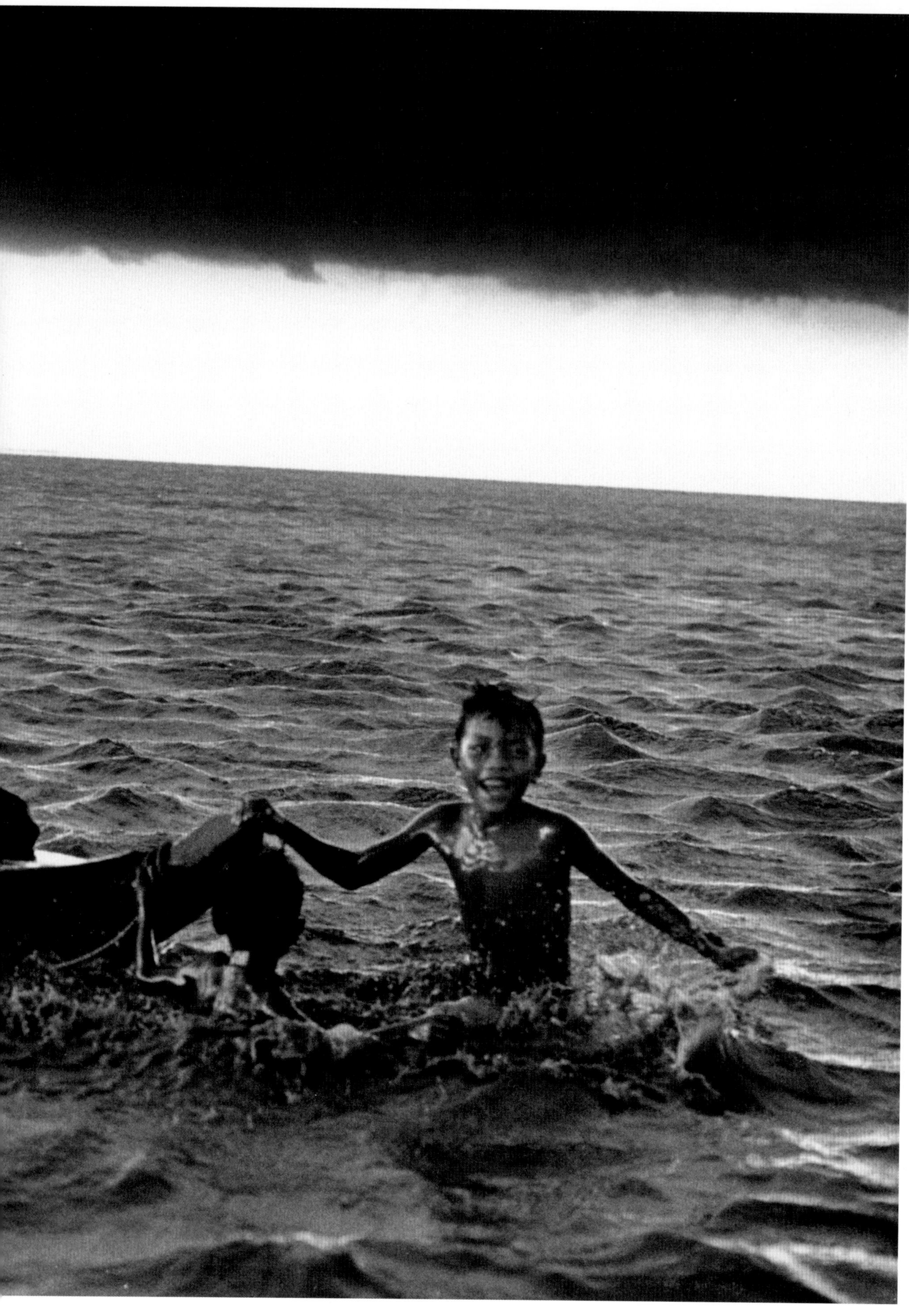

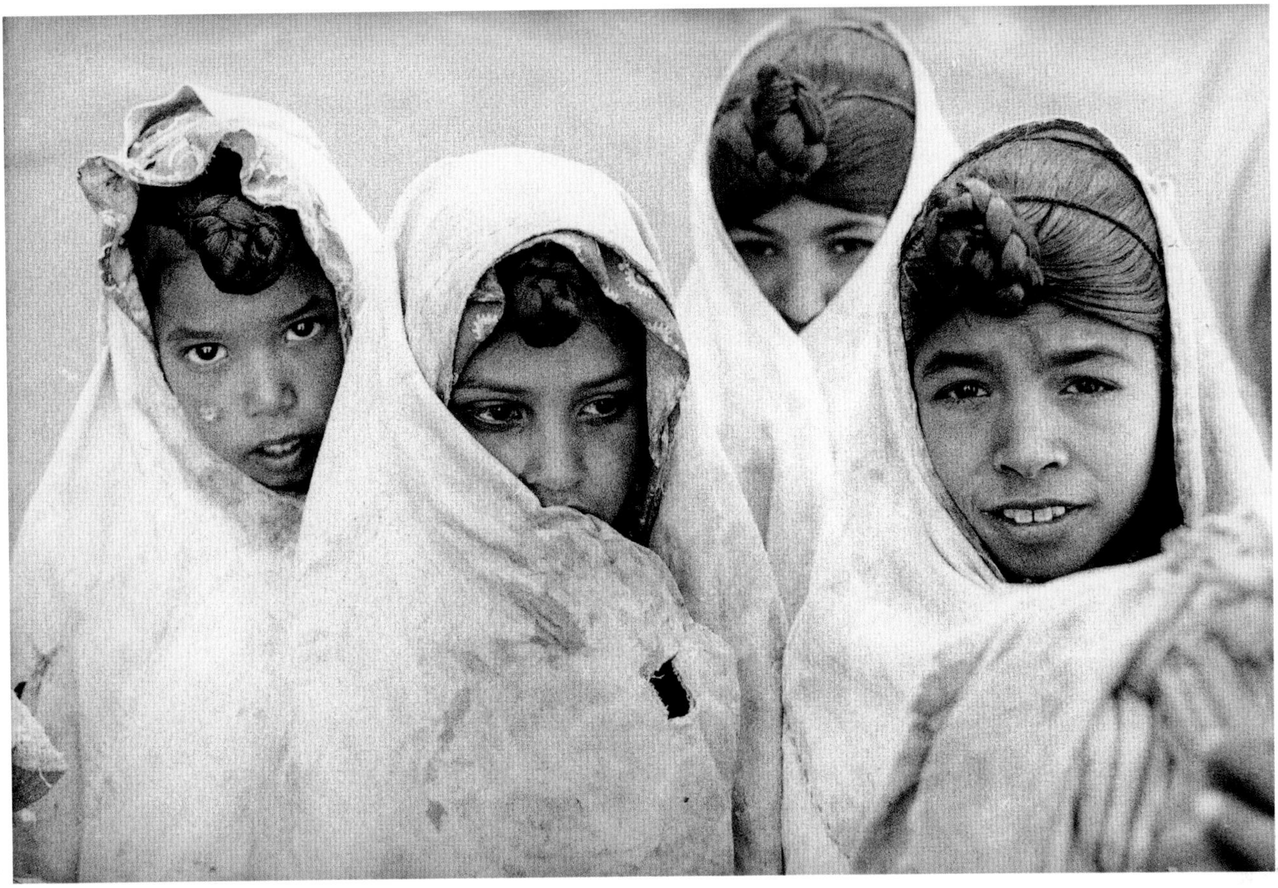

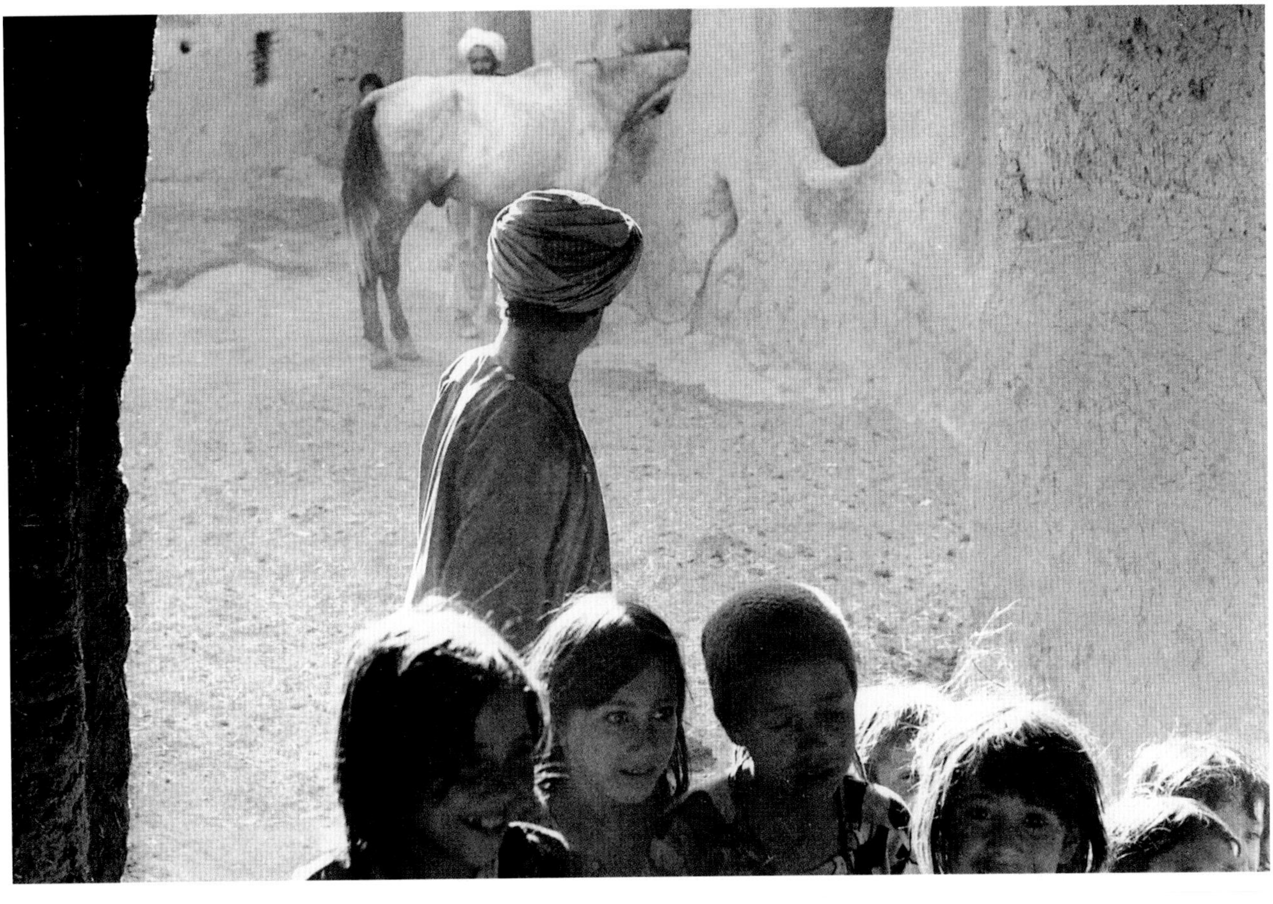

Mount Sinai, Egypt, 1960 / Herát, Afghanistan, 1977

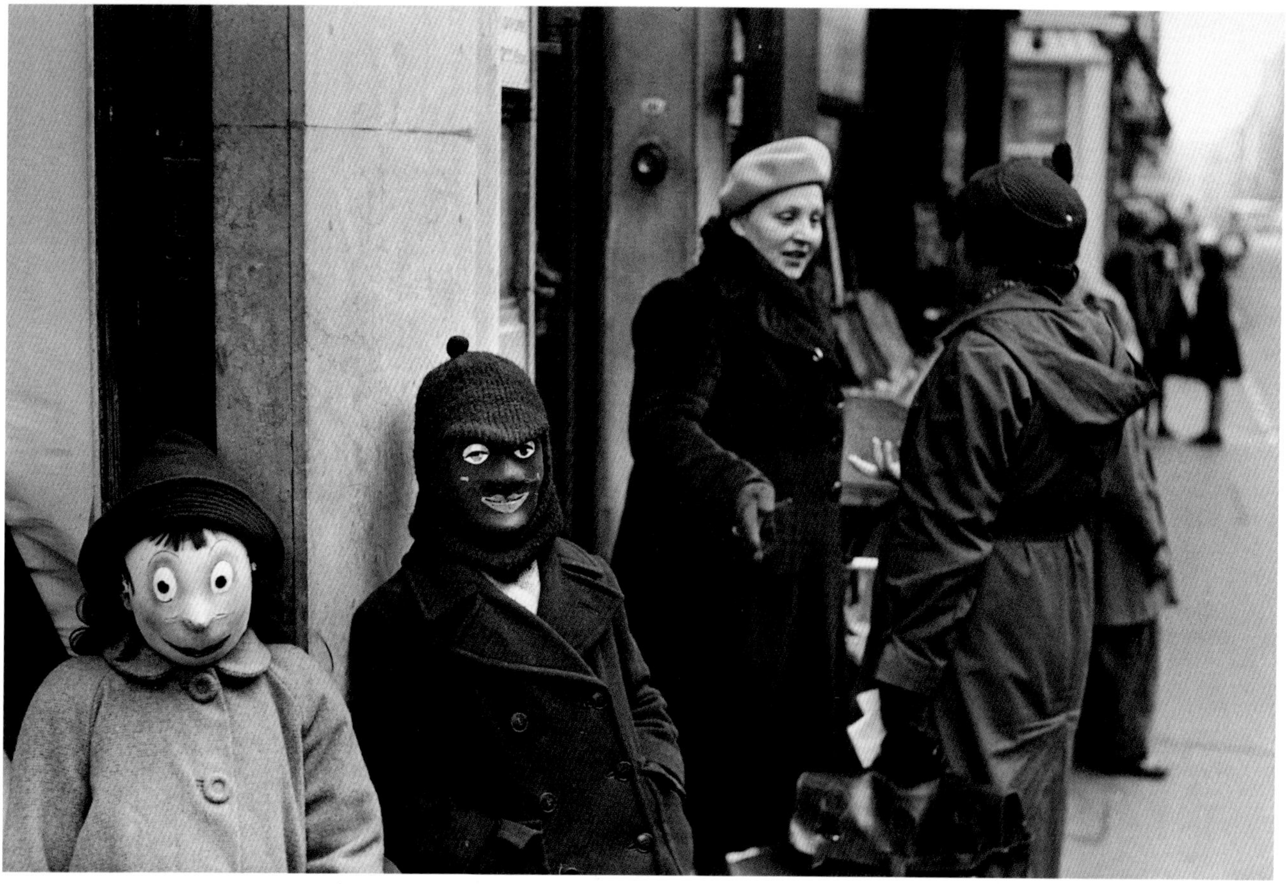

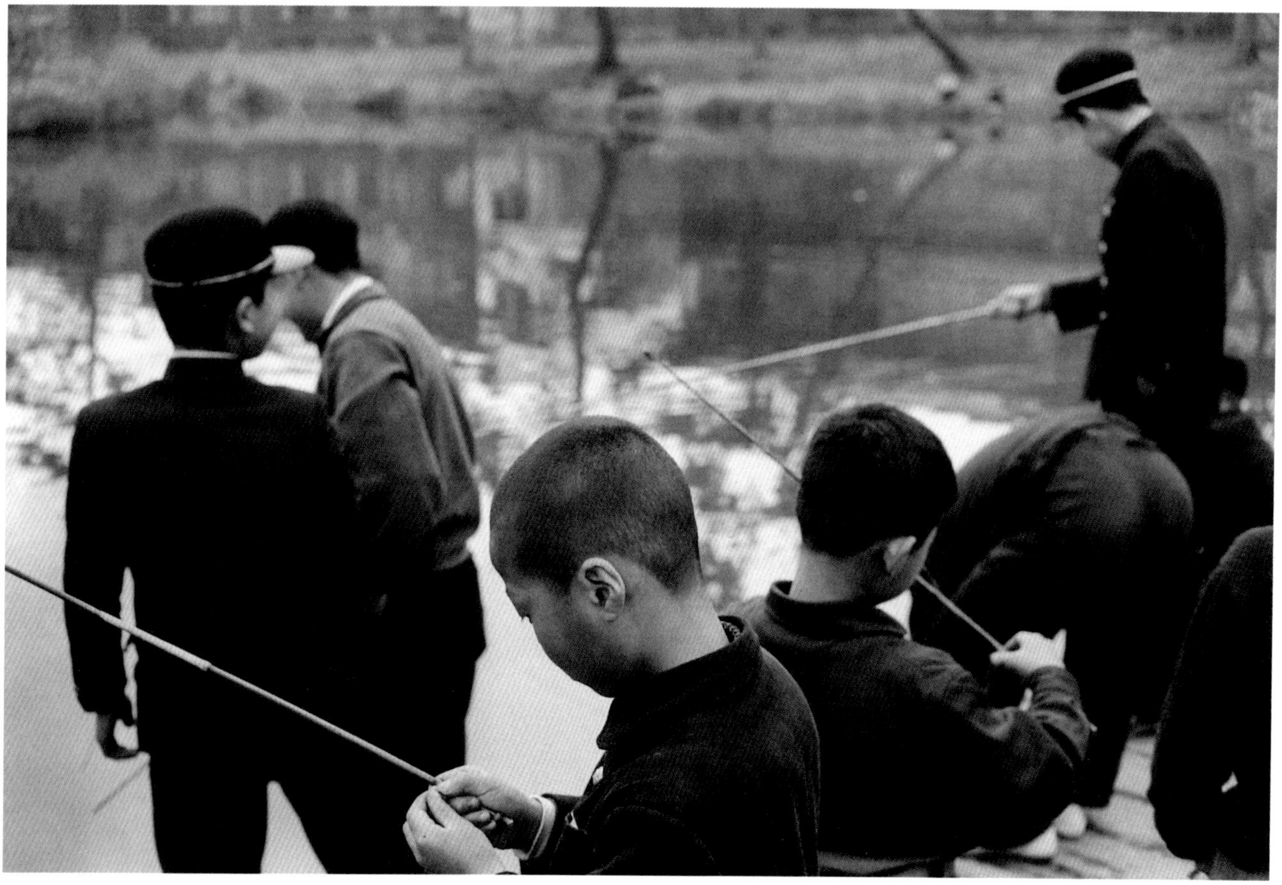

Paris, 1949 / *Tokyo, 1960*

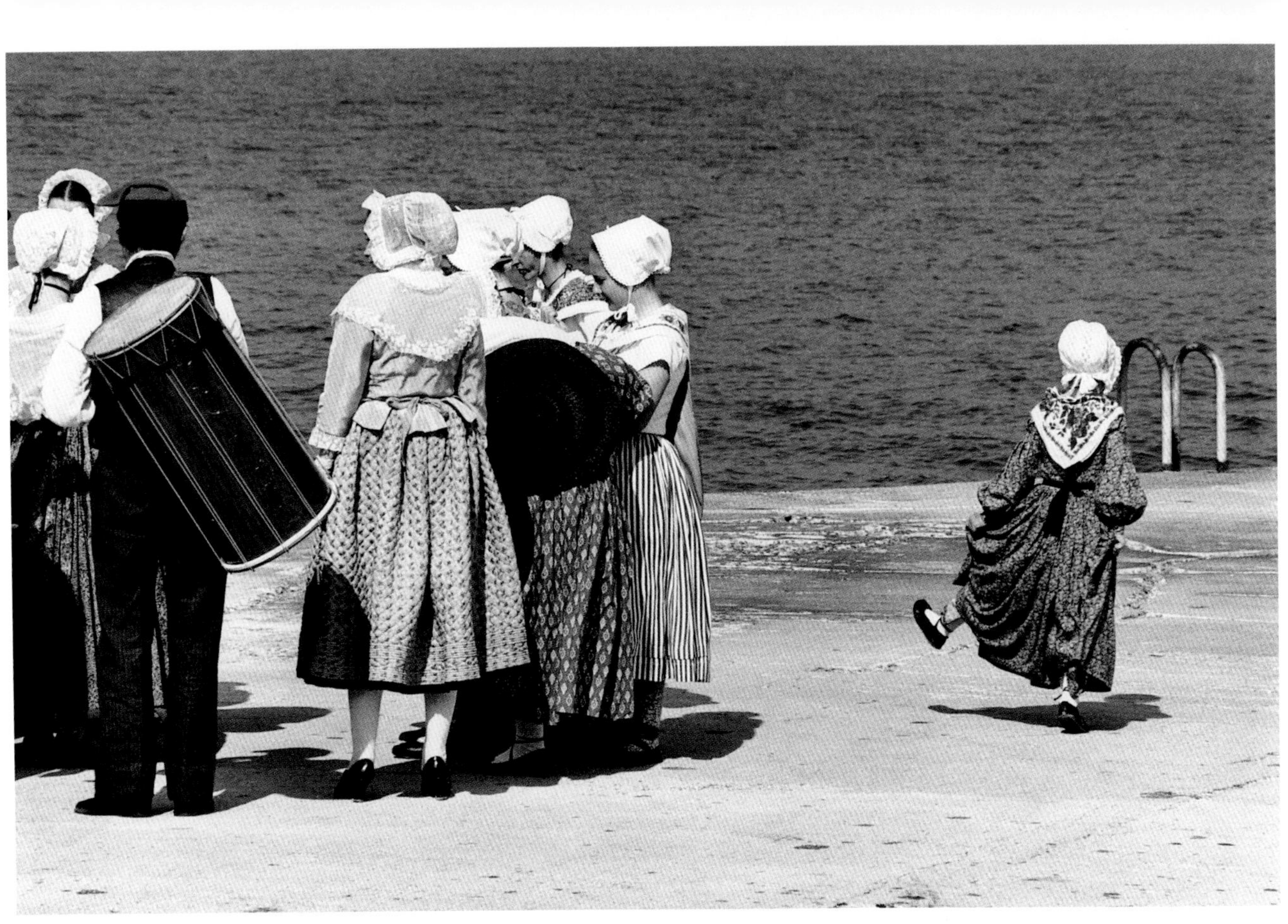

St Tropez, France, 1979

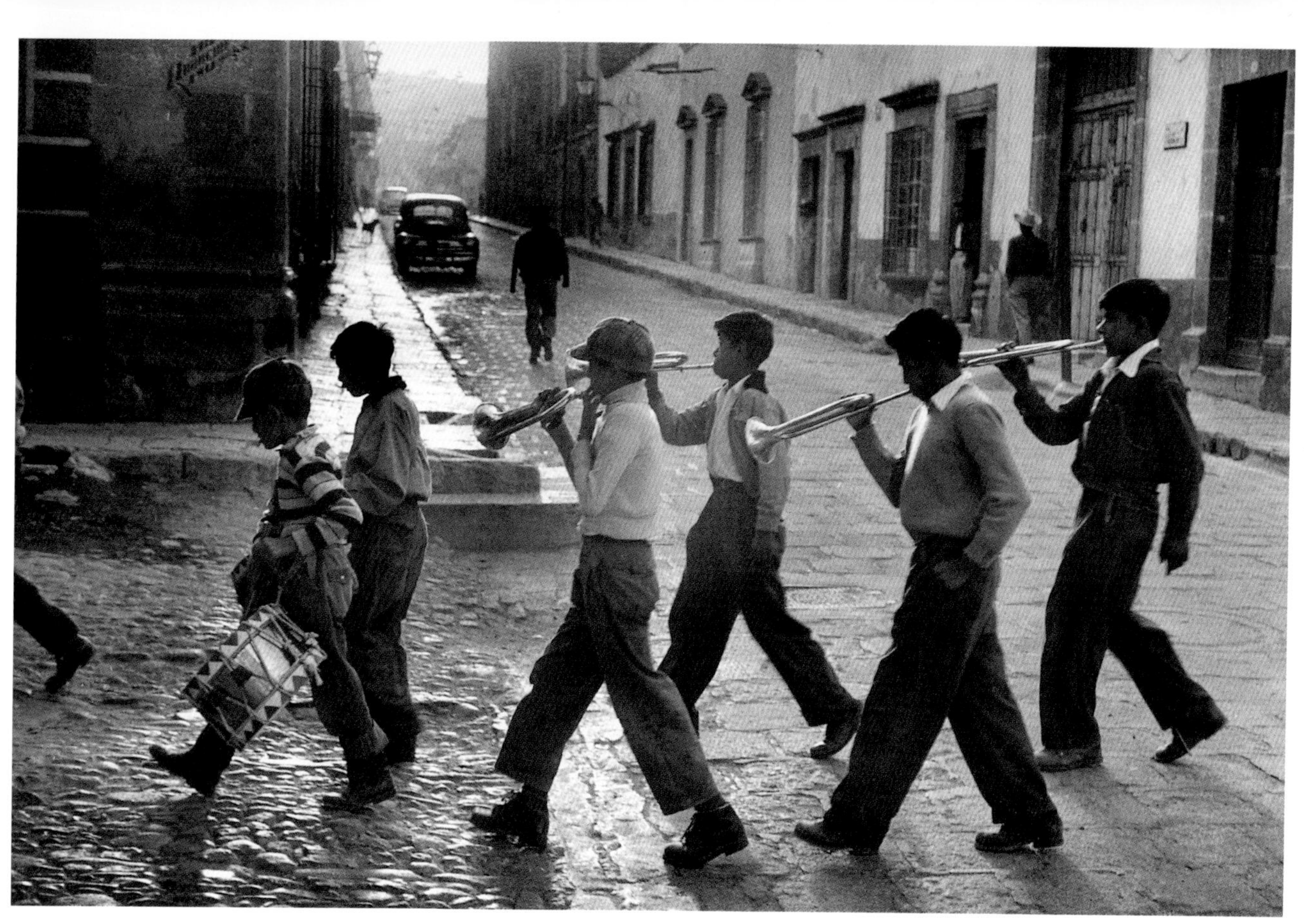

San Miguel de Allende, Mexico, 1957

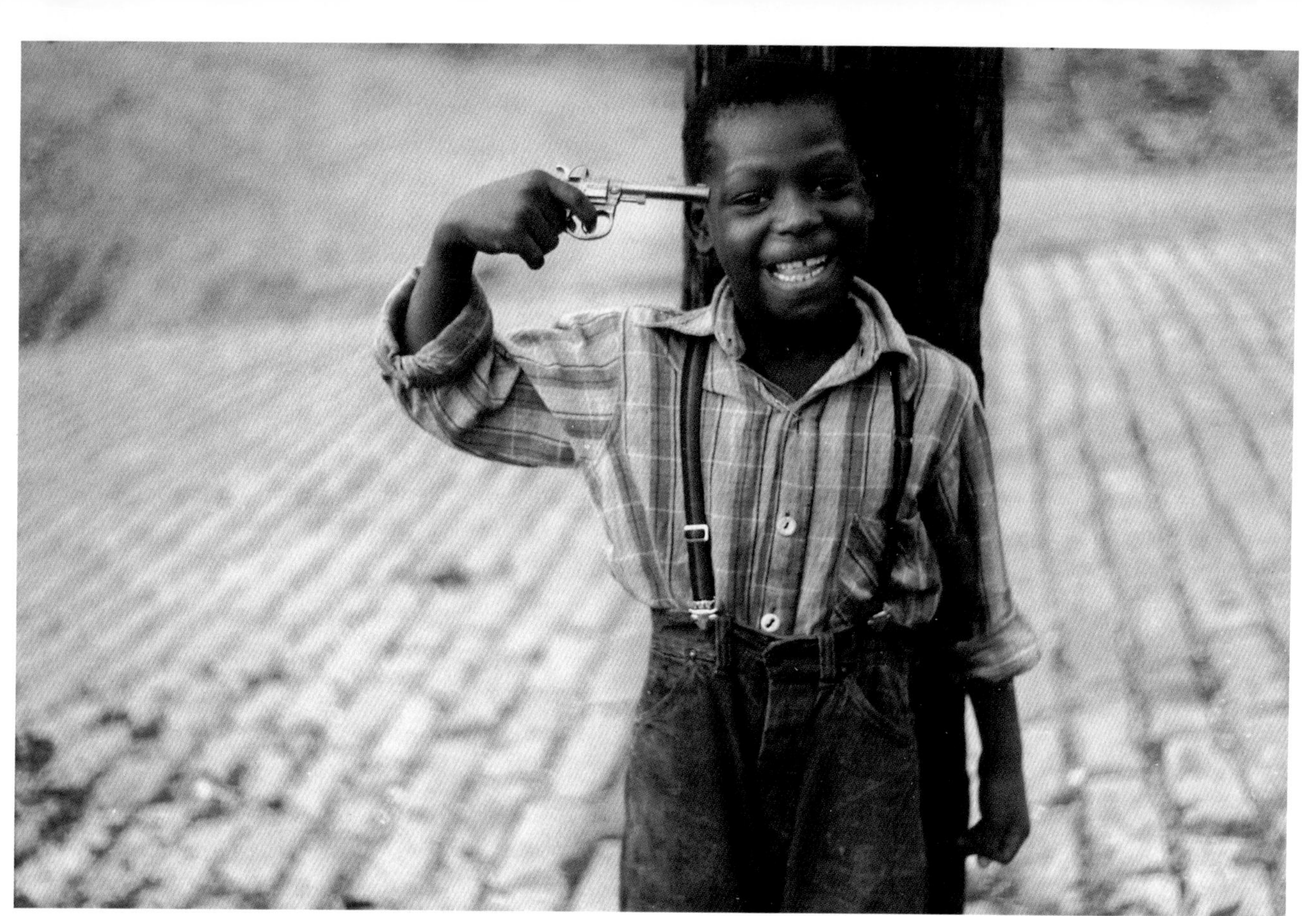

Pittsburgh, Pennsylvania, 1950

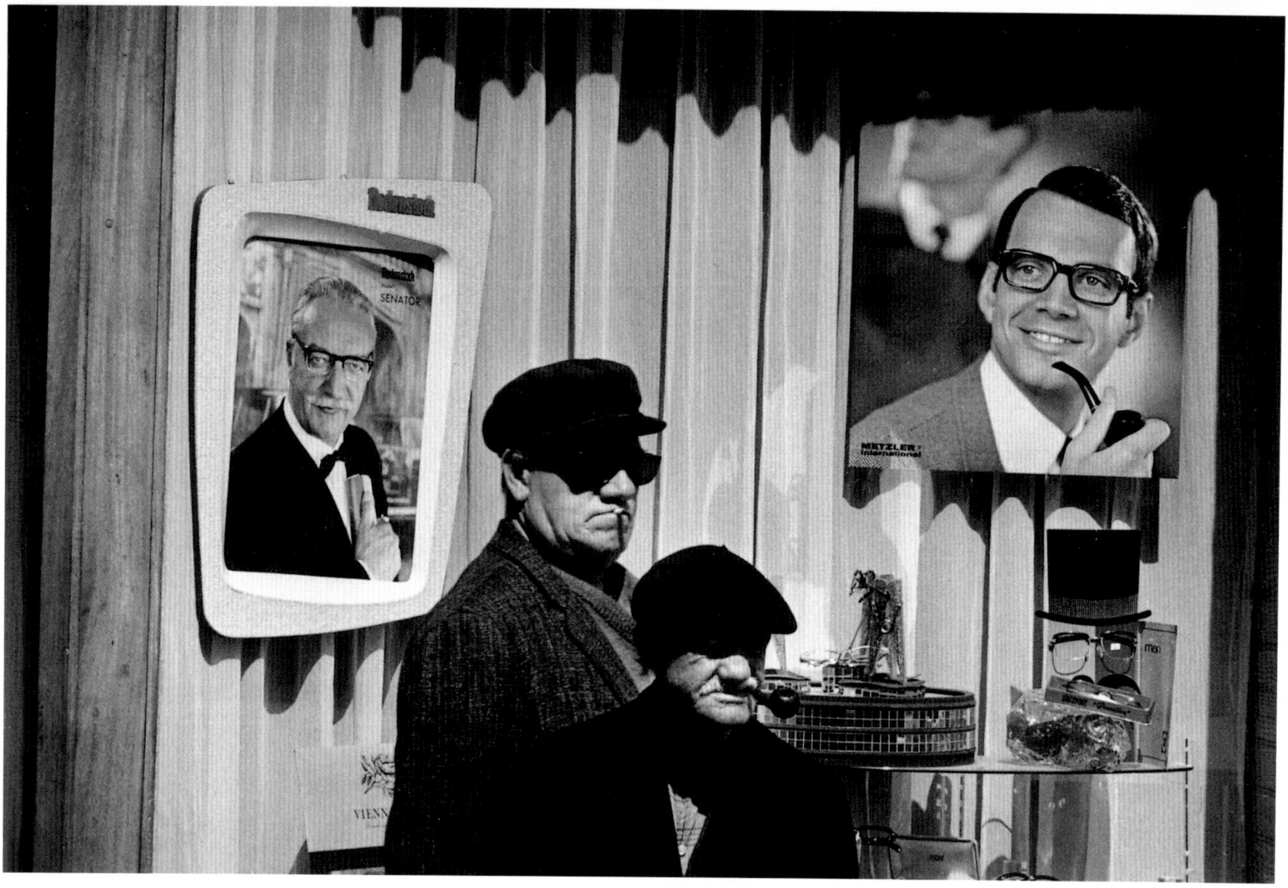

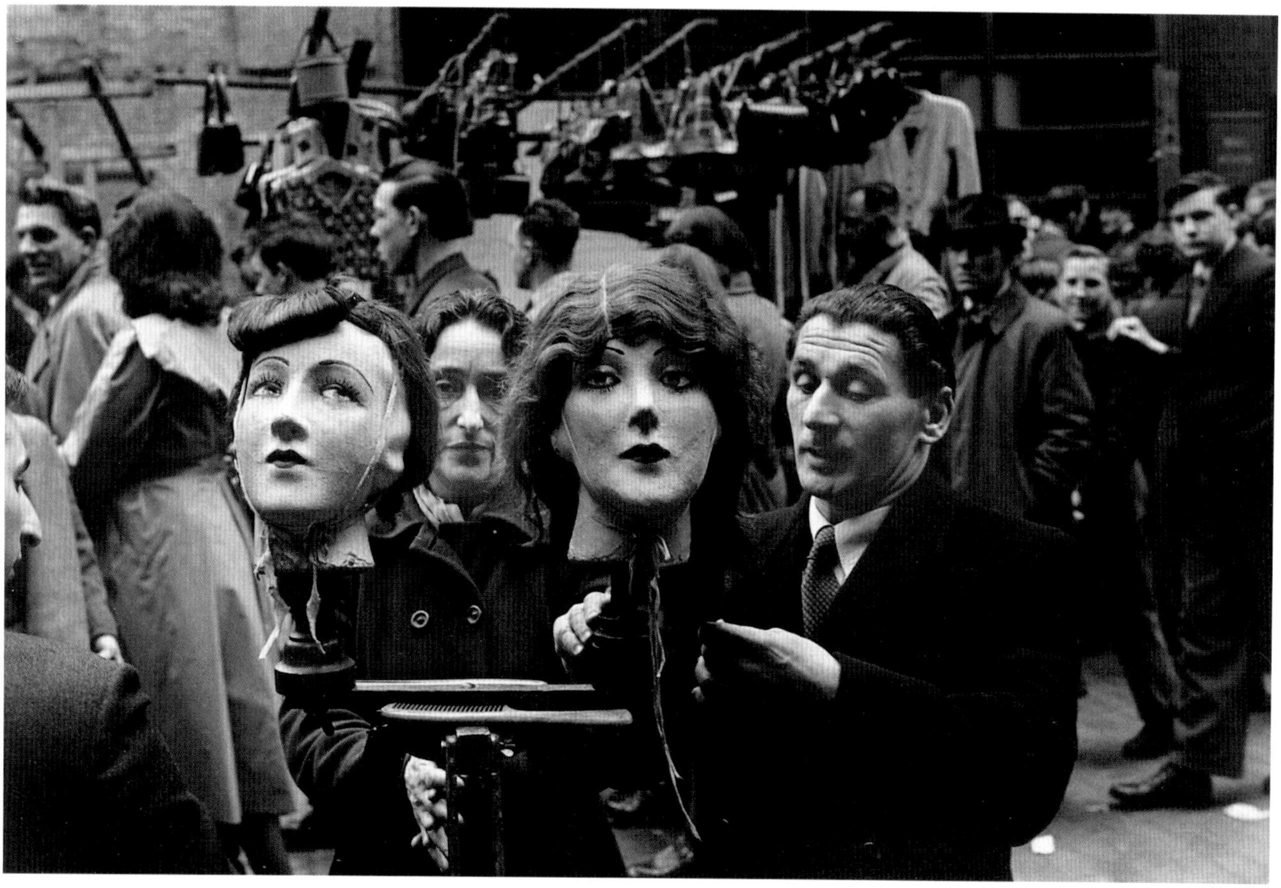

Amsterdam, 1968 / *London, 1952*

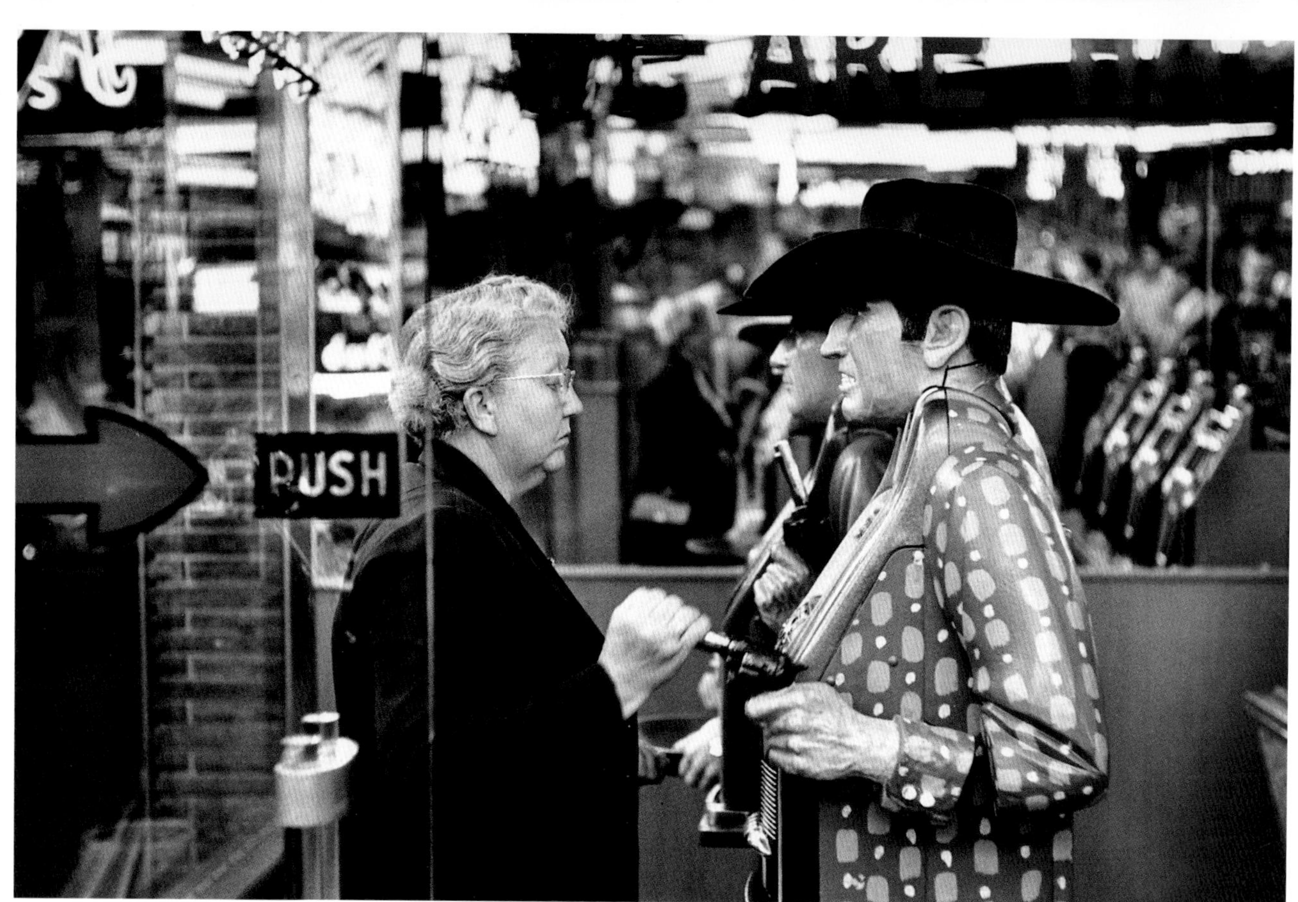

Las Vegas, 1954

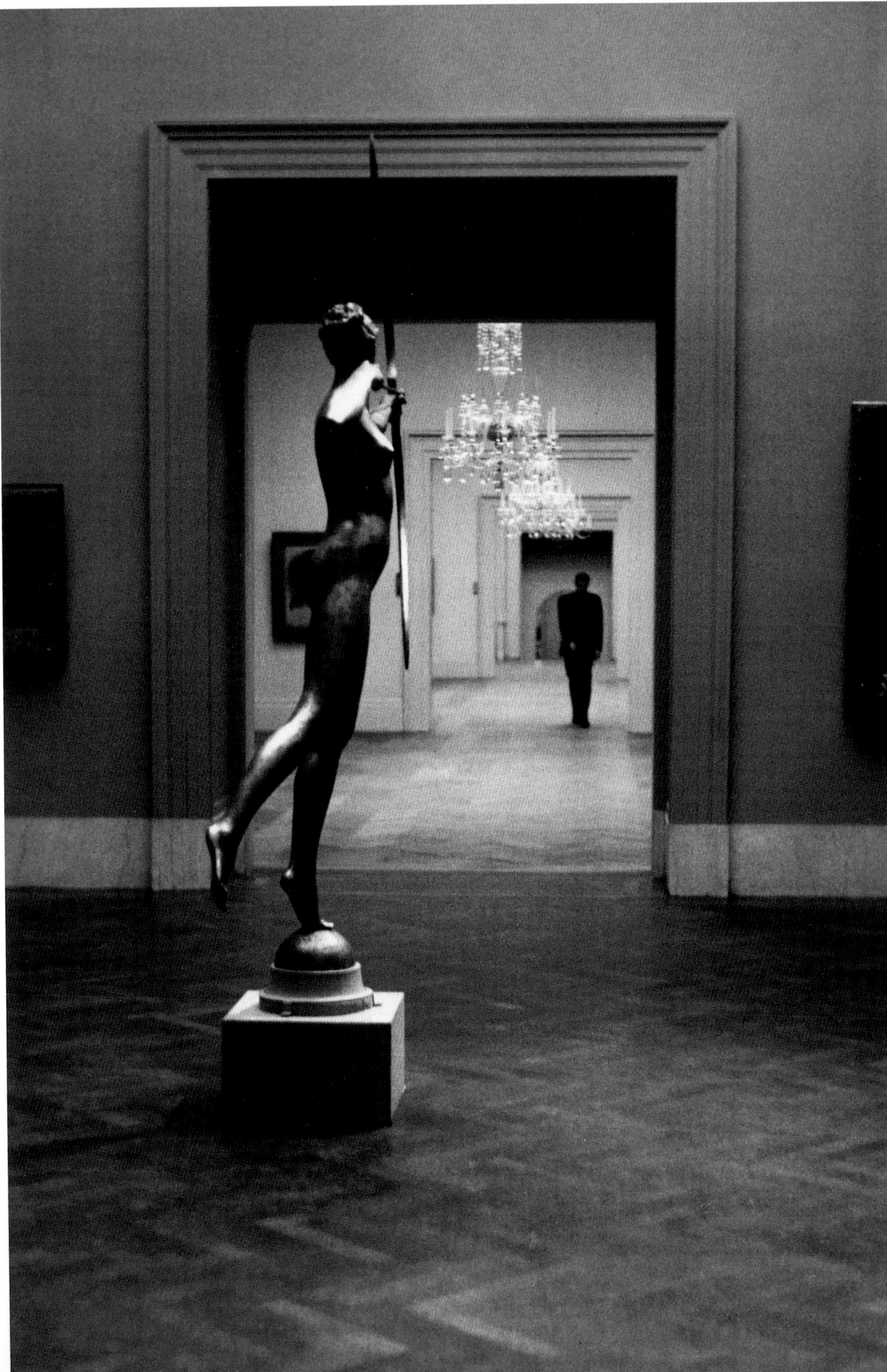

Metropolitan Museum of Art, New York, 1949

California, 1955

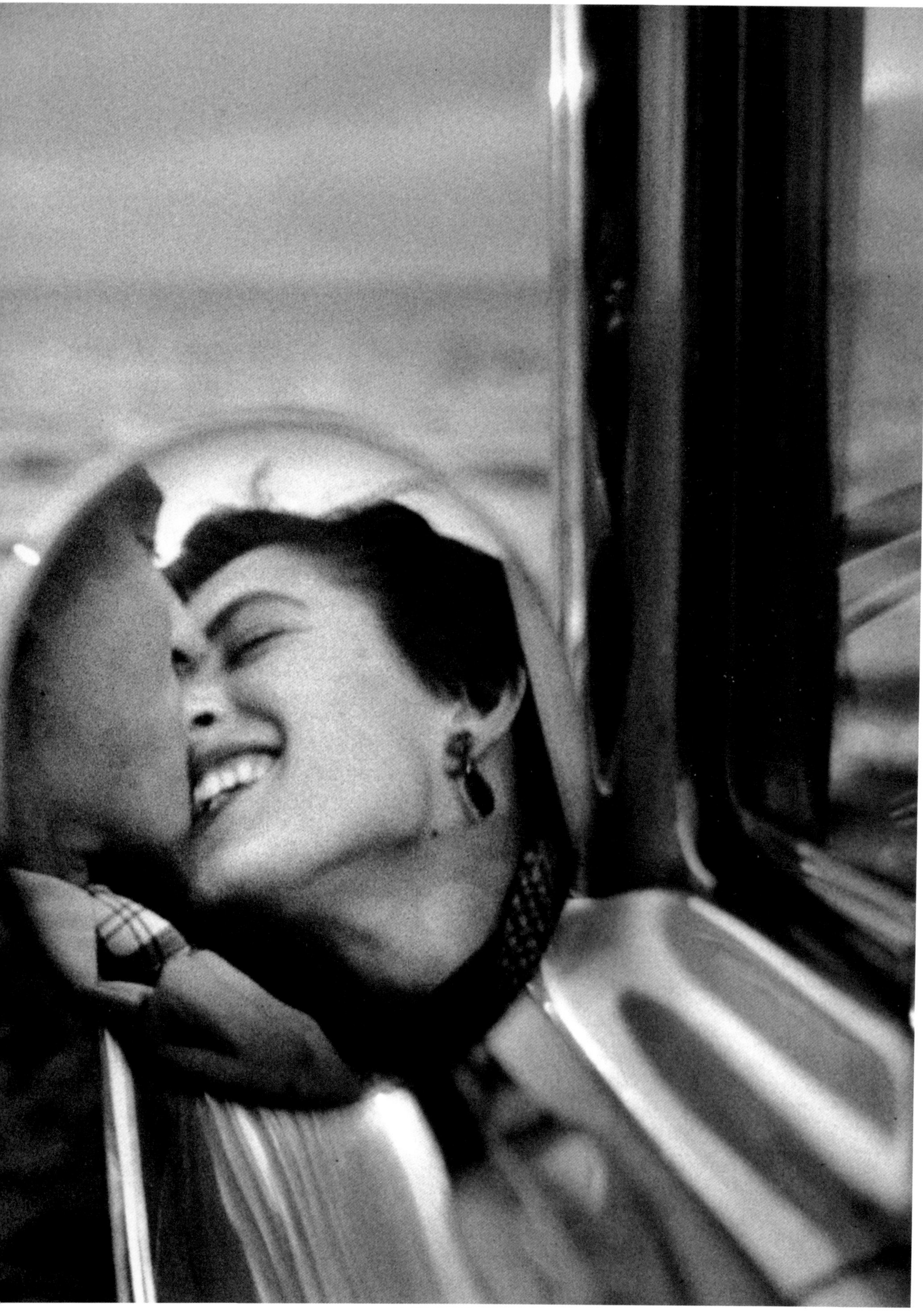

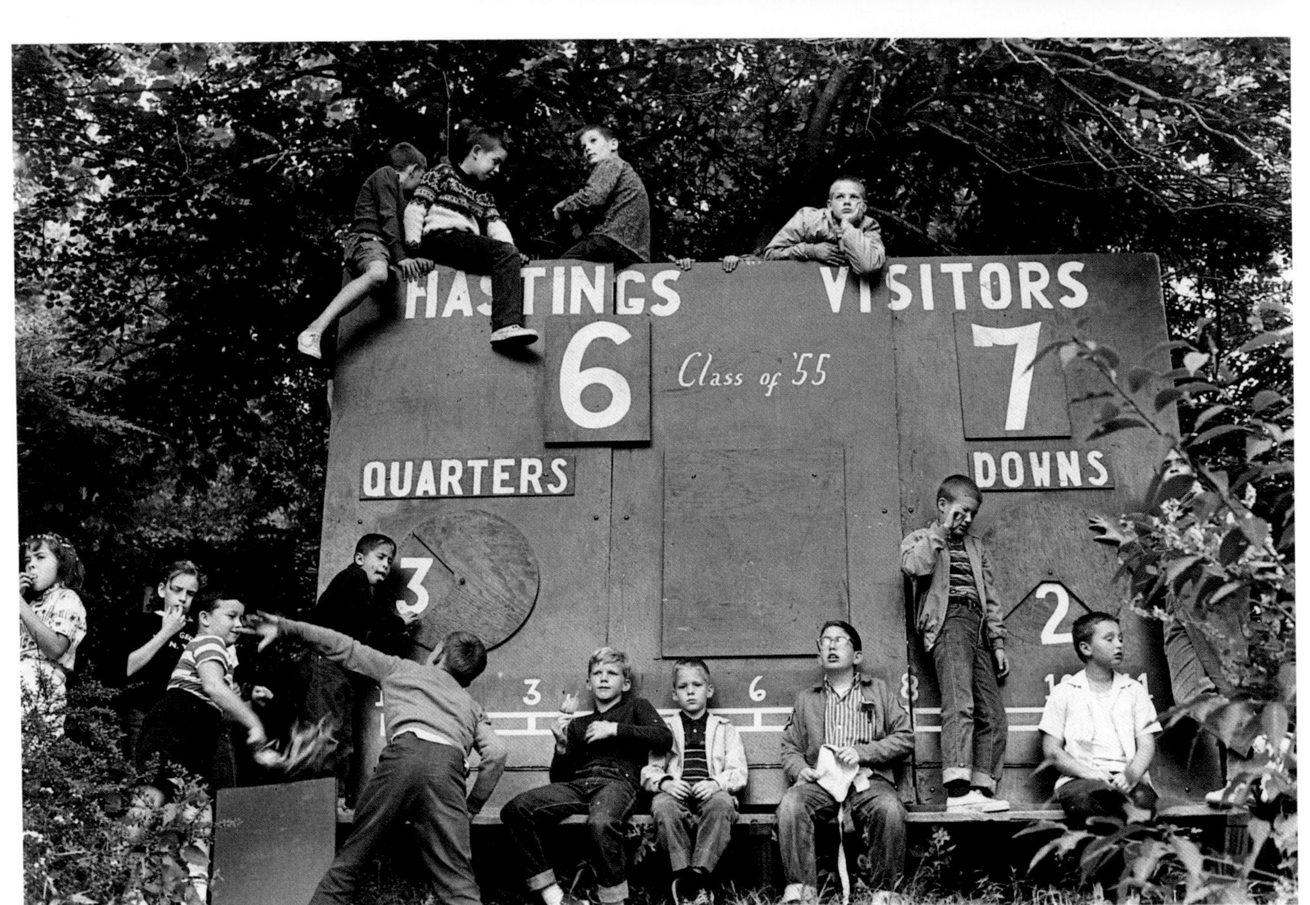

Hastings-on-Hudson, New York, 1962

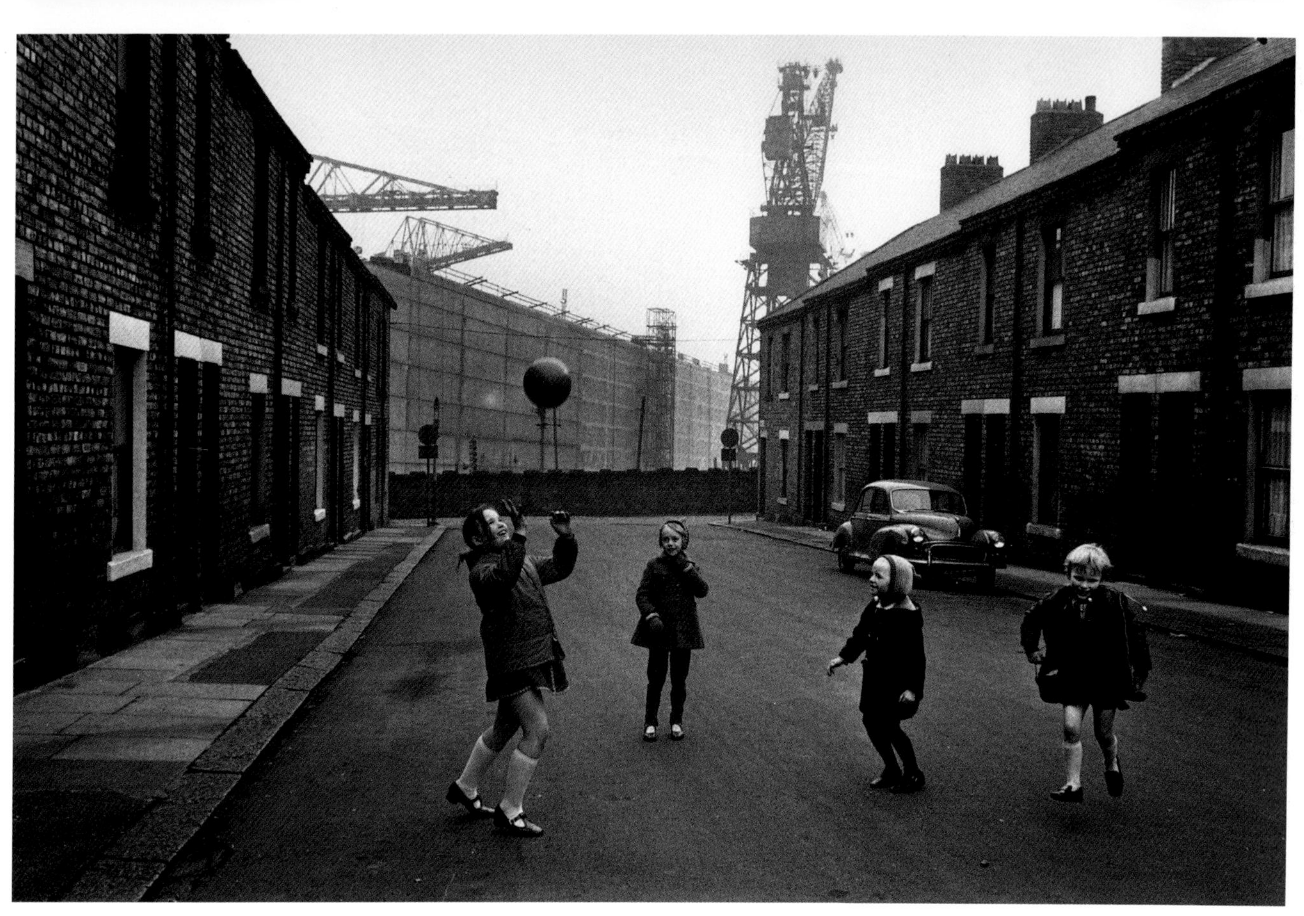

Newcastle, England, 1969

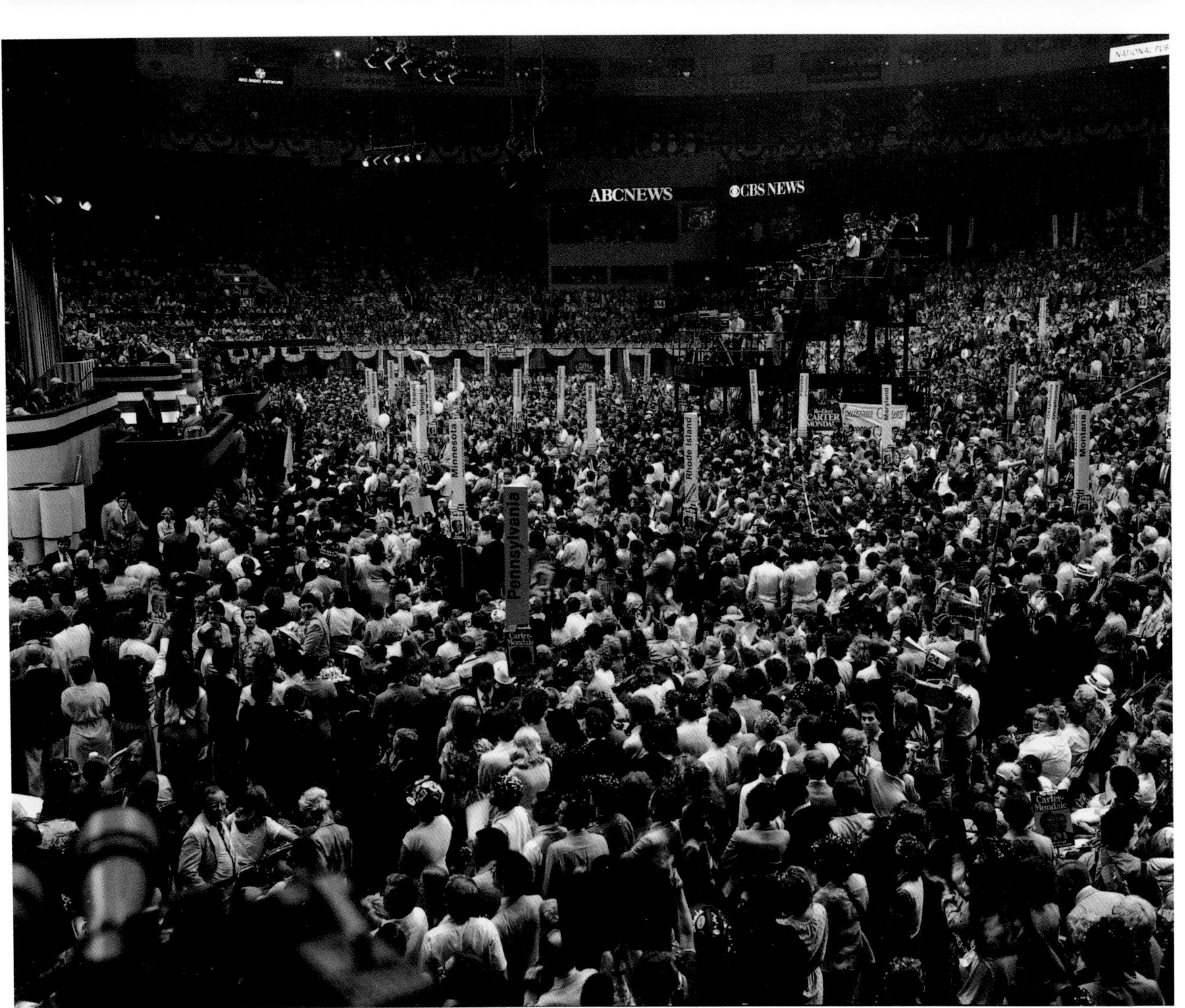

New York, 1980

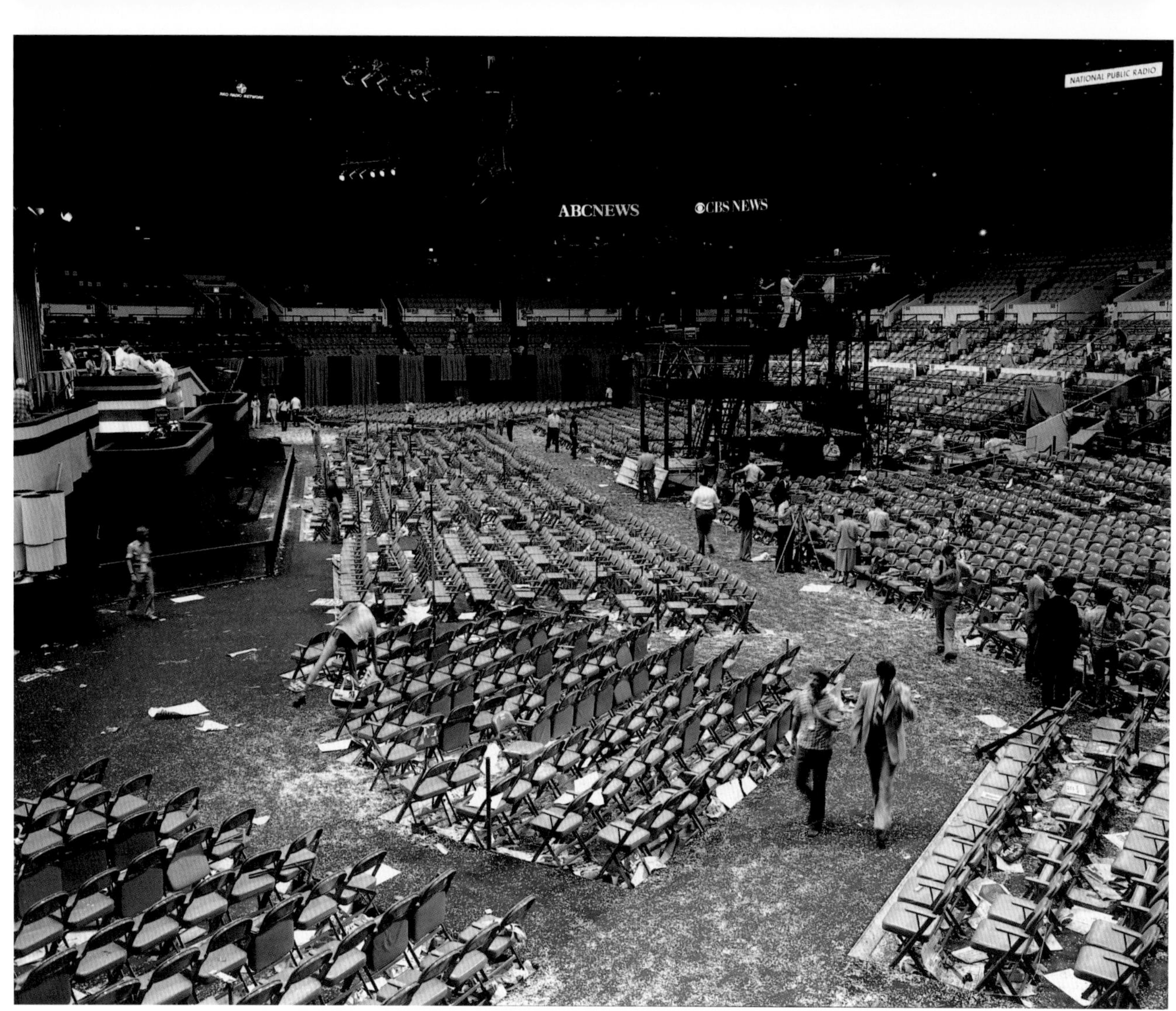

New York, 1980

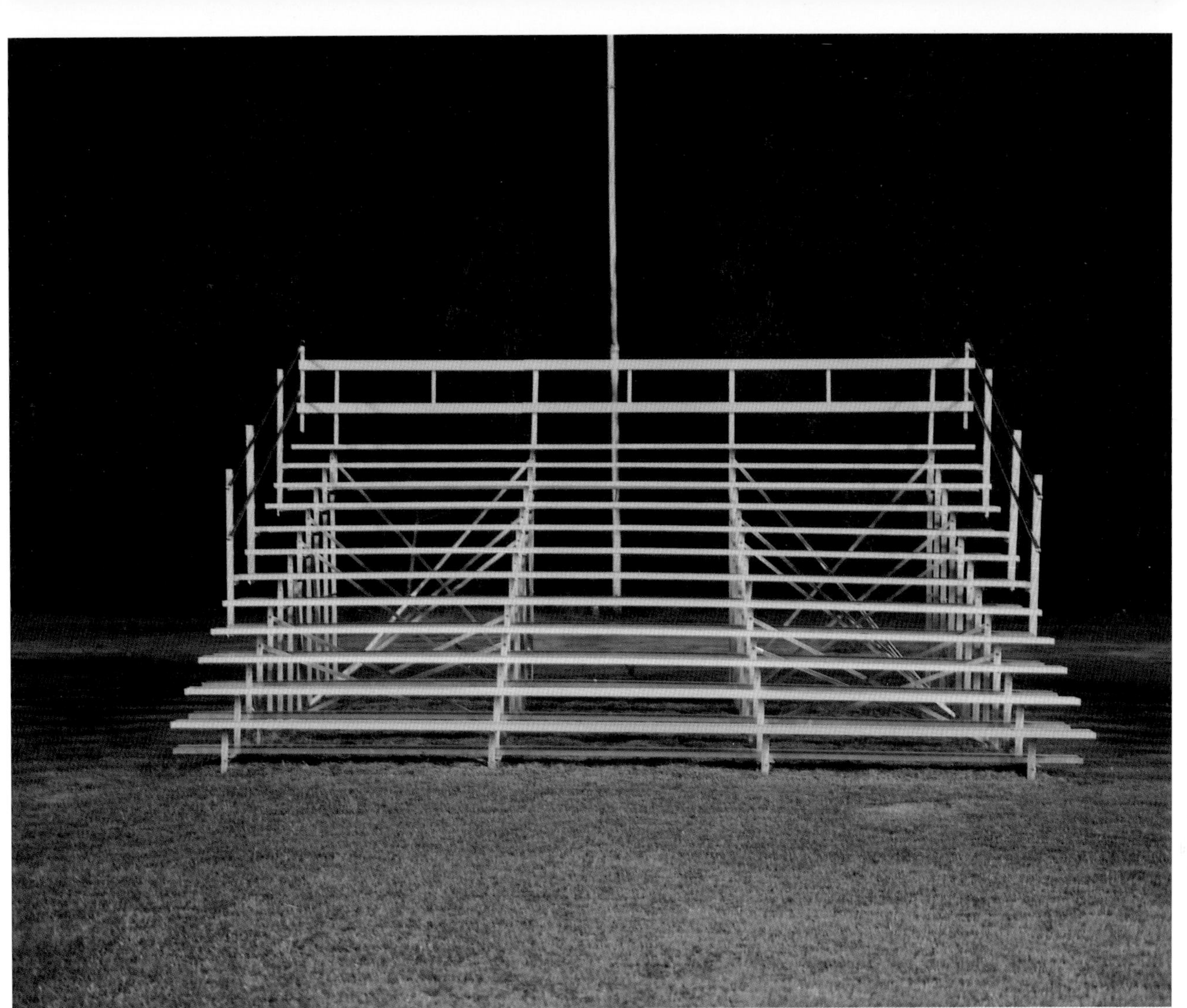

Tallahassee, Florida, 1980

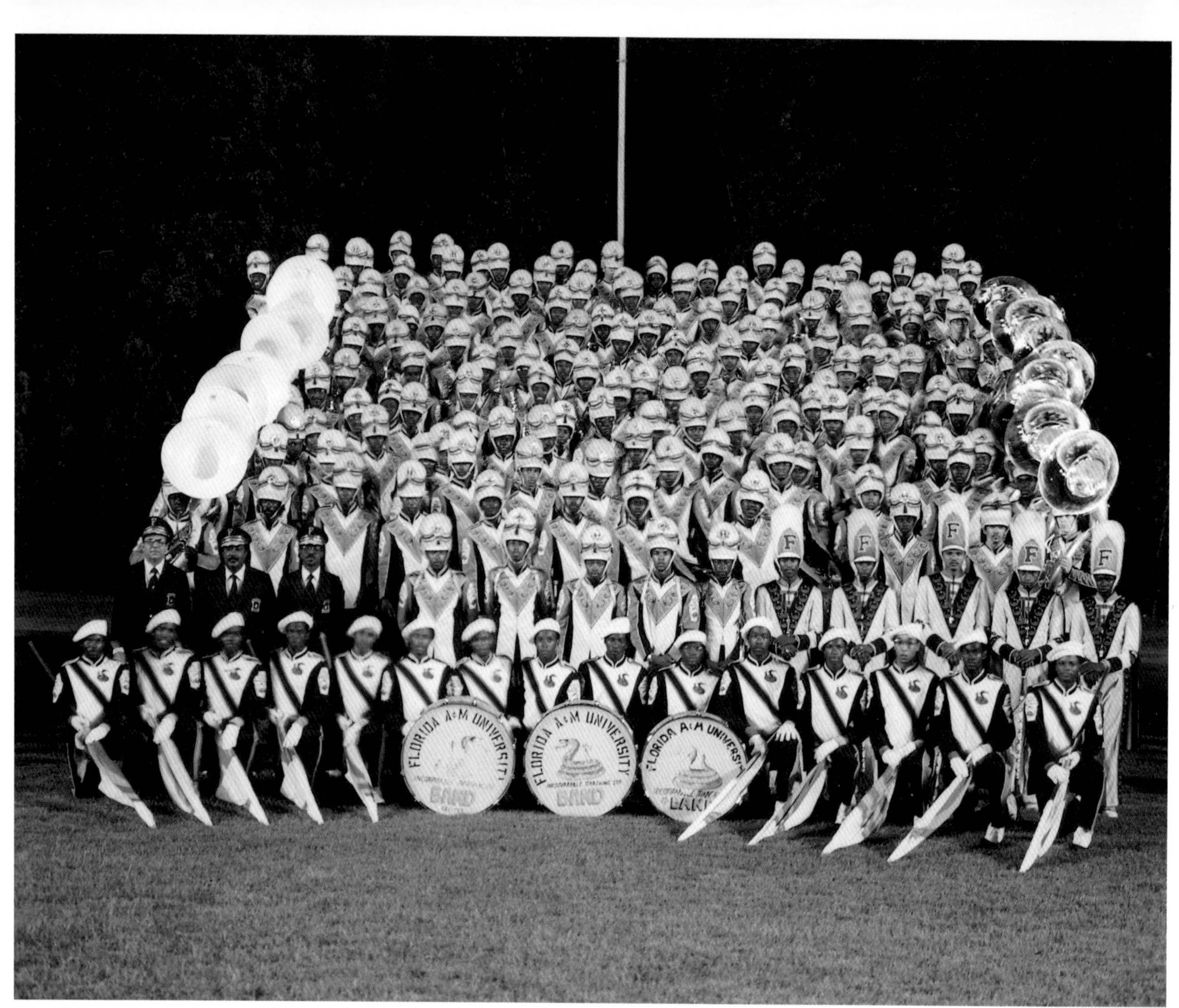

Tallahassee, Florida, 1980

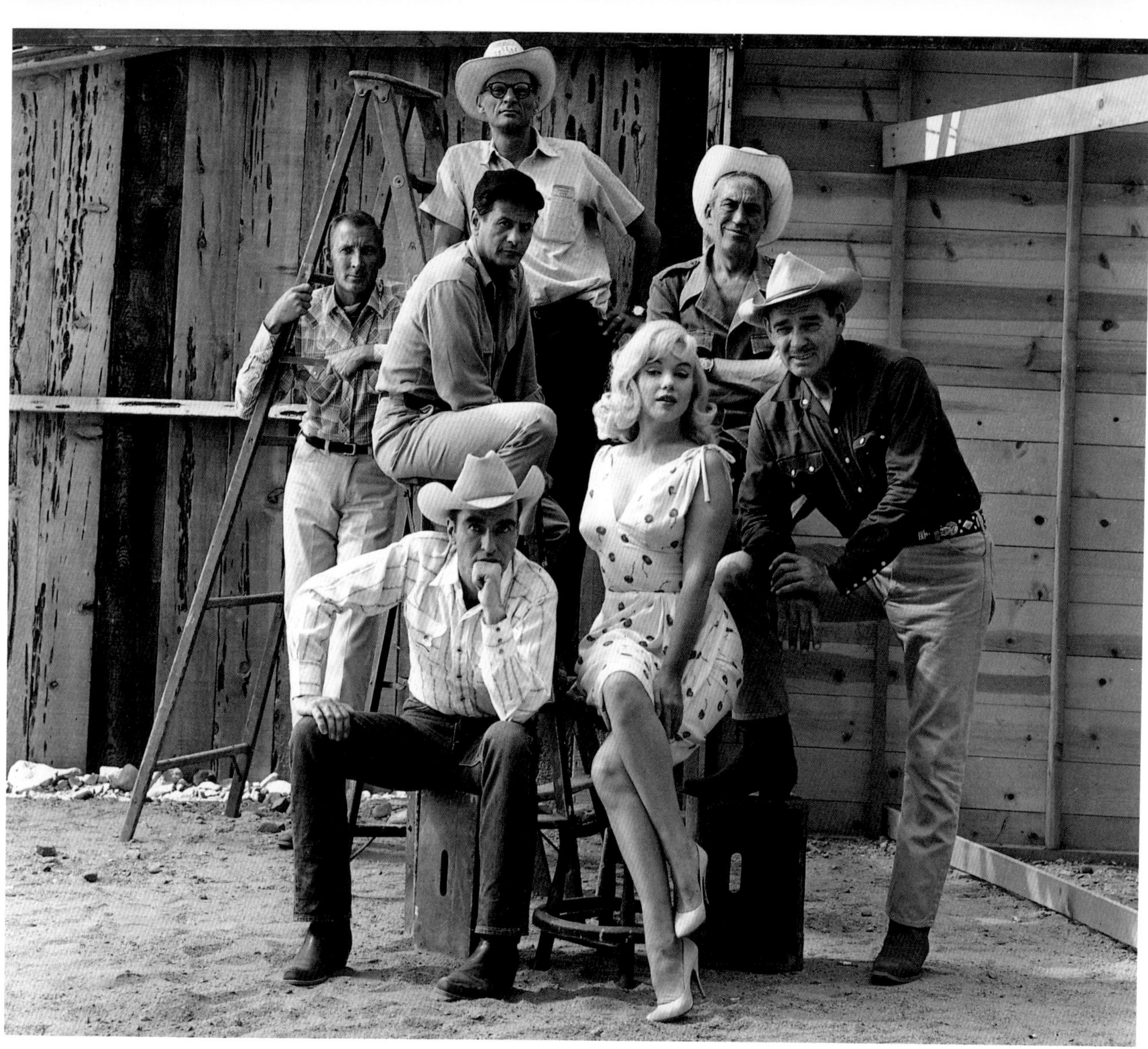

On the set of 'The Misfits', Reno, Nevada, 1960
overleaf *Rio de Janeiro, 1961* / *Des Moines, Iowa, 1955*

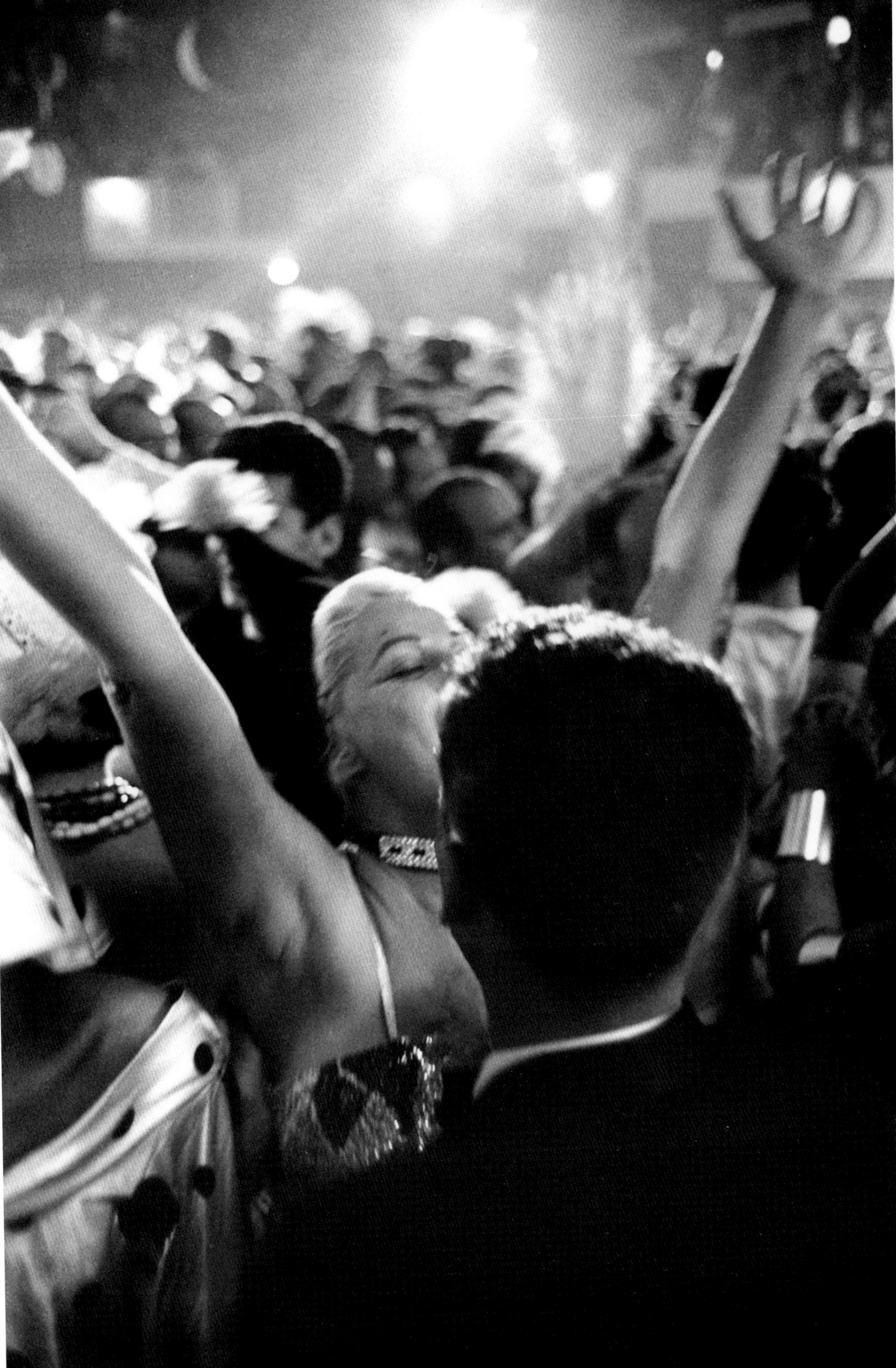

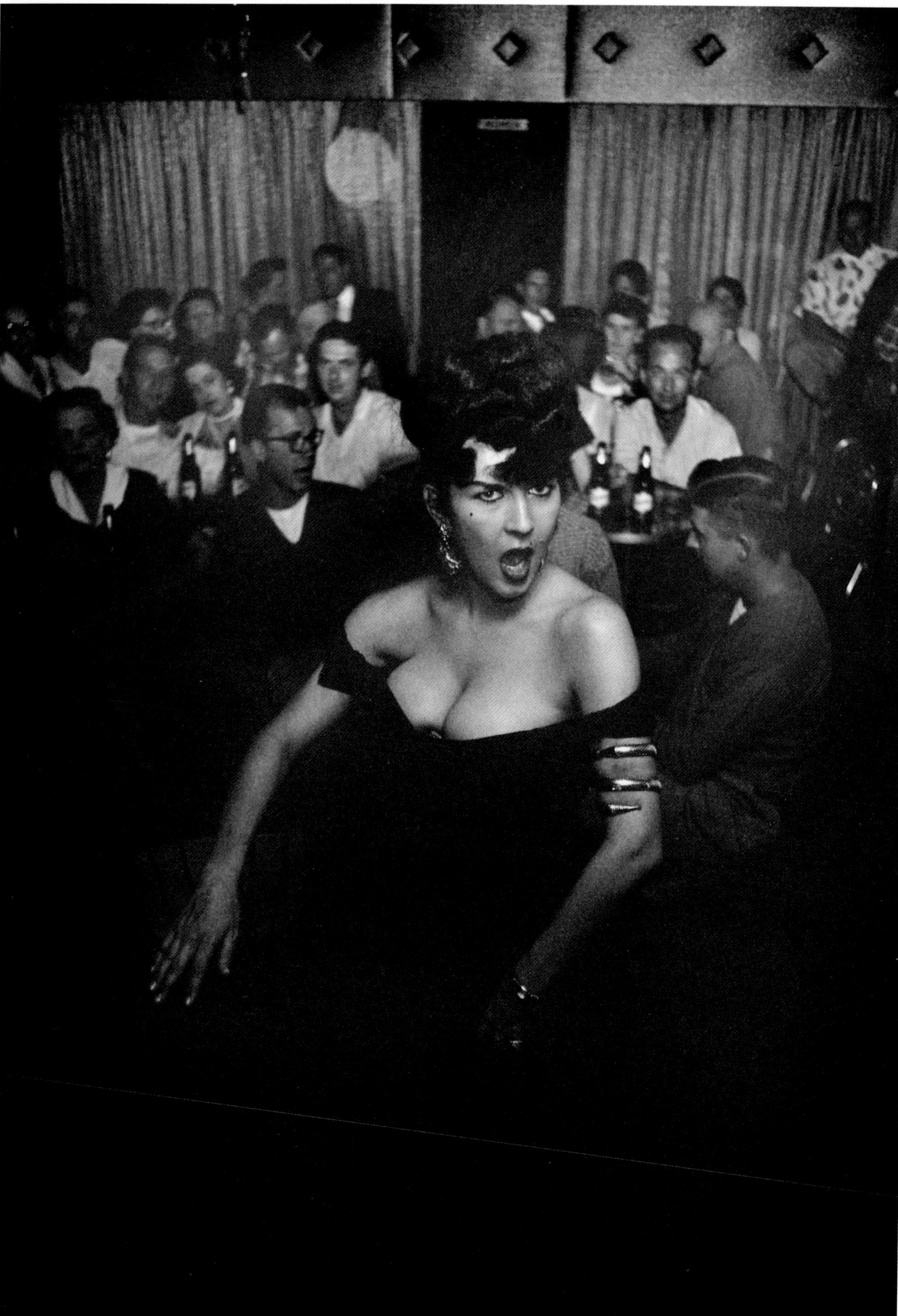

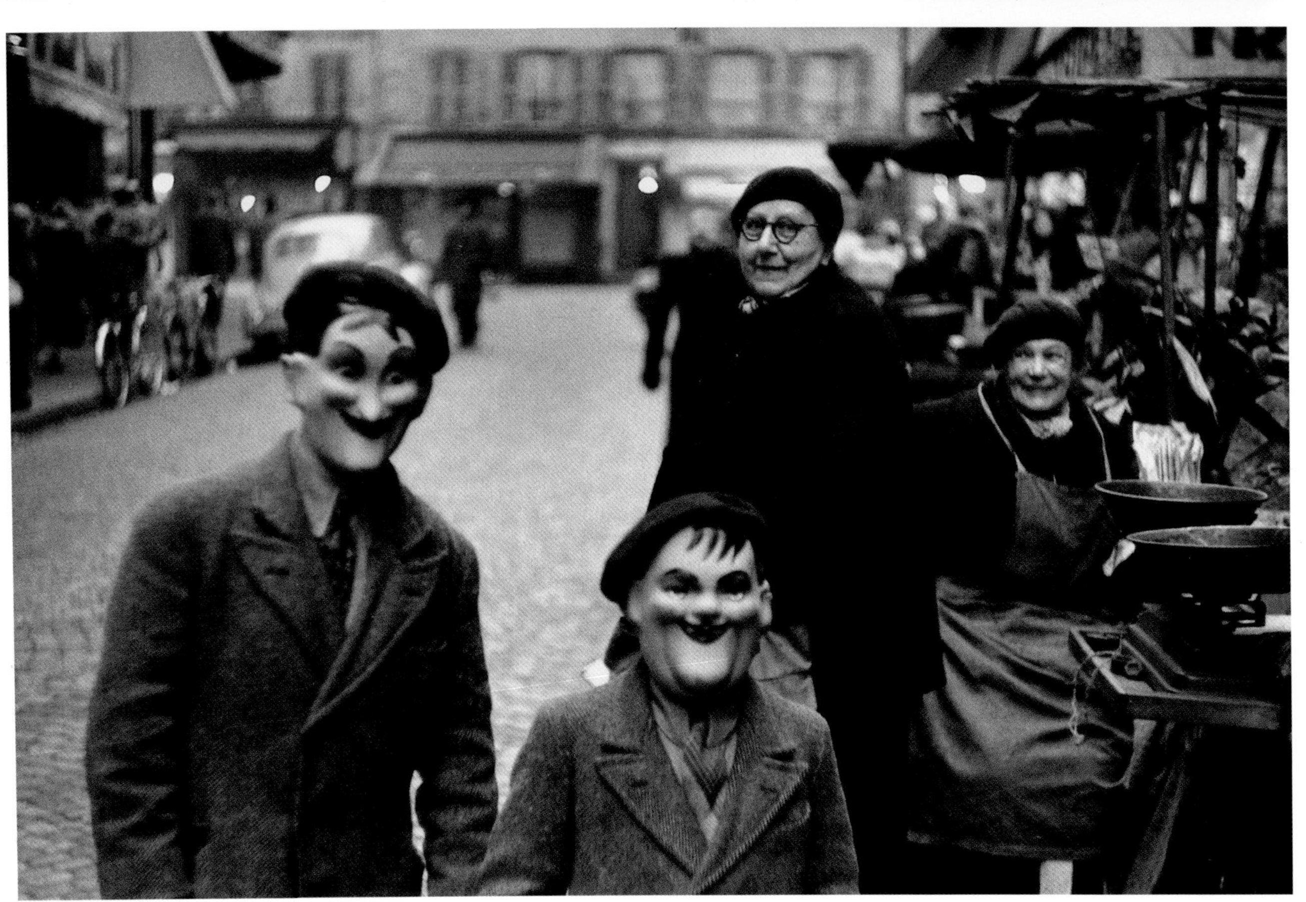

Paris, 1949

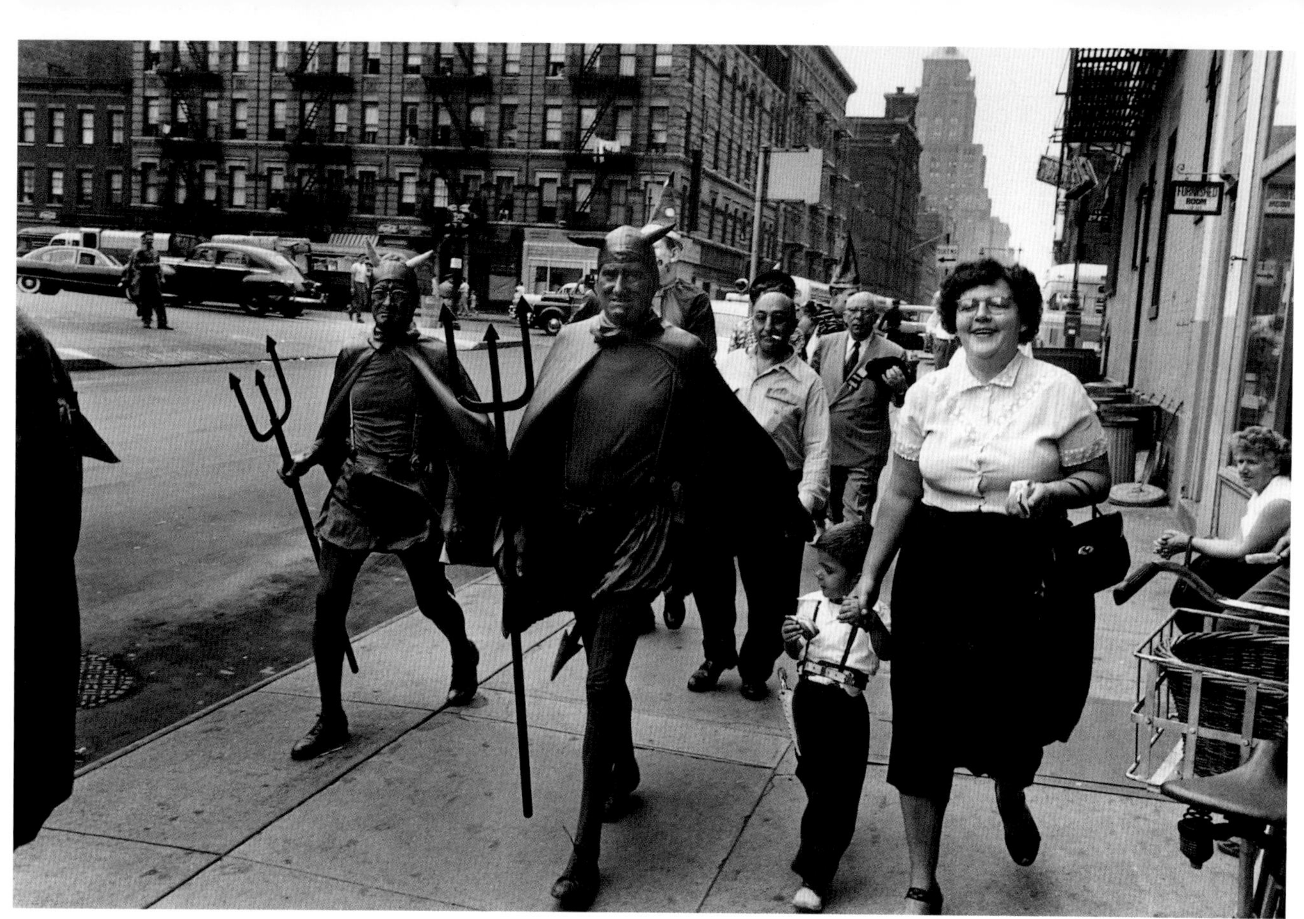

New York, 1953

overleaf *Rio de Janeiro, 1961* / *Valencia, Spain, 1951*

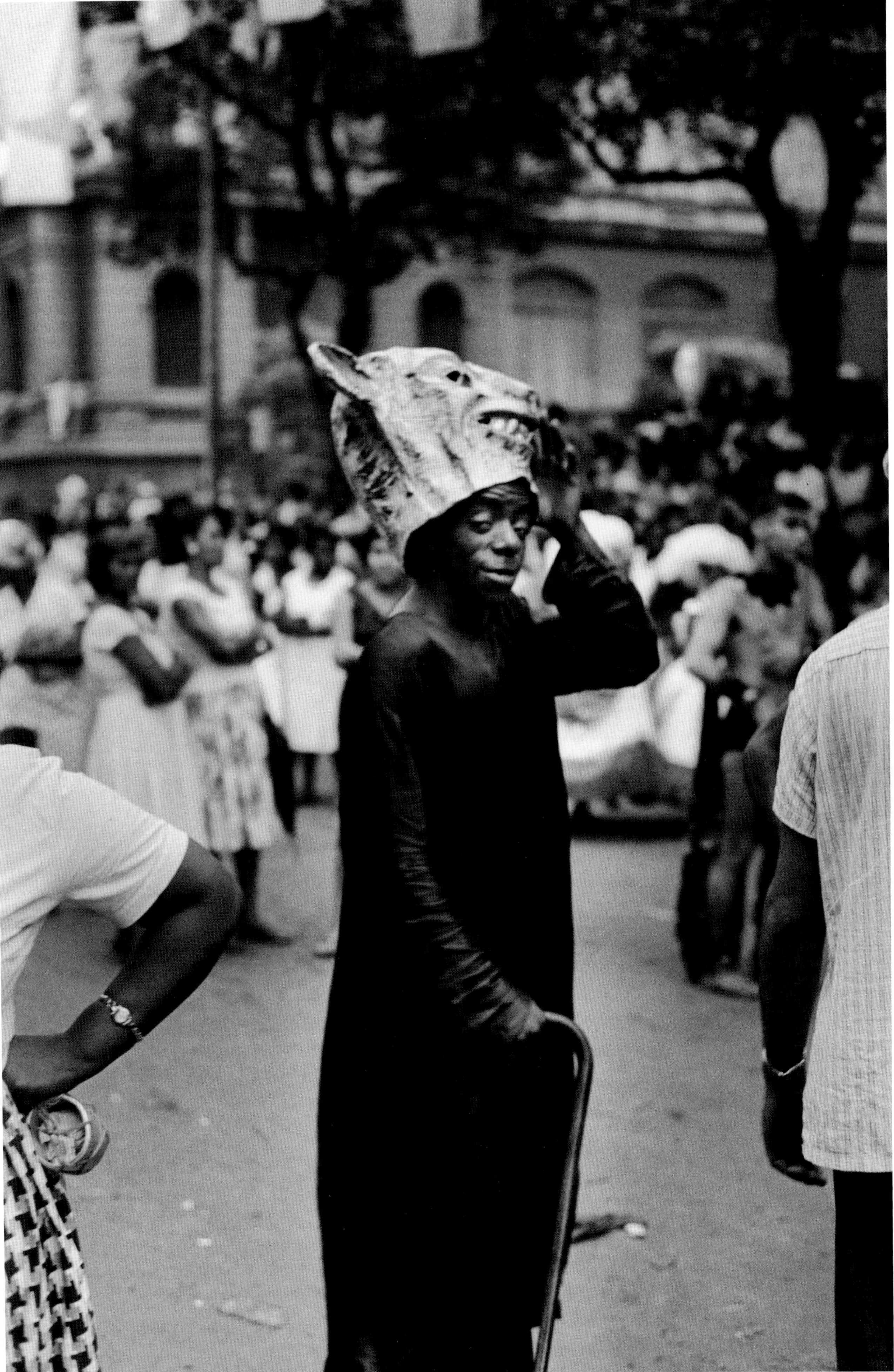

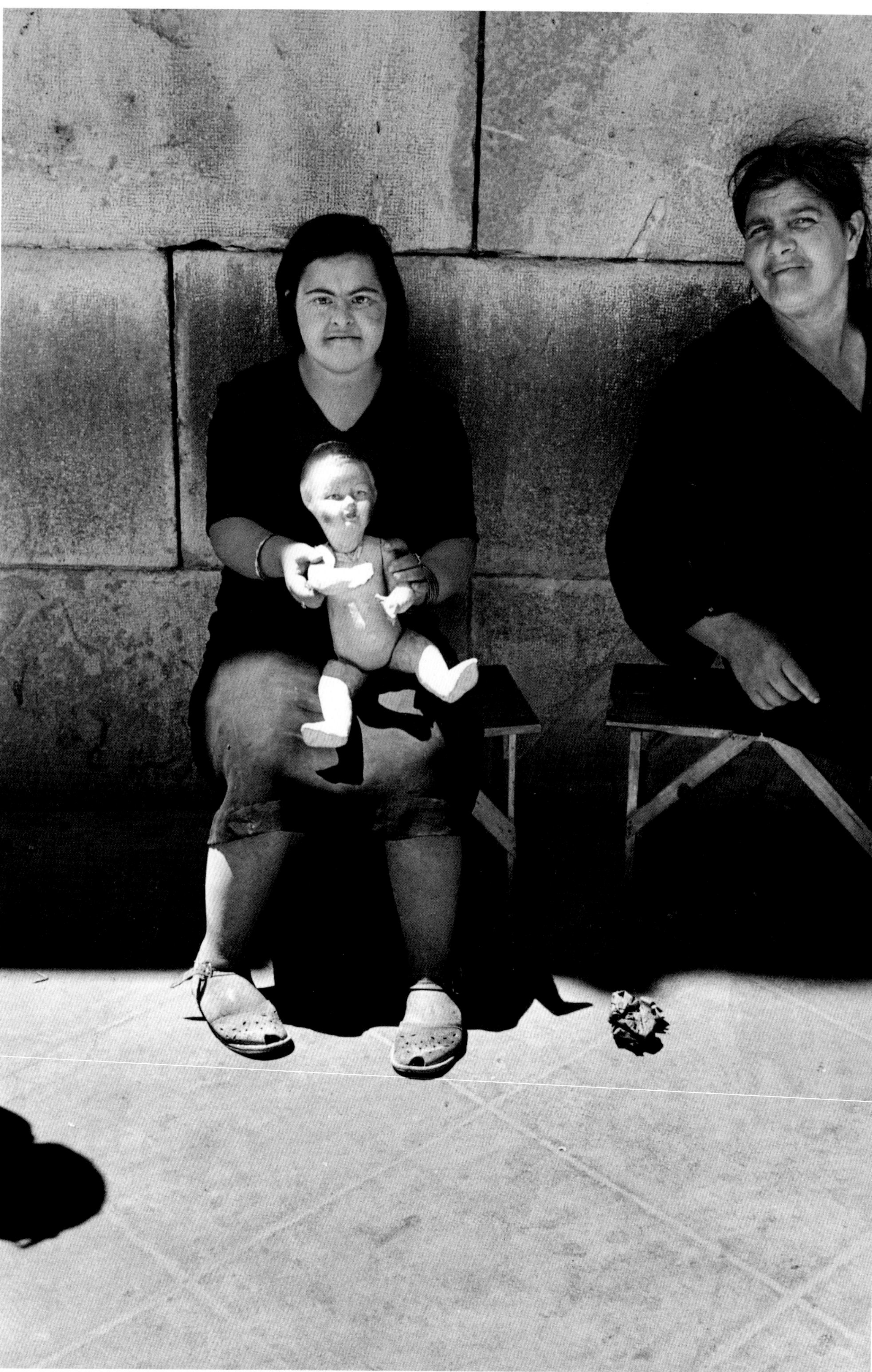

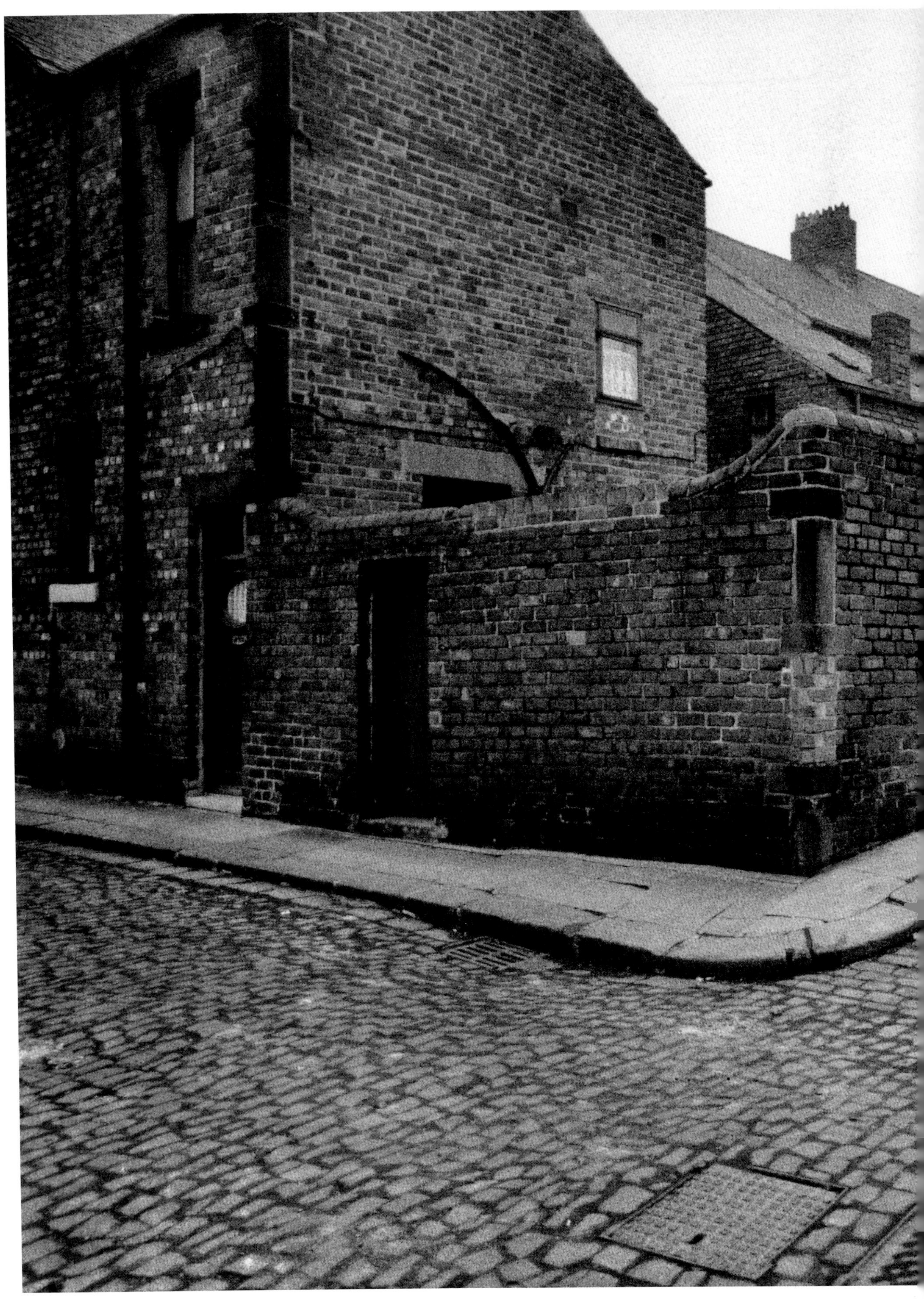

Newcastle, England, 1969

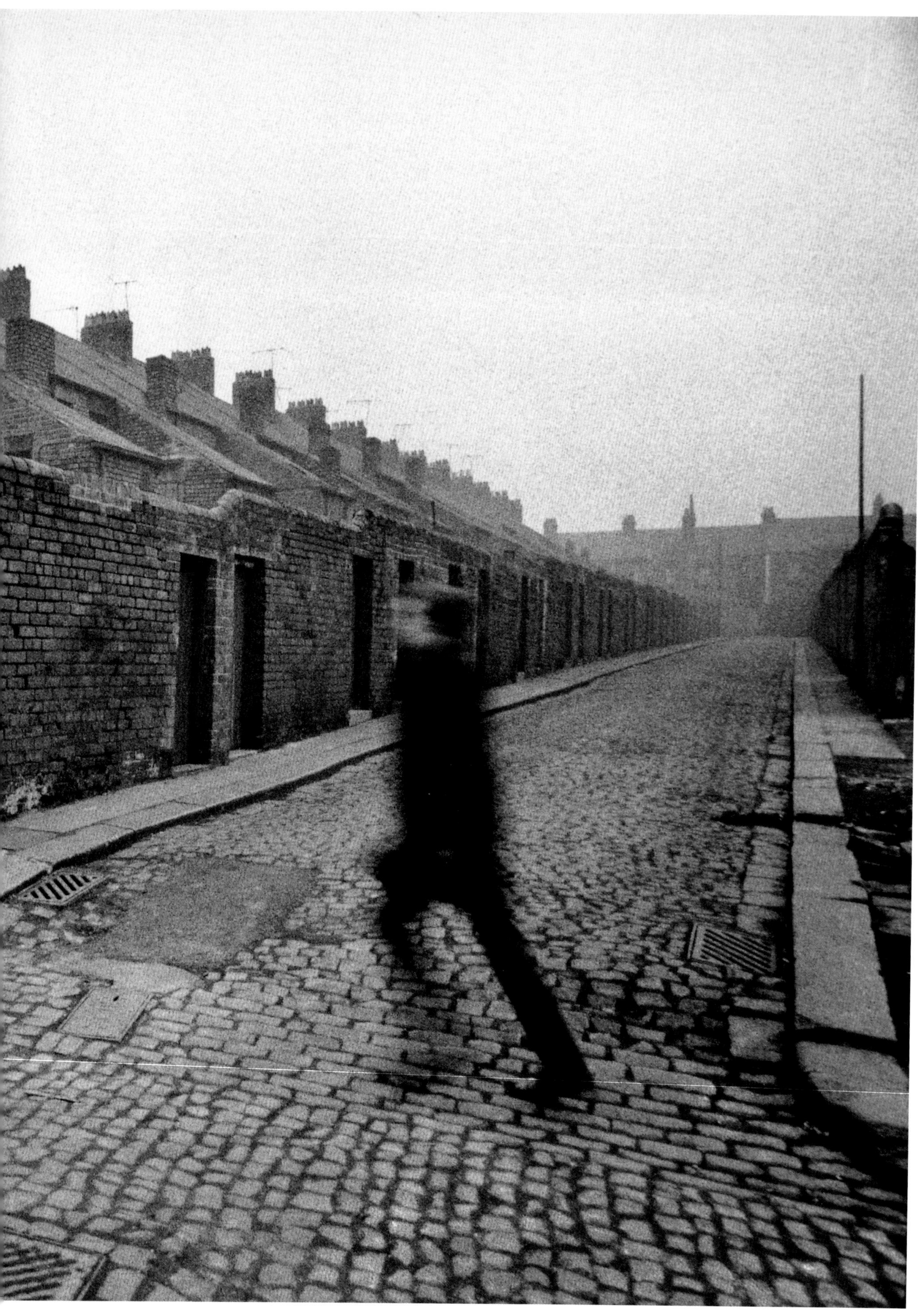

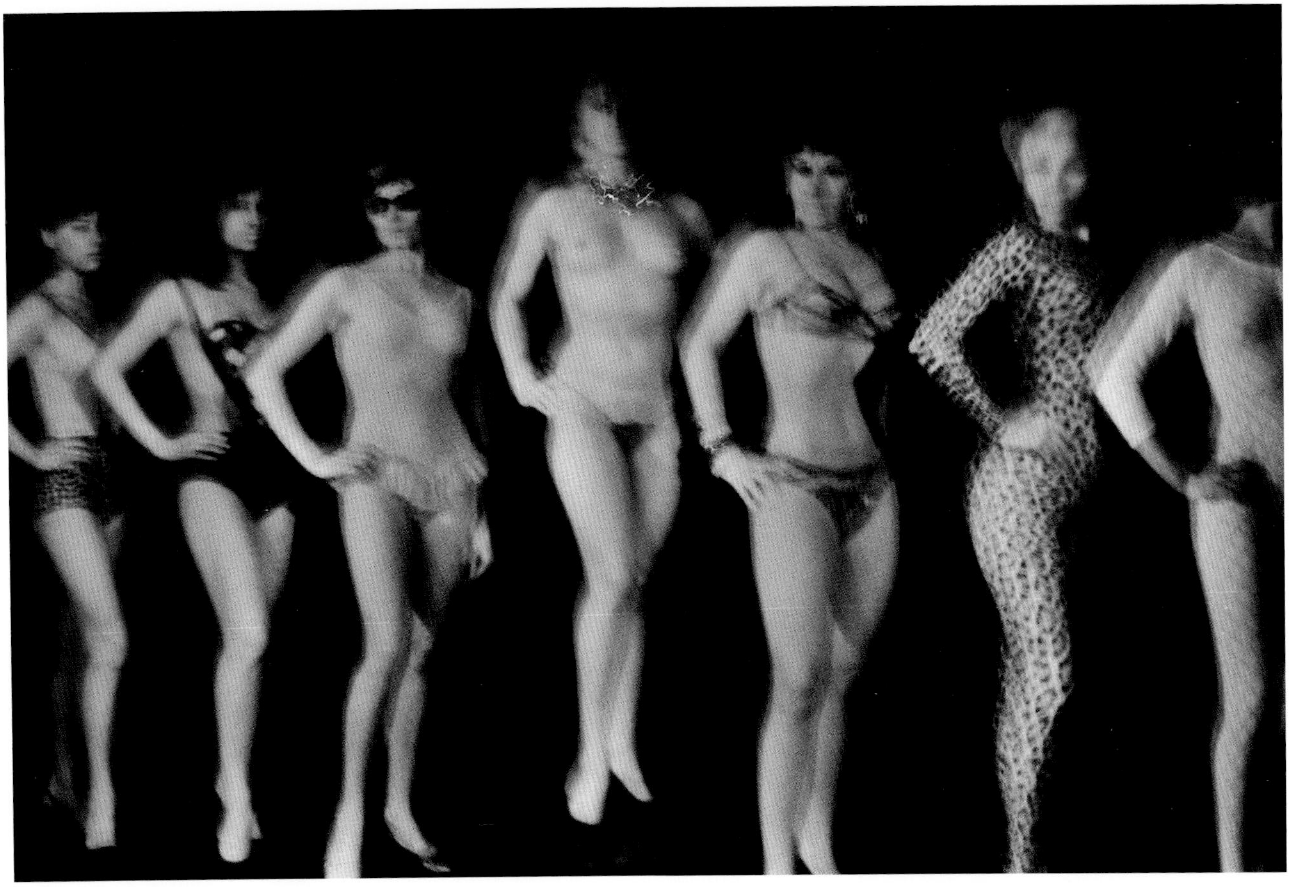

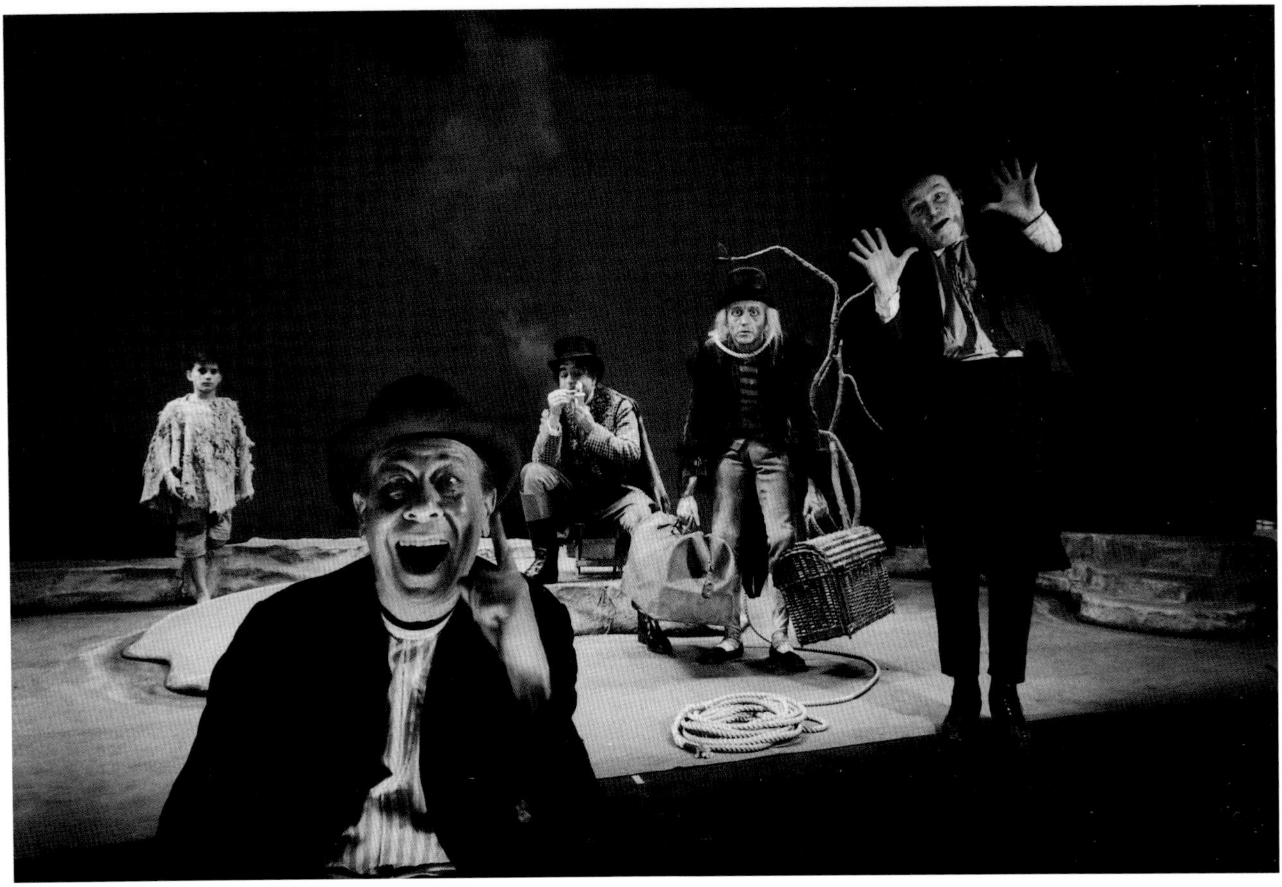

Paris, 1965 / *New York, 1956*

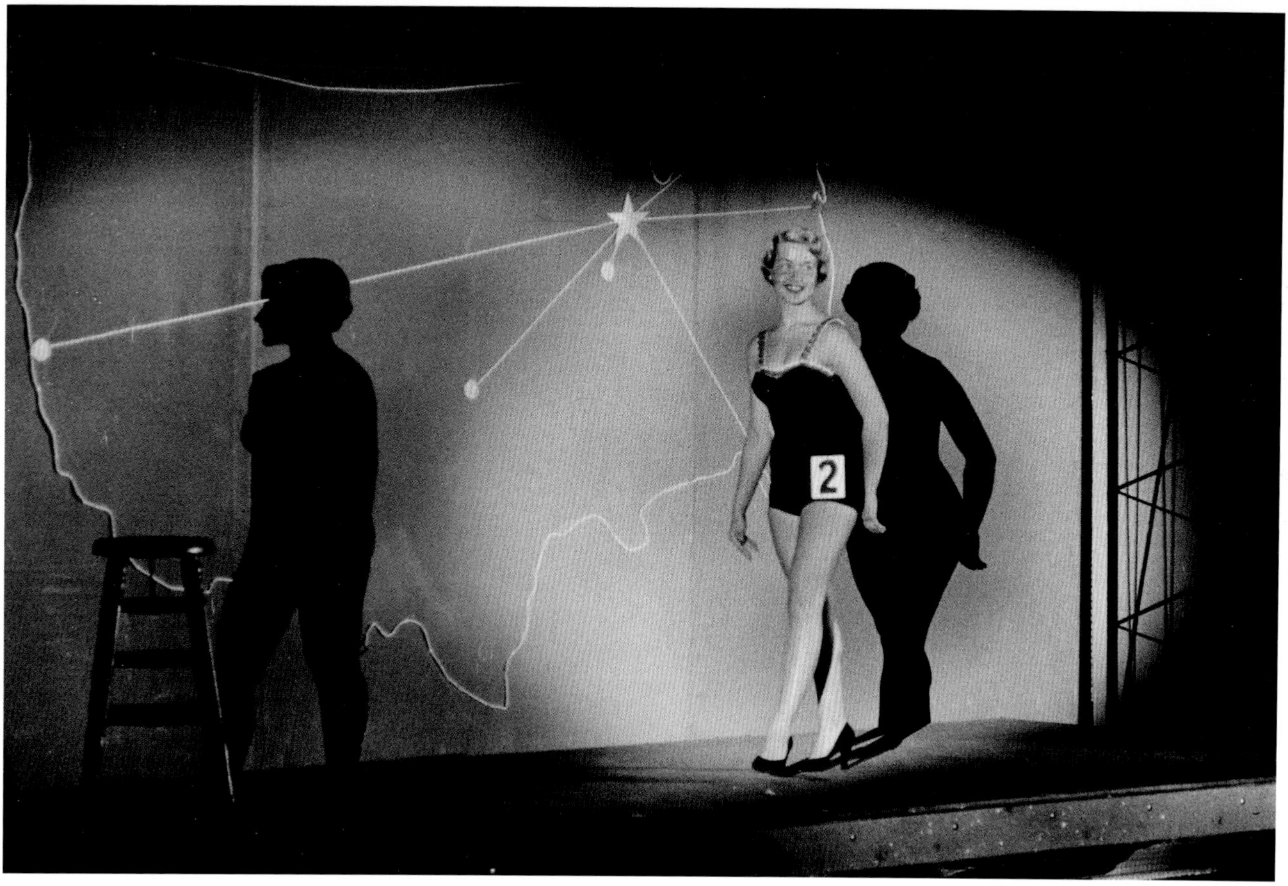

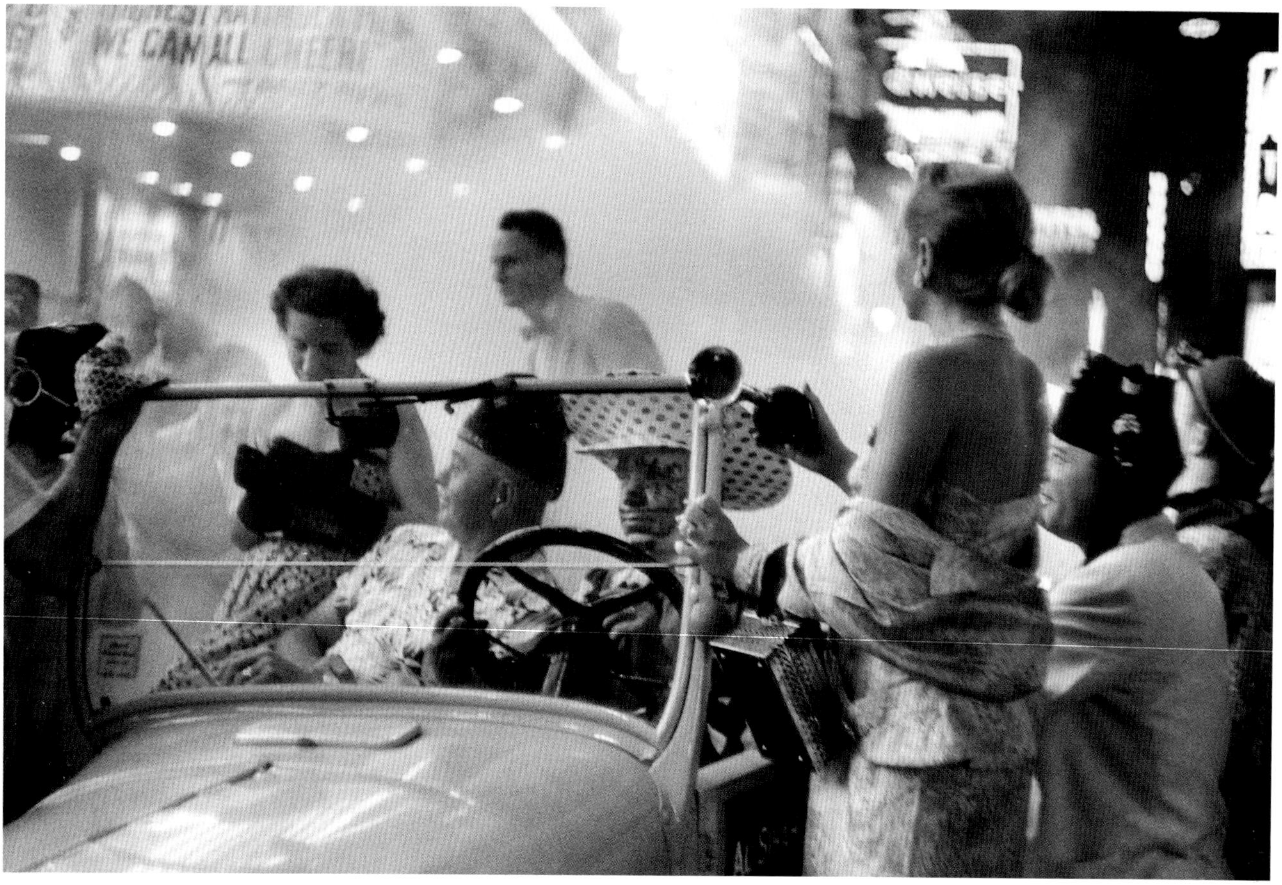

Iowa, 1956 / *New York, 1953*

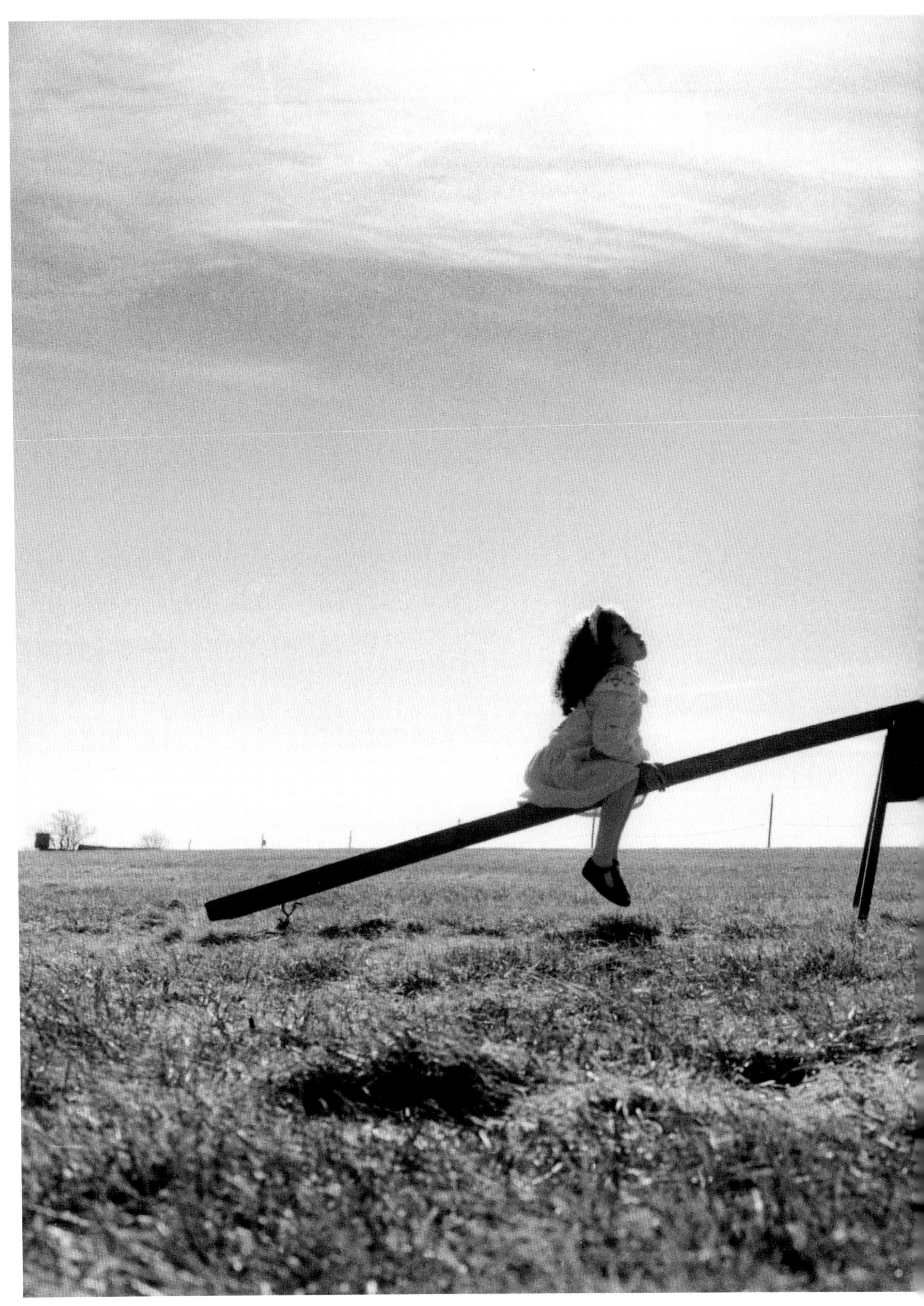

Bridgehampton, New York, 1990

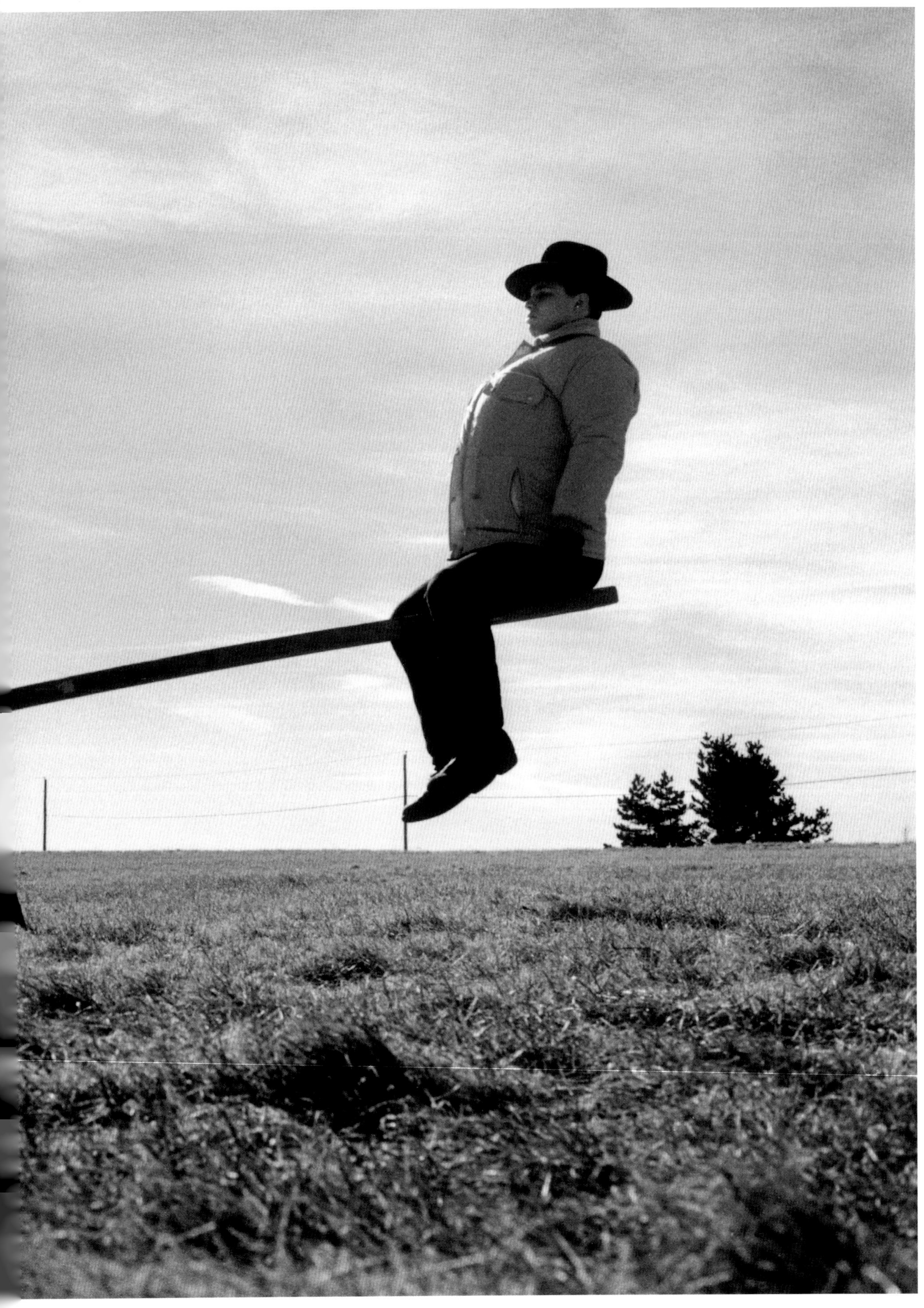

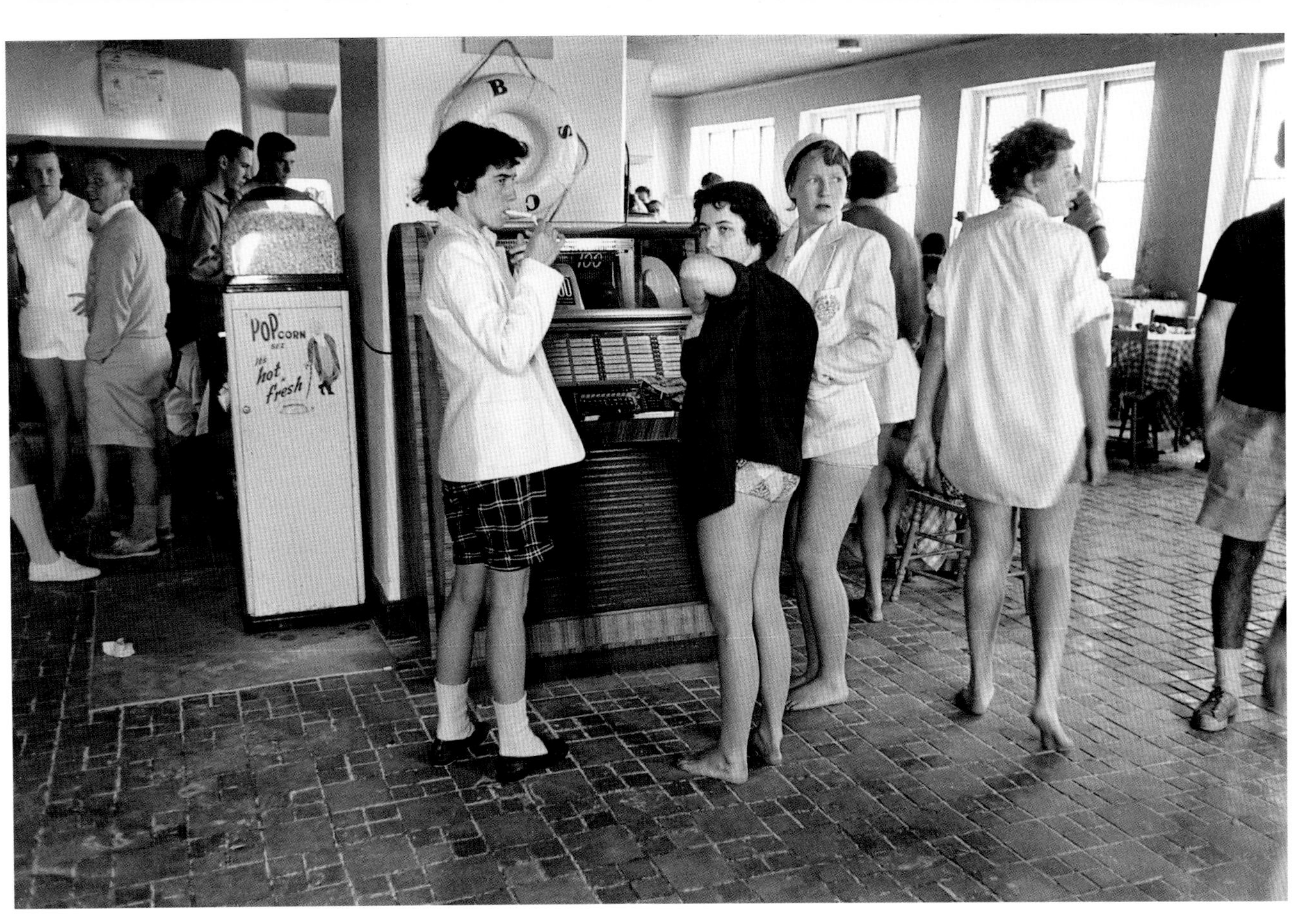

Hamilton, Bermuda, 1953

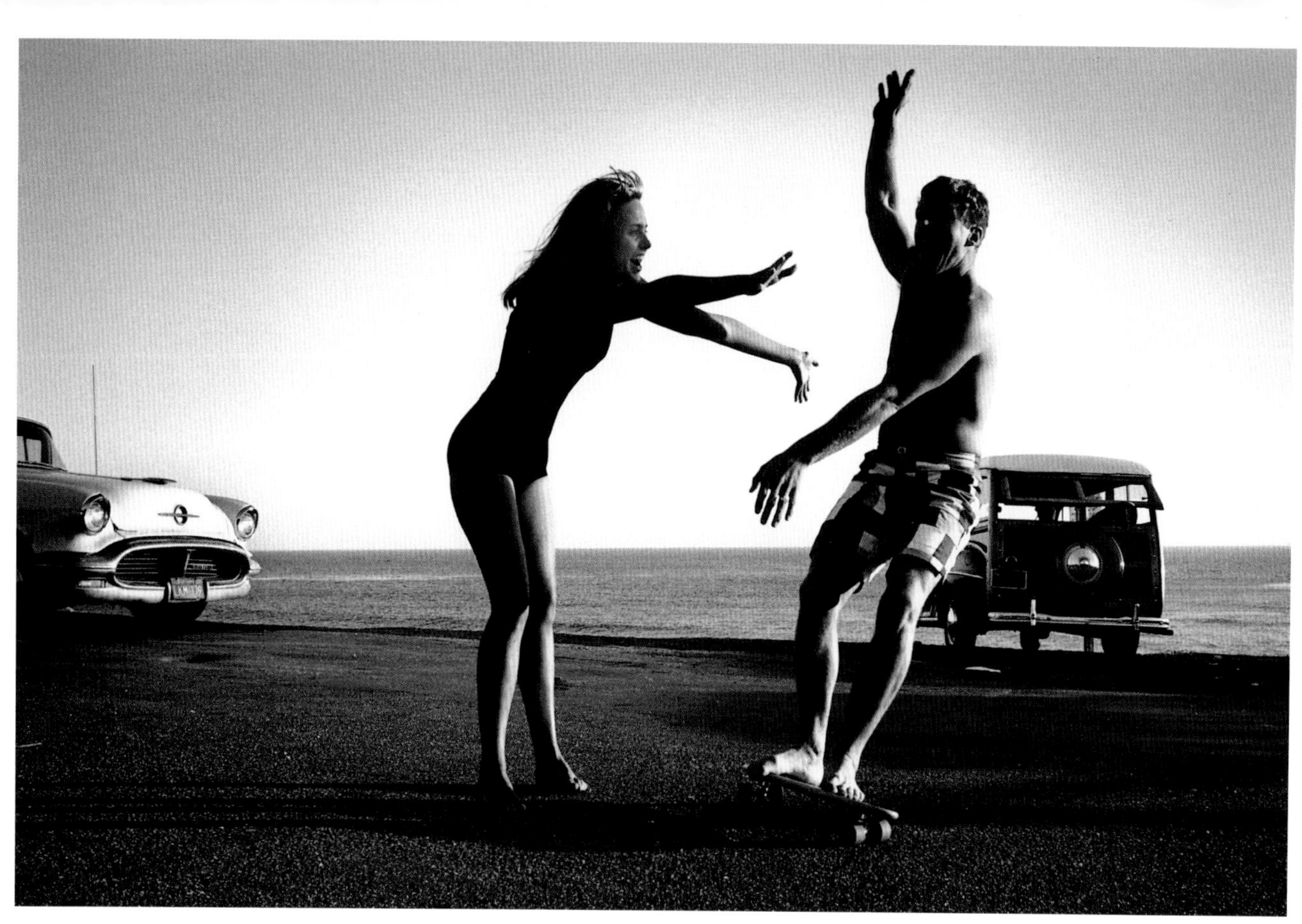

Pacific Palisades, California, 1964

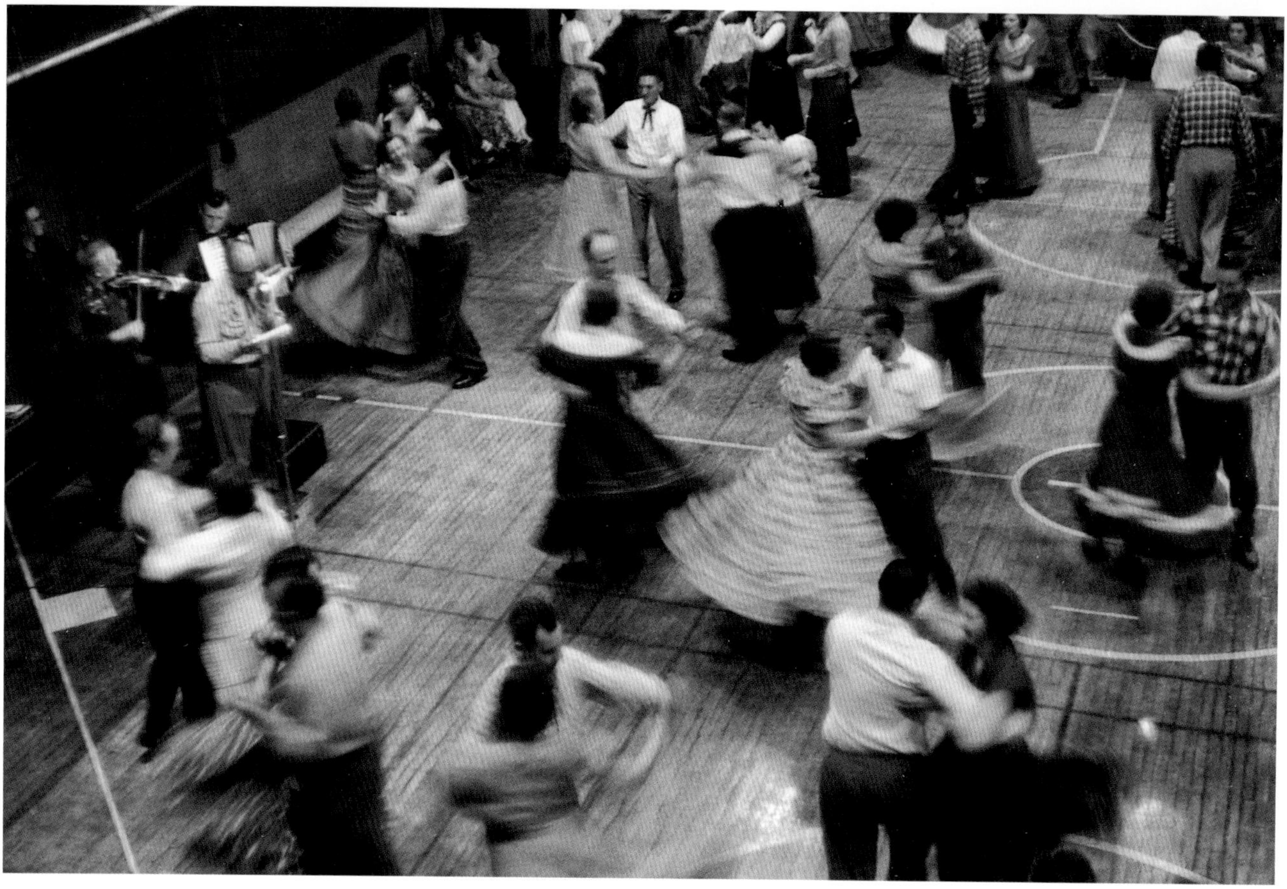

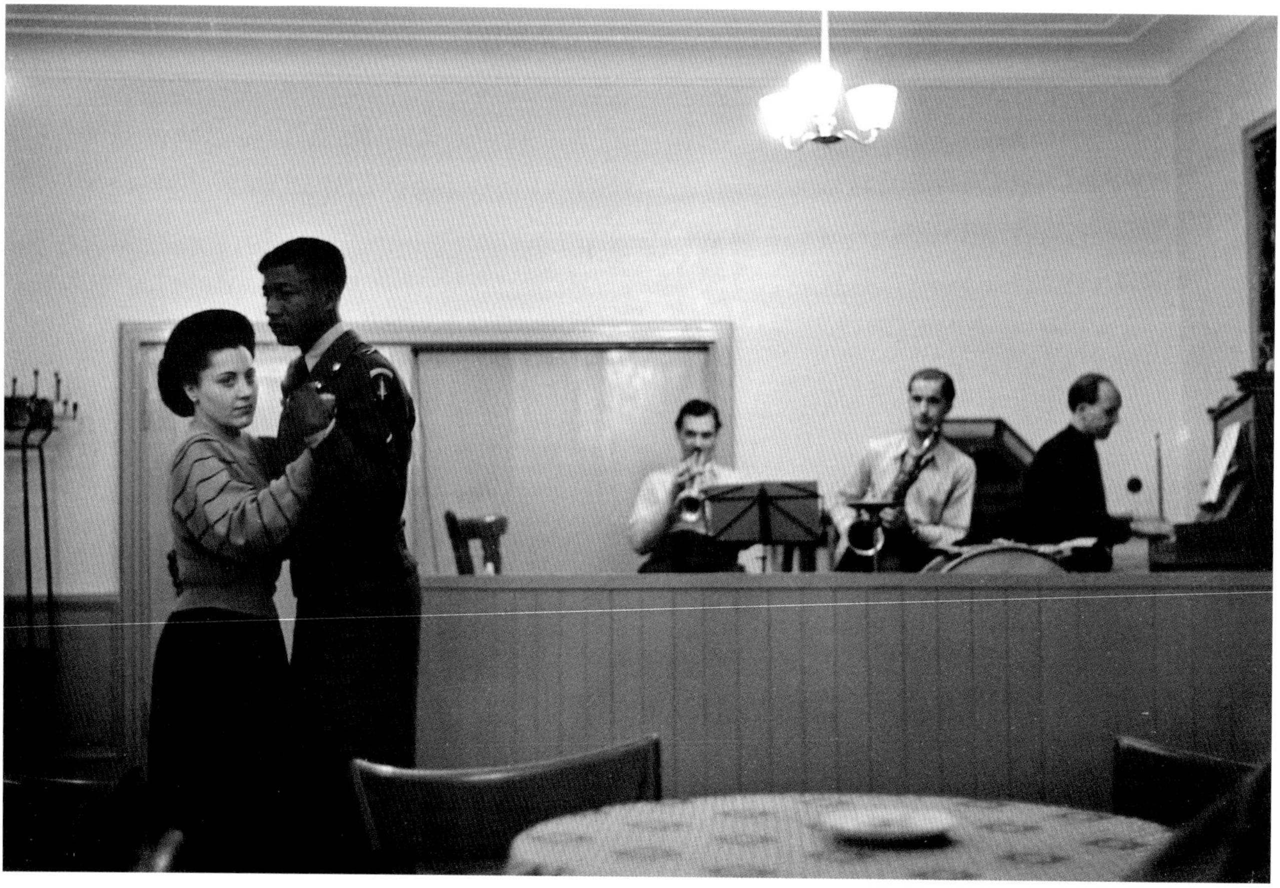

Dubuque, Iowa, 1955 / *Bremerhaven, Germany, 1951*
overleaf *Jackie Gleason, New York, 1944* / *Marlene Dietrich, New York, 1959*

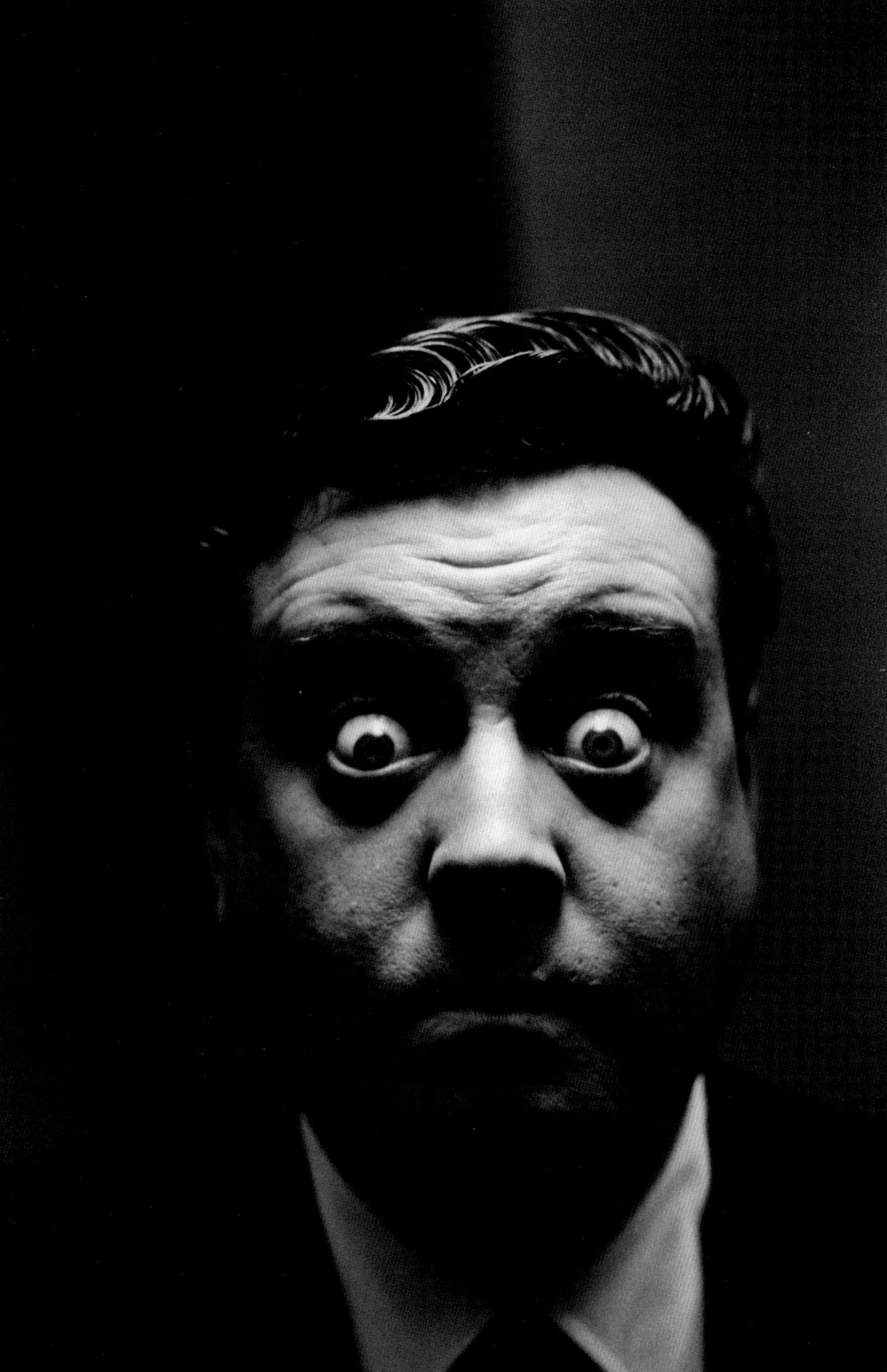

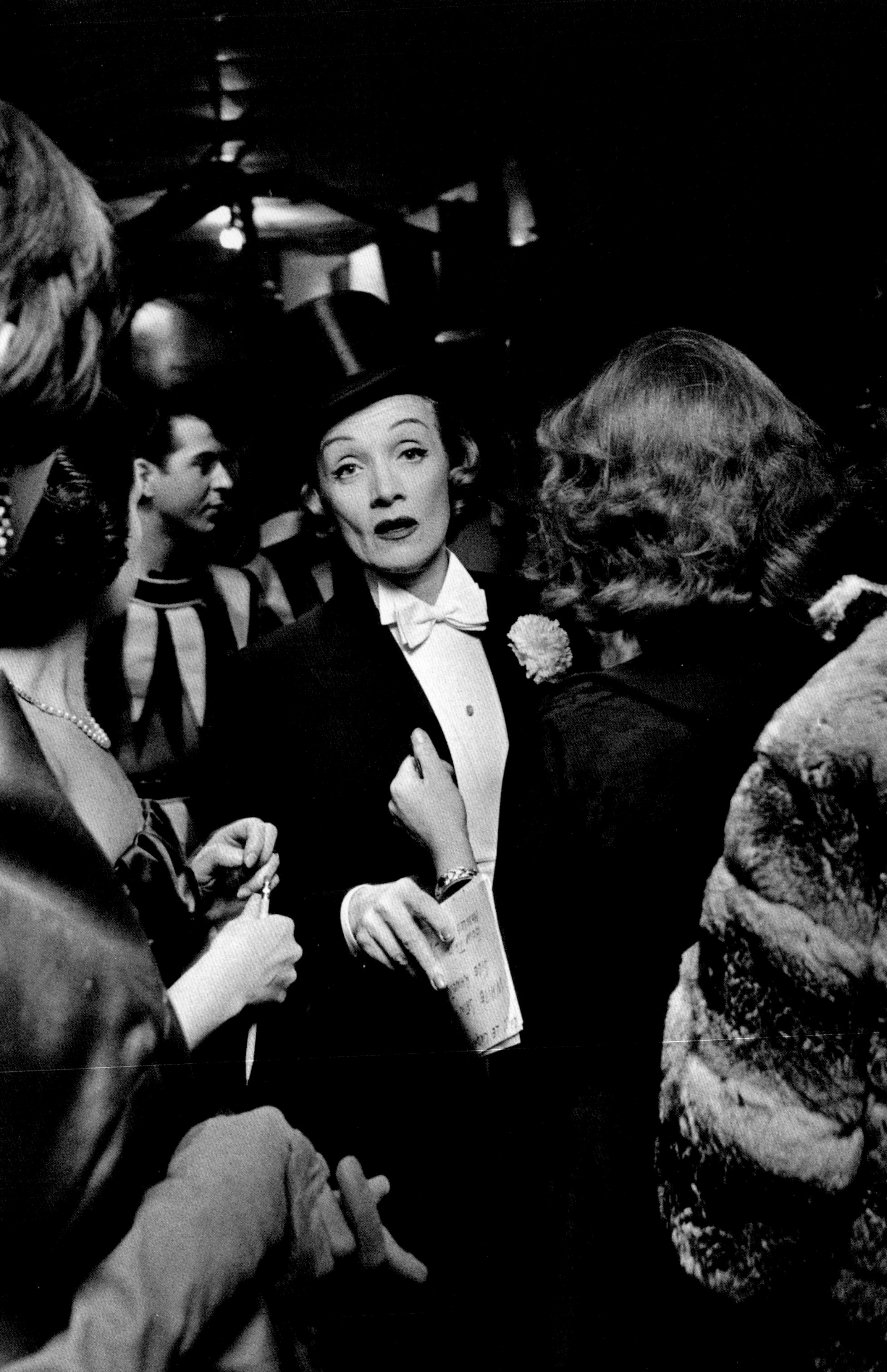

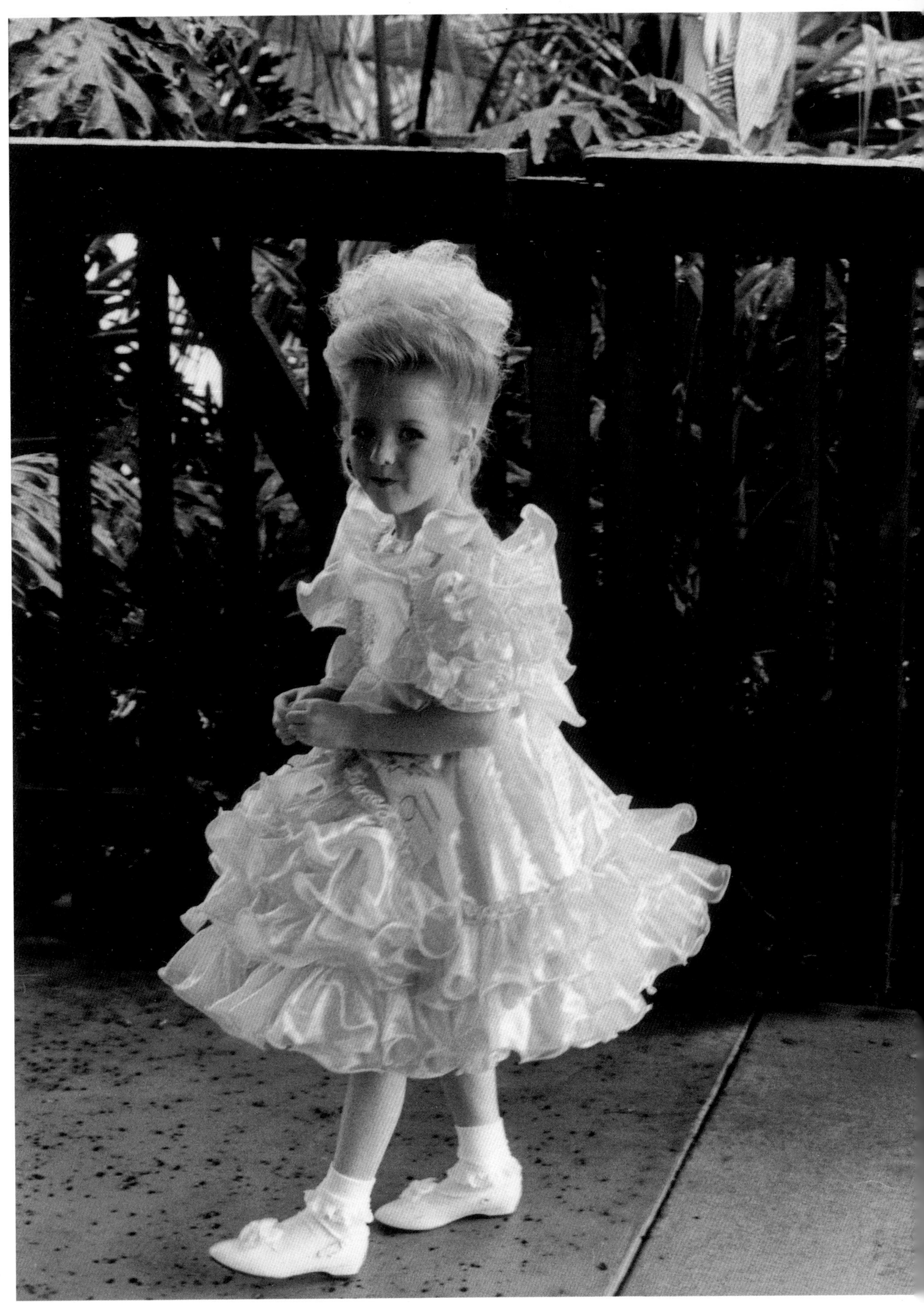

Kissimmee, Florida, 1997

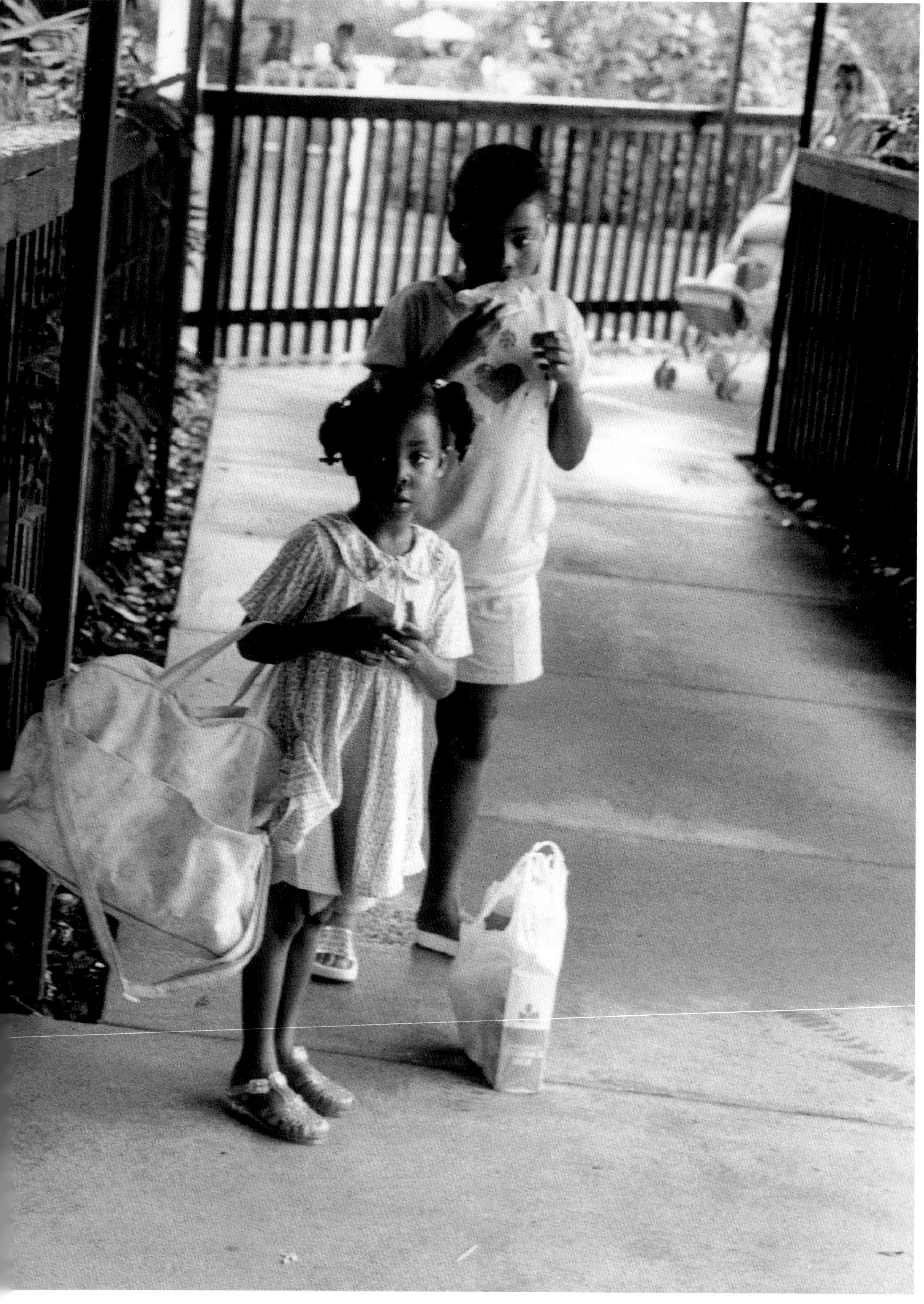

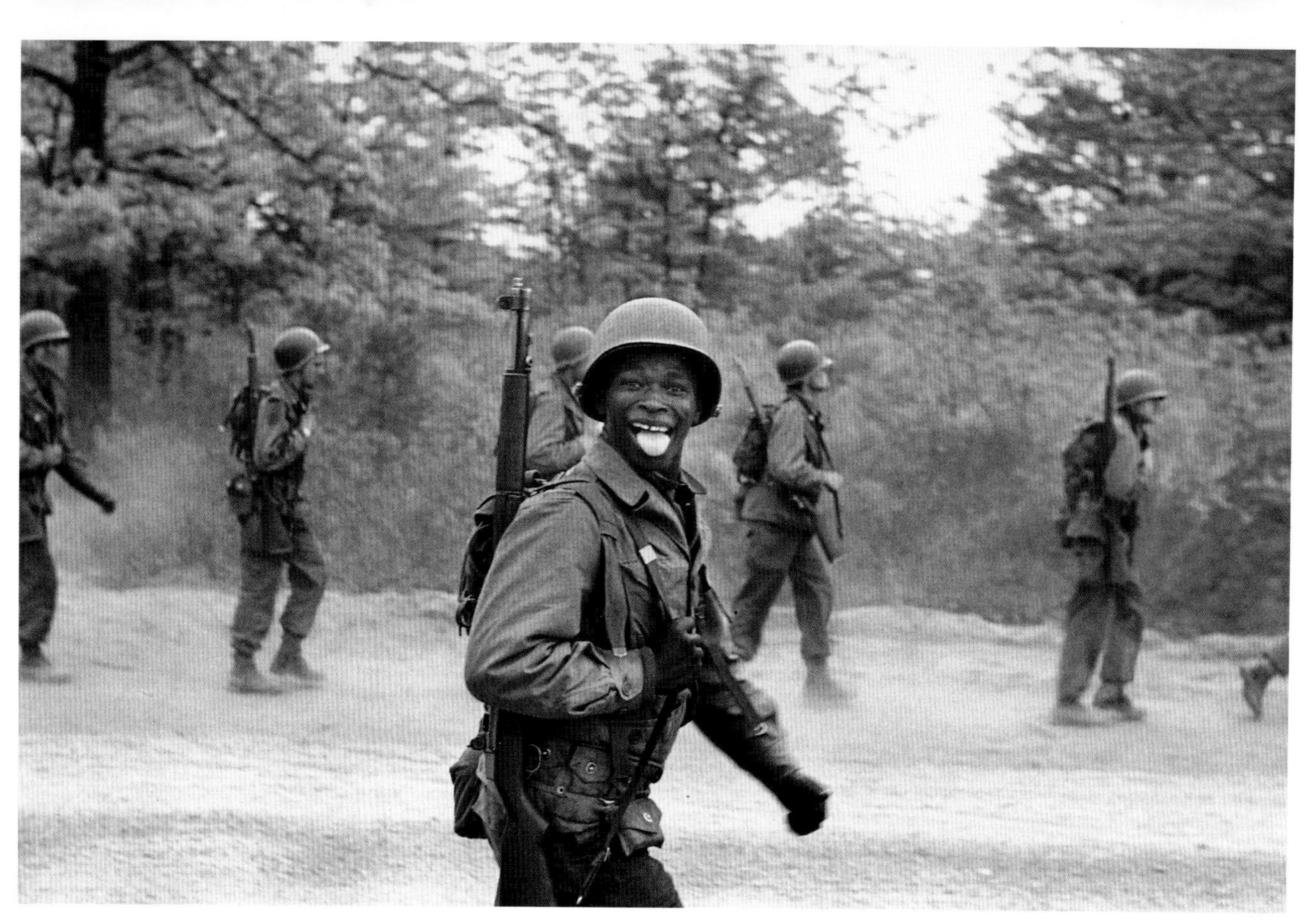

Fort Dix, New Jersey, 1951

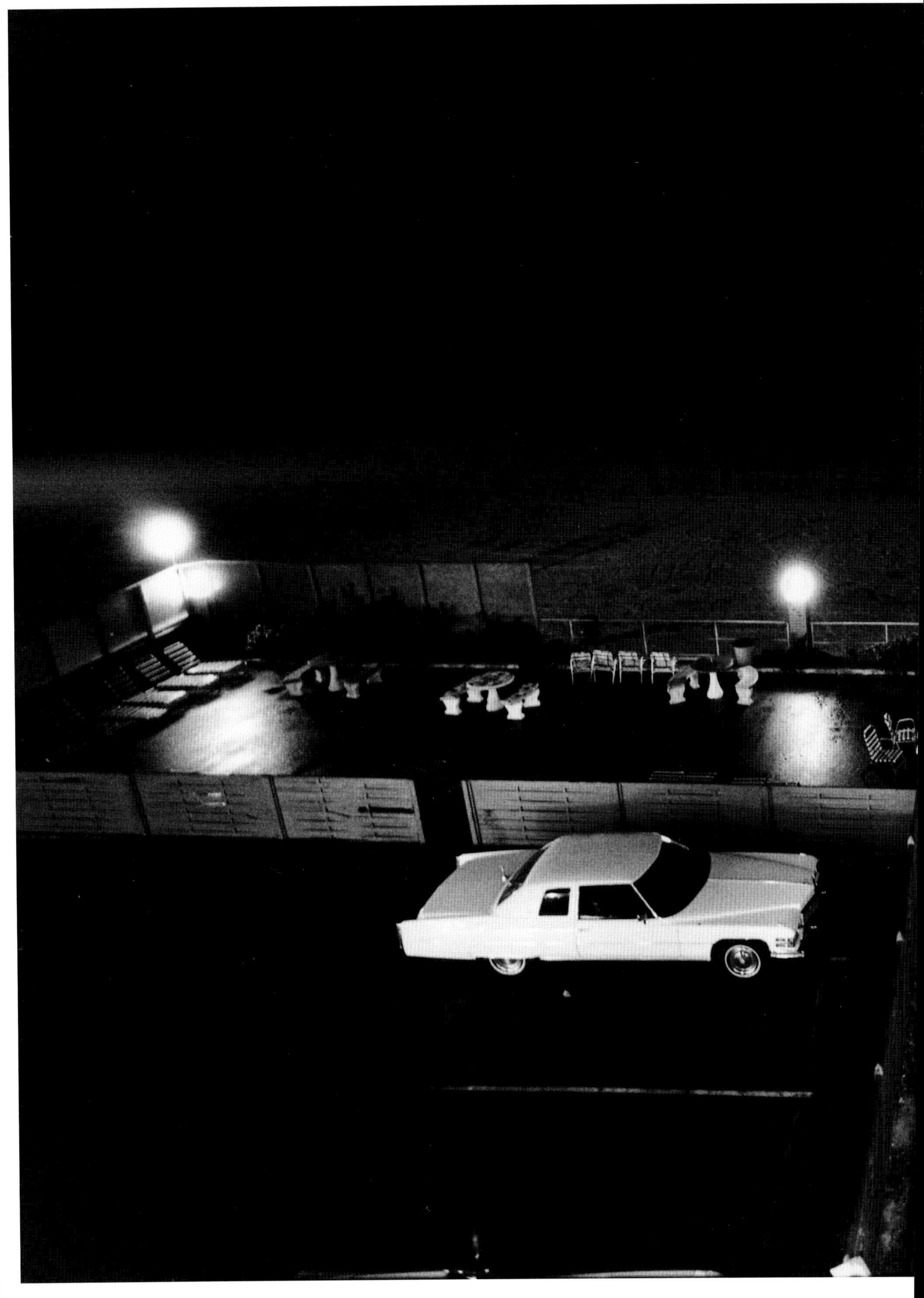

Jacksonville Beach, Florida, 1975

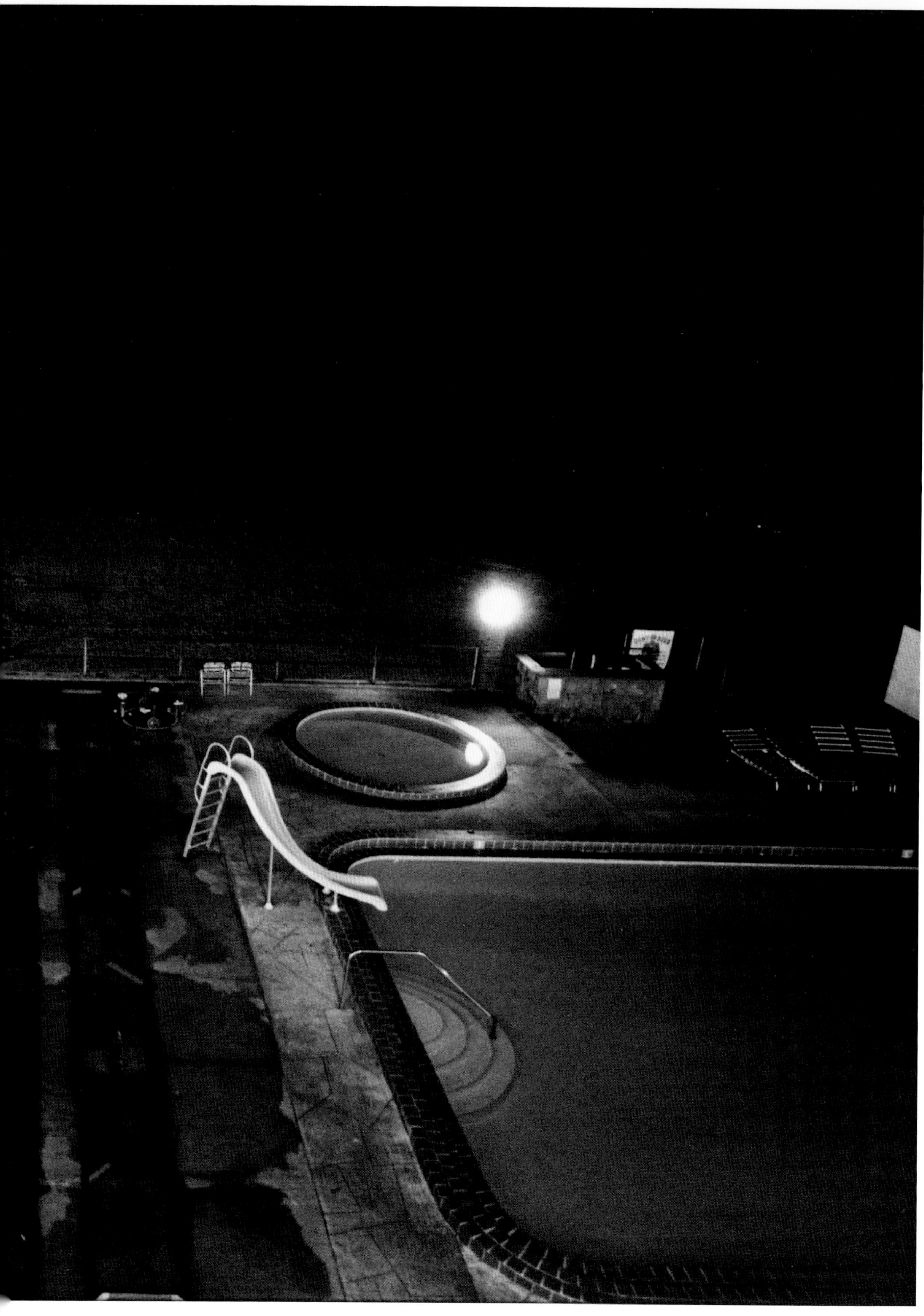

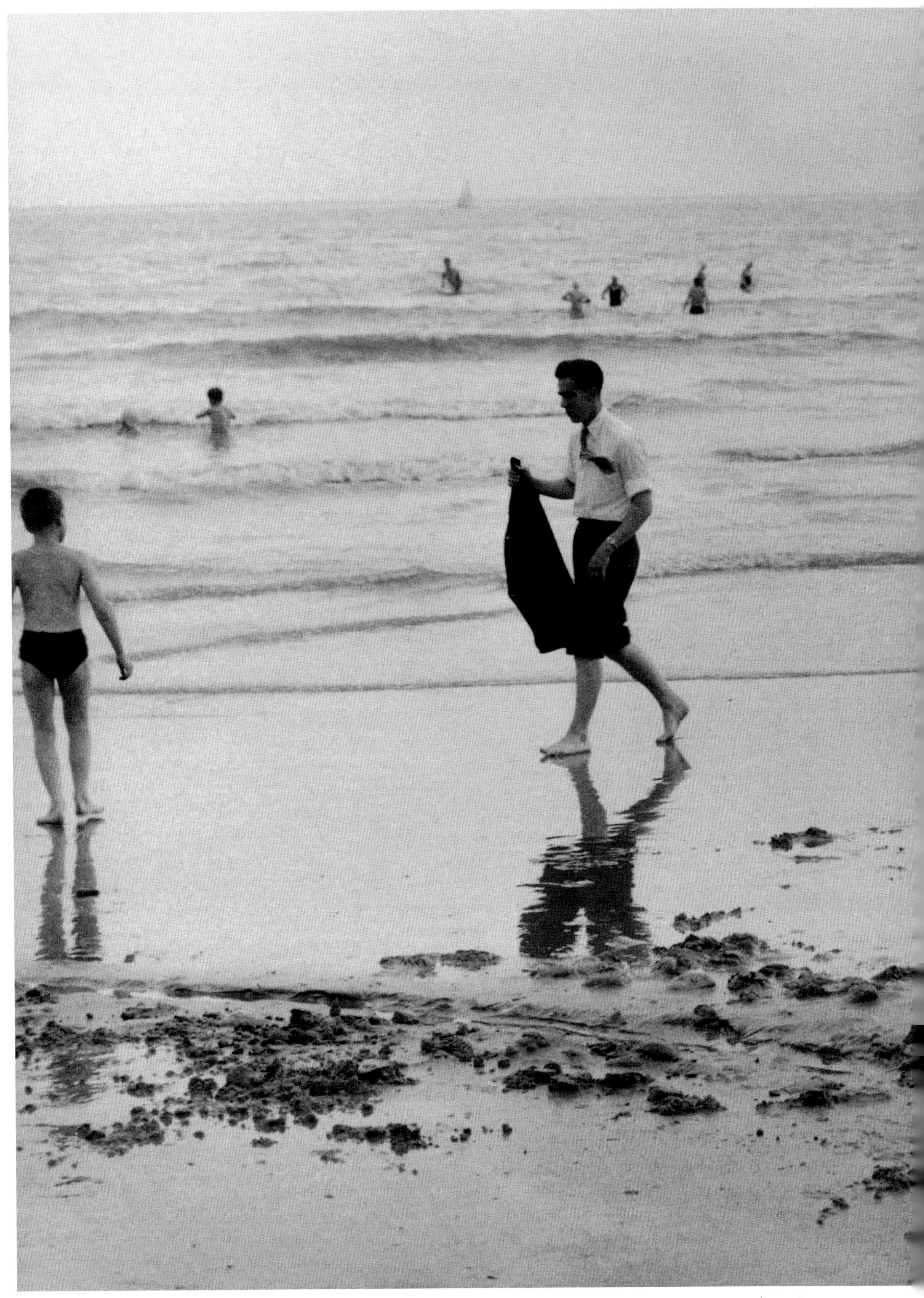

Brighton, England, 1956

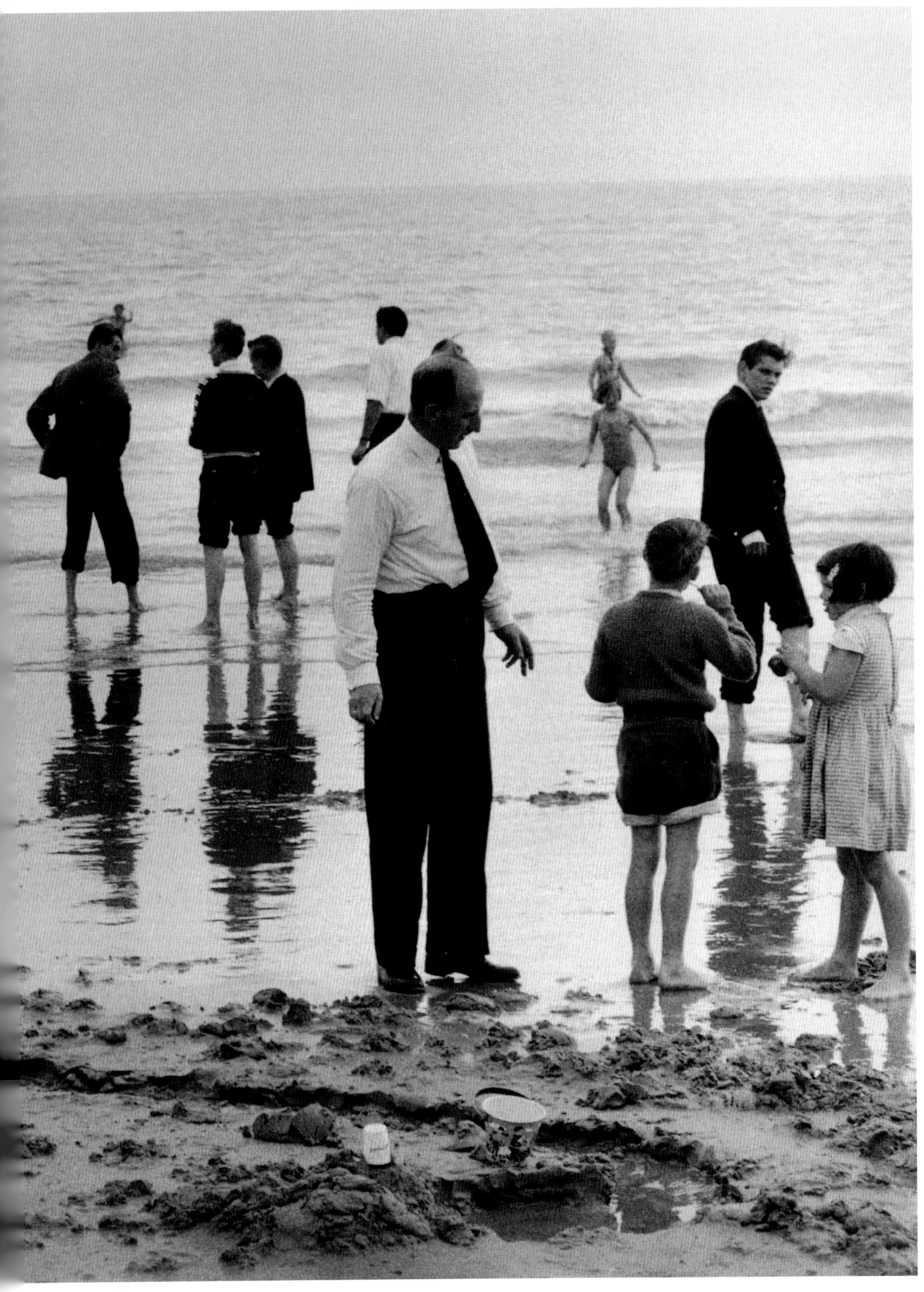

Chigasaki, Japan, 1977

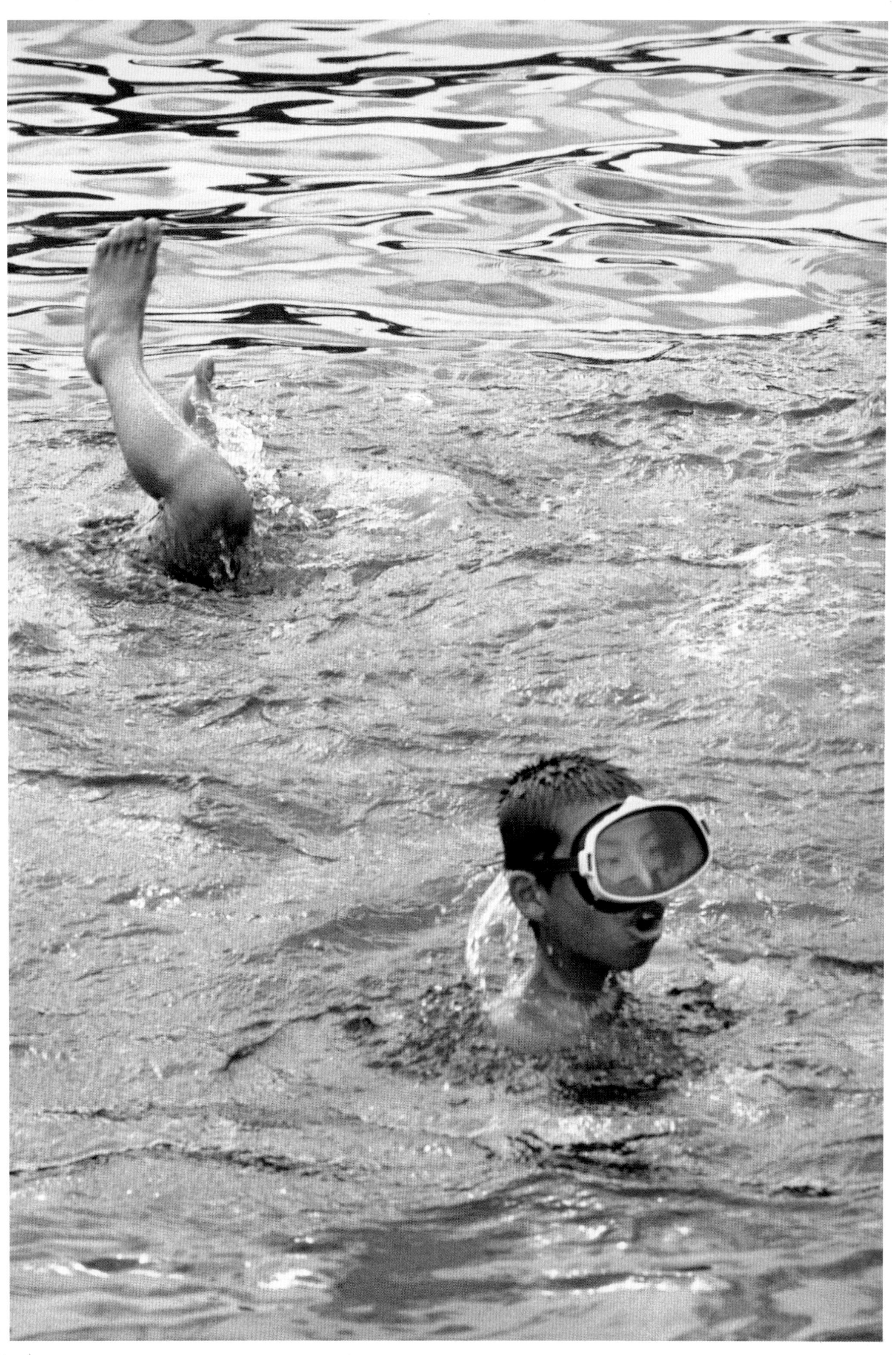

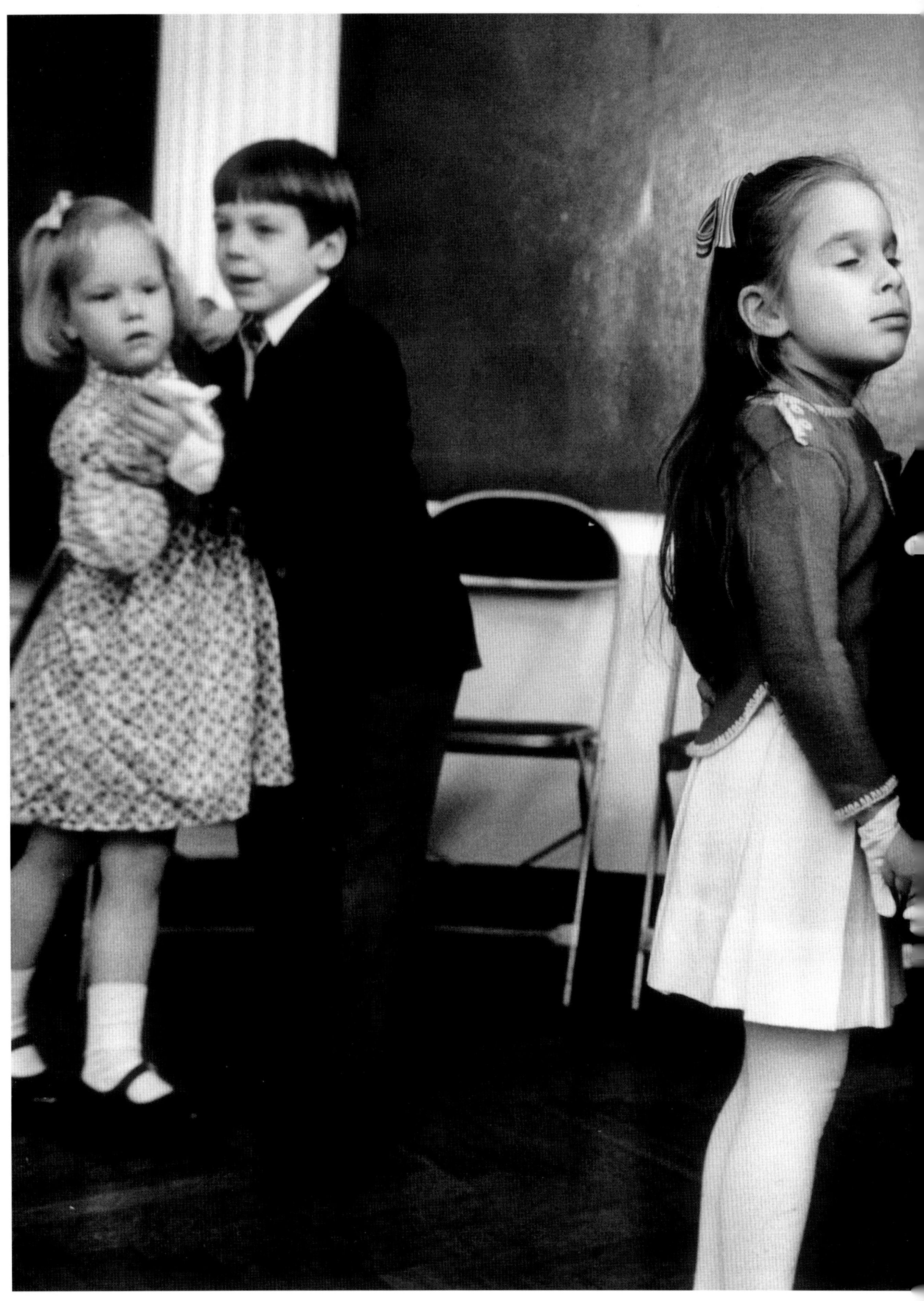

New York, 1977

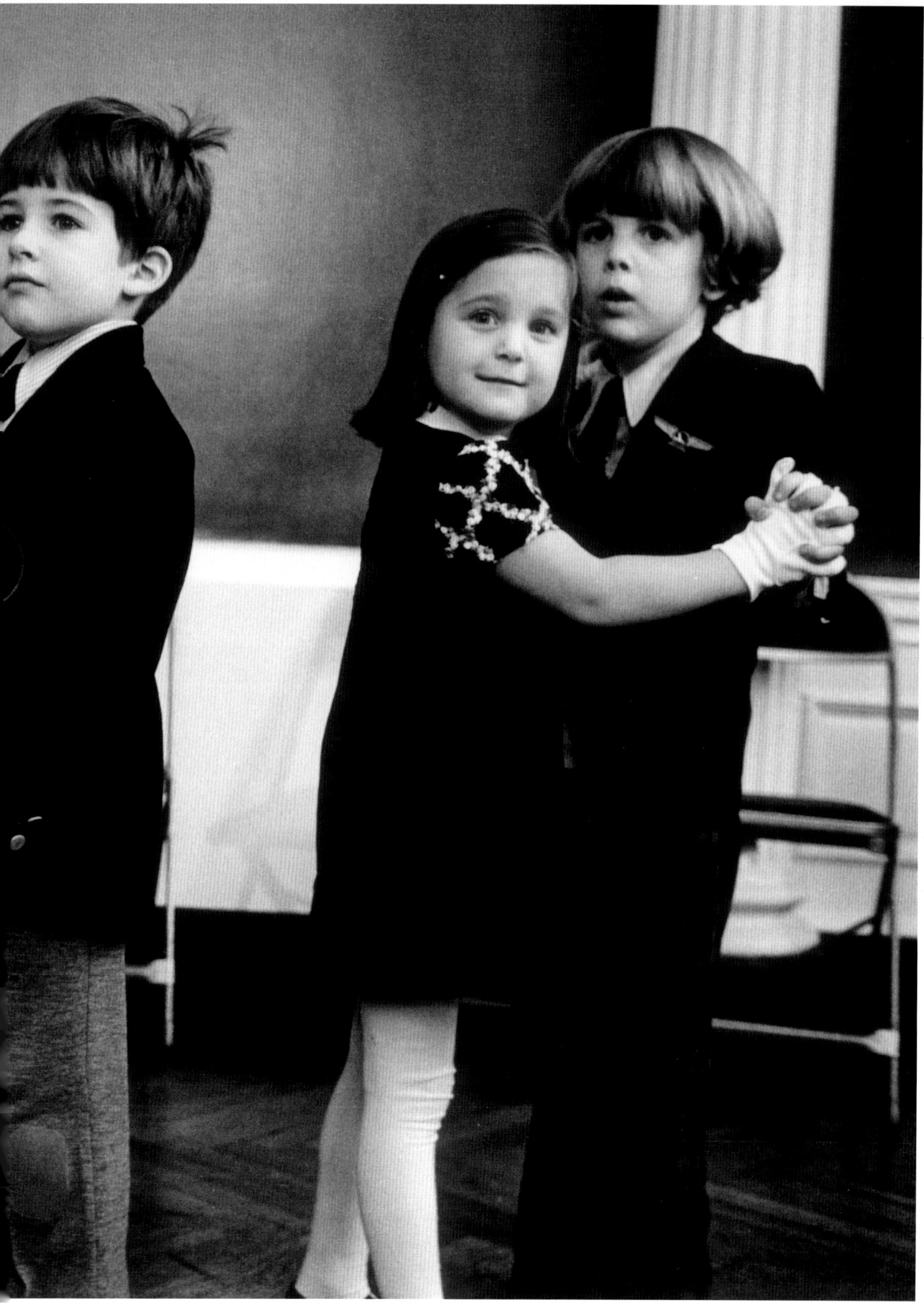

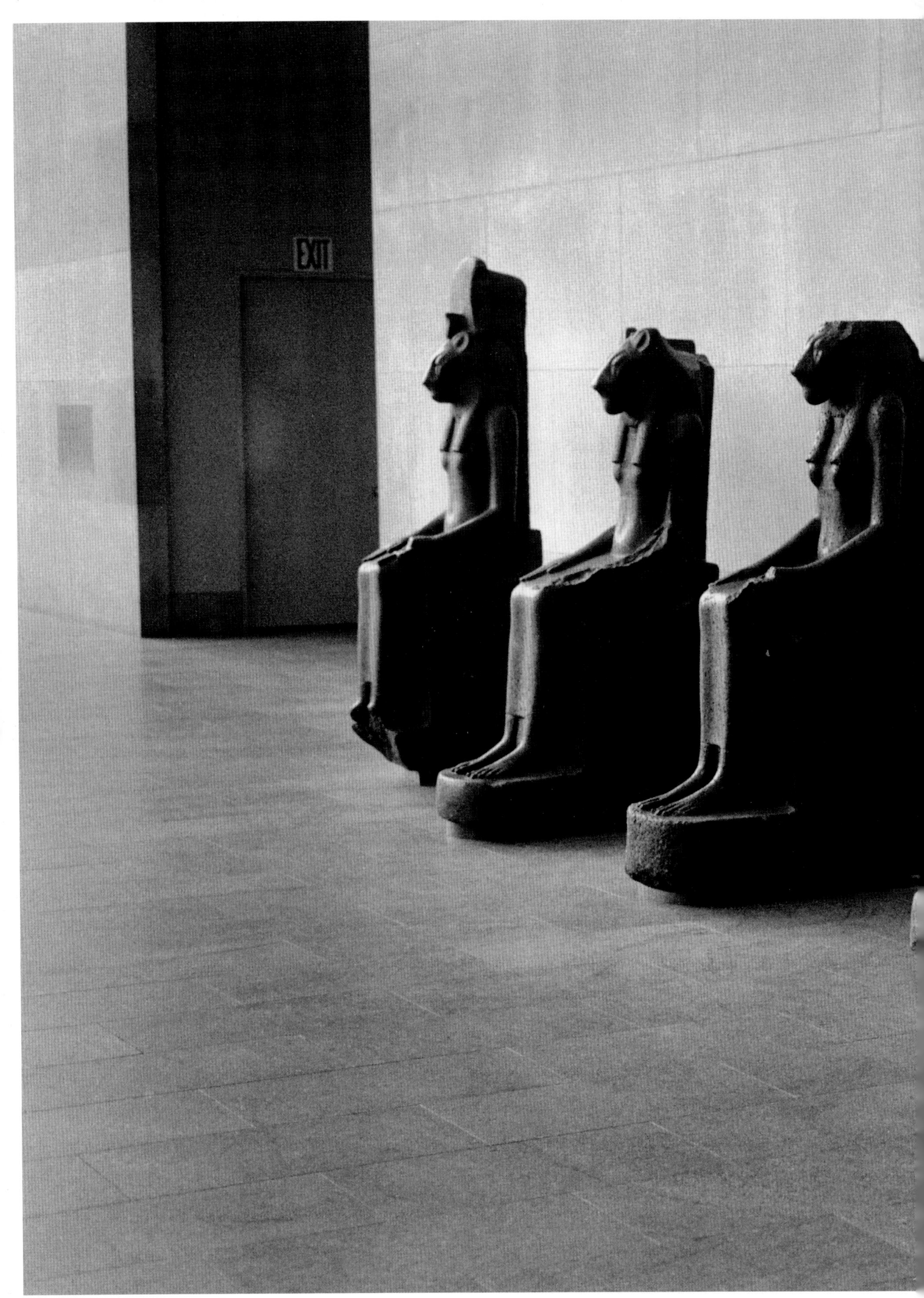

Metropolitan Museum of Art, New York, 1988

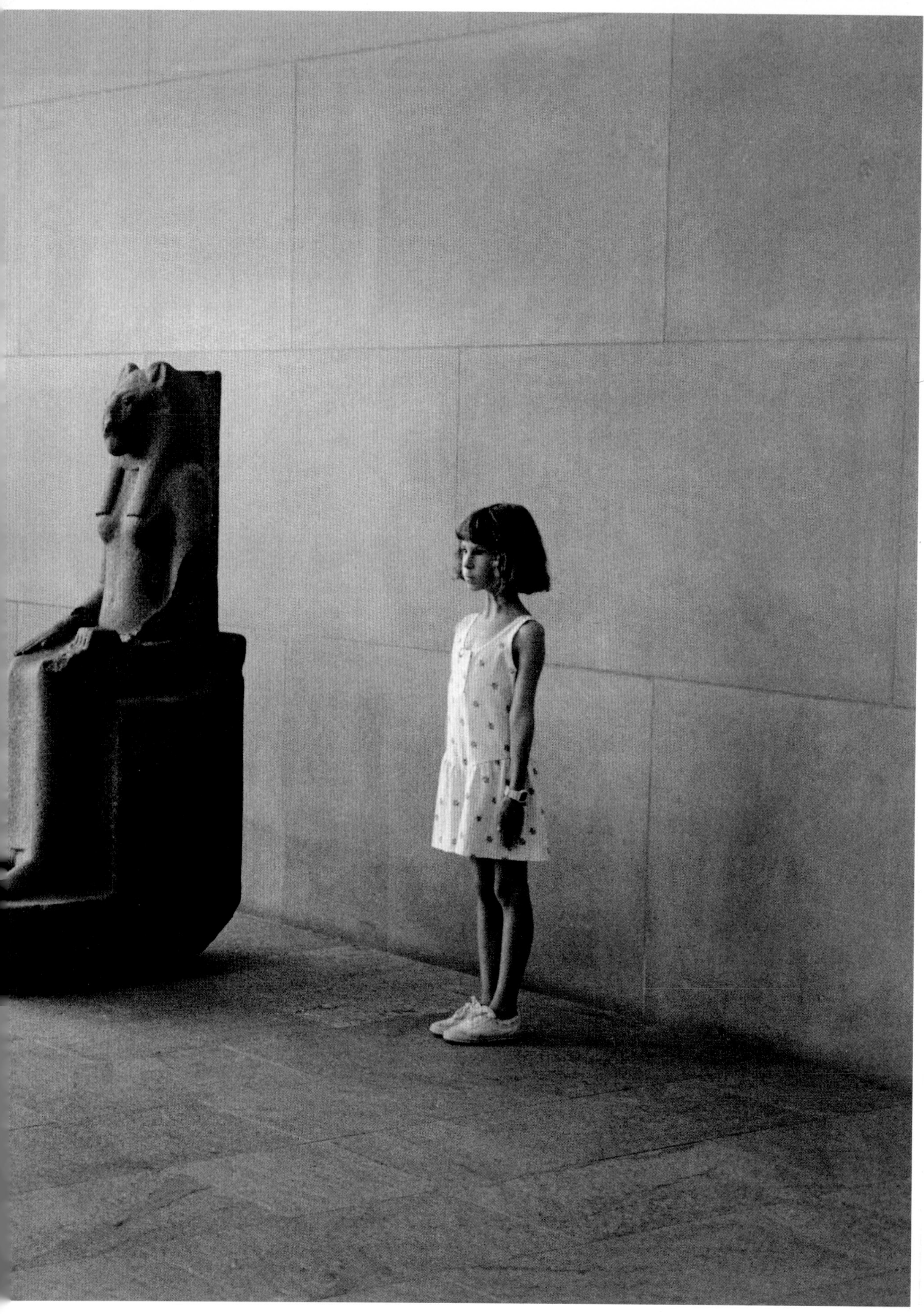

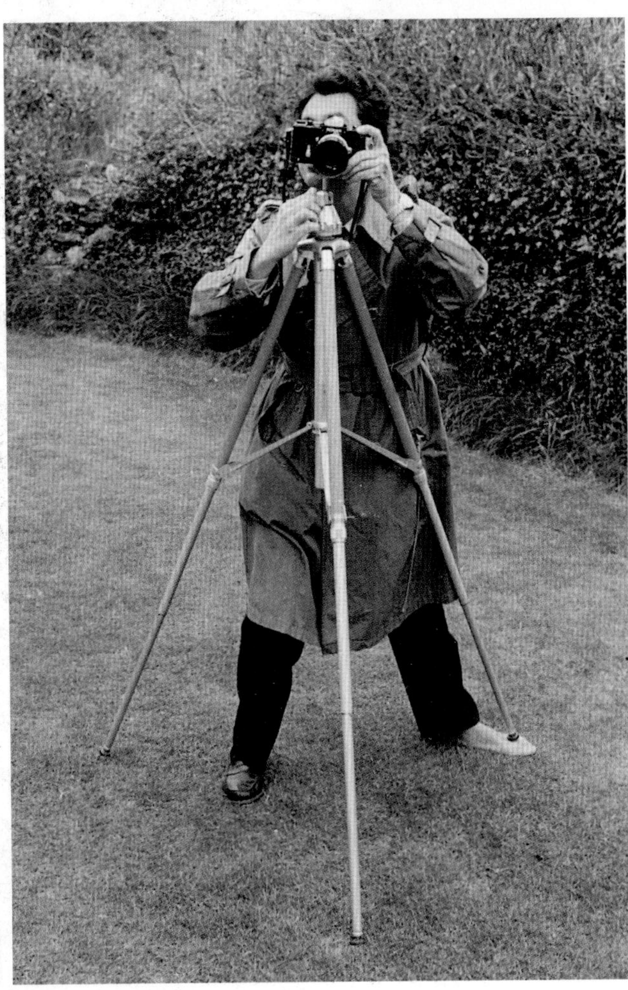

For my wife Pia and for her charming smile.

With thanks to hundreds of my witting and unwitting subjects and the numerous friends, clients and editors who have made my peregrinations possible and to my family who has had to put up with me. And to Stuart Smith, Liz Grogan, Jeff Ladd, Chris Boot, Neil Baber, Amanda Renshaw, Frances Johnson, Alexia Turner, Yayoi Sawada, Charles Flowers, Murray Sayle, Richard Schlagman, and to my colleagues and staff at Magnum Photos London, Paris, New York and Tokyo.

None of the photographs in this book have been electronically altered or manipulated.

Phaidon Press Limited
Regent's Wharf
All Saints Street
London N1 9PA

Phaidon Press Inc.
180 Varick Street
New York, NY 10014

www.phaidon.com

First published 2001
Reprinted in paperback 2003

ISBN 0 7148 4330 X

A CIP catalogue record for this book is available from the British Library.

Designed by SMITH
Printed in Hong Kong